W. H. AUDEN

PROSE

VOLUME III: 1949–1955

THE COMPLETE

WORKS OF

W. H. AUDEN

POEMS

PLAYS (WITH CHRISTOPHER ISHERWOOD)

LIBRETTI (WITH CHESTER KALLMAN)

PROSE

W. H. AUDEN

PROSE

VOLUME III

□

1949 – 1955

EDITED BY

Edward Mendelson

PRINCETON UNIVERSITY
PRESS

Published by Princeton University Press, 41 William Street,
Princeton, New Jersey 08540

ALL RIGHTS RESERVED

Library of Congress Catalog Card Number 2007920515
ISBN-13: 978-0-691-13326-3

This book has been composed in New Baskerville

Printed on acid-free paper. ∞
press.princeton.edu

Printed in the United States of America

2 4 6 8 10 9 7 5 3 1

CONTENTS

PREFACE

THIS volume, the fifth to be published in a complete edition of Auden's works, includes the essays, reviews, and other prose that he published or prepared for publication from 1949, when he wrote his first book of critical prose, *The Enchafèd Flood,* through December 1955, shortly before he was elected Professor of Poetry at Oxford and began the series of lectures that he published, with much else, in *The Dyer's Hand.* Further volumes of Auden's prose are projected. They will be followed by a complete edition of Auden's poems. The four volumes in the edition already published contain his complete plays, libretti, and other dramatic writings, and his prose works and travel books written from 1926 through 1948. The texts throughout this edition are, wherever possible, newly edited from Auden's manuscripts, and the notes report variant readings from all published versions.

ACKNOWLEDGEMENTS

THE TEXT and notes in this volume have benefitted from the learning and intelligence of John Fuller, Nicholas Jenkins, Arthur Kirsch, and many other friends and colleagues. The entire edition continues to be based ultimately on years of research by B. C. Bloomfield, followed by many more years of his advice.

For help with major and minor problems, I am grateful to Alan Ansen, John Ashbery, Jacques Barzun, George Bradley, John Bodley, Katherine Bucknell, Thekla Clark, Valerie Eliot, Sir Frank Kermode, Samuel Hynes, Christopher Isherwood, Arthur Krystal, Ursula Niebuhr, Adrienne Rich, Elisabeth Sifton, Stan Smith, James Stern, and Tania Stern. Corinne Chesnot and Joëlle Gardes-Tamine of the Fondation Saint-John Perse provided the text of the unpublished first version of "Nature, History and Poetry". *The Enchafèd Flood* is reprinted with the kind permission of the University Press of Virginia.

Much of my work on this volume was conducted in the generous company of librarians and curators. I am indebted above all to Isaac Gewirtz, Stephen Crook, and Philip Milito at the Henry W. and Albert A. Berg Collection of the New York Public Library; the curators and staff of all the many departments of the Columbia University Library; Judith Tydeman at the Britten-Pears Library; and the expert staff of the BBC Written Archives Centre. I am grateful for courtesies received from librarians and curators at the American Academy of Arts and Letters, Barnard College Library, Fordham University Library, Harvard College Library and the Harvard University Archives, the Huntington Library, Indiana University Library, the Library of Congress, Mount Holyoke College Library, the Museum of Television and Radio, the New York Public Library Manuscripts and Archives Division, New York University Library, the Library of the University of North Carolina at Chapel Hill, Northwestern University Library, Princeton University Library, the Schlesinger Library at Harvard University, Smith College Library, Sussex University Library, Swarthmore College Library, Sweet Briar College Library, Syracuse University Library, the Harry Ransom Humanities Research Center at the University of Texas at Austin, the University of Virginia Library, and the Yale University Library. I am grateful also to the archivists of the National Broadcasting Company and the Viking Press (now Viking Penguin).

Auden's readers will share my continuing gratitude to Jan Lilly for the clarity and elegance of this edition and to Princeton University Press for the intelligence and care with which it has published this and all previous volumes.

AUDEN wrote his prose so that he would be able to write his poems, and the benefits of writing prose were both financial and intellectual. In a letter written from Italy in 1955, he explained: "The winter months are those in which I earn enough dollars to allow me to live here in the summer and devote myself to the unprofitable occupation of writing poetry." During his winters in New York, punctuated by lecture tours and visiting professorships in American college towns, he wrote the commissioned essays and reviews that paid for his summers in Ischia. No matter what the nominal subject of those essays might be, he used them as exercises in which he explored whatever moral, intellectual, literary, or prosodic issues concerned him most in the poems he was writing or planning. During the late 1940s and early 1950s he wrote a sequence of poems largely about history, "Horae Canonicae", and another sequence largely about nature, "Bucolics". He developed the structure of ideas that holds them together by writing essays and reviews on the theme indicated by the title of one of them: "Nature, History and Poetry".

Auden enjoyed deflating romantic images of inspired poets driven only by their genius. He made a point of praising the bourgeois virtues—directly in his essays, indirectly in poems such as "Under Sirius", "Cattivo Tempo", "Sext", and "Mountains". He also made a point of practicing those virtues. After agreeing to write an introduction or essay or review, he typically finished the job weeks or months ahead of his deadline. For an anthology of English poetry and a collection of Elizabethan verse and music he used original texts rather than later reprints, and was impatient with collaborators who were less responsible and punctual than he was. As a public lecturer he gave value for money with his lucid and substantial talks. During the early 1950s he finally outgrew his intermittent temptation to pose before academic audiences as a severe philosopher, and his prose style achieved the urbane, inclusive ease that it maintained for the rest of his career.

Before this, during Auden's first years in America from 1939 to around 1947, his work and thought had focused on lonely inward crises and existential choices of the kind he wrote about in his longer poems from "New Year Letter" in 1940 through *The Age of Anxiety* in 1944–46. In the later 1940s he began to seek a less narrow and intense approach to experience, and explored ways of thinking that were more social and collective, and more aware of the common world of the body. In the early 1940s he had found the structure of his thought in the work of Søren Kierkegaard. In 1955, while still acknowledging his debt to Kierkegaard, he pointed toward "what seems to be his great limitation, a limitation which characterizes Protestantism generally. A planetary visitor could read through the whole of his voluminous works without discovering that human beings are not ghosts but have bodies of flesh and blood."

Auden first visited Italy in 1948. For the next ten years he settled into a routine of summers in a rented house in Ischia and winters in an apartment in New York. He countered the urgent and severe Protestantism of his thought in the earlier 1940s with what he half-seriously called a "counter-Reformationary" Catholicism. His poem "In Praise of Limestone," written in 1948, was an emphatic hymn of praise to the human body and the Mediterranean landscapes in which it was most at home. During the next few years he wrote sympathetically about the differences between Italian and northern European societies and cultures, especially about the lucid fatalism of Giovanni Verga's fiction and the operas based on Verga's stories. Also in 1948 he resumed his earlier practice of collaboration with other writers and artists by inviting Chester Kallman to join him in writing the libretto for Igor Stravinsky's opera *The Rake's Progress*.

In the summer of 1948 he was invited by the University of Virginia to deliver the 1949 Page-Barbour Lectures, an endowed annual series that required the lecturer to publish his lectures as a book. (T. S. Eliot's Page-Barbour lectures for 1933 were published as *After Strange Gods*.)* Auden chose for his subject the romantic and nineteenth-century image of the sea, and the contrary image of isolation, the desert, illustrated by examples from Wordsworth to Rimbaud. He titled the series (and the resulting book) *The Enchafèd Flood: The Romantic Iconography of the Sea*, after a fragment from *Othello*: "I never did like molestation view / On the enchafèd flood." The underlying theme of his lectures was the myth of the heroic artist as a solitary voyager in the realm of consciousness, a potentially redemptive figure who finds new territories of experience that he reveals to an audience too timidly bourgeois to make such explorations for themselves. Auden had repeatedly been tempted by this myth in earlier years; his lectures served as a final exorcism of it.

The Enchafèd Flood is a backward-looking book, both in its implicit renunciations and in its explicit themes. Auden's survey of literary images of the

---

* The first lecture series that Auden gave in America seems to have been the Turnbull Lectures in poetry at Johns Hopkins in January 1940. When Harvard invited him to lecture in December 1948, he may or may not have been told that the faculty intended to decide afterward whether to offer him the Charles Eliot Norton Chair in Poetry for 1950–51, a series of six lectures intended for publication as a book. He gave his talk on *Don Quixote*, "The Ironic Hero", perhaps the most probing and sympathetic reading of the book ever written in English (a published version appears in *Prose II*), but he began by joking that, like everyone else in the room, he had never finished reading it. The contents of the lecture proved the joke to be untrue, but Harry Levin and others took offense, and Thornton Wilder was chosen instead. Auden was eventually offered the Norton chair in the 1960s but declined; he told friends that he had nothing to say.

sea and the desert arranges in systematic form the imagery of "The Sea and the Mirror", the long poem he wrote in 1942–44. All the sentences in the book are new, but the content restates much that Auden had written in essays and reviews earlier in the 1940s, notably his Kierkegaardian account of aesthetic, ethical, and religious authority and his readings of Don Quixote as a religious hero and of Melville's Ishmael as an explorer of possibility. The last pages of the book turn away from all that: "We live in a new age," he wrote, and his phrase refers both to public culture and to his private interests. This new age is one in which

> the necessity of dogma is once more recognised, not as the contradiction of reason and feeling but as their ground and foundation, in which the heroic image is not the nomad wanderer through the desert or over the ocean, but the less exciting figure of the builder, who renews the ruined walls of the city. . . . We are less likely to be tempted by solitude into Promethean pride: we are far more likely to become cowards in the face of the tyrant who would compel us to lie in the service of the False City. It is not madness we need to flee but prostitution.

These new temptations became a recurring theme. Later in 1949 he contrasted the situation of nineteenth-century poets and that of his contemporaries: "The former were either admired or left alone; the latter are suspect, and the campaign to control them by bribes or threats is likely to intensify." He now began to write systematically about the ways in which poetry allowed itself to be tempted by these bribes and threats and the ways in which it might learn to resist them.

At the center of his thinking was his idea of history, a word he began using in 1949 in a special idiosyncratic sense. History, as he described it, was the realm of unique, voluntary, irreversible events that occur in linear time. Nature, in contrast, was the realm of recurring, involuntary, reversible events that occur in cyclical time. Human experience occurs in both these realms. Sexual desire is historical to the degree that it focuses on a unique person to the exclusion of all others, and natural to the degree that the instincts that drive it could equally be satisfied by almost anyone else.

The moral point of the distinction between nature and history was that public life, especially in a world increasingly dominated by the machine, tends to treat human beings in statistical and generalizing ways, as if they were predictable elements of the realm of nature. The impersonal power of government or the machine operates in the realm of nature, not history, and the reason that modern governments distrust the arts is that the arts are products of personal, historical choices. A work of art, no matter how much it owes to an anonymous cultural climate or literary tradition, bears witness to the historical realm of individual choices.

In 1951, when Auden was helping to prepare *The Rake's Progress* for its première, he applied these ideas in a series of essays on music. Music was the purest expression of "irreversible historicity" and of all that historicity implies about freedom and self-determination. "Every high C accurately struck utterly demolishes the theory that we are the irresponsible puppets of fate or chance." Auden's interest in music had always been inseparable from his curiosity about historical changes in theme and style. He and Kallman had adopted an eighteenth-century style for the libretto of *The Rake's Progress*; in 1952 they wrote another libretto in an even more archaic Tudor style, *Delia, or A Masque of Night* (which Stravinsky declined to set, having been introduced to the twelve-tone scale whose enthusiasts had declared it the style of the future). In 1953 Auden began collaborating with an early-music group, the New York Pro Musica, founded by Noah Greenberg, and at some of their concerts read the Tudor verses that the group then sang. These concerts issued in an anthology of words and music, *An Elizabethan Song Book*, with an introduction by Auden and Kallman and Greenberg's musical transcriptions.

For Auden, in many essays and reviews from the early 1950s, the great prophet of individual history was Sigmund Freud. Freud's greatness, Auden wrote, did not depend on the validity or cohesiveness of his theories—whose revolutionary significance Freud himself often failed to understand. "In fact, if every one of his theories should turn out to be false, Freud would still tower up as the genius who perceived that psychological events are not natural events but historical and that, therefore, psychology as distinct from neurology, must be based on the pre-suppositions and methodology, not of the biologist but of the historian."

Another name for individual historicity was the human face, the visible sign of uniqueness that was never exactly the same from one moment to the next, but was always a sign for the same individual person. In 1950 Auden wrote a poem, "Numbers and Faces", about the madness of those who prefer the statistical, anonymous world of numbers to the personal world of faces. The title and much of the content derived from a book written in 1919 by the Austrian thinker Rudolf Kassner, *Zahl und Gesicht*, which became central to Auden's thinking around 1950, although he seems to have encountered the book a few years earlier. (As a phrase, Kassner's title means quantity and quality; as separate words, *die Zahl* means number and *das Gesicht* means face or physiognomy.) As Kassner's "face" corresponded to Auden's "history", so Kassner's "number" corresponded to Auden's "nature".

Kassner used the term "Physiognomik" for his whole intellectual and moral enterprise, in which he contrasted, on one hand, unique individuality, finite human flesh, truth as something to be witnessed or exemplified, and, on the other, collective identity, indifferent fate, and truth as something impersonal that can be taught like a method. For Kassner this was the contrast between the Christian and classical worldviews, and Auden's poem "The Shield of

Achilles" in 1952 portrayed a modern world of statistical impersonality shaped by the same worldview that shaped the fated cruelties of the *Iliad*.

Faces and persons are characterized by their uniqueness as themselves; they are not sets of more or less widely distributed qualities such as beauty, strength, intelligence, or wit. Only a person has a physiognomy; a set of qualities has none. The classical gods have qualities such as shrewdness or strength; the Christian God has a face. The distinction between persons and qualities is a theme that pervades Auden's poems in the early 1950s, and he spelled out the distinction in a review of George Santayana, who, he suggested, sometimes lost sight of the difference:

> The natural human, or at least masculine, tendency, both in love and friendship, is to be attracted by qualities rather than persons. We like people not for what they are in themselves but because they are beautiful or rich or amusing, so if they lose their looks or their money or their wit, we lose our interest. . . .
>
> Plato, if I understand him rightly, took our romantic interest in qualities as his starting point and sought to show, by analysis, that on the temporal level it was self-defeating; if qualities, not persons, are what we want, then the proper place to look for them is in Heaven, among the Universals.

This is perhaps a generous reading of Socrates' report in the *Symposium* of what Diotima had told him about love; Auden privately referred to Plato as "a man of genius who's always wrong"—a view that emerged more visibly in Auden's later work.

To the degree that the modern artist resists the faceless impersonality of the machine, he is right to do so, but if his resistance is merely nostalgic, he may embrace the error that he hopes to escape. Auden borrowed from Henry Adams's *Mont-Saint-Michel and Chartres* the distinction between the Dynamo and the Virgin, between the natural world of involuntary recurrent events and the historical world of voluntary unique events; but, Auden wrote, for Adams himself, and for many who shared Adams's nostalgia, the Virgin was not the source and protector of individual lives but another name for the anonymous and impersonal nature-goddess. As Auden wrote in his poem "Nocturne" around 1951, this goddess was not the unique historical Mary but the cyclical lunar Venus, "Whose majesty is but the mask / That hides a faceless dynamo." And in a paragraph published in 1962 but probably first written in the early 1950s:

> Henry Adams thought that Venus and the Virgin of Chartres were the same persons. Actually, Venus is the Dynamo in disguise, a symbol for an impersonal natural force, and Adams' nostalgic preference for Chartres

to Chicago was nothing but aestheticism; he thought the disguise was prettier than the reality, but it was the Dynamo he worshiped, not the Virgin.

Starting from the idea of historical uniqueness, Auden developed an elaborate vocabulary for different kinds of social order and for the analogous kinds of formal order that give shape to poems. Unique persons create different kinds of social order from those generated by impersonal forces. Historical individuals, Auden wrote, join into communities united by their shared voluntary love of something; a community is historical because it has no bureaucratic impersonal structure. Communities tend to create societies that can carry out their purposes; societies are natural, not historical, because they have a bureaucratic structure in which individual members have roles distinct from their unique personalities. A group of music-lovers is a community but its love accomplishes nothing; a string quartet is a society that puts into effect the community's love.

A crowd, unlike a society or community, is a mere plurality of things that happen to be together. "The subject matter of poetry", Auden wrote in 1949, "is a crowd of past historic occasions of feeling", some portion of which the poet hopes to convert into a community; but the poem in which that community is embodied is a society, something that the poet must assume will remain unchanged and eternal once it is written. Crowds of feelings are not especially dangerous; but in the real world the extreme version of the crowd was the Public, that faceless purposeless mass that anyone can join when one is no one in particular.

The Public has always existed, but one effect of the mass media is to make it easier than ever to be faceless and impersonal. The culture of celebrity is one result of the growth of the Public: "the public instinctively worships not great men of action or thought but actors, individuals who by profession are not themselves." The moral consequences are all too clear: "The public, therefore, can be persuaded to do or believe anything by those who know how to manage it. It will subscribe thousands of dollars to a cancer research fund or massacre Jews with equal readiness, not because it wants to do either, but because it has no alternative game to suggest."

Auden had included sweeping historical summaries in his poems and prose from the start of his career, and since 1946 he had borrowed the Swiss-American historian Eugen Rosenstock-Huessy's outline of the past thousand years as a series of revolutions against local and sectarian authority. In 1949 he wrote the introductions to a five-volume anthology, *Poets of the English Language*, which he was editing for the Viking Portable Library in collaboration with an American professor, Norman Holmes Pearson. The introductions took the form of a history of English poetry that was also a compressed history of the revolutionary changes in literary, psychological, and political pre-suppositions over five centuries. Auden's four-part poem "Memorial for the City", written around the same time, retold much of this history in allusive verse. Also around this time, Auden began writing the sequence "Horae Canonicae", in which the events of a single Good Friday echo the historical events from birth to death, from the rise to the fall of a civilization, and from the Creation to the Apocalypse.

In 1951 Auden published *Nones*, one of the mostly quinquennial volumes of verse in which he collected his recent shorter poems. The book took its title from the central poem in "Horae Canonicae" (he had at this point fin-ished only two of the seven poems in the sequence). Auden tended to orga-nize his collections of shorter poems and volumes of longer poems with nu-merological precision, and the exact center of *Nones* was the historical survey in "Memorial for the City".

Historical intelligence, in Auden's criticism and reviews, was analogous to moral intelligence. His review of Isaiah Berlin's *The Hedgehog and the Fox*, a book built on the distinction between those whose historical understanding is based on a unified vision and those who perceive multiple purposes and ends, proposed a deeper, more morally unsettling distinction between two kinds of contemporary intellect. Borrowing from *Alice in Wonderland*—Auden wrote repeatedly about the moral seriousness of Lewis Carroll's fan-tasies—he distinguished between tough-minded Alices, who have nerves and courage but are tempted to imagine themselves the Queen of Heaven, and the weak-minded Mabels, increasingly common in intellectual life, who adopt "a grotesquely tough, grotesquely 'realist' attitude" as a mask over their weakness and terror.

Auden's exasperation at Albert Camus's well-meant confusions in *The Stranger* (in a review titled "Fog in the Mediterranean") was prompted largely by Camus' idea of history in which the only significant events occurred in France and revolutionary changes elsewhere were ignored. His pleasure in J.R.R. Tolkien's *The Lord of the Rings* arose largely from its historical imagi-nation. "If a feigned history is to seem real," Auden said in a broadcast about Tolkien's trilogy, "it must be shown as the joint product of individual char-acter and circumstances, neither, that is, as the operation of a few great men nor as the inevitable result of the play of impersonal forces. The present must have an intelligible relation to the past, neither inevitable nor arbitrary, and the future must appear open; that is, characters in this history may make guesses about what will happen which will turn out to be correct, but, in general, the outcome of their actions will be different from what they either hope or fear." Auden especially praised Tolkien's invention of the many plau-sible and varied languages and verse-forms that were essential to his invented history. Tolkien, in effect, had written an imaginary version of Auden's historical accounts of English metre in his *Poets of the English Language* and his lengthy, detailed, and politely devastating review of the historical account in *Rhythm and Tempo,* by the musicologist Curt Sachs.

Some of the most vexing literary questions that Auden was obliged to confront during the 1940s and 1950s were raised by the case of Ezra Pound. In 1946, after Pound was charged with high treason for his broadcasts from Italy during the Second World War, Auden's American publisher, Bennett Cerf at Random House, announced that Pound's work would be dropped from an anthology of American poetry. Auden severed relations with Random House until Cerf reversed this policy: "Begin by banning his poems not because you object to them but because you object to him, and you will end, as the Nazis did, by slaughtering his wife and children." Auden's view had nothing to do with his opinion of Pound's poems; "I do not care for them myself particularly," he told Cerf. He again acted against his literary opinions in 1948 when he defended the award of the first Bollingen Prize to Pound's *Cantos* by a committee of which he himself had been a member. (He seems to have preferred William Carlos Williams for the prize, but finally voted with the majority for Pound.) In the next few years Auden found occasions to praise Pound, not for his poems, but for the knowledge of literary history through which he introduced English poetry to styles and techniques that had not been available to it before: "it might be said of his translation of *The Seafarer* that its effect was to make the spondee respectable in English verse".

Auden focused on revolutionary changes whenever he wrote about large-scale history, but he refused the temptation to think of himself and his art as revolutionary, or to think of his own era as a unique moment of crisis when the moral and aesthetic concerns of calmer eras must be suspended or abandoned. "Revolutionary changes in sensibility or style are rare", he wrote at the start of *The Enchafèd Flood*; he cited only the twelfth-century conception of *"amor"*, the sixteenth-century abandonment of allegory as a common literary genre, and the eighteenth-century rise of Romanticism. Elsewhere, he emphasized that the current artistic climate was invented by an earlier generation of revolutionaries, not by himself and his contemporaries, about whom he made an elaborate show of modesty. He listed the birth years of great modernists from W. B. Yeats (1865) to T. S. Eliot (1888), the youngest of them almost twenty years older than himself, and observed:

> These are the figures whom we still think of as the creators and masters of the "modern style": none of them seems old-fashioned. . . . It is clear, then, that so far as the arts are concerned we are not . . . living at the beginning of a new era but in the middle of one. Poets of my generation and of the next, therefore, are in the position, whether we like it or not, of being colonisers rather than explorers. It would be as wrong-headed for us to attempt to make a radical break with the style of our immedi-

ate predecessors as it was right for them so to break with their Victorian elders.

> A coloniser is a less romantic and less heroic figure than an explorer, but his task is necessary and perhaps it is easier.

This restates the argument at the end of *The Enchafèd Flood* about the contemporary hero as no longer the romantic nomad but the builder who renews the city walls. Auden's prose leaves mostly unsaid the claim he made in many of his poems: that, for better or worse, the builder and colonizer is more densely engaged in moral complexities and emotional depths than the nomadic explorer, that his work is less spectacular but more profound. He makes no claim that the builder-poet is more virtuous or pure than the lonely explorer; instead, he acknowledges that the builder is more deeply implicated in social and political guilt. The builder who "renews the ruined walls of the city" in *The Enchafèd Flood* is the citizen-poet of "Vespers" (part of the "Horae Canonicae" sequence) who admits complicity in the injustice that sustains any civilization, even the mildest: "For without a cement of blood (it must be human, it must be innocent) no secular wall will safely stand."

Auden wrote the history of his own career, his development as a colonizer and builder, largely in indirect terms, by clarifying his differences with his great poetic predecessors, first Yeats, then Eliot. Both poets embodied temptations that Auden had overcome only after years of struggle. Yeats was the model for political and oratorical poetry, such as "Spain" and "September 1, 1939", that Auden was now ashamed to have written. In the early 1940s he wrote that Yeats's poetry was "lacking in seriousness, which, of course, has nothing to do with solemnity": Yeats's passionate engagement with recurring moments of strong feeling, and his temptation to treat art as a religious ritual, protected him from any serious risk of failure. Auden made no claim to have risked that kind of failure by writing poems that were concerned as much with the truths of history as with the timeless order of poetry, but he knew that he had written greater poems than Yeats's by having done so.

T. S. Eliot offered the subtler temptation to withdraw into the lonely vision of a superior intellect, and Auden had half-yielded to that temptation while reacting against those offered by Yeats. He overcame this temptation by the late 1940s, and during the next few years he found occasions to point out, with the greatest possible courtesy, Eliot's imaginative failings. As an editor at Faber & Faber, Eliot had accepted Auden's first book for publication when Auden was twenty-three, and throughout the 1930s Auden spoke and wrote about Eliot with reverent gratitude. When Auden returned to the Anglican Communion in 1940, he identified his religious views as being close to Eliot's, and echoed Eliot's "Ash-Wednesday" and "Burnt Norton" in the poetry he wrote after his conversion.

Auden soon realized that the focus of his religion was the worldly com-

mandment to love one's neighbor as oneself—something very different from
Eliot's unworldly, idealizing religion of a still point and a rose-garden never
entered. By writing "In Praise of Limestone" in 1948 he made clear to him-
self the differences between his own religious emphasis on the sacred importance of the body and Eliot's revulsion from the body's sordidness. When
Eliot's *Notes towards the Definition of Culture* was published a few months later,
Auden reviewed it for the *New Yorker*, where he treated the book partly as a
deliberate joke against liberal pieties—a polite way of dismissing most of
Eliot's arguments—and partly as a pharisaic misreading of history in which
Eliot credited a privileged social class with the transmission of culture that
had in fact been transmitted by the Church. "The value of Mr Eliot's book is
not the conclusions he reaches, most of which are debatable, but the questions he raises."

In 1951, reviewing Eliot's *Poetry and Drama*, Auden questioned Eliot's competence as a prosodist and hinted at a lack of imagination in his use of Broadway and West End conventions in his poetic drama. Auden spelled out the
moral and theological implications of this lack when he reviewed Eliot's *Complete Poems and Plays* two years later. He again pointed to this lack in Eliot's
plays and offered a slightly disingenuous apology for it:

> If in *The Family Reunion* and *The Cocktail Party*, one hears an occasional
> discordant snobbish note, I believe that this is not a matter of sensibility
> but of technique. While concentrating upon the problem of how to write
> dramatic verse which shall not be "Little Theatre" and arty, Mr Eliot has
> postponed the problem of dramatic convention, i.e. he has simply taken
> on unchanged the conventions of English "High" Comedy that have ex-
> isted from Congreve down to Noel Coward, under which the decor and
> the main characters are aristocratic. So long as the dramatic subject is
> one of the various worldly self-affirmations, like love between the sexes,
> and the moral values implied are social, the convention is perfectly sat-
> isfactory; wealth and good-breeding are quite adequate symbols for gifts
> and virtues. But when the theme becomes one of spiritual election, of
> the radical gulf between the Christian faith and *all* worldly values, the
> symbolism breaks down. I am absolutely certain that Mr Eliot did not in-
> tend us to think [in *The Family Reunion*] that Harry is called and not John
> because John is stupid, or [in *The Cocktail Party*] that Celia is called and
> not Lavinia because she is of a higher social class, but that is exactly what
> the comedy convention he is using is bound to suggest.

A few months later, in a review of Eliot's *Selected Essays*, Auden dismissed
Eliot's "efforts to be the Matthew Arnold of our time, to diagnose and prescribe
for the ills of modern civilization, his defense of dogmatic and organized Christianity against Liberal Protestantism and the Higher Thought". Eliot was not
at fault, he suggested, for his failure to influence anyone who did not already

share his views: the fault lay in the difficulty of the problems involved. The complexity of the questions "demands an investigation on a scale larger than that of the occasional essay which is all Mr Eliot has had the time, and, probably, the ambition to write." In Eliot's essays on liberal humanism, "I cannot help feeling that . . . Mr Eliot is flogging a horse which not only is dead but was never alive" and that Eliot avoids more-difficult problems because "such a job would take a long time and Mr Eliot has other and, for lovers of poetry, better things to do." Later the same year, Auden returned to Eliot's imaginative failings in a parenthetical remark on the difficulty of writing nature poetry: "A writer today may believe, if he is a Christian like T. S. Eliot or Graham Greene, that the temporal world is an analogue of the eternal . . . but it is very difficult for him to imagine what he believes, to portray, for instance a temporal relationship like marriage as anything but sordid and corrupting."*

Auden's theology was more social than solitary, and its social vision was more concerned with equality than with hierarchy. In 1950 he wrote a systematic theological statement in the form of a lecture for a conference at the Yale Divinity School which he later published in the learned Anglican journal *Theology* as "The Things Which Are Caesar's." It closed with these remarks on "the besetting temptations for the Christian layman in relation to the evils of the historical order":

> Laziness acknowledges the relation of the present to the past but ignores its relation to the future; impatience acknowledges its relation to the future but ignores its relation to the past; neither the lazy nor the impatient man, that is, accepts the present instant in its full reality and so cannot love his neighbour completely.
>
> In our age it is impatience, perhaps, which is the more characteristic temptation, partly because the historical situation is rather desperate, but mainly because for us the problem of faith is not of lapsing into a childish magical conception of God but of despair, of believing that God has abandoned us. "Trust in God and take short views", wrote Sydney Smith. In mid-Victorian England this may have had too Whiggish a ring to be sound advice, but as a motto for the laity in 1950 I cannot imagine a better one nor a more terrifying.

During these years Auden worked increasingly at the social tasks of literature: editing anthologies, judging competitions, introducing younger or forgotten writers. He continued to edit the Yale Series of Younger Poets, a job

---

* Auden was not the only actor in the Oedipal drama implied in his remarks on Eliot. Eliot's dustjacket blurbs for the Faber editions of Auden's books took away as much as they gave. In Eliot's letter to Auden on 3 February 1948, suggesting that Faber should now publish a volume of Auden's collected poems, he added: "Any season in which there was no new book of poems by you would be a good season for us." Auden's reply included a page on which he had pasted that sentence from Eliot's letter with the comment: "Oh Tom! What a *naughty* freudian error!"

he had begun in 1946. At first his work on the series had been desultory and not entirely successful. The series was intended partly to provide young poets with a starting point for a career, but the first poet whom Auden chose for the series had died some years earlier. His next two choices were poets whose work tended toward rhapsodic nonsense; conceivably he chose them out of a sense of obligation to find poets entirely unlike himself. (Both were associated with a San Francisco–based group of poets who called themselves Activists; the name referred to the nervous energy of their style and had no political significance.)

In 1949 the head of the Yale University Press hinted repeatedly that Auden might prefer to resign from the series, but Auden ignored the hints and became more assertive and confident in his editorship. Having accepted the least bad of the two or three manuscripts that survived the Press's preliminary screening in 1948, he now rejected all the manuscripts submitted in 1949. Starting in 1950, he chose poets who had learned much of their craft by reading and imitating Auden himself, but who proved to have enough individuality to diverge from his style in their later work. Auden's three earliest choices were largely forgotten; of his eight later choices, seven (one died young) went on to distinguished, productive careers. Auden's introductions to each book focused on the details of the young poet's work in the context of his own current concerns. In 1950 he prefaced Adrienne Cecile Rich's poems with reflections on revolutionary changes in literature. In 1951 his foreword to W. S. Merwin's poems considered the ways in which poems combine unique and recurring experiences. In 1952 he introduced Edgar Bogardus's poems with thoughts on whether the writing of poetry can be taught (a theme developed in detail a few years later in his fantasy of a "training school for poets"). In 1953 he prefaced Daniel G. Hoffman's poems with thoughts about nature and the machine. In 1955 (he again made no selection in 1954) he prefaced John Ashbery's poems with questions about the difficulty of translating a private mythology into publicly available verse.

In 1951 he began a dozen years of collaboration with Jacques Barzun and Lionel Trilling as editors of two subscription book clubs, first The Readers' Subscription, later The Mid-Century Book Society. The editors jointly chose the titles that would be offered to subscribers and divided among themselves the task of writing brief reviews of their selections for a monthly newsletter. After first refusing, Auden let himself be persuaded by Barzun, whose company he enjoyed and whose learning and enthusiasm he admired. With Trilling he was always cordial, but he seems to have been put off by Trilling's humorlessness, and he said privately that Trilling did not like literature. Auden's reviews for The Readers' Subscription newsletter *The Griffin* covered social and political subjects that other magazines might not have assigned to a poet, and gave him a chance to write about previously published books that continued to interest him. The Readers' Subscription was conceived and managed by a former student of Barzun and Trilling at Columbia, Gilman Kraft, who had already begun a predatory career in publishing and whose sharp practices led to the editors' joint angry resignation in 1959; Auden was clear-sighted enough to foresee the crisis when Barzun and Trilling refused to hear anything against someone who had studied at their feet.

In his early forties (he was born in 1907) Auden had the status of an elder statesman, invited to speak at solemn conferences and symposia. He seems to have shored up his courage at such events by adopting a style intended to dispel suspicions that poets were frivolous by nature. The lectures he wrote for *The Enchafèd Flood* in 1949 were compressed, allusive, and partly written in the philosophical shorthand of postwar secular existentialism. Auden had long since tried to avoid obscurity in his poems, but he was still pursuing it in his academic prose. During a visit to Mount Holyoke for a two-lecture series in 1950 he wrote to Kallman: "The first lecture was last night and the most severe I have ever given—a cross between Whitehead and Heidegger—but my Dickens-Firbank one will be gentler." All his later lectures were gentler than his severe one at Mount Holyoke, partly because he felt increasingly comfortable in his role of public sage while he taught himself to speak moral truths in a diffident, sometimes comic manner that achieved authority by refusing to claim it.

Auden's severe lecture at Mount Holyoke reused some of the densely philosophical *pensées* he had written in 1949 as reflections on poetry for a tribute to Saint-John Perse. Their layout and manner echoed those of Paul Valéry's notebooks (for which Auden wrote an introduction in 1955), which in turn echoed the *pensées* of Pascal. Because Auden's 1949 essay said nothing about Saint-John Perse, it was omitted from the tribute, but he expanded it into a new version, retaining the title "Nature, History and Poetry", and gave it to his friend Fr. William J. Lynch, the editor of *Thought*, a quarterly devoted largely to Roman Catholic theological studies, published by Fordham University, a Jesuit institution. The essay appeared in *Thought* in 1950, followed at two-year intervals by two further essays, "Notes on the Comic" and "Balaam and the Ass: The Master-Servant Relationship in Literature", each less severe than the last. A few traces of Auden's academic manner survived in "Notes on the Comic" but it was absent from "Balaam and the Ass", which included material from Auden's "gentler" lecture on Dickens and Firbank in 1950.

"Notes on the Comic" and "Balaam and the Ass" are serious manifestos against high seriousness. Each finds in low characters and comic situations expressions of the greatest moral truths. "Notes on the Comic", after considering inside-out umbrellas, sexual jokes, banality, Spoonerisms, puns, parody, flyting, satire, *Twelfth Night*, *Charley's Aunt*, and *Der Rosenkavalier*, ends with a section headed "Falstaff, or the Comic Presentation of the State of Grace". It concludes: "In his own way, Falstaff is, like Don Quixote, the Knight of the Doleful Countenance, the Suffering Servant who sacrifices his life for the sake of others." "Balaam and the Ass" pointedly ignores the economic and political relation of the master-servant relation in real life, and considers instead its literary expressions as instances of mutual love and voluntary commitment. The essay explores a dozen varieties of the master-servant relation from Shakespeare's plays, Mozart's operas, *Don Quixote*, and the inner relations among different aspects of a single person, illustrated by a brief comic dialogue about someone whose foot is stepped on in a train. The final section analyses the master-servant relations in *Around the World in Eighty Days* and P. G. Wodehouse's novels, ending with this comment on an exchange between Bertie Wooster and Jeeves: "So speaks comically—and in what other mode than the comic could it on earth truthfully speak?—the voice of Agapé, of Holy Love."

In 1939 Auden had renounced the politically engaged role that he had earlier both embraced and rejected—often in the same poem or essay—but his public reputation was still that of a politically minded radical writer rather than that of an ethically and religiously minded liberal one. When Auden wrote for left-leaning magazines in the 1940s and 1950s, he tended to provide a mild disruption of political orthodoxies. In 1950 the editors of *Partisan Review* worried in print over the new interest in religion that they observed among their intellectual contemporaries; Auden was one of about thirty writers who responded to the editors' invitation to comment, and his remarks focused on the editors' coarse misunderstanding of religion itself. A few months later, reviewing a biography of Oscar Wilde for *Partisan Review*, he dismissed the anarchist author's account of Wilde as a political thinker and social victim:

> Nothing is clearer in the history of the three trials than his unconscious desire that the truth should come out. This desire was not caused by guilt in the conventional sense but by the wish to be loved as he really was. One suspects that his secret day-dream was of a verdict of guilty being brought in whereupon Judge, Jury and public would rise to their feet, crown him with flowers and say: "We ought, of course, to send you to gaol, Mr Wilde, but we all love you so much that in this case we are delighted to make an exception."

The review ends by praising *The Importance of Being Earnest* in much the same terms Auden used when praising Falstaff and Jeeves as examples of holy love: "Wilde, like anyone who has been exposed to the culture of Christendom, knew, however unconsciously, that pleasure and happiness are distinct, and that happiness does not depend upon power but upon love". The subtitle of the review, "St Oscar, the Homintern Martyr", was meant to annoy Auden's acquaintances who thought of homosexuality in terms of its outcast social status rather than as a variety of love with the same kinds of temptations and rewards as any other. (The Homintern, an echo of the Comintern, was the term used among Auden's circle to refer to homosexual chauvinists.)

In the farther-left weekly pages of the *Nation*, around the same time, Auden praised Tocqueville as a "counter-revolutionary", one who defends the just causes of a revolution better than the revolutionaries themselves can do:

> De Tocqueville stands out as one of the noblest examples of an attitude which may be called the Counter-Revolution. This must not be confused with Reaction, which refuses to recognize the just element in the Revolution and wishes to regard it as a simple rebellion. The Counter-Revolutionary has no wish to return to the condition which preceded the outbreak of revolution; he wishes rather to save the revolution from failure through the inevitable over-emphasis and over-simplification of the revolutionary party.

This states in political terms the argument that Auden made elsewhere about revolutionaries and colonizers in the arts. Auden concluded his review of Tocqueville with a variation on the theme of nature and history:

> The central issue of the world revolution at present in progress is the right of every human body to the food, light, housing, medical attention, and so forth necessary for health. . . . The body knows nothing of freedom, only of necessities, and these are the same for all bodies. Hence the tendency of the revolutionary party in concentrating on this one goal to deny all liberty and all minority rights. In so far as we are bodies, we are or ought to be revolutionaries; in so far, however, as we are also souls and minds, we are or ought to be counter-revolutionaries . . .

Auden endorsed the counter-revolutionary position in a long essay on Sydney Smith (apparently an early version of his introduction to a selection from Smith that finally appeared in 1956) in which he defined Smith's politics in these terms:

> Sydney Smith is a perfect expression of the Whig mentality, of that English form of Liberalism which has always perplexed and sometimes enraged Continental observers both on the political Right and on the political Left. European liberalism, which has normally been anti-clerical, republican, and materialist, finds it bewildering that social reform in England should owe so much to religion—that the British Labour Party, for example, should be so closely associated with the Evangelical movement, and the increasing concern with juvenile delinquency and other cultural problems of urbanisation with Anglo-Catholicism . . .

In "The Things Which Are Caesar's" Auden had cited Sydney Smith's advice, "Trust in God and take short views", as a motto against impatience and laziness in relation to history. He made the same point in his essay on Smith in

terms of social justice: "Both his character which accepted the duty of the moment and then tried to get the most fun out of it, and his practical experience of the problems of the poor, made him an ideal person for attacking injustice."

One common form of laziness and impatience in twentieth-century liter-
ary culture was contempt for the bourgeois. Auden's defense of Smith's
Whiggism was one version of his defense of the bourgeois, as in a review of
Dostoyevsky's travel diaries:

> Poor Bourgeois! No other social class has ever caught it so hot in litera-
> ture. To begin with, nearly all writers have come from it . . . It is only nat-
> ural that writers should attack most violently the faults of which they have
> first-hand experience from childhood on. And then, to look at, the bour-
> geois is, it must be admitted, an unattractive object. He is a windbag, he
> worries about the future and what his neighbors are saying, he doesn't
> know how to wear clothes, he is either too fat or too thin. Even his virtues
> of industry and prudence are dull. . . .
>
> But when he is considered morally, the bourgeois has some questions
> to put to his critics. . . . If Dostoevsky could return to earth and visit such
> countries as England or the United states, he would not like us any bet-
> ter than before, but he would have to admit that it has been in precisely
> those countries where the bourgeoisie were strongest that they have
> been able to impose limitations and discipline themselves, while those
> countries with an aristocratic ruling class resisted all reform until it was
> too late. In a time of rapid historical change, the very vagueness and flu-
> idity of the bourgeois, his lack of a clearly defined notion of his class to
> which he must be loyal, is an advantage both practically and morally.

Auden refused partisan, ethnic, and ideological loyalties in the morals and
politics that he derived from his sense of historical uniqueness and the universality of the body. He knew that he had been helped toward his adult understanding of these matters by the bourgeois values that he had rebelled
against as an adolescent.

One step toward this mature understanding had been Auden's renunciation, during his first years in America, of the political loyalties that he had
ambivalently adopted in the 1930s. Soon after he arrived in New York he
began to praise Henry James as an heroic example of an artist who never wa-
vered in his service to his art, and whose elaborate style was the moral instrument through which James examined the finest details of nuance and
scruple. Then, around 1948, Auden learned from the newly published *Notebooks of Henry James* that this style was not the instrument with which James
had organized the subtleties of his fiction but the means by which he thought
and wrote about everything. James had not limited his aestheticism to his art,
where it belonged, but extended it into his life. As Auden told his secretary

and scholarly assistant Alan Ansen: "the *Notebooks* show that he was writing like that all the time. And I find that a very suspect attitude for an artist."

James now became one of Auden's illustrations of the ways in which writers can evade responsibilities by not noticing that they exist. He wrote in a review of Keats's letters:

> Dedicated artists are liable to suffer from two complaints, a humorless over-earnest attitude toward art, and a lack of ordinary social responsibility, a feeling that what they are doing is so important that it is the duty of others to support them. Reading Rilke's letters or the Journal of Henry James, for example, there are times when their tone of hushed reverence before the artistic mystery becomes insufferable and one would like to give them a good shaking; similarly, the incessant harping on money in the correspondence of Baudelaire or Wagner provokes in the most sympathetic admirer the reaction of a sound bourgeois—"Why doesn't he go and look for a job?"
>
> From both of these defects Keats is completely and refreshingly free. . . .

In 1946, in an introduction to a reprint of James's *The American Scene,* Auden had written at length about the differences between American and European writers. He resumed this theme in 1949 when the Jewish immigrant writer Anzia Yezierska pestered him into writing an introduction to her memoir *Red Ribbon on a White Horse.* Yezierska's career had included a sudden rise to fame, a disastrous summons to Hollywood, and an episode when she perhaps had been John Dewey's lover; she now hoped Auden would write a lyrical celebration of her genius, and was loudly horrified to read his sober analysis of the temptations faced by writers and immigrants in America. (Auden placated her by agreeing to wholesale cuts, which are restored in this edition.)

In later essays he used Oliver Twist and Huckleberry Finn as exemplars of the moral and emotional differences between Europeans and Americans. Europeans, he wrote, believe in some form of unchanging natural law that can be codified and explained by professionals, whereas Americans find it hard "to believe that there is anything in human nature that will not change" and so refuse to grant authority to any professional clerisy. Huckleberry Finn's decision to take Jim into safety "is a pure act of moral improvisation", based on no general law and providing him with no template for future actions; Americans tend never to rely on general principles in art or morals. Auden had noted in his introduction to *The American Scene* that American writers tended to be utterly unlike each other in ways that the writers of any European country were not; now he understood this variety in terms of America's moral improvisation, its refusal of precedent and professionalism.

In 1953 T. S. Eliot commissioned Auden to compile a *Faber Book of Modern*

American Verse. "What a way to make enemies", Auden wrote in a letter to Norman Holmes Pearson, although his choices seem to have been evenhanded enough to satisfy everyone except Laura Riding, who for years had refused permission to reprint anything she had written. Auden's selection of eighty-one poets began with Edwin Arlington Robinson and Edgar Lee Masters (both born in 1869) and ended with Robert Horan (one of his early selections for the Yale Series of Younger Poets) and Anthony Hecht, both born in 1922; Auden excluded anyone younger than thirty at the time he began compiling the book. The poetic styles represented in the book ranged from the formal elegance of Yvor Winters through the comic doggerel of Ogden Nash to the laconic rhapsodies of Robert Duncan; the only noteworthy style that was absent was the unreadable sub-Poundian avant-garde that emerged in the 1920s. Auden gave nine or more pages to Robert Frost, Vachel Lindsay, Wallace Stevens, William Carlos Williams, Ezra Pound, Marianne Moore, and Allen Tate; his generosity to Stevens, Pound, and Tate was perhaps more diplomatic than committed, but he genuinely admired the others.

His introduction praised American poetry for its openness and curiosity (qualities exemplified by his own selection) despite individual poets' tendency toward a narrowness of tone:

> There is much in Tennyson that Longfellow would never have dared to write, for the peculiar American mixture of Puritan conscience and democratic licence can foster in some cases a genteel horror of the coarse for which no Englishman has felt the need. On the other hand Longfellow had a curiosity about the whole of European literature compared with which Tennyson, concerned only with the poetry of his own land and the classical authors on whom he was educated, seems provincial.

After *The Enchafèd Flood* Auden wrote lengthy essays and series of connected essays, but he did not publish another separate book of prose until *The Dyer's Hand* in 1962. Much of that book was made up of material from Auden's lectures during his five-year term as Professor of Poetry at Oxford that began in 1956; much of the rest was rewritten from essays, lectures, and *pensées* written in the late 1940s and early 1950s, not all of which had been published at the time. Auden had been planning for some years to put together a book based on this material. An editorial note in the Fordham University quarterly *Thought* reported in 1952 that Auden was working on "a commentary on many things called *Thinks*". Perhaps around 1954 he wrote out a list of nine titles of essays that might be included in such a book, some already published, some delivered as lectures, some perhaps never written. The first item was "Hic et Ille", a title that did not appear in print until 1956, but which was probably his original title for a set of notes and aphorisms published only in a French translation in 1952 under the title "De Droite et de Gauche". Other items on the list matched more or less closely the titles of published works: "Nature, History and Poetry", "Notes on the Comic", and "Notes on Opera". Others corresponded to lectures that Auden gave on his annual speaking tours starting in 1950: "Dingley Dell and the Fleet" and "The Hero" (titled in the lecture hall "The Hero in Modern Poetry"). Two others, "Pothooks and Hangers" and "The Word and the Tribe", seem to have used (or were intended to use) extracts and notes from his reviews and *pensées* ("pothooks and hangers" refers to the ill-formed letters of a scrawled handwriting; Eliot had paraphrased Mallarmé on the "language of the tribe").

Another title on the list was "The Dyer's Hand" (a phrase from Shakespeare's sonnet 111). Auden used this title for a series of three broadcast lectures in 1955 that brought together many recurring themes from the past half-dozen years. The first of these lectures modified his earlier contrast of nature and history by juxtaposing two ideal, imaginary figures, the Poet and the Historian, who exist in uneasy tension in almost all real poets of the past nineteen hundred years. The contrast between them summarizes the moral and literary dilemmas that Auden had been exploring throughout his recent work.

The Poet, he explained, is that aspect of every real poet which celebrates power, beauty, cleverness, wisdom, and all other gifts of fate. He is interested in visible deeds, not invisible choices, because the characters in his poems can never be anything other than what they are. He charms his audience into forgetting themselves in their fascination with the timeless, imaginary world evoked by his poems. He is fascinated by the magical properties of numbers. The Historian, in contrast, is interested in the way in which his characters become themselves when they could have become something else; he does not distinguish between the gifted and the ungifted but between "those who are faithful to the True Voice, however difficult its commands or promises, and so become what they ought to become; and those who, through indifference or through believing the Lying Voices, which may be more plausible than the True, are unfaithful and fail to fulfil their proper destiny." His audience believes his stories not because they become unaware of anything else but "because they recognise in what they hear something which they know to be true about themselves." The Historian is indifferent to all numbers except One, the only number that to him is real.

These imaginary figures collaborated in the making of almost all of Auden's poems, but one or the other took charge of each individual poem. The Poet seems to have written "Precious Five", which ends by acknowledging "that singular command / I do not understand / *Bless what there is for being*"; in the same year, 1950, the Historian seems to have written "The Chimeras", which ends in a different kind of acknowledgement about the historical failure of those who voluntarily shed their personal selves: "It is good that they are but not that they are thus." In his essays and lectures throughout the 1950s Auden tended to adopt the voice of either the Poet or the Historian, the first when he wanted to emphasize art's indifference to politics and morals, the second when he wanted to emphasize art's ability to clarify moral dilemmas without pretending to solve them.

Auden gathered the shorter poems he had written from 1951 through 1954 in *The Shield of Achilles*, which appeared in 1955. The book opens with the sequence of seven "Bucolics"; then a group of shorter poems, many of them variations on the theme of personal speech and its relation to impersonal performance and personal choice; then the full sequence of "Horae Canonicae" including the two poems already printed in *Nones*. Almost all the poems Auden wrote in 1955 were meditations on history: "Makers of History", "The Old Man's Road", "The Epigoni", and "Homage to Clio". The last of these (which gave its name to Auden's next collection of poems, published in 1960), was a lightly disguised hymn to the Virgin as the source and defender of historical uniqueness, and the poem deliberately combined Protestant and Roman Catholic theology.

Auden's published prose expressed personal commitments and alluded to personal feelings, but was seldom autobiographical in any explicit way. Auden was especially reticent in his prose in the 1940s, although at times he hid personal secrets where an attentive and sympathetic reader might find them. In 1948, for example, he wrote a poem titled "A Household" (first published in *Nones* in 1951), about a successful businessman and his harridan mother and crybaby son, with no hint of any deeper meaning. Perhaps a few months later, he began his *New Yorker* review of Eliot's *Notes towards the Definition of Culture* with the conceit that "Like most important writers, Mr T. S. Eliot is not a single figure but a household". That household, he continued, had three permanent residents: the archdeacon, a violent passionate grandmother, and a boy who plays practical jokes. Without this oblique clue that the real subject of Auden's "A Household" was another, unnamed poet, similarly imagined as a household of three persons from three generations, the poem's autobiographical code could never have been deciphered.

Then, in the early 1950s, Auden began writing about his past in a less indirect way, but also in a way that treated his experiences as generic to his class rather than unique to himself. A review-essay in 1952, "Our Italy," begins with reminiscences of his contemporaries' attitudes toward different European cultures. Three years later, his review of Leslie Fiedler's *An End to Innocence*, "Authority in America", explored the motives and nuances of his and his friends' politics in the 1930s.

In 1955 Auden wrote his first extended autobiographical prose since 1940 as a contribution to *Modern Canterbury Pilgrims*, a book of twenty-three essays by converts to the Anglican Communion. It opened by stating the connection between Christianity and individual history: "The Christian doctrine of a personal God implies that the relation of every human being to Him is unique and historical, so that any individual who discusses the Faith is compelled to begin with autobiography." The essay weaves together a personal interpretation of Christian doctrines and a history of Auden's changing attitudes toward them. After losing his childhood faith based on magical rituals, he went through a period of indifference, until, in his thirties, he discovered an adult faith that combined Protestant doctrines of man as "a spirit, a conscious person endowed with free will," who has "a unique 'existential' relation to God" and Catholic doctrines that "stress the physical reality of the flesh into which the Word was made." The closing paragraph sidesteps the problem of choosing between these two sets of doctrines: "Into the question of why I should have returned to Canterbury instead of proceeding to Rome, I have no wish to go in print. The scandal of Christian disunity is too serious." The unwritten answer to this question seems to have had something to do with his understanding of Anglicanism as a unique combination of Catholicism and Protestantism, his memory of the Anglo-Catholicism of his childhood, and his continuing sense that the most dangerous temptations of his age were the temptations to accept authority.

Around the same time, Auden wrote a seriously comic counterpart to this essay in the form of a questionnaire—to which he supplied his own answers—on the nature of one's private image of Eden; he published it in the magazine of the prep school he had attended in his teens. The title of the questionnaire was a fragment from the *Purgatorio: "Qui è l'uom' felice"* ("here man is happy"); its double subtitle was "Everyman in His Eden: A Psychological Parlour-Game for a Wet Sunday Afternoon". The questionnaire asked, "In your Eden what is its . . .", followed by a list of twenty-six items, including landscape, climate, methods of lighting and heating, forms of public entertainment, and much else. Auden's answers resembled the account he gave of his private Eden in "Vespers"; to his final question, "Any feature, important to you, not covered by your answers to the preceding questions", his answer was "*Censored.*"

In August 1955, not long after writing these two pieces, he received a letter from Enid Starkie, whose biography of Rimbaud he had reviewed in 1939 but whom he seems never to have met, asking whether he would agree to be nominated for the chair of Professor of Poetry at Oxford, the only professorship chosen by an election in which all Oxford M.A.'s were eligible to vote. The winner would be obliged to give three lectures during each of the five years of his term. Auden at first refused. His American citizenship, he said, would prevent his election either on statutory or political grounds; and he could not afford to give up his winters writing for money in New York in order to be in Oxford during all three academic terms. Starkie persisted, and in November Auden finally agreed to be nominated for the election scheduled for February 1956, which he won by a small margin. His mixed feelings about his victory, and about his inaugural lecture scheduled for June 1956, prompted him to find new ways of speaking to an audience, and new ways of both hiding and revealing.

REFERENCES

Page xiii

> *The winter months*   Letter to Enid Starkie, 5 August 1955 (St Anne's College, Oxford; quoted in Joanna Richardson, *Enid Starkie* [1973], p. 196)

Page xx

> *Begin by banning*   Letter to Bennett Cerf, 29 January 1946 (Columbia University Library)

Page xxi

> *Lacking in seriousness*   *Prose II*, p. 174

Page xxix

> *the* Notebooks *show*   Alan Ansen, *The Table Talk of W. H. Auden* (1990), p. 95 (entry for 31 January 1948)

THE TEXT OF THIS EDITION

THIS volume includes all the prose that Auden wrote for publication from 1949 through 1955, including one essay, "L'Homme d'Esprit," that did not appear in print until many years later, and two essays written for, but not published by, the *New Yorker*: "A That There Sort of Writer" and "Bile and Brotherhood".

A few essays that first appeared in print during the years covered by this volume were written earlier and may be found in earlier volumes of this edition. These include, among others, "The Ironic Hero", "Yeats as an Example", "Opera Addict", the introduction to *Tales of Grimm and Andersen*, and the foreword to *The Grasshopper's Man*, by Rosalie Moore, all of which may be found in *Prose II*. The essay "Alexander Pope", reprinted in *Essays in Criticism*, July 1951, was first published in 1937 and may be found in *Prose I*.

Two ephemeral pieces about the opera *The Rake's Progress* are omitted from the present volume but may be found in the volume titled *Libretti* in this complete edition; the two pieces are "Com'è Nato il Libretto dell'Opera 'The Rake's Progress'" (written for the festival magazine of the Biennale di Venezia, where the opera had its première in 1951) and "The Met at Work: Writing a Libretto" (a program note written for the American première in 1953).

Some of Auden's prose pieces were originally printed exactly as he wrote them; others were cut and reshaped by editors; and it is often impossible to say how closely a printed text represents what Auden wrote. In the few instances where a manuscript exists, and where the printed version closely resembles it, the text in this edition has been newly edited from the manuscript. In all other cases, the printed text has been reprinted with a minimum of regularization. With the exception of two footnotes that indicate that the text in this edition has been retranslated from French translations of lost originals, all footnotes and square brackets in the main text (but not those in the titles, appendices, or notes) are Auden's own. Auden's manuscripts generally indicate footnotes with asterisks, and these have been used in place of the numbers added by some publishers and editors.

Many of the reviews and some of the essays in this volume were almost certainly given their titles by the editors of the magazines and books in which they appeared. Reviews that originally appeared without a title have been supplied with titles in the form "A Review of . . .". Subtitles and breaks that were obviously inserted by newspaper and magazine subeditors in order to break up long columns of type have been omitted; such subtitles and breaks appeared in almost all of Auden's work that first appeared in newspapers or in *Encounter* and some other magazines.

At the head of each book review is a listing in a consistent format of the title, author, publisher, and price of the book reviewed. The format of these headings in the original publications varied according to the style sheets of the magazines and newspapers in which the reviews appeared; some magazines used footnotes instead of headings. Auden's errors (or those of his editors) in transcribing the author or title of the books reviewed have been retained in the text and in the subheading that lists the title, publisher, and price of the book. The correct versions are given in the notes and in any titles supplied for this edition in the form "A Review of . . .".

The essays and reviews are arranged as closely as possible in chronological order of composition. In most cases, however, no direct evidence of the date of composition survives, and chronological order of publication has been used instead. The original date and place of publication is printed at the end of each work, together with the date of composition when this is known to have been much earlier than the publication date. The dates in the running heads are dates of composition, if known.

Auden almost invariably made minor errors when copying extracts from other authors. The text in this volume corrects the obvious misspellings that the original editors could reasonably be expected to have caught, but in all other instances I have preferred to print the text that Auden wrote instead of the text that he perhaps ought to have written. The text that Auden wrote includes the words that he thought he found on the page from which he was copying, which was not always the text that was in fact printed there. I have, however, corrected errors that are clearly the work of a typist or compositor working from Auden's hand. The textual notes indicate all significant deviations from the originals.

Auden subdivided many of his essays by using headings and outline levels. The indents and spacing in this edition have been very slightly regularized. In some instances, the punctuation of outline numbers has been changed from a style evidently introduced by a publisher to a style that more closely represents the typical punctuation in Auden's prose manuscripts. Auden generally circled the numbers and letters of his outline headings; these circles are represented here by pairs of parentheses, thus: (1). Where a surviving typescript has only a closing parenthesis after a number in a heading, an opening parenthesis has been added.

Some of the daily newspapers and weekly magazines to which Auden contributed were edited hurriedly, and I have in rare instances silently supplied a comma where the original has an incomplete pair of commas around a subordinate clause, and have made other similarly trivial corrections. Auden's erroneous "*acte gratuite*" has been altered to "*acte gratuit*". In some of his manuscripts Auden inconsistently used double quotation marks to set off quoted extracts and single quotation marks to set off concepts and abstractions; every competent editor normalized the inconsistency by using the same style of quotation marks for both extracts and concepts. I have normalized the rare instances where Auden's practice slipped through to the printed text, but have indicated these instances in the notes. Substantial emendations are listed in the textual notes.

The textual notes also explain some references that would have been familiar to Auden's contemporaries but are now obscure, and provide brief accounts of the magazines to which Auden contributed; more detail is provided for lesser-known publications than for familiar ones, and little or no description is provided for magazines described in notes to earlier volumes.

THE ENCHAFÈD FLOOD

The Enchafèd Flood

or

The Romantic Iconography of the Sea

———————————

[*1949*]

FOR

ALAN ANSEN

Étude de la grande maladie de l'horreur du domicile.
BAUDELAIRE, *Mon Coeur Mis à Nu.*

ACKNOWLEDGMENT

I wish to express my thanks to the University of Virginia and the trustees of the Page-Barbour Lecture Foundation under whose auspices the contents of this book were given in lecture form during March, 1949.

Thanks are also due to the following for the use of their translations in quotation: Kathleen Freeman (*Pre-Socratic Philosophers*), Margaret Williams (*The Wanderer and the Sea-Farer*), Alexander Dru and Walter Lowrie (Kierkegaard), Christopher Isherwood (Baudelaire's *Journals*), Helen Zimmern (Nietzsche), Helen Rootham, Norman Cameron and Delmore Schwartz (Rimbaud), Edwin Muir (Kafka).

W. H. A.

CONTENTS

ONE

The Sea and the Desert

ADAMA: O Adam, when blew God that bitter breath
On Earth's Plain; blew He likewise on sea-deep?
ADAM: I wiss not. Like to cragged desolate waste,
We lately passed, is sea-steep's haggard face.

— C. M. Doughty, *Adam Cast Forth*

Revolutionary changes in sensibility or style are rare. The most famous is, perhaps, the conception of "*amor*" which appeared in Europe in the twelfth century. The disappearance, during the sixteenth, of allegory as a common literary genre is another. The complex of attitudes and styles which emerges towards the end of the eighteenth century and is called, more conveniently than accurately, Romanticism is a third.

These chapters are an attempt to understand the nature of Romanticism through an examination of its treatment of a single theme, the sea.

★   ★   ★

Near the beginning of the fifth book of *The Prelude*, Wordsworth describes in some detail a dream. It is, perhaps, an indication that, to him, this dream was of particular importance, that the 1805 and the 1850 versions differ. In the first it is assigned to a friend, in the second to Wordsworth himself. This is the 1805 text.

> . . . once upon a summer's noon,
> While he was sitting in a rocky cave
> By the sea-side, perusing, as it chanced,
> The famous History of the Errant Knight
> Recorded by Cervantes, these same thoughts
> Came to him; and to height unusual rose
> While listlessly he sate, and having closed
> The Book, had turned his eyes towards the Sea.
> On Poetry and geometric Truth,
> The knowledge that endures, upon these two,
> And their high privilege of lasting life,
> Exempt from all internal injury,
> He mused: upon these chiefly: and at length,
> His senses yielding to the sultry air,
> Sleep seiz'd him, and he pass'd into a dream.
> He saw before him an Arabian Waste,
> A Desert; and he fancied that himself
> Was sitting there in the wide wilderness,

Alone, upon the sands. Distress of mind
Was growing in him, when, behold! At once
To his great joy a Man was at his side,
Upon a dromedary, mounted high.
He seem'd an Arab of the Bedouin Tribes,
A Lance he bore, and underneath one arm
A Stone; and, in the opposite hand, a Shell
Of a surpassing brightness. Much rejoic'd
The dreaming Man that he should have a Guide
To lead him through the Desart; and he thought,
While questioning himself what this strange freight
Which the Newcomer carried through the Waste
Could mean, the Arab told him that the Stone,
To give it in the language of the Dream,
Was Euclid's Elements; "and this," said he,
"This other," pointing to the Shell, "this Book
Is something of more worth." And, at the word,
The Stranger, said my Friend continuing,
Stretch'd forth the Shell towards me, with command
That I should hold it to my ear; I did so,
And heard that instant in an unknown Tongue,
Which yet I understood, articulate sounds,
A loud prophetic blast of harmony,
An Ode, in passion utter'd, which foretold
Destruction to the Children of the Earth,
By deluge now at hand. No sooner ceas'd
The Song, but with calm look, the Arab said
That all was true; that it was even so
As had been spoken; and that he himself
Was going then to bury those two Books:
The one that held acquaintance with the stars,
And wedded man to man by purest bond
Of nature, undisturbed by space or time;
Th' other that was a God, yea many Gods,
Had voices more than all the winds, and was
A joy, a consolation, and a hope.
My friend continued, "strange as it may seem,
I wonder'd not, although I plainly saw
The one to be a Stone, th' other a Shell,
Nor doubted once but that they both were Books,
Having a perfect faith in all that pass'd
A wish was now ingender'd in my fear
To cleave until this Man, and I begg'd leave

To share his errand with him. On he pass'd
Not heeding me; I follow'd, and took note
That he look'd often backward with wild look,
Grasping his twofold treasure to his side.
—Upon a Dromedary, Lance in rest,
He rode, I keeping pace with him, and now
I fancied that he was the very Knight
Whose Tale Cervantes tells, yet not the Knight,
But was an Arab of the Desert, too;
Of these was neither, and was both at once.
His countenance, meanwhile, grew more disturb'd.
And looking backwards when he look'd, I saw
A glittering light, and ask'd him whence it came.
"It is," said he, "the waters of the deep
Gathering upon us," quickening then his pace
He left me: I call'd after him aloud;
He heeded not; but with his twofold charge
Beneath his arm, before me full in view
I saw him riding o'er the Desert Sands,
With the fleet waters of the drowning world
In chase of him, whereat I wak'd in terror,
And saw the Sea before me; and the Book,
In which I had been reading, at my side.

(Book V. 56–139)

Here are three pairs of symbols:

(1) The desert and the sea.
(2) The stone of abstract geometry, and the shell of imagination or instinct, which between them offer alternative routes of salvation from the anxiety of the dreamer, a promise which is not realised.
(3) The double-natured hero, half Bedouin, i.e. Ishmael, the exile, the Wandering Jew, the Flying Dutchman, and half Don Quixote, i.e. the dedicated man, the Knight of Faith who would restore the Age of Gold.

THE SEA

The second verse of the first chapter of the Book of Genesis runs as follows:

And the earth was without form, and void; and darkness was upon the face of the deep. And the Spirit of God moved upon the face of the waters.

On the first day God said, Let there be light, on the second He

made the firmament, and divided the waters which were under the firmament from the waters which were above the firmament.

And on the third He gathered the waters under the heaven

unto one place, and let the dry land appear; and the gathering together
of the waters called he Seas.

Similarly in one of the Greek cosmologies, the beginning of everything was
when Eros issued from the egg of Night which floated upon Chaos.

The sea or the great waters, that is, are the symbol for the primordial undif-
ferentiated flux, the substance which became created nature only by having
form imposed upon or wedded to it.

The sea, in fact, is that state of barbaric vagueness and disorder out of
which civilisation has emerged and into which, unless saved by the effort of
gods and men, it is always liable to relapse. It is so little of a friendly symbol
that the first thing which the author of the Book of Revelation notices in his
vision of the new heaven and earth at the end of time is that "*there was no more
sea.*"

In consequence, though the metaphor of the ship of state or society appears early, it is only employed when society is in peril. The ship ought not
to be out of harbor. Thus Horace writes

> *O navis, referent in mare te novi*
> *fluctus. O quid agis! Forliter occupa*
> *portum.*

O ship, new billows are carrying you out to sea. What are you doing?
Struggle to reach port.

(Odes I.14)

The ship, then, is only used as a metaphor for society in danger from within
or without. When society is normal the image is the City or the Garden. That
is where people want and ought to be. As to the sea, the classical authors
would have agreed with Marianne Moore. "It is human nature to stand in the
middle of a thing; But you cannot stand in the middle of this." A voyage,
therefore, is a necessary evil, a crossing of that which separates or estranges.
Neither Odysseus nor Jason goes to sea for the sake of the voyage; the former
is trying to get home and, if it were not for the enmity of Poseidon, the father of the monster Cyclops, it would be soon over, which is what Odysseus
most desires; the latter is trying to capture the Golden Fleece, which is in a
distant country, to bring back to his own. If it were nearer and no voyage were
necessary, he would be much relieved.*

---

* The Christian conception of time as a divine creation, to be accepted, and not, as in Platonic
and Stoic philosophy, ignored, made the journey or pilgrimage a natural symbol for the spiritual
life. Similarly the injunction "Whosoever will come after me, let him deny himself, and take up
his cross, and follow me" and the distinction between the Kingdom of Heaven and the Kingdom
of this world contradicts the classical hope of the perfect *polis*. But, so far as I know, the pilgrimage of the pious soul is never symbolised in early Christian literature by a sea-voyage.

The state ship that deliberately chooses the high seas is the state in disorder, the Ship of Fools, as in Barclay's adaptation of Brant's *Narrenschiff*:

> Lyke as a myrrour doth represent agayne
> The fourme and figure of mannes countenaunce
> So in our ship shall he se wrytyn playne
> The fourme and figure of hys mysgovernaunce.

What ship is that with so many owners and strange tackle? It is a great vessel. This is the ship of Fools where saileth both spiritual and temporal of every calling some. This ship wanteth a good pilot, the storm, the rocks and the wrecks at hand; all must come to naught for want of good government.*

Similarly in the Anglo-Saxon poems, *The Wanderer* and *The Seafarer*, the mariner is to be pitied rather than admired, for he

>   heart weary
> Over ocean streams   must for long
> Stir with hands   frost-cold sea
> Rove paths of exile.

>   No protecting kinsman
> Can bring comfort to the soul in loneliness.
> Full little he thinks who has life's joy
> And dwells in cities and has few disasters,
> Proud and wine-flushed, how I, weary often,
> Must hide my time on the brimming stream.

The sea is no place to be if you can help it, and to try to cross it betrays a rashness bordering on hubris, at which a man's friends should be properly concerned.

> *Nequicquam dues abscidit*
> *prudens Oceano dissociabili*

---

* This looks so similar to the behaviour of the Jumblies, but how differently the reader is expected to feel towards the latter.

> They went to sea in a sieve, they did.
>   In a sieve they went to sea:
> In spite of all their friends could say
> On a winter's morn, on a stormy day
>   In a sieve they went to sea!
> And when the sieve turned round and round
> And everyone cried, "You'll all be drowned!"
> They called aloud, "Our sieve ain't big,
> But we don't care a button! We don't care a fig!
>   In a sieve we'll go to sea."

> *terras si tamen impiae*
> *non tangenda rates transiliunt vada.*

Vain was the purpose of the god in severing the lands by the estranging sea, if in spite of him our impious ships dash across the depths he meant should never be touched.

(Horace, Odes I.3)

There is a famous passage in the 26th canto of Dante's *Inferno* which is interesting not only for its beauty, but because the legend of Ulysses' last voyage appears to be Dante's own invention.

Ulysses is in Hell for having been an Evil Counsellor. Dante begins rather mysteriously

> I sorrowed then, and sorrow now again when I direct my memory to what I saw; and curb my genius more than I am wont lest it run where Virtue guides it not.

Ulysses in describing his end says: "Neither fondness for my son nor reverence for my aged father, nor the due love that should have cheered Penelope could conquer in me the ardor that I had to gain experience of the world, of human vice and worth." To his fellow-mariners he had argued: "Consider your origin: ye were not formed to live like brutes but to follow virtue and knowledge."

Ulysses behaves like the typical Romantic Marine Hero, which in Tennyson's version of the same story he, indeed, becomes, but to Dante, clearly, his action was not only reprehensible but, as the last sentence shows, essentially the original sin of Adam, and in his speech to his fellows, he is once more, as earlier at Troy, the Evil Counsellor whose words echo the words of the Serpent to Eve. Perhaps, too, Dante's opening remarks indicate that the same temptation to the concupiscence of curiosity was his own.

The handling of the symbols of sea and storm by Shakespeare provides us with a bridge between what, for convenience, one may call the classic attitude and the romantic. The subject has been so exhaustively and sensitively studied by Mr Wilson Knight in *The Shakesperian Tempest** as to make much further comment superfluous. As Wilson Knight demonstrates, in most of Shakespeare's plays there are two antithetical symbolic clusters. On the one hand tempests, rough beasts, comets, diseases, malice domestic and private vice, that is, the world of conflict and disorder; on the other hand music, flowers, birds, precious stones and marriage, the world of reconciliation and order. In the earlier plays the stormy sea is more purely negative, a reflection of human conflict or the fatal mischance which provides evil with its opportunity (e.g. *Othello*). In the last plays, *Pericles, The Winter's Tale, The Tempest,*

* Oxford, 1932.

however, not only do the sea and the sea voyage play a much more important role, but also a different one. The sea becomes the place of purgatorial suffering: through separation and apparent loss, the characters disordered by passion are brought to their senses and the world of music and marriage is made possible. There is, however, one extremely important difference in the relation of the actors to the sea from that which our period exhibits, namely, that the putting to sea, the wandering is never *voluntarily* entered upon as a pleasure. It is a pain which must be accepted as cure, the death that leads to rebirth, in order that the abiding city may be built. Deliberately to seek the exile is still folly. Thus, in *The Winter's Tale* the good old counsellor Camillo advises the young lovers Florizel and Perdita to enlist the help of Leontes rather than to elope.

> A course more promising
> Than a wild dedication of yourselves
> To unpath'd waters, undream'd shores, most certain
> To miseries enough: no hope to help you,
> But as you shake off one to take another;
> Nothing so certain as your anchors, who
> Do their best office, if they can but stay you
> Where you'll be loath to be.
>
> (*The Winter's Tale*, IV.4)

The distinctive new notes in the Romantic attitude are as follows.

(1) To leave the land and the city is the desire of every man of sensibility and honor.

(2) The sea is the real situation and the voyage is the true condition of man.

> The port we sail from is far astern and, though far out of sight of land, for ages and ages we continue to sail with sealed orders and our last destination remains a secret to ourselves and our officers. And yet our final haven was predestined ere we stepped from the stocks of creation. Let us not give ear to the superstitious gun-deck gossip about whither we may be gliding for, as yet, not a soul on board of us knows—not even the commodore himself—assuredly not the chaplain—even our professors' scientific surmisings are vain. On that point, the smallest cabin boy is as wise as the captain.
>
> (*White Jacket*)

(3) The sea is where the decisive events, the moments of eternal choice, of temptation, fall, and redemption occur. The shore life is always trivial.

(4) An abiding destination is unknown even if it may exist: a lasting relationship is not possible nor even to be desired.

> *Les vrais voyageurs sont ceux-là seuls qui partent*
> *Pour partir; coeurs légers, semblables aux ballons,*
> *De leur fatalité jamais ils ne s'écartent,*
> *Et, sans savoir pourquoi, disent toujours: Allons!*
>
> (Baudelaire, *Le Voyage*)

THE DESERT

Like the sea, the desert is the nucleus of a cluster of traditional associations.

(1) It is the place where the water of life is lacking, the valley of dry bones in Ezekiel's vision.

(2) It may be so by nature, i.e. the wilderness which lies *outside* the fertile place or city. As such, it is the place where nobody desires by nature to be. Either one is compelled by others to go there because one is a criminal outlaw or a scapegoat (e.g. Cain, Ishmael), or one chooses to withdraw from the city in order to be alone. This withdrawal may be temporary, a period of self-examination and purification in order to return to the city with a true knowledge of one's mission and the strength to carry it out (e.g. Jesus' forty days in the wilderness), or it may be permanent, a final rejection of the wicked city of this world, a dying to the life of the flesh and an assumption of a life devoted wholly to spiritual contemplation and prayer (e.g. the Thebaid).

(3) The natural desert is therefore at once the place of punishment for those rejected by the good city because they are evil, and the place of purgation for those who reject the evil city because they desire to become good. In the first case the desert image is primarily related to the idea of justice, i.e. the home of the dragon or any lawless power which is hostile to the city and so be the place out into which the hero must venture in order to deliver the city from danger. An elaboration of this is the myth of the treasure in the desert guarded by the dragon. This treasure belongs by right to the city and has either been stolen by force or lost through the city's own sin. The hero then performs a double task. He delivers the city from danger and restores the precious life-giving object to its rightful owners.

In the second case, when the desert is the purgative place, the image is primarily associated with the idea of chastity and humility. It is the place where there are no beautiful bodies or comfortable beds or stimulating food and drink or admiration. The temptations of the desert are therefore either sexual mirages raised by the devil to make the hermit nostalgic for his old life or the more subtle temptations of pride when the devil appears in his own form.

(4) The natural wilderness may lie not only outside the city but also *be-*

tween one city and another, i.e. be the place to be crossed, in which case the image is associated with the idea of vocation. Only the individual or community with the faith and courage which can dare, endure, and survive its trials is worthy to enter into the promised land of the New Life.

(5) Lastly, the desert may not be barren by nature but as the consequence of a historical catastrophe. The once-fertile city has become, through the malevolence of others or its own sin, the waste land. In this case it is the opportunity for the stranger hero who comes from elsewhere to discover the cause of the disaster, destroy or heal it and become the rebuilder of the city and, in most cases, its new ruler.

The Romantic Sea and the Romantic Desert

Resemblances

(1) Both are the wilderness, i.e. the place where there is no community, just or unjust, and no historical change for better or for worse.

(2) Therefore the individual in either is free from both the evils and the responsibilities of communal life. Thus Byron writes of the ocean:

> Man marks the earth with ruin—his control
> Stops with the shore.
>
> (*Childe Harold*)

And Captain Nemo, the commander of the submarine *Nautilus* in *Twenty Thousand Leagues under the Sea*, cries:

> The sea does not belong to despots. Upon its surface men can still exercise unjust laws, fight, tear one another to pieces, and be carried away with terrestrial horrors. But at thirty feet below its level, their reign ceases, their influence is quenched, and their power disappears. Ah, sir; live, live in the bosom of the waters. There only is independence. There I recognize no master's voice. There I am free.

And so Carmen tempts Don José to leave the fertile plain for the barren lawless mountains.

> Tu n'y dépendrais de personne.
> Point d'officier à qui tu doives obéir
> Et point de retraite qui sonne
> Pour dire à l'amoureux qu'il est temps de partir.
>
> Le ciel ouvert
> La vie errante
> Pour pays l'univers

Et pour loi ta volonté
Et surtout la chose enivrante
La liberté.

(Meilhac and Halévy, *Carmen*)

Both, in fact, are characterised by the absence of limitations, of "*les arrêts de la vie,*" the Ocean-chart that the Bellman bought describes them well.

"What's the good of Mercator's North Poles and Equators,
    Tropics, Zones, and Meridian Lines?"
So the Bellman would cry: and the crew would reply
    "They are merely conventional signs!

"Other maps are such shapes, with their islands and capes!
    But we've got our brave Captain to thank"
(So the crew would protest) "that he's bought *us* the best—
    A perfect and absolute blank!"

(3) But precisely because they are free places, they are also lonely places of alienation, and the individual who finds himself there, whether by choice or fate, must from time to time, rightly or wrongly, be visited by desperate longings for home and company. So Ishmael, however he may convince himself that "in landlessness alone resides highest truth, shoreless, indefinite as God—so better is it to perish in that lonely infinite than be ingloriously dashed upon the lea, even if that were safety," nevertheless, as he squeezes out the whale sperm with his hands, he is compelled to reflect that "Happiness is not in the intellect or the fancy—but in the wife, the heart, the bed, the table, the saddle, the fireside, the country." So Ahab, on that final beautiful day before his encounter with Moby Dick, softens and calls despairingly to Starbuck: "Stand close to me, Starbuck; let me look into a human eye; it is better than to gaze into sea or sky; better than to gaze upon God. By the green land; by the bright hearthstone! this is the magic glass, man; I see my wife and my child in thine eye. . . . It is a mild, mild wind, and a mild-looking meadow; they have been making hay somewhere under the slopes of the Andes, Starbuck, and the mowers are sleeping among the new-mown hay." Even that most passionate Don Quixote of absolute freedom, the Rimbaud of *Bateau Ivre,* is forced to confess

Je regrette l'Europe aux anciens parapets

and to remember nostalgically a time of a more restricted loneliness when on a black cold pond

Un enfant accroupi, plein de tristesse, lâche
Un bateau frêle comme un papillon de mai.

And so too in his moment of greatest anguish when the Ancient Mariner
is

Alone, alone, all, all alone
Alone on a wide wide sea!

he looks up yearningly to the moon and the stars and the blue sky which,
says the Gloss, "belongs to them, and is their appointed rest, and their
native country and their own natural homes." And when he repents, and
the ship begins to move again, he is refreshed by the sound of the sails

A noise like of a hidden brook
In the leafy month of June,
That to the sleeping woods all night
Singeth a quiet tune.

Differences

As places of freedom and solitude the sea and the desert are symbolically
the same. In other respects, however, they are opposites. E.g. the desert is the
dried-up place, i.e. the place where life has ended, the Omega of temporal
existence. Its first most obvious characteristic is that nothing moves; the second is that everything is surface and exposed. No soil, no hidden spring. The
sea, on the other hand, is the Alpha of existence, the symbol of potentiality.

Thy shores are empires, changed in all save thee—
Assyria, Greece, Rome, Carthage, what are they?
Thy waters wash'd them power while they were free,
And many a tyrant since; their shores obey
The stranger, slave, or savage; their decay
Has dried up realms to deserts:—not so thou;—
Unchangeable, save to thy wild waves' play,
Time notes no wrinkle on thine azure brow:
Such as creation's dawn beheld, thou rollest now.
                                        (*Childe Harold*, Canto IV)

Its first most obvious characteristic is its perpetual motion, the violence of
wave as tempest; its power may be destructive, but unlike that of the desert,
it is positive. Its second is the teeming life that lies hidden below the surface
which, however dreadful, is greater than the visible: "As this appalling ocean
surrounds the verdant land, so in the soul of man there lies one insular Tahiti,
full of peace and joy, but encompassed by all the horror of the half-known
life." (*Moby Dick*)

The sea, then, is the symbol of primitive potential power as contrasted with the desert of actualised triviality, of living barbarism versus lifeless decadence.

The Oasis and the Happy Island

The sea and the desert are related to the city as its symbolic opposites. There is a third image, in the case of the sea the happy island and in the case of the desert the oasis or rose garden, which stands related to both. It is like the city in that it is an enclosed place of safety and like the sea-desert in that it is a solitary or private place from which the general public are excluded and where the writ of the law does not run. The primary idea with which the garden-island image is associated is, therefore, neither justice nor chastity but innocence; it is the earthly paradise where there is no conflict between natural desire and moral duty.

Thus Pindar sings in the second Olympian of the land of the Hyperboreans

> In sunshine ever fair
> Abide the Good and all their nights and days
> An equal splendour wear.
> And never as of old with thankless toil
> For their poor empty needs they vex the soil
>   And plough the watery seas
> But dwelling with the glorious gods in ease
>   A tearless life they pass.

And Euripides in *Hippolytus*

> To the strand of the Daughters of the sunset,
>   The apple tree, the singing and the gold;
> Where the mariner must stay him from his onset
>   And the red wave is tranquil as of old;
>   Yea beyond that Pillar of the End
>   That Atlas guardeth, would I wend.

And the same nostalgia is common among the romantics, for *l'innocent paradis, plein de plaisirs furtifs*, where

> *tout n'est qu'ordre et beauté*
> *Luxe, calme et volupté.*

This image, in its turn, has two possibilities. Either it is the real earthly paradise, in which case it is a place of temporary refreshment for the exhausted hero, a foretaste of rewards to come or the final goal and reward itself, where the beloved and the blessed society are waiting to receive him into their select company; or it is a magical garden, an illusion caused by black magic to tempt the hero to abandon his quest, and which, when the spell is broken, is seen to be really the desert of barren rock, or a place of horror like Calypso's island, Klingsor's garden, or the isle of Venus.*

THE ROMANTIC OASIS-ISLAND

The image of the happy Prelapsarian Place appears often enough in Romantic literature but charged usually with a hopeless nostalgia. The examples which the romantic actually encounters turn out to be mirages or disappointing and dangerous deserts like the *Encantadas* of which Melville writes:

> Change never comes, neither the change of seasons nor of sorrows. No voice, no low, no howl is heard: the chief sound of life here is a hiss. In no world but a fallen one could such lands exist.

Where the population consists of

Men	0
Ant-eaters	Unknown
Man-haters	Unknown
Lizards	500,000
Snakes	500,000
Spiders	10,000,000
Salamanders	Unknown
Devils	Do. Do.

Eldorado turns out to be a reef, the island of Cythera is

> *un terrain des plus maigres,*
> *Un désert rocailleux troublé par des cris aigres*
> (Baudelaire, *Voyage à Cythère*)

---

* An interesting example of the tempting island imagery because of the unusual twist given to it is Tennyson's *Voyage of Maeldune.* In this poem there are nine islands which I associate, perhaps rather arbitrarily, with certain ideas as follows.

The Silent Isle	Introversion
The Shouting Isle	Extroversion
The Isle of Flowers but no Fruits	Art
The Isle of Fruits	Science
The Isle of Fire	Materialism
The Isle under the Sea	Mysticism
The Beauteous Isle	Leisure
The Isle of Witches	Sex
The Isle of Double Towers	Religious and Political Fanaticism

Maeldune's crew, when they first sight these islands, expect to enjoy themselves, i.e. they expect to be tempted to stay and be untrue to their mission, which is one of vengeance. What happens, however, is that the islands turn out to be places of danger which make them kill each other or commit suicide, i.e. they turn their aggressive feelings away from the absent object against themselves. Thus the islands become the means by which Maeldune and they are taught through suffering from hate that hate is hateful.

When at last they landed on the shore where the Snarks were to be found

> the crew were not pleased with the view
> Which consisted of chasms and crags.

And the natural surroundings of Lady Jingly Jones are in keeping with her lovelorn condition

> On that coast of Coromandel
> In his jug without a handle
> > Still she weeps and still she moans,
> > On that little heap of stones.

The tempestuous liquid sea is dangerous enough but when it approaches the condition of the solid desert it is worse. E.g. the sand-bank of the Kentish Knock in *The Wreck of the Deutschland* and the iceberg in Melville's poem

> Hard Berg (methought), so cold, so vast,
> With mortal damps self-overcast;
> Exhaling still thy dankish breath—
> Adrift dissolving, bound for death;
> Though lumpish thou, a lumbering one—
> A lumbering lubbard loitering slow,
> Impingers rue thee and go down
> Sounding they precipice below,
> Nor stir the slimy slug that sprawls
> Along thy dead indifference of walls.

And the Ancient Mariner's punishment begins when the sea becomes a counterfeit desert.

> Day after day, day after day,
> We stuck, nor breath nor motion;
> As idle as a painted ship
> Upon a painted ocean.
>
> Water, water, everywhere,
> And all the boards did shrink;
> Water, water, everywhere,
> Nor any drop to drink.
>
> The very deep did rot: O Christ!
> That ever this should be!
> Yea, slimy things did crawl with legs
> Upon the slimy sea.

To the romantic, that is, childhood is over, its island is astern, and there is no other. The only possible place of peace now lies under the waters.

Where lies the final harbor whence we unmoor no more? Where is the foundling's father hidden? Our souls are like those orphans whose un-wedded mothers die in bearing them: the secret of our paternity lies in their grave, and we must there to learn it.

(Moby Dick)

The images of the Just City, of the civilised landscape protected by the Madonna, the *"Fior', frondi, ombre, antri, onde, aure soavi"* which look at us from so many Italian paintings, and of the rose garden or island of the blessed, are lacking in Romantic literature because the Romantic writers no longer be-lieve in their existence. What exists is the Trivial Unhappy Unjust City, the desert of the average from which the only escape is to the wild, lonely, but still vital sea. The Desert has become, in fact, an image of modern civilisation in which innocence and the individual are alike destroyed.

THE LEVEL DESERT

None of the writers we are discussing had much good to say for laissez-faire democracy. Rimbaud's poem on that subject expresses an attitude shared by most of them.

Democracy

The flag is in keeping with the unclean landscape, and our jargon drowns the sound of the drums.

At certain centres we will encourage the most cynical prostitution. We will crush logical rebellion.

Let us go to dusty and exhausted countries—put ourselves at the service of monstrous industrial or military exploitations.

"To our next meeting—here—no matter where!"

Conscripts of good intentions we shall have a ferocious philosophy. Dunces shall be devotees of knowledge, sybarites enthusiasts for com-fort; and for this busy world there shall be dissolution.

This is real progress! Forward! March!

(Les Illuminations)

And Baudelaire foresaw a democratic future when "the son will run away from the family not at eighteen but at twelve, emancipated by his gluttonous precocity; he will fly, not to seek heroic adventures, not to deliver a beautiful prisoner from a tower, not to immortalize a garret with sublime thoughts, but to found a business, to enrich himself and to compete with his infamous papa" and the daughter, "with an infantile wantonness, will dream in her cradle that she sells herself for a million." (*Fusées*)

They did not feel like this because they disbelieved in individual freedom but precisely because, passionately believing in it, they saw urban democracy as they knew it, destroying the heroic individual and turning him into a cypher of the crowd, or a mechanical cogwheel in an impersonal machine.

What Baudelaire stigmatises as *l'esprit belge*, what Jack Chase means when he says, "let us hate the public and cleave to the people," what Lear means by They in such a limerick as

> There was an old man of Whitehaven
> Who danced a quadrille with a raven
> They said: It's absurd
> To encourage this bird
> So they smashed that old man of Whitehaven.

is dealt with most fully by Kierkegaard:

> The man who has no opinion of an event at the actual moment accepts the opinion of the majority, or if he is quarrelsome, of the minority. But it must be remembered that both majority and minority are real people, and that is why the individual is assisted by adhering to them. A public, on the contrary, is an abstraction . . . A public is neither a nation, nor a generation, nor a community, nor these particular men, for all these are only what they are through the concrete; no single person who belongs to the public makes a real commitment; for some hours of the day, perhaps, he belongs to the public—at moments when he is nothing else, since when he is really what he is he does not form part of the public. Made up of such individuals, of individuals at the moments when they are nothing, a public is a kind of gigantic something, an abstract and deserted void which is everything and nothing.
>
> (*Thoughts on the Present Age*)

So, too, Wordsworth saw the London crowds:

> The slaves unrespited of low pursuits,
> Living amid the same perpetual flow
> Of trivial objects, melted and reduced
> To one identity, by differences
> That have no law, no meaning, and no end.
>
> (*Prelude*, VII.700–704)

Again, although it has struck many readers as unjust, Coleridge was imaginatively correct in allowing all the companions of the Ancient Mariner to die.

The latter has sinned by shooting the Albatross, but the sin is a personal act for which he can suffer and repent. The rest of the crew react collectively as a crowd, not as persons. First they blame him because they think he has killed the bird that made the breeze to blow, then they praise him for having killed the bird that brought the fog and mist, and then when the ship is becalmed, they turn on him again and hang the albatross around his neck. That is to say, they are an irresponsible crowd and since, as such, they can take no part in the Mariner's personal repentance, they must die to be got out of the way.

The Mechanised Desert

If, in the overlarge, industrialised cities against which the romantic poets protest, the masses during their hours of leisure lack any real common bond of love or commitment and turn into crowds, in their working hours they tend to become mere instruments of their particular function, to have no existence over and above what they do to earn their living.

With the exception of the Beaver, the Bellman's crew in *The Hunting of the Snark* have no names, only jobs, Boots, Maker of Bonnets and Hoods, Barrister, Broker, Billiard Marker, Banker, Butcher, and Baker (the reason why the last is said to have forgotten his name, we shall consider later). It is not that they are passionate about these jobs, dedicated to them by a personal choice, no, these are just what they happen to do. The best portrait of this depersonalised technician is the Carpenter of the *Pequod*, "a strict abstract" who "works by a deaf and dumb spontaneous literal process, a pure manipulator: his brain, if he had ever had one, must have early oozed along with the muscles of his fingers." He is a solitary who has no relationships with human beings, only with wood and his tools, without being a simple individual. Then he continually talks to himself, but is incapable of a real dialogue of self with self, only a meaningless stream of free associations set off by the actions of his fingers, soliloquising "like the whirring wheel—to keep himself awake."

Drat the file, and drat the bone! That is hard which should be soft, and that is soft which should be hard. So we go, who file old jaws and shinbones. Let's try another. Aye, now, this works better (*sneezes*). Halloa, this bone dust is (*sneezes*)—why it's (*sneezes*)—yes, it's (*sneezes*)—bless my soul, it won't let me speak! This is what an old fellow gets now for working in dead lumber. Saw a live tree, and you don't get this dust; amputate a live bone, and you don't get it (*sneezes*). Come, come, you old Smut, there, bear a hand, and let's have that ferule and buckle-screw; I'll be ready for them presently. Lucky now (*sneezes*) there's no knee-joint to make; that might puzzle a little; but a mere shinbone—why it's easy as making hop-poles; only I should like to put a good finish on. Time, time;

if I but only had the time, I could turn him out as neat a leg now as ever scraped to a lady in a parlor . . . There! before I saw it off, now, I must call his old Mogulship, and see whether the length will be all right; too short, if anything, I guess. Ha! that's the heel; we are in luck; here he comes, or it's somebody else, that's certain.

(*Moby Dick*, chapter CVIII)

What has happened, in fact, is the disappearance of a true community, i.e. a group of rational beings associated on the basis of a common love. Societies still exist, i.e. organisations of talents for the sake of a given function. Communities and societies are not identical, i.e. a cello player in a string quartet, who hates music but plays because he must eat and playing the cello is all he knows, is a member of a society; he is not a member of the community of music lovers, but in a healthy culture societies exist as differentiated units inside a common community.

In a society, where the structure and relation of its members to each other is determined by the function for which the society exists and not by their personal choice, the whole is more real than the sum of its parts. In a community, on the other hand, which is determined by the subjective verbs Love or Believe, *I* always precedes *We*. In a closed traditional community this fact is hidden, because the *I* is only potential. The believer by tradition is unconscious of any alternative to his belief—he has only heard of one kind of snark, and therefore cannot doubt. The further civilisation moves towards the open condition in which each man is conscious that there are snarks that have feathers and bite and snarks that have whiskers and scratch, the sharper becomes the alternative: *either* personal choice and through the sum of such choices an actual community *or* the annihilation of personality and the dissolution of community into crowds.

A cartoon by Charles Addams which appeared some years ago in *The New Yorker* illustrates admirably the urban situation in which individuality is lost. It shows a residential street in New York. Along the pavement a motionless line of spectators is staring at a little man with an umbrella engaged in a life-and-death struggle with a large octopus which has emerged from a manhole in the middle of the street. Behind the crowd two men with brief-cases are walking along without bothering to turn their heads and one is saying to the other: "It doesn't take much to collect a crowd in New York."

The cartoon contains three groups:

(1) The majority crowd, no member of which dares move unless the rest do so, so that all remain passive spectators and not one steps out to help the man in trouble and, by doing so, to become an individual.

(2) The minority crowd who are, indeed, acting (they are walking, not standing still) but whose actions and feelings are negatively conditioned

by the majority, i.e. what they do is not their personal choice, but whatever it may be that the majority does *not* do.

(3) The single man struggling with the octopus. He is a real individual, yet even with him, the question arises: "Would he be standing out there in the street by himself if the octopus had not attacked him?" i.e. if he had not been compelled by a fate outside his personal control to become the exceptional individual. There is even a suggestion about his bourgeois umbrella of a magician's wand. Could it be possible that, desiring to become an individual yet unable to do so by himself, he has conjured up a monster from the depths of the sea to break the spell of reflection, and free him from being just a member of the crowd?

It is not only the little man in the bowler hat, however, who is in danger of loss of individuality. As Nietzsche perceived, the brilliant scholarly mind is, in modern civilisation, even more threatened.

However gratefully one may welcome the objective spirit—and who has not been sick to death of all subjectivity and its confounded *ipsisimosity*—in the end, however, one must learn caution, even with regard to one's gratitude, and put a stop to the exaggeration with which the unselfing and depersonalising of the spirit has recently been celebrated, as if it were the goal in itself, as if it were a salvation and glorification—as is especially accustomed to happen in the pessimist school, which has also in its turn good reasons for paying the highest honours to "disinterested knowledge." The objective man, who no longer curses and scolds like the pessimist, the *ideal* man of learning in whom the scientific instinct blossoms forth fully after a thousand complete and partial failures, is surely one of the most costly instruments that exist, but his place is in the hand of one who is more powerful. He is only an instrument—we may say he is a *mirror*, he is no "purpose in himself." The objective man is in truth a mirror. Accustomed to prostration before everything that wants to be known, with such desires only as knowing and reflecting imply—he waits until something comes, and then expands himself sensitively, so that even the lightest footsteps and gliding past of spiritual beings may not be lost on his surface and film. Whatever "personality" he still possesses seems to him accidental, arbitrary, or still oftener disturbing; so much has he come to regard himself as the passage and reflection of outside forms and events. He calls up the recollection of "himself" with an effort. He readily confounds himself with other people, he makes mistakes with regard to his own needs, and here only is he unrefined and negligent. Perhaps he is troubled about the health, or the pettiness and confined atmosphere of wife and friend, or the lack of companions and society—and indeed, he sets himself to reflect on his suffering, but in vain! His thoughts already rove away to the *more general* case, and tomorrow he knows as little as he knew yesterday how to help himself. He does not now take himself seriously and devote time to himself: he is serene, *not* from lack of troubles, but from lack of capacity for grasping and dealing with *his* trouble. The habitual complaisance with respect to all objects and experiences, the radiant and impartial hospitality with which he receives everything that comes his way, his habit of inconsiderate good nature, of dangerous indifference to Yea and Nay . . . Should one wish Love or Hatred from him—and I mean Love and Hatred as God, woman and animal understand them, he will do what he can, and furnish what he can. But one must not be surprised if it should not be much—if he should show himself just at this point to be false, fragile, and rather *un tour de force*, a slight ostentation and exaggeration. He is only genuine so far as he can be objective; only in his serene totality is he still "nature" and "natural." His mirroring and eternally self-polishing soul no longer knows how to affirm, no longer how to deny; he does not command; neither does he destroy. "Je ne méprise presque rien"—he says with Leibnitz: let us not overlook nor undervalue the *presque*!

(*Beyond Good and Evil*)

If a community so dissolves, the societies, which remain so long as human beings wish to remain alive, must, left to themselves, grow more and more mechanical. And such real individuals as are left must become Ishmaels, "isolatoes, not acknowledging the common continent of men, but each isolatoe living in a separate continent of his own"; Hamlet is at the mercy of reflection and melancholia.

What it feels like to be such an isolatoe, who cannot take the crowd way and become a grain of the desert sand, but is left standing there alone in the wide waste, is described similarly by most of them.

Thus Coleridge:

> A grief without a pang, void, dark, and drear,
>   A stifled, drowsy, unimpassioned grief,
>   Which finds no natural outlet, no relief,
>   In word, or sigh, or tear—
> O Lady! in this wan and heartless mood,
> To other thoughts by yonder throstle wooed,
>   All this long eve, so balmy and serene,
> Have I been gazing on the western sky,
>   And its peculiar tint of yellow green:
> And still I gaze—and with how blank an eye!
> And those thin clouds above, in flakes and bars,
> That give away their motion to the stars;

Those stars, that glide behind them or between,
Now sparkling, now bedimmed, but always seen:
Yon crescent Moon, as fixed as if it grew
In its own cloudless, starless lake of blue,
I see them all so excellently fair,
I see, not feel, how beautiful they are!

("Dejection")

Thus Baudelaire:

Rien n'égale en longueur les boiteuses journées
Quand sous les lourds flocons des neigeuses années
L'ennui, fruit de la morne incuriosité,
Prend les proportions de l'immortalité.

—Désormais tu n'es plus, o matière vivante!
Qu'un granit entouré d'une vague épouvante,
Assoupi dans le fond d'un Sahara brumeux!
Un vieux sphinx ignoré du monde insoucieux,
Oublié sur la carte, et dont l'humeur farouche
Ne chante qu'aux rayons du soleil qui se couche!

(Spleen)

Thus Melville:

It is a damp drizzly November in my soul;—I find myself involuntarily
pausing before coffin warehouses, and bringing up the rear of every funeral I meet . . . it requires a strong moral principle to prevent me from
deliberately stepping into the street, and methodically knocking people's hats off.

(Moby Dick, chapter i)

And Mallarmé in a sentence:

La chair est triste, hélas! et j'ai lu tous les livres.

The grand explanatory image of this condition is of course Dürer's *Melancholia.* She sits unable to sleep and yet unable to work, surrounded by unfinished works and unused tools, the potential fragments of the city which she
has the knowledge but not the will to build, tormented by a batlike creature
with a board, bearing figures, and, behind her, a dark sea, a rainbow and a
comet.

What is the cause of her suffering? That, surrounded by every possibility,
she cannot find within herself or without the necessity to realise one rather
than another. Urban society is, like the desert, a place without limits. The city
walls of tradition, mythos and cultus have crumbled. There is no direction in

which Ishmael is forbidden or forcibly prevented from moving. The only outside "necessities" are the random winds of fashion or the lifeless chains of a
meaningless job, which, so long as he remains an individual, he can and will
reject. At the same time, however, he fails to find a necessity within himself
to take their place. So he must take drastic measures and go down to the waters, though in a very different sense from those of which St John of the Cross
speaks:

> Y el cerco sosegaba
> Y la caballería
> A vista de las aguas descendía

The siege was intermitted and the cavalry dismounted at the sight of the
waters.

> ("Song of the Soul and the Bridegroom")

For the waters to which Ishmael goes are bitter and medicinal.

> God help me! save I take my part
>   Of danger on the roaring sea,
> A devil rises in my heart
>   Far worse than any death to me.

> (Tennyson, "The Sailor Boy")

Fleeing to the ship where "the sons of adversity meet the children of calamity
and the children of calamity meet the offspring of sin," yet at least, facing a
common death, he and they are bound into a true community, so unlike the
landsmen children of Abel of whom Baudelaire says

> Race d'Abel tu croîs et broutes
> Comme les punaises des bois.

And then out to sea, for there in the ocean wastes, the Paternal Power may
still be felt though but as dreadful tempest, and there still dwells the Mother-
Goddess though she appear but in her most malignant aspects, as the cas-
trating white whale to Ahab, as the Life-in-Death to the Ancient Mariner

> Her lips were red, her looks were free
> Her locks were yellow as gold:
> Her skin was white as leprosy,

as the ghoul Ice-maiden to Gordon Pym.

And now we rushed into the embrace of the cataract where a chasm threw
itself open to receive us. But there arose in our pathway a shrouded
human figure, very far larger in its proportions than any dweller among
men. And the hue of the skin of the figure was of the perfect whiteness
of snow.

Or, worst of all, the dreadful Boojum of Nothingness. Shipwreck is probable, but at least it will be a positive Death.

> *Je partirai! steamer balançant ta mâture*
> *Lève l'ancre pour une exotique nature!*
> *Un Ennui, désolé par les cruels espoirs,*
> *Croit encore à l'adieu suprême des mouchoirs!*
> *Et, peut-être, les mâts, invitant les orages,*
> *Sont-ils de ceux qu'un vent penche sur les naufrages*
> *Perdus, sans mâts, sans mâts, ni fertiles îlots . . .*
> *Mais, ô mon coeur, entends les chants des matelots.*

(Mallarmé)

TWO

The Stone and the Shell

The Non-Limited is the original material of existing things;
further, the source from which existing things derive their
existence is also that to which they return at their destruction, according to necessity for they give justice and make
reparation to one another for their injustice, according to
the arrangement of Time. —Anaximander of Miletus

The nature of Number and Harmony admits of no Falsehood; for this is unrelated to them. Falsehood and Envy belong to the nature of the Non-Limited and the Unintelli-
gent and the Irrational. —Philolaus of Tarentum

The desert knight of Wordsworth's dream was hurrying away to hide two treasures, a stone and a shell, and the poet is quite explicit as to their significance.
The stone is geometric truth, which holds acquaintance with the stars and
weds man to man

> by purest bond
> Of nature undisturbed by space or time.

For it is

> An image, not unworthy of the one
> Surpassing life which out of space and time
> Nor touched by weltering of passion is
> And has the name of God.

And the shell is Poetic Truth, the truth built by

> passion which itself
> Is highest reason in a soul sublime

for it is   a god, yea many gods

has   voices more than all the winds

and is   a joy, a consolation and a hope

Further he says quite definitely that the shell is of more worth than the stone.

As symbolic object, the stone is related to the desert, which like the Ancient
Mariner's situation is a becalmed state when the distress is caused by lack of
passion, good or bad, and the shell is related to the sea, to powers, that is,
which, though preferable to aridity, are nevertheless more dangerous; the
shell is a consolation yet what it says is a prophecy of destruction by the wel-
tering flood; and only a sublime soul can ride the storm.

The poet himself indeed is often endangered by his shell, and in the

Seventh Book Wordsworth speaks of his interest in geometry in the following terms

> Mighty is the charm
> Of these abstractions to a mind beset
> With images and haunted by itself

and then compares himself with a shipwrecked mariner who passed the time on a desert island drawing diagrams with a stick, escaping from the distress of his corporal situation into

> an independent world
> Created out of pure intelligence.

The Whale of Truth is "for salamander giants only to encounter," and thinking can be as dangerous as feeling. He who is merely a provincial, one of those "romantic, melancholy, and absent-minded young men, disgusted with the carking cares of earth" must beware of gazing too long at the sea or the fire, for even as he takes "the mystic ocean at his feet for the visible image of that deep, blue, bottomless soul pervading mankind and nature" he is hovering over Descartian vortices

> and perhaps at midday, in the fairest weather, with one half-throttled shriek you drop through that transparent air into the summer sea, no more to rise for ever,
>
> (*Moby Dick*, chapter xxxv)

the fate, for instance, of the timid child Pip, who against his own will was cast into the sea, saw "God's foot upon the treadle of the loom" and went mad, the fate of the over-sensitive Cowper:

> No voice divine the storm allay'd
>   No light propitious shone,
> When, snatched from all effectual aid,
>   We perished, each alone:
> But I beneath a rougher sea
> And whelmed in deeper gulphs than he.
>
> ("The Castaway")

When the preself-conscious savage Tashtego falls into the cistern of the sperm-whale head and is nearly drowned, Ishmael remarks, "How many, think ye, have likewise fallen into Plato's honey head, and sweetly perished there?" Even the hero may perish: the baker for all his courage vanishes away when he encounters the Boojum; and tough Baudelaire notes in his journal, "I have cultivated my hysteria with delight and terror. Now I suffer continually from vertigo, and today, the 23rd of January 1862, I have received a singular warning. I have felt the wind of the wing of madness pass over me."

The Stone, the Shell and the City

In Wordsworth's dream, then, as in all dreams, there are a number of ambiguities.

(1) The stone and the shell are alike in that they both signify Truth. They are also opposites. The stone is valuable because it stands for freedom from disorder and passion. The shell is valuable because it stands for life-giving power. Incidentally, also, the stone stands for the Divine Unity, the shell for the Divine Multiplicity.

(2) Both are the means through which the True City is built. Men become brothers through the recognition of a common truth in their several minds, and through the experience of a common hope and joy in their several hearts. But at the same time both are dangers to the city. The truths of abstraction are unrelated to the historical reality of the human moment and distract from the historical task. The truths of feeling may overwhelm individual identity and social order in an anarchic deluge.

The Polemical Situation of Romanticism

For every individual the present moment is a polemical situation, and his battle is always on two fronts: he has to fight against his own past, not only his personal past but also those elements in the previous generation with which he is personally involved—in the case of a poet, for instance, the poetic tradition and attitudes of the preceding generation—and simultaneously he has to fight against the present of others, who are a threat to him, against the beliefs and attitudes of the society in which he lives which are hostile to his conception of art. In order to plunge straight away into this question, let us take a few statements by that highly polemical writer William Blake.

> Cowper came to me and said: O that I were insane always. . . . Can you not make me truly insane? I will never rest till I am so. O that in the bosom of God I was hid. You claim health and yet are as mad as any of us all . . . mad as a refuge from unbelief—from Bacon, Newton and Locke.

> Mock on, Mock on Voltaire, Rousseau:
> Mock on, Mock on: 'tis all in vain!
> You throw the sand against the wind,
> And the wind blows it back again. . . .
>
> The Atoms of Democritus
> And Newton's Particles of light
> Are sands upon the Red sea shore
> Where Israel's tents do shine so bright.

The bounded is loathed by its possessor. The same dull round, even of a universe, would soon become a mill with complicated wheels.

Doctor Thornton's Tory Translation, Translated out of its disguise in the Classical & Scotch languages into the vulgar English.

"Our Father Augustus Caesar, who are in these thy Substantial Astronomical Telescopic Heavens, Holiness to thy Name or Title, & reverence to thy Shadow. Thy Kingship come upon Earth first & then in Heaven. Give us day by day our Real Taxed Substantial Money bought Bread; deliver from the Holy Ghost whatever cannot be Taxed; for all is debts & Taxes between Caesar & us & one another; lead us not to read the Bible, but let our Bible be Virgil & Shakespeare; & deliver us from Poverty in Jesus, that Evil One. For thine is the Kingship, (or) Allegorical Godship, & the Power, or War, & the Glory, or Law, Ages after Ages in thy descendants; for God is only an Allegory of Kings & nothing Else.   Amen."

and finally

> That God is Colouring Newton does shew,
> And the devil is a Black outline, all of us know.

To Blake, then, the Enemy was the sort of conception of the universe which he associates with Newton, which he regards as having disastrous psychological, religious, political and artistic consequences.

Professor Whitehead has lucidly summarised the essential features of the Newtonian cosmology as follows:

(1) The universe consists of ultimate things, whose character is private, with simple location in space.
(2) On these is imposed the necessity of entering into relationships with each other. This imposition is the work of God.
(3) These imposed behaviour patterns are the laws of Nature.
(4) You cannot discover the natures so related by any study of the laws.
(5) You cannot discover the laws by inspection of the natures.

Associated with this conception there was also that of the Great Chain of Being, i.e. creation was complete, every kind of thing which could possibly exist was already there without room for the admission of any extra novelty, and arranged in an orderly and rationally comprehensible hierarchy of being.

Such a cosmology has important theological consequences. Like the orthodox Christian God and unlike the God of Plato and Aristotle, He is the creator of the world; but unlike the Christian God, and like that of Plato and Aristotle, God and the World have no real mutual relation. While the Greek Universe loves and tries to model itself on the unconscious self-sufficient god, the Newtonian Universe is the passive neutral stuff. God imposes rational order, which it obeys, but to which it does not respond, for the natural world is no longer thought of as an organism.

At first such a concept was not altogether unwelcome to theologians. To an age exhausted by religious wars, weary of unending dogmatic disputes and exasperated by fanatic individual interpretations of Scripture, here at last the possibility of peaceful consent seemed to open up. Here was a god the existence and nature of whom could be ascertained by the use of the human reason which in all sane men comes to the same conclusion, when freed from personal passion and prejudice.

Indeed through the latter half of the seventeenth century and the first half of the eighteenth, there is an attempt in every field, religion, politics, art, etc., to do for that time what their mediaeval predecessors had done for the twelfth and thirteenth centuries, i.e. to construct a new catholic church, catholic society, and catholic art, to found a new Good City on the basis of sound reason, common sense, and good taste.

If the Enlightenment was the precursor of the French Revolution, nothing could have been further from its intentions, which were profoundly conservative and pacifist. The Encyclopaedists did not dream of a new world arising out of the ashes of an old one, but of substituting reason for unreason in the ordering of a human nature and society which was permanently the same at all times. The only necessary change was to substitute for the magic-loving priest or irrational king the rational man of esprit as the leader of the good world society. As Figaro says in Beaumarchais' play:

> Par le sort de la naissance
> L'un est roi, l'autre est berger;
> Le hasard fit leur distance;
> L'esprit seul peut tout changer.
> De vingt rois que l'on encense
> Le trépas brise l'autel
> Et Voltaire est immortel.

The attempt failed, but the history of the preceding two hundred years shows that, insufficient for an ultimate basis as reason, sense and taste turned out to be, they were qualities of which the time stood very much in need.

It is difficult for us to be quite fair to deist theologians like Toland, the author of *Christianity Not Mysterious*, or to hymn-writers like Addison:

> What though in solemn silence, all
> Move round the dark terrestrial ball?
> What though nor real voice nor sound
> Amid their radiant orbs be found?
> In reason's ear they all rejoice,
> And utter forth a glorious voice,
> For ever singing as they shine,
> The hand that made us is divine.

or to the rather cheap sneers of Gibbon or Voltaire, unless we remember the actual horrors of persecution, witch-hunting, and provincial superstition from which they were trying to deliver mankind. Further, the reaction of the Romantics against them is a proof that up to a point they had succeeded. If the final result of their labors was a desert, they had at least drained some very putrid marshes.

However, as Whitehead wittily remarks, such a world view is very easy to understand and extremely difficult to believe.

A transcendent God of Nature of the Newtonian type can be related to the human reason by his intelligibility, and to matter by his power to command exact obedience; the trouble begins when the question is raised of his relation to the human heart, which can and does suffer, and to the human will, which can and does disobey.

Such a Supreme Being could be completely indifferent to human joy or misery, but then he cannot possibly be identified with the Christian God who cares for men and demands their love, worship, and obedience. The attempt so to identify them must result in the purely authoritarian Judge who decrees the moral law and impartially punishes the offender, in fact, the Jehovah, God of This World, whom Blake so detested.

If the moral law is to be completely rational, there can be no contradiction between virtue and practical utility, there cannot be a kingdom of heaven whose values are completely other than the kingdom of this world. In teaching the recalcitrant to resist temptation, it becomes almost inevitable that the reason given will be that virtue succeeds and that vice fails, the Parables offered will be, in fact, the progress of the Virtuous Apprentice who finally marries the master's daughter and the progress of the Rake who ends in Bedlam. Children will be made to pay special attention to such verses as:

> Like some fair tree which, fed by streams
>   With timely fruit doth bend;
> He still shall flourish, and success
>   All his designs attend.
>
> Ungodly men in their attempts
>   No lasting roots shall find
> Untimely, withered and dispersed
>   Like chaff before the wind.
>
> (Tate and Brady, Psalm 1)

With his usual unerring insight Blake saw that the crucial points at issue were the Incarnation of Christ and the Forgiveness of Sins. A Supreme Architect cannot incarnate as an individual, only as the whole building; and a pure Judge cannot forgive; he can only condemn or acquit.

Blake and the other romantics along with him tried in their reaction, not to overcome the dualism, but to stand it on its head,* i.e. to make God purely

---

* More accurately, they absolutise another mode of consciousness. The Deist God is an absolutisation of the ego's consciousness of itself as stretching beyond itself, of standing as a spectator

immanent, so that to Blake God only acts and is in existing beings and men, or is pantheistically diffused through physical nature, not to be perceived by any exercise of the reason, but only through vision and feeling.

So Coleridge writes:

> In the Hebrew poets each thing has a life of its own and yet they are all one life. In God they move and live and *have* their being; not *had*, as the cold system of Newtonian Theology represents, but *have*.

As to the Great Chain of Being, it is retained but in a quite different spirit. The fullness of the universe is felt to be irrational hut that is its charm. Thus Schiller writes:

> Every kind of perfection must attain existence in the fullness of the world . . . in the infinite chasm of nature no activity could be omitted, no grade of enjoyment be wanting in the universal happiness . . . the Great Inventor could not permit even error to remain unutilized in his great design . . . It is a provision of the supreme wisdom that erring reason should people even the chaotic land of dreams and should cultivate even the barren land of contradiction . . . *Life* and *Liberty* to the greatest possible extent are the glory of the divine creation; nowhere is it more sublime than where it seems to have departed most widely from its ideal.

So too with the problem of evil and suffering. The attempt to explain either in rational terms alone, i.e. as if the question "Why do they exist?" were one primarily raised by the intellect, the substitution for Providence and Wisdom of Economy and Utility, created mysteries more fantastic than any which it replaced, e.g. the suggestion of Soame Jenyns that there might be higher beings who torment us for their pleasure and utility in the same way that we hunt animals, in reply to which Dr Johnson composed a famous passage:

> As we drown whelps and kittens, they amuse themselves now and then with sinking a ship, and stand round the fields of Blenheim or the walls of Prague, as we encircle a cock-pit. As we shoot a bird flying, they take a man in the midst of his business or pleasure, and knock him down with an apoplexy. Some of them, perhaps, are virtuosi, and delight in the operations of an asthma, as a human philosopher in the effects of the air-pump.

---

apprehending an external reality. The romantic immanent God, on the other hand, is an absolutisation of the ego's consciousness of itself as self-contained, as embracing all of which it is aware in a unity of experiencing. In Hegel, the third mode of consciousness, the ego's consciousness of itself as striving towards is similarly exalted at the expense of the other two modes.

One might say that in Deist theology the Son is called the Father and the divinity of the Father is denied, while in romantic theology the divinity of the Son is denied and the Father might more properly be called the Mother.

For a discussion of these heresies in the light of the Catholic teaching of the analogical relation between the Deity and creation, see *Polarity* by Erich Przywara (Oxford, 1935), and for the relevance of the Athanasian creed to the artist *The Mind of the Maker* by Dorothy Sayers (Harcourt Brace, 1941).

To swell a man with a tympany is as good sport as to blow a frog. Many a merry bout have these frolick beings at the vicissitudes of an ague, and good sport it is to see a man tumble with an epilepsy, and revive and tumble again, and all this he knows not why. As they are wiser and more powerful than we, they have more exquisite diversions, for we have no way of procuring any sport so brisk and so lasting, as the paroxysms of the gout and stone, which undoubtedly must make high mirth, especially if the play be a little diversified with the blunders and puzzles of the blind and deaf.

If such were true, then the only decent human reaction can be that of Captain Ahab, defiance till death.

The Romantic reaction to this is twofold. When they are objecting to the moralist legalism which thought in terms of objective infractions of the moral law and its appropriate penalties, they produce the figure of the Prelapsarian savage (Queequeg), the innocent sailor (Budd), or the child of the Immortality Ode, whose heart is good though he does not consciously understand or even keep the moral law of the Pharisee. When, on the other hand, they are objecting to the rationlistic optimism which attributes evil to mental ignorance curable by education, they reassert the fallen nature of men and the necessity for conversion.

To the Deists, who thought, like John Sheffield, Duke of Buckingham:

> While in dark Ignorance we lay afraid
> Of Fancies, Ghosts in every empty shade,
> Great Hobbes appeared and by plain Reason's light
> Put such phantastick Forms to shameful Flight.
> Fond is their Fear who think Man needs must be
> To Vice enslaved, if from vain Terrors free:
> The Wise and Good, Morality shall guide
> And Superstition all the World beside.

Blake retorts:

> Man is born a Spectre or Satan and is altogether an Evil, and requires a New Selfhood continually, and must continually be changed into his direct contrary. But your Greek Philosophy (which is a remnant of Druidism) teaches that Man is Righteous in his Vegetated Spectre. . . . Voltaire Rousseau. . . . you are Pharisees and Hypocrites, for you are constantly talking of the Virtues of the Human Heart and particularly of your own, that you may accuse others.
>
> (*Jerusalem*)

And Baudelaire to the disciples of Voltaire:

> Belief in Progress is a doctrine of idlers and Belgians. . . . True civilisation is not to be found in gas or steam or table-turning. It consists in the diminution of the traces of original sin.
>
> (*Mon Coeur Mis à Nu*)

POLITICS AND INDIVIDUALISM

Just as it had sought to escape from sectarian fanaticism by establishing a catholic religion of the One Engineer, so the eighteenth century sought to escape from the arbitrariness of absolute monarchy by establishing a catholic society in which all men were equal because they all possessed a body and a mind which obeyed and recognised the same laws. But this over-simplified the nature of man; by denying him an individual soul or by identifying soul with mind, it did indeed make men equal, but with the equality of billiard-balls, not of individual persons. To such a doctrine of a natural law which self-interest guided by common sense will of course accept, the proper answer is that of the hero of Dostoevsky's *Notes from Underground*:

> You will scream at me (that is if you condescend to do so) that no one is touching my free will, that all they are concerned with is that my will should of itself, of its own free will, coincide with my own normal interests, with the laws of nature and arithmetic. Good heavens, gentlemen, what sort of free will is left when we come to tabulation and arithmetic, when it will all be a case of twice two makes four? Twice two makes four without my will. As if free will meant that.

Hence the Romantic reaction stressed the soul and its uniqueness; Herder propounds the uniqueness of the soul of a nation; Schlegel writes: "It is precisely individuality that is the original and eternal theory in men." Novalis declares: "The more personal, local, peculiar, of its own time a poem is, the nearer it stands to the centre of poetry."

Minds may be similar, but they are not the whole or even the chief element in a human being. "I would rather," says Ishmael, "feel your spine than your skull, whoever you are."

The Deist religion of reason had a catholic myth, that of the Goddess of reason, but no cultus, no specifically religious acts; all rational acts were worship of the Goddess.

The romantic reaction replaced the Goddess by a protestant variety of individual myths; but it, too, lacked a cult in which all men could take part. Instead, it substituted imagination for reason, and in place of the man of esprit the artist as the priest-magician.

> Art is the tree of life. Art is Christianity.
>
> says Blake.

> Poets are the unacknowledged legislators of the world.
>
> says Shelley.

And when Baudelaire says:

> There are no great men save the poet, the priest, and the soldier . . . the rest are born for the whip.
>
> (*Mon Coeur Mis à Nu*)

one is not convinced that he cares as much about the last two as about the first.

ROMANTIC AESTHETIC THEORY

Cartesian metaphysics, Newtonian physics and eighteenth-century theories of perception divided the body from the mind, and the primary objects of perception from their secondary qualities, so that physical nature became, as Professor Collingwood says, "matter, infinite in extent, permeated by movement, devoid of ultimate qualitative differences, and moved by uniform and purely quantitative forces," the colorless desert from which Melville recoils:

> All deified nature absolutely paints like a harlot, whose allurements cover nothing but the charnel house within; and when we proceed further, the palsied universe lies before us like a leper.
>
> (*Moby Dick*, chapter XLII)

Such a view must naturally affect the theory of artistic composition, for it involves a similar division between the thing to be expressed and the medium in which it is expressed.

> Memory [writes Hobbes] is the World in which the Judgement, the severer sister, busieth herself in a grave and rigid examination of all the parts of nature and in registering by letters their order, causes, uses, differences, and resemblances; whereby the Fancy, when any work of Art is to be performed, finding her materials at hand and prepared for use, needs no more than a swift motion over them, that what she wants and is there to be had, may not lie too long unespied.

And Dryden:

> Expression and all that belongs to words is that in a poem which coloring is in a picture . . . Expression is, in plain English, the bawd of her sister, the design . . . she clothes, she dresses her up, she paints her, she makes her appear more lovely than she is.
>
> (*Poetry and Painting*)

This makes artistic creation an entirely conscious process, and here again we shall not understand its appeal to such great poets as Dryden and Pope unless we understand their wish to escape from chaotic idiosyncrasies, their hope of establishing catholic and objective canons of good taste recognisable by poets and public alike. Given the subjects with which these poets were passionately concerned—e.g. Dryden was as moved by the play of dialectic as Wordsworth was by Nature, Pope saw in Dulness as great a threat to the City as Dante saw in Sin—the theory did no harm; indeed it did good, for there is a conscious side of creation, and it made the poets take pains at a time when such pains were needed.

> A Poem where we all perfections find
> Is not the work of a Fantastick mind:
> There must be Care, and Time, and Skill, and Pains;
> Not the first heat of unexperienced brains

is sound advice.

It was only when poets continued working on the same themes as Dryden and Pope but without their passion, or attempted other kinds of themes to which this diction and treatment were unsuited that the deficiencies of the theory became apparent.

The Romantic reaction, naturally, was to stress imagination and vision; i.e. the less conscious side of artistic creation, the uniqueness of the poet's individual experience, and the symbolic rather than the decorative or descriptive value of images. "What is the modern conception of Art?" asks Baudelaire. "To create a suggestive magic including at the same time object and subject, the world outside the artist and the artist himself." "What is a poet if not a translator, a decipherer?"

THE ROMANTIC USE OF SYMBOLS

To understand the romantic conception of the relation between objective and subjective experience, *Moby Dick* is perhaps the best work to study, partly because in certain aspects it includes preromantic attitudes and treatments which show off the former more clearly than a purely romantic work like *The Ancient Mariner* or *Gordon Pym*.

If we omit the White Whale itself, the whole book is an elaborate synecdoche, i.e. it takes a particular way of life, that of whale-fishing, which men actually lead to earn their livelihood and of which Melville had firsthand experience and makes it a case of any man's life in general. This literary device is an old one and can be found at all periods; indeed almost all literature does this.

E.g. (1) Whalemen kill for their living. So in one way or another must we all.

(2) The proprietors of the *Pequod* are Quakers, i.e. they profess the purest doctrine of non-violence, yet see no incongruity in this; though perhaps Peleg recognises the paradox indirectly when he says: "Pious Harpooners never make good voyages. It takes the shark out of them." So always in every life, except that of the saint or the villain, there is a vast difference between what a man professes and how he acts.

(3) The crew are involved in each other's actions and characters. So every world is a world of social relations.

(4) In their attitude towards their job of killing whales, they reveal their

different characters. Thus Starbuck is a professional who takes no risks unless he has to and will have no man in his boat who is not afraid of the whale. Stubb is a reckless gambler who enjoys risks. Flask follows the fish just for the fun of it.

Insofar as the book is this, any other form of activity or society which Melville happened to know well would have served his purpose.

Then *Moby Dick* is full of parable and typology, i.e. as X is in one field of experience, so is Y in another. E.g.

> All men live enveloped in whale-lines. All are born with halters round their necks; but it is only when caught in the soft, sudden turn of death that mortals realise the silent subtle ever-present perils of life.
>
> (Chapter LX)

or

> O men, admire—model thyself after the whale. Do thou too remain warm among ice. Do thou. too, live in this world without being of it. Be cool at the Equator, keep thy blood flow at the Pole and retain in all seasons a temperature of thine own.
>
> (Chapter LXVIII)

or again the characters and names of the nine ships (the number is symbol not allegory) which the *Pequod* encounters are, in their relation to Moby Dick, types of the relation of human individuals and societies in the tragic mystery of existence. I.e.

The *Goney*	The aged who may have experienced the mystery but cannot tell others. (The captain's trumpet falls into the sea.)
The *Town-Ho*	Those who have knowledge of the mystery but keep it secret. (No one tells Ahab the story of Radney and Steelkilt.)
The *Jeroboam*	Those who make a superstitious idolatry of the mystery or whom the mystery has driven crazy.
The *Jungfrau* and the *Rosebud*	Those who out of sloth and avarice respectively will never become aware of the mystery.
The *Enderby*	Those who are aware of the mystery but face it with rational common sense and stoicism. ("What you take for the White Whale's malice is only his awkwardness.")
The *Bachelor*	The frivolous and fortunate who deny the existence of the mystery. ("Have heard of Moby Dick but don't believe in him at all.")
The *Rachel*	Those who have without their understanding or choice become involved in the mystery as the innocents massacred by Herod were involved in the birth of Christ.

| The *Delight* | Those whose encounter with the mystery has turned their joy into sorrow. |

This analogical method was practised by the Church Fathers in their interpretations of Scripture, and analogies from nature have been common ever since, for example in the Mediaeval Bestiaries or Jonathan Edwards' *Images or Shadows of Divine Things*. It is a conscious process, calling for Judgment and Fancy rather than Imagination, and the one-to-one correspondence asserted is grasped by the reader's reason.

Lastly, in his treatment of the White Whale, Melville uses symbols in the real sense.

A symbol is felt to be such before any possible meaning is consciously recognised; i.e. an object or event which is felt to be more important than the reason can immediately explain is symbolic. Secondly, a symbolic correspondence is never one to one but always multiple, and different persons perceive different meanings. Thus to Ahab "All visible objects, man, are but pasteboard masks. To me the white whale is that wall shoved near to me. Sometimes I think there's naught beyond. I see in him outrageous strength with an insatiable malice sinewing it. That inscrutable thing is chiefly what I hate."

To Gabriel, the mad demagogue who terrorises the *Jeroboam*, its qualities are similar, but his attitude is one of positive idolisation. He worships it as an incarnation of the Shaker God. To Steelkilt of the *Town-Ho* it is the justice and mercy of God, saving him from becoming a murderer and slaying the unjust Radney. To Melville-Ishmael it is neither evil nor good but simply numinous, a declaration of the power and majesty of God which transcends any human standards of ethics. To Starbuck it signifies death or his fatal relation to his captain, the duty which tells him he cannot depart his office to obey, intending open war, yet to have a touch of pity.

THE SHIP AS SYMBOL

If thought of as isolated in the midst of the ocean, a ship can stand for mankind and human society moving through time and struggling with its destiny. If thought of as leaving the land for the ocean, it stands for a particular kind of man and society as contrasted with the average landdwelling kind. *The Hunting of the Snark* is a pure example of the first use, *Twenty Thousand Leagues under the Sea* of the second. In Melville's books, and this is one of the reasons for their fascination, there is a constant interplay between both.

THE SHIP AS MANKIND

A constant aesthetic problem for the writer is how to reconcile his desire to include everything, not to leave anything important out, with his desire for an aesthetic whole, that there shall be no irrelevances and loose ends. The picture has to be both complete and framed. The more society becomes differentiated through division of labor, the more it becomes atomised through urbanisation and through greater ease of communication, the harder it becomes for the artist to find a satisfactory solution.

For, of the traditional wholes, the family becomes representative of one class only, the village the exceptional way of life instead of the typical. The ship is one of the few possible devices left, because, while it is most emphatically a frame—no one can get off or on board once the ship has started—yet it permits of a great deal of variety and interpretation.

E.g. (1) The people on board can show every variety of character as individuals and every age of man from fourteen to seventy. "Wrecked on a desert shore, a man of war's crew could quickly form an Alexandria for themselves."

(2) There are a number of social grades: Captain—Mates—Harpooners—Seamen, so that the role of authority in human society and of its dialectical relation to character can be portrayed.

(3) A ship has a function to perform, to hunt whales, to fight battles etc., and each member of the crew has his specialised function. The carpenter must carpenter, the boatswain must flog, the chaplain must preach, the master at arms must spy, etc., which allow the exhibition of all the relations between functions, given or chosen, and the character which willingly or unwillingly performs it.

There can even be passengers without a function.

(4) Life on a ship exhibits the distinction and relation between society, i.e. human beings associated for an end, and community, human beings associated by the tie of a common love or interest. Thus on *The Neversink* there are a number of antagonistic communities within the common society, for instance, the officers versus the common seamen, the rulers whose orders cannot be questioned and the ruled who feel like Melville:

I was a Roman Jew of the Middle Ages confined to the Jewish quarter of the town and forbidden to stray beyond its limits.

By far the majority of the common sailors of the *Neversink* were plainly concerned at the prospect of war and were plainly averse to it. But with the officers of the quarterdeck it was just the reverse . . . Because, though war would equally jeopardise the lives of both, yet, while it held out to the sailor no promise of promotion, and what is called *glory*, these things fired the heart of his officers.

(*White Jacket*)

In the case of the *Pequod*, the situation at the beginning is this: All of the crew with the exception of the captain are a community in that they all want to hunt whales and make money; Ahab stands outside, having no wish to hunt any whale except Moby Dick. He is so far from wishing to make a profitable voyage that, when the barrels begin leaking he would prefer to let them leak rather than delay his quest and only yields to Star-buck's demand to "up Burtons" because he is afraid of mutiny. At the end, however, Ahab has so infected the crew with his passion that they have ceased to care what happens and are made one community with him.

> They were one man, not thirty. For as the one ship that held them all; though it was put together of all contrasting things—oak, and maple, and pine wood; iron, and pitch, and hemp—yet all these ran into each other in the one concrete hull, which shot on its way, both balanced and directed by the long central keel; even so, all the in-dividualities of the crew, this man's valor, that man's fear; guilt and guiltiness, all varieties were welded into oneness, and were all di-rected to that fatal goal which Ahab their one lord and keel did point to.
>
> (*Moby Dick*, chapter CXXXIV)

(5) As a society which, once you are in (the question of how you get in is only raised when the ship is used in the second symbolic sense of a spe-cial kind of life) you cannot get out of, whether you like it or not, whether you approve of it or not, a ship can represent either:

(a) The state of being human as decreed by God. Mutiny then is a sym-bol of the original rebellion of Lucifer and of Adam, the refusal to ac-cept finitude and dependence.

(b) The *civitas terrena*, created by self-love, inherited and repeated, into which all men since Adam are born, yet where they have never totally lost their knowledge of and longing for the Civitas Dei and the Law of Love. From this arise absurd contradictions, like the chaplain on a man-of-war who is paid a share of the reward for sinking a ship and cannot condemn war or flogging, or the devout Baptist who earns his bread as captain of a gun.

To be like Christ, to obey the law of love absolutely, is possible only for the saint, for Billy Budd, and even for him the consequence is the same as for Christ, crucifixion. The rest of us cannot avoid disingen-uous compliances. Thus, in his dissertation on Chronometricals and Horologicals in *Pierre*, Melville writes:

> Bacon's brains were mere watch-maker's brains; but Christ was a chronometer . . . And the reason why His teachings seemed folly to the Jews, was because he carried that Heaven's time in Jerusa-lem, while the Jews carried Jerusalem time there . . . as the China

watches are right as to China, so the Greenwich chronometers must be wrong as to China. Besides, of what use to the Chinaman would a Greenwich chronometer, keeping Greenwich time, be? Were he thereby to regulate his daily actions, he would be guilty of all manner of absurdities:—going to bed at noon, say, when his neighbors would be sitting down to dinner.*

. . . one thing is to be especially observed. Though Christ encountered woe in both the precept and the practice of His chronometricals, yet did He remain throughout entirely without folly or sin. Whereas, almost invariably, with inferior beings, the absolute effort to live in this world according to the strict letter of the chronometricals is, somehow, apt to involve those inferior beings eventually in strange, *unique* follies and sins, unimagined before.

The Ship versus the City

In so far as a ship and its crew sail, whether gladly or sadly, away from the land, where all were born, and leave the majority, whether friends or foes, behind on shore, the mariner image has a different constellation of meanings.

(1) *The Search for Possibility and the Escape from Necessity*

Land is the place where people are born, marry, and have children, the world where the changing seasons create a round of different duties and feelings, and the ocean, by contrast, is the place where there are no ties of home or sex, only of duty to the end for which the voyage is undertaken, the world where the change of seasons makes no difference to what the crew must do and where there is no visible life other than theirs, so that to leave land and put out to sea can signify the freeing of the spirit from finite nature, its ascetic denial of the flesh, the determination to live in one-directional historical time rather than in cyclical natural time.

E.g.   *Verse-nous ton poison pour qu'il nous réconforte!*
           Nous voulons, tant ce feu nous brûle le cerveau
           Plonger au fond du gouffre, Enfer ou Ciel, qu'importe
           Au fond de l'Inconnu pour trouver du nouveau.

                                                        (*Le Voyage*)

---

* Cf. the Snark:

> Its habit of getting up late you'll agree
> That it carries too far when I say
> That it frequently breakfasts at five-o-clock tea
> And dines on the following day.

i.e. the flight from infinite repetition to infinite novelty.

> *Plus douce qu'aux infants la chair des pommes sures,*
> *L'eau verte pénétra ma coque de sapin*
> *Et des taches de vins bleus et des vomissures*
> *Me lava, dispersant gouvernail et grappin.*
>
> (*Bâteau Ivre*)

> *Pour n'être pas changés et bêtes, ils s'envirent*
> *D'espace et de lumière et de cieux embrasés;*
> *La glace qui les mord, les soleils qui les cuivrent,*
> *Effacent lentement la marque des baisers.*
>
> (*Le Voyage*)

i.e. the purification from debauchery and sex.

The *Nautilus* is a place of refuge from those who, like its commander, have broken every tie upon earth.

i.e. the flight from injustice.

"Come hither, broken-hearted; here is another life without the guilt of intermediate death; here are wonders supernatural, without dying for them. Come hither! bury thyself in a life which, to your now equally abhorred and abhorring, landed world, is more oblivious than death. Come hither! put up *thy* gravestone, too, within the churchyard, and come hither, till we marry thee!"

Hearkening to these voices, East and West, by early sunrise, and by fall of eve, the blacksmith's soul responded, Aye, I come! And so Perth went a-whaling.

(*Moby Dick*, chapter CXII)

i.e. the flight from memory.

Away O soul! hoist instantly the anchor!
Cut the hawsers—haul out—shake out every sail!
Have we not stood here like trees in the ground long enough?
Have we not grovel'd here long enough, eating and drinking like
    mere brutes?
Have we not darken'd and dazed ourselves with books long enough?

Sail forth—steer for the deep waters only,
Reckless O soul, exploring, I with thee, and thou with me.
For we are bound where mariner has not yet dared to go.
And we will risk the ship, ourselves and all.

(*Passage to India*)

i.e. the rejection of conventional habit.

(2) *The Search for Necessity and the Escape from Possibility*

The fact that a ship is a strictly disciplined and authoritarian society as compared with normal life, and that a ship has a purpose for a voyage, means that ship and city can have almost exactly the opposite significance to the above, i.e. the land can be thought of as the

noir océan de l'immonde cité,

the place of purposelessness, of the ennui that comes from being confronted with infinite possibilities without the necessity to choose one.

So, for instance, in Ishmael's case, or in Melville's enlistment on the *Neversink*, their going to sea is a commitment to a necessity which, however unpleasant, is at least certain and preferable to the melancholia and accidie induced by the meaningless freedom on shore.

THE ENVIRONMENT OF THE SHIP

The ship, i.e. the human, individual or social, is related to two pairs of contrasting symbols, i.e.

A. The sky and its creatures,	vs.	The water and its creatures,
birds		fish, whales, octopuses, etc.
B. The day and the sun	vs.	The night and the moon

and to two scales of weather,

The degree of visibility from very clear to thick fog.
The velocity of the wind from typhoon to dead calm.

The symbolism is easier to grasp in the purely imaginary voyages like those of Coleridge, Baudelaire, and Rimbaud than in the work of Melville and Hopkins, where there is the extra complication of the relation of objective reality to subjective meaning.

A

Sky as contrasted with water = Spirit as contrasted with Nature.
What comes from the sky is a spiritual or supernatural visitation.
What lies hidden in the water is the unknown powers of nature.
E.g. Cp. the angelic spirits sent by the Moon, or Master of the sea, who move the Ancient Mariner's ship by removing the air in front of it, and the avenging spirit from the land of ice and snow which dwells nine fathoms below the surface and at their command unwillingly moves the ship up to the line.
Cp. the Albatross which is related to the Dove of the Holy Spirit, and through him to the innocent victim, Christ, and the water-snakes which

are that in nature, whether outside man or within himself, for which he feels aversion because he cannot understand them aesthetically or intellectually and despises because he cannot make use of them. But for the Fall (the shooting of the Albatross), Adam (The Ancient Mariner) would never have consciously learned through suffering the meaning of Agapé, i.e. to love one's neighbour as oneself without comparisons or greed (the blessing of the snakes), so that the Ancient Mariner might well say in the end, *O felix culpa.*

Similarly the hawk in *Moby Dick is* the messenger bird of Zeus who warns Prometheus = Ahab of his hybris when he cheats the lookout by snatching away his hat, i.e. his heroic crown, but whom in its last death-defiance the *Pequod* drags down with it. Contrasted with him is the great squid, messenger of the underworld, whose appearance frightens Starbuck more than the whale itself.

In *Un Voyage à Cythère*, the doves of Venus have been metamorphosed into ferocious crows who devour the male corpse.

B

Day and the Sun = Consciousness and the Paternal Principle as contrasted with

Night and the Moon = Unconsciousness and the Maternal Principle.

In his excellent essay on *The Ancient Mariner,** Mr Robert Penn Warren has pointed out how all the events of salvation take place under the influence of the moon, and that the sun is the hostile judge of conscience.

The Father Sun can appear at night in the form of lightning.

E.g.
> The thick black cloud was cleft, and still
> The Moon was at its side:
> Like waters shot from some high crag,
> The lightning fell with never a jag,
> A river steep and wide.

Here the Ancient Mariner, so afraid of the Father, is comforted by knowing that the Mother is still present. Again when Captain Ahab addresses the lightning, on a night without a moon, he says:

> Thou art my fiery father; my sweet mother I know not. What has thou done with her?

And Hopkins, addressing God:

---

* *The Rime of the Ancient Mariner* (Reynal & Hitchcock, 1946).

> I did say yes
> O at lightning and lashed rod;
> Thou heardst me truer than tongue confess
> Thy terror, O Christ, O God;
> Thou knowest the walls, altar and hour and night:
> The swoon of a heart that the sweep and the hurl of thee trod
> Hard down with a horror of height:
> And the midriff astrain with leaning of, laced with fire of stress.

VISIBILITY

The degree of visibility = the degree of conscious knowledge.
    I.e. fog and mist mean doubt and self-delusion, a clear day knowing where one is going or exactly what one has done.

THE WIND

The wind is always a force which the conscious will cannot cause or control. In the works we are considering which were written before the advent of the steamship, it is also the source, good or bad, of all the movements of life.
    In *The Ancient Mariner* there are four winds described.

(1) The tyrannous strong wind which chases the ship down to the dangerous land of icebergs, mist and snow, against her will.

> With sloping masts and dipping prow,
> As who pursued with yell and blow
> Still treads the shadow of his foe,
> And forward bends his head,
> The ship drove fast, loud roared the blast,
> And southward aye we fled.

Man, that is, is driven on by an irresistible rush of creative powers which he did not expect and which frighten him because he does not know where they are carrying him except that it is probably into a state of dread. The powers, however, are not necessarily evil. They only, as it turns out, drive him into temptation, for the icebergs represent that state of dread which Kierkegaard describes as the necessary precondition for the Fall.

> Dread is a desire for what one fears, a sympathetic antipathy; dread is an alien power which takes hold of the individual, and yet one cannot extricate oneself from it, does not wish to, because one is afraid, but what one fears attracts one. Dread renders the individual powerless, and the first sin always happens in a moment of weak-

ness; it therefore lacks any accountableness, but that want is the real snare.*

(The Concept of Dread)

(2) The good south wind which extricates them from the ice. This is not frightening because it takes the ego where the ego thinks it wants to go. In fact, it turns out to be, like the first elation of Adam and Eve after eating the apple, a delusion, for it disappears and leaves them in the absolute calm of guilt and despair, bereft of all power.

(3) The roaring wind which is only heard and never touches the Mariner or the ship, but brings rain, and at the sound of which angelic spirits occupy the bodies of the dead crew. To hear and not feel, means to intuit the possibility and hope for the coming of the new life which one still does not know as an actuality.

(4) Finally, when his repentance is complete, so that he can even look away from the dead men (the proof of his sin), then comes the gentle wind which fans his cheek and leads the ship back home, i.e. the powers of grace and blessing.

In *Bateau Ivre*, the wind is usually violent and inevitable, but the point is that the hero of the poem deliberately surrenders to it. He enjoys defiantly its irrationality and disorder, and speaks of

tohus-bohus . . . triomphants
La tempête a béni mes éveils maritimes.

J'ai suivi, des mois pleins, pareille aux vacheries
Hystériques, la houle à l'assaut des récifs,
Sans songer que les pieds lumineux des Maries
Pussent forcer le mufle aux Océans poussifs.

Des écumes de fleurs ont béni mes dérades
Et d'ineffables vents m'ont ailé par instants.

The final result, however, is exhaustion, the state of all-too-real calm, and lack of relation.

Mais, vrai, j'ai trop pleuré. Les aubes sont navrantes,
Toute lune est atroce et tout soleil amer . . .

Je ne puis plus, baigné de vos langueurs, ô lames,
Enlever leur sillage aux porteurs de cotons.

(*Bateau Ivre*)

In *Moby Dick*, where the weather is real weather in nature, the point is the relation of human nature to non-human nature, i.e. the kind of importance

---

*The Voyage of Maeldune begins with a similar violent wind which does just the opposite; it takes the hero intent on vengeance away from opportunity to become guilty.

that the human characters attribute to it. E.g. the typhoon is significant to two of the characters, Starbuck and Ahab.

> "Here!" cried Starbuck, seizing Stubb by the shoulder, and pointing his hand towards the weather bow, "markest thou not that the gale comes from the eastward, the very course Ahab is to run for Moby Dick? . . . The gale that now hammers at us to stave us, we can turn it into a fair wind that will drive us towards home."
>
> (Chapter CXIX)

His disapproval of Ahab's quest is strengthened by this omen to the point where he goes down to Ahab's cabin with the intention of killing him as a madman. Ahab, on the other hand, is tempted precisely because the Typhoon is in opposition to the way he has sworn to go.

> "I own thy speechless, placeless power; but to the last gasp of my earthquake life will dispute its unconditional unnatural mastery in me . . . Come in thy lowest form of love, and I will kneel and kiss thee; but at thy highest, come as mere supernal power; and though thou launches navies of full-freighted worlds, there's that in here that still remains indifferent."
>
> (Chapter CXIX)

A calm, such as the beautiful day, before the final chase begins, which offers no outside opposition, makes him think of wife and child, and nearly wins him over to Starbuck's side and to giving up the quest.

The use of the tempest in *The Wreck of the Deutschland* is still more complicated. We have the physical contrasted situation of Hopkins, the Jesuit novice

> Away in the loveable west,
> On a pastoral forehead of Wales,
> I was under a roof here, I was at rest,

and of the nuns

> And they the prey of the gales

and in counterpoint to this is the subjective contrast of their inner peace in the face of death:

> Ah! there was a heart right!
> There was single eye!
> Read the unshapeable shock night
> And knew the who and the why;
> Wording it how but by him that present and past,
> Heaven and earth are word of, worded by?
> The Simon Peter of a soul! to the blast
> Tarpeian-fast, but a blown beacon of light

with his inner tempest in his struggle to submit his self-will to the will of God, on the necessity of which St Ignatius lays so much importance.

> The frown of his face
> Before me, the hurtle of hell
> Behind, where, where was a, where was a place?

Both kinds of tempest are related as forms of suffering, but also carefully differentiated. The suffering that arises out of the relation of the soul to God only arises because of the human sin of which the climax was the Crucifixion:

> The dense and the driven Passion, and frightful sweat;
> Thence the discharge of it, there its swelling to be,
> Though felt before, though in high flood yet—
> What none would have known of it, only the heart, being hard at bay.

The relation was intended to be one of joy, and the intensity of the struggle is a direct indication of the amount of self-will to be overcome, i.e. spiritual suffering is to be treated as purgatorial, i.e. the sufferer must embrace it, saying, "I say pain but ought to say solace."

External suffering, on the other hand, is something different. No one who is shipwrecked or diseased is to be considered as more or less sinful than fortunate people. Nevertheless, nature is the handiwork of God.

> They fought with God's cold.

All that the individual can do is accept it as he or she must accept every other event pleasant or unpleasant that happens to him, as a challenge, not to despair like Starbuck, not to defy like Ahab, but as an occasion to ask what in this actual situation sent by God God requires.

In this case the nuns who are innocent exiles

> Loathed for a love men knew in them,
> Banned by the land of their birth,
> Rhine refused them. Thames would ruin them.

by their conduct in this disaster are a witness to their faith which in the very moment of physical destruction may have saved some souls from spiritual death.

> Well, she has thee for the pain, for the
> Patience; but pity for the rest of them!
> Heart, go and bleed at a bitterer vein for the
> Comfortless unconfessed of them—
> No not uncomforted: lovely-felicitous Providence
> Finger of a tender of, O of a feathery delicacy, the breast of the
> Maiden could obey so, be a bell to, ring of it, and

Startle the poor sheep back! is the shipwrack then a harvest, does
tempest carry the grain for thee?

THE STONE: THE ROMANTICS AND MATHEMATICS

Whereas the Neoclassical writers had been taught to observe particular natural objects carefully and accurately and then abstract the general from
them, the Romantics reverse the process. Thus Blake says: "All goodness resides in minute particulars" but "Natural objects always did and now do
weaken, deaden and obliterate imagination in me" and Coleridge writes in a
letter:

> The further I ascend from animated Nature [i.e. in the embracements
> of rocks and hills], from men and cattle, and the common birds of the
> woods and fields, the greater becomes in me the intensity of the feeling
> of life. Life seems to me then a universal spirit that neither has nor can
> have an opposite.

As long as images derived from observation of nature had a utility value for
decorating the thoughts of the mind, nature could be simply enjoyed, for Nature was not very important by comparison with human reason. But if there
is a mysterious relation between them, if

> La Nature est un temple où de vivants piliers
> Laissent parfois sortir de confuses paroles;
> L'homme y passe à travers des forêts de symboles
> Qui l'observent avec des regards familiers.
>
> Comme de longs échos qui de loin se confondent
> Dans une ténébreuse et profonde unité,
> Vaste comme la nuit et comme la clarté,
> Les parfums, les couleurs et les sons se répondent.
>
> (Baudelaire, *Correspondances*)

then the merely visual perception is not the important act, but the intuitive
vision of the meaning of the object, and also Nature becomes a much more
formidable creature, charged with all the joys, griefs, hopes and terrors of the
human soul, and therefore arousing very mixed feelings of love and hatred.

On the one hand, the poets long to immerse in the sea of Nature, to enjoy
its endless mystery and novelty, on the other, they long to come to port in
some transcendent eternal and unchanging reality from which the unexpected is excluded. Nature and Passion are powerful, but they are also full of
grief. True happiness would have the calm and order of bourgeois routine
without its utilitarian ignobility and boredom.

Thus the same Baudelaire who writes:

Why is the spectacle of the sea so infinitely and eternally agreeable?

Because the sea presents at once the idea of immensity and of movement . . . Twelve or fourteen leagues of liquid in movement are enough to convey to man the highest expression of beauty which he can encounter in his transient abode.

(*Mon Coeur Mis à Nu*)

and identifies human nature with the sea:

> *Vous êtes tous les deux ténébreux et discrets*
> *Homme, nul n'a sondé le fond de tes abîmes,*
> *O mer, nul ne connaît les richesses intimes*
> *Tant vous êtes jaloux de garder vos secrets!*
>
> (*L'Homme et la Mer*)

also exclaims:

> *Ah! ne jamais sortir des Nombres et des Êtres*

and likens Beauty to a dream of stone (cp. the stone of Wordsworth's dream):

> *Je hais le mouvement qui déplace les lignes,*
> *Et jamais je ne pleure et jamais je ne ris.*

And the amorous Henry Beyle who cannot live without a grand passion writes:

I used to imagine that the higher mathematics dealt with all, or almost all, aspects of things, and that, by proceeding to their study, I should arrive at a knowledge of all things that were certain, irrefutable, and demonstrable at will. I said to myself, "mathematics will get me out of Grenoble, out of that sickening morass."

So too in *The Hunting of the Snark* the Beaver and the Butcher, romantic explorers though they are, who have chosen to enter a desolate valley, where the Jub-Jub bird screams in passion overhead, and the creatures from *The Temptation of St Anthony* surround them, escape from the destructive power of sex sublimating it into arithmetical calculations based on the number 3.

And Melville, despite his love of physical beauty, in nature and in man, of

> our Pantheistic ports:
> Marquesas and glenned isles that be
> Authentic Edens in a Pagan sea.

can also note in revulsion:

> Found a family, build a state,
> The pledged event is still the same:

Matter in end will never abate
His ancient brutal claim.

Baudelaire's ideal man, the Dandy, is, from the point of view of the bourgeois, a wild figure who indulges in every kind of excess, but, from his own,
he is a fastidious ascetic who despises the bourgeois because they are "natural."

Woman is the opposite of the Dandy. Therefore she should inspire horror. Woman is hungry and she wants to eat, thirsty and she wants to drink.
She is in rut and she wants to be possessed. Woman is *natural*, that is to
say, abominable.

The Dandy should aspire to be uninterruptedly sublime. He should
live and sleep in front of a mirror.

The more a man cultivates the arts, the less he fornicates. A more and
more apparent cleavage occurs between the spirit and the brute.

(*Mon Coeur Mis à Nu*)

The Euclidean stone, the transcendent stable reality desired as a haven for
the storm-tossed mariner, is not, however, the Transcendental Newtonian
God but rather the Platonic Ideas. Geometry does not judge or interfere but
is beyond good and evil; it demands nothing but what the mind cares to give
it; moreover, it cannot be made use of, it is not one of those ignoble social
snarks, you cannot fetch it home and serve it with greens: it is not for striking a light, it is simply itself, and to be oneself is the aim of every romantic.

When Peer Gynt visits the land of the Trolls, the king puts him through a
catechism:

K. What is the difference between Trolls and Men?
P. There isn't any, as far as I can gather;
   Big trolls would roast and little ones would claw you—
   Just as with us if only we dared do it.
K. True; we're alike in that and other things too.
   Still, just as morning's different from evening,
   So there's a real difference between us,
   And I will tell you what it is. Out yonder
   Under the skies men have a common saying:
   "Man, to thyself be true!" But here, 'mongst Trolls
   "Troll, to thyself be—enough."

(*Peer Gynt*, II.6)

To be enough to oneself means to have no conscious ego standing over
against the self, to be unable to say no to oneself, or to distinguish fantasy
from reality, not to be able to lie, to have no name and answer to Hi or to any
loud cry. The siren voice of the poetic shell calls men to the sea, the double
kingdom, to put off their human nature and be Trolls. The prospect is as al-
luring to every man as it was to Faust:

Hier fass ich Fuss! Hier sind es Wirklichkeiten,
Von hier aus darf der Geist mit Geistern streiten,
Das Doppelreich, das grosse, sich bereiten.
So fern sie war, wie kann sie näher sein!
Ich rette sie und sie ist doppelt mein.

(*Faust*, Part II, 1.5)

yet every man makes his reservations like Peer Gynt.

I've taken a tail, it is true; but then
I can undo the knots that our friend has tied,
And take the thing off. I have shed my breeches;
They were old and patched; but that won't prevent me
From putting them on if I have a mind to.
I shall probably find it just as easy
To deal with your Trollish way of living.
I can easily swear that a cow's a maiden;
An oath's not a difficult thing to swallow.
But to know that one never can get one's freedom—
Not even to die as a human being—
To end one's day as a Troll of the mountains—
Never go back, as you tell me plainly—
That is a thing that I'll not submit to.

(*Peer Gynt*, II.6)

For to submit would be to be swallowed up in the waters, to be drowned in the deluge.

On the other side, the Euclidean stone speaks of a world of pure truth, the image to the weary mariner of all that is true to itself. It is, however, not truth which is enough to itself, and no man can be as a triangle any more than he can be as a troll, for he would have to lose his self and become a purely self-conscious ego whose motto would be "I to I be enough." This is the dilemma of the romantic hero.

THREE

Ishmael–Don Quixote

Mes soeurs, n'aimez pas les marins:
La solitude est leur royaume.
— Jean Cocteau

What is a hero? The exceptional individual. How is he recognised, whether in life or in books? By the degree of interest he arouses in the spectator or the reader. A comparative study, therefore, of the kinds of individuals which writers in various periods have chosen for their heroes often provides a useful clue to the attitudes and preoccupations of each age, for a man's interest always centres, consciously or unconsciously, round what seems to him the most important and still unsolved problem. The hero and his story are simultaneously a stating and a solving of the problem.

HEROIC AUTHORITY

The exceptional individual is one who possesses authority over the average. This authority can be of three kinds, aesthetic, ethical and religious.

AESTHETIC AUTHORITY

Aesthetic authority arises from a necessary inequality of finite individuals in relation to one another. The aesthetic hero is the man to whom fortune has granted exceptional gifts. These may be within himself, e.g. A is more beautiful or cleverer than B, or in the situation in which he is placed, e.g. A is a king, B is a slave.

The inequality is necessary in the first case because beauty or brains are given qualities which cannot be produced or exchanged by any voluntary decision on either side, and in the second because, at any given moment of time in the situation, authority is given to the one.

Since, by virtue of his superior gifts, the hero can do what the average cannot do for themselves, he must do precisely that to be recognised by them as a hero. Thus, if victory over their enemies is what they most desire, he must lead them in war; if victory over nature, he must construct bridges, drain swamps, etc. In return they must give him admiration and obedience. The natural threat to the aesthetic hero is the passing of time, culminating in the inevitable fact of death, which brings him to the same level of nullity as everyone else.

There are also dangers within himself and within the others. For him the danger is pride, i.e. thinking that his superior qualities are not given him by the gods or fate or nature, but earned by him, i.e. that he is not merely luck-ier than others but intrinsically morally better. If he yields to this, he becomes a tyrant who demands admiration in excess and is insolent towards the pow-ers that gave him his power. Vice versa, the danger for the average is envy, i.e. denying that the inequality is necessary, and wishing to take the hero's place or, if that is impossible, at least to bring him down to their level.

The aesthetic hero is naturally thought of as being happy, for all desire to be as he. He only becomes unhappy when he ceases to be superior, i.e. when he dies, or suffers some great misfortune.

The Homeric kind of hero is pathetic, i.e. his death happens to him with-out any fault on his part. The hero of Greek drama is tragic because his death is due to pride on his part, and envy on the part of the gods.

ETHICAL AUTHORITY

Ethical authority arises from an accidental inequality in the relation of indi-viduals to the universal truth. The ethical hero is the one who at any given moment happens to know more than the others. This knowledge can be any part of the truth, not only what is commonly called ethics.

> E.g. A is ethically superior in relation to B if he knows the multiplication
> table up to 11 when B only knows it up to 10, just as C is to D, if C
> knows that it is wrong to steal and D does not yet know it.

Here it is not a question of innate gifts (if A is cleverer than B he is aes-thetically superior) but a remediable accident of time and opportunity, i.e. the hero is not one who *can* do what the others cannot, but one who *does* know now what the others *do* not but can be taught by him, which is precisely what he must do if he is to be recognised by them as a hero. In return they give him their attention, as a bridge between them and the truth, for what is re-quired of both is exactly the same, to love and to learn as much about the truth as possible. It is quite possible, for instance, that if A teaches B the eleven times table, so making them equal, B now learns the twelves table be-fore A, and their positions are reversed. It is now B who is the hero.

Here again there are dangers both from without and within. "Without," however, now has a special sense, it means outside the mind, i.e. not from time or fate, but from matter, the needs and passions of the body which in-terfere with love and study of the truth.

The inner danger is the same for both hero-teacher and inferior pupil, namely, that they will both attempt to treat the situation as an aesthetic rela-tion between them and forget or deny their relations to the truth, which is the important thing. Thus the ethical hero, desiring aesthetic admiration, is tempted to refuse to surrender his superiority and refuse to share his knowl-edge, treating it instead as a hermetic mystery, the consequence of which is that, thinking always of his relation to the ignorant, he ceases to think about the truth. The inferior, desiring ease and bodily pleasure, are tempted either to refuse to learn from the hero or to adopt a passive attitude of admiration which takes what he says because he says it, and not because they can see for themselves that it is the truth.

The Ethical Hero, e.g. Socrates, is thought of as one who is happier than his inferiors because he is already in the movement away from the dark misery of ignorance and servitude to passion towards the bright joy of freedom in knowledge of the truth. Time is not the ultimately overwhelming enemy, but the temporary element through which men move towards immortality.

Religious Authority

Religious authority is like aesthetic authority in that it is not transferable from one individual to another and like ethical authority in that it arises, not from a relation between individuals, but from a relation to truth. But the religious definition of truth is not that it is universal but that it is absolute. The religious hero is one who is committed to anything with absolute passion, i.e. to him it is the absolute truth, his god. The stress is so strongly on the absolute that though he may be passionately related to what, ethically, i.e. universally, is false, he is a religious hero and has religious authority over the one who is lukewarmly or dispassionately related to what is true. Thus, the distinction between being absolutely committed to the real truth, and being absolutely committed to falsehood, is not between being a religious man or not being one, but between the sane and the mad.

In a sense, the religious hero is not related to others at all: his authority cannot command admiration, or transfer knowledge, it can only enkindle by example a similar absolute passion, not necessarily for the same god. (E.g. one has sometimes observed in education that a teacher with a passion for, say, mathematics, has aroused in an unmathematical pupil a passion for, say, Latin.)

The dangers for the religious hero are two: firstly, that he may lose his faith, and so cease to be absolutely committed, and secondly and much more seriously that while continuing to recognise the absolute commitment he should transmute its nature from positive to negative, so that he is committed to the truth in an absolute passion of aversion and hatred. In the first case, he simply ceases to be a religious hero; in the second, he becomes the negative religious hero, i.e. the devil, the absolute villain, Iago or Claggart. The temptation to either arises from expecting something in return for his commitment, i.e. the aesthetic hero may expect happiness so long as he possesses his gifts, but it is his happiness that is a temptation to pride, the ethical hero can look forward to more and more true happiness so long as he perseveres, but it is the pleasures of the body that tempt him to give up his quest, but the religious hero cannot demand happiness, except the happiness of the commitment itself, of love for love's sake. It does not follow that he must necessarily expect misery though, since few desire misery, it is usually misery and not happiness or pleasure that are his temptation; it is more correct to say that whatever he does not expect is temptation.

The Romantic Hero

In Wordsworth's dream, the hero is described as a combination of a Bedouin desert dweller and Don Quixote; his intention is to carry away symbols of imagination and abstract reason to hide them from the destructive deluge to come; his motive, to save them for future descendants of men, for the age after the Flood. His end is left in doubt, but it seems probable that it is tragic, that he is overwhelmed and fails to save the treasures entrusted to him. Why a Bedouin and why Don Quixote?

Ishmael

The Biblical story of the first Bedouin, Ishmael, is given in *Genesis* (chapters XVI and XVII, and chapter XXI). Abraham's wife Sarah is barren, so at her suggestion Abraham lies with a bond-maiden, Hagar. Sarah now becomes jealous and with Abraham's consent treats the pregnant Hagar so badly that she runs away into the desert. But there an angel speaks to her and tells her to return to her mistress, and prophesies:

> Behold, thou shalt bear a son, and shalt call his name Ishmael. He will be a wild man; his hand will be against every man, and every man's hand against him: and he shall dwell in the midst of all his brethren.

God also speaks to Abraham:

> Sarah thy wife shall bear thee a son indeed and thou shalt call his name Isaac . . . As for Ishmael . . . Behold, I have blessed him, and will make him a great nation. But my covenant shall be with Isaac which Sarah shall bear unto thee at this set time in the next year.

In due order first Ishmael and then Isaac are born, but Sarah is still jealous—in fairness to her she has both before and now caught Hagar mocking at her—and says to Abraham:

> "Cast out this bondwoman and her son; for the son of this bondwoman shall not be heir with my son, even with Isaac."
>
> And the thing was very grievous in Abraham's sight because of his son. And God said unto Abraham, Let it not be grievous in thy sight because of the lad, and because of thy bondwoman; in all that Sarah hath

said unto thee, hearken unto her voice; for in Isaac shall thy seed be called.

And also of the son of the bondwoman will I make a nation, because he is thy seed.

Abraham accordingly gives Hagar and Ishmael some bread and water and turns them out into the desert where they are about to die of thirst, when God shows her a well and tells her too that he will make a great nation of Ishmael.

And God was with the lad; and he grew, and dwelt in the wilderness, and became an archer.

Translating this story into terms of personality, we get someone who

(1) Is conscious of superior powers. (The first-born)

(2) Has a grievance, feeling that he is the victim of some wrong for which he is not responsible. (Illegitimate)

(3) Does not like and is not liked by the respectable fashionable and successful of this world (Sarah and Isaac). He despises them for not being gifted as he (Hagar's mocking of Sarah) and they envy and persecute him for the same reason. (Sarah's behaviour towards Hagar)

(4) In consequence he is socially an outcast and not easily employable. If he does fall in love, it is an unhappy love. (He dwells in the wilderness)

(5) He prefers to spend his time with other social outcasts like himself, with crooks, whores, impressed sailors, etc., of whom there are a good many. (A great nation)

(6) In solitude and low company he develops the qualities of courage and tough endurance. (An archer)

(7) He is unhappy and lonely, yet cherishes his unhappiness and loneliness as a proof of his superiority. (He chooses to live in the desert)

DON QUIXOTE

When we are first introduced to Don Quixote he is

(1) poor

(2) not a knight but only the plain Alonso Quixano

(3) has had a sort of inclination for a good country lass, though 'tis believed she never heard of it

(4) has nothing to do except hunt and read romances about Knight Errantry

(5) is slightly mad, i.e. he sells land to buy these books.

Suddenly he goes really mad: i.e. instead of being content to project himself in imagination into the heroes of the books, he sets out to become in reality what he admires and rides off to restore to the fallen world the golden age of chivalry, and to challenge all comers to admit that the obscure country girl is the Princess Dulcinea del Toboso, the most beautiful woman in the world. Naturally enough, he fails in everything. When he thinks he is attacking giants, heretics and heathens he is not only worsted in combat, but attacks innocent people and destroys others people's property.

Further, his madness has two aspects: firstly, the nature of his resolution and secondly the moments in which he sees people and objects as other than they are. The first is constant, the second intermittent. Yet when his vision is sane, i.e. when he sees that the windmills are windmills and not giants, it does not change his original conviction, for he takes his moments of sane vision to be mad and says, "These cursed magicians delude me, first drawing me into dangerous adventures by the appearances of things as they really are and then presently changing the face of things as they please." Even when they meet a plain country wench, whom Don Quixote correctly sees as such, and Sancho Panza for a joke describes her as his ideal lady, the Princess Dulcinea, he believes Sancho Panza against the evidence of his own feelings.

Finally, after many adventures, all of them unsuccessful, he falls sick, and suddenly he recovers his sanity. His friends wish him to go on being mad and to provide them with fresh amusement, but he says simply: "Ne'er look for birds of this year in the nests of the last: I was mad and am now in my senses: I was once Don Quixote de la Mancha but am now the plain Alonso Quixano, and I hope the sincerity of my words and my repentance may restore me the same esteem you have had for me before." Whereupon he dies.

Don Quixote is, of course, a representation, the greatest in literature, of the Religious Hero, whose faith is never shaken and whose characteristics we have already discussed. The only point to consider here is why Cervantes makes him recover his sanity at the end. Does this mean that he ceases to be a religious hero, that he loses his faith? No. It is because Cervantes realises instinctively that the Religious Hero cannot be accurately portrayed in art. Art is bound by its nature to make the hero interesting, i.e. to be recognisable as a hero by others. Both the aesthetic hero and the ethical hero are necessarily interesting and recognisable by their deeds and their knowledge, but it is accidental and irrelevant if the religious hero is so recognised or not. Unless Don Quixote recovers his senses, it would imply that the Religious Hero is always also an aesthetic hero (which is what his friends want him to be). On the other hand, once he does, he has to die, for he becomes uninteresting and therefore cannot live in a book.

ISHMAEL AND DON QUIXOTE COMPARED

(1) Both are solitaries, despised and rejected by the world. But while Ishmael retreats from society, Don Quixote seeks a relation with it and it is just this attempt that gets him into trouble. As long as he stayed in his library alone reading, he was free from misfortune.

(2) Both are unhappy. But while Ishmael has a grievance and is sorry for him-

self, Don Quixote is only unhappy because he is sorry the world is not the world which for its own sake it should be; he is not sorry for himself but ashamed of himself for being unable to cure the world of its sickness.

(3) Both are unsuccessful in love; but while Ishmael is sorry because his love is not returned, Don Quixote never thinks of reciprocation and is only ashamed because he cannot prove his love.

(4) Both consort with and enjoy low company; but while Ishmael enjoys it because it is low and vicious, Don Quixote enjoys it because he is persuaded that it is noble and virtuous.

(5) Both are brave and tough; but while Ishmael congratulates himself on this fact, Don Quixote takes it for granted without thinking.

(6) Both are wanderers; but while Ishmael is a wanderer because he lacks a definite commitment to any person or goal, it is just his mania of commitment which turns the peaceful stay-at-home Alonso Quixano into the pugnacious vagabond Don Quixote de la Mancha.

(7) Ishmael has gifts which he will not put at the service of others, i.e. he does not try to be recognised as the aesthetic or ethical hero which he is.

Don Quixote, on the other hand, has no gifts yet tries desperately to be of use. He is not an aesthetic or ethical hero but goes on trying, in the face of constant failure, to become one.

The crucial difference between them, in fact, is that Ishmael is self-conscious and Don Quixote is completely self-forgetful.

The Heroic Action

The heroes of Classical and Renaissance literature (with the exception of Hamlet) are recognisable as heroic through the nature of their relations to other men, i.e. of their social acts. The hero is the one who conquers and rules others, or who teaches others. If he suffers a tragic fall, it is a social fall, he is overthrown by a stronger hero, or commits crimes which arouse public horror, or, like Socrates, is executed for being a political danger.

But our dream Ishmael–Don Quixote is quite alone. He is plainly not a conqueror. He is related to knowledge, i.e. he is the sole guardian of the imagination and the reason, the two human forms of knowledge, but he does not teach anyone else; he keeps the shell and the stone to himself. He is apparently performing a social act; he is trying to save these treasures for the sake of the future world, but there is no one around to recognise what he is doing, and even the I of the dreamer loses sight of him and does not know his end, whether or not he succeeded.

Taking such a figure as an archetype, we may now consider the romantic writers, their critical statements and the heroes of their books, and ask: What role does Ishmael play in their work? What role does Don Quixote play? How are these two related? What is the romantic hero up to?

There is almost universal agreement that one of the distinguishing marks of the hero is that he is always unhappy. To be happy is almost a proof that one is not a hero. For instance:

I have found a definition of the Beautiful, of my own conception of the Beautiful. It is something intense and sad, leaving scope for conjecture ... A beautiful male head ... will suggest ardours and passions—spiritual longings—ambitions darkly repressed—powers turned to bitterness through lack of employment—traces, sometimes, of a revengeful coldness (for the archetype of the dandy must not be forgotten here), sometimes, also—and this is one of the most interesting characteristics of Beauty—of mystery, and last of all (let me admit the exact point to which I am a modern in my aesthetics) of Unhappiness. I do not pretend that Joy cannot associate with Beauty, but I will maintain that Joy is one of her most vulgar adornments, while Melancholy may be called her illustrious spouse—so much so that I can scarcely conceive (is my brain become a witch's mirror?) a type of Beauty which has nothing to do with Sorrow. In pursuit of—others might say obsessed by—those ideas, it may be supposed that I have difficulty in not concluding from them that the most perfect type of manly beauty is Satan—as Milton saw him.

(Baudelaire, *Fusées*)

The sun hides not the ocean, which is the dark side of this earth, and which is two thirds of this earth. So therefore, that mortal man who hath more of joy than sorrow in him, that mortal man cannot be true—not true, or undeveloped. . . . He who dodges hospitals and jails, and walks fast crossing grave-yards, and would rather talk of operas than hell; calls Cowper, Young, Pascal, Rousseau, poor devils all of sick men; and throughout a care-free lifetime swears by Rabelais as passing wise, and therefore jolly;—not that man is fitted to sit down on tomb-stones, and break the green damp mould with unfathomably wondrous Solomon.

(Melville, *Moby Dick*, chapter XCVI)

It is strange, too, that he most strongly enlisted my feelings in behalf of the life of the seamen, when he depicted his more terrible moments of suffering and despair. For the light side of the painting I had a limited sympathy. My visions were of shipwrecks, famines, of death and captivity among barbarian hordes, of a lifetime dragged out in sorrow and tears upon some gray and desolate wreck, in an ocean unfathomable and unknown.

(Poe, *Gordon Pym*)

This is something new in the conception of the hero: that he *ought* to be unhappy. Unhappiness, to the classical aesthetic hero, is the sign that he is ceasing to be one; and to the classical ethical hero the sign that he has not yet become one.

There is also an agreement that the hero should be solitary, or if he
does enter into relations with others, the relations should be very temporary.
E.g. *Childe Harold*:

> Where rose the mountains, there to him were friends;
> Where rolled the ocean, thereon was his home;
> Where a blue sky, and glowing clime, extends,
> He had the passion and the power to roam;
> The desert, forest, cavern, breaker's foam,
> Were unto him companionship; they spake
> A mutual language, closer than the tome
> Of his land's tongue, which he would oft foresake
> For Nature's pages gloss'd by sunbeams on the lake.

★   ★   ★

> But in Man's dwellings he became a thing
> Restless and worn, and stern and wearisome,
> Droop'd as a wild-born falcon with clipt wings
> To whom the boundless air alone were home.
> Then came his fit again, which to o'ercome
> As eagerly the barr'd-up bird will beat
> His breast and beak against the wiry dome
> Till the blood tinge his plumage, so the heat
> Of his impeded soul would through his bosom eat.
>
> (III. 13, 15)

And Childe Harold says of himself:

> I have not loved the world, nor the world me;
> I have not flatter'd its rank breath, nor bow'd
> To the idolatries a patient knee,
> Nor conn'd my cheek to smiles, nor cried aloud
> In worship of an echo; in the crowd
> They could not deem me one of such; I stood
> Among them, but not of them, in a shroud
> Of thoughts which were not their thoughts, and still could,
> Had I not filed my mind, which thus itself subdued.
>
> (III. 113)

So Baudelaire:

> Many friends, many gloves—for fear of the itch.

The Ancient Mariner has no use for marriage and though he speaks favorably of praying in company:

> O sweeter than the marriage-feast
> 'Tis sweeter far to me,

> To walk together to the kirk
> With a goodly company!

he really thinks that the hermit's solitary moss cushion in the wood is the proper church, and he himself wanders about and is only related to others when he tells them his story:

> I pass, like night, from land to land,
> I have strange power of speech;
> That moment that his face I see,
> I know the man that must hear me:
> To him my tale I teach.

He doesn't care whether or not the other wants to hear it, and, the moment he has finished, has no further use for him.

The same lack of any permanent interest in others and their opinions is equally apparent in those who are outwardly socially involved. Ahab is only interested in getting his crew to do what he wants; he is entirely indifferent to their opinion of him except insofar that he needs their approval or at least assent to carry out his scheme.

Goethe's Faust and Ibsen's Peer Gynt both meet a lot of people, but the whole point about these heroes is that they always leave the others behind.

The same is true of both Da Ponte–Mozart's *Don Giovanni* and Byron's *Don Juan*. At first sight it looks as if Don Giovanni, the seducer, must be intensely interested in women and in their opinion of him, but this is really not the case. He doesn't care what they look like, once is enough, and he has no wish to be remembered by them. Indeed, what causes his downfall is that some of them do. What he is really interested in, in fact, is not women, but his list of women seduced, the number of names in his private diary. Byron's Don Juan, who is always the seduced one, allows it to happen over and over again, not because he is interested in the lady but because it is a new experience to remember.

This again is novel. The classical aesthetic hero must command others' admiration as long as he can, the classical ethical hero must teach them all he can. If he were left alone without admirers or without pupils, he would cease to be himself.

The Grievance

The classical aesthetic hero is pleased with the past, with his own record and his ancestor. If something tragic happens to him it is because he has been too pleased, too arrogantly happy.

With the Romantic Hero it is not so. The proof that he is the exceptional hero is that he comes of neurotic stock.

My ancestors, idiots or maniacs, in the solemn houses, all victims of terrible passions.

(Baudelaire, *Fusées*)

or that his childhood was unhappy:

And lastly, if you are hungry or thirsty, there is someone who chases you.
(Rimbaud, *Les Illuminations*)

And if, having surprised him in immodest acts of pity, his mother was alarmed, the profound tendernesses of the child fastened upon this astonishment. That's how it was. She had the blue-eyed look—which lies.
(Rimbaud, *Les Poètes de Sept Ans*)

Something catastrophic has happened in the past to all of them. Even if, in the case of the Ancient Mariner, he alone is responsible for his catastrophe—through his criminal *acte gratuit* of shooting the Albatross—he only becomes a hero through it. Before that he was just anyone. He has long ago repented, done penance and been shriven by the hermit for his crime. Repentance, penance and pardon are usually thought of as putting an end to the matter. Now the sinner can forget the whole thing and be one of the family, of God's children, and of society. The Ancient Mariner does nothing of the sort. He has to confess over and over again to prove that he is interesting. He doesn't want to forget or to have others forget.

It is noteworthy that three of the Mariner heroes, the most dedicated, the most Quixotic, are dedicated to Revenge. Captain Ahab, to revenge the loss of his leg, Captain Nemo the loss of his wife and children, the hero of the *Voyage of Maeldune* the death of his father.

The avenging hero is, of course, a very ancient figure; but several significant changes have taken place.

In the *Oresteia*, for instance, Orestes avenges his father's death and is pursued by the Furies set on him by the ghost of his mother, and is finally absolved by the Divine Court of Justice. But it is important to note that

(1) His murder of Clytemnestra is not a free choice of his own will, but a duty imposed upon him through his duty to his father.
(2) The suffering he undergoes at the hands of the Furies is unexpected by him, is not due to anything in him, for they are set upon him from without.
(3) He does not repent but is acquitted, on the grounds that the duty to the father takes precedence over the duty to the mother.
(4) He is a hero put into a tragic predicament, but if the situation were not tragic, he would still be a hero, only a happy one.

In most Elizabethan drama the revenge situation is similar. Shakespeare, however, had a new vision of the nature of revenge, and transformed the old

Hamlet into the first hero of the romantic type. I.e. Shakespeare's Hamlet is made a hero by the situation in which he finds himself of having a mother who has committed adultery with his uncle, who has murdered his father. Before this happened he was no hero, just an ordinary pleasant young man. The result is that, instead of just avenging his father and getting it over with, he secretly cherishes the situation and cannot bear to end it, for who will he be then?

This conception of revenge as a vocation is made all the clearer when the revenge theme is combined with the quest theme. Traditionally, the quest is for some treasure, such as the water of life. Giants or dragons may get slain in the process because they stand between the hero and the treasure, but it is the obtaining of the treasure not the slaying of the dragon that is the hero's goal. The revenge as quest brings out the *value* of the hated object to the hero.

The Romantic Avenger Hero, in fact, is a person who is in dread of not having a vocation and yet is unable to choose one for himself as Don Quixote does (the proof that Don Quixote's decision to save the world is his own is that he has no idea what the world is like), and so has to be given it from without.

"My injury," he says, "is not an injury *to* me; it *is* me. If I cancel it out by succeeding in my vengeance, I shall not know who I am and will have to die. I cannot live without it." So not only does he cherish the memory of a catastrophic injury, but also he is not lured forward by the hope of happiness at some future date.

That Ethical Hero of the Enlightenment, Prince Tamino in *The Magic Flute*, braves suffering, the ordeal by fire and water, because he knows that on the other side of it wait the Palace of Wisdom and the Princess Pamina. The Religious Hero, Don Quixote, may accept suffering in the cause of duty cheerfully without thinking of any reward, but he would much rather not suffer, does not congratulate himself on suffering nor deliberately seek it.

But the Romantic Hero does not expect any ultimate relief. The hero of *Bateau Ivre* is not motivated by any hope of reaching the Islands of the Blessed; the Baker more than half suspects that the Snark may be a Boojum. Nor does Ahab believe for a moment that if he succeeds in killing the White Whale, he will be any happier.

Before discussing why this should be so, we should first see the hero in relation to those who are not, and perhaps the simplest way to do this is to take one group, the crew of the *Pequod*.

Ishmael-Melville

Ishmael cannot properly be called a member of the crew; for, from the moment that he steps on board, he only speaks or is spoken to once more when after his first ducking (baptism) he makes his will, i.e. consciously accepts the absolute finality of his commitment. From then on, he becomes simply the recording consciousness, the senses and the mind through which we experience everything.

This suggests that if we are identified with him then, we should also identify ourselves with him during the prologue when he does have a certain personal existence.

One day in Manhattan Ishmael resolves to go whaling. To this resolution he is pushed from behind by the need to escape from a spiritual condition of spleen and powerlessness—Manhattan is for him the *selva oscura* of the *Divine Comedy* and the Sargasso Sea of the Ancient Mariner; and he is lured from in front by a vague but haunting image. He has never consciously heard of Moby Dick yet:

> in the wild conceits that swayed me to my purpose, two and two there floated into my inmost soul, endless processions of the whale, and, midmost of them all, one grand hooded phantom, like a snow hill in the air.
>
> (1)

But between this initial resolve and the actual decision, the irrevocable commitment of signing on the *Pequod*, he has a preliminary journey to make, during which he is subjected to various initiations from any of which he could draw back and return to the city.

He begins to move away from the safe centre of normal routine, convention and status (he has been a schoolmaster, i.e. a conventional authority) towards the edge of the land to the port New Bedford. The first test is a shock of fright. Imagining it to be an inn, i.e. a place of shelter and friendly companionship, he pushes open the door of *The Trap* and finds himself in a Negro church when the minister is preaching about hell, the wailing and gnashing of teeth. This is a warning that in his state of spleen from which he is trying to escape, it is easy to take a wrong turning—into despair. he rejects this and enters the Spouter Inn whose proprietor has the ominous name of Coffin. (It is finally a coffin that saves him from drowning—death and rebirth are two aspects of the same thing. Who would save his life must lose it.) Here he has a brief glimpse of the Handsome Sailor, Bulkington, who will play no part in *Moby Dick*, but will appear as a protagonist in a later work of Melville's under the name of Billy Budd, and the whole Queequeg episode begins.

Ishmael is a white man and a Presbyterian: Queequeg is a South-Sea Islander and a Pagan, formerly a cannibal. The Christian world is the world of consciousness, i.e. the ethically superior world which knows the truth, both the artistic and scientific truths and the moral truth that one should love one's neighbor as oneself.

The pagan world is the unconscious world, which does not know the truth. The cannibalism it practises is a symbol of self-love, of treating one's neighbor as existing solely for one's own advantage. Queequeg left his island in order to become conscious of the truth, only to discover that those who are conscious of it do not obey it, and so has decided to live as a pagan in the Christian world.

Ishmael, like us, has two preconceived notions.

(1) That men who are not white are ugly, i.e. in a physical sense, aesthetically inferior. He has just had that notion reinforced by seeing the handsome white Bulkington.

(2) That pagans cannot obey the Christian commandment to love one's neighbor as oneself, because they have never heard the Word of the true God, i.e. they are ethically inferior.

Ishmael is disabused of both notions. He admits that Queequeg is beautiful, and that he loves his neighbor, in fact, more than most Christians. When on the short voyage from New Bedford to Nantucket Queequeg rescues from drowning—again a test of Ishmael's courage (can he face the possibility of drowning?)—the man who has just insulted him, saying "It's a mutual joint-stock world in all meridians. We cannibals must help these Christians," he exhibits Christian forgiveness and Christian *agape* without the slightest effort. He is a doer of the Word who has never heard the Word.

By accepting Queequeg—the symbolic act of acceptance is his joining in the worship of Queequeg's idol—Ishmael proves himself worthy of the voyage.

The last tests are the mysterious warning by Elijah not to sail on the *Pequod*, another test of courage, and the encounter with the owners, Captains Peleg and Bildad.

This pair are Quakers, i.e. people who consciously believe in applying the absolute law of love in time and the world. No man who is not a saint can do this; Ishmael has first to be made conscious through this pair of the discrepancy between Heaven's time and Jerusalem time, and then to be warned against falling into either of the two temptations which follow the moment one is so conscious, either of frivolity, i.e. taking the contradiction too lightly, which is what Peleg does, or, more seriously, of hypocrisy, i.e. of pretending that there is no contradiction and that one is living by Heaven's time, which is what Bildad does. Bildad's besetting vice is avarice, which is the spiritual version of cannibalism. He does not eat men, but he exploits them to the death. Avarice is worse than cannibalism because the latter is limited by natural appetite—you cannot eat more than a certain amount of flesh—but avarice has no limits—there is no end to the accumulation of money.

FATHER MAPPLE'S SERMON

Standing apart from Ishmael's other tests is Father Mapple's Sermon. This is not, as has sometimes been said, a magnificent irrelevance, but an essential clue to the meaning of the whole book. The story of Jonah is the story of a voyage undertaken for the wrong reasons, of learning repentance through suffering and a final acceptance of duty. Jonah has ethical authority, i.e. he knows the Word; he is called upon to become more than that, to become an ethical hero with absolute passion, i.e. a religious hero; he flees from the divine command out of aesthetic pride, a fear that he will not be listened to and admired, not be an aesthetic hero. He is punished for his refusal by being confronted with the really aesthetically great, the storm and the whale, compared with which the greatest emperor is a puny weakling, and then, in the whale's belly, he is deprived of even the one gift he had, his ability to hear the Word. Humbled, he does not despair but repents and trusts in the God whom he can no longer hear. God forgives him, he is cast up on the land, and sets off to fulfil his vocation.

In drawing the moral, Father Mapple says two apparently contradictory things.

(1) If we obey God, we must disobey ourselves; and it is in this disobeying of ourselves, wherein the hardness of obeying God consists.

(2) Delight is to him—a far, far upward and inward delight—who against the proud gods and commodores of this earth ever stands forth his own inexorable self.

This is the same thing that the Button-Moulder says to Peer Gynt:

> To be one's self is to slay one's self
> But as perhaps that explanation
> Is thrown away on you, let's say,
> To follow out, in everything,
> What the Master's intention was.

(V. 9)

Man's being is a copulative relation between a subject ego and a predicate self. The ego is aware of the self as given, already there in the world, finite, derived, along with, related and comparable to other beings. It is further aware of the self not only as existing but also as potential, as not fully actual but as a self which becomes itself.

Being of itself unaware of its potentialities, the self cannot become itself of itself, cannot initiate anything; all it desires is to be in equilibrium, a self-enjoying, self-sufficient self: the responsibility for self-realisation lies with the ego which can decide; the self can only welcome or resist the decision when it is taken.

The ego, on the other hand, has no potentialities, only existence. Further, it is isolated; it cannot compare its egoship with other egos, as it can compare the self it is related to with other selves.

The desire of the ego is a double one. As freely owning a self, it desires a self of which it can approve. As solitary it desires to be approved of for the

self it has. This approval must have absolute authority, for the approval of finite beings whom the ego can see are not self-existent posits an ultimate authority which approves of their approval, i.e. the ego desires a God.

The ego, therefore, has three tasks:

(1) To know the self and the world, as they exist now.
(2) To know the true God and what He requires the ego to realise in the
     self as he knows it.
(3) To obey these commands.

The ego may err in three ways:

(1) It may refuse to look honestly at its given self and prefer a vague or a
     fantastic conception to the truth. The temptation to do so arises from
     the fear that if it should know the truth about the self, it would find that
     it had a self of which it did not approve, i.e. not the sort of self it would
     like to have to develop.
(2) It may prefer a false god to the true God. The temptation to do this
     arises out of a fear that if it knew the true God, the ego would encounter
     disapproval. A false god or idol is always one which the ego believes it
     can manage through magic; upon whose approval, therefore, it can, if it
     is smart enough, depend.
(3) Knowing the self and what God requires to realise in the self, it may
     disobey negatively out of weakness, yielding to the opposition of the self
     to change, or positively out of defiance, in assertion of its autonomy.

The Voyage of the Pequod

The voyage of the *Pequod* is one voyage for Ishmael and with him us, and another for the rest of the crew.

For us the voyage signifies the exploration of the self and the world, of potential essences. Nothing happens to us, we survive, and we are the same people at the end as at the beginning except that we know ourselves and others
better. We had to be tested first to see whether we were capable of such an
exploration; once we have passed the tests, we have nothing to do but record.

For the rest of the crew, however, it is not the voyage of self-inspection before the act, but the act of historical existence itself. They learn nothing about
themselves, but they are changed before our eyes, and reveal themselves unwittingly in what they say and do.

When we have finished the book, we realise why Father Mapple's sermon
was put in where it was: in order that we might know the moral presuppositions by which we are to judge the speeches and actions of Ahab and the rest.

The crew of the *Pequod* are a society whose function is to kill whales. As
such each has a specialised function of his own, arranged in a hierarchy of
authority.

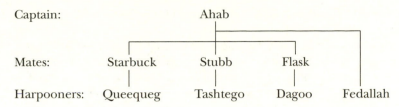

Captain: Ahab

Mates: Starbuck   Stubb   Flask

Harpooners: Queequeg   Tashtego   Dagoo   Fedallah

Then the crowd of seamen who man the whale-boats, of whom one or two appear for a moment, such as the old Manx sailor. Standing apart from them because their special functions are only indirectly connected with whales are:

Pip, Ahab's cabin boy
Perth, the Blacksmith
Carpenter

In their motives for going on the voyage:

Ahab wants to kill one particular whale.
The Blacksmith wishes to escape his memories.
The Carpenter wants to carpenter.
Pip doesn't want to go because he is terrified, but has no option.

The rest have a common motive which makes them a community, they want to earn their living, in a way for which they are fitted and which they enjoy. Since they are doing what they like and are good at it they are a happy community, and for them killing whales is morally permissible and indeed a much better job than most. It may sometimes tempt to unnecessary cruelty—as when Flask deliberately pricks the abscess of the old whale—but it encourages courage and democratic comradeship—the atmosphere on the *Pequod* is very different from that of the *Neversink*.

They are therefore in the right in going on the voyage. The only ones who should not have gone are firstly Ahab, because he has passed beyond killing whales in general, and secondly Pip, who lacks the courage which for whaling is essential, just as Captain De Deer of the *Jungfrau* and the captain of the *Rosebud* lack the necessary knowledge and skill.

THE FOUR SQUIRES

The four squires are representatives of the four non-white Pagan races.

Queequeg is   a South Sea Islander
Tashtego   a North American Indian
Dagoo   an African Negro
Fedallah   an Asiatic

Queequeg, Tashtego and Dagoo form a trio related to and contrasted with the white trio Starbuck, Stubb, and Flask, i.e. the three untormented by the problems of consciousness and the three who in different ways fail to live up to the challenge of consciousness.

Queequeg and Fedallah are opposites in their relation to Christianity. I.e. Queequeg is the unconscious Christian, Fedallah is the unconscious anti-Christian, the tempter of Ahab. In the Biblical story of Ahab, the Lord sends a lying spirit to entice him to his death. Such is Fedallah, who is Ahab's shadow and makes the *Macbeth*-like prophecies which finally persuade Ahab that he will succeed in killing the White Whale and survive. Fedallah alone, though he has not suffered Ahab's catastrophe, intuitively shares Ahab's attitude. Like Ahab he is a fire-worshipper.

> He was such a creature as civilized, domestic people in the temperate zone only see in their dreams, and that but dimly; but the like of whom now and then glide among the unchanging Asiatic communities, especially the Oriental isles to the east of the continent—those insulated, immemorial, unalterable countries, which even in these modern days still preserve much of the ghostly aboriginalness of earth's primal generations, when the memory of the first man was a distinct recollection, and all men his descendants, unknowing whence he came, eyed each other as real phantoms, and asked of the sun and the moon why they were created and to what end; when though, according to Genesis, the angels indeed consorted with the daughters of men, the devils also, add the uncanonical Rabbins, indulged in mundane amours.
>
> (L)

One thing all four have in common, a magnificent physique. To the romantics as a whole consciousness is usually held to upset the psychosomatic balance and to bring either ugliness or sickness. Those who are both beautiful and healthy belong to

> *ces époques nues*
> *Dont Phoebus se plaisait à dorer les statues.*
> *Alors l'homme et la femme en leur agilité*
> *Jouissaient sans mensonge et sans anxiété,*
> *Et, le ciel amoureux leur caressant l'échine,*
> *Exerçaient la santé de leur noble machine.*
>
> (Baudelaire)

In Father Mapple's terms, all four are themselves; but, since they are unconscious, i.e. since they have not begun Ishmael's voyage nor been called by the Lord like Jonah, they are only potentially themselves. Queequeg is not only himself but obeys God without having to disobey himself. Fedallah obeys himself and the Devil, i.e. denies the true God.

The Three Mates

None of the three mates is an evil man. All are physically brave, loyal and free from malice. Yet all suffer from spiritual sloth, which is a form of cowardice, so that none is his complete self; all have refused to grow up. They have, as it were, started on Ishmael's voyage and then tried to draw back, but that voyage is like a sea voyage in that once the boat has left the shore, you cannot get off, you can only play the child's game of "let's pretend we are on shore." Each of them in his own way takes ship from Tarshish to flee from the presence of the Lord.

Starbuck

Starbuck has gone farthest and is the most fitted for the voyage so that he suffers most from his refusal to go all the way.

He has a religious reverence for life and death; he knows that the fear of the Lord is the beginning of wisdom. That is why he will have no man in his boat who is not afraid of the whale.

He has mature self-control and authority in excitement.

> He did not say much to his crew, nor did his crew say anything to him. Only the silence of the boat was at intervals startlingly pierced by one of his peculiar whispers, now harsh with command, now soft with entreaty.
>
> (XLVIII)

He alone of the three has an inkling that Ahab's soul is in danger, and therefore looks at him not only with mingled fear and admiration but with pity and love.

He can tell Ahab the truth, as when he rebukes him for seeking "vengeance on a dumb brute that simply smote thee from blindest instinct," or again "Moby Dick seeks thee not. It is thou, thou that madly seekest him."

He knows that in obeying Ahab he is disobeying God, yet before Ahab's passion his knowledge and righteous fear are powerless: "I think I see his impious end, but feel that I must help him to it. 'Tis my miserable office to obey, rebelling."

Because fear may be the right way to begin, but it is not enough to go on with. For in the fear which is reverence is mixed the fear which is cowardice, the fear that the whole truth may be too much to encounter, that too much will be asked of me, that in fact God will not add His grace to one's own powers. Thus, Starbuck remains in the childish religious state of believing in omens like the Squid. "Almost rather had I seen Moby Dick and fought him, than to have seen thee, thou white ghost." He dare not look at the Doubloon too closely. "This coin speaks wisely, mildly, truly, but still sadly to me. I will quit it, lest Truth shake me falsely." And looking down into the Ocean on a beautiful calm day he sees belief and reason, faith and knowledge as contradictory. He keeps to his belief but at the cost of refusing to experience. His faith is insufficient for that.

> Loveliness unfathomable as ever lover saw in his young bride's eye!— Tell me not thou of thy teeth-tiered sharks, and thy kidnapping cannibal ways. Let faith oust fact; let fancy oust memory; I look deep down and do believe.
>
> (CXIV)

Stubb

It is characteristic of Stubb that, of the three of them, he should be the one who is always describing himself to himself to reassure himself.

> "I guess he's got what some folks ashore call a conscience, it's a kind of Tic-Dolly-Row they say—worse than a tooth-ache. Well, well, I don't know what it is, but the Lord keep me from catching it. Damn me, it's worth a fellow's while to be born into the world, if only to fall asleep. Damn me, but all things are queer, come to think of 'em. But that's against my principles. Think not, is my eleventh commandment, and sleep when you can is my twelfth."
>
> (XXIX)

> "A laugh's the wisest easiest answer to all that's queer."

> "I know not all that may be coming but be it what it will, I'll go to it laughing."

> "It's against my religion to get mad."

> "I am Stubb and Stubb has his history but here Stubb takes oaths that he has always been jolly."

For the comic always involves standing outside a situation, and so a man who makes a religion of the comic must be humorously self-regarding.

A man may laugh for pleasure or joy. Pleasure or joy are not comic, and the appropriate response is song, i.e. the expression of gratitude and praise. If a man lacks the gift of song, then he may laugh as a substitute. The substitute is acceptable because there is no suffering involved, except the comic contradiction of being unable to sing in a situation demanding song and in which laughter is actually ridiculous.

For what is the comic? The comic is a contradiction that does not involve suffering, either directly in the subject or indirectly by sympathetic identification with those involved in the contradiction.

There is, however, a particular religious form of the comic in which suffering is involved, i.e. a man may laugh at suffering on one condition that (1) it is he who suffers, (2) he knows that, ironically, this suffering is really a sign that he is in the truth, that he who suffers is really blest.

But the suffering must be real, i.e. not enjoyed. When Stubb thinks about his wife, he says:

> "What's my juicy little pear at home doing now? Crying its eyes out?— Giving a party to the last arrived harpooners, I dare say, gay as a frigate's pennant, and so am I—fa, la!"
>
> (XXXIX)

It looks at first as if this might be humorous resignation, but the end of the sentence gives him away. He is not suffering at the thought of his wife's infidelity, either because he no longer loves her, or because he is not really imagining a real scene, but a comic French farce in a theatre.

A man who makes a religion out of the comic is unable to face suffering. He is bound to deny it or to look the other way. When Stub looks at the Doubloon, he abstracts from it the features which can fit into his view of life and ignores the rest.

> "There's a sermon now, writ in high heaven, and the sun goes through it every year, and yet comes out of it all alive and hearty."

Stubb, however, is not soulless, i.e. he knows that suffering and mysteries which are not comic exist:

> "I wonder whether the world is anchored anywhere, if she is she swings with an uncommon long cable."

He senses, where Flask does not, the demonic qualities of Fedallah; but his solution is to put him away where he can't be seen:

> "Who's afraid of the devil except the old governor who dares not catch him and put him down in double darbies as he deserves."

And he gives himself away in his dream about Ahab, which is a terror dream, but on waking he does not meet this fact but says: "The best thing you can do, Flask, is to let that old man alone; never speak to him, whatever he says."

Starbuck fears God; Stubb fears suffering. Starbuck knows what he fears; Stubb doesn't, which makes him all the more insistent in his defence. As in a characteristic moment of frankness—the frankness itself is a defensive theatre—Stubb confesses to Starbuck: "I am not a brave man; never said I was a brave man; I am a coward; and I sing to keep up my spirits. And I tell you what it is, Mr Starbuck, there's no way to stop my singing in this world but to cut my throat."

When he does not or cannot sing, he turns away like a child from the frightening world to the comforting breast, i.e. to his pipe, which is never out of his mouth. The sight of the whale's blood is slightly disquieting to him so that he substitutes a pleasant image: "Would now it were old Orleans Whiskey," and his last thought in the moment of death is food. "Oh Flask, for one red cherry ere we die."

In his relations to his neighbor, he substitutes good-fellowship for love. "I never hurt when I hit, except when I hit a whale or something of that sort." His method of talking to his boat crew is one of good-tempered banter: "Pull, pull, my fine hearts—alive; pull, my little ones . . . Pull, then, do pull; never mind the brimstone—devils are good fellows enough."

The difficulty about good-fellowship as a principle of social conduct is that one's neighbor must also be a good-fellow, i.e. not a sufferer. Thus Stubb, who prides himself on his kindness, is the one who becomes guilty of destroying an innocent boy's sanity, for he cannot understand Pip's kind of fear, which cannot be laughed off. He does not guess what the consequences of leaving Pip in the water will be, because he has never really looked at him.

The best comment on Stubb is an aphorism of Kafka's:

> You can hold back from the suffering of the world, you have free permission to do so and it is in accordance with your nature, but perhaps this very holding back is the one suffering that you could have avoided . . .

FLASK

Flask is the least sympathetic of the three. Stubb, when confronted with mystery and suffering, looks the other way; Flask denies that it exists. Stubb would never laugh at the spectacle of a wrecked boat. Flask does. In relation to others he has the child's shamelessness and lack of dignity. For instance, his conduct in a whale-boat:

> "Lay me on—lay me on! O Lord, Lord! but I shall go stark, staring mad: See! see that white water!" And so shouting, he pulled his hat from his head, and stamped up and down on it; then picking it up, flirted it far off upon the sea; and finally fell to rearing and plunging in the boat's stern like a crazed colt from the prairie.

He is also the only one whom Peleg warns against fornication.

Towards animals he is cruel like a child.

> "A nice spot. Just let me prick him there once."

Towards the mysterious, however, instead of a child's reverence, he has developed the underdog's Philistinism; he trivialises everything. The whale is only a magnified water-rat; the doubloon is only a round thing made of gold worth sixteen dollars or nine hundred and sixty cigars.

His reaction to imminent death is equally characteristic. Starbuck says,

"May God stand by me now"; Stubb thinks of food; Flask thinks of his mother and money: "I hope my poor mother has drawn my part-pay ere this; if not, few coppers will now come to her for the voyage."

THE CARPENTER AND THE BLACKSMITH

Something has been said about these two in the first chapter, and there is not much to add here. If the harpooners have not started on Ishmael's voyage, and if the mates have started and tried to escape, for these all voyages are over. They are not children, nor childish, but senile. What catastrophe happened we do not know, for though we know that Perth's life went smash through drink, we do not know what made him a drunkard. Whatever the cause, though, they have lost themselves, and only exist in the tasks they are given to do. While Queequeg and Co. are potential selves, not consciously actual, the Carpenter and the Blacksmith have lost their actual selves, and there are no potentialities left. They are simply passively waiting for physical death to be superimposed on the spiritual death which has already taken place.

PIP

Pip is more significant, as his despair is dialectically related to Ahab's. Between them they represent the two opposite kinds of despair which Kierkegaard defines as:

| The despair of weakness | i.e. | The despair of willing despairingly not to be oneself |

and

| The despair of defiance | i.e. | The despair of willing despairingly to be oneself |

Pip is a slave, i.e. the one who has no authority, aesthetic, ethical or religious. He should never have been taken on this voyage at all, and he is innocent, for he never wanted to, knowing that he lacks the qualities required:

"Have mercy on this small Black boy down here. Preserve him from all men that have no bowels to feel fear."

His proper place is in a fairy story where fairy godmothers and animals assist him against all probability to vanquish the giant (who kills himself by mistake) and marry the Princess. But it has not been so. Papageno has been made to go through the ordeal and it has destroyed him.

He is bound to Ahab because they have both suffered a catastrophe, Ahab through his own deliberate original attack on the whale, Pip through the thoughtless action of the decent fellow Stubb. But Ahab is the exception, for

whom exceptional situations are made; Pip is not. Ahab, knowing that he is
the exception, is outraged by a catastrophe he was not powerful enough to
command; Pip is outraged by not being up to the command of the situation.
Thus Ahab's madness is directed against the whale; Pip's is directed against
himself. "Seek not Pip who's now been missing long. If ye find Pip, tell all the
Antilles he's a runaway; a coward, a coward, a coward. Tell them he jumped
from a whaleboat. I'd never beat my tambourine over Pip, and hail him general." Having lost himself, he can only exist through the self of another, and
where should he find that but in Ahab, the defiant self, so that he cannot bear
to be out of sight, and he only exists in obeying him.

> Here he this instant stood; I stand in his air,—but I'm alone. Now were
> even Pip here I could endure it, but he's missing . . . let's try the door.
> What? neither lock, nor bolt, nor bar; and yet there's no opening it. It
> must be the spell; he told me to stay here . . . Hist! above there. I hear
> ivory—Oh, master! master! I am indeed down-hearted when you walk
> over me. But here I'll stay, though this stern strikes rocks; and they bulge
> through; and oysters come to join me.
>
> (CXXIX)

Ahab on his side is bound to Pip, and to no one else, not even Starbuck.
As the conscious defiant despairer, he recognises that Pip is his antitype and
envies Pip's humility as Pip admires his strength. "There's that in thee, poor
lad, which I feel too curing for my malady. Like cures like; and for this hunt,
my malady becomes my most desired health."

If each could have had the qualities of the other added to his own, when
they encountered catastrophe, i.e. if Ahab had had Pip's humility as well as
his own strength and vice versa, both would have been saved.

AHAB

Kierkegaard defines defiant despair as follows:

> with hatred for existence it wills to be itself, to be itself in terms of its mis-
> ery; it does not even in defiance or defiantly will to be itself, but to be it-
> self in spite . . . Whereas the weak despairer will not hear about what
> comfort eternity has for him, so neither will such a despairer hear about
> it, but for a different reason, namely, because this comfort would be the
> destruction of him as an objection against the whole of existence. It is
> (to describe it figuratively) as if an author were to make a slip of the pen,
> and that this clerical error became conscious of being such—perhaps it
> was no error but in a far higher sense was an essential constituent in the
> whole exposition—it is then as if this clerical error would revolt against
> the author, out of hatred for him were to forbid him to correct it, and

were to say, "No, I will not be erased, I will stand as a witness against thee, that thou art a very poor writer."

(Sickness unto Death)

Of this despair, Ahab is a representation, perhaps the greatest in literature.

Before he was born there were prophecies of some extraordinary destiny, which caused his mother to name him Ahab, after the son of Omri, of whom it is written in the book of Kings that he "did evil in the sight of the Lord above all that were before him," that reared up an altar for Baal, that he made a grove, and constructed an ivory house.

He himself declares that the prophecy was that he should be dismembered. Now a prophecy is either true or false, and in either case the only thing to do is to ignore it. If it is true, then it will happen and must be accepted when it occurs, and it is defiance either to try to make it happen or to try to avoid it. If it is false, it will not happen, and if one makes it happen one is not really fulfilling a prophecy at all but doing what one has chosen to do.

As a symbol of his uniqueness, he is distinguished from the rest of mankind by a scar. About this there is a mystery. An Indian relative of Tashtego's says that Ahab was forty before he received it; the old Manx sailor, on the other hand, declares that Ahab was born with it. Ahab himself makes a mysterious statement during the thunderstorm:

> "Oh! thou clear spirit of clear fire, whom on these seas I as Persian once did worship, till in the sacramental act so burned by thee, that to this hour I bear the scar."

(CXIX)

Whether he was born marked, whether he received it by chance, or in some mysterious blasphemous rite is left vague. All we know for certain is that before his encounter with Moby Dick he was an exceptional man, an aesthetic hero.

So he encounters Moby Dick and loses a leg. That this is a castration symbol is emphasized by the story of how shortly before the present voyage he was found insensible in the street "by some unknown, and seemingly inexplicable, unimaginable casualty, his ivory limb having been so violently displaced that it had stake-wise smitten, and all but pierced his groin."* It is possible to attach too much importance to this as also to the sexual symbolism of the Whale as being at once the *vagina dentata* and the Beast with two backs or the parents-in-bed. The point is that the sexual symbolism is in its turn symbolic of the aesthetic, i.e. the Oedipus fantasy is a representation in aesthetic terms of the fantasy of being a self-originating god, i.e. of the ego

---

* Ahab's rival as an idolator of Moby Dick, Gabriel, worships the whale as the incarnation of the Shaker God, for whom the primal sin is sexual intercourse.

(Father) begetting itself on the self (Mother), and castration is the ultimate symbol of aesthetic weakness, of not being an aesthetic hero.

Ahab, then, the exceptional hero, suffers a tragic fall in the Greek sense, he is reduced to being lower than the average. In a Greek story this would be a punishment by the gods for hybris, and would come at the end of the book. Here, however, it comes before the book starts, so we must take it differently. How should Ahab react? Repent of his past pride? Perhaps, but the important thing is the future. What is the catastrophe telling him to become? Here again we can only answer negatively and say, "At least, not to go on whaling." One might hazard a guess and say, "To will to become nobody in particular in an aesthetic sense," i.e. to be a happy husband and father, to enter the cloister, the actual symbol does not concern us; the decisive difference is between the kind of individuality which is *being* what others are not, and that defined as "*becoming* what one wills or God wills for one."

Ahab does turn into such an individual but in a negative sense. He neither says, "I am justly punished" if he has been guilty nor "Though He slay me yet will I trust in Him" but "Thou art guilty and shalt be punished." His nature or self certainly does not wish to go rushing off in his aged maimed state round the world chasing a whale. It wants, as he himself admits, peace, family and, above all, happiness. It is as if, knowing that this is also what God wills him to become, he, his ego, defiantly wills to be always at every moment miserable. His extra wounding of himself, mentioned above, may well have been, at least unconsciously, not an accident, but a goading of himself to remember his vow. It is interesting to note the occasion during the voyage when he breaks his leg, jumping off the *Enderby*, whose captain has also lost an arm to Moby Dick without despairing and whose doctor ascribes Moby Dick's apparent malice to clumsiness. The example of sanity with authority is too much for Ahab, and he must again goad himself to his resolution.

So in his defiance he takes his vow: "I now prophesy that I will dismember my dismemberer. Now then, be this prophet and the fulfiller one. That's more than ye, ye great gods, ever were."

The defiant man and the obedient man use the same words "It is not I but Fate," but their meaning is opposite.

> The path to my fixed purpose is laid with iron rails, whereon my soul is grooved to run . . . The whole act's immutably decreed. I am the Fates' Lieutenant. I act under orders.

So too, as we follow him on his unnecessary voyage, unnecessary because he has been on it before and nothing new, as he well knows, can happen to him, only, possibly, to the whale, we watch him enact every ritual of the dedicated Don Quixote life of the Religious Hero, only for negative reasons.

His first act is to throw away his pipe, an act of ascetic renunciation. But what should be done, so as not to be distracted from the task set one by God, is done to prevent distraction from a task set by himself.

Next he sets up the Doubloon which is to be a prize for whoever sights Moby Dick first. The motive is simple enough—to inspire the crew in terms of their interests to work for his—actually, however, Ahab hasn't the slightest intention of letting anyone but himself be the first. At the same time he makes the harpooners swear an oath to pursue Moby Dick to the death.

Now an oath is an individual's commitment of his individual future. It is an aesthetic form of the ethical, for if later its fulfillment should turn out to involve violating ethics, the one who took the oath cannot release himself, which can only be done by the individual or his representative before whom the oath was made. It is right therefore to take an oath about a certain direction of the will, e.g. to vow at the altar that one will love one's wife till death. It would be all wrong to take an oath about a particular future act, e.g. that one will give one's wife a pound of candy every week, for the act which at this moment is an expression of one's love may not be tomorrow; she may get diabetes.

When it comes to persuading another to take an oath, not only must there be no coercion, the other must be completely free to refuse, but also he must understand exactly what is going on; he must have the right motive. Ahab violates these conditions both for himself and for the harpooners. He exercises his authority as captain, he weakens their will with drink, and they have no motives for taking the oath at all, nor could they understand his if he told them.

Later he goes further and baptises his harpoon itself. This is a perversion of the Knight Errant's act of dedicating his arms, so that he shall remember not to dishonor them. Ahab's act, however, is a pure act of black magic, an attempt to compel objects to do his will.

Three other acts are worth mention. He throws away the ship's quadrant with the words: "Science! Curse thee, thou vain toy; and cursed be all the things that cast man's eyes aloft to the heavens. . . . Level by nature to this earth's horizon are the glances of men's eyes; not shot from the crown of his head, as if God had meant him to gaze on his firmament." This is the defiant inversion in pride of the humility which resists the pride of reason, the theologian's temptation to think that knowledge of God is more important than obeying Him.

Next he places the child Pip in his place in the captain's cabin and takes the humble position of the lookout, an inversion of "He who would be greatest among you, let him be as the least."

Lastly, in refusing the call for help of his neighbor, the captain of the *Rachel*, whom he has known in Nantucket and who asks him to help look for his young son, he counterfeits the text:

If any man come to me and hate not his father and mother and wife and children and brethren and sisters, yea and his own life also, he cannot be my disciple.

His whole life, in fact, is one of taking up defiantly a cross he is not required to take up. Consequently, the normal reactions to pleasure and pain are reversed for him. Painful situations like the typhoon he welcomes, pleasant and happy ones like the calm day he regards as temptations. This is a counterfeit version of the saints' acceptance of suffering and distrust of pleasure. The aesthetic hero reacts normally, in that it is pleasure that tempts him to do wrong, and if he is doing wrong, suffering will dissuade him. Thus the hero of *The Voyage of Maeldune*, who is also bent on vengeance but not for himself but for his father, is brought to his senses by suffering, i.e. by the disasters that happen to his men on each of the islands they come to. The Religious Hero, however, is related in exactly the opposite way, and if his god be his own defiant will, it is pain that tempts him further, and pleasure that could save him.

In the same way Queequeg is a saint, but he is not the Christ incarnate, the second Adam, for, though he goes down with the rest of the crew, he does not suffer uniquely as an individual. For Melville's treatment of the Religious Hero and the Devil or the negative Religious Hero in their absolute form, we must now turn to his last work, *Billy Budd*.

BILLY BUDD

If, when we finish reading *Billy Budd*, we are left with questions which we feel have been raised but not answered, if so to speak the equation has not come out to a finite number, as in a work of art it should, this is not due to any lack of talent on Melville's part, but to the insolubility of the religious paradox in aesthetic terms.

For any writer who attempts a portrait of the Christ-like is faced with the following problems. His central figure

(a) must be innocent of sin, yet a man like us in all things tempted as we are. If he is given any aesthetic advantages, he at once ceases to be the God-Man and becomes the Man-God, the Aesthetic Hero, Hercules, who must be admired, but cannot be imitated. His sinlessness must be the result of faith, not of fortune.

(b) He must be shown as failing in a worldly sense, i.e. as coming into collision with the law of this world, otherwise there is no proof that his sinlessness is due, not to faith, but to mere worldly prudence.

(c) Failure and suffering, however, are in themselves no proof of faith, because the collision with the law may equally well be the result of pride and sin. The crucified Christ is flanked by two crucified thieves.

(d) The suffering must at one and the same time be willed and not-willed. If it seems entirely against the will of the sufferer, he becomes pathetic, if it seems entirely brought about by his own actions, he becomes tragic, and it is impossible to distinguish between pride and faith as the cause of his suffering.

We have seen how Cervantes tackled these problems. His ironically comic approach solved all the problems, I think, except the last one. As long as Don Quixote is mad, the suffering is not quite real, but if he becomes sane and still resists he becomes tragically proud.

Melville, on the other hand, solves this problem. The Passion of Billy Budd is convincing, but fails in respects where Cervantes succeeds, and the ways in which he fails are interesting for the light they throw on the romantic conception of life. Like many other romantics Melville seems to hold:

(1) That innocence and sinlessness are identical, or rather perhaps that only the innocent, i.e. those who have never known the law, can be sinless. Once a man becomes conscious, he becomes a sinner. As long as he is not conscious of guilt, what he does is not sin. This is to push St. Paul's remark "Except I had known the Law, I had not known sin" still further to mean that "Except I had known sin, I would not have sinned."* Thus when Billy Budd first appears he is the Prelapsarian Adam:

> Billy Budd in many respects was little more than a sort of upright barbarian, much such perhaps as Adam presumably might have been ere the urbane Serpent wriggled himself into his company.

He may have done things which in a conscious person would be sin—there appears to have been a certain Bristol Molly—but he feels no guilt.

(2) That the unconscious and innocent are marked by great physical beauty, and therefore that the beautiful are sinless. This is true for Billy Budd as it was for Bulkington and Queequeg.

If the story were to be simply the story of the Fall, i.e. the story of how the Devil (Claggart) tempted Adam (Budd) into the knowledge of good and evil, this would not matter, but Melville wants Budd also to be the Second Adam, the sinless victim who suffers voluntarily for the sins of the whole world. But in order to be that he must know what sin is, or else his suffering is not redemptive, but only one more sin on our part. Further, as long as Billy Budd is only the Prelapsarian Adam, our nostalgic image of what we would still be if we had not fallen, his beauty is a perfectly adequate symbol but the moment he becomes the Second Adam, the saving example whom we all should follow, this beauty becomes an illegitimate aesthetic advantage. The flaw of the stammer will not quite do, for this is only an aesthetic weakness, not a deliberate abandonment of advantages. It succeeds in making Billy Budd the innocent who "as a sheep before the shearer is dumb so openeth he not his mouth," but it makes his dumbness against his will not with it. We can never

---

* In the Barrister's dream in *The Hunting of the Snark* the pig is charged with deserting its sty, i.e. the crime is not the eating of the tree but the expulsion from Eden. The Snark who is officially the counsel for the defence is also the accuser-judge and the sentence is repetition of the offence. "Transportation for life."

look like that, any more than, once we have become conscious, we can go
back to unconsciousness, so how can we imitate his example? He becomes an
aesthetic hero to admire from a distance. Melville seems to have been aware
that something must happen to Billy to change him from the unconscious
Adam into the conscious Christ but, in terms of his fable, he cannot make
this explicit and the decisive transition has to take place off-stage in the final
interview between Billy and Captain Vere.

CLAGGART

Similar insoluble paradoxes are raised by the demonic, the religious passion
in reverse. For the demonic must be moved solely by pride, just as the religious must be moved solely by faith and love. Absolute pride cannot be manifested aesthetically because it tolerates no weakness except itself which
thinks of itself as absolute strength.

Absolute pride denies that the six other deadly sins are its children and despises them as weakness, being incapable of seeing that it is the source of all
weakness. The Devil, therefore, cannot himself be lustful, gluttonous, avari-
cious, envious, slothful, or angry, for his pride will not allow him to be anything less than proud. He can only pretend in disguise to be any of these without actually feeling them; he can only "act" them. His acts must appear to be
arbitrary and quite motiveless. No accurate aesthetic portrayal, therefore, is
possible; Iago has to be given some motive, yet if the motive is convincing, he
ceases to be demonic.

So with Claggart. Just as the bias in Melville's treatment of Billy Budd is a
tendency to identify consciousness and sin, so he makes Claggart identify innocence with love; "To be nothing more than innocent," he sneers on seeing Billy Budd. This is no doubt what the serpent says to Adam, but it is not
what he says to himself, which is rather "To be nothing more than loving."
For the difference between God and the Devil is not that God does not know
the meaning of good and evil and that the Devil does, but that God loves and
the Devil will not love. That is why the motive for Claggart's behaviour, half-
stated only to be withdrawn because no motive will really do, is homosexual
desire.

In *Moby Dick*, where Ahab's pride revolts against lack of absolute strength,
against being finite and dependent, the sexual symbolism centres round
incest and the Oedipus situation, because incest is the magic act of self-
derivation, self-autonomy, with the annihilation of all rival power.

In *Billy Budd*, the opposition is not strength/weakness, but innocence/
guilt-consciousness, i.e. Claggart wishes to annihilate the difference either
by becoming innocent himself or by acquiring an accomplice in guilt. If this
is expressed sexually, the magic act must necessarily be homosexual, for

the wish is for identity in innocence or in guilt, and identity demands the same sex. *

Claggart, as the Devil, cannot, of course, admit a sexual desire, for that would be an admission of loneliness which pride cannot admit. Either he must corrupt innocence through an underling or if that is not possible he must annihilate it, which he does.

THE ARTIST AS DON QUIXOTE

To understand the romantic identification of sin with consciousness, we must take it together with two other romantic characteristics, the romantic image of the hero as a mariner, an explorer of novelty, and the romantic contempt for the bourgeois and respectable, the churl who lives by conventional custom and habit. Is not this nostalgia for innocence precisely the characteristic of the man whose dedicated career is the exploration of the hitherto unknown and unconscious, who is by the very nature of his voyage travelling farther and farther away from unconsciousness; and would not the same man despise most those who have started, cannot go back, yet dare not go forward?

In earlier ages it was the business of the artist to record the great acts and thoughts of others. Hector and Achilles are the heroes; Homer records them. Later the hero might be Truth, and the poet's business to set down what has oft been thought but ne'er so well expressed. The contribution of the poet, that is, was his gift for language.

The characteristic of the Romantic period is that the artist, the maker himself, becomes the epic hero, the daring thinker, whose deeds he has to record. Between about 1770 and 1914 the great heroic figures are not men of action but individual geniuses, both artists and, of course, scientists (but they are not our province) with a religious dedication to furthering knowledge, and the kind of knowledge the artist could obtain was chiefly from himself. Characteristically, the subtitle of Wordsworth's epic poem is "The Growth of the Poet's Mind." Faust, Don Juan, Captain Ahab are not really the heroes of their respective books, but the imaginative projections of their creators, i.e. what they do is not really done as a man of action acts for the sake of the act, but in order to know what it feels like to act. Ahab is, so to speak, what it feels like to be Ishmael the recorder. The artist who has thus to be at once the subject of his experiment and the recorder enjoys excitement and suffers terrors

---

* It is not an accident that many homosexuals should show a special preference for sailors, for the sailor on shore is symbolically the innocent god from the sea who is not bound by the law of the land and can therefore do anything without guilt. Indeed, in a book like Genet's *Querelle de Brest*, the hero is at once god and devil. He is adored because, though he is a murderer and a police informer and sexually promiscuous in every sense, though, that is, he loves no one but himself, is, in fact, Judas, yet he remains Billy Budd, the beautiful god who feels neither guilt nor remorse, and whose very crimes, therefore, are a proof of his divinity.

hardly known before. He ceases to have an identity and becomes like the
Baker, who cannot remember his name and no longer bakes but hunts. He
used to bake bridecake, i.e. his recording of glorious deeds and thoughts
strengthened the bonds of community. Now he is a nomad explorer, whose
one virtue is his courage that can

> joke with hyaenas, returning their stare
> With an impudent wag of the head.

Further, to become so dedicated to a lonely task, done not for the public but
for the sake of the truth, mere talent is insufficient. The romantic artist is a
poète maudit, i.e. an individual marked out by some catastrophe like Ahab's
which supplies the driving passion to go ever forward, to the limits of exhaustion.

> Nothing was not to be known, nothing: hysteria, debauchery, disorder,
> grief, nor despair.

What Rimbaud said of himself in *Une Saison en Enfer* before bidding good-bye
to art is true, more or less, in one way or another, of them all.

> *Je m'habituai à l'hallucination simplex: je voyais très franchement une mosquée
> à la place d'une usine, une école de tambours faite par les anges, des calèches sur
> les routes du ciel, un salon au fond d'un lac; les monstres, les mystères; un titre
> de vaudeville dressait des épouvantes devant moi. Puis j'expliquai mes sophismes
> magiques avec l'hallucination des mots!*
>
>   *Je finis par trouver sacré le desordre de mon esprit. J'étais oisif, en proie à une
> lourde fièvre: j'enviais la félicité des bêtes,—les chenilles, qui représentent l'inno-
> cence des limbes, les taupes, le sommeil de la virginité.*
>
>   (*Une Saison en Enfer*)

Small wonder then if their capacity for experience was burned out quite
early, like Wordsworth's, or if the ability to express vanished in a welter of feelings, like Coleridge's, or if the man himself suffered from spleen, like Baudelaire. More remarkable is the realisation by some of them that the artist is not,
as he had thought, Don Quixote, the Religious Hero, but only Ishmael, the
explorer of possibility, for whom the Button-Moulder and the Boojum are
waiting at the next cross-roads where they will be asked to prove whether or
no they have become their actual selves.

Thus Melville:

> Round the world! There is much in that sound to inspire proud feelings;
> but whereto does all that circumnavigation lead? Only through num-
> berless perils to the very point whence we started, where those that we
> left behind secure were all the time before us.

Thus Rimbaud:

I! I who called myself magus or angel, dispensed with all morality, I am cast back to the soil, with a duty to seek, and enough actuality to grasp! Peasant!—I will ask pardon for having nourished myself on lies. And now, let us go.

(*Une Saison en Enfer*)

We live in a new age in which the artist neither can have such a unique heroic importance nor believes in the Art-God enough to desire it, an age, for instance, when the necessity of dogma is once more recognised, not as the contradiction of reason and feeling but as their ground and foundation, in which the heroic image is not the nomad wanderer through the desert or over the ocean, but the less exciting figure of the builder, who renews the ruined walls of the city. Our temptations are not theirs. We are less likely to be tempted by solitude into Promethean pride: we are far more likely to become cowards in the face of the tyrant who would compel us to lie in the service of the False City. It is not madness we need to flee but prostitution. Let us, reading the logs of their fatal but heroic voyages, remember their courage.

Melville once wrote a Requiem for soldiers lost in ocean transports, which seems to me no less fitting a requiem for him and his brethren in France, England and America.

> All creatures joying in the morn,
> Save them forever from joyance torn,
>   Whose bark was lost where now the dolphins play;
> Save them that by the fabled shore,
>   Down the pale stream are washed away,
> Far to the reef of bones are borne;
>   And never revisits them the light,
> Nor sight of long-sought land and pilot more;
>   Nor heed they now the lone bird's flight
> Round the lone spar where mid-sea surges pour.

ESSAYS AND REVIEWS

1949–1955

A Note on Graham Greene

In its form, Graham Greene's novel, *The Ministry of Fear*, is a thriller like John Buchan's *Thirty-nine Steps*. The thriller resembles the epic in that its subject is a war between two sides, but there are two important differences. First, the war is a secret undercover struggle. The outside sees only peace and there are no visible distinguishing marks to show who is friend and who is foe. Second, the reader is made a partisan of one side. In the *Iliad*, even though it is written by Greeks, the Trojans are depicted as equally noble but in a thriller *They*, the enemy, are always bad.

The secrecy is an added excitement, but the partisanship is apt to make the thriller a bit priggish.

As Graham Greene himself says, "none of the books of adventure one read as a boy had an unhappy ending. And none of them was disturbed by a sense of pity for the beaten side."

Graham Greene succeeds, I think, in avoiding this crudity without sacrificing the drama, by relating the thriller to another literary form, the allegory. His thrillers are projected into outer melodramatic action of the struggles which go on unendingly in every mind and heart. Maybe this is why we like reading thrillers because each of us is a creature at war with himself. Further he is a self-deceptive creature who thinks he is feeling one thing or acting from one motive when his real feeling and motive are quite different.

There is, therefore, not a good side and a bad, nevertheless it does matter who wins. Again victory does not finally solve anything. A dangerous attack has been defeated, perhaps we understand ourselves a little better: that is all. A future, as difficult as before, perhaps more so, still remains.

Graham Greene, then, employs a distinctive form: he also exhibits a distinctive concern. Just as Balzac came back again to avarice and Stendhal to ambition, so, in book after book, Graham Greene analyzes the vice of pity, that corrupt parody of love and compassion which is so insidious and deadly for sensitive natures.

The secret war in *The Ministry of Fear* is between those who pity and those who can bear pain—other people's pain—endlessly, the people who don't care. Yet both sides have a common bond; both have murdered. Arthur Rowe, the hero, has killed his wife to save her suffering from an incurable illness. Through his encounters with Hilfe, the Fascist agent, he is brought to realize that "it was her endurance and her patience which he had found most unbearable. He was trying to escape his own pain, not hers."

Behind pity for another lies self-pity, and behind self-pity lies cruelty.

To feel compassion for someone is to make oneself their equal; to pity them is to regard oneself as their superior and from that eminence the step to the torture chamber and the corrective labor camp is shorter than one thinks.

For providing us with such exciting reading and at the same time exposing so clearly a great and typical heresy of our time, Graham Greene deserves our lasting gratitude.

University Theatre, NBC Radio Network, 23 January 1949;
Renascence, Spring 1949

In Memoriam

A Letter to the Editor of *The New York Times Book Review*

To the Editor:

Every writer as he grows older faces a serious problem which I have rarely seen discussed; it becomes increasingly difficult for him to find persons to whom he can show his work in manuscript and obtain criticisms which convince him and upon which he can act.

When he started it was different; he was one of a band of eager and equally unknown young would-be writers who read each other's work with an interest all the more passionate because there was nobody else to read it. But time dissolves this company: some stop writing; those who go on and get published soon have little time or inclination to read their contemporaries' work, let alone give it serious critical attention. Reviewers, favorable or unfavorable, are rarely illuminating to the author to whom they are not addressed and, anyway, by that time it is too late; the book is out.

Where shall he find what he needs so badly—someone who is unselfish enough to take trouble with another's work, mature enough to trust, honest enough to be believed and friendly enough to convince the object of his home truths that they are not motivated by malice or envy? These reflections are occasioned in the present instance by the sudden and unexpected death of Prof. Theodore Spencer. Those who were associated with him as colleagues or pupils at Harvard can testify better than I to his work in education; I only wish to put on record my own less academic debt. I have not only lost a friend. I have lost a trusted and not easily replaceable literary confessor.

W. H. AUDEN

New York, N.Y.

The New York Times Book Review, 6 February 1949

Port and Nuts with the Eliots

Notes towards the Definition of Culture. By T. S. Eliot.
Harcourt, Brace. $2.50.

Like most important writers, Mr T. S. Eliot is not a single figure but a house-hold. This household has, I think, at least three permanent residents. First, there is the archdeacon, who believes in and practices order, discipline, and good manners, social and intellectual, with a thoroughly Anglican distaste for evangelical excess:

> . . . his conversation, so nicely
> Restricted to What Precisely
> And If and Perhaps and But.

And no wonder, for the poor gentleman is condemned to be domiciled with a figure of a very different stamp, a violent and passionate old peasant grand-mother, who has witnessed murder, rape, pogroms, famine, flood, fire, every-thing; who has looked into the abyss and, unless restrained, would scream the house down:

> Reflected in my golden eye
> The dullard knows that he is mad.
> Tell me if I am not glad!

Last, as if this state of affairs were not difficult enough, there is a young boy who likes to play slightly malicious practical jokes. The too earnest guest, who has come to interview the Reverend, is startled and bewildered by finding an apple-pie bed or being handed an explosive cigar.

From its rather formidable title, it is evident that Mr Eliot's latest essay is of-ficially from the pen of the Archdeacon, who is diffident about his powers but determined to do his social duty even under very unpropitious circumstances:

> In a society of smaller size (a society, therefore, which was less feverishly
> *busy*) there might be more conversation and fewer books; and we should
> not find the tendency—of which this essay provides one example—for
> those who have acquired some reputation, to write books outside the
> subject on which they have made that reputation.

With a proper caution and a schoolmaster's conscientiousness, the Arch-deacon begins by defining the various senses in which the word "culture" is used: to mean (1) the conscious self-cultivation of the individual, his attempt to raise himself out of the average mass to the level of the élite; (2) the ways of believing, thinking, and feeling of the particular group within society to which an individual belongs; and (3) the still less conscious way of life of society as a whole.

There are always two cultural problems: cultural innovation, i.e. how to change a culture for the better, however "good" may be defined; and cultural transmission, i.e. how to transmit what is valuable in a culture from one generation to the next. It is to the second problem that Mr Eliot addresses himself—and rightly, most people, I think, will agree, for in the unstatic and unstable societies of our age, transmission, or cultural memory, is the major problem. Starting from the premise that no culture has appeared or evolved except together with a religion, whichever may be the agent that produces the other, he states and develops the thesis that the transmission of any culture depends on three conditions: (1) the persistence of social classes; (2) the diversity of local or regional cultures within a larger cultural unit; (3) the diversity of religious cult and devotion within a large universality of religious doctrine. The premise is, I think, undeniable, even by the most violent atheist, for the word "religion" simply means that which is binding, the beliefs or habits of conduct that the conscience of an individual or a society tells him he should affirm, even at the cost of his life (and nobody has a personal identity without such). For example, a Logical Positivist is a person who is prepared to be shot rather than say that metaphysical statements about value are real statements. If he is not so prepared, or if, recanting under pressure, he is not ashamed, then he is not a Logical Positivist.

Nor will anyone quarrel, I think, with Mr Eliot's contention that in a civilized society religion and culture, though interdependent—"bishops are a part of English culture, and horses and dogs are a part of English religion"—are not and should not be identical; e.g. it is only in a barbarous society that to drive on the right or to eat boiled cabbage or to listen to the music of Elgar would be regarded not as matters of habit or convenience or taste but as matters of ultimate significance.

This, however, involves the conclusion that the religion of a civilized society is distinguished by the existence of dogma as separate from mythology and cult, and at this word "dogma" the hackles of the liberal are apt to rise. He immediately has visions of Torquemada and the stake, and, like Dr Humdrum, in Macaulay's poem, begins to wonder:

> . . . how we should dress for the show,
> And where we should fasten the powder,
> And if we should bellow or no.

Yet his experiences of the last twenty years have perhaps made him less likely to be alarmed by that word, for the all too successful anti-liberal heresies have compelled him to recognize that there is a liberal orthodoxy, of which he was unaware only because for so long it was never seriously challenged; he is forced to admit that there are beliefs from which, if he can, he must convert and which, if he cannot, he must, in however genteel a manner, persecute.

Nobody has ever really believed in Freedom of Religion. Where religion is concerned, the hardest virtue is tolerance, and to find out what a person's religion is one has only to discover what he becomes violent about. If one has never heard of a riot in the streets of New York between Greeks and Italians over the Filioque Clause, or of an elder from the Fifth Avenue Presbyterian Church defending Predestination with an umbrella against the Arminian onslaughts of a vestryman from Trinity, Wall Street, this means merely that to the majority of Americans today Christianity is not religion but only culture, and not an important aspect of that.

In a revolutionary age like the present, the greatest threat to freedom is not dogmas but the reluctance to define them precisely, for in times of danger, if nobody knows what is essential and what is unessential, the unessential is vested with religious importance (to dislike ice cream becomes a proof of heresy), so the liberal who is so frightened by the idea of dogma that he blindly opposes any kind, instead of seeing that nothing is made an article of faith that need not be so, is promoting the very state of tyranny and witch-hunting that he desires to prevent.

However, it is not Mr Eliot's views on religion that are going to get him into hot water with a great many people but his approval of hereditary classes and his doubts about universal education, for here the Archdeacon is from time to time replaced by the boyish practical joker, whose favorite sport is teasing the Whigs, particularly if they happen to be Americans:

> In a healthily *stratified* society, public affairs would be a responsibility not equally borne: a greater responsibility would be inherited by those who inherited special advantages and in whom self-interest, and interest for the sake of their families ("a stake in the country"), should cohere with public spirit.

> A high average of general education is perhaps less necessary for a civil society than is a respect for learning.

> In justice to Thomas Gray, we should remind ourselves of the last and finest line of the quatrain, and remember that we may also have escaped some Cromwell *guilty* of his country's blood. The proposition that we have lost a number of Miltons and Cromwells through our tardiness in providing a comprehensive state system of education cannot be either proved or disproved: it has a strong attraction for many ardent reforming spirits.

This is the hotfoot treatment, and the howls of anguish and rage that have already begun to go up are not altogether displeasing to at least one listener's ear, for one of the more unattractive characteristics of the Enlightened is their almost total lack of a sense of humor. The Archdeacon in me, however, must regret them, because an enraged audience will not listen, even to refute. The value of Mr Eliot's book is not the conclusions he reaches, most of which are debatable, but the questions he raises.

For instance, how has culture been transmitted in the past? If the methods of the past are no longer possible, how can it be transmitted now? Mr Eliot is only partly right, I think, in asserting that in the past the role of transmission was played by a class or by classes. For many centuries, it was transmitted by the Church; i.e. by an institution with a hereditary status whose members could be drawn from any social class. In England, it was only during the last two centuries or so that the responsibility for culture passed to social classes, first to the landed aristocracy, and then, when they became stockholders without responsibility, to the professional classes—the clergy, the doctors, the lawyers, etc. And even then it was certain institutions—the greater universities, the cathedral closes—that were really responsible. In Scotland, moreover, it was not only, or mainly, the rich who attended the universities.

The American problem has been unique. Jefferson and Hamilton read no different from Europeans; then, between 1830 and 1870, say, there emerged a culture that was definitely non-European but also entirely Anglo-Saxon; after that, in a sense, America had to begin all over again.

It was perhaps unfortunate that, with the exception of the Germans of '48 and the Jews who came to escape persecution, the stimulus to immigration from Europe during the nineteenth century was so simply poverty, for this meant that of, for instance, the Irish and Italians who came, few were conscious bearers of their native culture and few had many memories they wished to preserve.

This, and the absence of any one dominant church, has placed almost the whole cultural burden on the school, which has had to struggle along as best it could, with all too little help from even the family. It is a very encouraging sign that social groups within American society—the Labor Unions, for instance—are beginning to go into education instead of leaving it all to the state. I have never understood how a liberal, of all people, can regard State education as anything but a necessary and—it is to be hoped—temporary evil. The only ground for approval that I can see is the authoritarian ground that Plato gives—that it is the only way to insure orthodoxy. Well, if it comes to that, the gospel according to Teachers' Training College is not mine. Further, the more the total task of education can be shared among different groups, the smaller the educational unit can be. It is almost impossible for education organized on a mass scale not to imitate the methods that work so well in the mass production of goods.

The greatest blessing that could descend on Higher Education in this country would be not the erection of more class barriers but the removal of one; namely, the distinction drawn between those who have attended college and those who have not. As long as employers demand a degree for jobs to which a degree is irrelevant, the colleges will be swamped by students who have no disinterested love of knowledge, and teachers, particularly in the humanities, aware of the students' economic need to pass examinations, will lower their standards to let them.

So one could go on chatting and wrangling with the Archdeacon all evening. If, from time to time, a small head has popped around the door and shouted "Boo to Jefferson!" or "Excuse me, are you out of the top drawer?," it could be politely ignored. The talk has been stimulating, the port excellent. Do go on. I am not questioning the usefulness . . .

Ichabod! Ichabod!

(Heavens! *What* was that extraordinary noise?) You were saying, Sir, that the zealots of World Government seem to assume . . .

Mene, Mene, Tekel, Upharsin.

(There it goes again.)

The conversation trails off into silence. Whig? Tory? All flesh is grass. Culture? The grass withereth. One realizes that one is no longer reading lucid prose or following an argument; one has ceased trying to understand or explain anything; one is listening to the song of the third Eliot, a voice in Ramah, weeping, that will not be comforted.

The New Yorker, 23 April 1949

The Question of the Pound Award

(EDITORIAL NOTE.—*We are printing below a comment on William Barrett's editorial, "A Prize for Ezra Pound," which appeared in the April issue. A number of Bollingen jurors were invited to discuss the issues connected with the award, but at the time of going to press we had received replies only from Messrs Auden, Shapiro, and Tate. We would like to hear further from our readers on this subject.*)

W. H. AUDEN:

I fully share Mr Barrett's concern over the excessive preoccupation of contemporary criticism with Form and its neglect of Content. I am not sure however that this is the precise problem which his comment raises. In stating my own views, I should like to emphasize that I am speaking purely for myself and am not to be construed as representing any other colleague with whom at any time I may have been associated.

(1) According to one theory, art, both in intention and effect, is a means by which emotions are aroused in the spectator or reader, either in order

that, by re-living them imaginatively, he may get rid of them, or because he needs to be roused to feel in a certain way. If this theory is adopted, then it seems to me that Plato and Tolstoy are irrefutable. No works of art may be permitted which do not purge men of their bad feelings and stimulate good ones. The criterion of value may vary—Plato thought the supreme value was love of justice and loyalty to the Good State, Tolstoy thought it was love of one's neighbor—but the principle is the same. Applied to the present issue, the conclusion would be obvious—no prize; suppression.

(2) One may, on the other hand, hold another theory of art, that, in intention, at least, it is a mirror in which the spectator sees reflected himself and the world, and becomes conscious of his feelings good and bad, and of what their relations to each other are in fact. This theory presupposes, I believe certain other beliefs into which there is no time to go now, beyond baldly stating them:

(a) All created existence is a good.
(b) Evil is a negative perversion of created good.
(c) Man has free will to choose between good and evil.
(d) But all men are sinners with a perverted will.

An art which did not accurately reflect evil would not be good art.

(3) This does not dispose, however, of the question of censorship. Whatever its intention, a work of art cannot compel the reader to look at it with detachment, and prevent him from using it as a stimulus to and excuse for feelings which he should condemn. Everyone, I am sure, has had the experience of reading a book which he was aware, at the time or later, was bad for him personally, whatever its artistic merit, or however harmless it might be for others, because, in this case, he was not capable of exercising free will, and was therefore not reading it as a work of art. For instance, Baudelaire's poem *La Charogne* would not be healthy reading for a necrophilist. Anti-semitism is, unfortunately, not only a feeling which all gentiles at times feel, but also, and this is what matters, a feeling of which the majority of them are not ashamed. Until they are, they must be regarded as children who have not yet reached the age of consent in this matter and from whom, therefore, all books, whether works of art or not, which reflect feeling about Jews—and it doesn't make the slightest difference whether they are pro or anti, the *New York Post* can be as dangerous as *Der Stürmer*—must be withheld.

If it were to seem likely that the *Pisan Cantos* would be read by people of this kind, I would be in favor of censoring it (as in the case of the movie, *Oliver Twist*). That would not however prevent me awarding the *Pisan Cantos* a prize before withholding it from the public. But I do not believe that the likelihood exists in this case.

Partisan Review, May 1949

Introductions to *Poets of the English Language*

GENERAL PRINCIPLES

Selection

Literary judgment is neither completely conditioned by history nor completely autonomous. On the one hand, critical opinion as to which are the great masterpieces or upon the division between major and minor work remains substantially the same at all times: for example, *The Iliad, The Divine Comedy, Anthony and Cleopatra, War and Peace,* are great for every generation; on the other hand, the particular aspects of any great poet which elicit attention and the relative positions of writers of the second rank are always varying slightly. Tennyson enjoyed a period of great glory, then was for a time ignored, and now is once again admired. The same variation is exhibited by individual taste in any one period; while all agree that Shakespeare is a great dramatist, many differ as to which is his greatest play.

Although an anthology may be regarded as a public treasury, it can never include the total sum of poetical resources, or, invariably, the particular preferences of individuals. The creation of an anthology involves choice, and choice in turn involves the personalities of the editors. Impersonality is as dull in a book of this sort as it is in human beings. Nevertheless, a primary concern with the themes and craft of poetry in English serves as a controlling check against vagrant idiosyncrasy. What we have tried to give is a picture of the poetical tradition from Langland to the beginning of World War I. Langland has been chosen as a beginning, not because the tradition began with him, but because the language of earlier periods communicates directly only to those with scholarly training. We have ended the selections when we did because the practice of poetry from that time on is a matter of the present. *Poets of the English Language* is a presentation of our tradition, and should be received as such.

Arrangement

In general the poets have been presented in their historical order, but since there is no absolute value inherent in such a scheme we have departed from strict chronology whenever another kind of order seemed usefully suggestive. What is true of the arrangement of poets is also true of the arrangement of individual selections from the work of a single poet. Subsequent revisions of a poem destroy much of the significance of the original sequence of composition. We remember most poets in terms of the finally achieved body of their poetry rather than of its development. We have simply tried to present the poets and their poems at their best.

The divisions between individual volumes have inevitably been influenced by the number of pages available to us for each, but each volume represents a grouping which seems reasonable and natural. They are not, however, inevitable. The poetry of Edmund Spenser, for example, may be considered with equal justice to have ended one broad period of English poetry, or to have begun another. For the sake of those who are accustomed to regard Spenser's poetry as the beginning of what we call the English literary renaissance, we can say only that we have taken the point of view which sees it as the culmination of the use of allegory, which in this volume begins with Langland and *The Romance of the Rose*. We do so without quarreling with the second point of view and without any conviction that there is real justice in dichotomizing poetical tradition. For we hope that the reader of one volume will go on to the following ones with no more significant gap than will occur within his reading of any one of them. This is one reason why the separate volumes of *Poets of the English Language* have not been given categorizing titles, and why we prefer to think of the series as a unit. For the spirit of most groups is to be found latent in an earlier period and lingering on into the next. This is the way in which the consciousness of poets works.

Texts

The tendency of editors has been to present the poetry of earlier ages in modern spelling, punctuation, and capitalization. But this frequently does violence to both the meaning and the poetic effect of the lines. In using the contemporary appearance of poems we have followed the reasoning that important evidence has thus been retained as to pronunciation, syllabic values, emphasis, and breath pauses, as well as to the unit of phrasing. The following modifications have, however, been made:

(1) Letters which have fallen out of use have been replaced by their nearest equivalents in the standard alphabet.

(2) Where the spelling of a word in the original text seemed definitely confusing and could be altered without affecting either the meter or the pronunciation, we have altered it.

(3) Where the original punctuation seemed to nullify or badly obscure the meaning to the modern reader, we have changed it.

Supplementary Data

We have not tried to supply biographical data on the poets, although the dates of their births and deaths will be found with the poems, and those of their principal works in the charts which are a supplement to each volume. The amount of biographical data which could have been supplied within the volumes would in actuality have been meaningless. For such study there are published biographies which it would have been folly to attempt to summarize in a few lines. We have preferred to print more poems.

If there is anything in the nature of biography in the various volumes, it is the autobiography of the poetical imagination and fancy as it has been expressed in poems. Comments on this autobiography occur in the introductions to each volume, which are meant not to be definitive but to suggest as freshly as possible the problems with which poetry has coped. Instead of biographical data for each poet, therefore, we have drawn up tables in which, on one side, is given the direct course of poetry and, on the other, are to be found certain of the cultural and societal events which had formative effect. These will be of some help, we trust, toward seeing the course of poetry in historical perspective.

INTRODUCTION TO VOLUME I:
LANGLAND TO SPENSER

Language

Though the difficulties of appreciating Langland and Chaucer without special study of Middle English have perhaps been exaggerated by scholars, the reader will encounter in the poems at the beginning of this volume a language definitely different from his own. By the time he reaches the end, however, the language of the poets—of Sidney, for example—is in all essentials the one he reads and speaks himself. First, the question of what is to be regarded as standard English and what as dialect has been settled in favor of Southeast Midland or London English as the literary standard; second, with the disappearance of the þ and the ȝ the alphabet has become the one we now employ; and, third, the modern forms of the singular and plural of nouns and verbs, of the present and past participle, and of the personal and relative pronouns have been established.

The scholars are, of course, right in saying that for *complete* understanding linguistic study is required. The first thing that the average reader requires, however, is a conviction that the poetry deserves such trouble, and this conviction he can obtain, not simply by trusting the authority of others, but by reading for himself without worrying too much if he fails to understand every word. Once he has learned to like the poems, he will want to understand them fully.

The development of English out of an inflected language into an uninflected is already far advanced by the time Chaucer wrote, but there are enough inflections left to indicate some of the musical advantages which a language like Italian or German still possesses, and which every English song writer and composer of vocal music must envy. The writer of verses also may often envy an inflected language its greater richness in rhymes, for the few inflections remaining in English seem to have been left simply to annoy him. What poet has not at some time or other lost his temper over the unfortunate fact that the addition of *s* makes nouns plural but verbs singular? On the whole, however, the paucity of rhymes in English has not proved a disadvantage, for it has discouraged or at least instantaneously revealed the wrong kind of facility.

The real poetic advantage of an inflected language is of another kind. An inflected language implies that the nature of a thing is determined by its relations to other things, so that a change in its relations causes a change in its nature. In so far as poetry is concerned with emotions, this seems a more natural poetic attitude than that implied by an uninflected language, for I certainly feel myself to be a different person when I am kicking from the one I am when I am being kicked. Further, since the form of a word itself expresses its syntactical relations, it is possible for the poet by his choice of word order to obtain a double set of relations, those of syntax and those of neighborhood.

Every English Poet must regret that his language makes it impossible for him to secure effects such as these of Horace:

> *Nunc et campus et areae*
> *lenesque sub noctem sussuri*
> *composite repetantur hora*
>
> *nunc et latentis proditor intumo*
> *gratus puellae risus ab angulo*
> *pignusque dereptur lacertis*
> *aut digito male pertinaci*

There is a peculiar illusion that crops up from time to time on both sides of the English Channel that the English poets are nature's children "warbling their woodnotes wild" and that the others, the French for instance, care about the rules of art. "Formless," cries the one party: "Artificial," cries the other.

This of course is bosh: there is no such animal as a natural poet. The difference, if any, between English poetry and that of the rest of Europe is due to the former language's being a mongrel tongue containing elements of Anglo-Saxon, Scandinavian, French, and Latin.

This has two consequences. First, it makes for a large vocabulary. Where English has two words for two meanings, French, for instance, often has only one and must express the difference by two idiomatic constructions, with the result that the single word tends to become generalized in meaning, so that it is not altogether unfair to say that English is a more concrete language than French. This does not necessarily imply a better poetry, only a different kind. Neither a Shakespeare nor a Racine is translatable into the language of the other.

Second, a mongrel language inherits from its various ancestors their various metrical traditions. It is not true that the English poets have been less careful craftsmen than their European colleagues, but their tradition is perhaps more flexible. It is to be noted that when a French poet becomes dissatisfied with the classical French prosody, he is more likely than is an English poet in the same position to throw it over entirely and write prose poetry.

Prosody

This volume illustrates both the establishment of a standard language, and the settling down of English prosody into a norm which is still valid. To demonstrate what this norm is, a few general statements may not be out of place:

1. Nearly all poetry in the West has been written in verse, that is, in lines constructed out of a regular pattern of metrical units.

2. Each metrical unit, or foot, consists of an emphatic nuclear syllable and one or more unemphatic satellite syllables.

3. The criterion of emphasis can be (*a*) the length of the syllable, (*b*) the degree of vocal accentuation or (*c*) a mixture of both.

(*a*) In classical Greek and Latin poetry, the nucleus is a long syllable, which contains either a long vowel or a short vowel followed by more than one consonant, and the satellites are short syllables.

$$\text{Cēnā}\,|\,\text{bĭs bĕnĕ:}\,|\;\text{nām tŭ}\,|\,\text{ĭ Că}\,|\,\text{tŭllĭ}$$

Catullus

or

$$\text{Āll cŏm}\,|\,\text{pŏsed ĭn ā}\,|\;\text{mētrĕ}\,|\,\text{ŏf Că}\,|\,\text{tŭllŭs}$$

Tennyson

Such verse is called quantitative.

(*b*) In most English verse, the nucleus is an accented syllable and the satellites are unaccented syllables. Such verse is called qualitative. Compare a qualitative hexameter:

$$\text{Thìs ĭs thĕ}\,|\,\text{fòrĕst prì}\,|\,\text{mèvàl, thĕ}\,|\,\text{mùrmŭrĭnğ}\,|\,\text{pìnes ănd thĕ}\,|\,\text{hèmlŏcks}$$

Longfellow

with a quantitative

$$\text{Wōuldst thŏu}\,|\,\text{knōw whŏ}\,|\,\text{hĕre vĭsĭ}\,|\,\text{tĕth, dwēllĕth}\,|\,\text{ānd sīngĕth}\,|\,\text{ālsō}$$

Bridges

(*c*) In Anglo-Saxon verse, the emphatic element or lift is either a long accented syllable or a short accented syllable plus a short unaccented one.

It has been suggested, not implausibly, that a quantitative metric has its origin in song and dance, that is, in actions of ritual or play, and a qualitative metric in actions of work.

4. A quantitative metric was imposed on classical Latin poetry by Greek models, but in late Latin verse an accentual element reappeared. At first accent and length coincided.

$$\text{Crās ămĕt quĭ numquam ămāvĭt quĭque ămāvĭt crās ămĕt}$$

which scans the same by either rule. But in medieval Latin the quantitative element began to weaken, and a line like

Nobis datus, nobis natus, ex intacta virgine

Aquinas

can be scanned only accentually, as in English.

Lònely | iñ thẽ | Règeñt | Pàlače, | sìppiñg | à bǎ |nànǎ| blùsh

Betjeman

If accent tended to supersede length in Latin verse, it was all the more certain to do so in English with its inherited accentual tradition from Anglo-Saxon and—as it lost its inflections—its predominance of consonants, which makes so many short syllables long by position. From time to time experiments in quantitative English verse have been attempted, but the difficulties are so great that the experiments have remained curiosities or *tours de force*.

5. There are two opposite metrical extremes possible in English:

(*a*) To count only the accents in the line and to ignore the number of unaccented syllables, so that, with its three accents,

A pièd and peèled Mày

is regarded as equivalent to

Of his sodden with its sorrowing heàrt

Hopkins

(*b*) To count only the number of syllables in the line and to ignore their accented or unaccented quality, so that, with its fifteen syllables,

I recall their magnificence, now not more magnificent

is regarded as equivalent to

Wedge-shaped, slate-grey marks on their forelegs and the resolute tail

Marianne Moore

The bulk of English verse is written in a way that lies between these extremes, i.e. equivalent lines contain the same number of syllables and the same underlying regular pattern of metrical feet scanned qualitatively. But the musical art of the poet depends on his capacity to vary from this pattern without the sense of the pattern being lost:

> In tyme of trewe, on hawkyng wolde he ride
> Or elles honte boor, bere, or lyoun;
> The smale bestes leet he gon biside.
> And whan that he com ridyng into town,
> Ful ofte his lady from hire wyndow down,
> As fresshe as faucon comen out of muwe,
> Ful redy was hym goodly to saluwe.

Chaucer

The metrical base in all of these lines is the same—that is, each has five iambic feet, but only a child in the classroom would, in reading line 3, accent *leet,* or in line 4 accent *he* and *in,* so that only four accents are actually insisted on in the former, and only three in the latter.

> Thĕ sma̅|lĕ bĕs|tĕs lĕet | hĕ gŏn | bĭside.
> Ănd whān | thăt hĕ | cŏm rī|dy̆ng ĭn|tŏ tōwn.

The commonest kinds of feet in English verse are the iamb (˘-) and the trochee (-˘). Single dactyls (-˘˘) and anapests (˘˘-) often appear through an inversion of an iamb or a trochee, but as a metrical base they have played only a minor role.

What variations are possible depends on the poet's ear. The only rule seems to be an empirical and negative one, namely, that two successive accents cannot be suppressed or displaced without destroying the underlying pattern. Thus:

> Ĭ wānt | tŏ bĕ | ă gĕnŭine | sŭccĕss

or

> Gĭve mĕ | yŏur hănd; | prŏmĭse | yŏu'll stĭll | bĕ trŭe

will pass as iambic pentameters. But

> Ĭ wănt | tŏ bĕ | ĭn ăn | ĕxcĭt|ĕd state

or

> Lăy yŏur | knĭfe ănd | yŏur fŏrk | ăcrŏss | yŏur plāte

will not.

6. The tradition of Anglo-Saxon continued, particularly in the north, well into the fifteenth century, and shows itself not only in poems definitely written in Alliterative meter but also in the elaborate alliteration of poems written on French metrical models. If it was unable to hold its own, one of the reasons is that the writers of alliterative verse had lost a sense of what the original meter actually was, so that their verse represents a decadence without a development.

Compare

> Hie dy̆gel lond
> warigeath wulfhleothu,   windige næssas,
> frēcne fengelād,   thaer fyrgenstrēam
> under næssa genipu   nither gewiteth,
> flōd under foldan.
>
> *Beowulf*

with

> Thay bowen by bonkes wher bowes ar bare,
> Thay clomben by cliffes wher clenges the colde.
> The heven was up halt, bot ugly ther-under;
> Mist muged on the mor, malt on the mounte,
> Uch hille hade a hatte, a mist-hakel huge.
>
> *Sir Gawain and the Green Knight*

The rule that there be no alliteration in the last lift has been forgotten, a dactylic rhythm is no longer avoided, and no efforts are taken to counterpoint line structure and sentence structure. The meter has thus lost the gravity and subtlety of the original and actually increased the great drawback of all alliterative verse, a tendency to artificial diction.

The Middle Ages

Apart from any linguistic difficulties, the modern reader, particularly if his previous knowledge of poetry begins with the Romantic poets, may be puzzled by the content of medieval poetry. We are so accustomed to a culture in which poetry is the highbrow medium, to be employed only for communicating the most intense and subtle experiences, while the natural medium for everyday use is prose, that it is difficult for us to imagine a society in which the relative positions were the other way round, a time when verse was the popular medium for instruction and entertainment, and prose, mostly in Latin, the specialized medium for the intercourse of scholars.

If this anthology were being compiled by a contemporary of the poets themselves, the selection would certainly be very different and the impression we should get would be that they were very "impure" poets, always forsaking the poetry for moralizing or teaching. It is easier for us to understand the practical reasons why this should have been so—how, for instance, among a people without books and dependent on the oral transmission of culture, rhyme is a useful mnemonic device—than to appreciate it aesthetically.

Curiously enough, the lowbrow often has a much less inhibited attitude to *verse* than, shall we say, the middlebrow, as is evidenced by the popularity of limericks and those little moral and consolatory verses which are syndicated in newspapers. The highbrow may be right in purifying the poetry he himself writes from every "prosy" element, but one should, I think, have serious doubts of his poetic gift if he gets no personal pleasure from such poems as

> And masculine is found to be
> Hadria the Adriatic Sea

or

> Minus times minus equals plus;
> The reason for this we need not discuss.

It must be admitted that, to our taste, the medieval poets are frequently prolix and formless, but this is rather because they were too ambitious for their talents than because of any fault in their goal itself—too many average poets set out to write as all-embracing a masterpiece as *The Divine Comedy*. After the Middle Ages no one, not even Shakespeare or Milton, really attempts such a thing.

Allegory is so typical of medieval thinking and so untypical of ours—or, rather, when we are using allegory we are unconscious of the fact and believe we are thinking logically—that many people have difficulty in understanding medieval poetry because they do not grasp the principles of mythological and allegorical thought. Here are a few of them:

1. If an emotion or a concept is thought of as being absolute or given, that is, as being its own cause for being, then it may be represented as an immortal god or goddess.

2. If *A* is the logical ground of *B*—if *A*, for instance, is the general case of which *B* is the special case—*A* is represented as the parent of *B* (Aphrodite and Eros).

3. If *A* is the cause of *B*, *A* is represented as the social superior of *B*.

4. If *A* and *B* are equal and distinct but generally associated with each other, they are represented as having a sexual relation. If their association is considered socially desirable, this relation is one of marriage (Cupid and Psyche); if it is considered socially undesirable, it is one of adultery (Venus and Mars).

5. Consciousness or will is masculine.

6. Potentiality is young (the Future); actuality is old (Fate).

7. Moral goods and the goals of desire are physically beautiful. Moral evils and the objects of aversion are physically ugly. If the desire and the aversion are evil, then the beauty and the ugliness are enchanted simulacra.

8. Animal features indicate that what is represented cannot be fully grasped by consciousness.

9. Nature is heavy; the spirit is light. Therefore, to obey gravity is to follow natural desires; to climb or fly is to follow spiritual aspirations.

Anglo-Saxon poetry is the poetry of a tribe; Elizabethan poetry is the poetry of a nation; the poetry in this volume represents that portion of the poetry of Christendom which was written in English. Christendom was not a unity which grew out of the preceding unity of the Roman Empire, but a new structure created by the Papal Revolution of 1000–1200. The term "dark ages" has a real meaning in the sense that for more than five hundred years after the collapse of the Roman Empire there was no common Western culture, only scattered and isolated outposts of civilization, such as the Benedictine monasteries.

The Papal Revolution established once and for all that a man may have two loyalties, a local loyalty to the region where he is born, lives, and dies, and a universal loyalty to the truth which is the same for all. Whenever scientists and artists of different countries exchange periodicals they are enjoying a right won for them by the popes of the eleventh and twelfth centuries; whenever a national state keeps scientific discoveries secret or censors artistic creations for reasons of national security or public order, it is attempting to undo the revolutionary accomplishment of the Middle Ages. It is right and proper that the setting of *The Canterbury Tales* should be a pilgrimage in which all sorts and conditions of men are brought together away from their homes in a common intention to pay homage to one of the martyrs of that revolution, Thomas à Becket.

It would probably be a good thing if the word Renaissance were to disappear forever from our vocabulary, for few words have caused more popular misunderstanding. If our own experience is not untypical, the impression retained from the classroom is something like this: Modern Man was born around 1450, probably through the efforts of Greek refugees from Constantinople. Before that time there was Medieval Man, who dared not think for himself, did not look out objectively at the world of nature or consider his body with respect, but only looked inward to worry about the state of his soul. Suddenly, in the middle of the fifteenth century, the dreamer awoke and began to see reality for the first time, and to become an individual.

This is not only untrue in itself but diverts attention from the real revolutionary events, namely, the publication of Luther's ninety-five Theses in 1517, of Machiavelli's *Prince* in 1513, and of Descartes' *Discours de la Methode* in 1637. With these end five centuries of uninterrupted humanism, during which the energies of European civilization were directed toward making the whole of reality universally visible to the physical eye or the eye of reason, on the assumption that there was no truth, however mysterious, that could not be objectified in an image or a syllogism. This humanistic period begins with Anselm's ontological proof of the existence of God; it receives a temporary check with the condemnation of Abelard through the efforts of St Bernard; it is seriously challenged by the Cathar Movement with its doctrine that matter was incapable of salvation. But after the crusade against the Albigenses in 1226, the orthodoxy of Christian humanism remains secure until Luther. Its dramatic dates are 1215, when the mystery of the Mass was intellectually defined at the Council in Lateran; 1233, when it asserts its conviction of its rightness by establishing the Inquisition (whenever and wherever an individual denies what is held to be demonstrable, his denial is bound to be regarded as malice or lunacy, and persecution, however genteel its form, is inevitable); and 1264, when it shows its conscious awareness of its nature by the establishment of the feast of Corpus Christi. Its typical literary expressions are Courtly Love as a subject and Allegory as a form. It is not true that the literature of the Middle Ages is unconcerned with the individual; but it defines the individual not as a "character" but as a soul. All souls are equal in the sight of God; consequently, more than any before or since, medieval literature is democratic. Everyman is not a type, that is, a projection of a passion, but a complete individual who lives with others and dies alone; at the same time what he suffers is what we all suffer, whatever our differences in temperament, intelligence, and social situation. Troilus is an individual, but Chaucer's main concern is not with the way in which Troilus is peculiar as a lover but with how an individual falls in love.

One literary consequence of the conviction of the Middle Ages that everything could be made explicit is that, in their poetry, the treatment of the invisible sin of pride is perfunctory; in fact it is never pride itself that is described but only the visible and less serious sin of vanity. It is only after 1517 that the poets (Shakespeare, for example) study pride profoundly. It is significant that Dante and Milton are each strongest where the other is weakest: Satan is the least convincing figure in *The Divine Comedy*; God the least convincing figure in *Paradise Lost.*

It is to the end of the Middle Ages, not to the beginning of the next, that the Italian painters of the *quattrocentro* and the poets in this volume belong. It is not a new vision that they offer but illustrations of the *Summa*.

What happened was not the appearance of a new humanism—that was always there—but a fading away of its Christian base. The symptoms of the real break with the past appear with tragedy as a literary form, and baroque as an architectural style. Spenser, though he was not born till 1552 and was in belief an ardent Protestant, as an artist exhibits the old sensibility and is much nearer in spirit to the *Romaunt de la Rose* than he is to his contemporary, Fulke Greville. Again one has only to compare the love poetry of Wyatt with that of the Provençal poets four centuries earlier and with that of Donne less than a century later to see the continuity with the former and the radical break before the latter.

The Middle Ages believed that an ultimate and intelligible unity embraced all the diversity of existence.

> Within its depths, I saw ingathered, bound by love into one volume,
> the scattered leaves of the universe;
> Substance and accidents and their relations, as though together fused,
> after such fashion that what I tell of is one simple flame.
>
> Dante, *Paradiso*, canto xxxiii, lines 85–90

Faith in this unity, or rather faith in its intelligibility, was shattered in the sixteenth century. The causes of this breakdown were, as always, various: moral—the arrogance of the visible church in which, in the eyes of many thoughtful and thoughtless people, the corpus seemed to be smothering the Christus; economic—the dislocation of the traditional structure of society after the Black Death in 1381; and intellectual—the characteristic medieval method of demonstrating the unity of particulars and the relation of the invisible to the visible by *analogy* began to seem too easy to be true.

Nor is it true to say that the men of the Middle Ages did not observe nature, or cared only about their own souls, ignoring social relations: indeed it would be truer to say that their intellectual weakness was an oversimple faith in the direct evidence of their senses and the immediate data of consciousness, an oversimplification of the relation between the objective and subjective world. Believing that the individual soul was a microcosm of the universe and that all visible things were signs of spiritual truths, they thought that to demonstrate this, it was enough simply to use one's eyes and one's powers of reflection to perceive analogies. For example:

As the soul aspires to God, *so* the stone of the Gothic arch soars.
As individuals and armies fight for territory, *so* the virtues and vices struggle for the possession of the soul.
As indulgence money is a gift, *so* pardon is a gift.
As a noble man and woman love each other, *so* is the love that moves the sun and stars.

When Bacon defines science as putting nature to the question—that is, the torture—he is rebuking this trust in direct observation, for he implies that nature is secretive and must be compelled against her will to reveal the truth. Modern science begins when, instead of asking what a thing is like, for which simple observation is enough, one asks how long it is or how heavy, questions which cannot be answered without performing experiments. When the break came it was drastic. Luther denied any intelligible relation between Faith and Works, Machiavelli any intelligible relation between private and public morality, and Descartes any intelligible relation between Matter and Mind. Allegory became impossible as a literary form, and the human Amor seemed no longer a parable of the Divine Love but its blasphemous parody.

There has been no time since its own when the literature of the Middle Ages could appeal to readers as greatly as it can today, when the dualism inaugurated by Luther, Machiavelli, and Descartes has brought us to the end of our tether and we know that either we must discover a unity which can repair the fissures that separate the individual from society, feeling from intellect, and conscience from both, or we shall surely die by spiritual despair and physical annihilation.

The interest of modern poets in myths and symbols as devices for making their private and personal experiences public and typical, the tendency of modern novelists to take as their hero not the exceptional character, but the individual Everyman, Mr Earwicker, or K, are literary evidences of our search for a kind of unity similar to that which Christendom believed it had found. We must not, however, be nostalgic. Luther and Descartes, to whatever brink of disaster we may have allowed them to push us, stand, like the angels about Eden, barring the way back from an unintelligible dualism to any simple one-to-one relation. That way lies, not the Earthly Paradise, but a totalitarian hell.

INTRODUCTION TO VOLUME II: MARLOWE TO MARVELL

Language

The desire of the Protestants for a Bible and a liturgy in the vernacular, and the desire of the new aristocracy for secular culture combined to make the sixteenth and seventeenth centuries one of the great periods of translations. Translation is fruitful in two ways. First, it introduces new kinds of sensibility and rhetoric—for example, the Petrarchan love convention; and fresh literary forms—for example, the pastoral. It does not particularly matter if the translators have understood their originals correctly; often, indeed, misunderstanding is, from the point of view of the native writer, more profitable. Second, and perhaps even more important, the problem of finding an equivalent meaning in a language with a very different structure from the original develops the syntax and vocabulary of the former. It would be difficult to overestimate the debt which the technique of English verse owes to the exercise of making rhymed versions of the Psalms and translating Vergil and Ovid. Along with this interest in translation went an intense interest in words and verbal experiment. Theories about poetry, about prosody, about diction, affectations of every kind, flourished. The schoolmasters of literature frown on affectation as silly and probably unhealthy. They are wrong. Only stupid people are without affectations and only dishonest ones think of themselves as rational. In literature, as in life, there can be no growth without them, for affectation, passionately adopted and loyally obeyed, is one of the chief forms of self-discipline by which the human sensibility can raise itself by its own bootstraps.

The schoolmasters dismiss, for instance, the Euphuists and imagine that, because Shakespeare laughs at them in *Love's Labour's Lost* and *Hamlet*, they have him on their side. In fact, throughout his career, the diction, the figures of speech, the cadences of his poetry are profoundly indebted to the Euphuist movement, and he knew it.

Shakespeare's poetry exhibits, in its most fully developed forms, the characteristics of most of his contemporaries: the range of vocabulary from the most Latinate to the most vulgar, from

> I never did like mollestation view
> On the enchafed Flood.

to

> The Kitchen Malkin Pinnes
> Her richest Lockram 'bout her reechie necke.

the daring use of one part of speech as another,

> The smiles of Knaves
> Tent in my cheekes

> With every gale and vary of their masters

the concretion of abstractions,

> Murd'ring Impossibility, to make
> What cannot be, slight worke.

and the rapid shifting of metaphor to the edge of nonsense,

> The hearts
> That spaniel'd me at heels, to whom I gave
> Their wishes, do dis-Candie, melt their sweets
> On blossoming Cæsar; and this Pine is barkt
> That over-top'd them all.

Such a range of possibilities is dangerous, however, for all but the greatest artists. As Mr T. S. Eliot has remarked, if you try to imitate Dante and fail you will only be dull, but if you try to imitate Shakespeare and fail, you will make a fool of yourself. The lesser Elizabethan poets frequently do, and the reader must put up with a great many lines of fustian for the sake of a few lines of splendor.

The Lyric

In medieval English poetry, the poems are usually either short lyrics in the strict sense (poems intended to be sung), or long poems (allegorical, narrative, or didactic), intended to be recited or read over more than one evening. In the sixteenth century the sung lyric develops to keep pace with the development of music, both in solos and madrigals. The simple ballad measures develop into complicated variable stanzas with studied rhythmical tricks which depend on the music for their effect; for example:

> All you that love, or lov'd before,
>   The Fairie Queene Proserpina
> Bids you increase that loving humour more:
>   They that yet have not fed
> On delight amorous,
>   She vowes that they shall lead
>   Apes in Avernus.

> Campion, *A Booke of Ayres*

or,

> Slow, slow, fresh fount, keepe time with my salt tears;
>   Yet slower, yet, O faintly gentle springs:
> List to the heavy part the musique beares,
>   Woe weepes out her division, when shee sings.
>   Droupe hearbs, and flowres;
>   Fall griefe in showres;
>   Our beauties are not ours:
>   O, I could still
> (Like melting snow upon some craggie hill,)
>   Drop, drop, drop, drop,
> Since natures pride is, now, a wither'd daffodil.
>
>   Jonson, *Cynthia's Revels*

In addition, a new kind of poem develops, the poem of concentrated re-flection, lyric in length, but not for singing. Its archetype, both in manner and structure, is the Italian sonnet, which is then broken up into stanzas and extended. The development of the sonnet and the reflective lyric from Wyatt through Fulke Greville to Donne is an interesting example of the relation of poets to a convention. There can be no art without a convention which em-phasizes certain aspects of experience as important and dismisses others to the background. A new convention is a revolution in sensibility. It appeals to and is adopted by a generation because it makes sense of experiences which previously had been ignored. Every convention in its turn, when it has done its work, becomes reactionary and needs to be replaced. Its effects, however, do not disappear; its successor embodies them.

The Petrarchan love convention with which Tudor poetry begins, for in-stance, is not the same as the earlier Provençal convention. The Lady does not so much inspire noble actions in a warrior as be the cause of the emo-tions about which a poet writes. For such a convention, the most suitable kind of lady has a good character but says No, and the most suitable poet is one with introvert's capacity for deep and sustained emotion. When, either by temperament or on occasion, the poet's feelings are frivolous or transient, the convention of seriousness leads to the most boring kind of rhetoric. Nor is it well suited to situations in which the behavior of the beloved is such that there is as much hatred as love in the relation or in which the feelings of the lover are consciously and violently sensual.

Shakespeare in his sonnets and Donne in his early love lyrics wrestle with the convention and break through it, but at the same time neither of them can write as if the *Amor* religion of fidelity and deification of the beloved had never existed. It is precisely the conflict between their natural situation—that is, one that can always occur to lovers—and a historical ideal of love unknown to antiquity that is the new experience which their poetry expresses.

Blank Verse

It was perhaps more luck than deliberate choice which led to the adoption of unrhymed decasyllabics as the standard meter for drama. It might quite easily have been rhymed fourteeners. Further, the first essays in blank-verse drama did not look very promising. A playgoer familiar with the technical virtuosity of some of the rhymed miracle and morality plays, in which the kind of meter employed by a character was in itself revealing, might well have thought *Gorboduc*, with its monotonous iambic stomp, a lapse into barbarism.

Even when Marlowe has developed his mighty line, one wearies of a meter so continuously fortissimo, and is tempted to feel that the hero is a prisoner of the verse, compelled to be continuously grand and in a perpetual passion because that is all the meter is capable of. Certainly no one reading Surrey's translation of the *Æneid*:

> The Grekes toward the palace rushed fast,
> And, cover'd with engines, the gates beset,
> And rered up ladders against the walles;
> Under the windowes scaling by their steppes,
> Fencèd with sheldes in their left hands, whereon
> They did receive the darts, while their right hands
> Griped for hold th'embatel of the wall.
> The Troyans on the other part rend down
> The turrets hye and eke the palace roofe;
> With such weapons they shope them to defend,
> Seing al lost, now at the point of death.
> The gilt sparres and the beams then threw they down,
> Of old fathers the proud and royal workes

could have foreseen that within a generation this meter would become capable of such music and complexity as

>   Then beganne
> A top i' th' Chaser, a Retyre: Anon
> A Rowt, confusion thicke; forthwith they flye
> Chickens, the way which they stopt Eagles: Slaves,
> The strides the Victors made: and now our Cowards,
> Like Fragments in hard Voyages became
> The life o' th' need: having found the backe doore open
> Of the unguarded hearts: heavens, how they wound,
> Some slaine before, some dying; some their Friends
> O'er-borne i' th' former wave: ten chac'd by one,
> Are now each one the slaughter-man of twenty:
> Those that would dye or ere resist, are growne
> The mortall bugs o' th' Field.

>   Shakespeare, *Cymbeline*

or,

>   This deare hour,
> A doughtie Don is taken, with my Dol;
> And thou maist make his ransome, what thou wilt,
> My Dousabel: He shall be brought here fetter'd
> With thy faire lookes, before he sees thee; and throwne
> In a downe-bed, as darke as any dungeon;
> Where thou shalt keepe him waking with thy drum;
> Thy drum, my Dol, thy drum; till he be tame
> As the poore blackbirds were i' the great frost,
> Or bees are with a bason; and so hive him
> I' the swan-skin coverlid and cambrick sheets,
> Till he worke honey and waxe, my little Gods-guift.

Jonson, The Alchemist

Given that there were going to be Shakespeare and Jonson to use it, blank verse was a fortunate choice, for no other meter could have allowed so much freedom of inversion, elision, varying of the caesura, etc., without collapsing into doggerel or prose.

Freedom, however, is a snare for the second-rate. If, outside the plays of Shakespeare and Jonson, only one work of the period, *The Changeling*, approaches being a satisfactory stage play, if the average Elizabethan play is a hodgepodge containing a few magnificent scenes or poetic passages, the freedom permitted in its verse and its construction is in some measure responsible.

General

The sixteenth and seventeenth centuries cover a period of revolutionary change in our civilization. Revolutions are rare. Just as most illnesses are temporary derangements, recovery from which means a restoration of normal functioning as it was before the attack—and it is only on rare occasions that sickness is a symptom of a profound change in the organism after which health itself will have a new meaning—so, while a revolution is always accompanied by war, few wars are revolutionary.

Further, it is only after a revolution is over that it is recognizable as such; its contemporaries are always mistaken about what they are doing. The Revolutionary Party imagines that it is the revolution to end revolutions, that it is destined to make the world anew; the Counter-revolutionary Party imagines that what is happening is no revolution but a revolt which must and can be crushed without any radical change taking place.

Thus, the Reformers believed that the work of the previous Papal Revolution was to be swept from the earth, while the Papacy believed it was dealing with another heresy like the Albigensian revolt, which could be made to disappear. Neither anticipated or desired a Christendom in permanent schism, with all the consequences to life and thinking which this would involve for both.

As cultural examples of these consequences, take two: Catholic baroque art and Lutheran music. The Reformers denounced religious images; the Counter Reformation reaffirmed them more exuberantly than ever, but its conception of the nature of the image and its attitude towards the materials of which the image is made were very different from what they had been before the debate started. Previously the human figure had usually been thought of as we think of a friend—as a rational person to be encountered face to face; in baroque painting it becomes a natural object in space, to be regarded from any angle or perspective, and of which the eye is no more significant than the foot; it is the body in movement—or the will of man, rather than his reason—on which the interest is concentrated. Similarly, in baroque architecture the architect is no longer the midwife who brings forth from matter its latent soul but the potter whose will imposes on a neutral substance whatever shape he fancies. The defiant assertion in baroque of the visual simply as visual, its deliberate theatricality, its use of the *trompe l'oeil*, are signs that for Catholicism too the old confidence in a simple relation between Faith and Works has been lost. Nature can be exploited for religious purposes, but she herself is secular.

The Reformers, on the other hand, while depriving their congregations of visual images and pilgrimages, could not destroy the idea of Corpus Christi which the Papal Revolution had established; to hold their converts they had to replace the Catholic expressions of unity which they had destroyed with a new one, namely music, which goes further than they realized, for it transcends all doctrinal differences.

The political consequence of this revolution was the emergence of centralized national states and the exaltation of the power of the secular Prince. Luther deliberately glorified the Christian Magistrate, without whose support he could not have survived, and in defending itself the Papacy was compelled to do the same. The right of the subject to revolt against a prince who violates natural law, a doctrine held by St Thomas, was denied by both parties.

This political revolution went further in England than in any other country, and only in England did the political change precede the religious. The real symbolic revolutionary act of Henry VIII was not his severance from Rome but his execution of Sir Thomas More in 1535, for the Lord Chancellor was by tradition the King's conscience, the voice of natural law. This was going too far for the West, which has never been able to accept Byzantinism, and the excess was corrected in 1649 with the execution of Charles I, in whose person Sir Thomas More is avenged, and the voice of natural law returns as the Public Spirit of the House of Commons.

If the concept of the Machiavellian villain has more fascination for English dramatists than for French or Spanish, it is possible that this was because they had such first-hand experience under the Tudors of Machiavellian politics.

For political acumen combined with unscrupulousness, the Continent can show no figure before Richelieu to match Henry VIII or Burghley. Similarly, the emergence of a purely secular English drama with little overt reference to religious beliefs was perhaps encouraged by an unwillingness to look too closely at the reasons for the nation's having become Protestant. The new nobility, who patronized the players, was discharging one of the duties of the Church whose money it had stolen; a religious drama would have reminded men of events which were better forgotten.

The mythical hero of the Papal Revolution was the Knight-Errant, the epic hero who, tamed by Christianity and the love of a noble woman, fights and triumphs in the service of the law of justice and the faith of Mother Church. He is both good and successful. The representative heroes of the sixteenth century are three:

1. *The Machiavellian Prince* who believes neither in God nor in woman but only in himself. He has the secular virtues of will and cunning and is, unless or until he falls, successful. But good he is not. At his best he is Prince Hal, at his worst, Iago.

2. *Don Quixote*, the Knight of Faith, who has no epic virtues and knows it, but who believes he is called to perform the tasks of the Knight-Errant. He is like the Machiavellian Prince in that he is capable of acting. He is his opposite in that he does not love himself and his actions are totally ineffective. He is good and a worldly failure.

3. *Hamlet*, the man without faith either in himself or in God, who defines his existence in terms of others: "I am the man whose mother married his uncle who murdered his father." He would like to become what the Greek hero is, a creature of situation. Unable to achieve this, he cannot act, only "act" in the theatrical sense, that is, play at possibilities. He is neither good like Don Quixote nor evil like the Prince, because, unlike either of them, he is incapable of action; he can only reflect.

All three myths mark the emergence into consciousness of an attitude which Charles Williams has aptly called the "Quality of Disbelief." At its best this means an awareness and acceptance of the paradoxes involved in all human feelings, beliefs, and actions. The irony of Cervantes and Montaigne, the way in which Pascal examines his relation to God, and Donne his relation to women, have much in common. At its worst this attitude leads either to cheap complacency or to the nihilistic despair which produces the demonic Iago, who spends his destructive life proving that life has no meaning, or the paralyzed Hamlet, who will not wager but remains trapped in the snare of self-reflection.

Drama

Civilization appears to alternate between periods in which the dominating ideal is masculine and those in which it is feminine. The sixteenth century is marked by a revolt against *La donna gentile* and the Motherhood of the Church, in favor of the spectacular violent male and the Fatherhood of God. (In response to the rejection of the Madonna by the Reformation, Catholicism encouraged the cult of St Joseph.) The female does not come into her own again until the Romantic Movement. Perhaps drama, as distinct from ritual, only flourishes in such periods, and even then only so long as the emphasis is on the masculine will, for when, as in the eighteenth century, the ideal is the masculine reason, drama wanes.

Internal and External Drama. It is difficult, perhaps impossible, for any of us to form a complete picture of life, because, for that, we have to reconcile and combine two completely different impressions—that of life as each of us experiences it in his own person, and that of life as we observe it in others.

When I observe myself, the *I* which observes is unique, but not individual; it has only a power to recognize, compare, judge, and choose: the self which it observes is neither unique nor individual, but rather a succession of states of feeling or desire. Necessity in my world means two things, the givenness of whatever state of myself is at any moment present, and the obligatory freedom of my ego. Similarly, action in my world has a special sense; I act toward my states of being, not toward the stimuli which provoked them; *my* action, in fact, is the giving or withholding of permission to myself to act. It is impossible for me to act in ignorance, for any world is by definition that which I know; it is not even, strictly speaking, possible for me to be self-deceived, for if I know I am deceiving myself, I am at once no longer doing so; I can never believe that I do not know what is good for me. Again, I cannot say that I am fortunate or unfortunate, for these words apply only to my self.

If I try, then, to present my own experience of life in dramatic form, the play will be of the allegorical morality type, like *Everyman.* The hero will be the rational willing *I* that chooses, and the other characters, states of the self, pleasant and unpleasant, good and bad, for or against which the hero's choices are made. The aim of the hero is to attain true felicity; the play is a comedy if he succeeds and a tragedy if he fails. The plot can only be a succession of incidents in time, and the passing of time from birth to death the only necessity; all else is free choice.

If now I turn round and, deliberately putting aside anything I know about myself, scrutinize other human beings as objectively as I can, I see a very different world. I do not see states of being but individuals in states, say of anger, each of them different, and caused by different stimuli, that is, I see people acting in a situation, and the situation and the action are all I see; I never see another choose between alternative actions, only the action he does take. I cannot therefore tell whether he has free will or not, I only know that he is fortunate or unfortunate in his circumstances. I often see him acting in ignorance of facts about his situation which I know; I cannot, however, so long as I remain completely detached and objective, ever say for certain that in a given situation he is deceiving himself. To recognize self-deception I have to combine both the objective and subjective pictures—I learn to recognize self-deception in myself by observing others, and self-deception in others by observing myself.

If I try to present the objective version in dramatic form, the play will be of the type of Sophoclean tragedy, in which the hero is a man in an exceptional situation. The drama will consist, not in the choices he freely makes, but in the actions which the situation obliges him to take. His motive will not be ultimate felicity, but some concrete satisfaction of desire, and the tragedy will lie in the knowledge, granted to the audience but withheld from him, that in fact his actions are going to have the opposite effect.

The pure drama of consciousness, and the pure drama of situation, are alike in that their characters have no existence outside what they do and the situation they happen to be in. The audience knows all about them that there is to know. One cannot imagine, therefore, writing a book about the characters in Greek tragedy, or the characters in the morality plays; they themselves have said all there is to say. The fact that it has been and will always remain possible to write books about Shakespeare's characters, in which completely contradictory conclusions are reached, indicates that the Elizabethan play is different from either, being, in fact, an attempt to synthesize both into a new, more complicated type.

Actually, of course, the Elizabethan dramatists knew and owed very little to classical drama. The closet tragedies of Seneca may have had some influence upon their style of rhetoric, the comedies of Plautus and Terence provided a few comic situations and devices, but Elizabethan drama would probably be pretty much the same if they had never been known at all. Even the comedies of Ben Jonson, the most learned of all the playwrights, owe much more to the morality play than to Latin comedy. Take away Everyman, substitute one of the seven deadly sins as the hero, set the other six in league to profit from his obsession, and one has the basic pattern of the Jonsonian comedy of humors.

The link between the medieval play and the Elizabethan is the chronicle play. If few of the pre-Shakespearian chronicle plays except Marlowe's *Edward II* are now readable, nothing could have been more fortunate for Shakespeare's development as a dramatist than his being compelled for his livelihood—judging by the early poems his natural taste was for something much less coarse—to face the problems which the chronicle play poses.

The writer of a chronicle play cannot, like the Greek tragedians who have a significant myth as subject, select his situations; he has to take whatever history offers, the humdrum as well as the startling, those in which a character is the victim of a situation, and those in which he creates one. He can therefore have no narrow theory of aesthetic propriety which separates the tragic from the comic, no theory of heroic *areté* which can pick one historical character and reject another. Finally, the study of the human individual involved in political action, and of the moral ambiguities in which history abounds, cures any tendency toward a simple moralizing of characters into good or bad, or any equating of success and failure with virtue and vice.

The Elizabethan drama inherited from the mystery and morality plays three important and very un-Greek conceptions:

The significance of time. Whereas time in Greek drama is simply the time it takes for the situation of the hero to be revealed, in Elizabethan drama it is what the hero creates with what he does and suffers, the medium in which he realizes his potential nature.

The significance of choice. In a Greek tragedy everything that could have been otherwise has already happened before the play begins, and it is impossible at any point in the play to call out to the hero, "Don't choose this, choose that." He is already in the trap. In an Elizabethan tragedy, in *Othello,* for example, there is no point before he actually murders Desdemona when it would be impossible for him to control his jealousy, discover the truth, and convert the tragedy into a comedy. Vice versa, there is no point in a comedy like *The Two Gentlemen of Verona* where the wrong turning could not be taken and the conclusion be tragic.

The significance of suffering. To the Greeks suffering is retributive, a punishment for sin or vice. In tragedy the hero who suffers is the fortunate and gifted man whom everyone would like to be, and whose suffering therefore they sympathetically share. In comedy the hero, or rather the butt, is the ridiculous man who nobody wants to be, and whose suffering is, therefore, not felt by the audience. But in Shakespeare—Jonson's comedies are in this sense classical and non-Christian—suffering and misfortune are not in themselves a punishment. It is true that they would not exist if man had never fallen into sin, but precisely because he has, suffering is a necessary accompaniment to his salvation, to be accepted as an occasion for grace or as a process of purgation. Those who try to refuse suffering not only fail to avoid it but are plunged deeper into sin and suffering. Thus the difference between Shakespeare's tragedies and comedies is not that characters suffer in the one and not in the other, but that in comedy the suffering leads to self-knowledge, repentance, forgiveness, love, and in tragedy it leads in the opposite direction into self-blindness, defiance, hatred.

Even in so light-hearted a comedy as *Love's Labour's Lost* the decisive events involve real suffering. The princess is brought by the death of her father to the realization that she loves Biron, and at the same time to the insight that what he lacks, without which he cannot know the meaning of love, is a knowledge of suffering, hence the task of visiting hospitals for a year which she makes a precondition of their marriage.

If Shakespearean comedy is full of a sympathetic joy which classical comedy excludes, Shakespearean tragedy, on the other hand, is more terrifying than classical tragedy. In the latter the curtain falls on disaster, but also on justice done and knowledge of the truth gained; whereas in the former the disaster, for the hero, is in vain. He has suffered, but without gaining any comprehension of himself or his action, and he dies in despair, damned.

Whereas in Greek drama the hero and the chorus argue the truth out between them, in Elizabethan drama the hero receives no such help. He stands there alone, he makes his soliloquy to a silent chorus, the audience, who are expected by the playwright to supply the appropriate lines themselves. An Elizabethan play, therefore, is always at the mercy of the audience; if they are lazy or unperceptive, its significance and meaning are diminished and blurred.

The Metaphysical Poets

"Metaphysical" is a somewhat misleading term, for it suggests that the poets to whom it is applied had a unique interest in the science of Being, in contrast, say, to "Nature" poets. This is not the case: the subject matter of Donne and his followers is not essentially different from that of most poets. What characterizes them is, first, certain habits of metaphor: instead of drawing their images from mythology, imaginative literature of the past, or direct observation of nature, they take their analogies from technical and scientific fields of knowledge, from, for example, cartography.

> My face in thine eye, thine in mine appeares,
> And true plaine hearts doe in the faces rest,
> Where can we finde two better hemisphæres
> Without sharp North, without declining West?

> Donne

or mathematics:

> As Lines, so Loves oblique may well
> Themselves in every Angle greet:
> But ours so truly Paralel,
> Though infinite can never meet.

> Marvell

Secondly they are particularly intrigued by paradoxes, both of logic and emotion:

> For I
> Except you enthrall mee, never shall be free,
> Nor ever chaste, except you ravish mee.

> Donne

> My God, my God, though I be clean forgot,
> Let me not love Thee if I love Thee not.
>
> Herbert

Both the technical term and the paradox had appeared in poetry before Donne and were to continue after Traherne, but elsewhere they are peripheral, not central to the style.

It seems possible—it is not provable—that the disruption of traditional values, cosmological and political, which was occurring at the beginning of the seventeenth century encouraged this cast of mind and that metaphysical poetry is the reflection of a peculiar tension between faith and skepticism.

This would in part account for the rediscovery of these poets in our century after two centuries of neglect, a revival of popularity which has gone so far, indeed, that it is now not without its dangers. It has become necessary to remind readers that, great poets as Donne, Herbert, and Marvell are, their kind of poetry is not the only kind. The danger of thinking so has been increased by the development of certain methods of critical analysis which work particularly well with metaphysical poetry but perhaps not so well with other kinds. It is always wise to remember that, if a certain critical theory fails to do much with a certain kind of poetry, the fault may lie in the theory, not in the poetry. As one of the metaphysicals himself has said,

> Is all good structure in a winding stair?

Too exclusive a taste is always an indiscriminate taste. If a person asserts that he worships Donne but abhors Pope, or vice versa, one suspects that he does not really appreciate his favorite.

GENERAL PRINCIPLES

Selections

The exuberant richness of Christopher Marlowe's *Hero and Leander* serves as an introduction to this volume, somewhat as the sobered classicism of Marvell's "Horatian Ode" marks a point of departure. Midway, though not precisely halfway, comes the triumph of Shakespeare's *Anthony and Cleopatra*. With some polite and preliminary trepidation between themselves, the editors approached the choice of a single poetical drama to serve as outstanding and as an example of a genre in which the Elizabethan achievement has never been equaled in the English language. The same title came immediately to each mind. Additional space would have admitted Jonson's *The Alchemist* as a demonstration of a somewhat different success, yet his masque, *The Vision of Delight*, does help to widen the understanding of how brilliantly the Elizabethans realized the possibilities of the dramatic craft.

Fortunately it has been possible to include generous selections of longer poems from the period, and this should prove a welcome change from the usual emphasis on songs and briefer lyrics. Of this latter type, others than those selected for this volume might have been chosen from the almost anonymous wealth which its poets provided. But on this score anthologists must be permitted at least as much leeway as their critics, and freshness of choice may give refreshment to the reader.

Texts

As in the first volume of the series, the editors have retained the contemporary appearance of the texts of the poems, on the basis that modernization of spelling, punctuation, and capitalization detracts from the intended meaning and tonal qualities of the poem. Such variations from a true "diplomatic" text as exist have been made sparingly and only to avoid absolute misunderstanding. Thus the text of *Anthony and Cleopatra*, taken from the Second Folio, has been only minimally altered. In the enthusiasm of modern editors for modernizing punctuation and spelling, for example, they have in many instances, to all intents and purposes, substituted new lines.

The reader will be given useful, though not infallible, assistance in his reading—which should always be done with the ear as well as the eye—if he will remember that a capitalized word is usually stressed, and that spelling helps to give syllabic values, and that Elizabethan punctuation is not so much based on strict grammatical logic as on oratorical phrasing. For example, the progression of values of the comma, semi-colon, colon, and period (or "full stop" as the British call it) roughly follows a sequence of proportionally increasing rests or breath pauses. If the Elizabethans did not follow this absolutely, and though scholarship cannot accept the rule in finality, nevertheless it seems to work in practice.

Supplementary Data

We have not tried to supply biographical data on the poets, although the dates of their births and deaths will be found with the poems, and those of their principal works in the charts which are a supplement to each volume. The amount of biographical data which could have been supplied within the volumes would in actuality have been meaningless. For such study there are published biographies which it would have been folly to attempt to summarize in a few lines. We have preferred to print more poems.

If there is anything in the nature of biography in the various volumes, it is the autobiography of the poetical imagination and fancy as it has been expressed in poems. Comments on this autobiography occur in the introductions to each volume, which are meant not to be definitive but to suggest as freshly as possible the problems with which poetry has coped. Instead of biographical data for each poet, therefore, we have drawn up tables in which, on one side, is given the direct course of poetry and, on the other, are to be found certain of the cultural and societal events which had formative effect. These will be of some help, we trust, toward seeing the course of poetry in historical perspective.

INTRODUCTION TO VOLUME III: MILTON TO GOLDSMITH

Verse and Prose

During the latter half of the seventeenth century and the first half of the eighteenth, prose comes to rival verse as a popular medium. Moreover, a new kind of prose narrative, the novel, appears. In consequence the essential nature and possibilities of each become clearer.

Verse, owing to its greater mnemonic power, is the superior medium to prose for didactic instruction. Those who condemn didactic poetry can only do so because they condemn didacticism and must disapprove *a fortiori* of didactic prose. In verse, at least, as the Alka-Seltzer advertisements testify, the didactic message loses half its immodesty.

Verse is also certainly equal and perhaps superior to prose as a medium for the lucid exposition of ideas, because in skillful hands the form of the verse can parallel and reinforce the steps of the logic. Indeed, contrary to what most people who have inherited the romantic conception of poetry believe, the danger of argument in verse is that it will make the ideas too clear and distinct, more Cartesian than they really are. Pope's *Essay on Man* is a case in point.

On the other hand, verse is unsuited to controversy—to proving true or right some fact or belief which has been questioned or denied—because its formal nature then conveys a certain skepticism about its conclusions. The rhyme

> Thirty days hath September,
> April, June, and November

is valid because no one doubts its truth. Supposing, however, that there were a body of people who passionately denied it, the lines would be powerless to convince them, for formally it would make no difference if they ran

> Thirty days hath September,
> April, May, and December.

This becomes very clear in Dryden's poetry. We have no reason to doubt that the man who wrote *Religio Laici* and *The Hind and the Panther* was sincere in his beliefs, but these two great poems are not serious controversy in the sense that their poetic intention is to convert the reader to Anglicanism and Roman Catholicism respectively. Dryden the poet, like Shaw the playwright, exhibits that most skeptical of all mentalities, a passionate pleasure in argument for its own sake, in the play of dialectic irrespective of any conclusion. For, as Charles Williams says:

> Prose, especially sweet and rational prose, conceals its human limitations. It may argue or instruct or exhort, but all that while it subdues or hides from us the pattern which is our reminder that its conclusions are what they are because of its own limitations—which are its writer's—which are in the nature of man. . . . It is that fact which poetry willingly embraces, and from which prose, as it were, turns away. . . . It takes man's limitation and makes that explicitly a part of his total sensation. It avoids the last illusion of prose, which so gently sometimes and at others so passionately pretends that things are thus and thus. In poetry they also are thus and thus, but because the arrangement of the lines, the pattern within the whole, will have it so. . . . Exquisitely leaning to an implied untruth, prose persuades us that we can trust our natures to know things as they are; ostentatiously faithful to its own nature, poetry assures us that we cannot—we know only as we can.
>
> *Reason and Beauty in the Poetic Mind*

Controversy, then, requires prose. So does history, as distinct from myth. For the essential point about a historical fact is how and when it actually occurred, not how it ideally might have occurred. The novel differs from the epic or the tale in that it is an imitation of history: however unnaturalistic his technique, the novelist fails if he does not convince us while we are reading that his characters are historical characters, that this is what they actually said and did. The novel as a literary genre could not appear until men had become conscious of the peculiar nature of history.

Milton's Blank Verse

Milton is the ancestor of a kind of poet whom we associate with a much later period. He is, for example, the first poet in English literature whose attitude toward his art is neither professional like that of Ben Jonson and Dryden nor amateur like that of Wyatt, but priestly or prophetic. Poetry to him was neither an amusing activity nor the job for which he happened to be qualified, but the most sacred of all human activities. To become a great poet was to become not only superior to other poets but superior to all other men.

Again, he is the first English poet to set out deliberately to fashion a style for himself, for his own use alone. Whereas Shakespeare's blank verse is at the start indistinguishable from that of his contemporaries and develops as he develops, Milton's blank verse is, as it were, a medium which he had to invent before he could begin writing, and for its invention other English poets like Browne or Drummond were of much less assistance than Latin and Italian poets.

An idiosyncratic style, when it carries the authority of a great poet, is a dan-

ger to his successors, and in Milton's case particularly so. The most obvious
characteristic of his style is its uninterrupted grandeur, which is incapable of
any lighter tone, and the number of themes to which such a grand style is
suited is strictly limited. Milton's influence on later poets was principally
through his diction, which is precisely the element in his style which, when
the subject does not demand it, is most likely to fall into pomposity. Few, if
any, of them made use of his poetic syntax, his extraordinary way of arrang-
ing his clauses:

> Down a while
> He sate, and round about him saw unseen:
> At last as from a Cloud his fulgent head
> And shape Starr-bright appeer'd, or brighter, clad
> With what permissive glory since his fall
> Was left him, or false glitter: All amaz'd
> At that so sudden blaze the *Stygian* throng
> Bent thir aspect, and whom they wish'd beheld,
> Thir mighty Chief return'd: loud was th' acclaime:
> Forth rush'd in haste the great consulting Peers,
> Rais'd from thir *Divan*, and with like joy
> Congratulant approach'd him, who with hand
> Silence, and with these words attention won.
>
> *Paradise Lost,* Book X

This is a pity, because syntax, the structural element in style, is adaptable to
different subjects and different sensibilities in a way that diction is not.

The Couplet

At the mention of any poetry written between 1688 and 1776, our immediate association is likely to be with the heroic couplet. This is not quite just;
the period shows more metrical variety than we usually credit it with; there
are, for example, the meters of Prior, the octosyllabics of Swift and his irregular comic verse which anticipates Ogden Nash, stanzas of Gay which anticipate Byron, Charles Wesley's hymns, etc. It remains true, however, that during this period the heroic couplet was the dominating form for a poem of
any length. There is much to be said for a standard form, whether it be blank
verse, the couplet, or any other. Instead of searching for his own original form
and perhaps never finding it, the poet takes it as given and can concentrate
upon making it say what he has to say. The more original a poet is, the less—
barring a few exceptional cases—he feels it a limitation to use a form employed by others; further, continuous practice in the same form trains his
mind to think easily and naturally in it and makes him sensitive to the subtlest variations of which it is capable.

That the heroic couplet is capable of adapting itself to a wide range of topic and music can be seen from the following extracts.

> But this our Age such Authors does afford,
> As make whole Plays, and yet scarce write one word;
> Who, in this anarchy of Wit, rob all,
> And what's their Plunder, their Possession call:
> Who, like bold Padders, scorn by Night to prey,
> But rob by Sun-shine, in the Face of Day:
> Nay scarce the common Ceremony use
> Of Stand, Sir, and deliver up your Muse;
> But knock the Poet down, and, with a Grace,
> Mount Pegasus before the Owner's Face.
>
> Dryden, Prologue to Tomkis's *Albumazar*

> To happy Convents, bosom'd deep in vines,
> Where slumber Abbots, purple as their wines:
> To Isles of fragrance, lily-silver'd vales,
> Diffusing languor in the painting gales:
> To lands of singing or of dancing slaves,
> Love-whisp'ring woods, and lute-resounding waves.
> But chief her shrine where naked Venus keeps,
> And Cupids ride the Lion of the Deeps;
> Where, eas'd of Fleets, the Adriatic main
> Wafts the smooth Eunuch and enamour'd swain.
>
> Pope, *The Dunciad*, IV

> But few there are whom hours like these await,
> Who set unclouded in the gulfs of Fate.
> From Lydia's monarch should the search descend,
> By Solon caution'd to regard his end;
> In life's last scene what prodigies surprise,
> Fears of the brave, and follies of the wise?
> From Marlb'rough's eyes the streams of dotage flow,
> And Swift expires a driv'ler and a show.
>
> Johnson, *Vanity of Human Wishes*

In comparison with blank verse, its only serious rival in English verse as a standard form, the couplet has one disadvantage. The emphasis on the line structure which the rhymes produce, an emphasis so much stronger in an accented language like English than in French, is so powerful that it almost compels the sentence structure to conform to it, so losing a subtlety which can be one of the great charms of poetry—the opposition and interplay of the line stop and the sentence stop.

Of its comparative advantage, Dryden writes:

But that benefit which I consider most in it, because I have not seldome found it, is, that it Bounds and Circumscribes the Fancy. For Imagination in a Poet is a faculty so Wild and Lawless, that, like an High-ranging Spaniel it must have Cloggs tied to it, least it out-run the Judgment. The great easiness of blank Verse, renders the Poet too Luxuriant; He is tempted to say many things, which might better be Omitted, or at least shut up in fewer Words: But when the difficulty of Artfull Rhyming is interpos'd, where the Poet commonly confines his Sence to his Couplet, and must contrive that Sence into such Words, that the Rhyme shall naturally follow them, not they the Rhyme; the Fancy then gives Leisure to the Judgment to come in; which seeing so heavy a Tax impos'd, is ready to cut off all unnecessary Expences. This last Consideration has already answer'd an Objection which some have made; that Rhyme is only an Embroidery of Sence, to make that which is ordinary in it self pass for excellent with less Examination. But certainly, that which most regulates the Fancy, and gives the Judgment its busiest Employment, is like to bring forth the richest and clearest Thoughts.

Epistle Dedicatory to The Rival Ladies

The Battle of the Books

The characteristic which is common to the poets in this volume and distinguishes them from their predecessors (though Ben Jonson in some measure possesses it) is a consciousness of their historical position as poets. However different they may be in other ways, Milton and Pope are like each other and unlike Shakespeare in the kind of questions they ask themselves about their contemporary poetic task.

In addition to admiring the classical authors, they are conscious of them as writers of the past and of themselves as moderns. Reading a classical writer, therefore, they ask, "What has he accomplished once and for all, which it would therefore be useless repetition for me to attempt to repeat? What help as a model can he be to me in writing of experiences or subjects which are too modern for him to have known?" Thus Milton abandons his projected epic on King Arthur, not because the theme lacks personal appeal to him, but because the theme of Arthur is essentially the same as the theme of Aeneas; he is not satisfied until he alights on a subject which in relation to Vergil is modern, namely the Fall. Similarly Pope takes the *Iliad* and the *Aeneid* as his models, but, substituting for the gods and warriors of the one the Sylphs and visitors to a lady's drawing room, and for the prehistoric heroes of the other the literary hacks of a modern metropolis, he produces *The Rape of the Lock* and *The Dunciad*.

The mutual interaction of comparable memories is one of the greatest sources of civilized pleasure; just as one sees America differently after one has seen Italy, and vice versa, so, after one has read both the *Iliad* and *The Rape of the Lock*, one cannot help seeing the Baron in Hector and Hector in the Baron. Again, the differences between Samson's attitude to free will and sin and that of the Aeschylean tragic heroes, between their temptation to be insolent toward the gods and his to despair of God's goodness, are emphasized by the similarity of the dramatic form and make *Samson Agonistes* not only a tragedy but also a historical and critical comparison of the Greek and Biblical conceptions of life.

Both Milton and Pope consider and expect their audiences to consider their reading as a significant experience, comparable to, say, falling in love; literature is to them a natural part of life.

The Cavalier Poets

After the death of James I, the court ceased to be the symbolic center of the national life, and the poets associated closely with the court reflect the change. They are on the defensive; before the Civil War they try to believe that no serious change is going to take place, and after the Restoration they try to pretend that in fact no serious change has occurred, that the former status quo has been restored. Their poetry deliberately ignores history and public interests and as deliberately insists on the private life of leisure and pleasure. In technique they move away from the complicated stanzas and ingenious conceits of the metaphysical poets toward the simpler and more polite poetry of the coming age; in their subjects and sensibility, on the other hand, they represent the final development of the school which began with Wyatt. The wheel has with them turned a half-circle, so that now the Petrarchan convention is stood on its head; it is infidelity that is recommended, fidelity that is despised. But the Petrarchan sentiments are still there in a repressed form, and that is what gives these poets' work, Rochester's in particular, its unique flavor. They are not naïvely frivolous but defiantly so, debauched by a serious effort of will.

General

The Treaty of Westphalia in 1648 marks the end of the Lutheran revolution; neither Protestantism nor Roman Catholicism had succeeded in destroying the other; henceforth both were to live side by side. The problem facing Western civilization was how to find some principle of unity which could prevent a Christendom divided nationally and religiously from disintegration. In this attempt the lead was taken by England; between 1642 and 1776 England is the center of revolutionary and "progressive" ideas.

The actual period of revolution lasts from 1642–1688 and is best seen as one period, of which the Puritan Revolution and the Glorious Revolution are two complementary halves. The objective of this revolution is not to achieve freedom in either the Lutheran or the Jacobin sense, but rather to bring individual freedom into conformity with law. The slogans are Common Law, Common Sense, Public Spirit. Its first enemy is the claim of the king to be free to govern as he please; its second the claim of the sects—the Anabaptists, Anti-Scripturists, Chiliasts, Familists, Muggletonians, Old Brownists, Questionists, Sebaptists, Soul Sleepers, Traskites, etc.—to know the truth by private inspiration. Cromwell defeated the first; the Whigs of 1688 the second. Its viewpoint might be described as a sort of secular or at least non-sacramental Catholicism. The Whig families had no intention of undoing the Reformation to which they owed their fortunes, but their attitude to life was profoundly unprotestant. Whether in politics, religion, or art, whether in the mouth of a king or an oysterwoman, Luther's egotistic cry, "I can do no other," is to them the voice of the enemy, to be dealt with not by burning but by ridicule. The Parliament to which they gave sovereignty in civil and religious affairs is not only a collective body but an anonymous one; it is not an individual Mr Smith who speaks or votes but the Member for Middletown; the term Opposition is taken from astronomy, and signifies not irreconcileable conflict, but balance.

The hero of this revolution is the unarmed gentleman. The gentleman differs from the aristocrat in being distinguished not by birth but by breeding; anyone who can learn to acquire the habits and live according to the standards of the gentleman becomes one.

This revolution was catholic in another sense, namely that the views of the politicians were in harmony with those of the theologians, the scientists, and the writers.

Thus the Newtonian cosmology, in which the universe consists of things located in space upon which the laws of nature are imposed, requires the unitarian Deist God to impose the latter; for there is nothing in the nature of things to account for the laws they obey, and nothing in the laws to account for the things. The Deist God, for his part, need not reveal himself supernaturally to man; the public order and economy of the Newtonian universe are sufficient proof of his existence.

Similarly, in the aesthetic theories of the writers, there is no great mystery about poetic composition. It is the result of the cooperation of three mental faculties, memory, judgment, and fancy. Memory provides the raw material, judgment arranges all this into a coherent pattern, from which fancy can select whatever she needs for the task at hand. The first and last of these are private to the individual, but judgment is public and social; judgment is to art what public spirit is to politics, or the laws of nature to astronomy. Thus Addison writes:

> I shall add no more to what I have here offered, than that Musick, Architecture, and Painting, as well as Poetry, and Oratory, are to deduce their Laws and Rules from the general Sense and Taste of Mankind, and

not from the Principles of those Arts themselves; or, in other words, the Taste is not to conform to the Art, but the Art to the Taste.

The Spectator, no. 29

To be true to nature means to express what is enduring, essential, and comprehensible; the accidental or irregular is ugly and unnatural.

> There are two Causes of Beauty, natural and customary. Natural is from Geometry, consisting in Uniformity (that is Equality) and Proportion. Customary Beauty is begotten by the Use of our Senses to those Objects which are usually pleasing to us for other Causes, as Familiarity or particular Inclination breeds a Love to Things not in themselves lovely. Here lies the great Occasion of Errors; here is tried the Architect's Judgment: but always the true Test is natural or geometrical Beauty.
>
> Geometrical Figures are naturally more beautiful than other irregular; in this all consent as to a Law of Nature. Of geometrical Figures, the Square and the Circle are most beautiful; next, the Parallelogram and the Oval. Strait lines are more beautiful than curve. . . .
>
> Views contrary to Beauty are Deformity, or a Defect of Uniformity, and Plainness, which is the Excess of Uniformity; Variety makes the Mean.
>
> Variety of Uniformities make compleat Beauty: Uniformities are best tempered, as Rhimes in Poetry, alternately, or sometimes with more Variety, as in Stanzas.

Sir Christopher Wren, *Parentalia*

Eccentricity of emotion or diction, the elevation of private fancy over public judgment, are to be as condemned in poets as is the refusal of an individual member to accept the general verdict of the House of Commons:

> Beware what Spirit rages in your Breast;
> For ten Inspir'd ten thousand are possest.
> Thus make the proper Use of each Extream,
> And write with Fury, but correct with Pleam.

Roscommon

Conclusion

Such a view is most valid in political life, which by its nature is public, impersonal, secular, and practical. The lasting contribution of the English Revolution was neither the emancipation of a class nor the construction of a political theory, but the promulgation of a certain ideal of political conduct. If it would be partial to assert—as the writer believes—that "to behave like a gentleman" is the only possible ideal for sane politics in any kind of society, it is not too much to say that it is the ideal upon which the successful functioning of a democratic government, as the West understands the term, depends, even in, or rather most of all in, a situation of crisis.

In personal life, however, the religion of common sense and good taste is seriously defective. It can neither allow for nor comprehend those decisive once-for-all instants of vision in which a life is confronted by another, addressed by God, Nature, or a Beatrice—which, unique and momentary though they may be, are what make that life a person and give his normal day-to-day experiences their meaning.

It is a view which necessarily excludes some kinds of poetry, perhaps the greatest kinds. This does not mean, however, that it is of no use to poets or that the poetry written from it cannot be of a high order. Indeed, there is a good deal to be said for its aesthetic as a practical guide to poets. It may make out the creative act to be more conscious than in fact it is, but it encourages the poet to pay attention to that which is in his control. Inspiration is granted or withheld as the Muse, not he, disposes; all he can do is to see that his work is well made. If then he is not inspired—well, his work will be dull, but least it will not be chaotic rubbish.

If a style of poetry is valid, then there is an ideal subject for it, and we shall know its real possibilities only when that subject has been found. Luckily for our estimate of the Augustans it was. *The Dunciad* is not only a great poem but also the only poem in English which is at once comic and sublime. It should never be read with notes, for to think that it matters who the characters were or why Pope was angry with them is to miss the whole point of the poem, which is best appreciated by supplying one's own contemporary list of the servants of the Goddess of Dullness. No great poem can be written without genuine passion; hostile as the aesthetic of the Augustan might be to most kinds of passion, there was one it could and did encourage, a passion for the civilized intelligent life, and it is this which burns so fiercely throughout Pope's poem. To have seen Dullness, the goddess of minor and in themselves unimportant figures, as a really formidable and eternal threat to the City of Man was a vision in its own way as original and of as permanent value to the City as Dante's of Paradise or Wordsworth's of Nature.

GENERAL PRINCIPLES

Selections

The differing versions of Eden as remembered in Milton's *Paradise Lost* and in Goldsmith's *The Deserted Village* frame the present volume. Milton's concerns are not out of place as an introduction to a body of poetry so much influenced by his examples. *The Rape of the Lock* takes on fuller significance in juxtaposition to Milton's great poems, and *An Essay on Man* may be regarded with some justice as an eighteenth-century definition of post-lapsarian Adam. If cavaliers like Herrick, Carew, Suckling, Lovelace, and Waller seem strangers to the increasingly dominant mood, they serve as a reminder of what lingered after Milton but was ultimately abandoned.

Obviously no excerpts can replace *Paradise Lost* as a whole, though we have done what we could to suggest the whole. *Samson Agonistes* fortunately can be given in entirety. Pope's *The Rape of the Lock* and *An Essay on Criticism* are also printed without cutting, as are the individual books or essays from the other longer works of the man who took Milton's place as the chief poetic force of the advancing century. Johnson's *The Vanity of Human Wishes*, Smart's *A Song to David*, and Goldsmith's *The Deserted Village* also help to indicate the breadth of canvas preferred by poets. In these as elsewhere we have tried to overcome the tendency of anthologists to represent the past chiefly as a salon of miniatures.

Texts

Out of consistency to the principle of maintaining the contemporary appearance of the texts of the poems, we have tried to present them as they were known. Spelling and punctuation present no special problems, but the vagaries of contemporary capitalization, as they shift from one edition to another, are evidence that in this respect there is a decline in the reliance of either poets or public on capitalization as a guide. Capitalization apparently became little more than a sport for typesetters. We have nevertheless retained the contemporary appearance. The chief exception has been in the selections from Pope where we have generally used the texts of Warburton, since they contain Pope's own emendations, though the manner of capitalization is somewhat different from what Pope normally saw. Perhaps quixotically, but through a desire to show capitalization as it indicates the balance of a line, we have retained the early appearance of *The Rape of the Lock* and the "Epistle to Dr Arbuthnot," incorporating only the few verbal changes and altered punctuations which were later made.

William H. Bond and the Harvard College Library have generously permitted the use of excerpts from his forthcoming edition of Smart's *Jubilate Agno*, done from the original manuscript now in The Houghton Library of Harvard University. These versions, now published for the first time, are of real significance. Smart's trial essay toward *A Song to David*, whose composition it immediately preceded, has been hitherto considered as a disjunct series of separate poems. The reconstruction of the manuscript, however, shows Smart's design to have been that of paired poems in antiphonal relationship to each other. This structure we have stressed by printing them in alternate passages, though Smart originally arranged them on opposite sheets as in an antiphonary.* For the inimitable passages on Jeoffry, the cat, only one set of versicles now exists; but it is most probable that their missing counterparts in the other section of the poem bore little direct relationship to them, for by this time Smart's original design had begun to disintegrate.

---

* For a fuller discussion of the manuscript and Smart's intent, see Bond, William H., "Christopher Smart's *Jubilate Agno*," *Harvard Library Bulletin*, IV, i (Winter 1950), pp. 39–52.

Supplementary Data

We have not tried to supply biographical data on the poets, although the dates of their births and deaths will be found with the poems, and those of their principal works in the charts which are a supplement to each volume. The amount of biographical data which could have been supplied within the volumes would in actuality have been meaningless. For such study there are published biographies which it would have been folly to attempt to summarize in a few lines. We have preferred to print more poems.

If there is anything in the nature of biography in the various volumes, it is the autobiography of the poetical imagination and fancy as it has been expressed in poems. Comments on this autobiography occur in the introductions to each volume, which are meant not to be definitive but to suggest as freshly as possible the problems with which poetry has coped. Instead of biographical data for each poet, therefore, we have drawn up tables in which, on one side, is given the direct course of poetry and, on the other, are to be found certain of the cultural and societal events which had formative effect. These will be of some help, we trust, toward seeing the course of poetry in historical perspective.

INTRODUCTION TO VOLUME IV: BLAKE TO POE

The Romantic Definition of Man

What is man? How does he differ from the gods on the one hand and from nature on the other? What is the divine element in man? A different set of answers to such questions, or a shift of emphasis in the old answers, changes the style and subject matter of poetry and the poet's conception of his function.

For example, in the age of the heroic epic the difference between gods and men is that the former are immortal and the latter must finally all die like the beasts. In the meantime, however, some men are made godlike and separated from nature by the favor of the gods, becoming heroes who do great deeds. The poet, that is, the man inspired with the gift of tongues, celebrates the hero and his acts.

In the Middle Ages, the quality which man shares with God and which the creatures do not have is a will that can make free choices. What separates man from God is sin: that he can and does choose wrongly, love himself, act selfishly. The function of the poet is to exhibit the human soul tempted by competing loves, and to celebrate the ways in which she can be redeemed.

In the neoclassical period, the divine human quality is reason, the capacity to recognize general laws, and the function of the poet is to celebrate the Rational City and to pour scorn on its enemies.

Toward the end of the eighteenth century—Rousseau is one of the first symptoms—a new answer appears. The divine element in man is now held to be neither power nor free will nor reason, but self-consciousness. Like God and unlike the rest of nature, man can say "I": his ego stands over against his self, which to the ego is a part of nature. In this self he can see possibilities; he can imagine it and all things as being other than they are; he runs ahead of himself; he foresees his own death.

Hölderlin's poem *Der Mensch* is as complete and clear a definition as any.

> Soon he has grown up;
> The animals avoid him, for other than
> They is man; he does not resemble
> Thee, nor the Father, for boldly in him
>
> And alone are mingled the Father's lofty
> Spirit with thy joy, O Earth, and thy sorrow.
> Gladly he would be like the mother
> Of the gods, like all-embracing Nature!
>
> Oh, that is why his restless spirit drives
> Him away from thy heart, O Earth, and thy gifts
> Are in vain, and thy gentle fetters;
> And he seeks better things, the wild one!
>
> From the fragrant meadow of his shores, far out
> Into the flowerless water, Man must go
> And though, like the starlit night full of
> Golden fruit his orchard gleams, yet he digs
>
> Caves in the mountains and looks around the pit,
> Deeply hidden from his Father's cheerful light,
> Faithless also to the sun-god who
> Does not love the slave and scoffs at troubles.
>
> For more freely breathe the birds of the forest,
> And though Man's breast rises with greater splendour,
> And he sees the dark future, he must
> See death too, and he alone must fear it.
>
> —Translated by Michael Hamburger

If self-awareness and the power to conceive of possibility is the divine element in man, then the hero whom the poet must celebrate is himself, for the only consciousness accessible to him is his own. When Keats writes in his letters that the poet is the least poetical thing in existence because he has no identity, he is saying that the man of power who has this identity is less human, more like the sun or the birds of nature, which can only be themselves.

The romantic assertions of the supreme importance of art—for example, Blake's statement "Art is the tree of life. Art is Christianity," or Shelley's "Poets are the unacknowledged legislators of the world"—are not to be understood as vanity but as the inevitable conclusion to be drawn from the presupposition that consciousness is the noblest human quality.

Similarly, the romantic definitions of the poet and the poetic imagination—for example:

> . . . a disposition to be affected more than other men by absent things as if they were present; an ability of conjuring up in himself passions, which are indeed far from being the same as those produced by real events, yet (especially in those parts of the general sympathy which are pleasing and delightful) do more nearly resemble the passions produced by real events, than anything which, from the motions of their own minds merely, other men are accustomed to feel in themselves.
>
> Wordsworth, Preface to the *Lyrical Ballads*, 1800

> The primary Imagination I hold to be the living Power and prime Agent of all human Perception, and as a repetition in the finite mind of the eternal act of creation in the infinite I AM.
>
> Coleridge, *Biographia Literaria*, chapter xiii

seem meaningless so long as we think of the poet as a man with a gift for writing verse. They define, not the writer, but the hero about whom he writes, which for the Romantic are combined in the same person.

Thus, the subject of the greatest long poem of this period, *The Prelude*, is not a heroic action like the siege of Troy, nor a decisive choice like the Fall of Man, nor a threat to civilization like the Goddess of Dullness, but the Growth of a Poet's Mind.

The Romantic God and the Romantic Devil

Just as the reason which detects general laws governing the movements of natural bodies tends out of self-worship to create as an idol a purely transcendent and Unitarian god, so the idol of consciousness is a pantheistic god immanent in nature. For to my consciousness nature is a diversity of particular images present to it which have one thing in common, namely that they are *my* images: they are all flavored by the same invisible presence, myself.

Similarly, if the enemies of reason are passion and stupidity, which cause disorder, the enemies of consciousness are abstract intellectualizing and conventional codes of morality, which neglect and suppress the capacity of the consciousness to experience. Reason has to distinguish between true and false; the will, between right and wrong: consciousness can make no such distinctions; it can only ask "What is there?" For it, there is not an "either/or" but a "both-and."

The Romantic Hero

Wordsworth is an exceptional figure in that, like Dante, in addition to and quite distinct from his poetic gift, he was granted an extraordinary vision. The peculiar experience of Nature which came to him in childhood would have made him an exception even if he had never written a line. Whether or no similar experiences have befallen other poets they have seldom informed us. When we read Shakespeare, for instance, we are aware, not of his having enjoyed any out-of-the-way experience, but only of his unique poetic gift.

To demonstrate the identity of the romantic hero with the consciousness of the poet, therefore, it is more convincing to take works which are not professedly autobiographical, for example, Goethe's *Faust* and Byron's *Don Juan*. The Faust of Marlowe is simply an old professor who wants to be a godlike hero in the epic sense. He wants power to do great deeds and win glory, he wants to sleep with the most beautiful girls, he wants to be eternally twenty years old. Goethe's Faust has quite other aims. He doesn't want to *do anything*, he wants to *experience everything*. Hence the curious wager with Mephistopheles, for to cry to a moment of experience, "Stay: you are so beautiful," would be to renounce his quest, to exclude some possible future experience. He does not seduce Marguerite because he desires her or become a swamp-drainer because he wants to do good to mankind, but because he wants to know what it feels like to be a seducer and a benefactor. The definition of Mephistopheles as the spirit who denies would be meaningless if Faust were a hero of will, for the will is as much tempted by Yes as by No; it is only the consciousness, the imagination, which is tempted solely by refusal to accept what it experiences.

Similarly, the most obvious characteristic of Byron's hero is his passivity; it is he who is always the seduced one. *Don Juan* is as much the dramatized story of the education of Byron's mind as *The Prelude* is the direct account of the education of Wordsworth's.

One more example. The occurrence which begins the Ancient Mariner's redemption is no act of penance, is not even directly concerned with his sinful act, with the albatross; it is the acceptance of the water snakes by his consciousness which had previously wished to reject them.

Romantic Diction

More fuss has been made about this than it deserves. Wordsworth's would-be polemic expression "the language really used by men," which originally ran "the language of the middle and lower classes of society," is little more than an assertion that if a poet wishes to describe his own experiences, and happens, like Wordsworth, to belong to one of those classes, his diction, however elevated, will differ from that of a poet raised among the aristocracy. Much of Byron's hostility to Wordsworth seems to have been caused by his feeling that the latter was an inverted snob who in elevating into a general principle what was a personal need was claiming that the middle and lower classes were intrinsically better, more human, than the upper classes.

Symbol and Allegory

Consciousness cannot divide its *données* into the true and the false, the good and the evil; it can only measure them along a scale of intensity. Cer-

tain images present themselves charged with more affect than a rational inspection can account for. Such an image is a symbol. To the question "What
does it symbolize?" only multiple and equally partial answers are possible, for,
unlike an allegorical image, it has no one-to-one correspondence.

The allegorical method is to take two images, or an idea and an image, and
deliberately relate them. When Gavin Douglas writes

King Hart into his cumlie castell strang

we know without possibility of contradiction that King Hart is the soul and
his castle is the body. But there can be no method of symbolism. An image is
presented to the poet's consciousness either charged with symbolic affect or
not; all that the poet can do is to pick out one or several which are and
arrange them. We may say, if we like, that the sun and the moon in *The Ancient Mariner* symbolize respectively the punishing justice-demanding Father
and the forgiving merciful Mother; we are not wrong but we are very little
nearer understanding the poem, for a hundred equally valid allegorical identifications can be made.

Allegory is a form of rhetoric, a device for making the abstract concrete;
in nearly all successful allegory the images used do in fact have a symbolic
value over and above their allegorical use, but that is secondary to the poet's
purpose. In poetry of which the subject, the hero, is consciousness, the symbols are the primary material.

Organization

A poem that attempts to follow the motions of consciousness will have to
organize itself into a whole in ways which consciousness itself suggests, not as
logic dictates.

The real novelty in Romantic poetry is not its diction but its structure. If
the Romantic poets, after rejecting Pope and Dryden, did not rediscover
Donne and the metaphysical poets, this was because the latter, no less than
the former, organized their poems logically. For example, Marvell's poem
"To His Coy Mistress" is constructed syllogistically upon three conjunctions:
if–but–therefore. In contrast to this, take the structure of Keats's "Ode to the
Nightingale." The poem opens with a description of a state of feeling, a desire for death; it shifts to the nightingale singing of summer; it shifts back to
the "I" of the poem wishing for wine and the Golden Age; it returns to the
bird in the forest and what it does not know but the "I" describes: mortality,
sorrow, unrequited love; the "I" again is listening to the bird and desires again
to die; now the "I" disappears completely for a stanza and the bird is heard
singing to various others in the far past and faery lands forlorn. The word forlorn by its suggestion brings back the "I" to himself listening to the bird song
fading away. The roles of the nightingale and of the poet have kept varying
throughout the poem. Sometimes the bird has been contrasted with the con-

scious man; sometimes his bird's song has been considered not as distinct from the poet but as a part of his experience, and a symbol of himself as poet; sometimes again it is the poet who is singing of the bird and thereby doing what a bird cannot do, immortalizing the immediate moment.

Romanticism and Society

A new aesthetic is always accompanied by and related to religious and political changes, though none can be explained away in terms of another.

While the Pope couplet and the neoclassical aesthetic were still the poetic gospel, the Wesleyan religious revival cast doubts. Ignoring rational arguments, from design, for the existence of God, scorning utilitarian arguments for morality, it insisted upon a catastrophic personal experience of sin and divine redemption. To describe such experiences neither the form nor the diction of Pope would do, and the evangelical hymn writers like Charles Wesley were, in technique as well as in spirit, the forerunners of the English Romantic poets. This was, however, a local influence. The dominating event which affected all the Romantics is, of course, the French Revolution.

The uniqueness of this revolution is that it was the work of talented intellectuals, of orators and men of letters.* Its achievement was not the liberation of any social or economic class but freedom for the talented individual to profit from and earn full credit for his talents. Its hero is Figaro, the gifted barber of Beaumarchais' comedy, its enemy the count who claims privileges as a member of a social class to which his gifts as a natural individual do not entitle him. The French Revolution did not believe that all men were equal or should be equally rewarded by society, but that the inequalities should be natural, not artificial. In France the interest was concentrated upon politics and culture; in England the same principles were applied to economics: the mill owners of the North of England were the brothers of the Jacobins. Fouché's comment upon Napoleon at his fall *"C'est un acteur usé,"* was cruel but true. He had been not an emperor but an employee of the French Muse. His political achievement was nil, his cultural very great, for he created Europe, which is neither a political nor a geographical entity. Europe—and this is why England has never thought of herself as a part of Europe—is simply the area dominated by the ideals of French literature.

A revolution to emancipate the individual must necessarily regard tradition, the control of the present by the past, as its enemy; if the human individual is to be really free, then time must also be individualized into a succession of immediate moments. The kind of society, therefore, which it tends to create, is an atomized society of individuals, with neither a common myth nor a common cult, but united moment by moment by what they are reading.

---

* The Russian Revolution was the work of martyrs. Some of its leaders were intellectuals but it was not their intellects which gave them their authority, but the fact that they had suffered imprisonment and exile.

In France the danger of this was postponed by the importance to her economy of the peasant proprietor. In England, where the Industrial Revolution developed more rapidly, it was much sooner apparent. For the industrial system, by destroying the family as an economic unit, and converting the working individual into an impersonal labor force to be used like water or electricity for so many hours a day, destroys the one social bond which is natural—that is, independent of myth or cult and capable of surviving a change in or the disappearance of both. When it too is lost, then society degenerates into the city crowds described by Wordsworth:

> The slaves unrespited of low pursuits
> Living amid the same perpetual flow
> Of trivial objects, melted and reduced
> To one identity, by differences
> That have no law, no meaning, and no end.
>
> *The Prelude*

America

If we apply the term revolution to what happened in North America between 1776 and 1829, it has a special meaning.

Normally the word describes the process by which man transforms himself from one kind of man, living in one kind of society, with one way of looking at the world, into another kind of man, another society, another conception of life. So it is with the papal, the Lutheran, the English, and the French revolutions. The American case is different; it is not a question of the Old Man transforming himself into the New, but of the New Man becoming alive to the fact that he is new, that he has been transformed already without his having realized it.

The War of Independence was the first step, the leaving of the paternal roof in order to find out who one is; the second and more important step, the actual discovery, came with Jackson. It was then that it first became clear that, despite similarities of form, representative government in America was not to be an imitation of the English parliamentary system, and that, though the vocabulary of the Constitution may be that of the French Enlightenment, its American meaning is quite distinct.

The American had not intended to become what he was; he had been made so by emigration and the nature of the American continent. An emigrant never knows what he wants, only what he does not want. A man who comes from a land settled for centuries to a virgin wilderness where he faces problems with which none of his traditions and habits was intended to deal cannot foresee the future but must improvise himself from day to day. It is not surprising, therefore, that the first clear realization of the novelty and importance of the United States should have come not from an American but from outsiders, like Crèvecoeur and de Tocqueville.

In a society whose dominant task is still that of the pioneer—the physical struggle with nature, and a nature, moreover, particularly recalcitrant and violent—the intellectual is not a figure of much importance. Those with intellectual and artistic tastes, finding themselves a despised or at best an ignored minority, are apt in return to despise the society in which they live as vulgar and think nostalgically of more leisured and refined cultures. The situation of the first important American poets—Emerson, Thoreau, Poe—was therefore doubly difficult. As writers, and therefore intellectuals, they were without status with the majority; and, on the other hand, the cultured minority of which they were members looked to England for its literary standards and did not want to think or read about America.

This dependence on English literature was a hindrance to their development in a way which it would not have been had they lived elsewhere. A poet living in England, for instance, might read nothing but French poetry, or he might move to Italy and know only English, without raising any serious barrier between himself and his experiences. Indeed, in Europe whenever some journalist raises the patriotic demand for an English or French or Dutch literature free from foreign influences, we know him at once to be a base fellow. The wish for an American literature, on the other hand, has nothing to do, really, with politics or national conceit; it is a demand for honesty. All European literature presupposes two things: a nature which is humanized, mythologized, usually friendly, and a human society in which most men stay where they were born and do not move about much. Neither of these presuppositions was valid for America, where nature was virgin, devoid of history, usually hostile; and society was fluid, its groupings always changing as men moved on somewhere else.

The European Romantics may praise the charms of wild desert landscape, but they know that for them it is never more than a few hours' walk from a comfortable inn: they may celebrate the joys of solitude but they know that any time they choose they can go back to the family roof or to town and that there their cousins and nephews and nieces and aunts, the club and the salons, will still be going on exactly as they left them. Of real desert, of a loneliness which knows of no enduring relationships to cherish or reject, they have no conception.

The achievement of Emerson and Thoreau was twofold: they wrote of the American kind of nature, and they perceived what qualities were most needed by members of the American kind of society, which was threatened not by the petrified injustice of any tradition but by the fluid irresponsibility of crowd opinion. Their work has both the virtues and the vices of the isolated and the protestant: on the one hand it is always genuine and original, it is never superficial; on the other it is a little too cranky, too earnest, too scornful of elegance. Just as in their political thinking Americans are apt to identify the undemocratic with monarchy, so in their aesthetics they are apt to identify the falsely conventional with rhyme and meter. The prose of Emerson and Thoreau is superior to their verse, because verse in its formal nature protests against protesting; it demands that to some degree we accept things as they are, not for any rational or moral reason, but simply because they happen to be that way; it implies an element of frivolity in the creation.

Poe, on the other hand, has nothing to say directly about nature or society. He is the first poet to create an entirely imaginary landscape, a subjective *paysage moralisé*, the implication of which is that, where nature is not humanized, where there is no common mythology, each poet has to invent one for himself—nature by herself is meaningless. His love stories, without any conscious intention on his part, are terrible warnings of what can happen in a society where human relations are few in number and character, and where in consequence the whole range of human emotions may attach themselves to a single relation. One has often to decipher his work in order to see that, for all its cheapness and flashiness of execution, it is intensely serious. He may strike dramatic attitudes, but behind them there is a man who is really in great pain.

As the nineteenth century progressed, the destruction of the popular mythographic imagination by popular science and the spread of universal suffrage and the influence of the press made conditions in Europe to approximate more and more closely to the American case, and European writers came to see in Poe the heroic forerunner who had suffered and understood, who had really been what Byron, for instance, never was, the *poète maudit*, the alienated dandy.

GENERAL PRINCIPLES

Selections

The central cluster of poets represented in this volume marks the Romantic movement at the period of its greatest vigor, though as always there are strains other than the dominant one which had persisted or were being initiated. American verse, in this volume, begins to assume dimensions of some significance, and the intermingling of American with British poems from the same age should be variously suggestive. Certain cultural lags as well as certain distinctions in diction are apparent. Ordinarily one is accustomed, in anthologies, to find the two poetries completely separated, as though they were distinct and self-sufficient, but it is time for us to recognize how the poetical consciousness and training in craft depends upon a common or at least a joint tradition. The separation of British and American strains provides some useful insights, but we need to be reminded that poets did not work that way as poets.

Supplementary Data

We have not tried to supply biographical data on the poets, although the dates of their births and deaths will be found with the poems, and those of their principal works in the charts which are a supplement to each volume.

The amount of biographical data which could have been supplied within the volumes would in actuality have been meaningless. For such study there are published biographies which it would have been folly to attempt to summarize in a few lines. We have preferred to print more poems.

If there is anything in the nature of biography in the various volumes, it is the autobiography of the poetical imagination and fancy as it has been expressed in poems. Comments on this autobiography occur in the introductions to each volume, which are meant not to be definitive but to suggest as freshly as possible the problems with which poetry has coped. Instead of biographical data for each poet, therefore, we have drawn up tables in which, on one side, is given the direct course of poetry and, on the other, are to be found certain of the cultural and societal events which had formative effect. These will be of some help, we trust, toward seeing the course of poetry in historical perspective.

INTRODUCTION TO VOLUME V:
TENNYSON TO YEATS

The limiting conditions for inclusion in this volume are two: the poet must have been born before 1870 and his poem must have been published before August 1914. These two dates have not been chosen at random. The first is doubly significant: it is the year of the Franco-Prussian War, when Europe, the City of *L'esprit français*, is challenged from within by the *Blut und Eisen* spirit of the Barracks;* and it is the year in which the dogma of Papal Infallibility is proclaimed, when the oldest and most powerful Christian Communion declares in the most spectacular way possible that in matters of Faith the Liberal conception of truth as conditional and arrived at by experiment and discussion has no place. As the year when the First World War broke out, 1914 marks the final break-up of Europe. The experiences of mass mechanical warfare and organized propaganda were proof that, whatever the nature of man might be, it was not what the European intellectuals as a group had said it was.

For America these dates are not exact but they are sufficiently close to its decisive years to be serviceable. In the Civil War of 1861–65 the United States had a foretaste of total war with modern weapons, and 1917 ended its isolation from the Old World. Henceforth, whatever kind of civilization was to emerge would be a joint creation.

The nineteenth century is the European century. In so far that neither England nor America is part of Europe, the poetry with which this volume is concerned can be called provincial. To say this is not in any way to detract

---

* In view of the subsequent history of Germany, it is important to remember that it was France, not Prussia, which declared war in 1870. The initial betrayal of Europe was the *coup d'état* of 1852, and Napoleon III, with his combination of force and appeal to the masses, was, as De Tocqueville realized, a novel and sinister phenomenon, the first dictator of the modern type.

from its value. In literature, indeed, one is inclined to feel that the really new, the revolutionary, works appear not in Europe proper but on the peripheries—the Russian novels and the plays of the Norwegian Ibsen—or outside her altogether, in America.

Whatever one may feel about Poe's own work, it is impossible not to see that he is the father of one kind of "modern" poetry. However little to one's taste both the manner and the content of Whitman's poetry may be, the revolution in sensibility which he effected is indubitable, and one is reluctantly compelled to agree with D. H. Lawrence:

> Whitman, the one man breaking a way ahead. Whitman, the one pioneer. And only Whitman. No English pioneers, no French. No European pioneer-poets. In Europe the would-be pioneers are mere innovators. . . . Whitman like a strange, modern, American Moses. Fearfully mistaken. And yet the great leader.
>
> *Studies in Classic American Literature*

In style and craftsmanship the poetry of the nineteenth and the twentieth centuries has extended, developed, and refined the discoveries of the early Romantics. To a degree hitherto unknown, each poet sets out, like Milton, to create a personal style; he invents a particular genre of poem suited to his cast of temperament—the Tennyson idyl, the Browning dramatic monologue, the Patmore ode; for each poem he tries to find the form uniquely suited to its subject and vice versa. No previous period can show such a wealth of variety in stanzas, newly contrived or revived from the past, such metrical invention, from classical meters to sprung rhythm to dithyrambic free verse. The advantages of this variety and individual freedom are obvious, its disadvantages perhaps less so: a personal form and manner sometimes become more of a prison than would a traditional style shared in common, precisely because they are the poet's own; what was once his face can, if he himself change, turn into a mask without his realizing it.

If, then, we look for any point of division, any sign of a decisive change, in the period between, say, Wordsworth and the present day, we shall not find, as we find between Pope and the Romantics, any startling break in style. The dividing line between "Victorian" (to use an English term internationally) poetry and "modern" poetry lies between the poets for whom the ideas and hopes of liberal Christian humanism are still valid, and those for whom they are not. Thus Browning, Hugo, Longfellow are Victorian; Hopkins, Baudelaire, and Whitman are modern.

The Liberal Bard

The poets I have called for convenience Victorian inherit the beliefs of Romanticism and the French Revolution and become their official spokesmen; they are listened to by the general public in a way that their predecessors were

not, for the revolution has succeeded and is therefore now respectable.*
There are, of course, differences between the various countries: in Catholic
countries like France, liberalism is more directly political and anti-clerical,
more explicitly concerned with *Liberté, Egalité, Fraternité*; in Protestant countries, the liberalism is more concerned with religion. The poets preach a religion in which the values and even the cult are to remain Christian but the
Christian dogmas are to be regarded as myth, that is, poetic truth. If this is
the case, then the poets are, of course, the real priests of society, the oracles
on all social problems and values.

Their trouble was that they could never quite believe it; they were all
haunted men, with a room in the house which was kept locked and from which
they had to detract the attention of visitors. It is significant that the poem of
theirs which opens that room most dramatically professes to be a nonsense
poem, "The Hunting of the Snark." The snark, that is, the meaning of existence, turns out to be a Boojum—existence is meaningless. They were all of
them uneasily aware of the possibility that the liberal creed might only hold
for talented and successful people like themselves, for men who might speculate upon the meaning of existence in general but never had to put the personal question "Why do I exist?" because they were enjoying themselves in the
exercise of their talents and the glory such exercise brought them. However
many adoring disciples might sit at their feet, outside the cozy circle there was
a shadow who was by no means friendly, to whom their genius for inspiring
speech was a joke, and who spoke himself in a very different vein.

> I am a sick man. . . . I am a spiteful man. I am an unattractive man. I be-
> lieve my liver is diseased. However, I know nothing at all about my dis-
> ease, and do not know for certain what ails me. I don't consult a doctor
> for it, and never have, though I have a respect for medicine and doctors.
> Besides, I am extremely superstitious, sufficiently so to respect medicine,
> anyway (I am well-educated enough not to be superstitious, but I am su-
> perstitious). No, I refuse to consult a doctor out of spite. That you prob-
> ably will not understand. Well, I understand it, though. Of course, I can't
> explain who it is precisely that I am mortifying in this case by my spite: I
> am perfectly well aware that I can't "get even" with the doctors by not
> consulting them; I know better than anyone that by all this I am only in-
> juring myself and no one else. But still, if I don't consult a doctor it is
> out of spite. My liver is bad, well—let it get worse!
>
> Dostoevski, *Notes from Underground*

* In America, with its relative provincialism and its proliferating sects, the sermon of the Liberal Bard was concerned less with religious doubts than with the importance of culture. One
should never underestimate the value of Longfellow's attempt to secure democratic respect for
smoothness, correctness, and craftsmanship in poetry and through translation to make European
literature available to the youth of the Republic.

So speaks the victim of the French Revolution and liberalism. Emancipated from the traditional beliefs of a closed society he can no longer believe simply because his forefathers did—and he cannot imagine not believing—yet has found no source or principle of direction to replace them. He is not a genius, he is not socially gifted, his work is not important or interesting, so that self-love and the thirst for glory cannot motivate his life; his self-consciousness can only turn in destructively on himself, his freedom waste itself in freakish, arbitrary, spiteful little acts. "I swear, gentlemen," he says, "that to be too conscious is an illness—a real out-and-out illness."

Liberalism is at a loss to know how to handle him, for the only thing liberalism knows to offer is more freedom, and it is precisely freedom in the sense of lack of necessity that is his trouble. When a man knows what he wants, liberalism can help him—when a peasant exploited by his landlord desires a farm of his own, for example, liberalism can fight for land reform. But ask this man what he wants and his only answer is a fantastic daydream.

> Then the band would play a march, an amnesty would be declared, the Pope would agree to retire from Rome to Brazil: then there would be a ball for the whole of Italy at the Villa Borghese on the shores of the Lake of Como (the Lake of Como being for that purpose transferred to the neighborhood of Rome); there would come a scene in the bushes, and so on, and so on. . . .
>
> Dostoevski, *Notes from Underground*

He is a dangerous customer because he is desperate and can only imagine destructive change. Moreover, the real object of his resentment is not any exploiting class or concrete injustice but the man of talent who enjoys and profits from the consciousness that makes him suffer. He is anti-humanist, anti-liberal, in terms of democracy, above all anti-intellectual. The thought of a tyrant who will provide him with a myth of terror, of the prospect of a total war as a cult, are not unwelcome to him.

The confidence of the liberal humanist was not seriously shaken by the natural sciences, which were based on the presupposition that, whatever his origin, whatever the relation of his mind to matter, man was capable of a disinterested search for an objective truth which was universally valid. The dangerous assault came later from the half-sciences, like sociology, anthropology, and psychology, which are concerned with man as an interested actor. Their exhibition of the mind's capacity for self-deception, of the unconscious effect upon its thinking of social status and sex, their demonstration that the customs and beliefs of other peoples could not be dismissed as merely savage, irrational, and quaint but must be accepted as rival civilizations complete in themselves, cast doubts on the finality of any truth.

Again, in practical politics, the pure liberal doctrine of laissez-faire was proving unworkable. The Companies Act of 1862 in England and the legal advantages conferred by the American courts on corporations were symptoms of a modification of the liberal gospel; the gradual appearance of the social welfare state, first in Bismarck's Prussia, was another.

The Modern Poet

The break with liberal humanism exhibits itself in various ways. In France the poets rejected the political ideals of the French Revolution; "*l'esprit belge*," Baudelaire called it. And they rejected the notion of the poet as bard, of poetry as a popular religion. Poetry was, for them, to be a religion for poets only. The others must find their salvation with the priest or the philosopher. The poets are no longer interested in the others. In the Protestant countries, aestheticism did not come on so quickly or go to quite the same lengths. The notion of the bard persisted, but the myth was no longer liberal Christianity.

Wagner was the first, as Yeats has been the latest, to create a whole cosmology out of pre-Christian myth, to come out openly for the pagan conception of the recurrent cycle as against the Christian and liberal humanist conception of historical development as an irreversible process. Though the characters in *The Ring* wear primitive trappings, they are really, as Nietzsche pointed out, contemporaries, "always five steps from the hospital," with modern problems, "problems of the big city." Other poets turned to Stoicism or Platonism; a few were converted to orthodox dogmatic Christianity.

The Whitman Myth

Whitman's polemic exaltation of the human body is directed not against the Puritan ascetic, but against the emancipated liberal intellectual. To the former the body with its passions is a formidable enemy who threatens the salvation of his soul; his error lies in his taking the body too seriously. To the latter, on the other hand, the body is a mere thing, of no importance in itself whatever except as the instrument which feeds his mind with experiences; while working he forgets to feed and rest it, when in search of "copy" and inspiration he drives it into debauchery.

As against the intellectual's dogma that what all men have in common is a consciousness of possibilities and consequently a capacity to make history by realizing them, Whitman asserts that all men, whatever their talents, education, or race, are equal in the flesh; each has a body which needs the same things and suffers in the same way and does not partake in history but goes through the same cycle in every generation.

The good of the body is health, which cannot be thought of in liberal terms, for words like freedom or possibility do not apply to it. To sustain physical health so much food, shelter, light, and so on, neither more nor less, are *necessary*.

In their re-emphasis on the sacredness of the flesh, Whitman, Nietzsche, and other protestants were not alone; the cult of the Sacred Heart and the dogma of the Immaculate Conception were expressions of a similar insight on the part of the Catholic Church.

Epilogue

In 1914 a revolution was set in motion which has involved the whole world and is still going on. If every revolution can be represented graphically by a symbolic figure—the Papal Revolution by a twin Warrior-Priest, the Lutheran by a God-fearing paterfamilias, the English by a country gentleman, the American by a pioneer, the French by an intellectual—then the contemporary symbol is a naked anonymous baby. It is for the baby's right to health, not for the freedom of any person or class to act or think—for a baby is not yet a person and cannot choose or think—that the revolution is being fought everywhere in one way or another. A baby has to be controlled, it has to be indoctrinated, it cannot be told more of the truth than it can profitably understand, so the present revolution is authoritarian and believes in censorship and propaganda. Since its values are really derived from medicine, from a concept of health, it is hostile to any nonconformity, any deviation from the norm. It is precisely, therefore, the exceptional man, the man of talent, the man who works alone, the man whom the French Revolution liberated and admired, who has become the object of greatest suspicion.

The difference between the poets in this volume and the contemporary poet is in their relation to the state and society. The former were either admired or left alone; the latter are suspect, and the campaign to control them by bribes or threats is likely to intensify.

What will happen is anybody's guess. Perhaps history is forcing the intellectual, whether scientist or artist, into a new conception of himself as neither the respectable bard nor the anarchic aesthete, but as a member of the Loyal Opposition, defending, not for his own sake only but for all, the inalienable rights of the individual person against encroachment by an overzealous government, with which, nevertheless, even though the latter deny it, he has a bond, their common love for the Just City.

GENERAL PRINCIPLES

Selections

Selections from Tennyson appropriately begin the last of a series of volumes which have attempted to present the common tradition of poetry in the English language. The more difficult problem was where to end it, and William Butler Yeats' Prologue to "Responsibilities" can be taken more as a challenge to the future than as a conclusion to anything. It was also a challenge to himself in his role of a late pre-Raphaelite, and one which he met with major distinction.

The poetry in English which comes after this volume makes another story, not of tradition but of the present. To tell this would have required at least a further volume, one in which the problem of representing poets who are still actively writing becomes infinitely confusing and the result little more than temporary in its assessments. Everyone will wish to add some such collection to accompany *The Poets of the English Language*, changing this volume every few years to accommodate the rapid shifts. But it is hoped that *The Poets of the English Language*, because it does not encroach on such territory, will have a more permanent life.

Iteration and reiteration will perhaps never make clear to the casual reader why certain of Yeats' brilliant successes have not been included, nor why the selections from Robinson stop where they do, nor why Frost, for example, should not have been represented if Robinson is. With Robinson and Yeats, as with others, we have given only those poems which were printed before 1914, and given them in the versions then published. Many of his early poems Yeats later revised, but the revisions came from the pen of a post-1914 poet. Frost, Pound, Eliot, and others had written before 1914, but the dominance of their work is appropriate to the period which came after World War I.

This, at any rate, is the principle on which we have worked, and on which we have excluded certain poets and certain poems. What we have given we have tried to give substantially. To have done otherwise would have left us nowhere. There is no attempt on the part of the editors to belittle the present. Our concern with it and our pride in its poetry should be sufficiently known. Neither of us, however, believes in a provincialism of the present. The personal value to ourselves in the preparation of *The Poets of the English Language* has been the refreshening of a sense of the involvement of the present with the past and an understanding of the importance of an awareness of tradition which these volumes, we hope, may bring to their readers.

Supplementary Data

We have not tried to supply biographical data on the poets, although the dates of their births and deaths will be found with the poems, and those of their principal works in the charts which are a supplement to each volume. The amount of biographical data which could have been supplied within the volumes would in actuality have been meaningless. For such study there are published biographies which it would have been folly to attempt to summarize in a few lines. We have preferred to print more poems.

If there is anything in the nature of biography in the various volumes, it is the autobiography of the poetical imagination and fancy as it has been expressed in poems. Comments on this autobiography occur in the introductions to each volume, which are meant not to be definitive but to suggest as freshly as possible the problems with which poetry has coped. Instead of biographical data for each poet, therefore, we have drawn up tables in which, on one side, is given the direct course of poetry and, on the other, are to be found certain of the cultural and societal events which had formative effect. These will be of some help, we trust, toward seeing the course of poetry in historical perspective.

Poets of the English Language, edited by W. H. Auden and
Norman Holmes Pearson, 1950

Sixty-Six Sestets

An Acre in the Seed. By Theodore Spencer.
Harvard University Press. $2.50.

Of all poetic genres the very short poem is perhaps the hardest to master. The poet who attempts it starts with everything weighted against him. To begin with, his poem will probably be read, as all poetry should be read but very rarely is, with complete critical attention. Few readers, even among the most practised, can sustain the highest pitch of concentration beyond a page without relaxing, but almost anyone can do so for eight lines.

In consequence, blemishes, which in a longer poem only learning by heart and frequent recitation would disclose, betray themselves at a first reading. Further, a very short poem cannot compensate for any weakness in diction or rhythm with structural interest. No ingenious approaches and transitions, no amusing vistas, no elaborate decoration, no architecture are possible; it must make its whole effect with a single point, a simple contrast, a solitary image, make it immediately and be still.

It is hardly surprising, then, if few very short English poems have become famous. Only two poets, Landor, whom Professor Spencer (the late Boylston Professor of Rhetoric and Oratory at Harvard) mentions at the beginning of his volume, and Herrick, should owe much of their reputation to their productions of this kind.

An Acre in the Seed consists of sixty-six poems, each of them six lines long, all of them rhymed, and most of them written in four-foot iambics or trochaics.

In these poems, subtitled "Sestets for a Summer," the New England landscape provides a unifying background to their reflections on Life and Art and Love and Death. As an example of their style and range, let me quote three (for the reviewer, at least, the short poem is a godsend).

September Caterpillars

The cars squash flat on every road
Inch-sized bears in fur brown dress;
A muted million die like this,

Trundling to what they have to do
As fall, assuming summer's load,
Assumes her vague compulsions too.

Walt

The photographs of Whitman show
Eyes as cold as those of a cat,
Eyes like a cold fish, glass eyes,
But this should nourish no surprise
In those whose heart has taught them that
From ice love's warmest falsehoods grow.

The Neurosis

Little did that godmother know
Who, grinning vilely, slipped the pea
Under the mattresses, that she
(Wicked creature that she seems)
Would to the world a princess show
And fill her sleep with marvelous dreams.

I have selected these particular examples because, while I find them successful and moving, there is in each, I think, a questionable detail.

September Caterpillars, l. 3: Had the rhythm not demanded the extra syllable, would not the poet have written *mute*, not *muted*, for caterpillars have no voice to be deprived of?

Walt, ll. 2–3: Were it not for the formal necessity of a six-line poem, would he not have condensed these lines into one, for the multiplication of comparisons is redundant?

The Neurosis, l. 5: Had the rhyme not demanded the inversion, would he not have written, *Would show a princess to the world*, for the style of the poem is a "natural" one in which the words follow in their conversational order?

That it should be possible to pick such holes in the work of so conscious a craftsman as Professor Spencer is some indication of the general difficulty of writing good verse and of the particular risk, referred to above, which the writer of the short poem incurs.

By tradition the commonest subjects for the short poem are the epitaph, the satirical epigram, and the amorous compliment, but Professor Spencer rarely attempts these, I think wisely.

Such of his sestets as are "personal" are concerned with a serious relationship in which conceits would be out of place, and the few which are satirical attacks, e.g. "The Statistician" or "To John Dewey," do not come off because his poetic temperament lacks the necessary sadistic malice. Though he is capable of writing an admirable epigram, e.g.

History

Admiral That and General This
Met in a mere parenthesis.
Each thinking he deserved a page
They almost roared to death with rage.
What can be done to help their plight
(For history erred, and they were right)?

the note he most naturally and successfully strikes is neither of humor nor of rage but of the sympathetic observer, stoic, ironic, and rather sad.

Daily Greeting

Comes regularly every day
Close to this hour of ten o'clock,
The man for the milk-cans in his truck,
We wave, but have no more to say,
Each traveling upon his way
Regularly every day

In a period when the poetic fashion both in technique and topic combine to make the besetting temptation of the contemporary poet one of trying to write more profoundly and complexly than his actual vision justifies, one welcomes a poet who has the strength of character to resist and to risk a charge of triviality rather than face an inner conviction of dishonesty; indeed *An Acre in the Seed* has better right to be called "experimental" than many a more spectacular work, i.e. over and above their intrinsic worth, these sestets should suggest possibilities to other poets which they have no found hinted at in the recent past elsewhere.

This is a posthumous volume: where Professor Spencer would have proceeded from here, had he not died suddenly in his early forties, it is idle to speculate, but that his devotion to the Muse would have continued as faithful and untiring no one who knew him can doubt.

The New York Times Book Review, 9 October 1949

Notebooks of Somerset Maugham

A Writer's Notebook. By W. Somerset Maugham. Doubleday. $4.

A career as long, as productive and as successful as Somerset Maugham's earns a writer his membership in that select and curious group which Jean Cocteau has aptly named *Les monstres sacrés.* When Maugham publishes a new book, therefore, it would be dishonest of the critic to pretend that he either

can or wishes to read it as if it were by an unknown writer or to judge it by esthetic standards alone; in addition to any literary merit, it has inevitably and,
I think, quite properly a historic interest as the act of a person in whom one
has long been interested. Having for us a history, the author has become not
only a novelist but also a character in our novel, and a platitude or a blind
spot is scarcely less revealing (and therefore fascinating) than an insight or
an area of enthusiasm.

In describing *A Writer's Notebook* it may be as well to begin by saying what it
is not. It is not—no one who is familiar with Maugham's work would expect
it to be—a series of personal confessions. I have found only five in the whole
book: that he always expected to be successful, that he has a recurrent dream
of the City of God, that the famous rumor of his fainting at the sight of the
Yogi is untrue, that he can never remember the order of the letters in the alphabet, and that he still has twenty-six of his own teeth. Nor is it a collection
of practical tips for the would-be writer; I have found only one and that for
his parents—"Give him a hundred and fifty a year [pre-war pounds] for five
years and tell him to go to the devil."

It is the condensation of fifteen volumes of notes begun when he was eighteen years old in which, as he says in his preface (which contains, by the way,
an acute comparison of the English and the French literary life): "I never
made a note of anything that I did not think would be useful to me at one
time or another in my work, and though, especially in the early notebooks, I
jotted down all kinds of thoughts and emotions of a personal nature, it was
only with the intention of ascribing them sooner or later to the creatures of
my invention. I meant my notebooks to be a storehouse of materials for future use and nothing else."

Their primary fascination for any reader of a younger generation than
Somerset Maugham's derives from the fact that, while the problem of every
man and writer is at all times essentially the same, namely, first to learn to be
himself and then to learn to be not himself, its specific content changes
rapidly and radically.

For example, Maugham grew up during the Eighteen Nineties, when the
fashion in literature was the Wildean epigram and the Pateresque jeweled
prose, for neither of which, as it happened, he had a talent, yet began by trying dutifully to produce, as a young writer today might attempt the stichomythia of Hemingway or the dialectic of Kafka. Gradually, through his
own experience of life and his contact with other styles like those of Voltaire
and Matthew Arnold, he learns where his real interests lie and what he can
do well. Even more striking, perhaps, than the difference in literary climate
is the difference in the theological and moral climate between the bourgeois,
Erastian, largely deist Anglicanism of the prosperous England in which he
was raised and the pseudo-scientific nihilism of the ruins which surround
us now.

No young writer today would set down as a significant reflection—"Even if it held that pure unselfishness without afterthought gives most pleasure and brings the greatest rewards, that pleasure and those rewards are still its justifications"—not because hedonism is any less true or false than it then was, but because it is no longer a battle-cry of liberation from hypocritical relatives but merely an echo of the flat, dreadful, familiar voice of our jailers. Similarly, he will scarcely find it necessary to demand more sexual freedom; his aphorisms, if he makes them at all, are much more likely to concern the lack of a limiting principle to give his passions order and meaning. (How few of us have the strength of character to be even capable of the sustained folly of the hero in *Of Human Bondage*?)

Of himself as a writer Maugham says: "My native gifts are not remarkable, but I have a certain force of character which has enabled me in a measure to supplement my deficiencies. I have common sense. Most people cannot see anything, but I can see what is in front of my nose with extreme clearness; the greatest writers can see through a brick wall. My vision is not so penetrating."

Like nearly all self-analyses, this is at once too modest as regards the gifts and too proud as regards the character, for what lies in front of one's nose depends upon the direction in which one chooses to look. The greatest writer cannot see through a brick wall, but, unlike the rest of us, he refuses to erect them. The writer to whom we find it most difficult to be fair, whom we accuse of knowing nothing about "Life"—in Maugham's case he seems to be Henry James—is the one whose particular brick wall happens to be different from one's own wall, which stands unrecognized behind our vision precisely because it is self-made or unconsciously inherited.

The criticism which can be made of Maugham, as it must of all but the great masters, is that, having succeeded in becoming himself, he has been, as a writer and on the whole, content to remain so.

All through *A Writer's Notebook* there appear Theophrastian character sketches and anecdotes recorded because they struck the author as potential material for stories. What strikes the reader is their similarity. The ironic contradiction of character occurs time and time again: the teetotal philanthropist turns out to be a secret drinker, the brutal resident in Malaya becomes genteel in Cheltenham, the formidable mother-in-law is found naked in a hotel, murdered by a piece of trade—such are typical of the kind of "life" which he succeeds in portraying.

There are indications, however, that they are not the only kind of story he would like to tell. "Fiction," he says, "has never enriched the world with a more delightful character than Alyosha Karamazov," and one suspects that the deepest wish of a writer who has so often been called cynical has, all along, been to write a story about heroic goodness. He notes down two suggestions for such and in both cases, with an honesty as admirable as it must, for him, be sad, adds a note: "It was too difficult for me to cope with and I never wrote it."

I think many readers are going to be surprised—I certainly was—to learn that Somerset Maugham, of all people, believes "that the value of art lies in its effects . . . not in beauty but in right action."

A Writer's Notebook ends on a valedictory note: "I am like a passenger waiting for his ship at a wartime port. I do not know on which day it will sail, but I am ready to embark at a moment's notice. . . . I read the papers and flip the pages of a magazine, but when someone offers to lend me a book I refuse because I may not have time to finish it, and in any case with this journey before me I am not of a mind to interest myself in it. I strike up acquaintances at the bar or the cardtable, but I do not try to make friends with people from whom I shall so soon be parted. I am on the wing."

To which we can only answer: "We shall miss you. Of course we shall find new writers to read, but art, like friendship, is personal, that is, unique, and no writer is replaceable by or even comparable with another. Thank you for having given us so much pleasure for so long, for having never been tedious"—and so wish him Godspeed.

The New York Times Book Review, 23 October 1949

Firbank Revisited

Five Novels of Ronald Firbank.
Introduction by Sir Osbert Sitwell. New Directions. $5.

The nine or ten short novels—what a shame it is that the publishers have only been able or seen fit to include five in this volume—of Ronald Firbank are, for me, an absolute test. A person who dislikes them, like someone who dislikes the music of Bellini or prefers his steak well-done, may, for all I know, possess some admirable quality but I do not wish ever to see him again.

Ronald Firbank, who is generally believed to be the original of Lucius Orme in Harold Nicolson's *Some People*, was the son of a baronet who made "beautiful railways." Educated privately and at Cambridge, he spent most of his time traveling about Europe and the Middle East and died in Rome in 1926 at the age of 39. He was delicate, pathologically shy and an eccentric of whom many stories are told, some of which appear in Sir Osbert Sitwell's amusing and affectionate introduction.

"Novel" is a misleading term to apply to the works of this extraordinary writer, for "novel" suggests a plot and what is the plot of any Firbank novel, of say, *The Artificial Princess*? A Princess dispatches by a baroness an invitation to a saint to attend her party that evening. The invitation never reaches him and the Princess mistakes a gate-crasher with wavy hair and a gardenia for her sacred lion.

The Firbank plot is, clearly, simply a pretext, deliberately flimsy, for the existence of his characters, and the same is true of the Firbank setting—England, Spain, or the tropics—it is only a backdrop before which his characters behave.

Again, it is a pure accident that a character appears in one novel rather than in another; Lady Parvula de Panzoust might just as well have turned up in the Duguesa's drawing room as in Mrs Hurstpierpoint's, and if Master Charlie Mouth ever gets tired of the Café de Cuna he can always get a job in the Haboubet of Egypt.

All that really matters, in fact, is that the Firbank world should exist, a world in which a country church can have "the scheming look of an ex-cathedral" and a choir-boy who has been taking the lead in a mass of Palestrina's "the vaguely distraught air of a kitten that had seen visions," in which an enflamed girl can "leave the room warbling softly 'Depuis le jour,'" and a queen "motor for hours and hours with her crown on—it was quite impossible not to mistake her," in which one can be introduced to a lady wearing "a gown of ivory-black with heavy golden roses and a few of her large diamonds of ceremony."

Firbank's extraordinary achievement was to draw a picture, the finest, I believe, ever drawn by anyone, of the Earthly Paradise, not, of course, as it really is, but as, in our fallen state, we imagine it to be, as the place, that is, where, without having to change our desires and behavior in any way, we suffer neither frustration nor guilt.

The first axiom of such an Eden is that it is a world of pure being; what people are and what they want or ought to become are identical. From this it follows that character is identical with name, e.g. Madame Wetme, Eva Schnerb, Dr Cuncliffe Babcock, Monsignor Silex, are, like pets, described by their names.

The second is that there is no law and no super-ego; few Firbank characters confine their affections to a single object or a single sex, even fewer can say no, but nobody is shocked and nobody gets hurt. Religious exercises are practised extensively but, since God is loving without being a judge, they are all, even those of mortification, pure fun. A police-dog is baptised in white crême-de-menthe. Where all are innocent, what difference is there between a dog and a baby?

Not only is there no moral law to limit behavior, but characters wander at will from a crucifix to a gardener's legs, to a sunset, and their conversation skips like quanta of energy from one subject to another.

Everyone is welcome, but on one condition, that they are not in earnest; thus, when Laura de Nazianzi falls seriously in love with His Weariness the Prince, she ceases to belong and must leave. Poor Pope Tertius II is, to his regret, prevented by his office from entering.

Escape literature? Nonsense. There is only honest literature and dishonest. The latter pretends that an impossible world is the real one and, in consequence, is always solemn. The fact that Firbank's novels are so funny is proof that he never lets us forget the contradiction between life as it is and life as we should like it to be, for it is the impossibility of that contradiction which makes us laugh.

To employ a serious responsible tone in speaking of Firbank would be false to him, but I am prepared to be bold and say that his books have as permanent an importance as, say, *Alice in Wonderland*. An ideal Christmas present, but not a book for the guest room; it will "get lost" very soon.

The New York Times Book Review, 20 November 1949

Nature, History and Poetry

(For Saint-John Perse)

Events may be divided into two classes: natural events and historical events.

★   ★   ★

A natural event is (*a*) recurrent, (*b*) occurs according to laws. An historical event is (*a*) unique or once only, (*b*) is responsible for the occurrence of subsequent historical events, not by causing them necessarily to occur but by providing them with a motive for choosing to occur.

★   ★   ★

Natural time in which natural events occur is reversible and cyclical. Historical time which historical events create by their occurrence is irreversible and moves in a unilinear direction.

★   ★   ★

To be comprehensible an event must be relatable to some law. Laws may be divided into two classes, laws-of, according to which events occur and by which therefore they are described, and laws-for, under which events occur and by which therefore they are judged. A law-of can only be stated in the indicative, a law-for only in the imperative mood.

★   ★   ★

A law-of presupposes that, at any given instant, only one event will occur; a law-for presupposes that, at any given instant, two events are possible. About a law-of it may only be said that its formulation is true or false; about a law-for it may only be said that its persuasion is just or unjust.

★   ★   ★

The laws of nature are laws-of; they are what the scientist in time discovers, but are themselves at all times. Laws-for have power of persuasion only over historical events, providing them with motives for choosing to occur in this way rather than that. Of a motive it may be said that it is good or evil, of a choice that it is right or wrong. A just law is one which provides good motives for choices, not one which demands right choices. Being themselves historical events, existing at-such-a-time, laws-for can be changed.

★   ★   ★

For a law to be discoverable or for a law to exist, the actual or the possible occurrence of at least three events, i.e. a plurality, to which it is relatable, must be known.

Pluralities may be divided into three classes: crowds, societies and communities.

A crowd is a group characterised by togetherness and nothing else. It is countable but not comprehensible, for it is relatable to no law and has only an arithmetical existence.

A society is a group characterised by a specific kind of behavior as a whole. It has a definite or an optimum size and a definite structure and the character of the whole is not the arithmetical sum of the characters of its several members.

A community is a group characterised by a love for something other than itself. Its unity arises from the fact that what any one member loves is identical with what any other member loves. It has therefore no definite size or structure, for the addition or subtraction of one member does not alter its character. Thus, while a society cannot come into being until all its members are present, a single individual can be the potential beginning of a community.

★   ★   ★

In a society the will of the individual member is subordinate to the general will of the society.

In a crowd neither the individual integer nor the totality has a will.

In a community, since the will of the individual member and the will of the whole are identical, there can be no question of subordination, for to will something else means that the individual is a member of another community.

Of a crowd it can be said that it is large or small; of a society that it is strong or weak, effective or ineffective; of a community that its love is good or evil.

★   ★   ★

In nature where all events occur according to law, there are no real crowds, only apparent ones whose laws of occurrence have yet to be discovered. Nor, since in nature there is no choice and hence no distinction between doing and loving—a natural thing loves what it does—can there be communities. In nature there are only societies.

★   ★   ★

Man is both a natural and a historical being. As the latter he has real individuality and is therefore capable of forming communities.

A community united by a love which it wishes to express or satisfy creates societies for the purpose, e.g. a community of music-lovers creates a society, a string quartet, to play a certain kind of music.

Though these societies have a historical function, they have themselves a natural not a historical existence. A string quartet is as natural, of as fixed a character, as a molecule of water.

Since one is historical and the other natural, a community and a society can never be identical. They may coincide but not necessarily; one member of a string quartet, for example, may dislike music and be only playing to earn his living.

★   ★   ★

The subject matter of poetry is a crowd of past historic occasions of feeling. The poet's intention in making a poem is to convert some portion of this crowd into a community. Since the subject matter is historical events which do not happen necessarily according to a law-of, but according to provocation under a law-for, any number of communities are possible and so new works of art are always possible and no new work supersedes a previous one.

★   ★   ★

The poem by which a crowd of feelings is converted into a community is in itself a verbal society; i.e. it exists naturally not historically. In writing a poem, the poet has to assume that language has no history (or at least that its history is at an end), that the meaning of any word he uses will be perpetually recurrent.

★   ★   ★

The poet has at his disposal two crowds, the crowd of his occasions of past feeling and the crowd of his vocabulary, and his task is to organize the relevant members of the latter into a structure which will embody a community of the former.

In composing he can work in two ways: starting from an intuitive idea of the kind of community he desires to call into being, he may work backwards from that idea in search of the structure which will most justly incarnate it; or, starting with a certain kind of structure, he may work forward in search of the community which that structure is capable of incarnating most truthfully. In practice, he usually works simultaneously in both directions, modifying his idea of the ultimate character of the community at the immediate suggestions of the structure, and modifying the structure in response to the lure of his idea.

★   ★   ★

During the process of composition, the poetry, i.e. the verbal society, is coercive upon the feelings it is being asked to embody; all that it cannot embody truthfully it excludes.

The crowd of feelings, i.e. the potential community, are passively resistant to all claims of the poetry to embody them which they do not recognize as just; they decline all unjust persuasions.

*   *   *

When a poem is read, it orders into one possible community, out of many, some part of the crowd of the past occasions of feeling of the reader; i.e. a poem is a means whereby the setting in order of one past may become responsible for the setting in order of any other past. Its power of persuasion, however, is always over the past and its actual effect only one out of many possible effects. It has no power of persuasion over the present instant of historical choice; it does not introduce any new element into the reader's present which was not previously there other than a consciousness of his past set newly in order; it provokes no decision towards the future. Language can on occasion so provoke—e.g. a man is converted by reading the Bible or sexually aroused by reading a pornographic book—but such effects are magical not poetic. Of magic it may be said that it is White or Black, of poetry that it is beautiful or ugly.

*   *   *

The co-inherence of Truth and Justice in nature is Beauty; the co-inherence of Truth and Justice in the historical moment is Goodness.

> Written 1949 for, but not published in,
> a 1950 special number of *Les Cahiers de la Pléiade*
> devoted to Saint-John Perse

Then and Now: 1935–1950

In February 1935 I was just turning twenty-eight. I might therefore, had I been born a lady and an American, have well been one of the original readers of *Mademoiselle*. Let me try to imagine what I should have been like.

I see myself with parents who had been well enough off to give their children an expensive education and even an allowance to an elder brother on which to live in Paris writing novels. Shortly after I was graduated, however, they lost most of their money; my brother had to come home and I had to get a job, which was not easy. Even in 1935 a degree from Vassar or Bryn Mawr was a useful asset toward becoming a salesclerk in a department store at eighteen bucks a week. Things were improving, however; writers and painters I knew who had nearly starved had just found employment in the newly formed WPA. Their stories of the confusion in the office, of the peculiar assignments they were sometimes given and of the eccentric characters whom they met on the Project were extremely funny, but at least they could eat and were engaged as artists, not sent to build roads, and that a government should consider art as an occupation had never occurred in history before. At our parties, which were usually bottle parties, the quarrels which were not personal were mostly political; in high-brow circles like mine the majority opinion was a long way left of center, but if a Stalinist and a Trotskyite could be got together a jolly evening could be counted upon. Not many of us had actually read Marx but we all talked about him and some of us had even taken our places in a picket line; in our select group we knew that bankers and industrialists were bad men and that the worst thing that could be said of a writer was that he lived in an ivory tower.

Unable to go to Europe ourselves, we depended for our knowledge upon that successor to the expatriate, the international journalist, or men like Vincent Sheehan and John Gunther whose *Personal History* and *Inside Europe* were just coming out. From them and from warnings like Sinclair Lewis' *It Can't Happen Here*—warned, too, by such indigenous phenomena as the late Huey Long—we realized that Hitler was a danger, but most of us were still, I think, isolationist and certainly pacifist. Even during the next few years when the Spanish Civil War and the Sino-Japanese War were in full swing, when bottle parties became political parties to collect money for the Spanish Republicans and the Chinese, and World War II became a real possibility, we would have regarded all proposals to increase the budget for the Armed Forces as a reactionary plot.

"Wait a moment!" I hear a voice saying. "You are describing a small high-brow set, not the average reader of *Mademoiselle* in 1935 at all. The complaint is just, but in contrasting one period with another, the advantage of taking the special high-brow case is that it exhibits in an exaggerated, dramatic way the changes that have taken place more quietly and less obviously in the population as a whole. What, then, whether pro or anti New Deal (I am sure, by the way, that in 1936 my parents would have voted against Mr Roosevelt), were our amusements?

Well, a year ago a lot of people had bought *Ulysses*, this year a lot were reading *Seven Pillars of Wisdom* and (not me, however) *Of Time and the River*, a lot more *Goodbye, Mr Chips* and its sponsor, Alexander Woollcott, and in another year there would be a copy of *Gone with the Wind* in homes which had not seen a new book for years. Of course there were also in 1935 as in 1950 those same mysterious millions, whom somehow one never meets, who read Lloyd Douglas.

In the theatre Clifford Odets held the place now occupied by Tennessee Williams, and Orson Welles was beginning his remarkable career as an actor-director with the Federal Theatre Project. You could go and see *Waiting for Lefty, Awake and Sing!* and *Dead End* if you felt like earnest entertainment, Madame Flagstad at the Metropolitan if you cared for singing, and *Three Men on a Horse* or Beatrice Lillie in *At Home Abroad* if you wanted to laugh. If you were interested in modern music there were the concerts at the New School where you could hear works by young American composers like Aaron Copland and Virgil Thomson. And, of course, there was always burlesque.

Movies? Popular songs? To avoid a tedious catalogue let me simply point out a few differences. The biographical film à la Paul Muni and the rotten heroine à la Bette Davis—as distinct from the Garbo-Dietrich femme fatale who can't help the destruction she causes—were still to come. As for the songs, speaking as a passionate hater of the juke box and television, I can only say that singers still took them at a civilized human pace and had not yet developed the encephalitis-lethargica manner.

But enough. I was born neither a lady nor an American, and for me 1935 was the year when I decided to give up a full-time job as a teacher in a boys' boarding-school and risk a free-lance life, little dreaming that in less than four years this would lead me to the States.

It is interesting, at least to me, to recall how this country looked to us then from across the Atlantic. Visiting Republicans were often puzzled by the admiration for Roosevelt and the New Deal shown by Englishmen, whom from their class and interests the Republicans expected to find as bitterly hostile as themselves. We saw the States as a country plunged into a revolutionary situation and coping with it sensibly while other countries, notably Germany, were heading hysterically for disaster. England was at that time a country to which no catastrophe had yet occurred. During the twenties there had been no boom comparable to the American boom—no undergraduates wore fur coats, no office boys or doctors speculated on the Stock Exchange—and when the Depression hit, in England it was principally the working classes, particularly in the heavy industries, who felt it acutely; the middle class went on much as before—no brokers jumped out of windows; a college graduate could still expect the sort of job for which he had been trained. However far to the left we middle-class intellectuals were, I don't think we saw the political changes we advocated as involving any change in our standard of living. We did not study what was happening in America as seriously as we should— Europe seemed more interesting—but it seemed to us that Roosevelt was the only adventurous and inspiring political leader on our side, and that what happened in America would be decisive.

Since I came to this country and have got to know people who went through the Depression, I find that we had not been mistaken in thinking that the second half of the thirties here was a time of hope, when it was felt that the worst had happened and it had not been fatal, and a time of democratic fellowship—for everybody had suffered in one way or another and recognized the fact. Comparing the English middle-class intellectual with his American colleague during the period of social consciousness, I think we were at once more frivolous—our way of life had not been disturbed—and more pessimistic—no European finds it easy to believe that progress is likely. (However loudly a Republican may declare that the Democrats are steering the country straight toward Communism, or a Democrat prophesy that a return to power of the Republicans would mean a return to the Middle Ages, both of them are really convinced that the future will be better than the past.)

In other ways we were pretty much alike. Looking back now, we must all blush at some of our follies; nevertheless we learned one thing then of value which we must not forget, namely, to take a serious interest in history instead of thinking only about our own work and having a good time. We began to ask questions about how historical changes occur and to what extent we are each of us responsible, and the fact that our first answers were wrong matters very much less than the development of enough interest to go on asking such questions, for no democracy can function properly if politics are left to organizations and the individual is politically apathetic.

Precisely because the thirties are now in disrepute, it is important to give them credit where it is due and, on the other hand, to look critically at the present.

Setting Mademoiselle of 1950 beside her predecessor of 1935, how does she shape up? Despite the rise of living costs, she is better off; her clothes are not very different—I speak under feminine correction—but she looks tidier and her make-up is less artificial. If she has a job it is by necessity rather than choice; she would rather be married and looking after her home. On the other hand, if she is still at college she works harder than she used to do. A Phi Beta Kappa key is no longer an ambition confined to girls with thick ankles and convex glasses.

If she has dates, she finds the boys less slavishly attentive than they used to be; they will no longer fetch and carry and buy expensive dinners in return for one good-night kiss. One reason for this is that most of the boys have been in Europe, or have friends who have, where they encountered other cultural standards in the relations between the sexes.

Thanks to the GI Bill of Rights and the exchange, it is once more possible and popular to live in Europe, and Mademoiselle's younger brother may well be there now—though, if he is chic, he will be living in Rome rather than Paris.

Still speaking in terms of the limited intellectual group with which I started, if she finds life difficult, if she can't keep her man or her job, she does not attribute this to the social system or some outer, easily rectifiable error like the wrong toilet soap but thinks there must be some fault in herself for which she is responsible. She worries about her femininity and her boy friend is equally concerned about his masculinity. It is extremely probable, therefore, that she (and he) is paying visits to a psychiatrist or psychoanalyst, or, if she goes to books for help, they will not have titles like *How to Win Friends and*

Influence People or *Think and Grow Rich* but like *Peace of Mind* or *How to Stop Worrying and Start Living.*

The new novels she reads reflect this interest in the inner life; they are likely to be more fantastic than naturalistic and to show the influence of writers like Henry James and Kafka. At her parties existentialism has replaced Marxism as a conversational topic; her notions of what Kierkegaard, Heidegger, Sartre, et cetera, actually wrote are probably vague but she knows it has something to do with anxiety, guilt and making choices.

Though the chances of her actually being a church member are about the same as before, theological arguments in her presence will not embarrass her and the notion of the Contemplative Life will no longer seem a madness of the Dark Ages. Her political attitude, if she has one, is probably what has been described as slightly west of center.

That it is right of her to feel responsible for her inner life is obvious. What, then, should she beware of? As always, the short cut and the lack of patience and courage which tempt us to look for one. If it is true, as they say, that she feels a growing nostalgia for the twenties (mine is for the European eighteen-thirties and -forties) she should watch it carefully. In the twenties people were prosperous and arrogantly certain that no misfortune could overtake them; today they are prosperous again but they know that misfortune is always possible and in some ways they are more afraid of the future, I think, than they were fifteen years ago. This is all to the good in so far as it makes them walk, like Agag, delicately, but it must not get out of hand. The danger for Mademoiselle is that, faced with the immense complexities of the postwar world, she may say to herself, "There is nothing I can do about it; 'they' decide the course of history; all I can do is find a safe little corner and personal happiness," that the only "public" concerns in her head may be reduced to supporting rent control and hating Russia. It would be lovely if this were possible, but, unfortunately, the personal life and the impersonal cannot be cultivated apart; without a concern for both, neither can bear edible fruit.

But this has got much too serious. What shall we do tonight, Mademoiselle? Go dancing? The ballet? *Gentlemen Prefer Blondes?* I should like to see Bobby Clark myself.

Mademoiselle, February 1950

Jean Cocteau

Most artists devote themselves to one medium; whether their complete *oeuvre* is a single masterpiece, as in the case of Proust, or a succession of works, as in the case of Dickens, it is comparatively easy to grasp as a whole. There, in a uniform edition, is a row of books, The Collected Works. There is nothing left out. Both the general reader and the critic have a manageable task.

Now and then, however, an artist appears—Jean Cocteau is, in our time, the most striking example—who works in a number of media and whose productions in any one of them are so varied that it is very difficult to perceive any unity of pattern or development. To enclose the collected works of Cocteau one would need not a bookshelf, but a warehouse, and how then could one catalogue such a bewildering assortment of poems, plays in verse, plays in prose, mythologies, natural histories, travels, drawings, tins of film, phonograph records, etc.?

Both the public and the critics feel aggrieved. If they know about the drawing they resent the existence of the drama on which they are not experts, and vice versa, and are tempted to say "a dilettante" and pass on to someone from whom they know better what to expect. His fellow artists who know how difficult it is to succeed in one medium are equally suspicious and jealous of a man who works in several. I must confess that I found myself opening Cocteau's last volume of poems half hoping that they would be bad. They were not.

In addition to all this, Cocteau labors under the disadvantage of having become a public legend at a very early age and of having remained so ever since. One is usually right to distrust an artist who is notorious, for notorious people nearly always begin soon to act their own role and become fakes. In Cocteau's case, however, I believe one is wrong; he is the exception, thanks to his extraordinary lack of artistic vanity and self-regard. He has always been a poet in the Greek sense: a maker who forgets himself in a complete absorption with the task in hand.

His attitude is always professional, that is, his first concern is for the nature of the medium and its hidden possibilities: his drawings are drawings, not uncolored paintings, his theatre is theatre, not reading matter in dialogue form, his films are films, not photographed stage effects.

With this professional attitude goes a readiness to regard any task as interesting and worth doing: ask Cocteau for a detective story and he will immediately write you one which will be what you asked for and yet at the same time quite fresh and unexpected. One has the impression that half of his work has been done in this way, at the request of his friends.

A person who is so open to the outside world, so little concerned with "self-expression," is naturally responsive to the present moment and liable, therefore, to incur the charge of wanting, at all costs, to be chic. To this one can only answer, that to be "timely" is not in itself a disgrace: Cocteau has never followed fashion though he has sometimes made it.

The lasting feeling that his work leaves is one of happiness; not, of course, in the sense that it excludes suffering, but because, in it, nothing is rejected, resented or regretted. Happiness is a surer sign of wisdom than we are apt to think, and perhaps Cocteau has more of it to offer than some others whose claims are louder and more solemn.

Flair, February 1950

Religion and the Intellectuals

A Symposium

I. (A.) *Cause.*

Assuming that the editors are convinced of the truth and adequacy of some form of naturalism as the true religious Faith (of which more in a moment), then, of course, they must look for extra-religious reasons why any person should become, say, a Christian. From the point of view of the latter, however, the situation looks quite different; what to him calls for explanation are the reasons which previously prevented him from seeing the truth and allowed him to be satisfied with, say, a naturalism which he now sees to be false.

Thus, though both sides will readily agree that the breakdown in the West of the radical political movement and the rather eschatological situation of our civilization are "causes" in the conversion of some people to Christianity, we shall differ very much as to the meaning and significance of the word in this context.

Christianity, of all religions, attaches a unique importance to history; e.g. the clause in the creed "He suffered under Pontius Pilate" expresses the belief that, for God, a particular moment in history when the Jews had reached a certain point in their development, religious, intellectual, political, and the gentiles in theirs, was "the fullness of the time," the right moment for the eternal vow to be made Flesh and the Divine Sacrifice to take place. If such a god does exist, then all the historical realities of that time, the Roman Empire, the Mystery Cults, etc., must have been known to Him as characteristics of the fullness of time.

Again, in *The Confessions*, St Augustine gives a detailed account of his personal historical situation, his parents, his friends, his intellectual development, his character; but to him they are relevant, not as causes of his conversion, but as evidences that the God of love must permit his creations free will which can refuse the grace at the same time that they are seeking it.

(B.) *Naturalism and Religion.*

One must distinguish between faiths and Faith. Every co-ordinated pattern of human thought or behavior requires a faith, i.e. one or more absolute presuppositions without which it wants not to exist or take place in that way. E.g. a natural scientist as a scientist presupposes that there is a world of nature which is a world of events which cannot be produced or prevented by any-body's art, that this world is made up of many different realms, each com-posed of a class of things peculiar to itself to which events of a peculiar kind happen but that, nevertheless, the peculiar laws of these realms are modifi-cations of universal laws according to which all movements and events in spite of all differences agree in happening.

None of these presuppositions is a demonstrable proposition but without them there would be no natural science as we know it, e.g. to a person who believed that natural events were caused or prevented by personal magic, sci-ence would have no rationale and to one who believed that the world of na-ture was not real but an illusion, science might be possible but only as a friv-olous amusement like solitaire.

One cannot call such presuppositions hypotheses which are temporarily entertained till their truth or falsehood is established, for a scientist cannot seriously entertain the possibility that his life-vocation is absurd.

As distinct from a faith which applies to some specialized activity, there is the Faith by which a man lives his life as a man, i.e. the presuppositions he holds in order that (1) he may make sense of his past and present experience; (2) he may be able to act toward the future with a sense that his actions will be meaningful and effective; (3) that he and his world may be able to be changed from what they are into something more satisfactory. Such a faith can only be held dogmatically, for in man's historical and mortal existence, no experiment is ever identically repeatable.

Naturalism as it is used by the editors is used as a term for a religious Faith. It is necessary to know which particular kind of Naturalism is being referred to, for there are as many kinds as there are sciences. Historically, natural reli-gion has taken its presuppositions successively from mathematics, physics, bi-ology, psychology and history, and applied these analogically as key-concepts for accounting for the whole of reality and arrived in each case at very differ-ent conclusions. Similarly, even if they are all false, one cannot lump all the supernatural religions together. Thus in the rest of this article I shall substi-tute for the word religion as used by the editors the word Christianity, i.e. I shall not be thinking of Mohamedanism or Confucianism or Buddhism or even Quakers or Unitarians, but people who believe the dogmas expressed in the Apostles' creed, the Nicene creed and the Athanasian creed and who are members of an organized church with an ordained ministry which preaches the gospel and administers the sacraments.

II. *The credibility of certain mysteries like the Incarnation and the Trinity would cer-tainly not seem to be changed by any new data, scientific or otherwise; but there may be other parts of religion whose general credibility is changed by fundamental changes in the climate of opinion.*

It is precisely because such a climate is perpetually changing that carefully formulated creeds are necessary for heresy, as distinct from unbelief, is nearly always an over-emphasis of one part of the truth at the expense of the whole, and every age has its typical heresies. At any given historical moment, some article seems harder to accept than others because it runs completely counter to the prevailing ideology to which all, Christians and non-Christians alike, are at that moment exposed.

Thus in the second century when the prevailing tendency was to think of matter as more evil than mind, the Incarnation was the stumbling block; that the Logos should become real flesh seemed too infradig to be credible and too easy to confuse with those polytheistic myths in which some god appears in the simulacrum of a man or an animal. In the twelfth century the obstacle had become the doctrine of the divine creation of the world, so that even St Thomas Aquinas was forced to admit that to his natural reason the Aristotelian doctrine of the eternity of the world seemed more probable. In the seventeenth and eighteenth centuries, the object had become the Doctrine of the Trinity, for the Newtonian cosmology with its notion of imposed law and its lack of any concept of process seemed to require, to quote an epigram of Whitehead's, "at most one God."

Today, the prevailing ideology as regards matter and movement almost ensures that if a person can believe the Christian Faith at all, he will hold the orthodox Nicene Doctrine of the Trinity. Our stumbling blocks are different. The principal one, I suspect, is the acceptance of miracles affecting the natural order, e.g. the Virgin Birth and the Resurrection which would not have bothered a second century catechumen for five minutes. With this goes an all too easy acceptance of the Doctrine of Original Sin. But to believe that "I am shapen in iniquity and in sin hath my mother conceived me" and that "we have no power of ourselves to help ourselves" without at the same time believing "as in Adam all sleep even so in Christ shall be made alive" is, of course, not Christianity at all, but simply another variant of the pessimism we find in Homer.

I do not know if it was easier to believe the Christian Faith in the past than now, but I do know that Christians and the Church today share with everyone else in our civilization the experience of "alienation," i.e. our dominant religious experience—and this is why, I think, we find miracles so difficult—is of our distance from God. Hence the typical "modern" heresy is not a mechanized magical sacramentalism, or any form of Pantheism, but a Barthian exaggeration of God's transcendence which all too easily becomes an excuse for complacency about one's own sins and about the misfortunes of others. The abandonment of hope for a general social improvement which the editors suggest as a possible cause for a religious revival will lead a man not to Christianity but to one of those religions which hold that time is an illusion or an endless cycle. To the degree however that a would-be Christian believes in his depravity without believing in the miracle of his redemption, his religion is, what the Communists say it must be, opium for himself and the people.

III. *Objective and Subjective.*

All of us have suffered in recent history the experiences of what can happen when mathematical quantitative notions of mass and number or biological notions like species or class are applied as absolutes to human life. No reader of *PR*, I imagine, is going to accept any religion, naturalistic or otherwise, which does not allow and account for our experience of ourselves and our friends as being, not only individual members of class, but also persons, each a member of a class of one, i.e. no religion is credible today which lacks an existentialist aspect.

On the other hand we also live in a historical period of rival fanatical faiths, a religious period in the existentialist sense in which martyrdom has once more become a familiar event, and we cannot, any of us, really accept a religion which provides no criteria for distinguishing one of these faiths from another. Kierkegaard's statement that a passionate commitment to an untruth is religiously superior to a lukewarm interest in the truth is excellent polemics in a situation where both parties are agreed as to what the truth is. When they are not, it is highly dangerous. To kick a beggar or to give him a dime may both be existentially "authentic" choices of oneself, but we need to know in what respects they differ.

A purely existentialist attitude, since it has no conception of the universal or the eternal, cannot be Christian, to whom the existential is only one, admittedly very important, aspect of his situation. Atheist existentialism, while more logical, suffers under the disadvantage that, like Stoicism, it can only be held either by madmen, to whom the choice of "engagement" is arbitrary, or by the fortunate, i.e. those whose "engagement" has been chosen for them by their natural gifts and the chance of history. Existentialism has, as Baudelaire said of Stoicism, one sacrament for the sinner—suicide.

Apologetics by their nature can arrive at little more than negative conclusions, i.e. the most an apologist can hope to demonstrate is that his opponent's conclusions do not answer certain questions which they both agree must be answered. For instance, if we take one problem, not necessarily the most important, that of ethics: can naturalism provide both an acceptable theory of Right, i.e. of what is universally and eternally good, and an acceptable theory of Duty, i.e. of what in a given historical situation a given individual ought to do, and further establish an intelligible relation between the two?

I am willing to concede that naturalism might some day bring Right and Duty together in the sense that it might be possible to demonstrate that all offences against the Right were also offences against oneself (e.g. that envy injures the brain). There would still remain however the problem of temptation, i.e. if I know *what* I ought to do, how is it possible for me to do anything else? or if it is possible for me to do what I know I ought not, how do I overcome this?

IV. *Science, Art, Christianity.*

A Christian is committed to believing: (a) that there is one God, (b) that He is the source of all truth, (c) that He created the natural universe. From this it follows that any proposition about nature which can be proved to be true is *ipso facto* a revelation of the work of God and that, *a priori*, there can be no contradiction between true science and true Faith. So far, there has been no genuine advance in scientific knowledge which has not in the end been found by the Christian to confirm and clarify his faith.

In the short run, of course, from the time of Averroes to our own, Christianity and Science have repeatedly believed they were deadly enemies. Christians on the one side have confused the Christian dogmas with certain propositions which they have come through cultural habit to associate with them, so that they have reacted to new knowledge like most people react to modern art, and some scientists, on the other side (which makes the behavior of the Christians more sensible if not more excusable), have imagined that in disproving the propositions they would disprove the dogmas.

Let us take the most extreme case, that of the Biblical Scholarship and "Higher Criticism" of the past century and a half. A Christian is committed to believing that the Bible is an inspired book, i.e. that it is a unique revelation of the nature, acts and purposes of God in a way that no other history is, and that it is the clue by which all other history may be understood; further, that the life, passion and resurrection of Jesus as recounted in the gospels are not mythical events like the life of Hercules or Adonis but actual historical occurrences.

Before the development of Biblical Scholarship, perhaps the majority of uneducated Christians identified this belief with believing that the Bible was a succession of true propositions dictated by God to the "authors" of its various books without their conscious thought or control. When historical research into the biblical documents began, many Christians feared that if it were shown that every sentence in the Bible was not true in the sense that a geometrical theorem can be true, then they could lose their faith; conversely, some of the scholars certainly hoped that, in making literal fundamentalism untenable, they would destroy the historical evidence for Christianity and prove Jesus to be a myth. What in fact has been proved? All investigation into the history of the Jews and all comparative studies of Jewish history and religion with those of their contemporaries have confirmed the peculiar a-typical character of the former. All research into the gospel narratives has demonstrated that one cannot deny that the resurrection occurred on historical grounds, but only on the dogmatic assumption that it could not have occurred, and that the historian who makes this assumption is faced with the problem of explaining exactly why and how the apostles were deceived into a conviction that it did occur and, moreover, regarded it, not merely as the apotheosis of a hero which only concerned him and his glory, but as an event which should and did transform their lives.

In the, at present, purely hypothetic case of a modern state and a majority of its population becoming devoutly and orthodoxly Christian, what are the chances of scientific research being restricted or persecuted? One cannot say definitely that there would be none—stupid, suspicious, frightened churchmen always exist, and so do arrogant scientists who draw unscientific conclusions from scientific facts, but on the whole, in respect to science, I think the Church has probably learned her lesson. Even if she has not, I think one can confidently assert that a naturalistic religion like Marxism which holds certain scientific propositions dogmatically or certain presuppositions valid for one science as absolute for all is really threatened by advances in scientific knowledge in a way that Christianity is not, however Christians may be tempted to imagine sometimes that it is, and that the chances of persecution by the former are, at least, greater.

In actual fact, I foresee much more trouble between the Church and the Arts. The editors of *PR* find it suspicious that at present it seems to be literary folk who form the majority of those intellectuals who have been converted to some kind of supernatural religion. I think the Church would agree with them and so would I. It is easier for an artist to see the inadequacies of naturalism because in his professional work he is occupied with the personal and the existential which are his subject matter. On the other hand, he is also occupied in his profession in converting this subjective material into an a-historical objective form, its actual disorder into one possible order among others. This means that the artist *qua* artist is of all people the most skeptical, because in his art he does not have to believe what he says, only entertain it as a possibility: e.g. if he writes a poem about the Crucifixion, there is no means of knowing from the poem whether he believes in it as a Christian must believe or is using it as a convenient myth for organizing the emotions his poem expresses, for in poetry dogma and myth are identical.

The Christian, on the other hand, who is not an artist is inclined to forget that, as Cardinal Newman wrote, "There cannot really be a Christian literature for all literature is literature about the natural man," and therefore to condemn literature which describes sinful emotion and behavior or the triumph of the sinner in this world. Further the relative subjectivity of aesthetic values tempts the average man, Christian or not Christian, to suspect all art which he does not like or understand of being heretical and subversive.

V. *Prophetic and Institutional Religion.*

Man is both a historical creature creating novelty and a natural creature suffering cyclical recurrence and no religion is viable which does not do justice to both aspects.

A prophet is one through whom God speaks to awaken the Church to a consciousness of its contemporary historical mission. For this purpose it is not even necessary that the prophet himself be a Christian; indeed, during the past two hundred years most of the great prophets, e.g. Voltaire, Marx, Freud, Nietzsche, have been actively hostile to Christianity and even those who, like Kierkegaard and Dostoievsky, were members of a Christian Church, have been of very doubtful orthodoxy.

Their *raison d'être* depends on the existence of an institutional religion by whom they may be heard. This institution with its unchanging cycle of ritual and sacrament exists and must exist because men are born, bear children and die and "human nature," as we say, remains the same, through all historical change. Without prophets religion degenerates into popular natural habit. Without a church, it degenerates into a succession of highbrow spiritual fashions reflecting the ideology of the moment. Without both, in fact, religion becomes identical with culture, either the culture of the masses or the culture of the elite.

I have intentionally kept the argument limited to the conception of the Church as an institution, as this was the question raised. In fact, of course, it is no more simply an institution than the United States is its organized government. It is, and thinks of itself as being, the community of all the souls of the faithful living and dead, past and to come.

VI. *Orthodoxy and Heresy.*

In any future that we can envisage, we seem likely to live increasingly in a word of one culture and many faiths, (assuming, that is, that Communism does not succeed in conquering the world). In such a world the heretic is not the man who chooses his own truth, but the man who insists on his own taste, who, say, dislikes ice-cream or Italian opera in English. The likelihood of this condition does not, for me at any rate, make it desirable. A faith, on the other hand, which really is a faith and believes, therefore, that it is in possession of the truth, is by necessity missionary and must intend to convert the world.

The Church has, I think, learned one lesson the hard way, that persecution makes no converts. She is only beginning to learn that, as Newman also said, "it is as foolish to try and argue a man into belief as it is to try and torture him into it." Perhaps one should amend this slightly and say that fruitful argument is only possible between friends and that two people cannot become friends unless they can share each other's culture: my friend is one who understands my jokes. Thus, wherever the Church desires to preach the gospel, whether to savages, the industrial working class or intellectuals, she must in everything that does not concern faith and morals "go native."

In theory she has always held that every other religion was a revelation, partial or distorted but real, of the true God, that she must always say, like St Paul on the Acropolis, "He whom ye ignorantly worship, Him I declare unto you." In practice she has all too often denied this out of cultural pride so that the unbeliever has heard, not the good news itself, but the superior accents of the European and the white gentleman in which it was uttered.

Partisan Review, February 1950

Introduction to *Red Ribbon on a White Horse,* by Anzia Yezierska

Reading Miss Yezierska's book sets me thinking again about that famous and curious statement in the Preamble to the Constitution about the self-evident right of all men to "the pursuit of happiness," for I have read few accounts of such a pursuit as truthful and moving as hers.

To be happy means to be free, not from pain or fear, but from care or anxiety. A man is so free when (1) he knows what he desires and (2) what he desires is real and not fantastic. To know what one desires means either to desire one specific good exclusively—I want X and nothing else—or to have a definite preference at this time for one good rather than another—I want X more than Y now. A desire is real when the possibility of satisfaction exists for the individual who entertains it and the existence of such a possibility depends, first, on his present historical and social situation—a desire for a Cadillac which may be real for a prosperous American businessman would be fantastic for a Chinese peasant—and, secondly, on his natural endowment as an individual—for a girl with one eye to desire to be kept by a millionaire would be fantastic, for a girl with two beautiful ones it may not. To say that the satisfaction of a desire is possible does not mean that it is certain but that if the desire is not satisfied, a definite and meaningful reason can be given. Thus if the American businessman fails to get the Cadillac he desires and asks himself, "Why?" he has a sensible answer, say: "My wife had to have an emergency operation which took my savings"; but if the Chinese peasant asks, "Why cannot I buy a Cadillac?" there are an infinite number of reasons which can only be summed up in the quite irrational answer, "Because I am I." The businessman suffers disappointment or pain but does not become unhappy; the peasant, unless he dismisses his desire as fantastic, becomes unhappy because to question his lack of satisfaction is to question the value of his existence.

So long as it is a matter of immediate material goods, few sane individuals cherish fantastic desires after the age of puberty, but there are desires for spiritual goods which are much more treacherous, e.g. the desire to find a vocation in life, to have a dedicated history. "What do I want to be? A writer? A chemist? A priest?" Since I am concerned not with any immediate objective good but with pledging the whole of my unknown future in advance, the chances of self-deception are much greater because it will be years before I can be certain whether my choice is real or fantastic. Nor can any outsider make the decision for me; he can only put questions to me which make me more aware of what my decision involves. Thus Dr Cushing, the famous surgeon, once dissuaded a promising student who wanted to specialize in surgery by asking him one question: "Do you enjoy the sensation of cutting through flesh with a knife?" To make matters worse, it is quite possible and, maybe, even usual for the reasons for my decision now to be fantastic and yet for my decision to turn out to have been the right one. In his fascinating autobiography *A Mathematician's Apology* Professor G. H. Hardy tells how he decides to take up mathematics after reading a moral tale about two brothers in which the bad one ends up in Africa and the good one in a Cambridge Senior Common Room, and that it was only after he had won his Fellowship to Trinity that he realized what being a mathematician meant.

Miss Yezierska's book is an account of her efforts to discard fantastic desires and find real ones, both material and spiritual.

She began life in a Polish ghetto, i.e. in the bottom layer of the stratified European heap. In the more advanced countries of Europe, like England, it had become possible for a talented individual to rise a class a generation, but in Russia, above all for a Jew, it was still quite impossible; if once one had been born in the ghetto, then in the ghetto one would die. For its inhabitants extreme poverty and constant fear of a pogrom were normal, and even so humble a desire as the wish to eat white bread was fantastic. So it had been for centuries until, suddenly, a possibility of escape was opened—immigration to America. What America would provide positively in place of the ghetto remained to be seen, but at least it would be different and any sufferings she might inflict would, at the very least, not be worse.

So Miss Yezierska and her family came and found themselves on the Lower East Side. Here was poverty still but less absolute, exploitation but the possibility of one day becoming an exploiter, racial discrimination but no pogroms. Was their new condition an improvement on their former one? It was hard to be certain. Where poverty is accepted as normal and permanent, the poor develop a certain style of living which extracts the maximum comfort from the minimum materials, but where poverty is held to be temporary or accidental, the preoccupation with escape leaves no time for such amenities; every European visitor to the States, I think, receives the impression that nowhere else in the world is real poverty—admittedly, rarer here than anywhere else—so cheerless, sordid, and destitute of all grace.

Moreover, in the "bad old days" of which Miss Yezierska writes—a more lively social conscience and a slackening of the immigrant stream have largely put a stop to it—in no European country, it seems, were the very poor treated with such a total disregard of their human rights. In Europe the rich man and the poor man were thought of as being two different kinds of men; the poor man might be an inferior kind but he was a man: but here the poor man was not, as such, a man, but a person in a state of poverty from which, if he were a real man, he would presently extricate himself. The newly arriving poor, to judge from Miss Yezierska's description of the sweatshop, were treated by their predecessors, it seems, like Freshmen by Upper Classmen, i.e. subjected to a process of "hazing" so as to toughen their character and stiffen their determination to rise to a position of immunity.

For the older generation particularly, who, in any case, had usually immigrated for the sake of their children, not of themselves, the new life often seemed only a little better materially, and spiritually very much worse. The fellowship of suffering lasts only so long as none of the sufferers can escape. Open a door through which many but probably not all can escape one at a time and the neighborly community may disintegrate, all too easily, into a stampeding crowd. Those who had learned how to be happy even in prison and could neither understand nor desire another life stood abandoned, watching the stampede with bewilderment and horror.

Some, like Boruch Shlomoi Mayer, simply wanted to go back:

> To me, America is a worse *Goluth* than Poland. The ukases and pogroms from the Czar, all the killings that could not kill us gave us the strength to live with God. Learning was learning—dearer than gold. . . . But here in New York, the synagogues are in the hands of godless lumps of flesh. A butcher, a grocer, any moneymaker could buy himself into a president of a synagogue. With all that was bad under the Czar, the synagogue was still God's light in time of darkness. Better to die there than to live here.

Others continued to live their old life with uncompromising indifference to the new world. Miss Yezierska's father, for instance, had a vocation, the study of the Torah, which involved his being supported by his wife and children. He had expected them to do so in Plinsk, he expected them to continue doing so in New York. But what they had accepted in Poland as an extra burden, worth bearing for the honor in which a learned and holy man was held by the community, was bound to seem intolerable in America, where not only was a non-earner regarded as an idler but also the possibility for the family of acquiring status existed in proportion to their earning capacity.

His daughter, however, as she later realized, was more like him than either of them at the time could perceive. Had she been less like him, had she simply desired money and a good marriage, there would have been less friction between them but she, too, was seeking for a dedicated life of her own, which in his eyes was impious, for all vocations but one were for men only.

"A woman alone, not a wife and not a mother, has no existence." She, however, wanted a vocation all to herself and thought she had found it in writing. She began, as she tells us, with the hope that "by writing out what I don't know and can't understand, it would stop hurting me." At the same time, of course, she wanted money to satisfy her needs. This is any artist's eternal problem, that he needs money as a man but works for love. Even in the case of the most popular writer, money is not the purpose for which he writes, though popularity may be.

So she begins; she writes a book *Hungry Hearts* about the life of a poor immigrant, which is well reviewed but does not sell; then, suddenly, the American Fairy—whether she is a good or a wicked fairy, who knows?—waves her
wand and she is transported in an instant from Hester Street to Hollywood;
from one day to the next, that is, suffering is abolished for her. How does she
feel? More unhappy than she has ever been in her life. To have the desires of
the poor and be transferred in a twinkling of an eye to a world which can only
be real for those who have the desires of the rich is to be plunged into the
severest anxiety. The foreshortening of time which is proper to a dream or a
fairy story is a nightmare in actual life.

Further, to be called to Hollywood is not like winning a fortune in the Calcutta sweepstake; money is showered upon one because it is believed that one
is a valuable piece of property out of which much larger sums can be made.
For a writer this is only bearable if he knows exactly what he wants to write
and if what he can write happens to pay off the investors as they expect. Miss
Yezierska was too young to be the former and, by snatching her away from
Hester Street and the only experiences about which she knew, the film mag-
nates effectively destroyed the possibility that their expensive goose might lay
another golden egg. In fact, they gave it such a fright that it stopped laying
altogether.

The sudden paralysis or drying up of the creative power occurs to artists
everywhere but nowhere, perhaps, more frequently than in America; nowhere else are there so many writers who produced one or two books in their
youth and then nothing. I think the reason for this is the dominance of the
competitive spirit in the American ethos. A material good like a washing-
machine is not a unique good but one example of a kind of good; accordingly one washing-machine can be compared with another and judged better or worse. The best, indeed the only, way to stimulate the production of
better washing-machines is by competition. But a work of art is not a good of
a certain kind but a unique good so that, strictly speaking, no work of art is
comparable to another. An inferior washing-machine is preferable to no
washing-machine at all, but a work of art is either acceptable, whatever its
faults, to the individual who encounters it or unacceptable, whatever its merits. If the former, the existence of other works of art cannot replace it; if the
latter, their absence cannot make it do in their stead. The writer who allows
himself to become infected by the competitive spirit proper to the production of material goods so that, instead of trying to write *his* book, he tries to
write one which is better than somebody else's book is in danger, because of
the unreality of such an attempt, of trying to write the absolute masterpiece
which will eliminate all competition once and for all and, since this task is totally unreal, his creative powers cannot relate to it, and the result is sterility.

As she ceased to write and be a public success, Miss Yezierska found herself
being avoided by those who had previously sought to be her friends. Such be-

haviour is, of course, base, but one would be wrong to suppose that, if it is a little more common in the States than elsewhere, Americans are baser than others. In other and more static societies an individual derives much of his sense of identity and value from his life-membership in a class—the particular class is not important—from which neither success nor failure, unless very spectacular, can oust him, but, in a society where any status is temporary and any variation in the individual's achievement alters it, his sense of his personal value must depend—unless he is a religious man—largely upon what he achieves: the more successful he is, the nearer he comes to the ideal good of absolute certainty as to his value; the less successful he is, the nearer he comes to the abyss of nonentity.

No man naturally desires either to suffer or to be anxious, and will, by nature, seek to avoid the threat of either. A suffering individual is not avoided and may arouse compassion in others because suffering is not contagious, but an anxious individual is always avoided because anxiety, even more than fear (which requires the presence of a third factor, the fearful object), is always catching if the second party has any latent anxiety, which he nearly always has. If, in America, the failure finds himself without friends, this is not really because he is a failure but because failure has made him anxious.

So, after a fairy tale, Miss Yezierska woke into a realistic novel of the dreariest kind, "years without event" save of increasing poverty and isolation, and then came another translation, this time into farce. With the coming of the Depression she ceased to be a solitary failure and became one of millions who could not be called failures, because the positions in which they could succeed or fail no longer existed. It was surely the height of irony that in a country where the proof of one's importance had been that one was rich and popular, people should suddenly, in order to prove that they were important enough to eat, have to go to elaborate lengths to establish that they were penniless and friendless.

The Arts Project of W.P.A. was, perhaps, one of the noblest and most absurd undertakings ever attempted by any state. Noblest because no other state has ever cared whether its artists as a group lived or died; other governments have hired certain individual artists to glorify their operations and have even granted a small pension from time to time to some artist with fame or influence, but to consider, in a time of general distress, starving artists as artists and not simply as paupers is unique to the Roosevelt Administration. Yet absurd, because a state can only function bureaucratically and impersonally—it has to assume that every member of a class is equivalent or comparable to every other member—but every artist, good or bad, is a member of a class of one. You can collect fifty unemployed plumbers, test them to eliminate the unemployable, and set the remainder to work on whatever plumbing jobs you can find, but if you collect fifty unemployed writers, ex-professors, New England spinsters, radicals, bohemians, etc., there is no test of their abilities which applies fairly to them all and no literary task you can devise which can be properly done by even a minority of them. While only the laziest and most inefficient of your plumbers will let you down, because the jobs you give them are the jobs for which they have been trained and regard as theirs, only the writers with the strictest sense of moral, as distinct from professional, duty will fail to cheat you if, as must almost inevitably be the case, the literary job you offer them is one in which they take no interest, not because writers are intrinsically lazier or more dishonest than plumbers, but because they can see no sense in what you ask them to do.

Miss Yezierska, for instance, was set to work counting the trees in Central Park for the New York Guide (I myself know of a young man who was sent round the public schools of the city measuring the size of the filing cabinets in the Principals' offices); her natural lack of interest in this occupation was not dispersed by the knowledge that most of the information would never be used and that the Director had hired, as, of course, he was bound sooner or later to discover that he must, a couple of specialists to write the Guide itself.

It is easy for the accountant to frown on W.P.A. for its inefficiency and for the artists to sneer at it for its bureaucracy, but the fact remains that, thanks to it, a number of young artists of talent were enabled, at a very critical time in their lives, to get started on their creative careers. As for the rest, the executive might just as well—and I dare say would have been glad to—have been honest, given them their weekly checks and sent them home, but the legislature which could endure such honesty could exist only in Heaven.

Among her companions in poverty and comedy, Miss Yezierska felt once more to some degree that happiness of "belonging" which, years before, she had felt in Hester Street, though she realized it only after she had left. But belonging to some degree is not enough; one must belong completely or the feeling soon withers. Once again the lack of a common memory of the past and a common anticipation of the future was a fatal barrier, not only for her but for most of her fellows.

> The word "home" raised a smile in us all three,
> And one repeated it, smiling just so
> That all knew what he meant and none would say.
> Between three counties far apart that lay
> We were divided and looked strangely each
> At the other, and we knew we were not friends
> But fellows in a union that ends
> With the necessity for it, as it ought.

No, the accidental community of suffering was not the clue to happiness and she must look further; where she went and what she found the reader can learn for himself.

As an account of the experiences of an early twentieth-century immigrant

Miss Yezierska's book naturally sets one wondering how they compare with those of the post-Hitler immigrant. The typical representation of the former was a member of the working class, who had never been anyone in particular and who came to the States by choice in the hope that here he would find the opportunity to become someone. The typical representative of the latter, on the other hand, is a member of the professional class, who was of some, often, indeed, of great consequence in his native land and who never wanted to come to the States and would never have done so but for Hitler and Mussolini. For him the problem of adaptation to America is quite different. As a conscious bearer of his culture it is harder for him to make necessary changes but he is less likely to lose what he had without acquiring anything in its stead; as a person who has known success the problem for his ego is not the sudden opening of unlimited possibilities to one who has hitherto only known a single fate, but the transition, for all but the few internationally famous, from being of considerable consequence to being of little consequence. Let us hope that he will someday write as honest an account of his experience as Miss Yezierska has of hers. Native-born Americans who are sometimes, understandably enough, irritated by a too insistent harping on the *bei uns* note and may even be tempted to sigh for the old days when immigrants were seen but not heard and voted as their ward-boss told them to, should remember that if his criticisms of America are louder and shriller than those of his predecessor, his direct positive contribution to American life—one has only to think of the colleges—has been greater.

Miss Yezierska's autobiography, however, has a deeper and more general significance for us than its relevance to the problems of the actual immigrant, for the immigrant is coming more and more to stand as the symbol for Everyman, as the natural and unconscious community of tradition is rapidly disappearing from the earth.

It becomes increasingly clear that the eighteenth-century identification of pleasure with happiness makes nonsense of both. Pleasure and pain are given states of immediate feeling which cannot provide an explanation of why they are or whether they should be, and it is upon the convinced possession of such an explanation or the lack of it that a person's happiness or unhappiness depends.

One cannot speak of the right to pursue pleasure, for if one means that no individual has a right to make his neighbor suffer for his own pleasure, that implies the right of an individual to choose to suffer for his neighbor's sake. On the other hand, while, if I suffer, the responsibility may not be mine but another's, if I am unhappy nobody is responsible but myself. In reference to happiness the phrase "the right to pursue" is a curious way of describing obligation, for to be happy is not my right but my eternal duty.

Only the fortunate man is free from suffering but only the religious man, i.e. the individual whose life is grounded in an absolute concern—assuming (a big assumption) that he believes a concern to be absolute which in fact is not so does not matter—can be happy. The unconscious acceptance of an authority as absolute is rapidly becoming impossible and the choice of faiths open to men in any larger numbers seems to be narrowing down to a choice between a supernatural religion and a political one. Judging from statements made or reported by some of the Press, it seems necessary to observe that such a choice is not necessarily exclusive. It is meaningful to say, as the communist does, "Not God but Communism," or "Not God but Democracy," as the liberal rationalist does, but "God and Democracy" is no human speech but an animal outcry, an emotive noise.

Red Ribbon on a White Horse, by Anzia Yezierska, 1950

A Playboy of the Western World:
St Oscar, the Homintern Martyr

The Paradox of Oscar Wilde. By George Woodcock. Macmillan. $3.50.

What a subject for a Big Feature Movie and, in these days—who knows?—if pedantically introduced by Dr Kinsey, it might even be made. It has just about everything. For location, Dublin, Oxford, Greece, the Cultured East, the Wild West, drawing rooms in Belgravia, private rooms at the Savoy, the Old Bailey, Reading Gaol, Paris cafés; for supporting cast Sir William, unwashed, skirt-chasing, but a great surgeon, Lady "Speranza" Wilde, her broad chest covered with large miniatures of family portraits which made her look like a walking museum, Pater lecturing inaudibly, Ruskin with pick and shovel, Bosey Douglas and his dotty choleric papa, bloody-but-unbowed Henley, Frank Harris, editor and romancier, Carson the prosecutor who nearly became guilty of treason over Ulster; and for big scenes, the hero dusting his clothes after Oxford hearties had dragged him up a hill with ropes and remarking "Yes, the view from here is very fine," his drinking Arizona cowboys under the table, his reception of Queensberry's card on which tradition has it that the operative word was misspelt *sondomite*, the plot of his friends to get him out of England in a balloon, his arrest in a bedroom of the Cadogan Hotel, his oration at the first trial on the love-that-dare-not-speak-its-name and the unexpected appearance at the second of the "gilded snakes" with Cockney accents, the whores dancing in the street on the night of the verdict, the jeering crowd on the platform of Reading station, the curious crowd outside the Dieppe brothel waiting to hear his opinion ("it was like cold mutton"), his death and burial, etc. Is there another life-story in history to compete with it? Moreover, would there be much of importance about Wilde which a movie could not show? Byron's life was sensational, too, but measured against *Don Juan* it is a small matter. The traditional view is that there is little of Wilde's literary work which is worth much, that Wilde the conversationalist and behaver is the significant figure. Tradition is often wrong and it is important that the facts should from time to time be re-examined to check it. This Mr Woodcock has painstakingly done but the results of his re-examination of Wilde's writing and ideas seem to confirm, even, I suspect, for Mr Woodcock himself, the traditional view, i.e. that all that is worth reading of Wilde is *The Importance of Being Earnest*, the letters to the *Daily Chronicle* on prison conditions, some stanzas from *The Ballad of Reading Gaol*, and a passage here and there from *The Decay of Lying* and *The Critic as Artist*.

When Yeats said of Wilde that he was by nature a man of action who "might have had a career like that of Beaconsfield, whose early style resembles his, being meant for crowds, for excitement, for hurried decisions, for immediate triumphs," he was right in the negative sense that Wilde was not by nature an artist, but positively he was wrong, for the politician and the artist are alike in that both are primarily interested in deeds and only secondarily interested in securing the approval of others, whereas Wilde is the classic case of a man who is completely dominated by the desire to be loved for himself alone. The artist does not want to be accepted by others, he wants to accept his experience of life which he cannot do until he has translated his welter of impressions into an order; the public approval he desires is not for himself but for his works, to re-assure him that the sense he believes he has made of experience is indeed sense and not a self-delusion Similarly, the politician solicits public approval not for his own sake but because, without it, he is impotent to do what he thinks should be done.

Writing for Wilde, on the other hand, was, as he himself admitted, a bore because it was only a means to becoming known and invited out, a preliminary to the serious job of spell-binding. Most great talkers have probably belonged to this psychological type but in Wilde's case his peculiar kind of conversation makes it particularly clear; his real forte was not intellectual wit, like Talleyrand or Sidney Smith, but the inspired and good-natured nonsense of a precocious child, a gift which had, it is reported, the power to charm away heartaches and melancholy. A person with this passionate need to be loved has constantly to test those around him by unconventional and provocative behavior, for what he does or says must be admired not because it is intrinsically admirable but because it is *his* act or remark. Further, a person with a need to be loved universally is frequently homosexual. The sexual act comes to play the same role vis-à-vis those with a lesser degree of consciousness, the young, the working-classes etc. that conversation plays vis-à-vis those with an equal degree; it becomes a magic role of initiation into worlds which one cannot approach on a conscious level. In a homosexual of this kind—corresponding to the test of eccentric behavior in the drawing-room—one usually finds a preference for "trade," i.e. sexually normal males, because, if another homosexual yields to him, he is only one of a class, but if he can believe that an exception is being made in his case, it seems a proof that he is being accepted for himself alone.

Had Wilde only desired to be accepted by one world or the other, he would probably have kept out of trouble but he wanted to be accepted by all worlds and that was his ruin. Nothing is clearer in the history of the three trials than his unconscious desire that the truth should come out. This desire was not caused by guilt in the conventional sense but by the wish to be loved as he really was. One suspects that his secret day-dream was of a verdict of guilty being brought in whereupon Judge, Jury and public would rise to their feet, crown him with flowers and say: "We ought, of course, to send you to gaol, Mr Wilde, but we all love you so much that in this case we are delighted to make an exception." Mary McCarthy in her excellent, though I thought a bit governessy, *PR* review of Gielgud's production of *The Importance of Being Earnest* a few years back pointed out that Lady Bracknell is really Britannia, the moral Dragon whose capitulation to the hero's charms is the supreme victory. At the end all secrets are out, there is no need for Mr Bunbury and Lady Bracknell surrenders. In the Eden of Wilde's Hertfordshire all things are possible; in the late-Victorian Old Bailey, unfortunately, they were not.

Mr Woodcock who is, one gathers, an anarchist, does his best to show us what Wilde's ideas on Religion, Art, and Politics were, and to make of him an apostle of individualism, but it is difficult to take ideas as serious or contradictions as important paradoxes which seem so clearly to be simply strategies for an occasion. Of all men Wilde was least in the position to say: "the real weakness of England lies . . . in the fact that her ideas are emotional and not intellectual" for in few cases is the emotional root of thinking so obvious as in his.

Thus when, like all the nineteenth century literary *école païenne*, he extols the Greeks, the Great God Pan, and the Beautiful Pagan Life, any resemblance to the historical reality is accidental and all he seems to mean is: "I should like a world without Sunday closing, damp weather and overcooked vegetables but with plenty of sunshine and lots of yummy scantily-clad teenagers who can't say No." When he calls Sin "an essential element in progress," this has nothing to do with the serious Antinomian heresy, "Sin the more that grace may abound";—if one were to substitute a specific sin, say, cruelty, which Wilde really believed to be wicked, he would be horrified—the statement is simply one kind of seducer's patter like promising the young lady marriage.

And when he preaches individualism, e.g.

The development of the race depends on the development of the individual, and where self-culture has ceased to be the ideal, the intellectual standard is instantly lowered.

or

> There was to be a new hedonism that was to re-create life. It was to have
> its service of the intellect, certainly; yet it was never to accept any theory
> or system that would involve the sacrifice of any mode of passionate ex-
> perience. . . . Of the asceticism that deadens the senses, as of the vulgar
> profligacy that dulls them, it was to know nothing.

he is not advocating either of the two possible religions of self-development,
the concentrated discipline of one's nature in a chosen direction, like Mar-
cus Aurelius, nor the planned exploration of all experience like Faust, but expressing the simplest and oldest of all wishes, "let's have fun," which may not
be so impressive as a philosophy of life but is ever so much more sympathetic.
I am deeply shocked when Mr Woodcock condemns Wilde's affairs as "ridiculous and sordid" as if his hero should have devoted himself to the Higher Pleasures, and regrets his attachment to Alfred Douglas as an object "meanly unworthy of his admiration" as if he should have selected his friend for his virtue.
Surely, the really nice thing about Wilde is that his life is so much more honest than his writings; after all the high-falutin' talk about Beauty and the New
Hedonism, it is such a relief to discover that Wilde was just an ordinary sinner like you and me who liked his greens and wasn't too particular about the
restaurant. He was a phoney prophet but a serious playboy; even serious
prophets are not ideal guests for a party, but a good playboy is always welcome,
except to those who have murdered the child in themselves.

As for Wilde's political views, they are about as valuable as those of most literary men, i.e. his criticisms of the existing state of affairs are often just, if a
bit obvious, his practical suggestions merely silly. The nature of the literary
profession the influence of which, if any, is spiritual not material, renders
men of letters incapable of understanding the role of power in society and
their social position which, like that of the gypsies, is interstitial, prevents
their having a subjective understanding of social and economic relations. To
do Wilde justice he seldom indulges in the all-too-easy role of political satirist.
When, for instance, in *An Ideal Husband,* Lord Chiltern, in a fit of emotional
remorse, resolves to quit public life it is Wilde's alter-ego Lord Goring who
dissuades him, knowing that Chiltern is by nature a politician and would be
miserable doing anything else. This is not satire but sound sense.

Concerning the one work of Wilde's upon the excellence of which we can
all agree, *The Importance of Being Earnest,* Mr Woodcock's own social interests
make him see in Lady Bracknell "a satire on the snobbish values of the upper-
classes" and in Miss Prism and Dr Chasuble respectively "Wilde's contempt
for the educational system and the Church of his day." This seems to me a
complete misrepresentation of what Wilde is trying to do, namely, to portray
the Garden of Eden as a spot quite different from the pagan island of the
blessed.

The tough and pessimistic Greek who identified pleasure and happiness knew that pleasure depends upon power; accordingly his Happy Place is inhabited only by the beautiful, the strong and the wise; the weak, the ugly, the poor, the old, the stupid are excluded. But Wilde, like anyone who has been exposed to the culture of Christendom, knew, however unconsciously, that pleasure and happiness are distinct, and that happiness does not depend upon power but upon love. In his day-dream, therefore, Eden is the place where everyone is happy, poor Miss Prism, silly Dr Chasuble and old Lady Bracknell just as much as the young lovers, where everyone loves everyone else and where, though the laws of nature operate—people have the same nature that they have in the real world—their operation causes neither conflict nor suffering. Given his nature, it is not surprising that this subject should have excited Wilde to write a masterpiece, for on this subject as on no other is the playboy, who is always an "alienated" soul who craves to belong, truly earnest.

Partisan Review, April 1950

Of Poetry in Troubled Greece

Modern Greek Poetry. Translated and edited
by Rae Dalven. Gaer Associates. $3.50.

Translation of poetry is, strictly speaking, impossible because it involves separating two elements, the form and the words, which in poetry are inseparable. It is only in cases so rare as to be miraculous that a translator hits upon the form in the new language which is a true analogy of the original form; usually, either an identical form is adopted and the language distorted in consequence, or a literal word by word and line by line translation of the words is made and the form in consequence not distorted but destroyed.

Rae Dalven has chosen the second method as the lesser of two evils and, I think, rightly. However, if lack of space and the public's unfamiliarity with the Greek alphabet made her decide against accompanying her translations with the original texts, one would have welcomed at least a short account of the principles of modern Greek verse. Is it scanned by quantity, as in classical Greek, or by accent or both? Is it rhymed? What are the commonest forms for narrative, reflective and lyric poetry, etc.? Without such information one is too completely at the translator's mercy and, while it is obvious that Miss Dalven has tried to make her translation as scrupulously accurate as possible, her ear for the rhythms of the English language is defective.

Modern Greek Poetry falls into two parts, the first consisting of extracts from traditional folk songs and folk epics, and the second of selections from forty-three poets, beginning with Rhigas Pheraios, born in 1751, and ending with Odysseus Elytis, born in 1912; three-quarters of them belong to the last hundred years.

Of these, only one, Cavafy, is familiar to this reviewer, to whom he seems one of the most important and original European poets of the early twentieth century. Among the others, introduced by Miss Dalven, Kazantzakis' Nietzschean version of the *Odyssey* makes an immediate impression, so do Solomos, Malakassis, Griparis, Varnalis and Kariotakis; on the other hand, some poets whom she evidently considers important—e.g. Calvos, Palamas and Sikelianos—do not seem, at least at the first few readings, to get across.

Taking the volume as a whole, one has the impression that it is unfortunate for its poets when a country is continually in a state of political excitement, whether the cause be national hatred of a foreign ruler or internal faction, for such a condition, when permanent, tends to drive the poet to one extreme or the other, either to writing rhetorical calls to battle or to an over-fastidious apolitical estheticism: the muse does not like being forced to choose between Agit-prop and Mallarmé.

Greece has been particularly unlucky in that language itself has been a political issue. Miss Dalven gives a fascinating account of this in her preface. To those who have grown up in a less controversial atmosphere it sounds very odd indeed to hear that, as late as 1901, there were street riots and bloodshed in Athens over the publication of a demotic, or popular, translation of the New Testament. Again, it must, one feels, be very difficult to be a Greek student when every few years the language taught in the schools is changed by Government orders. At the present moment, according to Miss Dalven, who is herself a passionate partisan of the demotic, "the purist is in order. A student who writes his high school entrance examinations in the demotic risks failure." One cannot help wondering, if, when the demotic party is in power, the same risk is run by the student who writes in purist.

The difficulty for the outsider, who knows neither language, is that he is incapable of judging their rival literary merits. Miss Dalven is convinced that there can only be one answer.

In the meantime, we should be very grateful to Miss Dalven for introducing to us a world of poetry which has been closed to us. Every translator is an international agent of good-will.

The New York Times Book Review, 2 April 1950

A Guidebook for
All Good Counter-Revolutionaries

The Recollections of Alexis de Tocqueville.
Translated by Alexander Teixeira de Mattos.
Edited with many additions from the original text and an
introduction by J. P. Mayer. Columbia University Press. $5.

Since the *Recollections* cover only two years of de Tocqueville's political career, it may be well to give a resumé of that career as a whole.

Elected a deputy in 1839, de Tocqueville's talents were soon recognized by the Chamber, for he was entrusted with introducing a motion for the abolition of slavery in the colonies and, in 1840, with the question of prison reform. In 1846, he was made chairman of a Committee on African Affairs and in 1849, despite the fact that he had voted against Louis Napoleon, he entered the Cabinet as Minister for Foreign Affairs. During his term of office he was twice confronted with international disputes, once between Austria and Piedmont and once between Russia and Turkey, which might have led to a European war, and by his firm and adroit diplomacy preserved the peace. In 1851, it was largely his speech which persuaded the Chamber to vote against the reelection of Louis Napoleon. This he regarded as the great political blunder of his life:

> Our intention was not subtle and quick enough to realize that, from the moment that it has been decided that the public themselves were to choose the President directly, it was only making matters worse to thwart the people's choice so recklessly.

The result was the coup d'état at which De Tocqueville immediately resigned and retired into private life until his death in 1859.

This is a record that the most practical of men would not be ashamed of. De Tocqueville knew well that a politician must utilize the passions and issues of the moment or else he is impotent; on the other hand he believed that only barbarians consider politics purely practical and without any principles, his own aim being "balance, regular liberty, held in check by religion, custom, and law; the attractions of this liberty had become the passion of my life."

A small incident he relates illustrates like a parable his own practice of politics as the art of the possible ideal:

> No sooner was the hall recaptured, than General Courtais, the original author of our danger, had the incomparable impudence to present himself; he was seized and dragged to the rostrum. I saw him pass before my eyes, pale as a dying man among the flashing swords. Thinking they

would cut his throat, I cried with all my might, "Tear off his epaulettes, but don't kill him!" which was done.

Similarly, as a historian, he had an equal dislike for absolute systems of historical interpretation with their "false air of mathematical certainty," on the one hand, and for the "positivist" view, on the other, which would reduce the writhing of history to a meaningless catalogue of chance facts.

> I firmly believe that chance does nothing that has not been prepared beforehand. Antecedent facts, the nature of institutions, the cast of minds, and the state of morals are the materials of which are composed those impromptus which astonish and alarm us. The Revolution of February, in common with all other great events of this class, sprang from general causes, impregnated, if I am permitted the expression, by accidents; and it would be as superficial a judgment to ascribe it necessarily to the former or exclusively to the latter.

One is curious to know if the Abbé Lesueur ever read Thucydides with his young pupil, for De Tocqueville's whole approach to the Revolution of 1848 is startlingly similar to the approach of the great historian to the Peloponnesian War. Their historical method is really derived from medicine. For De Tocqueville, the norm of political health is a love of freedom, an honest obedience of law, and an unselfish respect for the rights of others. The revolutionary attack is then examined as follows: first comes the *catastasis*, or description of the general conditions preceding the outbreak—the state of France since the triumph of the middle class in 1830; then the *semeiology*, or detailed observation of the symptoms from day, to day, watching all the time for the crisis—the initial crisis which ousted Louis Philippe in February was not the real one which occurred in the following June, after which there was a final feeble crisis in the next year; then the *prognosis*, or forecast of the outcome—the revolution would not be fatal but the love of independence was to be followed by a dread of, and perhaps a distaste for, free institutions; and, lastly, the *therapeutics*, or the measures recommended for restoring and preserving health. For De Tocqueville, these included a second chamber and decentralization of the government. neither suggestion was followed, and the patient fell into what was in his eyes an ever more serious state. "Do you not realize," he wrote to his brother in 1852,

> that this government is as excessive in its way, indeed much more so, than that which it succeeded, that all its means are revolutionary, borrowed from the worst periods of the Revolution, and that the sole difference is that they are being employed against our enemies and no longer against us?

De Tocqueville's extraordinary, perhaps unique, merit as a historian is that he combines in equal measure the philosopher's capacity for drawing general conclusions and the novelist's eye for the particular and grotesque. His long-range forecasts are famous, his power of describing scenes and characters perhaps less so.

> Barrot at last appeared. He was out of breath, but not alarmed. Climbing the stairs of the tribune: "Our duty lies before us," he said; "the Crown of July rests on the head of a child and a woman."
>
> The Chamber, recovering its courage, plucked up heart to burst into acclamations, and the people in their turn were silent. The Duchesse d'Orleans rose from her seat, seemed to wish to speak, hesitated, listened to timid counsels, and sat down again: the last glimmer of her fortune had gone out. . . . At that moment, the crowd filling the semi-circle were driven back, by a stream from outside, towards the center benches, which were already almost deserted: it burst and spread over the benches. Of the few deputies who still occupied them, some slipped away and left the House, while others retreated from bench to bench, like victims surprised by the tide, who retreat from rock to rock always pursued by the rising waters.
>
> All this commotion was produced by two troops of men, for the most part armed, which marched through the two lobbies, each with officers of the National Guards and flags at their head. The two officers who carried the flags, of whom one, a swaggering individual, was, as I heard later, a half-pay colonel called Dumoulin, ascended the tribune with a theatrical air, waved their standards, and with much skipping about and great melodramatic gestures, bawled out some revolutionary balderdash or other. The President declared the sitting suspended, and proceeded to put on his hat, as is customary; but, since he had the knack of making himself ridiculous in the most tragic situations, in his precipitation he seized the hat of a secretary instead of his own, and pulled it down over his eyes and ears.

The *Recollections* are full of such scenes. As a study of the first tremors of the world revolution we are now living through, they are of immense importance. De Tocqueville stands out as one of the noblest examples of an attitude which may be called the Counter-Revolution. This must not be confused with Reaction, which refuses to recognize the just element in the Revolution and wishes to regard it as a simple rebellion. The Counter-Revolutionary has no wish to return to the condition which preceded the outbreak of revolution; he wishes rather to save the revolution from failure through the inevitable over-emphasis and over-simplification of the revolutionary party.

The central issue of the world revolution at present in progress is the right of every human body to the food, light, housing, medical attention, and so forth necessary for health. Its symbols are the naked anonymous baby and the tomb of the Unknown Soldier. The body knows nothing of freedom, only of necessities, and these are the same for all bodies. Hence the tendency of the revolutionary party in concentrating on this one goal to deny all liberty and all minority rights. In so far as we are bodies, we are or ought to be revolutionaries; in so far, however, as we are also souls and minds, we are or ought to be counter-revolutionaries, and in our struggle, the books of De Tocqueville belong, together with Thucydides, the Seventh Epistle of Plato, and the plays of Shakespeare, in the small group of the indispensable.

The Nation, 8 April 1950

The Score and Scale of Berlioz

Berlioz and the Romantic Century.
By Jacques Barzun. Little, Brown. 2 vols. $12.50.

First and foremost, this book is a love-child, the consequence of a *grande passion* of twenty years' standing. Such books are always fascinating to read, even when the objects of devotion are unworthy, for the devotion transforms them. They are also slightly comic at moments (even when the devotion is completely merited), for to the true lover any act or word of the beloved is more important than the greatest deeds of anyone else.

Jacques Barzun, professor of History at Columbia, is humorously aware of his condition and advises the individual reader to pick out the bits which interest him personally; the range of material that he offers is so astonishingly wide that every reader will find something to absorb him. The professional musician, for example, will find in an appendix a list of all the errors in the published Berlioz scores, the amateur listener will find clear and not too technical descriptions of every important Berlioz composition, while those who are interested in cultural history will find, interleaved between the accounts of Berlioz' life (1803–69) and work, thoughtful and stimulating studies of the nature, rise and fall of romanticism.

"Romanticism," Mr Barzun writes, "had to reabsorb the realities which the preceding two centuries had quite literally put out of court—wild nature, passion, superstition, myth, history and 'foreign parts.' . . . In sheer amount of intellectual gifts, few epochs can match that which stretches from the birth of Goethe in 1749 to the death of Berlioz 120 years later. . . . Romanticism did not merely oppose or overthrow the neoclassic 'Reason' of the Age of Enlightenment but sought to enlarge its vision and fill out its lacks by a return to a wider tradition—national, popular, medieval and primitive as well as modern, civilized and rational."

Mr Barzun's primary purpose, of course, is not to discuss romanticism but to get more people to listen to Berlioz' music; if, in his attempt at persuasion, he sometimes seems a fanatic to whom Berlioz is the only composer who ever lived, against whom the slightest criticism is blasphemy, it must be remembered that propagandizing for a composer is a very different job from recommending an author.

In the first place, music is a performed art, performances cost money and an unfamiliar program is a serious financial risk. In consequence, "At any time, the repertory of music resembles, not a body of literature, nor even a well-stocked library, but a one-volume anthology. . . . We see this in the relentless repetition of a piece that 'represents' a given composer to the exclusion of his other work."

In Berlioz' case, the *Symphonie Fantastique* and the *Rakoczy March* have got into the repertory everywhere; *The Damnation of Faust* is popular in France, and *Harold in Italy* is becoming known on records, and that is all, though all of these are early works. The large-scale compositions of his maturity, for chorus and orchestra and for the operatic stage, are hardly ever given and, even when they are, not as the composer wrote them nor in the way he intended them to be performed.

After quoting several instances of critics who have completely reversed their original verdict, Mr Barzun comments justly: "The sincere critic who formerly ignored and dismissed Berlioz has a sudden revelation, and the revelation is nothing more nor less than a good performance in full."

In the second place, the most obvious and effective way to convince others of the value of some artist's work is to give examples of it, but not only is the number of persons who can read music very limited but also the cost of reproducing musical quotations is prohibitive today. The propagandist is thrown back on verbal descriptions which, even when they are as well done as Mr Barzun's, are difficult to translate into sounds which one can judge; the best he can hope for is that his enthusiasm will make the composition sound so exciting that the reader will want to hear it too.

Since so little of Berlioz' music is widely known, the clichés about it remain undissipated. The two main ones are, firstly, that he loves noise for its own sake. This was already current in his lifetime, and the composer himself, who had frequently criticized Rossini for an inordinate use of the big drum, records a conversation with the Austrian statesman Metternich:

"Is it not you who compose music for five hundred players?"

"Not always, monseigneur; I sometimes write for four hundred and fifty."

If he sometimes wanted a large orchestra and chorus for large works, it was not for din but for smoothness, not for *ff*'s but for *pppp*'s. Indeed, many listeners, accustomed to the thick impasto tone of the Wagner-Strauss orchestration, at first find Berlioz' sound disappointingly thin, consisting as it does of "concerto-like sections framed within more massive yet always aerated ensembles."

The second, more serious cliché, is that Berlioz wrote "programme" music. Strictly speaking, this word should mean music which was a univocal sign of non-musical events, just as "pure" music should mean sounds without any analogy to any human experience. Even the purest music, as the West understands music, however, is analogous to history; i.e. to motivated free choice. On the other hand, if a composer writes a storm piece, however programmatic he tries to be, his musical storm is personal, purposeful, historical, more like a battle than any purely rational phenomenon.

Berlioz himself was well aware of the limits of musical representation. While defending expressiveness against convention: "In music I am a skeptic or, to speak more correctly, I belong to the religion of Beethoven, Weber, Gluck and Spontini, who believed and proved through their work that *everything is good* or *everything is bad*, the effect produced by a combination being that which alone ought to sanction or condemn it."

He was equally on the defense against those who would subordinate the formal unity of music to stage effects or poetry. "Wagner," he complains, "wants to dethrone music and reduce it to expressive accents. This is to outdo the system of Gluck (who most fortunately did not succeed in following his own impious theory.)"

Mr Barzun interestingly compares the orchestration of Wagner and Berlioz in expressing similar subjects. In the chorus in Act III of *Parsifal*, Wagner uses real bells; in the Easter chorus in the *Damnation*, Berlioz uses plucked notes on the basses. This comparison should not involve (as it so often has and, try as he may to be fair, Mr Barzun himself succumbs) using Berlioz as a stick with which to beat Wagner or vice versa.

The original cause of the Berlioz-Wagner feud was not really an esthetic matter but a matter of practical business. Large-scale dramatic works are so expensive that there is not room for two such composers at the same time. Wagner, who was both more unscrupulously selfish and stronger in will power, saw this more clearly than Berlioz, he knew that it would be hard enough for one of them to become a "bard," the equivalent in music of what Victor Hugo was in literature, and he set to work to see that the one should at least be himself.

No one can tell exactly how much Wagner believed in his talk about the Music of the Future; what is certain is that he was determined that his music should be the music of the present, and thanks to his amazing political skill, he succeeded: his Bayreuth became a real place, while Berlioz' Euphonia remained a daydream.

From our present perspective we should be able to see that all comparisons of Wagner with other composers make little sense, for, like Milton before him and Joyce after, he is one of those freak geniuses who stand altogether outside the common tradition and whose achievement is exhaustive: would-be heirs can only imitate or water down.

My only serious criticism of Mr Barzun is that, in discussing opera, he should devote so little attention to Verdi. Though they started from different points, Berlioz from outside the Italian tradition of Bellini and Rossini, and Verdi from within it, both were similarly concerned in developing an opera which was dramatically expressive throughout but in which the situations should remain truly musical, and the Shakespearean quality which Mr Barzun notes in Berlioz is characteristic in Verdi too. Though he might have thought the language a little excited, Verdi would certainly have agreed with the sense of Berlioz' words:

> Modern music is like the antique Andromeda, chained to a rock on the edge of a boundless sea; she waits the conquering Perseus who will break her chains and destroy the Chimera named Routine. Neighboring satyrs cry, "Leave her in chains. How do you know that once freed she will be yours? In bondage she is easier to possess." He will save Andromeda chastely and would even give her wings to augment her liberty.

There is no room in a review to discuss all the important questions raised by Mr Barzun (I sincerely hope that his wish to see opera transferred from the stage to the screen is never realized, but that is by the way), so one must conclude with the hope that his scholarly and passionate plea will be heard and a Berlioz society formed to insure the recording of all his principal works. For, whatever our final judgment may be, it is clearly necessary to know all the works of a composer concerning whom the opinions given by capable scholars show that every one of his dozen great works appears to some as his greatest, while the rest are unhesitatingly dismissed as inferior. If all the negative votes are correct, Berlioz is no good at all; if all the positive are correct, then he ranks among the very greatest.

The New York Times Book Review, 14 May 1950

The Things Which Are Caesar's

Whenever one glances over a list of titles to religious books, one realizes how almost impossible it is for writers on such topics to avoid sounding like salesmen of quack medicines. Even a phrase like *The Ministry of the Layman* suggests that the reader is to be offered a portable guidepost or a neatly packed message.

Even if I had one, which I certainly have not, I am sceptical of the value of such utensils. In the remarks which follow the questions I shall try to answer are more theoretical than practical—namely, What is the Laity? What is the distinction between the Laity and the Priesthood? What is the relation of each to the temporal order? If it is possible to reach conclusions on such matters, which are general, then the question of duty which is always n individual matter may be easier to answer.

For the general duty of the Christian, layman or priest, is as succinct as it is difficult—to love God with all his mind, heart, and soul, and to love his neighbour as himself, which in terms of the individual can also be expressed in the words of the Anglican Catechism: "To do my duty in that state of life, unto which it shall please God to call me."

The distinction between the layman and the priest is peculiar to Christianity, and must therefore arise out of the peculiar meanings given by Christianity to such terms as God, neighbour, love, life, and calling. Let us, then, begin at the beginning with Genesis.

The creation of man is described as a double act. First, "The Lord God formed man of the dust of the ground." Man, that is to say, is a natural creature subject like all other creatures to the laws of the natural order. Secondly, "The Lord God breathed into his nostrils the breath of life; and man became a living soul." Man, that is, is also a unique creature made in the image of God with self-consciousness and free-will, capable, therefore, of making history.

Because of this uniqueness he is given the power to understand and control the natural order and the responsibility to God for it.

> Have dominion over the fish of the sea, and over the fowl of the air, and over every living thing that moveth upon the earth.
>
> And out of the ground the Lord God formed every beast of the field and every fowl of the air and brought them unto Adam to see what he would call them; and whatsoever Adam called every living creature, that was the name thereof.
>
> And the Lord God took the man and put him in the Garden of Eden to dress and to keep it.

The creation of the sexes and thus of human relationships is likewise described as twofold.

> Male and female created he them. And God blessed them and God said unto them: Be fruitful and multiply.

That is to say, as a natural creature, man is related impersonally to others by natural needs which are not his but function through him to maintain life and perpetuate his species. He must devour others to live; if a male he seeks a female to mate with.

> And the Lord God said. It is not good that man should be alone; I will make him a help meet for him.

As a historical creature made in the image of God, man is also a person—i.e. a member of a class of one—desiring and capable of entering into unique relations with other unique persons. Here the relationship itself is its own reason for being rather than any function beyond itself, and consequently there is no limit to the possible number of such relationships.

If the sexual relationship is a special one, if a man may have only one wife at a time but should have many friends, this is because sexual appetite is the only natural need of his which is at once constant and involves another person, but like all natural appetites is indifferent to the person of the other.

In some circles recently there has been a tendency to see the notion of love as eros (or desire for getting) and the notion of love as agape (or free-giving) as incompatible opposites and to identify them with Paganism and Christianity respectively. Such a view seems to me a revival of the Manichean heresy which denies the goodness of the natural order; if it were true all natural affection, all admiration for the strong, all desire to protect the helpless, all wish for self-improvement, would be valueless. This seems not only contrary to common sense, but directly denied by the gospel definition of a neighbour as one who needs you. Further, the very sacrament of Agape, the Holy Eucharist, is in its outward and visible sign an act of eating, the most impersonal and naturally selfish of all acts.

Agape is the fulfilment and correction of eros, not its contradiction. When we speak of eros or natural desire we mean desire which necessarily seems right to us. What the gospel asserts is not that natural desire is necessarily wrong, but that, since man is a historical creature as well as a natural creature, furthermore since he is a fallen creature, the experience of a desire as natural or unnatural is not a sufficient guide.

As a natural creature man has, indeed, not desires but needs. Since nature is at once the realm of necessity and the creation of God, these needs cannot be wrong. As a historical creature man experiences these needs as desires which are historically conditioned; e.g. when hungry he does not desire what he needs, which is so-and-so many calories, but a certain kind of food which by culture and personal history he has come to like. Since history is at once the realm of man's freedom and of his sin, the desires which he feels to be natural are not necessarily good.

The command to love my neighbour as myself commands just that and no more; it does not say that those occasions when the command seems natural to me and I enjoy obeying it (e.g. in loving my wife or my family or my friends) are in any way inferior to those occasions when I find it unnatural (e.g. in loving my enemies). By the phrase "as myself" it cautions me, however, that in the cases where I am "getting" something, my love may not be as "natural" as I think.

Dominion over the natural order and the power to create a history for themselves was granted Adam and Eve, but two trees were forbidden them, the Tree of Life and the Tree of the Knowledge of Good and Evil. (Actually in the biblical story the Tree of Life is prohibited only after the Fall.) The former is a symbol common to most pagan mythologies and its appearance in Genesis is perhaps a survival from a pagan stage. At any rate, it is the second tree which is the fatal temptation.

> And when the woman saw that the tree was good for food and that it was pleasant to the eyes and a tree to be desired to make one wise, she took of the fruit thereof, and did eat.

It is to be noted that the story does not say that as a natural fruit this tree looked any more tempting than other trees which were permitted. Were it naturally more desirable than others, then God Himself would be the tempter in forbidding it and at the same time creating a natural order with a bias towards disobedience; were it less desirable man would not have been the image of God, but an animal defended from sin by his nature, and the prohibition would have been unnecessary. What is asserted is that man's real temptation, to disobey in order to become wise, was neither hindered nor provoked by his physical nature.

If one feels that the tree of life has no business to be in the garden of Eden at all, it is because it is incompatible with the notion of God as the creator of man. Its proper place is in pagan cosmologies, where the difference between gods and men is that the former are by fate permitted to eat of the tree of life, and the latter are not. If the gods were to be prevented from eating it, they would become mortal men and die; vice versa, if a man could succeed in eating it he would become an immortal god. To wish to eat of the tree of life, therefore, means to wish to become a god along with the other gods, to be related to them as equal to equal, instead of as slave to master. The master may, out of snobbery and jealousy for his superior position, try to prevent the slave from eating of the tree, but if the latter once succeeds in outwitting him there is nothing the former can do about it but accept the new relationship with a good grace.

If God is the creator of all things out of nothing, then the Tree of Life has no *raison d'être*. God does not need it to be God, for He made it, and, forbidden or not, it is impossible for man to eat of it, since a creature cannot become his Creator.

To wish, as Adam and Eve did, to eat of the tree of the knowledge of good and evil, on the other hand, is not a desire for equality or even superiority, but for autonomy. It is a desire to become one's own source of value, to become *as* God while still remaining a man, so that whether God exists or not is unimportant, since now any relationship to Him is unnecessary.

The one thing forbidden man, but which he insisted upon trying to take, was the right to love or not love as he chose. The immediate consequence of his disobedience was not suffering or any imposed punishment—these were to come later—but unhappiness; the relationship of Adam and Eve to God and to each other was not severed, but instantaneously altered from one of love and trust to one of guilt and anxiety.

> And the eyes of them both were opened, and they knew that they were naked; and they sewed fig leaves together, and made themselves aprons;
> And they heard the voice of the Lord God walking in the garden in the cool of the day: and Adam and his wife hid themselves from the presence of the Lord God.
> And the man said: The woman whom thou gavest to be with me, she gave me of the tree, and I did eat.
> And the woman said, The serpent beguiled me, and I did eat.

The sufferings which God predicts will follow are not so much imposed by Him from without, but are self-provoked consequences of man's unhappiness. God does not destroy man or take from him the powers with which He created him. The relation between man and nature may have become one of conflict instead of harmony, but man retains his dominion over the latter. Even as a sinner man is to be personally related to others, to make his history and create his culture. Further, the natural order, including the natural element in man, is to remain what it was in spite of sin. Whether we take the story of God's covenant with Noah in the ninth chapter of Genesis literally as a historic decision by God or figuratively as a historic human insight into God's nature, the meaning is the same: namely, that it is God's will that natural events should occur not arbitrarily but according to intelligible laws. The sun is to shine equally on the just and the unjust, and natural accidents like the fall of the tower at the pool of Siloam are not to be taken as divine moral judgments.

★   ★   ★

One consequence of the Fall was natural religion, i.e. man's own efforts to escape from the state of anxiety into which the Fall had plunged him. Such efforts were bound to be self-frustrated, since they were rooted in a self-contradictory desire to find an Absolute which at the same time should be controllable by man, a desire, in fact, to find the tree of life and eat of it.

Natural religions are of two kinds, polytheistic-magical and monistic-rational. Contradictory as they are in many respects, they have two features in common: to neither is God the creator of the world and to both happiness is identical with pleasure.

In the polytheistic cosmology, nature is the common origin of both gods and men.

> There is one
> race of men, one race of gods; both have breath
> of life from a single mother. But sundered power
> holds us divided, so that the one is nothing, while for the other the
>   brazen sky is established

their sure citadel forever. Yet we have some likeness in great
intelligence or strength to the immortals,
though we know not what the day will bring, what course
after nightfall destiny has written that we must run to the end.

(Pindar, *Nemean* vi)

The existence of nature is necessary to the gods, as they need it for their playground, but their existence is not necessary to nature. Men are similar in essence to the gods, only subject to time and death. There seems no reason why the gods should be concerned with human affairs, but the uncertainties of human life, its unpredictable and inexplicable triumphs and disasters, seem a proof that they do. Human suffering (i.e. the frustration of his desires) seems the result of the withdrawal of the gods' concern or their active antagonism, human pleasure or happiness the result of their favour. The task of human religion is to persuade them to take a favourable interest and dissuade them from hostility, so that man may prosper in his undertakings. If the only alternative man can see is between being destroyed by their disfavour and enduring a certain degree of suffering, he will accept the latter, but in his heart only as a temporary measure. The ultimate goal of religion is the discovery of the infallible magic which will compel the gods to help man to succeed without his having to sacrifice anything in return.

In the monistic cosmology nature is coeternal with God, from whom she derives not her existence but such order as she possesses. The existence of God therefore is necessary to nature, for without him she would be a chaotic welter of meaningless events, but the existence of nature is neither necessary nor of concern to God, who is the perfectly self-sufficient being. Man is capable of getting to know God through the exercise of the divine element in him, his reason. Till he does he is doomed to suffer, because suffering is the product of his incarceration in matter and time. Once he has, he will be immune from suffering. While the polytheistic gods were happy because they and only they could enjoy any particular pleasure they desired when they wanted it, the philosophical God has only one pleasure, the true pleasure of contemplation which is to be called happiness, compared with which all other pleasures are lower or unreal.

The task of human religion is the ascent from ignorance to knowledge of the truth which once known will be as binding on the will as the truths of mathematics.

The polytheistic priest could keep his magic secret from the unqualified masses; the philosopher, on the other hand, is first of all the teacher who shows others at a lower stage the way to the truth, and secondly, to the degree that they cannot or will not learn, the ruler who lays down the principles for every kind of human activity.

In neither kind of natural religion, therefore, is there a conception of the laity and the priesthood as two orders with distinct functions and equal importance. To the polytheistic religion, the priest is a specialised layman whose choice of profession is derived from his natural skill in magic or his inherited membership in a priestly caste, to be consulted by others when and only when they are in need of his special services, i.e. when they wish to be successful in some enterprise, like war or love. In the monistic religion the philosopher is the only complete man; if he be thought of as a priest and the uninstructed as the laity, then ideally there should be no laity and in practice the laity are to be ruled by the priest.

★   ★   ★

Beside and in contradistinction to the development of Natural Religion, there is discernible in history, or so Christians believe, another factor, the Religion of Revelation, i.e. God's movement to redeem the fallen world by revealing His nature to man. This may be called a consequence of the Fall in the sense that had the latter not occurred man would never have lost his vision of the true God, but not in the sense that it was inevitable as natural religion was; the revelation was the free work of God's mercy and love.

A religion of revelation is inseparably bound up with the notion of vocation or calling. While in a natural religion the presence of God is identified with the experience of a sudden access in power or a sudden lucidity of understanding—in a revealed religion it is experienced as a voice which issues a command, "Go get thee up." "Follow me." A command is addressed not to the emotions nor to the understanding, but to the will, and it implies that the person addressed is capable of obedience or disobedience; one does not issue commands to a thing.

The history of Revelation is divided into parts, the history of a nation (the Jews, as set forth in the Old Testament) and the history of a person (our Lord, as set forth in the New). Similarly the conception of divine calling is twofold; there is the calling of the Jewish people by God and the calling of the twelve Apostles by Christ. The relation in fact between the Jewish nation and the Gentiles before the Incarnation is analogous to the relation between the priesthood and the laity after it.

The calling of the Jews and the calling of the Apostles are similar in this respect, that if one asks the question, Why did Jehovah call the Jews rather than any other nation? or, Why did Christ call the Apostles He did call rather than any other individuals He encountered during His ministry? one can give no answer.

In neither case can it be said that those chosen possessed natural endowments which made them exceptional, nor that they were more or less sinful than others; it cannot even be said that God loved them more; it can only be said that He chose them for an exceptional task.

The Jews were called collectively to experience a peculiar revelation of God through their history; they were not to teach or preach, they were not to speculate about the universe or observe the history of others, but to be exclusively absorbed in reflection upon what happened to themselves.

While God permitted—would it be too much to say that He willed?—the Gentiles to use their natural gifts of imagination and reason and power which came from Him to explore to the limit the possibilities of natural religion, so that it should be impossible later to say that Human Culture, the attempt to establish happiness and goodness on earth through art or philosophy or politics, had not failed, but had merely not been carried far enough, He reserved to the Jews His revelation of Himself as the Creator of the world and the Lord of history, so that when in the fullness of time the Word should be made flesh, and be slain for the redemption of man, it should be an act possible both to believe and to believe without misunderstanding.

It was to the Jews that God revealed that in relation to Him man is a free son, not a slave, and that though he must obey God, because in obedience lies his own happiness, yet with both his reason and his emotions he may argue with and protest against God's commands. Even in the presence of his master he is to be honest.

It was to the Jews also that God revealed the essential difference between happiness and pleasure, despair and pain. Happiness consists in a loving and trusting relation to God; accordingly we are to take one thing and one thing only seriously, our eternal duty to be happy, and to that all considerations of pleasure and pain are subordinate. Thou shalt love God and thy neighbour and Thou shalt be happy mean the same thing.

Pleasure and suffering are given states of feeling which have no significance except in relation to happiness. As a consequence of man's fall, the pleasure he finds in loving himself frequently conflicts with the duty to love in which lies his happiness, so that doing his duty involves accepting suffering. On the other hand, suffering and failure are not to be taken in themselves as proofs of punishment for sin; they may equally well be tests of faith. We must accept suffering if and when it comes, not because suffering is a morally superior condition we can pretend that we desire, nor that any pleasure is an illusion we can pretend to despise, but because our duty to be happy is the only matter we have to consider.

★   ★   ★

Just as Jehovah calls the Jews from among the other nations, so Christ calls the Apostles out from other individuals, engaged in lay activities like fishing and tax-collecting. This time, however, their task is to go out among others and preach the coming of the Kingdom of God, and after His death and resurrection to preach the Risen Lord and to administer His sacraments to the faithful.

While the priestly function of the Jewish nation had been exercised not by any specifically religious acts or preaching to the Gentiles, but by their history as a people, the gradual and continuous development among them of the consciousness that God is not to be manipulated by magic nor possessed by reason, but is a Father who loves His children even when they sin, for the Apostles and their successors the history of religion is ended and their function is to be means of grace entrusted to them by Christ, are preserved and transmitted to the end of time. The Incarnation does not put an end to the history of the world but only to the history of religion, and the priest is then in the world yet detached from the historical order as a witness that this is so. Thus, while all lay occupations continue to exhibit historical development both for the individual during his lifetime and from one generation to the next, so that we may continue to speak of the history of art, science, law, etc., or of the development of an artist's work or a scientist's ideas, from the moment that a priest is ordained he ceases to have a history. Every priest is a witness in his time and place to the fact that the events which redeem history have already occurred once and for all. The Gospel he preaches, the sacraments he administers are already there, unchanged by any subsequent historical events.

★   ★   ★

Again, since a priest is only an instrument, in addition to renouncing a history he renounces all personal relations to others. When he preaches the Gospel, it is the Gospel itself, not his skill in preaching it, which has authority; when he administers Holy Communion, it is the Blessed Sacrament that the communicant encounters, not him; when he absolves the penitent in the confessional, it is not a personal act, as when one person forgives another, but God making use of his tongue.

Thus, while of any man practising a lay vocation like medicine or law it is possible to say that he is a good doctor or a bad or a better or a worse lawyer than another lawyer, of a priest it is possible to say only that he is one, i.e. that he has been ordained. Like some mass-produced utensil, any priest is interchangeable with any other. While there may be only one surgeon in the world who can perform the operation which can save my life, the most ignorant country curé can absolve me of a deadly sin.

The argument for a celibate priesthood is not based on any theory that virginity is intrinsically morally superior to marriage, but on the fact that in marriage two individuals have a unique relation to each other and a priest *qua* priest has no relation to others but is only a means to a relation between them and God. Strictly speaking, a priest does not even have neighbours, or one could put it differently and say that whereas the needs which a layman satisfies are temporal needs, so that any individual, Christian or non-Christian, whose needs he is in a position to satisfy is his neighbour, a priest is a neighbour only to Christians. Even if he is a missionary preaching to the heathen he becomes related to them only if and when they recognize the need for the Word of God and the sacraments, which he is the means of satisfying.

If the Apostles were not called by Christ on the basis of exceptional natural gifts, neither were they called because they were better than others. If they ended their lives as saints, that is another matter; they began as Apostles. It must not be forgotten that Judas who betrayed Christ and hanged himself was none the less an Apostle and received the same commission as the others. Sanctity is not a specific calling in the world. It is, no doubt, commanded and offered to us all, laity and priests alike, and refused by all but a very few through lack of faith. After considerable controversy the Early Church wisely established the principle that the efficacy of a priest is independent of his moral character. In judging a layman we make a distinction between his moral character and his ability at his job, but this distinction is never absolute. In relation to any lay activity there are certain traits of character which are relevant and others which are not, e.g. it does not matter very much if a soldier is a heavy drinker, but it matters a great deal if he is a coward; a bank manager may be a jealous man if he likes, but he must not be dishonest. In the case of a priest, on the other hand, no moral failing is more or less relevant to his office than another, so that we must either make the distinction between the man and the office absolute or make the absurd and, considering our own sinfulness, impious demand that no one shall officiate as a priest who is not a saint. The religious authority of the priest is an authority of office only; he is the medium *through* which men receive divine grace: we have no right to demand that in addition he shall have the religious authority of the saint so that we confront God *in* his person.

★   ★   ★

In the case of both lay vocations and the vocation of the priest, the decisive question for the prospective candidate is "Is my belief that this is to become my vocation real or fantastic?"

In the case of lay vocations, this question is comparatively easy to answer, since it depends on the presence or absence of a natural gift and temperament. The famous brain surgeon Dr. Cushing relates how, when an excellent student came to consult him about whether or not he should become a surgeon, he settled the matter in the negative by asking one question: "Do you enjoy the sensation of cutting through flesh with a knife?"

This is right and proper in relation to a lay activity, for there natural ability and pleasure in exercising it go hand in hand, but in the case of a vocation to the priesthood, where it is a matter of being called not by one's gift but by God directly, what human test could ever be devised to prove or disprove it? If God has indeed called a man, he cannot, any more than Abraham or Moses or Jacob or the Apostles, excuse himself on the ground of his incapacity.

A shrewd judge of men may suspect that in such and such a candidate for Holy Orders the vocation is spurious, not real, and have a nine to one chance of being right, but the single chance of being wrong remains. It might be wise practically to discourage candidates from entering the priesthood before they have had some experience in a lay occupation. The one fatal course for the Church to take is to play safe and, using the standards of this world, accept only the "healthy" and the "normal." I have heard, for example, that one Protestant denomination puts all its candidates through a series of psychological tests to eliminate the "maladjusted." One cannot help wondering how St Paul or St Augustine or St Francis would have scored on such a test.

If discouragement and delay seem the only possible human test, this is because the spiritual danger in which the priest always stands is one with which psychology is not equipped to deal.* In the case of the layman there are three factors in the situation, God, his gift, and his ego; in the case of the priest only two, God and his ego. The layman, an author let us say, may forget that his gift comes from God, but in that case he starts to idolize his gift, not himself; when he says "I wrote that" he cannot ever forget that he mans "My gift wrote that." If a priest, on the other hand, forgets God he is left only with his ego, so that when he says "*Ego te absolvo*" he really thinks that he *is* God.

★   ★   ★

Whenever and wherever the Church wields temporal power and exerts a cultural influence the priest discharges lay functions as well as his own. Thus in the Middle Ages the priesthood was responsible for practically all of the things of Caesar but agriculture, commerce, and war; up to the end of the nineteenth century in the country districts of most countries, Catholic and Protestant, the local priest or minister was the one permanent resident with some degree of learning and manners; and in the future as in the past it is probable that theology will continue to be the work of priests, though, strictly speaking, it is, as distinct from dogma, a lay activity, for to say that someone is a good or a bad theologian is quite different from saying that he is orthodox or heretical. But to-day in many countries, among them the U.S., the general spread of education among the laity has considerably changed the whole situation and, provided that those of the laity who profess and call themselves Christians do their duty, the change can be of advantage to the mission of the Church. Catholicism and Protestantism have shown the two opposite kinds of temptation which a mixed calling runs. In Catholicism, where the uniqueness of the priestly vocation has been safeguarded, the danger has been an improper extension of the dogmatic principle to lay affairs. When a man acts or judges as a layman, it is his act, the exercise of his natural gifts of body and mind which are limited and the movement of his will which, but for grace, is corrupt: everything he does and says is fallible and open to discussion and the highest praise we can give him is that he is doing his best; but the acts of

---

* In doubtful cases, tossing a coin would seem to be the only procedure for which there is apostolic authority. See Acts i, 23–26.

a priest are not his but God's and, therefore, to a Christian, infallible. Whenever a priest has also to function as a layman, therefore, he is tempted to claim for his lay judgment the infallibility which belongs to his priestly acts alone. In Protestantism, on the other hand, it is the layman's engagement in the historical order which has improperly extended itself into the historically detached or completed function of the priest and the Christian faith has been perverted into an ideology conforming to the spirit of the times.

★　★　★

At this point, perhaps, we should mention a third activity, the prophetic, because it belongs neither to the laity nor to the priesthood. A prophet is any individual who at one moment or from time to time is inspired by the Holy Spirit to speak. While the priest is called by God and the layman by his gift, the prophet is not called at all, for his ego is, as it were, by-passed; it is meaningless for a man to say "I am a prophet"; it is only the hearers who can recognize the Holy Spirit speaking through him and say "At this moment he is a prophet."

> Behold, are not all these which speak Galilaeans? And how hear we every man in our own tongue, wherein we were born . . . them speak the wonderful works of God.

Whenever a man speaks and the effect on his hearers is to wake them to repentance or to the praise of God, that man is a prophet. What he consciously thinks he is doing is irrelevant. He may think he is talking atheism, but if the Christian ear hears the tongue of God saying "Thus saith the Lord," he is a prophet.

The laity, then, inherit the role of the Gentiles, i.e. the responsibility for the natural and historical order. While it may be said that there would never have been a chosen people or a priesthood but for the Fall, the task entrusted to the laity is that entrusted to Adam in the garden of Eden. It is their task by virtue of the nature with which God endowed man at his creation and of which, despite the Fall and the certainty that, without divine grace, he would use it perversely, God did not deprive him. The difference between the Gentiles and the laity is defined by Christ in the famous words: "Render unto Caesar the things which are Caesar's and unto God the things that are God's." Hitherto the Gentiles had thought of their cultural task as being also a religious task. Henceforth culture and religion were to be seen as distinct, since religion as a natural quest for God by man was finished. The text has often been quoted and rightly against the idolatrous pretensions of the state. The Christian layman should also remember that it asserts that there is no such thing as a Christian politics, or a Christian art, or a Christian science, any more than there is a Christian diet. There is only politics, or art, or science, which are natural activities concerned with the natural and historical man.

The standards of efficacy, beauty and truth, by which they are measured, are valid irrespective of faith, but the Christian layman is conscious of exercising his natural gifts in the presence of God.

* * *

It may be said of the vocation of the priesthood that it is intrinsically serious; of all lay vocations it may be said that they are in themselves frivolous; for what a layman should do is answerable in terms of his individual gifts and his particular historical situation. Since these conditions are different for every individual, since gifts are greater or less, the taking seriously of a lay vocation in itself would mean that God loved some more than others. The belief that God is love involves the conclusion that what is serious must be something which is the same in all men, namely their free-will. What is serious for the layman is not his occupation, to which, if it be the right occupation for him, natural interest will make him devote himself, but the intention of his will, which is equally difficult for all men, gifted or ungifted, to love God and his neighbour as himself. "Though I speak with the tongues of men and of angels and have not charity, I am become as a sounding brass." Others hear the tongues of men and angels and profit from it, but as far as I am concerned my action is a tinkling cymbal, valueless before God. Vice versa, I may fail completely at what I undertake, and even by my failure do my neighbours harm, but if I have honestly intended good, God will judge my intention, not the result.

The Christian layman is a member of two communities: the Church, which includes the souls of all the faithful departed, living, and to be born, and the historical community of his neighbours. The pattern of relationships that this involves for him, and the problems involved, vary, of course, with his time and place, and it is possible to speak only of what one knows by direct experience.

For example, one can say of the layman in the U.S. to-day:

(1) That it is probable that within that sphere of the temporal where his work lies he can speak with some authority, a greater authority, probably, than that of the priest whose church he attends.

(2) Most of his neighbours are probably not professing Christians, or, if they are, belong to some other denomination.

The particular problem he faces to-day, therefore, is the lack of overlap between the two communities, and his minority position in the second.

His constant association with non-Christian neighbours, who, if he is honest, he is bound to admit are often more gifted and nicer than he, is a temptation, if he is one kind of man, to lose interest in the Christian faith and adopt, almost unconsciously, non-Christian beliefs. If he is another kind of man, the temptation is to become conceited about his minority position and think of himself as one of the superior élite. Because of these dangers there has probably never been a time when it was more necessary for the layman to be theologically educated, to know what the dogmas of the Church are, and how they relate to his professional life.

Further, the scandal of Church disunity, the tragedy that the body of Christ is broken in pieces, is becoming more and more a scandal to the laity. If ecumenicity is ever to be achieved, it will have to start from the intention of the laity that it shall, because it is the laity, not the clergy, who meet those of other Christian communions as neighbours. Mutual love and sympathy have to precede theological agreement; otherwise what are cultural misunderstandings and hostilities will defeat the possibility of agreement before discussion begins.

★   ★   ★

When the Christian layman prays "Thy Kingdom come, Thy will be done on earth as it is in heaven" he implies that the coming of the Kingdom is to be God's decision, not his. He is not to forget, first, that no man can choose when and where he is born and, secondly, that the act of faith is a free act. The Christian creed begins in the first person singular. It is every man's natural right as God made him to refuse grace and be damned. The ultimate goal of achievement in the historical order which the layman can imagine is not a world in which all men are necessarily Christians and it is impossible to sin—even in Heaven some angels fell—but a world in which faith in Christ or the rejection of Christ, the choice of loving or not loving, was for every individual a free act of conscious choice for which he would be and know himself to be responsible.

A Christian is at once commanded to accept his creatureliness, both natural and historical, not to attempt to escape into a fantastic world untrammelled by the realities of space and time, and forbidden to make an idol of nature or history. It might be said that for him only two temporal categories are significant, the present instant and eternity. The present instant is, of course, the result of the past; the command to accept this result exactly as it is without bowdlerization would be impossible but for the promise that our sins can be forgiven, for the burden of guilt for one's own sins and of resentment for the sins of others which have made the present instant what it is would be intolerable.

Similarly, the present instant is creating the future, and it is impossible to act now without some faith which makes action meaningful so that the actor must put his faith either in an idol, his reason, his power, the wave of the future, etc., or in the living Christ.

Apart from the self-love which either fears to lose by change or hopes to gain, the besetting temptations for the Christian layman in relation to the evils of the historical order with which it is his duty to deal are laziness and impatience.

Laziness acknowledges the relation of the present to the past but ignores its relation to the future; impatience acknowledges its relation to the future but ignores its relation to the past; neither the lazy nor the impatient man, that is, accepts the present instant in its full reality and so cannot love his neighbour completely.

In our age it is impatience, perhaps, which is the more characteristic temptation, partly because the historical situation is rather desperate, but mainly because for us the problem of faith is not of lapsing into a childish magical conception of God but of despair, of believing that God has abandoned us. "Trust in God and take short view," wrote Sidney Smith. In mid-Victorian England this may have had too Whiggish a ring to be sound advice, but as a motto for the laity in 1950 I cannot imagine a better one nor a more terrifying.

Theology, November and December 1950

A That There Sort of Writer

Byron: A Self-Portrait, Letters and Diaries, 1798 to 1824.
Edited by Peter Quennell. Charles Scribner's Sons. 2 vols. $10.

I dream that I am twenty years old and have just had a slim volume of poems published by a printer in Basingstoke. Harold Nicolson is taking me to Holland House, a Yale-Library-like building on the Grand Canal where Lady Melbourne is to introduce me to the great poet. We are just entering the drawing-room when, to my horror, Wordsworth appears, greets me effusively, and thrusts an inscribed copy of *Ecclesiastical Sonnets* into my unwilling hands. Before I can drop them behind a rubber plant, Lady Melbourne, who looks like Marianne Moore, is leading me by the arm up to my idol; she says something to him I cannot catch, and then I hear that fruity *milord anglais* voice saying: "Who? Auden? Is he a bore?"

This word, which seems to me one of the chief clues to Byron's work and life, is of great cultural interest for, so far as I know, the noun does not exist in other languages and in American usage, again so far as my limited experience goes, to say "X is a bore" is equivalent to saying "X bores me." But in England the noun stands for an objective judgment, as I hope the following examples will show.

> Seldom boring (to me) but bores: Henry James, Beethoven's last quartets, Cézanne.
> Sometimes boring (to me) but not bores: Shakespeare, The Art of the Fugue, Degas.
> Not boring (to me) and not bores: Pope, Verdi, Giorgione.
> Boring (to me) and bores: Shelley, Brahms, Rembrandt.

Classes of bores (the living tactfully omitted): All German writers except
Heine, all American writers except Scott Fitzgerald.
The absolutely boring but absolutely not a bore: the time of day.
The absolutely unboring but absolute bore: God.

Anyone who wishes to discover why so many Englishmen attach so much importance to this term, will find no better source than Byron's letters and diaries. The Bore-hater he will discover there is at once a sensitive extrovert, a man with an acute sense of the reality of time, and a frightened melancholic.

Sensitive extroverts make the best letter-writers because they have a keen sense of the person to whom they are writing and of the occasion: introverts are either frightened by the other and take refuge in stilted commonplaces or ignore his or her existence and talk into the bathroom mirror. "My correspondence since I was sixteen," wrote Byron, "has not been of a nature to allow of any trust except to lock and key," but it was only pious indignation he had to fear, not derision; the introvert is not always so fortunate—think of the so kickable whine of Poe's correspondence or the awful whiff, compounded of incense and stale underwear, emitted by Rilke's.

Byron is often frank but never indecently exposed; even in his diary he never bares his breast to show his spots and every letter he ever wrote is a social act, a performance in a particular situation, so that the manner as well as the matter varies with each correspondent. When he is having a row with his father-in-law, the style is high eighteenth-century, antithetical, rotund.

I will not, however, detain you longer than I can help, and as it is of some importance to your family, as well as to mine, and a step which cannot be recalled when taken, you will not attribute my pause to any wish to inflict farther pain on you or yours—although there are parts of your letter which, I must be permitted to say, arrogate a right which you do not possess; for the present at least, your daughter is my wife; she is the mother of my child, and till I have her express sanction of your proceedings, I shall take leave to doubt the propriety of your interference.

To his wife at the same time, the style is similar but the rhythm and pace are different; the Judge has changed into the Counsel for the Defense.

It is now a fortnight, which has been passed in suspense, in humiliation, in obloquy, exposed to the most black and blighting calumnies of every kind, without even the power of contradicting conjecture and vulgar assertion as to the accusations, because I am denied the knowledge of all, or any, particulars from the only quarter that can afford them. In the meantime I hope your ears are gratified by the general rumours. I have invited your return; it has been refused. I have requested to know with what I am charged; it is refused. Is this mercy or justice? We shall see.

So, too, in his informal letters to his intimates, it would usually be possible to guess the correspondent if the name were missing.

> So Scrope is gone—down-diddled—as Doug K writes it, the said Doug being like the man who, when he lost a friend, went to the Saint James' Coffee House and took a new one; we could have better spared not only a "better man", but "the best of men." Gone to Bruges where he will get tipsy with Dutch beer and shoot himself the first foggy morning.
>
> (To Hobhouse)

> Have you seen ——'s book of poesy? and, if you have seen it, are you not delighted with it? And have you—I really cannot go on: there is a pair of great black eyes looking over my shoulder, like the angel leaning over St Matthew's, in the old frontispieces to the Evangelists,—so that I must turn and answer them instead of you.
>
> (To Moore)

> I have been in some danger on the lake (near Meillerie), but nothing to speak of; and, as to all these "mistresses," Lord help me—I have had but one. Now don't scold; but what could I do?—a foolish girl, in spite of all I could say or do, would come after me, or rather went before—for I found her here—and I have had all the plague possible to persuade her to go back again; but at last she went. Now, dearest, I do most truly tell thee, that I could not help this, that I did all I could to prevent it, and have at last put an end to it.
>
> (To Augusta)

> P.S.—There is a certain O—I feel it in the note itself—and very much yes—Greet both the Gambas—I value their good graces. That blessed villa is being got ready—as quickly as possible on account of the two little girls—Allegra—and *you*.
>
> (To Teresa)

This sureness of touch takes training as well as a natural gift. The extrovert writer only develops through wide social experience, as contrasted with the introvert writer who draws on a few decisive experiences. When Byron asserts that "half of these Scotch and lake troubadours are spoilt by living in little circles and petty societies," he is assuming, mistakenly, that they were the same kind of writer as himself. For Byron, High life, Low life, and solitude— he spent more of the day alone than one would have expected—were essential and he was singularly fortunate in getting them all. To be elected a member of Alfred's Club, acquainted from the age of nineteen with the "keeping" side of town, to go on a Grand Tour to the Near East and return with a phial of Attic hemlock and four tortoises, to be a drawing-room lion in England and a Cavalier Sirvente in Italy, to mediate a duel over a whore between a clergyman and a guardsman, to have affairs with termagant peasant girls and hysterical society women, to be left by one's wife, to have an illegitimate daughter, to buy arms for revolutionaries, to learn Armenian, what better education could a writer of his gifts have had, and he knew it.

> As to "Don Juan," confess, confess—you dog and be candid—that it is the sublime of *that there* sort of writing—it may be bawdy but is it not good English? It may be profligate but is it not *life*, is it not *the thing*? Could any man have written it who has not lived in the world?—and fooled in a post-chaise?—in a hackney coach? in a gondola?—in a vis-à-vis?—on a table?—and under it?

Again, like all good extrovert writers, Byron accepts the conventions of the world he finds himself in; he may be wicked but he is never cranky. His daughter was going to be educated in a convent; he wasn't going to have her brought up by the Shelleys "to perish of starvation, and green fruit, or be taught to believe that there is no Deity." The crank always ignores the fact that the world exists in time, not eternity, and few writers have been as conscious as Byron of natural time; of historical time, the time created by unique experiences, he was less aware and for that one must go to Dante or Wordsworth. Though he had 20/20 vision, Byron's eyes were like those of some animal which can only see objects when they move; his visual descriptions of scenery or architecture are not particularly vivid but in descriptions of things in motion his only rivals are Shakespeare and Homer, and his gift for observing the *passage* of thought and feeling matches his eyes.

> Hear the carriage—order pistols and great coat as usual—necessary articles. Weather cold—carriage open, and inhabitants somewhat savage—rather treacherous, and highly inflamed by politics. Fine fellows, though—good materials for a nation. Out of chaos God made a world, and out of high passions comes a people.
>
> Clock strikes—going out to make love. Somewhat perilous, but not disagreeable. Memorandum—a new screen put up to-day. It is rather antique, but do with a little repair.

The juxtaposition of ideas in the last paragraph is characteristic. Byron never lets the reader forget how time and circumstance limit his ideal intentions, how the most abstruse cogitations are interrupted by a pretty face, the most ardent passion transformed into a need for lunch, and that in times of Revolution one's thoughts may dwell less on the glorious cause of liberty than on the problem of how to get some more of Waite's red tooth powder. That is why the Brooks-Warren kind of critical approach will never work with Byron's poetry. Stop on a word or a line and the poetry vanishes—the feeling seems superficial or even false, the rhyme forced, the grammar all over the place—but start the reading up again and the conviction of watching the real thing instantaneously returns, a conviction which many writers of profounder insight fail to inspire, for, though movement is not the only or even the fundamental characteristic of life, it is an essential one.

Perhaps all writers with this gift have, like Byron, been manic-depressives. He suffered from bad dreams, he felt blue when he woke up, he had a sissy stomach which could not tolerate bacon and eggs, alcohol made him sullen and savage. Violent exercise, swimming, riding, boxing, helped a bit; violent passions and personal crises helped a lot so that all the women who mattered in his life were "daggery and divorcy." The essential thing to avoid was introspective reflection which might uncover something terrible and send him mad; hence all introspective writers were his deadly enemies, and he could smell one of them a mile off without having to read him. The savagery of his attacks on Wordsworth, that "Jacob Behmen," and Keats, "viciously soliciting his own ideas into a state which is neither poetry nor any thing else but a Bedlam vision produced by raw pork and opium," are not to be taken as literary criticism but as the reflex of panic at the suggestion of *stopping* to think. One would not have expected it, but Byron was shocked by Burns' pornographic poems. "It is by veiling these ideas, by forgetting them altogether, or, at least, never naming them hardly to one's self, that we alone can prevent them from disgusting."

An extrovert, then, but nevertheless, a romantic not an augustan, for unlike his beloved Pope, the hero of whose poetry is a universal abstract, the Man of Reason and Good Taste, and like his introverted contemporaries, the hero of Byron's poetry is his own personal consciousness. If *Don Juan* had a sub-title it might well be *What Goes On in a Poet's Mind*.

In conclusion a word about this edition. It contains fifty-six new letters, all interesting, one a letter to Coleridge admiring the "Ancient Mariner" and "Cristabel," and thirty-six restored passages in old ones. A few indecencies are still omitted and indicated by asterisks. I must admit that I find this modern method of reconciling the reticence of propriety with the honesty of scholarship, too comic, e.g.

> * called to-day in great despair about his mistress, who has taken a freak of *

> * I have heard, also, many other things of our acquaintances, which I did not know; amongst others, that *

I can only presume that the frontispiece to Volume Two, a drawing by Richard Westwall in which the poet looks like the Principal Boy in a Christmas Pantomime, has been inserted as a camp, for anything less like the figure disclosed by the text it would be impossible to conceive. Mr Quennell has performed his editorial duties like a gentleman, accurately, adequately and unobtrusively, and a big bouquet must be offered to Scribners for producing—not, thank God, a fine edition—but as handsome a real book as I have seen in a long time. Which reminds me that I have a brickbat—a little one— to throw at Random House for their Modern Library *Don Juan*. My enthusiasm in acquiring at long last a single-column edition with which I could travel has subsequently been a little dampened by the discovery that it was never proofread.

Unpublished; written April 1950 for *The New Yorker*

Introduction to *Selected Prose and Poetry* *of Edgar Allan Poe*

What every author hopes to receive from posterity—a hope usually disappointed—is justice. Next to oblivion, the two fates which he most fears are becoming the name attached to two or three famous pieces while the rest of his work is unread and becoming the idol of a small circle which reads every word he wrote with the same uncritical reverence. The first fate is unjust because, even if the pieces known are indeed his best work, the reader has not earned the right to say so; the second fate is embarrassing and ridiculous, for no author believes he is that good.

Poe's shade must be more disappointed than most. Certain pieces—how he must hate these old war horses—are probably more familiar to non-Americans than are any pieces by any other American author. I myself cannot remember hearing any poetry before hearing "The Raven" and "The Bells"; and *The Pit and the Pendulum* was one of the first short stories I ever read. At the same time, the known works of no other author of comparable rank and productivity are so few and so invariably the same. In preparing to make this selection, for example, I asked a number of persons whom I knew to be widely read, but not specialists in American letters, if they had read *Gordon Pym* and *Eureka*, which seem to me to rank among Poe's most important works; not one of them had. On the other hand, I was informed by everyone that to omit *The Cask of Amontillado*, which for my taste is an inferior story, would be commercial suicide. Poor Poe! At first so forgotten that his grave went without a tombstone twenty-six years—when one was finally erected the only American author to attend the ceremony was Whitman; and today in danger of becoming the life study of a few professors. The professors are, of course, very necessary, for it is through their devoted labors that Poe may finally reach the kind of reader every author hopes for, who will read him all, good-humoredly willing to wade through much which is dull or inferior for the delight of discovering something new and admirable.

The Tales

Varied in subject, treatment, style as Poe's stories are, they have one negative characteristic in common. There is no place in any of them for the human
individual as he actually exists in space and time, that is, as simultaneously a
natural creature subject in his feelings to the influences and limitations of the
natural order, and an historical person, creating novelty and relations by his
free choice and modified in unforeseen ways by the choices of others.

Poe's major stories fall roughly into two groups. The first group is concerned with states of willful being, the destructive passion of the lonely ego
to merge with the ego of another (*Ligeia*), the passion of the conscious ego
to be objective, to discover by pure reason the true relationships which sensory appearances and emotions would conceal (*The Purloined Letter*), self-
destructive states in which the ego and the self are passionately hostile (*The
Imp of the Perverse*), even the state of chimerical passion, that is, the passionate unrest of a self that lacks all passion (*The Man of the Crowd*). The horror
tales and the tales of ratiocination belong together, for the heroes of both
exist as unitary states—Roderick Usher reasons as little as Auguste Dupin
feels. Personages who are the embodiment of such states cannot, of course,
change or vary in intensity either through changes in themselves or their environment. The problem in writing stories of this kind is to prevent the reader
from ever being reminded of historical existence, for, if he once thinks of real
people whose passions are interrupted by a need for lunch or whose beauty
can be temporarily and mildly impaired by the common cold, the intensity
and timelessness become immediately comic. Poe is sometimes attacked for
the operatic quality of the prose and *décor* in his tales, but they are essential
to preserving the illusion. His heroes cannot exist except operatically. Take,
for example, the following sentence from *William Wilson*:

> Let it suffice, that among spendthrifts I out-heroded Herod, and that,
> giving name to a multitude of novel follies, I added no brief appendix
> to the long catalogue of vices then usual in the most dissolute university
> of Europe.

In isolation, as a prose sentence, it is terrible, vague, verbose, the sense at the
mercy of a conventional rhetorical rhythm. But dramatically, how right; how
well it reveals the William Wilson who narrates the story in his real colors, as
the fantastic self who hates and refuses contact with reality. Some of Poe's successors in stories about states of being, D. H. Lawrence for example, have
tried to be realistic with fatal results.

In the second group, which includes such tales as *A Descent into the Mael-
strom* and *Gordon Pym*, the relation of will to environment is reversed. While
in the first group everything that happens is the consequence of a volition
upon the freedom of which there are no natural limits, in these stories of
pure adventure the hero is as purely passive as the I in dreams; nothing that

happens is the result of his personal choice, everything happens *to* him. What the subject feels—interest, excitement, terror—are caused by events over which he has no control whatsoever. The first kind of hero has no history because he refuses to change with time; this kind has none because he cannot change, he can only experience.

The problem for the writer of adventure stories is to invent a succession of events which are both interesting and varied and to make the order of succession plausible. To secure variety without sacrificing coherence or vice versa is more difficult than it looks, and *Gordon Pym*, one of the finest adventure stories ever written, is an object lesson in the art. Every kind of adventure occurs—adventures of natural origin like shipwreck; adventures like mutiny, caused by familiar human beings, or, like the adventures on the island, by strange natives; and, finally, supernatural nightmare events—yet each leads credibly into the next. While in the stories of passionate states a certain vagueness of description is essential to the illusion, in the adventure story credibility is secured by the minutest details, figures, diagrams, and various other devices, as in Poe's description of the mysterious ravines.

> The total length of this chasm, commencing at the opening *a* and proceeding round the corner *b* to the extremity *d*, is five hundred and fifty yards.

Both these types of Poe story have had an extraordinary influence. His portraits of abnormal or self-destructive states contributed much to Dostoevski, his ratiocinating hero is the ancestor of Sherlock Holmes and his many successors, his tales of the future lead to H. G. Wells, his adventure stories to Jules Verne and Stevenson. It is not without interest that the development of such fiction in which the historical individual is missing should have coincided with the development of history as a science, with its own laws, and the appearance of the great nineteenth-century historians; further, that both these developments should accompany the industrialization and urbanization of social life in which the individual seems more and more the creation of historical forces while he himself feels less and less capable of directing his life by any historical choice of his own.

Poe's minor fiction also falls into two groups. The first is composed, not of narratives, but physical descriptions of Eden, of the Great Good Place *The Domain of Arnheim*. Such descriptions, whoever they may be written by, are bound to be more interesting as revelations of their authors than in themselves, for no one can imagine the ideal place, the ideal home, except in terms of his private fantasies and the good taste of his day. In Poe's case, in particular, his notions of the stylish and luxurious, if they are not to seem slightly vulgar and comic, must be read in the light of his history and the America of the first half of the nineteenth century. And, lastly there is the group of humorous-satiric pieces unrepresented in this selection. Though

Poe is not so funny in them as in some of his criticism, at least one story, *A Predicament*, is of interest. A parody of the kind of popular horror story appearing in *Blackwood's*, it is, in a sense, a parody of Poe's serious work in this vein; and it actually uses the same notion of the swinging descending knife which he was later to employ in *The Pit and the Pendulum*.

The Poems

Poe's best poems are not his most typical or original. "To Helen," which could have been written by Landor, and "The City in the Sea," which could have been written by Hood, are more successfully realized than a poem like "Ulalume," which could have been written by none but Poe.

His difficulty as a poet was that he was interested in too many poetic problems and experiments at once for the time he had to give to them. To make the result conform to the intention—and the more experimental the intention, the more this is true—a writer has to keep his hand in by continual practice. The prose writer who must earn his living has this advantage, that even the purest hack work is practice in his craft; for the penniless poet there is no corresponding exercise. Without the leisure to write and rewrite he cannot develop to his full stature. When we find fault with Poe's poems we must never forget his own sad preface to them.

> In defence of my own taste, it is incumbent upon me to say that I think nothing in this volume of much value to the public, or very creditable to myself. Events not to be controlled have prevented me from making, at any time, any serious effort in what, under happier circumstances, would have been the field of my choice.

For faulty they must be admitted to be. The trouble with "The Raven," for example, is that the thematic interest and the prosodic interest, both of which are considerable, do not combine and are even often at odds.

In *The Philosophy of Composition* Poe discusses his difficulties in preventing the poem from becoming absurd and artificial. The artificiality of the lover asking the proper series of questions to which the refrain would be appropriate could be solved by making him a self-torturer. The difficulty of the speaker of the refrain, however, remained insoluble until the poet hit on the notion of something nonhuman. But the effect could still be ruined unless the narration of the story, as distinct from the questions and answers, flowed naturally; and the meter Poe chose, with its frequent feminine rhymes, so rare in English, works against this and at times defeats him.

> Not the least obeisance made he; not a minute stopped or stayed he;
> But with mien of lord or lady, perched above my chamber door.

Here it is the meter alone and nothing in the speaker or the situation which is responsible for the redundant alternatives of "stopped or stayed he" and "lord or lady."

Similarly, "Ulalume" is an interesting experiment in diction but only an experiment, for the poem is about something which never quite gets said because the sense is sacrificed to the vowel sounds. It is an accident if the sound of a place name corresponds to the emotion the place invokes, and the accidental is a comic quality. Edward Lear, the only poet, apparently, to be directly influenced by Poe, succeeds with such names as "The Hills of the Chankly Bore" because he is frankly writing "nonsense" poetry, but "Ulalume" has a serious subject and the comic is out of place. "The Bells," though much less interesting a conception than "Ulalume," is more successful because the subject is nothing but an excuse for onomatopoeic effects.

There remains, however, *Eureka*. The man who had flatly asserted that no poem should much exceed a hundred lines in length—"that music (in its modifications of rhythm and rhyme) is of so vast a moment to Poesy as never to be neglected by him who is truly poetical," that neither Truth, the satisfaction of the Intellect, nor Passion, the excitement of the Heart, are the province of Poetry but only Beauty, and that the most poetical topic in the world is the death of a beautiful woman—this man produces at the end of his life a work which he insists is a poem and commends to posterity as his crowning achievement, though it violates every article in his critical creed. It is many pages in length, it is written in prose, it handles scientific ideas in the truth of which the poet is passionately convinced, and the general subject is the origin and destiny of the universe.

Outside France the poem has been neglected, but I do not think Poe was wrong in the importance he attached to it. In the first place, it was a very daring and original notion to take the oldest of the poetic themes—older even than the story of the epic hero—namely, cosmology, the story of how things came to exist as they do, and treat it in a completely contemporary way, to do in English in the nineteenth century what Hesiod and Lucretius had done in Greek and Latin centuries before. Secondly, it is full of remarkable intuitive guesses that subsequent scientific discoveries have confirmed. As Paul Valéry says:

> It would not be exaggerating its importance to recognise, in his theory of consistency, a fairly definite attempt to describe the universe by its *intrinsic properties*. The following proposition can be found toward the end of *Eureka*: "Each law of nature depends at all points on all the other laws." This might easily be considered, if not as a formula, at least as the expression of a tendency toward generalized relativity.
>
> That its tendency approaches recent conceptions becomes evident when one discovers, in the poem under discussion, an affirmation of the *symmetrical* and reciprocal relationship of matter, time, space, gravity, and light.

Lastly, it combines in one work nearly all of Poe's characteristic obsessions: the passion for merging in union with the one which is at the root of tales like *Ligeia,* the passion for logic which dominates the detective and crypto-graphic studies, the passion for a final explanation and reconciliation which informs the melancholy of much of his verse—all are brought together in this poem of which the prose is as lucid, as untheatrical, as the best of his critical prose.

The Critical Writings

Poe's critical work, like that of any significant critic, must be considered in the literary content which provoked it. No critic, however pontifical his tone, is really attempting to lay down eternal truths about art; he is always polemical, fighting a battle against the characteristic misconceptions, stupidities, and weaknesses of his contemporaries. He is always having, on the one hand, to defend tradition against the amateur who is ignorant of it and the crank who thinks it should be scrapped so that real art may begin anew with him and, on the other, to assert the real novelty of the present and to demonstrate, against the academic who imagines that carrying on the tradition means imitation, what modern tasks and achievements are truly analogues to those of the past.

Poe's condemnation of the long poem and of the didactic or true poem is essentially a demand that the poets of his time be themselves and admit that epic themes and intellectual or moral ideas did not in fact excite their poetic faculties and that what really interested them were emotions of melancholy, nostalgia, puzzled yearning, and the like that could find their proper expression in neither epic nor epigram but in lyrics of moderate length. Poe was forced to attack all long poems on principle, to be unfair, for example, to *Paradise Lost* or *An Essay on Criticism,* in order to shake the preconceived notions of poets and public that to be important a poet must write long poems and give bardic advice.

His rejection of passion is really a variation of Wordsworth's observation that, to be capable of embodiment in a poem, emotion must be recollected in tranquility; immediate passion is too obsessive, too attached to the self. Poe's attack is further directed against the popular and amateur notion of poetic inspiration which gives the poet himself no work to do, a reminder that the most inspired poem is also a contraption, a made thing.

> We do not hesitate to say that a man highly endowed with the powers of Causality—that is to say a man of metaphysical acumen—will, even with a very deficient share of Ideality, compose a finer poem than one who without such metaphysical acumen, shall be gifted, in the most extraordinary degree, with the faculty of Ideality. For a poem is not the Poetic faculty, but the *means* of exciting it in mankind.

Through its influence on the French, Poe's general aesthetic is well known. The bulk of his critical writing, and perhaps that which was of the greatest service, is concerned with poetic technique and practical criticism of details. No one in his time put so much energy and insight into trying to make his contemporary poets take their craft seriously, know what they were doing prosodically, and avoid the faults of slovenly diction and inappropriate imagery that can be avoided by vigilance and hard work.

If Poe never developed to his potential full stature as a critic, this was entirely his misfortune, not his fault. Much of his best criticism will never be read widely because it lies buried in reviews of totally uninteresting authors. If he sometimes overpraised the second-rate like Mrs Osgood or wasted time and energy in demolishing nonentities like Mr English, such are inevitable consequences when a critical mind, equipped by nature for digesting the toughest of foods, is condemned by circumstances to feed on literary gruel. The first-rate critic needs critical issues of the first importance, and these were denied him. Think of the subjects that Baudelaire was granted—Delacroix, Constantin Guys, Wagner—and then of the kind of books Poe was assigned to review:

> *Mephistopheles in England, or the Confessions of a Prime Minister*
> *The Christian Florist*
> *Noble Deeds of Women*
> *Ups and Downs in the Life of a Distressed Gentleman*
> *The History of Texas*
> *Sacred Philosophy of the Seasons*
> *Sketches of Conspicuous Living Characters in France*
> *Dashes at Life with a Free Pencil*
> *Alice Day; A Romance in Rhyme*
> *Wakondah; The Master of Life*
> *Poetical Remains of the Late Lucretia Maria Davidson*

One is astounded that he managed to remain a rational critic at all, let alone such a good one.

The Man

If the Muses could lobby for their interest, all biographical research into the lives of artists would probably be prohibited by law, and historians of the individual would have to confine themselves to those who act but do not make—generals, criminals, eccentrics, courtesans, and the like, about whom information is not only more interesting but less misleading. Good artists— the artist *manqué* is another matter—never make satisfactory heroes for novelists, because their life stories, even when interesting in themselves, are peripheral and less significant than their productions.

As a person, for example, Poe is a much less interesting figure than is Griswold. Since Professor Quinn published side by side the original versions of Poe's letters and Griswold's doctored versions, one is left panting with curiosity to know more about the latter. That one man should dislike another and speak maliciously of him after his death would be natural enough, but to take so much trouble, to blacken a reputation so subtly, presupposes a sustained hatred which is always fascinating because the capacity for sustained emotion of any kind is rare, and, in this instance, particularly so since no reasonable cause for it has yet been found.

In his personal reputation, as in so much else, Poe has been singularly unfortunate. Before the true facts were known, he was dismissed by respectable men of letters as a dissolute rake and hailed by the antirespectable as a romantically doomed figure, the Flying Dutchman of Whitman's dream.

> In a dream I once had, I saw a vessel on the sea, at midnight in a storm . . . flying uncontrolled with torn sails and broken spars through the wild sleet and winds and waves of the night. On the deck was a slender, slight, beautiful figure, a dim man, apparently enjoying all the terror, the murk, and the dislocation of which he was the centre and the victim.

Today this portrait has been shown to be false, but the moral climate has changed, and Poe would be more respected if it had been true. Had he been a really bad lot like Villon or Marlowe or Verlaine, someone who drank like a fish and was guilty of spectacular crimes and vices, we should rather admire him; but it turns out that he was only the kind of fellow whom one hesitates to invite to a party because after two drinks he is apt to become tiresome, an unmanly sort of man whose love-life seems to have been largely confined to crying in laps and playing house, that his weaknesses were of that unromantic kind for which our age has least tolerance, perhaps because they are typical of ourselves.

If our present conception of Poe as a person is correct, however, it makes Poe the artist a much odder figure. Nobody has a good word to say for his foster father, John Allan, who certainly does not seem to have been a very attractive gentleman; but if we imagine ourselves in his place in the year 1831, what sort of view would we have taken of Poe's future?

Remembering his behavior at the university, his pointless enlistment in the army, his behavior at West Point, his behavior to ourselves, would he not have seemed to us an obvious case of a certain kind of neurotic with which we are quite familiar—the talented youngster who never comes to anything because he will not or cannot work, whose masterpieces never get beyond the third page, who loses job after job because he cannot get to work on time or meet a deadline? We might find psychological excuses for him in his heredity and early childhood—the incompetent, irresponsible father, the death of his mother when he was two—but our prognosis for his future not only as a man but also as a writer would hardly have been sanguine. At the very best we might have hoped that in the course of a lifetime he would produce one or two exquisitely polished lyrics.

But what in fact did happen? While remaining in his personal life just as difficult and self-destructive as we foresaw, he quickly became a very hard-working and conscientious professional writer. None of his colleagues on magazines seems to have had any professional difficulty with him. Indeed, when one compares the quality of most of the books he had to review with the quality of his reviews, one is inclined to wish that, for the sake of his own work, he had been less conscientious. The defects we find in his work are so often just the defects we should have least expected—the errors of a professional who is overtaxed and working against the clock.

As to his private life and personality, had it been more romantically wicked, his work would not have the importance it has as being, in some senses, the first modern work. He was one of the first to suffer *consciously* the impact of the destruction of the traditional community and its values, and he paid the heaviest price for this consciousness. As D. H. Lawrence says in an essay conspicuous for its insights:

> Poe had a pretty bitter doom. Doomed to seethe down his soul in a great continuous convulsion of disintegration, and doomed to register the process. And then doomed to be abused for it, when he had performed some of the bitterest tasks of human experience, that can be asked of a man. Necessary tasks too. For the human soul must suffer its own disintegration, consciously, if ever it is to survive.

To which one might add: "Abused?" No, a worse doom than that. Doomed to be used in school textbooks as a bait to interest the young in good literature, to be a respectable rival to the pulps.

Still, he has had some rewards. Not many authors have been invoked as intercessors with God in an hour of need, as Poe was named by Baudelaire when he felt himself going mad; not many have been celebrated in poems as beautiful as Mallarmé's Sonnet, of which this is Roger Fry's translation.

The Tomb of Edgar Poe

Such as to himself eternity's changed him,
The Poet arouses with his naked sword
His age fright-stricken for not having known
That Death was triumphing in that strange voice!

They, with a Hydra's vile spasm at hearing the angel
Giving a sense more pure to the words of their tribe
Proclaimed aloud the sortilege drunk
In the dishonored flow of some black brew.

Oh, Grief! From soil and from the hostile cloud,
If thence our idea cannot carve a relief
Wherewith to adorn Poe's shining tomb

Calm block fallen down here from some dark disaster
May this granite at least show forever their bourn
To the black plights of Blasphemy sparse in the future.

Selected Prose and Poetry of Edgar Allan Poe, 1950

Foreword to *A Change of World,*
by Adrienne Cecile Rich

Reading a poem is an experience analogous to that of encountering a person. Just as one can think and speak separately of a person's physical appearance, his mind, and his character, so one can consider the formal aspects of a poem, its contents, and its spirit while knowing that in the latter case no less than in the former these different aspects are not really separate but an indissoluble trinity-in-unity.

We would rather that our friends were handsome than plain, intelligent than stupid, but in the last analysis it is on account of their character as persons that we accept or reject them. Similarly, in poetry we can put up with a good deal, with poems that are structurally defective, with poems that say nothing particularly new or "amusing," with poems that are a bit crazy; but a poem that is dishonest and pretends to be something other than it is, a poem that is, as it were, so obsessed with itself that it ignores or bellows at or goes on relentlessly boring the reader, we avoid if possible. In art as in life, truthfulness is an absolute essential, good manners of enormous importance.

Every age has its characteristic faults, its typical temptation to overemphasize some virtue at the expense of others, and the typical danger for poets in our age is, perhaps, the desire to be "original." This is natural, for who in his daydreams does not prefer to see himself as a leader rather than a follower, an explorer rather than a cultivator and a settler? Unfortunately, the possibility of realizing such a dream is limited, not only by talent but also by time, and even a superior gift cannot cancel historical priority; he who today climbs the Matterhorn, though he be the greatest climber who ever lived, must tread in Whymper's footsteps.

Radical changes and significant novelty in artistic style can only occur when there has been a radical change in human sensibility to require them. The spectacular events of the present time must not blind us to the fact that we are living not at the beginning but in the middle of a historical epoch; they are not novel but repetitions on a vastly enlarged scale and at a violently accelerated tempo of events which took place long since.

Every poet under fifty-five cherishes, I suspect, a secret grudge against Providence for not getting him born a little earlier. On writing down the obvious names which would occur to everyone as those of the great figures in "modern" poetry, novels, painting, and music, the innovators, the creators of the new style, I find myself with a list of twenty persons: of these, four were born in the sixties, six in the seventies, and ten in the eighties. It was these men who were driven to find a new style which could cope with such changes in our civilization as, to mention only four, the collapse of the liberal hope of peaceful change, of revolution through oratory and literature; the dissolution of the traditional community by industrial urbanization; the exposure of the artist to the styles of every epoch and culture simultaneously; and the skepticism induced by psychology and anthropology as to the face value of any emotion or belief.

Before a similar crop of revolutionary artists can appear again, there will have to be just such another cultural revolution replacing these attitudes with others. So long as the way in which we regard the world and feel about our existence remains in all essentials the same as that of our predecessors we must follow in their tradition; it would be just as dishonest for us to pretend that their style is inadequate to our needs as it would have been for them to be content with the style of the Victorians.

Miss Rich, who is, I understand, twenty-one years old, displays a modesty not so common at that age, which disclaims any extraordinary vision, and a love for her medium, a determination to ensure that whatever she writes shall, at least, not be shoddily made. In a young poet, as T. S. Eliot has observed, the most promising sign is craftsmanship for it is evidence of a capacity for detachment from the self and its emotions without which no art is possible. Craftsmanship includes, of course, not only a talent for versification but also an ear and an intuitive grasp of much subtler and more difficult matters like proportion, consistency of diction and tone, and the matching of these with the subject at hand; Miss Rich's poems rarely fail on any of these counts.

They make no attempt to conceal their family tree: "A Clock in the Square," for instance, is confessedly related to the poetry of Robert Frost, "Design in Living Colors" to the poetry of Yeats; but what they say is not a parrotlike imitation without understanding but the expression of a genuine personal experience.

The emotions which motivate them—the historical apprehension expressed in "Storm Warnings," the conflict between faith and doubt expressed in "For the Conjunction of Two Planets," the feeling of isolation expressed in "By No Means Native"—are not peculiar to Miss Rich but are among the typical experiences of our time; they are none the less for that uniquely felt by her.

I suggested at the beginning of this introduction that poems are analogous to persons; the poems a reader will encounter in this book are neatly and modestly dressed, speak quietly but do not mumble, respect their elders but are not cowed by them, and do not tell fibs: that, for a first volume, is a good deal.

Adrienne Cecile Rich, A *Change of World*, 1951

Nature, History and Poetry

I

Temporal events may be divided into two classes: natural events and historical events.

A natural event (*a*) is recurrent, i.e. a member of a class of similar events;
    (*b*) occurs necessarily according to law.

An historical event (*a*) is once only, i.e. the unique member of a class of one;
    (*b*) occurs not necessarily according to law but voluntarily according to provocation;
    (*c*) is a cause of subsequent historical events by providing them with a motive for occurring.

Of a natural event it can only be said that it is what it is; of an historical event it can be said that it could have been otherwise.

Natural events are related by the principle of Identity; historical events by the principle of Analogy.

Natural time in which natural events occur and which they measure is reversible or cyclical; historical time which historical events create is irreversible and moves in a unilinear direction.

To be intelligible an event must be related to some law. Laws may be divided into two classes: Laws-of and Laws-for.

A Law-of is stated in the indicative mood; it presupposes that at any given instant only one event can occur: About a Law-of, therefore, it can only be said that its formulation is true or false. A Law-for is stated in the imperative mood; it presupposes that at any given instant at least two events are possible and asserts that one is more probable or preferable: About a Law-for it can be said that its command is just or unjust.

Natural laws are Laws-of and are what the scientist in time discovers. Laws-for only apply to historical events and are what the historian at a time judges them by. Of the motive for choosing to occur with which a Law-for provides an historical event, it may be said that it is good or evil, of the choice itself that it is right or wrong. A just law is one which provokes good motives, not one which compels right choices.

II

For a law to be discoverable, at least three events, i.e. a plurality, must be known to which it is relatable. Pluralities may be divided into three classes: crowds, societies, and communities.

A crowd consists of n members where $n > 1$, whose sole characteristic in common is togetherness. A crowd loves neither itself nor anything other than itself. It can only be counted; its existence is chimerical. Of a crowd it can be said either that it is not real but only appears to be or that it should not be.

A society consists of x members, i.e. a certain finite number, united in a specific manner into a whole with a characteristic mode of behavior which is different from the behavior of its several members in isolation (e.g. a molecule of water or a string quartet). A society has a definite size, a specific structure and an actual existence. It cannot come into being until all its component members are present and properly related. Add or subtract a member, or change their relations, and the society ceases to exist or is transformed into another society. A society is a system which loves itself. To this total self-love, the self-love of its members is totally subordinate. Of a society it may be said that it is effective or ineffective.

A community consists of n members, all of them rational beings united by a common love for something other than themselves (e.g. a group of music-lovers). Like a crowd and unlike a society the number of members is indefinite, for its character is not changed by the addition or subtraction of a member. It exists, not like a crowd by chance nor like a society actually, but potentially, i.e. that $n = 1$ is possible. To attain actual existence it must embody itself in societies which express the love which is its *raison d'être*, and of these there may be an infinite number. The actualization of a community in a social system is an order.

   A community may be closed or open. A closed community is one the members of which are unaware of the existence, actual or potential, of rival communities united by another love; an open community is one the members of which are aware of the existence of rival communities but choose to belong to this one and to refuse membership in the others. Absolute closure or absolute openness are hypothetical, every community is more or less closed, less or more open. Of a community it may be said that its love is more or less good.

In nature there exists only the total system of partial social systems and no community; i.e. we cannot say of a natural event that it occurs for the love of anything other than itself; it only enjoys its self-occurrence. The natural social system is therefore fully describable in terms of laws-of, and terms like freedom and unfreedom, good and evil, have no relevance. It is only in history that one can speak of communities as well as societies, or make a distinction between an order and a system.

In a system freedom and unfreedom appear as each other's boundaries and good and evil as real opposites striving to annul each other like positive and negative numbers. If one member of a string quartet refuses to play Mozart and the others insist, they annul each other.

 In a community unfreedom and evil appear as the denial of freedom and goodness; i.e. freedom and goodness are not annulled but the denial testifies to their existence. If nine people prefer beef to mutton and one person prefers mutton to beef, there is not one community containing a dissident member but two communities. The antithesis of a community, therefore, is not another community with a different love, but a crowd.

Wherever rival communities compete for embodiment in the same society, there is either unfreedom or disorder. In the chimerical case of a society completely embodying a crowd there would be a state of total unfreedom, i.e. Hell.

A perfect order, i.e. one in which a community was perfectly and completely embodied in a system, could be described in terms of a law-of but the description would be irrelevant. For a perfect order the relevant description would be "Love is the fulfilling of the Law." Only in Paradise is this the case. In historical societies, where the order is always imperfect, for community and system never coincide, the obligation to approximate to such a coincidence is felt as the command of a law-for.

III

Man exists as a unity in tension of four modes of being, Soul, Body, Mind and Spirit.

As a soul and a body he is an individual person; as mind and spirit, a conscious member of a community. Were he only soul and body, his only relation with others would be numerical and a poem would be comprehensible only to its author. Were he only mind and spirit, men would only exist collectively as the system Man, and there would be nothing for poetry to be about.

As body and mind, man is a natural creature; as soul and spirit, an historical creature. Were he only body and mind his existence would be one of everlasting recurrence and only one good poem could exist. Were he only soul and spirit, his existence would be one of perpetual and absolute novelty and every new poem would supersede all previous poems, or rather a poem would be superseded before it could be written.

Man's consciousness of himself exists as a unity-in-tension of three modes of awareness:

(*a*) the consciousness of the self as self-contained; as embracing all of which it is aware in a unity of experiencing. This mode is undogmatic, amoral and passive. Its good is the enjoyment of being, its evil the fear of nonbeing.

(*b*) the consciousness of beyondness, of the ego standing as a spectator over against both itself and the external world. This mode is dogmatic, amoral, objective. Its good is the perception of true relations, its evil the fear of chance or nonrelation.

(*c*) the ego's consciousness of itself as striving towards, as desiring to transform the self, to realize its potentialities. This mode is moral and active. Its good is not present but propounded, its evil the present actuality.

Were the first mode absolute, man would inhabit a magical world of idols in which the image of an object, the emotion aroused by the object and the word signifying the object were all identical, a world where past and future, the living and the dead were united. Language in such a world would consist only of proper names which would not be words in the ordinary sense but sacred syllables, and in the place of the poet there would be the magician whose task is to discover and utter the truly potent spell which can compel what-is-not to be. It seems probable that, historically, poetry was born out of magic of this kind, hence the myth of Orpheus. Whenever this mode of consciousness predominates, it can be exploited; propaganda is the employment of magic by those who do not believe in it over against those who do.

Were the second mode absolute, man would inhabit a world which was a pure system of universals. Language would be a kind of algebra and there could exist only one poem of absolute banality expressing the system. Whenever this mode of consciousness is predominant we find a poetry in which poetic forms in the abstract, monotonous rhythms and conventional rhymes tyrannize over the would-be poet and dictate what he says.

Were the third mode absolute, man would inhabit a purely arbitrary world, the world of the clown and the actor. The ugliest person would be the nicest and vice versa. In language there would be no relation between thing and word; all rhymes would be comic, e.g. love would rhyme with indifference, and all poetry would be nonsense poetry. Whenever this mode of consciousness is predominant we find a fantastic contradiction between the emotions and ideas displayed in a poet's work and the emotions and ideas he displays in his life, and a fanatical religion made of a sense of humor.

Thanks to the first mode of consciousness every poem is unique; thanks to the second the poet can embody private experience in a public poem which can be read by others in terms of their private experiences; thanks to the third both poet and reader desire that this be done.

IV

The subject matter of the natural scientist is a crowd of disordered natural events at all times. He assumes this crowd to be not real but apparent and attempts to discover the true system concealed beneath this appearance. The subject matter of the poet is a crowd of historic occasions of feeling in the past. He accepts this crowd as real and attempts to transform it into a community, i.e. to give it a possible instead of a chimerical existence.

The Muses are, as the Greeks said, the daughters of Memory, but Memory is not herself a Muse. When we recall an occasion of past feeling, we recall the occasion, not the feeling itself; desire is seen, as it were, in a mirror detached from its roots in appetite and passion; it is no longer *ours*. Were this not so, it would be impossible to detach it from the past, relate it to other emotions and embody them in a poem. There are cases where the recall of the occasion is accompanied by a repetition of the original emotion but such are of no practical value to the poet and of interest only to the psychiatrist. For poetry the emotion must, as Wordsworth said, be recollected in tranquillity.

The transformation of a crowd of feelings into a community is effected by translating the former into words that embody the latter. The poem itself is a linguistic society or verbal system. As such it is a natural, not a historical being. Every poem presupposes that the history of language is at an end. A poem, therefore, cannot properly be said to exist except when it is being read or remembered. At all other times it is only on hand. But, unlike the fleeting occasions of feeling from which it is derived, it is persistently on hand. When a poem is read it orders into a possible community a crowd of past historic occasions of the reader's feeling, not identical with but analogous to those of the author. For the reader as for the author it is only past occasions which are so transformed; a poem has no power of persuasion over the present moment of historical choice, it introduces no novel emotion into the reader's now other than the satisfaction which accompanies every such transformation of disorder into order, the satisfaction we imply when we say that something is beautiful. Language can be used to introduce novel emotion into the present, e.g. in pornography, but such use is magical, not poetical.

It has been said that a poem should not mean but be. This is not quite accurate. In a poem as distinct from many other verbal societies, meaning and being are identical. Like an image in the mirror, a poem might be called a pseudo-person, i.e. it has uniqueness and addresses the reader as person to person but, like all natural beings and unlike historical persons, it cannot lie. It is not possible to say of a poem that it is true or false for one does not have to go to anything except itself to discover whether or not it is in fact an order, a community of feelings truly embodied in a verbal society. If it is not, if unfreedom or disorder is present, the poem itself reveals this on inspection. We may be and frequently are mistaken in a poem but the cause of the mistake is our self-deception, not the poem.

V

In sitting down to write a poem, the poet has at his disposal two crowds, the crowd composed of the total number of occasions of past feeling he can recall, and the crowd composed of the total number of words in his vocabulary. His task is to organize the relevant members of the latter into a society which will embody as many members of the former as it can transform into one community.

The nature of the final order is the outcome of a dialectical struggle between the feelings and the verbal system.

As a society the verbal system is actively coercive upon the feelings it is attempting to embody; what it cannot embody truthfully it excludes. As a potential community the feelings are passively resistant to all claims of the system to embody them which they do not recognize as just; they decline all unjust persuasions. As members of crowds, every feeling competes with every other, demanding inclusion and a dominant position to which they are not necessarily entitled, and every word demands that the system shall modify itself in its case, that a special exception shall be made for it and it only.

In a successful poem society and community are one order and the system may love itself because the feelings which it embodies are all members of the same community, loving each other and it. A poem may fail in two ways; it may exclude too much (banality), or attempt to embody more than one community at once (disorder).

In writing a poem, the poet can work in two ways. Starting from an intuitive idea of the kind of community he desires to call into being, he may work backwards in search of the system which will most justly incarnate that idea, or, starting with a certain system, he may work forwards in search of the community which it is capable of incarnating most truthfully. In practice, he nearly always works simultaneously in both directions, modifying his conception of the ultimate nature of the community at the immediate suggestions of the system, and modifying the system in response to his growing intuition of the future needs of the community.

A system cannot be selected completely arbitrarily nor can one say that any given system is absolutely necessary. The poet searches for one, which imposes just obligations on the feelings. "Ought" always implies "can" so that a system whose claims cannot be met must be scrapped. But the poet has to beware of accusing the system of injustice when what is at fault is the laxness and self-love of the feelings upon which it is making its demands.

VI

Every poet, consciously or unconsciously, holds the following absolute presuppositions as the dogmas of his art.

(1) An historical world exists, a world of unique events and unique persons, related by analogy not identity. The number of events and analogical relations is potentially infinite. The existence of such a world is a good, and every addition to the number of events, persons and relations is an additional good.

(2) The historical world is a fallen world, i.e. though it is good that it exists, the way in which it exists is evil, being full of unfreedom and disorder.

(3) The historical world is a redeemable world. The unfreedom and disorder of the past can be reconciled in the future.

It follows from the first presupposition that the poet's activity in creating a poem is analogous to God's activity in creating man after his own image. It is not an imitation for, were it so, the poet would be able to create like God *ex nihilo*; instead, he requires pre-existing occasions of feeling and a pre-existing language out of which to create. It is analogous in that the poet creates not necessarily according to a law of nature but voluntarily according to provocation.

It is untrue, strictly speaking, to say that a poet should not write poems unless he must; strictly speaking it can only be said that he should not write them unless he can. The phrase is sound in practice, because only in those who can and when they can is the motive genuinely compulsive.

In those who profess a desire to write poetry, yet exhibit an incapacity to do so, it is often the case that their desire is not for creation but for self-perpetuation, that they refuse to accept their own mortality, just as there are parents who do not really wish to beget children, new persons analogous to themselves, but to prolong their own existence in time. The sterility of this substitution of identity for analogy is expressed in the myth of Narcissus. When the poet speaks, as he sometimes does, of achieving immortality through his poem, he does not mean that he hopes, like Faust, to live for ever, but that he hopes to rise from the dead. In poetry as in other matters the law holds good that he who would save his life must lose it; unless the poet sacrifices his feelings completely to the poem, so that they are no longer his but the poem's, he fails.

It follows from the second presupposition that a poem is a witness to man's knowledge of evil as well as good. When we say that poetry is beyond good and evil, we simply mean that a poet can no more change the facts of what he has felt than, in the natural order, parents can change the inherited physical characteristics which they pass on to their children. The judgment good-or-evil applies only to the intentional movements of the will. Of our feelings in a given situation which are the joint product of our intention and the response to the external factors in that situation it can only be said that, given an intention and the response, they are appropriate or inappropriate. Of a recollected feeling it cannot be said that it is appropriate or inappropriate because the historical situation in which it arose no longer exists.

Every poem, therefore, is an attempt to present an analogy to that paradisal state in which Freedom and Law, System and Order are united in harmony. Again, an analogy not an imitation; the harmony is possible and verbal only; a poem is a natural, not an historical object.

It follows from the third presupposition that a poem is beautiful or ugly to the degree that it succeeds or fails in reconciling contradictory feelings in an order of mutual propriety. Every beautiful poem presents an analogy to the forgiveness of sins, an analogy not an imitation, because it is not evil intentions which are repented of and pardoned but contradictory feelings which the poet surrenders to the poem in which they are reconciled.

The effect of beauty, therefore, is good to the degree that, through its analogies, the goodness of created existence, the historical fall into unfreedom and disorder, and the possibility of regaining paradise through repentance and forgiveness are recognized. Its effect is evil to the degree that Beauty is taken, not as analogous to but as identical with Goodness, so that the artist regards himself or is regarded by others as God, the pleasure of beauty taken for the joy of Paradise, and the conclusion drawn that, since all is well in the work of art, all is well in history. But all is not well there.

Thought, September 1950

Young Boswell

Boswell's London Journal, 1762–1763. Edited with an introduction and notes by Frederick A. Pottle. McGraw-Hill. $5.

Certain unfortunates among the famous dead seem doomed to be kept turning in their graves by the folly of imitation they provoke in their living admirers. One cannot visit the Zoo in Central Park without encountering Beethoven scowling at the monkeys or Goethe speculating profoundly upon a giraffe; one cannot frequent any of the better University Clubs without, sooner or later, having to endure the anecdotes of a reincarnate Lincoln or the Old Guard Republican opinions of a latter-day Dr Johnson.

One may safely assert, however, that James Boswell has enjoyed his century and a half of rest without so much as a single rotation, for to imitate him a man would have to become deliberately what every man is by nature born and no man ever wishes to remain—a bounder. To cultivate aggressive bad manners or even some peculiar nervous tic is easy and has its attractions, but to cultivate a lack of dignity that results in being teased and tickled in the ribs by one's juniors, intentionally to commit social gaffes for which one is very properly snubbed, to be merely afraid of the dark like a child or a peasant are beyond the power or the courage of any human being. As for Boswell's sex life, any accurate imitation would, in the illuminated and patrolled streets of today, quickly land the imitator in jail.

The fascinating story of the discovery of the Boswell Papers is well known and is excellently told by Mr Christopher Morley in his preface, so there is no need to retell it here. I would merely remark that it is perhaps the only instance in history when an anonymous-letter writer has done nothing but good.

This journal, which has been admirably edited and annotated by Frederick A. Pottle, begins with Boswell's departure from Edinburgh in November 1762 to take up residence in London, and ends on the eve of his departure for the Continent the following August. He had visited London before, but this was the first visit since he had attained his majority—he was now twenty-two—and a modest independence, his father having given him an allowance of two hundred pounds a year. During these nine months, two events of crucial importance occurred: On June 8th, Boswell decided to follow his father's advice and abandoned his intention of becoming a Guards officer; on July 14th, after they had consumed two bottles of heavy port, Dr Johnson (their first meeting had been in May) took Boswell's hand cordially and said, "My dear Boswell! I do love you very much." On the former date, Boswell decided, consciously or unconsciously, to give up trying to become a gentleman and to be himself instead; on the latter, he discovered his vocation.

For the rest, the journal is a day-to-day account, written to amuse his friend John Johnston, of a young man who has come up from the provinces, armed with a few introductions, to make good in the Big City, anxious, like every young man, to make a favorable impression, to do the proper thing, to be liked by the right people, and determined, now that he has escaped the paternal eye at last, to have lots and lots of sex. His experiences are those of most young men in such circumstances. He wants to buy a very expensive suit but has to be content with a "plain suit of a pink color, with a gold button"; he settles on the coffeehouse he is going to frequent; he has an affair with a minor actress and catches gonorrhea; he picks up whores in the Park; he has a row with his landlord; he has good days, when he is convinced that he is a great genius, and bad days, when he is equally certain that he is an utter failure.

Autobiographies fall into three classes. First, there are the self-histories in the proper sense: the record, that is, of decisive events, internal and external—the events that have been responsible for the course of a man's life. Such histories are rare, because the man with a significant internal history, like Augustine or Newman, is the exception, and the public hero of war or peace seldom has the time or the talent to write a true historical account of himself. Second, there are the histories of a vocation; e.g. Wordsworth's *The Prelude*, or Berlioz' *Mémoires*, in which the only facts recorded are those relevant to a man's work. Last, there are the self-portraits, in which an attempt is made to set down truthfully all experiences, irrespective of their historical or career importance. The extreme difficulty of such self-portraiture is that a man who has reached the degree of self-consciousness presupposed by the desire to paint his own portrait has almost invariably also developed an ego-consciousness that paints himself painting himself and inevitably produces a theatrical image. Boswell, indeed, is perhaps the only one of the My-Heart-Laid-Bare boys who reached the one without developing the other. When we read Rousseau or Stendhal or Gide, we are conscious of artful highlights and shadows, and keep asking ourselves, "Now, just what was his secret motive for confessing this or recalling that?" But when we read Boswell, the character presented is as complete and transparent as a character in a novel by Defoe or Dickens; we cannot imagine there being any more to know than we are told.

Take, for example, the following extract:

> When I got home, I was shocked to think that I had been intimately united with a low, abandoned, perjured, pilfering creature. I determined to do so no more; but if the Cyprian fury should seize me, to participate my amorous flame with a genteel girl.

An ego-conscious writer like Stendhal would never have allowed himself to write phrases like "the Cyprian fury" or "my amorous flame;" he would have reflected, "These are clichés. Clichés are dishonest. I must put down exactly what I mean in plain words." But he would have been mistaken, for everyone's self, including Stendhal's, does think in clichés and euphemisms, not in the style of the Code Napoléon; in self-portraiture, nature and art are incompatible.

In a sense, Boswell triumphs as a writer because in all other respects he is such a thoroughly ordinary man. He is not clever; he never astonishes us with an observation we could not have had the insight to make; he is not abnormal; his feelings and behavior are never such that we cannot easily imagine ourselves feeling and doing the same. Consequently, in reading Boswell each of us is confronted by himself. Who does not recognize his own youth in confessions like these:

> I dreamt that Johnston did not care for me. That he came to see me set off on a long journey, and that he seemed dissipated and tired, and left me before I got away. I lay abed very gloomy. I thought London did me no good. I rather disliked it; and I thought of going back to Edinburgh immediately.

> From having been so long and so lately under strict family discipline at home, whenever I have been a little too late about at night, I cannot help being apprehensive that Terrie my landlord will reprove me for it next morning.

> Another shocking fault which I have is my sacrificing almost anything to a laugh, even myself. . . . I am firmly resolved to amend it. I shall be most particularly wary.

> I was well-dressed and in excellent spirits, neither muddy nor flashy. I sat with much secret pride, thinking of my having such a company with me. I behaved with ease and propriety, and did not attempt at all to show away.

> I can with pleasure trace the progress of this intrigue to its completion. I am now at ease on that head, having my fair one fixed as my own. . . . I really conducted this affair with a manliness and prudence that pleased me very much. The whole expense was just eighteen shillings.

Like every ordinary man, Boswell wanted desperately to become a conventional man; that is to say, to lose his humanity and become a mechanical doll. What makes him so extraordinary is that this transformation, which most ordinary men go through with the greatest ease, was entirely beyond his powers. Over and over again, he vows to look dignified, not to giggle, to shake off old friends who are not out of the top drawer, but it is no use. One wink, one dig in the ribs, one knock at the door, and his attempt to be grown-up collapses, for his childlike appetite for the immediate moment is too strong. A child he remains to the end of his days in all respects but one; a child is incapable of a sustained and faithful affection, and in his devotion to Dr Johnson, a devotion as remarkable in its way as Dante's to Beatrice, Boswell displays a maturity he shows nowhere else. One rather doubts whether the later journals will add much to his self-portrait in this first volume, for after 1763 his real interest is centered not on himself but on his friend; this volume, however, is an indispensable prologue to the *Life*.

The book-designing departments of publishers move in a mysterious way. In the present instance, after taking enormous pains with the paper, the type, the end-papers, the binding, etc., they seem, on coming to the jacket, to have gone suddenly mad, for they have concealed what is really a very handsome book indeed beneath a completely banal water color of Temple Bar, of which the only interesting detail, the traitors' heads over the gate, is obliterated by the title.

The New Yorker, 25 November 1950

Some December Books Chosen for the Trade Book Clinic

My only qualifications—and I doubt whether either is valid—for sitting in judgment on the make-up of books are, firstly, that I write books myself and, secondly, that I am a voracious, I should say gluttonous, consumer of this commodity.

A writer's task in such matters is apt to be parochial, too colored by his conceptions of how he would like his own wares to look. As a writer of poetry, for example, I have a violent prejudice against arty paper and printing which is too often considered fitting for unsalable prestige books, and by inverted snobbery I favor the shiny white paper and format of the textbook. Further, perhaps because I am near-sighted and hold the page nearer my nose than is normal, I have a strong preference for small type.

On the other hand, like all persons who buy books to read and not to give as presents, I have a horror of expensive fine editions which one dare not read without first washing one's hands; I drop ash between pages, I leave books lying open on the floor, and my first prerequisite is that they shall not come to pieces under brutal treatment.

What follows, therefore, must be taken for what it is, the opinion of an uninstructed amateur, intoxicated with the heaven-sent opportunity, which may never come again, to have his little say on other people's business.

Incidentally, anyone who has done reviewing can imagine the joy of being allowed to talk about books without having to read them.

My one real criticism of bookmaking in the United States is that it tries to do too much; it seems to assume that format is a competitive asset. This I do not believe. The public may buy apples for their appearance rather than their flavor, but a person buys a book because it is about some subject in which he is interested, or because it is by an author whom he admires or has been told to admire; it is only in cases where the same book is offered in different editions that a superior format can affect his choice.

My vision of the book designer in any of the better American houses is of a very able young man who is terrified of losing his job unless he produces an original idea with every new book. Consequently, while his basic conception is nearly always straightforward and good, he dare not leave it at that and all too often ruins it by meaningless additions for the sake of making something different. American publishers do not need better designers; they need lazier ones who take less benzedrine. As for jackets, the sooner they are handed over to the typographer, the better.

In making my selections, I have ignored all fine editions in the strict sense and tried to pick books which seemed to me good examples of their class.

I. Fiction

The Cometeers by Jack Williamson (Fantasy Press, $3). Of all types of book-consumer, the novel reader cares least about format and demands little more than that the print shall not be actually smudged or show through from the other side of the page. A decently got-up novel, therefore, should be counted unto the publisher for pure righteousness.

My choice comes from a field in which one would least expect trouble to be taken, namely, science-fiction. In this case paper and type are such that no parent need worry about the eyesight of his twelve-year-old son even if he reads in bed. There is one illustration only, which is just as well, for that art seems to have vanished with the disappearance of the wood-engraving. I doubt if we shall ever see anything as beautiful and exciting again as, for example, the plates in the old editions of Jules Verne.

II. Scholarly Nonfiction

The Letters of Benjamin Franklin and Jane Mecom, edited by Carl Van Doren (Princeton University Press, $5). A collection of letters in eighteenth-century English with editorial notes could easily be exhausting to read. The publishers have overcome this problem very happily by combining a fairly substantial page, $7 \times 4\frac{1}{4}$ inches of text, with a wider-than-average spacing of lines. The binding is a handsome, conservative green, embossed with one of Franklin's own stencils.

III. Art Books

Primitive Painters in America 1750–1950 by Jean Lipman and Alice Winchester. (Dodd, Mead, $6). The illustrations, both in color and in black-and-white are excellently reproduced and the page-size, $10 \times 6\frac{3}{8}$, is large enough for clarity and small enough for easy holding. I find the system of placing the illustrations so that they bleed off the top and side leaving a wide bottom margin most attractive.

IV. Children's Books

Horses Are Folks by C. W. Anderson (Harper, $3.50). I could find nothing for this month in the strictly juvenile field. So many illustrators of children's books seem to imagine that children like their own drawings. But children only draw that way because they lack technical skill; if they could, they would draw like Landseer or Dali. Despite its revolting title (one foresees a whole series, *The Underprivileged Horse, Delinquent Horses, Peace of Horse*, etc). *Horses Are Folks* is illustrated by enchanting and naturalistic full-page lithographs of its subject at all ages and in all postures. Faced with the problem of a page wider than it is high, the publishers have daringly but most successfully arranged the text in double 4¼-inch columns with a half-inch inter-margin.

V. Educational Books

Oil for the World by Stewart Schackne and N. D'Arcy Drake. (Harper, $2.50). I am, personally, a little suspicious of visual aids to learning, whether in book form or in documentary films, but the method is here to stay and the above volume displays it to its fullest advantage. Every trick, the striking "still" of machinery, the geological map, the explanatory diagram of technical processes, even the homely vignette sketch is used and most effectively so that the attention of the most scatterbrained student may be held. The wide outer margin allows the placing of subject headings where they are most easy to find.

VI. Cheap Books

The American Arts Library: *Early American Firearms, American Glass, American Rugs, American Silver, Pennsylvania Dutch Art* (World Publishing Company, $1 each). These little books, which each run to some sixty-odd pages of text and illustrations, have been as carefully and beautifully got up as if they were to sell at ten times the price. But why, oh, why, blemish such an achievement by inserting end-papers which look like an insipid wallpaper? Somebody worked too hard.

VII. Mad Books

My choice is divided between two: *Treasury of Early American Automobiles 1877–1925* by Floyd Clymer (McGraw-Hill, $5), and *The Swiss Family Perelman* by S. J. Perelman, drawings by Hirschfeld (Simon and Schuster, $2.95). This class of book is the only one in which the designer becomes almost as important as the author and the more extravagant the former can be the better. The first of my choices is a hagiography by a most sympathetic maniac to whom the automobile is a numinous object and the most trivial fact concerning that vehicle of religious importance. For five dollars the reader can become the owner of a vast museum of period photographs, advertisements, technical drawings, fashion-plates, poems and jokes concerning the primordial motor-car and the primordial motorist, male and female. How the publishers can offer so much at the price I do not know. Again, I feel the end-papers are out of period and style with the rest, but this is a small detail. Ideal bathroom reading.

Mr Perelman, as to our joy we all know, is a zany of the first water, and it is fitting that he should be illustrated and produced in a dotty manner. The great rectangular washes of violent pink, blue, yellow or green, planked down unpredictably on the drawings, sometimes managing to cover them, sometimes missing, are delightful. Finally, of all the books before me, this one is superior in a virtue which I believe to be unduly neglected by publishers—it has the nicest smell.

Publishers' Weekly, 6 January 1951

In an Age Like Ours, the Artist Works
in a State of Siege

Old Friends and New Music. By Nicolas Nabokov. Little, Brown. $3.50.

Everyone who is friendly disposed toward contemporary art but dissatisfied with its products and every young person considering an artistic career should read Mr Nabokov's book. Upon finishing it, the former, instead of grumbling because music, literature, and painting today are not better than they are, will, I think, be left wondering that any exists at all. The latter will have got some inkling of the iron nerves and strength of character he will need, for, lacking them, no matter how great his talent, he is doomed to failure.

From the artist's point of view, the worst feature of this age is not its horrors—every age has been full of them—but the acceleration of its historical tempo.

In the first chapter of *Old Friends and New Music* we are rattling through a country estate in a fancy victoria upholstered in dark red velvet on our way to pick mushrooms. The scene swarms with servants, priests, obscure relatives, governesses. The atmosphere is charged with custom, piety, reverence for rank, space and leisure.

Four chapters later we are in a theatre on the Riviera at three o'clock in the morning. There is still plenty of luxury; a few titles are still around, but no relatives. Few of the men and women are legally married and those who are have no children. Custom has been replaced by fashion and the icon to which incense is burned is that of the Muse who Astonishes. As for leisure, the following incident is descriptive.

> Diaghilev asked me to bring over the score and the orchestra parts and told me that the orchestra had twenty minutes of free time and could read it through. I tried to dissuade him by saying that "Ode" was forty minutes long and that, besides, the parts were still full of mistakes. He replied that Scotto, the conductor, would read it through in a fast tempo. . . . Every time I wanted to jump up from my seat, the heavy hand

of Diaghilev kept me back. "Don't disturb them. They haven't much time."

A few more chapters and we are, first, buried in a small college in northern New York State teaching counterpoint and directing plays, then whisked to Hollywood to hear Stravinsky say of the Berkshire festival: "Why should contrabasses practice outdoors under pine trees? After all, they are not herbivorous instruments." And then, finally, we are driving through the ruins of Berlin in a looted automobile with a fresh caviar Russian colonel who addresses us thus:

A man with your name and intelligence should be wearing our uniform or should be teaching in one of *our* conservatories. Of course you wouldn't hope to find right away a teaching post in Moscow or Leningrad, or even Kharkov or Kiev, but in one of those new Siberian towns. . . .

Rank has returned with a new face. "His head was clean shaven and had large protruding ears. It sat, totally neckless, on a short, well-built body. When he smiled, his eyes took on a shy and somewhat foxy expression." Piety, too, has returned but the name of its god is Power.

And how much time has it taken to get from Miss Slipcover, the governess, to Colonel Tulip of the N.K.V.D.? Five hundred years? Less than fifty. How, at that speed, can any artist be expected to make the slow sustained effort necessary to create a masterpiece?

Mr Nabokov's description of Stravinsky's workroom and working habits gives some hints. To achieve anything today, an artist has to develop a conscious strictness in respect of time which in former ages might have seemed neurotic and selfish, for he must never forget that he is living in a state of siege.

His workroom has also to be a fortress; the stop-watch and the metronome are his shield and buckler. Similarly, in a howling storm, a theatrical and purple artistic style is ridiculous; only clarity and economy will work as charms against the void. Intervals, as Stravinsky says, must be treated like dollars.

We must pass quickly over the second obstacle, how to get the dollars. I have often wondered how writers and composers would both feel if the prevailing situation in each field were reversed, if at parties, that is, people would, in discussing music, talk only of the latest teen-age composer who had made Mozart a back number but, in discussing literature, would speak of no one but Dante, Shakespeare and Goethe. Think of the awed servility and cutthroat intrigue with which novelists would approach the Koussevitzky of the publishing world; think of the embittered demodé composer who was the rage five years ago.

And so we come to the class war between the highbrow and the middlebrow (the lowbrow is a modest good-natured man who would live and let live). This war cuts across all political and ideological differences. There is one subject—I am surprised that the diplomats have not thought of it—upon which Senator McCarthy and Mr Molotov would find themselves in enthusiastic agreement, the effrontery and downright wickedness of "modern" poetry, painting and music, and, conversely the sort of pictures they would like for their own houses. As critical terms, communistic and cosmopolitan, Christian Americanism and Socialist Realism, are interchangeable.

The odd and frightening thing about the provincial middlebrows is the intensity of their hostile interest in the highbrow. Even Mr Churchill, I am sorry to say, for he ought to know better, wanted to kick Picasso. It isn't as if there weren't plenty of people producing work with the kind of "melodichna" they like, but that is not enough for them. They find it insulting and subversive that anyone should dare to have independent tastes. When I read Zhdanov's purge speech, every word was already familiar; it was the voice of my old housemaster publicly rebuking me for my lack of team spirit.

Three cheers, then, for Democracy because, though many Congressmen would like to do to us what the Politburo has done to Prokofiev, they can't, bless their hearts. And now, in thanks to Mr Nabokov for his witty and penetrating book, let us rise and join in a toast. I give you "Highbrows of the world, unite."

The New York Times Book Review, 4 February 1951

Aeneid for Our Time

The Aeneid of Virgil. A verse translation by Rolfe Humphries.
Charles Scribner's Sons. $3.50.

Virgil's reputation, like Milton's, has for some time been rather under a cloud. The prevailing opinion regards Catullus, Horace, Propertius as the true Latin poets and Virgil as little more than a skilful rhetorician, capable of some admirable effects but really an academic old bore, "a Tennysonized Homer," as Ezra Pound once called him.

Unjust as, of course, this is, it is perhaps understandable, for we live in an age where the notion of official art has such repugnant connotations that it is difficult for us to believe that a State Bard, which Virgil was, could possibly be any good. In a world where

> The best lack all conviction and the worst
> Are full of passionate intensity

a poet like Lucretius, who preaches salvation through knowledge, is easier for us to take than a poet like Virgil, who preaches salvation through willpower and whose hero is a man with a political mission.

If, however, we are not completely pessimistic about the human enterprise, if we have any faith that historical decisions are meaningful, that we are not merely the puppets of chance and immediate self-interest, that a just and peaceful world is a possibility, admittedly remote, which it is our duty to try to realize, we owe that faith as much to Virgil as to anyone or anything else.

To imagine a world in which that hope has not yet been born, one has only to go back to Homer and hear, for instance, Achilles speaking to Priam, who has come to beg the body of Hector.

> Here, far from home, I sit in Troy, afflicting you and your children.

Why? For no reason. That is how things are. Does it matter if the Trojans win the war or the Greeks? Not in the least. One can be brave, one can be cowardly, but one can't change anything.

Virgil's conscious imitation of Homer is, of course, not due to a lack of invention; indeed, it is often precisely when he copies most closely that the novelty of his vision is clearest. Odysseus and Aeneas are both wanderers who are driven off their course. But while the goal of Odysseus is fixed by the past—he knows exactly what he wants, to get home—the goal of Aeneas is set by a future of which he is only dimly cognizant. His experiences in Crete and Carthage have a moral as well as an adventure interest; he is not only delayed by forces outside his control but also he delays when he should not. Odysseus has bad luck, Aeneas makes mistakes. Again, Hephaestus fashions a shield for Achilles, so does Vulcan for Aeneas. The figures on the former represent life as it always is, the earth, the besieged city, the dancing floor, the plow, and so on: the figures on the latter portray

> the stock to come
> The wars, each one in order, all the tale
> Of Italy and Roman triumphs. . . .
> All this Aeneas
> Sees on his mother's gift, the shield of Vulcan,
> And, without understanding, is proud and happy
> As he lifts to his shoulder all that fortune,
> The fame and glory of his children's children.

The *Iliad* is poetry of the highest order, but it is the poetry of barbarians, of a tribal culture; the *Aeneid* is the poetry of civilization, of world history. A child can enjoy Homer; anyone who has come to appreciate Virgil has already grown up.

Mr Humphries writes that it has become the practice in American schools to read only Books, I, II, IV, and VI. To read snippets of great poems is always bad, but in the case of the *Aeneid* it is fatal. It is possible to read selected passages from the *Iliad* and gain a fairly accurate picture of what is going on, but unless one reads the whole of the *Aeneid* one completely misses the point. In the vast stretch of time which elapses between the moment when Aeneas carries Anchises on his shoulders out of blazing Troy to the moment when the Fury, disguised as a little owl, is beating its wings against the shield of Turnus, everything that happens, happens in a definite order, so that the meaning of any event depends upon what precedes it and what follows it.

The first problem of the verse translator is the choice of an equivalent meter. The length of a line is a matter not only of the number of syllables or accents it contains but also of the number of verbal notions it expresses: thus twelve syllables of an inflected tongue like Latin will often sound shorter than twelve syllables of an uninflected tongue like English. Further, it is impossible to ignore the position occupied by any given meter in the poetic tradition of a given language. The hexameter was the conventional meter in Latin for a long poem; in English, even in the rare cases where successful hexameters have been written, they sound eccentric. The same holds good for other formal questions, such as the choice between rhymed and unrhymed verse. If Gavin Douglas and Dryden chose the rhymed couplet as the metrical form for their translations of the *Aeneid*, this was not because they were unaware of the compulsion to alter and pad the original which rhyme would involve but because they felt that in their times and for their readers the rhymed couplet held a position analogous to that held by the hexameter for the Romans and that this fact more than compensated for its drawbacks.

Today, when our ears are accustomed to unrhymed verse and irregular feet, the balance is the other way, and it is unlikely that a contemporary translator would consider using either rhyme or regular iambics.

Indeed, there would seem to be virtually only two sensible choices—either a loose six-beat line as used by Mr Day Lewis in his translation of the *Georgics*:

> And now, the time when a vineyard puts off its reluctant leaves
> And a bitter north wind has blown away the pride of the woodland,
> Even now the countryman actively pushes on the coming
> Year and its tasks, attacking the naked vine with a curved
> Pruning-knife he shears and trims it into shape.

or a loose blank-verse pentameter such as Mr Humphries has chosen for the *Aeneid*.

> They reach the mountain height, the hiding places
> Where no trail runs; wild goats from the rocks are started,
> Run down ridges; elsewhere, in the open
> Deer cross the dusty plain, away from the mountains.

The second problem, which today, in the case of an epic like the *Aeneid*, is even harder to solve, is that of style and diction. The epic poem is a solemn rite and written in an elevated liturgical style, but in modern society the sense of ceremony and rite has atrophied—that is why verse epics can no longer be written.

This difficulty had already begun to arise even in Milton's time, so that the elevated style of *Paradise Lost* seems already peculiar and removed from normal sensibility in a way that the Virgilian style does not. Mr Humphries has decided, very wisely in my opinion, to cut our losses and make no attempt to reproduce the pomp of the epic manner but to concentrate instead on its matter and movement; we do inevitably lose something by this, particularly, I feel, in the speeches, but the loss is infinitely preferable to the pseudo-Miltonic pomposity of some translations.

Nothing is easier than to pick on some particular line and find fault with the translator for his rendering: I would prefer, for instance, a more literal translation of *hoc solum nomen quoniam de coniuge restat* than "I must not call you husband any longer," but a translation must be judged in the large, and, so considered, Mr Humphries' version is an extraordinarily fine achievement. Further I am amazed, on checking passages here and there, at his skill in detail. Thus, for the famous onomatopoeic lines

> *libravit dextra media inter cornua caestus,*
> *arduus, effractoque inlisit in ossa cerebro:*
> *sternitur exanimisque tremens procumbit humi bos,*

he has

> Drew back his right hand, posed it, sent it smashing
> Between the horns, shattering the skull, and splashing
> Brains on the bones, as the great beast came down, lifeless

and I cannot imagine a happier transliteration of

> *tum vero exarsit iuveni dolor ossibus ingens,*
> *nec lacrimis caruere genae, segnemque Menoeten,*
> *oblitus decorisque sui sociumque salutis,*
> *in mare praecipitem puppi deturbat ab alta;*

than

> Then Gyas really was burnt-up; he was crying
> In rage; to hell with pride, to hell with safety!
> He grabbed that cautious pilot of his, and heaved him
> Over the stern.

In making it not only possible but also agreeable for those who cannot read Latin to read straight through the *Aeneid*, Mr Humphries has done this generation and, I hope and believe, several generations to come a service for which no public reward could be too great.

The Nation, 10 March 1951

Address to the Indian Congress for Cultural Freedom

If I ask myself the justification of this Congress, the answer lies first of all in the answer to other questions. The first question is, why is it that all of us here at this moment, whether sitting on the floor, or on the platform, are bored to death and wanting to go home. Why are they bored? Why are we bored? Because this is a public meeting, that is to say, an occasion upon which nobody meets anybody! The reason for this Congress is that we are threatened by forces which would turn the whole of human existence into a continuous public meeting in which anyone who yawned would be deprived of his ration card, anyone who fell asleep shot without trial. Again, if when asked, if I were to say that any of us should go away, as I shall go away, glad that this conference was held, it will be for us not so much any resolutions that may have been drawn up, or even any practical effect they may have, it will not even perhaps be anything particular that was said by anyone. Speaking for myself, what I shall take away will be the memory of certain real faces, certain real encounters, over, I am sorry to say, non-alcoholic beverages, with real persons. Perhaps we shall never meet again, but a real encounter with anyone, if only for a second, and even if later consciously forgotten, enters once and for all into the structure and fabric of one's being.

Again the reason for this conference is the thought that we are threatened by forces which would create a world in which—even supposing they could, which they cannot, fulfill their promises of making us all as plump as turkeys—real encounters would be prohibited as not increasing production, and anyone caught off his guard with a real expression would be condemned as dangerous to the State and sent to a camp for "re-education."

I have been introduced to you as a poet. What does that mean? First of course it means somebody who makes something and who therefore has a duty to see that what is made is well, and not shoddily, made. Secondly, because what I make are verses which say something, it is my duty to see that so far as I know and so far as it goes, what they say is true and not false. How important the truth may be is not for me to say. Indeed if I once started thinking about importance I shall immediately start lying. Why do I do this? Certainly not because I must, as I must eat in order to live, nor because I ought for the pleasure of others, because other people cannot know whether it will give them pleasure until they have it. I do it for the same reason that Professor Mueller, for example, does his researches in genetics, because we are both in love—he with the muse of genetics, and I with the muse of poetry. Professor Mueller of course hopes that his discoveries may be of value to mankind, but that is not the reason why he does them. I hope that my verses may give pleasure, that again is not the reason why I do them. If a boy and a girl fall in love, they do not ask themselves what good to humanity it will be if they marry and rear a family, they just try to get married.

Freedom for me personally, then, means three things, I think—freedom to publish what I write, if I can please sufficient persons to make it worth the publishers' while; the freedom of reviewers to pass honest judgment on what they think of what I do; the freedom of readers to procure what I write if they want it, and to buy something else if they don't. The word freedom, as Señor Madariaga said on the first day, implies freedom to err, that is to say, tempta-tion. Now, apart from laziness, what are the temptations that might seduce me from the muse? Well, chiefly vanity, which would like mass applause, greed, which would like large houses, expensive automobiles. They might suggest, for example, that I should work for the movies or write some little book, a best seller on "How to stop worrying in twenty easy lessons." Now if I yield, I am free in so far that if I yield to these, I have no one to blame but myself.

Now, in the societies in which so far I have lived, I have enjoyed these free-doms. No one has even suggested, far less commanded, that I write an ode to General MacArthur or a greeting song to the Coca Cola Company. No re-viewer, so far as I know, has ever been ordered either to praise or blame my work at the risk, in case of disobedience, of losing his job.

Well, let me compare my case with the case of another writer, a Russian woman poetess, Akhmatova. Akhmatova came of a bourgeois origin. She stayed on in Russia at the revolution, lived in obscurity, quietly. Suddenly when the war began and the government wished to make use of everybody, someone suddenly remembered that she had a reputation. She was whisked, so to speak, out of the dustbin, given an apartment, a special ration card, her collective works were brought out, they were enthusiastically reviewed. A friend of mine visited her in 1946 and brought her the first copy of the Poems of Eliot that she had ever seen.

In February 1947, Zhdanov opened his attack on the Leningrad writers, specifying Akhmatova. What happened? Overnight all the reviewers attacked her, the edition was withdrawn, she lost her ration card, she lost her apart-ment, and went back to the dustbin. Why? Because of nothing or anything positive, her poems were about the personal life, they were not about the no-bility of Stalin, or shop-workers, or cement, or glue.

Now, you notice here three things, the absolute, arbitrary nature of a de-cree from above—a person is used when they are useful and discarded when they are not, as if they were a thing; the complete terrorization of the press, so that what is good one day has to become bad the next day; the extension of the punishment from the books themselves to the obliteration of the writer as a person. I do not think one has to be an expert in economics or political science to know that a form of society in which such a thing can occur is a wicked form. I say of course, "a form of society" to be relevant to the fact that it happened in Russia. It happened under a particular form. The potentialities of good and evil, the types of men are the same in America, in Britain, in India, in Russia, everywhere. We can all recognize, and probably have all met, our potential Zhdanovs. That is why forms of state are not just an academic matter for the expert, but of the utmost concern to us amateurs.

There is a great lie in the world which confuses everybody, which seeks to make a false antithesis between the individual and society, the private and the public. To some—shall we say to the Manchester Economist—the individual is good; perhaps to the Marxist only the public is good. This is an unreal division. There are two real worlds and we inhabit both of them. One, the natural material world, the physical world, the world of mass, of number, not of language. A world in which freedom is indeed consciousness of necessities, a world in which justice means equality before the law of physics, chemistry, physiology. And then there is the other world, the historical community of persons, the world of faces, the world of language where necessity is the consciousness of freedom and justice is the command to love my neighbour as myself, that is to say, as a unique, irreplaceable being.

Unreality comes when either world is treated as if it were the other one. The ancient unreality was to treat the natural world as if it were a world of faces producing a magic polytheism. The new modern unreality, and even more dangerous, is the treatment of persons as if they belong to the world of numbers, as if they were only documents. And with that unreality, needless to say, back come the fetishists, the orgiasts.

The new form of totalitarianism is, in fact, animism stood on its head.

We hear a good deal about the gulf between the intellectual and the masses. We do not hear enough about the ways in which they are alike. Why is it, for example, that, if I have got the pronunciation right, Mr Ramagu and his wife Shatama from the village of Vadgaon, who to the eye are brownish, undernourished objects with bad teeth, and Mr W. H. Auden, B.A., Oxford, with a publisher in New York City, who to the eye is a pale, over-corpulent object with well-made American teeth, why is it that when we both, both they and I, meet a public official, we both have the same feelings, namely that we will not trust him further than we can throw a grand piano? Why is it that when we go into a public building we both are struck by the same feeling of apprehension that perhaps we shall not get out? Because, whatever the differences in culture between us, we know, we sense in an official world the smell of that unreality in which people are not treated as people, but as numbers.

It would be well in any government, I think, if in every single Minister's office there are two inscriptions. One is a poem of Ogden Nash's: "As I sit in my office on the corner of 23rd Street and Madison Avenue, I say to myself, you've a responsible position, haven't you?" The other, a remark: "We are all here on earth to help others; what on earth the others are here for, I don't know."

I have a small reason for thinking that artists and poets may have some political value at this time. The only reason I have for thinking so is that among all official circles in all countries they arouse a certain suspicion. I don't know of a country where the suspicion doesn't occur. That is why, selfishly, it is very important that the suspicion does not take too violent a form. Perhaps as long as artists exist doing what they like, they remind people who govern of what they do not like to be reminded, that the government are people and not numbers. After all, I can read any day in the paper, as I read the other day, about a lakh of refugees—now that may be an actual number, the real numbers are, am I right in saying, a hundred thousand ones. Then it is easy to read that 15½% died of starvation in some province. Now that statement cannot be accurate for, unlike a ton of rice, if you cut a man in half he dies. I think that as long as there are works of art which are, each of them, unique, they are a witness, whether people understand them or not, to the world of humanity that they reflect. The fact that a starving refugee is not a number but a real person, and that though you may feed him, you feed him as a number—he is not so far gone that he is barely human; the moment your back is turned, he will quite rightly spit!

Well, the poet may, as I say, have this small political value of being an irritant reminder. That is not very much, because after all the tyrant may suspect the artist—he also despises him because it is the tyrant, who has the police and the tanks, and the artist has only his talents. There are only two things really that the tyrant fears. He worships the dynamo, and one of his fears is the rival worshipper of the dynamo who may have two dynamos to his one. There is only one thing that he grades absolutely and his rival grades it equally, therefore, and that is the martyr. It is fitting, I think, that I should mention the martyr in this land where the most famous martyrdom of our times took place—I mean the dead Gandhi.

One of the great changes in sensibility is signified, I think, by the sudden discovery at the First World War of the idea of the Unknown Soldier. The Unknown Soldier, the monument not to the victorious general but to the person who is nameless but one person. Of course ideally I should know what one has to assume, that the Unknown Soldier volunteered and sacrificed himself willingly. The martyr's act is a free act, a martyr is someone who chooses out of love for others to sacrifice his natural body and his historical person to the force of mass and number. No physical miracle occurs, he is destroyed, he becomes a thing. His name is not actually important for there is no talent for martyrdom.

It is no easier or no harder for Gandhi or for an unknown figure in a concentration camp to sacrifice his life for another. The martyr cannot become a subject for poetry, because all that matters is the fact that the martyr is the only thing that the tyrant grades absolutely, it is because before the actual martyrdom—whatever our differences, whether we are lettered or unlettered, scientists, artists, religious or rationalists—we all are united equally in reverence. And when that happens the dynamo is seen for what it is, an ingenious piece of machinery, and the wicked priest of that blood-stained temple flees away into the night pursued by boos and Bronx cheers into the night, where I trust he hangs himself.

Indian Congress for Cultural Freedom, March 28–31, 1951

Some Reflections on Opera as a Medium

Every artistic medium reflects some area of human experience. These areas often overlap but never coincide, for if two media could do the same thing equally well one would be unnecessary.

When someone, like myself, after years of working in one medium, essays another for the first time, he should always, I believe, try to discover its proper principles before starting work. Otherwise he is in danger of carrying over assumptions and habits of mind which have become second nature to him into a field where, as a matter of fact, they do not and cannot apply.

★　★　★

What is music about? What, as Plato would say, does it "imitate"? Choice. A succession of two musical notes is an act of choice; the first causes the second not in the scientific sense of making it occur necessarily, but in the historical sense of provoking it, of providing it with a motive for occurring. A successful melody is a self-determined history: it is freely what it intends to be yet is a meaningful whole not an arbitrary succession of notes.

★　★　★

Music as an art, i.e. music that has come to a conscious realization of its true nature, is confined to Western Civilization alone and only to the last four or five hundred years at that. The music of all other Cultures and epochs bears the same relation to Western music that magical verbal formulae bear to the art of poetry. A primitive magic spell may be poetry but it does not know that it is, nor intend to be. So, in all but Western music, history is only implicit; what it thinks it is doing is furnishing verses or movements with a repetitive accompaniment. Only in the West has chant become song.

★　★　★

Lacking a historical consciousness, the Greek theories of music tried to relate it to Pure Being, but the becoming implicit in music betrays itself in their theories of harmony in which mathematics becomes numerology and one chord is intrinsically "better" than another.

Western music declared its consciousness of itself when it adopted time-signatures, barring and the metronome beat. Without a strictly natural or cyclical time, purified from every trace of historical singularity, as a framework within which to occur, the irreversible historicity of the notes themselves would be impossible.

★   ★   ★

A verbal art like poetry is reflective; it stops to think. Music is immediate, it goes on to become. But both are active, both insist on stopping or going on. The medium of passive reflection is painting, of passive immediacy the cinema, for the visual world is an immediately given world where Fate is mistress and it is impossible to tell the difference between a chosen movement and an involuntary reflex. Freedom of choice lies, not in the world we see, but in our freedom to turn our eyes in this direction or in that, or to close them altogether.

Because music expresses the opposite experience of pure volition and subjectivity (the fact that we cannot shut our ears at will allows music to assert that we cannot not choose), film music is not music but a technique for preventing us using our ears to hear extraneous noises and it is bad film music if we become consciously aware of its existence.

★   ★   ★

All of us have learned to talk, most of us, even, could be taught to speak verse tolerably well, but very few have learned or could ever be taught to sing. In any village twenty people could get together and give a performance of *Hamlet* which, however imperfect, would convey enough of the play's greatness to be worth attending, but if they were to attempt a similar performance of *Don Giovanni*, they would soon discover that there was no question of a good or a bad performance because they could not sing the notes at all. Of an actor, even in a poetic drama, when we say that his performance is good, we mean that he simulates by art, that is, consciously, the way in which the character he is playing would, in real life, behave by nature, that is, unconsciously. But for a singer, as for a ballet dancer, there is no question of simulation, of singing the composer's notes "naturally"; his behaviour is unabashedly and triumphantly art from beginning to end. The paradox implicit in all drama, namely, that emotions and situations which in real life would be sad or painful are on the stage a source of pleasure becomes, in opera, quite explicit. The singer may be playing the role of a deserted bride who is about to kill herself, but we feel quite certain as we listen that not only we but also she is having a wonderful time. In a sense there can be no tragic opera because whatever errors the characters make and whatever they suffer, they are doing exactly what they wish. Hence the feeling that *opera seria* should not employ a contemporary subject, but confine itself to mythical situations, that is, situations which as human beings we are all of us necessarily in and must, therefore, accept, however tragic they may be. A contemporary tragic situation like that in Menotti's *The Consul* is too actual, that is, too clearly a situation some people are in and others, including the audience, are not in, for the latter to forget this and see it as a symbol of, say, man's existential estrangement. Consequently the pleasure we and the singers are obviously enjoying strikes the conscience as frivolous.

★ ★ ★

On the other hand, its pure artifice renders Opera the ideal dramatic medium for a tragic myth. I once went in the same week to a performance of *Tristan und Isolde* and a showing of *L'Eternel Retour*, Jean Cocteau's movie version of the same story. During the former two souls, weighing over two hundred pounds apiece, were transfigured by a transcendent power, in the latter a handsome boy met a beautiful girl and they had an affair. This loss of value was due not to any lack of skill on Cocteau's part but to the nature of the cinema as a medium. Had he used a fat middle-aged couple the effect would have been ridiculous because the snatches of language which are all the movie permits have not sufficient power to transcend their physical appearance. Yet if the lovers are young and beautiful, the cause of their love looks "natural," a consequence of their beauty, and the whole meaning of the myth is gone.

★ ★ ★

If music in general is an imitation of history, opera in particular is an imitation of human wilfulness; it is rooted in the fact that we not only have feelings but insist upon having them at whatever cost to ourselves. The moment a person starts to sing, he becomes a monomaniac. Opera, therefore, cannot present character in the novelist's sense of the word, namely, people who are potentially good *and* bad, active *and* passive, for music is immediate actuality and neither potentiality nor passivity can live in its presence. This is something a librettist must never forget. Mozart is a greater composer than Rossini but the Figaro of the *Marriage* is less satisfying, to my mind, than the Figaro of the *Barber* and the fault, is, I think, Da Ponte's. His Figaro is too interesting a character to be completely translatable into music so that co-present with the Figaro who is singing one is conscious of a Figaro who is not singing but thinking to himself. The barber of Seville, on the other hand, who is not a person but a maniacal busybody, goes into song exactly, with nothing over.

Again, I find *La Bohème* inferior to *Tosca*, not because its music is inferior, but because the characters, Mimi in particular, are too passive; there is an awkward gap between the resolution with which they sing and the irresolution with which they act.

The quality common to all the great operatic roles, e.g. Don Giovanni, Norma, Lucia, Tristan, Isolde, Brünnhilde, is that each of them is a passionate and wilful state of being. In real life they would all be bores, even Don Giovanni.

In recompense for this lack of psychological complexity, however, music can do what words cannot, present the immediate and simultaneous relation of these states to each other. The crowning glory of opera is the big ensemble.

★   ★   ★

The chorus can play two roles in opera and two only, that of the mob and that of the faithful, sorrowing or rejoicing community. A little of that goes a long way. Opera is not oratorio.

★   ★   ★

Drama is based on the Mistake. I think someone is my friend when he really is my enemy, that I am free to marry a woman when in fact she is my mother, that this person is a chambermaid when it is a young nobleman in disguise, that this well-dressed young man is rich when it is really a penniless adventurer, or that if I do this such and such a result will follow when in fact it results in something very different. All good drama has two movements, first the making of the mistake, then the discovery that it was a mistake.

In composing his plot, the librettist has to conform to this law but, in comparison to the dramatist, he is more limited in the kinds of mistakes he can use. The dramatist, for instance, procures some of his finest effects from showing how people deceive themselves. Self-deception is impossible in opera because music is immediate not reflective; whatever is sung is the case. At most self-deception can be suggested by having the orchestral accompaniment at variance with the singer, e.g. the jolly tripping notes which accompany Germont's approach to Violetta's death-bed in *La Traviata*, but unless employed very sparingly such devices cause confusion rather than insight.

Again, while in the spoken drama the discovery of the mistake can be a slow process and often, indeed, the more gradual it is the greater the dramatic interest, in a libretto the drama of recognition must be tropically abrupt, for music cannot exist in an atmosphere of uncertainty; song cannot walk, it can only jump.

On the other hand, the librettist need never bother his head, as the dramatist must, about probability. A credible situation in opera means a situation in which it is credible that someone should sing. A good libretto plot is a melodrama in both the strict and the conventional sense of the word; it offers as many opportunities as possible for the characters to be swept off their feet by placing them in situations which are too tragic or too fantastic for "words." No good opera plot can be sensible for people do not sing when they are feeling sensible.

The theory of "Music-drama" pre-supposes a libretto in which there is not one sensible moment or one sensible remark: this is not only very difficult to manage though Wagner managed it, but also extremely exhausting on both the singers and the audience, neither of whom may relax for an instant.

In a libretto where there are any sensible passages, i.e. conversation not song, the theory becomes absurd. If, for furthering the action, it becomes necessary for one character to say to another "Run upstairs and fetch me a handkerchief," then there is nothing in the words, apart from their rhythm, to make one musical setting more apt than another. Wherever the choice of notes is arbitrary, the only solution is a convention, e.g. *recitativo secco*.

★   ★   ★

In opera the orchestra is addressed to the singers, not to the audience. An opera-lover will put up with and even enjoy an orchestral interlude on condition that he knows the singers cannot sing just now because they are tired or the scene-shifters are at work, but any use of the orchestra by itself which is not filling-in time is, for him, wasting it. Leonora III is a fine piece to listen to in the concert hall, but in the opera house, where it is played between scenes one and two of the second act of *Fidelio*, it becomes twelve minutes of acute boredom.

★   ★   ★

In opera the Heard and the Seen are like Reality and Appearance in philosophy; hence the more frankly theatrical and sham the sets the better. Good taste is not in order. A realistic painted backdrop which wobbles is more satisfactory than any conscientiously three-dimensional furniture or suggestive non-representational objects. Only one thing is essential, namely, that everything be a little over life size, that the stage be a space in which only the grand entrance and the grand gesture are appropriate.

★   ★   ★

If the librettist is a practising poet, the most difficult problem, the place where he is most likely to go astray, is the composition of the verses. Poetry is in its essence an act of reflection, of refusing to be content with the interjections of immediate emotion in order to understand the nature of what is felt. Since music is in essence immediate, it follows that the words of a song cannot be poetry. Here one should draw a distinction between lyric and song proper. A lyric is a poem intended to be chanted. In a chant the music is subordinate to the words which limit the range and tempo of the notes. In song, the notes must be free to be whatever they choose and the words must be able to do what they are told.

Much as I admire Hofmannsthal's libretto for *Rosenkavalier*, it is, I think, too near real poetry. The Marschallin's monologue in Act I, for instance, is so full of interesting detail that the voice line is hampered in trying to follow everything. The verses of *Ah non credea* in *La Somnambula* on the other hand, though of little interest to read, do exactly what they should, suggest to Bellini one of the most beautiful melodies ever written and then leave him completely free to write it. The verses which the librettist writes are not addressed to the public but are really a private letter to the composer. They have their moment of glory, the moment in which they suggest to him a certain melody: once that is over, they are as expendable as infantry to a Chinese general: they must efface themselves and cease to care what happens to them.

★   ★   ★

The golden age of opera, from Mozart to Verdi, coincided with the golden age of liberal humanism, of unquestioning belief in freedom and progress. If good operas are rarer today, this may be because, not only have we learned that we are less free than nineteenth century humanism imagined, but also have become less certain that freedom is an unequivocal blessing, that the free are necessarily the good. To say that operas are more difficult to write does not mean that they are impossible. That would only follow if we should cease to believe in free-will and personality altogether. Every high C accurately struck utterly demolishes the theory that we are the irresponsible puppets of fate or chance.

Tempo, Summer 1951

The Philosophy of a Lunatic

Wisdom, Madness and Folly. By John Custance.
Foreword by L. W. Grensted. Gollancz. 16s.

Mr Custance is a manic-depressive of fifty-one who suffered his first attack in 1936; his longest manic phase lasted six months, his longest depressive fifteen, the intervals between the two from one month to four years.

In his first four chapters he describes in fascinating detail what he experiences in each state. When manic he inhabits a universe of bliss; all sensations of colour, touch and taste are intensely vivid; he can concentrate anywhere, his ideas flow easily, and he develops powers of drawing, singing and reading without spectacles which, when "normal," he does not possess; no dirt seems repulsive, no act forbidden, and he himself is a very important person indeed.

> I hold imaginary conversations—which appear absolutely real to me— with all my favourite historical characters, notably anima figures like Cleopatra and Mary Magdalen. . . . I feel so close to God, so inspired by His Spirit, that in a sense I am God. I see the future, plan the Universe, save mankind.

Unfortunately, the behaviour which accompanies such feelings is liable to get him into trouble. During one attack he gave away three hundred pounds to whores, and when the Christian Science Church in Curzon Street refused to give him money for the same purpose he started to wreck the place.

When the depressive phase comes on, he is plunged into a universe of horror and despair. He feels unclean and must wash all the time; he sees devils everywhere. Worst of all, he is convinced that he is damned; "because I was such an appalling sinner, the worst man who had ever existed. I had been chosen to go alive through the portals of Hell. . . . I was a sort of opposite of Jesus Christ." His behaviour in this state is what one would expect; he lies in bed with his head under the blankets or he tries to kill himself.

Of the various treatments he received, neither psychological analysis nor narcosis were much help. The present improvement in his condition—during the last four years the depressions have ceased to be serious—seems to have been brought about mainly by his own efforts at self-understanding. About the doctors and nurses with whom he came into contact, Mr Custance does his best to be fair; he realises that they are overworked and underpaid and that the behaviour of the mentally ill would often try the patience of a saint, but he cannot forget how much bureaucratic injustice and even personal sadism lunatics have to endure.

Out of his experiences Mr Custance has developed a kind of psychological cosmology phrased in Jungian terms. Two great powers are at work in the universe, a Positive or dividing power and a Negative or uniting power. The sun, the Father god, intellect, science, Protestantism, Communism, the future are expressions of the Positive; the moon, the Mother goddess, instinct, art, Catholicism, monarchy, the past are Negative. The present age is one in which, after centuries of dominance by the Positive power, the long repressed Negative forces are returning and, unless we accept them consciously and gladly, their mood will be one of revenge.

There is no space in a review either to do justice to Mr Custance's theory or to make adequate criticism. As he himself admits, the author is a "negative" and, consequently, he can only think about the Positive in negative terms, e.g. as male when it would think of itself as neuter. His depressive universe is really just as negative as his manic, for both are animistic and magical, all things have faces, impersonal necessity is absent, and, whether it be in love or in hatred, the patient's ego and the universe are of the utmost concern to each other. For a "positive" personality, the contrasting states are quite different. The elated state is one in which the ego rejoices at being detached, liberated from both attraction and aversion, and the depressed state one in which the ego feels that the universe is not hostile, but absolutely indifferent to his fate. A similar difference shows in his behaviour; it is the elated positive who takes a pride in cleanliness and chastity, for both express his feeling of being in control, and the depressed positive who neglects his personal appearance—nobody cares—and becomes a Don Juan; i.e. his sexual promiscuity is motivated by will not feeling, an attempt to compel the universe to be interesting and interested.

In conclusion, since Mr Custance tells us that he is a Christian, it seems fair to point out that the Christian conception of a unique revelation in history is as incompatible with Jung as it is with Marx, with cyclical theories of time as with doctrines of the Wave of the Future, with the imagination's idolatry of images as with the reason's idolatry of number. One cannot, for instance, identify the cult of the Earth Mother with the cult of the Madonna; the former is a dynamo in disguise, the falsely personal image of the impersonal forces of nature; the latter, through her actual personal historical existence on earth, has become the type and pledge of the redemption of the natural order.

The Observer, 10 June 1951

Eliot on Eliot

Poetry and Drama. By T. S. Eliot. Faber & Faber. 7s 6d.

The best artists rarely print their own thoughts about their productions, some because they are modest, some because they are preoccupied with work in progress. This is a pity. Though criticism must begin and end with interjections of approval or disapproval which it is the business of the reader rather than the author to utter, in between lie all the questions which make criticism interesting, such a question, for example, as this: "What particular problems was the author trying to solve in this particular work and how far has he succeeded?" Here the author himself, unless he is abnormally deficient in self-judgment, is better qualified to give an answer than any outsider. Henry James does more in his prefaces to make one understand what he is up to in his novels than any other critic, however perceptive, could have hoped to do.

In inaugurating the annual lecture in memory of his old friend Professor Theodore Spencer, Mr Eliot has very happily chosen to speak on a personal topic, that of his own plays, and in a manner freer, more personal and, incidentally, more humorous than he has ever allowed himself before. The task of the poet-dramatist, as he sees it, is "to bring poetry into the world in which the audience lives and to which it returns when it leaves the theatre; not to transport the audience into some imaginary world totally unlike its own, an unreal world in which poetry is tolerated." He opens his lecture with a discussion, illustrated by quotations from *Hamlet*, of the nature of dramatic verse. People do not come to the theatre to hear poetry, as people go to a volume of lyrics; they come to witness characters in action. But if the poetry is integrated with the action, they can be dramatically affected by it. Dramatic verse, therefore, must be capable of every degree of intensity from the most "prosaic" to the most "poetical." It must permit the characters to transcend their individualised practical selves when the emotional situation demands it and also permit them to resume themselves without a noticeable jolt. It must be able to sing and able to converse.

Mr Eliot then gets down to his own plays. *Murder in the Cathedral* was a period piece on a religious subject. For a beginner this had its advantages; "period costume renders verse more acceptable," and "people who go deliberately to a religious play at a religious festival expect to be patiently bored." The disadvantage was that the kind of versification, based on *Everyman*, which Mr Eliot devised was suitable only to a play set in that particular historical period. Further, the use of the chorus as pure spectators of the action, though effective in this case, was, he felt, a snare, a temptation to evade a real integration of poetry and action. In his next play, therefore, he decided to take a contemporary subject, to devise a verse rhythm close to contemporary speech and to use the characters themselves as commentators. In *Family Reunion* he came a long way towards solving the problem of versification. The line he devised is, according to him, one with three stresses and a strongly marked caesura. Here I must confess myself baffled. Opening the play at random I read:—

> WARBURTON. I wonder what he wants. I hope nothing has happened
>   To either of your brothers.
> HARRY.   Nothing can have happened
>   To either of my brothers. Nothing can happen
>   If Sergeant Winchell is real. But Dennian saw him.

I must have a tin ear for, try as I may, I cannot for the life of me read any of these lines with less than four stresses and line three sounds to me as if it had five. But then prosody is to poets what laying a fire is to married couples, a matter on which nobody is right but oneself.

With other aspects of the play, Mr Eliot felt less satisfied. The use of the characters as commentators had proved even more artificial than the frank employment of a chorus, he had failed to make anything happen on the stage till the last few minutes and his hero had turned out "an insufferable prig." As for the Furies:—

> We put them on the stage, and they looked like uninvited guests who had strayed in from a fancy dress ball. We concealed them behind gauze, and they suggested a still out of a Walt Disney film. We made them dimmer, and they looked like shrubbery just outside the window.

In the next play, then, no chorus, no overt reference to mythology and plenty of action, even if that meant playing down the poetry. In *The Cocktail Party* he succeeded at last in challenging the prose drama on its own grounds. What his next step is to be, Mr Eliot, naturally, is not telling. He only expresses the hope that one day he will be sufficient master of his medium to give the poetry its head without fear of the drama suffering. Mr Eliot speaks with the

authority of achievement. I am not quite convinced, however, that it is necessary to accept the *verismo* of the contemporary West End play (which even
condemns the formalised plot) as a premise for all poetic drama even if Mr
Eliot feels it to be for his own. I think of two dramatic forms, the pantomime
and the opera, which, though totally unrealistic, compete successfully with
prose drama for popular appeal and, far from presenting an "unreal world,"
are, at least to me, a better "imitation" of life as we experience it subjectively
than any naturalistic reflection can hope to be.

Mr Eliot's path may well prove the highway, but it would be a pity if his authority should cause others to be left unexplored. With the ideal poetic
drama which he envisages as the goal of all paths, none, I think, will disagree:
"a design of human action and words which will present at once the two aspects of dramatic and of musical order without losing contact with the ordinary everyday world" with which all the arts must ultimately come to terms,
for to elicit, "by imposing a credible order upon ordinary reality, some perception of an order in reality" is precisely their function.

The Observer, 28 October 1951

Foreword to *A Mask for Janus,*
by W. S. Merwin

In every successful poem the reader encounters, at one and the same time,
a historically unique experience—what occurs in the poem has occurred for
the first and last time—and an experience which is universally significant—
analogous experiences have always occurred and will continue to occur to all
men. In respect of these two elements, most poems fall into one of two classes,
those in which the historic occasion is, so to speak, on the outside and the
general significance on the inside, and those in which their positions are the
other way round. In the first kind of poem, the overt subject of the poem is
a specific experience undergone by the "I" of the poem at a specific time and
place—whether the experience actually occurred to the poet or was invented
makes no difference—and the universal significance is implied, not stated
directly. In the second kind, the overt subject is universal and impersonal, frequently a myth, and it is the personal experience of the poet which is implied.
Most of the poems of Robert Frost belong to the first category, those of Paul
Valéry to the second, while Yeats alternates between writing "occasional" and
"mythological" poetry.

Neither kind, of course, is better or greater than the other, but each has its
peculiar danger. In uninspired hands, the occasional approach degenerates
into triviality and journalism—the occasion described is without significant

resonance—while the mythological approach becomes "literary" in the bad sense, a mere elegant manifestation of the imaginative work of the dead without any live relation to the present of the writer or his reader.

Silly and tiresome as is that favorite question of reporters, "What are the trends in poetry today?" it is impossible, if one compares a contemporary issue of any literary magazine with an issue of fifteen years back, not to recognize certain changes in content, and among these the most obvious is the increase of interest shown today, both by poets and critics, in myth, and a corresponding turning away, on the part of the poets at least, from occasional subjects whether political or private.

The shift of concern is probably a fortunate one, particularly for a young poet, like Mr Merwin. To be able to speak in one's own person and directly in terms of one's own experience without making a fool of oneself requires a wisdom and assumed authority which is more likely to come, if it comes at all, in later life, but the profundity and eternal relevance to the human condition of the great myths cannot fail to instill the most immature writer who reflects upon them with that reverence and wonder without which no man can become wise.

One of Mr Merwin's best poems, "Dictum: For a Masque of Deluge" is based upon the myth of the Flood. The historical experience which is latent in the poem is, I fancy, the feeling which most of us share of being witnesses to the collapse of a civilization, a collapse which transcends all political differences and for which we are all collectively responsible, and in addition feeling that this collapse is not final but that, on the other side of disaster, there will be some kind of rebirth, though we cannot imagine its nature. By translating these feelings into mythical terms, the poet is able to avoid what a direct treatment could scarcely have avoided, namely, the use of names and events which will probably turn out not to have been the really significant ones.

With his concern for the traditional conceptions of Western culture as expressed in its myths, Mr Merwin combines an admirable respect for its traditions of poetic craftsmanship. His carols show how carefully he has studied Spanish versification, and in poems like "For a Dissolving Music" and "A Dance of Death" he has not been ashamed to write what are frankly technical exercises. Apart from the fact that works which set out to be exercises in technique often end by being works of art as well, e.g. the Chopin *Etudes*, the mastery of his medium through diligent practice is of incalculable value to any artist. Technique in itself cannot make a good poem, but the lack of it can spoil one. The final stanza of "Dictum" shows the reward that Mr Merwin has earned by his studies.

> A falling frond may seem all trees. If so
> We know the tone of falling. We shall find

> Dictions for rising, words for departure;
> And time will be sufficient before that revel
> To teach an order and rehearse the days
> Till the days are accomplished: so now the dove
> Makes assignations with the olive tree,
> Slurs with her voice the gestures of the time:
> The day foundering, the dropping sun
> Heavy, the wind a low portent of rain.

No one who had not previously trained himself thoroughly in the mechanics of verse could have varied so skillfully the position of the caesura from line to line, a variation on which so much of the poetic effect depends.

In conclusion, reflecting upon the general tenor of Mr Merwin's poetry as an example of the younger generations of American poets, I am reminded of a remarkable prophecy in de Tocqueville's *Democracy in America* concerning the poetry of the future. Of its accuracy I must leave the reader to judge.

> When skepticism had depopulated heaven . . . the poets . . . turned their eyes to inanimate Nature. As they lost sight of Gods and heroes, they set themselves to describe streams and mountains, . . . Some have thought this . . . the kind of poetry peculiar to democratic ages; but I believe it only belongs to a period of transition.
>
> I am persuaded that in the end democracy diverts the imagination from all that is external to man, and fixes it on man alone. . . .
>
> . . . [The] poets living in democratic ages will prefer the delineation of passions and ideas to that of persons and achievements. The language, the dress, and the daily actions of men in democracies are repugnant to ideal conceptions. . . . This forces the poet constantly to search below the external surface which is palpable to the senses, in order to read the inner soul. . . .
>
> . . . The destinies of mankind—man himself, taken aloof from his age and his country, and standing in the presence of Nature and of God, with his passions, his doubts, his rare prosperities, and inconceivable wretchedness—will become the chief, if not the sole theme of poetry among these nations.*

W. S. Merwin, *A Mask for Janus*, 1952

* Alexis de Tocqueville, *Democracy in America*, tr. Henry Reeve, ed. Henry Steele Commager (New York, Oxford University Press, 1947), pp. 290–294.

Keats in His Letters

The Selected Letters of John Keats. Edited by Lionel Trilling.
Farrar, Straus and Young. $3.50.

This volume is a model example of what the Great Letters series should be.
All the important letters are included and without cuts; following the Mau-
rice Buxton Forman edition of 1931, the letters are printed in their original
spelling and punctuation, which is more important than one might think, for
normalization of such matters ruins Keats's peculiar epistolary style; the footnotes are helpful and modest, and Professor Trilling's introduction is, for its
length, one of the best essays on Keats that I have read. Against certain of the
Romantic writers the charges of moral woolliness and self-idolatry brought by
Irving Babbitt and others are, I believe, legitimate, but I fully share Professor
Trilling's conviction that Keats is not among them.

The distinction which Keats drew between the poet who is unpoetical because he has no identity of his own and poetical things like the sun, the moon,
and men and women who are creatures of impulse and action, is applicable to
people's letters, including his own. There are two kinds of letters, those in which
the writer is in control of his situation—what he writes about it is what he
chooses to write—and those in which the situation dictates what he writes. The
terms personal and impersonal are here ambiguous; the first kind of letter is
impersonal in so far as the writer is looking at himself in the world as if he were
a third person but personal in so far as it is his personal act so to look—the signature to the letter is really his and he is responsible for its contents; vice versa,
the second kind is personal in that the writer is identical with what he writes,
but impersonal in that it is the situation not he which enforces that identity.

The second kind are what journalists call "human documents" and most
of the letters written by Keats after his first serious hemorrhage belong to it.
I am not sorry that they have been published but I am sorry that they were
not published anonymously, for in them Keats has, as it were, ceased to be a
poet and become a poetic subject, human nature in an extreme existential
situation of suffering and despair. Phrases like "You must be mine to die upon
the rack if I want you" or "You may have altered—if you have not—if you still
behave in dancing rooms and other societies as I have seen you—I do not
want to live," or "I should like to die. I am sickened at the brute world which
you are smiling with. I hate men and women more," strike the heart with pity
and fear; nobody but a priggish fool would censure the man who wrote them
for they themselves pass judgment on our "poor impassioned clay."

Any discussion of Keats's letters, therefore, should confine itself to those
written before February 3, 1820.

I wonder if school children are still taught, as I was, the ridiculous myth
that Keats was killed by a bad review. I wonder, furthermore, how much Shel-

ley, who is largely responsible for it, actually believed what he wrote in *Adonais*; one cannot help suspecting that subconscious jealousy of Keats's superior gifts and resentment at his lack of admiration for Shelley's own poetry played a role in his portrait of Keats as a lovable weakling, a sort of male and literary *Dame aux Camélias*. Had it been true, Byron's sneers in *Don Juan* would have been fully deserved, but both the poems and the letters prove it to be a fantastic distortion.

Adonais is a sensitive plant without an idea in his head; Keats's mind, on the other hand, was a rare combination of witty and original intelligence with common sense. There are lines in his poetry with which one can find fault, there are statements in his letters which one may wish to question, but I cannot remember anything in either which one could call just silly. There are very few poets of any period—none of Keats's contemporaries are among them—of whom this can be said. Even the two sentences for which he has most frequently been attacked, the conclusion of the *Ode on a Grecian Urn* and the "O for a life of Sensations rather than Thoughts" in the letter to Bailey have only to be read in their context to see that they do not mean what their hostile critics say they mean.

A small but revealing example of Keats's maturity of outlook is his political attitude. Politics is a subject upon which poets are peculiarly liable to make asses of themselves. Keats moved in a circle with strong liberal views and a young man of twenty-three might most excusably have became hot-headed and exaggerated in his expressions; in fact, the few political comments that he does make are extraordinarily cool and sensible.

> Notwithstanding the part which the Liberals take in the Cause of Napoleon I cannot but think he has done more harm to the life of Liberty than anyone else could have done; not that the divine right Gentlemen have done or intend to do any good—no they have taken a Lesson of him, and will do all the further harm he would have done without any of the good—The worst thing he has done is, that he has taught them how to organise their monstrous armies.

This maturity seems all the more remarkable when on considers his lack of educational or social advantages. Like Blake, he attended neither a public school nor a university, and his circle of friends could hardly be described as distinguished, either artistically or socially—his family, a curate, a clerk in an insurance office, a navy Pay Officer. The only "names" he knew intimately were the painter Benjamin Haydon, who was dotty and unsuccessful, and Leigh Hunt whom everybody, Keats included, seems to have found a ridiculous bore.

> He understands many a beautiful thing; but then, instead of giving other minds credit for the same degree of perception as he himself possesses—he begins an explanation in such a serious manner that our taste and

self-love is offended continually. Hunt does one harm by making fine things petty and beautiful things hateful—Through him I am indifferent to Mozart, I care not for white Busts—and many a glorious thing when associated with him becomes a nothing.

Given Keats's age and gifts this confinement to the outskirts of literary and social life was probably advantageous. It is always dangerous for a young writer to be taken up by the fashionable world before he has discovered his own values, and a mind which is original and self-critical often finds the company of those among whom, because they are not its intellectual equal, it is not afraid to think aloud, more helpful than one more brilliant. Many of the famous passages in the letters on art and life seem just such thinking aloud, i.e. they are not addressed to anyone in particular; had he been writing to someone else at the moment, another correspondent would have received them. As time went on, however, one gets the impression that Keats was beginning to feel a certain constriction and loneliness. Writing to his brother (How much, one wonders, did George understand of the extraordinary letters he received?) he complains

> They do not know me, not even my most intimate acquaintance—I give in to their feelings as though I was refraining from irritating a little child . . . everyone thinks he sees my weak side against my will, when in truth it is with my will . . . I am content to be thought all this because I have in my own breast so great a resource . . . It is one reason they like me so; because they can all show to advantage in a room, and eclipse from a certain tact one who is reckoned to be a good poet.

In the case of a poet's letters our first interest, naturally, is in what they reveal about his attitude toward poetry, his admirations and distastes, his conception of his own work. References to poets other than Shakespeare are not very frequent in Keats's letters. He admired Wordsworth while thinking that he was a freak genius, "an egotistical sublime" whose didacticism had to be accepted in him but not as an example to be imitated; while he is not malicious about either, it is clear that he did not think much of the Byron and the Shelley he had read, and equally clear that there was nobody among his contemporaries whose judgment on his own poetry he really trusted or respected.

Keats is as indisputable an example as any of which we have record of a man with a vocation, whose life was consciously dedicated to poetry:

> The only thing that can ever affect me personally for more than one short passing day, is any doubt about my powers for poetry—I seldom have any, and I look with hope to the nighing time when I shall have none.

He can even put his work before writing to Fanny Brawne:

I would feign, as my sails are set, sail on without an interruption for a Brace of Months longer—I am in complete cue—in the fever; and shall in these four Months do an immense deal—This Page as my eye skims over it I see is excessively unloverlike and ungallant—I cannot help it— I am no officer in yawning quarters; no Parson-romeo . . . My heart seems now made of iron—I could not write a proper answer to an invitation to Idalia.

Dedicated artists are liable to suffer from two complaints, a humorless over-earnest attitude toward art, and a lack of ordinary social responsibility, a feeling that what they are doing is so important that it is the duty of others to support them. Reading Rilke's letters or the Journal of Henry James, for example, there are times when their tone of hushed reverence before the artistic mystery becomes insufferable and one would like to give them both a good shaking; similarly, the incessant harping on money in the correspondence of Baudelaire or Wagner provokes in the most sympathetic admirer the reaction of a sound bourgeois—"Why doesn't he go and look for a job?"

From both of these defects Keats is completely and refreshingly free. As convinced as any writer of the seriousness and value of art, he never sounds like an abbé of the aesthetic, and, though frequently in financial difficulties, he is never extravagant with money he has been given and never forgets the reality of the situation. Thus he writes to Brown:

I am getting into an idle-minded, vicious way of life, almost content to live upon others . . . I have not known yet what it is to be diligent. I purpose living in town in a cheap lodging, and endeavouring, for a beginning, to get the theatricals of some paper. When I can afford to compose deliberate poems, I will . . . I had got in the habit of mind of looking towards you as a help in difficulties . . . You will see it is a duty I owe myself to break the neck of . . .

Few solid citizens of his age, let alone artists, have shown a greater sense of family responsibility; for instance, at the same time that in a letter to his grown-up brother he is expressing heterodox theological opinions, in answer to some questions by his adolescent sister, he sends—O admirable insincerity!—a set of conventionally orthodox answers.

Lastly, the literary style of Keats's letters is of exceptional interest. In the case of most poets or novelists whose correspondence has been preserved, there is an obvious similarity between their studied compositions and their epistolary style; the Byron of *Don Juan* and the Byron of the letters are recognizably the same person, so that, reading the one, one could make a good guess, not, of course, at the quality but at the manner of the other. In Keats's case there is no such likeness; no one who had read the Odes, so calm and majestic in pace, so skillfully and tightly organized, could possibly foresee the helter-skelter rush of the letters in which the thoughts tumble over each other, defying the laws of grammar, spelling and punctuation.

It is in the letters, indeed, rather than in the poems, that one is constantly reminded directly of his idol, Shakespeare, the Shakespeare who wrote the prose of the Comedies. Passages such as the following would not seem out of place in *Much Ado* or *Twelfth Night.*

> Had England been a large devonshire we should not have won the Battle of Waterloo. There are knotted oaks—there are lusty rivulets such as are not—there are vallies of femminine Climate but there are no thews and Sinews—Moor's Almanack is here a curiosity—Arms Neck and Shoulders may at least be seen there, and the Ladies read it as some out of the way romance . . . A Devonshirer standing on his native hills is not a distinct object—he does not show against the light—a wolf or two would disposses him.

> . . . ready to tumble into bed so fatigued that when I am asleep you might sew my nose to my great toe and trundle me round the town like a Hoop without waking me.

> . . . you had better each of you take a glass of cherry branday and drink to the health of Archimedes who was of so benign a disposition that he never would [leave] Syracuse in his Life so kept himself out of all Knight errantry—this I know to be a fact for it is written in the 45 Book of Winkine's treatise on Garden rollers that he trod on a fisherwoman's toe in Liverpool and never begged her pardon. . . . the Life of Man is like a great Mountain—his breath is like a Shrewsbury Cake—he comes into the world like a shoeblack and goes out of it like a Cob[b]ler—he eats like a Chimneysweeper drinks like a Gingerbread Baker and breath[e]s like Achilles.

I am inclined to believe that, as a rule, artists, even Mozart, have not died before they have completed their work (many, of course, have only too often gone on living and producing long after they had nothing left to say). On the evidence of his letters Keats was the rare and tragic exception of a man who died before he had found a style and form in which he could incarnate all sides of his sensibility. One cannot resist the temptation to speculate about what the work of his maturity might have been. Despite his interest in drama, the times in which he lived make it unlikely, I think, that he would have become a dramatist; the narrative poem seems a more promising medium. The narrative poems, e.g. *The Eve of St Agnes*, which he did write, though beautiful in their descriptive details, suffer from a lack of narrative and character interest; the actors and their actions are too stock. Had he lived, he might well have learned how to use all the psychological insight, wit and irony which his letters show him to have possessed, in writing tales which would have made him the equal of and only successor to Chaucer.

Partisan Review, November–December 1951

A Review of *Short Novels of Colette*

Short Novels of Colette.
With an introduction by Glenway Wescott. Dial Press. $5.

For years I resisted every recommendation to read her. Her name conjured up for me the conventional anglo-saxon images of Paris as the city of the Naughty Spree—*Le Vie Parisienne, Les Folies Bergères*, Madamoiselle Fifi, bedroom mirrors and bidets, lingerie and adultery, the sniggers of school boys and grubby old men. I was further suspicious because she was so often recommended to me for her prose style and it has generally been my experience that when a writer is praised for style it is because there is little else to praise.

I mention this because my prejudice seems to be common; all the five novels in this collection were published in the States between 1929 and 1936, unpropitious years maybe, without attracting much attention. Since I have now come to agree wholeheartedly with Mr Glenway Wescott who, in his masterly introduction, declares without equivocation that Colette is the greatest living French fiction writer, I am convinced that others have only to read her work to experience the same conversion.

Her subject matter is exactly what one's hostile preconception imagined it to be. Her world has the same limited concerns as the naughty French farce, food, money, and l'amour, the same limited professions; one can be kept, one can have something to do with the stage, one can speculate on the Bourse, once can have independent means—and the same limited range of roles, more star parts for actresses than for actors, bit parts for servants and an occasional adolescent but none for small children. Yet out of this specialized, slightly shop-soiled stuff she has managed to create works of art the significance of which is profound, tragic and universal.

For Colette, as for any other writer, this alchemy was a process which took her time to learn. The publishers here wisely put the earliest novel of their collection last and the reader should follow their order. He should read the productions of her maturity, the two *Chéri* novels, *Duo* and *The Cat* before he reads *The Indulgent Husband*, if he is to get a proper measure of her growth. Technical skill she displayed from the very first, but the development in her imagination and moral insight is astounding.

The Indulgent Husband smells, at least to me, a little gamey, not because of its "daring" theme but because Claudine, the heroine and narrator, instead of being honestly absorbed in her story, is too reader conscious; there are moments when, as it were, she turns in the midst of an embrace to wink at the audience and whisper, "Aren't I a naughty girl." For instance her insight into her corrupt husband, Renaud, is so penetrating that her decision to return to him at the end, or rather the reason she gives for it, is incredible and outrageous.

Yet there are glimpses in this book already of a great artist: when Claudine runs back to the Eden of her childhood, to her eccentric professor father and the countryside round Montigny, all giggles are hushed, and there are pages which are so beautiful one could cry.

> So many roses! I'd like to say to the bush, "Take a rest, my dear, you have bloomed enough, worked enough, given lavishly of your strength and your perfume." The bush would never heed me. It wants to beat the record for roses as to both quantity and fragrance. It has endurance and speed, it gives every ounce that is in it.

When we come to *Chéri*, this pure awareness has enlarged and includes not only the world of innocence but also the worlds of sin and grief.

As in all tragedy, the final outcome is the result of an interaction between fate and free-will. Fate for Chéri is the world of high-class successful courtesans to which his mother and her friends belong. It is a world without fathers; the male exploits or is exploited but in either case his presence is temporary; he passes across the stage and exits, but the women remain. They leave or are left by their lovers but the bond between them is unbreakable, the unfriendly intimacy of kept women, the peevish affection of rivals stalking each other's first wrinkle or white hair, the comradeship of women with highly-developed characters, shrewd at gathering in the cash. Like every other world it has its own standards. Watch your figure. Guard your bank balance. Enjoy yourself when you can. Don't fall in love if you can help it but if you do never give yourself away. Love passes but good cuisine is a joy for ever. Never pity yourself. Fear nothing. As in a Greek tragedy, the decisive events have already occurred when the story opens: Chéri has had his childhood, by turns adored and forgotten, matured among blotchy maids and tall sardonic valets, his liaison with Léa has lasted six years, and, though neither he nor the others realize it, he is already doomed.

During their affair, both Léa and Chéri have imagined that they were blissfully happy and not too involved with each other, but Colette indicates very subtly that something was wrong. In a relationship between a boy of seventeen and a wise experienced woman of forty-three, there is only one level, the physical, on which he can meet her as an equal. Chéri's fussing over the household accounts is really a pathetic attempt to be the adult husband in some sphere other than the bed. It is no use; the women treat it as a joke. His only defense against the feeling of being the inferior is to retreat from consciousness into his senses; all his maturity, his sensitivity, his goodness is buried in his body: his mind remains that of a spoilt child, just as greedy. He is a splendid animal, but his animality is not natural; dogs and horses scent this and he can never make friends with one. Only the vegetable and mineral worlds are unafraid of him. Colette tells us how, when he was a soldier in the trenches, "his fingers, black with mud and his own grime, were still able to distinguish, by a single sure touch, medals and coins, to recognize by stem or leaf plants the very names of which he did not know." Later, when he visits a hospital with his wife, though consciously he is indifferent to the suffering of the wounded, his senses know better than the doctors what could be done to make them more comfortable.

For one brief moment when he sees that Léa is getting old and she, realizing this, insists on a final break, he seems to be in the superior position, and she the victim.

> Léa let the curtain fall. But she still had time to see that Chéri lifted his head toward the spring sky and the flowering chestnut trees and that in walking he filled his lungs with air like a man escaping from prison.

But in the terrible and magnificent scene in the second book when he comes to see her again after a lapse of five years, we discover that it is she who has escaped. He is still a young man haunted by her image, but she has grown stout, simple and "merry, like an old man"; nature has delivered her. Once again she is as she was in the beginning, the victor and he the vanquished. Realising that their relative positions are now irrevocable, Chéri surrenders to his obsession with its inevitable end.

Looking back to discover where and why the fatal error was made, one can see that if the affair between Léa and Chéri had only lasted one year, the tragedy would not have occurred. Chéri would probably then have developed, as his wife developed, into a shrewd tough acquisitive creature at home in his own world, a true son of his mother. But for Léa to have broken off the relationship in time, she would have had to be either as cold-hearted as her friends or gifted with supernatural charity; being neither, she followed the natural promptings of her heart and it is precisely her genuine love for Chéri that destroys him.

Had Edmée married another husband, she might have turned into a decent person, but whoever Chéri married, his marriage would have been bound to be a failure, for he was already incapable of loving anyone but Léa. Mr Wescott hints, and I agree with him, that, after what has happened, the only escape for Chéri would have been the cloister.

In the little space left to me, rather than an inadequate discussion of *Duo* and *The Cat*, both of them masterpieces, I will conclude with two quotations to illustrate Colette's depth of psychological insight and the economy and felicity with which she can express it.

On Desmond, a night-club proprietor who has just discovered the joys of making money:

> He bathed in an enamelled zinc tub beside a frieze of water plants painted on the tiles, and the decrepit water-heater snored and wheezed like an old bull-dog. But the telephone shone like some cherished weapon in daily use.

On Copine, an old prostitute:

> She had brought a pipe for smoking opium, a lamp, a little jar of the drug, a silver snuff-box full of cocaine—a pack of fortune teller's cards, a case of poker chips and a pair of spectacles. She looked up with eyes like those of an indulgent grandmother who spends all her money on toys for the children.

Worlds apart as they may be in many respects, when I read such sentences, I am reminded of only one other novelist, Tolstoy.

The Griffin, [December 1951]

The World That Books Have Made

"Of the making of books there is no end," sighed the Preacher more than two thousand years ago. "We read many books because we cannot know enough people," said Mr Eliot wryly only three years ago. "They are so right," I say to myself this morning. But how is it that I am able to agree with them? Because I have bought and read their books. There is a real case to be made out against reading, but the prosecutor has to have had direct experience of what he is talking about, which puts him in the paradoxical position of Carlyle, who is said to have extolled the virtues of silence in nineteen volumes.

The principal charges brought against books are two. The first is the psychologist's assertion that all imaginative literature, fiction or verse, indulges day-dreaming and makes it difficult for its devotees to adjust to the demands of reality. There is a small grain of sense in this position, but only a small one. Let us, however, swallow it whole; it still betrays a false identification of human weakness with a particular means of indulging it; like all puritanical reformers, the ascetic preacher of the Reality Principle argues that, if the means of indulgence are cut off, the desire will wither away, a doubtful proposition. I often spend time reading detective stories when I ought to be answering letters, but, if all detective stories were suppressed, I see no reason to believe that I should not find some other device for evading my duty.

The second, and more serious, objection to the printed word is that the language, sensibility and wisdom of literate persons is, in so many cases, inferior to that of the illiterate—the D. H. Lawrence pro-peasant position. How much substance is there in this? It is nonsense to talk of the "secondhand" experience gained from books in contrast to the "firsthand" experience gained from the bookless life, for human beings are not born, like the insects, fully equipped for life, but have to learn almost everything secondhand from others. If we were limited to our firsthand, that is, our sensory experience, we should still be living in trees on a diet of raw vegetables. If a literate person seems inferior to an illiterate, this means that the quality of experience he is gaining from his reading is inferior to that which a peasant gains from talking to his father or his neighbors. The remedy is not to stop him reading but to persuade him to read better books.

The pro-illiteracy position confuses symptom and cause. The real disease in our technological civilization is the ever-widening gap between the size and nature of the social organization required for the mass production of cheap consumer goods, and the size and nature of a psychologically and politically healthy community. When Aristotle asserted that a viable community is one in which everybody can recognize the faces of his neighbors, and when Plato set the population figure of the ideal community at 5,040, they based their conclusions on an estimate of man's spiritual and political nature which history has, till now, confirmed. How the problem of cheap goods versus a civilized community is to be solved, few would dare to pretend that they know; I only know that the abolition of books would solve nothing.

The what-would-happen-if game is always amusing to play. Suppose, then, our society exactly as it is except for the printed word, an industrial society without printing presses, typewriters or mimeograph machines. Two things would certainly vastly improve: our memory and our handwriting. From our earliest years we should be trained to learn great masses of material by heart, and the person whose hand was illegible would be at a grave economic disadvantage. Skilled occupations would become more and more specialized and probably hereditary. The necessity of either keeping all the knowledge requisite to one's job in one's head or of having access to rare and costly manuscripts would narrow the field in which anyone could hope to be an expert, and the personal intimacy between teacher and pupil which the oral transmission of knowledge demands would have to be so close and last so long that it would inevitably tend to become a family affair.

Mass entertainment, movies, radio, television, would not be immediately much affected, but, in the long run, the same symptoms would appear and there would grow up a caste of professional storytellers with very rigid and conservative conventions. Politically, whatever the form of state in theory, we should, in practice, be governed by a small conservative oligarchy. Indeed, every would-be dictator must dream of a world in which the means of entertainment and popular instruction are restricted to the screen and the loudspeaker. Movies require a lot of apparatus, time and money to make and exhibit, an opposition radio station can readily be jammed, a street-corner orator cannot attract a following without the knowledge of the police, but books and pamphlets are relatively cheap to produce and easy to carry and conceal. In an industrialized society, no printing press, no minority, is an axiom.

Thank God, then, for the printing press, and thank God for books, even for the publishers' free copies which keep piling up in my closet and on which I can never give an opinion because I shall never read them, just as I shall never read *Kalevala, The Anatomy of Melancholy* or *Pamela.* The annual tonnage of publications is terrifying if I think about it, but I don't have to think about it. That is one of the wonderful things about the written word; it cannot speak until it is spoken to. (Imagine the horror of life if bars had literary equivalents to Muzak and the juke-box.) In theory I may feel that there are too many books, but in practice I complain that there are not enough—when, for instance, I try to obtain the collected works of some favorite author and find that half of them are out of print, or when I try to find exactly the right book as a Christmas gift to a friend. Of course a great many of the books I do read are mediocre or dull, but life, as Henry James remarked, is, luckily for us, only capable of splendid waste, and every now and then I am rewarded by one which gives such happiness and excitement that the memory of every wasted or tedious hour is soon obliterated.

Finally, and most fervently of all, thank God for books as an alternative to conversation. People may say all they like about the plethora of books, their low quality and the damage they do, but the same charges, only ten times more strongly, can be brought against that unruly member, the human tongue. What has been said of youth applies, unfortunately, to most of us: "How wonderful we should be if we could not hear what we said." Luckily we forget ninety-nine per cent of it immediately; otherwise we should very soon find ourselves restricted to the company of our cats and dogs. I have what I believe is an invaluable suggestion to offer to any hostess. Buy a stack of writing pads and pencils and then throw a dumb cocktail party. Even the most hardened bore who thinks nothing of trapping an unfortunate fellow guest in a corner and asking him "What do you think of Modern Poetry?" would lose his nerve, I think, if he had to commit himself on paper.

The New York Times Book Review, 2 December 1951

Portrait of a Whig

I

The wit and pamphleteer who is the subject of this essay was an Anglican Clergyman of middle-class origin who was born in 1771, two years after the invention of Watt's steam-engine and one year after Goldsmith's *Deserted Village*, that vivid description of the effects of land enclosure. It was still dangerous to walk through the streets of London after dark, there were no waterproof hats, no braces, no calomel, no quinine, no clubs, no savings banks, the government was completely in the hands of great landowners, and, in the best society, one third of the gentlemen were always drunk. He died in 1845, which was also the year in which Engels' *State of the Working Classes in England* was published and Newman was received into the Roman Church. The American Revolution, the French Revolution, the Napoleonic wars, the Romantic Movement had all occurred, there was gaslight in houses, there were railways through the country, the Victorian proprieties were firmly established (Bowdler's *Shakespeare* appeared in 1818) and public opinion had forced Parliament to soften the rigors of pure laisser-faire (the first Factory Act was passed in 1833).

Most of Sydney Smith's writings are polemical; they are intended, of course, to please and amuse, but that intention is secondary to the intention of influencing historical action in the issues which provoked them. In studying a poet or a novelist, we need only study his writings themselves and compare them with writings by others and no consideration of the author as a person can add to our comprehension and appreciation; in studying a polemical writer, this is not the case. A knowledge of the historical issue involved is a sine qua non and, in addition, there are questions about the author which it is relevant to ask. These, in decreasing order of importance are: (1) Whom was he in the habit of reading? (2) How did he live and who were his friends? (3) What peculiarities of character and temperament did he exhibit? Let us take these in reverse order.

II

Sydney Smith's mother, Maria Olier, was of French Huguenot stock and he seems to have loved her; with his father he seems to have had less sympathy. Robert Smith Senior was an eccentric unstable man who left his bride at the church door and departed to America for several years, spent the rest of his life in travel and unsuccessful speculation, and insisted on the family sitting over the dinner-table in the half-dark for hours. Three of his four sons went to India where one died young and the other two made fortunes (his only daughter, of course, stayed at home), and Sydney, his second son, ended up as a Canon of St. Paul's.

Physically, Sydney Smith was swarthy, sturdy, tending to stoutness, and suffered in later life from gout. Mentally, like the majority, perhaps, of funny men, he had to struggle against melancholia: he found it difficult to get up in the morning, could not bear dimly-lit rooms—"Better," he wrote, "to eat dry bread by the splendour of gas, than to dine on wild beef with wax-candles"—and music in a minor key upset him. Writing to a friend who was similarly afflicted, he gave his own recipe for combating it, of which the following are some clauses.

(1) Go into the shower-bath with a small quantity of water at a temperature low enough to give you a slight sensation of cold, 75° or 80°.

(2) Short views of human life—not further than dinner or tea.

(3) Be as busy as you can.

(4) See as much as you can of those friends who respect and like you, and of those acquaintances who amuse you.

(5) Attend to the effects tea and coffee produce upon you.

(6) Avoid poetry, dramatic representations (except comedy), music, serious novels, sentimental people, and everything likely to excite feeling and emotion, not ending in active benevolence.

(7) Keep good blazing fires.

(8) Be firm and constant in the exercise of rational religion.

This helps us to understand certain of his biases. For example, in the *Peter Plymley Letters* and in his attack on the Arminian Bishop of Peterborough, one is conscious, apart from his fully justified dislike of intolerance and persecution, of a distrust of all theology which makes me wonder a little whether he could have explained why he was an Anglican and not, say, an Unitarian. Again, his criticisms of the Methodists and the Puseyites are acute enough, yet one cannot help feeling that it was their devotional intensity as much as their follies which aroused his hostility. As a young man his ambition was to read for the Bar and it was only lack of money which compelled him to take Holy Orders. I do not mean in any way to suggest that he was secretly a sceptic,—all his friends were convinced of the seriousness of his faith—only that, being aware of his fear of metaphysical speculation, he would have preferred a profession in which good works are all to one in which some intellectual consideration of doctrine cannot be avoided.

On the other hand, his need for company and activity made him an excellent father to his country parish and, by sharpening his sense of the mentality and reactions of others, developed in his writing that quality which is essential in polemics, an exact sense of the proper style for any given occasion and audience. Thus, in *The Peter Plymley Letters* or the *Letters to Archdeacon Singleton*, the vocabulary, the references, the arguments are designed for an average clergyman, not very intelligent or well-informed but, still, one who has attended Oxford or Cambridge, prejudiced but capable of recognising logical or moral absurdities, e.g.:

> Is it necessary that the Archbishop of Canterbury should give feasts to Aristocratic London; and that the domestics of the Prelacy should stand with swords and bag-wigs round pig and turkey, and venison, to defend, as it were, the Orthodox gastronome from the fierce Unitarian, the fell Baptist, and all the famished children of Dissent.

Compare this with his *Advice to Parishioners*:

> I don't like that red nose, and those blear eyes, and that stupid, down-cast look. You are a drunkard. Another pint, and one pint more; a glass of gin and water, rum and milk, cider and pepper, a glass of peppermint, and all the beastly fluids which drunkards pour down their throats. . . . It is all nonsense about not being able to work without ale, and gin, and cider, and fermented liquors. Do lions and cart-horses drink ale? It is mere habit. . . . I have no objection, you will observe, to a moderate use of ale, or any other liquor you can *afford* to purchase. My objection is, that you cannot afford it; that every penny you spend at the ale-house comes out of the stomachs of the poor children, and strips off the clothes of the wife—

and this with a letter to a young girl:

> Lucy, dear child, mind your arithmetic. You know, in the first sum of yours I ever saw, there was a mistake. You had carried two (as a cab is licensed to do) and you ought, dear Lucy, to have carried but one. Is this a trifle? What would life be without arithmetic but a scene of horrors? . . . I now give you my parting advice. Don't marry any body who has not a tolerable understanding and a thousand a year, and God bless you, dear child.

III

The finances of the Church Visible are always a fascinating topic. Being a state church, the revenues of the Church of England are derived, partly from property which it owns, and partly from taxation, but very little from the contributions of its members. Patronage, however, is only in part in the gift of the Crown; some livings are bestowed by bishops, some by cathedral chapters, and many by private patrons. With its money it has to pay for the upkeep of churches and parsonages and secure for every parish, if it can, a vicar of good manners and well-educated, with habits and appearance above those of the farmers or workers to whom he preaches and who, since Anglican ministers are normally married men, must not only support himself but rear and educate his family.

In Sydney Smith's time, by his own calculations, the total revenues of the Church would, if divided up equally, have provided each minister with an annual income of £250, "about the same as that enjoyed by the upper domestic of a nobleman." Needless to say, its revenues were not so divided, but ranged from rich sees like Canterbury, worth £25,000, to poor country livings worth no more than £125. In the competition for preferment, those who had sufficient private means to endure the rigors of their early clerical years, and those with good social connections who could gain the ear of the disposers of patronage, had a great advantage. It was not, however, impossible for a person of lowly social origin to succeed. Sydney Smith paints the following picture of the ecclesiastical career of a baker's son:

> Young Crumpet is sent to school—takes to his books—spends the best years of his life, as all eminent Englishmen do, in making Latin verses— knows that the *crum* in crum-pet is long, and the *pet* short—goes to the University—gets a prize for an Essay on the Dispersion of the Jews— takes orders—becomes a Bishop's chaplain—has a young nobleman for his pupil—publishes an useless classic, and a serious call to the unconverted—and then goes through the Elysian transitions of Prebendary, Dean, Prelate, and the long train of purple, profit, and power.

It is not hard to deduce from this description the personal attributes best fitted for a rise from obscurity to a mitre: an unoriginal brightness of intellect which is good at passing examinations but not at thinking for itself, a proper respect for persons of rank, a talent for flattery, a solemn countenance and, above all, strictly Tory political opinions.

Sydney Smith possessed none of these: intellectual ability he had in abundance but of a dangerously lively kind; though he came to number many titled and rich people among his friends, he was utterly without snobbery and incapable of flattery; he was continually making jokes and, worst of all, he was a convinced Whig. Yet, starting from the bottom—with an income of £100 a year and no influential friends—he rose, if not to a bishopric, to a residential canon of St Paul's at a salary of £2,000 a year. It may be not without interest to consider how he did it. His career began with a stroke of good luck: the local squire of the Wiltshire village where he was a young curate took a shine to him and asked him to accompany his son as a tutor on the Grand Tour. Sydney Smith recommended Weimar but the outbreak of war made it impossible and they went to Edinburgh instead. There he met Jeffrey, Brougham, and Francis Horner and started with them *The Edinburgh Review*, devoted to the criticism of contemporary literature and the furthering of Whig policies. The review was an instantaneous success and Smith began to be talked about. In 1800 he married for love and the marriage seems to have remained a singularly happy one. The only gift he had for his bride was six worn silver tea-spoons and she, though she possessed some small means of her own, had presently to sell her mother's jewelry to meet expenses. In 1803 the couple moved to London, where he managed to live by preaching at the Foundling Hospital and lecturing on Moral Philosophy at The Royal Institution. Through his elder brother he was introduced into the Holland House circle, the centre of Whig society, of which he quickly became a popular and admired member. He was still, however, too poor to afford an umbrella, far less a carriage; moreover, his new friends, while cultivated and rich, belonged to the party which was out of power and likely to remain so. Again, he had a stroke of luck for, after Pitt's death, the Whigs came into power for a few months, just long enough to appoint him to the living of Foston in Yorkshire, worth £500 a year. Foston had not had a resident vicar since the reign of Charles II and Smith had no intention of leaving the social amenities of London which he loved for the country which he regarded as "a healthy grave" and where it seemed to him as if "the whole creation were going to expire at tea-time." In 1808, however, a Tory government passed the Clergy Residence Bill and he was banished, at the age of thirty-eight, to a village "twelve miles from a lemon," its existing parsonage a brick-floored kitchen with a room above it, there to do duty for the next twenty years.

Any man might have quailed at the prospect but for an intellectual and man-about-town like Smith, anonymous author of *The Peter Plymley Letters* which had electrified the public and enraged the government, accustomed to the best tables, the best conversation, the most elegant ladies and gentlemen, it must have seemed the end, and a stranger might well have expected him to lapse into despondency and drink. He did nothing of the kind. He kept up his reading, his reviewing, and his large correspondence; he designed a new parsonage for himself and got the local carpenter to furnish it; he devised all sorts of ingenious gadgets—devices for adding draught to the fires, devices to prevent smoky chimneys, lamps burning mutton-fat to save the expense of candles, a special scratcher pole for all his animals etc., and, far from neglecting his parish duties, became one of the best county vicars of whom there is record, and the idol of his parishioners. Church services were only a small part of his ministrations: he started small vegetable gardens, let out to the laborers at very low rents, to help them augment their food supply; he experimented with diets to discover which were both cheap and nourishing; he acted as their doctor and, as a local magistrate, saved many of them from going unjustly to gaol.

Both his character which accepted the duty of the moment and then tried to get the most fun out of it, and his practical experience of the problems of the poor, made him an ideal person for attacking injustice. In his articles he is never, like too many liberals, utopian and given to large generalisations; he always attacks a specific abuse and the reform he proposes is equally specific and always possible to realise. In attacking the Game Laws, for instance, he does not raise any question about the justice or injustice of private property and its unequal distribution but sticks to immediate issues about man-traps and spring-guns and then points out that, besides being cruel, they are not necessary if a few simple alterations are made in the law, namely, giving every landowner the right to kill game, not only the large landowners, making game private property like geese and ducks, and allowing game to be bought by anybody and sold by its lawful possessors since, as long as the sale of game is forbidden, and there are rich men who desire to buy it, a black market supplied by poachers is inevitable.

Knowing both the world of the rich and the world of the poor, he was aware that many injustices to the poor exist, not because the rich are deliberately malicious but because they are unaware of them. In attacking the law which denied defence counsel to prisoners accused of a felony, a left-over from feudal times when a defence of prisoners accused by the Crown was felt to imply disloyalty to the Crown, he explains very simply why, though this attitude no longer existed, the law still remained on the Statute Books.

To ask why there are not petitions—why the evil is not more noticed, is mere parliamentary froth and ministerial juggling. Gentlemen are rarely hung. If they were so, there would be petitions without end for counsel.

His views on Prison reform may shock the humanitarian liberal, for he was opposed to model prisons in which the conditions would be more agreeable than the prisoners were accustomed to outside; he believed that hard labor should be monotonous and disagreeable—he even approved of the treadmill—he believed in solitary confinement but not in darkness. The chief abuses in the prison system current in his day, as he saw them, were, firstly that untried prisoners were treated in the same way as those already condemned, violating the principle that a man is innocent until he is proved guilty and lessening his chances of appearing to his best advantage when finally brought into court, secondly that treatment in prisons was grossly unequal, for those who had friends and money could procure excellent food and drink from outside, and, thirdly, that sentences in general were too long. He recommended short sentences but a treatment in prison which, while doing no injury to health, should be disagreeable enough to give the offender a healthy fear of returning there again. Here again he sticks to the immediately possible: he would not have denied that bad social conditions are a factor in making criminals but they can only be changed in the long run and the question at issue is what to do with criminals now; he would never have agreed with those who hold that the criminal should not be punished because he is not a free moral agent responsible for his actions.

During the first half of his residence at Foston, he was never free from financial anxiety—during the bad harvest year of 1816, for instance, he could no more afford to buy white flour than could his parishioners—but in 1820 an unexpected legacy from an aunt lightened his burden and in 1828, as in 1808, a brief Coalition Ministry including Whigs remembered him and procured him a canonry at Bristol, and the living of Combe Florey in Somerset, which, though it did not increase his income, was a step up in the Ecclesiastical Hierarchy.

From then on his life was smooth sailing: two causes in which he was a leader triumphed—the Catholic Emancipation act was passed in 1829 and the Reform Bill in 1832,—his services were rewarded in his sixty-first year by a canonry at St Paul's, and then his unmarried younger brother died, leaving him a third of his very large fortune. He was now rich, popular, and famous. A letter he wrote shortly before his death aptly describes the last fourteen years of his life:

> Being Canon of St Paul's in London, and a rector of a parish in the country, my time is divided equally between town and country. I am living among the best society in the Metropolis, and at ease in my circumstances; in tolerable health, a mild Whig, a tolerating Churchman, and much given to talking, laughing, and noise. I dine with the rich in London, and physic the poor in the country; passing from the sauces of Dives to the sores of Lazarus. I am, upon the whole, a happy man, have found the world an entertaining place, and am thankful to Providence for the part allotted to me in it.

It will be observed that his knowledge of poverty was confined to rural poverty, to the poor clergy and the poor agricultural laborer; of industrial poverty, of the abuses in factories and mines, he had no direct experience. This may partly account for his opposition to a bill reducing working-hours from twelve to ten; in agriculture, the limitation of working-hours was, and still is, as doubtful a good as it is an obvious one in industry.

For a man with as wide a circle of friends as Sydney Smith, it is surprising how few of them were fellow writers. The only writers he seems to have known intimately were old members of the Holland House set, like Samuel Rogers and Tom Moore, and towards the end of his life he became acquainted with Dickens. Though an omnivorous reader, poetry, other than Greek and Latin, drama and fiction, seem to have interested him very little, and his principal concerns throughout his life were politics and history. Presumably he must have read the letters of Junius, whose style is the closest to his own, but I can find no record of his having done so. His cast of mind was that, typical of *The Edinburgh Review*, which was almost always as reactionary and wrong in its literary judgments as it was liberal and right in its political.

IV

Some of Sydney Smith's wittiest and most charming writing occurs in his private correspondence, a definitive collection of which is long overdue. Apart from his articles in *The Edinburgh Review* his principal works are the ten *Letters on the subject of the Catholics to my brother Abraham who lives in the country by Peter Plymley* (1807–8), the speeches in support of the Reform Bill (1831), the three *Letters to Archdeacon Singleton on the Ecclesiastical Commission* (1837), a pamphlet opposing the replacement of the open ballot by a secret one (1839), and two letters occasioned by the repudiation of its public debt by the state of Pennsylvania (1843).

Polemical writings on issues no longer alive are seldom interesting to anyone but a historian. Sydney Smith's are the happy exception; they can still be read today with admiration and delight by the most general reader. As a writer of forensic prose, his only equal in English Literature is Bernard Shaw. He is always lucid, well-informed, fair to his opponents, never ill-tempered or abusive, equally at home with the long period and the short, the ornate vocabulary and the plain, and a master of every rhetorical effect, e.g., of the satirical inversion:

> Their object is to preserve game; they have no objection to preserve the lives of their fellow creatures also, if both can exist at the same time; if not, the least worthy of God's creatures must fall—the rustic without a soul—not the Christian partridge—not the immortal pheasant—not the rational woodcock, or the accountable hare—

the ironic description of shocking facts in tea-table terms:

> one summer's whipping, only one: the thumb-screw for a short season; a little light easy torturing between Lady-day and Michaelmas—

the homely simile:

> You may not be aware of it yourself, most reverend Abraham, but you deny their freedom to the Catholics upon the same principle that Sarah your wife refuses to give the receipt for a ham or a gooseberry dumpling: she refuses her receipts, not because they secure to her a certain flavour, but because they remind her that her neighbors want it: a feeling laughable in a priestess, shameful in a priest; venial when it withholds the blessings of a ham, tyrannical and execrable when it narrows the boon of religious freedom—

and the ringing peroration of righteous anger:

> If I lived at Hampstead upon stewed meats and claret; if I walked to church every Sunday before eleven young gentlemen of my own beget-

ting with their faces washed, and their hair pleasingly combed; if the Almighty had blessed me with every earthly comfort—how awfully would I pause before I sent forth the flame and the sword over the cabins of the poor, brave, generous, open-hearted peasants of Ireland. . . . The vigour I love consists in finding out wherein subjects are aggrieved, in relieving them, in studying the temper and genius of a people, in consulting their prejudices, in selecting proper persons to lead and manage them, in the laborious, watchful, and difficult task of increasing public happiness by allaying each particular discontent. . . . But this, in the eyes of Mr Percival, is imbecility and meanness: houses are not broken open— women are not insulted—the people seem all to be happy: they are not rode over by horses, and cut by whips. Do you call this vigour? Is this government?

His command of comic effects is equally extensive and masterly. Many of his conversational puns are still remembered, such as his remark on hearing two women screaming insults at each other from upper stories on opposite sides of a narrow street in Edinburgh:

Those two women will never agree: they are arguing from different premises.

His particular forte was the treatment of analogical situations as identical; during the period of the Luddite riots he wrote to a friend:

What do you think of all these burnings? and have you heard of the new sort of burnings? Ladies' maids have taken to set their mistresses on fire. Two dowagers were burned last week, and large rewards are offered! They are inventing little fire-engines for the toilet table, worked with lavender water!

Lastly, he can create pictures in what might be called the ludicrous baroque style, as surely as Pope:

Frequently did Lord John meet the destroying Bishops; much did he commend their daily heap of ruins; sweetly did they smile on each other, and much charming talk was there of meteorology and catarrh, and the particular cathedral they were pulling down at the time; till one fine morning the Home Secretary, with a voice more bland, and a look more ardently affectionate, than that which the masculine mouse bestows on his nibbling female, informed them that the Government meant to take all the Church property into their own hands, to pay the rates out of it, and deliver the residue to the rightful possessors. Such an effect, they say, was never before produced by a *coup de théâtre*. The Commission was separated in an instant: London clenched his fist; Canterbury was hurried out by his chaplains, and put into a warm bed; a solemn vacancy spread itself over the face of Gloucester; Lincoln was taken out in strong hysterics.

V

Sydney Smith is a perfect expression of the Whig mentality, of that English form of Liberalism which has always perplexed and sometimes enraged Continental observers both on the political Right and on the political Left. European liberalism, which has normally been anti-clerical, republican, and materialist, finds it bewildering that social reform in England should owe so much to religion—that the British Labour Party, for example, should be so closely associated with the Evangelical movement, and the increasing concern with juvenile delinquency and other cultural problems of urbanisation with Anglo-Catholicism—and that the English Liberal who desires the abolition of the Crown or the House of Lords should be so rare a bird. Liberals like Godwin and H. G. Wells are very a-typical, and much closer to the European mind.

For the European who knows a little history, it is all the more puzzling, since he is aware that Voltaire and the French Encyclopaedists of the Enlightenment who were the founders of continental Liberalism were inspired by and took many of their ideas from Locke, the Deists, and the Whig authors of the Glorious Revolution of 1688. If he is a pro-clerical monarchist, he is apt to conclude that the English Liberal is a materialist at heart who is only using religious sentiments as a smoke-screen, and to point to the ambiguities of the Thirty-Nine Articles as proof that an Anglican does not know what he believes; if he is an anti-clerical rationalist, he is apt to come to similar conclusions about the Englishman's Liberal convictions and cite, in evidence, his devotion to irrational political institutions.

The clue to the difference is to be found in the difference in meaning of the word Revolution as applied to the events which took place in France in 1789 and as applied to the events which took place in England in 1688. In the former case the word means a radical transformation, the birth of a new society, in the latter, it is a metaphor from astronomy, meaning a restoration of proper balance.

The radical transformation of the whole structure of English social and cultural life which corresponds to that effected in France between 1789 and 1833 was the work of the Tudors. The execution of Charles I was not, like the execution of Louis XVI, a revolutionary breach with the conservative past, but the restoration of a conservative idea, namely that the ruler is not above but subject to Natural Law; Charles had to pay with his life for the revolutionary act of his ancestor Henry VIII in 1535 when he executed Sir Thomas More who as Lord Chancellor was the Keeper of the King's Conscience.

From their experiences under the Protectorate, Englishmen learned that the dangers of arbitrary power were not removed by abolition of the crown, that the claims of religious sects to know by divine inspiration what the good life should be and their consequent right to impose it on others were as great a threat as any theory of the Divine Right of Kings. The monarchy was restored but it presently became apparent that the Stuarts had not learned their lesson; they tried to behave as if Cromwell had never existed or the Civil War taken place; with surprisingly little fuss they were sent packing.

Attitudes of mind seem to resemble persons in that the events of their early life, the circumstances which first brought them into being, are never outgrown. Thus, while all Liberals, by definition, agree that freedom is a good which should be defended and promoted, they differ in their notions of what constitutes the greatest threat or obstacle to freedom. The historical experience with which the Whigs of 1688 had to cope was a century and a half of bitter quarrels and drastic changes imposed on the public by individuals or minorities, who believed that they were right. Consequently the way of thinking characteristic of English Liberalism goes something like this:

(1) All people differ from each other in character, temperament, etc. therefore any attempt to impose an absolute uniformity on them is tyranny.

(2) On the other hand, there can be no social life unless the members of a society hold certain beliefs in common, and behave towards each other in certain commonly accepted ways.

(3) The doctrines which it is necessary to hold in common must therefore be so defined that differences of emphasis are possible, and the laws which regulate social conduct must be such that they command common consent. A minority has no right to impose a law, even if it be just, on the majority who do not appreciate its justice. Vice versa, the majority has no right to impose its will on a minority, unless it can be clearly demonstrated that the latter is a public menace.

(4) The way in which a reform is effected is just as important as the reform itself. Violent change is as injurious to freedom as inertia.

Compare this with the experience of the French enlightenment which was confronted with a static society in which nothing had changed, except that the withdrawal of the Court from Paris to Versailles had severed relations between the political life of the country and its intellectual and its economic life. To the French Liberal, nothing could seem to matter except that a change should occur, and the threat to freedom was not arbitrary individual power but the imprisonment of the individual in an arbitrary status. Materialism was a natural philosophy for French Liberalism to adopt since its enemy was the aristocrat, who claimed privilege on biological grounds (very few of the English peerages were more than two centuries old); it was no less natural that this materialism should be militantly dogmatic since the philosophy it associated with the old order, the theology of the Roman Catholic Church, was rigid and uncompromising. This division has been one of the great disasters of Europe, for the materialism of its Liberals has often forced the Church into accepting the political conservatism of those who accepted Her theology.

In their strategy Sydney Smith's campaigns are typical of the English tradition.

The situation he faced when he wrote the Peter Plymley's letters was as follows: Laws prohibiting Catholics from voting or holding public offices which when they were originally passed may have had some justification—an attempt to bring back the Stuarts might have met with their support—were still in effect, long after any such danger had passed. Sydney Smith assumes that the vast majority of those who opposed their repeal were capable of seeing that they were unjust, if he can demonstrate that there was no danger incurred by removing them. With the inveterately stupid or demagogic minority, his argument is different; he warns them of the unpleasant material consequences to themselves which will follow if they refuse to listen to their conscience.

In the case of the Singleton letters, his enemies are not those who refuse to make a needed reform but who would impose a necessary reform from above in a hasty and unjust manner. What right, he asked, have the bishops to make changes without consulting the lower clergy who will be most affected by them and whose experience of parochial life makes them better equipped to make concrete judgements about abuses instead of generalisations. Further he complained that much of the plan for reform was utopian, since to do what it was intended to do would require a sum of money which the Church did not possess.

In his opposition to secret ballot, later experience has shown us that he was mistaken, because he did not forsee—neither, for that matter, did his opponents—a day when there would arise one-party governments prepared to use all the instruments of coercion at their disposal to ensure an overwhelming vote in their favour. Even so, he makes two points in his pamphlet which no liberal democracy should forget; firstly, that the free voter must hold himself responsible for the consequence of his vote:

> Who brought that mischievous profligate villain into Parliament? Let us see the names of his real supporters. Who stood out against the strong and uplifted arm of power? Who discovered this excellent and hitherto unknown person? . . . Is it not a dark and demoralising system to draw this veil over human actions, to say to the mass, be base, and you will not be despised; be victorious and you will not be honored—

and secondly that the free voter is the voter whose choice is determined by what he believes to be in the best interest of the country and by nothing else.

> The Radicals are quite satisfied if a rich man of popular manners gains the votes and affections of his dependents; but why is not this as bad as

intimidation? The real object is to vote for the good politician, not for the kind-hearted or agreeable man: the mischief is just the same to the country whether I am smiled into a corrupt choice, or frowned into a corrupt choice.

The age in which we live is not one in which liberalism can flourish because the liberal is only effective within a society which holds certain values in common. The liberal logic begins by assuming that its opponent believes in a certain concept of truth and justice and then demonstrates that his behavior is inconsistent with this belief; but when his opponent holds totally different beliefs, this logic is powerless. It is serious enough that the civilisation of the West in which the liberal tradition developed should be opposed by powers with which rational discussion appears to be impossible; it is even more serious, perhaps, that many of us appear to be forgetting that rational discussion is desirable, and that liberty is not just an abstract value of which one approves, but has, to be real, to be embodied in one's own person and daily acts. Indeed, the more critical a situation, the less the opinions a man expresses matter in comparison to his behavior. As a warning and a guide in these times of trouble, we could do worse than listen to Sydney Smith's definition of *A Nice Person*:

A nice person is neither too tall nor too short, looks clean and cheerful, has no prominent feature, makes no difficulties, is never displaced, sits bodkin, is never foolishly affronted, and is void of affectations. . . . A nice person is clear of little, trumpery passions, acknowledges superiority, delights in talent, shelters humility, pardons adversity, forgives deficiency, respects all men's rights, never stops the bottle, is never long and never wrong, always knows the day of the month, the name of every body at table, and never gives pain to any human being. . . . A nice person never knocks over wine or melted butter, does not tread upon the dog's foot, or molest the family cat, eats soup without noise, laughs in the right place, and has a watchful and attentive eye.

English Miscellany, 1952

Introduction to *The Living Thoughts of Kierkegaard*

I am not Christian severity contrasted with Christian leniency. I am . . . mere human honesty. — Kierkegaard

Though his writings are often brilliantly poetic and often deeply philosophic, Kierkegaard was neither a poet nor a philosopher, but a preacher, an expounder and defender of Christian doctrine and Christian conduct. The

near contemporary with whom he may properly be compared is not someone like Dostoevski or Hegel, but that other great preacher of the nineteenth
century, John Henry, later Cardinal, Newman: both men were faced with the
problem of preaching to a secularized society which was still officially Christian, and neither was a naïve believer, so that in each case one is conscious
when reading their work that they are preaching to two congregations, one
outside and one inside the pulpit. Both were tempted by intellectual ambition. Perhaps Newman resisted the temptation more successfully (occasionally, it must be confessed, Kierkegaard carried on like a spiritual prima
donna), but then Newman was spared the exceptional situation in which
Kierkegaard found himself, the situation of unique tribulation.

Every circumstance combined to make Kierkegaard suffer. His father was
obsessed by guilt at the memory of having as a young boy cursed God; his
mother was a servant girl whom his father had seduced before marriage; the
frail and nervously labile constitution he inherited was further damaged by
a fall from a tree. His intellectual precociousness combined with his father's
intense religious instruction gave him in childhood the consciousness of an
adult. Finally he was fated to live, not in the stimulating surroundings of Oxford or Paris, but in the intellectual province of Copenhagen, without competition or understanding. Like Pascal, whom in more ways than one he resembles, or like Richard III, whom he frequently thought of, he was fated to
be an exception and a sufferer, whatever he did. An easygoing or prudent
bourgeois he could never become, any more than Pascal could have become
Montaigne.

The sufferer by fate is tempted in peculiar ways; if he concentrates on himself, he is tempted to believe that God is not good but malignantly enjoys making the innocent suffer, i.e. he is tempted into demonic defiance; if he starts
from the premise that God is good, then he is tempted to believe that he is
guilty without knowing what he is guilty of, i.e. he is tempted into demonic
despair; if he be a Christian, he can be tempted in yet a third way, because of
the paradoxical position of suffering in the Christian faith. This paradox is
well expressed by the penitent shade of Forese when he says to Dante:

> And not once only, while circling this road, is our pain renewed:
> I say pain and ought to say solace.

For, while ultimately the Christian message is the good news: "Glory to God
in the highest and on earth peace, good-will towards men"; "Come unto me
all that travail and are heavy laden and I will refresh you"—it is proximately
to man's self-love the worst possible news—"Take up thy cross and follow me."

Thus to be relieved of suffering in one sense is voluntarily to accept suffering in another. As Kafka says: "The joys of this life are not its own but our
dread of ascending to a higher life: the torments of this life are not its own
but our self-torment because of that dread."

If the two senses of suffering are confused, then the Christian who suffers is tempted to think this a proof that he is nearer to God than those who suffer less.

Kierkegaard's polemic, and all his writings are polemical, moves simultaneously in two directions: outwardly against the bourgeois Protestantism of the Denmark of his time, and inwardly against his suffering. To the former he says, "You imagine that you are all Christians and contented because you have forgotten that each of you is an existing individual. When you remember that, you will be forced to realize that you are pagans and in despair." To himself he says, "As long as your suffering makes you defiant or despairing, as long as you identify your suffering with yourself as an existing individual, and are defiantly or despairingly the exception, you are not a Christian."

Kierkegaard and the Existential

However complicated and obscure in its developments it has become, Existentialism starts out from some quite simple observations.

(a) All propositions presuppose the existence of their terms as a ground, i.e. one cannot ask, "Does X exist?" but only, "Has this existing X the character A or the character B?"

(b) The subjective presupposition "I exist" is unique. It is certainly not a proposition to be proven true or false by experiment, yet unlike all other presuppositions it is indubitable and no rival belief is possible. It also appears compulsive to believe that other selves like mine exist: at least the contrary presupposition has never been historically made. To believe that a world of nature exists, i.e. of things which happen of themselves, is not however invariably made. Magicians do not make it. (The Christian expression for this presupposition is the dogma, "In the beginning God created the Heaven and the Earth.")

(c) The absolute certainty with which I hold the belief that I exist is not its only unique characteristic. The awareness of existing is also absolutely private and incommunicable. My feelings, desires, etc., can be objects of my knowledge and hence I can imagine what other people feel. My existence cannot become an object of knowledge; hence while, if I have the necessary histrionic imagination and talent I can act the part of another in such a way that I deceive his best friends, I can never imagine what it would be like to *be* that other person but must always remain myself pretending to be him.

(d) If I take away from my sense of existence all that can become an object of my consciousness, what is left?

(1) An awareness that my existence is not self-derived. I can legitimately speak of *my* feelings. I cannot properly speak of *my* existence.

(2) An awareness that I am free to make choices. I cannot observe the act of choice objectively. If I try, I shall not choose. Doctor Johnson's

refutation of determinism, to kick the stone and say, "We know we are free and there's an end of it" is correct, because the awareness of freedom is subjective, i.e. objectively undemonstrable.

(3) An awareness of being *with* time, i.e. experiencing time as an eternal present to which past and future refer, instead of my knowledge of my feelings and of the outer world as moving or changing *in* time.

(4) A state of anxiety (or dread), pride (in the theological sense), despair or faith. These are not emotions in the way that fear or lust or anger are, for I cannot know them objectively; I can only know them when they have aroused such feelings as the above which are observable. For these states of anxiety or pride, etc., are anxiety about existing, pride in existing, etc., and I cannot stand outside them to observe them. Nor can I observe them in others. A gluttonous man may succeed when he is in my presence in concealing his gluttony, but if I could watch him all the time, I should catch him out. But I could watch a man all his life, and I should never know for certain whether or not he was proud, for the actions which we call proud or humble may have quite other causes. Pride is rightly called the root of all sin, because it is invisible to the one who is guilty of it and he can only infer it from results.

These facts of existence are expressed in the Christian doctrines of Man's creation and his fall. Man is created in the image of God; an image because his existence is not self-derived, and a divine image because like God each man is aware of his existence as unique. Man fell through pride, a wish to become God, to derive his existence from himself, and not through sensuality or any of the desires of his "nature."

Kierkegaard's Three Categories

Every man, says Kierkegaard, lives either aesthetically, ethically, or religiously. As he is concerned, for the most part, with describing the way in which these categories apply in Christian or post-Christian society, one can perhaps make his meaning clearer by approaching these categories historically, i.e. by considering the Aesthetic and the Ethical at stages when each was a religion, and then comparing them with the Christian faith in order to see the difference, first, between two rival and incompatible Natural Religions and, secondly, between them and a Revealed Religion in which neither is destroyed or ignored, but the Aesthetic is dethroned and the Ethical fulfilled.

The Aesthetic Religion (e.g. The Greek Gods)

The experience from which the aesthetic religion starts, the facts which it sets out to overcome, is the experience of the physical weakness of the self in the face of an overwhelmingly powerful not-self. To survive I must act strongly and decisively. What gives me the power to do so? Passion. The aesthetic religion regards the passions not as belonging to the self, but as divine visitations, powers which it must find the means to attract or repel if the self is to survive.

So in the aesthetic cosmology, the gods are created by nature, ascend to heaven, are human in form, finite in number (like the passions) and inter-related by blood. Being images of passions, they themselves are not *in* their passion—Aphrodite is not in love; Mars is not angry—or, if they do make an appearance of passionate behaviour, it is frivolous; like actors, they do not suffer or change. They bestow, withhold or withdraw power from men as and when they choose. They are not interested in the majority of men, but only in a few exceptional individuals whom they specially favour and sometimes even beget on mortal mothers. These exceptional individuals with whom the gods enter into relation are heroes. How does one know that a man is a hero? By his acts of power, by his good fortune. The hero is glorious but not re-sponsible for his successes or his failures. When Odysseus, for instance, suc-ceeds, he has his friend Pallas Athene to thank; when he fails, he has his enemy Poseidon to blame. The aesthetic either/or is not good or bad but strong or weak, fortunate or unfortunate. The temporal succession of events has no meaning, for what happens is simply what the gods choose arbitrarily to will. The Greeks and the Trojans must fight because "hateful Ares bids." To the aesthetic religion all art is ritual, acts designed to attract the divine favours which will make the self strong, and ritual is the only form of activity in which man has the freedom to act or refrain from acting and for which, therefore, he is responsible.

The facts on which the aesthetic religion is shattered and despairs, pro-ducing in its death agony Tragic Drama, are two: man's knowledge of good and evil, and his certainty that death comes to all men, i.e. that ultimately there is no either/or of strength or weakness, but even for the exceptional individual the doom of absolute weakness. Both facts it tries to explain in its own terms and fails. It tries to relate good and evil to fortune and misfortune, strength and weakness, and concludes that if a man is unfortunate, he must be guilty. Oedipus' parricide and incest are not really his sins but his pun-ishment for his sin of *hubris*. The Homeric hero cannot sin, the tragic hero must sin, but neither is tempted. Presently the observation that some evil men are fortunate and some good men unfortunate brings forth a doubt as to whether the gods are really good, till in the *Prometheus* of Aeschylus it is openly stated that power and goodness are not identical. Again, the aesthetic religion tries to express the consciousness of universal death aesthetically, that is, individually, as the Fates to which even the gods must bow, and betrays its failure to imagine the universal by having to have three of them.

The Ethical Religion (The God of Greek Philosophy)

To solve the problem of human death and weakness, the ethical religion begins by asking, "Is there anything man knows which does not come and go like his passions?" Yes, the concepts of his reason which are both certain and independent of time or space or individual, for the certainty is the same whether a man be sick or well, a king or a slave.

In place of the magnified passions of the aesthetic religion, the ethical sets up as God, the Ideas, the First Cause, the Universal. While to the former, the world begot the gods who then ruled over it because they were stronger than any other creature, in the latter God and the world are coeternal. God did not create the world of matter; he is only the cause of the order in it, and this not by any act of his—the neuter gender would be more fitting to him—for to be divine means to be self-sufficient, "to have no need of friends." Rather it is matter which, wishing to escape from the innate disorder of its temporal flux, "falls in love" with God and imitates his unchangeableness in such ways as it can, namely by adopting regular movements. (Plato's introduction of a mysterious third party, the Demiurge who loves the Ideas and then imposes them on matter, complicates but does not essentially alter the cosmology.) Man, however, being endowed with reason, can apprehend God directly as Idea and Law, transcend his finite bodily passions, and become like God.

For the aesthetic either/or of strength or weakness, fortune or misfortune, the ethical religion substitutes the either/or of Knowledge of the Good or Ignorance of the Good. To the aesthetic, evil was lack of power over the finite world, for all finiteness, all passion is weakness, as goodness is gained by transcending the finite world, by a knowledge of the eternal and universal truths of reason which cannot be known without being obeyed. To the aesthetic, time was unmeaning and overwhelming; to the ethical, it is an appearance which can be seen through. The aesthetic worshipper was dependent on his gods who entered into relationship with him if and when he chose; the ethical worshipper enters into relationship with his god through his own efforts and, once he has done so, the relationship is eternal, neither can break it. The ethical hero is not the man of power, the man who does, but the philosopher, the man who knows.

Like his predecessor, however, he is not tempted and does not choose, for so long as he is ignorant he is at the mercy of his passions, i.e. he *must* yield to the passion of the moment, but so soon as he knows the good, he must will it; he can no more refuse assent to the good than he can to the truths of geometry.

As in the case of the aesthetic religion, there are facts with which the ethical religion cannot deal and on which it founders. Its premise "Sin is ignorance; to know the good is to will it" is faced with the fact that all men are born ignorant and hence each individual requires a will to know the universal good in order to will it. This will cannot be explained ethically, first because it is not a rational idea so that the ethical has to fall back on the aesthetic idea of a heavenly Eros to account for it. Secondly, it is not a universal; it is present or appeals to some individuals and not to others, so that the ethical has to call in the aesthetic hero whom it instructs in the good, and who then imposes justice by force. Art to the elect is no longer a religious ritual, but an immoral sham, useful only as a fraudulent but pragmatically effective method of making the ignorant masses conform to the law of virtue which they do not understand.

Lastly, there comes the discovery that knowledge of the good does not automatically cause the knower to will it. He may know the law and yet not only be tempted to disobey but yield to the temptation. He may even disobey deliberately out of spite, just to show that he is free.

Revealed Religion (Judaism and Christianity)

A revealed religion is one in which God is not present as an object of consciousness, either as a feeling or a proposition. He is not begotten by the world, nor does he impose order on its coeternal flux but creates it out of nothing, so that while God and the world are at every moment related, God is not knowable as an object. While in the aesthetic religion the feelings, and in the ethical religion, the ideas *were* the presence of God, they are now only *my* feelings, *my* ideas and if I believe that what I feel (e.g. God is present) or think (e.g. God is righteous) is caused by my relation to God, this belief is a revelation, for the cause is outside my consciousness. As one term of a relation, the other term of which is God, I cannot overlook the whole relation objectively and can only describe it analogically in terms of the human relation most like it, e.g. if the feeling of which I have immediate certainty is one which I would approximately describe as sonship, I may speak of God as Father.

There is no longer a question of establishing a relation between God and myself for as my creator he is necessarily related to his creature and the relation is presupposed by my existence; there is only a question of the right relation. The uniqueness of the relation is that it is a relation to an Other yet at the same time as continuous and inescapable as my relation to myself. The relation of the aesthetic worshipper to his gods is intermittent and depends on their pleasure—they do not have to get in touch with him at all. The relation of the ethical worshipper to the Ideas is intermittent or not depending on his pleasure. They are always there to be contemplated if he choose, as a river is always there to be drunk from if one is thirsty, but if he doesn't choose to contemplate them, there is no relation. But the relation to the creator God of revealed religion is unbreakable: I, his creature, can forget it as I can forget my relation to myself when I am thinking of other things, but it is permanently there, and, if I try to banish it permanently from consciousness, I shall not get rid of it, but experience it negatively as guilt and despair. The wrath of God is not a description of God in a certain state of feeling, but of the way in which I experience God if I distort or deny my relation to him. So Dante inscribed on the portals of Hell: "Divine Power made me, Wisdom supreme and Primal Love"—and Landor justly remarked about the Inferno that its inhabitants do not want to get out. To both the aesthetic and the ethical religion, evil was a lack of relation to God, due in the one case to the God's will, in the other to man's ignorance; to the revealed religion, evil is sin, that is to say, the rebellion of man's will against the relation.

The aesthetic commands cannot be codified because they are arbitrary commands of the gods and always novel. The ethical commands ought to be able to be completely codified as a set of universal moral laws. Revealed religion shows why this is impossible. A law is either a law *of* or a law *for.* Laws *of,* like the laws of science, are patterns of regular behaviour as observed by a disinterested observer. Conformity is necessary for the law to exist, for if an exception is found, the law has to be rewritten in such a way that the exception becomes part of the pattern, for it is a presupposition of science that events in nature conform to law, i.e. a physical event is always related to some law, even if it be one of which scientists are at present ignorant. Laws *for,* like human legislation, are patterns of behaviour imposed on behaviour which was previously lacking in pattern. In order for the laws to come into existence, there must be at least some people who do not conform to them. Unlike laws *of* which must completely explain how events occur, laws *for* are only concerned with commanding or prohibiting the class of actions to which they refer, and a man is only related to the law when it is a question of doing or not doing one act of such a class; when his actions are covered by no law, e.g. when he is sitting alone in his room, he is related to no law at all.

If the commands of God were laws *of* man, then disobedience would be impossible; if they were laws *for* man, then his relation to God would not be permanent but intermittent. The commands of God are neither the aesthetic fiat, "Do what you must" nor the ethical instruction, "These are the things which you may or must not do," but the call of duty, "Choose to do what at this moment in this context I am telling you to do."

Christ the Offence

To one who believes that Jesus was what he claimed to be, the incarnation as an existing individual of the Son of God begotten of his Father before all worlds, by whom all things were made, his birth, life and death are, first, a simultaneous revelation of the infinite love of God—to be righteous means to love—and of the almost infinite sinfulness of man—without the gift of the Holy Spirit it is impossible for him to accept the truth; secondly, a revelation that God is related to all men, but to each of them uniquely as an existing individual, i.e. God is the father of all men, not of a chosen people alone, and all men are exceptions, not aesthetically, but as existing individuals—it is their existence not their natures which makes each of them unique; thirdly, a revelation that the Life is not an object for aesthetic admiration nor the Truth an object for ethical appropriation, but a Way to be followed, an inclination of the heart, a spirit in which all actions are done. In so far as collectively they considered their relation to God to be aesthetically unique, and individually an ethical relation to his Law, this revelation is an offence to the Jews; in so far as it proclaims that God the Father is not *a* God but *the* God, that Christ is not a teacher of truths but the Truth, it is an offence to the Gentiles.

The Jews would have welcomed a Messiah for them alone, but not one who demanded that they give up their claim to be the unique people of God or their belief that the Law covers the whole duty of the individual; the Gentile imagination could have accepted another culture-hero to add to its old ones, the Gentile reason, another teacher to add new stores to its knowledge, but could not accept one who was a passive sufferer, put faith before reason, and claimed exclusive attention. The Jews crucified Jesus on the serious charge that he was a blasphemer, the Gentiles, on the frivolous charge that he was a public nuisance.

Preaching to the Non-Believer

"It is," Newman observed, "as absurd to argue men, as to torture them, into believing." However convincing the argument, however holy the arguer, the act of faith remains an act of choice which no one can do for another. Pascal's "wager" and Kierkegaard's "leap" are neither of them quite adequate descriptions, for the one suggests prudent calculation and the other perverse arbitrariness. Both, however, have some value: the first calls men's attention to the fact that in all other spheres of life they are constantly acting on faith and quite willingly, so that they have no right to expect religion to be an exception; the second reminds them that they cannot live without faith in something, and that when the faith which they have breaks down, when the ground crumbles under their feet, they *have to* leap even into uncertainty if they are to avoid certain destruction.

There are only two Christian propositions about which it is therefore possible to argue with a non-believer:

(1) That Jesus existed; (2) That a man who does not believe that Jesus is the Christ is in despair.

It is probably true that nobody was ever genuinely converted to Christianity who had not lost his "nerve," either because he was aesthetically unfortunate or because he was ethically powerless, i.e. unable to do what he knew to be his duty. A great deal of Kierkegaard's work is addressed to the man who has already become uneasy about himself, and by encouraging him to look more closely at himself, shows him that his condition is more serious than he thought. The points that Kierkegaard stresses most are, firstly, that no one, believer or not, who has once been exposed to Christianity can return to either the aesthetic or the ethical religion as if nothing had happened. Return he will, if he lose his Christian faith, for he cannot exist without some faith, but he will no longer be a naïve believer, but a *rusé* one compelled to excess by the need to hide from himself the fact that he does not really believe in the idols he sets up.

Thus the aesthetic individual is no longer content with the passive moderation of paganism; he will no longer simply obey the passions of his nature, but will have by will power to arouse his passions constantly in order to have something to obey. The fickle lover of paganism who fell in and out of love turns into Don Giovanni, the seducer who keeps a list so as not to forget. Similarly, the ethical philosopher will no longer be content to remain a simple scientist content to understand as much and no more than he can discover; he must turn into the systematic philosopher who has an explanation for everything in existence except, of course, his own existence which defeats him. Nothing must occur except what he can explain. The multitude of ordinary men and women cannot return to the contented community of the Greek chorus for they cannot lose the sense that they are individuals; they can only try to drown that sense by merging themselves into an abstraction, the crowd, the public ruled by fashion. As Rudolf Kassner says in his fascinating book, *Zahl und Gesicht*:

> The pre-christian man with his Mean (*Mitte*) bore a charmed life against mediocrity. The Christian stands in greater danger of becoming mediocre. If we bear in mind the idea, the absolute to which the Christian claims to be related, a mediocre Christian becomes comic. The pre-christian man could still be mediocre without becoming comic because for him his mediocrity was the Mean. The Christian cannot.

To show the non-believer that he is in despair because he cannot believe in *his* gods and then show him that Christ cannot be a man-made God because in every respect he is offensive to the natural man is for Kierkegaard the only true kind of Christian apologetics. The false kind of apologetics of which he accuses his contemporary Christians is the attempt to soft-pedal the distinction between Christianity and the Natural Religions, either by trying to show that what Christians believe is really just what everybody believes, or by suggesting that Christianity pays in a worldly sense, that it makes men healthy, wealthy, and wise, keeps society stable, and the young in order, etc. Apart from its falsehood, Kierkegaard says, this method will not work because those who are satisfied with this world will not be interested and those who are not satisfied are looking for a faith whose values are not those of this world.

Preaching to Believers

The danger for the Christian in an officially Christian society is that he may think he is a Christian. But nobody except Christ and, at the end of their lives perhaps, the saints *are* Christian. To say "I am a Christian" really means "I who am a sinner am required to become like Christ." He may think he believes as an individual when all he is doing is believing what his parents said, so that he would be a Mohammedan if they had been. The task of the Christian preacher is therefore first to affirm the Christian commands and arouse the consciousness of sin, and secondly to make the individual's relationship with Christ real, that is, contemporary.

The world has changed greatly since Kierkegaard's time and all too many of his prophetic insights have come to pass. The smug bourgeois Christendom he denounced has crumbled and what is left is an amorphous, despairing mass of displaced persons and paralyzed Hamlets. The ubiquitous violence of the present age is not truly passionate, but a desperate attempt to regress from reflection into passion instead of leaping forward into faith. The worst feature, for example, of the massacre of the Jews by the Nazis is not its cruelty but its frivolity; they did not seriously believe that the Jews were a menace as the Inquisition believed about heretics; no, it was rather a matter of "We must do something. Why not kill all the Jews?"

It is almost bound to be the fate of Kierkegaard, as of so many polemical writers, to be read in the wrong way or by the wrong people. The contented will not read him or read him only scientifically as an interesting case history. The unhappy and, for the most part, agnostic intellectuals who will read him, will confine themselves to his psychological analyses like *The Sickness unto Death* or his philosophical polemics like *Concluding Unscientific Postscript*, which they will read poetically as sympathetic and stimulating reflections of their feelings and thoughts, but they will fight shy of books like *Training in Christianity* or *The Works of Love*, either because they are not as unhappy as they pretend or because they really despair of comfort and cling in defiance to their suffering.

Kierkegaard is particularly vulnerable to such misunderstanding because the only force which can compel us to read an author as he intends is some action of his which becomes inexplicable if we read him any other way, e.g. Newman's conversion to Roman Catholicism. In Kierkegaard's case there is indeed such an action, but the action is another book, *The Attack upon "Christendom."* The whole of his writings up to this one, written in the last year of his life, even the sermons, are really "poetical," i.e. Kierkegaard speaks in them as a genius not as an apostle, so that they all might have been published, as many of them were, anonymously. *The Attack upon "Christendom,"* on the other hand, is that contradiction in terms, an "existential" book. What for the author was the most important book of his life is for us, as readers, the least, for to us the important point is not what it contains, but the fact that Kierkegaard wrote it. For this reason, no selection from it appears here.

The Living Thoughts of Kierkegaard, presented by
W. H. Auden, 1952

Some Reflections on Music and Opera

What is music about? What, as Plato would say, does it "imitate"? Choice. A succession of two musical notes is an act of choice; the first causes the second not in the scientific sense of making it occur necessarily, but in the historical sense of provoking it, of providing it with a motive for occurring. A successful melody is a self-determined history; it is freely what it intends to be, yet is a meaningful whole not an arbitrary succession of notes.

★   ★   ★

Music as an art, i.e. music that has come to a conscious realization of its true nature, is confined to Western civilization alone and only to the last four or five hundred years at that. The music of all other cultures and epochs bears the same relation to Western music that magical verbal formulae bear to the art of poetry. A primitive magic spell may be poetry but it does not know that it is, nor intend to be. So, in all but Western music, history is only implicit; what it thinks it is doing is furnishing verses or movements with a repetitive accompaniment. Only in the West has chant become song.

★   ★   ★

Lacking a historical consciousness, the Greek theories of music tried to relate it to Pure Being, but the becoming implicit in music betrays itself in their theories of harmony in which mathematics becomes numerology and one chord is intrinsically "better" than another.

Western music declared its consciousness of itself when it adopted time-signatures, barring and the metronome beat. Without a strictly natural or cyclical time, purified from every trace of historical singularity, as a framework within which to occur, the irreversible historicity of the notes themselves would be impossible.

In primitive proto-music, the percussion instruments which best imitate recurrent rhythms and, being incapable of melody, can least imitate novelty, play the greatest role.

★   ★   ★

The most exciting rhythms seem unexpected and complex, the most beautiful melodies simple and inevitable.

★   ★   ★

Music cannot imitate nature: a musical storm always sounds like the wrath of Zeus.

★   ★   ★

A verbal art like poetry is reflective; it stops to think. Music is immediate, it goes on to become. But both are active, both insist on stopping or going on. The medium of passive reflection is painting, of passive immediacy the cinema, for the visual world is an immediately given world where Fate is mistress and it is impossible to tell the difference between a chosen movement and an involuntary reflex. Freedom of choice lies, not in the world we see, but in our freedom to turn our eyes in this direction or that, or to close them altogether.

Because music expresses the opposite experience of pure volition and subjectivity (the fact that we cannot shut our ears at will allows music to assert that we cannot not choose), film music is not music but a technique for preventing us from using our ears to hear extraneous noises and it is bad film music if we become consciously aware of its existence.

★   ★   ★

Man's musical imagination seems to be derived almost exclusively from his primary experiences—his direct experience of his own body, its tensions and rhythms, and his direct experience of desiring and choosing—and to have very little to do with the experiences of the outside world brought to him through his senses. The possibility of making music, that is, depends primarily, not upon man's possession of an auditory organ, the ear, but upon his possession of a sound-producing instrument, the vocal cords. If the ear were primary, music would have begun as programme pastoral symphonies. In the case of the visual arts, on the other hand, it is a visual organ, the eye, which is primary, for without it, the experiences which stimulate the hand into becoming an expressive instrument could not exist.

★   ★   ★

This difference is demonstrated by the difference in our sensation of motion in musical space and visual space.

An increase in the tension of the vocal chords is conceived in musical space as a going "up," a relaxation as a going "down." But in visual space it is the bottom of the picture (which is also the foreground) which is felt as the region of greatest pressure and as the eye rises up the picture, it feels an increasing sense of lightness and freedom.

The association of tension in hearing with up and in seeing with down seems to correspond to the difference between an experience of the force of gravity in our own bodies and an experience of it in other bodies. The weight of our own bodies is felt as inherent in us, as a personal wish to fall down, so that rising upward is an effort to overcome the desire for rest in ourselves. But the weight (and proximity) of other objects is felt as weighing down on us; they are "on top" of us and rising means getting away from their restrictive pressure.

★   ★   ★

All of us have learned to talk, most of us, even, could be taught to speak verse tolerably well, but very few have learned or could ever be taught to sing. In any village twenty people could get together and give a performance of *Hamlet* which, however imperfect, would convey enough of the play's greatness to be worth attending, but if they were to attempt a similar performance of *Don Giovanni*, they would soon discover that there was no question of a good or a bad performance because they could not sing the notes at all. Of an actor, even in a poetic drama, when we say that his performance is good, we mean that he simulates by art, that is, consciously, the way in which the character he is playing would, in real life, behave by nature, that is, unconsciously. But for a singer, as for a ballet dancer, there is no question of simulation, of singing the composer's notes "naturally"; his behavior is unabashedly and triumphantly art from beginning to end. The paradox implicit in all drama, namely, that emotions and situations which in real life would be sad or painful are on the stage a source of pleasure becomes, in opera, quite explicit. The singer may be playing the role of a deserted bride who is about to kill herself, but we feel quite certain as we listen that not only we but also she is having a wonderful time. In a sense, there can be no tragic opera because whatever errors the characters make and whatever they suffer, they are doing exactly what they wish. Hence the feeling that *opera seria* should not employ a contemporary subject, but confine itself to mythical situations, that is, situations which as human beings we are all of us necessarily in and must, therefore, accept, however tragic they may be. A contemporary tragic situation like that in Menotti's *The Consul* is too actual, that is, too clearly a situation some people are in and others, including the audience, are not in, for the latter to forget this and see it as a symbol of, say, man's existential estrangement. Consequently the pleasure we and the singers are obviously enjoying strikes the conscience as frivolous.

★   ★   ★

On the other hand, its pure artifice renders Opera the ideal dramatic medium for a tragic myth. I once went in the same week to a performance of *Tristan und Isolde* and a showing of *L'Eternel Retour*, Jean Cocteau's movie version of the same story. During the former two souls, weighing over two hundred pounds apiece, were transfigured by a transcendent power, in the latter a handsome boy met a beautiful girl and they had an affair. This loss of value was due not to any lack of skill on Cocteau's part but to the nature of the cinema as a medium. Had he used a fat middle-aged couple the effect would have been ridiculous because the snatches of language which are all the movie permits have not sufficient power to transcend their physical appearance. Yet if the lovers are young and beautiful, the cause of their love looks "natural," a consequence of their beauty, and the whole meaning of the myth is gone.

★   ★   ★

The man who wrote the Eighth Symphony has a right to rebuke the man
who put his raptures of elation, tenderness, and nobility into the mouths
of a drunken libertine, a silly peasant girl, and a conventional fine lady,

instead of confessing them to himself, glorying in them, and uttering
them without motley as the universal inheritance.

—Bernard Shaw

Shaw, and Beethoven, are both wrong, I believe, and Mozart right. Feelings
of joy, tenderness and nobility are not confined to "noble" characters but are
experienced by everybody, by the most conventional, most stupid, most depraved. It is one of the glories of opera that it can demonstrate this and to
the shame of the spoken drama that it cannot. Because we use language in
everyday life, our style and vocabulary become identified with our social character as others see us, and in a play, even a verse play, there are narrow limits to the range in speech possible for any character beyond which the playwright cannot go without making the character incredible. But precisely
because we do not communicate by singing, a song can be out of place but
not out of character; it is just as credible that a stupid person should sing
beautifully as that a clever person should do so.

★   ★   ★

If music in general is an imitation of history, opera in particular is an imitation of human wilfulness; it is rooted in the fact that we not only have feelings but insist upon having them at whatever cost to ourselves. Opera, therefore, cannot present character in the novelist's sense of the word, namely,
people who are potentially good *and* bad, active *and* passive, for music is immediate actuality and neither potentiality nor passivity can live in its presence. This is something a librettist must never forget. Mozart is a greater composer than Rossini but the Figaro of the *Marriage* is less satisfying, to my mind,
than the Figaro of the *Barber* and the fault, is, I think, Da Ponte's. His Figaro
is too interesting a character to be completely translatable into music so that
co-present with the Figaro who is singing one is conscious of a Figaro who is
not singing but thinking to himself. The barber of Seville, on the other hand,
who is not a person but a maniacal busybody, goes into song exactly, with
nothing over.

Again, I find *La Bohème* inferior to *Tosca*, not because its music is inferior,
but because the characters, Mimi in particular, are too passive; there is an
awkward gap between the resolution with which they sing and the irresolution with which they act.

The quality common to all the great operatic roles, e.g. Don Giovanni,
Norma, Lucia, Tristan, Isolde, Brünnhilde, is that each of them is a passion-
ate and wilful state of being. In real life they would all be bores, even Don
Giovanni.

In recompense for this lack of psychological complexity, however, music
can do what words cannot, present the immediate and simultaneous relation
of these states to each other. The crowning glory of opera is the big ensemble.

★   ★   ★

The chorus can play two roles in opera and two only, that of the mob and that of the faithful, sorrowing or rejoicing community. A little of that goes a long way. Opera is not oratorio.

★ ★ ★

Drama is based on the Mistake. I think someone is my friend when he really is my enemy, that I am free to marry a woman when in fact she is my mother, that this person is a chambermaid when it is a young nobleman in disguise, that this well-dressed young man is rich when he is really a penniless adventurer, or that if I do this such and such a result will follow when in fact it results in something very different. All good drama has two movements, first the making of the mistake, then the discovery that it was a mistake.

In composing his plot, the librettist has to conform to this law but, in comparison to the dramatist, he is more limited in the kinds of mistakes he can use. The dramatist, for instance, procures some of his finest effects from showing how people deceive themselves. Self-deception is impossible in opera because music is immediate not reflective; whatever is sung is the case. At most self-deception can be suggested by having the orchestral accompaniment at variance with the singer, e.g. the jolly tripping notes which accompany Germont's approach to Violetta's death-bed in *La Traviata*, but unless employed very sparingly such devices cause confusion rather than insight.

Again, while in the spoken drama the discovery of the mistake can be a slow process and often, indeed, the more gradual it is the greater the dramatic interest, in a libretto the drama of recognition must be tropically abrupt, for music cannot exist in an atmosphere of uncertainty; song cannot walk, it can only jump.

On the other hand, the librettist need never bother his head, as the dramatist must, about probability. A credible situation in opera means a situation in which it is credible that someone should sing. A good libretto plot is a melodrama in both the strict and the conventional sense of the word; it offers as many opportunities as possible for the characters to be swept off their feet by placing them in situations which are too tragic or too fantastic for "words." No good opera plot can be sensible for people do not sing when they are feeling sensible.

The theory of "Music-drama" presupposes a libretto in which there is not one sensible moment or one sensible remark: this is not only very difficult to manage, though Wagner managed it, but also extremely exhausting on both the singers and the audience, neither of whom may relax for an instant.

In a libretto where there are any sensible passages, i.e. conversation not song, the theory becomes absurd. If, for furthering the action, it becomes necessary for one character to say to another "Run upstairs and fetch me a handkerchief," then there is nothing in the words, apart from their rhythm, to make one musical setting more apt than another. Wherever the choice of notes is arbitrary, the only solution is a convention, e.g. *recitativo secco*.

★   ★   ★

In opera the orchestra is addressed to the singers, not to the audience. An opera-lover will put up with and even enjoy an orchestral interlude on condition that he knows the singers cannot sing just now because they are tired or the scene-shifters are at work, but any use of the orchestra by itself which is not filling-in time is, for him, wasting it. Leonora III is a fine piece to listen to in the concert hall, but in the opera house, where it is played between scenes one and two of the second act of *Fidelio*, it becomes twelve minutes of acute boredom.

★   ★   ★

In opera the Heard and the Seen are like Reality and Appearance in philosophy; hence the more frankly theatrical and sham the sets the better. Good taste is not in order. A realistic painted backdrop which wobbles is more satisfactory than any conscientiously three-dimensional furniture or suggestive non-representational objects. Only one thing is essential, namely, that everything be a little over life size, that the stage be a space in which only the grand entrance and the grand gesture are appropriate.

★   ★   ★

If the librettist is a practicing poet, the most difficult problem, the place where he is most likely to go astray, is the composition of the verse. Poetry is in its essence an act of reflection, of refusing to be content with the interjections of immediate emotion in order to understand the nature of what is felt. Since music is in essence immediate, it follows that the words of a song cannot be poetry. Here one should draw a distinction between lyric and song proper. A lyric is a poem intended to be chanted. In a chant the music is subordinate to the words which limit the range and tempo of the notes. In song, the notes must be free to be whatever they choose and the words must be able to do what they are told.

Much as I admire Hofmannsthal's libretto for *Rosenkavalier*, it is, I think, too near real poetry. The Marschallin's monologue in Act I, for instance, is so full of interesting detail that the voice line is hampered in trying to follow everything. The verses of *Ah non credea* in *La Somnambula* on the other hand, though of little interest to read, do exactly what they should, suggest to Bellini one of the most beautiful melodies ever written and then leave him completely free to write it. The verses which the librettist writes are not addressed to the public but are really a private letter to the composer. They have their moment of glory, the moment in which they suggest to him a certain melody: once that is over, they are as expendable as infantry to a Chinese general: they must efface themselves and cease to care what happens to them.

★   ★   ★

There have been several composers, Campion, Hugo Wolf, Benjamin Britten,
for example, whose musical imagination has been stimulated by poetry of a
high order. The question remains, however, whether the listener hears the
sung words as words in a poem, or, as I am inclined to believe, only as sung syllables. A Cambridge psychologist, P. E. Vernon, once performed the experiment of having a Campion song sung with nonsense verses of equivalent syllabic value substituted for the original; only six per cent of his test audience
noticed that something was wrong. It is precisely because I believe that, in listening to song (as distinct from chant), we hear, not words, but syllables, that
I am violently hostile to the performances of operas in translation. Wagner in
Italian or Verdi in English sounds intolerable, and would still sound so if the
poetic merits of the translation were greater than those of the original, because
the new syllables have no apt relation to the pitch and tempo of the notes with
which they are associated. The poetic value of the words may provoke a composer's imagination, but it is their syllabic values which determine the kind of
vocal line he writes. In song, poetry is expendable, syllables are not.

★   ★   ★

The golden age of opera, from Mozart to Verdi, coincided with the golden
age of liberal humanism, of unquestioning belief in freedom and progress.
If good operas are rarer today, this may be because, not only have we learned
that we are less free than nineteenth-century humanism imagined, but also
have become less certain that freedom is an unequivocal blessing, that the
free are necessarily the good. To say that operas are more difficult to write
does not mean that they are impossible. That would only follow if we should
cease to believe in free will and personality altogether. Every high C accurately struck utterly demolishes the theory that we are the irresponsible puppets of fate or chance.

Partisan Review, January–February 1952

The Adult Voice of America

The New Yorker 25th Anniversary Album. Hamish Hamilton. 30s.

Mr Harold Ross, the creator and sustainer of the *New Yorker*, died last month.
It is not for a stranger to write an obituary, but I cannot review this volume
of comic cartoons without reminding those who will laugh at them that the
New Yorker is not merely a funny magazine; for years its reports on the political and social scene in the United States and abroad have been among the
most honest and best written of any journal in the world, and the editorial

comments in "Talk of the Town" among the sanest. In addition, if Mr Ross had not been a great editor he would still go down to history as the knight in white armour who led and won the battle to defend what advertisers call The Captive Audience against the broadcasting of commercials in Grand Central Station; for that alone the ears of New Yorkers shall bless him and magnify him for ever.

That the *New Yorker* is the best comic magazine in existence I have not the slightest doubt, and it is encouraging to note the influence it has begun to exert on comic magazines elsewhere, notably on *Punch.* Nothing is more difficult to discuss than humour in the absence of the concrete examples, but I must do my best. This album opens in the period when, if a mother said "I'd trust my little girl anywhere," her short-skirted daughter would snort: "Well, mother, I like *that*!" and a guest, who was invited to mix his own drink, was confronted with bottles of alcohol, citric acid, glycerine, orange juice and distilled water. Presently one apple-seller is saying to another: "Well, so long. I'll see you at the Bankers' Club"; intellectuals are saying: "Oh, it's very simple. Our little group simply seize the power-houses and the radio stations," and those who still have tuxedos to wear are going off to newsreels to hiss Roosevelt. Then uniforms begin to appear, an exasperated sergeant is appealing to a squad of draftees: "Hereafter, if there's anything you don't like, come to me—don't write to Mrs Roosevelt"; and the only man-power available for a bowling-alley is a chimpanzee. The war ends, and in almost no time a lady looking out at a beautiful landscape is sighing: "Oh dear. I'd really be enjoying this if it weren't for Russia." And so to the concluding cartoon, apt and ominous, of the animals entering, two by two, a space-rocket Ark.

But through all these changes certain comic worlds persist beyond the touch of time: the Thurber war between the sexes—"Well, who made the magic go out of our marriage, you or me?"; the Helen Hokinson Ladies' Club—"Now, Mezzos, let me hear the thunder of hoofs"; the Charles Adams suburbia of Gothic horror; the Hoff apartment in the Bronx; the histrionic Steig children; and a dozen others.

If an ancient Greek or a European from any century previous to this were to appear and ask us to explain contemporary American humour, it would probably be easiest to begin with examples from a comic genre popular in all ages, the animal parable:—

> Two horses quizzically regarding a third which is tossing its head and showing its profile: "Oh, she's been acting that way all day. Someone told her she looks like Katharine Hepburn."

> A worried pair of rabbits: "Of course, we could adopt some."

> A penguin wearing loud checks to his shocked friend: "I just got damn well fed up with being formal all the time."

One hanging sloth to another: "For heaven's sake stop worrying; you're *supposed* to feel sluggish."

Boy llama to girl llama: "I llove you."

A sociologist, David Riesman, in a fascinating book, *The Lonely Crowd*, has defined American culture (and, by implication, all modern culture) as Other-directed, i.e. the source of authority as to what the individual ought and ought not to think and do is not codified tradition as in a static hierarchical society nor private conscience as in Protestant *laissez-faire* capitalism, but his contemporaries as a group; success depends neither upon obeying the divinely inspired laws of society nor upon developing a strong character but upon possessing a winning personality, and failure arouses feelings not of shame or guilt, but of anxiety. In a traditional culture poverty is accepted as the will of God, in *laissez-faire* capitalism it is the unnecessary result of laziness and stupidity; only in an Other-directed culture could a cartoon be shown of a pavement beggar with a placard round his neck reading "Maladjusted." Again, the Wife-Mistress opposites are traditionally a matter of course, and in a Puritan acquisitive culture a guilty secret, but to-day the roles are indistinct and both a cause for worry, so that a cartoon can appear in a respectable paper showing an elderly man with his elderly wife on his knee, saying, "Martha, my secretary doesn't understand me."

An Other-directed culture contains many factors which encourage a sense of humour; the idea of a moral norm which is statistical is comic in itself— "You're one of the lucky few who have a normal skin"; the necessity of responding in time to changes of fashion puts a premium upon quick and accurate observation of other personalities; and, since what is commanded as normal is always changing, no specific failure to obey can be tragic—"Well, back to the old drawing-board," says the aeroplane designer as he leaves the blazing wreck behind him.

Most anti-American feeling in Europe is based on two illusions, a snobbish self-deception which likes to pretend that Europe is still a traditional or a private-conscience culture, and a conception of the Booster personality as being the acknowledged American ideal, which is as fantastic as thinking that what all Englishmen mean by "a strong character" is Colonel Blimp. If I had any say in American propaganda to Europe and Russia, I would have copies of the *New Yorker* dropped from the air all over; her friends might learn that the inhabitants of the United States are not as uncritical, conformist and depersonalised as they fear, and her foes that they are a great deal tougher, in the real not the phoney anti-sissy sense, than they would like to believe.

The Observer, 6 January 1952

While the Oboes Came Up,
the Bagpipes Went Down

A Composer's World: Horizons and Limitations. By Paul Hindemith.
Harvard University Press. $3.75.

It would be hard to think of a happier choice for the Charles Eliot Norton
lectures than Paul Hindemith. His long and distinguished career as a
"maker" of music allows him to speak of its nature with an authority no listener or performer can claim, his scholarship and experience as a teacher
are worthy of a great academic setting, and his concern for the social position and moral influence of music entitle him to the attentive respect of a
public audience.

He opens with a discussion of the musical theories of Augustine, to whom
the musical order was analogous to the moral order, creating in the listener a
desire to better his soul; of Boethius, to whom it was a platonic imitation of
the order of the universe; and of Sextus Empiricus, to whom it was a mere play
of tones and forms, indicative of nothing beyond itself. This last view implies
that the sensuous pleasure aroused by the sounds is the sole criterion of value,
but there are dangers of overemphasis in the other, more serious, theories;
pushed too far, the Augustinian view leads to rejection of actual physical
sounds altogether, the Boethian view to an intellectual and arid formalism.

From this Hindemith passes to a consideration of the psychology of music,
of the roles played by the intellect and the emotions in absorbing it. While
music is a unique art, I think he exaggerates the difference between music
and the other arts when, after saying: "the emotions released by music are no
real emotions, they are mere images of emotions that have been experienced
before"—which I believe—he goes on to assert: "paintings, poems, sculp-
tures . . . speak to the real, untransformed and unmodified feelings. Gaiety
released by examples of these arts is real gaiety . . . sadness is real sadness."

As far as poetry, at least, is concerned, I can assure him that its effect, in
this respect, is no different from that of music. What makes music unique is
the uniquely intimate group of experiences which is its human ground, our
immediate acquaintance with ourselves, with the rhythms and tensions of our
own bodies, the contradictions of needs and desires and the leaps of choice;
alone among the arts it does not call upon our experience of the not-self so
that, while in the other arts, a sense organ, the eye or the ear is primary and
an expressive organ, the hand or the tongue is secondary, in music their relative positions are reversed and primacy lies with the vocal chords. Hence the
impossibility of a musical imitation of nature, for music cannot but sound voluntary; hence also the association, to which Mr Hindemith draws attention
in a fascinating chapter on musical space, of increase in tension of the vocal

cords with going *up*, whereas in visual space tension increases as the eye goes *down*, for in the first case the association is with gravity as we feel its force in our own bodies, in the second with gravity as we experience it second-hand through the impact of other bodies upon us.

On intervals and tonal systems Mr Hindemith has many wise things to say. He reminds us that our feeling for the purity of intervals can no more be altered than our ability to recognize colors; that the practical advantages of equal temperament should not blind us to its artifice and compromise; and that tonal systems grow and live like languages and cannot be manufactured like motors or crackers or enforced like laws.

He is convinced that music has now reached a state comparable to that of poetry in that its language, so to speak, is now known and should be taken for granted; a frantic search for novel harmonic combinations, a willful invention of a priori systems like the twelve-tone system, are, in his opinion, as doomed to failure as would be a poet's attempt to invent a new tongue.

His middle chapters are devoted to performers and instruments and their curious fluctuations in musical and social prestige through the centuries. Oboes and bassoons, for instance, have come up in the world; bagpipes, reed-organs and harps have gone down, and the horns have passed the trumpets; organists have slipped way behind; singers, though they still keep a high prestige, now rank below the conductor whose appeal, Mr Hindemith very plausibly suggests, is to the dictator fantasies of the modern public—in the person of the conductor every listener enjoys by proxy absolute power yet creates a welcome effect. The days of the violin as we know it are, he fears, numbered; the instrument is too small for the large concert halls in which it is now played and for the loudspeaker tone which is now preferred, and the present methods of securing tone-volume by using strings reinforced with metal and a hacking bow technique are ruining it.

The concluding chapters, at once amusing and moving, deal with the contemporary situation—with the enslavement of the composer to the whims of performers, conductors, and publicity agents, and with the drugging of the public into a tasteless passivity through an unending stream of would-be musical noise. The worst symptom of this general malaise is, Mr Hindemith believes, the virtual disappearance of the amateur musician, of the man who grew up in a family which made music as a matter of course, who played in orchestras beside the professionals, sang in choruses, and for whom all chamber music was written.

He estimates that, whereas in the eighteenth century the proportion of passive listeners to amateurs to professionals was about 5 to 90 to 5, it is now about 95 to 1 to 4. As long as such proportions hold, there is no place where musical talent can form and be tested; the young man who today presents himself at a school of music to study composition is rarely one who has grown up from infancy playing instruments and singing in ensembles; all too often, he is one who owns a radio and a phonograph and has decided that he, like Beethoven, is a genius.

Reform will not be easy, but Mr Hindemith believes that composers should initiate it by writing chamber music and vocal ensembles for amateur performance, consciously bearing in mind the limitations of amateur musical understanding and technique; as long as music is written for virtuoso professionals, whether soloists or orchestras, the child who begins studying an instrument in school or who joins a choir, will give up and become a passive listener when he realizes that he cannot hope to perform such music even passably.

This move away from the large-scale and public professional to the small and personal group, seems to me as desirable as, in the long run, it is inevitable. The chief obstacle at the moment would seem to be financial: can amateurs afford to pay composers adequately and, if not, how are the latter to live? A contemporary composer makes more money conducting professional orchestras in a performance of his work than he makes by composing it.

Here I feel Mr Hindemith is a little unjust to the foundations which give grants and the colleges which offer sinecure posts. A time when the number of active amateurs demanding new work will be great enough to support half-a-dozen composers without outside subsidy is far off; state patronage, however well-meaning, is too impersonal and too subject to extra-musical pressures to be anything but a disaster; as long as patronage for composers is necessary— the question does not affect Mr Hindemith's recommendations as to the sort of music composers should write—foundations which are independent of politics and colleges which are small and local seem the best solution.

The New York Times Book Review, 14 February 1952

Notes on the Comic

I

General Definition of the Comic

A contradiction in the relation of the individual or personal to the universal or impersonal which does not involve the spectator in suffering or pity.

★   ★   ★

When we consider the history of epic or tragic or lyric art, we see change but no progress; *Paradise Lost* is different from *The Iliad* but no better. When, however, we consider comic art, it seems to us that the progress has been immense. The jokes in ancient literature seem singularly unfunny and there is hardly a line written before the middle of the eighteenth century which, on reading, can make us laugh out loud.

⋆   ⋆   ⋆

A sense of wit and humor develops in a society to the degree that its members are simultaneously conscious of being each a unique individual and of being all in common subjection to unalterable laws.

Among primitive peoples the sense of individuality is weak, and is only aroused by exceptional suffering; they only perceive a contradiction between the individual and the universal when it is a tragic contradiction—(any comic contradiction which they do perceive is of the most obvious kind).

In our own society, those individuals, like gamblers and dabblers in spiritualism, who believe in chance or magic, not in impersonal law, are usually humorless.

⋆   ⋆   ⋆

The Hierarchy of Universals

Every man as a person, a unique singular, is related to a variety of universals.

(1) As a being formed out of matter to the laws of physics and chemistry.
(2) As a living being, to the needs common to all organic life, hunger, reproduction, etc.
(3) As a rational being to the laws of logic.
(4) As a social and historical being to the laws of his city, i.e. the conception of the order of moral goods held by his community.
(5) As a spiritual being to the absolute good, the real and eternal hierarchy of values to which the laws of his city are at most an approximation.

Of these,

(1) is the realm of pure necessity. Disobedience is impossible. No man can add a cubit to his stature or fly out of the window. However, because he can become conscious of these laws, he can make use of them to his advantage. He can make growth-inducing hormones and aeroplanes.
(2) is a realm of necessity which cannot be disobeyed but can be modified, i.e. the necessary need is always experienced by man as a historically conditioned desire. His hunger, his need for x calories is experienced as a desire for this or that kind of food.
(3) is also a realm of necessity, in the sense that, once the data are present in consciousness, man's reason necessarily draws the conclusions. Disobedience, however, is possible because man is free to refuse to admit these data to consciousness.
(4) is largely a realm of freedom in that obedience or disobedience is a matter of individual choice. The element of necessity which remains is the passion of fear or desire for social approval which the city is able to arouse in the individual in favor of obedience.
(5) is entirely free. The choice of obedience or disobedience is a purely personal act.

Some Types of Comic Contradiction

(1) The operation of physical laws upon inorganic objects associated with a person in such a way that it is they who appear to be acting from personal volition and he who is or appears to be the helpless thing.

Examples

A man is walking in a storm protected by his umbrella when a sudden gust of wind blows it inside out. This is comic for two reasons:

(a) an umbrella is itself a mechanism designed by man to function in a particular manner. Its existence and its effectiveness as a protection depend upon man's understanding of physical laws. An umbrella turning inside out is funnier than a hat blowing off because an umbrella is made to be opened, to change its shape when its owner wills. It now continues to change its shape, in obedience to the same laws, but against his will.

(b) The activating agent, the wind, is invisible so that the cause of the umbrella turning inside out appears to lie in the umbrella itself. It is not particularly funny if a tile falls and makes a hole in the umbrella, because the cause is visibly natural.

When a film is run backwards, reversing the historical succession of events, the flow of volition is likewise reversed and proceeds from the object toward the subject. What was originally the action of a man taking off his coat becomes the action of a coat putting itself on its man.

The same contradiction is the basis of most of the comic effects of the clown. In appearance he is the clumsy one whom inanimate objects conspire against to torment; this in itself is funny to watch, but our profounder amusement is derived from our consciousness that it is only an appearance, that, in reality, the accuracy of the objects in tripping him up or hitting him on the head is caused by the clown's own skill.

(2) A clash between the laws of the inorganic which have no *telos* and the laws of the organic which do.

Example

A man walking down the street, with his mind concentrated on the purpose of his journey, fails to notice a banana skin, slips and falls down. Under the obsession of his goal, he ignores his subjection to the law of gravity.

The goal need not necessarily be a unique and personal one; he may simply be looking for a public lavatory. All that matters is that he should be ignoring the present for the sake of the future.

A child learning to walk, or a grown man picking his way carefully over the icy surface, are not funny if they fall down, because they are conscious of the present.

★   ★   ★

Comic Situations in the Relationships between Sexes

Sex is a sphere peculiarly rich in comic possibilities precisely because of its sacred nature, its size as a social fact, and the intense personal relationship it involves. A special comic possibility in the sex relation comes from the contradiction between man as a natural creature and man as a historical person.

As a natural creature man is born either male or female and endowed with an impersonal tendency to reproduce his kind by mating with any member of the opposite sex who is neither immature nor senile. ("Male and female created he them. . . . Be fruitful and multiply.") In this tendency the relation between a given male and a given female is subordinated to its general reproductive function.

As a historical person, every man and woman is a unique individual capable of entering into a unique relation of love with another person. As a person, the relationship takes psychological precedence over any function it may also have ("It is not good for man to be alone").

The ideal of marriage is a relationship in which both these elements are synthesized; husband and wife are simultaneously involved in relations of physical love and the love of personal friendship.

This synthesis might be easier to achieve, if the two elements remained distinct, if the physical, that is, remained as impersonal as it is among animals, and the personal relation was completely unerotic. In fact, however, the physical is always a natural and general principle modified by social and personal history—such as a preference for pretty blond ladies under forty.

Sex on the level of nature is impersonal in that it lacks all consideration for the person who belongs to our type, but personal in that our type is our personal and free taste and election, not a blind need.

This contradiction is fertile ground for self-deception. It allows us to persuade ourselves that we value the person of another, when in fact we only value her or him as a sexual object, and it allows us to endow her or him with an imaginary personality which has little or no relation to the real one.

> For each an imagined image brings
> And finds a real image there.
> —W. B. Yeats

★   ★   ★

Comic Travesties

I. *Twelfth Night.* The pattern of relationships is as follows:

(1) Viola (Caesario) is wholly in the truth. She knows who she is, she knows that the Duke is a man, that she feels a personal love for him and her passionate image of him corresponds to the reality.

(2) The Duke is in the truth in one thing; he knows that he feels a per-

sonal love for Caesario (Viola). This is made easier for him by her boy-like appearance—did she look like a grown-up man, she would fall into a class, the class of potential rivals in love. The fact that he feels personal affection for the illusory Caesario guarantees the authenticity of his love for the real Viola as a person, since it cannot be an illusion provoked by sexual desire.

His relation to Olivia, on the other hand, is erotic-fantastic in one of two ways and probably in both: either his image of her does not correspond to her real nature, or, if it does correspond, it is fantastic in relation to himself, i.e. the kind of wife he really desires is not what he imagines. The fact that, though she makes it clear that she does not desire him, he still continues to pursue her, and by devious strategies, demonstrates that he has no real respect for her as a person.

(3) Olivia has an erotic-fantastic image of Caesario (Viola). Since she is able to transfer her image successfully to Caesario's double, Sebastian, and marry him, we must assume that her image was only accidentally fantastic, that the image of the kind of husband she desires is real in relation to herself and only fantastic because, as it happens, Caesario is not a man, but Viola in disguise.

(4) The illusion of Antonio and Sebastian is not concerned with the erotic relationship but with the problem of body-soul identity. They make the assumption which is usually correct, that a face is the creation of its past, but are met by the exceptional case which proves that this assumption is not universally true. When Viola is dressed as a man, she and her brother appear to be identical twins, and the existence of identical twins proves that it is possible for two different pasts to produce almost the same face.

It is essential to the play that Viola's disguise be perfect. If she looks like a girl dressed up as a boy, if she shows the slightest hint of physical femininity, there will be a false suggestion of sexual perversity about the feelings she arouses in the Duke and in Olivia, and Antonio will appear signally short-sighted.

II. *Der Rosenkavalier* and *Charley's Aunt.* In Baron Lerchenau, the seduction of young chambermaids has become a habit, i.e. what was once a combination of desire and personal choice has now become an automatic reflex with little relation to either. A costume suggests to him the magic word "chambermaid" and the word issues the command, "Seduce her." To make this clear, Octavian's disguise in the third act should be patently absurd, so that only a man at the mercy of habit could fail to see through it.

In *Charley's Aunt*, a different situation demands the same absurdity of disguise. The fortune-hunting uncle is not, like Baron Lerchenau, a slave of habit; he really does care about marrying a rich widow, but this desire is so strong that it has the same effect—the words "rich widow" issue the command, "Marry her." He has been told he is going to meet an old rich widow; he sees widow's weeds and this is sufficient to set him in motion, though it is patent to any other eye that the widow is really a young undergraduate dressed up.

★   ★   ★

The Comic Contradiction of the Lover vs. the Citizen

Since the relation between the sexes has the reproductive function of producing more people, it not only concerns the man and woman themselves but society, so that it involves not only their physical desires and their personal feelings for each other, but also their class feelings of social status and prestige.

Don Pasquale. A rich old man plans to marry a young girl against her will, for she is in love with a young man of her own age, and is foiled.

For this to be comic, it is essential that Don Pasquale feel no real desire for Norina, that his motive be a social one, to be able to boast to the other old men that he can get a young wife when they cannot. He wants the prestige of parading her and of appearing still both attractive and passionate. If he really feels desire, then he really suffers and the situation is either tragic or satiric.

Sam Weller and the Widows. Here it is the woman who pursues and, again, not for reasons of love but for reasons of prestige. The widows who pursue Sam Weller do not desire him in particular, they merely want to be Mrs X instead of Miss Y.

★   ★   ★

The Law of the City and the True Law

Example. Falstaff's Honor speech (*Henry IV.* Act V. scene 5).

If the warrior ethic of honor, courage and personal loyalty were the perfect expression of the moral law, as it was held to be in Homeric society, the speech would not be sympathetically comic, but a satirical device by which Falstaff was held up to ridicule as a coward. If, on the other hand, the warrior ethic were totally false, if there were not occasions when it was a true expression of moral duty, the speech would be, not comic, but a serious piece of pacifist propaganda.

The speech has a sympathetically comic effect for two reasons, the circumstances under which it is uttered, and the character of the speaker.

Were the situation one in which the whole united community seemed to be threatened, e.g. in the field of Agincourt, the speech would be out of place, but the circumstances are those of civil war, a struggle for power between the feudal nobility in which the claims of both sides to be the legitimate rulers are pretty equal—Henry IV himself was once a rebel who deposed his king—a struggle in which their feudal dependents are compelled to take part and risk their lives without having a real stake in the outcome. Irrespective of the speaker, the speech is a comic criticism of the feudal ethic as typified by Hotspur. Courage is a personal virtue but its misapplication can be a social evil; unnecessary warfare creates the paradox that personal cowardice becomes a public virtue.

That it should be Falstaff who utters the speech increases the comic effect. Falstaff has a fantastic conception of himself as a daredevil who robs purses and is a law unto himself, which, if it were real, would require exceptional physical courage. He tries to keep up this illusion but it is always breaking down because of his moral courage which keeps forcing him to admit that he is afraid. (In this he contrasts with Pistol, who shares his illusion but does not admit that he is a coward.) Further, though he lacks physical courage, he exemplifies the other side of the warrior ethic, personal loyalty, as contrasted with Prince Hal's Machiavellian manipulation of others.

When Falstaff is rejected by the man to whom he has pledged his whole devotion, his death may truly be called a death for the sake of his wounded honor.

★   ★   ★

The Banal

The human person is a unique singular, analogous to all other persons but identical with none. Banality is an illusion of identity, for, when people describe their experiences in clichés, it is impossible to distinguish the experience of one from the experience of another.

The cliché-user is comic because the illusion of being identical with others is created by his personal act. He is the megalomaniac in reverse. Both have fantastic conceptions of themselves but, whereas the megalomaniac thinks of himself as being somebody else—Julius Caesar, Napoleon, Michael Angelo, etc.—the banal man thinks of himself as being everybody else, that is, nobody in particular.

★   ★   ★

The Comic and the Witty Contradiction

The comic is an actual contradiction which is not intentionally created by the person or persons involved in it. The witty contradiction is intentionally created by the wit (the clown is the wit of action) and may be imaginary. Thus one of the most fruitful devices of wit is the imaginary treatment of analogous situations as if they were identical. During a period of riots and social unrest when the mob had set fire to hayricks all over the country, Sydney Smith wrote to his friend Mrs. Meynell:

> What do you think of all these burnings? and have you heard of the new sort of burnings? Ladies' maids have taken to set their mistresses on fire. Two dowagers were burned last week, and large rewards are offered! They are inventing little fire-engines for the toilet table, worked with lavender water.

Metaphor (the relation by analogy) is pushed to the absurd point where it is made to appear as exact concrete description. A similar process is at work in Oscar Wilde's epigram:

Twenty years of romance make a woman look like a ruin; twenty years of marriage make her look like a public building.

The term "ruin" is commonly used metaphorically, the term "public build-ing" only concretely. The juxtaposition removes the metaphorical meanings of "ruin" and restores it to its exact descriptive meaning.

★   ★   ★

The Spoonerism and the Pun

Spoonerism.

> Your tutor tells me that you have hissed all the mystery lectures and tasted nearly three worms.

or, We will now sing Hymn 366. "Shoving leopard of my sheep."

Pun.

> When I am dead I hope it may be said:
> His sins were scarlet but his books were read.
>
> —Hilaire Belloc

The origin of the comic effect is the same in both cases, namely that mere chance, a slip of the tongue, an accidental homophone, appears as provi-dence and, instead of resulting in unintelligibility, makes unexpected sense.

In the spoonerism, however, the meaning created is only meaning in a for-mal syntactical sense; the sentence is made of real words and is grammatically correct, but otherwise nonsense, and it is important for the comic effect that the intended sentence shall not be immediately obvious to the listener, but require thought to discover, while in the pun both meanings of the homo-phone are simultaneously present and both make equally good sense.

The spoonerism is comic and should at least appear to be involuntary; the pun is witty and should appear to be deliberate.

★   ★   ★

Literary Parody

Example

> As we get older we do not get any younger.
> Seasons return, and to-day I am fifty-five,
> And this time last year I was fifty-four,
> And this time next year I shall be sixty-two.
>
> —Henry Reed (parodying T. S. Eliot)

Just as a human face is an unique modification of the flesh common to all faces, created by the human spirit within, so the style of every poem is an unique modification of the language common to all poems, created by the special vision of the poet.

The art of literary parody consists in dividing the substance from the spirit.

It takes the style and even exaggerates its originality and it limits the subject matter to the area of concern most typical of the poet and in which he has displayed the deepest insights; but then it makes the statements in that style and on that subject as banal as possible. The comic effect lies in the contradiction that a highly original style and original attitude to life are employed to make statements that only require a banal style and a dull concern.

★   ★   ★

Flyting

An exchange of insults between cab-drivers or in verse form between poets (e.g. *The Flyting of Dunbar and Kennedy*) is comic because the insulting nature of what is said appears to indicate a passionate relation of hostility and aggression while the calculated skill of expression indicates that the protagonists are not thinking about each other but about the language and their pleasure in employing it skillfully. The relation between the two of them is impersonal for all that is needed is some stimulus to imagination and any other person would do as well. A man who is really in a state of passionate hatred for another is speechless and can only express it by physical violence.

All poetry is emotion recollected in tranquillity; in flyting, the emotion concerned is anger, and the association of anger with tranquillity is a comic contradiction.

★   ★   ★

Satire

The Object of Satire. The comic butt of satire is a person who, though in possession of moral faculties, transgresses the moral law beyond the normal call of temptation.

Thus the lunatic cannot be an object for satire because he is not responsible for his actions, nor can the devilish be an object because, while responsible, he lacks the normal faculty of conscience.

Any person who causes serious suffering to the innocent partakes of the devilish and is the object, not of satire, but of prophetic denunciation. For example, a black marketeer in sugar is satirizable because the existence of such a black market depends upon the greed of others and to do without sugar is not a serious suffering; a black marketeer in penicillin is not satirizable because those who need it are innocent and, if they cannot pay his prices, die.

The mere fact of transgressing the moral law is not enough to make a person the object of satire, for all men do so, but the average man's transgression is tempered by various considerations, conscience, prudence, reason, competing desires. Most men, for example, desire wealth and are sometimes unscrupulous in their means of obtaining it, but their desire is tempered by laziness. A miser is satirizable because his desire for money overrides all other desires, such as a desire for physical comfort or love for his family. The commonest object of satire is a monomaniac.

The Satirical Strategy. There is not only a moral norm but also a normal way of transgressing it. At the moment of yielding to temptation, the normal human being has to exercise self-deception and rationalization, he requires the illusion of acting with a good conscience; after the immoral act, when desire is satisfied or absent, he realizes the nature of his act and feels guilty. He who feels no guilt after transgressing the moral law is mad, and he who, at the moment he is transgressing it, is completely conscious of what he is doing is demonic.

The two commonest satirical devices, therefore, are as follows:

(1) to present the object of satire *as if* he or she were mad, i.e. as unaware of the nature of his act.

> Now Night descending, the proud scene was o'er,
> But liv'd in Settle's numbers, one day more.
>
> —Pope

The writing of poetry which, even in the case of the worst poets, is a personal and voluntary act is presented as if it were as impersonal and necessary as the revolution of the earth, and the value of the poems produced which, even in a bad poet, varies, is presented as invariable and therefore subject to a quantitative measurement like dead matter.

The satiric effect presupposes that we know that Settle in real life is not a certifiable lunatic for real lunacy overcomes a man against his will; Settle is, as it were, a self-made lunatic.

(2) To present the object of satire *as if* he or she were demonic, i.e. completely conscious.

> Although, dear Lord, I am a sinner,
>   I have done no major crime;
> Now I'll come to Evening Service
>   Whensoever I have time.
> So, Lord, reserve for me a crown,
> And do not let my shares go down.
>
> —John Betjeman

Again, the satiric effect depends upon our knowing that in real life the lady is not wicked, for if she really were as truthful with herself as she is presented, she could not go into a Christian church but would have to attend the Temple of Mammon, and become a formidable criminal.

Satire flourishes in a homogeneous society with a common conception of the moral law, for satirist and audience must agree as to how normal people can be expected to behave, and in times of relative stability and contentment, for satire cannot deal with serious evil and suffering. In an age like our own it cannot flourish except in private circles as an expression of private feuds;

in public life, the serious evils are so importunate that satire seems trivial and the only suitable kind of attack prophetic denunciation.

II

Falstaff, or the Comic Presentation of the State of Grace

> — Now, Hal, what time of day is it, lad?
> —What a devil hast thou to do with the time of day.
> *—Henry IV.* Part I. Act I. scene 2

Not to know the time of day is to be governed, like animals and children, by the immediate mood of the self. To know the time of day, to structure the passage of time, is to submit the self to the ego which takes purposive decision with a view to attaining some future good; it signifies that a person is conscious of a vocation, of the kind of person he intends to become. This is equally true for the saint who intends to love God and his neighbor and for the worshipper of the Prince of this world whose goal is power and success. He who does not know the time of day is either the child who has not yet tasted of the tree of the knowledge of good and evil or one in a state of salvation whose sins have been forgiven.

★　★　★

> I prithee, sweet wag, shall there be gallows standing in England when thou art king? and resolution thus fubb'd as it is with the rusty curb of old father antic the law?
> —Act I. scene 2

> What? A young knave a begging? Is there not wars? Doth not the king lack subjects? Do not the rebels need soldiers?
> —Part II. Act II. scene 2

Falstaff thinks of himself as Mr Worldly Wiseman, learned in the smart ways of the big city. In reality he is, like Shallow and Silence, a country boy who can only conceive of the world as a child conceives of it, as a place where all relations are personal. Toward the impersonal, law and politics, his attitude is one, not of rebellious hatred (the attitude of the criminal) but of incomprehension—what is impersonal is dream-like and does not exist.

★　★　★

> I have foresworn his company hourly any time this two and twenty years and yet I am bewitched by the rogue's company.
> —Part I. Act II. scene 2

> The young prince hath misled me. I am the fellow with the great belly, and he my dog.
> —Part II. Act 1. scene 2

I shall be sent for soon at night.

—Part II. Act V. scene 4

Falstaff thinks of the Prince as his ideal self, like himself, but young, not old, the future King of England not a bankrupt knight. What he never realizes is that Prince Hal, unlike himself, really is Mr Worldly Wiseman who will attain success in this world because he will never let personal feeling for others interfere with his ambition; others are to him only means to his end. Unwittingly Falstaff passes a final judgment on him.

Thou art essentially mad, without seeming so.

—Part I. Act II. scene 4

★   ★   ★

Falstaff fornicates promiscuously, lives at other people's expense and tries to steal purses. In real life fornication and theft are sins because they involve selfishness and aggression, either hating our neighbor or treating him as a thing.

In the comic mirror, however, where nobody is seen to suffer as a consequence, promiscuity becomes a symbol of loving all one's neighbors as oneself, and debt and theft a symbol of our mutual interdependence—we are all members one of another. (Thus the Hostess may grumble at having to feed Falstaff at her own expense but she would never let him starve, and Doll Tearsheet is willing to give her professional services free.) Falstaff's conduct is play, not reality, for he is without a trace of aggression. (His physical cowardice is a symbol for this.) On two occasions he acts with apparent aggression, when he drives the drunken Pistol out of the inn and when he stabs the dead Hotspur. In the first case he is defending the women and displays no personal animus toward Pistol, who is his friend, and, in the second, stabbing a corpse is only aggression when it expresses a fanatical hatred pursued beyond death which is not so in his case.

With this lack of aggression goes an *agapé* without distinction of persons.

—I never did see such pitiful rascals.
—Tut, tut! good enough to toss: food for powder, food for powder. They'll fill a pit as well as better. Tush, man, mortal men, mortal men.

—Part I. Act IV. scene 2

A plague on sighing and grief! It blows a man up like a bladder.

—Part I. Act II. scene 4

Thou seest I have more flesh than another man, and therefore more frailty.

—Part I. Act III. scene 3

I have a whole school of tongues in this belly of mine, and not a tongue of them all speaks any word but my name.

—Part II. Act IV. scene 3

Falstaff's drinking and its physical consequence are his means of preserving his childish innocence, of preventing his seeing this world as it really is, a place governed, not by personal affection, but by love of power. Should he allow himself to see the truth, he would either turn into the Machiavellian man of the world, like Prince Hal, and become a success, or, finding himself without the necessary talent and position for that, become an embittered failure; in either case he would cease to love others. A fat man is, in the eyes of a child, a big man. Obesity is, for innocence, the playful symbol of contented importance. Falstaff suffers from melancholia which is the most typical suffering of childhood when it has come to sense that all is not well in the world without knowing the facts. Thanks to alcohol he remains at this point of not knowing the facts, in order that he may continue to love others. He keeps his melancholy at bay by drink in order that he may not become a bore but go on amusing others and remaining lovable. In his own way, Falstaff is, like Don Quixote, the Knight of the Doleful Countenance, the Suffering Servant who sacrifices his life for the sake of others.

Thought, Spring 1952

Our Italy

Rome and a Villa. By Eleanor Clark. Doubleday. $4.

My first image of Italy is associated with an aunt whose devotion to the country led her into building her dream Italian house in one of the wettest parts of England. It was dreadfully damp and draughty and the veranda shut out the sun; even so, I thought it beautiful. My aunt was a spinster who devoted her life to looking after an elder sister: how she came to go to Italy in the first place I do not know—her favorite saint, St Francis, had something to do with it and, I suspect, Ruskin also—but Italy had come to represent for her rare wonderful holidays when for a few weeks one could ride a bicycle where one chose and not have to be unselfish. Shocked as she would have been at the idea, I can easily imagine her as the heroine of *A Room with a View*.

After this introduction, however, Italy vanished from the imagination and the conversation in the circles I knew. True, one of the writers we most admired, D. H. Lawrence, lived there and wrote wonderfully about it, and one of my contemporaries, Adrian Stokes, began his passionate love-affair with Italian stone, but they failed to rouse in most of us any desire to go there. For my immediate elders there was one culture, French, and one city, Paris— there was intellectual excitement, there one could learn how to write. In reaction to them, and with some prophetic intuition of the future, maybe, I and some of my friends deserted Paris for the much grimmer and disturbing but, at least, uncartesian world of Berlin. The idea of Rome never entered any heads till 1945, and then it entered a great many other heads besides. It is tempting to ascribe this neglect to distaste for Mussolini but up until the Abyssinian war, I doubt if Italian fascism would have been an effective deterrent had we felt a strong interest.

As a rule the best writers and the purest hack journalists have one thing in common; their books are timely. I intend a compliment therefore, when I say that *Rome and a Villa* is timely for it is about *our* Italy, the Italy of those, like myself, whose interest in and knowledge of the country postdates the Second World War.

Apart from a chapter about Salvatore Giuliano, the Sicilian bandit— which, as a matter of fact, I feel does not quite belong to the book—there is little in Miss Clark's record that is "news." What she asks us to notice has always been there to be noticed. We stand on the Campodoglio and look out over Rome; "the heterogeneous city" as Henry James called it.

> The scorn of neatness, the deep fantasy of juxtaposition are there, beyond the power of any poet or period; nobody could be so ruthless. The author of this creation is time, in collaboration with aesthetic judgment and energy, which has smashed and transgressed in one way or another at every point as art always does, until the fine and the atrocious are a joint essence of the one always contemporary work.

We walk through the streets, haunted by images of water and attracted in our interested Protestant modesty by the noise and the public gregariousness.

> It is like a party all the time; nobody has to worry about giving one or being invited; it is going on every day in the street and you can go down or be part of it from your window: nobody eats alone in the cafeteria, reading a book. A sickbed is another public gathering; there is a ritual of moaning, question and response; everybody must crowd in.

Our guide, thank goodness, does not try to make us see everything. She knows that, to carry away a real impression of a place, you must never allow the thought that you may never visit it again to enter your head: if the Trevi fountain catches your eye; very well, look at it as long as you like, even if that means that you never set eyes on the Coliseum. So, following her as house-guests rather than tourists, we "do" St Peter's, (by luck, it happens to be Holy Year), the Palaces, some Berninis and Caravaggios, we pause to admire the tribe of cats in the Piazza Vittorio, we leave the city and spend a whole day at Tivoli among the ruins of Hadrian's Villa, we come home to spend the evening thumbing through Belli who wrote two thousand sonnets in Roman dialect about the life of the city, a poet unpublished in his lifetime but come now to be regarded as one of the greatest poets of the nineteenth century. Well, what does it all add up to? Miss Clark's real service to us had been, I think to make each of us ask ourselves a question which is perhaps unanswerable, but which will not let us rest: "Why did I come here? Why here rather than somewhere else?"

If one is an artist, a negative answer, at least is clear: One has not come to Italy, as artists used to go to Paris, for intellectual conversation and technical discovery; Italy may stimulate the imagination, but there is nobody there from whom one can learn *how* to write or paint. Nor anywhere else in Europe, for that matter. If exchange of ideas and contact with intelligent minds is what one wants, one had better stay in New York.

For liberty from puritanical morals, to believe in as one could not or would not dare believe at home?

Hardly. Morals are so lax everywhere today that what may have constituted a powerful attraction to some people fifty years ago has lost its force. I suspect that the uninhibited easy-going sensuality of the emancipated puritan acts rather as a sedative and that many Americans live more chastely in Italy than they do in the States.

In days when Protestants were convinced that theirs was the only real Christianity and that Catholics were heathens, the emancipated Protestant who had read the Higher Criticism was drawn to Italy as to a pagan Eden. That attraction still persists, I believe, but with an important shift in emphasis. If Italy were really pagan, if Diana and Apollo had not been transformed—dare one say redeemed?—into Catholic saints, the most ardent agnostic would not enjoy it. It is an essential element of their charm that the easy-going ritual, the fireworks, the brass-bands, the votive models of limbs and eyes, the whole hodgepodge of worship and superstition, faith and cynicism, should be committed, however stagily and superficially, to belief in God who is not a poetic symbol for natural phenomena but their creator who became historical flesh and died to save mankind. Take away St Peter and there is nothing left in Italy either to love or hate except the classical ruins and the Fascist sport stadium. Even the baroque fountains are meaningless apart from the presence of the Church, shabby maybe, a menace if you choose to think so, but close and visible.

The Classical ruins. To one of them Miss Clark devotes her longest and most complicated chapter which is very courageous of her for many writers would not have dared attempt a theme which sounds so cliché.

Gibbon, I think, would be very shocked. To him, as to the other children of the enlightenment, the imperial ruins stood as witnesses to a golden age, peaceful, orderly, rational, and to its tragic end when the stoic virtues went down before the forces of Gothic barbarism and superstition. Now (in the eighteenth century), however, the Goddess of Reason has returned to earth, the hideous tyranny of the Papal throne was losing its power, and a new Antonine Age would presently be ushered in.

To Miss Clark and to all of us, I believe, in the middle of the twentieth century, the Roman Empire is like a mirror in which we see reflected the brutal, vulgar, powerful yet despairing image of our own technological civilization, an imperium which now covers the entire globe, for all nations, capitalist, socialist and communist, are united in their worship of mass, technique and temporal power. What fascinates and terrifies us about the Roman Empire is not that it finally went smash, but that, away from the start, it managed to last for four centuries without creativity, warmth or hope.

The Emperor Hadrian was individually what we now are collectively, Lord of the World; what we are collectively, each of us can in fantasy see himself as individually.

Hadrian's Villa, as Miss Clark shows it to us, is an expression of that fantasy in all its monstrosity, the more frightening because Hadrian was not personally a monster, like Nero, but an extremely capable and cultivated man. His incredible building which he was at for twenty-one years, to be stopped only by death, illustrates the law that where, in fact or in fantasy, power is unlimited, relations with other persons and with nature vanish and the victim is condemned to an unending dialogue with himself on the subject of death, unreal, theatrical, mad. Love for another is not possible, only the love of loving; the loss of the love-object, Antinous or another, be it never so precious, is nothing compared with the power to embody grief in dead matter.

> The main thing is to keep building, for one's very point of rest to be always in motion, a thrusting out of the ailing ego which must have recognition and more and more is forced to make it for itself in its own empyrean; if it stopped building its own temple, it would die.

> There seems to be no private space at all, at least it is hard to imagine a private life in any of it. Almost everything is either too light and large or too dark and small, and all of it pours into the hemmed-in outdoors as in a hopeless cross between claustrophobia and agoraphobia.

> What is shared with Versailles and the Palaces of the Czars, the lavishness and the arrogance of the dimensions, becomes something more insidious here. Not the simple effrontery of despotism . . . but the innermost statement of a mind, a true Folly, just the opposite of innocent Versailles.

> What is not fake is the expression; the need is real. The staginess is of his deepest nature . . . he has to build himself a plain of philosophy, a valley of the dead, guarded by a stone Cerberus; if he is not on a stage he is nothing, he will lose all belief in himself.

But this memorial to folly unlimited stands now, ruined, in the middle of a poor country without natural resources, without sufficient rainfall, and inhabited by a people with whom, of all the western peoples, it seems to have least to do, Mussolini notwithstanding. Measured beside the great creators of State Power, like Richelieu in France or the Tudors in England, or his contemporaries in Russia and Germany, Mussolini seems only a bad joke.

It is we who have drunk that poison, so no wonder we are drawn to Italy as to an Eden, idyllic because it is poor and its public life is intimate and local, and the eyes that meet ours are friendly but distant, like those of a grandmother who has survived too much to entertain false hopes.

The Griffin, [April 1952]

[Hic et Ille]*

"The name of the song is called '*Haddocks' Eyes.*'"

"Oh, that's the name of the song, is it?" Alice said, trying to feel interested.

"No, you don't understand," the Knight said, looking a little vexed. "That's what the name is *called.* The name really *is* '*The Aged Aged Man.*'"

"Then I ought to have said 'That's what the *song* is called?'" Alice corrected herself.

"No, you oughtn't: that's quite another thing. The *song* is called '*Ways and Means*': but that's only what it's *called,* you know!"

—Lewis Carroll, *Through the Looking Glass*

I

Criticism is tradition defending itself against the three armies of the Goddess Stupidity: the army of amateurs who are ignorant of tradition; the army of conceited eccentrics who believe tradition should be suppressed by a stroke of the pen in order that true art may begin with them; and the army of academicians who believe they maintain tradition by a servile imitation of the past.

★   ★   ★

The desire to link art to life, beauty to truth, justice to goodness, almost infallibly leads criticism to utter a host of stupidities; a critic who ignores or represses this concern and contents himself with being no more than an amateur or an historian of art, avoids covering himself with ridicule, but at what cost. No one reads him.

★   ★   ★

Judging a work of art is virtually the same mental operation as judging human beings, and requires the same aptitudes: first, a real love of works of art, an inclination to praise rather than blame, and regret when a complete rejec-

---

* [Retranslated for this edition by Richard Howard from "De Droite et de Gauche", a French translation by Christine Lalou of the lost English text. The French text is reprinted in the Textual Notes, together with comments on the title and other details of the retranslation.]

tion is required; second, a vast experience of all artistic activities; and last, an awareness, openly and happily accepted, of one's own prejudices. Some critics fail because they are pedants whose ideal of perfection is always offended by a concrete realization. Others fail because they are insular and hostile to what is alien to them; these critics, yielding to their prejudices without knowing they have them and sincerely offering judgments they believe to be objective, are more excusable than those who, aware of their prejudices, lack the courage to enter the lists to defend their personal tastes.

★   ★   ★

The best literary critic is not the one whose judgments are always right, but the one whose essays compel you to read and reread the works he discusses; even when he is hostile, you feel that the work attacked is important enough to be worth the effort—e.g. *Nietzsche contra Wagner*, or D. H. Lawrence against Fennimore Cooper. There are other critics who, even when they praise a book, cancel any desire you might have to read it.

★   ★   ★

The terms *classical* and *romantic* are misleading terms for two poetic parties which have always existed: the Aristocratic and the Democratic. Every poet belongs to one or the other, though he may switch his party allegiance, or, on some specific issue, refuse to obey his party Whip.

The Aristocratic Principle as regards subject matter:

> Poetry will treat no subject matter which it cannot digest.
> Thereby poetry is safeguarded from prosaic journalism and didacticism.

The Democratic Principle as regards subject matter:

> Poetry will exclude no subject matter which it cannot digest.
> Thereby poetry is safeguarded from narrow or false definitions of poetic material.

The Aristocratic Principle as regards treatment:

> The poem will treat none of the side-issues of the subject in question.
> Thereby the poem's unity is preserved and kept from being shapeless and diffuse.

The Democratic Principle as regards treatment:

> Nothing which can have the slightest relation to the subject will be neglected.
> Thereby the poem's richness and variety is preserved and kept from being impoverished and arid.

★   ★   ★

The terms "young" and "old" can be applied only within a closed system. In all matters subject to historical development, such as art or civilization, only the terms "before" and "after" may be applied. The *Iliad* precedes the *Aeneid*, but it is meaningless to say that it is older. Furthermore, it is no less absurd to say that works of art are immortal; the persistence of the work of art is not in the object's material duration but in its lifegiving quality for a spectator or a reader living in a given historical period. The *Iliad* in 1950 is not identical to the *Iliad* in 1750, but it is not older.

Traditional taste does not signify a preference for ancient art, but a just appreciation of historical order, of the relations between ancient and modern.

It can be said that a poem ages only when the language in which it is written undergoes certain transformations, while evidently remaining the same language. Strictly speaking, "Old English" should be called "Young English."

★   ★   ★

Works of art are closer to each other than they are to their creators; a poet's library will enlighten us about his poems infinitely more than his childhood or his love affairs.

★   ★   ★

If it is true, as seems likely, that childhood experiences mark the personality more deeply than experiences of adulthood, the nursery library of a future writer may be the surest guide in exploring his work; by "library" I mean the books he read with passion before acquiring the first critical notions.

My Nursery Library

Fiction: Complete works of Beatrix Potter; *Alice's Adventures in Wonderland* and *Through the Looking Glass* (Lewis Carroll); *The Little Mermaid* (Hans Andersen); *Icelandic Legends*; *The Princess and the Goblin* (George Macdonald); *The Rose and the Ring* (Thackeray); *The Child of the Cavern* (Jules Verne); *The Cruise of the Cachalot* (Ballantyne); *The Adventures of Sherlock Holmes* (Conan Doyle).

Poetry: *Struwwelpeter* (Hoffmann); *Hymns Ancient & Modern*; the mnemonic couplets in Kennedy's *Latin Primer*.

Non-Fiction: *Underground Life*; *Machinery for Metalliferous Mines*; *Lead and Zinc Ores of Northumberland and Alston Moor*; *Dangers to Health* (a Victorian treatise on plumbing); *The Edinburgh School of Surgery*.

When, at the age of fifteen, I began to be consciously interested in poetry, my taste was formed by reading Walter de la Mare's anthology *Come Hither*, which still seems to me the best possible introduction to poetry. (I have never held in my hands a book with a more exquisite smell.) When, some years later, I began to read literary critics, the two who most impressed me—and I have not changed my opinion of either of them—were Dr Johnson and Professor W. P. Ker.

★   ★   ★

All works of art are commissions, by the simple fact that the idea which incites the artist to create a given work "comes" to him from outside. Among the works which fail because their point of departure is false or inadequate, the number of works one commissions from oneself is greater than the number of works commissioned by a patron or a friend.

The artistic faculty that neoclassic critics call Judgment is the capacity to distinguish between blind chance and Providence. E.g.

> I was composing the G minor chorus (the Prayer, in *Moses in Egypt*), when I happened to thrust my pen into my medicine bottle instead of my inkwell; this produced a blot, and when (blotting paper not yet having been invented) I dried it with sand, the blot assumed the shape of a natural sign which instantaneously suggested the effect to be produced by the transition from G minor to G major; it is therefore this blot which deserves whatever merit the piece possesses. (Letter from Rossini to Louis Engel)

★   ★   ★

In a work of art, the effect of surprise is "fortunate" only if, on reflection, it appeared inevitable where any other procedure would have provoked an "unfortunate" surprise. Similarly, in life, when we recall an unfortunate choice, it seems to us that a fortunate choice would have been easier to make than the one we had decided on.

★   ★   ★

In the course of many centuries a few labor-saving devices have been introduced into the mental kitchen—alcohol, coffee, tobacco, benzedrine, etc.— but these mechanisms are very crude, liable to affect the health of the cook, and constantly breaking down. Artistic composition in the twentieth century A.D. is pretty much the same as it was in the twentieth century B.C.: nearly everything has still to be done by hand.

★   ★   ★

If works of art could be created by means of "inspiration" alone, i.e. automatically, in the course of a trance, creation would become an operation so boring and unpleasant that only substantial compensations of cash or honors could incite a man to become an artist.

★   ★   ★

The Pythoness claimed to give those who consulted her good advice for their future life; she never claimed to be giving poetry readings.

★   ★   ★

A work of art which was entirely profound, and from which everything obvious and banal was excluded, would inevitably be a fake.

★   ★   ★

If very few people, in the presence of a fine building, ask the architect's name, while the majority, hearing a lovely piece of music, ask the composer's name, it is not because music is a more personal art, but only because the architect must unite utilitarian goals to esthetic ones, while music is only a gratuitous game.

When we see a building, we know that, beautiful or hideous, it is there for a precise purpose; but when we hear a piece of music, we know that its only raison d'être is to please, and if we are pleased we instinctively feel a need to thank the person responsible. Furthermore, arts such as music or spoken poetry which exist only in the present and during performance seem to us more likely to be intended for our personal pleasure than the visual arts which are permanently there—always ready to give pleasure to the first passerby. Yet this impression does not confer a more personal character upon the act of hearing.

★   ★   ★

Sincerity is like sleep. Normally, we should assume that, of course, we will be sincere, and not give it a second thought. Most of us, however, suffer from bouts of hypocrisy as we suffer from bouts of insomnia; in both cases, the remedy is generally quite simple: in the case of insomnia, a change of diet; in the case of hypocrisy, a change of company.

★   ★   ★

What English-language poet has not at times rebelled against a language in which the suffix "s" makes a noun plural and a verb singular?

Art requires not only conventions of form, but also conventions of rhetoric.

There can be no art without a convention which emphasizes certain aspects of experience as important and dismisses others to the background. A new convention is a revolution in sensibility. It appeals to and is adopted by a generation because it makes sense of experiences which had hitherto been ignored. Every convention, in its turn, when it has done its work, becomes reactionary and needs to be replaced. Its effects, however, do not disappear. Its successor embodies them.

The Petrarchan love convention with which Tudor poetry begins, for instance, is not the same as the earlier Provençal convention. The Lady does not so much inspire noble actions in a warrior as be the cause of the emotions about which a poet writes. For such a convention, the most suitable kind of lady has a good character but says No; and the most suitable poet is one with a gentle and rather passive temperament, but with the introvert's capacity for deep and sustained emotion. When, either by temperament or on occasion, the poet's feelings are frivolous or transient, the convention of

Love's seriousness leads him to the most boring kind of rhetoric. Nor is it well suited to situations in which the behavior of the beloved Lady is such that there is as much hatred as love in the relation or in which the feelings of the lover are consciously and violently sensual. Shakespeare, in his earlier sonnets, and Donne in his early lyrics, wrestle with the convention and break through it, but at the same time neither of them can write as if the *Amor* religion of fidelity and deification of the beloved had never existed.

In the poetry of their successors, the Cavalier Poets—a poetry which excludes social upheavals, which deliberately ignores the public interests and as deliberately insists on the private life of leisure and pleasure—the wheel has turned a half-circle, so that the Petrarchan convention is stood on its head. It is now infidelity which is recommended, fidelity which is despised. But the Petrarchan sentiments are still there in a repressed form; and this is what gives these poets' works, Rochester's in particular, its unique flavor. They are not naïvely frivolous but defiantly so, debauched by a serious effort of will.

★   ★   ★

When a reviewer declares a book to be "sincere", we know immediately: (*a*) that it is not sincere, and (*b*) that it is badly written.

A mannered style (that of Gongora or the later Henry James, for example) is like an eccentric garment. Very few writers can carry it off, but if they do, we are enchanted.

Rhymes, meters, stanzas, etc., are like servants. If the master is just enough to win their affection and firm enough to command their respect, the result is an orderly happy household. If he is too tyrannical, the servants give notice; if he is too weak, they turn slovenly, impertinent, drunk and dishonest.

The poet who writes "free verse" is like Robinson Crusoe on his island: he must do all his cooking, laundry, darning, etc. In a few exceptional cases this manly independence produces something original and impressive, but more often the result is squalor: empty bottles on the unswept floor, dirty sheets on the unmade bed.

There is much to be said in favor of an established form, whether blank verse, heroic couplet, or any other. Instead of striving for an original personal form, at the risk of achieving no such thing, the poet employs a given form; he may then devote all his efforts to making it express everything he has to say. With rare exceptions, the more original a poet is, the less he considers it a limitation to employ a given form; furthermore, by continually working with the same form, he will exercise his mind to think easily and naturally within it and will become sensitive to the subtlest variations of which this form is capable.

★   ★   ★

If it were true that the purest poetry is the poetry that most closely approaches music, then the purest of all would be tea-table conversation; for in such conversation words have no meaning in themselves; their meaning depends entirely on the vocal modulations of those who are speaking. "What a lovely day!" can mean, according to the tone of voice, "And what do you think?" or "Admire me!" or else "Help me!" or even "Blah-blah-blah!," "Bah!," etc.

★   ★   ★

Owing to its superior power as a mnemonic, verse is better than prose for didactic purposes. Those who condemn didacticism must condemn *a fortiori* didactic prose. In verse, at least (as is often proved by advertising slogans) the didactic message loses half its immodesty.

In the same way, verse is certainly equal and probably superior to prose for the lucid exposition of ideas, since, in skillful hands, the verse form can parallel and reinforce the steps of the logic.

Indeed, contrary to what most people who have inherited a romantic conception of poetry believe, the danger of argument in verse is that it renders ideas *too* clear and distinct, more Cartesian than they really are. Pope's *Essay on Man* is an example.

On the other hand, verse is unsuited to controversy—to the defense of a truth or a belief which has been called into doubt or contested—because its artificial nature conveys a certain skepticism about its conclusions.

Thirty days hath September,
April, June and November

is valid because nobody doubts its truth. If, however, there existed a body of people who denied this affirmation, the verses would be powerless to convince them because, formally, one might just as well say:

Thirty days hath September,
April, May and December.

★   ★   ★

Poe's theory about the necessity of writing short poems is in accord with the industrial revolution. As societies grow, their poems tend to grow shorter. A peasant will listen to interminable epic poems in the village square; the literary man in big cities reads sonnets in his bath.

★   ★   ★

It is sometimes easier to enjoy wholeheartedly a fine poem that expresses convictions we do not share than a fine poem that expresses our own convictions, for the skepticism pertaining to poetic form in itself disturbs us only insofar as the subject treated is really important to us.

Poetry in primitive societies—more static in their structure and more immediately governed by ritual practices—expresses simple things in a contorted manner; the sentiments are direct, the poetic form is complicated and complex. The poetry of our disintegrated society, which has little respect for ritual, seeks a direct expression for complicated things; the sentiments are subtle and ambiguous, the poetic form is "everyday language."

★   ★   ★

British English is the only language which distinguishes what is boring from
what is a bore. Similarly, *boring* expresses a subjective judgment which means
boring-to-me; the expression *a bore* claims to be objective, universally valid, a
true judgment.

> Not boring but a bore: Henry James, the last quartets of Beethoven,
> Michelangelo's frescoes in the Sistine Chapel.
> Sometimes boring but not a bore: Bach's "Art of Fugue," Shakespeare,
> Degas.
> Not boring and not a bore: Pope, Verdi, Giorgione.
> Boring and a bore: Shelley, Brahms, David.
> Absolutely boring but absolutely not a bore: the time of day.
> Absolutely not boring but an absolute bore: Eternity.

★   ★   ★

I am indebted to my friend Chester Kallman for having invented a new critical classification which has become a precious resource to me. Works of art
can be classified not only as *good* and *bad*, but also as *good, bad,* and *theoretical.*

The difference may be better understood through a culinary example: the
usual method of cooking Brussels sprouts in our country is an example of
bad cooking; i.e. the English cook intends to serve a savory vegetable, but she
fails, and the reason for her failure is that she boils them too long. Certain
salads eaten in the United States by the ladies in Helen Hokinson cartoons
are examples of "theoretical" cooking; they are good to look at, they contain
all the necessary vitamins, and if we could absorb them through the eyes or
ingest them by means of an esophageal tube, they would be perfect. Unfortunately they must pass over the taste buds, and that is something one doesn't
care for. It cannot be said that they are a failure, since there has been no intention to make them agreeable to the taste; and for this very reason it is impossible to give advice to the cook about how to improve them.

Similarly, when a work of art is bad, we can discern the maker's intentions
and where he went wrong; when it is a theoretical work, this becomes impossible. An average critic can always detect a work of bad art, but even the
most experienced critic will sometimes find his skill fail him and be taken in
by a theoretical work of art.

> *Examples of theoretical art*: About half of Petrarch's sonnets, Meredith's nov-
> els (not his poems), the paintings of Ingres, Rachmaninoff's Third Piano
> Concerto.

Touchstones

It is all well and good that Matthew Arnold recommends the use of selected
bits of sublime poetry as models for the poets and as criteria for critics; the

problem is that the sublime is all too easily recognized. Starting from the zenith is the same thing as giving a child the solution of a problem in arithmetic: the solution may be correct, but it does not follow that the child has understood the reasoning by means of which it has been found.

When you want to know a reader's genuine reaction to a work (even a work by a very great poet), you must offer him passages he does not already know; and in selecting such passages you must take into account the tendencies of public taste in that reader's country and period. For instance, in the nineteenth century, a passage of Donne would have been a good touchstone because metaphysical poetry was very little known or admired; but in our day, a reader's reaction to the same passage would have very little to tell us because it is fashionable to admire metaphysical poetry. Fifteen years ago Pope might have served the purpose; today such a passage is unlikely to be of much use. I should like to propose the following tests, in America, in this year 1951:

(1) The *Iliad*, second half of the second canto (the catalogue of ships and their crews).
(2) A dialogue in stichomythia setting forth the situation in any Greek tragedy.
(3) A passage of Dante, such as: *In quel loco fu 'ia Pier Damiano* . . .
(4) Spenser: the end of *The Faerie Queen* (Canto VII and the unfinished Canto VIII).
(5) Dryden: "To Her Grace the Duchess of Ormond."
(6) Dr Johnson: "On the Death of Dr Robert Levet."
(7) William Barnes: "The Little Sister."
(8) Any canto of Drayton's *Polyalbion*, etc.

II

The dialectical relation between art and science is as follows: Replying to art's effort to answer the question: "Who am I?" by the truism: "I am what I am," science objects that my "oneness" is relative, that I can be considered as the child of my parents, as a mammal, etc.

Replying to science's effort to drown the subject in its attributes, art objects that the self cannot be reduced to a pure epistemological subject, but that it remains stubbornly enthralled by its own existence.

★　★　★

Every work of art is an answer to the same unformulated question: "Who goes there?" and its answer is always: "Me."

In art, action and signification are united, and the artist's or performer's intention is of no importance. If a mistake is made, the effect fails to come off.

In a religious rite, action and signification do not depend upon exactness of execution, but on the believer's intention.

★   ★   ★

If art were magic, if the purpose of a love-song was to incite the Cruel Fair to entrust the poet with the key to her bedroom, a magnum of champagne would be more beautiful than a sonnet.

★   ★   ★

Propaganda is the use of magic by those who no longer believe in it against those who still do.

★   ★   ★

Catharsis is properly effected, not by works of art, but by religious rites. It is also effected, less properly, by bullfights, professional football matches, bad movies, military bands, and monster rallies at which ten thousand Girl Guides form themselves into a living flag.

★   ★   ★

Hamlet is a myth only for actors. Every actor (and actress) identifies himself (and herself) with Hamlet and wants to play the part; but the greater his (or her) talent, the more disastrous the failure. A great actor can play any character except an actor's; yet that is precisely what Hamlet is.

Having seen a number of great actors fail in the role, I cannot help thinking that Shakespeare has deliberately played a good trick on an institution from which he had certainly suffered a good deal.

★   ★   ★

The old prejudices against the theatre are not totally unjustified, for the representation of characters by flesh and blood individuals gives rise to dangerous ambiguities, even more severe in the audience than among the actors.

I am at the theatre where I see a valiant and talented hero fall tragically from the summits of happiness to the depths of misery, and a stupid and weak character paradoxically rise from obscurity to fortune and glory; whereupon I say to myself: "What a charming fairy tale!" In real life, unfortunately for me, belonging as I do to the category of the weak, it is the strong man who wins the princess and a million dollars; it is the weak one who dies in poverty and scorn. But here what I see, after all, is only theatre. The tragic hero whose suicide we have just observed will appear in a moment to greet the public, and the imbecile who has married the princess will return, after the performance, to his furnished rooms for bachelors.

If this is how I conceive of theatre, I have simply abandoned myself to my dream of being counted among the powerful and of seeing those I envy reduced to poverty. In order to grasp the truth the theatre claims to illustrate, I must, on my own initiative, make a correction which the theatre is impotent to impose upon me. The unreality (because this is only theatre) of the tragic hero's sufferings and the comic hero's triumph prove, not that the tragic hero does not suffer in actuality, nor that the comic hero is not really happy, but that suffering and happiness are not what I choose to believe them to be. The distressing tragic truth is this: "This hero is either what I am, or what I would like to be; and I am told here that as long as I am like him or like whom I desire to be, I shall proceed, unknowingly, to a miserable death." The distressing comic truth is concealed, since the comic hero is just as happy when he is a nobody as when he is the husband of the princess: "Here's a man I shouldn't like to be, or whom I would be ashamed of being; yet I am told that he is blessed because he considers himself happy in a situation I consider miserable. Only he who can accept suffering is, in reality, the princess's bridegroom."

★   ★   ★

Music is the whiskey of the damned. (Bernard Shaw)

The danger of identifying oneself with the unreal is even greater in the case of music than in that of the theatre. On the one hand, the ear is a passive organ; on the other, music is, above all, dynamic; it reflects will and choice. Those who suffer from a lack of resolve and determination in life can, at a stroke, abandon themselves passively to music and, by identifying themselves with it, can lead vicariously an imaginary life of triumphant affirmation.

★   ★   ★

A photograph in which the characters' poses are nicely studied always has an artificial look, and a modern photograph of this same type, utilizing the fastest film and the fastest shutter, seems even more artificial than an elaborately posed daguerreotype. A scene synthesizes history's unfolding in an instant, and composition is the means employed to achieve this synthesis, but a photograph composes nothing whatsoever; it offers an exact reproduction of a real historical moment which is never composed because it is an unfolding between past and future.

The camera cannot lie; but since the truth it preserves is the truth of an ephemeral moment, excluded from past and future alike, its signification is determined by the past and future attributed to it by the man who provides it with a title and by the man who watches it—a signification which cannot help being false.

A photograph shows us a man, perched on a tractor, smiling broadly; but the reason this man, in this field, was smiling at this moment, the photograph cannot show us. The observer of the photograph can invent any reason he likes, without fear of contradiction.

There exists no country in the world, nor even a single community, in which an unprejudiced camera cannot take two series of pictures one of which would show a paradise and the other a hell.

★   ★   ★

In a photograph, differences between a crag, a marble column, an oak, a frog and a human face are merely differences in shape and texture.

From the height of ten thousand feet, the earth appears to the human eye as it appears to the eye of the camera; that is to say, all history is reduced to the accidents of nature. This has the salutary effect of making historical evils, like national divisions and political hatreds, seem absurd.

I look down from an aeroplane upon a stretch of land which is obviously continuous. That, across it, marked by a tiny ridge or river or even by no topographical sign whatever, there should run a frontier, and that the human beings living on one side should hate or refuse to trade with or be forbidden to visit those on the other side, is, from the height where I find myself, revealed to me as ridiculous. Unfortunately, I cannot have this revelation without having the illusion that there are no historical values.

From this same height I cannot distinguish between an outcrop of rock and a magnificent cathedral, or between a happy family playing in a backyard and a flock of sheep; so that I am unable to feel any difference between dropping a bomb to destroy the cathedral, the happy family, or even the rocks or the flock. If the effects of distance between the observer and the observed were mutual, so that as the objects on the ground shrank in size and lost their uniqueness, the observer in the aeroplane felt himself shrinking and becoming more and more generalized, we should either give up flying or create a heaven on earth.

Those who accuse the movies of having a deleterious moral effect, of dividing families and increasing youthful crime, may well be right, but not for the reasons they usually give. It is not what movies are about—gangsters or adultery—which does the damage, but the naturalistic nature of the medium itself which encourages a fantastic conception of time. In all narrative art, the narration of the action takes less time than it would take in real life; but in the novel or drama, even when they are naturalistic, the passage of time is abridged, i.e. placed in perspective. For example, a man woos a woman; in the theatre this scene may last perhaps ten minutes; but the audience will have the sense that the scene took place over a period of two hours. The absolute naturalism of the camera destroys this sense: the illusion of real life is so strong that the audience begin to be convinced that, in real life as on the screen, the conquest of a woman takes forty minutes. When, leaving the movies for real life, they become aware that this takes two hours, they lose patience. Make movies as moral as you like, in their subject matter or their tone, they will still be harmful; because, if they seek to inculcate a taste for virtue, they cannot prevent themselves from bearing witness that virtue can be acquired in only a few minutes. When he grows impatient, the movie addict does not cry "Hurry!"; he cries "Cut!"

Preuves, May 1952

Keeping the Oriflamme Burning

Henry Irving: The Actor and His World. By Laurence Irving.
Macmillan. $10.

The biographer whose subject rises from poverty and obscurity to wealth and fame must envy the writer of fairy stories. The latter, once he has brought the poor woodcutter's son safely through all his trials into the arms of the beautiful princess, can write, "And so they lived happily ever after," and break off, confident that his hero has never lost the reader's sympathy. The biographer, on the other hand, is compelled to tell the story of the marriage as well, which, if it be indeed a happy one, means almost inevitably that the second half of his biography will be less interesting than the first. It is not our innate kindness that makes us enjoy the rise of a man from rags to riches, nor is it our innate malice that makes us enjoy equally his fall from glory to misery; it is simply that peripety in either direction is a law of dramatic interest.

The biographer of an actor is at a particular disadvantage in that if an actor succeeds at all, he does so fairly early in life. At the start of *Henry Irving: The Actor and His World*, the task of his grandson, Mr Laurence Irving, is easy, for from 1851, when John Brodribb, then in his teens, sees his first *Hamlet*, until 1871, when Henry Irving, the new star from Manchester, appears in the first performance of *The Bells* and has all theatrical London at his feet, the story is pure fairy tale. Every circumstance seems against the poor boy from Somerset who has made up his mind to become a great actor; he stammers, his legs are too long and too thin, without spectacles he is as blind as a bat, his mother is a devout Methodist who believes that all actors are eternally damned. But he sticks to his decision. Ignoring his mother's tears and saving his pennies, he visits the theatre constantly, takes elocution lessons, appears in amateur productions, and manages to get introduced to his idol, Samuel Phelps, only to be told, "Sir, do not go on the stage; it is an ill-requited profession."

The fairy godmother, disguised as an uncle, appears with a hundred pounds, enabling him to leave Thacker, Spink & Co., East India merchants, to buy wigs, buckles, laces, feathers, sham jewelry, and three swords, and to secure, for three guineas, the leading role in an amateur production of *Romeo and Juliet*, at the Soho Theatre, billed under his newly adopted stage name. Wisely, he decides not to hang about the London theatres but to learn his trade in the provinces, and departs for Sunderland. One night, during his first week as a professional,

> . . . when he came upon the stage as Cleomenes in *The Winter's Tale* to describe Leontes' discovery of his daughter, no words came from his lips. His fellow-actors waited in awkward dismay. The prompter groaned his cue in tones that were heard all over the house. Irving was paralysed with

horror. Then, with a tremendous effort of will, he managed to blurt out, "Come to the market place and I will tell you further!" and, leaving the astonished actors, who knew of no such market place, to pick up the threads of the play as best they could, he rushed to his dressing room, angry and ashamed, with the hisses of the audience buzzing in his burning ears.

Miraculously, he is not dismissed, and stays on, at a salary of twenty-five shillings a week, singing in opera, dancing in burlesque, and generally making himself useful until the end of the year, when he is offered a job at the Theatre Royal, in Edinburgh. Conditions in a repertory company at that time were certainly good training in versatility. In the course of the next three years, he plays over four hundred parts, including Venoma, a female fairy. In an appendix, Mr Laurence Irving lists the titles of the dramas; the "F"s run as follows:

> The Fairy Circle, The Falls of Clyde, A Fascinating Individual, Fazio, The Fire Raiser, The Flowers of the Forest. The Flying Dutchman, The Fortunes of Nigel, Forty and Fifty, The Foundling of the Forest, Frankenstein, Fraud and Its Victims, Frederick of Prussia, French Before Breakfast, The French Spy.

The next few years are ups and downs. He makes an attempt on London and fails (the largest part he is offered is Osric); he goes to Dublin, where he has his troubles with a hostile audience; he goes to Manchester, where he achieves great success and has his first stab at *Hamlet*. Nevertheless, he is still so poor that he bursts into tears when a fellow-actor makes him a present of woollen underclothes, a luxury beyond his means. He has a row with the Manchester management and leaves, finds it difficult to get employment, and by Christmas, 1865, is stranded, penniless, in Liverpool. Once again the fairy godmother intervenes:

> As he turned his back on the theatre, the stage-doorkeeper hurried out with a letter which he had forgotten to give him. Irving opened it absent-mindedly—it was probably a bill—no—it bore a Manchester postmark. He took a hasty glance at the signature—Dion Boucicault. The writer was about to produce a play in Manchester in which he believed there was a good part for him.

The play, *The Two Lives of Mary Leigh*, or *Hunted Down*, in which Irving played Rawdon Scudamore, "a polished and villanous adventurer," was a smashing hit in Manchester, and it was decided to take it to London. George Eliot attended the first night. As she left, she asked G. H. Lewes, editor of the *Fortnightly Review*, what he thought of Irving.

"In twenty years," replied Lewes, "he will be at the head of the English stage." "He is there, I think, already," murmured the novelist.

Anyway, with the public he is now an important star. He begins to have a social and personal life. He falls in love with an actress, Nellie Moore, but she dies. A Miss Florence O'Callaghan falls in love with him and marries him, but it is soon apparent that their temperaments are incompatible. A reading of Thomas Hood's poem *Eugene Aram* so impresses Hezekiah Bateman, the lessee of the Lyceum Theatre, that he offers to make Irving his leading comedian and character actor at a salary of fifteen pounds a week, an offer Irving accepts on condition that should the opportunity arise, Bateman will produce a melodrama called *The Bells*. The opportunity does arise, and on Saturday, November 25, 1871, the life of Henry Irving reaches its dramatic climax, both professionally and personally. He is driving home with his wife. For the last few hours, he has known that he has accomplished his boyish ambition; he is now acknowledged as the greatest actor in England.

> He laid his hand on Florence's arm, saying, "Well, my dear, we too shall soon have our own carriage and pair!" . . . "Are you going on making a fool of yourself like this all your life?," she asked. They were crossing Hyde Park Corner. Irving told the driver of the brougham to stop. Without a word he got out and left his wife to continue the journey alone. He never returned to his home and he never spoke to her again.

What a final curtain! But this is biography, not drama; we are only at page 200, with nearly five hundred pages more to go. Hitherto we have been too absorbed in the story to notice the style, but now we begin to be conscious of Mr Laurence Irving's prose, which is that of a rather good old-fashioned provincial newspaper, dignified but terribly stodgy. To Henry Irving, the struggling young actor, we have given our unwavering support, but of the Sir Henry to be—"The Chief," artistic dictator of the Lyceum, member of the Garrick Club, member of the Athenæum Club, D.Litt. [Cantab.], welcome at Marlborough House—of Irving the public institution, we are prepared to be highly critical.

It is greatly to Mr Laurence Irving's credit that while he is absolutely convinced of the greatness of his grandfather, he gives all the facts on which his critics based their complaints. To begin with, there were his eccentric habits of pronunciation: "go" was "gaw," "good" was "god," "sight" was "seyt," "smote" was "smot," "hand" was "hond" or "hend," "war" rhymed with "far," and "trammel up the consequence" became "trammele up-p the cunsequence"; then, there was his peculiar voice, which Augustin Daly compared to "a man speaking half of a long sentence while drawing in his breath and letting the other half fly out while he expels his breath."

Henry James was always, perhaps, a bit prissy as a critic, but after reading the descriptions of performances in this book I suspect that his verdict on Irving, whom in many respects he admired, was probably just:

His strong points are intellectual. He is ingenious, intelligent, and fanciful; imaginative he can hardly be called. . . . It is, of course, by picturesqueness that Mr Irving has made his place; by small ingenuities of "business" and subtleties of action; by doing as a painter does who goes in for colour when he cannot depend upon his drawing.

The plays in which, once he was his own master, Irving chose to star fall into three classes. First, there were the melodramas, *The Bells, The Lyons Mail, The Dead Heart,* etc., which made no literary pretensions and were intended only to be vehicles for bravura acting. These, I am sure, would delight us as much as they did Irving's contemporaries. Despite James's horror, I would add *Faust,* with

the angelic visions, the heavenward ascents, the descents into sulphurous infernos, the magical appearances and trap-door vanishings, the lycopodic brimstone, the gauzy treacle, the new-fangled battens of electric lights, the calcium arcs, the sub-stage generation of steam, the daring use of electric fluid (under the personal supervision of Colonel Gourand— the partner of the great Mr Edison).

Any relation to Goethe must have been so purely accidental that it seems pointless to call it a travesty; why should one not have sat back and enjoyed it for the preposterous pantomime it was?

The second class comprised the plays of Shakespeare. As theatregoers, we are now accustomed to seeing Shakespeare played more or less as written, so we should probably complain more than the Victorians at Irving's cuts and changes. It seems, however, that in comparison to his predecessors his practice was almost pedantic; for example, he played *Richard III* without Colley Cibber's interpolations. As for his interpretations, it is a great tribute to the detail and vividness of Mr Laurence Irving's descriptions that we can consider forming an opinion at all. On the whole, I think we should agree with the most intelligent critics of his time; that is to say, we should admire his Shylock (enormously), Richard III, Iago, Benedick, Iachimo, and Cardinal Wolsey, have our doubts about his Hamlet and Macbeth, and dislike his Othello, Romeo, Lear, and Coriolanus.

But our real quarrel with him would be over the third class of his preferred plays, to which belonged the Higher Drama of the Poet Laureate Tennyson, Bulwer-Lytton, William Wills, and Comyns Carr. As acting vehicles, they were inferior to the melodramas, and as literature, they were beneath contempt. What are we to think of the taste of a man who will have nothing to do with Ibsen yet sees nothing incongruous in reciting Shakespeare one night and the next night such lines as these, from Bulwer-Lytton:

> With this
> I at Rochelle did hand to hand engage

> The stalwart Englisher—no mongrels, boy,
> Those Island mastiffs—mark the notch—a deep one—
> His casque made here—I shore him to the waist!
>
> (*Richelieu*)

or these, from William Wills:

> I saw a picture once, by a great Master,
> It was an old man's head,
> Narrow and evil was its wrinkled front—
> Eyes closed and cunning: a dull vulpine smile,
> 'Twas called a Judas, wide that painter erred;
> Judas had eyes like thine, of candid blue,
> His skin was smooth, his hair of youthful gold;
> Upon his brow shone the white stamp of truth,
> And lips, like thine, did give the traitor kiss.
>
> (*Charles I*)

On one of the rare occasions when anyone saw Irving drunk, he was heard declaiming, "The Oriflamme! We must keep—the Oriflamme—burning brightly!" One knows, alas, only too well what he meant.

Shaw's apparent indifference to Shakespeare as a poet, his curious illusion that anybody can write blank verse, may well have been largely Irving's fault; his ear deafened by the thunders of the Lyceum, all iambic pentameters sounded the same to him. Of the famous Shaw-Irving feud, it is impossible for us not to think that on almost every point Shaw was in the right; if he was unfair to Irving, it was in demanding more of him than he had a right to expect.

Irving came to maturity as an actor at the beginning of a period of revolutionary change, at a time, that is, when the only persons who had sensed what was about to happen were the producing artists; the performing artists and the public were still unaware of any change. (Perhaps they were dimly aware, but the only symptom of this was an increased passion for the good old past.) Like all performers, Irving knew the kind of thing he liked and could do well, but like nearly all performers, he could not distinguish between a genuine example of that kind and a counterfeit; it was his misfortune rather than his fault that after 1870 a play that was at once genuine and suitable for the Lyceum was not, and could not be, written; the only genuine art possible was iconoclastic both in subject and style. A man as intelligent as Shaw must have known that it was hopeless to bother Irving with Ibsen or his own plays and that the most sensible critical advice to offer would have been to say, "Stick to Shakespeare and melodrama, and leave contemporary drama alone." Had Irving been simply an actor, Shaw would, I daresay, have said just that, but he was not simply an actor; he was also a Victorian monument and, as such, he had to be demolished.

Despite their apparent undiminished glory, Irving's concluding years are sad, and our exasperation at the public figure gives way to sympathy for the dying lion. His audiences are still as enthusiastic as ever, but he is losing the younger generation and he knows it. All his stock of scenery is lost in a fire. The Lyceum goes bankrupt and closes. But the final scene is all that a great actor could wish. He has died in the lobby of a Bradford hotel after a performance of *Becket*:

> Alexander and a few of Irving's close friends so gauged public feeling that they asked the Dean of St. Paul's if they might bury their dead leader in his cathedral. Their request was refused. They waited upon Dr Armytage Robinson, the Dean of Westminster. . . . The Dean had been threatened with blindness and lay in a darkened upper room attended by his sister, in whom the old prejudices against players and playhouses lingered. When she heard the purpose of the petition she protested vehemently against the burial of any more actors in the Poets' Corner. The members of the deputation were still waiting for an answer when Sir Anderson Critchett, who had become the leading oculist in the country, passed through the room in which they sat, on his way to see his patient. Recognizing several of his friends, he asked what they were waiting for. When he heard the purpose of their mission, he promised he would do all he could to help them. He reminded the Dean that, when he had saved his sight, he had asked what return he could make as a token of his gratitude. Now, said Critchett, was the time and opportunity to make that return by granting the request of the gentlemen waiting below. The Dean's sister repeated her protest—"No actors! No actors!"—but in vain. The Dean honored his debt.

This is better even than a fairy tale; this is grand opera.

The New Yorker, 12 July 1952

Sigmund Freud

Today, thanks to Freud, the man-in-the-street knows (to quote by an inaccurate memory from *Punch*) that, when he thinks a thing, the thing he thinks is not the thing he thinks he thinks, but only the thing he thinks he thinks he thinks. Fifty years ago, a girl who sprained her ankle on the eve of a long-looked-forward-to ball, or a man who suffered from a shrewish wife, could be certain of the neighbors' sympathy; today the latter will probably decide that misfortune is their real pleasure. The letter of apology to the hostess whose dinner invitation you have forgotten is much more difficult to write than it used to be. If an Isolde worries all day lest her absent Tristan should be run over by a bus, the dumbest Brangaene could warn her that her love includes a hope that he will never return. As for parents, not only the few who have read up on the Oedipus Complex and Erogenous Zones, but also the newspaper-reading mass, the poor things are today scared out of their wits that they will make some terrible mistake; the Victorian, even the Edwardian, paterfamilias who knew what was right is almost extinct, which is, perhaps, a pity. (However, if the bearded thunder god has turned into a clean-shaven pal, there is still the iron-toothed witch).

It always comes as a shock to me to remember that, when Freud was born, *The Origin of Species* had not yet appeared, and that he was in his fortieth year before he published his first "freudian" papers. Freud's formative years, that is, were a time when the great intellectual battle was between Science and the sort of bourgeois idealist manicheeism of which, in 1875, Mrs Eddy became Popess. The feeling that matter and the body are low or unreal and that the good and the real are spiritual or mental is always likely to become popular in a society where wealth and social prestige go to those who work with their heads; as long as the aristocracy thinks of itself as the warrior class, it is protected from this heresy because, while it may despise manual labor, athletic fitness is a badge of class: further, as long as their work is really manual, the market value of physical strength and manual skill prevents the working-classes from underestimating the body, but with the coming of the machine which can be minded perfectly well by an unskilled child, white-collar manicheeism infects them as well. The great dramatic interest of the second half of the nineteenth century lies in the fact that, at the very time when the scientific advances which were being made in the natural sciences like chemistry and biology seemed to suggest that all reality might ultimately be explicable in terms of quantity and necessity, the development of society was making the notion of any relation of the good and the beautiful to matter peculiarly repugnant. One cannot read either the scientists or the naturalistic novelists of the period without feeling, in the very passion with which they assert that man is *only* an animal, their selection for portrayal of the ugliest "nature" they can find, the same horror as was exhibited by their episcopal opponents; they see themselves as preaching the truth, but none of them thinks that the truth is good news. Freud is no exception; the very man who has done most to free us from a manicheean horror of sex quotes more than once, with an unmistakable shudder of distaste, the Church Father who pointed out that we are born *inter urinas et faeces*. Some wag once summed up the message of psychoanalysis as saying: "We are born mad; we grow sane and unhappy; then we die." There are photographs of Freud in which he almost looks as if he would agree.

In this battle between those who asserted that the egg is only a dream of the hen and those who asserted that the hen is only a dream of the egg, Freud certainly thought of himself as a dyed-in-the-wool egg-fancier. He observes all the egg-fancier tabus; Beatrice, for instance, becomes the Love Object and the four-letter words always appear veiled in the decent obscurity of the Latin language. (The child-like faith of even the most anti-clerical members of the medical profession in the magical properties of that tongue is extremely comic and warrants psychoanalytic investigation.)

But Freud is a clear and beautiful example of a revolutionary thinker—it probably holds good for them all—who is much more revolutionary and in quite another way than he himself realizes.

Had one asked a doctor in the '80s and '90s to forecast the future of psychology, he would almost certainly have replied somewhat as follows:

> It seems probable that we shall soon be able to describe all mental events in terms of physical events in the brain, but even if we cannot, we may safely assume:
>
> 1. Like the human body, the human mind has a constant nature, typical for the species; individual variations are either pathological or insignificant.
>
> 2. The behavior of this mind can be explained in terms of stimulus and response. Similar stimuli will necessarily produce similar responses. Both are quantitatively measurable in terms of intensity and duration.
>
> 3. Mental development is like physical growth, i.e. the mind passes from a younger or earlier phase into an older or later one. This process can be arrested or become morbid, but two phases cannot exist simultaneously any more than an oak can be an acorn at the same time.
>
> 4. The neuroses and psychoses must be typical diagnostic entities, identical in every patient. To discover a cure for one means to discover the procedure which is effective independently of the individual doctor or the individual patient.

One has only to read a few lines of Freud to realize that one is moving in a very different world, one in which there are decisive battles, defeats, victories, decisions, doubts, where things happen that need not have happened and even things which ought not to have happened, a world where novelties exist side by side with ancient monuments, a world of guilt and responsibility, a world, heaven help us, that has to be described with analogical *metaphors.* The Master may sometimes write as if he thought that saying a three-year-old child wishes to commit incest with his mother were the same kind of statement as saying he wishes to go to the bathroom, but we are not deceived. Whatever we may think of that famous trio Ego, Super-Ego and Id, we can see that they are like Prince Tamino, Sarastro, and The Queen of The Night and not like mathematical equations. We may find the account of the Fall in *Totem and Taboo* more or less plausible than the account in Genesis (the Bible version which makes the psychological sin, and therefore the sense of guilt, prior

to the moral crime seems to me the more "freudian"), but we shall not dream
of applying the standards of "scientific" evidence employed in Chemistry or
Biology to either.

In fact, if every one of his theories should turn out to be false, Freud would
still tower up as the genius who perceived that psychological events are not
natural events but historical and that, therefore, psychology as distinct from
neurology, must be based on the pre-suppositions and methodology, not of
the biologist but of the historian. As a child of his age who was consciously
in a polemic with the "idealists" he may officially subscribe to the "realist"
dogma that human nature and animal nature are the same, but the moment
he gets down to work, every thing he says denies it. In his theories of infantile sexuality, repression, etc., he pushes back the beginnings of free-will and
responsibility earlier than even most theologians had previously dared; his
therapeutic technique of making the patient re-live his past and discover the
truth for himself with a minimum of prompting and interference from the
analyst (meanwhile, one might add, doing penance by paying till it hurts),
the importance of Transference to the outcome of the therapy, imply that
every patient is a unique historical person and not a typical case.

Freud is not always aware of what he is doing and some of the difficulties
he gets into arise from his trying to retain biological notions of development
when he is actually thinking historically. For example, he sometimes talks as
if civilization were a morbid growth caused by sexual inhibition; at other
times he attacks conventional morality on the grounds that the conformists
exhaust in repression the energies which should be available for cultural
tasks: similarly, he sometimes speaks of dream symbolism as if it were pure allegory, whereas the actual descriptions he gives of the dreaming mind at work
demonstrate that, in addition to its need to disguise truth, it has an even
greater need to create truth, to make historical sense of its experience by discovering analogies, an activity in which it shows the most extraordinary skill
and humor. In a biological organism, everything was once something else
which it now no longer is, and change is cyclical, soma-germ-soma; a normal
condition is one that regularly re-occurs in the cycle, a morbid one is an exception. But history is the realm of unique and novel events and of monuments—the historical past is present in the present and the norm of health
or pathology cannot be based on regularity.

Freud certainly expected opposition and obloquy from the conventional
moralists and the man-in-the-street for his theories about human sexuality;
in actual fact, the general public took him to their bosoms rather less critically, perhaps, than they should have done, while the real opposition came
and still comes from the behaviorists, the neurologists and all the schools of
psychiatry that regard their subject as a natural science and are therefore outraged by the whole approach of the psychoanalysts, irrespective of any particular theory they may hold.

The opposition can certainly find plenty of ammunition in psychoanalytic literature; for, while it is possible to do important work (though not, I believe, the greatest) in the natural sciences without being a wise and great man, the most routine exercises in a field that involves the personal and historical demand wisdom, and a psychoanalyst who lacks it cannot write a five-minute paper without giving himself away as a vulgar nincompoop.

The same holds for the reader; a man may fail to understand a text-book of physics but he knows he has not understood it and that is the end of the matter; but he may read a psychoanalytical treatise and come out more of a damned fool at the end than he was before he began it. Or more of a crook— every defense lawyer in a seemingly hopeless criminal case knows how to instruct his client in his unloved childhood to embarrass Bench and Jury.

In the long run, however, the welcome given to psychoanalysis by the public is based on a sound intuition that it stands for treating every one as a unique and morally responsible person, not as a keyboard—it speaks of the narcissism of the Ego, but it believes in the existence of that Ego and its capacity to recognize its own limitations—and that in these days is a great deal. The behaviorists are certainly right in one thing; the human mind does have a nature which can be tampered with: with a few drugs and a little regular torture every human mind can be reduced to a condition in which it is no longer a subject for psychology.

Psychoanalysts and their patients may sometimes seem funny little people, but the fact that they exist is evidence that society is still partly human.

The New Republic, 6 October 1952

Foreword to *Various Jangling Keys*, by Edgar Bogardus

> Robins and pens, poets and scribes, remain
> Sweet enemies, often in the same
> Witched head, and yet how many notes contain
> More heart than the poetry of easy fame
> They try to annotate, having cost more pain,
> Having cost more pleasure. We think the scholar tame,
> And yet how often has it been that he,
> Unlike his poet, dealt strongly with the sea.
>   "In Memory of Robert Menner"

It is novel and refreshing to find a poet whose attitude toward critics of poetry is not the conventional contempt— "Bald heads forgetful of their sins"— but one of praise and love, and who openly dedicates his book to Mr John

Crowe Ransom not as the poet but as "the teacher." Such statements encourage me to believe that Mr Bogardus will not take it amiss if I take his poems as an opportunity to consider a question which I think of some concern, namely, how far and in what ways it is possible to "teach" the art of poetry and how, in fact, the traditions of their "mystery" are transmitted from one generation of poets to the next.

The notion of the original iconoclastic genius, springing full grown from the head of Apollo, owing the past nothing but scorn, is a very recent one, and no practicing poet, however revolutionary, can ever have seriously entertained it. In all ancient cultures a young man was not admitted to the rank of poet until he had qualified himself by years of arduous training under the tutelage of his elders, and when later such personal apprenticeship was given up, authority remained as the body of "classical" models which he was required to know intimately and by the standards of which he was to be judged. We are all inclined, particularly if we are paid to give them, to sneer at creative writing courses but, if any of the great poets of the past were to visit one, though no doubt he would laugh with and at us over the follies of our practice, he would regard the principle as only natural and proper. He might also, after forcing us to admit the relative superiority of scientific achievement to artistic during the last hundred years, point out that in scientific research the master-apprentice relationship is still the rule.

In any teaching the first problem is how to eliminate the unteachable, how to distinguish between lack of knowledge or experience and plain lack of capacity. Here I can only give my own opinion for what it may be worth. In my first reading of a batch of poems I look for one thing and one thing only, a few lines which are really lines and not arbitrary choppings. Poetry may be rhymed or unrhymed, metrically strict or free, but what distinguishes it as a medium from prose is that the words organize themselves into lines rather than into sentences. He who can produce such a line, which need not necessarily be very "poetic," has at least *some* poetic gift; he who cannot, however remarkable his writing in other respects, is not and never can become a poet. I do not, in a young writer, demand very many such lines—it takes years of practice to learn how to enjamb with perfect safety—but if he has any, he can be taught to correct those which are defective by appealing to those in which he has been successful. Thus, glancing through Mr Bogardus' poems, I find lines like the concluding couplet of the stanza quoted above or

> I love the whole unfaithful world but you

or

> . . . like any ignorant janitor
> Whose dogma is the dogged way he's dumb . . .

That is enough for me: he can come in.

Any fairly instructed reader who comes on this last line or such a stanza as

> But, mother, that athletic youth
> So rudely runs from key to key,
> From white to black leaps furiously,
> And skips some tough and senseless truth:
> Soft harmonies can hardly be
> Good guards against such ruthless ruth.

will not need Mr Bogardus' dedication to guess in what school he has found guidance and illumination. It may be, and probably is, true that the poetic imagination is an inborn gift, but we can only recognize that someone has it when it is brought out into the open, and this bringing out is very largely the work of others, of reading or personal contact. I have often wondered, for example, how I should have made out if, at the time when I first began writing poetry, I had not come across Walter De la Mare's unique anthology *Come Hither*, or, when I first began to read criticism, the writings of W. P. Ker. Whether I should have been better or worse off with someone else is not, of course, for me to say, but I cannot believe that I should be the same poet.

Ascribe it to prevenient grace, intuition, or sheer luck as you will, one of the surest signs of genuine talent seems to be a capacity to meet the right helper at the right time. There are some unfortunate or self-destructive writers who show as unerring a flair for always choosing what, for them, are the wrong influences as some men show for choosing the wrong girl. I have even, I must confess, come across trainees of the Kenyon School who I felt would have been better off elsewhere—the varieties of imaginative talent are such that it would be a very grave criticism of Mr Ransom and his colleagues if one had not—but reading these poems convinces me that Mr Bogardus is one of the favored ones who knows exactly where to find what he is looking for.

I cannot think of any other mentors who could have made him discover his bent for wit, both verbally and stylistically. If a rival pedagogue dare offer a suggestion, it is this: Mr Bogardus' personal style of wit, e.g.

> But love wants balconies and paint
> Before surveying and cement

> I wish that love were a spring ignored
> And not a well in the world's backyard

> I take you for my lawless wedded life
> To hold and to have
> As wrong as we both shall lie

seems to me closer to Byron than to the Metaphysicals, in the light of which my prescription would be: no Donne or Yeats for a season but a good strong dose of *The Ingoldsby Legends* and Saintsbury's *History of English Prosody*. I have sufficient confidence in Mr Bogardus to entertain no fear that my advice will be followed if it is bad.

Various Jangling Keys, by Edgar Bogardus, 1953

Foreword to *The Desire and Pursuit of the Whole,* by Frederick Rolfe, Baron Corvo

A gift for literary expression can embarrass its owner for it is always revealing his nature to others without his consent or even his knowledge. Banalities and platitudes are effective masks which can be worn by any face and it is impossible to guess the character of the wearer through them; but a genuine style, however "artificial" or "impersonal", however intended to conceal, is the creation of the unique face behind it and its "unlikeness" to the latter is never arbitrary. *The Desire and Pursuit of the Whole* is as striking a proof of this as I know. In writing it, Rolfe certainly expected that his readers would see life as Crabbe sees it, that they would take his side, agree that he was the innocent genius victim of a gang of malicious boobies, "bullocks stamping on the fallen", and share his indignation. Thanks to Rolfe's remarkable talent, however, the reader has the very different and, for him, much more interesting experience of knowing that he is looking at the world through the eyes of a homosexual paranoid: indeed, so brilliantly does the author draw his own portrait that one is more likely to be unjust to him and dismiss all his grievances as imaginary which, in one instance at least, the behaviour of Bonsen (Benson), was not the case.

I would strongly advise anyone who has not read A. J. A. Symons' fascinating biography *The Quest for Corvo* to postpone that pleasure until he has read both of Rolfe's fictionalised autobiographies, *Hadrian the Seventh* and this book. He will then be surprised, I think, when he comes to the historical facts, to discover how much he has already inferred from the literary fictions.

The Desire and Pursuit of the Whole interweaves a nightmare and a daydream. The figures in the nightmare really existed in Venice or England but appear distorted into sinister shapes by Crabbe's rage and suspicion: Zildo never was on land or sea but is as accurate, as "realistic" a revelation as one could find anywhere of what, in all its enormity, every human ego secretly demands of life. One of the triumphs of the book, one which Rolfe certainly did not consciously intend, is that, though Zildo and the "enemies" never meet, the relation between the two worlds is made so clear: a person who surrenders himself so completely to such a day-dream without acknowledging its absurdity is bound to make his daily life in the world a nightmare.

I cannot agree with Mr Symons that the Zildo story is "exquisite" and "romantic"; to me it is quite terrifying. Crabbe begins by telling us, blandly, that for a long time he could not make up his mind whether his Other Half was a person or a position, a statement which is surely as brutal as anything in Rochefoucauld. Granted that Half-Two is a person, what properties must "It" possess? Well, physically, of course, It must be a seventeen-year-old boy because that is Crabbe's physical type; but a boy, unfortunately, is not capable of an absolute and life-long devotion to a middle-aged man with no money, a boy will grow up and become hirsute and coarse-featured and, furthermore, neither Church nor State will permit you to marry one; consequently, Zildo, the boy, is declared Zilda, the girl, by fiat: It throws snowballs overarm but knows when to stop because Half-One is getting bored. It must be a poor orphan because It must owe Its life, livelihood and education to Half-One; but, since It must be worthy of such a union, It must be descended from a Doge. Lastly, It must be, like the Miltonic Eve, a servant but by choice not fate, finding in the service of Its master Its "perfect freedom".

The characteristics of this day-dream which are abnormal and peculiar to Crabbe should not conceal its generic likeness to the reader's; on the contrary, they should help to prevent the latter from thinking of his own as "romantic".

A paranoid goes through life with the assumption: "I am so extraordinary a person that others are bound to treat me as a unique end, never as a means". Accordingly, when others treat him as a means or are just indifferent, he cannot believe this and has to interpret their conduct as malignant; they are treating him as an end, but in a negative way; they are trying to destroy him.

The "normal" person knows that, as a matter of fact, in most of our relations most of the time, we are doing no more than make use of each other, as a rule with mutual consent, as a means to pleasure, intellectual stimulus, etc., but keeps up the convention, both with himself and others, that we love and are loved for "ourselves alone", a fiction which is probably wise for, not only would social life be unbearable without it, but also the possibilities of genuine agape which, rare and delicate as they may be, do exist, would wither without its protective encouragement.

But it is a salutary experience also that, every now and then, we should have it stripped from us and that is what the paranoid does. His inordinate demand that we love him very much and his accusation when we do not that we hate him very much compel us to realise that we very rarely love or hate anybody; on the contrary, we can only stand each other in small doses without getting bored. The paranoid is the epitome of the bore. Crabbe was mistaken in thinking that the British colony in Venice hated him, but he was quite correct in thinking that they would be highly relieved to hear that he was dead.

Any paranoid is a nuisance, but a penniless one is a torment. The average person, if he has enough money in his pockets to be comfortable, will feel an obligation to help an acquaintance in a financial jam such as being unable to pay a hotel bill, but he hopes that will be the end of the matter and he certainly does not expect it to be taken too personally. Personally, however, is just how the paranoid takes it; he will never leave a benefactor alone because, to him, the important thing is not his hotel bill but the interest another has shown in him by paying it; consequently, he will soon create another crisis as a test and continue until the wretched benefactor can bear no more and the inevitable explosion occurs.

Anyone who has had personal experience of a paranoid, will sympathise with the Thiasarkh's final remark to Crabbe when, out of sheer despair, he reveals himself as a Pharisee:

> "Oooh, my dear person, what are you going to do?"
>
> "Leave, when you leave. I suppose you won't be long".
>
> "But—look at the rain. Where will you go?"
>
> "I haven't quite made up my mind".
>
> The Warden emitted a noise like "Oooooeughph", which was a sort of mixture of a snarl and a growl and a screech strangulated in twisted guts.
>
> "Dear me!" said Crabbe, eyeing him fastidiously.
>
> "Of course, you know, I'm not really bound to help you, seeing that you're not a co-religionist", screamed the infuriated self-condemner.
>
> "Comfort yourself, o blessed of God, with that beautiful thought", said Crabbe—and went out.

Rolfe-Crabbe had every right to be proud of his verbal claws. Like most suspicious people, he had a sharp eye; more than most he knew how to describe what he saw. For instance, the "blubber-lipped Professor of Greek with a voice like a strangled Punch" happens to be a friend of mine and I can vouch for the remarkable accuracy, within its unkind limits, of the description. A large vocabulary is essential to the invective style, and Rolfe by study and constant practice became one of the great masters of vituperation; when he uses a rare word or a neologism such as "banausic" or "bestemmiating" it is never out of place, and he is equally at home in ornate abuse.

> Some coarse, raucous, short-legged hockey—or hunting—female hideous in hairy felt—some bulgy kallipyg with swung skirts and cardboard waist and glass-balled hatpins and fat open-work stockings and isosceles shoes—some pink-nosed and round-eyed and frisky, as inane and selfish and snappy-mannered as a lapdog—some leek-shaped latest thing, heaving herself up from long tight lambrequins to her own bursting bosom and bonneted with a hearse-plumed jungle-crowned bath;

and in the plainest of "plain-speaking".

> As for your letter, let me congratulate you (from a literary point of view) on having produced a masterpiece of hypocrisy. Thank you very much,

but I firmly refuse to oblige by going and dying on someone else's doorstep, even with my clothes washed. You don't seem to understand that I take a fierce (but purely academic) interest in you, for I really did not believe that such dreadful people existed outside Ouida's *Friendship* and *In a Winter City*. Erastians one knows, metoikoi one has heard of, but what the devil you are will be my pleasing pastime to determine. And, as perhaps it will suit you (as well as me) if I make the break between us as inviable as possible, kindly note that you are prohibited from mentioning my name or work in the preface of your book. I'm going to choose my company, for future; and I don't choose to appear in connection with a character like yours.

Safely inside a novel, such letters are fun to read—if the series to Caliban are a bit wearisome to us, it is because The Order of Sanctissima Sophia is not the sort of private world that is now in fashion—but in real life it is said that the recipients trembled when they saw an envelope or "a severe postcard" addressed in Rolfe's handwriting.

If there were nothing in *The Desire and Pursuit of the Whole* but Rolfe's nightmare and his daydream, it might be too depressing to read except as a clinical study; luckily there is a third story behind both which is a real love story, the story of Rolfe's love for Venice. Just when we are beginning to think that we cannot take any more clapper-clawing and megalomania, Crabbe suddenly notices where he is and becomes quiet, self-forgetful, truthful and happy.

He slowly paced along cypress-avenues, between the graves of little children with blue or white standards and the graves of adults marked by more sombre memorials. All around him were patricians bringing sheaves of painted candles and gorgeous garlands of orchids and everlastings, or plebeians on their knees grubbing up weeds and tracing pathetic designs with cheap chrysanthemums and farthing night-lights. Here, were a baker's boy and a telegraph messenger, repainting their father's grave-post with a tin of black and a bottle of gold. There, were half a dozen ribald venal dishonest licentious young gondolieri, quiet and alone on their wicked knees round the grave of a comrade.

Rolfe arrived in Venice in the summer of 1908 and never left it again till his death in October, 1913. The only money he earned during those five years was an odd guinea here and there from a magazine; his friends in England were willing to help if he returned but he absolutely refused to budge; he would sponge, he would starve, but he would not leave Venice.

Whatever else about him was distorted or sham, his passion for the city was genuine. Sex had something, no doubt, to do with it. After years of chastity— if Crabbe's vow is autobiographical, as it very well may be—Rolfe let go with a vengeance and was leading a life which he could neither have dated nor afforded to lead in England. But this was not the only nor, I think, the most important attraction. Venice was for him The Great Good Place, a city built by strong and passionate men in the image of their mother, the perfect embodiment of everything he most craved and admired, beauty, tradition, grace and ease.

As we read the extraordinary and magnificent twenty-fifth and twenty-sixth chapters of this book, in which Crabbe, friendless, homeless, penniless, delirious for lack of food, wanders day and night through the streets, we cease to laugh at or pity him and begin to admire. Faced with the choice of going home or dying in the place that he loves, he will choose to die, and behind all his suffering there is a note of exaltation. Like his author, Crabbe is more than a little crazy, more than a bit of a scoundrel, and a most dreadful nuisance, but he is neither a wet-leg nor ignoble.

The Desire and Pursuit of the Whole, by Frederick Rolfe,
Baron Corvo, 1953

The Rake's Progress

"The Rake's Progress," as depicted by Hogarth, is a bourgeois cautionary tale; its twin is the story of The Virtuous Apprentice who is never late for work, saves his pennies and finally marries the master's daughter. Wine, Women and Cards are to be avoided, not because debauchery is wrong in itself but because it lowers the bank balance; Chastity is the child of Economic Abstinence. Hogarth's Rake, that is, is not a demonically passionate man like Don Giovanni but a self-indulgent one who yields to the temptation of the immediate moment. Consequently in the engravings, the décor is more significant than the protagonist. In an opera this is impossible, for music is, par excellence, the expression of subjective activity; a character in opera can never appear the victim of circumstance; however unfortunate, he or she is bound to seem the architect of fate. When we look at a picture of a couple embracing, we know for certain that they are interested in each other, but are told very little about what each is feeling; when we listen to a love duet on the opera stage, it is just the other way round; we are certain that each is in love; but the cause of that love will seem to lie in each as subject not as an object. On the other hand, though a single picture defines the relations between its component figures, a story told in a succession of pictures is a succession of static tableaux in which the present supersedes the past; what is portrayed in one picture is not the cause of what is portrayed in the next but is merely previous to it.

In writing our libretto, therefore, Mr Kallman and I were faced with two problems: how to make Tom Rakewell a singing being, and how to make him a dramatic being with a coherent life story and a sustained involvement with others. Our Tom Rakewell is a man to whom the anticipation of experience is always exciting and its realization in actual fact always disappointing; temperamentally, therefore, he is a manic-depressive, elated by the prospect of the future and then disgusted by the remembrance of the recent past. To define and differentiate the stages of his flight from reality, we have employed the familiar fairy-story device of the three wishes (which are spoken not sung); these, in his case, are, successively, to be rich, to be happy and to make the world a utopia. The real world from which he flies but can never forget is represented by Anne Trulove (soprano) with whom, when the curtain rises, he is singing a love duet in an idyllic garden; the instigator and director of his flight is personified in Nick Shadow (baritone), whom his first wish causes to appear with the news that an unknown uncle has left him a fortune. Rakewell engages Shadow as his servant and, at the latter's suggestion, promises to pay whatever shall seem a just wage at the end of a year and a day. Shadow is, of course, a Mephisto disguised as a Leporello, who brings into Rakewell's consciousness what is already latent there. He leads him to a brothel where he loses his innocence. When Rakewell tires of pleasure and utters his second wish, Shadow suggests that he commit an absolutely gratuitous act, namely, marry Baba the Turk, a bearded lady from the circus. (In Hogarth, he marries an ugly old woman for her money.) When this joke palls and Rakewell utters his third wish, Shadow enters with a fake machine for turning stones into bread. (One Hogarth engraving is concerned with The Philosopher's Stone.) Ruined and hunted by those he has ruined, Rakewell is led by Shadow to a graveyard. The year and a day are up, Shadow reveals himself and forces Rakewell to play a card game with the latter's soul as the stake. Thanks to the Devil's traditional overconfidence and the Divine intervention of Anne, Shadow loses his prey but before disappearing strikes Rakewell insane. The last scene takes place (as in Hogarth) in Bedlam. Rakewell believes himself to be Adonis and Anne, who comes to see him, to be Venus. They sing a duet of forgiveness and he dies.

Harper's Bazaar, February 1953

T. S. Eliot So Far

The Complete Poems and Plays. By T. S. Eliot, Harcourt, Brace. $6.

It is high time that the book-buying public started protesting against a practice of publishers which borders on the dishonest, namely, their habit of labelling a collection of past work by a still living author as *the* collected etc., or "complete." In the case of the volume before us, for instance, the title will be a lie by the fall of this year. Apart from the misrepresentation, such titles encourage the tendency of most readers to forget that no judgment about a contemporary work can be more than tentative. The more important a writer, the more his separate productions are, like the movements of a symphony, subordinate parts of his whole "oeuvre" and cannot be seen in proper perspective until that is complete. *The Waste Land*, for example, read very differently in 1925 when its only successor was *The Hollow Men* than it reads today in the light of *Four Quartets*.

> . . . every sentence is an end and a beginning
> Every poem an epitaph.

The trouble is that, at the time, no one, not even the poet himself, can tell exactly what birth and what death it signifies. The poet, at least, knows this; his critics are apt to be less diffident.

To become a poet of the first rank, great talent is not enough; one must also get born at the right time and in the right place. To become a great revolutionary innovator, for example, a man must come to manhood just as historical circumstances have created a real break in sensibility; those who are born earlier have no stimulus to break with their immediate past, those who are born later find the innovations already made.

To have had a chance of becoming a real explorer in the arts, it would seem that one had to be born between 1870 and 1890; the eighties were particularly favorable, producing, among others, Picasso, Stravinsky, Joyce and Eliot. Those of us who were born later have to put up with the less heroic but, I hope, useful role of colonisers.

Further, so far as English poetry was concerned, it was important *not* to be born in England itself and, of all other places, the United States seems to have been the best. Leaving Eliot's influence aside, we should not have had the poetry of Edward Thomas without Robert Frost, the later poems of Robert Graves without Laura Riding and, probably, not even the later poems of Yeats without Ezra Pound.

The poets in England at the turn of the century lay imprisoned in the poetic conventions, both of sensibility and technique, created by the Romantic Movement, confined to the territory opened up by Wordsworth, Coleridge, Keats and Shelley and colonised by Tennyson, Browning and Arnold. They sensed that they were in bondage, that these conventions no longer corresponded to their real needs, but they were too habituated to be able to see where true liberation lay. Swinburne and the Pre-Raphaelites had tried to escape into an aesthetic universe where the novelty consisted in a total divorce from the contemporary material universe. Three very remarkable poets, Hardy, Hopkins and Doughty, had found other routes, but for themselves alone; their work, fine as it is, is cranky.

American writers, just because they inherit no long indigenous tradition, have always been more curious than their English cousins about the poetry of other traditions than just the English; compare, for example, the interest shown by even so genteel a poet as Longfellow, in the poetry of Europe, with the insularity, tempered only by his classical education, of Tennyson. Further, they could look at even the English tradition with a fresh detachment. The impact of *The Sacred Wood*, for example, was caused not so much by the critical remarks it contained, as by its revelatory quotations. Mr Eliot has told us that the chief influences in forming his style were the late Elizabethan dramatists like Webster and the French Symbolists like Laforgue. Many British poets had sought inspiration in the Elizabethan drama but without success because they could only hear the verse through the ears of the Romantics, just as they could only hear Baudelaire through the ears of Swinburne.

Prufrock came upon English poetry like a bombshell (it is difficult now to realise how great the shock was, to remember that one outraged critic referred to Mr Eliot as "a drunken helot"). Here, in one poem, a satisfactory solution had been found to the three main problems that were baffling poets, the prosodic problem of how to escape from the iambic convention, the organisation problem of how to escape from stanzaic succession, and the problem of diction and imagery, of how to integrate the traditional "poetic" properties with the properties of contemporary industrial civilisation.

What has struck me most on rereading his poems straight through is how little, stylistically, Mr Eliot has changed. (In the plays, of course, there is a change, but it is mostly a technical one, an adaptation of the style to the stage.) We already find, fully developed in *Prufrock* and *Portrait of a Lady*, the imagery, the elderly hero in whom desire has failed, the nostalgic vision, the intimate voice—no other poet so gives a reader the sense that he is alone in the room with it—and even such little tricks as epanorthosis on words like *time*. The change in the later poems is not stylistic but a change brought about by a steady maturing and purification of the poet's vision of life, in particular a conquest of the aesthetic dandy in him.

In most of the poems up to and including *The Waste Land*, we find two figures opposed to each other as hero to churl, the sad elderly sensitive cultural observer—Prufrock, the Lady's Friend, Gerontion, Burbank, Tiresias—and the vulgar active greedy man of this world—Sweeney, Bleistein, the carbuncular house agent, whom the former is at once disgusted by and envious of. What is disagreeable about this hero is his mixture of self-pity and conceit. Sweeney steals his girl, he is very upset, but he comforts himself that he is better educated and wears cleaner linen. One is sometimes tempted to say, even to Tiresias: "Really, why don't you stop moping and go out and play with the other boys."

But the "I" of *Ash-Wednesday* and *Four Quartets*, the "chosen" individuals of the plays, Becket, Harry, Celia, no longer masochistically indulge their pain but accept it as a means of grace and a hope of glory, a signpost pointing to a special vocation: the old Tiresias had to do nothing but shore up fragments against his ruins, the new Tiresias has to become an explorer,

> . . . still and still moving
> Into another intensity

a journey which may end in a martyr's death.

Sweeney, if he appears at all, appears transformed, no longer a monster without feeling, but just an average human being, the Johns and Edwards who carry on, making the best of a bad job,

> Maintain themselves by the same routine,
> Learn to avoid excessive expectation,
> Become tolerant of themselves and others,
> Giving and taking, in the usual actions
> What there is to give and take.

If in *Family Reunion* and *The Cocktail Party*, one hears an occasional discordant snobbish note, I believe that this is not a matter of sensibility but of technique. While concentrating upon the problem of how to write dramatic verse which shall not be "Little Theatre" and arty, Mr Eliot has postponed the problem of dramatic convention, i.e. he has simply taken on unchanged the conventions of English "High" Comedy that have existed from Congreve down to Noel Coward, under which the decor and the main characters are aristocratic. So long as the dramatic subject is one of the various worldly self-affirmations, like love between the sexes, and the moral values implied are social, the convention is perfectly satisfactory; wealth and good-breeding are quite adequate symbols for gifts and virtues. But when the theme becomes one of spiritual election, of the radical gulf between the Christian faith and *all* worldly values, the symbolism breaks down. I am absolutely certain that Mr Eliot did not intend us to think that Harry is called and not John because John is stupid, or that Celia is called and not Lavinia because she is of a higher social class, but that is exactly what the comedy convention he is using is bound to suggest. Now that he has pretty well solved his verse problem, he has time to consider, as I am sure he is, the problem of "setting." That is one reason, surely, why we look forward so eagerly to *The Confidential Clerk*.

The Griffin, [March 1953]

Two Sides to a Thorny Problem

Exploring below Surface of Shakespeare's "Merchant"

Of all dramatists Shakespeare is, perhaps, the most "lifelike." His plays may be in verse and, therefore, anything but "naturalistic," yet no one else conveys so perfectly the double truth that, while each man is a unique individual responsible for the choices he makes and not an impotent victim of circumstance, at the same time we are all members one of another, mutually dependent and mutually responsible. No man is what he is or chooses what he chooses independently of the natures and choices of those with whom he is associated.

That is why our primary social duty is to forgive our neighbor; if he were not responsible, forgiveness would be meaningless—one does not forgive the banana skin on which one slips—and if we were totally innocent, directly or indirectly, forgiveness would be unjust.

"Star" (as distinct from "character" actors) do not willingly play a role which will arouse hostile reactions from the audience, yet the role of Shylock, whom nobody would call a "nice" person, has always attracted them because they sense that Shakespeare has written the part in such a way that, without in any way playing down Shylock's moroseness, avarice and murderous hatred, they can be sure of securing for him the audience's sympathy.

Superficially, *The Merchant of Venice* presents a simple black-and-white contrast of two worlds—the money-grubbing, loveless "Jewish" world of Shylock who hates music (the characteristic Shakespearean symbol for balance and concord):

> Lock up your doors; and when you hear the drum
> And the vile squeaking of the wry-necked fife,
> Clamber not you up to the casements then,
> Nor thrust your head into the public street
> To gaze on Christian fools with varnished faces

and the generous loving world of the "Christians" who delight in it:

> The man that hath no music in himself
> Nor is not moved with concord of sweet sounds,
> Is fit for treason, stratagems, and spoils . . .
> Let no such man be trusted. Mark the music.

A more careful reading, however, reveals that the horrid and the nice are not two separate worlds, but parts of one whole; neither could exist without the other. Take, for instance, the question of usury. In an economy based on agriculture and production for use, and in which supply and demand are more or less constant, wealth is the reward for hard work, and the average man will not get into debt except through an act of God, like a fire or a bad harvest, or through, what for him is the same thing, malice domestic or restraint of princes. To charge interest on a loan in such circumstances is to profit from an innocent man's misfortune, which is immoral; hence the church's condemnation of usury, which went hand in hand with her theory of the just price.

But the economy of Shakespeare's Venice is based on mercantile speculation; money is invested in buying goods here and now in the hope of selling them elsewhere and later at a great profit: luck may make a man suddenly rich and misfortune may beggar him, but it is a misfortune he has deliberately chosen to risk. In such an economy it is only the man with capital resources today who has a chance of making a profit tomorrow; money, in fact, and as the church was to discover, does breed money.

The Venice of the play is a city of *nouveaux riches* and ostentatious luxury. It is a characteristically subtle touch of Shakespeare's to make Bassanio, whose debts involve Antonio with Shylock, not a merchant but the impoverished son of an old family who is living beyond his means in an attempt to keep up with the new and higher living standard of his friends in trade.

Again, the first thing that Jessica learns from her Gentile lover is conspicuous waste, moreover, of wealth she has stolen from her father.

> Your daughter spent in Genoa, as I heard, one night fourscore ducats. . . . One of them showed me a ring that he had of your daughter for a monkey.

The jolly spendthrift is, naturally, an aesthetically more agreeable figure than the sour-faced miser, but it is thanks to the latter's economic abstinence that the former is able to please and, as Dante knew, both end up in the same circle in Hell.

Antonio is a "good" man but he is also a very rich one who does not realize that, without his wealth, he could not practise "the ancient Roman Honor" in which he believes. His hatred of Shylock is really a projection of his distaste for the whole society in which he lives, a distaste which makes him a melancholic. The first line of the play—so often in Shakespeare an important clue—is his:

> In sooth I know not why I am sad.

and in the trial scene he remarks:

> Grieve not that I am fall'n to this for you:
> For herein Fortune shows herself more kind
> Than is her custom. It is still her use
> To let the wretched man outlive his wealth
> To view with hollow eye and wrinkled brow
> An age of poverty.

Shylock should, of course, have forgiven Antonio and canceled the bond, but Antonio should also have realized that he needed to be forgiven. I think that his magnanimity toward Shylock at the end is meant to imply such a realization (typically enough, it is the frivolous Gratiano, who has not suffered, who would insist on punishment) and his demand that Shylock become a Christian probably did not seem such a cynical insult to an Elizabethan audience, who believed in the sacramental efficiency of the mere baptismal act, as it does to the average man today.

In a Shakespeare play the subplot usually has important implications for the main action and the wooing of Portia in *The Merchant of Venice* is no exception. The peace and concord which should inspire the Just City, the celestial harmony of which music is the terrestrial image, is the product of the right kind of love, and in the choice between the three caskets we are told what that kind is.

Morocco chooses gold to "gain what many men desire," in other words, power for the self over others, the desire which animates the Venice of this world, its Gentiles no less than its Jews. Arragon chooses silver to "get as much as he deserves," that is, he thinks of love as something which is given not to a person but to some quality he or she possesses, beauty or wit or niceness or what have you. Both of them fail because the true lover neither seeks self-aggrandizement nor calculates whether its object is worth loving, but recklessly—how superficially similar to and how profoundly different from the recklessness of the speculative capitalist—"gives and hazards all he hath."

If self-aggrandizement were all, then Shylock would be right and Antonio wrong; if merit were the criterion, who can say that Antonio does not merit Shylock's hatred and vice versa. But it is not so. Without self-forgetfulness and mutual forgiveness, all the music in the world is not an image of universal harmony but a frivolous pastime of the fortunate.

One can imagine, if one likes, the management of The Globe Theatre putting Shakespeare onto the subject of *The Merchant of Venice* in the expectation of getting another crude anti-Semitic farce like *The Jew of Malta*. But that is not what they got.

The New York Times, 1 March 1953

Cav & Pag

While we all know that every moment of life is a living moment, it is impossible for us not to feel that some moments are more lively than others, that certain experiences are clues to the meaning and essential structure of the whole flux of experience in a way that others are not. This selection is, in part, imposed by experience itself—certain events overwhelm us with their importance without our knowing why—and in part the result of a predisposition on our side, by personal temperament and by social tradition, to be open to some kinds of events and closed to others. Dante's encounter with Beatrice, for example, was *given* him, but he would probably not have received or interpreted the revelation exactly the way that he did if the love poetry of Provence had never been written. On the other hand, many people before Wordsworth must have experienced feelings about Nature similar to his, but they had dismissed them as not very relevant.

Every artist holds, usually in common with his contemporaries, certain presuppositions about the real *Nature*, concealed behind or within the stream of phenomena, to which it is his artistic duty to be true, and it is these which condition the kind of art he produces as distinct from its quality.

Suppose that a dramatist believes that the most interesting and significant characteristic of man is his power to choose between right and wrong, his responsibility for his actions; then, out of the infinite number of characters and situations that life offers him, he will select situations in which the temptation to choose wrong is at its greatest and the actual consequences incurred by the choice are most serious, and he will select characters who are really free to choose, who are least in the position to blame their choice afterwards on circumstances or others.

At most periods in history he could find both of these most easily among the lives of the rich and powerful, and least among the lives of the poor. A king can commit a murder without fear of punishment by human law; a poor man cannot, so that, if he commits one, we feel he must be mad and therefore not responsible, and if he refrains we feel that the law, not he, is largely responsible. A king who steals a country is more interesting dramatically than a starving peasant who steals a loaf, firstly because the country is so much bigger, and secondly because the king is not driven, like the peasant, by an impersonal natural need outside his control, but by a personal ambition which he could restrain.

For many centuries the dramatic role of the poor was to provide comic relief, to be shown, that is, in situations and with emotions similar to those of their betters but with this difference that, in their case, the outcome was not tragic suffering. Needless to say, no dramatist ever believed that in real life the poor did not suffer but, if the dramatic function of suffering is to indicate moral guilt, then the relatively innocent cannot be shown on the stage as suffering. The comic similarity of their passions is a criticism of the great, a reminder that the king, too, is but a man, and the difference in destiny a reminder that the poor who, within their narrower captivity, commit the same crimes, are, by comparison, innocent.

Such a view might be termed the traditional view of Western culture against which naturalism was one form of revolt. As a literary movement, nineteenth century naturalism was a corollary of nineteenth century science, in particular of its biology. The evidences of Evolution, the discovery of some of the laws of genetics, for example, had shown that man was much more deeply embedded in the necessities of the natural order than he had imagined, and many began to believe that it was only a matter of time before the whole of man's existence, including his historical personality, would be found to be phenomena explicable in terms of the laws of science.

If the most significant characteristic of man is the complex of biological needs he shares with all members of his species, then the best lives for the writer to observe are those in which the role of natural necessity is clearest, namely, the lives of the very poor.

The difficulty for the naturalistic writer is that he cannot hold consistently to his principles without ceasing to be an artist and becoming a statistician, for an artist is by definition interested in uniqueness. There can no more be an art about the common man than there can be a medicine about the uncommon man. To think of another as common is to be indifferent to his personal fate; to the degree that one loves or hates another, one is conscious of his or her uniqueness. All the characters in literature with universal appeal, those that seem to reveal every man to himself, are in character and situation very uncommon indeed. A writer who is committed to a naturalist doctrine is driven by his need as an artist to be interesting to find a substitute for the tragic situation in the pathetic, situations of fantastic undeserved misfortune, and a substitute for the morally responsible hero in the pathological case.

The role of impersonal necessity, the necessities of nature or the necessities of the social order in its totality, upon the human person can be presented in fiction, in epic poetry and, better still, in the movies, because these media can verbally describe or visually picture that nature and that order; but in drama, where they are forced to remain off-stage—there can be no dramatic equivalent to Hardy's description of Egdon Heath in *The Return of the Native*—this is very difficult. And in opera it is impossible, firstly, because music is in its essence dynamic, an expression of will and self-affirmation and, secondly, because opera, like ballet, is a virtuoso art; whatever his role, an actor who sings is more an uncommon man, more a master of his fate, even as a self-destroyer, than an actor who speaks. Passivity or collapse of the will cannot be expressed in song; if, for example, a tenor really sings the word *Piango* (*I'm crying*), he does not cry, a fact of which some tenors, alas, are only too aware. It is significant as a warning sign that the concluding line of *Cavalleria Rusticana*, "Hanno ammazzato compare Turiddu" ("They've killed our friend Turiddu"), and the concluding line of *Pagliacci*, "La commedia è finita" ("The comedy is over"), are spoken, not sung.

In practice, the theory of *verismo*, as applied to opera, meant substituting, in place of the heroic aristocratic setting of the traditional *opera seria*, various exotic settings, social and geographic. Instead of Gods and princes, it gave us courtesans (*La Traviata, Manon*), gypsies and bull-fighters (*Carmen*), a diva (*Tosca*), bohemian artists (*La Bohème*), the Far East (*Madama Butterfly*), etc., social types and situations every bit as unfamiliar to the average operagoer as those of Olympus or Versailles.

Giovanni Verga was no doctrinaire naturalist. He wrote about the Sicilian peasants because he had grown up among them, knew them intimately, loved them and therefore could see them as unique beings. The original short story *Cavalleria Rusticana* which appeared in *Vita dei Campi* (1880) differs in several important respects from the dramatized version which Verga wrote four years later, and upon which the libretto is based. In the short story the hero Turiddu is the relatively innocent victim of his poverty and his good looks. Santuzza is not the abused defenseless creature we know from the opera but a rich man's daughter who knows very well how to look after herself. Turiddu serenades her but he has no chance of marrying her since he has no money and though she likes him, she does not lose her head. Her betrayal to Alfio of Turiddu's affair with Lola is therefore much more malicious and unsympathetic than it is in the opera. Finally, the reason that Turiddu gives Alfio for insisting upon a fight to the death is not Santuzza's future—he has completely forgotten her—but the future of his penniless old mother.

Santuzza's seduction and pregnancy, Turiddu's brutal rejection of her, her curse upon him, his final remorse were all added by Verga when he had to build up Santuzza into a big and sympathetic role for Duse. As a subject for a short libretto, it is excellent. The situation is strong, self-contained and immediately clear; it provides roles for a convenient number and range of voices; and the emotions involved are both singable emotions and easy to contrast musically. The psychology is straightforward enough for song but not silly: how right it is, for instance, that Turiddu should reproach Santuzza for having let him seduce her—"pentirsi è vano dopo l'offesa" ("Repentance after the offense is futile"). Thanks to the swiftness with which music can express a change in feeling, even Turiddu's sudden switch of attitude from contempt to remorse becomes much more plausible in the opera than it seems in the spoken drama. Targioni-Tozzetti and Menasci quite rightly stuck pretty closely to Verga's story, their chief addition being the lines in which Turiddu begs Lucia to accept Santuzza as a daughter. But, having at their disposal as librettist what a dramatist no longer has, a chorus, they took full advantage of it. The choral episodes, the chorus of Spring, the mule-driving song, the Easter hymn, the drinking song take up more than a quarter of the score. It might have been expected that, particularly in so short a work, to keep postponing and interrupting the action so much would be fatal; but, in fact, if one asks what was the chief contribution of the librettists towards giving the work the peculiar impact and popularity it has, I think one must say it was precisely these episodes. Thanks to them, the action of the protagonists, their personal tragedy, is seen against an immense background, the recurrent death and rebirth of nature, the liturgical celebration of the once-and-for-all death and resurrection of the redeemer of man, the age-old social rites of the poor, so that their local history takes on a rhythmical significance; Turiddu's death is, as it were, a ritual sacrifice in atonement for the sins of the whole community. One of the most moving moments in the opera, for example,— and nothing could be less *verismo*—occurs when Santuzza, the excommunicated girl who believes that she is damned, is translated out of her situation and starts singing out over the chorus, like Deborah the Prophetess, "Innegiamo il Signor non è morto!" ("Let us sing! Christ is not dead!").

If the interplay of rite and personal action which is the secret of *Cavalleria Rusticana* is not a typical concern of the *verismo* school, the libretto interest of *Pagliacci* is even less naturalistic, for the subject is the psychological conundrum—"Who is the real me? Who is the real you?" This is presented through three contradictions. Firstly, the contradiction between the artist who creates his work out of real joys and sufferings and his audience whom it amuses, who enjoy through it imaginary joys and sufferings which are probably quite different from those of its creator. Secondly, the contradiction between the actors who do not feel the emotions they are portraying and the audience who do, at least, imaginatively. And lastly the contradiction between the actors as professionals who have to portray imaginary feelings and the actors as men and women who have real feelings of their own. We are all actors; we frequently have with others to hide our real feelings and, alone with ourselves, we are constantly the victims of self-deception. We can never be certain that we know what is going on in the hearts of others, though we usually overestimate our knowledge—both the shock of discovering an infidelity and the tortures of jealousy are due to this. On the other hand, we are too certain that nobody else sees the real us.

In the *Prologue* Tonio, speaking on behalf of Leoncavallo and then of the cast, reminds the audience that the artist and the actor are men. When we reach the play within the play all the contradictions are going simultaneously. Nedda is half actress, half woman, for she is expressing her real feelings in an imaginary situation; she is in love but not with Beppe who is playing Harlequin. Beppe is pure actor; as a man he is not in love with anybody. Tonio and Canio are themselves, for their real feelings and the situation correspond, to the greater amusement of the audience for it makes them *act* so convincingly. Finally there is Nedda's lover Silvio, the member of the audience who has got into the act, though as yet invisibly. When Nedda as Columbine recites to Harlequin the line written for her "A stanotte e per sempre sarò tua!" ("Till tonight, then! And forever I'll be yours!"), Canio as Pagliaccio is tortured because he has heard her use as herself these identical words to the lover he has not seen. One has only to imagine what the opera would be like if, with the same situation between the characters, the *Commedia* were omitted, to see how much the interest of the opera depends on the question of Illusion and Reality, a problem which is supposed only to concern *idealists*.

About the music of these two operas, I can, of course, only speak as a layman. The first thing that strikes me on hearing them is the extraordinary strength and vitality of the Italian operatic tradition. Since 1800 Italian opera had already produced four fertile geniuses, Bellini, Rossini, Donizetti and Verdi, yet there was still enough left to allow, not only the lesser but still formidable figure of Puccini, but also the talents of Ponchielli, Giordano, Mascagni and Leoncavallo to create original and successful works. Today, indeed—it may have seemed different in the nineties—we are more conscious in the works of these later composers of the continuity of the tradition than of any revolutionary novelty. We do not emerge from the house, after hearing *Cavalleria* or *Pagliacci* for the first time, saying to ourselves, "What a strange new kind of opera! How shall I classify it? I've got it. *Verismo*.": No, before the first ten bars are over, we are thinking; "Ah, another Italian opera. How jolly!"

Comparing one with the other (a rather silly but inevitable habit), Leoncavallo strikes me as much more technically adroit. One of the strange things about Mascagni is the almost old-fashioned simplicity of his musical means; he writes as if he were scarcely aware of even the middle Verdi. There are dull passages in *Cavalleria Rusticana*; the music of the mule-driving song and the drinking song seem to me pretty *imaginary*. Yet, in the dramatic passages, the very primitive awkwardness of the music seems to *go with* the characters and give them a conviction which Leoncavallo fails to give to his down-at-heel actors. For instance, when I listen to Turiddu rejecting Santuzza in the duet, *No, no! Turiddu, rimani (No, no! Turiddu! Remain)*, I can believe that I am listening to a village Don Giovanni, but when I listen to Silvio making love to Nedda in the duet, *Decidi, il mio destin (Tell me my fate, I pray)*, I know that I am listening to a baritone. As a listener, then, I prefer Mascagni; if I were a singer, I dare say my preference would be reversed.

In making their way round the world, *Cav & Pag* have had two great advantages; they are relatively cheap to produce and the vocal writing is effective but does not make excessive demands so that they are enjoyable even when performed by provincial touring companies, whereas works like *La Gioconda* or *Fedora* are intolerable without great stars. Take, for example, the famous aria *Vesti la giubba*: if the singer is in good voice, he has a fine opportunity to put it through its paces; if his voice is going, he can always throw away the notes and just bellow, a procedure which some audiences seem to prefer.

The idea of *verismo* may have meant a lot to Mascagni and Leoncavallo; I don't know. All the various artistic battle-cries, Classicism, Romanticism, Naturalism, Surrealism, The-language-really-used-by-men, The-music-of-the-future, etc., are of interest to art-historians because of the practical help which, however absurd they may seem as theories, they have been to artists in discovering how to create the kind of works which were proper to their powers. As listeners, readers and spectators, we should take them all with a strong dose of salt, remembering that a work of art is not *about* this or that kind of life; it *has* life, drawn, certainly, from human experience but transmuted, as a tree transmutes water and sunlight into treehood, into its own unique being. Every encounter with a work of art is a personal encounter; what it *says* is not information but a revelation of itself which is simultaneously a revelation of ourselves. We may dislike any particular work we encounter or prefer another to it but, to the degree that our dislike or our preference are genuine, we admit its genuineness as a work of art. The only real negative judgment—it may be we, not the work, that are at fault—is indifference. As Rossini put it: "All kinds of music are good except the boring kind."

Libretto booklet accompanying a recording of *Cavalleria Rusticana* and *I Pagliacci*, RCA Victor Records, 1953

Through the Collar-Bone of a Hare

My Host the World. By George Santayana.
Charles Scribner's Sons. $3.

The Middle Span ended in 1912 with Santayana shaking the dust of Harvard from his feet to engage thenceforth in "a voluntary study, a satirical survey, a free reconsideration" as "a spirit, the spirit in a stray individual." *My Host the World* leaves off in 1942 with its author come finally to rest in Rome. In the meantime, he has visited the Near East, he has resided in both Oxford and Cambridge, he has found temporary lodgments in Paris, Madrid, and Cortina, and, of course, he has written a number of books. It would be unfair to expect the last third of a philosopher's memoirs to be as fascinating as the first two. Elderly men have been known to be transformed in character by an illness, or to undergo a religious conversion, or suddenly to commit some appalling folly, but they are the exceptions. Normally, what is interesting about a grown-up writer is not his life but his books, and the most significant fact about Santayana during the years covered here is that in them he wrote his best work, *The Last Puritan.*

Nevertheless, *My Host the World* is less interesting than it need have been. A stranger to our planet, though he would find the two world wars mentioned by name, could never guess that the Russian Revolution, Mussolini, Hitler, and the Spanish civil war had taken place or that the private lives of human beings during the last fifty years had been in any way different from what they were in, say, the nineties.

It is not that one expects or even wants long political disquisitions upon a scene with which we are all too familiar and about which we have read more than enough, and, in any case, if we want to know Santayana's political theory, we can read *Dominations and Powers*. Nor is one really curious to know upon which side, if any, his immediate sympathies, intellectual or animal, lay.

> Neither tribal nor commercial morality inspired me with particular horror. I knew that the first was brutal and the second vulgar; but they both were intelligible phases in human civilization, just as Catholicism was; and it was an accident of temperament or circumstances how far my sympathies were enlisted on one or the other side.

Such a detachment could have told us much. What, for instance, would be more fascinating and illuminating than a history of these years as seen through the eyes of a precocious child, a maître d'hôtel, or a high-class courtesan? But that a man who was in an especially fortunate position to hear and see what was happening in Europe, not in chancelleries but to the daily lives of old ladies, tradesmen, doctors and lawyers, even philosophers, should not have found a single anecdote of such nature worth recording in his memoirs is, surely, rather strange, particularly when one cannot say that such abstention is due to an overwhelming wealth of other material.

Santayana was not a "visual type" or one who responded immediately and originally to the unfamiliar. He needed time to react; consequently, he had no natural gift for travel writing. The whole chapter on the "origin" countries—Egypt, Palestine, and Greece—might well have been omitted, for its only real contribution is the self-revealing comment:

> Of all periods in history the Hellenistic, between Alexander and Caesar, corresponds best to my feeling. . . . With Alexander a great part of the East, in fact, and the whole world in prospect, were introduced into the sphere of the West, into the narrow military life of the ancient city: yet the gods of the city were not abandoned; but exalted into gods of the open rational philosophic mind, they were retained to preside over a universal empire.

Again, he fails to make us see the architecture of Venice and Rome, perhaps because he likes them too whole-heartedly, for he is at his best when his feelings are mixed and admiration is crossed with malice, as in his description of King's College Chapel:

> Here concentration is perfect, the whole court drawn up in order, waiting; only the monarch is late. Meantime the arrangements continue to suggest his presence, and we may study them the more freely while we postpone our acts of homage.

For this reason, by far the most interesting chapter is the one on Earl Stanley Russell, that wonderful monster who so beguiled us when we first met him in the earlier volumes, almost as perfect a gift to a writer of memoirs as Sir George Sitwell. The reader has no doubt that Santayana was devoted to him, but his account of the Earl's love life is uproarious. Few novelists would dare invent a character who, when turned down by a lady to whom he had proposed while still married to another and having promised to marry a third when free, could write:

> It was very painful . . . and yet the relief was immense. . . . Veronica saved the situation by cutting the knot—what I regret is that fear and pique were the cause of the step. I wish I could attribute it to unselfish consideration of Martha's interests.

The friendship between Santayana and Russell had begun in youth. On Santayana's side, at least, it was genuine, and their final estrangement—not through a quarrel but through a withering of Russell's interest to the point where he kept calling Santayana Sargeaunt, the name of a Latin master at Westminster "who no doubt had been a friend of Russell's at school or in Oxford. . . . They had nothing now in common save that old sense of familiarity"—is sad.

With most of the other characters mentioned, Santayana became acquainted only later in life, and we are more conscious of his malice than of his admiration. The former is entertaining enough so long as it is directed at little foibles like Robert Bridges' detestation of hot water:

> His hands . . . were not dirty: but they hadn't the nursery-maid's pink cleanliness produced by soap and hot water. The nails were gray and thick, like talons. Admirable, no doubt, for certain purposes; but in ages when hot water is available for the toilet, delving is no longer done with the claws.

But his inability to praise anyone wholeheartedly without some derogatory comment, deserved though it often may be, leaves an unpleasant taste in the mouth. If one has claimed for oneself a praiseworthy broadmindedness by saying, "I had always been on pleasant terms with the Babe, liked him, and didn't despise him for not being intellectual or for letting Howard adopt and support him," one cannot add, two sentences later, "The Babe was certainly a minor personage and feeble." One cannot call Lytton Strachey obscene, cite as proof his leaving a pornographic book in Lady Ottoline's drawing room, and then continue:

> Naturally I read on in it, for I like obscenity well enough in its place, which is behind the scenes, or bursting out on occasion in a comic, rollicking, enormously hearty mood as in Aristophanes . . . but he might have put it in his pocket, and not left it lying in the drawing room.

Hoity-toity, Professor.

The continual reiteration of his intellectual independence, of his lack of any desire to have disciples, of his resistance to "human contagion, except provisionally, on the surface, and in matters indifferent to me" becomes suspicious. As in the case of Henry Adams, whom in many ways he resembles, one begins to wonder if all these protests are not a cover-up for disappointed ambition, for a feeling that his real superiority has not been properly recognized by his equals. King's College was disappointing ("the birds were not worthy of their cage"); Corpus would never do because of two faculty members, Warren and Schiller, "individuals that a novelist might like to study, interesting cases; but to be sandwiched between them as if intellectually I were such another tramp (as externally indeed I was) would have been a perpetual mortification;" after a lecture in the Natural History Museum "several dusky youths brought me books to be autographed. Did they feel that I was one of them at heart? We might have been in Singapore"; the atmosphere of the Riviera was disagreeable—too many Americans.

> I like to be a stranger myself, it was my destiny; but I wish to be the only stranger. For this reason I have been happiest among people of all nationalities who were not of my own age, class, or family circle; for then I was a single exceptional personage in their world, and they a complete harmonious milieu for me to drop into and live with for a season.

This publican confession is engaging and the conscience of many of us must second it; what repels is the pharisaic excuse "It was my destiny," though it has comic possibilities. Two Free Spirits who have arrived separately but simultaneously in an Italian village are sitting at neighboring tables in the only café, glaring at each other. Presently the wine takes effect.

> 1ST F.S.: What the devil are you doing here?
> 2ND F.S.: Pardon me, Prof. I was just about to ask you the same question.
> 1ST F.S.: How dare you! This milieu is my destiny this season. I, sir, am The Wanderer (*hands his card*).
> 2ND F.S.: Wanderer schwanderer. That's me (*hands his card*).
> 1ST F.S.: This is an outrage. I must ask you to retire immediately to the Oxford Common Room, where you belong.
> 2ND F.S.: Look who's talking. Go home yourself, Princeton.

Similarly, none of us has a right to frown on Santayana for being episodic in his affections for persons and places, but one has a right to object to the platonic window dressing:

> I saw only the gifts and virtues of which, perhaps for the first time, they gave me a clear idea. They become to that extent my local shrines or the saints for that day in my calendar; but never did the places or the per-

sons turn into idols for my irrational worship. . . . I gladly recognize the good and the beautiful in unexpected quarters; and I am not in the least daunted in my cult of those divine essences when I find that they have disappeared from a place or a person that had once seemed to possess them.

The natural human, or at least masculine, tendency, both in love and in friendship, is to be attracted by qualities rather than persons. We like people not for what they are in themselves but because they are beautiful or rich or amusing, so if they lose their looks or their money or their wit, we lose our interest. We could probably never learn to correct this tendency and love persons for themselves if life did not impose on us relationships with parents, brothers and sisters, wives, children, colleagues at work, and so on, from which, whatever our emotions, we cannot escape.

Plato, if I understand him rightly, took our romantic interest in qualities as his starting point and sought to show, by analysis, that on the temporal level it was self-defeating; if qualities, not persons, are what we want, then the proper place to look for them is in Heaven, among the Universals. Moreover, he was concerned with the education of the political élite, whose duties in this world demanded an otherworldly detachment from personal and family ties; the governed were to be content with the unromantic pattern of family and social relations prescribed for them. If one substitutes materialist presuppositions for the idealist presuppositions of Plato, then I cannot see that the cult of divine essences becomes anything more than a genteel description of feelings that are natural and common enough but not particularly laudable: Gather ye divine essences while ye may. . . . Ah me, that delicious divine essence I met in Shanghai in 1906. . . . This divine essence isn't fun any more. I guess I better beat it.

"To possess [things or persons] physically or legally," writes Santayana, "is a burden and a snare." Quite so, but it is equally true that it is only through such possessions that most men can learn loyalty and responsibility. The danger is equally an opportunity, and to refuse to risk the one is to miss the other. Santayana's besetting sin, both in his life and in his thinking, seems to be a refusal to take risks, an abnormal horror of being "had." Hence his theory of religion as "valid poetry." Having recognized that nearly all theological statements are metaphorical, not literal, he would regard them as interchangeable. They are interchangeable—in poetry—because the world of poetry is a mirror world outside which we stand as spectators. The myth of the Apple of Discord is as valid in Homer as the myth of Adam and Eve is in Milton. Both are possible worlds. But I cannot be a spectator to my own life, and, as presuppositions concerning the cause of evil as I experience it in actual existence, they cannot be equally valid, for they impose on me completely different conclusions as to how I am to behave. To vary an analogy of Kierkegaard's, religious dogmas are to the good life as the laws of grammar are to a language. A master does not need to think about them and may sometimes shock the orthodox by his daring, but the beginner must bear them in mind. An ungrammatical, misspelled letter may have inspired life in it and a formally faultless editorial be quite dead, but the grammatical facts are not affected thereby.

Santayana tries to warn us off beliefs by pointing to the spectre of fanaticism, as if the belief that you had seen the light and were convinced that those who had not yet seen it were in darkness was in itself "Subjective Egoism." But the reason I may not torture my neighbor into believing anything, even if it is true, is that it will be I, not the truth, that is doing the torturing, and therefore, if he submits, it will be to *my* truth, not *the* truth. The fanatic is the one who secretly believes that the truth or falsehood of a belief is affected by the number of people who believe it; his is the skepticism of the minority. The fanatics of our age would never have succeeded as they have but for the skepticism of the majority, which suspects that one gospel is as good as another, a characteristic well understood by the fanatic, who knows that he is not secure unless he can keep his people in total ignorance of all gospels but his.

"Skepticism is the chastity of the intellect" is one of Santayana's most admirable epigrams. But chastity is meaningless except in relation to passion, and his own brand seems to me little more than intellectual old-maidishness fittingly expressed in that genteel—and soporific—style for which he is famous. No wonder he was averse to the novels of Stendhal and to my favorite landscape, the North of England. You know, I don't think I really like him.

The New Yorker, 2 May 1953

Transplanted Englishman Views U.S.

The other day, for the first time since I was a boy, I re-read *Huckleberry Finn*, and ever since I have been trying to imagine how it would read to a fairly intelligent Englishman of forty-six with as little knowledge of the United States as I had at sixteen.

To begin with, he will not know which surprises him most, the violence of the experiences Huck undergoes or the stoic matter-of-factness with which he accepts them. That a fourteen-year-old should have seen so much of the seamy side of life, had so revolting a father, been a key-witness in a murder case, watched a massacre of his friends, etc., without being either corrupted or frightened out of his wits, will seem to him incredible. Secondly, he will find the natural background, though beautiful, too big, too uncosy, very scary; wild nature, for him, is fun to take a peep at provided that you can return in a few hours to the home fireside, gardens and well-kept woods. Thirdly, and more important, the description of Huck's moral decision to help Jim escape will puzzle him.

The idea of a boy who has been taught the difference between right and wrong overcoming temptation and choosing the right is familiar enough; the notion of a boy who has been brought up, say, by thieves, making the discovery for himself that stealing is wrong is also possible. Indeed, when I first read the book, that is how I took Huck's decision—brought up in a slave-owning state, he suddenly realized the truth, namely that slavery is wicked.

Consequently, I took the wonderful passage in which he wrestles with his "conscience" as simple abolitionist satire put into his mouth by Mark Twain. What we are really shown, however, and this is what it will be so hard for my adult Englishman to understand, is a pure moral improvisation: nothing in Huck's past experience can tell him what he should do, and he cannot draw from his choice any general conclusions as to how he or others ought to behave in future situations; morally, he must always be an amateur. In terms of Ethics, there is no relation whatsoever between Right and Duty.

Whatever Clemens' views on slavery may have been, from Mark Twain one can only draw two conclusions; either a relativist one, that every form of society, slave-owning or free or blood-feuding, is a way of life which is agreeable to its members and which, therefore, an outsider has no right to judge, or an anarchist one, that all public social values are false and useless to the individual in discovering what is true which he can only discover by himself. Lastly, my Englishman will be surprised, since he has always understood that Americans are cheerful and optimistic, at finding the book so sad.

All human affections, it seems to say, are the creatures of some occasion and perish with it; the strongest tie in time becomes a burden; love and freedom are incompatible. He might think, by comparison, of an English novel with a boy hero, *Oliver Twist*. Like Huck, Oliver is a social waif, runs away, gets involved with crooks, is befriended by strangers and unexpectedly comes into money, yet how different their two histories are.

Oliver's small fortune is his by legal right of inheritance, Huck's by sheer luck—he happens to be the first to discover the robbers' cache and its rightful owners cannot be traced. The widow Douglas wants to do for Huck at the very beginning what Mr Brownlow does for Oliver at the very end, give him a loving home and a stable place in society but, while for Oliver this is the uttermost fulfillment of his dreams, for Huck it is only a disagreeable restraint; even the company of his papa, unloving and awful as he is, is preferable for, with him, at least, he can keep all hours, smoke, go barefoot and not be forced to study. So does the Artful Dodger enjoy the company of Fagin but, in Dickens, there hangs over such freedom the shadow of the gallows, and, for all his charm and courage, the Artful Dodger is corrupt.

When we close *Oliver Twist*, we know that all the friends he has made during his adventures will remain his friends for life, but when we finish *Huckle-berry Finn*, we feel that even Jim, with whom he has enjoyed a friendship more intense than any of Oliver's, is going to be left behind the moment they get back to Missouri. The conclusions of the two novels draw a sharp contrast between the English and the American day-dream:

> Mr Brownlow went on from day to day, filling the mind of his adopted child with stores of knowledge, and becoming attached to him more and more, as his nature developed itself, and showed the thriving seeds of all he wished him to become.

> I reckon I got to light out for the Territory ahead of the rest, because Aunt Sally she's going to adopt me and sivilize me, and I can't stand it. I been there before.

A New World! World, because it was vast and virtually unoccupied; new, because nothing had been done to it, nothing had been taken out of it, no one had consecrated it and the Nature which confronted the Seventeenth Century European minds of the first settlers was of a sort which had not existed since prehistoric times: neither their past experience nor their inherited associations could teach them what to do or how to feel.

The primary freedom conferred by America has little to do with democracy; it is the freedom to make experiments. Indeed the first two experiments were anything but democratic; an experiment in a theocracy in the North, an experiment in an archaic form of society, one based on slavery, in the South. Yet the slave-owners who signed the Declaration of Independence and helped draw up the Constitution were not hypocrites.

Democracy was to come later as the only political form for what America had been from the beginning, a pluralist nation, religiously, socially and, later, ethnically. No one had had the space before to attempt a pluralist experiment. The European situation might be described as follows: an old, a middle-aged and a young man are sharing a single room. The first hates music, the second loves classical records, the third has a passion for jazz. There are no other rooms because there is no space on which to build them.

What is to happen? The oldest may, by the authority of his age, insist upon complete silence—that is Conservatism; the youngest may knock the other two down and turn on the radio—that is Revolution; or, on the advice of the middle-aged one, the three may work out a compromise, allotting so many hours a day to the tastes of each—that is Democracy.

Transfer the room to America. At the moment the three are still sharing it, either because other rooms have not yet been built or because it is the most comfortable room in the house.

What will happen? Probably, I think, the two who share a common preference for sound to silence will effect a compromise over their differing musical tastes, and then say to the old man: "If you don't like music, why don't you move to another room or build one?"

A pluralist nation and a nation of amateurs, with a deep-seated distrust for professional authority, for the man who claims that he knows the law, in theology, politics, economics, technique or what-have-you. By a professional, I mean a member of a professional body; not necessarily bookish—he may be a skilled craftsman—and not necessarily unoriginal, but he will be hesitant about any discovery or innovation he makes until he has secured the approval of his colleagues. By an amateur, I mean a solitary individual whose knowledge is, in the main, the result of his personal experience; he is not necessarily without book-learning, but his reading list has not been prescribed by others but by chance and personal choice.

When conditions are really new so that the collective experience of the past is little guide, the amateur has as good, indeed, since his eyes are fresh, often a better chance of solving a problem than the professional; further, even if the amateur should be wrong, in so large and wealthy a country, his mistake is a local error and will not seriously damage the whole of society. That the people have a right to make their own mistakes is a fine maxim and the single most admirable trait in the American character is the courage and lack of fuss with which it picks itself up after a failure and starts all over again; but the maxim and, maybe, the character too, require a very large and wealthy space. Perhaps the time has already come when, even in the States, professional caution has become a virtue. Life will be much less fun, but some kinds of fun are getting too risky.

There has never been a time when it was so essential to the future of mankind that America and Europe should co-operate. The greatest obstacles to co-operation are not conscious differences of doctrine or opinion but feelings and attitudes which have become so much second nature to each party that they imagine they are universal and have never tried to formulate them. As a person who was born and bred in England, who is an American citizen with fourteen years of residence here, and who loves both countries very much, I can only try my best to discover what they are. In the limited space I have I shall confine myself to two, the respective attitudes of the European and the American towards Time and towards Nature.

Let A be an historical situation in the past and B an historical situation now, and let us suppose that, in fact, the two are analogous. Both the European and the American may fail to realize this, the former because his tendency is to see B, not as analogous to, but as identical with A—he fails to see the element of novelty in B—the latter because his tendency is to see no relation whatever between them—he fails to see the element of repetition in B.

Every European, therefore, whatever his religion or politics, believes, consciously or unconsciously, that Man, as a history-making person as well as a physical organism, is subject to Natural Law, that there is such a thing as an essential human nature which persists unaltered through all changes. If he is a Conservative, he believes that this Natural Law has already been discovered and embodied in the social order; if he is a Revolutionary, he believes that the true law has at last for the first time been discovered by him and that it is his task to embody it in the new social order for all time; if he is a Liberal, he believes that, though both knowledge of the Law and its social embodiment are still incomplete, full knowledge and perfect embodiment will be achieved in time; none of them, however, doubts that the Law exists.

The average American, on the other hand, finds it very difficult to believe in the existence of such a law, to believe that there is *anything* in human nature which is not plastic and changeable. Americans are supposed to be, and often think of themselves as being liberal optimists, who believe that the world will slowly get better and better, but their literature and the very aggressiveness with which they often voice optimistic sentiments makes me suspect that, in their heart of hearts, they feel, not that the good will necessarily triumph over the evil, but that all things pass; the evils we know will pass but so will the goods we know. New, utterly unforeseen goods and evils will take their place.

I do not find Americans either optimistic or pessimistic; I find them adventurous and anxious. The American is saved by his attitude from the European vice of idolatry, idolatry of some particular social structure or theory; on the other hand, it makes it hard for him to think about anything but immediate and local problems, and hard not to be impatient and demand immediate solutions. There is a story, alas, I fear apocryphal, that a bill was once introduced into a State Legislature to declare Pi equal to 3 on the grounds that the exact fraction was too difficult for the school children to learn. If the problem of the mathematical education of children had no connection to anything else in the universe, the suggestion would have been perfectly reasonable; unfortunately, it does have a connection. At times Europeans are afraid that American Foreign Policy is just such an improvisation.

So much for Time. What, then, about Nature? The primitive religion of Europe, which neither the Greek philosophers nor the Church have ever succeeded in completely eradicating, was a polytheistic, magical worship of Nature.

Nature was alive, immensely powerful, capricious. Man was at her mercy, and his fate depended upon securing her good favor; if she were against him, no practical activity of his could succeed. The bad side of this is obvious, an acceptance of disease, poverty, social injustice, etc., as the divine will, instead of as problems God requires man to solve. But it also had a good side; it inculcated a reverence for Nature, a sense that man has a duty towards things as well as towards his human neighbors. In the States, on the other hand, Nature is seen as the Other, the blind neuter savage realm of necessity against which man must pit his will and his wits; Nature, so to speak, is the dragon and Man St George.

To fight the dragon is the test of his manhood, but, when you have conquered a dragon, what can you do with it except enslave it? The trouble about this is that, while you can respect an as yet unconquered enemy, a slave is a mere thing to exploit. Hence the frightening waste of natural resources in America, and the even more frightening day to day, household by household, waste of materials and food, a waste which has nothing to do with a high standard of living. When Europeans call Americans materialistic, what they ought to say is that Americans don't respect matter enough.

This has been realized by thoughtful Americans, of course, for some time, but the fact that Government officials and private citizens like Bernard De Voto have still to fight so hard to protect forests, grazing lands, etc., from spoliation is proof that the feeling for Nature as a sacred trust, has not become general enough.

The threat which hangs over Western Civilization means that Europe and America are going to have to be allies, whether they like it or not.

But the alliance can either be, what at present, I am afraid, it largely is, an alliance imposed by a common fear, suspicious, unstable and liable to panic, or it can be an alliance founded on mutual respect, a desire to learn from each other, using our very differences as opportunities to correct our respective biases. I am enough of an old-fashioned liberal to believe that the second alternative is possible.

St Louis Post-Dispatch, 13 December 1953

Verga's Place

The House by the Medlar Tree. By Giovanni Verga. Grove Press. $3.50.

Giovanni Verga is an excellent witness to the creative role of style and form. In a biographical note to *Mastro-Don Gesualdo*, D. H. Lawrence has quoted him as saying:

> I had published several of my first novels. They went well: I was preparing others. One day, I don't know how, there came into my hand a sort of broadside, a halfpenny sheet sufficiently ungrammatical and disconnected, in which a sea-captain succinctly related all the vicissitudes through which his sailing ship had passed. Seaman's language, short, without an unnecessary phrase. It struck me, and I read it again; it was what I was looking for without definitely knowing it. Sometimes, you know, just a sign, an indication, is enough. It was a revelation.

As long, that is, as he wrote in the conventional literary Italian of his time he was compelled to write about the subjects that such a style suggested and for the treatment of which it had been created, namely, stories of amorous intrigues in high life. The subjects he knew and loved best, the life in the villages of Sicily went untouched, not because he had not realized their value but because he had not discovered the proper method of treatment. The richest ore must remain unmined till a correct process of smelting has been invented. Needless to say, the captain's letter was only a stimulus to the creation of a style which is very far from being artless and naive.

Verga is generally classified by critics as a member of the Verismo school. If all that is meant by that is that he wrote about poor people speaking a heightened version of what they actually speak, the classification will stand but means very little. All valid art is true to "Nature," i.e. the most interior allegory must reveal something about everyday life and the most detailed rapportage reveal himself to a reader who has never known the society reported on.

But if what is meant is that Verga wrote, like Zola, according to a particular doctrine of naturalism, it is not true. Doctrinaire naturalism was a corollary of nineteenth-century science, in particular of its biology. Believing that man was the creature of his biological needs and that "Nature" knows nothing of morality, it chose to write about the lives of the destitute, the oppressed, the pathological, less out of personal interest and love than as a matter of principle and duty, for it is precisely among such people that the role of physical and social necessity is greatest, and freedom of choice least. If there was any hope it lay in the future, either, as for Zola, through scientific mastery over nature, or, as for Hardy, through progressive evolution—"Consciousness the Will informing, till it fashion all things fair"; but the present was bleak. Verga has hardly any of this; very occasionally he drops a bitter comment: for example,

> He won't write for money while he's away, the old man said to himself. If God grants him long life, he'll set the house by the medlar tree on its feet again! But, just because he was made of that stuff, God did not grant him long life.

but he never shows a superior pity for his characters; it is always the compassion of an equal. The reader never feels that he has consulted governmental Blue Books in libraries; everything has been observed at first-hand with the loving attention one gives to a way of life which, whatever its sorrows and crimes, is worth living.

The House by the Medlar Tree is the first volume of an intended trilogy (Verga never finished the third volume) to be called *The Defeated*, dealing in turn with the poor peasant, the rich peasant, and the aristocrat. Its central theme is the effect of exceptional misfortune upon the various members of a fisherman's family. Since it is a novel and not real life, the misfortunes which in the latter would be distributed among several families are concentrated upon one. The family consists of Grandfather 'Ntoni, his son Bastiano, his daughter-in-law Maruzza, and his five grandchildren, 'Ntoni, Luca, Mena, Alessio and Lia.

By the end of the novel, Bastiani has got drowned, Maruzza has died of cholera, young 'Ntoni has gone to jail, Luca has been killed in a naval battle, Mena has had to refuse to marry the man she loves for his sake, Lia, unable to bear the shame of a false accusation of having had an affair, has run away and become a whore, Grandfather 'Ntoni has died in the poor house, and only Alessio with his future bride Nunziata are left to start rebuilding the house of the Malavoglia.

So summarized the book sounds terribly depressing; in fact, it is nothing of the kind and one is left with a feeling of tragic exaltation which only great art can arouse.

In a society as poor as that to which the Malavoglia belong, success or failure must, for the majority, depend upon the caprices of Mother Nature. A good anchovy season makes it possible to pay off debts and even save a little; a storm wrecks a boat and one is worse off than ever. Wherever chance is so powerful—as, for instance, in Hollywood—misfortune is regarded as infectious and the unlucky are shunned by their neighbors. It is possible for an individual to escape from the see-saw but the cost is high; he must deny himself rest and pleasure, and he must ruthlessly take advantage of every weakness and misfortune of others. If, like Uncle Crocifisso, he is prepared to do this, his wealth and power will increase in geometrical progression, for to have capital in a society where most have none makes one a king. It is, however, virtually impossible to be wealthy and nice at the same time; Verga's prosperous peasants are unhappy and deservedly unloved, obsessed with the craving for possession—were they not obsessed they would never have succeeded—and tormented by the thought that they cannot keep what they have gathered when they die. In two stories Verga tells of a rich peasant who, feeling the approach of death, tries to slaughter his animals and destroy his trees so that no one else shall have them. The tragedy of 'Ntoni the younger is that he is too decent to behave like Uncle Crocifisso but not morally brave enough like his grandfather and his brother Alessio to accept his lot. His time of service in the Navy has unsettled him, for he has seen places where life was quite different from that in his village. He wants to go away and make a fortune:

"... I'm sick and tired of this life! I want to change my condition, my own and the whole family's. I want mother and you and Mena and Alessi and all of us to be rich."

Master 'Ntoni's eyes opened wide. He seemed to want to chew over the words he had just heard before he could swallow them.

"Rich!" he exclaimed. "Rich! And what shall we do when we are rich?"

'Ntoni scratched his head and started racking his brains trying to think what they would do when they were rich.

"We shall do what the others do," he said. "We shan't do anything at all! . . . We shall go and live in town, and do nothing, and eat macaroni and meat every day!"

That is not the way a person thinks who is really going to get on in the world and we are not surprised when 'Ntoni returns to the village with his tail between his legs. With extraordinary delicacy and skill Verga portrays his downfall, his drinking, his outbursts of resentment, how he slips from lounging about the tavern to smuggling in the hope of making easy money, an activity in which his innate innocence and trustfulness ensure that he will get caught.

In Hardy's novels one sometimes feels that the author's personal philosophy influences what happens to his characters, in Verga's never; he never stands between the reader and his characters and the only point he can be said to make is that what matters is not success or failure but honor and courage. Few novelists can reveal character so economically: for example,

> The boy, who was as sensible as his grandfather, rolled up the bottoms of his trousers on the balcony, although he was going to be put into uniform and wouldn't be wearing them again.

"But all the newspapers say that we've lost!"
"Lost what?" said Uncle Crocifisso, putting his hand to his ear.
"A battle."
"Who lost it?"
"I, you, everybody, the whole of Italy," said the chemist.
"I haven't lost anything!" replied Dumbbell shrugging his shoulders.

Verga never indulges in long descriptions but through the dialogue the physical presence of Sicily, the heat, the sea, the lava, the smells are always vividly present. I do not understand why *The House by the Medlar Tree* has not been made into a movie. If the reverence were given to the text that it deserves, it could make a magnificent one.

The Griffin, July 1953

Zahl und Gesicht

Forio d'Ischia. June 1953

An invitation—an honor indeed—to contribute to a Festschrift in celebration of the 80th birthday of Rudolf Kassner arrived too late for me to write anything remotely worthy of the occasion. All I can offer is a simple historical fact. Among all the books which a writer reads over the years, the number which have so essentially conditioned his vision of life that he cannot imagine who he was before he read them is, naturally, very small. But every now and then, perhaps by pure accident, he picks up a volume, opens it at random, and is immediately overwhelmed by the feeling that this voice is adressed to him personally, so much so that he is jealous lest it should speak to others.

Zahl und Gesicht has been for me, and still is, such a book: in such a case, discussion is not called for, only gratitude and homage.

W. H. AUDEN

Rudolf Kassner zum achtzigsten Geburtstag: Gedenkbuch,
herausgegeben von A. Cl. Kensik und D. Bodmer, 1953

Huck and Oliver

About six months ago I re-read *Huckleberry Finn*, by Mark Twain, for the first time since I was a boy, and I was trying when I read it to put myself back in the position of what it would seem like to re-read the book without knowing the United States very well. Because *Huckleberry Finn* is one of those books which is a key book for understanding the United States; just as I think one could take other books, English books—shall I say *Oliver Twist?*—as corresponding pictures of a British attitude.

When you read *Huckleberry Finn*, the first thing maybe that strikes somebody who comes from England about it is the difference in nature and in the attitude towards nature. You will find the Mississippi, and nature generally, very big, very formidable, very inhuman. When Oliver goes to stay in the country with Mrs Maylie, Dickens writes:

> Who can describe the pleasure and delight and peace of mind and tranquillity the sickly boy felt in the balmy air, and among the green hills and rich woods of an inland village.

All very human, very comforting. Huck describes how he gets lost in a fog on the Mississippi, and he writes as follows:

> I was floating along, of course, four or five miles an hour; but you don't ever think of that. No, you *feel* like you are laying dead still on the water; and if a little glimpse of a snag slips by, you don't think to yourself how fast *you're* going, but you catch your breath and think, my! how that snag's tearing along, If you think it ain't dismal and lonesome out in a fog that way, by yourself, in the night, you try it once—you'll see.

One of the great differences between Europe in general and America is in the attitude towards nature. To us over here, perhaps, nature is always, in a sense, the mother or the wife: something with which you enter into a semi-personal relation. In the United States, nature is something much more savage; it is much more like—shall we say?—St George and the dragon. Nature is the dragon, against which St George proves his manhood. The trouble about that, of course, is that if you succeed in conquering the dragon, there is nothing you can do with the dragon except enslave it, so that there is always the danger with a wild and difficult climate of alternating, if you like, between respecting it as an enemy and exploiting it as a slave.

The second thing that will strike any European reader in reading *Huckleberry Finn* is the amazing stoicism of this little boy. Here he is, with a father who is a greater and more horrible monster than almost any I can think of in fiction, who very properly gets murdered later. He runs into every kind of danger; he observes a blood feud in which there is a terrible massacre, and he cannot even bear, as he writes afterwards, to think exactly what happened. Yet, in spite of all these things, which one would expect to reduce a small child either into becoming a criminal or a trembling nervous wreck, Huck takes them as Acts of God which pass away, and yet one side of this stoicism is an attitude towards time in which the immediate present is accepted as the immediate present; there is no reason to suppose that the future will be the same, and therefore it does not, perhaps, have to affect the future in the same kind of way as it does here.

Then, more interestingly, the European reader is puzzled by the nature of the moral decision that Huck takes. Here Huck is with his runaway slave, Jim, and he decides that he is not going to give Jim up, he is going to try to get him into safety. When I first read *Huckleberry Finn* as a boy, I took Huck's decision as being a sudden realisation, although he had grown up in a slave-owning community, that slavery was wrong. Therefore I completely failed to understand one of the most wonderful passages in the book, where Huck wrestles with his conscience. Here are two phrases. He says:

> I was trying to make my mouth say I would do the right thing and the clean thing, and go and write to that nigger's owner and tell where he was; but deep down inside I knowed it was a lie, and He knowed it. You can't pray a lie—I found that out.

He decides that he will save Jim. He says:

> I will go to work and steal Jim out of slavery again; and if I could think up anything worse, I would do that, too; because as long as I was in, and in for good, I might as well go the whole hog.

When I first read the book I took this to be abolitionist satire on Mark Twain's part. It is not that at all. What Huck does is a pure act of moral improvisation. What he decides tells him nothing about what he should do on other occasions, or what other people should do on other occasions; and here we come to a very profound difference between American and European culture. I believe that all Europeans, whatever their political opinions, whatever their religious creed, do believe in a doctrine of natural law of some kind. That is to say there are certain things about human nature, and about man as a historical creature, not only as a natural creature, which are eternally true. If a man is a conservative, he thinks that law has already been discovered. If he is a revolutionary he thinks he has just discovered it; nobody knew anything in the past, but now it is known. If he is a liberal, he thinks we know something about it and we shall gradually know more. But neither the conservative, nor the revolutionary, nor the liberal has really any doubt that a natural law exists.

It is very hard for an American to believe that there is anything in human nature that will not change. Americans are often called, and sometimes even believe themselves to be, liberal optimists who think that the world is gradually getting better and better. I do not really believe that is true, and I think the evidence of their literature is against it. One should say, rather, that deep down inside they think that all things pass: the evils we know will disappear, but so will the goods.

For that very reason you might say that America is a country of amateurs. Here is Huck who makes an essentially amateur moral decision. The distinction between an amateur and a professional, of course, is not necessarily a matter of learning; an amateur might be a very learned person, but his knowledge would be, so to speak, the result of his own choice of reading and chance. *Vice versa*, a professional is not necessarily unoriginal, but he will always tend to check his results against the past and with his colleagues. The word "intellectual" in Europe has always meant, basically, the person who knew what the law was, in whatever sphere, whether it was religion, medicine, or what have you. There has always been a distrust in the States of the person who claimed in advance to know what the law was. Naturally, in any country where people are faced with situations which are really new, the amateur often is right where the professional is wrong; we sometimes use the phrase "professional caution", and that sometimes applies when situations are quite different. On the other hand, the amateur tends, necessarily, to think in terms of immediate problems and to demand immediate solutions, because if you believe that everything is going to be completely different the day after tomorrow, it is no good trying to think about that.

A third thing, coupled with that, is that on reading *Huckleberry Finn* most Europeans will find the book emotionally very sad. Oliver Twist has been through all kinds of adventures; he has met people who have become his friends, and you feel they are going to be his friends for life. Huck has had a relationship with Jim much more intense than any that Oliver has known, and yet, at the end of the book, you know that they are going to part and never see each other again. There hangs over the book a kind of sadness, as if freedom and love were incompatible. At the end of the book Oliver the orphan

is adopted by Mr Brownlow, and that is really the summit of his daydream—
to be accepted into a loving home. Almost the last paragraph of *Oliver Twist*
runs:

> Mr Brownlow went on, from day to day, filling the mind of his adopted
> child with stories of knowledge . . . becoming attached to him, more and
> more, as his nature developed itself, and showed the thriving seeds of all
> he wished him to become . . .

How does Huck end:

> I reckon I got to light out for the Territory ahead of the rest, because
> Aunt Sally she's going to adopt me and sivilise me, and I can't stand it. I
> been there before.

In that way, of course, he is like a character in *Oliver Twist*—the Artful
Dodger. But in the case of the Artful Dodger, Dickens shows us this charming young man as nevertheless corrupt, and over him hangs always the
shadow of the gallows; he is not the natural hero, as Huck is in *Huckleberry
Finn*.

In addition to the attitude towards nature, the attitude towards natural law,
there are two more things one might take up briefly; the attitude towards
time, and the attitude towards money. Imagine two events in history, (*a*) followed by (*b*), which in some way are analogous. The danger to the European
will be to think of them as identical, so that if I know what to do over (*a*), I
shall know exactly what to do with (*b*). The danger in America will be to see
no relation between these things at all, so that any knowledge I have about
(*a*) will not help me to understand (*b*). The European fails to see the element of novelty; the American fails to see the element of repetition. You may
remember that both Oliver and Huck come into some money. In Oliver's case
it is money that is his by right of legal inheritance. In Huck's case, it is pure
luck. He and Tom Sawyer found a robber's cache. The money came to them
only because it could not be restored to its rightful owners. The money, therefore, is not something that you ever think of inheriting by right.

One might put it this way: in Europe, money represents power—that is to
say, freedom from having to do what other people want you to do, and freedom to do what you yourself want to do; so that in a sense all Europeans feel
they would like to have as much money themselves as possible, and other people to have as little as possible.

In the States, money, which is thought of as something you extract in your
battle with the dragon of nature, represents a proof of your manhood. The
important thing is not to have money, but to have made it. Once you have
made it you can perfectly well give it all away. There are advantages and disadvantages on both sides. The disadvantage in Europe is a tendency towards
avarice and meanness; the danger in America is anxiety because, since this

quantitative thing of money is regarded as a proof of your manhood, and to make a little more of it would make you even more manly, it becomes difficult to know where to stop. This ties up with something that always annoys me: when I see Europeans accusing Americans of being materialists. The real truth about Americans is they do not care about matter enough. What is shocking is waste; just as what shocks Americans in Europe is avarice.

I have mentioned a few of these things because we live in a time when it has never been so important that America and Great Britain should understand each other. Many misunderstandings arise, not over concrete points, but over a failure to recognise certain presuppositions or attitudes which we all take, according to our upbringing, in such a way that we cannot imagine anybody taking any other one. When those are understood, it is much more possible to help each other's strong points and weaknesses by exchanging them to our mutual profit.

In so far as that can be done, and I am sufficiently much of a liberal optimist to believe it can, the alliance between the States and Great Britain can become a real and genuine and mutually self-critical thing, instead of the rather precarious relationship forced by circumstances which it seems to be at present.

BBC Third Programme, 27 September 1953;
The Listener, 1 October 1953

Selected Essays of T. S. Eliot

Selected Essays: New Edition. By T. S. Eliot. Harcourt, Brace. $4.50.

As a critic, Mr Eliot has, from the beginning, consistently manifested two concerns: what one might call the selfish concern of a practising poet, and the public-spirited concern of a man who believes that poets, along with priests, lawyers, doctors, etc., are members of the order of "clerks," those who, in one way or another, know the Law, and whose social function, therefore, is to expound it to the ignorant and defend it against the heretic and the barbarian.

In reading the poetry of the past, a practising poet does not ask, "Is this poem good or bad? Is this poem better than that?"; he asks, "Given the present historical situation of myself and my colleagues, from what works can we derive most help in solving our contemporary poetic problems, and what works, on the other hand, are dangerous hindrances?"

Thus in his Dante essay, Mr Eliot's main point is to demonstrate the greater utility for the would-be poet of the Dantesque style and the allegorical method compared with the Shakespearean. Though his knowledge of classical literature is, I am sure, profound, his only two essays in this field are both concerned with the problem of translation, with how, that is, the past can be made, truthfully and vitally, contemporary. Again, his essays on English literature are all confined to the seventeenth and nineteenth centuries; he has nothing about the Middle Ages or the eighteenth century, not, obviously, because he considers the writers in these periods boring or worthless, but because, in his opinion, they are less practically relevant.

To a practising poet, a few lines of an author may be quite enough to give him the clue he is looking for, and Mr Eliot has always been a great anthologist: indeed, if, after reading his essays on the Elizabethan dramatists, one turn to the dramatists themselves—Tourneur or Massinger, for instance—one is apt to find that he has picked out the only good passages.

Similarly, his occasional summary words of disapproval, like his famous strictures on Milton, are not as arrogant as they sound. What Mr Eliot is really saying is: "For me, personally, and, I believe, for my contemporaries, Milton cannot help but only hinder. I don't want to waste more time on this, as it is more profitable to spend it studying what is positively valuable to me." The unwary reader may be misled, even dangerously, by the sober, "impersonal" style of his prose into thinking that Mr Eliot is a calm, cool, dispassionate man; the truth is that Mr Eliot is every bit as violently polemical a writer as, say, D. H. Lawrence. I say "dangerously misled" because it is possible to become his partisan or his enemy without knowing what his cause is: thus, the young admirer of Mr Eliot's poetry may conclude that Milton, whom he has not read, is not worth reading, and a more elderly admirer of Milton's poetry that a poet who can see no good in Milton cannot be worth reading.

The enormous and almost wholly beneficial influence of Mr Eliot's efforts "to purify the dialect of the tribe" shows how great an advantage a critic who is by vocation a poet, and a good one, has over a critic who is not. The latter, should he find the contemporary literary scene distasteful, is apt—and who can blame him?—to leave it to stew in its juice while he devotes his attention to those periods and authors whom he finds congenial; but the former is compelled, if he is to write at all, to seek a cure for the malaise of the present. Further, the fact of having written authentic poetry himself lends to his critical opinions an authority (not always, alas, justified) which the other cannot—however sound his taste and great his learning—hope to have. Professors W. P. Ker and George Saintsbury declared that Dryden and Pope were great poets but the poetry reading public continued to regard them as "classics of our prose"; the author of "Prufrock" said the same thing and that public pricked up its ears.

If Mr Eliot's other concern, his efforts to be the Matthew Arnold of our time, to diagnose and prescribe for the ills of modern civilization, his defense of dogmatic and organized Christianity against Liberal Protestantism and the Higher Thought, have, as I suspect, had little influence except with those who

already share his beliefs, this is mainly due, of course, to the vastly more serious nature of the problems involved: a single quotation may be enough to
transform a man's literary taste but it is doubtful that any one was ever argued into a religious conversion, though such a one may sometimes ascribe
to logical cogency what in reality is due to the personality or sanctity of the
arguer. (One has to assume, for instance, that T. E. Hulme was such a personality for, to one who is acquainted only with his published work, Mr Eliot's
opinion of him seems a fantastic overvaluation.) Further, the complexity of
the questions, the impossibility of treating any one in isolation, demands an
investigation on a scale larger than that of the occasional essay which is all
Mr Eliot has had the time, and, probably, the ambition to write. Thus his
finest essay of this kind seems to me to be "Thoughts after Lambeth" precisely because it is, in the best sense, parochial; in it he is speaking not to the
world in general but as an educated layman to his fellow Anglicans. Excellent
as they may be, I cannot help feeling that in his essays on Humanism Mr Eliot
is flogging a horse which not only is dead but never was alive. It is amusing
to see poor little Professor Foerster torn to pieces, but would it not be more
useful to have a careful, and no doubt duller, investigation of that much more
dangerous because much greater man, John Dewey, or, for that matter, of
Bernard Shaw, who is not so easily dismissed as Mr Eliot sometimes seems to
think. (Shaw is not Wells.) And then there is that greatest heathen of them
all, Goethe. What would one not give for a study of Goethe similar to Nietzsche's *The Case of Wagner*, a critique which even in attack should reveal the
greatness of the antagonist. However, such a job would take a long time and
Mr Eliot has other and, for lovers of poetry, better things to do. It is surely
more than enough that one cannot read one of these short essays without
coming across some striking observation:

> Rational assent may arrive late, intellectual conviction may come slowly,
> but they come inevitably without violence to honesty or nature. To put
> the sentiments in order is a later and an immensely difficult task: intel-
> lectual freedom is earlier and easier than complete spiritual freedom.

Or some remarks that are really funny:

> Mr Thomson is a metaphor-addict and his mind is ridden by images of
> underground passages (very short ones), ferries, wherries, and other fig-
> ures of easy transport from Canterbury to Rome. He remarks for in-
> stance: "And the careers of several prominent Anglo-Catholics served to
> strengthen the general suspicion. For they had a habit of using the
> Church of England as a junction and not as a terminus." I cannot see
> how *several* can form a habit; unless Mr Thomson wishes to suggest that
> Father Knox and Father Vernon have formed the "habit" of leaving the
> English Church.

I must end on a querulous note. The translator of Baudelaire's *Intimate Journals*, referred to on page 371 of both this and the earlier edition, is not a mysterious "Christopher Sherwood," but Christopher Isherwood, the novelist and my good friend.

The Griffin, October 1953

The Greatness of Freud

Sigmund Freud: Life and Work. Vol I: The Young Freud, 1856–1900.
By Ernest Jones. Hogarth Press. 27s. 6d.

"To relate Freud's personality and the experiences of his life to the development of his ideas" is a formidable task but Dr Jones has proved himself fully equal to it. His book, thank goodness, is a work of love not of idolatry. If, occasionally, the style gets a little "high-powered", the selection and organisation of the material could not be better done. One does not know which to admire more, Dr Jones' instinct for the relevant document to quote, or the skill with which he weaves it into his own text. How interesting it is, for example, to be given the actual passage from an essay of Ludwig Börne, written in 1823, which provided Freud with his first hint for free-association (though he could not remember it later):

Take a few sheets of paper and for three days in succession write down without any falsification or hypocrisy everything that comes into your head. Write what you think of yourself, of your women, of the Turkish War, of Goethe, of the Fonk criminal case, of the Last Judgment, of those senior to you in authority—and, when the three days are over, you will be amazed at what novel and startling thoughts have welled up in you.

Even an odd little fact, like Freud's belief in the Earl of Oxford Theory of Shakespeare, or a comic story, like that of how a patient secured Freud his professorial chair by persuading her aunt to sell the Minister of Education a Böcklin he coveted, are always more than just amusing gossip. If the subsequent volumes maintain the standard of this one, Dr Jones will have written a biography of the first rank.

The present volume covers the first forty-four years of Freud's life up to the publication of *Die Traumdeutung* in 1899; it includes, that is, his marriage, his years as a neurologist, first in the laboratory and then in private practice, his collaborations with Charcot and Breuer in the study of hysterias, his very strange friendship with Fliess, his self-analysis and his formulation of the Oedipus theory.

The artist, scientist, or philosopher, who makes his original discoveries as late in life as Freud, is uncommon, but Freud's case seems almost unique. The usual history of the late developer is one of false starts. He tries one thing after another and makes a mess of them all, till his friends despair of his ever amounting to anything. Freud's "false start" in neurology, on the other hand, was not only not a failure but very nearly a great triumph. He enjoyed his work, he was highly thought of; he almost discovers the neurone theory, he *almost* discovers the anaesthetic use of cocaine: that is, he discovers all the facts necessary to draw the correct conclusion and then, mysteriously, loses interest.

In contrast with the ease and pleasure with which he attacks neurological problems, when he begins his true career as a psychologist he moves slowly and uncertainly: it takes him eight years to abandon all use of electricity and hypnotism and to trust his free-association technique alone; it takes him four years to realise that a child's memories of seduction may be phantasy not fact, although he knew this to be so in the case of adult hysterics, and he never loses a certain nostalgia for the world he has left behind. "In the summer", he writes to Fliess in 1894, "I hope to return to my old pursuit and do a little anatomy; after all, that is the only satisfactory thing"; years later, he expresses to Dr Jones a hope that it will become possible "to cure hysteria by administering a chemical drug without any psychological treatment".

Further, every step he takes is accompanied by great psychological distress, attacks of indigestion, "intellectual paralysis . . . curious states of mind which one's consciousness cannot apprehend: twilight thoughts, a veil over one's mind, scarcely a ray of light here and there".

Much of this reluctance to enter "forbidden ground" must, of course, have been due to a normal human fear of discovering unpleasant truths about oneself, but there was, in Freud's case, I believe, a particular historical factor. The great revolutionary step taken by him, one that would make him a very great man still if every one of his theories should turn out to be false, was his decision—I am not perfectly sure that he ever quite realised what he had done—to treat psychological facts as belonging, not to the natural order, to be investigated according to the methodologies of chemistry and biology, but to the historical order.

For a man, piously brought up on the firm rock of the Helmholtz Faith—

No other forces than the common physical and chemical ones are active within the organism. In those cases which cannot be explained by these forces, one has either to find the specific way or form of their action by means of the physical-mathematical method or to assume forces equal in dignity to the chemical-physical forces inherent in matter.

—to take such a step was to enter a ground forbidden, not by conventional prudery but by his God; for the historical world is a horrid place where, instead of nice clean measurable forces, there are messy things like mixed motives, where classes keep overlapping, where what is believed to have happened is as real as what actually happened, a world, moreover, which cannot be defined by technical terms but only described by analogies.

No wonder Freud was frightened, for the people he was going to outrage were not the general public but the very men whom, intellectually, he most admired; what could anyone who thought of science as physics and chemistry possibly say of *Die Traumdeutung* but "uncritical minds will be delighted to join in this play with ideas and will end up in complete mysticism . . ."? No wonder that, during the crucial years, his only intellectual companion was a numerological crank.

Freud could hardly have dared or succeeded had he not been endowed by nature with a historian's type of mind rather than an exact scientist's. Dr Jones says of him:

> His great strength, though sometimes also his weakness, was his quite extraordinary respect for the *singular fact* . . . the idea of collecting statistics was quite alien to him . . . he was apt to be careless and imprecise in his use of technical terms.

One is not surprised to learn that his hobby was collecting antiquities, and it is significant that "The microscope was his only tool: physiology meant histology to him"; in comparative anatomy he could gratify his historical interest but in a "safe" way, for there the past and present, e.g. reptiles and mammals, exist side by side, but do not affect each other as they do in history proper.

In devising a therapeutic technique in which the doctor was to say and do as little as possible while the patient worked out his own salvation, in his distaste for "ruling, educating, curing", Freud accepted the moral consequences of his intellectual position. I say "I have a toothache", meaning that my aching tooth is something distinct from myself and for which, since I can now do nothing to alter it, I am not responsible. Accordingly, I put myself passively in the hands of my dentist and, when I wake from the gas, the pain and the tooth are gone, but I am still myself. But I do not say "I have a depression", I say "I am depressed", meaning that I cannot be cured without becoming a different person, and, whatever help I may seek, I remain responsible for myself. The treatment of the mentally ill by hypnotism, drugs, shocks, or any other method in which the patient is purely passive, is morally revolting in the same way as is the maintenance of social order by the Criminal Courts. It may—after a fashion—work, it may be necessary for the sake of others, but only one's sadism can possibly approve.

I have no idea how many people have been "cured" by psychoanalysis—I have a suspicion that it demands of a patient a courage and strength of character almost equal to that of its founder, which cannot be very common— but one of the proofs of Freud's greatness is that he as good as said that he didn't care. No one can resist trying to cure by force, no one can allow another his right to himself, even to his misery, who has not learned to love: Dr Jones' chapters on Freud's courtship and marriage leave one in no doubt where he learned it.

The Listener, 8 October 1953

Translation and Tradition

The Translations of Ezra Pound. With an introduction by Hugh Kenner. Faber and Faber. 30s.

It was a happy thought to collect these translations, most of which have for years been hard to obtain. Here are the Cavalcanti poems, the Arnaut Daniel, *The Seafarer*, the Chinese poems, the Noh plays, and, for good measure, some *pensées* of Remy de Gourmont written just before his death. I am sorry that the editors have decided against including *Homage to Sextus Propertius*. Technically, of course, they are right—it is not a translation—but the time has passed when anyone would attempt to read it as such, and since it was not included in the *Selected Poems*, it would have been nice to have it available again.

Though the translation of poetry from one tongue into another is, as everybody knows, impossible, for the poetic unity of sensibility, diction, and rhythm cannot be taken apart and reassembled in exactly the same way in the new language, nevertheless the influence of such translations on poets has probably been greater than the influence of translations of prose works upon prose writers, and in those periods when English poetry, for example, seemed to have arrived at an impasse, it was always translation that came to the rescue. So it was when the original Anglo-Saxon poetic tradition broke down, so it was at the beginning of the sixteenth century when linguistic changes had destroyed the Chaucerian prosody and the allegorical habit of thinking had gone stale, and so it was in the late seventeenth century when dramatic blank verse and the emotional conventions associated with it collapsed.

Translation can have various kinds of effect. Sometimes, as in Chaucer's translation of *Le Romaunt de la Rose*, it introduces both a new kind of sensibility, the Allegory of Love, and a new rhythm, the strict octosyllabic couplet. Sometimes, as in Dryden's translations from the classics, it is the means whereby the poet discovers and develops the full possibilities of a verse medium, the heroic couplet, which he already has in his own tongue, when it is the very difference of this medium from the original which is the fruitful challenge.

Pound began his translations in just such another period of uncertainty. The Romantic conception of poetry and of the self was ceasing to seem adequate, and the prosodic convention based on the iamb and the anapæst had been brought to a pitch of virtuosity by Tennyson and Swinburne beyond which no development seemed possible. It was the latter which was first realised to be a problem, and by the late 1870s poets were seeking a solution, Hopkins in "sprung rhythm," Bridges in the theories of Spedding and Stone about classical metres (people who find his poetic personality unsympathetic should not let this blind them to the great rhythmical interest of Bridges' later work), and Doughty was conducting a heroic but doomed one-man campaign to restore the diction of Spenser.

The importance of Pound's translations of Cavalcanti lies in their rhythmical novelty. The sensibility expressed in the poems, the cult of *Amor* and *La Donna gentile*, is nothing new—indeed, its vulgar corruption in cheap fiction has made it unusable—while the diction of the translations is embarrassingly pre-Raphaelite, quaint and diffuse, the very opposite of the directness of the Italian. Thus:

> *Io vidi donne con la donna mia:*
> *Non che niuna mi sembrasse donna;*
> *Ma simigliavan sol la sua ombria* (Ballata II)

(I saw ladies with my lady,/not that any seemed to me a lady,/but they resembled her shadow)

becomes

> Fair women I saw passing where she passed;
> And none among them women to my vision;
> But were like nothing save her shadow cast

and

> *E po mj conta sj d'amore il vero* (Sonnetto II)

(and then told me such of the true love)

becomes

> With such deep parlance of love's verities.

But Pound had set himself one task, that of reproducing in English the cadence of the Italian hendecasyllabic in general, and of Cavalcanti's in particular, a cadence which does not correspond to the five foot iambic line of the normal English sonnet, and to achieve this, he was bound, given the nature of the two languages, to sacrifice the diction. What a refreshing shock it must have been for a reader in 1910 to come across such lines as

> Who is she that comes, making turn every man's eye
> And making the air to tremble with a bright clearnesse
> That leadeth with her Love, in such nearness
> No man may proffer of speech more than a sigh?

> Ah God, what she is like when her owne eye turneth, is
> Fit for Amor to speake, for I can not at all;
> Such is her modesty, I would call
> Every woman else but a useless uneasiness.

(Sonnet VII)

for he was hearing cadences which had not been heard in English poetry since Wyatt, e.g.

> Wherewith love to the hart's forest he fleeth
> Leaving his enterprise with pain and cry,
> And there him hideth and not appeareth.
> What may I do? when my master feareth,
> But in the field with him to live and die,
> For good is the life ending faithfully.

and Wyatt, it will be remembered, was still appearing in the *Oxford Book of English Verse* in a prosodically doctored version. It is only fair to say that, in Wyatt's case, these cadences were more the accidental effect of uncertainty than consciously intended, and that Spenser's prosodic reforms were necessary, but by Pound's time the situation was quite different, and the music of his Cavalcanti translations could suggest all kinds of new and exciting possibilities for English poetry. Here was a seed which was to bear as fruit such a movement as that of the lines in *Little Gidding*, beginning

> In the uncertain hour before the morning

Similarly, it might be said of his translation of *The Seafarer* that its effect was to make the spondee respectable in English verse, and of his Arnaut Daniel translations that they delivered complicated verse forms from their unfortunate association, thanks to French verse and the poets of the nineties, with elegant tea-table trifling. (I have tried to find a use for the triolet that was not indecent, but in vain.)

The influence of Pound's Chinese translations and—for he must share the honours—of Arthur Waley's, on the other hand, has been due, not to their form but to their revelation of a new kind of poetic sensibility. The average reader cannot know what relation the forms and rhythms of these English poems have to their Chinese originals—I suspect none—but he can easily imagine with what delight a young poet, who was tired of the prolixity and moralising of nineteenth century poetry, tired of its methods of poetic organisation, tired of its conception of the poetic subject, yet unable to see what to put in their place, would pounce on such a poem as the following:

> The Dai horse neighs against the bleak wind of Etsu,
> The birds of Etsu have no love for En, in the north,
> Emotion is born out of habit.

Yesterday we went out of the Wild-Goose gate,
To-day from the Dragon-Pen.
Surprised. Desert turmoil. Sea sun.
Flying snow bewilders the barbarian heaven.

Lice swarm like ants over our accoutrements.
Mind and spirit drive on the feathery banners.
Hard fight gets no reward.
Loyalty is hard to explain.
Who will be sorry for General Rishogu,
                the swift moving,
Whose white head is lost for this province?

The dramatic conventions of a culture, like its music, seem to resist transplantation or grafting much more than its poetry or its painting. Pound's translations of the Noh plays are fascinating to read, and some of them, e.g. *Nishikigi*, very beautiful, but I am not convinced, despite Yeats' efforts, that they can contribute much to our spoken drama, to opera libretti, perhaps.

As for the Remy de Gourmont, I am a pushover for *pensées* even when they are second-rate, as most of these are; there are, however, at least five really good ones, e.g.

The greater number of skeptics whom I have known were of the type in fashion in the eighteenth century, who if it thundered while they were eating ham-omelette on Good Friday would hurl the plate through the window, saying: "What a fuss about a mere omelette!"

All in all a very good thirty shillings' worth. Mr Pound has every right to say that he has done the State of Letters some service and that they, or at least some of them, know it.

Encounter, December 1953

Speaking of Books

A few weeks ago Mr Winston Churchill had a birthday, and a poetic competition was held in England to celebrate the occasion. I do not think that anybody will be surprised to learn that none of the entries was of the slightest poetic merit. However different from each other in outlook and style they may be, all modern poets seem to agree on one thing—that the successful public figure is not a possible poetic subject.

The persons, for example, whom Yeats celebrates in "Easter 1916" were, firstly, personal acquaintances; secondly, men who became involved in a life of action not by their natures but by historical events outside their control, and, thirdly, men who died defeated in this world. Even when the hero of modern poetry is not the sensitive passive observer, he is someone who is unsuccessful by the standards of our society, the solitary stoic endurer, the gypsy, the fool, the child, and the only successful kind of action which the poets seem able to praise is the action of the great artist himself, his transmutation of "the fury and the mire of human veins" into "a starlit or a moonlit dome."

In former ages victory in war was celebrated by triumphal arches and statues of great generals: today we all feel that real homage can be paid only to The Unknown Soldier, to the individual, that is, about whom nothing is known whatsoever except that he was killed, and it is irrelevant if the war in which he was killed ended in victory or defeat.

The ideal subject of artistic celebration combines three qualities: personality, power and excellence. What cannot be experienced as a personal encounter belongs not to Art but to Science; what has no power cannot be made public and manifest; though flawed excellence is one of the great artistic themes, that which has no excellence to be flawed is, at most a subject for satire. The effect of technological progress has been to make power impersonal and to divorce it completely from excellence. Nature, as man encountered her for centuries in the rhythmical succession of the seasons and the motions of the stars, could be thought of as living, personal and holy; natural forces as exploited by man through machines cannot. However heroic Mr Churchill may have been, however he inspired the English people, it would have all gone for nothing without planes, tanks, etc.; without, that is, the machine which is the absolute mercenary.

In former ages when all work was done by hand and in the time of nature or the worker, the way in which the artist worked was no different from anybody else's, but in a technological civilization the artist is one of the very few who still work by hand and in their own time while the vast majority must work as the machine decides. In the past there was an art for the elite and a popular art, but they were both produced in the same kind of way; what is called popular art today is not only different in style or content but made in a completely different way. It is hardly surprising, then, if the gap between "highbrow" and "popular" art becomes increasingly wider. "Modern" art is often criticized, and with justice, for being private and introspective, but such characteristics are almost bound to appear when the way in which the artist works is, by comparison with the way in which most of his neighbors work, so peculiar.

If it were only the modern artist who was adversely affected by a technological civilization, it would not matter much—the world could get on perfectly well for a time without him; the serious question is how the majority, the white-collar and industrial workers, are affected. The only serious study of this that I know is Simone Weil's account of her year in the Renault plant.

Is she talking nonsense when she says that it is impossible to work on a production line without depersonalizing one's self? If she is not, and if certain
goods like tractors and refrigerators are real social goods and can be produced economically only in this manner, what, if anything, can be done?

One would like to know, for a start, for how many hours a day, for how many
days, a man can work in such a plant before depersonalization sets in. And
there is a second question. In the case of goods which are not material like refrigerators—e.g. the goods of the word—is there something about the machine which is incompatible with them? Is there, for example, something
about the way in which the modern newspaper, films, radio, etc., are produced
which nullifies the very best intentions of their producers? Let me give one little example. Amid the crowd of advertising posters in the subway, one finds
here and there one recommending racial tolerance or church-going, but the
nature of the advertising medium as such has the effect of putting this appeal
on exactly the same level as appeals to buy a new deodorant or a special brand
of mustard. I do not know what can be done about it, but I know that there is
something wrong with a civilization where such a leveling happens.

The New York Times Book Review, 20 December 1953

Ballet's Present Eden
Example of The Nutcracker

Every artistic medium has its peculiar nature which allows it to express some
things better than any rival medium and prohibits it from expressing other
things altogether. The medium of ballet is the human body moving in rhythmical balance within a limited area of space. What it can express is whatever
is immediately intelligible in terms of variety of motion—fast-or-slow, to-and-
fro, round-and-round, up-and-down; and variety of spatial relations—absent-
or-present, face-to-face, back-to-back, side-by-side, above-below, at-the-center,
on-the-outside, far-or-near, approaching-or-receding, etc.

Ballet time, that is, is a continuous present; every experience which depends on historical time lies outside its capacities. It cannot express memory,
the recollection of that which is absent, for either the recollected body is on
stage and immediate or it is off and non-existent. Memory distinguishes between the object and its invoked image; ballet deals only in the object. No
character in a ballet can grow or change in the way that a character in a novel
changes; he can only undergo instantaneous transformations from one kind
of being to another. Ballet can show A protecting and comforting B, but it
cannot tell us whether A is the mother, the aunt or the fairy godmother of B.
These observations, it should be said, refer to the forming principles of

ballet; as with the other media, tension and excitement come from pushing against the form. A choreographer may take this risk again and again, but he will watch closely, being careful to make himself clear. And he will return in good time to safe ground.

In its dazzling display of physical energy, on the other hand, the ballet expresses, as no other medium can, the joy of being alive. Death is omnipresent as the force of gravity over which the dancers triumph; everything at rest is either a thing, or it is asleep, enchanted or dead. If it moves, it comes to life, and its kind of life—man, bird or animated toy—is a minor matter, to be indicated by slight details of costume, compared to the fact of life itself which dancing expresses. The more energy implied by an emotion, the more danceable it is. Thus defiance can be danced but despair is impossible, and joy is the most danceable of all. Since suffering, as human beings understand it, depends on memory and anticipation which are alien to the medium, it may be said that nobody suffers in ballet: if they did, their movement would become unbalanced and ugly.

When ballet portrays funeral rites for the death of a hero, the glory and the pleasure in the rite itself are what it conveys. In other words, all real ballets take place in Eden, in that world of pure being without becoming and the suffering implied by becoming, a world where things, beasts and men are equally alive, a world without history and without seriousness. The ballet character who becomes serious must either come to rest and die or he must exit. One could turn *Pickwick Papers* into a ballet up to the point where Mr Pickwick enters the Fleet Prison (The Fallen World), but neither the Fleet, nor Mr Pickwick after he has been in it and tasted of the fruit of the knowledge of good and evil, are ballet subjects. It is not an accident that so many of the most successful ballets are based on fairy stories.

E.T.A. Hoffmann who wrote the original story (in 1816) on which *The Nutcracker* is based, was haunted by nostalgic visions of a childhood Eden with its magical wonder. At the same time he was haunted by terrors and visions of evil. Black magic was as real to him as white. His Drosselmeyer is a much more complex and sinister character than Drosselmeyer in the ballet; the horrid things that happen to Princess Perribou and to Nutcracker, or to Crosselmeyer Jr, have quite rightly been kept off the stage, and the ballet battle is not the sadistic thing it is in the story.

Dumas turned Hoffmann's often fierce German tale into *Casse-Noisette*, a story for French children. Since children's stories also take place in a present Eden, he thus tended to preserve the incidents that Petipa and Ivanov could use for their scenario. What comes down to us now in dance are most of the ceremonial scenes like the Christmas party and the festivities in Confectionland. All the history of Nutcracker and Clara is telescoped into one ballet and a transformation scene; the long romantic journeys of the story are represented by the lovers in a snow storm. Certain charming scenes had to be left

out, not only on account of length, but also because they are too literary. For
example, the sausage feast in which the King rushes from a Privy Council
meeting to see how things are going in the kitchen:

> "Gentlemen!" he cried, rising from the throne, "will you excuse me? I
> will return in a minute."
>
> Then, hardly able to prevent himself from running to the door, he
> rushed to the kitchen, where, after embracing the Queen many times,
> he began to stir the contents of the cauldron with his sceptre. Afterwards
> he put it in his mouth, and, in a calmer state of mind, returned to his
> Privy Council, where, though still a little absent-minded, he succeeded
> in taking up the question of foreign policy where he had left it.

Some of this, e.g. "hardly able to prevent himself from running," is mimeable
though not danceable, but not even mime can take up foreign policy; that
requires words, as do Hoffmann's philosophic reflections on the difference
between the ideal and the real. In ballet only the ideal remains.

In order of composition, *The Nutcracker* is the last of three full-length ballets which Tchaikovsky wrote. There is beautiful ballet music in the operas of
classical composers like Gluck and Mozart, there are mid-nineteenth century
ballet scores of great charm like those of Adam and Delibes, but Tchaikovsky
was the first to raise ballet music to its present status as a serious orchestral
form equal to that of the symphony. Before Tchaikovsky the choreographer
and the composer had little to do with each other: the former told the latter
what kind of dances he wanted and how many bars long they should be, and
the composer went off and wrote them without bothering to find out what
actions were to accompany his music. Tchaikovsky wrote to Petipa's orders,
but he also wrote to sense and in his ballet scores the music is always appo-
site to the scenario. The very difficulties which Tchaikovsky found in training his musical imagination to the traditional sonata and symphony forms
may well have been an advantage when he came to write ballet music, which
makes such different formal demands. Today, many of us find his compositions in this form his best music, the closest in spirit (though completely original) to the work of Mozart who was his confessed idol.

Outside Russia, where it has become popular, the ballet has hardly been
seen, and only the orchestra suite Tchaikovsky made out of some of the music
is well known. After seeing the Vic-Wells 1934 revival, Cyril Beaumont complained in his *Complete Book of Ballets* that the first scene was suitable only to
a juvenile audience and that the character dances in the last scene were
ridiculous, but praised highly the solo numbers.

Apart from the fact that it requires a number of professionally trained children which most ballet companies do not possess, *The Nutcracker* is not suitable for a company built, like the majority, around a few star soloists and with
a corps de ballet capable of little more than calisthenics. George Balanchine

has always set his face against such a structure. The ideal he has worked for is a company in which every member is technically capable of dancing a solo role: in his choreography, instead of the conventional corps de ballet acting in unison, every one has his unique part to play. Balanchine sees *The Nutcracker* as a festival of joy, a sort of Christmas pantomime, and only those who have lost their sense of joy and for whom, consequently, ballet is a meaningless art will find that juvenile.

Center: A Magazine of the Performing Arts, February 1954;
souvenir program of *The Nutcracker*, City Center of Music
and Drama, New York, 2 February 1954

Foreword to *An Armada of Thirty Whales*,
by Daniel G. Hoffman

Reading Mr Hoffman's poems, I find myself asking a very silly question: "Is there going to be a revival of 'Nature' poetry and, if so, how will it differ from nature poetry in the past?" It is significant, I think, that until quite recently nobody would have dreamed of asking such a question but that now, silly though I know it to be, I cannot help asking it.

It has always been difficult to write well, but, in a technological civilization, it is becoming increasingly difficult, in addition, to find themes worth writing about. One of the principal functions of poetry—of all the arts, for that matter—is the preservation and renewal of natural piety toward every kind of created excellence, toward the great creatures like the sun, moon, and earth on which our lives depend, toward the brave warrior, the wise man, the beautiful woman. Sometimes poetry regards the excellence of its subjects as self-derived, at other times as an outward and visible sign of an invisible uncreated Good, but in either case it is with the outward, concrete, and visible that it is concerned. Further, the subject of poetic celebration must possess at least two qualities, one of which is an invariable, power; it must, that is, be a real subject, a cause, not an effect. On the other hand, though poetry cannot praise weakness, it cannot praise pure force either. The Earth Mother may be mysterious and at times cruel in her dealings with men, but unless there were a pattern discernible in her ways, she could only be hated and defied; the Hero must be strong, but he also must be brave or magnanimous or wise; the Beloved must inspire, not simply enslave, if she is to be called beautiful.

Technology, by transferring power from nature to the social collectivity, has deprived power of a face and left all personal excellence without visible power. Even when the collectivity is beneficent, showering on us some unequivocal blessing like the refrigerator, poetry cannot thank it as it might thank a king who made wine flow in the streets; and when it does harm it cannot be attacked, for it is faceless and makes no conscious choices: in antiquity a tyrant could be satirized for his vices, but a modern dictator cannot really be praised or blamed, because he is an official or a medium rather than a person. Courage, wisdom, beauty continue, of course, to exist but, as it were, in private, and poetry finds it very difficult to communicate the excellence of anything that is not publicly visible. A writer today may believe, if he is a Christian like T. S. Eliot or Graham Greene, that the temporal world is an analogue of the eternal, or, if he is a platonist, that it is a parody, but it is very difficult for him to imagine what he believes, to portray, for instance a temporal relationship like marriage as anything but sordid and corrupting.

Further, the way of life which the machine imposes on us, replacing the rhythmical recurrences of Nature by mathematically identical "soulless" repetitions, has developed in us a horror of all recurrence and a corresponding obsession with novelty. The resistance of most people to poetry, the lack of interest displayed by many contemporary poets in the art of "numbers," is due, I believe, to their association of repeated pattern with all that is boring and disagreeable in their lives. Similarly, while novelty is a good—even the most traditional cultures have demanded that a work of art be in some sense "original" and not a mere copy—the idolatry of novelty is more destructive than any traditional idolatry and harder to cure. Tristan may be led to see that there is something excessive about his love for Isolde by being reminded that she will die; Don Giovanni cannot be cured in this way, because you cannot tell him that the supply of ladies will run out.

Still, Nature, however we may ignore or exploit her, is all about us, and, so long as we have bodies, however we may maltreat them, our relation to her has not been severed. The ever growing popularity of hunting, fishing, and mountain climbing are evidence of this but I am not sure that the experiences which such sports provide, precious though they may be, are, at least for poets, the most desirable. Insofar as they make the relation to Nature one of contest, the goal of which is human victory, and limit contacts with her to those of the greatest dramatic intensity, they may exacerbate rather than cure that unnatural craving for excess and novel thrills which is the characteristic urban disease. What is really needed is a much more modest, passive, and reverent kind of approach. One does not have to agree with all of his doctrines to think that Robert Graves' manual, *The White Goddess*, should be required reading for all poets.

A poet today, particularly perhaps if he is an American like Mr Hoffman, who sets out to take his themes from Nature is in a very different and much more difficult situation than a Romantic poet like, say, Wordsworth. By the end of the eighteenth century the Newtonian cosmology had destroyed the ancient beliefs in Nature as the abode of actual spirits good or bad, so that the continued use in poetry of Greek mythology had degenerated into genteel periphrasis. At the same time, life was still rural enough for men to feel instinctively that Nature was numinous. Wordsworth's achievement in poetry, parallel to that of Kant in philosophy, was to preserve the validity of this feeling by describing it, not in the traditional mythological terms, but in terms of the psychology of his time. But the poet today is faced not only with the question of contemporary expression but also with the task of recovering the feeling which he and the public have largely lost, that Nature is numinous. He has to make a much more conscious and deliberate effort. At this point I hear the Accuser adopt his "honest Iago" voice: "This is sentimental rubbish. You don't feel that Nature is holy and as a modern man you never can. Genuine art is the mirror of genuine feelings, and the only real feelings you have are of self-pity at your alienation. So be frank, be modern. Express your pity for your self in the rhythmless language really used by metropolitan man." The only way to counter this lie is to realize its half-truth, namely, that our conception of Nature cannot be that of some prescientific magician, nor our modes of poetic expression those of some agricultural community without a written literature.

Mr Hoffman has not been led astray by the Accuser. While admitting the pains and tragedies of life, he can find joy in life and say so. Nor, on the other hand, does he try to pretend to a Wordsworthian intimacy with Nature. He knows that, for any member of our urban culture, such intimacy is not given but is a prize slowly and patiently to be won: we all start as outsiders. Sometimes, as in "An Armada of Thirty Whales," he uses natural objects as heraldic symbols, but more often starts with direct observation and description. Such an approach produces, I feel, more interesting results. There is always a danger of becoming whimsical in using some animal as a symbol when you have no personal experience of it as an animal.

A number of Mr Hoffman's poems are concerned with the same kind of place, the frontier between earth and water, and with the creatures associated with it, and they are written in the same kind of meter, a loose couplet, stopped between the lines and sometimes employing internal rhymes in lieu of end rhymes; e.g.:

> All shrinks in the rage of the sun
>   save the courage of clams, and their faith:
>
> Sacrificing the water they breathe
>   seems to urge the tall moon from her orbit;
>
> she tugs ocean, cubit by cubit
>   over killdeer's kingdom
>
> and ends parched freedom.
>   Moon, with sky-arching shell
>
> and bright snout nine thousand miles long
>   and anemones in her kelp hair

that gleam in the heaven around her,
    responds with the wave of their prayers

or sucks the sea unawares.

("The Clams")

The skeptical caution of the last line seems to me right, but so does the analogy Mr Hoffman perceives between the clams and human ritual. Indeed if such
analogies are not valid, no art is possible. As Malcolm de Chazal has written:
"Symbolism was born when Adam, wishing to tell Eve with a single gesture of
the immensity of his love for her, pointed with his hand to the disk of the sun."

An Armada of Thirty Whales, by Daniel G. Hoffman, 1954

Words and Music

Rhythm and Tempo: A Study in Music. By Curt Sachs. Dent. 42s.

I cannot imagine anyone who is interested in either of the metrical arts not
being fascinated by Dr Curt Sachs' recent book: *Rhythm and Tempo: A Study
in Music History.* Immensely learned though he is, Dr Sachs has a gift for clear
exposition with which scholars are not always endowed and, except for a few
pages on Proportional Signatures which, I must confess, made my poor head
go round, the reader with only an amateur knowledge of music will find him
quite easy to follow.

To read any history of music is to be unpleasantly reminded of the fantastic narrowness of the conventional concert repertoire. Despite the curse of
Babel, it is much easier to get to know foreign and ancient literature than it
is to hear any music other than that composed in Europe after 1600. Of
course it is always *possible* that we are not missing much. Musicologists have
their own and, for them, quite proper approach to music, but it does not always coincide with the listener's. I am tantalised, for example, by the few bars
quoted by Dr Sachs from the French manneristic composers of the fourteenth century, but when I find that Dr Sachs admires Edgar Varèse's *Ionisa-
tion*, a work which I have had the misfortune to hear, I get worried.

Dr Sachs recognises two basic kinds of rhythm, divisive and additive. Divisive rhythm is based on the human stride and is therefore 2/4 or 4/4 time.
The East knows no other and cannot recognise a rhythm in triple time. Additive rhythm, which Dr Sachs believes to be associated with the "tension and
relaxation that we experience in breathing in and out," can be on the other
hand, and generally is, in triple time, for its patterns are not based on "a certain duration to be divided into equal parts, but rather a grouping composed
of longer and shorter elements, such as 2+1 or 3+2 units, or any other

arrangements of shorts and longs." In poetry the approximate equivalents are the purely accentual prosody of, say, Anglo-Saxon poetry on the one hand, and the strictly quantitative metres of Greek poetry on the other. French and Italian poetry, which reckon by the number of syllables, are, presumably, more additive than divisive. Where English poetry should be placed, which, since *Ormulum*, is composed of feet, but feet which are made by accent not by length, I am not quite sure.

In music, according to Dr Sachs, "any rhythm related to harmony must be of a divisive kind. Additive rhythm belongs to civilisations without harmony." The former he associates with classicistic cultures and a feeling in the visual arts for perspective, the latter with more other-worldly cultural phases. Thus, in the Gothic Middle Ages, ternary time and counterpoint are dominant; in the High Renaissance, 4/4 time and harmony carry all before them; since 1900, Dr Sachs sees a return to additive rhythms.

The association of accentual double time with perspective is a fascinating one, but when Dr Sachs says "Greek-Roman art took an important turn to perspective, imperfect, it is true, at the beginning of the Common Era, as evidenced in the paintings of Pompeii and Herculaneum. There is a strong possibility that the change from metre to accentual rhythm in later antiquity was a kindred phenomenon," I become suspicious. Early Latin poetry, like vulgar-spoken Latin, was an accentual tongue, upon which, during the classic period of Latin poetry, a Greek prosody was imposed. If Dr Sachs' generalisations were always true, then it would follow that in their early days, the Romans were interested in perspective: and what about the Germanic peoples who always had an accentual verse?

By the time a language can have a literature, it is more or less a fixed medium and its rhythmic possibilities are much more limited, much more resistant to cultural changes than music, so that exact parallels are difficult to draw. Compare, for instance, the influence of sixteenth-century classical humanism on music with its influence on English verse. It affected the former to such an extent that "most of the metrical songs written between 1500 and 1600 are strictly note against note and syllabic with their longs and shorts in the regular ratio 2 : 1"; but the poets like Sidney, Spenser, and Campion who, under the same influence, attempted to write in classical metres abandoned them in a few years, for it was immediately obvious that such a prosody ran counter to the nature of the English language. In comparison with music, the difference between the "freest" kind of verse line, e.g. that of Shakespeare's late blank verse, and the strictest, e.g. that of the Pope couplet, is very slight indeed.

Dr Sachs is on much safer ground, I think, in his parallels between music and architecture, e.g. when he sees in both the Gothic cathedral and the isorhythms of the thirteenth-century composers a common "spiritualisation and abstraction of tone or stone under the sign of abstract number," or the same short sudden flurry of restlessness at the beginning of the fifteenth century in Italian music and the work of Jacopo della Quercia in Bologna.

One of the many pleasures his book affords is similar to that of watching a film in which a flower grows up in a few minutes; one sees history pulsating, becoming itself rhythmical. In the fourteenth century the North is complicated, rapid, ternary in time, while Italy is slower, more lyrical, binary; the Italian style triumphs over the Northern but then, in the last third of the fifteenth century, a new, excited period returns, to be again overcome by the stateliness and binary time of the High Renaissance; by 1600 polyphony is being attacked for destroying the metrical values of words, but by 1680 the Italians are beginning to tire of *Stile Recitativo* and to prefer the Neapolitan *da capo* aria; in the same century ternary time predominates over binary; in 1700 Italy is the home of *cantabile*, expressiveness and wide tempo range, while Germany is the home of polyphony and moderate tempi, but by 1750 the positions are reversed; the dynamism of Baroque music shows itself in its fondness for entrances on an upbeat, the elegance of Rococo music in its reluctance to approach a note directly and its tendency, particularly in France, to dotted notes, i.e. to lengthening the "good" notes and shortening the "bad"; and so it goes on.

I hope Dr Sachs will forgive me if I now give up trying to review his excellent book, and concern myself with a problem, which is not his subject, but which his book necessarily raises, namely the relation between musical rhythm and verse rhythm, a relation which is of importance to anyone, who, like myself, is interested in the musical setting of words. I must, of course, confine myself to the English language.

Rhythm and Measurement

On page 68 Dr Sachs makes a statement which amazes me because it seems to run contrary to the whole argument of his book:

> Philologists have been asking why rhythmical poetry, as opposed to music, is allowed to violate the evidently fundamental quality of all rhythm: the exactly equal distance between stimuli or groups of stimuli.

This assumption is utterly false. It is a fundamental law of rhythm, as of any æsthetic quality, that it is *perceptible* but *not* mathematically measurable. If the distance between stimuli were *exactly* equal, there would be no rhythm whatsoever, any more than there is in the noise of a road drill. Rhythm is to time what symmetry is to space. We call the human face symmetrical—two eyes at equal distance from the nose, two ears at the same level, etc.—and in books on anatomical proportions mathematical norms are given, but any face in which the symmetry were really mathematically exact, in which, for instance, the two eyes were *identically* the same size and shape, would appear to us, not as a face, but as a lifeless mask.

It certainly looks, at first sight, as if musical rhythm was based on identity. On paper, if one is given the metronome marking, all quarter notes are identical in length, but if the work could be played, which is doubtful, exactly as it appears on paper, it would not sound rhythmical but mechanical like a musical box. The reason why this fact is so easy to see in verse and so difficult to see in music is, probably, because in music there are so many other variables like pitch, volume, colour, the range in permissible "rubato" beyond which a rhythmical pattern becomes unrecognisable, is so much narrower in the latter art. In a line of verse like Prior's

The gōd. | ŏf ŭs vērse | mĕn, yŏu knōw, | chĭld, thĕ sūn

the unaided human ear can perceive the difference in exact length between the two similar rhythmical units *the god of* and *you know, child,* while it would probably take a very sensitive instrument to detect the bar to bar variations in a performance of a Mozart symphony.

Music and Verse Quantity

Though neither musical nor verse rhythm are based on identities, the differences between them are so great as to make it impossible to express one in terms of the other. If this has not always been clear, the probable reason is that most primitive poetry is not spoken but chanted or recited to a musical accompaniment. When Plato laid down the rule that "Rhythm and harmony are regulated by the words, and not the words by them," he was really only objecting to a style of music in which the distortion of verbal rhythm by musical rhythm was greater than he was accustomed to. Indeed it is difficult to see how the basic principle of quantitative prosody, namely, that all syllables may be divided into long and short, the former being twice as long as the latter, could have been arrived at except through music for, even in a language with little accent like Greek, it would be obvious in speaking that all long and all short syllables were not the same length. It is only by singing them that they can be made to appear so.

If one asks, for example, why the *ā* in *fāther* is called long and the *ă* in *făthom* is called short, one cannot help noticing that it is much easier to sustain a note on the first than on the second.

Tempo in Music and Verse

Dr Sachs tells us the tempo range in music from Adagio to Prestissimo is about 1 : 4. Taking the Nightmare Song from *Iolanthe* as an example of a verse Prestissimo, and *Tears, idle tears* as an Adagio, I find that, in a given period, I recite about twice as many syllables of the former as of the latter. However, much of this difference is due, not to a faster delivery of the syllables themselves, but to the absence of rests, of the cæsuras I make in the Tennyson. The widest tempo range in verse, that is, is less than 1 : 2.

Further, this range lies in the rapid half of the musical tempi. Thus, if I recite a hymn at the pace at which it is normally sung, the verse rhythm disappears. The iambs of *Now Thank we all our God*, for instance, turn into spondees, the dactyls of *Sun of my soul* into molossoi.

The slowest tempo at which it is possible to take spoken verse is, musically, an Allegretto.

Quantitative and Accentual Feet

I am not sure that Dr Sachs is fully aware of how completely different a rhythmical significance the prosodic terms dactyl, anapæst, trochee, iamb, have in an accentual prosody from that they have in a quantitative. In this he is not alone; the medieval composers who were setting accentual Church Latin, continued to scan it as if it were Vergil.

Thus Dr Sachs believes that dactyls and anapæsts are in binary time, trochees and iambs in ternary. So they are in classical Greek and Latin, but in an accentual tongue like English, the exact opposite is the case: it is the trochees and iambs that are in binary time.

To demonstrate this, let me take the musical examples given on pp. 22–23 of Dr Sach's book and try fitting English words to them.

Ex. 2. Beethoven. Seventh Symphony. Slow movement.

Musically and quantitatively, this is, as Dr Sachs says, an adonic. But when I try to sing to it an English adonic, e.g. *beau-ti-ful | ball-pen*, the second beat of the bar confers too much accent on the *ti*. the nearest approximation I can find makes the first foot a bacchic, e.g. *Come, come a | way, dear.*

Ex. 4. Beethoven. Ninth Symphony. Scherzo.

Quantitatively, cyclic dactyls. But this time there is an excess of accent on the third syllable, so that the accentual dactyl *beautiful* becomes a cretic, *beau-ti-ful.* Actually, in this case, it is not the temporal value of the notes themselves that is at fault, but the rest: had the phrase been repeated without interruption, English dactyls could be sung to it.

Ex. 5. Bach. Brandenburg Concerto #3

Anapæsts, says Dr Sachs; so I try

The Assyr | ian came down | like a wolf | on the fold

and the music makes it sound like this, a set of cretics.

The Ăssȳr | iăn cáme dōwn | lĭke ă wōlf | ōn thĕ fōld.

Ex. 6. Brahms. Deutsches Requiem. Second movement.

Iambs to Dr Sachs. But set to it

Mў mō- | thĕr grōaned, | mў fā- | thĕr wēpt

and the accented syllables are dragged out to a disproportionate length. On the other hand, if I turn the half notes into quarters, the Byron anapæsts, which would not go with the previous example, go very nicely.

Finally, an example of my own. Bach. Fugue in G minor.

Dr Prout, the famous Victorian organist, composed words for this which are prosodically admirable

Ō | Ē -bĕ- | nē-zĕr | Prōut
Yŏu | are ă | fŭn-nȳ | mān;
Yŏu-oŭ | makē | Bāch fūgues
Jŭst ăs | sīl -lȳ | as yŏu | căn.

From this I conclude:

1. An exact identity of English verse rhythms and musical rhythms is impossible.

2. In setting accentual verse, the distortion is least when accented syllables are allotted to down-beats, unaccented to up-beats.

3. The approximate musical values of the commonest English feet are as follows. The tempo in all cases is an Allegro.

Iamb

Anapæst

Cyclic Anapæst

(E.g. *Beggar's Opera*: "*How happy could I be with either.*")

Apt Distortion

Because some distortion is inevitable, it does not follow that the composer is free to ignore the verbal prosody altogether, nor that he is bound at all times to adopt the most "natural" method, setting all iambic verse in binary time and all anapæstic in ternary. An apt setting of a line is one which achieves a just balance between its rhythm and its content. In English verse, with its large number of common syllables, it is often impossible to know the correct scansion of a line without knowing its context, and the sense of the words is often that which settles rival claims. E.g.

> Come away, come away, death,
>   And in sad cypress let me be laid;
> Fly away, fly away, breath:
>   I am slain by a fair cruel maid.

The fourth line of this can only be scanned as anapæsts.

Ĭ ă̄m slāin | bў ă fāir | crŭ-ĕl māid

But lines one and three could, in theory, be scanned in three ways:
As anapæsts

Cŏme ă-wāy, | cŏme ă-wāy, | dēath

As trochees with catalexis

Cōme ă- | wāy, | cōme ă- | wāy, | dēath

As dactyls

Cōme ă-wăy, | cōme ă-wăy, | dēath

In fact, however, the first alternative, which is the one Dr Sachs chooses, is impossible, because the spacing of the unaccented and accented syllables will make the line sound, spoken or sung, like an impatient nursemaid calling a disobedient child. (Had the line run

Cŏme ă-wāy, | cŏme ă-wāy | tŏ the fīelds | ănd the wōods

an anapæstic scansion, on the other hand, would be the only possible one.) A composer could, I believe, use the second scansion, if it suited him; but the third scansion is the only possible one for speaking.

In *Dido and Æneas* occurs the following couplet:

> Fear no danger to ensue,
> The hero loves as well as you

If nothing but the rhythm be considered, the aptest setting would be to some four-four tune like Tallis' Canon, but the result would be lacking in the martial vigour which the meaning of the words requires. Purcell, accordingly, sets it to a syncopated 3/4 time, thus

♩	♩ ♩	♩	♩ ♩	♩ ♩	♩.
The	he - ro	loves as	well as	you.

Substitute a heroine for a hero and the syncopation might seem out of place, and more fitting a straightforward waltz time, thus

The | la - dy | loves | her | faith - ful | swain.

English Verse and Additive Rhythms

In so far that English feet are based on accent not length, and that the predominant rhythm in English verse is iambic (musically, that is, in binary time), one must class its poetic rhythms as divisive.

The language, however, permits certain licences which often give an additive effect. Inversion of an iamb into a trochee has always been permitted and, except between 1700 and 1780, the substitution of trisyllabic feet, limited only by the proviso that the underlying iambic basis must not be destroyed; further, unlike French verse, English verse not only permits but prefers a constant shift in position of the cæsura from line to line.

> He ended, and the heav'nly Audience loud
> Sung Halleluia, as the sound of seas,
> Through multitude that sung. Just are thy ways,
> Righteous are thy decrees on all thy Works;
> Who can extenuate thee? Next, to the Son,
> Destined restorer of Mankind, by whom
> New Heav'n and Earth shall to the Ages rise,
> Or down from Heav'n descend.
>
>   (*Paradise Lost.* Book X.)

It would be very difficult, if the fifth line of this passage were quoted by itself, to guess that the base is iambic, for, if it be read in strict conformity with its norm, the result is a monstrosity.

Who *căn* | ĕxtēn | wăte thēe? | Nĕxt *tō* | thē Sōn

It can, however, be read naturally and its variations explained.

Whō căn | ĕx-tēn- | ŭ-ăte thēe | ? Nēxt | tŏ thē Sōn

First foot. Inversion. Trochee for iamb.
Second foot. Iamb.
Third foot. Substitution. Anapæst for iamb.
Fourth foot. Catalectic iamb. The "rest" of the cæsura replacing the unaccented syllable.
Fifth foot. Substitution. Anapæst for iamb.

This is an extreme case, but in even the most "regular" verse, the emphasis on the accented syllables varies, so that one of them very often almost becomes unaccented, e.g. in the second line of

> Those ghosts of beauty ling'ring there abide
> And haunt the places where their honour died.
>
>   (Pope.)

the accent of *where* is very nearly suppressed, making the iamb *-es where* almost a pyrrhic.

The effect, in the Milton passage, of the constant cæsura shift is to provide two sets of foot groupings: on the one hand there is the recurrent symmetrical grouping by line—5 : 5 : 5 : 5 . . . ; on the other asymmetrical grouping by pause—$1\frac{1}{2} : 3\frac{1}{2} + 2\frac{1}{2} : 2\frac{1}{2} : 3 : 2 : 3 : 2 : 4 : 1 + 2 : 3$.

That is enough, or more than enough, for now. No quarrels are as bitter as those of persons whose prosodic theories differ: I like to think this testifies to the interest of the subject.

Encounter, January 1954

A Message from W. H. Auden

The first and most fundamental duty of the poet is, I believe, to praise what is excellent. In a technological civilization such as ours this is not easy for, while in earlier times excellence could be married to power, today the machine has utterly estranged them from each other.

Dylan Thomas, however, to a greater degree, perhaps, than most of his contemporaries, was faithful to this duty. The excellence of which he had so clear and rich a vision was the magical world of childhood, that Eden in which man and nature are united in innocence and love, and to the celebration of its joys he devoted all his genius. How triumphantly he succeeded, those—and they are fortunately many—who have read his work, know well and will be grateful in that knowledge all their lives long.

New York, January 1954

Souvenir programme booklet for *Homage to Dylan Thomas*,
Globe Theatre, London, 24 January 1954

A Contemporary Epic

The Anathemata. By David Jones. Faber & Faber. 25s.

Am I dotty? For some fifteen years now Mr David Jones has made me ask myself this question. When *In Parenthesis* came out in 1938, I thought it—I think so still—the greatest book about the First World War that I had read. But nobody seemed to notice or write about it. Having lived with *The Anathemata* for the last ten months, I feel as certain as one can feel of anything that it is one of the most important poems of our time. But where are the bells? Where are the cannon? I have given it to friends whose literary taste I have always found reliable (true, they are Americans), and they seem to be completely baffled by it. I cannot, therefore, write an evaluatory review, for that presupposes, or should presuppose, that the public are well acquainted with the text: I can only attempt to describe the sort of poem it is, the sort of thing I believe Mr Jones is trying to do. Let us consider the style first.

Before the drift
          was over the life-face.
Sometime between the final and the penultimate débâcle.
          (Already Arcturus deploys his reconnoitering chills in
     greater strength: soon his last *Putsch* on any scale.)
Before this all but proto-historic transmogrification of the land-face.
Just before they rigged the half-lit stage for dim-eyed Clio to step with
     some small confidence the measures of her brief and lachrymal pavan.

                              ★   ★   ★

                              Plucked with his jack bucket from
the Punic foreshore b' a bollocky great Bocco procurer, or I weren't christed Elen Monica in Papey Juxta Muram. 'V'a mind to sign him Austin Gregorians in Thames-water, an' ransom him with m'own woman's body.

                              ★   ★   ★

          Within, with lights brighted
                    under the dressed beam
     all can eat the barley-cake
     and sisters dear
                    may plait him bearded
     for their hair
     and all can sing:
                    Fol the dol the didiay
     but he
                    he must be broken off at knee.
     Within, in the lighted *sacellum*
     as yet the *signum*
                    shorn soon
                    draggled at Black Fosse
                    lopped at the *agger*
     stands dressed—reg'mental
                    and the binding *sacramentum*
     is reaffirmed upon it.

> Down the traversed history-paths
> > his stumbling *Grenadiere*
> in the communication-ways
> > his burdened infants
> shall learn like vows to take.

Joyce certainly, and Dante probably, have had a hand in Mr Jones' development, but his style is in no sense an imitation. Nor is this verse as "free" as at a superficial glance it looks. Mr Jones is not a Welshman for nothing. Welsh poetry is famous for its use of internal rhyme and assonance, and a careful examination of the last quotation, for example, will disclose similar subtleties. Like Joyce, Mr Jones uses a very wide vocabulary; like Joyce and Dante his poem is full of riddles which require considerable erudition to solve: unlike Joyce and Dante, however, he accompanies his text with his own commentary notes. In his introduction he says: "I ask the reader, *when actually engaged upon the text*, to consult these glosses mainly or only on points of pronunciation. For other purposes they should be read separately." Speaking for myself, I can only say that I have frequently found this advice impossible to follow. When the riddles depend on geological knowledge, I can solve them as I read, but when I come to such lines as the following about Abraham and Isaac

> Take the lamb that you do love
> > — his mother's boy
> get north-east by north
> > by way of Liknites' cave of bread, past anemone-
> dell where poor Ishtar is a-weeping in the burning sun of day
> > where her precious
> bloods the flowery carpet she shall kneel
> > at the turn of the hog-track.

to me they are nonsense poetry like Edward Lear's, until I consult the accompanying note:

> . . . To get to it [Mount Moriah] from Beersheba one would, and the ancient track did, go via Bethlehem (House of Bread, or with equal significance *Beit Laham*, House of Flesh), a place sacred to Adonis for whom *Es Sitt*, "the lady" (in this case Ishtar), weeps. The anemones in part of Palestine are still said to be red with his blood that was shed by the boar's tusks. The name Liknites was applied to Dionysius and other cult-figures and could signify "crib-born".

Once I have been informed, the lines not only cease to be nonsense, but become right and inevitable. My own advice to a reader, therefore, would be to read a section the first time very slowly, consulting *every* note, and then a second time without looking at one.

T. S. Eliot, Marianne Moore, William Empson (and Coleridge one might add) have supplied notes to their poems, but none of them to anything like the same degree as David Jones, and *The Anathemata* raises as never before the question whether a poem can be good which cannot be understood without them. One must begin by distinguishing between riddle which is, I believe, a fundamental element in poetry, and obscurity, which is an æsthetic vice. Every crossword-puzzle addict (it is curious that it should so often be precisely he who objects most violently to puzzles in poetry) knows the difference: when, having failed to get a word, he looks at the answer next week, he says either "What a fool I was. Of course that's it," or "The clue was unfair. Four or five other words would fit it equally well."

Yet the same man, when he comes to a line in a poem which he finds difficult, is apt to accuse the poet of making fun of him out of conceit, of sneering at his lack of knowledge or sensibility, when, in fact, the poet is only trying to give him fun. If a poet hesitates to add an explanatory note, his hesitation often arises from the same neighbourly feeling which restrains a man, looking over the shoulder of a fellow clubman as he does his weekly crossword, from telling him the answers. To be laughed at for not knowing something is not nearly so insulting as having one's ignorance falsely assumed and being informed of what one knows already.

While the riddle element has always existed in poetry, the disappearance of a homogeneous society with a common cult, a common myth, common terms of reference, has created difficulties in communication for the poet which are historically new and quite outside his control. The poet—and each one of his readers—is a particular man; none of them can become a generalised type. As Mr Jones says in his introduction:

> The poet may feel something with regard to Penda the Mercian and nothing with regard to Darius the Mede. In itself that is a limitation, it might be regarded as a disproportion; no matter, there is no help—he must work within the limits of his love. There must be no mugging-up, no "ought to know" or "try to feel"; for only what is actually loved and known can be seen *sub specie aeternitatis*. The muse herself is adamant about this: she is indifferent to what the poet may wish he could feel, she cares only for what he in fact feels.

The question then arises whether a reader is entitled to retort: "It so happens that Darius means a lot to me and Penda nothing. I can only read about what I love and know."

If, as I believe, the reader is not entitled to this retort, it is because of a fundamental difference between the imaginative activity of making and that of reading. If the poet can only make a living work out of what he knows and loves, it is only a living work that the reader can, and with much less difficulty than one might suppose, translate and understand in terms of his own, different yet analogous, love and knowledge. The Darius-loving reader is able to see his hero in the poet's Penda because, and only because, the latter is a creation of love.

This applies not only to the subject of a poem as a whole but also to every detail in it.

> The words "May they rest in peace" and the words "Whosoever will" might, by some feat of artistry, be so juxtaposed within a context as not only to translate the words "Requiescat in pace" and "Quicunque vult" but to evoke the *exact historic over-tones and under-tones* of those Latin words. But should some writer find himself unable by whatever ingenuity of formal arrangement of contextual allusion to achieve this identity of content and identity of evocation, while changing the language, then he would have no alternative but to use the original form . . . , it is not a question of "translation" or even of "finding an equivalent word," it is something much more complex. "Tsar" will mean one thing and "Caesar" another to the end of time.

To return to my American friends who have such difficulty in "getting" *The Anathemata*, their problem is not, I think, the introduction of strange historical proper names or the employment of foreign words, but the fact that what Mr Jones calls "The Break," which occurred in Europe towards the end of the nineteenth century as a result of the technological revolution, occurred in America when the *Mayflower* landed on its shores. It would have made little difference if the first settlers had been Catholics instead of Protestants; they were faced with a continent with which the gods and goddesses of pre-Christian Europe had no relation, and too late in time for there to be any Christian absorption of whatever Indian myths there may have been. As an epigraph for his poem, Mr Jones might have put "Behold, I make all things new"; i.e. his attitude is very different from that expressed by Milton in his Nativity Ode, in which one consequence of the Incarnation is that, somewhat to the poet's regret, the mythological gods, the household spirits, the local geniuses are once and for all abolished: for Mr Jones the consequence is not their abolition but their redemption; when the Word is made Flesh a possibility of redemption is offered to all speech and to all bodies, to both the natural and the historical order (which is why the elements offered in the Mass are not corn and grape-juice but bread and wine, the product of human work). But on the North American continent there was neither a Nature nor a History to be redeemed from magic and idolatry; Nature in America was from the beginning what it had only lately become in Europe, naked, faceless, "unnuminous" Force, Henry Adams' Dynamo. The patron saint of the Italian island where I am writing this review is a lady whom I strongly suspect of having once had a tail and who is apt to send a sirocco whenever the Madonna has a feast; the Madonna of an American Catholic has never had such a rival.

Communication between persons with "unshared Backgrounds" is always possible if they have had analogous experiences—Welsh mythology, for example, is not one of my own "deposits," but thanks to other mythologies which are, I have little difficulty in acquiring it from the poet: but I can see that, for someone to whom *all* myths are stories mugged up at school from Bullfinch, very serious difficulties must arise. Since, however, everyone has, at least in his childhood, inhabited a magic mythological universe, I do not believe that difficulty means impossibility; the problem for an American or for most young townspeople today anywhere is how they are to recognise their own private and contemporary signs for such a world in Mr Jones's historic signs.

The Anathemata is not an easy poem to describe. Imagine that, in the middle of the twentieth century, in a world of atom-bombs, posters, and gossip-columnists, a man is attending Mass. This man is Adam, a European, a Welshman, a Londoner, a poet, himself. Some phrase or other from the rite catches his attention and his mind goes wool-gathering. And why not? Is not the rite he is attending itself a rite of anamnesis? The language sounding now in his physical ear is remote from the present age, formal, humourless, the creation of a vanished kind of society. The anathemata he thinks about,

> the blessed things that have taken on what is cursed and the profane things that somehow are redeemed: the delights and also the "ornaments" . . . things dedicated after whatever fashion . . . things . . . that partake of the extra-utile and of the gratuitous; things that are the signs of something other . . . signs that . . . are themselves . . . what they signify.

all belong to the remote past—none of them is younger than the Roman Empire—but the language in which he thinks about them is the complex, ironical, historically conscious, informal language of our own time.

His wool-gatherings are divided into eight heaps, which, with childish crudeness, I should describe as follows:

(1) *Rite and Fore-Time.* Pre-history. The fashioning of the continents. The appearance of Nature's "adaptable, rational, elect and plucked out otherling." His earliest magical and artistic factures.

(2) *Middle-Sea and Lear-Sea.* The rise of coherent cultures, e.g. the Bronze Age culture of the Mediterranean and its diffusion by maritime trade.

(3) *Angle-Land.* The appearance of the Englishman as the result of a cross between Celtic and Teutonic stocks.

(4) *Redriff.* I am not sure what this is about. The Norse Invasions?

(5) *The Lady of the Pool.* The founding of London, of the English polis. The taking of "barbaric" Britain into the Roman civitas.

(6) *Keel, Ram, Stauros.* A very difficult section. I *think* it is about the conversion of Britain by Christian missionaries; the planting on her shores of the Cross.

(7) *Mabinog's Liturgy.* The coming of the God-Man in the fullness of time.

(8) *Sherthursdaye and Venus Day.* The redemption of time by His sacrifice.

Mr Jones has set out to write a poem which should be at once epic, contemporary, and Christian. It would be interesting, on another occasion, to compare *The Anathemata* with another poem which is epic and contemporary, but religiously excludes any religious references whatsoever, St Jean Perse's *Vents.* Something has already been said about the problems of a contemporary epic; the peculiar and paradoxical relation, for a poet who is a Christian, between his art and his faith raises all kinds of other fascinating questions. Is all "Christian" poetry, for example, necessarily and profoundly, a joke? Is it possible, in poetry, to speak of God the Father without making him indistinguishable from Zeus, or of God the Son without making him into another culture-hero like Dionysus or Hercules? If it is not possible, does it matter? But a review is not the place to discuss such matters. I can only conclude by reiterating my profound admiration for this work and expressing the hope that many others will come to share it.

Encounter, February 1954

The Man Who Wrote *Alice*

The Diaries of Lewis Carroll. Edited and supplemented by Roger
Lancelyn Green. Oxford University Press. 2 vols. $8.50.

These volumes give us Charles Dodgson's account of his whole life from his becoming a fellow of Christ Church at the age of twenty-three until his death at the age of sixty-five, with the exception of part of the summer of 1867 (when he visited Russia), the last three months of '55 and the years '58 to mid-'62 (the journals for which are lost). He did not write them with an eye to publication or treat them as a private confessional, and, to be frank, I think only the most devoted Lewis Carroll fans—luckily, there are many thousands of us—will be able to get through them for, considered simply as a diary, it is probably the dullest ever published.

Roger Green has done his best, by adding explanatory comments, quotations from letters, reminiscences by others and seventeen of Dodgson's magnificent portrait photographs: this editorial material is inserted into the original text in the same size of type, separated from it only by brackets which one frequently overlooks, but, since it is usually more interesting than the text, this procedure seems to me justified.

Mr Green tells us that he has cut nothing of importance but he reproduces a facsimile page from the diaries which he has cut in his text, containing observations about visual perception which are more interesting than much which he has retained. I would rather hear about Dodgson's mathematical concerns, assuming that he entered them in his diary, than about all those farces he went to see. Or to learn that, after the performance of *Il Flauto Magico* which he attended, the national anthem was played.

I would go even further, personally, since I share the same obsessions, and say that I would rather know, for example, the departure hour of the Oxford-Paddington express in the Sixties, or the temperature in Dodgson's rooms on any one day, than be told that he was glad to have the opportunity of discussing slavery with a slave-holder without being told what either party said.

Despite all this, Lewis Carroll so fascinates me, that I have enjoyed reading every word. July 4th is as memorable a day in the history of literature as it is in American history; Dodgson's entry for that date in the year 1862 runs as follows:

> Atkinson brought over to my rooms some friends of his, a Mrs and Miss Peters of whom I took photographs, and who afterwards looked over my album and stayed to lunch. They then went off to the Museum, and Duckworth and I made an expedition *up* the river to Godstow with the three Liddells: we had tea on the bank there, and did not reach Christ Church again till quarter past eight, when we took them to my rooms to see my collection of micro-photographs and restored them to the Deanery just before nine.

That is all, yet it was on that afternoon picnic that he composed, extempore, the greater part of what is now acknowledged the world over to be a masterpiece. That we possess *Alice in Wonderland* at all must be ascribed to Divine Providence, for, had the break between Dodgson and Mrs Liddell occurred before instead of just after that date, the picnic would probably never have taken place. On Oct. 28 of the same year Dodgson writes: "I have been out of her good graces ever since Lord Newry's business" (nobody seems to know what that was); on Nov. 13: "Returning to Christ Church I found Ina, Alice and Edith in the quadrangle, and had a little talk with them—a rare event of late. Began writing the fairy-tale for Alice." After that he records only one happy reunion, and then comes this sad entry.

> May 12, 1864. During these last few days I have applied in vain for leave to take the children on the river; i.e. Alice, Edith and Rhoda: but Mrs Liddell will not let any come in future—rather superfluous caution.

Mrs Liddell was not to be the only mother with whom he would have trouble:

Brought in "Atty" Owen and her little brother, to wait in my rooms until Owen was at leisure. She does not look 14 yet, and when, having kissed her at parting, I learned (from Owen) that she is 17, I was astonished, but I don't think either of us was much displeased at the mistake having been made! Wrote a mock apology to Mrs Owen, assuring her that the incident has been "as distressing to her daughter as it was to myself"! but adding that I would kiss her no more. (The next day). Mrs Owen treats the matter quite seriously! She adds "we shall take care it does not recur."

Whether these Victorian mammas had any justification for their suspicions or not—his fondness for photographing little girls in the nude at least makes them understandable—is no business of ours, beyond hoping, for his sake, that they had none. For a man with as strict a conscience as Dodgson, to be the innocent victim of suspicion would be painful enough but, if he were in the slightest degree guilty, he must have suffered tortures.

To write so unique a book as *Alice in Wonderland* is astonishing enough, but to write a second one which is, if possible, even better seems miraculous. *Alice Through the Looking-Glass*, unlike its predecessor, was no extempore work but took Dodgson more than two years to write and between the day when the last line of *The Hunting of the Snark* came into his head and his completion of the poem lay some eighteen months.

Though he met a great many people, he seems to have had few close adult friends, but among them was that saintly character and now shamefully neglected writer George Macdonald. Dodgson stuttered, he was a boring lecturer, he was always complaining about the College servants and at Common Room meetings, if one was on the other side in an issue, he must have been extremely tiresome, as one can imagine from such an entry as: "One regrettable change was made—the substitution of The Sunday Times (said to be a disreputable paper) for The Observer."

Irene Vanbrugh, who met him when she was a child actress, even thought that, though he had a great love for children, he did not understand them very well, and one can believe, after reading Miss Edith Olivier's vivid description of him, that the more unruly kind of child might feel ill at ease with his little orderly manias:

Dinner was at seven, and at half past six, he always appeared at St Hugh's to walk with me to Christ Church. The walk took exactly half an hour, and at the end of the evening, my host timed our return to St Hugh's to synchronize with the ringing of the ten-thirty bell, in the passages. . . . The food was always the same. Only two courses—first, some well-cooked mutton chops, and then, meringues. A glass or two of port followed, and, an hour after dinner, we had tea. Mr Dodgson never spoke of *Alice in Wonderland*; but there were three other things in his life of which he seemed really proud. He spoke of them every time we had dinner together. They were his kettle, his logic, and his photographs.

Was this strange man happy? His diaries do not say; they only tell of a regular, busy life, teaching, engaging in university controversies, arguing with the illustrators of his books, attending the theatre and opera, inventing cyphers, new croquet games, a substitute for gum, a method of controlling the traffic at Covent Garden, binding books after removing their objectionable pages and so on, nothing, that is, to indicate that their writer was a genius but, for us, who know that he was, such reticence is itself a fascination.

The New York Times Book Review, 28 February 1954

Handbook to Antiquity

Ancilla to Classical Reading. By Moses Hadas.
Columbia University Press. $4.75.

Though the number of college students studying Greek and Latin is still, I understand, on the decline, there are some indications that the great wave of reaction against a Classical education and all the cultural attitudes that went with it, is already beginning to slacken. However much some of us may have deplored it, we must admit, I think, that this reaction was inevitable and, in some respects, even salutary.

Until the break-up of Christendom into national states at the end of the middle ages, Latin was the international language for theology, law, medicine and every intellectual activity, and learning it, therefore, as vocational an education for the "clerk" as learning to guide a plough was for the serf or learning to handle weapons was for the feudal knight. The Classics, i.e. the literature of ancient Greece and Rome as a special and superior culture, the ideal model to which all culture worth the name must try to approximate, was a discovery of the Renaissance at the same time that, for practical purposes, Latin was beginning to be displaced by national vernaculars. A Classical education, therefore, became "polite learning," the proper training for a young gentleman who would not have to earn his living but would be expected to take his place in society and the government of his country. The contemporary atmosphere makes this view so strange that one is apt to forget how recently it was held. When I first went to school, all there was a Classical side and a Modern side; while all "modern" subjects were regarded as inferior, mathematics and history were just respectable, but the sciences, comprehensively known as "Stinks," were outside the pale, fit only for board school boys and boys who were going into "trade." Even when I was an undergraduate, the allotment of marks in the Civil Service examinations were so weighted in favor of those with a classical education that a candidate who had not taken Mods and Greats would have to be exceptionally brilliant to succeed. It is right, though easy, to laugh at such snobbery, so long as we remain dissatisfied with what has taken its place. There are a number of careers— that of the politician is one—for which no kind of formal education is clearly vocational and for which, therefore, the accepted kind will always remain to some degree a social convention. In the States, for instance, the conventional choice is the study of law, but it is permissible to doubt whether a Senate or a House of Representatives composed of lawyers is necessarily a wiser and more efficient body than it would be if composed of Classics majors. Further, even in the case of professions like medicine or engineering, where the nature of the vocational training required is obvious, there is considerable evidence that an exclusively vocational education does not produce the best results. The Bell Telephone Co., for example, is now experimenting with a course in the humanities for its most promising young executives, because its experience has been that a bright young man who has only studied engineering goes ahead very quickly at first but reaches the limit of his capacities around forty, while one who has had a good general education in addition to training in his special field continues to develop.

Since words and numbers are the two media of human thinking, without a proper training in language and mathematics no man, however intelligent, can think clearly and communicate his thoughts accurately. An old reactionary like myself ascribes the general deterioration in the handling of the English language during the past twenty years—a deterioration which few will deny—to the abandonment of the teaching of Latin and Greek in schools, since he believes that there is no better way of learning to use one's native tongue than the practise of translation out of and into languages which are completely different in their structure. I am under no illusions that a restoration of the dead languages to the normal school curriculum will happen in my lifetime, but some day—who knows?

In the meantime the appearance of new and excellent translations from the classics—many of them in pocket book editions—of books on classical mythology and archaeology for the general reader, and a book like this *Ancilla* by Mr Hadas, testify to a revival of interest in the cultures of Greece and Rome which is most encouraging. The abandonment of the Classics as the conventional "paideia" for the ruling class at least enables us to look at the classics with fresh eyes and not through the spectacles of our own cultural prejudices: we are less tempted than our fathers to see Cicero, for instance, as a Gladstonian Liberal or Plato as a German professor. Further, since we are not limited by the needs of a curriculum, we are free to study the period or figure who catches our interest, archaic sculpture rather than Pheidias, Ionia rather than Athens, the Silver poets rather than the Augustans, etc.

Though it is true, as Mr Hadas says, that "With the Greeks we feel an immediate kinship, and in their works we recognise the cultural stream in which
we ourselves move and live. Greek literature is European in a sense in which
its Near Eastern predecessors are not", I think that the chief difference between the attitude of our time towards both Greece and Rome and that of
the nineteenth century is that we—Nietzsche is our spiritual father in this respect—are much more conscious of the difference between the Ancients and
ourselves, of how strange, almost incomprehensible, their ways of thinking
often are to us, so that when Mr Hadas says that a Greek author "offers no
greater obstacles to understanding than does a modern French or Russian
author" I cannot follow him and would cite his own book as evidence to the
contrary.

Let me give an example. Though written literature comes into existence
very early, and though by the Hellenistic period there were large libraries and
a kind of literary scholarship which seems very similar to our own, it was not
till the final days of the Roman empire, as proved St Augustine's surprise
when he saw St Ambrose doing it, that reading in our sense, silently by eye,
was thought of. The lack of subjectivity which this implies, is something we
can hardly imagine.

The second part of *The Ancilla* is mainly devoted to literary gossip and
brings out in an unexpected way the gulf between the classical sensibility and
our own. For, though the malice and envy are, of course, the same, the kind
of story by which they are expressed are not. The kind of gossip which interests us most involves a paradoxical relation between the outer and the inner,
the public life and the private, e.g. that a famous philanthropist undertips
waitresses or that a writer who advocates free love in his books has never
looked at any woman but his wife. The typical gossip of the Ancients was the
reverse of this; most of their stories, true or false, assert an identity; Euripides who wrote in his plays about conjugal unhappiness was unhappy at home;
the hedonist philosopher Epicurus was a drunkard, and so on.

In the first part of his book Mr Hadas gives us, among many other things,
an excellent and succinct summary of Greek theories concerning the function of art and its relation to the good life; what makes these theories, even
Aristotle's, so bewildering to us is that, while the arguments are logical, the
underlying presuppositions are those of a magical culture in which name and
thing, visible beauty and invisible goodness are identical, and the concept of
analogy in the modern sense is unknown. Plato may hold that finite material
beauty is an imperfect copy of the ideal good, but the former is of the same
order; he who perceives a beautiful thing has thereby a direct knowledge of
goodness. For the same reason no Greek could have conceived of a plain Narcissus who fell in love with his reflection not because it was beautiful but because it was his, or of an unfortunate man becoming guilty of hybris.

I mention such matters because, light in tone and agreeable to browse in, as the *Ancilla* is, it is never trivial but is always forcing one to think. When one is tired of thinking, however, there is always some odd piece of information to amuse one; indeed I cannot imagine a more useful addition to the libraries both of those who compose cross-word puzzles and of those who solve them. Here you will discover, for instance, who it was:

Who made the first library catalogue.
Who made the first critical edition of an author.
Who was the first aggressive low-brow.
Who was the first psychiatrist.
Who was the first playwright to direct his plays.
Who was the first to give a grant for scientific research.
Who was the first to hire salaried state teachers.
Who died in a fit of temper at losing his luggage.

While those who think literary follies are something confined to the avant-garde of our age, the following information may come as something of a disappointment.

Tryphiodorus wrote a "lipogrammatic" Odyssey; that is, the poem was rewritten so that in each book the use of the letter by which the book was numbered was avoided: there was no alpha in Book I, no beta in Book II, and so on.

The Griffin, March 1954

A Consciousness of Reality

A Writer's Diary. By Virginia Woolf. Harcourt, Brace. $5.

It is, probably, already too late to hope that someone will write a definitive history of Bloomsbury, that fascinating cultural milieu which formed itself around 1910, exercised its greatest influence during the twenties, and came to an end with the death of Virginia Woolf. There is an excellent account of the intellectual influences from which it was born in a posthumous essay by Maynard Keynes; for its later history we shall have to rely upon the memoirs of David Garnett, which are now appearing in England, and the journals of Virginia Woolf, of which *A Writer's Diary* is, we hope, only the first installment.

Bloomsbury was not a "school" in any literary sense—there is no common Bloomsbury style or subject—nor was it centered on any one salon, like the Holland House set of the nineteenth century, or the Garsington set, to which many of its members also belonged. It included novelists, critics, painters, college dons but, curiously, no important poet (if one counts Virginia Woolf as a novelist) or composer. Nearly all its members had been to Cambridge and came from distinguished upper-middle-class families; i.e. without being aristocrats or large landowners, they were accustomed to efficient servants, first-rate meals, good silver and linen, and weekends in country houses. In rebellion against the rhetoric and conventional responses of their Victorian parents, hating dogma, ritual, and hypocritical expressions of unreal feelings, they, nevertheless, inherited from the Victorians a self-discipline and fastidiousness that made bohemian disorder impossible. "I have," writes Virginia Woolf—and most of them could have written the same—"an internal, automatic scale of values; which decides what I had better do with my time. It dictates 'This half hour must be spent on Russian,' 'This must be given to Wordsworth.' Or 'Now I'd better darn my brown stockings,'" and it is characteristic that the word she should find to express her critical reservations about *Ulysses* is "underbred." Politically a little to the left of center, they all shared a deep distrust of Parties and the State, believing passionately in the supreme importance of personal relations: "If I had to choose between betraying my country and betraying my friend, I hope I should have the guts to betray my country," wrote E. M. Forster, and during the spring of 1940, when invasion seemed imminent, Virginia Woolf refused to be distracted from writing her life of Roger Fry: "It's the vastness, and the smallness, that makes this possible. So intense are my feelings (about Roger); yet the circumference (the war) seems to make a hoop round them. No, I can't get the odd incongruity of feeling intensely and at the same time knowing that there's no importance in that feeling. Or is there, as I sometimes think, more importance than ever?"

It was, I feel, a very happy idea to confine the selections from her diary to her reflections on her own career as a writer. Henry James in his notebooks, letters, and prefaces may have said more interesting things about literary technique, but I have never read any book that conveyed more truthfully what a writer's life is like, what are its worries, its rewards, its day-by-day routine. Some readers, apparently, have been shocked to find how anxious and sensitive Virginia Woolf was about reviews, and how easily commendation of others could make her envious, but most writers, if they are honest, will recognize themselves in such remarks as "No creative writer can swallow another contemporary. The reception of living work is too coarse and partial if you're doing the same thing yourself. . . . When Desmond praises 'East Coker,' and I am jealous, I walk over the marsh saying, I am I," and even in her reflection on her father's death: "Father . . . would have been 96 . . . and could have been 96, like other people one has known: but mercifully was not. His life would have entirely ended mine."

Some of us keep up an air of stoic indifference to reviews, some avoid distress by refusing to read them, but we all care, and for good reasons. Every writer who is original is often doubtful about the value of a work; praise from a critic whom he respects is a treasured reassurance, silence or blame a confirmation of his worst fears: "So I'm found out and that odious rice pudding of a book is what I thought it—a dank failure." Then there are those critics who have made up their minds, for reasons of jealousy or fashion, about his work before they have read it, and the readers of those critics—rival contemporaries or the ambitious young—who are glad to hear that his work is bad: "I dislike the thought of being laughed at: of the glow of satisfaction that A., B., and C. will get from hearing V. W. demolished." In Virginia Woolf's case, the fact that she was a woman was a further aggravation. She belonged to a generation in which a woman had still to fight to be taken seriously as a writer. For her, therefore, good notices and brisk sales meant financial independence and masculine admission of her sex as a literary equal; when she writes, "I'm out to make £300 this summer by writing and build a bath and hot-water range at Rodmell," she is thinking of the satisfaction it will give her, as a wife, to contribute substantially to the family budget.

Sensitive as she was to attacks, she was never too vain to deny any truth there might be in even the most prejudiced: "The thing to do is to note the pith of what is said—that I don't think—then to use the little kick of energy which opposition supplies to be more vigorously oneself. . . . To investigate candidly the charge; but not fussily, not very anxiously. On no account to retaliate by going to the other extreme—thinking too much."

These selections from Virginia Woolf's diary begin in the last year of World War I, when, in spite of it, England still seemed to be pretty much the same country it had been before 1914, and end, a few days before her death, in the darkest days of World War II, when her London house had been destroyed by bombs and the future of England was problematic: "A kind of growl behind the cuckoos and t'other birds. A furnace behind the sky. It struck me that one curious feeling is, that the writing 'I' has vanished. No audience. No echo. . . . We live without a future. That's what's queer: with our noses pressed to a closed door."

At the beginning, her literary reputation is just established—"I get treated at great length and solemnity by old gentlemen." During the twenties, she is universally admired; then, in the thirties, the wiggings start—she is bourgeois, oversensitive, out of date, and so on—and then she dies before she could become (what may well be the most painful fate of all) a sacred cow of whom everyone speaks in tones of hushed and bored reverence, but not before she has finished *Between the Acts*, which, in my opinion, is her masterpiece.

With the exception of a description of an eclipse of the sun, which is as beautiful as any of the best pages in her novels, and an occasional comment, usually rather malicious, on people she knew, these selections are devoted to her thoughts upon the work in hand. Like every other writer, she was concerned about what particular kind of writer she was, and what her unique contribution could and should be. "My only interest as a writer lies, I begin to see, in some queer individuality; not in strength, or passion, or anything startling. Peacock for example: Borrow; Donne. . . . Fitzgerald's Letters." This is true if strength and passion are taken to mean what they conventionally mean when speaking of novelists. What she felt and expressed with the most intense passion was a mystical, religious vision of life, "a consciousness of what I call 'reality': a thing I see before me: something abstract; but residing in the downs or sky; beside which nothing matters; in which I shall rest and continue to exist. . . . How difficult not to go making 'reality' this and that, whereas it is one thing. Now perhaps this is my gift: this perhaps is what distinguishes me from other people: I think it may be rare to have so acute a sense of something like that—but again, who knows? I would like to express it too." Moreover, as is true of most mystics, she also experienced the Dark Night when "reality" seemed malignant—"the old treadmill feeling, of going on and on and on, for no reason . . . contempt for my lack of intellectual power; reading Wells without understanding. . . . society; buying clothes; Rodmell spoilt; all England spoilt: terror at night of things generally wrong in the universe."

What is unique about her work is the combination of this mystical vision with the sharpest possible sense for the concrete, even in its humblest form: "One can't," she observes, "write directly about the soul. Looked at, it vanishes; but look at the ceiling, at Grizzle, at the cheaper beasts in the Zoo which are exposed to walkers in Regent's Park, and the soul slips in." In preserving this balance, her sex was probably a help; a man who becomes interested in the Ground of Being all too easily becomes like Lowes Dickinson—"Always live in the whole, life in the one: always Shelley and Goethe, and then he loses his hot-water bottle; and never notices a face or a cat or a dog or a flower, except in the flow of the universal." A woman who has to run a house can never so lose contact with matter. The last entry in Virginia Woolf's diary is typical: "And now with some pleasure I find that it's seven; and must cook dinner. Haddock and sausage meat. I think it is true that one gains a certain hold on sausage and haddock by writing them down."

Though she took extraordinary pains over each book, she was a born spontaneous writer who never seems to have known periods when she was without a fresh idea; even while she was in the middle of writing one book, she got ideas for the next, and her output shows a greater variety than she is sometimes credited with. Each book set its particular problem and provoked in the author its particular psychosomatic reactions: "While I was forcing myself to do *Flush* my old headache came back—for the first time this autumn. Why should *The Pagiters* [*The Years*] make my heart jump; why should *Flush* stiffen the back of my neck?"

Within the years covered by this diary, Virginia Woolf wrote what her husband believes to be, and I agree with him, her three best books, *To the Light-*

house, The Waves, and *Between the Acts,* and the fortunate reader is able to follow the writing of each. Here, for example, is the history of *The Waves*:

1926 [She is finishing To the Lighthouse]:

SEPTEMBER 30. It is not oneself but something in the universe that
one's left with. It is this that is frightening and exciting in the midst of
my profound gloom, depression, boredom, whatever it is. One sees a fin
passing far out. What image can I reach to convey what I mean?

1927 [the year of Orlando]:

FEBRUARY 21. Why not invent a new kind of play; as for instance:
Woman thinks . . . He does. Organ plays. She writes. They say: She sings.
Night speaks. They miss.

JUNE 18. A man and a woman are to be sitting at a table talking. Or
shall they remain silent? It is to be a love story; she is finally to let the last
great moth in.

1928:

NOVEMBER 28. The poets succeeding by simplifying: practically
everything is left out. I want to put practically everything in: yet to satu-
rate. . . . It must include nonsense, fact, sordidity: but made transparent.

1929:

JUNE 23. I think it will begin like this: dawn; the shells on a beach: I
don't know—voices of cock and nightingale; and then all the children
at a long table—lessons. . . . Could one not get the waves to be heard all
through?

[*On September 10th, she begins writing.*]

SEPTEMBER 25. Yesterday morning I made another start on "The
Moths," but that won't be its title. . . . Who thinks it? And am I outside
the thinker?

DECEMBER 26. I wish I enjoyed it more. I don't have it in my head all
day like *The Lighthouse* and *Orlando.*

1930:

JANUARY 12. I can now hardly stop making up *The Waves.* . . . What is
essential is to write fast and not break the mood.

MARCH 17. The test of a book (to a writer) is if it makes a space in
which, quite naturally, you can say what you want to say. As this morning
I could say what Rhoda said.

APRIL 9. It is bound to be very imperfect. But I think it possible that
I have got my statues against the sky.

APRIL 29. The greatest stretch of mind I ever knew. . . . I suspect the
structure is wrong. Never mind.

[*She begins her second version of* The Waves]

AUGUST 20. *The Waves* is I think resolving itself into a series of dramatic soliloquies.

DECEMBER 22. . . . merge all the interjected passages into Bernard's final speech and end with the words O solitude.

1931:

[*On January 20th, she gets the idea, in her bath, for* Three Guineas.]

FEBRUARY 7. I wrote the words O Death fifteen minutes ago, having reeled across the last ten pages with some moments of such intensity and intoxication that I seemed only to stumble after my own voice, or almost, after some sort of speaker. . . . Anyhow it is done; and I have been sitting these fifteen minutes in a state of glory, and calm, and some tears. . . . How physical the sense of triumph and relief is! . . . I have netted that fin in the waste of water which appeared to me over the marshes out of my window at Rodmell.

I do not know how Virginia Woolf is thought of by the younger literary generation; I do know that by my own, even in the palmiest days of social consciousness, she was admired and loved much more than she realized. I do not know if she is going to exert an influence on the future development of the novel—I rather suspect that her style and her vision were so unique that influence would only result in tame imitation—but I cannot imagine a time, however bleak, or a writer, whatever his school, when and for whom her devotion to her art, her industry, her severity with herself—above all, her passionate love, not only or chiefly for the big moments of life but also for its daily humdrum "sausage-and-haddock" details—will not remain an example that is at once an inspiration and a judge. If I had to choose an epitaph for her, I would take a passage from *The Waves*, which is the best description of the creative process that I know:

There is a square: there is an oblong. The players take the square and place it upon the oblong. They place it very accurately; they make a perfect dwelling-place. Very little is left outside. The structure is now visible; what is inchoate is here stated; we are not so various or so mean; we have made oblongs and stood them upon squares. This is our triumph; this is our consolation.

The New Yorker, 6 March 1954

The Word and the Machine

Two themes, which in the past had always been fruitful sources of inspiration to poets, have almost vanished from the poetry written in the last fifty years, namely, the public figure as a hero for panegyric or a villain for satire, and the *polis*, the particular political-economic-religious organism in which any given poet happens to be a cell. Most living English poets probably admire Sir Winston Churchill more than Dryden admired Charles II, but the thought of writing a poem about him does not occur to them; one has no right to suppose that all the poets in Russia who wrote hymns to Stalin had their tongues in their cheeks, yet their efforts were uniformly worthless as poetry. Most poets in the West believe that some sort of democracy is preferable to any sort of totalitarian state and accept certain political obligations, to pay taxes, to vote for the best man or programme, to serve as jurymen, to write letters of protest against this or that act of injustice or vandalism, but I cannot think of a single poet of consequence whose work does not, either directly or by implication, condemn modern civilisation as an irremediable mistake, a bad world which we have to endure because it is there and no one knows how it could be made into a better one, but in which we can only retain our humanity in the degree to which we resist its pressures.

Justified or unjustified, this negative attitude raises some interesting questions about the nature of poetry. For poetry to take an interest in and be capable of dealing with a subject, the latter must possess three qualities: personality, power, and virtue or wickedness. Thus, to be a poetic hero, a man must intend to do something and be able to do it; the consequences of his act may be contrary to his intention, but if they are, it is because he has misused his power, not because he lacked it, so that he must accept responsibility.

As long as he only possessed tools and no machines, man could think of natural forces as personal: Nature, as he encountered her, was more powerful than he, variable from day to day, but rhythmical and consistent in the long run—she might send a drought one year but she would never make Autumn precede Summer. Similarly, without machines, the public relations between men as citizens, producers, and consumers, and their private relations as families and friends were of the same order; the power which one man could exert over another was determined in both cases by his personal magnetism, his personal achievements, and the *numen* attributed to his status as father, king, priest, etc.

But the machine divorced power from person: nature becomes an impersonal slave, but the slave not of this or that person but of man-in-general, the impersonal collective. Poor morale can still lose a war, but no excellence of morale can win one without machines which take no oaths of loyalty. The good or evil a man can do depends not on the intensity of his intention but the power of the machines which carry out his intention for him. If I stab another with a spear, the act of killing is clearly mine; if I drop a bomb on a city, *my* act consists in pressing a button, and it is the bomb which does the killing. Even the personal influence a public figure can exert depends less on his personality than on the printing-presses and loud-speakers he can command.

The position of the poet in a technological civilisation, therefore, is doubly difficult. A natural ease of communication between artist and audience requires that the unity of power and person which is the æsthetic subject be publicly manifest, but in such a civilisation they are united only on the private level. In previous times, the way in which the poet worked was essentially the same as that of everybody else—writing a poem and digging a ditch were both done by hand, and the poet and the ditcher were both personally responsible for the result; but today, the poet has become an eccentric figure, not through any intention on his part but simply because the way in which he works, by hand, by himself, has become eccentric.

The "courtly" bard might look down on the "popular" ballad singer, but he recognised him as a brother: today "high-brow" art and the "mass-entertainment" of film, radio, and television are so separated by their methods of production that no comparison is possible—they belong to different worlds.

Anyone whose social position is eccentric is apt to compensate for his feelings of loneliness by assertions of superiority, but in the case of the modern poet this tendency is aggravated by his feeling that he is one of the lucky few whose work is still personally meaningful and not so and so many hours of meaningless activity spent to acquire the means to live a real life after they are over. Those whom he envies are not the rich or the powerful but the scientists, doctors, machine designers, etc., for whose happiness our age seems designed as earlier ages were designed for great landowners, for these people enjoy the satisfaction both of meaningful work and of an unequivocal social position. When I am in the company of scientists I feel like a curate who has strayed into a drawing-room full of dukes.

If the attitude of poets towards our civilisation is purely negative, this is mainly because they know that poetry can do nothing to solve the problems of a machine culture and the people who might be able to do so seem hardly aware that these problems exist. Let me mention two.

The kitchen refrigerator seems to me an unqualified material good, so that it would be good if every household on earth possessed one. To produce refrigerators at a price which would make this possible, mass-production methods must, I assume, be employed. Here the problem is the spiritual welfare of the workers in the refrigerator factory. While a great deal of research has been done to discover how the worker can economise time and effort, what incentives appeal to him most, what physical and psychological conditions in the plant will keep him contented, almost nothing, so far as I know, has been done to find out for how many hours it is possible for the average person to work in this way before permanent depersonalisation sets in. Such research cannot be done by poets.

The second problem is much more serious and much harder to find an answer to, for it is concerned with the role of the machine, of radios and gramophones, for example, in the production not of material but of spiritual goods, and its effect not only on those who make them but also those who enjoy their use. Is there something in the essential natures of the machine and the Word which makes them incompatible, so that at the slightest contact with the former the Word turns into lifeless words? Is even the mechanical printing press, but for which I should never have been able to read the books which have formed my life, nor, for that matter, be writing this article now, an evil? Sometimes I have an uneasy suspicion that it is.

Encounter, April 1954

A European View of Peace

The Century of Total War. By Raymond Aron. Doubleday. $4.75.

Books and articles about "The Situation" pour off the presses in such volume that we are tempted, since we know that we cannot read them all, to read none, and, for those of us whose direct political activity is confined to voting in elections, the depressing nature of the subject and the distressing absence of clear-cut solutions enhance this reluctance. Every now and again, however, a book like this book of Mr Raymond Aron's appears which even the most literary-minded will feel rewarded by reading.

The Century of Total War is primarily addressed to an European audience, but since the problems of Europe are willy-nilly also American problems, it is essential that we understand them. The word Europe no longer has nor can recover the meaning it had between the Fall of the Bastille and the outbreak of World War I. "At the present moment," as Mr Aron says, "what remains of Europe west of the Iron Curtain has no chance of independence. Either it will be a part of a whole of which the Atlantic forms the centre just as the civilisation of the ancients had the Mediterranean for its centre; or it will be incorporated in the Continental empire of which the Soviet Union is the central directing element . . . Eliminate the United States and Europeans will not suddenly become secure; on the contrary, they will be doomed to Sovietisation, perhaps without a general war, but quite certainly not without pain." The idea of Europe as a neutral Third Force, mediating between Washington and Moscow would be a fine one, but Force means what it says and, to realise the idea, Europe would have to possess the means and the will to become a military force of the first order.

Mr Aron begins by analyzing the novel elements in modern wars. Serious as they are, the losses in life and wealth which they incur are not the most serious results; the restoration of population was slower after the Thirty Years War and the economic cost of the 1930–1938 crisis in France was as great as that of the war.

The really catastrophic effects are moral and political; modern technological warfare demands a collectivisation of society, a centralisation of state power which is much easier to establish than to get rid of and, unless an immediate decision is arrived at, it must inevitably turn into "hyperbolic war" in which the efforts demanded and the suffering endured are so great that the only war-aim which can seem to justify them is total victory and the unconditional surrender of the enemy. But for any state which is not simply out for aggressive conquest, which today means world conquest, the only proper war-aim should be "the establishment of international relations in a balance that would favor world peace." World peace *might* be secured through the absolute domination of the planet by a single power but it is doubtful if any power which claimed to be a democracy could attempt it or remain a democracy for very long if it did; the only other alternative is a balance of Powers and the more of these there are, the less temptation there is for any one of them to embark on aggressive adventures. This involves an awareness that the historical future is open, so that your enemy of today may become your ally tomorrow and vice versa.

In Mr Aron's opinion, the British by their indiscriminate strategic night bombing of Germany and the Americans by their total lack of caution in dealing with the Russians are largely responsible for the post-war difficulties. However, it is useless to reflect on what-might-have-happened-if; given the circumstances, what is possible now? The unification of Germany? Not unless the Soviets are willing to withdraw their troops which appears highly unlikely. An acceptance of the status quo by Russia with a corresponding slackening of revolutionary missionary fervor? It is the day-dream, probably, of all of us that a settlement be arrived at similar to that of the Treaty of Westphalia in which both parties realise that they cannot obliterate the other and must live side by side. But what reason has the Kremlin to think so? Between 1918 and 1939 despite the depression of the thirties, no other country turned Communist; since 1945 Communism has had one triumph after another but, as the Kremlin knows very well, there were not ideological but military: given the backing of Russian troops it was possible for a militant minority to seize the power which the majority would never have voted them; indeed, there are probably more uncynical believers in the communist idea on our side of the Iron Curtain than on theirs where the alternative society offered in contrast to capitalist or Labour Party democracy is real and not some ideal mythical society. As an antidote to pessimism about the human race and as a warning against defeatist notions of the "wave-of-the-future," we should all do well to ponder the following remarks by Mr Aron:

Even in the twentieth century there is no instance of universal suffrage ever having given an absolute majority to a revolutionary party (of Right or Left) where the freedom of the vote was respected. Though the electorate is less conservative than in the last century, it has not yet become revolutionary.

The trumpets of propaganda are not sufficient to bring down walls. There are traitors to be found who will hand the keys of the city to the besiegers. The revolution comes after the seizure of power, and the violence most frequently comes from the State itself.

To which one should perhaps add that by traitors Mr Aron does not mean only or primarily those who share the besiegers' beliefs, but those who, out of cowardice or a mistaken hope that the barbarian can be tamed and made use of, admit to the city that which, in their heart of hearts, they know is evil.

The real danger for Europe is not the existence, in France and Italy, of large well-heeled communist parties but the lack of any military force and the weakness of the pluralist democratic governments which have not succeeded in convincing their nations that they are "legitimate," i.e. that they represent, not merely a certain form of government but a way of collective existence. It begins to look as if a democratic form of government is not viable unless there are not more than, at most, three parties, and unless the elected representatives, whatever their party, whether in power or in opposition, in the debating chamber or the corridors, have learnt to behave like gentlemen. The British Parliamentary system was fortunate enough to be born in a period when all its members, whatever their views, belonged to the same class, so that, by the time that other classes began to be represented, a style of behaviour was already set. The United States has been fortunate in possessing a two-party system in a country so vast that neither could stand consistently for any one ideological point of view. For a stable democracy it is probably important that the number of "independent" voters be small, that the majority should usually vote for a party because their fathers did or the region in which they are living does.

It is difficult for even a strong democratic government to put through a program which is unpopular but necessary; for a weak one it is almost impossible. With the average voter, the unpopularity of a policy is, naturally and inevitably, in direct proportion to its cost and personal inconvenience. To maintain, for many years to come, a standing army large enough to deter the Communists from starting any limited wars like that in Korea will be both expensive and disagreeable, yet in Mr Aron's view it is the only policy for Europe to take. "The one place where the European idea is capable of being

realised within a limited time is in the armed forces. Logically, political institutions should come first; in practice they will emerge from the requirement
of common defense. The General Staff will precede The Defense Department." One alternative, that the United States maintain a similar body of
troops in Europe, is politically impossible for both. The other is to do nothing and piously hope that because, as is probably true, the Kremlin is afraid
of setting off a global war, it will, contrary to its theory and its past practice,
refrain from trying to weaken and overthrow the democratic regimes of the
West. And, should the Kremlin not refrain, and should it meet with any success, what can the United States do? Ignore it, or treat it as a *casus-belli* and
atom bomb Russia?

Atomic weapons have put the States at a disadvantage in every situation but
one in which an aggressor has already used them. It would be, as Mr Aron remarks, "indispensable, but singularly difficult to convince the masses in the
Soviet Union that the West bears no ill-will except towards their tyrants, if
atom bombs unite in death Stalinists and their opponents: women, children,
and the secret police."

It is a little difficult to understand why communism should continue to attract large sections of the working class in Western Europe when the realities
of communist society are no longer far-off in a distant Russia but next door,
yet the attraction is a fact. "The French worker, for a shorter working day, receives real payment higher than in 1913. Yet he says and frequently believes
(and intellectuals keep repeating for him) that he has nothing to defend.
Thirty years ago, he had no doubt that he had something to defend, something that he called *la patrie* or *la France*." One reason may be that, in Europe,
industrialism has not gone far enough. It has destroyed, as industrialism always does, traditional attitudes and loyalties without attaining, as it has in the
States, a productivity which creates, not merely a quantitatively higher standard of living, but a qualitatively different way of living. If European workers,
in defiance of the material and spiritual facts, still seek refuge in the Red Metropolis, it is because they hate the society in which they live.

In his economic views Mr Aron would prefer, when and where possible,
free-trade and convertible currencies. He believes, for example, that the
problem of the dollar shortage could be solved if the United States would
abolish all their customs duties and invest abroad a sum similar to the annual
loans made by Europe before 1914, and he is suspicious of grandiose schemes
for universal security and nationalisation of industry which arise, he thinks,
not from the demands of the workers themselves but from the doctrinal, sys-
tematizing or demagogic mentality of a few leaders. At the same time he is
no doctrinaire who cries "Red Communism!" at the slightest interference of
the State in finance, housing or trade. He knows that no political society
today can tolerate a high figure of unemployment, and he sees no reason to
think that a mixed economy is incompatible with democracy.

While he has many criticisms to make of America policy, he has nothing but contempt for those European intellectuals who refuse to see that, when it comes to the essential values, freedom from arbitrary police power, freedom of thought, speech and reading, freedom of worship, Europe and America are in one camp, and the Soviet Union in the other. "When Europeans who boast of democratic values denounce the American way of life, they do so at bottom in the name of aristocratic values," or again, "It is difficult to understand why the people who are moved by the sufferings of the non-privileged give their sympathy to a system that begins by multiplying sufferings on pretense of lessening them."

A state of partial mobilisation and cold war calls for even greater faith and courage than a "hyperbolic war" but why should America and the West not have faith in what they stand for? "Whenever the battle of ideas has been waged with equal weapons, the West has won consistently."

The Griffin, April 1954

England: Six Unexpected Days

I have devised a cultural-psychological test which I am seriously thinking of patenting. This takes the form of a questionnaire about the subject's conception of Eden, his Innocent Place where no contradiction has yet arisen between the demands of Pleasure and the demands of Duty. What is its landscape, the ethnic origin of its inhabitants, its religion, its form of state, its architecture, its system of weights and measures, et cetera? To the first of these questions, the answer, in my own case, is a landscape like that of the Pennines, that chain of limestone hills which runs due North up the centre of England from Derbyshire to Northumberland.

I mention them with mixed feelings: on the one hand I want all worthy people to agree with me about their beauty; on the other, I have a feeling of personal possession which makes me jealously afraid of unworthy or unappreciative intruders. It is not an area for those who like their landscape cozy. To qualify, one must have a proper moral sense about the points of the compass; North must seem the "good" direction, the way towards heroic adventures, South the way to ignoble ease and decadence. Nor, however, will it do for those who crave the romantically wild, jagged precipices, Salvator Rosa gorges, Wagnerian tempests. Visually, the nearest approach to it that I have seen in this country is the sagebrush uplands one sees from the train between Denver and Laramie; to the feet, though, they would seem very different, for the climate of the Pennines is—well, British and often wet.

To the usual visitor in the United Kingdom the North means the Lake District and Scotland. If he goes to Scotland direct, by the London-to-Glasgow train, he will get two glimpses of the Pennines; about half an hour after leaving Carnforth, he will see the steep humps of the Sedbergh Fells close on his right, and during the long descent from Shap to Penrith, if he is lucky enough to get a clear day, he will see a great unbroken wall of grey fells towering up on the eastern edge of the lush sandstone valley of the Eden, where the Pennine range reaches its greatest height and behind which lie its wildest and loneliest moors.

To an American ear two thousand feet must sound puny, but the impression of size is a matter of scale and, in England, two thousand feet create a mountainous effect which, in the States, would require at least ten. In this age of rapid transportation, landscapes like the English which are built on a small scale are at a disadvantage. A passion for walking is not a conspicuous American trait, but if anyone really wants to get the full flavour of the English countryside, he has, I am afraid, no choice.

Such advice is, I know, too utopian to be followed, so I shall assume I am writing for an American Visitor to Great Britain whose main northern objective is to see Scotland, but who is not too hurried or too incurious to make detours if there is any scenery worth inspecting on the way.

For the traveller with a car and six days to spare, the following route will give a pretty good idea of what there is to see. (The A.A. road map and guide will show him how to avoid built-up areas.)

First Day

London to Uttoxeter, via Oxford, Banbury, Daventry and Burton-upon-Trent. This last, as famous for breweries as Milwaukee, is one of the most horrible towns in England, but can be skirted. Uttoxeter lies just to the south of the Peak District and (a point of interest to those who, like myself, have a taste for grim industrial landscapes) just to the east of the Potteries, those Five Towns which Arnold Bennett wrote about. An American, homesick for a cold Martini, might find it worth his while to stop, not at Uttoxeter, but some fifty miles further east at Ashby de la Zouch where, by some miracle, the chief hotel has an honest-to-goodness American bar.

Second Day

Uttoxeter to Appletreewick in Wharfedale. One can begin by visiting either Dovedale or the Manifold valley; the former, thanks to Izaak Walton, is apt to be crowded; the latter, which, in my opinion, is just as pretty, is practically unknown. From either, one climbs up onto limestone moors—if this is your country, you are a person who is thrilled when hedges start to be replaced by stone walls—then up and down through Bakewell, Eyam, and Tideswell to the Hope valley. Those with an interest in great old country houses can detour east to see Chatsworth and Haddon Hall. At Hope, turn left to Castleton whose caverns, the Peak, the Speedwell, and the Blue John Mine, though now, alas, more organized for the tourist trade than they were in my youth, have not yet developed the horrors of Carlsbad. Turn back again through Hope and then north over the Hathersage moors where the limestone is hidden under millstone grit, a dark grim stone out of which so much of the northern towns is built. Though it is possible to avoid both Sheffield and Leeds, during this part of the journey one is bound to go through an industrial area. Personally, I find the early nineteenth-century architecture of the woollen mills, which resemble the paper mills at Holyoke, very beautiful in their stark utilitarian way. The road passes through Haworth where the Brontës lived; their house, the only literary shrine in the Pennines, is open to visitors. After Keighley the real scenery begins. The high moors are brown covered with peat and heather and haunted by curlews; lower they turn to green turf out of which the white limestone keeps cropping. These hills have one advantage over the hills of New England, beautiful as they are: their outlines are not hidden by trees; and, compared with the bare hills of the far West, spectacular as they are, there is soil and life, and the sound of running water. Owing to the porousness of limestone, the streams cut deep ravines or ghylls, homes of the hearts-tongue fern and the rock-rose, and keep disappearing underground. At Appletreewick there is only one inn, but a good one.

Third Day

Appletreewick to Keld in Swaledale. This is a short run but the scenery is worth taking slowly. The road goes up Wharfedale past Kettlewell, then over high ground and down to Hawes in Wensley Dale. Wensley Dale is famous for its blue cheese, highly prized, incidentally, by Mr T. S. Eliot. However, the tourist must beware. Finding himself in the Dale, a friend of mine bought a cheese as a present for the Master who took one glance at it and pronounced—"This is a store cheese." From Hawes the road climbs over the Buttertubs Pass, so called because of a cluster of swallow-holes near the summit, and descends to Muker from which it is only some three miles to Keld which lies just below the main road beside a very pleasant little waterfall. Swaledale is not as pretty as Wharfedale but I find its wildness and remoteness more satisfying. Rather than stay at the inn which is not in the village, inquire for people who let rooms.

Fourth Day

Keld to Dufton. A mile east of Keld turn sharp right up a steep gradient to Tan Hill, the highest inn in England, bear left till the road joins the old Roman Road of Watling Street, then left again to Brough-under-Stainmore and on down into the Eden Valley through Appleby to Dufton. Laid out in a rectangle around its green, and nestling at the foot of the volcanic dome of Dufton Pike, Dufton is one of the quietest and loveliest villages that I know.

Another short run, but it will give an early starter time to take an afternoon walk up the fells. If he is feeling very energetic, he might get as far and as high as High Cup Nick, a great cleft with a rim of precipices eight hundred feet high. At Dufton there is an inn and a youth hostel.

Fifth Day

Dufton to Blanchland. A warren of country lanes running along the foot-hills of the Pennine escarpment leads into the Penrith-Alston road which was built by Macadam himself. In this final stretch the land has something of the shape of a wave rising northeast and breaking southwest. On reaching its crest from the breaking side the eye is confronted by an enormous sweep of whaleback moors. Today they produce little but sheep and grouse, but from Roman times down to the end of the nineteenth century, this was the richest lead-mining field in the country. Relics of its vanished wealth, derelict shafts, abandoned washing-floors, decayed water wheels, solitary chimneys sticking up in the midst of nowhere abound and give that same melancholy fascina-tion which one finds among the ghost towns in the West. To get its full flavour, take the road from Alston to Nenthead, the highest village in the Kingdom, turn right to Coalclough, bear left by a rather rough road till the river Allen is reached, then right to Allenheads, then left over into Rookhope, the most wonderfully desolate of all the dales, and finally, on reaching the Wear at East-gate, turn left for Stanhope. The valley widens and the landscape becomes gentler; in the words of a Victorian visitor, "its umbrageous riches and deep seclusion afford the highest delight to a lover of nature," but on turning north one reenters the fells before reaching Blanchland. Blanchland was once a monastery and one enters the village through a battlemented arch. It is a number of years now since I stayed at the Lord Crewe Arms, but no other spot brings me sweeter memories.

Sixth Day

Blanchland to Hawick and Edinburgh, via Hexham and Bellingham. The "sights" on this trip are Hexham Abbey and Hadrian's Wall. The best parts of the latter are at Housesteads and Sewing Shields to the west of Corbridge and a detour should be made. The road now runs up the North Tyne valley, up over Scots Gap and down into the Walter Scott country. Of all the approaches to Scotland, this is the wildest, most beautiful, and least known.

I hope you will have luck with the weather, but if the Pennines are really your dish you won't care.

Vogue, 15 May 1954

Introduction to *An Elizabethan Song Book*

BY W. H. AUDEN AND

CHESTER KALLMAN

The Poems

WORDS AND NOTES

All the songs in this collection were written in a space of only twenty-five years, and the whole period of the English madrigalists and lutanists is no more than forty. What makes this brief moment one of the most extraordinary events in cultural history is the miraculous coincidence of composers and lyric poets of equal high quality. Moreover, the former did not have to depend on one or two poets; more than half the lyrics they set come down to us unsigned, yet even these, in all their stylistic variety, are no whit inferior to those written by the identifiable or the famous.

There is no better period, therefore, to study if one is interested in the relation between poetry and music, and in the influence, if any, which they exert on each other. There are two schools of thought which either deny or deplore their relation. The first is made up of persons who love poetry but have no feeling for the human singing voice, though they may claim to admire instrumental music. They base their objection to vocal music upon observations which are, in themselves, correct: that, whenever verse is set to notes, its rhythm is distorted and that, however precise a singer's diction, a listener who is not already familiar with the words will at best catch half of them.

The second, made up of singing fans, observing, again correctly, that very beautiful arias have been written to trivial or downright silly verses, conclude that all a composer requires from a poet are so and so many syllables of such and such a quality, and that their meaning is irrelevant. They quote Rossini's remark, "Give me a laundry-list and I will set it," unaware, apparently, that a laundry-list, or any list for that matter, has a poetic value, and one which is exceptionally translatable into musical terms. It might be difficult, however, to resist their arguments were there, in the period we are covering, many examples like Byrd's "Although the heathen poets," where an unresolved subordinate clause has been set quite happily. Mercifully, it is very much an exception.

Then, to confuse matters, there are the crank prosodists who attempt to scan verse by musical notation, provoking the orthodox, like Sir George Saintsbury, to conclude that the less a poet knows about music, the better; indeed it is probably best for him to be, like Shelley, tone-deaf.

Yet the output of vocal music between 1588 and 1632 remains. Here are scores of poems, the poetic quality of which satisfies the most exacting of the song-hating school, which were written directly for the purpose of being set, and would not have come into being had the composers not existed to set them; here are scores of part-songs and solos, the musical value of which satisfies the most exacting of the syllable-for-voice school, the stimulus to which was, nevertheless, a good poem.

It is always possible, of course, to assert—because the assertion cannot be proved or disproved—that the poets would have written better if they had written only for the speaking voice, and that the composers would have done as well or better with bad verses, but one thing is certain: both the poems and the music would have been different.

The questions which will naturally arise in the literary reader's mind are two: From an examination of these poems, is it possible to learn what characteristics a good poem must possess in order to be settable? and: Are some of the characteristics of these poems, which, read apart from the music, make them good, the result of their having been written to be set?

Any consideration of such questions must begin with the difference between musical rhythm, in any style of music, and verse rhythm, in any language. In music a difference in temporal duration between two notes is more noticeable than a difference in accentuation; musical "prosody," so to speak, is always quantitative, not qualitative, and in a much stricter way than any spoken verse can be which, like Greek or classical Latin, is scanned quantitatively. If in quantitative scansion syllables are classified as either long or short, every long syllable being temporally equivalent to two short syllables, this classification, when applied to a spoken language, is, strictly speaking, a fiction, for probably no two spoken syllables are of exactly the same length. But in music, for any given metronome marking, all quarter notes, say, are identical in duration. Also, instead of there being only two kinds of lengths, there are infinite possibilities of sustaining or subdividing notes. When, therefore, a line of verse in any language, no matter what its prosodic principle, is sung, the rhythm the ear perceives is based on differences in length. Differences in accent are also often perceptible, but they are always secondary. Further, the ear's judgment of tempo when hearing music is quite different when hearing speech: a tempo of spoken syllables which feels like an adagio would, if the syllables were musical notes, feel like an allegretto.

By the end of the sixteenth century the English language and the prosodic principles governing its verse had become, in all essentials, what they are today. It had already been established that the normal scansion of English verse should be by feet, not by accent only, like Anglo-Saxon verse, nor by the number of syllables only, like French, but that these feet should consist of various combinations of accented and unaccented syllables, not of the "long" and "short" syllables of classical poetry. Further, it had become clear that the language was favorable to certain kinds of feet and hostile to others. Even at the height of his folly about classical meters in English, Campian noted:

The heroical verse that is distinguisht by the *Dactile* hath bene oftentimes attempted in our English toong, but with passing pitiful successe; and no wonder, seeing it is an attempt altogether against the nature of our language. For both the concourse of our monasillables make our verse unapt to slide, and also if we examine our polysillables, we find few of them by reason of their heaviness, willing to serve in place of a Dactile . . . . . our English monasillables enforce many breathings which no doubt greatly lengthen a verse, so that it is no wonder if for these reasons our English verses of five feete hold pace with the Latines of sixe.

—*Observations in the Art of English Poesie,* 1602

When poets discover that their language is most easily organized rhythmically by using certain kinds of feet and certain kinds of meters, they tend to fall into the habit of using these exclusively, as if no other kinds were possible. To this habit, a familiarity with the art of vocal music can be a valuable corrective. For, while listening to a song, the verses of which were written, say, in iambics, one hears not only iambics, but any number of other feet, amphibrachs, cretics, tribrachs, spondees, etc., which can suggest to the poet all kinds of rhythmical possibilities for spoken verse. This is particularly true, perhaps, in the case of English, owing to its large number of monosyllabic words, the metrical value of which is not innate but depends on their position in the line. In a language like German, for example, which has an accentual prosody and many polysyllabic words, metrical innovations are much more difficult, for one polysyllabic word in a line can dictate the meter of the rest of the words in it.

If the lyrics of the Elizabethan poets are rhythmically more interesting than those of other periods, it is difficult to escape the conclusion that the close association of poets with musicians of high caliber was largely responsible.

Dryden and Burns are excellent song writers, but their songs have a metrical conventionality from which the Elizabethans were free; and it is to be noticed that those Romantic lyrics which are most exciting rhythmically, like some of Blake's and Beddoes', are consciously modeled on the Elizabethans. The normal conventions of spoken English verse make small provision for monosyllabic feet or for the spondee, and frown on changes of metrical base within a stanza. In these songs we find such things constantly, and very effective they sound when only spoken, e.g.:

> Deare, sweet, faire, wise, change, shrinke nor be not weake

> Not a friend, not a friend greet
> My poor corpse, where my bones shall be throwne.
>   A thousand thousand sighes to save, lay me o where
>   Sad true lover never find my grave, to weepe there.

> But if you let your lovers mone,
>   The Fairie Queene Proserpina,

> Will send abroad her Fairies ev'ry one,
>   That shall pinch blacke and blew,
>   Your white hands, and faire armes,
>   That did not kindly rue
>   Your Paramours harmes.

Such lines have indeed, as Saintsbury declares, their own vocal music, but their authors would not have found it, had they not been writing songs.

This seems the right point at which to digress and put in a good word for the "classical" metrical experiments of the Cambridge School, to which Campian belonged. Their attempt, out of a Renaissance idolization of the Ancients, to write in the meters of Greek and Latin poetry, whether quantitatively in exact imitation or in some accentual substitute, was defeated by the nature of the English language. And their rejection of rhyme, from the same motive, though possible, turned out to be an unnecessary deprivation. But English poetry owes much to their forlorn attempt. In art, as in science and almost every human activity, men should never be discouraged from going up blind alleys. They will not find what they are looking for, but they may discover something which a more orthodox investigator would never have come upon. But for this particular blind alley, we should lack certain beautiful poems—for example, that charming lyric of Campian's, *Rose-cheeked Laura, come*, and the magnificent choruses in *Samson Agonistes*. What is more important, it might have taken English poetry a much longer time to escape from the metrical anarchy of the fifteenth and early sixteenth centuries. As that most implacable foe of all "classicizing" has chivalrously admitted:

> It is at least possible that Spenser might not have been what he most assuredly is, the founder of modern English prosody and modern English poetic diction alike, had he not gone through this "distemper" . . . If there is one thing that a study of the classics indicated more than another, it was the necessity of a certain "standardisation"—the law that verse *has* laws, and cannot be made by merely pitchforking together unselected words, and leaving the heaps to correspond at the hazard of the pitchfork . . . The less definitely the example was taken, the more entirely literal acceptance of the precepts was avoided, the better; but example, and even precept to some extent, could not but establish an atmosphere—set up a tendency and a habit—in the sphere of poetic working.
>
> —Saintsbury, *History of English Prosody*

Returning to the influence of music upon verse: this influence affects not only the rhythms of the latter but also its style and content.

Though words take time to say, as notes take time to play, words do not, as notes do, express themselves merely as sounds in temporal motion; they express their meanings as well. In music, that is, the movement is the expression; in poetry it is but a very small part of it. The elements of the poetic vocabulary, therefore, which are best adapted for musical setting are those which require the least reflection to comprehend—its most dynamic and its most immediate. For example: interjections, which in one's mother tongue always sound onomatopoeic (fie, O, alas, adieu); imperatives; verbs of physical motion (going, coming, hasting, following, falling) or physical concomitants of emotions (laughing, weeping, frowning, sighing); adjectives denoting elementary qualities (bright, hard, green, sad); nouns denoting states of feeling (joy, love, rage, despair) or objects, the emotional associations of which are common to all, and strong (sea, night, moon, spring). On the other hand, complicated metaphors which, even if the words are heard, take time to understand and didactic messages which demand assent or dissent are unsuitable. Again, since music, generally speaking, can express only one thing at a time, it is ill adapted to verses which express mixed or ambiguous feelings, and prefers poems which either express one emotional state or successively contrast two states.* Lastly, since words take much longer to sing than to speak, even without the repetitions that music so often requires, poems intended for songs must be short. Ballads and epic chants, in which the music is a subordinate carrier for the words, are another matter.

The poet who would write songs is denied many poetic virtues, but he is also guarded from many poetic vices; he cannot be prolix or private or preachy or obscure. When one compares the poetry of the preceding age, so crowded with endless maundering allegories, with the poems in these song books, one cannot but thank God for men like Byrd and Dowland, in response to whose demands the poets were compelled to practice the virtues of graceful ease and conciseness. In illustration of this, let us quote some of the madrigal verses, since these are not represented in this collection.

> Thus Bonny-boots the birthday celebrated
>   Of her his lady dearest,
> Fair Oriana, which to his heart was nearest.
>   The nymphs and shepherds feasted
> With clouted cream were, and to sing requested.
>   Lo here the fair created,
>   Quoth he, the world's chief goddess.
> Sing then, for she is Bonny-boots' sweet mistress,
>   Then sang the shepherds and nymphs of Diana:
>   Long live fair Oriana.

---

* It is difficult to imagine an adequate musical setting of Shakespeare's "Farewell, thou art too dear for my possessing," for example. The ambiguous feeling, developed throughout, hinges on the word "dear," with its two meanings of "high in merit" and "expensive"; and one could not expect music to express the simultaneous abnegation and sour mockery of the text.

> Weep, O mine eyes, and cease not;
> Your spring-tides, out alas, methinks increase not.
> O when, O when begin you
> To swell so high that I may drown me in you?
>
> Tan ta ra: cries Mars on bloody rapier.
> Fa la la: cries Venus in a chamber.
> Toodle loodle loo:
> Cries Pan, that cuckoo,
> With bells at his shoe,
> And a fiddle too.
> But I, alas, lie weeping,
> For Death has slain my sweeting,
> Which hath my heart in keeping.

Minor poetry, if you like: but how perfect of its kind, how novel and how irreplaceable.

THE TEXT

No one today can concern himself with the Elizabethan song writers without being aware that he is working in the shadow of that great scholar, Dr Fellowes, and should he feel obliged, as we have felt, to differ from him on some points, it must be with humility and the knowledge that the differences are of minor importance.

In his now classic collection, *English Madrigal Verse*, Dr Fellowes modernized the spelling and punctuation of the poems. There is much to be said in favor of this course. His book, like ours, was intended not only for scholars, but also, and primarily, for the general reader.

The language of the Elizabethan poets is, in all essential respects, that of our own day. Whereas you cannot modernize a line of, say, Chaucer without destroying both the sound and the rhythm, in the case of these songs it makes almost no difference to what a reader will recite or a singer sing if you print a modernized text or the original. One cannot say that there is a consistent principle which governs the highly erratic spelling of the period when the same word can appear in a poem several times with a different spelling each time. Occasionally, though, modernization can lessen the effect. For example:

> Noe noe it is the rule to learne a man to woe.
> I pray quoth he, nay nay quoth shee,
> I pray you let me goe.

Modernize *woe* to *woo*, and you spoil a rhyme and lose a pun.

The unconventional, by modern standards, punctuation has, at least in the case of the songs, a definite purpose as phrasing direction to the singer, and as a pointer to oratorical pauses it is not simply arbitrary even for spoken verse.

Our decision to print, as far as possible, the original texts has been based on two judgments, a negative and a positive: we believe that the average reader will have no difficulty in following them and that he will find it fun to see what the Elizabethans actually wrote.

However, bearing in mind that this collection is intended for the general public, we have followed modern orthographical practice in the writing of *s* and *v*, and where the original punctuation or spelling (e.g. *then* for *than*) seemed likely to cause a confusion of sense, we have changed it.

In his layout of the stanzas Dr Fellowes followed nineteenth-century convention; every rhyme word marks the end of a line and indentation is strictly according to line length. Further—though it must be remembered that he was printing the poems without the music—all refrains are reduced to their essential elements.

We have printed the stanzas in the shape in which they appear under the music, not out of mere archaeological piety, but because it seems to us aesthetically better. For instance, where Dr Fellowes prints

> Thus, dear damsels, I do give
> > Good night, and so am gone.
> With your hearts' desires long live,
> > Still joy and never moan.
> > > Lullaby, lullaby
> > > > Hath pleased you
> > > > And eased you,
> > > And sweet slumber seized you
> > > And now to bed I hie!

the song book has

> Thus deare damzells I do give
> Good night and so am gone:
> With your hartes desires long live,
> Still joy, and never mone.
> Lulla lullaby, Lulla lullaby
> Hath pleasd you and easd you, & sweet slumber sezd you,
> And now to bed I hie.

The difference is not, of course, very important, but it is real.

Three of the lyrics in this collection raise textual problems which merit a special note.

I. Morley–Breton, Faire in a morne

The text in *The First Book of Ayres* (1600) runs thus:

Faire in a morne oh fairest morne was ever morne so faire,
When as the sun but not the same that shined in the air,
And on a hill, oh fairest hill was never hill so blessed,
There stood a man was never man for no man so distressed.

But of the earth no earthly Sunne, and yet no earthly creature,
There stoode a face was never face, that carried such a feature.
This man had hap O happie man, no man so hapt as he,
For none had hap to see the hap, that he had hapt to see.

And as he, behold, this man beheld, he saw so faire a face,
The which would daunt the fairest here, and staine the bravest grace,
Pittie, he cried, and pittie came, and pittied for his paine,
That dying would not let him die, but gave him life againe.

For joy whereof he made such mirth, that all the world did ring,
And *Pan* for all his *Nimphs* came forth, to hear the shepherds sing,
But such a song song never was, nor nere will be againe,
Of *Philida* the shepheards Queen, and *Coridon* the swaine.

In the miscellany *England's Helicon* (1600), under the title *Astrophell his song of Phillida and Coridon,* appears the following poem by Nicholas Breton.

Faire in a morne, (o fairest morne) was never morne so faire:
There shone a Sunne, though not the Sunne, that shineth in the ayre.
For the earth, and from the earth, (was never such a creature:)
Did come this face, (was never face,) that carried such a feature.
Upon a hill, (o blessed hill, was never hill so blessed)
There stoode a man, (was never man for woman so distressed.)
This man beheld a heavenly view, which did such vertue give:
As cleares the blind, and helps the lame, and makes the dead man live.
This man had hap, (o happy man more happy none then hee;)
For he had hap to see the hap, that none had hap to see.
This silly Swaine, (and silly Swaines are men of meanest grace:)
Had yet the grace, (o gracious guest) to hap on such a face.
He pitty cried, and pitty came, and pittied so his paine:
As dying, would not let him die, but gave him life againe.
For joy whereof he made such mirth, as all the woods did ring:
And *Pan* with all his Swaines came foorth, to heare the Sheepheard sing.
But such a Song sung never was, nor shall be sung againe:
Of *Phillida* the Sheepheards Queene, and *Coridon* the Swaine . . .

One can only describe the relation between these two versions by saying that Morley's song must be derived from Breton's poem. It is as if someone,

Morley or a friend, with a good sense of poetry but poor verbal recall, had attempted to reproduce from memory a poem read and admired some time back. Even at that, one cannot be altogether certain that some of the changes—*no man* instead of *woman*, for example—were not made deliberately. If, as is also quite possible, a copyist then made errors of his own in transcribing this recalled version, it is beyond the powers of any human editor to pick them out from the other differences. By what principle, for example, did Dr Fellowes decide to restore *Sunne* in place of *same* in line 2, but retain *world* instead of *woods* in line 13? We have felt justified in making only two emendations, and these without any certainty that a singer in Morley's time would have made either. Believing that, even in a song, sense is preferable to nonsense, we have, as Dr Fellowes did, interchanged lines 3 and 4 with lines 5 and 6; and, on musical grounds—the original is possible to sing, but awkward—we have deleted the *And* from the beginning of line 9.

II. Rosseter–Campian, When Laura Smiles

In *A Booke of Ayres* (1601), stanza 2, line 1, runs:

> The sprites that remaine in fleeting aire

but from the other stanzas it is clear that the line should be an iambic alexandrine. Having noticed, one imagines, that in stanza 4, line 4, occurs the phrase *heav'nly spirits,* Dr Fellowes takes *sprites* to a copyist's error and prints the line thus:

> The spirits that remain in fleeting air

which restores an iambic rhythm, but still lacks a foot. In a note, he suggests that the line may have run

> The wanton spirits that remain in fleeting air.

This emendation is open to two objections. The adjective *wanton* has already been employed in stanza 1, line 2, and Campian was too careful an artist to make it likely that he would use the same adjective again so soon. Secondly, and more seriously, Rosseter's music demands that the line split up into three phrases of four syllables each, a requirement which Dr Fellowes' line fails to meet. We make no claims for our own restoration

> The daintie sprites that still remaine in fleeting aire

beyond the fact that it changes no words and fits the notes.

III. Melvill–Anon., O Lusty May

The only known manuscript of David Melvill's *Booke of Roundels* (1612) is in Australia, and we have been unable to secure a microfilm. All we have had to work with is a modernized transcription.

In the case of this particular song, there are some lines which in their mod-

ernized form will not do. For instance, the rhyme scheme of the stanzas is
aabab, but the transcription of the first two lines of stanza 3 runs

> Birds on boughs of every sort
> Send forth their notes and make great mirth.

The O.E.D. gives *sorth* as a variant for *sort*, but only for the fifteenth century.
Lacking a better idea, we have decided to risk it.

Metrically, the lines are iambic tetrameters, but stanza 5 is transcribed

> Of all the months of the year,
> To mirthful May there is no peer,
> Then glistering garments that are so gay,
> Ye lovers all make merry cheer
> Through gladness of this lusty May.

Since even the transcribers have archaistically given the noun *balme* two syllables under the music, we have ventured to do the same with months, thus
filling out the line. The third line of the stanza, as transcribed, neither keeps
the meter nor makes sense. On our own responsibility, therefore, we have
emended it to

> Then glist'ring garments are so gay.

W. H. AUDEN
CHESTER KALLMAN

An Elizabethan Song Book: Lute Songs, Madrigals and Rounds,
music edited by Noah Greenberg, text edited by
W. H. Auden and Chester Kallman, 1955

Balaam and the Ass

The Master-Servant Relationship in Literature

And the angel said to him: "Why beatest thou thy ass these
three times? I am come to withstand thee, because thy way
is perverse, and contrary to me: And unless the ass had
turned out of the way, giving place to me who stood against
thee, I had slain thee, and she should have lived."
Balaam said: "I have sinned." —Numbers, Chap. XXII

I

"Friend, I do thee no wrong. Didst thou not agree with me
for a penny?" —Matthew, XX

The relation between Master and Servant is agnatic, not cognatic; that is to say, it is not given by nature or fate but comes into being through an act of conscious volition. Secondly, it is not erotic; an erotic relationship, e.g. between man and wife or parent and child, comes into being in order to satisfy needs which are, in part, given by nature; the needs which are satisfied by a master-servant relationship are purely social and historical. By this definition, a wet nurse is not a servant, a cook may be. Thirdly, it is contractual. A contractual relationship comes into being through the free decision of both parties, a double commitment. The liberty of decision need not be, and indeed very rarely is, equal on both sides, but the weaker party must possess *some* degree of sovereignty. Thus, a slave is not a servant because he has no sovereignty whatsoever; he cannot even say, "I would rather starve than work for you." A contractual relationships not only involves double sovereignty, it is also asymmetric; what the master contributes, e.g. shelter, food and wages, and what the servant contributes, e.g. looking after the master's clothes and house, are qualitatively different and there is no objective standard by which one can decide whether the one is or is not equivalent to the other. A contract, therefore, differs from a law. In law all sovereignty lies with the law or with those who impose it and the individual has no sovereignty. Even in a democracy where sovereignty is said to reside in the people, it is as a member of the people that he has a share in that, not as an individual. Further, the relationship of all individuals to a law is symmetric; it commands or prohibits the same thing to all who come under it. Of any law one can ask the aesthetic question, "Is it enforceable?" and the ethical question, "Is it just?" An individual has the aesthetic right to break the law if he is powerful enough to do with impunity, and it may be his ethical duty to break it if his conscience tells him that the law is unjust. Of a contract, on the other hand, one can only ask the historical question, "Did both parties pledge their word to it?" Its justice or its enforceability are secondary to the historical fact of mutual personal commitment. A contract can only be broken or changed by the mutual consent of both parties. It will be my ethical duty to insist on changing a contract when my conscience tells me it is unfair only if I am in the advantageous position; if I am in the weaker position I have a right to propose a change but no right to insist on one.

When the false oracle has informed Don Quixote that Dulcinea can only be disenchanted if Sancho Panza will receive several thousand lashes, the latter agrees to receive them on condition that he inflict them himself and in his own good time. One night Don Quixote becomes so impatient for the release of his love that he attempts to become the whipper, at which point Sancho Panza knocks his master down.

> DON QUIXOTE. So you would rebel against your lord and master, would you, and dare to raise your hand against the one who feeds you.

SANCHO. I neither make nor unmake a king, but am simply standing
up for myself, for I am my own lord.

Similarly, when Mr Pickwick, on entering the Debtors' Prison, attempts to dismiss Sam Weller because it would be unjust to the latter to expect him to accompany his master, Sam Weller refuses to accept dismissal and arranges to get sent to jail himself.

Lastly, the Master-Servant relationship is between real persons. Thus we do not call the employees of a factory or a store servants because the factory and the store are corporate, i.e. fictitious, persons.

II

Who is there?
I.
Who is I?
Thou.
And that is the awakening—the Thou and the I.
— Paul Valéry

Man is a creature who is capable of entering into Thou-Thou relationships with God and with his neighbors because he has a Thou-Thou relationship to himself. There are other social animals who have signal codes, e.g. bees have signals for informing each other about the whereabouts and distance of flowers, but only man has a language by means of which he can disclose himself to his neighbor, which he could not do and could not want to do if he did not first possess the capacity and the need to disclose himself to himself. The communication of mere objective fact only requires monologue and for monologue a language is not necessary, only a code. But subjective communication demands dialogue and dialogue demands a real language.

A capacity for self-disclosure implies an equal capacity for self-concealment. Of an animal it is equally true to say that it is incapable of telling us what it *really* feels, and that it is incapable of hiding its feelings. A man can do both. For the animal motto is that of the trolls in Ibsen's *Peer Gynt*—"To thyself be enough"—while the human motto is, "To thyself be true." Peer is perfectly willing, if it is convenient, to swear that the cow he sees is a beautiful young lady, but when the Troll-King suggests an operation which will take away from Peer the power of distinguishing between truth and falsehood so that if he wishes that a cow were a beautiful girl, the cow immediately appears to him as such, Peer revolts.

To present artistically a human personality in its full depth, its inner dialectic, its self-disclosure and self-concealment, through the medium of a single character is almost impossible. The convention of the soliloquy attempts to get round the difficulty but it suffers from the disadvantage of *being* a convention; it presents, that is, what is really a dialogue in the form of a monologue. When Hamlet soliloquizes, we hear a single voice which is supposed to be addressed to himself but in fact is heard as addressed to us, the audience, and it is impossible not to suspect that he is not disclosing to himself what he conceals from others, but only disclosing to us what he thinks it is good we should know, and at the same time concealing from us what he does not choose to tell us.

A dialogue requires two voices, but, if it is the inner dialogue of human personality that is to be expressed artistically, the two characters employed to express it and the relationship between them must be of a special kind. The pair must in certain respects be similar, i.e. they must be of the same sex, and in others, physical and temperamental, polar opposites—identical twins will not do because they inevitably raise the question, "Which is the real one?"—and they must be inseparable, i.e. the relationship between them must be of a kind which is not affected by the passage of time or the fluctuations of mood and passion, and which makes it plausible that wherever one of them is, whatever he is doing, the other should be there too. There is only one relationship which satisfies all these conditions, that between master and personal servant. It might be objected at this point that the Ego-self relationship is given while the master-servant relationship, as defined above, is contractual. The objection would be valid if man, like all other finite things, had only the proto-history of coming into being and then merely sustaining that being. But man has a real history; having come into being, he has then through his choices to become what he is not yet, and this he cannot do unless he first chooses himself as he is now with all his finite limitations. To reach "the age of consent" means to arrive at the point where the "given" Ego-self relationship is changed into a contractual one. Suicide is a breach of contract.

III

> CRICHTON. There must always be a master and servants in
> all civilised communities, for it is natural, and whatever
> is natural is right.
> LORD LOAMSHIRE. It's very unnatural for me to stand
> here and allow you to talk such nonsense.
> CRICHTON. Yes, my lord, it is. That is what I have been
> striving to point out to your lordship.
> —J. M. Barrie, *The Admirable Crichton*

Defined abstractly, a master is one who gives orders and a servant is one who obeys orders. This characteristic makes the master-servant relationship peculiarly suitable as an expression of the inner life, so much of which is carried on in imperatives. If a large lady carelessly, but not intentionally, treads on my corn during a subway rush hour, what goes on in my mind can be expressed dramatically as follows:

SELF (*in whom the physical sensation of pain has become the mental passion of anger*). Care for my anger! Do something about it!

COGNITIVE EGO. You are angry because of the pain caused by this large lady who, carelessly but not intentionally, has trodden on your corn. If you decide to relieve your feelings, you can give her a sharp kick on the ankle without being noticed.

SELF. Kick her.

SUPER-EGO (*to simplify matters, let us pretend that super-ego and conscience are identical, which they are not*). Unintentional wrongs must not be avenged. Ladies must not be kicked. Control your anger!

LADY (*noticing what she has done*). I beg your pardon! I hope I didn't hurt you.

SELF. Kick her!

SUPER-EGO. Smile! Say "Not at all, Madam."

VOLITIONAL EGO (*to the appropriate voluntary muscles*).

either   Kick her!

or   Smile! Say "Not at all, Madam!"

Of my five "characters," only one, my cognitive ego, really employs the indicative mood. Of the others, my self and my super-ego cannot, either of them, be a servant. Each is a master who is either obeyed or disobeyed. Neither can take orders. My body, on the other hand (or rather its "voluntary muscles"), can do nothing but what it is told; it can never be a master, nor even a servant, only a slave. While my volitional ego is always both, a servant in relation to either my self or my super-ego and a master in relation to my body.

The "demands" of reason are not imperative because, although it is possible not to listen to them and to forget them, as long as we listen and remember, it is impossible to disobey them, and a true imperative always implies the possibility of either obeying or disobeying. In so far as we listen to reason, we are its slaves, not its servants.

IV

> I care for nobody, no, not I
> And nobody cares for me.
> — "The Miller of Dee"

> But my five wits nor my five senses can
> Dissuade one foolish heart from serving thee,
> Who leaves unswayed the likeness of a man,
> Thy proud heart's slave and vassal wretch to be.
> —Shakespeare, Sonnet CXLI

Because of its double role the volitional ego has two wishes which, since the Fall, instead of being dialectically related, have become contradictory opposites. On the one hand it wishes to be free of all demands made upon it by the self or the conscience or the outer world. As Kierkegaard wrote:

> If I had a humble spirit in my service, who, when I asked for a glass of water, brought me the world's costliest wines blended in a chalice, I should dismiss him, in order to teach him that pleasure consists not in what I enjoy, but in having my own way.

When Biron, the hero of *Love's Labor Lost*, who has hitherto been free of passion, finds himself falling in love, he is annoyed.

> This senior junior, giant dwarf, Dan Cupid,
> Sole emperor and great general
> Of trotting paritors (O my little heart)
> And I to be a corporal of his field
> And wear his colours like a tumbler's hoop.

On the other hand, the same ego wishes to be important, to find its existence meaningful, to have a *telos*, and this *telos* it can only find in something or someone outside itself. To have a *telos* is to have something to obey, to be the servant of. Thus all lovers instinctively use the master-servant metaphor.

> MIRANDA.   To be your fellow
>   You may deny me; but I'll be your servant,
>   Whether you will or no.
> FERDINAND.   My Mistress, dearest,
>   And I thus humble ever.
> MIRANDA.   My husband then?
> FERDINAND. Aye, with a heart as willing
>   As bondage e'er of freedom.

And so, with calculation, speaks every seducer.

> BERTRAM. I prithee do not strive against my vows.
>   I was compelled to her, but I love thee
>   By love's own sweet constraint, and will for ever
>   Do thee all rights of service.
> DIANA.   Ay, so you serve us
>   Till we serve you.

To be loved, to be the *telos* of another, can contribute to the ego's sense of importance, provided that it feels that such giving of love is a free act on the part of the other, that the other is not a slave of his or her passion. In practice, unfortunately, if there is an erotic element present as distinct from *philia*, most people find it hard to believe that another's love for them is free and not a compulsion, unless they happen to reciprocate it.

Had man not fallen, the wish of his ego for freedom would be simply a wish not to find its *telos* in a false or inferior good, and its wish for a *telos* simply a longing for the true good, and both wishes would be granted. In his fallen state, he oscillates between a wish for absolute autonomy, to be as God, and a wish for an idol who will take over the whole responsibility for his existence, to be an irresponsible slave. The consequence of indulging the first is a sense of loneliness and lack of meaning; the consequence of indulging the second, a masochistic insistence on being made to suffer. John falls in love with Anne who returns his love, is always faithful and anxious to please. Proud and self-satisfied, he thinks of *my Anne*, presently of *my wife* and finally of *my well-being*. Anne as a real other has ceased to exist for him. He does not suffer in any way that he can put his finger on, nevertheless he begins to feel bored and lonely.

George falls in love with Alice who does not return his love, is unfaithful and treats him badly. To George she remains Alice, cruel but real. He suffers but he is not lonely or bored, for his suffering is the proof that another exists to cause it.

The futility of trying to combine both wishes into one, of trying, that is, to have a *telos*, but to find it within oneself not without, is expressed in the myth of Narcissus. Narcissus falls in love with his reflection; he wishes to become its servant, but instead his reflection insists upon being his slave.

V

Das verfluchte Hier
— Goethe, *Faust*

Goethe's *Faust* is full of great poetry and wise sayings but it is not dramatically exciting; like a variety show, it gives us a succession of scenes interesting in themselves but without a real continuity; one could remove a scene or add a new one without causing any radical change in the play. Further, once the Marguerite episode is over, it is surprising how little Faust himself actually does; Mephisto creates a new situation and Faust tells us what he feels about it. I can well imagine that every actor would like to play Mephisto, who is always entertaining, but the actor who plays Faust has to put up with being ignored whenever Mephisto is on stage. Moreover, from a histrionic point of view, is there ever any reason why he should move instead of standing still and just delivering his lines? Is not any movement the actor may think up arbitrary?

These defects are not, of course, due to any lack of dramatic talent in Goethe but to the nature of the Faust myth itself, for the story of Faust is precisely the story of a man who refuses to be anyone and only wishes to become someone else. Once he has summoned Mephisto, the manifestation of possibility without actuality, there is nothing left for Faust to represent but the passive consciousness of possibilities. When the Spirit of Fire appears to Faust, it says:

> Du gleichst dem Geist, den du begreifst,
> Nicht mir.

and in an ideal production, Faust and Mephisto should be played by identical twins.

Near the beginning of the play Faust describes his condition:

> Zwei Seelen wohnen, ach! in meiner Brust,
> Die eine will sich von der andern trennen;
> Die eine hält, in derber Liebeslust
> Sich an die Welt mit klammernden Organen;
> Die andre hebt gewaltsam sich vom Dust
> Zu den Gefilden hoher Ahnen.

This has nothing to do, though he may think it has, with the conflict between pleasure and goodness, the kingdom of *this* world and the kingdom of Heaven. Faust's *Welt* is the immediate actual moment, the actual concrete world now, and his *hohe Ahnen* the same world seen by memory and imagination as possible, as what might have been once and may be yet. All value belongs to possibility, the actual here and now is valueless, or rather the value it has is the feeling of discontent it provokes. When Faust signs his contract with Mephisto, the latter says:

> Ich will mich hier zu deinem Dienst verbinden,
> Auf deinen Wink nicht rasten und nicht ruhn;
> Wenn wir uns drüben wieder finden,
> So sollst du mir das Gleiche tun.

to which Faust replies airily:

> Das Drüben kann mich wenig kümmern
> Schlägst du erst diese Welt zu Trümmern,
> Die andre mag darnach enstehen.

because he does not believe that *Das Drüben*, the exhaustion of all possibilities, can ever be reached—as, indeed, in the play it never is. Faust escapes Mephisto's clutches because he is careful to define the contentment of his last moment in terms of anticipation:

> Im Vorgefühl von solchem hohen Glück
> Geniess' ich jezt den höchsten Augenblick.

But, though Faust is not damned, it would be nonsense to say that he is saved. The angels bearing him to Heaven describe him as being in the pupa stage, and to such a condition Judgment has no meaning.

Mephisto describes himself as:

> ein Teil des Teils, der Anfangs alles war,
> Ein Teil der Finsternis, die sich das Licht gebar

as, that is to say, a manifestation of the rejection of all finiteness, the desire for existence without the limitation of essence. To the spirit that rejects any actuality, the ideal must be the *Abgrund*, the abyss of infinite potentiality, and all creation must be hateful to it. So Valéry's serpent cries out against God:

> Il se fit Celui qui dissipe
> En conséquences son Principe,
> En étoiles son Unité.

Mephisto describes himself as:

> ein Teil von jener Kraft,
> Die stets das Böse will und stets das Gute schaft,

but it is hard to see what good or evil he does to Faust. Through his agency or his suggestion, Faust may do a good deal of harm to others, but Faust himself is completely unaffected by his acts. He passively allows Mephisto to entertain him and is no more changed in character by these entertainments than we are by watching the play.

Faust may talk a great deal about the moral dangers of content and sloth, but the truth is that his discontent is not a discontent with himself but a terror of being bored. What Faust is totally lacking in is a sacramental sense,* a sense that the finite can be a sign for the infinite, that the secular can be sanctified; one cannot imagine him saying with George Herbert:

> A servant with this clause
> Makes drudgery divine;
> Who sweeps a room as for Thy laws
> Makes that and the action fine.

In this lack Faust is a typical modern figure. In earlier ages men have been tempted to think that the finite was not a sign for the holy but the holy itself, and fell therefore into idolatry and magic. The form which the Devil assumed in such periods, therefore, is always finite; he appeared as the manifestation of some specific temptation, as a beautiful woman, a bag of gold, etc. In our age there are no idols in the strict sense because we tire of one so quickly and take up another that the word cannot apply. Our real, because permanent, idolatry is an idolatry of possibility. And in such an age the Devil appears in

---

* If Faust holds any theological position, it is pantheist. The pantheist believes that the universe is numinous *as-a-whole.* But a sacramental sign is always some particular aspect of the finite, *this* thing, *this* act, not the finite-in-general, and it is valid for this person, this social group, this historical epoch, not for humanity-in-general. Pansacramentalism is self-contradictory.

the form of Mephisto, in the form, that is, of an actor. The point about an actor is that he has no name of his own, for his name is Legion. One might say that our age recognized its nature on the day when Henry Irving was knighted.

VI

Voglio far il gentiluomo
E non voglio più servir.
— Da Ponte, *Don Giovanni*

Dein Werk! O thör'ge Magd
— Wagner, *Tristan and Isolde*

The man who refuses to be the servant of any *telos* can only be directly represented, like the Miller of Dee, lyrically. He can sing his rapture of freedom and indifference, but after that there is nothing for him to do but be quiet. In a drama he can only be represented indirectly as a man with a *telos*, indeed a monomania, but of such a kind that is clear that it is an arbitrary choice; nothing in his nature and circumstances imposes it on him or biases him toward it. Such is Don Giovanni. The *telos* he chooses is to seduce, to "know" every woman in the world. Leporello says of him:

Non si picca, se sia ricca
Se sia brutta, se sia bella,
Purchè porti la gonnella.

A sensual libertine, like the Duke in *Rigoletto,* cannot see a pretty girl, or a girl who is "his type" without trying to seduce her; but if a plain elderly woman like Donna Elvira passes by, he cries, "My God, what a dragon," and quickly looks away. That is sensuality, and pains should be taken in a production to make it clear why the Duke should have fallen into this particular idolization of the finite rather than another. The Duke must appear to be the kind of man to whom all women will be attracted; he must be extremely good-looking, virile, rich, magnificent, a grand seigneur.

Don Giovanni's pleasure in seducing women is not sensual but arithmetical; his satisfaction lies in adding one more name to his list which is kept for him by Leporello. Everything possible, therefore, should be done to make him as inconspicuous and anonymous in appearance as an F.B.I. agent. If he is made handsome, then his attraction for women is a bias in his choice, and if he is made ugly, then the repulsion he arouses in women is a challenge. He should look so neutral that the audience realizes that, so far as any finite motive is concerned, he might just as well have chosen to collect stamps. The Duke does not need a servant because there is no contradiction involved in sensuality or indeed in any idolatry of the finite. The idol and the idolater between them can say all there is to say. The Duke is the master of his ladies and the slave of his sensuality. Any given form of idolatry of the finite is lacking in contradiction because such idolatry is itself finite. Whenever we find one idol we find others, we find polytheism. We do not have to be told so to know that there are times when the Duke is too tired or too hungry to look at a pretty girl. For Don Giovanni there are no such times, and it is only in conjunction with his servant, as Giovanni-Leporello, that he can be understood.

Don Giovanni is as inconspicuous as a shadow, resolute and fearless in action; Leporello is comically substantial like Falstaff, irresolute and cowardly. When, in his opening aria, Leporello sings the words quoted at the head of this section, the audience laughs because it is obvious that he is lacking in all the qualities of character that a master should have. He is no Figaro. But by the end of the opera, one begins to suspect that the joke is much funnier than one had first thought. Has it not, in fact, been Leporello all along who was really the master and Don Giovanni really his servant? It is Leporello who keeps the list and if he lost it or forgot to keep it up to date or walked off with it, Don Giovanni would have no *raison d'être* for existing. It is significant that we never see Don Giovanni look at the list himself or show any pleasure in it; only Leporello does that: Don Giovanni merely reports the latest name to him. Perhaps it should have been Leporello who was carried down alive to hell by the Commendatore, leaving poor worn-out Giovanni to die in peace. Imagine a Leporello who, in real life, is a rabbity-looking, celibate, timid, stupendously learned professor, with the finest collection in the world of, say, Trilobites, but in every aspect of life outside his field, completely incompetent. Brought up by a stern fundamentalist father (Il Commendatore) he went to college with the intention of training for the ministry, but there he read Darwin and lost his faith. Will not his daydream versions of his ideal self be someone very like Don Giovanni?

It is fortunate for our understanding of the myth of Tristan and Isolde that Wagner should have chosen to write an opera about it, for the physical demands made by Wagnerian opera defend us, quite accidentally, from an illusion which we are likely to fall into when reading the medieval legend; the two lovers, for whom nothing is of any value but each other, appear on the stage, not as the handsomest of princes and the most beautiful of princesses, not as Tamino and Pamina, but as a Wagnerian tenor and soprano in all their corseted bulk. When Tamino and Pamina fall mutually in love, we see that the instigating cause is the manly beauty of one and the womanly beauty of the other. Beauty is a fine quality which time will take away; this does not matter in the case of Tamino and Pamina because we know that their romantic passion for each other has only to be temporary, a natural but not serious preliminary to the serious unromantic love of man and wife. But the infinite romantic passion of Tristan and Isolde which has no past and no future outside itself cannot be generated by a finite quality; it can only be generated by finiteness-in-itself against which it protests with an infinite passion of rejection. Like Don Giovanni, Tristan and Isolde are purely mythical figures in that we never meet them in historical existence: we meet promiscuous men like the Duke, but never a man who is absolutely indifferent to the physical qualities of the women he seduces; we meet romantically passionate engaged couples, but never a couple of whom we can say that their romantic passion will not and cannot change into married affection or decline into indifference. Just as we can say that Don Giovanni might have chosen to collect stamps instead of women, so we can say that Tristan and Isolde might have fallen in love with two other people; they are so indifferent to each other as persons with unique bodies and characters that they might just as well—and this is one significance of the love potion—have drawn each other's names out of a hat. A life-long romantic idolatry of a real person is possible and occurs in life provided that the romance is one-sided, that one party plays the Cruel Fair, e.g. Don José and Carmen. For any finite idolatry is by definition an asymmetric relation: my idol is that which I make responsible for my existence in order that I may have no responsibility for myself; if it turns round and demands responsibility from me it ceases to be an idol. Again, it is fortunate that the operatic medium makes it impossible for Wagner's Tristan and Isolde to consummate their love physically. Wagner may have intended, probably did intend, the love duet in the Second Act to stand for such a physical consummation, but what we actually see are two people singing of how much they desire each other, and consummation remains something that is always about to happen but never does, and this, whatever Wagner intended, is correct: their mutual idolatry is only possible because, while both assert their infinite willingness to give themselves to each other, in practice both play the Cruel Fair and withhold themselves. Were they to yield, they would know something about each other and their relation would change into a one-sided idolatry, a mutual affection or a mutual indifference. They do not yield because their passion is not for each other but for something they hope to obtain by means of each other, Nirvana, the primordial unity that made the mistake of begetting multiplicity, "der Finsternis die sich das Licht gebar."

Just as Don Giovanni is inseparable from his servant Leporello, so Tristan and Isolde appear flanked by Brangaene and Kurvenal. It is Kurvenal's mocking references to Morold that make Isolde so angry that she decides to poison Tristan and herself, in consequence of which Tristan and she are brought together; otherwise he would have kept his distance till they landed. It is Brangaene who substitutes the love-potion for the death potion so that Tristan and Isolde are committed to each other not by their personal decisions but by an extraneous factor for which they are not responsible. It is Brangaene who tells King Mark about the love-potion so that he is willing to forgive the lovers and let them join each other, but tells him too late for his decision to be of any practical help. And it is Kurvenal's leaving of his master to greet Isolde that gives Tristan the opportunity to cause his death by tearing off his bandages. Kurvenal obeys his friend like a slave who has no mind of his own.

> Dem guten Marke,
> dient'ich ihm hold,
> wie warst du ihm treuer als Gold!
> Musst' ich verathen
> den edlen Herrn,
> wie betrogst du ihn da so gern!
> Dir nicht eigen,
> einzig mein.

Tristan tells him, but then points out that Kurvenal has one freedom which he, Tristan, can never have. He is not in love.

> Nur—was ich leide,
> das—kannst du nicht leiden.

As in the case of Don Giovanni and Leporello, one begins to wonder who are really master and mistress. Imagine a Kurvenal and a Brangaene who in real life are an average respectable lower middle-class couple (but with more children than is today usual), living in a dingy suburban house. He has a dingy white-collar job and has a hard time making both ends meet. She has no maid and is busy all day washing the diapers of the latest baby, mending the socks of older children, washing up, trying to keep the house decent, etc. She has lost any figure and looks she may once have had; he is going bald and acquiring a middle-aged spread. Their marriage, given their circumstances, is an average one; any romantic passion has long ago faded but, though they often get on each other's nerves, they don't passionately hate each other. A couple, that is, on whom the finite bears down with the fullest possible weight, or provides the fewest of its satisfactions. Now let them concoct their daydream of the ideal love and the ideal world, and something very like the passion of Tristan and Isolde will appear, and a world in which children, jobs, and food do not exist. His Boss and her husband will appear as King Mark, an old beau of hers (to him) and an old disreputable drinking crony of his (to her) as Morold, the scandal-mongering neighbors next door as Melot. They cannot, however, keep the sense of reality out of their dream and make everything end happily. They are dreamers but they are sane dreamers, and sanity demands that Tristan and Isolde are doomed.

VII

> The fool will stay
> And let the wise man fly.

> The knave turns fool who runs away,
> The fool, no knave perdy.
> —Shakespeare, *King Lear*

According to Renaissance political theory, the King, as the earthly representative of Divine Justice, is above the law which he imposes on his subjects. For his subjects the law is a universal, but the King who makes the law is an individual who cannot be subject to it, since the creator is superior to his creation—a poet, for instance, cannot be subordinate to his poem. In general, the Middle Ages had thought differently; they held that not even the King could violate Natural Law. In English history, the transition from one view to the other is marked by Henry the Eighth's execution of Sir Thomas More who, as Lord Chancellor, was the voice of Natural Law and the keeper of the King's Conscience. Both periods believed that, in some sense, the King was a divine representative, so that the political question, "Is the King obliged to obey his law?" is really the theological question, "Does God have to obey His own laws?" The answer given seems to me to depend upon what doctrine of God is held, Trinitarian or Unitarian. If the former, then the Middle Ages were right, for it implies that obedience is a meaningful term when applied to God—The co-equal Son obeys the Father. If the latter, then the Renaissance was right, unless the sacramental theory of kingship is abandoned, in which case, of course, the problem does not arise.* An absolute monarch is a representative of the deist God. The Renaissance King, then, is an individual, and the only individual, the superman, who is above the law, not subject to the universal. If he should do wrong, who can tell him so? Only an individual who, like himself, is not subject to the universal because he is as below the universal as the King is above it. The fool is such an individual because, being deficient in reason, subhuman, he has no contact with its demands. The fool, is "simple," i.e. he is not a madman. A madman is someone who was once a normal sane man but who, under the stress of emotion, has lost his reason. A fool is born a fool and was never anything else; he is, as we say, "wanting," and, whereas a madman is presumed to feel emotions like normal men, indeed to feel them more strongly than the normal man, the fool is presumed to be without emotions. If, therefore, he should happen to utter a truth, it cannot be *his* utterance, for he cannot distinguish between truth and falsehood, and he cannot have a personal motive for uttering what, without his knowing it, happens to be true, since motive implies emotion and the fool is presumed to have none. It can only be the voice of God using him as His mouthpiece. God is as far above the superman-King, whose earthly repre-

---

* Or does it? In recent years we have seen the emergence, and not only in professedly totalitarian countries, of something very like a doctrine of the Divine Right of States, though the adjective would be indignantly denied by most of its exponents.

sentative he is, as the King is above ordinary mortals, so that the voice of God is a voice, the only one, which the King must admit that it is his duty to obey. Hence the only individual who can speak to the King with authority, not as a subject, is the fool.

The position of the King's Fool is not an easy one. It is obvious that God uses him as a mouthpiece only occasionally, for most of the time what he says is patently nonsense, the words of a fool. At all moments when he is not divinely inspired but just a fool, he is subhuman, not a subject but a slave with no human rights, who may be whipped like an animal if he is a nuisance. On the occasions when he happens to speak the truth, he cannot, being a fool, say, "This time I am not speaking nonsense as I usually do, but the truth"; it rests with the King to admit the difference and, since truth is often unwelcome and hard to admit, it is not surprising that the fool's life should be a rough one.

> FOOL. Prithee, nuncle, keep a schoolmaster that can teach thy fool to lie.
> LEAR. An you lie, sirrah, we'll have you whipped.
> FOOL. I marvel what kin thou and thy daughters are. They'll have me whipped for speaking true; thou'lt have me whipped for lying; and sometimes I am whipped for holding my peace. I had rather be any kind of thing than a fool. And yet, I would not be thee, nuncle.

It was said above that the cognitive ego never uses the imperative mood, always the indicative or the conditional: it does not say, "Do such-and-such!"; it says, "Such-and-such *is* the case. *If* you want such-and-such a result, you can obtain it by doing as follows. What you want to do, your emotive self can tell you, not I. What you ought to do, your conscience can tell you, not I." Nor can it compel the volitional ego to listen to it; the choice of listening or refusing to listen lies with the latter.

> Truths a dog must to kennel; he must be whipped out when Lady the brach may stand by the fire and stink.

We are told that, after Cordelia's departure for France after Lear's first fatal folly, his first "mad" act, the fool started to pine away. After the Third Act, he mysteriously vanishes from the play, and when Lear appears without him, Lear is irremediably mad. At the very end, just before his death, Lear suddenly exclaims "And my poor fool is hanged!" and it is impossible for the audience to know if he is actually referring to the fool or suffering from aphasia and meaning to say Cordelia whom we know to have been hanged.

The fool, that is, seems to stand for Lear's sense of reality which he rejects. Not for his conscience. The fool never speaks to him, as Kent does, in the name of morality. It was immoral of Lear to make the dowries of his daughters proportionate to their capacity to express their affection for their father, but not necessarily mad because he (and the audience) has no reason to suppose that Cordelia has any less talent for expressing affection than her sisters. Rationally, there is no reason why she should not have surpassed them. Her failure in the competition is due to a moral refusal, not to a lack of talent. Lear's reaction to Cordelia's speech, on the other hand, is not immoral but mad because he knows that, in fact, Cordelia loves him and that Goneril and Regan do not. From that moment on, his sanity is, so to speak, on the periphery of his being instead of at its center, and the dramatic manifestation of this shift is the appearance of the fool who stands outside him as a second figure and is devoted to Cordelia. As long as passion has not totally engulfed him, the fool can appear at his side, laboring "to outjest / His heart struck injuries." There is still a chance, however faint, that he may realize the facts of his situation and be restored to sanity. Thus when Lear begins to address the furniture as if it were his daughters, the fool remarks:

> I cry you mercy. I took you for a joint-stool.

In other words, there is still an element of theater in Lear's behavior, as a child will talk to inanimate objects as if they were people, while knowing that, in reality, they are not. But when this chance has passed and Lear has descended into madness past recall, there is nothing for the fool to represent and he must disappear.

Frequently the fool makes play with the words "knave" and "fool." A knave is one who disobeys the imperatives of conscience; a fool is one who cannot hear or understand them. Though the cognitive ego is, morally, a "fool" because conscience speaks not to it but to the volitional ego, yet the imperative of duty can never be in contradiction to the actual facts of the situation, as the imperative of passion can be and frequently is. The socratic doctrine that to know the good is to will it, that sin is ignorance, is valid if by knowing one means listening to what one knows, and by ignorance, willful ignorance. If that is what one means, then, though not all fools are knaves, all knaves are fools.

LEAR. Dost thou call me fool, boy?
FOOL. All thy other titles thou hast given away; that thou wast born with.
KENT. This is not altogether fool, my lord.
FOOL. No, faith, lords and great men will not let me. If I had a monopoly on't; they would have part of it.

Ideally, in a stage production, Lear and the fool should be of the same physical type; they should both be athletic mesomorphs. The difference should be in their respective sizes. Lear should be as huge as possible, the fool as tiny.

VIII

BODY. O who shall me deliver whole
From bonds of this tyrannic soul?

> Which, stretcht upright, impales me so
> That mine own precipice I go. . . .

SOUL. What Magick could me thus confine
Within another's grief to pine?
Where whatsoever it complain,
I feel, that cannot feel, the pain. . . .

—Andrew Marvell

VALENTINE. Belike, boy, then you are in love; for last morning you could not see to wipe my shoes.

SPEED. True sir; I was in love with my bed. I thank you, you swinged me for my love, which makes me the bolder to chide you for yours.

—Shakespeare, *Two Gentlemen of Verona*

The Tempest, Shakespeare's last play, is a disquieting work. Like the other three comedies of his late period, *Pericles, Cymbeline* and *A Winter's Tale*, it is concerned with a wrong done, repentance, penance and reconciliation; but, whereas the others all end in a blaze of forgiveness and love—"Pardon's the word to all"—in *The Tempest* both the repentance of the guilty and the pardon of the injured seem more formal than real. Of the former than real. Of th former, Alonso is the only one who seems genuinely sorry; the repentance of the rest, both the courtly characters, Antonio and Sebastian, and the low, Trinculo and Stephano, is more the prudent promise of the punished and frightened, "I won't do it again. It doesn't pay," than any change of heart: and Prospero's forgiving is more the contemptuous pardon of a man who knows that he has his enemies completely at his mercy than a heartfelt reconciliation. His attitude to all of them is expressed in his final words to Caliban:

> an you look
> To have my pardon trim it handsomely.

One must admire Prospero because of his talents and his strength; one cannot possibly like him. He has the coldness of someone who has come to the conclusion that human nature is not worth much, that human relations are, at their best, pretty sorry affairs. Even toward the innocent young lovers, Ferdinand and Miranda, and their "brave new world," his attitude is one of mistrust so that he has to preach them a sermon on the dangers of anticipating their marriage vows. One might excuse him if he included himself in his critical skepticism but he never does; it never occurs to him that he, too, might have erred and be in need of pardon. He says of Caliban:

> born devil on whose nature
> Nurture can never stick, on whom my pains,
> Humanely taken, all, all lost, quite lost.

but Shakespeare has written Caliban's part in such a way that, while we have to admit that Caliban is both brutal and corrupt, a "lying slave" who can be prevented from doing mischief only "by stripes not kindness," we cannot help feeling that Prospero is largely responsible for his corruption, and that, in the debate between them, Caliban has the best of the argument.

Before Prospero's arrival, Caliban had the island to himself, living there in a state of savage innocence. Prospero attempts to educate him, in return for which Caliban shows him all the qualities of the isle. The experiment is brought to a halt when Caliban tries to rape Miranda, and Prospero abandons any hope of educating him further. He does not, however, sever their relation and turn Caliban back to the forest; he changes its nature and, instead of trying to treat Caliban as a son, makes him a slave whom he rules by fear. This relation is profitable to Prospero:

> as it is
> We cannot miss him. He does make our fire,
> Fetch in our wood, and serve us in offices
> That profit us.

but it is hard to see what profit, material or spiritual, Caliban gets out of it. He has lost his savage freedom:

> For I am all the subjects that you have
> Which first was mine own king.

and he has lost his savage innocence:

> You taught me language and my profit on't
> Is, I know how to curse.

so that he is vulnerable to further corruption when he comes into contact with the civilized vices of Trinculo and Stephano. He is hardly to be blamed, then, if he regards the virtues of civilization with hatred as responsible for his condition:

> Remember
> First to possess his books, for without them
> He's but a sot, as I am.

As a biological organism Man is a natural creature subject to the necessities of nature; as a being with consciousness and will, he is at the same time an historical person with the freedom of the spirit. *The Tempest* seems to me a manichean work, not because it shows the relation of Nature to Spirit as one of conflict and hostility, which in fallen man it is, but because it puts the blame for this upon Nature and makes the Spirit innocent. Such a view is the exact opposite of the view expressed by Dante:

> Lo naturale è sempre senza errore
> ma l'altro puote errar per male obbietto
> o per poco o per troppo di givore.
>
>   —*Purgatorio* XVII

The natural can never desire too much or too little because the natural good is the mean—too much and too little are both painful to its natural well-being. The natural, conforming to necessity, cannot imagine possibility. The closest it can come to a relation with the possible is as a vague dream; without Prospero, Ariel can only be known to Caliban as "sounds and sweet airs that give delight and hurt not." The animals cannot fall because the words of the tempter, "Ye shall be as gods," are in the future tense, and the animals have no future tense, for the future tense implies the possibility of doing something that has not been done before, and that they cannot imagine.

Man can never know his "nature" because knowing is itself a spiritual and historical act; his physical sensations are always accompanied by conscious emotions. It is impossible to remember a physical sensation of pleasure or pain, the moment it ceases one cannot recall it, and all one remembers is the emotion of happiness or fear which accompanied it. On the other hand, a sensory stimulus can recall forgotten emotions associated with a previous occurrence of the same stimulus, as when Proust eats the cake.

It is unfortunate that the word "Flesh," set in contrast to "Spirit," is bound to suggest not what the Gospels and St Paul intended it to mean, the whole physical-historical nature of fallen man, but his physical nature alone, a suggestion very welcome to our passion for reproving and improving others instead of examining our own consciences. For, the more "fleshly" a sin is, the more obviously public it is, and the easier to prevent by the application of a purely external discipline. Thus the sin of gluttony exists in acts of gluttony, in eating, drinking, smoking too much, etc. If a man restrains himself from such excess, or is restrained by others, he ceases to be a glutton; the phrase "gluttonous thoughts" apart from gluttonous acts is meaningless.

As Christ's comment on the Seventh Commandment indicates, the sin of lust is already "unfleshly" to the degree that it is possible to have lustful thoughts without lustful deeds, but the former are still "fleshly" in that the thinker cannot avoid knowing what they are; he may insist that his thoughts are not sinful but he cannot pretend that they are not lustful. Further, the relation between thought and act is still direct. The thought is the thought of a specific act. The lustful man cannot be a hypocrite to himself except through a symbolic transformation of his desires into images which are not consciously lustful. But the more "spiritual" the sin, the more indirect is the relation between thought and act, and the easier it is to conceal the sin from others and oneself. I have only to watch a glutton at the dinner table to see that he is a glutton, but I may know someone for a very long time before I realize that he is an envious man, for there is no act which is in itself envious; there are only acts done in the spirit of envy, and there is often nothing about the acts themselves to show that they are done from envy and not from love. It is always possible, therefore, for the envious man to conceal from himself the fact that he is envious and to believe that he is acting from the highest of motives. While in the case of the purely spiritual sin of pride there is no "fleshly" element of the concrete whatsoever, so that no man, however closely he observe others, however strictly he examine himself, can ever know if they or he are proud; if he finds traces of any of the other six mortal sins, he can infer pride, because pride is fallen "spirit-in-itself" and the source of all the other sins, but he cannot draw the reverse inference and, because he finds no traces of the other six, say categorically that he, or another, is not proud.

If man's physical nature could speak when his spirit rebukes it for its corruption, it would have every right to say, "Well, who taught me my bad habits?"; as it is, it has only one form of protest, sickness; in the end, all it can do is destroy itself in an attempt to murder its master.

Over against Caliban, the embodiment of the natural, stands the invisible spirit of imagination, Ariel. (In a stage production, Caliban should be as monstrously conspicuous as possible, and, indeed, suggest, as far as decency permits, the phallic. Ariel, on the other hand, except when he assumes a specific disguise at Prospero's orders, e.g. when he appears as a harpy, should, ideally, be invisible, a disembodied voice, an ideal which, in these days of microphones and loud-speakers, should be realizable.

Caliban was once innocent but has been corrupted; his initial love for Prospero has turned into hatred. The terms "innocent" and "corrupt" cannot be applied to Ariel because he is beyond good and evil; he can neither love nor hate, he can only play. It was not sinful of Eve to imagine the possibility of being as a god knowing good and evil: her sin lay in desiring to realize that possibility when she knew it was forbidden her, and her desire did not come from her imagination, for imagination is without desire and is, therefore, incapable of distinguishing between permitted and forbidden possibilities; it only knows that they are imaginatively possible. Similarly, imagination cannot distinguish the possible from the impossible; to it the impossible is a species of the genus possible, not another genus. I can perfectly well imagine that I might be a hundred feet high or a champion heavyweight boxer, and I do myself no harm in so doing, provided I do so playfully, without desire. I shall, however, come to grief if I take the possibility seriously, which I can do in two ways. Desiring to become a heavyweight boxer, I may deceive myself into thinking that the imaginative possibility is a real possibility and waste my life trying to become the boxer I never can become. Or, desiring to become a boxer, but realizing that it is, for me, impossible, I may refuse to relinquish the desire and turn on God and my neighbor in a passion of hatred and rejection because I cannot have what I want. So Richard III, to punish existence for his misfortune in being born a hunchback, decided to become a villain.

Imagination is beyond good *and* evil, but it is only with the help of imagination that I can become good *or* evil. Without imagination I remain an innocent animal, unable to become anything but what I already am. In order to become what I should become, therefore, I have to put my imagination to work, to limit its playful activities to imagining those possibilities which, for me, are both permissible and real; if I allow it to be the master and play exactly as it likes, then I shall remain in a dreamlike state of imagining everything I might become, without getting round to ever becoming anything. But, once imagination has done its work for me to the degree that, with its help, I have become what I should become, imagination has a right to demand its freedom to play without any limitations, for there is no longer any danger that I shall take its play seriously. Hence the relation between Prospero and Ariel is contractual, and, at the end of the drama, Ariel is released.

If *The Tempest* is overpessimistic and manichean, *The Magic Flute* is overoptimistic and pelagian. At the end of the opera a double wedding is celebrated; the representative of the spiritual, Tamino, finds his happiness in Pamina and has attained wisdom while the chorus sing:

> Es seigte die Stärke und Krönet zum Lohn.
> Die Schönheit und Weisheit mit ewigen Kron.

and, at the same time, the representative of the natural, Papageno is rewarded with Papagena, and they sing together:

> Erst einen kleinen Papageno
> Dann eine kleine Papagena
> Dann wieder einen Papageno
> Dann wieder eine Papagena.

expressing in innocent humility the same attitude which Caliban expresses in guilty defiance when Prospero accuses him of having tried to rape Miranda,

> O ho, O ho! Would't had been done.
> Thou didst prevent me; I had peopled else
> This isle with Calibans.

Tamino obtains his reward because he has had the courage to risk his life undergoing the trials of Fire and Water; Papageno obtains his because he has had the humility to refuse to risk his life even if the refusal will mean that he must remain single. It is as if Caliban, when Prospero offered to adopt him and educate him, had replied: "Thank you very much, but clothes and speech are not for me; It is better I stay in the jungle."

According to *The Magic Flute*, it is possible for nature and spirit to coexist in man harmoniously and without conflict, provided both keep to themselves and do not interfere with each other, and that, further, the natural has the freedom to refuse to be interfered with.

The greatest of spirit-nature pairs and the most orthodox is, of course, Don Quixote–Sancho Panza. Unlike Prospero and Caliban, their relationship is harmonious and happy; unlike Tamino and Papageno, it is dialectical; each affects the other. Further, both they and their relationship are comic; Don Quixote is comically mad, Sancho Panza is comically sane, and each finds the other a lovable figure of fun, an endless source of diversion. It is this omnipresent comedy that makes the book orthodox; present the relationship as tragic and the conclusion is manichean, present either or both of the characters as serious, and the conclusion is pagan or pelagian. The man who takes seriously the command of Christ to take up his cross and follow Him must, if he is serious, see himself as a comic figure, for he is not the Christ, only an ordinary man, yet he believes that the command, "Be ye perfect," is seriously addressed to himself. Worldly "sanity" will say, "I am not Christ, only an ordinary man. For me to think that I can become perfect would be madness. Therefore, the command cannot seriously be addressed to me." The other can only say, "It is madness for me to attempt to obey the command, for it seems impossible, nevertheless, since I believe it is addressed to me, I must believe that it is possible"; in proportion as he takes the command seriously, that is, he will see himself as a comic figure. To take himself seriously would mean that he thought of himself, not as an ordinary man, but as Christ.

For Christ is not a model to be imitated, like Hector, or Aristotle's megalopsych, but the Way to be followed. If a man thinks that the megalopsych is a desirable model, all he has to do is to read up how the megalopsych behaves and imitate him, e.g. he will be careful, when walking, not to swing his arms.

But the Way cannot be imitated, only followed; a Christian who is faced with a moral problem cannot look up the answer in the Gospels. If someone, for instance, were to let his hair and beard grow till he looked like some popular pious picture of Christ, put on a white linen robe and ride into town on a donkey, we should know at once that he was either a madman or a fake. At first sight Don Quixote's madness seems to be of this kind. He believes that the world of the Romances is the real world and that, to be a knight-errant, all he has to do is imitate the Romances exactly. Like Lear he cannot distinguish imaginative possibilities from actualities and treats analogies as identities; Lear thinks a stool is his daughter, Don Quixote thinks windmills are giants, but their manias are not really the same. Lear might be said to be suffering from worldly madness. The worldly man goes mad when the actual state of affairs becomes too intolerable for his amour-propre to accept; Lear cannot face the fact that he is no longer a man of power or that he has brought his present situation upon himself by his unjust competition. Don Quixote's madness, on the other hand, might be called holy madness, for amour-propre has nothing to do with his delusions. If his madness were of

Lear's kind, then, in addition to believing that he must imitate the knight-errants of old, he would have endowed himself in his imagination with all their gifts, e.g. with the youth and strength of Amadis de Gaul: but he does nothing of the kind; he knows that he is past fifty and penniless, nevertheless, he believes he is called to be a knight-errant. The knight-errant sets out to win glory by doing great deeds and to win the love of his lady, and whatever trials and defeats he may suffer on the way, in the end he triumphs. Don Quixote, however, fails totally; he accomplishes nothing, he does not win his lady, and, as if that were not ignominious enough, what he does win is a parody of what a knight-errant is supposed to win, for he does, in fact, become famous and admired—as a madman. If his were a worldly madness, amour-propre would demand that he add to his other delusions the delusion of having succeeded, the delusion that the welcome he receives everywhere is due to the fame of his great deeds (a delusion which his audience do everything to encourage), but Don Quixote is perfectly well aware that he has failed to do anything which he set out to do.

At the opposite pole to madness stands philistine realism. Madness says, "Windmills are giants"; philistine realism says, "Windmills really exist because they provide me with flour; giants are imaginary and do not exist because they provide me with nothing." (A student of psychoanalysis who says, "Windmills and giants are only phallic symbols," is both philistine and mad.) Madness confuses analogies and only admits identities; neither can say, "Windmills are like giants."

At first sight Sancho Panza seems a philistine realist. "I go," he says, "with a great desire to make money"; it may seem to the reader hardly "realistic" of Sancho Panza to believe that he will gain a penny, far less an island governorship, by following Don Quixote, but is not the philistine realist who believes in nothing but material satisfactions precisely the type to whom it is easiest to sell a non-existent gold mine?

The sign that Sancho Panza is not a philistine but a "holy" realist is the persistence of his hope of getting something when he has realized that his master is mad. It is as if a man who had been sold a nonexistent gold mine continued to believe in its existence after he had discovered that the seller was a crook. It is clear that, whatever Sancho Panza may say, his motives for following his master are love of his master and that equally unrealistic of motives, love of adventure for its own sake, a poetic love of fun. Just as Don Quixote wins fame, but fame as a madman, so Sancho Panza actually becomes the Governor of an island, but as a practical joke; as Governor he obtains none of the material rewards which a philistine would hope for, yet he enjoys himself enormously. Sancho Panza is a realist in that it is always the actual world, the immediate moment, which he enjoys, not an imaginary world or an anticipated future, but a "holy" realist in that he enjoys the actual and immediate for its own sake, not for any material satisfactions it provides.

Don Quixote and Sancho Panza are both inveterate quoters: what the Romances are to the one, proverbs are to the other. A Romance is a history, feigned or real. It recounts a series of unique and extraordinary events which have, or are purported to have, happened in the past. The source of interest is in the events themselves, not in the literary style in which they are narrated; as long as the reader learns what happened, it is a matter of indifference to him whether the style is imaginative or banal. A proverb has nothing to do with history for it states, or claims to state, a truth which is valid at all times. The content of "A stitch in time saves nine" belongs to the same class as a statement of empirical science like "bodies attract each other in direct proportion to their masses." The interest of a proverb, therefore, lies not in its content but in the unique way in which that content is expressed; the content is always banal because it is a statement of empirical science, and a scientific statement which was not banal would not be true.

Proverbs belong to the natural world where the Model and imitation of the Model are valid concepts. A proverb tells one exactly what one should do or avoid doing whenever the situation comes up to which it applies: if the situation comes up the proverb applies exactly; if it does not come up, the proverb does not apply at all. Romances, as we have seen, belong to the historical world of the spirit, where the Model is replaced by the Way, and imitation by following. But in man, these two worlds are not separate but dialectically related; the proverb, as an expression of the natural, admits its relation to the historical by its valuation of style; the romance, as an expression of the historical, admits its relation to the natural by its indifference to style.

Don Quixote's lack of illusions about his own powers is a sign that his madness is not worldly but holy, a forsaking of the world to follow, but without Sancho Panza it would not be Christian. For his madness to be Christian, he must have a neighbor, someone other than himself about whom he has no delusions but loves as himself. Without Sancho Panza, Don Quixote would be without neighbors, and the kind of religion implied would be one in which love of God was not only possible without but also incompatible with love of one's neighbor.

IX

He that is greatest among you, let him be as the younger;
and he that is chief, as he that doth serve. — Luke, XXII

ché per quanti si dice più lì nostro
tanto possiede più di ben ciascuno.
— Dante, *Purgatorio*, XV

When a lover tells his beloved that she is his mistress and that he desires to be her servant, what he is trying, honestly or hypocritically, to say is something as follows: "As you know, I find you beautiful, an object of desire. I know that for true love such desire is not enough; I must also love you, not as an object of my desire, but as you are in yourself; I must desire your self-fulfillment. I cannot know you as you are nor prove that I desire your self-fulfillment, unless you tell me what you want and allow me to try and give it to you."

The proverb, "No man is a hero to his own valet," does not mean that no valet admires his master, but that a valet knows his master as he really is, admirable or contemptible, because it is a valet's job to supply the wants of his master, and, if you know what somebody wants, you know what he is like. It is possible for a master to have not the faintest inkling of what his servant is really like—unless his servant loves him, it is certain that he never will—but it is impossible for a servant, whether he be friendly, hostile or indifferent, not to know exactly what his master is like, for the latter reveals himself every time he gives an order.

To illustrate the use of the master-servant relationship as a parable of agapé. I will take two examples from books which are not great works of art but for that very reason present the parable in a clear, simplified form, *Round the World in Eighty Days* by Jules Verne and the *Jeeves* series by P. G. Wodehouse.

Mr Fogg, as Jules Verne depicts him in his opening chapter, is a kind of stoic saint. He is a bachelor with ample private means and does no work, but he is never idle and has no vices; he plays whist at his club every evening but never more or less than the same number of hands, and, when he wins, he gives the money to charity. He knows all about the world for he is a religious reader of the newspapers, but he takes no part in its affairs; he has no friends and no enemies; he has never been known to show emotion of any kind; he seems to live "outside of any social relation." If "apathy" in the stoic sense is the highest virtue, then Fogg is a saint. His most striking trait, however, is one which seems to have been unknown in Classical times, a ritual mania about the exact time, an idolatry of the clock—his own tells the second, the minute, the hour, the day, the month and the year. He not only does exactly the same thing every day, but at exactly the same moment. Classical authors like Theophrastus have described very accurately most characterological types, but none of them, so far as I know, has described The Punctual Man (the type to which I personally belong), which cannot tell if it is hungry unless it first looks at the clock. It was never said in praise of any Caesar, for instance, that he made whatever was the Roman equivalent for trains run on time. I have heard it suggested that the first punctual people in history were the monks— at their Office hours. It is certain at least that the first serious analysis of the human experience of time was undertaken by St Augustine, and that the notion of punctuality, of action at an exact moment, depends on drawing a distinction between natural and historical time which Christianity encouraged if it did not invent.*

By and large, at least, the ancients thought of time either as oscillating to

---

* The Greek notion of *kairos*, the propitious moment for doing something, contained the seed of the notion of punctuality, but the seed did not flower.

and fro like a pendulum or as moving round and round like a wheel, and the notion of historical time moving in an irreversible unilateral direction was strange to them. Both oscillation and cyclical movement provide a notion of change, but of change *for-a-time*; this *for-a-time* may be a long time—the pendulum may oscillate or the wheel revolve very slowly—but sooner or later all events reoccur: there is no place for a notion of absolute novelty, of a unique event which occurs once and for all at a particular moment in time. This latter notion cannot be derived from our objective experience of the outside world—all the movements we can see there are either oscillatory or cyclical—but only from our subjective inner experience of time in such phenomena as memory and anticipation.

So long as we think of it objectively, time is Fate or Chance, the factor in our lives for which we are not responsible, and about which we can do nothing; but when we begin to think of it subjectively, we feel responsible for *our* time, and the notion of punctuality arises. In training himself to be superior to circumstance, the ancient stoic would discipline his passions because he knew what a threat they could be to the apathy he sought to acquire, but it would not occur to him to discipline his time, because he was unaware that it was his. A modern stoic like Mr Fogg knows that the surest way to discipline passion is to discipline time: decide what you want or ought to do during the day, then always do it at exactly the same moment every day, and passion will give you no trouble.

Mr Fogg has been so successful with himself that he is suffering from *hybris*; he is convinced that nothing can happen to him which he has not foreseen. Others, it is true, are often unreliable, but the moment he finds them so, he severs relations with them. On the morning when the story opens, he has just dismissed his servant for bringing him his shaving water at a temperature of 84° instead of the proper 86° and is looking for a new one. His conception of the just relation between master and servant is that the former must issue orders which are absolutely clear and unchanging—the master has no right to puzzle his servant or surprise him with an order for which he is not prepared—and the latter must carry them out as impersonally and efficiently as a machine—one slip and he is fired. The last thing he looks for in a servant or, for that matter, in anyone else is a personal friend.

On the same morning Passepartout has given notice to Lord Longsferry because he cannot endure to work in a chaotic household where the master is "brought home too frequently on the shoulders of policemen." Himself a sanguine, mercurial character, what he seeks in a master is the very opposite of what he would seek in a friend. He wishes his relation to his master to be formal and impersonal; in a master, therefore, he seeks his opposite, the phlegmatic character. His ideal of the master-servant relation happens, therefore, to coincide with Fogg's, and to the mutual satisfaction of both, he is interviewed and engaged.

But that evening the unforeseen happens, the bet which is to send them both off round the world. It is his *hybris* which tempts Mr Fogg into making the bet; he is so convinced that nothing unforeseen can occur which he cannot control that he cannot allow his club mates to challenge this conviction without taking up the challenge. Further unknown to him, by a chance accident which he could not possibly have foreseen, a bank robbery has just been committed, and the description of the thief given to the police plus his sudden departure from England have put him under suspicion. Off go Mr Fogg and Passepartout, then, pursued by the detective Fix. In the boat train Passepartout suddenly remembers that in the haste of packing he has left the gas fire burning in his bedroom. Fogg does not utter a word of reproach but merely remarks that it will burn at Passepartout's expense till they return. Mr Fogg is still the stoic with the stoic conception of justice operating as impersonally and inexorably as the laws of nature. It is a fact that it was Passepartout, not he, who forgot to turn off the gas; the hurry caused by his own sudden decision may have made it difficult for Passepartout to remember, but it did not make it impossible: therefore, Passepartout is responsible for his forgetfulness and must pay the price.

Then in India the decisive moment arrives: they run into preparations for a suttee, against her will, of a beautiful young widow, Aouda. For the first time in his life, apparently, Mr Fogg is confronted personally with human injustice and suffering, and a moral choice. If, like the priest and the levite, he passes by on the other side, he will catch the boat at Calcutta and win his bet with ease; if he attempts to save her, he will miss his boat and run a serious risk of losing his bet. Abandoning his stoic apathy, he chooses the second alternative, and from that moment on his relationship with Passepartout ceases to be impersonal; *philia* is felt by both. Moreover, he discovers that Passepartout has capacities which his normal duties as a servant would never have revealed, but which in this emergency situation are particularly valuable because Mr Fogg himself is without them. But for Passepartout's capacity for improvisation and acting which allow him successfully to substitute himself for the corpse on the funeral pyre, Aouda would never have been saved. Hitherto, Mr Fogg has always believed that there was nothing of importance anyone else could do which he could not do as well or better himself; for the first time in his life he abandons that belief.

Hitherto, Passepartout has thought of his master as an unfeeling automaton, just, but incapable of generosity or self-sacrifice; had he not had this unexpected revelation, he would certainly have betrayed Mr Fogg to Fix, for the detective succeeds in convincing him that his master is a bank-robber, and, according to the stoic notion of impersonal justice which Mr Fogg had seemed to exemplify, that would be his duty, but having seen him act personally, Passepartout refuses to assist impersonal justice.

Later, when the Trans-American express is attacked by Indians, it is Passepartout's athletic ability, a quality irrelevant to a servant's normal duties, which saves the lives of Mr Fogg and Aouda at the risk of his own, for he is captured by the Indians. In such an act the whole contractual master-servant relation is transcended; that one party shall undertake to sacrifice his life for the other cannot be a clause in any contract. The only possible repayment is a similar act, and Mr Fogg lets the relief train go without him, sacrificing what may well be his last chance of winning his bet, and goes back at the risk of his life to rescue Passepartout.

Like Mr Fogg, Bertie Wooster is a bachelor with private means who does no work, but there all resemblance ceases. Nobody could possibly be less of a stoic than the latter. If he has no vices it is because his desires are too vague and too fleeting for him to settle down to one. Hardly a week passes without Bertie Wooster thinking he has at last met The Girl; for a week he imagines he is her Tristan, but the next week he has forgotten her as completely as Don Giovanni forgets; besides, nothing ever happens. It is nowhere suggested that he owned a watch or that, if he did, he could tell the time by it. By any worldly moral standard he is a footler whose existence is of no importance to any-body. Yet it is Bertie Wooster who has the incomparable Jeeves for his servant. Jeeves could any day find a richer master or a place with less arduous duties, yet it is Bertie Wooster whom he chooses to serve. The Lucky Simpleton is a common folk-tale hero; for example, the Third Son who succeeds in the Quest appears, in comparison with his two elder brothers, the least talented, but his ambition to succeed is equal to theirs. He sets out bravely into the un-known, and unexpectedly triumphs. But Bertie Wooster is without any am-bition whatsoever and does not lift a finger to help himself, yet he is rewarded with what, for him, is even better than a beautiful Princess, the perfect om-niscient nanny who does everything for him and keeps him out of trouble without, however, ever trying, as most nannies will, to educate and improve him.

> —I say, Jeeves, a man I met at the club last night told me to put my shirt on Privateer for the two o'clock race this afternoon. How about it?
> —I should not advocate it, sir. The stable is not sanguine.
> —Talking of shirts, have those mauve ones I ordered arrived yet?
> —Yes, sir. I sent them back.
> —Sent them back?
> —Yes, sir. They would not have become you.

The Quest Hero often encounters an old beggar or an animal who offers him advice: if, too proud to imagine that such an apparently inferior crea-ture could have anything to tell him, he ignores the advice, it has fatal con-sequences; if he is humble enough to listen and obey, then, thanks to their help, he achieves his goal. But, however humble he may be, he still has the dream of becoming a hero; he may be humble enough to take advice from what seem to be his inferiors, but he is convinced that, potentially, he is a superior person, a prince-to-be. Bertie Wooster, on the other hand, not only knows that he is a person of no account, but also never expects to become anything else; till his dying day he will remain, he knows, a footler who requires a nanny; yet, at the same time, he is totally without the envy of others who are or may become of some account. He has, in fact, that rarest of virtues, humility, and so he is blessed: it is he and no other who has for his servant the god-like Jeeves.

> —All the other great men of the age are simply in the crowd, watching you go by.
> —Thank you very much, sir. I endeavor to give satisfaction.

So speaks comically—and in what other mode than the comic could it on earth truthfully speak?—the voice of Agapé, of Holy Love.

Thought, Summer 1954; *Encounter*, July 1954

The Freud-Fliess Letters

The Origins of Psycho-Analysis: Letters to William Fliess, Drafts and Notes, 1887–1902. By Sigmund Freud. Edited by Marie Bonaparte, Anna Freud, Ernest Kris. Basic Books. $6.75.

These letters tell two stories, one happy, the other sad. The former is the history of a man who succeeds in making revolutionary and important discoveries. When the letters begin, Freud is thirty-one; he has given up his previous career as a comparative anatomist and neurologist, in which he had achieved a considerable reputation, and has set up as a specialist in nervous disorders. He has already come to the conclusion that sexual factors are decisive in hysterias and obsessional neuroses (though one would not have guessed this from his collaboration with Breuer published several years later), but in therapy, he still relies mainly on electrical treatment and hypnosis. When the letters end fifteen years later, he has already published both *The Interpretation of Dreams* and *The Psycho-pathology of Everyday Life*; the basic and pioneer discoveries of psychoanalysis have been made, its fundamental dogmas established. From these letters we learn, for instance that the notion of dreams as wish-fulfillments came to Freud on July 24th, 1895, that, while in January of 1897, he was still firmly convinced that all memories of seduction in childhood were memories of real events, by September he had abandoned this hypothesis.

> Let me tell you straight away the great secret which has been slowly dawning on me in recent months. I no longer believe in my *neurotica*. . . . It is

curious that I feel not in the least disgraced, though the occasion might seem to require it. Certainly I shall not tell it in the land of the Philistines— but between ourselves I have a feeling more of triumph than defeat.

In the same year, while he was engaged on his auto-analysis, the following extracts tell their own story.

Hostile impulses against parents (a wish that they should die are also an integral part of neuroses. . . . It seems as though in sons this death wish is directed against their father and in daughters against their mother. (May 31st)

. . . later (between the ages of two and two-and-a-half) libido towards *matrem* was aroused; the occasion must have been the journey with her from Leipzig to Vienna, during which we spent a night together and I must have had the opportunity of seeing her *nudam*. (Oct. 3rd)

Only one idea of general value has occurred to me. I have found love of the mother and jealousy of the father in my own case too, and now believe it to be a general phenomenon of early childhood. . . . If that is the case, the gripping power of *Oedipus Rex*, in spite of all the rational objections to the inexorable fate that the story presupposes, becomes intelligible. . . . Every member of the audience was once a budding Oedipus in phantasy, and this dream-fulfillment played out in reality causes everyone to recoil in horror, with the full measure of repression which separates his infantile from his present state. (Oct. 15th)

Scientists are less apt than artists to keep personal accounts of their progress. These letters are, therefore, all the more fascinating as a demonstration that, despite all differences in subject matter and methodology, the process of creative work in the scientist and the artist are strikingly similar. In both cases advance is never in a straight line or at an even pace; circuitous routes are taken, blind alleys run into; there are good days

One strenuous night last week when I was in the stage of painful discomfort in which my brain works best, the barriers suddenly lifted, the veils dropped. Everything fell into place.

and bad days

it suddenly broke down for three days, and I had the feeling of inner binding about which my patients complain so much, and I was inconsolable.

there are moments of triumph

I cannot give you any ideas of the intellectual beauty of the work.

and moments of disappointment

> No critic can see more clearly than I the disproportion between the prob-
> lems and my answers to them, and it will be a fitting punishment for me
> that none of the unexplored regions of the mind in which I have been
> the first mortal to set foot will ever bear my name or submit to my laws.

and those of us whose activities are artistic may be consoled to learn that,
when it comes to jealousy of one's contemporaries, scientists are every bit as
bad.

> I picked up a recent book of Janet's on hysteria and *idées fixes* with beat-
> ing heart, and laid it down again with my pulse returned to normal. He
> has no suspicion of the clue. . . . When I read the latest psychological
> books and see what they have to say about dreams, I am as delighted as
> the dwarf in the fairy tale because "the princess doesn't know."

The second, the sad, story is that of a deep friendship, the deepest, apparently in Freud's life, which lasted fifteen years and then ended in total estrangement, lacking even the resignation expressed in these lines of Edward
Thomas':

> We were divided and looked strangely each
> At the other, and we knew we were not friends
> But fellows in a union that ends
> With the necessity for it, as it ought.

It is sad, not only because of the persons involved, but also for what it reveals
about human nature in general, for its unwelcome evidence that, in any
friendship between comrades-in-arms, (both Freud and Fliess were married
men with families) the persistence of the relationship is threatened in direct
proportion to its intensity. What the Oedipus myth signifies for the parent-
child relationship, the Cain-Abel or Romulus-Remus myth signifies for the
heroic partnership (each partner, of course, playing both roles.)

Fliess' side of the correspondence is missing and few people—the reviewer
is not among them—have read his books, so that any attempt to understand
what happened must rely a good deal on guesswork.

Two years younger than Freud, Fliess was, during all the years of their
friendship, outwardly, the successful one. While Freud was having a hard time
making both ends meet in Vienna, Fliess quickly built up a flourishing practice in Berlin and also married a rich wife. Freud was ill-at-ease with others
and full of self-doubts while Fliess gave an impression of great self-confidence
and soon had a circle of devoted admirers. One gets the impression—again
without having read his work—of a clever, widely read, imaginative, amusing,
but fundamentally frivolous man who was induced to adopt ideas because he
found them entertaining rather than because he was convinced that they
were true, and one suspects that his air of self-confidence was a defensive
mask behind which lay a deep uncertainty about the value of his work.

Until the break came, however—and it was Fliess, incidentally, who took the initiative in that—it was Freud who was in the dependent position. He is the one who has to write first, the first to use *Du*, the one who asks if he may call his next baby, should it be a boy, Wilhelm.

> I feel very isolated, scientifically blunted, stagnant and resigned. When I talked to you, and saw that you thought something of me, I actually started thinking something of myself, and the picture of confident energy which you offered was not without its effect. (Aug. 1890)

> I hope you will explain the physiological mechanism of my clinical findings from your point of view; secondly I want to maintain the right to come to you with all my theories and findings in the field of neurosis; and thirdly, I still look to you as the Messiah who will solve the problem I have indicated. (Oct. 1893)

> I hope you will allow me to go on taking advantage of your good nature as an indulgent audience, because without such a thing I cannot work. (May 1897)

and even after they have quarreled, and despite the evidence of his own dreams that he wants to sever relations, he cannot bring himself to do it. The letter of Sept. 1902 which begins with—

> There is no concealing the fact that we have drawn somewhat apart from each other. By this and that I can see how much. . . . In this you came to the limit of your penetration, you take sides against me and tell me that "the thought reader merely reads his own thoughts into other people," which deprives my work of all its value.

and ends with the suggestion that they collaborate on a book. To understand Freud's sense of isolation from his colleagues, his desperate need for an intimate listener, who would understand and appreciate what he was doing, one should, I think, bear in mind, firstly the intellectual atmosphere in which he was educated, its presuppositions as to the nature of science and secondly, the complete denial of their validity in the field of psychology which psychoanalysis, if its findings are true and its therapy successful, implies. Freud was brought up in and, with a part of his mind, continued until the end of his life stubbornly to believe, what might be called the Helmholtz faith, namely that real knowledge can only be obtained by the methods of the natural sciences, physics, chemistry, biology etc. Thus he opens his *Project for a Scientific Psychology* with a definition of his aim:

> . . . to represent psychical processes as quantitatively determined states of specifiable material particles and so to make them plain and void of contradictions.

In fact he did nothing of the kind. Freud's greatest achievement was not the hitherto unsuspected facts about the life of the mind but his discovery of the only method by which they could be found. If every one of his findings should turn out to need modification, he would remain the genius who made real knowledge of the psyche possible by regarding mental events, not as natural events, but as historical events to be approached by the methods of the historian. In the historical order every event is unique and related to others by the principle of analogy, not, as in the natural order, by the principle of identity, which means that they are not quantitatively measurable: say that A is the cause of B means in the historical order that A provides B with a motive for occurring, i.e. A makes B possible or likely but not inevitable; further, while change is reversible in the inorganic order and cyclical in the organic, historical change is irreversible yet every new event changes all past events; lastly, while in the natural order what is real must necessarily be true, in history a deliberate lie, a mistaken notion, are as real and important as the truth.

Instinctively Freud knew quite well what he was doing and where the attacks would come from.

> I still find it a very strange thing that the case histories I describe read
> like short stories and lack, so to speak, the serious imprint of science.

It was not only or mainly to his assertion of the importance of sexuality that his colleagues were going to object—had he for instance claimed that all mental life was determined by the sexual hormones he would have been listened to seriously—but to his whole approach to the subject. It has not been the priests who have been most shocked by psychoanalysis; it has been, and still is, the neurologists.

Part of Fliess' attraction for Freud lay in the fact that he was an organologist, i.e. concerned with the "safe science" of biology so that he looked to Fliess to provide the biological proofs of his psychology. Since his own discoveries were so startling, the new biology ought to be startling too, and Fliess' ingenious speculations had the sort of novelty demanded. Unfortunately, it seems that Fliess' theories were not true and that Freud instinctively knew this. While he is loud in praise of Fliess' work in general, whenever it comes to discussing a specific point, he excuses himself by saying that he does not understand figures. Biological life is cyclical and there was no inherent impossibility that Fliess' cycles should apply there, but again, with his extraordinary flair, Freud sensed that the historical life of the mind is not cyclical and would have nothing to do with them in psychology.

That Fliess should have accused Freud of "merely reading his own thoughts into other people" and that Freud should have taken offense is profoundly ironical and significant. What Freud should have replied is something as follows: "Apart from the *merely*, which shows that you have not understood me, you are perfectly right. In investigating the life of the mind, not only is it permissible to read one's thoughts in another person because they are there, but also it is the only way in which any knowledge whatsoever of other minds can be gained. Imagination may, all too easily, err, but for the psychologist there is no other instrument. In studying the life of the body, of events in the central nervous system, shall we say, one is not permitted to read one's own thoughts into them because they do not think, and I am sorry to say so, my dear Wilhelm, but that is just what, with your numerological calculations, your Holy Numbers, I suspect you of doing in your organology. What is the correct scientific procedure in my field is *fantastica fornicatio* in yours."

The letters leave one feeling very sorry for Fliess who had to suffer the fate which always befalls a man of talent who associates with a genius. Geniuses are apt to leave destruction and resentment in their wake because they cannot help assimilating everything from those around them which is potentially valuable and turning into gold what they could have turned into silver. This kind of assimilation has nothing to do with plagiarism—Freud was always scrupulous about acknowledging any suggestion he was aware of having been given by another—but the unfortunate man of talent is left with a feeling of having been robbed without being able rationally to justify it.

I am not sure that it was wise of the editors to follow the Letters with the hundred page *Project for a Scientific Psychology* which Freud sent to Fliess in 1895. It might have been better to publish it separately because, while the letters are of universal interest, the Project presupposes a considerable knowledge of neurology, and the average reader is going to find it very stiff going indeed. Still, what does it matter? Those who cannot follow it can leave it alone, and, for those who can, it is an additional pleasure.

The Griffin, June 1954

Introduction to *The Visionary Novels of George Macdonald*

For the writing of what may comprehensively be called Dream Literature, though it includes many works, like detective stories and opera libretti which are, formally, "feigned histories," the primary requirement is the gift of mythopoeic imagination. This gift is one with which criticism finds it hard to deal for it seems to have no necessary connection with the gift of verbal expression or the power to structure experience. There have been very great writers, Tolstoy, for example, who appear to have been without it; on the other hand, because they possessed it, writers like Conan Doyle and Rider Haggard, whom nobody would call "great," continue to be read.

A genuine "mythical" character like Sherlock Holmes can always be recognized by two characteristics: his appeal, at least within a given culture, transcends all highbrow-lowbrow, child-adult differences of taste, and his nature is independent of his history; one cannot imagine Anna Karenina apart from what we are told happened to her, but no adventure can change Mr Pickwick—if he changes he ceases to exist,—the number of adventures which might happen to him are potentially infinite, and every reader can imagine some which Dickens, as it were, forgot.

George Macdonald is pre-eminently a mythopoeic writer. Though he has very considerable literary gifts in the usual sense, his style sometimes lapses into Ossian Gothic and Victorian sentimentality (the baby talk of The Little Ones in *Lilith* is, frankly, shy-making, though partly redeemed by the fact that they represent not real children but people who, afraid of the risks and suffering involved in becoming adult, refuse to grow up) and, in reissuing *Phantastes*, the editors have been wise, I think, in their decision to omit most of the hero's songs, for George Macdonald was not endowed with that particular verbal gift which the writing of verse requires. In his power, however, to project his inner life into images, events, beings, landscapes which are valid for all, he is one of the most remarkable writers of the nineteenth century: *The Princess and The Goblins* is, in my opinion, the only English children's book in the same class as the Alice books, and *Lilith* is equal if not superior to the best of Poe.

The Scylla and Charybdis of Dream Literature are incoherence and mechanical allegory. Without some allegorical scheme of meaning—it is not always necessary that the reader know what it is—the writer has no principle by which to select and organize his material and no defense against his private obsessions; on the other hand, if he allows the allegory to take control so that symbol and thing symbolized have a mere one-to-one correspondence, he becomes boring. In the supreme master of the dream, Dante, we find simultaneously an inexhaustible flow of images of the profoundest resonance and a meticulous logical and mathematical structure which even dictates the number of verses. If *Lilith* is a more satisfactory book than *Phantastes*, one reason is that its allegorical structure is much tighter: there seems no particular reason, one feels, why Anodos should have just the number of adventures which he does have—they could equally be more or less—but Mr Vane's experiences and his spiritual education exactly coincide. The danger of the chain adventure story is that perpetual novelty gives excitement at the cost of understanding; the landscape of *Lilith* becomes all the more vivid and credible to the reader because he is made to repeat the journey Adam's-Cottage to Bad-Burrow to Dry-River to Evil-Wood to Orchard-Valley to Rocky-Scaur to Hot-Stream to Bulika-City several times.

In comparison with his colleague, the novelist of our social waking life, the novelist of dream life is freer in his choice of events but more restricted in his choice of characters, for the latter must all be variations on a few "archetypes," the Wise Old Man, the Wise Old Woman, the Harlot-Witch, the Child-

Bride, the Shadow-Self, etc., and it is no easy matter to present these types in unique and personal figures. George Macdonald, however, almost invariably manages to do so: there is a clear affinity between Lilith and the Alder Witch, between Eve and the old woman in the cottage with four doors, yet each is herself, and not a mere repetition.

But his greatest gift is what one might call his dream realism, his exact and profound knowledge of dream causality, dream logic, dream change, dream morality: when one reads him, the illusion of participating in a real dream is perfect; one never feels that it is an allegorical presentation of wakeful conscious processes. Nobody can describe better that curious experience of dreaming that one is awake:

> . . . looking out of bed, I saw that a large green marble basin, in which I was wont to wash, and which stood on a low pedestal of the same material in a corner of my room, was overflowing like a stream; and that a stream of clear water was running over the carpet, all the length of the room, finding its outlet I knew not where. . . . Hearing next a slight motion above me, I looked up, and saw that the branches and leaves designed upon the curtains of my bed were slightly in motion. Not knowing what change might follow next, I thought it high time to get up; and, springing from the bed, my bare feet alighted on a cool green sward; and, although I dressed in all haste, I found myself completing my toilet under the boughs of a great tree.

To describe how a dreamer reasons without making him sound either too arbitrary or too logical is not easy, but Macdonald's characters always argue like real dreamers:

> I saw, therefore, that there was no plan of operation offering any probability of success but this: to allow my mind to be occupied with other thoughts, as I wandered around the great center-hall; and so wait till the impulse to enter one of the others should happen to arise in me just at the moment when I was close to one of the crimson curtains.

Like real dreamers, too, their consciences are aware of ambiguities of feeling and motive before and during their actions in a way that, when we are awake, we can only become aware, if at all, after we have acted.

> But a false sense of power, a sense which had no root and was merely vibrated into me from the strength of the horse, had, alas, rendered me too stupid to listen to anything he said.

In waking life, it would be psychologically false to make the rider so aware of his self-deception at the moment of choice; in a dream it is true.

As for his power of exact dream description, one can open his books at random and find passage after passage like this:

We rushed up the hills, we shot down their further slopes; from the rocky chasms of the river-bed he did not swerve; he held on over them in his fierce terrible gallop. The moon, half way up the heaven, gazed with a solemn trouble in her pale countenance. Rejoicing in the power of my steed and in the pride of my life, I sat like a king and rode.

We were near the middle of the many channels, my horse every other moment clearing one, sometimes two in his stride, and now and then gathering himself for a great bounding leap, when the moon reached the key-stone of her arch. Then came a wonder and a terror: she began to descend rolling like the nave of Fortune's wheel bowled by the gods, and went faster and faster. Like our own moon, this one had a human face, and now the broad forehead now the chin was uppermost as she rolled. I gazed aghast.

Across the ravines came the howling of wolves. An ugly fear began to invade the hollow places of my heart; my confidence was on the wane. The horse maintained his headlong swiftness, with ears pricked forward, and thirsty nostrils exulting in the wind his career created. But there was the moon jolting like an old chariot-wheel down the hill of heaven, with awful boding. She rolled at last over the horizon-edge and disappeared, carrying all her light with her.

The mighty steed was in the act of clearing a wide shallow channel when we were caught in the net of the darkness. His head dropped; its impetus carried his helpless bulk across, but he fell in a heap on the margin, and where he fell he lay. I got up, kneeled beside him, and felt him all over. Not a bone could I find broken, but he was a horse no more. I sat down on the body, and buried my face in my hands.

Descended from one of the survivors of the Massacre of Glencoe, George Macdonald was born in 1824, took a degree in Chemistry and Natural Philosophy and entered the Congregational Ministry in which he soon acquired a considerable reputation as a preacher.

Presently, however, like many of his contemporaries, he was suspected, with reason, of holding unorthodox theological opinions—in his case the orthodoxy was Calvinist—and in 1850 he abandoned pastoral work in order to devote himself to literature. His first book was a long poem *Within and Without* which aroused the admiration of Tennyson and Lady Byron. In addition to the dream stories for which he is best known, he wrote a number of realistic stories about Scotch peasant life some of which, like *Alec Forbes* and *Robert Falconer*, deserve to be better known. By all accounts a saintly and lovable man, he was a friend of most of the famous mid-Victorian writers, among them Lewis Carroll. In 1872 he made a successful lecture tour through the United States. Delicate health obliged him to spend much of his later years in Bordighera. He died in 1905.

If unorthodox on certain points—for example, he believed, like Origen, in the ultimate salvation of the Devil—he never, like many "liberals" of his day, abandoned the Christian doctrines of God, Sin and Grace for some vague emergent "force making for righteousness" or a Pelagian and secular belief in "Progress." *Lilith* is a surprisingly tough book. Bulika, its *civitas terrenae*, where all human beings are born, is a nightmare of suspicion, greed, sterility and cruelty, and, if in Mr Vane's dream it is captured by the innocent, it is, one feels, only in his dream; the reader is not left with the impression that Bulika has ceased to exist for others. The life-giving waters are restored to the Waste Land, but evil is not thereby abolished:

> We came to the fearful hollow where once had wallowed the monsters of the earth: it was indeed, as I had beheld it in my dream, a lovely lake. I gazed into its pellucid depths. A whirlpool had swept out the soil in which the abortions burrowed, and at the bottom lay visible the whole horrid brood: a dim greenish light pervaded the crystalline water, and revealed every hideous form beneath it. . . . Not one of them moved as we passed. But they were not dead.

When Mr Vane comes to in his library, his life is only just beginning; he has now to start obeying the advice which the raven gave him when they first met:

> "The only way to come to know where you are is to begin to make yourself at home."
> "How am I to begin that when everything is so strange?"
> "By doing something."
> "What?"
> "Anything, and the sooner you begin the better! for until you are at home, you will find it as difficult to get out as it is to get in. . . . Home, as you may or may not know, is the only place where you can go out and in. There are places you can go into, and places you can go out of; but the one place, if you do but find it, where you may go out and in both, is home."

The Visionary Novels of George Macdonald, edited by
Anne Fremantle, 1954

How Cruel Is April?

The difference between any two poets of the same nationality, between, say, Robert Frost and Marianne Moore or William Empson and Dylan Thomas, is immediately obvious and fairly easy to describe, but I very much doubt if it is possible to say what qualities the American or the British pair have in common which they do not share with their cousins, even though a sensitive reader may feel sure that such qualities exist. One can only approach the problem indirectly by asking if there are any experiences peculiar to each country but common to all its inhabitants, irrespective of temperament, occupation or social status. Anybody who has visited both countries can think of two: Englishmen live in a mild climate of "weather," Americans in a climate of violent extremes; in England there is no primitive wilderness left and no uninhabitable area, but within fifty miles of New York City you can get fatally lost in the woods, and a breakdown of its irrigation system would turn most of Southern California into desert within a few days.

The Arcadian conception of Nature as friendly and humanised is as natural to all Englishmen (except, perhaps, the very poor) as it is incomprehensible to any American. I am quite prepared to be told that the first line of *The Waste Land* is adapted from the French, but I shall continue to think that Eliot's reaction to the fourth month is as American as Browning's is British. In his story *The Domain of Arnheim* Poe describes an American Arcadia but its construction and upkeep require the total resources of the richest man in the world; in any British detective story the same kind of scenery is within the means of the village curate. In England, even when, as in Thomas Hardy's poem *Yell'ham-Wood's Story*, the message of Nature is a stern one, "Life offers—to deny!", her voice is still human and intelligible; she may have read Darwin and Schopenhauer but she is still recognizably Rhea: in the United States she is apt to become either Adams' Dynamo or Melville's White Whale, the inhuman Other against which he must pit his manhood. There are millions of devout Catholics in the States but I doubt if any of them anticipate a day when there will be pilgrimages to the shrine of, say, Our Lady of Kalamazoo.

American Nature may be numinous but she is not to be propitiated by prayers or rites, and he who loves her must learn stoically to endure her indifference and not confuse courage with a romantic lack of caution; if she is in a temper he had better arm himself with an unchivalrous bulldozer or hide. The same attitude, Frost suggests in his poem *A Drumlin Woodchuck*, is the wisest one for the individual to adopt towards our modern egalitarian society.

> All we who prefer to live
> Have a little whistle we give,
> And flash, at the least alarm
> We dive down under the farm
>
> . . . And if after the hunt goes past
> And the double-barreled blast
> (Like war and pestilence
> And the loss of common sense),

> I can with confidence say
> That still for another day,
> Or even another year,
> I will be there for you, my dear,
>
> It will be because, though small
> As measured against the All,
> I have been so instinctively thorough
> About my crevice and burrow.

If America is a land of heat waves, cold waves, tornadoes, droughts, floods, it is also, as a land only half-full and half domesticated, still a land of the Open Road, where the openness of the future does not seem wholly dependent on technological advance and political wisdom. It is true that Huckleberry Finn can no longer light out for a Wild West, but he still feels that if to-day he fails, he can make a wholly new start somewhere else to-morrow; he can remember the past if he likes but he doesn't have to, and its only meaning to him is its relevance to the present.

Literature of any value cannot, of course, be written without reverence for the past, but an idolatry of the past as past can be equally stultifying and from that Americans are spared. Her best writers and critics have been able to look at our common literary heritage with a freshness and lack of provinciality which Europeans must envy. The latter may laugh, and rightly, at the anachronisms of Hollywood movies (*Cleopatra*: "Take a letter to Caesar. To Caesar, Rome. Dear Caesar . . .") but in a country where such things were impossible, the creative use of tradition by such poets as Eliot and Pound, to which Europe owes so much, would probably have been impossible too.

"American Writing Today", a supplement to
The Times Literary Supplement, 17 September 1954

Holding the Mirror Up to History

The Hedgehog and the Fox: An Essay on Tolstoy's View of History.
By Isaiah Berlin. Simon & Schuster. $2.50.

I have never been able to agree with those literary critics who, following Turgenev, have deplored the historical disquisitions in *War and Peace* as inartistic irrelevancies; they have always seemed to me not only of great interest in themselves but also an essential element in the novel. I am naturally delighted, therefore, to find my opinion confirmed by so eminent an authority as Mr Isaiah Berlin in his beautifully written and suggestive essay on Tolstoy, *The Hedgehog and the Fox*.

Every good novel gives us the illusion that we are reading history; it makes us believe that the happenings in it really happened as described, and it makes them intelligible to us; if a character acts in a certain way, we perceive his motive, and if the consequences are not what he intended, we understand why. The more talented a novelist, the more conscious he must be of the simplifications—the selection of suitable characters, the exclusion of everything that might compromise the unity of pattern—that enable him to give us this illusion, and the more ambitious he is, the more he will feel the writing of actual history, from which all such easy conveniences are banned, as a challenge to his powers. Tolstoy was both immensely gifted and immensely ambitious, and *War and Peace* might be called a prolegomenon to a work he never managed to produce but considered the only literary task really worth doing ("To write the genuine history of present-day Europe: there is an aim for the whole of one's life"), all the more so because, on reading the accepted and respected professional historians, he found them guilty of a glibness and superficiality no reader would tolerate in a third-rate novel.

Mr Berlin has two theses, a major and a minor. The first is that, while unexcelled as a negative critic of historical theories, demolishing one after the other the attempts to explain history by Great Men, Ideas, and Forces, Tolstoy failed to arrive at a positive theory of his own because he was a man divided against himself. One part of him, the part that included all his natural gifts, saw the multiplicity of life too clearly to accept any pattern that might overlook its full concreteness; the other part yearned for some single and absolutely simple principle that would make sense of everything. Such a principle was not granted him through either an intellectual or a mystical vision, but, refusing to admit this and determined to banish the sense of meaninglessness by which he was haunted, he ended up adopting by force of will a simplification that satisfied neither his head nor his heart.

In his view of history—and this is Mr Berlin's minor thesis—the writer Tolstoy most closely resembles, despite the difference in their conclusions, is de Maistre; both have the same genius for destroying liberal optimistic hopes for a planned rational society, and though Tolstoy adopts a sort of Primitive Gospel Anarchy and de Maistre an Ultramontane Catholicism, in both cases the position is assumed out of defiant despair rather than heartfelt conviction.

All men, Mr Berlin suggests, can be divided into two classes—hedgehogs and foxes. The hedgehogs

> relate everything to a single central vision, one system less or more coherent or articulate, in terms of which they understand, think and feel

while the foxes

> pursue many ends, often unrelated and even contradictory, connected, if at all, only in some *de facto* way, for some psychological or physiological cause, related by no moral or aesthetic principle.

Examples are given:

HEDGEHOGS	FOXES
Dante	Herodotus
Plato	Aristotle
Lucretius	Montaigne
Pascal	Erasmus
Hegel	Molière
Dostoevsky	Goethe
Nietzsche	Pushkin
Ibsen	Balzac
Proust	Joyce

Tolstoy and de Maistre, says Mr Berlin, were like each other in that both were by nature foxes but both wanted and tried desperately, though unsuccessfully, to become hedgehogs.

I find this classification entertaining and illuminating, but I think it needs elaboration. Are there not artists, for example, who, precisely because they can perceive no unifying hedgehog principle governing the flux of experience, are aesthetically all the more hedgehog, imposing in their art the unity they cannot find in life? Is not Joyce such an artist, or Henry James, who possessed, in Mr Eliot's famous epigram, "a mind so fine that no idea could violate it"? Conversely, are there not hedgehog visionaries—Heraclitus? Nietzsche?—whose vision by its nature forbids any presentation in a systematic hedgehog form? Further, must one not consider also the kind of activity either temperament is engaged in? Mathematics would seem to be a field forbidden to foxes, while no pure hedgehog could ever succeed as a novelist or a historian, though he might as a poet.

If we leave Tolstoy's theories for a moment and look at *War and Peace* as a historical novel, what conception of the historian's purpose is implied by what he actually writes? Certainly not the discovery of laws that would make the future scientifically predictable, or the reduction of infinitesimals to statistical probabilities. Tolstoy's purpose seems to be what I suspect always is and must be the purpose of any historian who goes beyond mere documentation, pedagogical and moral. All the forces of his genius are employed to persuade the reader that Napoleon, Anatole Kuragin, Princess Helena are the sort of people he should not imitate and that Kutuzov, Platon Karataev, Natasha are the right kind of model, that military glory and salon triumphs are a pseudo-life as compared with the real life of work and marriage as led finally by the Rostovs and the Bezukhovs. Tolstoy attacks the Great Man theory of history so violently precisely because "greatness" is the only thing he really cares about, and what all the historians call great he finds a wicked sham. Though wars and the military virtues are in themselves part of the sham life, so long as they are admired there will be wars and the question

"What is the good kind of soldier?" must arise. Kutuzov is one because it is impossible to think of him as the head of an invading army; he does nothing that is not purely defensive and has no aim in fighting beyond ridding his country of the invaders with the least loss of life.

Some of the theoretical difficulties with which Tolstoy is confronted are self-created; in his determination to demolish the legend about the fellow once and for all, he portrays Napoleon as a man with neither talent, character, nor personal magnetism. So when, for instance, he tells how a troop of Polish uhlans, who had barely escaped drowning while fording the perilous Vistula under Napoleon's eyes, had, "as soon as they had got out, in their soaked and streaming clothes, shouted 'Vivat' and looked ecstatically at the spot where Napoleon had been but where he no longer was, and considered themselves happy," their behavior seems not understandable but foolish, like Prince Andrew's musings—"I want glory, want to be known to men, want to be loved by them . . . want nothing but that and live only for that"; it seems inhuman, impersonal lunacy. Tolstoy is not content to point out that many of Napoleon's orders at the battle of Borodino could not be executed; he has to deny him any role whatsoever: "Had Napoleon forbidden them to fight the Russians, they would have killed him and have proceeded to fight the Russians because it was inevitable."

It is impossible for the average reader to know to what extent Tolstoy's portrait of Napoleon is a distortion, but by watching Tolstoy at work in a field he can check against his own experience, he can gain an insight into Tolstoy's satiric technique. For various reasons, Tolstoy disapproved of opera, and in Book VIII, Chapters 8 and 9, he describes one attended by Natasha. The description is perfectly truthful but for one little omission; he tells you exactly what you would experience at the opera if you were healthy, intelligent, with twenty-twenty vision, but stone-deaf. This technique, which Tolstoy inherited from the writers of the Enlightenment, creates, unfortunately, an imaginary human being, half purely rational and absolutely free, half purely emotional and the creature of blind forces; if the satirist should now turn philosopher, he is faced with the insoluble task of putting the halves together again. When Tolstoy comes to discuss Free Will and Determinism, he is committed to some absurd positions—that, for instance, the better you understand a man's motive for acting, the less free you think his act, or that the farther back into history you go, the more fated actions appear, because you cannot imagine what the present would be like had they not occurred as they did.

Despite the two men's common scorn of smart, town-bred intellectuals and their common conviction that reason and calculation play a small part in the causation of historical events, I am not completely persuaded by Mr Berlin's contention that de Maistre had a considerable direct influence on Tolstoy. There are two passages in *War and Peace* which, I admit, do sound like pure de Maistre:

The cannon-balls flew just as swiftly and cruelly from both sides, crushing human bodies, and that terrible work, which was not done by the will of a man, but at the will of Him who governs men and worlds, continued.

Why did millions of people kill one another when it has been known since the world began that it is physically and morally bad to do so? Because it was such an inevitable necessity that in doing it men fulfilled the elementary zoological law which bees fulfill when they kill each other in autumn, and which causes male animals to destroy one another.

The reader notices them immediately, because in their pessimistic obscurantism they are so unlike the rest of Tolstoy's comments.

Mr Berlin derives his two classes of men from Archilochus; I would like to suggest a classification of my own, derived from *Alice in Wonderland*:

And she began thinking over all the children she knew that were of the same age as herself, to see if she could have been changed for any of them.

"I'm sure I'm not Ada," she said, "for her hair goes in such long ringlets, and mine doesn't go in ringlets at all; and I'm sure I can't be Mabel, for I know all sorts of things, and she, oh, she knows such a very little! . . . I'll try if I know all the things I used to know." (*Alice fails to remember anything properly and starts to cry.*) "I must be Mabel after all, and I shall have to go and live in that poky little house, and have next to no toys to play with, and oh, ever so many lessons to learn! No, I've made up my mind about it; if I'm Mabel, I'll stay down here!"

If all men may be divided into hedgehogs and foxes, they may also be divided into Alices and Mabels. Examples follow:

ALICES	MABELS
Thucydides	Tacitus
Horace	Juvenal
Marvell	Donne
Leibnitz	Schopenhauer
Jane Austen	Richardson
Verdi	Wagner
Henry James	Dostoevsky
de Tocqueville	de Maistre
Tolstoy	Joyce

All Alices have strong nerves. When he has to describe a flogging or a lynching, Tolstoy is as coolly detached as Homer. What shocks him most about human nature is not its love of violence, its capacity for hatred, but its willful stupidity, its preference for illusions to the truth. De Maistre, on the other hand, seems to me to belong to a type that is becoming, unfortunately, commoner—the intellectual with weak nerves and a timid heart, who is so appalled at discovering that life is not sweetly and softly pretty that he takes a grotesquely tough, grotesquely "realist" attitude. He would like William Godwin to be right and man to be perfectible; if that cannot be, then man must be utterly depraved—de Maistre is much more Calvinist than Thomist—and the public executioner is the saviour of society. One cannot imagine de Maistre, the advocate of punishment, beating up a peasant with his own hands, like Pierre Bezukhov, and then being humanly ashamed of himself. The "real life" led by Nicholas and Princess Mary on their country estate presupposes neither an Inquisition nor Spiritual Exercises but only obedience to the same principles, stoic but cheerful, that the Red Queen recommends to Alice:

> "Speak in French when you can't think of the English for a thing—turn out your toes as you walk—and remember who you are!"

Like all Alices, Tolstoy possessed a morality that was aesthetic. What is most noticeable about Napoleon and Pfuel as he describes them is not that the one is insanely ambitious and the other absurdly pedantic but that both are ill-bred; Kutuzov may be a general and Platon only a private, but both have the assurance of the gentleman. Even in *What is Art?* Tolstoy appears more motivated by a distaste for the vulgar airs of self-importance put on by artists than by a disapproval of art itself.

In his last years, Tolstoy adopted a position that to almost everybody else seems false and in contradiction to his nature, and about which it is hard not to think like D. H. Lawrence:

> The big flamboyant Russia
> Might have been saved, if a pair
> Of rebels like Anna and Vronsky
> Had blasted the sickly air
> Of Dostoevsky and Tchekov,
> And spy-government everywhere.

> But Tolstoy was a traitor
> To the Russia that needed him most,
> The clumsy, bewildered Russia
> So worried by the Holy Ghost.
> He shifted his job on to the peasants
> And landed them all on toast.

Mr Berlin's comparison of Tolstoy in his old age to Oedipus at Colonus is singularly felicitous, suggesting that Tolstoy's tragic flaw was not Christian pride, from which we all suffer, but pagan *hybris*, into which only the strong and exceptionally fortunate can be tempted. Tolstoy was, and knew himself to be, an aristocrat, a superb animal, and one of the most intelligent men who ever lived. Indeed, I cannot think of anyone else in history upon whom Providence showered so many gifts. It is hardly surprising, then, if he was tempted to think that he was a superman to whom no problem was insoluble. Behind his chapters on the nature of history, one feels his baffled fury that he, Tolstoy, should be no more able to find a satisfactory explanation of why and how historical events occur than all the little men whose ridiculous presumption he had exposed. De Maistre preached a theocracy as the only possible form of society, but he preached it as a theory he never expected would be put into practice—one suspects he would have been rather annoyed if anyone had seriously tried—but the moment Tolstoy comes to his theoretical conclusion, the times and the rest of society are ignored with a fantastic aristocratic arrogance, and he sets to work immediately to turn the Tolstoy estate into the New Jerusalem. What he lacked was not so much a hedgehog vision of unity as humility. It is proper that Alice should remember that she is not Mabel, but when she begins to believe that she is the Queen of Heaven, she, too, forgets her station.

The New Yorker, 25 September 1954

The Hero Is a Hobbit

The Fellowship of the Ring. Being the First Part of The Lord of the Rings.
By J. R. R. Tolkien. Houghton Mifflin. $5.

Seventeen years ago there appeared, without any fanfare, a book called *The Hobbit* which, in my opinion, is one of the best children's stories of this century. In *The Fellowship of the Ring*, which is the first volume of a trilogy, J.R.R. Tolkien continues the imaginative history of the imaginary world to which he introduced us in his earlier book but in a manner suited to adults, to those, that is, between the ages of twelve and seventy. For anyone who likes the genre to which it belongs, the Heroic Quest, I cannot imagine a more wonderful Christmas present. All Quests are concerned with some numinous Object, the Waters of Life, the Grail, buried treasure etc.; normally this is a good Object which it is the Hero's task to find or to rescue from the Enemy, but the Ring of Mr Tolkien's story was made by the Enemy and is so dangerous that even the good cannot use it without being corrupted.

The Enemy believed that it had been lost forever, but he has just discovered that it has come providentially into the hands of the Hero and is devoting all his demonic powers to its recovery, which would give him the lordship of the world. The only way to make sure of his defeat is to destroy the Ring, but this can only be done in one way and in one place which lies in the heart of the Enemy's country; the task of the Hero, therefore, is to get the Ring to the place of its unmaking without getting caught.

The hero, Frodo Baggins, belongs to a race of beings called hobbits, who may be only three feet high, have hairy feet and prefer to live in underground houses, but in their thinking and sensibility resemble very closely those arcadian rustics who inhabit so many British detective stories. I think some readers may find the opening chapter a little shy-making, but they must not let themselves be put off, for, once the story gets moving, this initial archness disappears.

For over a thousand years the hobbits have been living a peaceful existence in a fertile district called the Shire, incurious about the world outside. Actually, the latter is rather sinister; towns have fallen into ruins, roads into disrepair, fertile fields have returned to wilderness, wild beasts and evil beings on the prowl, and travel is difficult and dangerous. In addition to the Hobbits, there are Elves who are wise and good, Dwarves who are skillful and good on the whole, and Men, some warriors, some wizards, who are good or bad. The present incarnation of the Enemy is Sauron, Lord of Barad-dûr, the Dark Tower in the Land of Mordor. Assisting him are Orcs, wolves and other horrid creatures and, of course, such men as his power attracts or overawes. Landscape, climate and atmosphere are northern, reminiscent of the Icelandic sagas.

The first thing that one asks of an adventure story is that the adventure should be various and exciting; in this respect Mr Tolkien's invention is unflagging, and, on the primitive level of wanting to know what happens next, *The Fellowship of the Ring* is at least as good as *The Thirty-Nine Steps*. Of any imaginary world the reader demands that it seem real, and the standard of realism demanded today is much stricter than in the time, say, of Malory. Mr Tolkien is fortunate in possessing an amazing gift for naming and a wonderfully exact eye for description; by the time one has finished his book one knows the histories of Hobbits, Elves, Dwarves and the landscape they inhabit as well as one knows one's own childhood.

Lastly, if one is to take a tale of this kind seriously, one must feel that, however superficially unlike the world we live in its characters and events may be, it nevertheless holds up the mirror to the only nature we know, our own; in this, too, Mr Tolkien has succeeded superbly, and what happened in the year of the Shire 1418 in the Third Age of Middle Earth is not only fascinating in A.D. 1954 but also a warning and an inspiration. No fiction I have read in the last five years has given me more joy than *The Fellowship of the Ring*.

The New York Times Book Review, 31 October 1954

A World Imaginary, but Real

The Fellowship of the Ring. Being the First Part of
The Lord of the Rings. George Allen and Unwin. 21s.

I suppose readers exist who do not enjoy Heroic Quests, but I have never met them. For many of us they are so much the most delicious form of literature that we can devour one even when our critical faculties tell us it is trash. Those who remember *The Hobbit* as the best children's story written in the last fifty years will open any new work by Professor Tolkien with high hopes, but *The Fellowship of the Ring* is better than their wildest dreams could have foreseen; if he is not a rich man by next Christmas, I shall be surprised.

In discussing a book of this type, a reviewer is at a disadvantage because he must not spoil the reader's pleasure by giving away what happens, which—in this case—is at least as exciting as the story of *The Thirty-Nine Steps*. In the normal Quest plot there is a numinous object which has either fallen into the hands of the Enemy or is protected from the unworthy by terrifying guardians; none but the predestined hero can find it, but it is good that he should. In *The Fellowship of the Ring* the numinous object, which is like the Ring of the Niebelungs only even more sinister, is in the possession of the hero at the start. The Enemy who made the evil thing but believed that it had been lost for ever has just discovered its whereabouts and is devoting all his demonic powers towards its recovery. Since even the good cannot use the Ring without becoming evil, it must be destroyed but this can only be done in one way and in one place which, unfortunately, lies in the centre of the Enemy's kingdom; the aim of the Quest, therefore, is to get the Ring to the place of its unmaking, without getting caught.

This quest takes place in an imaginary world of Mr Tolkien's invention with its own landscape, history, and inhabitants. In its general characteristics this world is Celtic and Scandinavian rather than Mediterranean. The hero, Mr Frodo Baggins, belongs to a race of beings called Hobbits, who may be only three feet tall and have hairy feet, but in their thinking and sensibility closely resemble those arcadian villagers who so frequently populate British detective stories. For more than a thousand years they have been enjoying an idyllic rural existence in a fertile region called the Shire, unaware of, and incurious about, the world beyond its borders. Actually, the Shire is a tiny oasis in a world which has known better days; great cities of old are now ruins, fertile plains have become barren wastes, roads and bridges have fallen into disrepair, wild beasts and malignant powers stalk abroad. Besides Hobbits with their child-like innocence, there are Elves, who know good and evil but are creatures of an unfallen world, there are Dwarves, and there are Men, good and bad. Some of these are heroic warriors, descended from ancient kings, some are wizards. The latest incarnation of the Enemy is Sauron, Lord of Barad-dûr, the Dark Tower in the Land of Mordor; he commands the services of Trolls, Orcs, and some much more deadly creatures and is daily increasing his hold on the hearts of men.

For a contemporary writer who sets out to create a convincing imaginary world, the task is much more formidable than it was for the authors of the Courtly Romances, since he can neither write nor expect to be read as if the naturalistic novel and scientific historical research did not exist. It may give some indication of Mr Tolkien's astonishing powers that I can only find two questions of probability to raise, just as the questions themselves may illustrate the difference between a mid-twentieth-century reader and a contemporary of Spenser. We are told that the Hobbits have lived for many generations immune from war, pestilence, and famine; and that, normally, they have large families and are long-lived. In that case, I do not quite understand why population pressure has not forced them to emigrate from the Shire. Secondly—a minor point—the drying up of the Sirannon river is explained by the fact that it has been dammed; but the lake so formed has been full for years—where is the water going to?

The first problem for the maker of an imaginary world is the same as Adam's in Eden; he has to invent names for everything and everyone, and these names must be both apt and consistent with each other. It is hard enough to find the "right" names in a comic world; in a serious one, success seems almost magical. I can only say that in the nominative gift Mr Tolkien surpasses any writer known to me, living or dead. The landscape of his tale is an extensive one—East to West, from The Iron Hills to The Gulf of Lune, some twelve hundred miles, and North to South, from Carn Dûm to the delta of the Anduin, some eleven hundred. This area contains a number of verbalising species, each with its own nomenclature and its own family and political history, yet the author, without, apparently, the slightest difficulty, finds names which always seem inevitable. Of course, he is a famous philologist, but what colleague of his could invent such convincing examples of a "good" and a "bad" language as the following quotations?

> *A Elbereth Gilthoniel,*
> *silivren penna míriel*
> *o menel aglar elenath!*
> *Na-chaered palan-díriel*
> *o galadhremmin ennorath,*
> *Fanvilos, le linnathon*
> *nef aear, si nef aearon!*

Ash nazg durbatulûk, ash nazg gimbatul, ash nazg thrakatelûk agh burzum-ishi krimpatul.

Again, what other creator of imaginary landscapes has possessed so acute a topographical eye? For a journey to seem real, the reader must be convinced that he is seeing the landscape through which it passes as, given his mode of locomotion and the circumstances of his errand, the traveller himself saw it. By the end of the volume Frodo Baggins has covered some thirteen hundred miles, much of it on foot, and with his senses kept perpetually sharp by fear, watching every inch of the way for signs of his pursuers, yet Mr Tolkien succeeds in convincing us that there is nothing which his hero noticed which he has forgotten to describe; indeed, so exact is he that a reader who consults the beautiful map at the end of the book will observe immediately that the course of the road between Hoarwell Bridge and Bruinen Ford is erroneously drawn.

In a heroic romance where the situations are those of elemental crisis to which the possible reactions are few, to stand one's ground or to flee, to be faithful or to betray, subtleties of character drawing are neither possible nor relevant. The characters must be representative specimens of a few archetypes, the Wise man, the Strong man, the Cheerful man, the Cautious man, the Lady of Light, the Lord of Darkness, etc. Mr Tolkien manages very cleverly to give his types an uncommon depth and solidity by providing each of them with a past which is more that of the group to which he belongs than a personal one; what Aragorn, for instance, talks about is the history of the Rangers, not of himself. Only one character, and this may be an idiosyncracy of my own, does not come off. Sam Gamgee, the faithful squire, is certainly a very estimable person and I think that we are meant to love him; but, in me, he arouses a strong desire to kick him all round the block.

Perhaps Mr Tolkien's greatest achievement is to have written a heroic romance which seems wholly relevant to the realities of our concrete historical existence. When reading medieval examples of this genre, enjoyable as they are, one is sometimes tempted to ask the Knightly hero—"Is your trip necessary?" Even in the Quest for the San Graal, success or failure is only of importance to those who undertake it. One cannot altogether escape the suspicion that, in relation to such knights, the word "vocation" is a high-faluting term for a game which gentlemen with private means are free to play while the real work of the real world is done by "villains."

In *The Fellowship of the Ring*, on the other hand, the fate of the Ring will affect the daily lives of thousands who have never heard of its existence. Further, as in the Bible and many fairy stories, the hero is not a Knight, endowed by birth and breeding with exceptional *aretè*, but only a hobbit pretty much like all other hobbits. It is not the wise Gandalf or the mighty Aragorn but Frodo Baggins who is called to undertake this deadly dangerous mission which he would much rather avoid, and if one asks why he and not one of a hundred others like him, the only answer is that chance, or Providence, has chosen, and he must obey.

If there are any people for whom it would be dangerous to read *The Fellowship of the Ring*, and I think there may be some, they will be those who draw too literal a parallel between it and our present historical situation. In a romance it is right and proper that evil ideas should be incarnate as evil beings; in history it is a disastrous notion. We live in a time, unfortunately, when, if one is thinking of evil ideas, one can locate on the atlas the positions of Dol Guldur and Barad-dûr (I think I can identify Minas Tirith, though the *New Statesman* would not agree with me), but it will go ill with us if, in consequence, we regard all who live East of the Anduin as Orcs to be exterminated.

I have nothing more to say about this wonderful story except that it is very inconsiderate of the publishers not to have issued simultaneously the two volumes which are to follow, *The Two Towers* and *The Return of the King*; the suspense of waiting to know what happens to the Ring Bearer is intolerable. I hope that, in the second edition, they will place the topographical map in a pocket instead of gumming it to the inside cover, for most readers are going to do what I did, tear it out in order to follow with the text, which involves the risk of its getting lost. Finally, those who, like myself, have some dwarf blood in their veins, would be delighted if Mr Tolkien could see his way to providing us with a geological map as well.

Encounter, November 1954

The Private Diaries of Stendhal (1801–1814)

The Private Diaries of Stendhal (Marie-Henri Beyle). Edited and translated from the French by Robert Sage. Doubleday. $7.50.

These diaries were kept by Stendhal between the ages of eighteen and thirty-one. Stendhal was an unusually slow developer; it seems strange to us now that a man whose temperament and talents were so obviously those of a novelist, should not have published his first novel till he was forty-seven, and that during most of the period covered by these diaries he should have been under the illusion, singular in one without the slightest interest in verse as such, that his medium was to be poetic drama.

In place of his Russian diary for 1812 which was unfortunately lost during the retreat from Moscow, Mr Sage, the editor and translator, has, very happily, given us extracts from letters Stendhal wrote to friends during the campaign. Apart from these, with their general historical interest, the diaries are, in the strict sense, private.

Stendhal's intention was neither to give a day-by-day account of his doings nor to write a personal history of the not unexciting times in which he was living, but to discover who he really was. Whatever the content of the entries, his travels, his love affairs, his critical opinions, he makes them in order to keep a chart of his development, as a social being, as a lover, as a writer. "This hodge-podge," he says, "is an *anatomical* work solely for my enlightenment. I was born violent; in order to mend my ways, I have been counselled to know myself."

In a work of the kind, it seems to me better to give some typical extracts and let the reader judge for himself, rather than to talk about them.

Self-Analysis—

When I lack money, I'm bashful wherever I go; since I lack it frequently, the bad tendency to find reasons for my bashfulness in everything I see has become almost a habit with me. I must absolutely get over it. The best way would be to carry a hundred gold louis in my pocket every day for at least a year. The constant weight of the gold would destroy the root of the evil. (1804)

If I live, my conduct will show that there never has been a man whose pity is as easily aroused as my own: the tiniest thing moves me, brings tears to my eyes. My sensation invariably triumphs over my perception, thus preventing me from carrying out the slightest plan. In a word, they'll realize that there never has been a man with a better disposition than mine. (1805)

. . . for the first time in my life, I was brilliant with prudence and not in the least with passion; I was aware of what I was doing all the time, but without being bothered because of that . . . I was wearing a waistcoat, silk breeches and black stockings, with a cinnamon-bronze coat, a very well arranged cravat, a superb frill. Never, I believe, was my homeliness more effaced by my character. (1805)

Generally speaking, I am immensely lacking in wisdom; the fact is that I don't know what I want. In general: Paris, Auditor, eight thousand livres a year, life in the best society and having women from it. (1806)

Shortcomings: (1) I reflect on everything I see, I sometimes devote too little time to observation. When reading the newspapers I frequently skip words or parts of words. (2) Excessive enthusiasm. (1806)

I don't at all desire war . . . but, once this business is decided, I'd be delighted if it were waged and I was there. This is a case where it may nearly always be said, "You'll never see again what you've already seen," and I'm beginning to notice that this is the only thing that makes three quarters of men and things bearable. (1808)

. . . the folly of amusing myself by imagining that I have been insulted so I can compose some very haughty and insolent replies and picture myself handing out insults in return. This morning, as I was going to the shooting range at seven o'clock, I discovered myself indulging in this folly. (1811)

Women—

. . . it's a curious experience to be present casually at the toilette of a pretty woman. For her, it's a matter of the greatest importance; she's herself, and you are in a position to judge her. All that I saw was: an insensitive soul, absence of gentle passions, cruelty. (1805)

Between the ages of sixteen and thirty-one, Martial has had about twenty-two women, of whom a dozen came after a genuine love affair. I'm twenty-five years old; in the next six years I'll probably have six. (1808)

I need a woman with a lofty soul, and all of them are like novels—interesting as far as the denouement, and, two days later you're surprised at having been able to be interested in things so common. (1809)

In order that I may experience pleasure with a woman, nothing must intervene to disturb the illusion I've formed; at the first low thought my little grisette permitted me to have, my impulse would be to give her a frock and see her no more . . . (1810)

For me, love would be a far keener pleasure if, like Signor Lechi for instance, when I'm with my mistress, I thought of nothing else. (1811)

At a quarter to ten, I went into the little church on the corner of the Via dei Mervigli. I wasn't able to hear ten o'clock strike. I went by at five minutes after ten by my watch; no paper. I went by again at twenty minutes after ten; she signaled to me. After a very serious moral conflict, in which I shammed unhappiness and almost despair, she was mine at half-past eleven. (Sept. 21st, 1811)

Literature—

Of all writers, I should be the one who offends the vanity of my readers the least, I should appear completely natural to them without their noticing it. (1804)

O divine Shakespeare, yes, thou art the greatest bard in the world. And yet his work is almost prose to me. Consequently, it's possible to be a poet in prose; but verse gives an added charm. (1805)

It's very difficult to describe from memory what has been *natural* for you: the *factitious*, the *shammed*, is described much more easily because the effort that's been made to sham it has engraved it on the memory. (1805)

My style will have a character all its own by scoffing a bit at everyone; it will be apt and concise, and it won't put the reader to sleep. (1808)

I'm thinking of returning to my true talent, if I have a talent, that of comic bard. (1810)

I'm obliged to force myself to read Corneille and Racine, I find fault with them at every step. (1810)

I'm convinced that a comic bard ought to arrange his life in a manner quite different from that of Alfieri. He'd have had more intelligence, talent and happiness if he hadn't attempted to struggle proudly against institutions that can't be changed; what he ought to have done was to look at life as a masked ball in which a prince isn't offended in the least when a wigmaker in domino crosses in front of him. (1811)

Mme de Stael makes me sick. That stilted style, the least fault of which is to strive to command admiration continually, that wit which lays claim to the honors of genius and doesn't realize that the latter's most salient quality (naturalness) is entirely lacking in it, that farce which ridicules what I love most, makes me acutely ill. (1811)

I was reading Rousseau's *Confessions* a week ago. It was uniquely through the lack of two or three rules of *Beylism* that he was so unhappy. The mania of seeing duties and virtues everywhere put pedantry in his style and unhappiness in his life. He'd ally himself with a man for three weeks: boom, the *duties* of friendship, etc.! Two years later, this man no longer thinks of him; he looks for some sombre explanation of that. *Beylism* would have said to him, "Two bodies come together, heat and fermentation are produced, but every state of this kind is temporary. It's a flower that must be enjoyed sensually, etc." (1812)

I'm probably the opposite of J.-J. Rousseau in many things, and especially in that I can only work when I am far from the sensation. It's not while strolling through a delightful forest that I'm able to describe this happiness; it's shut up in a bare room, where there's nothing to distract my attention, that I'm able to accomplish something. (1813)

Chateaubriand's history of France will at best be good only for women. There will be some *fine pages*, a form of praise that is a criticism in itself, in my opinion. (1813)

Music and Painting—

Mozart, a musician born for his art, but a soul of the North, better fitted to depict unhappiness or the tranquility produced by its absence than the ecstacies and gracefulness that the mild climate of the South bestows upon its inhabitants. As a man of ideas and sensibility, he's infinitely to be preferred, the artists say, to all the mediocre Italian composers; but, as a rule, he's far beneath Cimarosa. (1807)

Delightful sensation at the *Nozze di Figaro* during the voluptuous duet in which the count asks his wife for the key to the closet where Susanna has just hidden herself. My heart, stirred by the contemplation of the beautiful bosom of Mme Lacvée and the beautiful face of Mme Pallavacini, drank in these sounds with avidity. (1810)

My sentiments embellish that part of a song which, according to the dominant passion, may provide my soul the most pleasure; I'm unable to embellish the verse of the best French play in this manner. (1811)

I was all aflutter for two hours. I'd been told that this picture was by *Guerchino*; I worshipped this painter from the bottom of my heart. Not at all; I was told two hours later that it was by Agnolo Bronzino, a name unknown to me. This discovery annoyed me a great deal. I was also told that the coloring was pale. At that I thought of my eyes.

My eyesight is tender, nervous, apt to become agitated, sensing the slightest nuances, but shocked at the dark and harsh tones of the Carrachis, for example. The pale manner of Guido Reni is almost in harmony, not with my manner in judging the arts, but with my eyesight. (1811)

What I require is either expression or beautiful female figures. (1811)

The lower extremities of (Ligozzi's) St Lawrence are pock-marked; outside of that, he's a handsome young man. His loins are beginning to sizzle; he's looking up at the sky all right, but he hasn't a quarter of the expression that the first monk you might burn would have. It might be said that he's a long way from having the sublime expression of which the subject is capable. (1811)

The Griffin, November 1954

Fog in the Mediterranean

The Rebel. By Albert Camus. Translated from the French
by Anthony Bower. Alfred A. Knopf. $4.

I

The stimulus that led Mr Camus to write this well-meaning but maddeningly woolly and verbose essay is his horror at the spectacle of our era "which dares to claim that it is the most rebellious that ever existed but only offers a choice of various types of conformity. The real passion of the twentieth century is servitude". Like all decent people, he hates injustice, cruelty, and the inquisitor type who would compel others by force and fear of death to accept his version of the true and the good. Is there, he asks, any alternative between passive acceptance of evil and the mass murders of organized revolution; is it possible, through an examination of the history of rebellion, to discover "a sign at least concerning our right, or duty, to kill"; can it "furnish the principle of a limited culpability"?

One would have thought that such an enquiry would have to go back a long way, but for Mr Camus history begins in 1789. He considers literary figures like Rousseau, Sade, Dostoievski, Hegel, Marx, commissar prototypes like St Just and Netchaiev, and the Russian anarchists like Kaliayev, who, alone among political types, seem to him worthy of admiration.

By the time he has finished the book, a non-French reader will find himself wondering why its title should be *The Rebel* (*L'Homme Revolté*) for it seems a curious term to apply to a person whom Mr Camus defines as one who is able "to learn to live and to die, and in order to be a man, refuse to be a god"; a Christian may well ask, "Why doesn't he write 'to learn to live and to die, and, admitting that he cannot become a god, accept the limitations of being a man'".

The reason why he has to cast his definition in a negative form is, I believe, the same as that which makes a right wing political party in France call itself Radical Socialist. For most Frenchmen history begins with the French Revolution, that is, with saying No to the past. Despite its acknowledged horrors, this, for the vast majority, was a good thing—only a tiny minority have ever wished for a restoration of the *Ancien Régime*. Consequently, they instinctively think of the right act as rebelling against evil rather than as an obeying of the good. Hence the ambivalence of feeling towards Communism among French intellectuals. However horrified they may be morally, they cannot help feeling that to be against any revolution is reactionary and un-French.

II

It is impossible to understand the nature of revolution from an examination of only one, because what every revolution claims to be doing, establishing the New Jerusalem, is never what it is doing, which is establishing once and for all time in men's minds a particular freedom. That is why each revolution creates its own symbolic figure whose name is usually untranslatable and its own symbolic institution which is usually inimitable. In the case of the English Revolution of 1688, for example, these are the gentlemen and Parliament; in the case of the French Revolution they are *l'homme d'esprit* and *l'Ecole Normale*. The particular freedom won by the French Revolution was *la carrière ouverte aux talents*, the right of the best man to rise to the top irrespective of his social origin, and to follow the guidance of his own intelligence and heart rather than the set form of tradition.

Every revolution is of particular and even excessive benefit to some class, and in the case of the French Revolution this class is made up of writers and painters.

What seems so odd about many French writers on historical matters is, not that they should think French history the most important—all nationalities do that—but that they should so ignore their own history before 1789. Mr Camus, for instance, writes as if the French had always had an absolute Monarch, as if Philip V had held the same view of his function as Louis XIV, forgetting that the Byzantine notion of the priest-king was only introduced into the West at the end of the Middle Ages when feudal civil wars and religious schism had made many ready to welcome a strong central authority at whatever cost. Had had considered medieval theories of sovereignty, Mr Camus would have been compelled to recognize the contribution to human liberty made by the Papacy, and for an anti-clerical that might have been embarrassing. For it was the Popes of the eleventh and twelfth centuries who, by claiming the superiority of the spiritual to the temporal power, established the principle of double loyalty, to the universal truth on the one hand, and to one's native soil and community on the other, a principle which it is now clear is essential to freedom, and, lacking which, a secular or a theocratic absolutism is inevitable. As has happened all too often in revolutions, the theoreticians of the French Revolution, like Rousseau and St Just, accepted without question the most pernicious premises of their enemies, i.e. instead of denying the whole idea of absolute sovereignty, they merely transferred it from the Crown to the People. Similarly, it never occurred to Marx, for all his insight into the influence on thought and behaviour of modes of production, to ask whether there might not be something hostile to life in the factory system as such, which no change from private to state ownership could cure, an oversight which was later to cost millions of peasants their lives.

III

Towards Christianity Mr Camus is tolerant which is a pity for all; those like Blake and Nietzsche who have reacted violently have always done the Church a great service for their notion of orthodox Christian doctrine, though false, is derived from observing Christians in their age. There is no doubt, for example, that in Blake's time many Anglicans, while dutifully reciting the Nicene formulas, really thought of God in Arian terms, just as the sense of Nature declaring the glory of God and of the holiness of the flesh which the Christian doctrines of the creation and the Incarnation imply, were probably not conspicuous among Nietzsche's bourgeois Lutheran contemporaries.

Had Mr Camus sought for and found the characteristic heresy of Christians in 1950, which must certainly exist, he could have helped us a great deal; in fact, he takes his notion of Christianity from its nineteenth century opponents. It is one thing to detest the Inquisition and to sympathize with its victims; it is another to describe a manichean type of heresy as follows: "Hellenism, in association with Christianity, then produces the admirable efflorescence of the Albigensian heresy . . . But with the Inquisition and the destruction of the Albigensian heresy, the Church again parts company with the world and with beauty, and gives back to history its pre-eminence over nature."

The antithesis Nature-History is very important to Mr Camus, but when one tries to discover what precisely he means by either, one runs into an impenetrable fog. Apparently, the right attitude, which is held by the Greeks and the Mediterranean mind, is that nature should be obeyed in order to subjugate history; the wrong attitude, which is held by present-day Christians and Communists, and is all the fault of those nasty nordics, is that nature should be subjugated in order to obey history. But, unless he is an animist or a polytheist, what can Nature as distinct from History mean for him but that order of events which recur necessarily according to law and which man, since he participates in Nature, cannot disobey however hard he tries? Conversely, since he is not a communist but believes passionately in the reality and value of personal freedom, why should Mr Camus defeat himself, by accepting the Hegelian-Marxian use of the word History which robs it of all meaning, since for them all historical events are natural events? To believe in freedom and the reality of the person means to believe that there is an order of unique (though analogous) events which occur, neither necessarily nor arbitrarily, but voluntarily, according to motive and provocation and for which, therefore, the actor is responsible, (since history is something man *makes*, it is meaningless to talk of *obeying* it,) that there is an historical order as distinct from a natural order, and that man participates in both. I am convinced that Mr Camus does in fact believe this, in which case, he is bound to admit that the historical is superior to the natural in the sense that the former is responsible for the latter.

"One can reject," he writes, "all history and yet accept the world of the sea and the stars," and quotes with approval an apothegm by René Char, "Obsession with the harvest and indifference to history are the two extremes of my bow." But what do these statements mean if not that an individual can take an historical decision to ignore politics (and the sufferings of his neighbor) and devote himself to astronomy or farming. This may or may not be the wisest course to take in this age, but it hardly seems more rebellious than the Christian precept "Resist not evil but . . ." of which Mr Camus seems to disapprove. As a model for political action he offers us the Russian martyr-assassins like Kaliayev who "kill and die so that it shall be clear that murder is impossible". It is certainly admirable about these brave men and women that they accepted responsibility for their acts, though both the wisdom and the morality of killing another not because you disapprove of him personally but because you disapprove of his function is questionable. Then why must Mr Camus rob their act of all significance by saying: "The sole but invincible hope of the rebel is incarnated, in the final analysis, in innocent murderers", which is precisely what they refused to be? The only innocent murderer in peace time is the public executioner.

Since Mr Camus speaks so snootily of the North in contrast to the Mediterranean where "intelligence is intimately related to the blinding light of the sun," I shall be snooty in return; I think it a pity that he was not born an Englishman. Had he been, he would know what his real political position is, liberal-conservative; he might well be a Christian; and he would certainly have written a more lucid book.

The Christian Scholar, December 1954

The Pool of Narcissus

The Private Diaries of Stendhal (Marie-Henri Beyle). Edited and translated from the French by Robert Sage. Doubleday. $7.50.

Could he return to earth, Stendhal would get a shock. Instead of being greeted by a "Happy Few," he would find himself the lion of every literary circle in Europe and invited to lecture at every college in America. The writer who thought of himself as a daring and dangerous original has become a touchstone of respectable good taste. If one is asked in strange company to name a novelist whom one admires, the safest answer is Stendhal. Whether this is to his credit or to ours, I am not certain.

The Private Diaries are the preliminary essay in what was to be Stendhal's lifelong preoccupation, the study of himself. The first modern writer in so many ways, in none was Stendhal more so than in his use of the medium of the novel as fictional autobiography; all his characters are portraits either of an imaginary version of himself or of the people by whom he would have liked to be admired or loved, and the actions in his novels are confined to those in which he could fancy himself playing a part. He is the father of everyone who thinks of fiction as a means of self-expression.

The diaries cover his life between the ages of eighteen and thirty-two—the period, that is, of his career as a man of action, the commissary of Brunswick, the Auditor of the Council of State, the wholesale grocer of Marseille, the period of the Moscow campaign, of his discovery of the charms of Italy, and of his affairs with Mélanie Guilbert, Angiola Pietragrua, and Angèline Bereyter. What strikes the reader most forcibly is the evidence they offer of how early Stendhal assumed the Stendhalian style and attitudes and how little he really changed. The boy of eighteen who is under the extraordinary illusion that he is to write dramas in alexandrines is, as a diarist, already the anti-heroic, irreverent apostle of "sincerity" that he was to remain till the end of his days, though he did not publish a novel till he was forty-four.

By a very early age, Stendhal seems to have acquired the habit that makes him the most "interesting" of writers, the habit of observing himself, of being at once on the stage and beside the reader as a fellow-spectator, so that one never knows exactly how seriously to take what he says or exactly how far to believe or disbelieve him. When one reads, say, the *Journals* of Boswell, one is sometimes aware that Boswell is deceiving himself; one says, that is, "He thinks he feels X but he really feels Y." In Stendhal's case, there is a duplication of reflection to deal with, so that one can find oneself saying either "He thinks he thinks he feels Z when he really thinks he feels X and really feels Y" or "He thinks he thinks he feels Y when he really thinks he feels X and really feels Y." In the second instance, what is said is true, but the truth has been arrived at accidentally, as it were, by the mutual cancelling out of two falsehoods.

A man, for example, who was either really paranoid or obsessed with playing the role of a paranoid would have kept his diaries locked up or written them in as impenetrable a code as he could devise; how are we, then, to take Stendhal, who, like the schoolboy who writes in his Latin grammar

> Black is the raven and black is the rook
> But blacker the fiend who steals this book

excites the hypothetical snooper to read his diary by warning him not to, and employs ciphers that any child of ten could solve?

On one day, he will write, "I was born violent;" on another, "There has never been a man whose pity is as easily aroused as my own: the tiniest thing moves me, brings tears to my eyes. . . . There has never been a man with a better disposition than mine." Which is true? Are both? Is neither? At what level?

Again, on returning to his beloved Milan he notices that what moves him most is a smell of manure in the streets. A man of romantic or conventional sensibility who refused to admit this to himself would be understandable, but one would expect a man who realized the truth to set it down simply as an interesting example of psychological association. Yet Stendhal has to preface it with "Dare I say what moved me the most upon arriving at Milan? It's obvious that this is written for no one but myself." How can admitting anything to oneself be daring? And is the observation so shocking anyway?

The same ambiguity characterizes Stendhal's record of his relations with women. At one moment, he represents himself as the romantic idealist who sees in every woman a goddess until she says something "low," whereupon he immediately loses all interest; at the next, he is being the calculating seducer—"I went by again at twenty minutes after ten; she signaled to me. After a very serious moral conflict, in which I shammed unhappiness and almost despair, she was mine at half-past eleven"—and he is not quite convincing in either role. For in love, as in everything else, Stendhal was not a selfish man (that is to say, a man who seeks to satisfy his desires at whatever cost to others) but an egoist (that is, a man whose primary interest is not in objects or persons outside himself but in his own thoughts and feelings). To a selfish or a proud man, triumph is pleasant and defeat painful, but to an egoist, both are equally interesting, for what matters is not the content of the experience but the fact that it is *his*, and he is always making little experiments with himself and others, less out of desire than out of curiosity to see what will happen—"M . . . was reading, she was holding a bouquet negligently in her right hand, this bouquet was right beside me. I began to stroke it, and, true to my romantic character, I experienced a lively pleasure; finally, after being conscious for some time of my action, she gave me a tap on the fingers."

There could be no better definition of an egoist than Stendhal's self-constructed epitaph, "*Visse, Scrisse, Amò*," in which living is made a kind of personal activity, distinct from but of a similar nature to writing and loving. To live is normally thought of as the necessary ground for activity; in the Stendhalian dictionary it means the job of making and finding oneself unique. Coming to maturity in the Napoleonic period, when *liberté, égalité, fraternité* had lost its appeal in favor of *la carrière ouverte aux talents*, and an individual with the requisite energy, suppleness, and lack of scruple could win high position, wealth, and fame irrespective of his social origin, the young Stendhal indulged, understandably, in daydreams of "Paris, Auditor, eight thousand livres a year, life in the best society and having women from it," and the influence of his relative Pierre Daru gave him the opportunity, had he really wanted that sort of worldly success, to climb a great deal higher. In fact, however, he was too interested in too many things, too nervous and too self-indulgent for a sphere of action where the prizes go to ruthless, single-minded efficiency. How, then, was ambition to be satisfied? The substitute that Stendhal employed—others may have discovered it before him, but he was the first to record it—was originality; if one cannot be above everybody else, one can be completely different from everybody else, one can practice Mocenigo or Beylism. (Who, before Stendhal, would have dreamed of calling his view of life an ism and, as though he were his own posthumous critic, naming it after himself?) For this, the first prerequisite is total irreverence toward the past. Montaigne was possibly a greater skeptic than Stendhal—he would certainly have smiled at the latter's enthusiasm for Destutt de Tracy's Idéologie—but his skepticism was rooted in humility, in a distrust of the claim of the human intellect to solve all mysteries, so that in matters about which certainty is impossible, his advice was to obey custom and do as your old nurse did. Neither the age nor Stendhal's temperament could have found such piety tolerable; whatever might be true, at least all past views were false. Stendhal was the first writer in history to show a conscious dislike of poetry. He imagined that he admired Shakespeare, but admits, "His work is almost prose to me. Consequently, it's possible to be a poet in prose." For poetry demands that the poet piously submit his precious personality to impersonal limitations; he cannot say anything he likes but only what they permit him to say. In poetry, *le mot juste* is not only one that expresses a certain shade of meaning but also one with a certain number of syllables, its main accent in a certain place, and perhaps rhyming with another word. Stendhal is also the first writer to think of style as a personal property; instead of beginning with subjects that excite him and then trying to find the style they require, he decides at the age of twenty-five, before he has written anything, "My style will have a character all of its own by scoffing a bit at everyone, it will be apt and concise, and won't put the reader to sleep."

As for the arts of painting and music, though he took a great interest in both, he regarded them not as arts in their own right but as stimulants to literature. The writer who hated Chateaubriand and modelled his own writing on the dry restraint of the Code Napoléon required from painting "either expression or beautiful female figures" and explained his love for music as follows: "My sentiments embellish that part of a song which, according to the dominant passion, may provide my soul the most pleasure."

There are some writers, among them all the greatest, of whom one feels that writing was their vocation; that is what they were born into the world to do; for them writing and living are the same thing. There are others who, one feels, became writers by accident; their books are the fruit of some exciting or catastrophic experience which happened to them and but for which they would not have written. Stendhal does not quite fit into either category; one feels, rather, that he said to himself, "In order to be myself, in order to be a complete Beylist, I must, among other things, like having some love affairs, write some books." Again, he is the first person I know of—today the type is common—who makes me believe that, excellent as his novels are, I would rather spend an evening with their author than read them. Stendhal is endlessly fascinating, like a precocious child; only immaturity is so terrified of being a bore. But who are we to judge him? Which of us is more mature and which of us is half as amusing?

As editor, Mr Robert Sage has done a good job: when, as in 1803, the entries in the diaries are scanty or, as in 1812, lost, he has inserted some of Stendhal's letters of the period, and his biographical introductions to each section give the reader a clear picture of where Stendhal was and what he was doing at any given time. As a translator, Mr Sage is not quite so successful. He conveys the meaning of the original pretty accurately for the most part, but too often his sentences, though grammatically correct in a formal sense, are, in their rhythm and structure, simply not English. I also think that the publishers have made a mistake in using capital type for those phrases that Stendhal wrote in English; by a convention too strong to be ignored, capitals express an exclamatory emphasis that is foreign to the author's intention.

The New Yorker, 18 December 1954

Introduction to *The Faber Book of Modern American Verse*

One often hears it said that only in this century have the writers of the United States learned to stand on their own feet and be truly American, that, previously, they were slavish imitators of British literature. Applied to the general reading public and academic circles this has a certain amount of truth but, so far as the writers themselves are concerned, it is quite false. From Bryant on there is scarcely one American poet whose work, if unsigned, could be mistaken for that of an Englishman. What English poet, for example, in need of emotive place-names for a serious poem, would have employed, neither local names nor names famous in history or mythology, but names made up by himself as Poe did in *Ulalume*? Would an English poet have conceived the idea of writing a scientific cosmological prose poem and of prefacing it thus: "I offer this Book of Truths, not in its character of Truth-teller, but for the Beauty that abounds in its Truth, constituting it true . . . *What I here propound is true*: therefore it cannot die . . . Nevertheless it is as a Poem only that I wish this work to be judged after I am dead." (Poe, Preface to *Eureka*)?

Maud, The Song of Hiawatha and the first edition of *Leaves of Grass* all appeared in the same year, 1855: no two poets could be more unlike each other than Longfellow and Whitman—such diversity is in itself an American phenomenon—yet, when compared with Tennyson, each in his own way shows characteristics of the New World. Tennyson and Longfellow were both highly skilful technicians in conventional forms and both were regarded by their countrymen as the respectable mouthpieces of their age, and yet, how different they are. There is much in Tennyson that Longfellow would never have dared to write, for the peculiar American mixture of Puritan conscience and democratic licence can foster in some cases a genteel horror of the coarse for which no Englishman has felt the need. On the other hand Longfellow had a curiosity about the whole of European literature compared with which Tennyson, concerned only with the poetry of his own land and the classical authors on whom he was educated, seems provincial. Even if there had been Red Indians roaming the North of Scotland, unsubjugated and unassimilable, one cannot imagine Tennyson sitting down to write a long poem about them and choosing for it a Finnish metre. Leaving aside all questions of style, there is a difference between Tennyson's *Ode on the Death of the Duke of Wellington* and Whitman's elegy for President Lincoln *When lilacs last in the dooryard bloom'd* which is significant. Tennyson, as one would expect from the title of his poem, mourns for a great public official figure, but it would be very hard to guess from the words of Whitman's poem that the man he is talking of was the head of a State; one would naturally think that he was some close personal friend, a private individual.

To take one more example—two poets, contemporaries, both women, both religious, both introverts preoccupied with renunciation—Christina Rossetti and Emily Dickinson; could anyone imagine either of them in the country of the other? When I try to fancy such translations, the only Americans I can possibly imagine as British are minor poets with a turn for light verse like Lowell and Holmes; and the only British poets who could conceivably have been American are eccentrics like Blake and Hopkins.

Normally, in comparing the poetry of two cultures, the obvious and easiest point at which to start is with a comparison of the peculiar characteristics, grammatical, rhetorical, rhythmical, of their respective languages, for even the most formal and elevated styles of poetry are more conditioned by the spoken tongue, the language really used by the men of that country, than by anything else. In the case of British and American poetry, however, this is the most subtle difference of all and the hardest to define. Any Englishman, with a little effort, can learn to pronounce "the letter *a* in psalm and calm . . . with the sound of *a* in candle", to say *thumb-tacks* instead of *drawing-pins* or twenty-minutes-*of*-one instead of twenty-minutes-*to*-one, and discover that, in the Middle West, *bought* rhymes with *hot*, but he will still be as far from speaking American English, as his Yankee cousin who comes to England will be from speaking the King's. No dramatist in either country who has introduced a character from the other side, has, to my knowledge, been able to make his speech convincing. What the secret of the difference is, I cannot put my finger on; William Carlos Williams, who has thought more than most about this problem, says that "Pace is one of its most important manifestations" and to this one might add another, Pitch. If undefinable, the difference is, however, immediately recognizable by the ear, even in verse where the formal conventions are the same.

> He must have had a father and a mother—
> In fact I've heard him say so—and a dog,
> As a boy should, I venture; and the dog,
> Most likely, was the only man who knew him.
> A dog, for all I know, is what he needs
> As much as anything right here today,
> To counsel him about his disillusions,
> Old aches, and parturitions of what's coming,—
> A dog of orders, an emeritus,
> To wag his tail at him when he comes home,
> And then to put his paws up on his knees
> And say, "For God's sake, what's it all about?"
> (E. A. Robinson, "Ben Jonson Entertains A Man From Stratford")

Whatever this may owe to Browning, the fingering is quite different and un-British. Again, how American in rhythm as well as in sensibility is this stanza by Robert Frost.

> But no, I was out for stars:
> I would not come in.
> I meant not even if asked;
> And I hadn't been.
>
> ("Come In")

Until quite recently an English writer, like one of any European country, could presuppose two conditions, a nature which was mythologized, humanized, on the whole friendly, and a human society which had become in time, whatever succession of invasions it may have suffered in the past, in race and religion more or less homogeneous and in which most people lived and died in the locality where they were born.

Christianity might have deprived Aphrodite, Apollo, the local genius, of their divinity but as figures for the forces of nature, as a mode of thinking about the creation, they remained valid for poets and their readers alike. Descartes might reduce the non-human universe to a mechanism but the feelings of Europeans about the sun and moon, the cycle of the seasons, the local landscape remained unchanged. Wordsworth might discard the mythological terminology but the kind of relation between nature and man which he described was the same personal one. Even when nineteenth century biology began to trouble men's mind with the thought that the universe might be without moral values, their immediate experience was still of a friendly and lovable nature. Whatever their doubts and convictions about the purpose and significance of the universe as a whole, Tennyson's Lincolnshire or Hardy's Dorset were places where they felt completely at home, landscapes with faces of their own which a human being could recognize and trust.

But in America, neither the size or condition or climate of the continent encourages such intimacy. It is an unforgettable experience for anyone born on the other side of the Atlantic to take a plane journey by night across the United States. Looking down he will see the lights of some town like a last outpost in a darkness stretching for hours ahead, and realize that, even if there is no longer an actual frontier, this is still a continent only partially settled and developed, where human activity seems a tiny thing in comparison to the magnitude of the earth, and the equality of men not some dogma of politics or jurisprudence but a self-evident fact. He will behold a wild nature compared with which the landscapes of Salvator Rosa are as cosy as Arcadia and which cannot possibly be thought of in human or personal terms. If Henry Adams could write:

When Adams was a boy in Boston, the best chemist in the place had probably never heard of Venus except by way of scandal, or of the Virgin except as idolatry. . . . The force of the Virgin was still felt at Lourdes, and seemed to be as potent as X-rays; but in America neither Venus nor Virgin ever had value as force—at most as sentiment. No American had ever been truly afraid of either.

the reason for this was not simply that the *Mayflower* carried iconophobic dissenters but also that the nature which Americans, even in New England, had every reason to fear could not possibly be imagined as a mother. A white whale whom man can neither understand nor be understood by, whom only a madman like Gabriel can worship, the only relationship with whom is a combat to the death by which a man's courage and skill are tested and judged, or the great buck who answers the poet's prayer for "someone else additional to him" in *The Most of It* are more apt symbols. Thoreau, who certainly tried his best to become intimate with nature, had to confess

> I walk in nature still alone
>   And know no one,
> Discern no lineament nor feature
>   Of any creature.
> Though all the firmament
>   Is o'er me bent,
> Yet still I miss the grace
> Of an intelligent and kindred face.
> I still must seek the friend
> Who does with nature blend,
> Who is the person in her mask,
> He is the man I ask. . . .

Many poets in the Old World have become disgusted with human civilization but what the earth would be like if the race became extinct they cannot imagine; an American like Robinson Jeffers can quite easily, for he has seen with his own eyes country as yet untouched by history.

In a land which is fully settled, most men must accept their local environment or try to change it by political means; only the exceptionally gifted or adventurous can leave to seek his fortune elsewhere.

In America, on the other hand, to move on and make a fresh start somewhere else is still the normal reaction to dissatisfaction or failure. Such social fluidity has important psychological effects. Since movement involves breaking social and personal ties, the habit creates an attitude towards personal relationships in which impermanence is taken for granted.

One could find no better illustration of the difference between the Old and the New World than the respective conclusions of *Oliver Twist* and *Huckleberry Finn*, the heroes of which are both orphans. When Oliver is at last adopted by Mr Brownlow, his fondest dream, to have a home, to be surrounded by familiar friendly faces, to receive an education, is realized. Huck is offered adoption too, significantly by a woman not a man, but refuses because he knows she would try to "civilize" him, and announces his intention to light out by himself for the West; Jim, who has been his "buddy" in a friendship far closer than any enjoyed by Oliver, is left behind like an old shoe, just as in *Moby Dick* Ishmael becomes a blood-brother of Queequeg and then forgets all about him. Naturally the day-dream of the life-long comrade in adventure often appears in American literature:

> Camerado, I give you my hand!
> I give you my love more precious than money,
> I give you myself before preaching or law;
> Will you give me yourself? will you come travel with me?
> Shall we stick by each other as long as we live?
>   (Whitman, "Song of the Open Road")

but no American seriously expects such a dream to come true.

To be able at any time to break with the past, to move and keep on moving lessens the significance not only of the past but also of the future which is reduced to the immediate future, and minimizes the importance of political action. A European may be a conservative who thinks that the right form of society has been discovered already, or a liberal who believes it is in process of being realized, or a revolutionary who thinks that after long dark ages it can now be realized for the first time, but each of them knows that, by reason or force, he must convince the others that he is right; he may be an optimist about the future or a pessimist. None of these terms applies accurately to an American, for his profoundest feeling towards the future is not that it will be better or worse but that it is unpredictable, that all things, good and bad, will change. No failure is irredeemable, no success a final satisfaction. Democracy is the best form of government, not because men will necessarily lead better or happier lives under it, but because it permits constant experiment; a given experiment may fail but the people have a right to make their own mistakes. America has always been a country of amateurs where the professional, that is to say, the man who claims authority as a member of an élite which knows the law in some field or other, is an object of distrust and resentment. (In the field with which we are here concerned, one symptom of this is that curious American phenomenon, the class in "Creative Writing".)

> Amerika, du has es besser
> Als unser Kontinent, der alte,
> Hast keine verfallenen Schloesser
> Und keine Basalte.*

---

* Things are easier for you, America, than for this old continent of ours; you have no ruins of fortresses, no basalt intrusions.—GOETHE

wrote Goethe, by *Keine Basalte* meaning, I presume, no violent political revolutions. This is a subject about which, in relation to their own histories, the English and the Americans cherish opposite fictions. Between 1533 and 1688 the English went through a succession of revolutions in which a church was imposed on them by the engines of the State, one king was executed and another deposed, yet they prefer to forget it and pretend that the social structure of England is the product of organic peaceful growth. The Americans on the other hand like to pretend that what was only a successful war of secession was a genuine revolution.* There is indeed an American mentality which is new and unique in the world but it is the product less of conscious political action than of nature, of the new and unique environment of the American continent. Even the most revolutionary feature of the Constitution, the separation of Church and State, was a recognition of a condition which had existed since the first settlements were made by various religious denominations whose control of the secular authority could only be local. From the beginning America had been a pluralist state and pluralism is incompatible with an Established Church. The *Basalt* in American history, the Civil War, might indeed be called Counter-Revolution, for it was fought primarily on the issue not of slavery but of unity, that is, not for a freedom but for a limitation on freedom, to ensure that the United States should remain pluralist and not disintegrate into an anarchic heap of fragments. Pluralist and experimental: in place of *verfallene Schloesser* America has ghost towns and the relics of New Jerusalem which failed.

Whatever one may feel about Whitman's poetry, one is bound to admit that he was the first clearly to recognize what the conditions were with which any future American poet would have to come to terms.

> Plenty of songs had been sung—beautiful, matchless songs—adjusted to other lands than these . . . the Old World has had the poems of myths, fictions, feudalism, conquest, caste, dynastic wars, and splendid exceptional characters, which have been great; but the New World needs the poems of realities and science and of the democratic average and basic equality. . . . As for native American individuality, the distinctive and ideal type of Western character (as consistent with the operative and even money-making features of United States humanity as chosen knights, gentlemen and warriors were the ideals of the centuries of European feudalism) it has not yet appeared. I have allowed the stress of my poems from beginning to end to bear upon American individuality and assist it—not only because that is a great lesson in Nature, amid all her generalizing laws, but as counterpoise to the levelling tendencies of Democracy.

---

* 1829, though bloodless, was a more revolutionary year than 1776.

The last sentence makes it quite clear that by the "average" here who was to replace the "knight" Whitman did not mean the mediocre, but the individual whose "exceptional character" is not derived from birth, education or occupation, and that he is aware of how difficult it is for such an individual to appear without the encouragement which comes from membership in some *élite*.

What he does not say, and perhaps did not realize, is that, in a democracy, the status of the poet himself is changed. However fantastic, in the light of present-day realities, his notion may be, every European poet, I believe, still instinctively thinks of himself as a "clerk", a member of a professional brotherhood, with a certain social status irrespective of the number of his readers (in his heart of hearts the audience he desires and expects are those who govern the country), and taking his place in an unbroken historical succession. In the States poets have never had or imagined they had such a status, and it is up to each individual poet to justify his existence by offering a unique product. It would be grossly unjust to assert that there are fewer lovers of poetry in the New World than in the Old—in how many places in the latter could a poet demand and receive a substantial sum for reading his work aloud?—but there is a tendency, perhaps, in the former, for audiences to be drawn rather by a name than a poem, and for a poet, on his side, to demand approval for his work not simply because it is good but because it is *his*. To some degree every American poet feels that the whole responsibility for contemporary poetry has fallen upon his shoulders, that he is a literary aristocracy of one. "Tradition", wrote Mr T. S. Eliot in a famous essay, "cannot be inherited, and if you want it you must obtain it by great labour." I do not think that any European critic would have said just this. He would not, of course, deny that every poet must work hard but the suggestion in the first half of the sentence that no sense of tradition is acquired except by conscious effort would seem strange to him.

There are advantages and disadvantages in both attitudes. A British poet can take writing more for granted and so write with a lack of strain and over-earnestness. American poetry has many tones, a man talking to himself or one intimate friend, a prophet crying in the wilderness, but the easy-going tone of a man talking to a group of his peers is rare; for a "serious" poet to write light verse is frowned on in America and if, when he is asked why he writes poetry, he replies, as any European poet would, "For fun," his audience will be shocked. (In this Cambridge-on-the-Cam is perhaps a few leagues nearer Gambier, Ohio than is Oxford-on-Thames.)

On the other hand a British poet is in much greater danger of becoming lazy, or academic, or irresponsible. (One comes across passages, even in very fine English poets, which make one think: "Yes, very effective but does he believe what he is saying?": in American poetry such passages are extremely rare.) The first thing that strikes a reader about the best American poets is how utterly unlike each other they are. Where else in the world, for example, could one find seven poets of approximately the same generation so different as Ezra Pound, W. C. Williams, Vachel Lindsay, Marianne Moore, Wallace Stevens, e. e. cummings and Laura Riding? The danger for the American poet is not of writing like everybody else but of crankiness and a parody of his own manner.*

Plato said that when the modes of music change the walls of the city are shaken. It might be truer to say, perhaps, that a change in the modes gives warning of a shaking of the walls in the near future. The social strains which later break out in political action are first experienced by artists as a feeling that the current modes of expression are no longer capable of dealing with their real concerns. Thus, when one thinks of "modern" painting, music, fiction or poetry, the names which immediately come to mind as is leaders and creators are those of persons who were born roughly between 1870 and 1890 and who began producing their "new" work before the outbreak of World War I in 1914, and in poetry and fiction, at least, American names are prominent.

When a revolutionary break with the past is necessary it is an advantage not to be too closely identified with any one particular literature or any particular cultural group. Americans like Eliot and Pound, for example, could be as curious about French or Italian poetry as about English and could hear poetry of the past, like the verse of Webster, freshly in a way that for an Englishman, trammelled by traditional notions of Elizabethan blank verse, would have been difficult.

Further, as Americans, they were already familiar with the dehumanized nature and the social levelling which a technological civilization was about to make universal and with which the European mentality was unprepared to deal. After his visit to America De Tocqueville made a remarkable prophecy about the kind of poetry which a democratic society would produce.

> I am persuaded that in the end democracy diverts the imagination from all that is external to man and fixes it on man alone. Democratic nations may amuse themselves for a while with considering the productions of nature, but they are excited in reality only by a survey of themselves . . .

---

* The undeniable appearance in the States during the last fifteen years or so of a certain literary conformity, of a proper and authorized way to write poetry is a new and disquieting symptom, which I cannot pretend to be able to explain fully. The role of the American college as a patron of poets has been discussed a good deal both here and in England. Those who criticize it, often with some reason, fail to suggest a better alternative. It would be nice if the colleges could ask no more from the poets in return for their keep than occasional pieces, a Commencement Day masque or an elegy on a deceased trustee; if that is too much to ask, then the poets themselves should at least demand that they give academic courses in the literature of the dead and refuse to have anything to do with modern literature or courses in writing. There has been a vast output of critical studies in contemporary poetry, some of them first rate, but I do not think that, as a rule, a poet should read or write them.

The poets who lived in aristocratic ages have been eminently successful in their delineations of certain incidents in the life of a people or a
man; but none of them ever ventured to include within his performances the destinies of mankind, a task which poets writing in democratic ages may attempt . . .

It may be foreseen in like manner that poets living in democratic times
will prefer the delineation of passions and ideas to that of persons and
achievements. The language, the dress, and the daily actions of men in
democracies are repugnant to conceptions of the ideal. . . . This forces
the poet constantly to search below the external surface which is palpa-
ble to the senses, in order to read the inner soul; and nothing lends itself more to the delineation of the ideal than the scrutiny of the hidden
depths in the immaterial nature of man. . . . The destinies of mankind,
man himself taken aloof from his country and his age, and standing in
the presence of Nature and of God, with his passions, his doubts, his rare
prosperities and inconceivable wretchedness, will become the chief, if
not the sole, theme of poetry.

If this be an accurate description of the poetry we call modern, then one
might say that America has never known any other kind.

Exigencies of space have compelled me to draw a line which is necessarily arbitrary, excluding all poets born after 1923. This does not mean, of course,
that I think no one under thirty worthy of inclusion.

Two obvious omissions will be noted. If the decisive factors in determining
the sensibility of a poet belong to the first twenty years of his life, then Mr
T. S. Eliot is an American poet whatever his citizenship. I have, however, with
his consent, left him out of this collection because, since its primary purpose
is to give the English reader a broad picture of American poetry, the space
that could be gained for less familiar work by omitting one whose work is as
well known in England as his seemed to justify such a course. The second
omission, at her insistence and to my regret, is Miss Laura Riding.

Anchor Review, 1955; *The Faber Book of Modern American Verse*,
edited by W. H. Auden, 1956

"I Am of Ireland"

The Letters of W. B. Yeats. Edited by Allan Wade. Macmillan. $9.50.

I do not understand why publishers should be exempted from obeying the
law that requires other manufacturers to label their wares accurately. Seeing
a volume entitled *The Letters of W. B. Yeats*, a customer who puts the natural

construction upon the use of the definite article will imagine that the collection he is being offered is complete; it is not. Quite aside from the letters to George Moore, A.E., Lionel Johnson, and Maud Gonne that have been destroyed or lost, there are no letters to Bernard Shaw, Ezra Pound, Gordon Craig, or Mrs Yeats, and only one to James Joyce, because for one reason or another the editor, Mr Allan Wade, could not obtain them, and he has decided (on various grounds, among them the fact that both have already been in print) to omit the correspondence with Sturge Moore and to include only a selection from the letters to Lady Dorothy Wellesley.

However, the letters he does use make a volume of over nine hundred pages. It opens with the youth of twenty-one, as yet unpublished, saying, "The only business of the head in the world is to bow a ceaseless obeisance to the heart," and it closes with the grand old man of seventy-three saying, "The abstract is not life and everywhere draws out its contradictions. You can refute Hegel but not the Saint or the Song of Sixpence."

Yeats was not, like Keats or Byron, a born letter writer; the correspondence of a man of genius who has varied and exciting experiences cannot fail to contain many good things, but, given who Yeats was and the life he led, these letters are surprisingly dull. One remark attributed to him—"A man has no friends: he has women and the men who talk to him about women"—is no doubt apocryphal, but it is certainly noticeable that, apart from the letters to his father and one to O'Casey explaining why *The Silver Tassie* was no good, all the best letters in this volume were written to women—Katharine Tynan, Olivia Shakespear, Florence Farr, Lady Gregory, Edith Shackleton Heald, Dorothy Wellesley, Ethel Mannin. None of these are love letters in the conventional sense. Indeed, today, when first names and salutations like "darling" or "with love" are freely used without any passionate intention, it seems very odd that anyone should sign letters to his most intimate friends, even to his own father, with "Yours W. B. Yeats."

Few readers, I fancy, will share all of Yeats' enthusiasms. In my own case, I am temperamentally incapable of considering theosophy or spiritualism as anything but a joke; every generation has its own brand of snobbery, and, to mine, reciting poems to the psaltery or a bamboo flute, and verse playlets for dancers, are madly unchic. I know that the poems of Yeats I admire owe much to all of these, but I don't want to hear about them; the day-to-day fortunes of the Abbey Theatre may be of great importance to a theatrical historian, but they leave me cold. There are long stretches of this correspondence, therefore, that I have merely skimmed over in search of matters in which I take an interest.

Encounters with eccentrics and curious anecdotes always make good reading, and everyone, I think, will enjoy hearing about Althea Gyles, who "brought a prosperous love-affair to an end by reading Browning to the poor man in the middle of the night," or the middle-aged Englishman in Nice who "led about a wooden dog on wheels and addressed all his conversation to the dog. Sometimes he took a photograph, then he would explain to the dog why it must stand in the foreground." And the following anecdote may be a chestnut, but it is new to me:

> Adah Menken was given £5 a week by Prinsep and others to seduce Swinburne. She said at the end of a couple of weeks that she had always been an honest woman and could not accept the money. "We have been constantly together for two weeks and nothing has happened except that he has bitten me twice."

It is also nice to learn that Yeats, whose manner was often somewhat hierophantic, was capable of making fun of himself:

> George consulted the stars and they said quite plainly that if I went to the London operator I would die, probably of hemorrhage. Then later we did another figure to know should I go to the Dublin operator. Then the stars were as favorable as possible—Venus, with all her ribbons floating, poised upon the mid-heaven! We went to Dublin, Gogarty, with his usual exuberant gaiety, removed my tonsils. As long as I retained consciousness he discussed literature, and continued the discussion when I awoke. He would probably have continued it most of the afternoon . . . but I had a hemorrhage and was preoccupied with my possible end. I was looking, secretly, of course, for a dying speech. I rejected Christian resignation as too easy, seeing that I no longer cared whether I lived or died. I looked about for a good model (I have always contended that a model is necessary to style), but could think of nothing save a certain old statesman who, hearing a duck quack, murmured "Those young ducks must be ready for the table," and added to that "Ruling passion strong in death." Then I wondered if I could give the nurses a shock by plucking at the bedclothes.

Writing poetry and criticizing it are separate activities, and an equal talent for both is rarely found in the same person. As a critic, a practicing poet has the advantages and disadvantages of being "existentially" related to the art. For example, only a practicing poet, I think, could have made this observation, which Yeats made when he visited Oxford:

> How very unlike Ireland this whole place is—like a foreign land (as it is). One understands . . . English poetry more from seeing a place like this. I only felt at home once—when I came to a steep lane with a stream in the middle. The rest one noticed with a foreign eye, picking out the stranger and not as in one's own country the familiar things for interest— the fault, by the way, of all poetry about countries not the writer's own.

Yeats' judgments of poetry may be partial, but they are always honest and unaffected by respectable or fashionable canons of good taste; William Mor-ris is today almost unread, and I hope that those for whom Yeats has authority will take his admiration seriously.

Poets are notoriously unreliable in their judgments on their contemporaries because, being preoccupied with their own work and often as jealous of rivals as children, they seldom read the work of their colleagues unless, for some particular reason, they are obliged to. Yeats' comments while he was editing *The Oxford Book of Modern Verse* are fairer and more catholic in taste than one might have expected. Granted his bias in favor of song rhythms and "the syntax and vocabulary of common personal speech," his remarks to Dorothy Wellesley about Laura Riding and other "difficult" poets show considerable generosity:

> This difficult work, which is being written everywhere now . . . has the substance of philosophy and is a delight to the poet with his professional pattern. . . . We can learn from poets like —— ————, they purify diction, though they contort it, and see what we in our swift movement forget. Let us even imitate them, precisely because we cannot do so, swiftness and the lilt of songs in our blood.

The only poet toward whom he shows definite spite is Wilfred Owen, and it is not hard to guess why. When the *Oxford Book* came out, the omission of Owen was the point most widely criticized, and Yeats suspected, perhaps with reason, that some of his critics were motivated by political rather than aesthetic considerations; if he dug his toes in and refused to admit he could have been mistaken, that was only human. That he should have cited the large sale of his anthology as proof of its virtues, a type of defense utterly out of character, betrays his uneasiness. Given a particular poem to criticize, Yeats, like most practicing poets, offers excellent specific advice, as, for example, in this letter to A.E.:

> I do not agree with you about the ancient "planets." The word "seven" throws the imaginative strength back to the time when the planets were gods. The planets of science are round objects flattened a little top and bottom and quite without feet. To write of a material object being "fiery footed" is almost always to write from the phantasy rather than the imagination. The imaginative deals with spiritual things symbolized by natural things—with gods and not with matter. The phantasy has its place in poetry but it has a subordinate place.

But by far the greatest contribution poets can make to criticism lies in the corrections they make in their own lines as they work, for nothing can give better insight into the nature of the creative process. Yeats was not one of those poets—if such have ever existed—who produce perfect results at the first go; indeed, there have been few about whom we have evidence who had to work harder and revise more often in order to get a poem right. Here are stanzas by Yeats, first in their early version, as they appear in his letters, and then in their final published form:

(a) I will arise and go now and go to the island of Innisfree
And live in a dwelling of wattles, of woven wattles and woodwork
    made.
Nine bean rows will I have there, a yellow hive for the honey-bee
And this old care shall fade.

(b) I will arise and go now, and go to Innisfree,
And a small cabin build there, of clay and wattles made:
Nine bean rows will I have there, a hive for the honey-bee,
And live alone in the bee-loud glade.

(a) I laid a hand upon that head
Of blossom tinted stone
And can neither work nor play
Since the deed was done:
O but hands are lunatic
That travel on the moon.

(b) But since I laid a hand thereon
And found a heart of stone
I have attempted many things
And not a thing is done,
For every hand is lunatic
That travels on the moon.

Poets are always fascinating when they talk about technique, so the absence from this volume of Yeats' letters to Pound, which must surely contain many such discussions, is particularly regrettable. It is interesting to find Yeats writing to Bridges, "Though I work very hard at my rhythm, I have but little science on the matter and as a result probably offend often. Without a consistent science it is difficult to distinguish between licence and freedom."

I strongly suspect that Yeats could not tell one note from another—his conception of song implies the complete subordination of the composer to the poet—but his interest in relating words, about which he knew a very great deal, to music, however imaginary his notions of music may have been, bore good fruit, and the extraordinary rhythmical beauty of some of his last poems, like "News for the Delphic Oracle," owes much to it.

All my life I have tried to get rid of modern subjectivity by insisting on construction and contemporary words and syntax. . . . Unfortunately it was only about a year ago that I discovered that for sung poetry (though not for poetry chanted as Florence Farr chanted) a certain type of "stress" was essential. . . . It was by mastering this "stress" that I have written my more recent poems which have I think, for me, a new poignancy.

The status of most poets who have lived till seventy would not be seriously impaired had they died at forty-five. By that age, many have already written their finest work; a few, like Milton, have not, but we should acknowledge the author of "On the Morning of Christ's Nativity," "Lycidas," and "Comus" as a major poet. Yet if Yeats' last volume had been *In the Seven Woods*, we should think of him now as a good minor poet whose compositions were charming and excellently made but not of great importance. No one could have foreseen the astonishing increase in power that was suddenly to appear in *The Wild Swans at Coole*, published when Yeats was fifty-four, and to continue increasing till the end, twenty years later. It would be absurd to attempt to explain this miracle, but it is safe to say, I think, that the political events which took place in Ireland between 1916 and 1922 were a contributing cause. Yeats is probably the only poet in this century who has written great poetry on political subjects. In this, luck played as large a part as genius. If most modern poets refuse to write on political themes or try to and fail, this is not because they think politics beneath their dignity—how could they when, as never before, the daily lives of millions depend upon political decisions?—but because the scale of the political has become so great that a personal relation with it is impossible, and no theme, however important, to which one can only have an impersonal relation is capable of poetic treatment. That is why, when asked for a war poem at the outbreak of World War I, Yeats wrote:

> He has had enough of meddling who can please
> A young girl in the indolence of her youth,
> Or an old man upon a winter's night

and why, on the even of World War II, having just written some ballads about Roger Casement, a political subject, he drew the following distinction:

> In [these ballads] I defend a noble-natured man, I do the old work of
> the poets but I will defend no cause. . . . All Germany on [one] side and
> kept there by rhetoric and manipulated news; all England on the other
> side and kept there by rhetoric and manipulated news. When the rivers
> are poisoned, take to the mountain well; or go with Dante into exile.

But the Irish Rebellion and Civil War were another matter. Yeats knew most of the principal actors, the places where the events happened had been familiar to him from childhood, he witnessed in a woman he loved the unhappy effects of fanatical devotion to a cause, and he was able to perceive on a local, comprehensible scale the neo-barbarism that has disgraced the earth in our time:

> Democracy is dead and force claims its ancient right, and these men,
> having force, believe that they have [the] right to rule. With democracy
> has died too the old political generalizations. Men do not know what is,
> or is not, legitimate war.

Consequently Ireland provided him with themes for poetry that were denied poets who were citizens of the Greater Powers, and in old age he could truthfully say:

> I am reading Roger Fry's translation of Mallarmé. . . . I find it exciting, as it shows me the road I and others of my time went for certain furlongs. It is not the way I go now, but one of the legitimate roads. He escapes from history; you and I are in history, the history of the mind. Your "Fire" has a date or dates, so has my "Wild Old Wicked Man."

As yet there has been no dispassionate consideration, to my knowledge, of Yeats' political views. During the thirties, when those who admired his poetry most were well to the left of center, these views were passed over in pained silence; the postwar shift in opinion, particularly in this country, may have made them more dangerous. In justice to a great poet, we have no right to whitewash them; had Yeats been as young as Ezra Pound and as lacking in worldly prudence (of which, as it happens, he possessed a very great deal), he might well have found himself today in the same situation. It must first be remembered that Yeats was an Irishman, and one can no more expect an Irishman to respond enthusiastically to the word "Democracy," which he associates with oppression by the English, than one can expect it of an Asiatic, who associates it with the arrogance of the white races. Nor can one expect someone to whom the Independence of Ireland was dear to overlook the fact that gunfire succeeded where parliamentary procedure had failed. Yeats distrusted causes precisely because he felt their temptation, having inherited the "fanatic heart" of his countrymen. The man who wrote in 1900:

> Whoever is urged to pay honour to Queen Victoria to-morrow morning should remember this sentence of Mirabeau's—"The silence of the people is the lesson of kings." She is the official head and symbol of an empire that is robbing the South African Republics of their liberty, as it robbed Ireland of theirs

had not forgotten his historic grudge in 1937:

> I am an old Fenian and I think the old Fenian in me would rejoice if a Fascist nation or government controlled Spain, because that would weaken the British Empire, force England to be civil to Indians, perhaps to set them free and loosen the hand of English finance in the far East.

Secondly, it must be remembered that Yeats was a poet with the normal aesthetic bias of his calling. Democracy has many virtues, but aesthetic appeal is hardly one of them. No poet has ever been a democrat by instinct; observation and experience may convince him that, in practice, Democracy is the least vicious form of government, but his heart will not exactly glow at the idea; any aesthetic approach to political theory will come to conclusions similar to Plato's. The lesson is, of course, that politics must not be approached aesthetically and that the political pronouncements of artists should be heard with great caution. This does not mean that they should be totally ignored, for though most of what they say may be rubbish, it often contains insights from which more sensible but less talented citizens can profit.

At the very end of his life, in pamphlets like *On the Boiler*, Yeats came out into the open. "I must lay aside the pleasant paths I have built up for years and seek the brutality, the ill-breeding, the barbarism of truth." This is just what old age and only old age has a right to do. In youth it is impossible to be honest either with oneself or with others; in middle age it becomes possible to be honest with oneself, but there are many things that prudence and modesty alike forbid one to say in public; only within the shadow of the grave can one be perfectly frank and reveal, for better or for worse, one's naked self. It is not romantic Romeo or intellectual Hamlet but mad old King Lear whom it befits to cry, "Off, off, you lendings! Come, unbutton here."

The New Yorker, 19 March 1955

[A Tribute to Paul Claudel]*

Despite the ideological abyss separating Whitman and Claudel, I have often been struck by the similarity I found in the way they expressed their thoughts, and sometimes in those thoughts themselves. Of course Whitman's mysticism claimed a human and Claudel's a divine source. But their common intensity flowed in the same vein and from the same heart. . . .

Le Figaro Littéraire, 5 March 1955

Authority in America

An End to Innocence. By Leslie A. Fiedler. Beacon Press, $3.50.

The best compliment I can pay Mr Fiedler is to say that it took me much longer to read his book than most, since I found myself continually stopping to compose one of my own, not in order to rebut his arguments but because the questions he raises seem to me the most important questions and his approach to them the most fruitful.

Mr Fiedler has divided his essays into three groups. The first is concerned with the strains and dangers of contemporary American political life which

---

* [Retranslated into English by Richard Howard from the French text probably based on a lost original; the French text is reprinted in the Textual Notes.]

are manifested by such cases as Alger Hiss, the Rosenbergs and McCarthy; the second describes his own experiences in Italy, and discusses the mutual misunderstandings which arise between Americans and Europeans owing to their respective myths about each other; the last is a study of the hero (and heroine) in American literature, as portrayed by such writers as Whitman, Melville, Mark Twain, Hemingway, Faulkner and Fitzgerald.

The theme common to all three might be stated as follows: hitherto, both in literature and in politics, the virtues and vices of Americans have been those of adolescence, but to-day adolescence in either is no longer tolerable; the literary gold which can be mined from boyishness has been exhausted by their predecessors and American writers must either discover more adult themes or be doomed to sterility; the rise of the United States to the position of a great Power and the simultaneous decline in power of Europe places a responsibility upon the former which, if she fails to live up to it, can result in world catastrophe.

Anyone who, like myself, was born and bred on the other side of the Atlantic and then comes to this country, soon discovers that certain important words have completely different meanings and associations for Americans than they have for him. Mr Fiedler, for example, describes himself as a liberal and an intellectual. To me a liberal can only be defined by his relation to a conservative, and represents, primarily, the point of view of the mercantile classes as opposed to the land-owners: he believes in laissez-faire, Free Trade and low taxes; if he is English he is probably a Low-Churchman or a Dissenter but as staunch a supporter of the Monarchy as his High-Church Conservative rival; if he is a European he is probably agnostic, anti-clerical and republican.

Liberalism, that is, as I was brought up to understand the term, is represented in the States by Old Guard Republicans like Senator Bricker. But of course that is not what liberalism means here, where a liberal is one sort of another of Utopian, someone who is dissatisfied with the present moral condition of America and believes that the world not only should but also can become a better place: that is why an American communist feels no incongruity in calling himself a liberal and why those whose idea of Utopia is very different do not know how to dissociate themselves from him without appearing to accept the immoral present.

Again, Mr Fiedler labels himself an intellectual and a writer; to me this suggests that, along with priests, doctors, scientists, lawyers, etc., he is a "clerk," a member of a professional body which claims authority as knowing the Law in its own field, in the case of the writer, the Law of right "making." In fact, however, I know perfectly well that no American intellectual thinks of himself as a member of a caste and would neither dare nor desire to lay down the law, for the law is exactly what he thinks of himself as questioning. The sense of discouragement and defeat which Mr Fiedler detected in European writers to-day is due to their waking up to the fact that their status is now the one to which American intellectuals from Emerson and Thoreau on have always been accustomed but for which Europeans are totally unprepared; hitherto every European writer has assumed, consciously or unconsciously, that he was writing primarily for those who govern the country; now, like his American colleague, he can only cry, "He that has ears to hear, let him hear," and he doesn't like it.

I have long been seeking for a cosy little definition of "The American" and at last, after reading Mr Fiedler, I have found it: An American is a person who is as reluctant to give orders as he is to obey them.

Americans are under the illusion that their pluralist society which they are correct in thinking a new kind and are justly proud of, is the result of their own revolutionary political actions when, in fact, it was created for the most part by Nature, by the unique conditions of a large, virgin, underpopulated continent with immense natural resources. To call their secession from allegiance to the British Crown a revolution is nonsense.

Suppose a large house tyrannised over by an old grandfather; if his sons suddenly decide that they have had enough, seize him and shut him up in the attic, or if the servants, exasperated with the whole family, rise and take possession of the drawing room, relegating their former masters to the servants' hall, that is revolution: authority has changed hands, but authority remains, for the house has to be kept running. But if outside the house there are, not other houses, but a seemingly endless open road, and one of the sons walks out of the house, slamming the door behind him, and sets off towards the horizon, there has been no revolution and so long as he can keep on moving, he has neither to command others nor obey them.

Europe has always envied America as the country where the serious problems were not political, that is, concerned with the relations of human beings to each other, but problems of engineering, of the relations, that is, of man to Nature. As Mr Fiedler realised when he visited Europe, much of its anti-American feeling comes from a disappointment that Americans are not as wonderful as, given the unique good-fortune of their natural circumstances, a European thinks they ought to be. In his heart of hearts, I suspect, the average European believes that America is too good for Americans, that, if *he* had had such a chance, he would have taken better advantage of it; that is why the most vociferous critics of America are often those who would most like to emigrate.

What they do not know, because they have never experienced it, is that the Open Road has its own forms of misery, in particular loneliness and anxiety. Further, they forget one great disadvantage with which America started and for which, incidentally, they were largely responsible. If, for the majority of Americans, life was an open road down which he could walk as far as he chose or had the strength, there was a minority who could not even stroll a yard.

The reluctance of Americans to claim or obey authority, which would exist anyway in such a continent, has been aggravated by their association of authority with its most arbitrary form, slavery. What makes *Huckleberry Finn* a profound masterpiece and not just a boys' adventure story is its ironic interweaving of the dream of the Open Road and the fact of slavery. For the same reason, despite recent efforts to discover one, there has never been a satisfactory American Conservatism because those, like Calhoun, who perceived the errors and weaknesses of Liberalism, found themselves obliged to defend a social institution which, in any civilisation which claims to be either Christian or enlightened, is indefensible.

In the relation between man and nature, the question of authority does not arise; there is the will of man on the one side and nature on the other which, being a realm of necessity, has no will of her own.

Further, in an age of advanced technology, man in his mastery of nature is rapidly approaching omnipotence; there seems no problem which he does not expect to lick in time. A nation, like the United States, which suddenly finds itself confronted with serious political problems when it has been accustomed to dealing with technological problems, has a hard time understanding and being understood by other peoples.

The slogan "A bigger bang for the Dollar" for instance which sounds to European ears so akin to "Might is Right" is really the expression of the American day-dream that creating a better world is a question, not of human relations, but of finding the right gadget.

For a man travelling along the Open Road with a buddy, the question of authority does not arise for, if they cannot agree, they can always part company; moreover if they make an error of judgment and get lost, they know that they have only themselves to blame and that no one else will suffer for their mistake. But among people who have to live in the same house, someone, if they disagree, has got to accept a common course of action against her will, and, if an error is made, the innocent will suffer with the guilty. Politically, the United States has had to come in off her Open Road and start living in the World House. Small wonder then, if she gets impatient with political negotiations and attributes to malevolence errors which are due to human fallibility.

My experience of the Popular Front days is English and I can only guess at what they were like there. Here as there, I gather, communism was largely a middle-class concern. Looking back, it seems to me that the interest in Marx taken by myself and my friends, by people, that is, who were liberals in the American sense of the word, was more psychological than political; we were interested in Marx in the same way that we were interested in Freud, as a technique of unmasking middle class ideologies, not with the intention of repudiating our class, but with the hope of becoming better bourgeois; our great error was not a false admiration for Russia but a snobbish feeling that noth-

ing which happened in a semi-barbarous country which had experienced neither the Renaissance nor the Enlightenment could be of any importance:
had any of the countries we knew personally, like France, Germany or Italy,
the language of which we could speak and where we had personal friends,
been the one to have a successful communist revolution with, as it now seems
probable, the same phenomena of terror, purges, censorship, etc., we would
have screamed our heads off. As it was, the similar phenomena of which we
had direct knowledge were the work of fascism. Nobody I know who went to
Spain during the Civil War who was not a dyed-in-the-wool stalinist came back
with his illusions intact.

I have a suspicion that, for American liberals, their image of Russia was
more utopian, that, aware of the inequalities in their own country, they en-
visaged the Soviet Union as the truly egalitarian society which America claims
to be and, compared with any other country, is, whereas no European, of
whatever class, wants equality because, in the poor, fully-populated countries
of Europe, no one can be his own boss unless he bosses other people.

This does not explain the treason of Hiss or the Rosenbergs but it does help
to understand the reluctance of American liberals to admit it. The European
uproar about the Rosenbergs, in so far as it was not simply the effect of Communist propaganda, was due to the lapse in time between the trial and the
execution which made it impossible to remember what the evidence was. It
makes me realise that, though I have always believed what I was told, that
Sacco and Vanzetti were innocent, I have never examined the actual evidence.

Mr Fiedler draws attention to the role played by the American press in Mc-
Carthy's rise to power. It is an unfortunate fact about mankind that it finds
bad news more interesting than good. Of the two statements "There are five
hundred communists in the State Department," and "there are no communists in the State Department," the first has more news value, irrespective of
which statement is true. The surrender of the whole of the American press
(including the most respectable like the *New York Times*) to this weakness is
not, I believe, just a cynical wish to make money by exploiting it, but largely
a reluctance to assert authority and deny the public what they want because
it is not good for them.

In describing the reactions of Americans to Europe, Mr Fiedler is under
the personal disadvantage of having, so far as I can detect, no feeling for landscape. Here again, I must draw on my own experience. When I lived in England, my reasons for going abroad were to get into the sun, to be able to
drink what I liked when I liked and in general have the kinds of fun I could
not have at home. Now when I go to Europe from the States, the great relief
is escaping from a non-humanised, non-mythologised nature and getting
back to a landscape where every acre is hallowed. This has nothing to do with
Culture with a capital C, but I think it is the real attraction for native-born
Americans as well as for myself. Architecture aside, there are very few artistic

experiences which any American who lives within range of a big city cannot enjoy as well or better at home, but for a civilised landscape he still must go elsewhere, since his own is still the wild country of the open road where no one expects to stay, physically or spiritually, in one place for long.

In his literary essays, apart from a deplorable habit of using the term poetry not as a contrast to prose but for some vague state of emotion, Mr Fiedler is at his freshest and best. Two World Wars and technological progress are making the spiritual climate of Europe and America more and more similar. The Open Road down which the American felt free to wander at will has vanished at the same time that the European House which might be cramped but was cosy has crumbled. All of us alike are on the move, not by our own personal volition, but propelled by machinery we cannot control at a most uncomfortable pace towards a sinister-looking future. The exaggerated, in my opinion, admiration of European intellectuals for American literature comes from their feeling that it describes their present condition better than their own writers. To the degree that this is true, they should take warning from what American literature comes from their feeling that it describes their present condition better than their own writers. To the degree that this is true, they should take warning from what American literature lacks, any portrayal of adult and stable relationships.

As Mr Fiedler points out, the girls in Hemingway and Fitzgerald might just as well be boys; they too are buddies for the road, not wives and mothers. Marriage involves children and children have to be given orders. Every woman knows this, so that if the American male refuses to claim authority she has no option but to become the American Mom; most of the available evidence would suggest that she doesn't enjoy that role very much.

The ordinary citizen in his human relations faces the same difficulty that the writer faces in his art; so much which previously was either given him by tradition or did not matter has now to be deliberately cultivated under circumstances which are very unpropitious, and the price of failure has gone up enormously. One curious, and perhaps encouraging fact is the strength and vitality shown during the last forty years by American poetry.

If much of even the best fiction written during the same period seems on re-reading a little dated, the same is not true of the poetry; what seemed good when it first appeared still stands up. I find this curious because if an American is, as Mr Fiedler describes him, someone who defines his destiny not by what he is at the moment but by what he dreams of becoming, one would not expect him to succeed in a medium which places such restrictions upon dreams; in prose a man can say anything that comes into his head, in poetry he can only say what the form he has chosen to obey, allows him to say. A good poem exhibits the kind of marriage between freedom and authority, far from tyranny as it is from anarchy, which one would like to see exhibited in personal and political life. That is why I think the existence of good American poets may be an encouraging sign. I hope Mr Fiedler will write us an essay on this subject soon. The number of critics who have something worth reading to say and at the same time are readable is not large; with this book Mr Fiedler has increased it by one, and we should all be grateful.

The Griffin, March 1955

Am I That I Am?

Cards of Identity. By Nigel Dennis. Weidenfeld and Nicolson. 15s.

I really have no business reviewing a work of fiction at all. In the first place, I can no more imagine myself writing one than I can imagine myself doing up a parcel properly. In the second, my tastes are much too limited. For me, a novel should be short—not more than 350 pages—and, preferably, funny. I like novels to be about my betters, in body, wit, energy, breeding, or bank balance; I know that there are many admirable persons who live in poky flats and drink cocoa but I don't want to hear about them. (The genius of Dickens, my favourite novelist, lies in his capacity to transform the lower middle class into an aristocracy which it would be a privilege for any Proust to enter.) When, therefore, as happens now and then, as happens in this case, I see before me a novel written by an old friend, it is with trepidation and the prayer "O God, please let me like it" that I take it up. Taking up *Cards of Identity*, I looked first to see how many pages I should have to get through—370. A bit on the long side, but possible. Then, like those who consult the Bible for guidance, I opened at three pages taken at random, one near the beginning, one near the end, and one somewhere in the middle, and a read a passage on each, a procedure which I have found infallible in judging a new volume of poetry but which is, I suppose, very unfair to a piece of fiction. I found:

> *Page 2*:   There was a time when you were *younger* and had more *spirit*, when you got the rich person *first* and the horse *second*. Often you found that the friendship could be made and kept without the help of a horse. Did Mr Truter, your bosom friend, have a horse? No. He had a Rolls. Did old Miss Mallet ride? Only in a bathchair. But you wheeled her in it.

> *Page 353*:   Without any disrespect to the present incumbent of the chair, I must say that I shall always think the defunct occupant was the better man. When the present incumbent passes on, I shall proceed to think that *he* was. I consider this perfectly natural. The car we used to have is always the one that started on a cold morning: we have to have a new car to appreciate this fact.

Page 239: I quite understand why it should be thought necessary to write this sort of obituary; the only thing I have against it is that it causes people to try and read between the lines, with the result that they often suspect the deceased of crimes of which he or she is completely innocent. Thus, it was no surprise to me to hear someone say, some months later, that Violet had been secretly married to a sheik, whom she had poisoned because he had betrayed her with other women; and that the master had spent a year in prison for importuning women in Shaftesbury Avenue. Such stories are harmful, because they arouse the passions of younger people, who unconsciously model themselves on the legendary identity and, later in life, are found performing acts of crime, such as poisoning and importuning, which they believe to be purely imitative, when in fact they are entirely original.

By this time I was certain I was going to enjoy Mr Dennis's book—it was clearly my sort of novel—but how excellent I was to find it when I had read the whole, I had not the remotest conception. Hoping that such praise from me is not the kiss of death, I can only say that I have read no novel published during the last fifteen years with greater pleasure and admiration.

In formulating the problem upon which *Cards of Identity* is based, Mr Dennis may have got suggestions from many foreign sources, Kafka, Pirandello, my *bête noir* Dostoievsky, even the "existentialists," but his treatment is purely English, in the tradition of writers like Ben Jonson, Peacock, and Wyndham Lewis. His book is very funny and unbelievably tough, a jolly farce which, nevertheless, makes all those naturalistic novels in which men beat each other up, women die of syphilis, and no lavatory would dream of flushing seem the work of vegetarian social workers. Mr Dennis has come to the same conclusion as the sociologist David Riesman, namely, that twentieth-century society is "other directed" and he does not approve. This society which he explores and exposes in all its aspects, its attitudes to class and culture, its sexual relations, its political behaviour, was foreseen by nineteenth-century figures like Kierkegaard and Nietzsche, and the following passages might well have served him as epigraphic texts.

> Just as the children's crusade may be said to typify the Middle Ages, precocious children are typical of the present age. In fact one is tempted to ask whether there is a single man left who, for once, commits an outrageous folly. Nowadays not even a suicide kills himself in desperation. Before taking the step he deliberates so long and so carefully that he literally chokes with thought.

> While the collective impression of such future Europeans will probably be that of numerous, talkative, weak-willed, and very handy workmen who *require* a master, a commander, as they require their daily bread;

while, therefore, the democratising of Europe will tend to the production of a type prepared for *slavery* in the most subtle sense of the term: the strong man will necessarily in individual and exceptional cases become stronger and richer than he has perhaps ever been before—owing to the unprejudicedness of his schooling, owing to the immense variety of practice, art, and disguise.

In *Cards of Identity*, there are two sets of characters, the slaves who are delighted to be provided with imaginary identities since they cannot believe in or accept the ones they have, and the masters, the members of the Identity Club, who have learnt how to manufacture imaginary persons to their profit. Thus the Mallets take charge of Henry Paradise, a former gentleman parasite on the rich who, since the war, can find no one on whom to practise his vocation, and turn him into Jellicoe, their overworked and underpaid butler.

> "I hope you have supplied him with a rich, full past," said Mrs Mallet.
> "Everything a respectable steward could want. As a lad, I decided, he ran away to sea. Twenty years of drink and women followed in all parts of the world. Now, at last, he is going straight and though we cannot *quite* assure him that he will ever atone for his sins we can at least assure him that he is no longer trying to escape reality."
> "Has he been with us long?"
> "A good many years. He came straight here from the Navy. I found him, dead-drunk, in a Portsmouth gutter."
> "I suppose he is still dreadfully ashamed."
> "Wouldn't you be? He owes me a debt he can never repay."
> "Does he still drink?"
> "We stumble upon him sometimes taking a secret pull."
> "He took well to a watery past, did he?" asked Beaufort.
> "He couldn't resist it. The internal struggle of it all fascinated him. I mean, the long healthy hours at sea, followed by the revolting excesses of shoreleave."

Such a situation can provide comedy enough but Mr Dennis does not stop there; he goes on to show something which Nietzsche did not guess, that maters who succeed in ruling by fraud must succumb to the same disease of unreality as their slaves. A tyrant who rules by force has only an objective enemy to fear, someone with greater force, but a tyrant who finds that he can make other people believe anything cannot escape the subjective demon of doubt which suggests that perhaps he only *believes* he wants to be a tyrant; every successful lie weakens the liar's hold upon reality. Whatever horrors may be in store for us, at least one nightmare, that of a world in which a small élite still speak among themselves a real language while they rule the masses by Double Talk, can never come true.

As this novel proceeds, therefore, we find that the Club members are just as ridiculous as their dupes, and just as unreal.

> Our first step to freedom was to depersonalise the patient by calling him Mr X or Miss Y. There is nothing like algebra in this respect. It really gives the brain a chance. But it was no final solution: our equation still had to wait for an X or Y before it could be printed in a book. So, in the end, we got rid of the patient altogether. We keep only enough to bring us in a small income and solve the servant problem. We write our case histories with a purity of invention and ingenuity impossible in the days when someone was always coming into the room. But this is where I wish to make my warning. I must remind you that liberty must not breed laziness. I expect the histories we are about to hear to be of a high order. They must be plausible. The invented patients must sound like real people.

Needless to say, neither the givers of the papers, Dr Bitterling the authority on symbols, Dr Shubunkin the sexologist, Father Golden Orfe, the ascetic who is a heavy drinker and has fixed his point of self-recognition precisely midway between religious faith and the hip-flask, nor the heroes of the stories they tell: the Co-warden of the Badgeries who eases a stuffed or token badger out of a symbolic den with a symbolical gold spade, the young gentleman who in certain moods thinks he is a normal husband crushed underfoot by a contemptuous wife and in others that he is that wife, dreaming nightly of abduction by a male gorilla, the ex-Communist secret agent who has become a monk and a professional writer of confessions—none of these could be described as a real person, but their various forms of unreality have become so common that few readers, I fancy, will not be made acutely uncomfortable by at least one of them.

Text-books on Child Psychology are legion, but in which of them can one find such insights as these?

> What fun it was in those dear, bygone days to hear mother and father talk sex! "Let's always," my father told her, "speak frankly about sex before the child, so that we don't give society a maladjusted dwarf." These words are my earliest recollection: I think I was about three at the time. They impressed me because I hated the thought of becoming a maladjusted dwarf, and it seemed that conversation about sex, whatever that might be, was the one thing that would make me grow.

> I would like to interject here a warning to parents. None of you, I am sure, wants to see your son become first a secret agent of Materialism and then a public-relations agent of the Incomprehensible. Well, you can prevent this from happening if you will only hold your tongue and stop bragging about the little chap. Whenever I felt lazy or vapid and put on a moon-face, my father always bellowed at the top of his voice: "Just look

at him! With the other children you always know where you are, but you
never know with him what's at the back of *his* mind!" It had not occurred
to me before that I *had* a back to my mind, but once this area had been
brought to my attention as the place where admiration is found, I took
a life-lease on the premises. When my parents said: "Well, boys, we have
a surprise today: we're going to take you to the circus," I never turned a
hair. While my brothers cat-called and hurrahed, I sat with a pudding-
face, looking, if anything, more depressed than pleased. My father was
enthralled. "Just look at the little b——!" he would shriek, "not a squeak
out of him! I wonder what's going on *inside—at the back?*" My mother
would tousle my hair and murmur fondly: "A mother *always* knows. He's
more thrilled than all the rest of them put together—that's why he's so
quiet."

Perhaps the most significant symptom of our age is that its love and admiration is given, not to those who do or make, but to those who perform, not
to soldiers, scientists, or artists but to film-stars, night-club singers, conductors, so that, today, a politician succeeds, not through the appeal of his
programme, but through his ability to put on a good act. An actor is, by definition, someone with no identity of his own. In the first work about an identity-
less hero, *Hamlet*, there is a play within a play, and *Cards of Identity* also contains one, a pseudo-Shakespearian Late Comedy written and performed by
middle-class persons who have been persuaded that they belong to the Servant's Hall and now imagine that they are servants playing at being medieval
Kings and Queens.

I have been allowed only forty-eight hours in which to read and review this
novel, which is not long enough to judge so daring a device as the introduction of a parody blank-verse drama. I am certain that the idea is right, but I
have not had the time to discover its exact effect on the characters in the
novel who perform it nor just what it reveals about them. For those who, like
myself, enjoy good parody, this does not matter so much; they will like it, relevant or irrelevant, for its own sake. I think it possible—this, mind you, is after
only one reading—that Mr Dennis has been a little self-indulgent and that
the play could be shorter. But good parody it surely is.

CATRIONA. Once, in a moral play, good ma'am,
    I was the part of a Lazarian nun.
    My eyes so low they bandied with my toes
    And all agreed I was the thing itself.
    But that's long since, and many a broad moustache
    Has rubbaged off the mantle of my bloom. Yet,
    I could feign once more.
HERMIONE. Nay, Catriona, nuns are grown naughty.
    At night, when all's asleep, the Abbess

Rises, and takes a pick and spade in hand.
Helped by her sisters, emulating moles,
They tunnel underground for leagues and leagues,
Come up at last i' the Bishop's cell
And ravish every friar.

CATRIONA. Is't so, Madam? Why, when
I've walked the meadows, I've remarked
How, underfoot, the ground springs up and down.
I'd not believe 'twas all athrob with nuns.

HERMIONE. Catriona, we must be friars.

CATRIONA. What, Madam? Do friars not tunnel too?

HERMIONE. Nay, 'tis woman's work, sappery.

CATRIONA. What of our beards, Madam? Can we raise them up
And set them to our chins?

HERMIONE. We'll be young friars, in whom the academy
Hath gaoled the refulgent whisker under skin.

CATRIONA. And what thereafter, ma'am, when we're made vicars?

HERMIONE. Thereafter comes hereafter, we shall see
What chance and skill provide. Attend
The chapel vestry, Catriona, bring two garbs.

Reading this sort of thing, I yearn for the good old days when one lived in
a real house instead of an apartment and there was mother's clothes-closet
to rifle for garbs.

Encounter, April 1955

Man before Myth

Young Sam Johnson: A Biography.
By James L. Clifford. McGraw-Hill. $5.75.

One cannot help wondering if the shades of Dr Johnson and Boswell are still
on speaking terms, for what could be more painful to an author's vanity than
to know that for one person who still reads his books there are ten who read
the biographer whose efforts have created for him a peculiar public. The
Johnsonian is not—as the Doctor, surely, must wish he were, someone who
reads and re-reads *Rasselas, The Vanity of Human Wishes, The Lives of the Poets*
etc. with ever growing admiration, but someone who wishes to know every
detail of their author's private life, including those details and traits of which
he himself was most ashamed. If, in a prophetic dream of a bookshop two
hundred years hence, I were to see a new volume about myself, I should, of

course, at first be delighted, but how, I wonder, should I feel if, on looking at the index, I were then to find such entries as the following:

> laziness; lessons, method of getting; masochistic traits; melancholia; memory; negligent pose; outsider, feeling of being; physical handicaps;

I do not honestly know what we can say to appease Johnson's indignant and unwieldy ghost except: "We can't help it. Our curiosity about you is stronger than our sense of good manners. It's your fault for having been in life so continuously and diversely fascinating." *Young Sam Johnson* deals with the first forty years of his life, ending, that is, just before his meeting with Boswell, while he was still a struggling and relatively unknown writer. (Incidentally, how typical of his peculiar position in literature it is that his latest biographer, Mr James Clifford, should be described on the jacket as the only Johnsonian who has been an engineer.)

Mr Clifford writes clearly and simply, is scholarly without being heavy and, where Johnson's nervous peculiarities are concerned, has very sensibly preferred to give the historical facts so far as they are known and let the reader interpret them for himself instead of indulging in any fancy psychology.

Any man who has managed to rise from obscurity to eminence must, on looking back, acknowledge that success owes as much to chance as it owes to talent, that, had he not met certain people or read certain books at certain moments and in certain places, had he not experienced, even, what, at the time, seemed failure or defeat, he would never have gotten where he has, and when we inquire into the history of such a man it is the providential elements about which we are most curious to learn.

After reading *Young Sam Johnson*, it seems to me that he was much luckier in his father than he himself realised. At a time when libraries were an aristocratic luxury, what better choice of parent, short of a lord, could a future man-of-letters have made than a bookseller? Indeed a bookseller was perhaps better than a lord, since it was not considered becoming in a gentleman to show more than a dilettante's interest in literature. Even Michael Johnson's love of making his precocious child perform, a trait which Samuel resented and modern psychologists deplore, did him more good than harm. It may have been partly responsible for the bouts of accidie from which Dr Johnson suffered all his life—sloth is frequently the result of a conflict between a high standard to which the sufferer feels he is expected to conform and a fear that his accomplishment will fall below it—but it also certainly implanted that sense of superiority and desire to excel without which there would have been no Johnsonian prose, no Johnsonian repartee.

Again, not many adolescents living in the country have had the good fortune to find such intellectual stimulus as the young Johnson found in the at once scholarly and worldly-wise company of his first cousin, Cornelius Ford, and the witty lawyer, Gilbert Walmesley. The public, familiar with a famous writer's work, are apt to forget that there was once a time when he had written little or nothing, but every writer himself knows what an eternal debt of gratitude he owes to the first person who took a chance on him and gave him work to do, even if it was sheer hack-work. Knowing how lucky Edward Cave was in having Johnson on the staff of the *Gentleman's Magazine*, we must not forget that there was a moment when the luck seemed all Johnson's. Moreover, Johnson was not one of those dedicated geniuses like Wagner or Proust, in whom the notion of the exact kind of work they wish to create and the passion to create just that kind and no other, at whatever cost, are so strong that, audience or no audience, published or unpublished, they go ahead and complete it; aside from the poems and the unreadable *Irene*, there is scarcely a page of Johnson's which was not commissioned. Given the multiple stimulus of a prescribed task, financial need and a deadline, he could write with great fluency and speed; without them he was in danger, like all melancholics, of day-dreaming about an infinity of projects and executing none, or of dissipating his imagination and talent in the intoxicating immediacy of talk. It is always an ominous sign when the list of works which a writer thinks he might some day do is large and heterogeneous, and Johnson's list was both.

> As the years progressed, his "designs" grew until there were almost fifty titles. There was a history of criticism from Aristotle to the eighteenth century, a history of the Revival of Learning in Europe, an edition of Chaucer from manuscripts and old copies, "with various readings, conjectures, remarks on his language", a translation of Aristotle's *Rhetoric* and his *Ethics*, a translation of Machiavelli's History of Florence, translations of Herodian, Claudian, Cicero, editions of such English writers as Oldham and Roscommon. In a separate category, he listed possible works of the imagination: a "Hymn to Ignorance," "The Palace of Sloth—a Vision", "Prejudice—a Poetical Essay", "The Palace of Nonsense—a Vision." Not one was ever completed in the exact form originally planned.

Johnson does not appear to have been seriously tempted to go drinking or whoring, but for someone of ready wit who is afraid of his own society, conversation can be an even more dangerous form of debauchery. A man who succumbs to it must, however innately respectable, soon find himself in disreputable and Bohemian society, for only in such circles are fellow talkers available at all hours. Many of Johnson's closest friends during the first forty years of his life were rascals: there was Richard Savage, a paranoid drunk, there was Samuel Boyse who could "spin verses as fast as most men write prose, but he only worked when he could not sponge off forgiving patrons and friends. He made use of the most disgraceful expedients to excite charity, sometimes raising subscriptions for nonexistent poems, and sometimes having his wife report that he was dying," there was George Psalmanazar who "as a young man pretended to be a native of Formosa and actually had gone so far as to invent an elaborate alphabet and grammar of the language and even to publish a historical and geographical description of the island. So little was known at that time about Formosa that he was invited to spend some months at Christ Church in Oxford teaching his pretended language to a set of gentlemen who planned to go out to convert the natives to Christianity." Johnson himself was anything but a rascal and far more talented than any of his cronies but they all shared one temperamental trait which can all too easily deny to talent any lasting achievement, a trait which nobody has described better than Johnson himself.

> As soon as I enter the door of a tavern, I experience an oblivion of care, and a freedom from solicitude: when I am seated, I find the master courteous, and the servants obsequious to my call; anxious to know and ready to supply my wants: wine there exhilarates my spirits, and prompts me to free conversation and an interchange of discourse with those whom I most love: I dogmatise and am contradicted, and in this conflict of opinions and sentiments I find delight.

Mr Clifford does not go in for detailed criticism of Johnson as a writer but by skillful documentation he shows in a most interesting way how early in life both his critical attitudes and his style were formed. The unknown hackwriter in his twenties who, on reading the line "Which of pure seraphim consumes and nourishes the soul?" commented thus; "Mr Crousaz is so watchful against impiety, that he lets nonsense pass without censure: Can anything consume and nourish at the same time?" and who could compose such a period as the following:

> Here are no Hottentots without religion, polity, or articulate language; no Chinese perfectly polite, and completely skilled in all sciences; he will discover, what will always be discovered by a diligent and impartial inquirer, that wherever human nature is to be found, there is a mixture of vice and virtue, a contest of passion and reason; and that the Creator doth not appear partial in his distributions, but has balanced, in most countries, their particular inconveniences by particular favors.

is, temperamentally and stylistically, little removed from the Grand Old Dictator who castigated *Lycidas* and wrote of Pope's incursion into landscape-gardening; "Where necessity enforced a passage, vanity supplied a grotto."

It is only Johnson the poet whom one can imagine developing otherwise than as he did. On the evidence of his poetic juvenilia like the hymn for the feast of St Simon and St Jude, and of later occasional poems like the memorial verses for Dr Levet and "Long-expected one-and-twenty," one is curious to know what he might have produced had he had the time and the inclination to depart more often and for more serious subjects from the heroic couplet.

The reader will find in *Young Sam Johnson*, if not all that he would like to know, all that is certain knowledge, and the value of the book is greatly enhanced by the excellent illustrations, not least the endpaper map of Lichfield in Johnson's time.

It is to be hoped that one result of reading it will be to send him back to Johnson's own writings, and not to *The Lives of the Poets* only. An author's valuation of his work is never to be ignored. Johnson thought *The Vision of Theodore, the Hermit of Teneriffe* the best thing he had ever written. How many people alive to-day have read it? It cannot be too strongly emphasised that Johnson and Boswell are not the same person and that Johnson is much too good and interesting a writer to be left to the Johnsonians.

The Griffin, April 1955

The Dyer's Hand

I   WHAT IS POETRY ABOUT?

I want to try to answer the question "What is poetry about? What is the poetic subject?"

Let me begin by trying to draw two Theophrastian sort of character sketches—portraits that is, of fictitious beings from whom every trait except the one they typify has been removed. The first I shall call *The Poet*.

Hearing me call him by a generic term he will immediately object and give his name, his genealogical tree, his place of birth, and his horoscope, but for which, he says, he would not be a poet, for he believes that every man is fated to be what he is and to act in conformity with his nature. In the rare cases which seem to be exceptions to this law—when, say, a man of honour does something dishonourable—the cause must lie outside himself; for instance, in a fit of madness put on him by a god. There are people whom the Poet despises or condemns, but it would never occur to him to think that they could be anything but despicable.

For him mankind are divided into two classes, the gifted few whom he admires because they are really themselves, and the average anonymous mass whom he considers beneath his notice because they are no one in particular. Thus he is interested in well-bred families with ancient titles, great warriors, athletes, beautiful heiresses, wise ancients of both sexes, all who exhibit daring and energy like big-time gangsters and speculators, and monomaniacs of all kinds like pathological misers and spendthrifts.

For him there is little or no difference in kind between the behaviour of men of power and the behaviour of other powerful creatures like the great beasts of prey or of the great forces of nature, the volcano, the ocean tempest, the forest fire. The only moral commandment which he takes seriously is: *Thou shalt keep thy word irrespective of the consequences.* Disloyalty is the unforgiveable sin. However, for one who emphasises loyalty so much, he has a curious trait. If some misfortune happens to his dearest friend, if he loses his job or falls ill, the Poet will drop him or avoid him, for the Poet agrees with Nietzsche that there must be something dreadful about anyone to whom dreadful things happen, and he has a superstitious horror of misfortune which he believes is infectious. This is not his only superstition. For him every number up to about twenty-four has a unique magical significance of its own, lucky, unlucky, weak, powerful, etc. Large numbers, on the other hand, mean nothing to him. He would never say, for instance: "Alexander conquered 1316 cities". He might say "Alexander conquered a thousand cities", but the number would simply be a term meaning *very many*; if he wished to be accurate he would give the names of every one of the 1316.

His attitude towards politics and jurisprudence is that of Blake: One law for the ox and the ass is oppression. He is not in the least shocked by cruelty or inequity so long as it is personal. He would have no objection, for instance, to some tyrant who, out of sheer whim, commanded his subjects on pain of death to wear crimson bowlers while he himself wore a black one; but the notion that a law should be obeyed not because the lawgiver is strong enough to enforce it but because it is just, is beyond the Poet's comprehension. On the other hand, when he plays games, he is a stickler for the rules; for him, the more complicated the rules, the greater the challenge to the player's skill, the better the game.

Should you ask him: "Do you believe in God?", he will reply: "I don't understand what you mean by believe. To me, a god is any power that unlike man is immortal and autonomous, able to do whatever he likes. I have only to use my five senses to know that a number of such gods and goddesses exist and that a man's success in life depends upon attracting their favour and avoiding giving them offence".

If you now ask him: "Do you think that you can affect the actions of the gods by composing poems?", I think his answer will be something like this: "My ancestors were magicians and believed that poetry had this power, and old country women to this day use verse charms; e.g. over a burned finger they will intone:

> There came two angels from the North,
> One was Fire, and one was Frost.
> Out Fire! In Frost!
> In the name of the Father, the Son, and the Holy Ghost.

But I myself do not think of poetry as that kind of magic. When, for example, I begin a poem with an invocation to Apollo, I do not believe that, in consequence, Apollo must inspire me, or that, should I omit such a prayer, he will refuse; I am only expressing my sense of the seriousness of the task before me. Life is fleeting and full of sorrow and no words can prevent the brave and beautiful from dying or annihilate a grief. What poetry can do is transform the real world into an imaginary one which is god-like in its permanence and beauty, providing a picture of life which is worthy of imitation as far as it is possible. It is not possible, of course, but without the attempt the real world would get even worse".

When the Poet tells a story one is overwhelmed by the power of his visual imagination and the grandeur of his language; while he is speaking, his audience forget time and themselves completely and see the events he is narrating taking place before them; if, for instance, he makes a digression from his main story, they are unaware that it is a digression, for the intensity of the present moment banishes both recollection and anticipation. For the same reason it never occurs to a listener to ask "Did these events actually happen, or is the poet making it up?", for it is incontrovertible that they are happening at this moment in the listener's mind. The only criticisms—if they are criticisms—which can be made about the Poet's stories is that they lack suspense and that they lack mystery. All the persons in his stories act so completely in character that one cannot imagine there is anything to know about them that we are not told, or even to reflect upon.

The nearest the Poet gets to the mysterious is in his love of riddles. But the point about a riddle is that its mysteriousness is only apparent, like that of a person wearing a mask. Once the solution is found or the mask removed, the mystery vanishes. In any actual writer of poetry born in the West during the last two thousand years, the Poet has had to cohabit with a second type whom, for want of a better term, I shall call *The Historian*.

The most obvious difference between the Historian and the Poet is that the Historian has no interest in nature, only in human beings, and that he is interested in them precisely because he does not believe that their lives are pre-ordained by fate but that, on the contrary, what their future is to be depends on the choices that they make, for which they are personally responsible. Thus, while the Poet, when he meets someone, thinks only in terms of the present moment and asks therefore "Who is he? What is he like? What does he do?", the Historian is interested in the present only as it relates the past to the future and will ask, "Where is he coming from? What is he heading towards?" The Poet judges by appearances. For him, therefore, if a man is fortunate, which is an objective fact, he must be good or in favour with the gods, and vice versa. The Historian will say: "You never can tell what any appearance is going to mean. This young man who has just inherited a hundred thousand pounds may before he dies regret it; this other young man who has just lost a leg may later discover that it was the best thing that could have happened to him". Similarly, while the Poet judges the importance of an action by its magnitude, the Historian treasures those actions, which may seem trivial but which reveal the direction in which the actor is already moving, unknown to himself or others.

Like the Poet, he does not believe that all men are alike; but he does not divide men into the gifted and ungifted, he divides them into those who are faithful to the True Voice, however difficult its commands or promises, and so become what they ought to become; and those who, through indifference or through believing the Lying Voices, which may be more plausible than the True, are unfaithful and fail to fulfil their proper destiny. Further, this division is never permanent; anybody in either class can at any moment cross over into the other. Therefore no numbers, big or small, mean anything to him, or rather you might say that only the number One has significance, not because it is in any way magical, but because it alone is real.

The Historian is no more interested in a law for everybody than the Poet—what the True Voice commands is unique for every individual. On the other hand, he does not share the Poet's admiration for arbitrary power. The True Voice is not to be obeyed because it is powerful—the Lying Voices may often seem much more compulsive—but because it is true. Thus it is not enough, for instance, that a warrior be brave; he must also be fighting for the right cause.

If the same theological question as was asked the Poet be put to the Historian, there are several possible answers he may give. He may say: "I believe in One God beside whom there are no others"; or "I believe in the Good God, and his eternal antagonist, the Evil God"; or "I believe there is no God, but I believe that there is, innate in man, a sense of what is truly excellent". But whatever answer he gives, he understands perfectly well what believing something means. Should you then ask him if he considers that the function of art is to make people listen to the True Voice and prevent them from listening to the false, he will answer: "No. Art cannot teach or even portray examples worthy of imitation. It can only hold a mirror in which each person sees his face reflected; it can, that is, make him conscious of what he is like, but what he is to do about it must be left to his choice to decide, since the way for every person is unique".

The Historian's method of story telling, therefore, is very different from that of the Poet. To begin with, he usually tells stories in prose, having a distrust of formal verse as falsifying the truth; but, if he does use verse, it is in a homely, not an elevated, style. In comparison with the Poet, he leaves such a lot out. He rarely tells you where things happened or describes the landscape. If natural objects play a role in the story, he is not specific; he will say, for instance, "Then Hans came to a tree", or "Then Jack saw a fish", where the Poet would have said "Then he came to a tall oak", or "Then he saw a red salmon". Sometimes, indeed, he does not even bother to give the hero's name, but will start off: "A certain man was about to be married".

The persons in his stories may come from any class, they may be gifted or ungifted; they may even be children, which is incomprehensible to the Poet; but something unexpected happens to all of them. They are always being tested or tempted, often without their being aware of it. Thus a young man is rude to a poor woman and as a result takes the wrong turning and is devoured by an ogre; his brother is courteous and in return she guides him to the enchanted palace.

His stories do not contain riddles, but instead are full of contradictions and paradoxes. To the Poet comedy is synonymous with satire: only inferiority causes laughter; in the Historian's tales, on the other hand, it is often the comic character who is superior to other characters. His characters remain mysterious, so that every listener interprets them slightly differently, as we all read faces differently.

If the Historian lacks the Poet's visual imagination and noble style, he has a better ear for how men who are not actually poets speak. Listening to him, his audience are not under the Poet's spell; they remember that they exist as an audience, they remember the part of the story that has already been told and they are conscious of wondering what is going to happen next. The Historian's spell is of a different character; he makes his audience believe, not that they are living an experience at this moment but that what they are hearing really happened, because they recognise in what they hear something which they know to be true about themselves. When the Poet has finished a tale, everybody remains silent, lost in admiration of the great persons and heroic deeds of which they have just heard: when the Historian finishes a tale, everyone jumps to his feet, saying, "That reminds me of another story".

I have described the Poet before the Historian, since before the Christian era most of the stories we know are his, but not all: whatever the actual date of Genesis, a story like that of Abraham and Isaac is the Historian's work. It would be incorrect, however, to say that the historical element in our literature comes solely through the Judaic-Christian tradition. *The Aeneid*, for example, already exhibits traces of it: the Trojan War has no significance except as an occasion for the heroes on both sides to manifest their heroic qualities; Aeneas, on the other hand, is not only a hero but has a mission as the founder of Roman civilisation. Thus, the pathos of Hector's death is simple; the noble character is slain: the pathos of Turnus' death is ironic; he is a more sympathetic character than Aeneas, but he is slain defending the wrong cause. It is better for the future of the world that Aeneas should win.

Perhaps it is just this historical element which prompted Virgil's supposed remark that he was working against the Muse. Though nearly all poems written in the last nineteen hundred years are the joint product of the Poet and the Historian, the collaboration is one of uneasy tension. The message of the Grecian Urn, as Keats realised, was that Beauty and Truth are identical; for

Keats himself, as for every modern poet, they are at odds. Essentially poetry is an affirmation of Being, and the main negative motive for writing it a dread of non-being. The Poet feels like St Augustine: "I would rather have been deprived of my friend than of my grief"; even when he says "Since never to have been born is beyond all comparison the best", he is rejoicing that he is alive to make that statement. For him, therefore, anything which has a history, which changes, contains an element of non-being, which resists poetic expression. His very medium, language, is ill-fitted to describe becoming. I can describe fairly accurately, for example, inorganic objects, like stones, which either are, or are not, by naming them and giving their shape and dimensions. Even their colour is not too difficult to specify for, if the colour vocabulary is limited, I can always use a comparison and say "green as grass" to indicate the exact shade I mean. Inorganic things can exist in different forms, like Water, Ice and Steam, but the forms do not overlap. But when I come to describe even the non-human organic world which does not even have a real history but only a cycle of growth, I run into difficulties. I may possess names for certain stages, e.g. acorn, sapling, oak, but the exact point at which I abandon one term to use the next is arbitrary.

Before discussing the poetic problems raised by the historical existence of human beings, however, let us compare a work in which the Poet has no Historian to contend with, and one in which they fight it out between them: for instance, Sophocles' *Oedipus Rex* and Shakespeare's *Macbeth*. I have selected these because in both of them there is a prophecy about the future which comes true. The notion pre-supposed by the Greek Oracle is that the future is pre-ordained; that is to say, there is no real future because it is already latent in the present. If one asks, therefore, what would have happened if Oedipus had remained in Corinth instead of running away, the only answer can be that, although the actual events would have been different, the results would have been the same; in the end he would have murdered his father and married his mother. What the Oracle says may be put in a riddle form, but, once this is deciphered, what it says is not a promise but a statement of fact like a statement of a scientific law, and there is no question of belief or disbelief. In the Old Testament, God promises that the Land of Canaan shall in the future belong to the Children of Israel, but the fulfilment of this promise depends upon their believing it, and when, as is told in the thirteenth chapter of the Book of Numbers, all but Joshua and Caleb, after spying out the land, say "We cannot attack such a people as this; they are too strong for us", God postpones the fulfilment of his promise to their children.

In *Macbeth* the witches prophesy that Macbeth shall become king. If he had listened to them as a Greek would have listened to the Oracle, then he would have been able to sit and wait until by necessity it came to pass. But he takes it as a promise with which he has to cooperate and which, in consequence, brings about his downfall, so that it is legitimate to say that Macbeth should not have listened to them, in which case he would not have become king, and they would have been proved to be what they were, lying voices.

One might say that, though there is a history of Oedipus, Oedipus himself has no history, for there is no relation between his being and his acts. When the play opens he has already committed parricide and incest, but he is still the same person he was before he had done so; it is only when he finds out that the old man whom he killed in a quarrel about precedence, a deed which neither he nor his audience are supposed to think wrong, was, in fact, his father, and that the Queen of Thebes to whom he has been happily married for years is, in fact, his mother, that there is a change, and even then this is a change not in him but in his status. He who formerly was a happy king beloved by his subjects is now a wretched outcast. In *Macbeth*, on the other hand, every action taken by Macbeth has an immediate effect upon him so that, step by step, the brave bold warrior we hear of in the first scene turns before our eyes into the guilt-crazed creature of the "Tomorrow and tomorrow and tomorrow" soliloquy.

At no point during the Greek tragedy is Oedipus faced with a choice so that one could say that he made the wrong one. If, for example, he accepts Tiresias' advice and drops his inquiry into who the criminal is who is responsible for the plague, the plague will continue. But Macbeth not only makes a series of wrong choices which he should not have made, but also, though the past exerts an increasing pressure on the present, at no point does it become necessity; however difficult it might have been, for instance, after the murder of Duncan, to repent and refrain from murdering Banquo, it was not impossible.

The parricide and incest committed by Oedipus are not his acts but things that happen to him, without his knowledge and against his desire, presumably as a divine punishment for his hubris; for thinking, that is, that he is so fortunate he is a god whom misfortune cannot overtake. Macbeth's acts are his own and not a punishment for, but the outcome of, his pride; of his believing, not that he is a god, but that he can do what he pleases irrespective of God's will.

Watching *Oedipus*, there is no question of the audience identifying themselves with the hero—all psychoanalytical explanations of the play are nonsense—for what they see is a unique case of spectacular misfortune. The majority know, like the members of the chorus, that they will never be great men, so such a thing could not happen to them: if there is an exceptionally fortunate man in the audience, the most he will say is, "I hope nothing like that ever happens to me", and has quite good grounds for his hope. Watching *Macbeth*, every member of the audience knows that the possibility of becoming a Macbeth exists in his nature. One cannot imagine Sophocles arriving at the idea of a play about Oedipus except from a knowledge of the myth, but the germ of Macbeth in Shakespeare's mind could perfectly well have been what Kipling suggests in his poem, "The Craftsman":

> How at Bankside, a boy drowning kittens
> Winced at the business; whereupon his sister—
> Lady Macbeth aged seven—thrust 'em under,
>   Sombrely scornful.

That is why no one would dream of writing a book about the characters in Greek tragedy: everything that can be said about them has been said in the plays themselves, but people have and will continue to write books about Shakespeare's characters and quarrel furiously about their rival interpretations. The characters in Greek literature are like Greek statues in which the face is no more significant than any other part of the body. For, like an animal, their nature is completely expressed in their actions; nothing is left to the imagination because there is nothing to leave; there is no inner life of possibilities which are implied in such a phrase as "I can read his character in his face".

It is possible to imagine a Shakespearean type of play using the premise of Oedipus. If Oedipus is to make certain of not fulfilling the prophecy, then he must take two vows: never to strike a man and never to sleep with a woman. Let us imagine, then, a man by nature highly choleric and passionate, and place him in two situations in which he is greatly tempted to break these vows; in the first, some man has done him a mortal injury, some serious treachery, perhaps; in the second, he falls violently in love with a woman who reciprocates equally violently. Naturally, he will do his best to persuade himself that the man could not possibly be his father or the woman his mother, but in this kind of play the author must show us the process of self-deception; that is to say, there must be elements in both situations which would make any impartial observer suspect that the man and the woman could very well be what anger and lust would persuade Oedipus they are not.

Such a treatment demands not only a different plot, but also a different formal structure and a different poetic style. In the original play it is natural that there should be only one place and no breaks in time, for the function of both is external: the action is the revelation of what has already happened, and all that is needed is a place where and a certain length of time in which this can occur.

In our new version such unities are highly unnatural and can be retained, if at all, only by a technical tour de force, for the decisive events and choices by which the innocent Oedipus becomes guilty cannot occur all at the same time and it is improbable that they could all occur in the same place. As to style, the unbroken elevation of the Greek version becomes unsuitable and needs to be replaced by something far more mixed, now high, now low like the porter in *Macbeth*. In a world of Being, where people are what they are by fate, the more intense the moment and the more magnificent their verbal response to it, the more they manifest their being, and every relaxation weakens the effect and should be eliminated. But in a world where people become by their choices what they previously were not, a moment in which the characters are emotionally relaxed may be just as significant as one in which they are emotionally stirred.

Further, while in the first world there is no essential difference between man and other creatures of nature, in the second man is unique as a conscious creature who is changed by his acts and at the same time as a physical being subject to the necessities of nature. He cannot choose to feel hungry or not hungry, sleepy or not sleepy, full of or free from sexual desire, and one function of a lowering of style is to express this creaturely framework within which his freedom of will operates. When this is ignored, as it is in French classical tragedy, the drama becomes pure theatre; that is to say, only great actors and actresses can make it real. If the cast is poor, the audience are reminded of human frailty and the elevated style and sentiments become absurd. The formal model for French tragedy is Greek tragedy, but it is about matters concerned with choices, not with necessity. In attempting to copy the Greek form, it leaves out necessity altogether. Its exalted personages are demi-gods without physical needs; even when they are in love, one cannot imagine them doing anything so vulgar and natural as going to bed together. This makes their diction suitable not for them but for the flesh and blood actors who play them. Opera is much safer from ridicule because singing is primarily a gift of nature, not of personality or skill. One might put it this way. If lions and tigers were granted the gift of speech, they would speak in the alexandrines of Racine; if angels had any need for words, they would speak in the inconsequential prose of Lady Bracknell or Cardinal Pirelli.

Returning to our imaginary version of *Oedipus*, let us suppose it is written by Shakespeare himself at the height of his powers, equal in poetic splendour to *King Lear* and *Antony and Cleopatra*. Compared with Sophocles it will be a more interesting, possibly more profound, play but it will be a less beautiful and less perfect work of art; for no matter how great the genius of its author, it will lack that exact correspondence of form and content which the Greek play possesses. The modern dramatist is faced with an insoluble problem: how to present a character who by a combination of circumstances and his own free choices becomes different. Becoming and choice are continuous processes, not a series of jumps from one state to another, but it is only as a series of jumps that the dramatist can portray becoming at all, and any answer to the question "How many different stages do I need to show?" must be arbitrary: there is no Shakespeare play which one cannot imagine either longer or shorter than it is.

Again, in the Greek world of Being, where people are neither more nor less than what they say and do, a character may be ignorant of the true situation, he may lie about it to others, but he cannot deceive himself or reveal anything about himself to others which he does not intend. In the modern world of historical becoming, in which what people say and do is not only expressive but significant of their hidden inner life, why they say something is as important as what they say. Unfortunately, the time it takes the spectator to guess the former is not the same as the time it takes to grasp the latter. As Mr Eliot has pointed out, Othello's final speech, "I have done the state some service and they know it", is harrowing because it reveals that, after everything, Othello still clings to illusion and is trying to cheer himself up. A spectator may fail to get this revelation, in which case the effect is lost; but if he does get it, he gets it in a flash which may occur at any time during the speech; once he has got it, the rest of the speech is, from the point of view of character revelation, redundant and undramatic, poetry for its own sake.

The same differences and difficulties can be seen in lyrical poetry; When Sappho writes:

> Some say that the fairest thing upon the dark earth is a host of foot-soldiers, and others again a fleet of ships, but for me it is my beloved—

she is thinking in terms of a world of Being in which one thing can be compared with another thing but cannot stand for it. The possibility that the beauty of the beloved could transform the being of the lover so that all things, including soldiers and ships, suddenly become more beautiful in his eyes, could not occur to her. There are plenty of Greek poems on the "Gather ye rosebuds while ye may" theme, but the passage of time is seen objectively. You are young and beautiful and desirable now; in a few years you will be less beautiful and desirable; so enjoy yourself. But there are none in which the present moment is felt subjectively as in this poem of Rochester's:

> The Time that is to come is not,
>> How can it then be mine?
> The present Moment's all my Lot,
> And that, as fast as it is got,
>> *Phyllis*, is only thine.

> Then talk not of Inconstancy,
>> False Hearts and broken Vows;
> If I, by Miracle, can be
> This live-long Minute true to thee,
>> 'Tis all that Heav'n allows.

Again, to the Greeks, the difference between animals and men was a difference in gift; men have the gifts of speech and reason, animals have not. Such a difference is no more radical than that between a beautiful and an ugly man, a wise man and a foolish man. In consequence, nature in their poetry could be a source of similes but not of symbols, of public omens but not of occasions of personally significant encounter.

The kind of experience described in Keats' "Ode to a Nightingale" or the famous passage in *The Prelude*, where, having borrowed a boat without leave, Wordsworth feels that the mountain peak is striding in his pursuit, is possible only to those who see a radical break between Man and nature. The significant difference is not that man has speech, but that he talks to himself, not that he has reason but that he reasons about reasoning.

Modern poetry—and by "modern", I mean poetry of the last fifteen centuries—is obscure in a special sense; it means and cannot help meaning more than and something different from what it expresses, so that the reader is required to play a creative role which the reader of ancient poetry is spared. I should like to end with one of Yeats' last poems, "The Circus Animals' Desertion", which describes the modern poet's predicament better than any other I know.

The Circus Animals' Desertion

I

I sought a theme and sought for it in vain,
I sought it daily for six weeks or so.
Maybe at last, being but a broken man,
I must be satisfied with my heart, although
Winter and summer till old age began
My circus animals were all on show,
Those stilted boys, that burnished chariot,
Lion and woman and the Lord knows what.

II

What can I but enumerate old themes,
First that sea-rider Oisin led by the nose
Through three enchanted islands, allegorical dreams,
Vain gaiety, vain battle, vain repose,
Themes of the embittered heart, or so it seems,
That might adorn old songs or courtly shows;
But what cared I that set him on to ride,
I, starved for the bosom of his faery bride.

And then a counter-truth filled out its play,
The Countess Cathleen was the name I gave it;
She, pity-crazed, had given her soul away,
But masterful Heaven had intervened to save it.
I thought my dear must her own soul destroy
So did fanaticism and hate enslave it,

And this brought forth a dream and soon enough
This dream itself had all my thought and love.

And when the Fool and Blind Man stole the bread
Cuchulain fought the ungovernable sea;
Heart-mysteries there, and yet when all is said
It was the dream itself enchanted me:
Character isolated by a deed
To engross the present and dominate memory.
Players and painted stage took all my love,
And not those things that they were emblems of.

III

Those masterful images because complete
Grew in pure mind, but out of what began?
A mound of refuse or the sweepings of a street,
Old kettles, old bottles, and a broken can,
Old iron, old bones, old rags, that raving slut
Who keeps the till. Now that my ladder's gone,
I must lie down where all the ladders start
In the foul rag-and-bone shop of the heart.

II   THE POETIC PROCESS

In my first talk I suggested that the primary intention of poetry, as of all the arts, is to affirm personal being and personal becoming and to defeat their enemies, the accidental and the fantastic. Now I am going to discuss the process of writing poetry but, before doing so, I should like to say something about the relation of Art to that other great activity of the human spirit, Science.

As a being composed of matter, Man is subject to all the laws of the inorganic universe, the laws of physics and chemistry; as a biological organism, he is subject to biological needs and the biological cycle of birth, growth, reproduction, death; as a conscious being with a personal self and free-will who makes his own history for which he is personally responsible, he is the subject of the historical order. For the purposes of this discussion, we can lump the physical and the biological together and say that Man inhabits simultaneously two worlds, for which I shall use names invented by Henry Adams, the World of the Dynamo, and the World of the Virgin. Any event which occurs in the World of the Dynamo is (*a*) recurrent, a member of a class of similar events to which it is related by the principle of Identity, and (*b*) occurs necessarily according to law. Of such an event it can only be said that it is what it is. Any event which occurs in the World of the Virgin is (*a*) once only, the unique member of a class of one, related to other classes by the principle of analogy, (*b*) occurs not necessarily according to law but voluntarily according to provocation, and (*c*) is a cause of subsequent events by providing them with a motive for occurring. Of such an event it can be said that it could have been otherwise.

The World of the Dynamo is describable, therefore, in terms of number, not language. In it Freedom is the consciousness of necessity, and Justice the equality of all before the law. The World of the Virgin is describable not by numbers but by metaphorical language. In it necessity is the consciousness of Freedom, and Justice the recognition of my neighbour as a unique irreplaceable being.

Since all human experience is that of conscious persons, it is not surprising that the existence of the World of the Dynamo, in which events happen of themselves and cannot be prevented by anybody's art, took time to discover, for man had first to learn to separate his perceptions from the emotions aroused by and accompanying them. Freedom is an immediate datum of consciousness; necessity is not.

Mankind needs both the artist and the scientist, not only because both their worlds of study are real, but also for protection against the hubris by which each is tempted, for both, if unchecked, will lay claim to total mastery and create a chimerical universe. Without the check of the scientist, the artist, attempting to treat the world of mass as a world of faces, creates a magical universe in which prayers are said to the Dynamo. Without the check of the artist, the scientist, by attempting to treat the world of faces as a world of number, creates a positivist universe in which the Virgin is a statistic. In the artist's chimerical universe there can be no notion of equality, in the scientist's no notion of liberty.

But God is not mocked: the punishment of hubris comes swiftly, a common madness in which the pseudo-artist and the pseudo-scientist are indistinguishable from each other, for the artist becomes as incapable of recognising beauty as the scientist of recognising truth. Marx claimed to have stood Hegel on his head: in fact, both were animists with their feet off the ground. At this moment it may look as if the artist's chance of dictatorship had passed for ever, and that the only danger in the future will come, as it comes now, from the scientist; but one should never be too sure; one could hardly call Nazism the work of scientists, whatever use it managed to make of them; and if a thermonuclear war were to destroy all the plumbing on earth tomorrow, who knows what strange sybils and shamans might walk abroad again the day after?

Any world comprises a plurality of events. Pluralities are of three kinds: crowds, societies, and communities.

A crowd is comprised of $n > 1$ members whose sole common character is togetherness. A crowd loves neither itself nor anything else. It can only be counted; its existence is chimerical. Of a crowd it may be said, either that it is not actual but only apparent, or that it should not be.

A society is comprised of a finite number of members, united in a specific manner into a whole with a characteristic mode of behaviour which is different from the behaviour of its members in isolation. A society has a definite size, a specific structure, and an actual existence. It cannot come into being until its component members are present and properly related. Add or subtract a member, change their relations, and the society either ceases to exist or is transformed into another society. A society is a system which loves itself. To this total self-love, the self-love of its individual members is totally subordinate. Of a society it may be said that it is more or less successful in sustaining its existence.

A community is comprised of *n* members, united, to use a definition of St Augustine's, by a common love of something other than themselves. Like a crowd, and unlike a society, its character is not changed by the addition or subtraction of a member. It exists neither by chance, like a crowd, nor actually like a society, but potentially, so that it is possible to speak of a community where $n = 1$. To achieve an actual existence it has to embody itself in a society or societies which can express the love which is its raison d'être. For example, a community of music lovers cannot just sit there loving music like anything; they have to form themselves into societies like choirs, symphony orchestras, string-quartets, etc., and make music. Such an embodiment of a community in a system is an order. Of a community it may be said that its love is more or less good.

Such a love, good or bad, presupposes choice, so that in the World of the Dynamo, the world of Nature, communities do not exist, only societies which are sub-members of the total system of nature, enjoying their self-occurrence.

Communities can only exist in the historical world of the Virgin but they do not necessarily exist there.

Whenever rival communities compete for embodiment in the same society there is either unfreedom or disorder. In the chimerical case of a society embodying a crowd there would be a state of total unfreedom and disorder: the normal term for this chimerical case is Hell. A perfect order—that is, one in which the community united by the best love were embodied in the most self-sustaining system—could be described in terms of scientific laws, but the description would be irrelevant, the correct description being "Her Love is the fulfilling of the law" or "In his Will is our Peace". The normal term for this is Paradise. In historical existence, where no love is perfect, no society immortal, and no embodiment of the one in the other precise, the obligation to approximate to the ideal is felt not as a law but as an imperative.

If the natural world were immediately intelligible, there would be no need for science, no impulse to become a scientist; if the historical world were the creation of saints only, there would be no need for art or impulse to become an artist. In fact, however, man is confronted in both worlds by a crowd of events, which provide the subject-matter and stimulus to science and art respectively. The subject-matter of the scientist is a crowd of natural events at all times; he presupposes that this crowd is apparent, not real, and seeks to discover their real place in the system of nature. The subject-matter of the artist is a crowd of historical events recollected from the past: he presupposes that this crowd is real but should not be, and seeks to transform it into a community.

Both science and art are spiritual activities, not practical, whatever practical applications may be derived from their results. Disorder, lack of meaning, are spiritual not physical discomforts; order and sense are spiritual not physical satisfactions.

The subjects and the methods of the scientist and the artist differ, but their impulse is the same, the impulse which is at work in anyone who, having taken the same walk several times, finds that the distance seems shorter; what has happened is that, consciously or unconsciously, he has divided the walk into stages, thus making a memorable structure out of what at first was a structureless flux of novelty.

Since in his work the scientist has to eliminate himself, reducing his person to a pure epistemological subject, all he requires qua scientist is technical skill and a knowledge of the work of other scientists past and present. The artist, on the other hand, needs all the self he can get; technique and familiarity with other works of art are by no means sufficient.

There have been times and places, medieval Wales, for example, when being a poet was a normal profession; that is to say, the poet enjoyed considerable social prestige and earned his living by the practice of his art. Whenever such conditions hold, poets are not left to educate themselves, but are systematically trained and admitted to the rank of poet only after meeting high professional standards, just as doctors are today. Such conditions are not going to recur in any future we can envisage, nor am I certain that it would be a good thing if they did. I suspect that poets are only granted such prestige when poetry is credited with magical powers. This doctrine, I believe, is not only false but usually associated with other equally false and much more pernicious doctrines.

A poet today has to educate himself and he has to keep himself, and most of us, I fear, as we get older and it is too late to rectify our mistakes, wish we had brought ourselves up differently. In my own case, I find my inability, through ignorance, to name and recognise plants and birds a serious handicap.

Ideally, a poet-to-be should be born to parents with varied interests. Two conditions are unfavourable: a too highly sophisticated or artistic home in which everything is in perfect taste, where the library contains the best literature and nothing else, is as dangerous as a Philistine home with no books at all. Similarly, it is better that he spend his childhood and adolescence in the country rather than in a town, particularly a metropolis. This is becoming extremely difficult, so that, I think, a poet today has deliberately to learn by study many things which a rural childhood would have taught him naturally.

Suppose some eccentric Texas billionaire were to give me carte blanche in running a training school for poets, I know what the curriculum would be. The technical side would consist of learning thirty lines of poetry a day by heart, and instruction in prosody, rhetoric, and the history of the language. Works of criticism would be banned from the school library. For the rest, courses in Natural History, Geology, Meteorology, Archaeology, Mythology, Liturgics, and Cooking. Further, every student would be expected to look after a domestic animal and a garden plot.

Since no poet can earn his living by poetry, he must either sponge or find a job. The ideal characteristics of such a job are easy enough to state: it should be

non-literary
not physically or mentally exhausting
well paid
one the poet can leave when he can afford it and return to when he must.

If such jobs are rare, the poet who is qualified to take one is rarer still. The only non-literary job for which the average poet is equipped is unskilled manual labor. Perhaps the time is coming when parents with intellectually or poetically minded children will see to it that, like rabbis in old times, they are taught some skilled trade.

But let us leave this depressing topic and return to the writing of poetry.

I suggested that the material with which the poet starts is a crowd of recollected historic occasions of feeling. Some of these may be called Outstanding, others Significant. An outstanding event is the sort one reads about in the newspapers or puts down in one's diary; a significant event is one which one may hardly notice at the time but which on reflection seems to hide some important secret. Marvell's "Cromwell Ode", for example, is about an outstanding event, Wordsworth's "The Highland Reaper" about a significant event, and Milton's "Lycidas" involves both.

This crowd of events the poet attempts to transform into a community by embodying it in a verbal society. Such a society, like the physical universe, can be described in terms of laws and structure. Prosody and syntax are to the one what physics and chemistry are to the other. Take this verbal society:

> There was a young man of Bengal
> Who went to a fancy dress ball;
> He went just for fun
> Dressed up as a bun,
> But a dog ate him up in the hall.

I can say about this: "This is a quintain, rhymed *aabba*. Each of the *a* lines is made up of three anapaests, each of the *b* lines of two," etc. Since any society cannot change without ceasing to be itself, the poet had always to assume that the history of the language is at an end, that words are as unhistorical as atoms, that the word *river*, for example, will never turn into an iamb or come to mean *mud*.

This assumption is necessary but, of course, not always valid: when Milton wrote

> And hears the unexpressive nuptiall Song.

he could not foresee the reversal in meaning that would take place in *unexpressive*, and Keats would be startled to learn what a slight change in association can make. A colleague of mine asked a student to explicate the lines

> The wakeful bloodhound rose, and shook his hide,
> But his sagacious eye an inmate owns,

the student said, "The poor dog was blind. Some lunatic had punched his eye out and kept it".

A poem is more like an organism, however, than a thing. For instance, it is rhythmical. The temporal recurrences of rhythm are never identical, as the metrical notation would seem to suggest. Rhythm is to time what symmetry is to space. Seen from a certain distance, the features of a human face seem symmetrically arranged and constant in size and position, so that a face with a nose a foot long or a left eye situated an inch away from the nose would appear a monstrosity. Close up, however, the regularity disappears; the size and position of the features varies slightly from face to face and, indeed, if a face could exist in which the symmetry was mathematically perfect, it would appear not a face, but a lifeless mask.

So with rhythm. A poem may be described as written in iambic pentameters, but if every foot in every line were identical, if all accented syllables carried identically the same weight of accent and all the unaccented were identically light, the poem would sound intolerable to the ear.

I am sometimes inclined to think that one of the reasons why poetry as a medium is unpopular today is that in a machine age all repetition is associated with the lifeless and the boring, with road drills and time-clock punching, all formal restrictions with bureaucratic regulations.

The nature of the final order of any poem is the outcome of a dialectical struggle between the events the poet wishes to embody and the verbal system.

As a society, the verbal system is actively coercive upon the events; those it cannot embody truthfully it excludes.

As a potential community, the events are passively resistant to all claims of the system to embody which they do not recognise as just; they decline all unjust persuasions. As a member of a crowd, every event competes with every other, demanding inclusion and a dominant position to which it is not necessarily entitled, and every word demands that the system shall modify itself in its case, that a special exception shall be made for it and it only. If the system is allowed to dictate to the events, the result is the kind of versifying satirised by Pope in the lines

> Where-e'er you find "the cooling western breeze",
> In the next line, it "whispers through the trees";
> If crystal streams "with pleasing murmurs creep",
> The reader's threaten'd (not in vain) with "sleep".

When the events are allowed to dictate, the consequence is formlessness and obscurity.

In writing a poem, the poet can work in two ways. Starting with an intuitive idea of the kind of community he desires to call into being, he may work backwards in search of the system which will most justly embody it; or, starting with a certain system, he may work forward in search of the community which it is capable of embodying most truthfully. In practice, he nearly always works simultaneously in both directions, modifying his conception of the ultimate nature of the community at the immediate suggestions of the system, and modifying the system in response to his growing intuition of the future needs of the community. After Tennyson had written

> All along the valley, where the waters flow,
> I walked with one I loved two and thirty years ago

it was pointed out to him that as a matter of historical fact, thirty-two years was inaccurate, but he decided to leave the figure that rhythm and sound demanded. On the other hand, here is "The Lake Isle of Innisfree" in its first and its final version.

> I will arise and go now and go to the island of Innisfree
> And live in a dwelling of wattles, of woven wattles and woodwork made.
> Nine bean-rows will I have there, a yellow hive for the honey-bee,
> And this old care shall fade.

becomes

> I will arise and go now, and go to Innisfree
> And a small cabin build there, of clay and wattles made;
> Nine bean-rows will I have there, a hive for the honey-bee,
> And live alone in the bee-loud glade.

Here the form has been changed in the interests of a more precise embodiment of the subject.

In any language the number of possible verbal societies is very high, but it is infinite in none. Thus Greek falls naturally into hexameters; English does not. A syllabically counted alexandrine with elision suits French, where the corresponding English line is an iambic pentameter with trisyllabic substitution. In English, unrhymed iambic pentameters sound like verse; but shorten the lines by a foot and they will sound like chopped-up prose. Further, even between two forms which are possible, one may be more beautiful than the other, irrespective of their subject. For instance, no skill can make this metre anything but monotonous.

> I am monarch of all I survey,
>   My right there is none to dispute,
> From the center all round to the sea,
>   I am lord of the fowl and the brute
> O Solitude! Where are the charms
>   That sages have seen in thy face?
> Better dwell in the midst of alarms
>   Than reign in this horrible place.

But add one more syllable to the odd lines, converting them from masculine rhymes into feminine, and the metre is transformed into a charming and musical vehicle:

> Good-night to the Season! the dances,
>   The filling of hot little rooms,
> The glancing of rapturous glances,
>   The fancying of fancy costumes . . .
> The female diplomatists, planners
>   Of matches for Laura and Jane,
> The ice of her Ladyship's manners,
>   The ice of his Lordship's champagne.

Again, in any language very many experiences may be embodied in poems, but not all. A French poet, for instance, can write

> La monde
> Est ronde.

which is meaningful. But the only statements on that subject in a similar form which an English poet can make are nonsense, e.g.

> The World
> Is curled.

or

> The Earth
> Is birth.

The poet's decision in any given case to employ this verbal society and no other is not arbitrary, but it is not absolutely necessary either. He searches for the one which imposes just obligations upon his material. Ought always implies Can, so that a society whose claims cannot be met must be scrapped. He must always, however, beware of accusing the society of injustice when it is his own laxness that is really at fault.

The process of composition is a process of civilising. What at first was a barbaric horde of experiences, incapable of ruling themselves, is transformed into a city, a true *polis*, the members of which are good citizens loving each other and it.

In the earlier stages of composition, the poet has to act like a Greek tyrant; the decision to write this rather than that must be largely his, for the demands of the poem are as yet inarticulate or contradictory. As composition proceeds, the poem begins to take over the job of ruling itself, the transient rule of the poet gets weaker and weaker, until in the later stages, he is like the elected representative in a democracy whose function is to execute the demands of the poem which now knows pretty well what it wishes to be. On completion, the poem rules itself immanently and the poet is dismissed into private life.

From all this it can be easily seen how dangerous are all theories of politics which conceive of the politician's function in terms of the poet's. A poet—Dylan Thomas in this case—may first write

> The mast-high anchor dives through a cleft,

change it to

> The anchor dives through closing paths,

then to

> The anchor dives among hayricks,

and finally to

> The anchor dives through the floors of a church.

A cleft and *closing paths* have been liquidated and *hayricks* deported to another stanza.

Any actual political society which was like a good poem would be a nightmare of tyranny; conversely, any poem which was like any actual democracy—there are, unfortunately, some—would be formless, banal, and very boring indeed.

Properly speaking, to say that a poem is inspired means no more than that it is good beyond hope or expectation. When, after reading a poem, a competent judge of poetry exclaims "I can't understand how the old boy could have written it", or when a poet, upon completing one, is justified in feeling, as Robert Frost has expressed it, "O what a good boy am I", they can, if they like, speak of inspiration. But this is not what most people who are not practicing poets think it means. To say that a poet is inspired means to them either that while composing he is in a state of wild excitement, or that he is merely a stenographer who takes down as fast as he can write what the Muse dictates. Neither supposition is true. Any poet, I think, could tell them of occasions when he felt great excitement yet, on looking at the result next day, found that it was rubbish, and of other occasions when writing seemed a dreary chore yet the result turned out excellent; and of course he could give examples where the contrary was true.

As for the poet as stenographer to the Muse, there do seem to be a few cases—"Kubla Khan" is one—in which the actual composition seems to have been an instantaneous process, but they are very rare, and, even then, one cannot tell how much preparatory work, conscious or unconscious, preceded the sudden solution. Further, if such cases were the norm, writing poetry would be so boring an activity that no poet would do it except for money. The law of pleasure for the mind is the same as it is for physical pleasures like evacuation or sex: without the building up of tension to the point almost of pain, the sensation of pleasure which accompanies release cannot come to be. Among the few sensible remarks ever made about poetry, these two, both by Paul Valéry, seem outstanding to me. "If a man's imagination", he says, "is stimulated by artificial and arbitrary rules, he is a poet: if it is stifled by such limitations, whatever other kind of writer he may be, a poet he is not". And again: "I would rather have composed a second-rate work while in full possession of my faculties than a masterpiece in a trance".

Most poets, I believe, if asked to describe the Muse and their relations with her, would reply somewhat as follows:

"Like Beatrice in *Much Ado* she is a formidable girl and will only give herself to a Benedict who can stand up to her. Feminine as she is, though she has little use for either, if she must choose between them, she prefers a wolf who whistles at her behind to a spaniel who fawns at her feet. She has been known to forget that she is a lady and turn into an aggressive Venus pursuing a reluctant Adonis, but very seldom and with unhappy consequences for both. As a rule, a wooer has to use all his powers of insistence and the most subtle strategies he can devise to get a word of sense out of her. Unless he refuses to let her go till she talks sense, she will put him off with nonsense, and if some poor lovelorn fool believes everything she says, how she leads him on."

An inspired work, that is, depends just as much on what the Augustan critics called Judgment as it does upon the Muse herself. Let me give you an example from another art. Rossini's opera, *Moses in Egypt*, contains a chorus in which there is a sudden and extremely effective modulation from minor to major. In a letter to a friend Rossini describes how this came about: "When I was writing the chorus in G minor, I suddenly dipped my pen into the medicine bottle instead of the ink-pot; I made a blot, and when I dried it with sand (blotting-paper was not invented then) it took the form of a natural, which instantly gave me the idea of the effect which a change to G major would make, and to this blot all the effect—if any—is due".

There is genius for you—the power to distinguish between Chance and Providence.

Poems belong to the historical order; therefore, unlike scientific discoveries, a later poem does not include and supersede an earlier, nor does the earlier remain unchanged. *The Iliad* is not replaced by *Paradise Lost*; nor, however, is it the same poem since *Paradise Lost* was written as it was before. Again, since every poem is a unique object, they are not comparable with each other. I may say that *The Divine Comedy* is a more important poem than some two-line epigram; I cannot say it is better. Value judgments about poems are of the same nature as value judgments about people. If I say Mr Smith is a bad man, I mean, or should mean, either Mr Smith is so unhuman that he should never have been born, or that Mr Smith, as he is now, is a bad version of the Mr Smith he could and should become; and to say that a poem is bad means the same. Similarly, if I say of a sunset or a machine "it is beautiful", I mean that it is what it ought to be. But if I say of a human face or a poem that it is beautiful, I mean not only that it is what it ought to be but that it might easily have been otherwise: that, indeed, all the chances were against it attaining this beauty; nevertheless, it succeeded.

Beauty, however, is not Goodness but its formal analogue. Art, as Ernst Cassirer has said, is an enjoyment not of life but of forms. Every poet, consciously or unconsciously, holds the following absolute presuppositions, as the dogmas of his art.

(1) A historical world of unique events and persons exists and that its existence is a good.
(2) This historical world is a fallen world, full of unfreedom and disorder. It is good that it exists but the way in which it exists is evil.
(3) This historical world is a redeemable world. The unfreedom and disorder of the past can be reconciled in the future. Every successful poem, therefore, presents an analogue of that Paradisal state in which Freedom and Law, System and Order are united, and contradictions reconciled and sins forgiven. Every good poem represents already very nearly Utopia.

An analogue to Utopia, however, not an imitation; the Utopia is possible and verbal only—holy perhaps, but only holy play. A poet, a scientist, too, for that matter, is, as Henry Thoreau said, a person who, having nothing to do, finds something to do; and I know of no better, because modest, description of what the greatest artist can achieve than this passage from Virginia Woolf's novel, *The Waves*.

There is a square. There is an oblong. The players take the square and place it upon the oblong. They place it very accurately. They make a perfect dwelling-place. The structure is now visible. What was inchoate is here stated. We are not so various or so mean. We have made oblongs and stood them upon squares. This is our triumph. This is our consolation.

III   ON WRITING POETRY TODAY

So far we have discussed what poetry is about and how it is written, matters which apply to all poets at all times. In this last talk I want to consider the special problem of poetry in the present age. The talk, I am afraid, will be rather gloomy.

Plato once remarked that when the modes of music change, the walls of the city are shaken. Perhaps one should slightly modify this—suggesting as it does that a change in modes is the cause of the shaking walls, this is to give art a greater importance than it deserves. Let us say, rather, that a change in the modes is the first symptom of an instability that will presently manifest itself in more material and political ways.

Those poets who, like myself, were born after 1900 are sometimes tempted to wish that we had been born some fifteen or twenty years earlier. Here are some birth dates which tell their own story:

1865	Yeats
1869	Matisse
1871	Valéry; Proust
1875	Schoenberg; Gertrude Stein; Rilke; Robert Frost
1881	Picasso
1882	Stravinsky; James Joyce; Virginia Woolf
1883	Kafka
1885	D. H. Lawrence; Ezra Pound
1887	Marianne Moore
1888	T. S. Eliot

These are the figures whom we still think of as the creators and masters of the "modern style": none of them seems old-fashioned, yet all were born before 1900 and had begun producing their characteristic work before 1914. It is clear, then, that so far as the arts are concerned we are not, despite two world wars, social revolutions, economic depressions, thermonuclear bombs, living at the beginning of a new era but in the middle of one. Poets of my generation and of the next, therefore, are in the position, whether we like it or not, of being colonisers rather than explorers. It would be as wrong-headed for us to attempt to make a radical break with the style of our immediate predecessors as it was right for them so to break with their Victorian elders.

A coloniser is a less romantic and less heroic figure than an explorer, but his task is necessary and perhaps it is easier. We know who succeeded in finding new methods of expression suited to the post-Victorian change in sensibility; but we do not know how many there were at that time who failed to realise their talents because they failed to find a way out but who, if born later, when this way had been found for them, might have produced excellent work.

The problems of the poets who came before us are still our problems and they are special aspects of a universal problem, how to live in an advanced technological society.

To begin with, it is technology that puts at our immediate disposal the arts of all ages and all cultures. The full impact of the machine in this respect is quite recent. My grandfather, for example, could live in a roomy house of his own while I must live in a rented apartment, but if he were left alone in the evening, he could not do as I do. He could not ask "What shall I do? Shall I open a volume of translations of Chinese poetry? Shall I look at reproductions of Negro sculpture? Or shall I put on an L.P. record of medieval church music?"

This has completely changed the meaning of the word Tradition. It no longer means a way of working handed down from one generation to the next. It means a consciousness of the whole of the past as present, yet at the same time as a structured whole whose parts are related in terms of before and after. Originality no longer means a slight modification in the style of one's immediate predecessors; it means the capacity to find in any work of any date or locality clues for the treatment of the present. The burden of choice and selection, therefore, is put squarely upon the individual poet himself and it is a heavy burden. The same thing happens when the poet leaves his library and walks out into the street. He is instantly bombarded by a stream of varied sensations which would drive him mad if he took them all in. It is impossible to guess how much energy we have to spend every day in not-seeing, not-hearing, not-smelling, not-reacting. What is worse, in addition to the energy it consumes, the habit of inattention tends to become so ingrown that we find it increasingly difficult to attend when we want to and need to.

Even harder, perhaps, on the nerves of any kind of artist is the ever-increasing acceleration in the rate of historical change.

The sense of security from which a poet can gain the patience to aim at artistic perfection is not so much a sense of personal security—the thought of his own death has often, indeed, been a stimulus—rather it is a trust that the sort of world and the sort of readers which will exist twenty, thirty, a hundred years ahead will be more or less the same as that which exists at the moment when he is writing. Lacking that trust as we all do, uncertain even that we ourselves will be the same people next year, the temptation either to be content with improvisations—to get something down before we find we no longer want to say it—or to follow fashion—if one can have no faith in the taste of the future, immediate success is better than none at all—these temptations become very strong.

The contemporary poet who claims to be impervious to fashion is fibbing, though he may demonstrate its effect upon him by being defiantly unfashionable. Nor, however dangerous fashion may be, should he, I think, be impervious. Fashion is the reflection of the immediate moment; to the degree that the immediate moment has a unique quality of its own, differing from both the past and the future, fashion has a real value, though the quantity of value is, naturally, very small. Whereas the artist of the past could accept most of the tradition into which he was born and needed to reject only a very little of it, the contemporary artist has to reject the greater part of fashion as dross and only retain its tiny particle of gold.

I suggested in my first talk that all the arts are primarily concerned with the praise and affirmation of Personal Being: I am that I am; or of Personal Becoming: I shall become that which I choose to or ought to become. In both cases one should also add "in spite of everything against me, in spite of the forces of non-being, in spite of the temptations to become unreal". With impersonal being: it is what it has to be; and with passive becoming: I am changed without my consent like a thing, the arts cannot deal. The investigation of the impersonal and the passive is the business of science.

In a more or less static world where next year is pretty much like last year, most of the answer to the question "Who am I?" consists of statements about my relation to other human beings: I am Saigon, king of Natrium, son of Harma, father of Ru—and the rest is made up of a list of my deeds; Slayer of Anacolouthon the Black Dragon, Reticulator of the Fens of Cush. In attributing the draining of the fens to myself, I do not of course mean that I dug the canals with my own hands. I mean that out of awe or love or fear of my person, my subjects obeyed my order that the fens be drained.

In a technological world very little of this has meaning any more. Last year is no longer like this year, and the world fifty years ago would scarcely recognise itself now. My genealogy, therefore, defines nothing about me; even my present status says little because it may be changed tomorrow. I may still be king but the meaning and function of monarchy will not be the same.

As to my deeds, the advent of the machine destroys that direct relation between what I intend and what actually happens—a relation which must exist if I am to speak of an act of my own. If I meet the dragon face to face and plunge my spear into his heart, I may legitimately say I slew him, but if I drop a bomb on him from an altitude of 20,000 feet, even though my intention— to slay the dragon—is the same as it was before, my act now consists in pressing a lever, and it is the bomb that actually does the killing. Again, if, at my command, ten thousand of my subjects toil for five years at draining the fens, this is only possible because I command the personal loyalty of enough persons to see that my orders are carried out. If my army, for instance, revolts, I am powerless. But when I can have the fens drained in six months by a hundred men with bulldozers, the whole situation is changed. I still need some personal authority, enough to persuade a hundred people to man the bulldozers—but that is all, the rest is the work of machines that know nothing of loyalty or fear—and if my enemy should get hold of them, they will work just as efficiently at filling up the canals as they have just worked at digging them. It is now becoming possible to imagine a world in which the only human work on such projects will be the operation of electric brains, reducing the number of persons who can choose to obey or disobey orders to a mere handful.

None of this, of course, says anything morally for or against technology. It means only that the range of events with which poetry can deal is very greatly reduced. There are some products of technology—kitchen refrigerators, for example—which seem to me an unqualified good; but however grateful I may feel towards mine at cocktail time, I cannot see myself writing a panegyric ode to it as I could have written centuries ago to a king who at his marriage ordered wine to flow from the public fountains. A savage might still write such an ode if he believed that the refrigerator was a god who produced ice-cubes faster if flattered and broke down if annoyed. Since I am past the stage at which such animistic beliefs are possible, I cannot.

Before the coming of the machine, a great, perhaps the greater, part of poetry concerned itself with what are called public figures and public events, with warriors and kings, with battles, the building of cities: great events, that is, in which person, excellence and power were combined together. But today public figures, however admirable they may be as persons, are first and foremost impersonal officials, and the good or harm they can do depends less upon their personality and their intention than upon the quantity of impersonal energy at their disposal, and it therefore becomes impossible for the poet to write about them. As for the public events, these now take place on a scale so great that the personal power of any one individual to shape them is very limited, and the personal experience which any one individual can have of them is confined to a tiny fragment which is meaningless by itself. It is quite unjust, I believe, to attribute the lack of patriotic or political poems to a snobbish lack of concern for the real world on the part of the poets. After all, what poet today does not know only too well that a political decision can overnight transform his existence? To how many of us would the choice between living in Moscow or living in London or Washington seem a matter of indifference? But all of us, including our unfortunate fellow poets on the other side of the Iron Curtain who are compelled to keep their knowledge to themselves, also know that all attempts to write poems about events, no matter how important they may be, to which a poet is not personally related, are doomed to failure.

Yeats could write great poetry about the Irish civil war because most of the protagonists were known to him personally:

> I write it out in a verse—
> MacDonagh and MacBride
> And Connolly and Pearse.

The places where the events happened were familiar to him from childhood and the history of Ireland was the history of his own people:

> When Pearse summoned Cuchulain to his side,
> What stalked through the post-office?

But the only person who could write great poetry about World War II would be God. The only possible human treatment is documentation: statistics, straightforward factual prose reporting, the eye-witness of the candid camera, and so forth. The personal excellence left for the poet's praise is today largely confined to the private life. The hero in modern poetry is generally not someone who wields power for the general good but someone who, by resisting the pressure of impersonal powers, preserves his integrity and remains himself. If the charge of being unnecessarily private and limited in subject-matter can legitimately be brought against modern poetry—I think that it sometimes can—the reason is again not that the poet is too conceited but that he is too timid. Knowing that he can only produce genuine work about events to which he has a personal relation, aware of the awful results of attempting to deal with anything else, he sticks for safety to some area in which he is sure of his personal relation, an area such as his childhood experiences, when, as a matter of fact, if he would take the risk, he would find that the possible area of the personal is larger than he supposes.

Besides this tendency to over-restrict his subject-matter, the modern poet has another tendency which he needs to watch, one which is more apparent perhaps to his fellow poets than to the reading public, the tendency to develop an over-personal style and to develop it much too early in life. The temptation to do this is the same, fear of not being truly himself. I can only be certain, he seems to argue, that I am being authentically myself if everybody must admit that what I write, whether it be good or bad, at least could have been written by nobody else on earth but me. The trouble about this is that a person can and ought to change; at any given time his being holds latent possibilities which are waiting their chance to realise themselves. An over-personal style, no matter how authentic so far as it goes, becomes a prison from which the poet cannot escape. I can think of several poets whose work I find admirable but who make me sad, because I feel that they have it in them to go further but never will, for the style they have developed will not permit it and they will never dare break with this style and make a new start. Whenever one's first reaction to a work is not "What a beautiful poem! Who wrote it?" but "Oh! That's by X. One of his best so far", one knows that the poor devil is in jail.

The poet has, however, good reason to be timid; what he dreads is a fate which can befall everyone equally easily if he relax his vigilance: the fate of becoming a member of the Public, that chimerical creature so admirably described by Kierkegaard in his essay *Thoughts on the Present Age*:

> Majority and minority are real people, and this is why the individual is assisted by adhering to them. A public on the contrary is an abstrac-

tion. . . . A public is neither a nation nor a generation, nor a community, nor a society, nor these particular men, for all these are only what they are through the concrete; no single person who belongs to the public makes a real commitment; for some hours of the day, perhaps, he belongs to the public—at moments when he is nothing else, since when he really is what he is, he does not form part of the public. Made up of such individuals, of individuals at the moments when they are nothing, a public is a kind of gigantic something, an abstract and deserted void which is everything and nothing.

The Public—in my last talk I called such a plurality a crowd—may have existed at other times in history but never has it become so formidable a phenomenon as in our own. When the individual cannot define who he is in terms of concrete objective qualities, when what he performs and what he is seem the consequence neither of his own choice nor the personal will of those who are stronger than he but of impersonal forces, the danger of giving up and joining the public is naturally very great. Since it is nothing in particular, the public is the least exclusive of clubs; anybody rich or poor, educated or unlettered, nice or nasty, can join in. It even tolerates a sort of pseudo-revolt against itself, that is, the formation inside itself of clique publics. The members of such a clique are no more themselves than the others, but instead of doing whatever the public in general does at any moment, they do the opposite. As any observer of literary cocktail-parties knows, the clique within the clique within the clique provides an illusion of great complexity, yet a simple unreality is common to all.

As D. H. Lawrence wisely wrote:

If you live along with all the other people
and are just like them, and conform, and are nice
you're just a worm—

and if you live with all the other people
and you don't like them and won't be like them and won't conform
then you're just the worm that has turned,
in either case, a worm.

The conforming worm stays just inside the skin
respectably unseen, and cheerfully gnaws away at the heart of life,
making it all rotten inside.

The unconforming worm—that is, the worm that has turned—
gnaws just the same, gnawing the substance out of life,
but he insists on gnawing a little hole in the social epidermis
and poking his head out and waving himself
and saying: Look at me, I am *not* respectable,

> I do all the things the bourgeois daren't do,
> I booze and fornicate and use foul language and despise your honest
>   man.—
>
> But why should the worm that has turned protest so much?
> The bonnie bonnie bourgeois goes a-whoring up back streets
> just the same.
> The busy busy bourgeois imbibes his little share
> just the same
> if not more.
> The pretty pretty bourgeois pinks his language just as pink
> if not pinker,
> and in private boasts his exploits even louder, if you ask me,
> than the other.
> While as to honesty, Oh look where the money lies!

It follows that all actions and words of the public are merely theatrical, and it is not surprising, though alarming, that the public instinctively worships not great men of action or thought but actors, individuals who by profession are not themselves. In previous ages the power to act aroused superstitious horror so that no actor could be buried in consecrated ground. Today he receives state decorations.

Moreover, it is not the actor as such that is worshipped but rather the star: that is, the actor or actress who takes various roles but does not really act, since he or she is the same in all of them. This allows the public who identifies itself with them the double luxury of playing at being different people and playing at being one's ideal self at the same time. The public, therefore, can be persuaded to do or believe anything by those who know how to manage it. It will subscribe thousands of dollars to a cancer research fund or massacre Jews with equal readiness, not because it wants to do either, but because it has no alternative game to suggest.

Between any two members of the public no personal encounter is possible and the function of words is not to convey meaning but to conceal by noise the silence and the solitude of which both members are secretly aware. Before people complain of the obscurity of modern poetry, they should first examine their consciences and ask themselves with how many people and on how many occasions they have genuinely and profoundly shared some experience with another; they might also ask themselves how much poetry of any period they can honestly say that they understand.

The degeneration of people into the public has been tremendously facilitated by the invention of mechanical means of communication, such as the high-speed printing press, the movies, and even those devices which enable me to broadcast. Neither the inventors nor those who developed these media intended harm; most were and are thoroughly well-intentioned people who at worst want to make a little money. It took some time indeed before the wicked realised what a weapon science had put at their disposal. Yet, whatever the intention, the destructive effect of the mass media is stronger than anyone's intentions, since it is inherent in the nature of the media themselves. Before their coming there existed popular art and art for the elite, different but only in the way that two brothers are different. The Athenian court may smile at the popular play of Pyramus and Thisbe, but they know it belongs to the same world as their own. Hippolyta may remark

This is the silliest stuff that ever I heard,

but she has to agree with the rejoinder of Theseus:

The best in this kind are but shadows; and the worst are no worse, if imagination amend them.

Court poetry and popular poetry are bound by the common tie that both are made personally by hand. The crudest ballad is as custom-built as the most esoteric sonnet.

But the moment the machine, which is never tired and so expensive that it can only pay its way by never being allowed to stop, the machine which is incapable of making mistakes, is introduced, entertainment becomes an industry and, no matter how well-intentioned its leaders, the impersonality of the means produces an impersonal result—the realm of the aesthetic is no different in this respect from the realm of morals or politics—and the result is nothing that you can call art, popular or highbrow, but a kind of entertainment offered for consumption like any other form of consumer's goods and to be judged in the same way. The real victim is not the highbrow artist but the popular artist; the highbrow can still work as he did a thousand years ago, because his audience is too small to interest the mass media, but the audience of the popular artist is the majority. This the mass media must steal from him if they are not to go bankrupt. The sad consequence is that, apart from a few comedians, the only good art today is highbrow art. This is bad for everyone: the lowbrow loses all genuine taste of his own, and the highbrow becomes a snob. The only places where genuine popular art still exists in the world today are poor and backward and unindustrialised countries. In the others the effect of the machine on taste cuts across all political and religious differences. For example, the same kind of painting is approved of by all the publics, be they Catholic, Protestant, Communist, Capitalist, Conservative, Labour, Democrat, Republican, and though their terms of disapproval may vary—where one cries "materialistic", another cries "Decadent Cosmopolitan" and a third "Communistic"—the kind of picture of which they disapprove is the same for them all.

We highbrow artists in the West are extremely fortunate. Not because there are not plenty of persons in our countries who would enjoy giving us the same treatment that highbrows have received in the East, but because, thanks to our political institutions, they are forbidden that fun—bless their bleak little hearts.

This seems a good point at which to discuss the question of propaganda, for without the mass media and without the transformation of people into a public, successful propaganda would not be possible. Propaganda, commercial or political, might be defined as the employment of magic by those who are not susceptible to its spells against those who are. Its aim, the aim of all magic, is to gain such power over the wills of others that the question of their personal assent or dissent does not arise. Naturally, its task is easiest when its victims do not care what they choose. Thus the success of advertising depends upon the truth of this proposition: "Most-people-in-most-cases-do-not-know-what-they-want". Toilet soap, for example, is something about which I have no preferences. I assume that the law protects me from being sold a product which is poisonous or which leaves me dirtier after use than before. So, when I go into a chemist to buy a cake of soap, I ask for the first brand that comes into my head, a name planted there by advertising; if the chemist is out of it, I take without hesitation whatever brand he suggests. So far as soap is concerned, I am not a person but a member of the public.

But when it comes to a field in which I take choice seriously, advertising is powerless. If I go into a bookstore and ask for, let us say, *The Collected Poems of Robert Graves*, I do so, not because I have seen his name on a hoarding, but because I have read and admired enough of his poems to desire his collected work. If the assistant says, "I'm sorry, we're out of stock of Graves, but we have just got in *The Collected Poems of X*"—a poet equally well known to me whose work I dislike—I shall leave the bookstore empty-handed.

In the case of a material good like toilet soap, the morality of advertising does not arise. But in the case of a spiritual good like books it does, for books are one of the means by which we acquire our beliefs and attitudes towards life, and there are some kinds—pornography, books which create irrational hatred of others—which do harm. Rationalist liberals sometimes overlook the fact that, since human beings are born as babies, whose power to make moral or rational or aesthetic choices is only potential, no human society could exist for five minutes without the use of verbal and other magic; every mother, for example, employs the magic of the clock, in the toilet training of her children, and no Christian parents will put off taking their offspring to church until they are capable of understanding the *Summa*. If asked to justify their actions, in the case of the toilet training the mother will say: "No circumstances can arise in which the ability to control one's acts of excretion is a disadvantage; therefore, the more instinctive the habit, the less choice and will-power are required, the better". In the case of church going, the parents will say, I think, something like this: "We, personally, believe that the Christian Faith is the true faith, and that all other faiths are false. But we also know that no adult can be compelled to accept a belief, true or false. There will come a time when our children will have either to accept or to reject the beliefs we have taught them on their own responsibility; in the meantime, what would you have us do—tell them what we believe, or say nothing, which can only give them the impression that the matter is of no importance?"

The essential evil of totalitarian propaganda is not that the doctrines it promulgates happen to be false, but that a small minority take it upon themselves to regard the rest of the population as children under the age of consent and to keep them there, so that even if the doctrines were true, which they are not, people would never be permitted to choose the truth; the admission of any facts or any feelings which would make doubt possible are forbidden.

I have gone into this at what you may think an unseemly length because I think that the arguments of those who, like Plato and Tolstoy, have condemned Art as immoral, the conception of the artist held by the rulers of the People's Democracies, namely that the function of the artist is to serve the Cause, to be in line with History, are unanswerable so long as one accepts their two premises: (1) that art is a kind of magic; and (2) that there is no significant moral difference between doing good and choosing to do good.

Leaving aside the question of his morality, one may say that anyone who tries to use a poet as a propagandist is very stupid, for of all people the poet will be the least efficient, since the formal nature of his medium turns every assertion he makes into a playful hypothesis. If he says:

> Thirty days hath September,
> April, June and November

the reader cannot help noticing that he might just as easily have said

> Thirty days hath September
> April, May and December.

Dryden's great poem, *The Hind and the Panther,* is an argument between an Anglican and a Roman Catholic, in which the R.C. has the best of it, but it is not propaganda. For purposes of conversion the arguments would be more effective in prose; in verse form they become play; whatever the religious convictions of the reader, he enjoys the wit, the give-and-take of the debate, for its own sake, and the more evenly-matched the opponents the better, and if he gives a vote at all at the end it will be to the cleverer of the two.

Yet, stupid or not, there are many States today where the authorities refuse to leave the poet alone. Nobody could call Miss Democracy anything but a plain girl, but when one compares her with the hags to whom millions are expected to pay court, she seems a very Helen. Her hair may be stringy but at least it is her own. I would advise any poet, when he feels depressed either by the smallness of his sales or by the goings on in Westminster or Capitol Hill, to read a book called *The Captive Mind* by Czeslaw Milosz, in which he tells what happened to three talented Polish writers who had been his personal friends. It was all very well for Yeats to write:

> The Muse is mute when public men
> Applaud a modern throne:
> Those cheers that can be bought or sold,
> That office fools have run,
> That waxen seal, that signature,
> For things like these what decent man
> Would keep his lover waiting?

Yeats was going to die very soon and the future could not harm him. But for those of us who are younger and know what could happen to us within a normal lifetime, there are occasions when every decent man must, with a sigh, keep both his lover and his Muse waiting, while he goes off drearily to vote, and to vote against any party, if I may say so, which permits one of its responsible spokesmen to declare, not that the nation can only afford an inferior kind of cheese, but that any kind of cheese is as good as any other.

I said I was going to be gloomy, yet in the gloomiest aspect of the present, this active hatred of the free artist, I see an encouraging sign. Why should the authorities feel that a highbrow artist is important enough to be worth destroying? It can only be because so long as artists exist, making what they please even if it is not very good, even if very few people appreciate it, they remind the management of something the management does not like to be reminded of, namely, that the managed people are people with faces, not anonymous numbers; it reminds them that *homo sapiens* is also *homo ludens* which, if admitted, makes nonsense of any doctrine of historical necessity.

We hear a lot about the gulf between the intellectual and the masses but not enough about the ways in which they are alike. If I meet an illiterate peasant we may not be able to say much to each other, but if we both meet a public official, we share the same feeling of suspicion; neither of us will trust him further than we can throw a grand piano. If we enter a government building together, we share the same feeling of apprehension that perhaps we shall never get out. Whatever the cultural differences between us, we both sniff in an official world the smell of that unreality in which persons are treated as statistics. The peasant may play cards in the evening while I write poetry, but there is one political principle to which we both subscribe, namely, that among the half-dozen or so things for which a man of honour must be prepared, if necessary, to die, the right to play, the right to frivolity, is not the least.

Ladies and Gentlemen, I give you a toast. I propose: Highbrows and Lowbrows of the World, unite!

BBC Third Programme, 8, 15, and 22 June 1955;
The Listener, 16, 23 and 30 June 1955

Qui è l'uom' felice

or

Everyman in His Eden

A PSYCHOLOGICAL PARLOUR-GAME FOR A WET SUNDAY AFTERNOON

Instructions

Before attempting to answer the questionnaire, it is important to realise that it is concerned with Eden *not* with New Jerusalem, a prelapsarian Arcadia, not a post-judgment-day Utopia.

In New Jerusalem the conflict between Pleasure and Duty has at last been solved. In Eden this conflict has not yet arisen.

In New Jerusalem only being and doing what you should is fun: in Eden having fun is your only duty.

In order to answer the questions truthfully, therefore, you must ignore your conscience completely and put down accurately what, in fact, you like and dislike.

Suppose, for example, that you happen to dislike the sight of people with red hair. Then your answer to Question 3 should include the statement "No Redheads." In general, do not forget that it is as important to state what and whom you exclude as what you want included.

In answering such a question as 23 (Sports) you do not necessarily have to practise any sport you mention. You can, of course, if you want to, but it can also be simply one you would like to watch. This applies to several other questions.

It has to be assumed that the laws of Nature and of Logic are a valid in your Eden as in the real world. Thus you cannot simultaneously demand a temperate climate and tropical flowers growing out of doors. Otherwise, there is no restriction whatever upon your fancies.

The answers to the Questionnaire given by its inventor (Farfield 1920–25) will be found on page 570.

Questionnaire

In your Eden what is its

1. Landscape.
2. Climate.
3. Ethnic origin of inhabitants.
4. Language.

5. Religion.
6. Form of State (if any).
7. Size of Capital City (if any).
8. Sources of natural power.
9. Industries (if any).
10. Means of access (i.e. how do you enter your Eden?).
11. Modes of transport (within Eden).
12. Architectural Styles: (*a*) State (*b*) Ecclesiastical (*c*) Industrial (*d*) Domestic.
13. Styles of interior decoration: (*a*) Ecclesiastical (*b*) Domestic.
14. Style of Gardens.
15. Methods of lighting.
16. Methods of heating.
17. Type of Cuisine.
18. Styles of dress for formal occasions.
19. Scales for weights, measures, currency, etc.
20. Calendar.
21. Educational system.
22. Hobbies.
23. Sports: (*a*) Winter (*b*) Summer.
24. Forms of Public Entertainment.
25. Sources of Public Information.
26. Any feature, important to you, not covered by your answers to the preceding questions.

QUI È L'UOM' FELICE

1. Limestone moors like those of the Pennines between Swaledale and Tynedale, bounded on one side by a large oak forest, on the other by the sea, into which the land falls in immense precipices.
2. British.
3. As in the U.S.A., a mixture of races, but with a slight dolichocephalic nordic predominance.
4. Italian.
5. Roman Catholic in an easy-going superstitious Mediterranean sort of way, but with Anglican Hymns and Psalms. Witches and Magicians have an official and much respected social status.
6. Absolute Monarchy. The Sovereign is chosen by lot. He or she reigns for one year.
7. About five thousand inhabitants.
8. Coal. Water. Wind. No oil.
9. Lead mining, Wire-drawing. Weaving. Sheep farming. Green-house horticulture.

10. Branch railway. Canal.
11. Litters. Donkey carts. Hansom cabs. Balloons. No motor cars.
12. (*a*) Baroque. (*b*) Romanesque. (*c*) Early nineteenth century cotton-mill style. (*d*) Eighteenth century country-house style.
13. (*a*) Baroque. (*b*) Heavy Victorian.
14. Formal. Many mazes, grottoes, ha-has etc.
15. Candles. Gas. No electricity.
16. Open fires. No central heating.
17. Basically French but Haute Cuisine with international trimmings such as American seafood, German white-wines, Chinese vegetables etc.
18. The Parisian fashions between 1830 and 1840.
19. Complicated and irrational. No decimal system.
20. Based on lunations, not on the motion of the sun.
21. Segregated boarding-schools run by wild eccentrics.
22. Archaeology. Bird-watching. Chamber music. No folk-dancing.
23. (*a*) Sheep-dog trials. Wrestling. (*b*) Swimming. Croquet.
24. Opera. Classical ballet. Religious processions. No movies.
25. Gossip. No newspapers, radio or television.
26. *Censored.*

The Grasshopper, Gresham's School, Holt, 1955

Speaking of Books

Human nature being what it is, there will probably always be fewer good critics than good poets or novelists, for, while the latter may and, indeed, while they are writing, should believe that what they are doing is the most important thing in the universe, the former must never forget that the work they are criticizing is more important than anything they may say about it, and such humility is one of the rarest virtues: if the occasional criticism of successful poets and novelists is, despite their lack of scholarship and their often absurd prejudices, usually readable and illuminating, one reason is that their vanity has been satisfied elsewhere.

Further, while a poem or a novel is frankly subjective, a certain vision of a certain field of experience, taking its place beside all the other poems and novels written and to-be-written without superseding or preventing any, a critical judgment must necessarily claim universal validity: if I say, for example, that I like "Lycidas" and dislike "Adonais," I am not stating a mere personal preference like saying I like coffee and dislike tea; I cannot help believing that anyone who disagrees with me is wrong. One curious consequence of this is that, while a wise man knows that a knowledge of an author's private life, upbringing, social position, would contribute nothing toward understanding his work—all that is relevant is already present in the work itself—in the case of a reviewer passing judgment on an author one has not read, one often feels that a knowledge of his taste in women or in wine would be a great help in deciding how far to trust him.

Works of art are "as if" persons, and the qualities required by a critic are analogous to those required by a judge of people; first and foremost, he must be so fond of works of art that he would rather there were imperfect ones than none at all; secondly, he should have the widest possible acquaintance with every kind of work, and thirdly, he must never allow his principles to deny his actual feelings in an encounter with a work.

A good critic is not someone who is always right but someone who always convinces us that the work he is criticizing deserves our attention and respect. When, for example, Nietzsche writes about Wagner or D. H. Lawrence about Fenimore Cooper, though much of what they say is a violent attack, the reader is left with a feeling that Wagner and Cooper were much greater figures than he had hitherto realized. On the other hand, one knows of all too many critics whose labored, interpretative praise of authors they admire would, if one had not previously read them for oneself, effectively prevent one from ever doing so.

Since he exists historically, not on some timeless Olympus, every critic is, consciously or unconsciously, engaged in a polemic. It is wrong to ask about any critic worth reading "Are his judgments true or false?" One must always ask "What overemphasized half-truth are they intended to counterbalance?" There has been a lot of discussion about the New Criticism, but I have not come across any impartial effort to understand why it should have come into being. It arose, I think, as a corrective against two kinds of critical procedure, the attempt to explain literary works in terms of the author's psychology or the social life of his age, and the treatment of works as representative specimens of their stylistic period without reference to their esthetic merit; the former procedure is always in danger of forgetting that there is a text to read, the latter of forgetting that the reader is alive in the present. Essentially, the New Criticism has been an attempt to train people to read carefully, and in our age of photographs and comic books, nothing could be more necessary for the young.

I would gladly see a New Critic in every public school and high school: at college level, however, the approach has serious limitations. For teaching people to read, the intensive study of a small number of texts selected for the problems of understanding which they present, is the correct method but it is deplorable when a person of twenty takes these texts as an official canon: it is right and proper that an undergraduate should have violent likes and dislikes in literature but when one hears him condemn works which he has not read one feels sorry for him. Some critical expositions of his school are exasperating because they impertinently try to do for an adult reader what he is perfectly capable of doing for himself. Furthermore, a total neglect of historical context is quite as mistaken as an exclusive concentration upon it. I have had undergraduates, and not stupid ones, tell me that *Pickwick Papers* was written in the Eighteen Nineties and that Debussy composed *L'Après-Midi d'un Faune* in the Eighteen Forties; so to lack any sense of historical order is just as great an obstacle to the enjoyment and understanding of literature as a tiny vocabulary.

The New York Times Book Review, 15 May 1955

[Contribution to *Modern Canterbury Pilgrims*]

The Christian doctrine of a personal God implies that the relation of every human being to Him is unique and historical, so that any individual who discusses the Faith is compelled to begin with autobiography.

So far as my own family is concerned, my generation is the first, I believe, in which no member wears a clerical collar: both my grandfathers and four of my uncles were Anglican priests. When I was born, the Church was still regarded as one of those professions, like the Army, the Navy, law, and medicine, which it was respectable for the middle-class to practise. One of my uncles, for example, would have preferred to go into the Army but there was not enough money to get him into a good regiment, so he was ordained instead.

The many clergy I met in my youth were, with very few exceptions, hardworking, decent-living men, trying to do their duty by their parishioners and educate their children on inadequate stipends, but one could not say that they gave an impression of following a unique vocation. Their virtues, which were many, were those of their class; so were their defects. This is not intended as a sneer or to suggest that a celibate priesthood is necessarily superior. So long as the vast majority of people thought of themselves as Christians and attended church regularly, the decision to take Orders could not seem so drastic as it seems today. Further, before the spread of general education and the development of transport and mass media of entertainment, the country clergy had many functions to fulfill besides their cure of souls, and the notion of having a "gentleman" in every parish was by no means contemptible. And today, when the worldly inducements to enter the priesthood are so small, who will assert that the spiritual level of candidates for ordination has greatly risen?

The atmosphere of my home was, I should say, unusually devout, though not in the least repressive or gloomy. My parents were Anglo-Catholics, so that my first religious memories are of exciting magical rites (at six I was a boat-boy) rather than of listening to sermons. For this I am very grateful, as it implanted in me what I believe to be the correct notion of worship, namely, that it is first and foremost a community in action, a thing done together, and only secondarily a matter of individual feeling or thinking.

It so happened that the bishop of our diocese was an extreme modernist who refused to visit the church we attended; consequently I was accustomed from my earliest years to doctrinal and liturgical controversy. Dissenters and Low Churchmen were known as "Prots" and accused of squatting instead of kneeling; on the other hand, a firm line was drawn between "Devotions," which were all right, and "Benediction," which was definitely over the Roman border. I grew up, therefore, with a conception of the Church which is, I suppose, uniquely Anglican, as a community in which wide divergences of doctrine and rite can and do exist without leading necessarily to schism or excommunication.

At thirteen I was confirmed. To say that shortly afterwards I lost my faith would be melodramatic and false. I simply lost interest. Cases may occur in which a dramatic decision is taken and a person says to himself, "Yesterday I believed the Creed; today I do not," but I am sure they are rare. In describing what usually happens in this age, so far as I can judge from my experience, I am not trying to excuse it. Essentially the reason why any person in any age who has been brought up a Christian loses his faith is that he wants to go his own way and enjoy the pleasures of the world and the flesh.

There are, however, certain aspects of the present age which have made the victory of the prince of this world easier than he has any right to expect. As he reaches adolescence, every boy or girl today begins to notice two phenomena, official religion and religiosity. Official religion is not the same as conventional religion. A conventional Christian is someone who does not distinguish between his faith and his culture; he believes in the Nicene Creed as unquestionably and in the same way as he believes that no gentleman wears a celluloid collar.

An official Christian, on the other hand, is someone who, for various reasons like setting an example to the young or doing business in his community, attends the rites and recites the formulas while knowing perfectly well that he, personally, does not believe in them. In the boarding schools I attended, chapel was compulsory for the masters as well as the boys, and one very soon realized that many of the former were definitely not Christians but that attending chapel was a condition of their employment. One could not call them hypocrites because this was an open secret which they made no serious effort to conceal.

At the same time, the adolescent begins to notice that, of those who take religion most ardently, a number are unfortunate in one way or another, suffer from physical or mental ill-health, or are unhappily married or too unattractive to get married. He may, as I did, go through a pseudo-devout phase himself and then realize that behind it lay a quite straightforward and unredeemed eroticism. He is apt, then, to draw the conclusion that people only love God when no one else will love them, a tendency, incidentally, which "Crisis" theology sometimes encourages, I think.

A more formidable difficulty for the Church today than either officialdom or religiosity is the gulf between the language and imagery of her liturgies and devotions and those of contemporary culture. Whatever drawbacks it may have, a liturgy in a dead language, like Latin, which the average worshipper does not understand or to which, at least, he has no personal relation, has one great advantage over a vernacular liturgy: it cannot strike him as comic.

Agnus Dei has the attraction, at least, of a magical and musical spell; *Lamb of God*, in a culture, mainly urban, to which the notion of animal sacrifice is totally strange, is liable to evoke ridiculous images.

In ages typified by personal rule and social hierarchies, it was natural to express awe and admiration by honorific titles like *King of Kings*, and to think of performing such extraordinary acts as that proposed in the hymn "Crown him with many crowns," but in an age when rulers are constitutional officials and the real power belongs to the lifeless machine, even the title *Lord* is excessive; in fact, the more we revere and admire someone today, the more we value our relation to him, the less likely we are to use any ceremonial forms of address; those we reserve for our business correspondence. Even the term *Our Father* as a metaphor for God's relationship to us has become awkward since the decline in spiritual authority of the male and of old age.

The clergy, I believe, underestimate the seriousness of this problem, since, for them, liturgical and devotional language is "shop talk," technical like the discourse of doctors among themselves. An adult layman with some imagination and some knowledge of cultural history can learn to use it with understanding as he can learn to understand Homer, but the adolescent is in a different situation.

Having just reached the age when personal belief becomes possible—hitherto it was not really he who believed but his parents and godparents who believed for him—when his relationship to God has to become contemporary, he finds that the terms in which the Church expects him to think about God (as distinct, of course, from *what* she expects him to think) are terms in which neither he nor any of his contemporaries, Christian or not, can think, sincerely or accurately, of anything. At the same time—I am thinking now of England in the twenties but, though the climate has changed a bit, it has not changed that much—he finds, whatever his interests may be, that most of the people who talk or write in terms which he does understand and which excite him are not Christians and are often actively hostile to the Christian Faith.

Writers did and do exist who, if not always, perhaps, completely orthodox, are effective Christian apologists, capable of showing the meaning and relevance of Christian dogmas to secular thought and action, but I never heard of them. I sometimes wonder, for example, what would have happened if, when I was at school or the university, a godparent or a friend had given me the works of Kierkegaard or Rudolf Kassner, both of whom were, later in my life, destined to play a great part. The only theological writer I knew of at that time whom I found readable and disturbing to my complacency was Pascal.

Today I find a certain element of fake in his writings, a kind of romantic indulgence in unhappiness not so far removed from *The Sorrows of the Young Werther*, which may well have been what attracted me at that time; but at least he did not talk like a parson and he prevented me from banishing the thought of God from my mind when I should very much have preferred to do so.

Two other pieces of good fortune exerted a similar saving influence on me as a boy and a young man. I was lucky enough to be born in a period when every educated person was expected to know the Bible thoroughly and no undergraduate could take a degree without passing a Divinity examination. In consequence, whatever attitude one might take towards the Bible, that it was great literature, an interesting anthropological document, or what have you, the events and sayings upon which Christianity is founded were as familiar to one as Grimm's fairy tales. In the United States today, even among students who come from Christian homes, I rarely find one with even the most elementary knowledge of the Bible, and this must make the task of the Church appallingly difficult.

Secondly, I was lucky enough to have a voice and a musical sense adequate to the modest demands of school choirs to which, first as a boy and later as a master, I belonged. In consequence, however bored I might be at the thought of God, I enjoyed services in His worship very much, more, probably, than many who were more devout than I but who had no active role to play. I can say this with some certainty because now, when I profess myself a Christian but, owing to circumstances, cannot be a choir member, I am often bored and distracted in church in a way that I never was when I had a function irrespective of my feelings or beliefs. I wonder if parish priests or church choir masters have ever considered one little fact, that the treble line of a hymn, the tune, after all, is too high for the male members of their congregations to sing. I have no idea how this problem is to be solved satisfactorily, but for those of us who can read music it would be a great pleasure if there were a few hymn books about with all four parts in them. This may sound a frivolous request but it is tied up with a very serious problem indeed for the life of the Church. As the late Dom Gregory Dix has shown so clearly in his wonderful book *The Shape of the Liturgy*, Christian worship is corporate action and anything which tends towards division, whether it be a Roman Catholic Low Mass in which the priest and acolyte perform the rite between them while the congregation occupy themselves with their private devotions, or an Anglican Matins in which the choir sings and the minister preaches while the rest listen, obscures the true nature of the Church as the mystical body of Christ and is a threat to its spiritual health.

The various "kerygmas," of Blake, of Lawrence, of Freud, of Marx, to which, along with most middle-class intellectuals of my generation, I paid attention between twenty and thirty, had one thing in common. They were all Christian heresies; that is to say, one cannot imagine their coming into existence except in a civilization which claimed to be based, religiously, on belief that the Word was made flesh and dwelt among us, and that, in consequence, matter, the natural order, is real and redeemable, not a shadowy appearance or the cause of evil, and historical time is real and significant, not meaningless or an endless series of cycles.

They arose, as I suspect most heresies do, as a doctrinal protest against what one might call a heresy of behavior exhibited by the orthodox of their day. By a heretic in behavior, I mean not simply someone whose conduct or thinking on secular matters is inconsistent with his faith, but someone who is quite honestly unaware that there is any inconsistency and defends his actions as Christian.

One is entitled to say of him, therefore, as one is not of a simple sinner, that, however orthodox he may imagine himself to be, in fact he holds some heretical doctrine of God, that in some way or another he is "dividing the Substance" and "confounding the Persons," for if this were not so, he would recognize the inconsistency and, though he might continue to act as before, he would know his actions to be sinful.

The doctrinal heretic perceives, usually more or less correctly, what doctrine is implied by the particular actions of which he more or less justly disapproves, and in protest propounds a doctrine equally one-sided in the opposite direction.

My own experience convinces me of the folly of trying to protect people from heresy by censorship or repression. In all the figures I have mentioned, I have come to realize that what is true in what they say is implicit in the Christian doctrine of the nature of man, and that what is not Christian is not true; but each of them brought to some particular aspect of life that intensity of attention which is characteristic of one-sided geniuses (needless to say, they all contradicted each other), and such comprehension of Christian wisdom as I have, little though it be, would be very much less without them.

What was one looking for at the time? Nothing is more difficult to recall than past assumptions, but I think the state of mind among most of my contemporaries was somewhat as follows. We assumed that there was only one outlook on life conceivable among civilized people, the liberal humanism in which all of us had been brought up, whether we came from Christian or agnostic homes (English liberalism had never been anti-clerical like its Continental brother).

To this the theological question seemed irrelevant since such values as freedom of the person, equal justice for all, respect for the rights of others, etc., were self-evident truths. However, the liberal humanism of the past had failed to produce the universal peace and prosperity it promised, failed even to prevent a World War. What had it overlooked? The subconscious, said Freud; the means of production, said Marx. Liberalism was not to be superseded; it was to be made effective instead of self-defeating.

Then the Nazis came to power in Germany. The Communists had said that one must hate and destroy some of one's neighbors now in order to create a world in which nobody would be able to help loving his neighbors tomorrow. They had attacked Christianity and all religions on the ground that, so long as people are taught to love a non-existent God, they will ignore the material obstacles to human brotherhood. The novelty and shock of the Nazis was that they made no pretense of believing in justice and liberty for all, and attacked Christianity on the grounds that to love one's neighbor as oneself was a command fit only for effeminate weaklings, not for the "healthy blood of the master race." Moreover, this utter denial of everything liberalism had ever stood for was arousing wild enthusiasm, not in some remote barbaric land outside the pale, but in one of the most highly educated countries in Europe, a country one knew well and where one had many friends. Confronted by such a phenomenon, it was impossible any longer to believe that the values of liberal humanism were self-evident. Unless one was prepared to take a relativist view that all values are a matter of personal taste, one could hardly avoid asking the question: "If, as I am convinced, the Nazis are wrong and we are right, what is it that validates our values and invalidates theirs?"

With this and similar questions whispering at the back of my mind, I visited Spain during the Civil War. On arriving in Barcelona, I found as I walked through the city that all the churches were closed and there was not a priest to be seen. To my astonishment, this discovery left me profoundly shocked and disturbed. The feeling was far too intense to be the result of a mere liberal dislike of intolerance, the notion that it is wrong to stop people from doing what they like, even if it is something silly like going to church. I could not escape acknowledging that, however I had consciously ignored and rejected the Church for sixteen years, the existence of churches and what went on in them had all the time been very important to me. If that was the case, what then?

Shortly afterwards, in a publisher's office, I met an Anglican layman, and for the first time in my life felt myself in the presence of personal sanctity. I had met many good people before who made me feel ashamed of my own shortcomings, but in the presence of this man—we never discussed anything but literary business—I did not feel ashamed. I felt transformed into a person who was incapable of doing or thinking anything base or unloving. (I later discovered that he had had a similar effect on many other people.)

So, presently, I started to read some theological works, Kierkegaard in particular, and began going, in a tentative and experimental sort of way, to church. And then, providentially—for the occupational disease of poets is frivolity—I was forced to know in person what it is like to feel oneself the prey of demonic powers, in both the Greek and the Christian sense, stripped of self-control and self-respect, behaving like a ham actor in a Strindberg play.

Much as I owe to Kierkegaard—among many other virtues, he has the talent, invaluable in a preacher to the Greeks, of making Christianity sound bohemian—I cannot let this occasion pass without commenting upon what seems to be his great limitation, a limitation which characterizes Protestantism generally. A planetary visitor might read through the whole of his voluminous works without discovering that human beings are not ghosts but have bodies of flesh and blood. (It is interesting to notice that while Kierkegaard shows great love of and insight into literature and music, he shows no interest in the visual arts whatsoever.)

As a spirit, a conscious person endowed with free will, every man has, through faith and grace, a unique "existential" relation to God, and few since St Augustine have described this relation more profoundly than Kierkegaard. But every man has a second relation to God which is neither unique nor existential: as a creature composed of matter, as a biological organism, every man, in common with everything else in the universe, is related by necessity to the God who created that universe and saw that it was good, for the laws of nature to which, whether he likes it or not, he must conform are of divine origin.

And it is with this body, with faith or without it, that all good works are done. All Catholic doctrines, such as the unity of the Two Natures, the special veneration due to the *Theotokos*, the Real Presence of Christ in the Mass, and Catholic practice, such as the liturgical use of the sensible—vestments, lights, incense—and the emphasis upon auricular confession, stress the physical reality of the flesh into which the Word was made. Admittedly this can and at times has led to an obscuring of the Word behind the splendors of the flesh, reduction of the spiritual life to a mechanical and automatic routine of physical acts against which the Reformers were fully justified in protesting, but their consequent denial of the value of anything visible and objective made the Christian Faith into something even more difficult than it is. It is easy to forget, particularly if I do not wish to remember, what I thought or felt yesterday, but it is difficult to forget what I did. Even mere routine has its value, as a reminder. A man may go to confession in a frivolous state of mind, rattle off some sins without feeling any real contrition, and go away to commit them again, but as long as he keeps up the habit he cannot forget that there are certain actions which the Church calls sinful, and that he has committed them; similarly, a man who likes Dover sole better than beefsteak may be a greater glutton on Friday than he was on Thursday, but as long as he observes the habit of ordering fish on Fridays, he cannot forget that Friday has a special significance.

Into the question of why I should have returned to Canterbury instead of proceeding to Rome, I have no wish to go in print. The scandal of Christian disunity is too serious. As Charles Williams has written:

> The separations in Christendom remain, nor will they be soon or easily ended. But the vocal disputes are a little suspended, and courtesies between the clamant bodies are easier. . . . It might be possible to "exchange" our ignorance, even if our decisions and certitudes must remain absolute. Those definitions apart, what is there anywhere but ignorance, grace, and moral effort? Of our moral effort the less said the better; grace is always itself alone, and demands only our adoration; and therefore it is between our ignorances that our courteous Lord might cause exchange to lie, till the exchange itself became an invocation of the adorable Spirit who has so often deigned to instruct and correct the Church by voices without as well as within the Church.*

Modern Canterbury Pilgrims: And Why They Chose the Episcopal Church, edited by James A. Pike, 1956

Foreword to *Some Trees*, by John Ashbery

A poet is perhaps the only kind of person who can say, honestly and knowing what he means, that he would rather have been born in an earlier age than the present. Very much earlier, for his golden age might be defined as the time when the statement "The real man speaks in poetry" was as self-evident as the statement "Men really speak in prose" is today.

Then, real meant sacred. From such a standpoint a man or woman is only real when he or she impersonates a god or goddess; in what we should call "themselves" they are of no account. Real events are sacred ritual actions, ritual marriages, sacrifices, and so on, by means of which the universe is sustained in being and repeatedly reborn: a rite is a public, not a private, act, not an act of personal choice but that which has to be done. An event that does not re-occur is nothing. The particular, the individual, the secular are nothing. Poetry, too, is a rite, which is why the poet speaks not in his own

---

* *The Descent of the Dove* (New York: Farrar, Straus and Cudahy, 1950), p. 232.

name but as a mouthpiece of the Muses. The ancient Greeks called the Muses the daughters of Memory, but memory meant something very different to them than it means to us. If we say someone has a good memory, we mean that he can recall the exact particulars of the past as they actually happened; to a Greek, remembering meant re-creating the past in what he would call its real form and we should call an ideal form. Particularity only appears as the particular details of a rite; it is important, for example, that Hercules should perform neither more nor less than twelve labors or that iambic verse should be used only for satires and curses.

Such a period is golden for the poet because he has no problem of subject matter, communication with his audience, or style, and, in addition, is a highly valued member of society.

How different such an age is from our own may best be seen in matters which, at first sight, seem to have changed least. To Roman Catholics, for example, the Pope is the Vicar of Christ, but the Pope is not crucified on Good Friday, and one can say of such and such a pope that he was a bad man. A few states are still monarchies and their kings or queens may be greatly loved by their people, but no one seriously regards them any longer as sacred; no one, for example, would expect them to touch for the King's Evil. A marriage may often still seem a significant ceremony, but what gives it significance, what makes it "holy," is for us not any special public status of the couple but the subjective relation between them, that they are in love.

For us, there is a sharp distinction between reality and meaning. Only concrete particulars seem real, and all concrete particulars seem equally real. Some may be brute fact without meaning beyond their occurrence, some may have a meaning known to God but imperceptible by us, in some we may perceive their true meaning, to others we may attribute a false meaning, but none of all this has anything to do with their reality. Human experience of time is an experience of a succession of unique moments, each of which is novel and will never recur. We may find one such moment uninteresting, we may forget it, but we cannot deny its importance, for if it had not existed we should not now exist. In their attitude toward the sacred, Christianity and materialism are agreed that created things and persons are not in themselves divine, though to Christianity they may become an outward and visible sign of the sacred to an individual; what the one condemns as idolatry the other condemns as irrational nonsense.

From Rimbaud down to Mr Ashbery, an important school of modern poets has been concerned with the discovery that, in childhood largely, in dreams and daydreams entirely, the imaginative life of the human individual stubbornly continues to live by the old magical notions. Its world is one of sacred images and ritual acts, the marriages of gods and goddesses, the recurrent sacrifices and rebirths of sacred kings, a numinous landscape inhabited by demons and strange beasts.

There is, however, a vast difference between these psychic worlds and the world of antiquity. The mythology of each of the former is unique—there are as many mythologies as there are individuals—and their origin, the experiences they are invented to explain, lie not, as for antiquity, in the recurrent events of Nature such as the rotation of the seasons or the movements of the heavenly bodies, but in the unique particulars of the individual's personal history. Magic numbers, for example, occur in dreams as they do in the old myths, but the reason why a dream number is magical may be hidden even from the dreamer himself. It is not difficult to perceive a relation between the twelve labors of Hercules and the twelve signs of the Zodiac, but if an ambitious young poet dreams of the number 37, it may take him considerable reflection before he remembers that Shakespeare wrote thirty-seven plays.

Every imagination has its holy places but they are its private property. In "The Instruction Manual" Mr Ashbery contrasts his historically real but profane situation, doing hackwork for his living, with his sacred memories of a Mexican town.

> How limited, but how complete withal, has been our experience of
>   Guadalajara!
> We have seen young love, married love, and the love of an aged mother
>   for her son.
> We have heard the music, tasted the drinks, and looked at colored
>   houses.
> What more is there to do, except stay? And that we cannot do.
> And as a last breeze freshens the top of the weathered old tower, I turn
>   my gaze
> Back to the instruction manual which has made me dream of
>   Guadalajara.

Reading this, I who have never been to Mexico nor wish to go there translate this into images of the happy life drawn from quite different cities. In this case, it is perfectly easy to do so, but even in the simplest case communication between poet and reader is indirect, demanding an active re-creation by the latter which ancient poetry with its public references does not.

Further, a modern poet who celebrates his inner mythological life cannot escape asking himself: "Do I really believe in my mythology and, if I do, ought I to believe it?"

The subject of Mr Ashbery's poem "Illustration" is a woman who acts out her private mythology and denies the reality of anything outside herself; that is to say, she is insane. As a ritual sacrificial act she jumps off a high building.

> For that the scene should be a ceremony
>
> Was what she wanted. "I desire
> Monuments," she said. "I want to move

> Figuratively, as waves caress
> The thoughtless shore. You people I know
>
> Will offer me every good thing
> I do not want. But please remember
>
> I died accepting them." . . .

She is mad, but is the kind of public sanity which regards nothing as sacred or even personal, the unauthentic life of the crowd watching her fall, not equally insane? Her action, crazy as it is, arouses a feeling of envy at her capacity so heroically to reject.

> . . . an effigy
> Of indifference, a miracle
>
> Not meant for us . . .

Every genre of poetry must find the style appropriate to it. When Rimbaud declared his intention of taking rhetoric and wringing its neck, he meant by rhetoric certain particular logical relations and conventional congruities of imagery which, however useful in describing some experiences, were bound to falsify those in which he, as a poet, was interested.

Where Wordsworth had asked the question "What is the language really used by men?" Rimbaud substituted the question "What is the language really used by the imagining mind?"

In "Les Illuminations" he attempted to discover this new rhetoric, and every poet who, like Mr Ashbery, has similar interests has the same problem. As Paul Valéry has said, every poem is made up of *given* lines and *calculated* lines; the former the poet has to improve, the latter he has to make sound "natural." A style of rhetoric expresses a notion of what is to be considered nature. If in the eighteenth century, with its interest in the general and universal, the danger for poets was a neglect of the singular, the danger for a poet working with the subjective life is the reverse; i.e. realizing that, if he is to be true to nature in this world, he must accept strange juxtapositions of imagery, singular associations of ideas, he is tempted to manufacture calculated oddities as if the subjectively sacred were necessarily and on all occasions odd.

At the same time he cannot avoid the question of how to reconcile truth to nature with accuracy of communication, for the writing of poetry presupposes that communication is possible; no one would write if he were convinced to the contrary.

It is not surprising, then, that many modern poems, among them Mr Ashbery's entertaining sestina "The Painter," are concerned with the nature of the creative process and with posing the question "Is it now possible to write poetry?"

Some Trees, by John Ashbery, 1956

Bile and Brotherhood

Winter Notes on Summer Impressions. By Fyodor M. Dostoevsky.
Translated from the Russian by Richard Lee Renfield.
Criterion Books. $2.75.

Perhaps the Iron Curtain is all Venice's fault. At least, any list of disastrous dates in modern history must include April 12th, 1204, when, encouraged by the Venetians, the Fourth Crusade turned aside and sacked Constantinople, making the schism between Rome and Byzantium irreparable and the ultimate defeat of the latter by Islam inevitable.

Had Byzantium remained as a bridge between East and West, Russia might well have shared in and made her unique contribution to such great historical changes as the Renaissance, the Reformation and the Enlightenment in which all the countries of Western Europe took part. In that case, attempts like that of Peter the Great to westernise her by force would not have seemed necessary and a reaction into Pan-Slavism would have been without point. But then we should not have Dostoevsky.

It is fitting that the introduction to these notes should be written by an American for, however different the historical causes may be, Americans and Russians both share the same ambivalent emotions about Europe, the same awe of its "Old Stones" and the same conviction that they are morally better than Europeans, if not in actuality, at least in what they aspire to be.

> Guidebooks in hand, they hungrily dash about to observe the curiosities in each city, and they do this as if by obligation, as if they were continuing to serve their native land; they do not miss a single three-windowed palace, provided it is mentioned in the guidebook. . . . They admire a side of beef by Rubens and convince themselves it is the Three Graces combined, because that is what the guidebook orders; they rush to the Sistine Madonna and stand before it in vague expectation: something will happen any second, someone will scramble out of the floor and dissipate their aimless melancholy and weariness. And they leave amazed that nothing happened.

Who, reading such a passage out of context, would not take it to be a malicious description of American tourists? And when Mr Saul Bellow writes, "Paris is revered by your American as something approximately sacred," he is saying something that Dostoevsky would understand very well, but which is incomprehensible to someone who, like myself, was born and bred in England.

An Englishman who likes paying visits to the Continent, knows pretty well what he is going for—to get out of the British climate, to have a respite from home cooking, to be able to have a drink at any time of the day, to enjoy a sexual freedom which is only possible when one has no "neighbors." Consequently, though he may be just as annoyed as Dostoevsky or Mr Bellow by foreign red-tape and cheating landladies and find the Frenchman's love of rhetoric or the vanity of the Italian male just as comic, he is not disillusioned for he has not come to find a holy place. It sometimes happens, of course, that some particular spot or even country (probably one of the odder ones like Bulgaria) becomes for him a holy place but this is his personal and unexpected discovery.

Not that Dostoevsky, by the time he paid his first visit to Europe, expected to find it a holy place; on the contrary, he was determined to find it hell. *Winter Notes on Summer Impressions* is a collection of articles which he wrote for a Russian periodical *Vremya* describing his impressions of France and England in 1862.

The fairness or unfairness of his remarks hardly matter to us, for Paris and London hardly matter to him except as a weapon with which to attack the westernising party in his own country. Since the end of the Crimean War, this party had been in the ascendancy and in the previous year Alexander II had liberated the serfs. This period, however, was nearly at an end: emancipation did not prove a cure-all, the Polish Revolt in 1863 gave the authorities a fright and after 1865 the Czar became and remained as pro-Slav and anti-West as even Dostoevsky could wish.

The real object of his polemic, to which the evils of Europe were subsidiary conveniences, was to ridicule those Russians "who stand furiously for foreign apron-strings", the one hundred thousand of the upper set who considered the fifty million Russians who stayed at home nobodies "whom our profound satirical journals ridicule to this day for not shaving off their beards."

It can hardly have been a novelty for a Russian citizen to be asked to register with the police: if Dostoevsky devotes a whole chapter to a very commonplace incident of this kind in Paris, one can only suppose that there were Russians who claimed that, if Russia would only adopt Western ideas, policemen and spies would disappear overnight.

Having told us himself how Gvozdilov, who was an officer and a gentleman, was in the habit of savagely beating his wife, he cannot have been as shocked as he pretends to learn that cockney costermongers beat their wives with pokers, but he is happy to show Russian liberals that wife-beating is not confined to Slavic countries.

What really and profoundly shocks Dostoevsky about Europe is not the injustice and suffering which he observes, but its bourgeois attitude to life.

In French nature, and in Occidental nature in general, you find a principle of individualism, a principle of isolation, of intense self-preservation, of personal gain, of self-determination of the *I*, of opposing this *I* to all

nature and the rest of mankind as an independent, autonomous principle entirely equal and equivalent to all that exists outside itself.

He is so obsessed by this, so fearful that the same spirit will infect Russia if the
westernisers get their way, that he can make no distinction between real faults
and harmless cultural habits.

> . . . both these needs—*voir la mer* and *se rouler dans l'herbe*—the Parisian
> usually permits himself only after he has amassed wealth or, in short,
> after he has begun respecting himself, taking pride in himself, consid-
> ering himself a human being. *Se rouler dans l'herbe* is twice, even ten times
> more delightful when it takes place on his own land, on land bought with
> the money he has labored to earn. When the bourgeois retires from busi-
> ness, he generally likes to buy a lot somewhere and build a house with a
> garden, a wall, chickens and a cow. And even if it is all on the most mi-
> croscopic scale, the bourgeois is carried away by a most childish and
> touching rapture.

A westerner cannot help asking: "And what is so wrong or funny about that?"
Again, because it is Western, the Roman Catholic Church must be corrupt,
but one is a little puzzled by the evidence of corruption which Dostoevsky
gives us:

> The Catholic priest himself tracks down poor workingmen and attempts
> to insinuate himself into their families. He may find, for instance, a sick
> man lying on a litter of straw on a damp floor, surrounded by children
> crazed with cold and hunger, and by a hungry and often drunk wife. He
> will nourish and dress them all, heat the house, care for the invalid, buy
> medicine, become a friend of the household, and end by converting
> them all to Catholicism. Sometimes, however, after the recovery they
> drive him away with oaths and blows. But he does not get discouraged
> easily, and goes on to others. They too drive him away, but he has infi-
> nite patience and invariably ends by taking a captive.

Surely, he could have found something more shocking to tell us.

In contrast to bourgeois Europe Dostoevsky offers the Russia of his grandfather's day.

> At that time, naturally, Europe came to us easily—in its physical aspects,
> of course. But, naturally, as for its moral aspects, the whip remained. We
> donned silk stockings and wigs and hung little swords on ourselves, and
> lo and behold, we were Europeans. This did no harm; it was even fun.
> In actual fact everything remained as before . . . Having taken off our
> glasses, we dealt with the house serfs just as before; we treated our fam-
> ilies just as patriarchally as before; out in the stable we flogged the small
> landowner who lived nearby if he was rude to us, just as before; and we

kowtowed just as obsequiously before higher placed personages. Even the peasant understood us better: we scorned him less, disdained his ways less, knew more about him, were less foreign to him, less German. And if we gave ourselves airs before him, so what? How could a master help but give himself airs; a master was made for that. Even if we flogged him to death, we somehow seemed nicer to the people than nowadays, because we were closer to them.

Dostoevsky is not sorry, of course, that, owing to Russia's peculiar history, liberal ideas could only be imported from abroad by a small cultured elite, causing an estrangement between them and the mass of the peasants: he is delighted that the peasants cannot understand them. What appalls him about Europeans is that the bourgeois attitude has triumphed so completely that there is no other.

The workers themselves are proprietors in their hearts; their sole desire is to become proprietors and amass all the possessions they possibly can. The Farmers? But French farmers are arch-proprietors, the most obtuse of proprietors, i.e. the best and fullest imaginable realization of the proprietor.

Dostoevsky was right about the triumph. Paris to-day is no longer the "still of orderliness" that it was under Napoleon III nor contemporary London the savage city of the sixties when on Saturday night in certain quarters every living soul was dead drunk and twelve year old girls offered themselves in the Haymarket, but both are still governed by what he would call the bourgeois attitude, and any changes which have been made have been made by it. One of the funniest passages in the *Notes* is a description of a typical romantic comedy in the Paris of the Empire.

Gustave is as proud and as disdainfully noble as always, but he swaggers more than he used to, for he is a soldier. Dearer to him than anything in the world is his cross which was bought with his blood, and "*l'épée de mon père.*" Of course he is penniless: that is the sine qua non. Madame Beaupré as usual is in love with him, as is Cecilia, but he has not the slightest suspicion that Cecilia loves him. Cecilia spends five acts groaning with love. Finally it snows or does something of the sort. Cecilia wants to jump out of the window. But under the window two shots ring out; everyone gathers around; Gustave slowly enters, ghostly pale and with his arm in a sling. Cecelia's calumniator and deceiver has been punished. Madame Beaupré is pale and frightened, and Gustave realises that she loves him. But another shot rings out. This time it is Monsieur Beaupré driven to suicide by despair. Madame Beaupré screams and rushes to the door, but in walks Monsieur Beaupré carrying a dead fox or something of the sort. The lesson has been learned; *ma biche* will never

forget him. She clings to *bribi* who forgives everything. But lo and behold! Cecilia suddenly inherits a million and Gustave rebels again. He
refuses to marry; Gustave makes faces; Gustave uses foul language. It is
indispensable that Gustave should use foul language and scornfully reject the million, for otherwise the bourgeois would never forgive him:
there would be an insufficiency of ineffable nobility. However, do not
think that the bourgeois has been untrue to his nature. Never fear; the
million will not by-pass the happy couple; it inevitably appears towards
the end in the guise of a reward for virtue. Gustave ends by taking the
million, that is, Cecilia, and this sets in motion the inevitable fountains,
cotton night-caps, gurgling of the water and so forth.

Compared with the productions of Hollywood or Messrs Rogers and Ham-
merstein, this may seem a little unsophisticated, but it clearly belongs to the
same world.

Poor Bourgeois! No other social class has ever caught it so hot in literature.
To begin with, nearly all writers have come from it; aristocrats regard writing
as beneath their dignity and peasants don't know how. It is only natural that
writers should attack most violently the faults of which they have first-hand
experience from childhood on. And then, to look at, the bourgeois is, it must
be admitted, an unattractive object. He is a windbag, he worries about the future and what his neighbors are saying, he doesn't know how to wear clothes,
he is either too fat or too thin. Even his virtues of industry and prudence are
dull. Aesthetically, it must be admitted that a static hierarchical society in
which who a person is depends not on himself but on fate is much nicer. The
aristocracy have the graces of those who are sure of themselves, and the peas-
antry are not envious because they cannot imagine the possibility of being
anything but what they are. Moreover, so long as nothing, no machinery for
instance, causes a change in the way men live, the relations between master
and servant, just because they are so clearly defined and have existed for so
long, may well be more "brotherly" than the relations in a society where no
one's position is certain or permanent.

But when he is considered morally, the bourgeois has some questions to
put to his critics. "Suppose," he may say, "you are right in saying that bourgeois freedom only means freedom for the individual who has made a million; is that necessarily a worse or more limited kind of freedom than that
which depends on inheriting a thousand acres? Suppose I do sell a shawl
worth 1500 francs for 12,000 in such a way that milady is completely satisfied?
Is that so much more ignoble than taking someone's land by force and making him a serf, or ruining tradesmen by running up debts which you have neither the means nor the intention to pay?" If Dostoevsky could return to earth
and visit such countries as England or the United States, he would not like
us any better than before, but he would have to admit that it has been in pre-

cisely those countries where the bourgeoisie were strongest that they have been able to impose limitations and discipline themselves, while those countries with an aristocratic ruling class resisted all reform until it was too late. In a time of rapid historical change, the very vagueness and fluidity of the bourgeois, his lack of a clearly defined notion of his class to which he must be loyal, is an advantage both practically and morally.

So long as he is on the attack, Dostoevsky is very funny and, so far as he goes, not inaccurate, but when he tries to make positive suggestions he gives himself away.

> If we transposed fraternity into rational conscious language, of what then would it consist? It would consist of this: each individual, of his own accord, without any external pressure or thought of profit, would say to society, "We are strong only when united; take all of me, if you need me; do not think of me when you make your laws; do not worry about me in the least; I cede all my rights to you and beg you to dispose of me as you see fit. My greatest joy is to sacrifice everything to you, without hurting you by so doing. I shall annihilate myself, I shall melt away, if only your brotherhood will last and prosper." But the Community should answer, "You offer us too much. What you offer we have no right to refuse, for you say it would be your greatest joy; but what can we do, when our constant concern is for your happiness. Take everything that is ours too . . ."

It is odd that Dostoevsky should repeat what had already been said by a Frenchman, Rousseau, and odder, after the French Revolution, that he should not have seen the fallacy, in any society larger than a small village, of crediting society with a personality of the same kind as that of an individual, as if he did not know how in fact laws are passed. The Christian commandment to love one's neighbor as oneself may be extremely difficult but it is meaningful because my neighbor is a concrete individual, but society is an abstraction which it is meaningless to talk of loving.

Bourgeois society is, as perhaps all societies have always been, in a mess, but it is not from Dostoevsky that we shall learn how to get out of it. And, if it comes to models, I would rather take that bourgeois hero, Sir Walter Scott, who worked himself to death to pay his creditors, than Alyosha or any other of Dostoevsky's seedy enthusiasts.

Unpublished; written June 1955 for the *New Yorker*

L'Homme d'Esprit

Introduction to Analects, *by Paul Valéry*

To discuss literature written in any tongue other than one's own is a questionable undertaking, but for an English-speaking writer to discuss a French writer to discuss a French writer borders on folly, for no two languages could be more different.

To discover the essential and unique qualities of a language, one must go to its poetry for it is the poet, as Valéry says, who attempts to remove all the noises from speech leaving only the sounds. The conventions of a poetry, its prosodic rules, the kinds of verbal ornamentation, rhymes, alliterations, etc., which it encourages or condemns can tell us much about the way in which a native ear draws this distinction. I very much doubt whether a Frenchman can ever learn really to hear a line of English verse—think of Baudelaire and Poe—and I am perfectly certain that no Englishman can learn to hear French poetry correctly. When I hear a native recite German or Spanish or Italian poetry, I believe, however mistakenly, that I hear more or less what he hears, but if the reciter is French, I know I am hearing nothing of the sort. I know, in an academic way, the rules of Classical French verse, but the knowledge does not change my habit of hearing. For example, to my ear, trained on English verse, the prevailing rhythm of the French alexandrine sounds like the anapaestic rhythm of

> The Assyrian came down like a wolf on the fold

thus

> Je suis belle, | ō mŏrtēls! | cŏmme uň rêve | dě pierre

I know this is all wrong but it is what I hear.* Further, most unfortunately, the nature of the English language forbids the use of anapaests for tragic subjects. I am convinced that, when he goes to hear *Phèdre* at the Comédie Française, an Englishman, however well he may know French, however much he admire the extraordinary varied and subtle delivery of the cast, cannot help finding Racine comic.

I have known Valéry's poem *Ebauche d'un serpent* for over twenty-five years, reread it often with increasing admiration and, as I thought, comprehension, only to discover the other day, on reading a letter by the poet to Alain, that I had missed the whole point, namely, that the tone of the poem is burlesque, that the assonances and alliterations are deliberately exaggerated, and that the serpent is intended to sound like Beckmesser in *Die Meistersinger*.

---

* Another difficulty for my ear is the caesura; an English poet works just as hard to vary its position from line to line as a French poet works to keep it in the same few places.

How could I, to whose ear all French verse sounds a bit exaggerated, hope to get this?

In prose, the difficulties of communication, though not so formidable, are still serious enough. It is not just a matter of the obvious translator's headaches, that there is no English equivalent to *esprit*, for instance, or that *amour* and *love* are not synonymous, but of the entirely different rhetorical structure of French and English prose, so that an English reader may entirely ignore some important effect and be over-impressed by another.

In writing about Valéry, therefore, I can only console myself with the thought that, if the Valéry I admire is in large measure a creation of my own, the man who wrote—"the proper object of thought is that which does not exist"—would be the first to appreciate the joke.

From the age of twenty, Valéry made it his daily habit to rise before dawn and spend two or three hours studying the interior maneuvers of his freshly-awoken mind. This habit became a physiological need so that, if circumstance made him miss these hours of introspection, he felt out of sorts for the rest of the day. The observations he made during this period he wrote down in notebooks, without a thought, he says, of their ever being read by another. From time to time, however, he was persuaded to publish selections. The reluctance he expresses seems more primadonna-ish than real.

> I never dreamt that one day I would have these fragments printed as they stood. Dr Ludo van Bogaert and M. Alexandre Stols had the idea for me. They tempted me to do so by pointing out the "intimate" quality of this little venture, and by the typographical perfection of the sample pages they showed me.

> There are times when one has to give way to the preposterous desires of lovers of the spontaneous and ideas in the rough.

This does not ring quite true, especially when one finds him writing privately to a friend (Paul Souday) that he considers his notebooks his real *œuvre*.

In any case, we may be very glad that he overcame his reluctance, for, taken together, these notes form one of the most interesting and original documents of "the inner life" in existence.

Much of such documents are concerned with the so-called personal, that is, with the confession of sins and vices, memories of childhood, the feelings of the subject about God, the weather, his mistress, gossip, self-reproach, and the ordinary motive for producing them is a desire to demonstrate that their author is more interesting, more unique, more *human* than other folks.

For the personal in this sense, Valéry had nothing but contempt. It is in what they show, he believed, that men differ; what they hide is always the same. Confession, therefore, is like undressing in public; everyone knows what he is going to see. Further, a man's secrets are often much more apparent to others than to himself.

One of Gide's most obvious traits, for example, was his tightfistedness; after reading his journals, one is curious to know if he was aware of this.

A cultivation of memory for its own sake, as in Proust, was incomprehensible to Valéry, who preferred to forget everything in his past that was just a picture, retaining only what he could assimilate and convert into an element of his present mental life. As for confiding one's sufferings to paper, he thought it responsible for all the worst books.

The task which Valéry set himself was to observe the human mind in the action of thinking; the only mind that he can observe is, of course, his own, but this is irrelevant. He is not a philosopher, except in the etymological meaning of that word, nor a psychologist in so far as psychology is concerned with hidden depths—for Valéry, humanity is confined to the skin and consciousness; below that is physiological machinery—but an amazingly keen and *rusé* observer of conscious processes of thinking. For this neither a special talent, like a talent for mathematics, nor esoteric learning is required, but only what might be called intellectual virtue, which it is possible for every man to develop, if he chooses.

For the cultivation of such an *Ethique spotive*, as Valéry once called it, one must develop a vigilance that immediately distinguishes between fictions and real psychic events, between the seen, the thought, the reasoned and the felt, and a precision of description that resists all temptation to fine literary effects. Hence Valéry's repeated attacks on the popular notion of "profundity." A thought, he says, can properly be called profound only if it profoundly changes a question or a given situation, and such a thought is never found at the bottom of the mind which contains only a few stock proverbs. Most people call something profound, not because it is near some important truth but because it is distant from ordinary life. Thus, darkness is profound to the eye, silence to the ear; what-is-not is the profundity of what-is. This kind of profundity is a literary effect, which can be calculated like any other literary effect, which can be calculated like any other literary effect, and usually deplorable. For Valéry, Pascal's famous remark about the silence of the eternal spaces is a classic instance of literary vanity passing itself off as observation. If Pascal was genuinely interested in stating a truth, then why, Valéry maliciously asks, did he not also write: "The intermittent hubbub in the small corners where we live reassures us."

After reading his notebooks, we know no more about Valéry as a person than before—we are not told, for example, that he suffered from depressions—he has only shown us that he was a good observer and that he expressed his observations in precise language. To judge if his observations are true or false, we have only to repeat the experiment on ourselves. For instance, he says that it is impossible consciously to put a distance between oneself and an object without turning round to see if one is succeeding. I try, and I find that Valéry is right.

Valéry's attitude to life is more consistent than he admits, and begins with a conviction of the essential inconsistency of the mind and the need to react against it. The following three notes might be taken as mottoes for all his work.

Cognition reigns but does not rule.

Sometimes I think; and sometimes I *am*.

I invoke no inspiration except that element of chance, which is common to every mind; then comes an unremitting toil, which wars against this element of chance.

Valéry's observations cover a wide range of subjects. As one might expect, the least interesting, the ones in which he sounds least like Valéry and most like just one more French writer of mordant aphorisms, are those concerned with love, self-love, good, and evil.

He has extremely interesting things to say about our consciousness of our bodies, about those curious psycho-physical expressions, laughing, crying, and blushing, about the physical behavior of people when they are concentrating on a mental problem. He is excellent on dreams—he observes, for instance, that in dreams there is "practically no present tense."

But for poets, naturally, and for many others too, I believe, his most valuable contributions are his remarks on the art of poetry. A critic who does not himself write poetry may be an admirable judge of what is good and bad, but he cannot have a first-hand knowledge of how poetry is written, so that not infrequently he criticizes, favorably or unfavorably, some poem for achieving or failing to achieve something that the poet was not interested in doing. Many poets have written defenses of poetry against charges that it is untrue or immoral, but surprisingly few have told us how they wrote. There are two reasons for this: the poets are more interested in writing more poems and, less laudably, they, like lawyers and doctors, have a snobbish reluctance to show the laity the secrets of their mystery. Behind this snobbery, of course, lies the fear that, if the general public knew what goes on, that a poem is not sheer logomancy, for instance, or that an intensely expressive love poem does not necessarily presuppose a poet intensely in love, that public would lose even the little respect for poets that it has.

It is unfortunate that one of Valéry's few predecessors, Poe, should have used as his case history of composition a poem, "The Raven", which does strike the reader as "contrived" in a bad way, which means that it is not contrived enough. The form Poe employed for the poem, which demands many feminine rhymes, has in English a frivolous effect out of key with the subject. A reader, who wishes to cling to a more magical view of the poetic process, can find reasons to confirm his illusion. Valéry's achievements as a poet make his critical doctrines harder to wish away. His statements are obviously intended to be polemical. He dislikes two kinds of writers, those who try to impress with sonorous or violent vagueness, and naturalistic writers who would simply record what the camera sees or their stream of accidental thoughts. For Valéry, all loud and violent writing is comic, like a man alone in a room, playing a trombone. When one reads Carlyle, for instance, one gets the impression that he had persuaded himself that it takes more effort, more *work*, to write *fortissimo* than *piano*, or *universe* than *garden*.

Of the Zola school of naturalism Valéry disposes very neatly, by asking what kinds of scents perfumers would bottle if they adopted this aesthetic.

For Valéry, a poem ought to be a festival of the intellect, that is, a game, but a solemn, ordered, and significant game, and a poet is someone to whom arbitrary difficulties suggest ideas. It is the glory of poetry that the lack of a single word can ruin everything, that the poet cannot continue until he discovers a word, say, in two syllables, containing P or F, synonymous with *breaking-up*, yet not too uncommon. The formal restrictions of poetry teach us that the thoughts which arise from our needs, feelings, and experiences are only a small part of the thoughts of which we are capable. In any poem some lines were "given" the poet, which he then tried to perfect, and others which he had to calculate and at the same time make them sound as "natural" as possible. It is more becoming in a poet to talk of versification than of mysterious voices, and his genius should be so well hidden in his talent that the reader attributes to his art what comes from his nature.

Needless to say, Valéry found very little in the French poetry of his age which seemed to him anything more than a worship of chance and novelty, and concluded that poetry was a freak survival, that no one today would be capable of arriving at the notion of verse if it were not already there.

In his general principles I am convinced that Valéry is right past all possibility of discussion, but I cannot help wondering if I should also agree in daily practice as much as I do, if I were a Frenchman trying to write French poetry. For polemical reasons, probably, Valéry overstresses, I think, the arbitrariness of poetic formal restrictions, and over-dramatizes the opposition between them and the "natural." If they really were purely arbitrary, then the prosodies of different languages would be interchangeable, and the experience which every poet has had, of being unable to get on with a poem because he was trying to use the "wrong" form for this particular poem until, having found the right form, the *natural* form, composition proceeded freely, would be unknown. While it is true that nothing which is without effort and attention is likely to be of much value, the reverse proposition is not true: it would take an immense effort, for example, to write half a dozen rhopalic hexameters in English, but it is virtually certain that the result would have no poetic merit.

To an English poet, French poetry seems to suffer from a lack of formal variety, as did English poetry between 1680 and 1780. Any form, be it the

French alexandrine or the English heroic couplet, however admirable a vehicle originally, tends to exhaust its possibilities in the hands of two or three
masters, and their successors must either find quite different forms or be
doomed to remain epigoni. If it is rare to find a modern French poem that
is not written in free verse (and one must not forget that Valéry himself wrote
quite a lot of what he called *poésie brute*), while formal poems are still common in modern English poetry, the lack of resilience in the official forms of
French verse may be partly responsible.* By comparison with French, English
seems an anarchic amateur language, but this very anarchy, if it stimulates
the proper revolt against it, can give rise to new and living structures. Would
Valéry, I sometimes patriotically wonder, have finished his poetic career so
soon if he had had the vast resources of *our* tongue, with all the prosodic possibilities which its common syllables permit, to play with?

But then, of course, we might not have got the notebooks. It is fitting that
the man whose critical banner might well have carried the device *Vade retro,
Musa*, should have written *Tes pas, enfants de mon silence*, one of the most beautiful invocations to the Muse in any language. His worshiped Muse, whom he
sometimes called Laura, was not, perhaps, the Muse of poetry or, if so, only
accidentally, but the Muse of insight and self-renewal whom he daily expected
in the dawn hours.

> My mind thinks of my mind,
> My past is foreign to me,
> My name surprises me,
> My body is a pure idea.
> What I was is with all other selves
> And I am not even what I am going to be.

Aside from the money, literary success can give but small satisfaction to an
author, even to his vanity. For what does literary success mean? To be condemned by persons who have not read his works and to be imitated by persons devoid of talent. There are only two kinds of literary glory that are worth
winning but the writer who wins either will never know. One is to have been
the writer, perhaps a quite minor one, in whose work some great master generations later finds an essential clue for solving some problem; the other is
to become for someone else an example of the dedicated life,

> being secretly invoked, pictured, and placed by a stranger in an inner
> sanctum of his thoughts, so as to serve him as a witness, a judge, a father,
> and a hallowed mentor.

---

* About some things it would seem that French taste is more indulgent than English. Thus
Valéry, while admitting that De Vigny's line *J'aime la majesté des souffrances humaines* is nonsense,
allows it, nevertheless, because of its beautiful sound. An English poet could never get away with
a similar line.

It was this role, rather than that of a literary influence, which Mallarmé played in Valéry's life, and I can vouch for at least one life in which Valéry does likewise. Whenever I am more than usually tormented by one of those horrid mental imps, *Contradiction, Obstination, Imitation, Lapsus, Brouillamini, Fange-d'Ame*, whenever I feel myself in danger of becoming *un homme sérieux,* it is on Valéry, *un homme d'esprit* if ever there was one, more often than on any other poet, I believe, that I call for aid.

Written 1955; *Hudson Review,* Autumn 1969; Paul Valéry,
Analects, translated by Stuart Gilbert, 1970

The History of an Historian

The Life and Work of Sigmund Freud. Vol. II: Years of Maturity,
1901–1919. By Ernest Jones. Basic Books. $6.75.

The First Act in the life-drama of anyone who, like Freud, makes a revolutionary discovery has a natural excitement that no bungler—and Dr Jones is anything but that—can destroy. The hero has the stage all to himself and the events, the false starts, the first glimmerings, the self-doubts when the data seem so at variance with everything he has been taught, the need for a confidante, carry the biographer and the reader along with them. The real test of the biographer's skill and understanding comes when the hero ceases to be a lonely pioneer and the story becomes one, not of sudden discovery, but slow development and modification. Dr Jones' second volume covers the period between 1901 and 1919, that is to say, the spreading of Freud's ideas from being his private property to being those of an international movement. The drama is now supplied by the appearance of schism and of persecution. In writing the history of this, Dr Jones has the advantages and disadvantages of one who played an important and active role in it: he has the advantage of first-hand experience of the facts and the disadvantage or, let us say, the danger of a deep emotional involvement. If he is a man of honor and intellectual integrity, as Dr Jones clearly is, he knows that he must suppress no fact which might seem detrimental to the side he takes on a controversial issue, at the same time that he knows it would be equally dishonest of him to pretend that he has no opinion.

One minor danger which Dr Jones does not completely escape, is that he knows too much. Thus, while I am fascinated to learn how Freud behaved during his summer holidays, that, for instance he had no sense of geographical location and a passion for hunting mushrooms, I have no particular wish to know exactly where he went to—unless, as in the case of his first visit to Rome, it is obviously relevant—still less, exactly which hotel he stayed in and how much he paid for his room.

The serious danger, of course, arises over the history of schism, the defections of Adler, Stekel, Jung etc.

In general Dr Jones' treatment of this period deserves the highest praise. Indeed, I think that some of the deficiencies I find in it may be due to his having been too much of a gentleman—the man who thought up the Council of Five to defend and help the Master like, as he himself admits, the Knights of old, will never lose his sense of chivalry, even in fighting the heathen—he knows, I am sure, more than he thinks it decent to tell. In consequence, when he does make a personal remark, the absence of detail makes it sound more malicious than it should. For instance he writes of Stekel that he "was a born journalist in a pejorative sense . . . and indeed he earned part of his living by writing regular feuilletons for the local press." To write feuilletons is, certainly, a journalistic act; whether it is also pejorative depends upon the quality of the feuilletons and of that we are not told.

Since Dr Jones is not writing a history of the psychoanalytical movement but a biography of its founder and, therefore, had no space to go into a detailed refutation of, say, Jung's theories, I think it a mistake to refer to psychological motives at all, important, of course, as we know them to be. If I believe something to be true, I am of necessity bound to think that my motive is love of truth: I can only be led to look for another motive when someone has convinced me that what I have previously believed is untrue.

It is not that I question Dr Jones' judgment but that I think the average lay reader of his book is not going to know enough about the theoretical differences or the evidence on which they are based, to know if it is just. It is curious to note that one of Freud's predictions, namely, that those psychologies like Jung's and Adler's which soft-pedal the importance of sexuality, would receive more popular support, has not come true: there are just as many, if not more, Freudian analysts as Jungian or Adlerian. Nor, on the other hand, have the latter disappeared as they would have if their therapeutic results had been nil. What bewilders the poor layman is that he knows of individual cases of therapeutic success and failure by all three schools. Truly, as Freud said, "The transference is altogether a curse."

In reviewing, elsewhere, the first volume of this biography, I suggested that the essential revolutionary discovery of Freud's was that psychology and neurology are different fields, that the life of the mind cannot be studied by the quantitative methods suitable to the study of brain events, for it is a historical life to be studied by the principles which govern historical research, which, since it contains both objective and subjective elements, is neither a strict science nor a pure art. The objective or "scientific" side of the historian's work consists in trying to find out what actually happened in the past. In this research he must eliminate so far as possible his personal hopes and fears and never accept second-hand evidence, like the accounts of previous historians, when there is available first-hand evidence, like documents contemporary to his period, by which to check the former.

Of course a lucky or shrewd guess may lead him to look for and find such evidence, hitherto unknown because no one had thought of looking for it, but either it is there or it is not.

So far the difference between a good and bad historian is a difference between carefulness or honesty and carelessness or dishonesty. Freud's surrender of his original belief that phantasies of seduction in childhood were accounts of historical fact is an example of the first; to write a paper, as Stekel apparently did, showing the influence of a person's name upon his character and life in which all the names were made up, is an example of the second.

In assessing the importance of his data, all historians are governed by the same general principle that the importance of an historical event is in proportion to its causal effect upon subsequent historical events which includes its influence upon later interpretations of the past, but, in history, to say that A causes B does not mean that if A occurs then B has to occur but only that A provides B with a motive for occurring. Dr Jones gives us some illuminating reflections of Freud's on his subject.

> He felt satisfied that he could trace back the causal links quite comprehensively from the end product to the very beginning, but he was equally clear that were one to proceed in the reverse direction there would be no such certainty. Over and over again one could see that such and such an aetiological factor might have led to several different effects, and one could only say in any particular case that it led to the one it actually did. Why it did so instead of leading to any of the other directions open to it no one could say. The explanation of the difficulty is simple enough. It is that our knowledge of the causal agencies is purely qualitative, and that we have at present no prospect of making it quantitative. If a given conflict ends in a certain way one can say that one side of it was stronger than the other, but there is no means of predicting this beforehand since we have no method for measuring the strength of mental "forces."

In the last three sentences one hears the nostalgia of the ex-neurologist for an "exact" science. Freud was probably overmodest when he described himself as having no talent at all "for the natural sciences; nothing for mathematics; nothing for anything quantitative," but we may be thankful that he had had such a great talent for the qualitative. One proof of his extraordinary courage is that he accepted the qualitative while at the same time thoroughly disliking it on philosophical grounds, that he could stick to being an analyst and at the same time say that the only possibility for real improvement in the world that he could see lay in the emergence of a new species or, of all things, selective breeding.

Taken off his guard, however, he could quite forget that he was supposed to be a determinist as when, on being told of a "paraprax" committed by Jung, he made a historian's judgment: "A gentleman should not do such things even unconsciously."

The historical discipline is the most difficult of all, since it lacks the demonstrable certainty of the natural sciences and at the same time cannot enjoy the luxury of the arts which are frankly subjective. A historian is bound to claim that the interpretation he gives to historical facts, the causal importance he attributes to them are the true ones, that his account of how the present has been born of the past is essentially the correct one and that all rival versions even if they are possible, are still wrong.

Thus, while in the natural sciences, controversies are short lived, for either one side is proved to be right or both sides are proved to be wrong, in the realm of the historical, be it what is normally called history, or psychoanalysis, or theology etc., controversy and schism are perpetual. This does not mean, of course, that everybody is equally right, but that in deciding between two sides, one has to make a qualitative judgment. If I say that I choose Freud as against Jung or Adler, I do not mean that I believe every word that Freud uttered as gospel, or that there might not be a detail of fact upon which he was wrong and his opponents right—I am, anyway, in no position to judge— I mean that, as a whole, his work feels or "smells" right to me, and that theirs does not. Into this feel aesthetic-ethical judgments enter and quite justifiably—I like Freud's face better, fussing with matters like alchemy seems to me plain silly etc. I must, in justice, add that, judging by their photographs, the only two of the six Paladins that I like are Dr Jones and Dr Abraham.

In reading Dr Jones' account of the opposition and downright persecution which Freud and his colleagues encountered—having grown up in a time when Freud has become part of our mental climate, one forgets that there was a time when a Geheimrat could bang the table and scream: "This is not a topic for discussion at a scientific meeting; it is a matter for the police," or that, when the first psychoanalytical paper was read in England, the audience of eight solemnly left the room when Dr Eder came to the sexual aetiology— one is immediately struck by how frequently the objection to the sexual is linked with an objection to the subjective. Freud's theories were not only dirty but also full of "mystical tendencies," "a modern form of witchcraft mania," "a simply gruesome old-wives psychiatry," my favorite being a Dr Collins, who after protesting against pornographic stories about pure virgins continued thus: "It is time the Association took a stand against transcendentalism and supernaturalism and definitely crushed out Christian Science, Freudism and all that bosh, rot and nonsense." (What would poor Mrs Eddy have felt at such a linkage?)

This amiable fellow was notorious, we are told, for his love of indecent jokes. In his case, certainly and, I suspect, in many other cases, indignation was not so much at having to admit the existence of the sexual as at having to take it seriously. We all tend, I think, and intellectual workers are particularly liable, to divide our activities into the field of our work, where our standards of truth and precision may be very high, and the field of play which is governed either by conventional rules or is a free-for-all anarchy.

If Freud was right, then the sexual was neither anarchic nor conventional, but governed by its own laws which could not be broken with impunity, and Dr Collins would have had to ask himself why he enjoyed dirty stories so much.

In discussing the works published by Freud, it is not easy, in a biography intended for the general reader, to gauge his previous acquaintance with them. The specialist, naturally knows the work already, and does not need to be told about it; on the other hand, since some of the material is highly technical, a reader who knows nothing may find an account too difficult and too condensed. Speaking for myself, I can only say that Dr Jones has struck as good a balance as is possible, so that, even a reader who doesn't understand it all will at least get a sense of the way in which Freud's thinking was developing. I think he dismisses the anthropologists' objections to *Totem and Taboo* too cavalierly, but I am not a competent judge.

The biographer of a historian is one of the luckiest of men. The private lives of natural scientists or of artists are of no public importance—the work of the former has no necessary relation to his life or, at least, is not required in order to judge the value of his work and since the work of the artist is openly subjective, a "feigned" history, what matters is not what happened to him but what he has made his experiences into. But in the case of a historian, curiosity about his person is legitimate for they are a help in assessing his work.

> "The unworthiness of human beings, even of analysts," wrote Freud once, "has always made a deep impression on me, but, why should analyzed people be altogether better than others? Analysis makes for *unity*, but not necessarily for *goodness*. I do not agree with Socrates and Putnam that all our faults arise from confusion and ignorance."

An excellent remark, but I think it probable that, wherever he may have to get his goodness from, an analyst has also to be a good person, which does not mean, of course, a faultless one.

As Freud's biographer, Dr Jones has, aside from his literary gifts, the great advantage of being the only one of his close friends who was neither Jewish nor Viennese.

The rest, including Freud himself, lived—and not entirely because they had to; they, also, rather enjoyed it—in a middle class ghetto, suspicious of the gentile world and even of Jews from other cultures. It is obvious, for instance, that, whatever blame attaches to Jung for the split, this suspicion played an unfortunate role. As a gentile (I am surprised that, as a Welshman, Dr Jones feels himself a member of an oppressed race, but I must take his word for it) and one who has traveled widely, Dr Jones has a certain detached eye which notes many things as interesting which the other members of the circle might have taken for granted. Why do so many Jews seem to have trouble with their "Konrad"? Why are so many Jewish men, like Freud, a combination of Poppa and a Queen-Bee? so that their friends never know quite where they stand: one may be out of favor or in without being conscious of having done anything?

A biographer requires knowledge, love and detachment: Dr Jones possesses them all and, in consequence, has succeeded brilliantly in painting us a portrait, human enough to be credible, yet unmistakably great and noble. He shows us, what are always observable in an outstanding man, the contradictions in Freud's character, his credulity and his scepticism, his secretiveness and his indiscretion, his capacity for affection and his fear of betrayal, yet these combine into a single real person. We see a man passionately devoted to his work and certain of its importance and for that very reason little interested in his personal fame and able to laugh at himself. How nice it is that one, whose psychology might be criticized for looking at life too exclusively from the male point of view, should himself have confessed: "The great question that has never been answered and which I have not yet been able to answer, despite my thirty years of research into the feminine soul, is 'What does a woman want?'" And one wishes that all those people who think of analysis as a device for getting a brand-new personality in place of their own would read Freud's warning: "A man should not strive to eliminate his complexes but to get into accord with them: they are legitimately what directs his conduct in the world." Freud cannot be blamed for what journalists and literary folk have done with his ideas, but there are too many persons to-day who believe they have Freud's sanction for measuring their value and state of psychological health by the quantitative amount of sexual gratification they are getting, just as there are others who imagine that an unhappy childhood relieves them of all obligation to behave well. For such people I can imagine no better corrective than reading Dr Jones' biography and discovering that Freud himself was an embodiment of the Bourgeois ideal at its best, hardworking, a good husband and parent, honest about money, unobtrusively charitable and with an aesthetic distaste for all pathological types and extremes. Our lives are more formed, for better or for worse, by the individuals upon whom we try to model ourselves than by any other factor, even if we belong to the minority with an interest in ideas: Dr Jones' biography is one of those books that will not only give much pleasure but will also do much good.

The Griffin, November 1955

A Self-Policing People

Exploring English Character.
By Geoffrey Gorer. Criterion Books. $8.50.

On December 31st, 1950, an article by Mr Gorer appeared in *The People*, a Sunday newspaper with a readership of some twelve million, in which he appealed for volunteers to fill up a questionnaire he had prepared. Within three weeks, nearly fifteen thousand had asked for it and then, most surprisingly, 75% answered it. Five thousand of these were selected and Mr Gorer's work began. As a sample, Mr Gorer confesses, the 18–34 age group is a little over-represented, the over-65 group and the top 10%, economically and socially, underrepresented. But, on the whole, he and we can be satisfied that the results obtained give an accurate picture of the attitude of the British People toward such matters as the family, neighbors, courtship, sex, marriage, bringing-up children, religion and law and order. The making up of such a questionnaire is, of course, a fiendishly difficult business. Different classes may understand a phrase differently. Thus, a number of the respondents made the statement that they knew more neighbors to speak to than they knew by sight, indicating that in some circles "to know someone by sight" must mean something more like knowing his name and family. Again, it is all too easy to forget a key question, as Mr Gorer forgot to ask for specific information on the control and management of the family budget, whether husband or wife have sole authority or share it, etc. Sometimes, of course, this information was offered voluntarily, but the lack of a definite question which would have elicited it from all turned out to be unfortunate, since one of the most frequent causes of marital quarrels is money.

I have no space in a brief notice like this to discuss in detail the information Mr Gorer received and the conclusions he draws from it, which is a good thing since reading his book has all the excitement of reading a detective story in which suspense is half the fun.

I will confine myself, therefore, to two points: the British attitude towards the bringing up of children, and their attitude towards the police.

English, as Mr Gorer points out, is the only language in which identically the same word is used for the place where children are reared and the place where plants are reared. A new-born child is not regarded as innocent, but rather as a wild plant which may well become a noxious weed unless it is pruned and civilized by its elders. Thus, to the question *When do you think toilet-training should begin?*, the answers ran as follows.

	Fathers %	Mothers %
from birth	50	25
before six months	45	69
before one year	60	84
between one and two	10	7

And here are the answers to *How do you think a really naughty child should be punished?*

	for boys	for girls
Deprivative (food, pocket-money etc.)	58	54
Restraint (sending to bed etc.)	10	10
Verbal	17	17
Slapping and Spanking	21	18
Caning and Thrashing	F. 21; M. 14	F. 11; M. 8

    (about 50% of the respondents, however, disapproved of this last form of punishment)

On the complementary question of rewards for good behaviour, a slight majority disapproved of them, and—a contrast to the States—nearly half disapprove of their children being paid money for doing chores for their neighbors.

Except in the lower working class, the form of naughtiness most expected and most frowned on is any form of aggression, bad temper, cruelty to animals or other children etc.

England must be the only country in the world where, among all age-groups and classes, even among those who have themselves been in trouble, the police are both admired and liked. But then the English Police Force is an unique institution. Unarmed except with a truncheon, living at home not in barracks, the average English policeman has spent some years in another job. Aside from certain age and height requirements, no special qualifications are demanded, and selection is made by personal interview alone. From the very beginning the character trait regarded as most essential in a candidate has been "a perfect command of his temper," something, evidently, that is not asked of a New York cop.

Whether or no the establishment of a police force of this kind has been, as Mr Gorer believes, its chief cause, there is no doubt that, during the last century, an astonishing change has come over the English: a revenant from Elizabethan, Hogarthian or even Dickensian London would find it difficult to recognize his descendants. "Where," he might ask, "is the bear-baiting, the public executions, the violence, the drunkenness, the jobs?" I don't know what the statistics are for other countries, but the following figures seem to me amazing. In 1841 the number of criminal commitments per hundred thousand of the population was 174.6; fifty years later it was 40, a drop of no less than 80%: moreover, in the single decade of 1851–61 there was a drop of 42%. Within a hundred years, the English have become, in large measure, a self-policing society. I myself witnessed a curious exhibition of this when, two or three years ago, I was in London at the time when meat was taken off rationing and price controls. Immediately, as in New York in 1946, the prices soared but within one week they had fallen to a slightly lower level than under rationing because, instinctively and without any organisation, housewives abstained from buying.

Naturally, as for all good things, the English have had to pay a price for this transformation. The unconscious energy they have to spend suppressing impulses towards aggression has made them, Mr Gorer thinks, a little slothful, uninterested in sexuality to the point where it is a danger to married life, and, perhaps, a little dull.

While the symptoms are obvious enough, I am not completely in agreement with Mr Gorer's psychological explanation, if I have understood it rightly. Every organism has a certain drive to preserve itself and to reproduce itself. The only reason for labelling this drive "aggressive" is that it is the source from which we can derive the psychic energy for aggression properly so-called, that is, the desire, from motives of revenge or to compensate for some feeling of inadequacy, to dominate or injure others. There are moments when Mr Gorer almost seems to suggest that the reason why the English have come to frown so on aggression is that, by nature, they are more liable to it than other societies. This I doubt. The negative aspects of their cultural attitude, which Mr Gorer notes, seem to me due to the unfortunate association habits of the unconscious, which, when told that aggression in the second sense as I have defined it is tabu, will extend this prohibition to aggression in the first sense—hence, for example, the notorious badness of English teeth.

Aggression feeds on aggression; the more I am kicked, the more likely it is that I shall want to kick others. Naturally, anybody in whom, for one reason or another, aggressive impulses are particularly strong will find English society difficult to live in, and may break out in sudden crimes of violence or, as some of Mr Gorer's respondents only too hideously suggest, may indulge their sadism with a good conscience in disciplining their children. I think however that such misfits are uncommon and becoming rarer—school-life for the upper middle classes has become very much gentler even since I was at school—and that the English have less trouble with aggression than many other societies because they have less cause to feel it. Many English mothers may still be starting toilet-training too early—that is a matter of ignorance—but their intention and guiding principle, to civilise the wild, is the only one upon which a civilised society can be founded. Long live the word "nursery."

The Griffin, December 1955

Reflections on *The Magic Flute*

Even the most ardent opera fans, who can easily take such absurdities as the plot of *I Puritani*, are apt to find the libretto of *The Magic Flute* hard to swallow, and I think with some justification, though they do not always know what upsets them. So long as an opera libretto is just that and no more, we ask of it only that it shall provide lyrical characters and lyrical situations; but if, whether by accident or design, it should have a significance in itself, apart from anything the composer may do with it, then any muddle or contradictions in the way the story is told cannot be covered up by the music, even when the latter is by Mozart.

It is highly dangerous for a librettist, unless he knows exactly what he is ding, which Schikaneder and Giesecke certainly did not, to make use of fairy-story material, for such almost always expresses universal and profound human experiences which will make a fool of any hack who ignores or trivialises them. If the libretto of *The Magic Flute* seems peculiarly silly, it is because a proper treatment of its material would have made it one of the greatest librettos ever written.

Don Juan is a character of profound extra-musical significance, but he cannot be said to have a story since, by definition, he cannot or will not change himself; he can only be shown as triumphant and invulnerable as in *Rigoletto* or in his fall as in *Don Giovanni*; he cannot be shown as both in the same opera, for the transition from triumph to ruin depends not on him but on the will of Heaven. The characters in *The Magic Flute*, on the other hand, have a real history in which what happens next always depends upon what they choose now.

To discover what, if anything, can be done to improve the libretto, one must begin by trying to detect what the elements of the story are about. It seems to me that there are two themes, both of great interest. The first and most basic of these is the story of a change in relation between the Dionysian principle and the Appollonian, Night and Day, the instinctive and the rational, the unconscious and the consciousness, here symbolised as female and male respectively.

What has hitherto been a relationship of antagonism, the war between the Queen and Sarastro, is finally replaced by a relationship of mutual affection and reconciliation, the marriage of Pamina and Tamino. (Before I knew any German, I always imagined that Sarastro was the estranged husband of the Queen. I seem to remember someone once telling me that Pamina's father was a renegade priest from Sarastro's Brotherhood, but I have never been able to find a text of *The Magic Flute* in which this information is given: all we are told is that he was the maker of the Flute itself.) Though the conscious and rational must take the responsibility for the instinctive and hence be the "superior" partner, neither can exist without the other. What the libretto fails to make clear is that, though the Queen must be defeated in order that the New Age may come, her defeat completes Sarastro's task; he must now hand on his crown to Tamino and pass away like Prospero in *The Tempest*, a work to which I shall have occasion to refer later. I suspect that Freemasonry is partly responsible for their vagueness on this point, but what is most surprising about the librettists is that they should have allowed the Queen to play such a positive role in the action to save Tamino's life, to give him Pamina's portrait and, even further, the magic flute without which he could never have gotten through the trials successfully. Again, whether by sheer luck or by sound instinct, the messengers of the Gods, i.e. the three Boy Spirits, are equally at home in the Queen's realm and Sarastro's.

I say surprising because to allow the Night a creative role is very untypical of Enlightenment doctrine and, had they denied it to the Queen, they would have spared themselves the most obvious criticism which is always brought against them, namely, that without any warning, the audience has suddenly to switch its sympathies at the end of the First Act. There seemed to Mr Kallman and myself nothing that we could do about that except retroactively, allowing Sarastro some lines in Act Two in which he reflects upon their relationship.

The other defect in the handling of this theme is one of taste rather than understanding; the perfectly proper symbolisation of the two Principles as male and female gave the librettists the opportunity which, alas, they could not resist, to make cheap vaudeville jokes about women. Lines like *Ein Weib tut wenig, plaudert viel*, or *hinab mit den Weibern zur Hölle*, or the whole duet *Bewahret euch vor Weibertücken*, therefore, we have changed to something which is, we hope, both more courteous and more psychologically accurate.

The second theme is an educational one: how does a person discover his vocation and what does this involve? At the beginning of the opera Tamino has been wandering about the desert without aim or direction, driven merely by vague dissatisfaction and, therefore, like all adolescents, in danger from forces in the depth of his nature which he does not understand or control (the serpent). Saved from this, he is shown the picture of Pamina and falls in love with it, i.e. he discovers, he believes, his future vocation, but only the future will show if this belief is genuine or fantastic; he has, as yet, no notion of what this vocation will involve. That is what Sarastro has to teach him, namely, that any vocation demands faith, patience, and courage: consequently he has to undergo the ordeal of doubt, the three ladies in the Quintet, *Wie, wie, wie*, the test of his patience, having to keep silence even though it makes Pamina suffer, and the test of his courage, the trials by Fire and Water.

Pamina, for her part, as the representative of the emotions has to learn humility through being pestered by Monostatos, acceptance of other values besides those of the emotions, by enduring Tamino's incomprehensible silence, the breaking of past ties, her mother's curse, and finally, in company with her lover, an equal courage. In Act II, as written, her troubles with Monostatos and the Queen precede her suffering caused by Tamino's silence and departure. We have reversed this order for the following reasons. It seems unnatural that, having seen her fall into his arms at the end of Act I, when we see her next she seems to have forgotten altogether about Tamino. Secondly, the effect upon her of Monostatos and her mother would be a much greater temptation to suicidal despair if it came after she imagines her lover has deserted her than before, when she could console herself with the thought of him or even call on him for help and guidance.

Thirdly, this order makes better sense of her appearance in the Finale with a dagger. As the libretto stands, the Queen gives her a dagger, Monostatos takes it away from her, a long interval elapses in which she and we forget all about the instrument and then, suddenly, there it is again. To make Tamino's now earlier farewell plausible, he does not, in our version, depart straight away for the trials but for a preparatory period of solitude and instruction, and, after *in diesen heiligen Hallen*, the First Priest comes to report to Sarastro on his progress.

Over against Tamino the Quest Hero, who has to *become* authentic, stands Papageno, the uncorrupted child of Nature, for whom authenticity means accepting the fact that he *is* what he is. Quite properly, his hut lies in the Queen's realm, not Sarastro's. He successfully passes his trial and is rewarded with his mirror image, Papagena, but since his trial takes place during the second piece of spoken dialogue in Act II which often gets cut, the audience does not always realise what it is. Asked if he is prepared to take the trials by Fire and Water like his master, he says no, they are not for the likes of him. Threatened then by the Priest that if he refuses he will never win Papagena, he replies, "In that case, I'll remain single." It is by this last answer that his humility is revealed and for which he receives his reward.

This clear division between the Hero who must be brave enough to dare and the Hero who must be humble enough to stay home, is smudged in the libretto owing to Schikenader's actor's vanity which wanted to be on the stage as much as possible and get laughs all the time. For example, it is absurd and embarrassing to have Papageno present and being "funny" during the pathetic climax of *Ach, ich fühl's*. Tamino can take vows because for him they have meaning and the audience has the dramatic excitement of wondering whether he will have the strength to keep them. A child of Nature cannot take vows because they apply to the future and he exists in a continuous present; there is no interest in hearing Papageno take a vow to silence which we know perfectly well in advance he will not keep because the notion of a vow is incomprehensible to him.

The only trial, therefore, we have allowed him is that of being frightened by the three ladies in the *Wie, wie, wie* Quintet, from which, anyway, for musical reasons, he cannot be absent. This fright confirms his decision not to accompany Tamino, he is officially excused from doing so, and the two friends say good-by to each other. Only after he has left, i.e. shortly before Pamina's entrance, is the vow of silence imposed upon Tamino. We then found that we could make use of his being on his own to solve a problem of action. With our re-arrangement of the order of the number, Pamina is left alone on stage after the Trio. *Soll ich dich, Teurer, nicht mehr sehn?*, and the next number, Monostatos' aria, *Alles fühlt der Liebe Freuden*, requires that she be asleep. Here Papageno and his glockenspiel came in handy.

A comedian, naturally, requires a companion as a foil so we have turned the Second Priest, who is appointed to look after him, into a comic character.

Beside Papageno, the uncorrupted child of Nature, stands Monostatos, his corrupted twin. Like Papageno, he is incapable of daring the trials by Fire and Water; unlike the former, however, he lacks the humility which would accept a variety of Papagena; no, he demands the heroine, Tamina. He is, in fact, clearly a brother of Caliban. It is impossible to remove entirely the feeling that Sarastro, the great educator, is rather careless in leaving Pamina in the hands of such a person even after in Act I he has discovered what he is like, but, in the scene where Sarastro banishes him, we have taken a cue from *The Tempest*, and attributed to the former the same motive for keeping Monostatos in his realm as Prospero gives for Caliban's presence.

We have written all the spoken dialogue in heroic couplets except for the wooing scene between Papageno and Papagena which is in fifteeners with end and internal rhymes. Verse seemed to us the right medium for the spoken word in an *opera magica* like this one: it obliterates any trace of *verismo* and it keeps the comic passages within decent bounds. Here, at least, the translator-adapter can be certain that, however feeble his effort, it cannot be worse than the original which is beneath contempt.

To clarify what I have written, let me finish by giving the order of the numbers in Act Two as arranged by Mr Kallman and myself, with the original order in figures on the right:

1.	Sarastro and Chorus, *O Isis und Osiris.*	1.
2.	Priests' Duet, *Bewahret euch.*	2.
3.	Three ladies, Tamino, Papagena, *Wie, wie, wie.*	3.
4.	Three spirits, *Seid uns zum zweitenmal.*	7.
5.	Pamina, *Ach, ich fühl's.*	8.
6.	Sarastro, Tamino, Pamina, *Soll ich dich, Teurer.*	10.
7.	Monostatos, *Alles fühlt der Liebe.*	4.
8.	Queen of the Night, *Der Hölle Rache.*	5.
9.	Sarastro, *In diesen Heiligen Hallen.*	6.
10.	Chorus, *O Isis und Osiris, welche Wonne.*	9.
11.	Papageno, *Ein Mädchen oder Weibchen.*	11.
12.	Finale.	12.

Center: A Magazine of the Performing Arts, December 1955

Putting It in English

A Translator Discusses the Problems of
Changing an Opera's Language

The task of the translator is simple enough to state. His version must convey the general sense of the original words and reproduce all points of emotional and dramatic intensity. It must conform to the musical prosody, be singable and, in addition, competent verse—not operese. And the literary style must be in keeping with the period in which the opera is set or felt.

In the case of the English language, his first difficulty is, of course, the scarcity of the pure open vowels required for a high tessitura. A translator of *The Magic Flute*, for instance, looks at a couplet that is easy to translate and scribbles down:

> Now let my approach be courageous and sure:
> My purpose is honest and noble and pure

only to find that he is expecting the poor tenor to sing "pure" on a sustained high G.

Fortunately for him, few librettos have the literary distinction of *Falstaff* or *Der Rosenkavalier*. Usually, in translating the arias, he has a free hand, provided he conveys the general emotion expressed. It is in dramatic interchanges, where the exact sense of a particular word may be the essential point, that the difficulties occur.

Thus, one of the most beautiful moments of *The Magic Flute* occurs in the finale of Act I, when, in reply to Papageno's frightened question as to what to say now, Pamina cries out: "Die Wahrheit!" Dramatically, nothing will do here but the literal sense: "The Truth." But the prosody demands an extra syllable. It is impossible to spread truth over two notes and sing "troo-hooth" without sounding funny. "Truthful" has no intensity and any word added for the second syllable detracts something. I do not believe any satisfactory solution is possible; we, certainly, have not found it.

In his relation to the composer, the translator is in a different position from the original librettist. The latter writes his verses without any notion of the music to which they are going to be set, but the translator knows the music already and probably knows it better than the text.

If, as one assumes, he is a competent versifier, he can, without too much difficulty, copy the form of the original verses, their metres, rhymes, etc., and know that, if he does this accurately, his words will conform to the notes. It does not necessarily follow, however, that he should be content with this. The ideal goal he should set himself, whether attainable or not, is to make the audience believe, when his version is performed, that his are the words that the composer actually set.

Since every language has its unusual peculiarities, this can mean that a too faithful copy of the original may sometimes be a falsification. In comparison with German, for example, English has far fewer syllables upon which a run can be made or that sound well when spread over more than one note.

Because of this fact, we have, in a number of places, supplied more syllables than exist in the original. If it be asked: "Is the effect on the ear the same?", the answer is: "No. The English sounds more staccato than the German." It is our view—debatable, of course—that, if it is to sound natural and, incidentally, audible, in English, it should be more staccato.

Whatever liberties he may take with the text, the first principle of a conscientious translator is: No tampering with the notes. He may, nevertheless, come to places where he feels that an exception ought to be made and that, could he summon the composer from the grave, the composer would approve of an alteration. If such an occasion does arise, it is always, I think, one in which the particular structure of the notes is, so to speak, an accident of the verbal prosody of the original libretto rather than an essential musical idea.

In the case of a work like *The Magic Flute*, it is very understandable if many ears are irritated by the slightest deviation from a score they have known and loved so well and for so long, just as my British ear is irritated when Americans pray, "Our Father, *who* art in Heaven" instead of "*which* art."

To such, one can only reply that one has every sympathy for them, but that *The Magic Flute* neither can nor ought to be identical with *Die Zauberfloete*, and that to judge the former, whether favorably or adversely, it should be listened to as if for the first time.

The New York Times, 8 January 1956

ADDENDA TO
PROSE II

Three items came to light after *Prose II* was published that would have been included in that volume had they been discovered earlier. The first was intended for publication in 1939 but is published here for the first time; had it been published as Auden intended it would have been included in the main text of *Prose II*. The remaining two items are additions to the appendices.

A further note may be added to the appendix in *Prose II* that lists Auden's unwritten or unpublished work. Gore Vidal alluded in "'Everything Is Yesterday,'" *New York Review of Books*, 28 February 2002, to "Auden whom *The New York Times* refused to take on as a columnist in its Sunday book section on the ground that he was sexually degenerate." In a letter to me on 26 February 2002 Vidal explained that after J. Donald Adams "let slip the feather" as the writer of the "Speaking of Books" column for the *New York Times Book Review* in 1947 or 1948, Auden proposed himself as Adams's successor but was turned down; Vidal learned this story from Christopher Isherwood (who was in New York in the summer of 1947), supplemented by a cryptic word or two from Auden. Adams in fact wrote the "Speaking of Books" column for many years before and after 1947–48, so this report may be only partly correct.

E. M. FORSTER

This brief note was evidently written for the same bookseller's catalogue of modern literature that included Auden's similar note, "Louis MacNeice" (see note to *Prose II*, p. 35). Forster is not one of the many authors listed in the catalogue, and Auden's contribution was never published. The text follows the manuscript (now in a private collection). Auden omitted the first word of the title *A Passage to India*.

E. M. Forster

Those who only know Mr E. M. Forster as the author of *Passage to India* may be misled into thinking that his primary concern is with Social Problems. Nothing could be further from the truth: in fact, his unsympathetic characters are precisely those nurses and schoolmasters who want to reform others. Differences of class, nationality, color, interest him, not in themselves, but in the test that they offer to the individual. They are like the witches and dragons in fairy stories whom only the true Prince can overcome, and by whom the selfish and cowardly are destroyed. To me, the peculiar quality of his books lies in the contrast between the triviality of their objective incidents—things that would earn at most a few lines in the social columns of a local paper—and their immense subjective significance to the actors involved. The Powers of the Air hover over the vicarage tea-table; a discussion between two ladies in a third-class railway carriage is attended by Lucifer, Son of the Morning.

In our age when so many artists identify importance with news value, tragedy with physical violence, this is refreshing. Mr E. M. Forster is my favorite living English novelist.

Written for, but not printed in,
We Moderns: Gotham Book Mart 1920–1940,
catalogue 42, December 1939

A Lecture in a College Course

Among the lectures listed in Auden's course "Poetry and Culture" at the New School for Social Research, spring term 1940, was "The lyric of condensed experience", delivered on 24 April 1940 (and listed in *Prose II*, p. 465). Marianne Moore took notes at the lecture and quoted them in a talk she delivered at the Grolier Club, New York, 21 December 1948, "Humility, Concentration, and Gusto"; her talk was printed in the *Gazette of the Grolier Club*, May 1949. She says in her talk: "a poem is a concentrate and has, as W. H. Auden says: 'an immediate meaning and a possible meaning; as in the line:

> Or wedg'd whole ages in a bodkin's eye

where you have forever in microscopic space; and when George Herbert says:

> I gave to Hope a watch of mine,
> But he an anchor gave to me,

the watch suggests both the brevity of life and the longness of it; and an anchor makes you secure but holds you back.'"

The first quotation (slightly emended) is from Pope's *The Rape of the Lock*; the second is from Herbert's "Hope". Moore quoted the same passage in a letter to Bryher [pseudonym of Winifred Ellerman], 7 May 1940, where she named Auden's lecture (Yale University Library).

An Endorsement

An advertisement for the American release of Jean Cocteau's film *The Eternal Return* (the English-language version of *L'Eternel retour*) at the 55th Street Playhouse, New York, in February 1948, included a comment by Auden, the source of which is unknown: "There could not be a better screen version of the Tristan and Isolde story." (I have omitted the exclamation point found at the end of all such comments in contemporary advertisements.) The advertisement appeared in the *New York Times*, 6 February 1948, and probably also in other newspapers. For another reference to this film, see "Some Reflections on Opera as a Medium" (p. 252).

APPENDICES

Record Sleeves and Program Notes

CAV AND PAG

Auden's essay published under this title was written for the libretto booklet that accompanied the RCA long-playing record album *Cavalleria Rusticana and I Pagliacci*, released in New York in 1953. Because it is an essay, not a set of notes, it appears in the main text of this volume, p. 358.

W. H. AUDEN READING

Caedmon Records was founded in 1952 by Barbara Cohen and Marianne Roneyill to produce recordings of poets reading their own poems. Their long-playing disc of Auden's reading, released in spring 1954 under the title above, was recorded on 12 December 1953. This was the first long-playing record devoted entirely to Auden's poems; he had made 78-r.p.m. recordings in 1940 for the National Council of Teachers of English; in 1941 for Harvard Vocarium Records; and in 1949 for the Library of Congress Recording Laboratory; and he had contributed two poems to an anthology recording, *Pleasure Dome*, edited by Lloyd Frankenberg, and released as a long-playing record and as three 78-r.p.m. discs by Columbia Records in 1949.

For the sleeve of the Caedmon recording Auden wrote the notes reprinted below. The poems gathered as "Five Lyrics" (only two of them named in the notes) were: "As I walked out one evening", "Jumbled in the common box", "Seen when night is silent", "My dear one is mine as mirrors are lonely" (identified as "Miranda's Song" only in Auden's notes), and "Sing, Ariel, sing".

In trying to think what I could say about these poems which would have any point or value, I have let myself be guided by my own experience in listening to other poets reciting their work. The formal structure of a poem is not something distinct from its meaning but as intimately bound up with the latter as the body is with the soul. When one reads a poem in a book one grasps the form immediately, but when one listens to a recitation, it is sometimes very difficult to "hear" the structure. If these notes sound a bit schoolmasterly, I am sorry, but it is very easy to ignore them.

In Memory of W. B. Yeats. An elegy in three parts. Part I is in unrhymed free verse, Part II, the shortest, in five-foot iambics, irregularly rhymed, Part III in rhymed four-foot trochaic quatrains.

In Praise of Limestone. This poem is a kind of prelude to the series of Bucolics on Side Two. Unrhymed, the odd lines contain thirteen syllables, the even eleven.

The Capital. Unrhymed quatrains; each line contains five stresses.

School Children. Unrhymed quatrains; the first three lines of each stanza have five stresses, the fourth three.

As He Is. A poem about the nature of man. In each stanza a word in the third line re-occurs in the fourth, and a word in the seventh re-occurs in the eighth.

Five Lyrics. Nothing needs, I think, to be said about these. *As I walked out one evening* is an attempt to write a poem in the folk-song style; *Miranda's Song* is a villanelle.

Precious Five. An address to the five organs, the nose, the ears, the hands, the eyes, the tongue, through which a man establishes relations with the outside world.

Bucolics. Seven poems entitled *Winds, Woods, Mountains, Lakes, Islands, Plains, Streams,* which have in common the theme of the relation of man, as a historical or history-making person, to nature.

Winds is unrhymed; in the first half lines of six syllables alternate with lines of seven, in the second half the order is reversed, and the sevens precede the sixes. Arthur O'Bower as a name for the wind is taken from a nursery riddle.

Woods. Six-line stanzas of five foot iambics, rhymes ababcc.

Mountains. The syllabic lengths of the lines in each stanza are 11, 7, 11, 7, 11, 13, 13, 9, 5, 11, 5. The two short pairs, the sevens at the beginning and the fives at the end, rhyme.

Lakes. Six-line unrhymed stanzas; the odd lines are six-foot iambics, the even five-foot; three lines in every stanza have feminine endings.

Islands. Traditional ballad metre with only the even lines rhyming.

Plains. Eight-line unrhymed stanzas with eleven syllables to each line.

Streams. In each quatrain, lines 1 and 2 have twelve syllables each and masculine endings, line 3 has nine syllables and a feminine ending. A syllable within line 1 rhymes with a syllable within line 3, the final syllable of line 2 rhymes with the penultimate syllable of line 4, and the penultimate syllable of line 3 rhymes with a syllable within line 4.

An Evening of Elizabethan Verse and Its Music

This recording was part of Auden's collaboration with Noah Greenberg and his early-music group the New York Pro Musica (described in *Libretti*, pp. 750–51). The group performed at the 92nd Street YM-YWHA in New York where Auden gave poetry readings, and they seem to have begun working together in 1953. Their first collaboration was a concert of Elizabethan verse and music performed on 30 and 31 January 1954, in which Auden read the text of each song and the group then performed the music. Out of that concert grew the anthology described on p. 633 and a Columbia long-playing record issued in 1955 with the above title; the performers are listed on the sleeve and label as "W. H. Auden and the New York Pro Musica, directed by Noah Greenberg".

Auden's untitled sleeve notes appear below. In the paragraph that begins "Fortunate for both" I have emended "controversy over an" to "controversy over and".

When one considers the English school of madrigals and lute songs, it is hard to say which is the more extraordinary, the number of good composers and their fertility, or the brevity of the period within which they flourished. Dr Fellowes' collection, *English Madrigal Verse*, includes the work of forty-five composers, and the printing of the verses which they set, the majority of which are quite short, requires some six hundred pages of close type; yet, between the first published music of this kind, *The Psalms and Sonnets* of William Byrd, in 1588, and the last, the *Madrigals and Airs* of Walter Porter, lie no more than forty-two years and, moreover, there is very little written after 1615—magnificent as it is, Tompkins' anthem on the death of Absalom (side 2, band 6) must already have sounded a bit old-fashioned to the ears of his contemporaries.

Most of the material set is secular and, indeed, the school begins just as the great period of English church music, which had exerted considerable influence on the continent, was coming to an end.

The initial stimulus came from Italy—some of the composers had studied there—but an indigenous style, suited to the English language, was developed very rapidly. At least one composer, John Dowland, was famous in Europe, but, on the whole, the school was little known outside England. One can never say with certainty just why a style should decline and disappear when it does. In the case of this late Elizabethan and early Jacobean music, changes in social habit due to the Puritans, the Civil War, and the Restoration, played a part, no doubt, but the spread of the baroque style from Italy was the most decisive factor.

There are two extreme schools of thought which disapprove of setting verses with real poetic merit to music. There are lovers of poetry who hold that not only can nothing be added to a good poem by music but also something must be lost, that music, by distorting the rhythms and tempi of the spoken word, is bound to ruin it. There are lovers of singing, on the other hand, (few of them, I suspect, are actually composers) who hold that all a composer requires are so-and-so-many syllables of such-and-such a quality, that their verbal meaning is irrelevant and that good poetry is too intractable, too insubordinate, to be settable.

Both doctrines are more popular, perhaps, in English-speaking countries than in others. One reason for this may be that it is harder for a solo singer or a choir to make English words audible than those of other European languages. In a polysyllabic language, the listening ear may miss a syllable but still get the word; in a language like English which abounds in monosyllables, a single syllable may be the key to the meaning of a whole sentence. Further,

English is relatively poor in words ending in a vowel. If a word ending in a consonant is being sung on a sustained note, it is difficult to complete it audibly without doing violence to the music. Take the word *dark*, for instance. A singer who cares most about his vocal effects will be tempted to sing *da . . .* ; if he thinks about enunciation, he is apt to finish with an explosive little accent which is musically not there and sing *da . . rkè*.

The fact remains however that, despite all such difficulties, during the period represented by this record, good composers deliberately chose good poems to set, and good poets were glad to write verses for them. Shakespeare did not write *Come away, come away, death* or *Full fathom five* to be recited, nor did Dowland think of *I saw my lady weeping* (side 1, band 7) as merely a series of vaguely sad syllables.

Of course, not all good poetry is settable. No composer in his senses, for instance, if he were writing an opera on *Troilus and Cressida*, would attempt to set such a complicated succession of metaphors and images as the following.

> . . . Keep, then, the path;
> For emulation has a thousand sons
> That one by one pursue: if you give way,
> Or hedge aside from the direct forthright,
> Like to an entered tide they all rush by
> And leave you hindmost;
> Or, like a gallant horse fall'n in first rank
> Lie there for pavement to the abject rear
> Oerrun and trampled on.

Even if the words could be heard, the strain of attending to their meaning and listening to the music at the same time would be too much. Generally speaking, since music is essentially immediate and dynamic, those elements in language, like metaphor, which require reflection in order to grasp them, are dangerous. The limit of what is settable is probably reached in the poem attributed to Raleigh and set by Gibbons, *What is our life? A play of passion* (side 2, band 3) the whole of which is an elaboration of a single metaphor. Rather surprisingly, a dialectical playing with words seems well suited to musical treatment. The logical movement, the antitheses and repetitions "translate" so to speak. Moreover, the musical translation may throw new light on the poem. For example, I, personally, had always thought of Donne's poem *The Expiration* as serious and intense, an expression of suffering, but after hearing Ferrabosco's setting, I see it now as he interprets it, as *galante* rather than passionate.

Again, if not all good poetry is settable, neither is all settable verse of first-rate poetic merit. No one would include in an anthology of great poetry, for example, such madrigal verses as *Flora gave me sweetest flowers* (side 1, band 3) or *Sweet honey-sucking bees* (side 1, band 8). Nevertheless, even such pieces are well worth study by any serious poet who is interested in writing words for music. Their conventional hellenistic paraphernalia may be a bit boring to read, but conventional properties can be very serviceable to a composer, precisely because, being conventional, they are instantaneously recognizable. A composer welcomes a poem which expresses either a single state of feeling or an obvious contrast of states and a diction centered round the dynamic elements of language, interjections, imperatives, verbs of motion, etc.

The couplet

> For if one flaming dart come from her eye,
> Was never dart so sharp, ah, then you die

may not seem poetically very distinguished, but when one hears what Wilbye makes of it, one realizes how admirable for music is its structure.

Moreover, anyone who reads through the first half of Dr Fellowes' collection, the half devoted to madrigals, will be struck by two things, firstly, by the surprising number of verses which are not just convenient and trifling musical vehicles but beautiful in themselves and, secondly, by the appearance of a kind of short poem which was quite new in English poetry at the time. *Tan ta ra cries Mars* (side 1, band 1) is a good example. This would never have been written except to be used as a madrigal, yet the result is a poem at once beautiful and strange.

Fortunately for both poets and composers, the period was one of controversy over and experimentation in prosody. Even when the prosodic notions were odd—the poet-composer Campion spent much time experimenting with classical metres in English—the conscious attention paid to metrical values bore fruit. Listening to almost any of the lute songs, for example, Dowland's *In darkness let me dwell* (side 2, band 2) one is amazed at how scrupulously the vocal line conforms to the natural rhythm of the words, yet, at the same time, the notes form a real melody not a recitative. There is no wrenching of the natural accent and no racking out of a syllable over several notes, as one finds in baroque arias and which, at its worst, can produce such monstrosities as

When the bloo-hoo-hoom is o-hon the rye.

There is no other period of English vocal music, perhaps, in which both the lover of words and the lover of song are so equally satisfied.

Auden as Anthologist and Editor

IN THE quarterly periodical *Perspectives*, published from autumn 1952 through summer 1956 by Intercultural Publications, supported by the Ford Foundation and secretly sponsored by the United States Central Intelligence Agency, Auden was listed as a member of the Editorial Board, although he seems to have had no active role. In Britain the magazine was published as *Perspectives USA*.

The anthology *Riverside Poetry—1953* was subtitled "Poems by Students in Colleges and Universities in New York City, Selected by W. H. Auden, Marianne Moore, Karl Shapiro," with an introduction by Stanley Romaine Hopper. The poets who selected the contents made no other contribution to this volume.

As noted in *Prose II*, the magazine *Contemporary Poetry*, published at the Johns Hopkins University in Baltimore, listed Auden as a member of the advisory board in the numbers dating from spring 1946 through 1965, although he was probably only intermittently active.

Auden's editions of selected works by Edgar Allen Poe and Søren Kierkegaard are described in the textual notes.

THE YALE SERIES OF YOUNGER POETS

Auden selected, edited, and introduced volumes 45 through 55 in this annual series published by the Yale University Press; his choices were published each year from 1947 through 1959, except in 1950 and 1955, when he found no suitable manuscripts. The first years of his editorship are described in *Prose II*, pp. 459–60. The following account of Auden's editorship is based largely on George Bradley's introduction to *The Yale Younger Poets Series Anthology* (1998) and on further information generously provided by him.

Around the end of 1948, Eugene Davidson, the editor in charge of the series at the Yale University Press, began discussing with his colleagues his dissatisfaction with Auden's stewardship of the series. As he wrote in an internal memo to the faculty committee on publication on 29 December 1948: "My criticism of his choices . . . is that they seem to stem from a relatively small proportion of his time and creative energy. His last choice [by Rosalie Moore], for example, was merely the best of the two or three manuscripts we weeded out of those submitted, and while both his earlier choices [by Joan Murray and Robert Horan] were manuscripts he himself brought in, we are under the impression that he is doing what for him is a perfunctory job." Davidson had sounded out Louise Bogan on the possibility that she might replace Auden; she replied that she and Auden were good friends, that he was incapable of choosing a bad book, and that she would be willing to take on the job only if he preferred to give it up.

In March 1949, Davidson proposed to Auden that they meet to talk about the future of the series, and they met in his New York apartment during the last days of the month, just before he left for Italy on 1 April. Davidson told Bogan on 5 April: "I had a chance to see Mr Auden . . . and we had a somewhat inconclusive talk. With all the packing boxes and signs of sailing, there wasn't much room for a basic discussion about the Series and its future, so it looks as though we'll have to defer getting his approval for a change in the editorship until his return" (Yale University Archives). Bogan again made clear that she would replace Auden only if he chose to resign, and effectively made it impossible for Davidson to fire him.

A series of accidental and deliberate misunderstandings followed. Davidson wrote to Auden on 3 May, apparently asking if he wanted the submitted manuscripts sent to him in Italy or if it might be more convenient to let someone else take on the editorship. Auden seems to have ignored the letter. Davidson wrote again on 2 June, apparently emphasizing how inconvenient it was for Auden to act as editor from Italy. Auden replied on 9 June: "I'm quite willing to read the manuscripts but, of course, I shall understand if you would rather get someone nearer home and so save all the bother of shipping. It is a pity that they come along when they do and not in the winter."

This was no help to Davidson, who wrote again on 6 July with a copy of his unanswered letter of 3 May, adding that it was essential to have Auden's decision whether he wanted the manuscripts forwarded to him, and if it were not convenient, could he let them know so that someone else could act as editor in his absence. Auden replied on 10 July: "I must have misunderstood as I have been expecting the Mss to arrive. Parcels are apt to take some time. If you are therefore in a great hurry, you had better get someone on the spot to judge. If not, send them and I will read them immediately."

Thoroughly defeated, Davidson sent the manuscripts, which Auden read as soon as they arrived. On 8 August he reported: "I have read through all the mss for the *Yale Younger Poets* several times, and have come to the conclusion that none of them will quite do. After our conversation last March, I have assumed that you want me to set the standard high and not accept anything in which I don't wholeheartedly believe." Davidson now accepted this decision, and Auden wrote again on 21 August: "I'm glad you agree. I dispatched the Mss back, overcoming to do so, the most fantastic difficulties as the local P.O. had never seen parcels of that size, so I hope they arrive safely. I wrote letters direct to the three best candidates; for the rest I enclosed rejection slips in the Mss." (When Auden first accepted the editorship he had asked that no more than six manuscripts be submitted to him; Auden's letter implies that the press no longer honored this limit.)

Further details of Auden's editorship may be found in the notes to his introductions to the book he selected in 1950, Adrienne Cecile Rich's *A Change of World* (1951, p. 224); the book he selected in 1951, W. S. Merwin's *A Mask for Janus* (1952, p. 259); the book he selected in 1952, Edgar Bogardus's *Various Jangling Keys* (1953, p. 344); and the book he selected in 1953, Daniel G. Hoffman's *An Armada of Thirty Whales* (1954, p. 396).

On 20 August 1954, he reported to Davidson on that year's set of submissions: "After reading them all several times, I have come to the conclusion that none of the mss submitted this year for the Yale Younger Poets will quite do. Three or four are highly competent, there are some good individual poems, but I cannot find one with an authentic note of its own, and I think we would be doing past and future contestants an injustice if we do not keep our standards as high as possible."

In 1955, Auden again found no manuscript worth printing among those the press sent him after its initial culling; the outcome of this is described in the notes to John Ashbery's *Some Trees* (1956, p. 580).

Auden's three final selections for the series are described in *Prose IV*.

POETS OF THE ENGLISH LANGUAGE

Plans for this multivolume anthology for the Viking Portable Library series seem to have taken shape while Auden's first volume for the series, the *Portable Greek Reader*, was in late stages of production. Auden probably suggested the project to the series editor, Pascal Covici, at one of their meetings about the Greek selection. Auden had earlier thought of his *Oxford Book of Light Verse* (1938) as a survey of a different poetic tradition from the lyric tradition emphasized in Sir Arthur Quiller-Couch's *Oxford Book of English Verse*, and now wanted to create a full-scale rival to the Quiller-Couch anthology.

Covici wanted Auden to work with an academic coeditor whose name could improve sales to the college market. Either Covici or, more probably, Auden suggested Norman Holmes Pearson, a Yale professor who had coedited with William Rose Benét *The Oxford Anthology of American Literature* (1938). Auden had met Pearson in 1940 through his friend Elizabeth Mayer; Pearson had helped make it possible for her to come to the United States as a refugee.

Auden and Pearson probably discussed the project when Auden lectured at Yale in February 1948. A final agreement was worked out at a meeting with Covici on 30 March. For both commercial and literary reasons, Pearson insisted that Auden should write the introductions himself; Auden did so, although the finished books give no indication that they are the work of only one of the two editors. Pearson wrote to Auden soon after the meeting, and Auden replied on 4 April 1948:

> Many thanks for your letter. I'm delighted too, about everything.
>
> Please don't do much work this summer on the selections because I shan't be able to, being out of reach of libraries and I don't want you to think I am just another lazy bohemian.
>
> My feeling at the moment is that our job is to concentrate on two things.
>
> > (1) The development of verse. (Chaucerian couplet, skeltonics, Wyatt, Sydney etc.)
> > (2) The dominant subject pre-occupations of the period (e.g. the Amor religion through Troilus to The Faerie Queen)
> > C. S. Lewis is an invaluable guide to the best passages in the minor writers like Hawes and Douglas.
>
> As to the introductions, whoever actually writes the words on paper, they must be real collaborations in the sense that everything that is said must be mutually agreed upon.

(Auden's letters to Pearson are in the Yale University Library.)

The original plan seems to have been for a four-volume anthology; Viking's cover letter to Auden on 6 April 1948, enclosing a contract, refers to volumes I through IV. Virtually all the planning, selecting, and writing for the anthology seems to have been done by Auden, while Pearson (whose career owed perhaps as much to his social connections as to his scholarship) commissioned Yale students to arrange for the Yale Library to make photocopies of the original texts of the older poems; Auden had insisted on using original versions rather than modernized reprints. Pearson's main contribution was to urge Auden to rethink some of his selections from American poets. Other suggestions came from Pearson's Yale colleagues whom he asked for help in locating some of the more obscure material.

Although Auden expected to do no work on the anthology during his summer in Italy in 1948, he evidently returned to New York with a list of selections. He reported to Pearson on 24 September 1948, "I have done quite a spot of work on suggested selections". Again on 7 November he reported "Have done a lot more work on the Anthologies", and two days later added, "I believe we are going to need 5 volumes." During the latter months of 1948 Auden sent or gave Pearson his lists of contents, frequently supplementing them afterward with additions and changes. Pearson seems to have been relatively inactive at this stage; Auden wrote him a worried note on 25 February 1949: "Hope you are not dead. When I am going to see you? Covici is stamping his feet."

Pearson became more active when Auden proposed his selections from nineteenth-century American poets, and one set of Pearson's comments prompted this undated reply from Auden:

You are a *beast*. My head is reeling and I feel I never want to read or write another line of poetry again, having just read through the *entire* poems of Bryant, Whittier and Lowell. (Goodness how prolific they were, too.). I got back [perhaps from a visit to the Harvard library in January 1949] only to realize that I'd forgotten Holmes who must wait for another day.

Bryant. I chose *Prairies* as his nature piece because of its local colour, and the Thanatopsis pseudo-philosophy is in it too. *The Snow-Shower* is technically nice and *To a Mosquito* though clumsy is an interesting attempt to be less refined than usual.

Whittier. They're all so *long*. *Invocation* admits a most unquakerish almost Cowperish melancholia [Whittier made a great point of his Quakerism] which makes me like him a bit better. The others, well, see for yourself.

Lowell. I see he's really the American Praed. *The Origin of Didactic Poetry* I particularly like and the two epigrams aren't at all bad. (His serious poems in the Queen's English won't do.)

Anyway, it looks as if we shan't be exactly copying the Oxford [*Anthology of American Literature*] Vol I.

An undated letter to Pearson reports: "Having at last obtained a copy of Thoreau's Poems and studied them carefully, I am dissatisfied with our selection"; this is followed by the original list and a proposed replacement, concluding "I do hope you will approve. (I *insist* that you do!)" Other lists sent by Auden include changes to the selections from Lowell, Holmes, Bryant, Whittier, Emerson, and Melville. All these lists differ greatly from the contents of the printed volumes, which were the product of much further cutting and changing.

Auden insisted on including a chronological table, similar to the one that Alan Ansen had prepared for *The Portable Greek Reader*. A preliminary typescript of the table, prepared by Ansen with extensive additions in Auden's hand, is among Auden's letters to Pearson in the Yale University Library; the preliminary version has five columns headed "General Events", "Church History", "Kings of England and Presidents of the United States", "Vital Statistics" (dates of writers' births and deaths), and "Time" (divided into twenty-five-year periods); because of the way the typescript is divided into multiple pages, it is unclear whether the first two of these headings were intended to precede or follow the next three. The beginning and ending of the part of the table intended for each volume is indicated in Auden's hand. In the published version, a part of this table appears after the introduction to each volume under the title "A Calendar of British and American Poetry", and the material in the typescript is reduced and rearranged into two outer columns headed "General Background" and "Direct History" and a central column headed "Date".

On 1 February 1949, while this chart was being prepared, Auden wrote to Pearson on another editorial question: "Am in complete agreement against *any* modernisation other than typographical þ, 3 and ? u for v)." (The question mark indicates doubt about substituting *u* for *v*.) In response to Auden's insistence on scholarly accuracy, Pearson commissioned his young Yale colleague E. Talbot Donaldson to emend the medieval texts and provide glosses for obscure words. Donaldson also provided a "Note on the Middle English Selections" that appeared in the first volume between the introduction and chronology.

Auden wrote the introductions in Italy in the late spring and early summer of 1949, and sent the manuscripts to Alan Ansen for checking and typing on 19 July. Pearson meanwhile continued to oversee the preparation of the texts of the poems. The original texts of many of the poems in the first two volumes could be found only in rare books that were not in the Yale Library, and Pearson asked Auden to write to Auden's friend John Hayward, the English bibliophile and scholar, for help in getting photocopies from perhaps a dozen such books. Hayward sent Auden a sharp reply on 29 October, suggesting that Professor Pearson ("I assume from his title that he is a scholar", Hayward wrote) should order the copies himself. Hayward, unlike Pearson, knew enough to consult catalogues of early printed books, and found that some of the titles that Pearson wanted Hayward to find for him in England could in fact be found only in American libraries. Auden forwarded this letter to Pearson, but Pearson's response is unknown; possibly he resorted to anthology texts rather than pursue the originals.

On 2 September 1949 Pearson reported to Auden that Malcolm Cowley, another editor at Viking, felt strongly that "we cannot afford to omit either Mrs Browning's *The Hounds of Heaven* [Pearson's muddle of Elizabeth Barrett Browning with Francis Thompson's *The Hound of Heaven*, an excerpt of which appears in the anthology] or the group around Dawson [his mistake for Dowson] who wrote at the close of the century." Auden held firm against both suggested inclusions.

Cowley also wanted biographical notes in the anthology; Pearson was prepared to accede and suggested to Auden that the table of dates be dropped. Auden replied to

Pearson later that month: "There are *under no circumstances* to be *any* biographical notes; and I am convinced that our [chronological] table is the proper way to handle all that. I think it is important to make a stand on this for the sake of the next generation of schoolteachers." Pearson seems again to have counselled retreat; on 8 November 1949, in a letter that included a long list of changes to the selections, Auden insisted:

> No, we must *not* give in about the biographies. (a) it is immoral. (b) an awful waste of our time. (c) we need every inch of space we have.
>
> Incidentally, I would like, but I suppose we couldn't do it, to date the poets not by their births and deaths but by the dates of their first and last volumes. Do you think we could dare?

Auden and Pearson ironed out further problems during meetings in the autumn. One confusion occurred when E. Talbot Donaldson questioned their choice of Book V (rather than III) of Chaucer's *Troilus and Criseide*. In fact, they had not chosen Book V; Auden had chosen all of Book III and about three hundred lines of Book V, but Pearson had included all of Book V by mistake. Auden explained in an undated letter: "I felt an awful pang when your M.E. friend wondered why we chose Book V of Troilus. Have just looked it up on my card which says *Book III* and also originally Book V (ll. 1538–1848). This must, at all costs, be changed." The printed book includes all of Book III and about five hundred lines from Book V.

Auden made some final changes to the contents in December 1949; a postcard to Pearson sent on 2 December is headed "Some last highhanded changes by W.H.A." Auden wrote to Chester Kallman on 27 December 1949: "The copy for the Viking Anthology has at last gone in and I believe that we are going to make lots of money but not this year" (Berg Collection). However, the contents were still subject to change; in a letter to Marianne Brock of the Mount Holyoke College English Department, Auden wrote: "am in the middle of a battle with Viking over cuts in our anthology, as we have exceeded our allotment of pages" (Mount Holyoke College).

The battle over excess pages seems to have been settled soon afterward. In a letter to Christopher Isherwood on 28 February 1950, Auden wrote: "Hope to be rich in a few years from a five volume anthology for Viking which I and a prof from Yale have just finished. I had to deal with the whole of English poetry in five introductions, an impossible job but I am not dissatisfied with my attempt" (Huntington Library).

Viking began sending galleys of the first volume early in 1950. On 18 February Auden reported to Pearson a blunder in the choice of texts:

> Have just been going through the galleys of Vol I. I imagine you, or probably Donaldson, will check them properly with the text.
>
> The only bad error I have found is in the Wyatt, where two of them, *My galley charged with forgetfulness*, and *They flee from me that sometime did me seek* have been copied from Tottel [*Tottel's Miscellany*] who altered lines ruining Wyatt's music. Have corrected these, but you better check.

Probably early in 1950, Auden wrote to Pearson:

> First a little anthology point to settle between us. I understand you want Index of First lines *and* titles together. This seems to me a little space-

filling and redundant if they have a list of contents at the beginning anyway but, perhaps, I am wrong. I should have thought first lines enough,
but let me know what you think.

The published indexes include both titles and first lines.

Viking remained unhappy with Auden's insistence that no biographical material
would be included. In April 1950 another Viking editor, Marshall Best, sent to a small
number of English professors (between twenty and thirty of them) the "Sample Pages"
from the anthology, as described in the textual notes (p. 710), together with a mar-
keting questionnaire asking for comments on the suitability of the books for college
courses. Best's cover letter asked especially for an opinion on whether or not to include biographical notes. A few weeks later Best reported to those who had replied
that the votes were divided on the question of biographical notes, and that Viking had
decided to offer a separate pamphlet of such notes, to be supplied to students at the
request of their teacher. Pearson supervised the preparation of the notes (probably
written by Yale graduate students) for this separate pamphlet, which was printed with
no indication of authorship. The biographical notes were incorporated into the five
volumes of the anthology when retitled paperback editions were published in 1957
(see p. 630).

Viking sent Auden galley proofs of the introductions in April and May 1950, when
he was again summering in Italy. He returned the introductions for volumes I and V
with an undated letter that asked, "Would you ask Professor Pearson to check the scansion of the Latin quotations in Vol I with an expert" (Viking Press archive). Auden
wrote to Pearson on 27 April 1950:

> As to your queries:
>
> (1) Introduction to Vol I. By all means cut "Totalitarian Hell". [But the
>   phrase remained as the final words of the introduction.]
> (2) Chapman's *Bismarck* [John Jay Chapman's "Lines on the Death of
>   Bismarck", first published in a magazine and shortened for book pub-
>   lication]. I think the reason why he cut the lines—the last three are
>   the published end—is obvious: they are inferior. My feeling is that
>   since it is a matter of lines *cut* after 1914, not of new lines added, we
>   should print the version the poet wished preserved. If we want to be
>   right donnish we can give a footnote.
>
> . . . . . .
>
> P.S. Viking sent me the galleys of the Introductions to Vols II and III
> which I have corrected and returned.
> P.P.S. If possible add to the charts:
>   1831. Bellini. *Norma.*

The addition to the chart was not made. On 6 June Auden wrote to Pearson from Italy,
"Still waiting to see the proofs of our famous chart."

Pearson then reported that Viking had asked the editors to arrange for dust-jacket
blurbs and had also asked for cuts that would permit the books to fit into multiples of
32-page signatures; also that manuscripts of Christopher Smart's poetry had been dis-

covered in the Harvard Library; unlike the reprinted texts of Smart that they had already chosen, these would not require payment to use. Auden replied on 6 July 1950:

> Your letter arrived yesterday overwhelming me with guilt and schadenfreude. Book-production remains a mystery to me—I cannot believe that *all* books published come out in multiples of 32 pages so why must we? Best is an idiot and Cowley just a deaf old imbecile. The Smart business sounds very interesting but I wish Harvard had discovered it in time to save our pockets. It seems that it will be years before we have paid off our debts. The only cuts that I am anxious about are in Vol III but I must wait now till I see them.
>
> On the blurb question I think we should get hold of a pliable medium and secure comments from the dead: e.g.
>
> > "The standard of taste and scholarship shown by the editors makes me realise the justice of my exclusion."
> > Elisabeth Barrett Browning
> >
> > "Gr-rr-r"
> > Robert Browning
> >
> > "Better than Tottell."
> > William Shakespeare
> >
> > "I salute that pair who by their compilation have put Viking above Oxford."
> > Dante
> > . . . . . .
>
> P.S. To be serious about the blurbs, I think we should get a word from a scholar for Vol I. For the others I don't know: Louis Untermeyer? Harry Levin? Clifton Fadiman? The Doctor of Renishaw [Edith Sitwell, who lived in Renishaw Hall and took pride in her honorary doctorate]? Old Possum [T. S. Eliot]?

The newly discovered manuscripts of Smart were not, in fact, discovered too late, and some of the material was published in the anthology for the first time.

The anthology was officially published on 29 September 1950. Having received his copies a few days earlier, Auden wrote to Pearson on 27 September:

> Thanks for your letter. I am delighted with the appearance of our five tomes. Have spotted one error. In the Emily Brontë selections, two poems are printed as one. Terrence Holliday (of the [Holliday] Bookshop) has also pointed out to me that our spelling of *Anthony* and Cleopatra is unelizabethan. Miss one or two dates in the calendar, notably the beginning of school classes in the 14th century. But I think—thanks, mostly, to you—we have done a good job. How *dare* the N.Y.

Times only give 500 words [for a review]! (By the way, I have given a copy
to Dr Edith [Sitwell]).

Auden was mistaken about the error that he thought he had spotted; the poems by
Emily Brontë were in fact printed as a single poem in many editions. Holliday was
wrong about "Anthony", which is the spelling in the First Folio (which however used
"Mark Antony" in *Julius Caesar*).

Reviewing the anthology in *The Nation*, 30 September 1950, Rolfe Humphries wrote
enthusiastically about Auden's taste, brilliance, scholarship and energy, noting that
"Mr Auden, to be sure, has had, in doing this work, the assistance of Norman Holmes
Pearson, and in the first volume also that of E. Talbot Donaldson, who has done the
special preparation necessary for the selections in Middle English. These gentlemen,
however—I suspect—are going to remain as uncredited, by and large, as Messrs. Mar-
tin and Pomeroy in that other field" (an allusion to the coauthors of the Kinsey report
on the sexual behavior of the American male). Pearson seems to have taken some offense at this, and Auden wrote to him on 2 October:

I never read reviews (nor *The Nation*, for that matter) so haven't seen
Humphries' article. What does he object to?
  Another error. Vol III. p. 458, ll 27 (Gay, *The Birth of the Squire*)

  Why dost thou glory in thy strength of beer.

is printed twice. (*That*, I *must* say, Viking should have caught.)
  Query? Vol II, p. 541, l 2. (Marvell, *The Garden*)

  Withdraws into it happiness

This is usually printed, I believe, as *its* happiness. Is our version the original text? If so, what fun for the Brooks-Warrens.
  Will drop Holliday a note on *Anthony*.

The error in the poem by Gay was corrected in later printings; the error (which was
in fact an error) in the poem by Marvell was not.

When the first paperback editions were printed in December 1957, Viking gave each
of the five volumes a categorizing title of the kind that, as Auden had written in his
"General Principles", the editors had chosen not to use. Volume I was retitled "Medieval and Renaissance Poets", with the series title "Poets of the English Language"
above this in smaller type and the names "Langland to Spenser" in small type below.
The remaining volumes were similarly retitled "Elizabethan and Jacobean Poets",
"Restoration and Augustan Poets", "Romantic Poets", and "Victorian and Edwardian
Poets". The biographical notes originally supplied in a separate unsigned pamphlet
were placed at the end of each volume. The new titles and the notes were also used in
later clothbound issues.

When the books were retitled for the paperback issue, Viking also quietly removed
from the statement of "General Principles" in Volume I the last three sentences of the
section headed "Arrangement" and the entire section headed "Supplementary Data".
The sections headed "Supplementary Data" were similarly removed from the "General Principles" sections in Volumes II, III, and IV, and the footnote in the introduc-

tion to Volume III, which was printed below the paragraphs about supplementary data, was removed by mistake. The entire "General Principles" section was dropped from Volume V, probably to make room for the biographical notes. The requirement to make room for the notes probably prompted the resetting of a few lines of the introduction to Volume IV, where, in the last phrase of the section "The Romantic Hero" (p. 141), the word "had" was cut, presumably by mistake.

THE READERS' SUBSCRIPTION

The Readers' Subscription was a book club intended for a more intellectual audience than that of the Literary Guild and The Book-of-the-Month Club. Auden and his coeditors Jacques Barzun and Lionel Trilling were associated with the club from its beginning in 1951 until they severed relations with it early in 1959 and founded a second club, The Mid-Century Book Society. (A book club is a subscription service of a kind introduced early in the twentieth century; each month, the "club," which is open to any paying customer, ships to its members one or two books chosen by a board of editors and sold at reduced prices; members receive a monthly bulletin announcing the next selection, which is then sent to them with an invoice unless they return a form indicating that they do not want it.)

The idea for The Readers' Subscription emerged from a conversation between Gilman Kraft (1926–99) and Trilling, his former teacher at Columbia, shortly after Kraft graduated in 1947 and founded a publishing house, the Fielding Press. Kraft formally organized the club, intending to call it The Bookman's Society; Trilling recruited his Columbia colleague Jacques Barzun as a second editor; Barzun proposed Auden as a third. Kraft told Barzun in April 1951 that Auden was unavailable for the job, but Barzun persisted; he arranged for Kraft to send a formal proposal to Auden in Italy and Barzun followed this with a telegram to Auden urging him to accept the formal offer. Auden responded to Barzun by telegram on 23 June 1951: "Proposal not yet received but favorable", and followed this (as Kraft reported to Barzun) with a letter to Kraft saying he was favorably inclined but wanted further details (Columbia University Library). He then agreed to become the third editor, and contracts were signed after his return to New York in September.

Diana Trilling gave the club its name and Kraft chose *The Griffin* as the name of the bulletin that would be published every four weeks, in which the editors would print reviews of the current selections. The club was designed to be profitable, and the editors received a sometimes irregular salary, but they hoped to provide value for money and did some of their best writing for *The Griffin*.

The club was officially founded in September 1951. During the first few years the editors seem to have chosen the club's selections and alternative offerings mostly by letter; Kraft sent them proofs of forthcoming books, and they reported their choices in reply. In later years they may have met more frequently, and certainly did so in the early years of their successor club, The Mid-Century. Barzun, who ascended to various posts as dean and provost at Columbia during the later years of the club, was the editor who kept closest watch over organizational and administrative matters. Auden was amused by what he called Barzun's donnishness, but admired his scholarship and enjoyed his company. Auden's relations with Trilling were cordial but not close, and a year or two after the club began, Auden told a friend that Trilling did not really like literature.

The first, undated, number of *The Griffin* was mailed to subscribers probably around November 1951. Auden's first contribution (p. 267) was to the second number, mailed the following month. The club's finances during the first few years were uncertain, and the editors often did not receive monthly payments. Whenever an editor complained, Kraft apologized, explained that he had kept quiet about the club's financial difficulties because he had hoped they would quickly improve, and promised (repeatedly) that the problem would never occur again. Auden did not see his coeditors for ten months after April 1952; when Trilling saw him again in February 1953, he learned that Auden had received no payments during this entire period.

Barzun recalls, however, that the club became successful under Kraft's financial management despite many practical difficulties in mailing books and handling accounts (tasks performed, often incompetently, by outside firms). While still managing The Readers' Subscription, Kraft bought the Broadway program magazine *Playbill* in 1957. At some point after this, the club again began to suffer severe financial troubles, and the editors formally severed their connection with it on 1 January 1959. The issue of *The Griffin* dated February 1959 (vol. 8, no. 2) was the last with material by the original three editors, who seem to have allowed their reviews to appear in order to avoid an interruption that might hinder the sale of the club and thus reduce their chances of receiving any last payments from Kraft. The club was quickly bought by the publisher Arthur Rosenthal, the founder of Basic Books, who continued to operate it under its original name, to the confusion of many subscribers.

Two contradictory accounts exist of the kinds of financial problems suffered by The Readers' Subscription (and later by The Mid-Century Book Society), one in Diana Trilling's *The Beginning of the Journey* (1993), the other in Jacques Barzun's "Foreword: Three Men and a Book" in *A Company of Readers*, a selection of reviews by the club's three editors, edited by Arthur Krystal (2001). Diana Trilling writes: "Only Auden, that most practical-minded of poets, was capable of making an objective assessment of the clubs' management. Because the men who had the business end of the clubs in their charge had once been their students, Lionel and Jacques would not question either their loyalty or their competence, and so great was the admiration for Lionel and Jacques of the supposedly tough-minded lawyer [James Grossman] whom they had engaged to guard their interests that he never questioned their judgment" (p. 266). Diana Trilling's allusion to the managers' questionable "loyalty" is consistent with other unpublished reports that Auden's coeditors ignored his warnings of ethical lapses in the clubs' financial management until the editors resigned *en masse* when the facts became too obvious to ignore. Diana Trilling's account is further confirmed by correspondence in the archive of one of the editors (not Auden) in the Columbia University Library, which includes a letter in which this editor reports to a friend that the other editors' connection with the club had "ceased early this year [1959] when it became apparent that the business side was up to some shenanigans".

In Barzun's published version of the story, written forty years after the fact, the editors' relations with Kraft were entirely harmonious. Nothing is said in Barzun's published version about shenanigans, nor about Kraft's recurring earlier lapses in paying the editors and informing them of the club's financial state. The only problems that

Barzun mentions in print are the "errors" committed by outside firms that handled distribution and billing. The club came to an end, Barzun writes, because it "did not meet Gilman Kraft's financial hopes or needs, and one day in early 1959 he told us that he had reluctantly decided to leave for greener pastures. He gave us time to find his replacement." Barzun recalls fondly that the editors "missed him," because Kraft was "always calm, friendly, and solicitous about our wants. . . . he was a thoughtful person whose Columbia College education had given him a solid grounding in literature and history" (pp. xii–xiii).

A different picture of the effect of a Columbia education emerges from letters and memos preserved among one of the editors' papers at Columbia; these documents include, in addition to Kraft's frequent letters of apology in the club's early years, a snarling exchange of letters between Kraft and the editors' lawyer after the sale of the club. The editors' lawyer demanded overdue payments from Kraft. Kraft countered that Barzun and Trilling had violated their contracts by republishing some of their *Griffin* essays, and that through this and other means they had caused him financial harm; he added, however, that their disputes were to be blamed on unnamed third parties who had misinformed all of them. The exchange ended when the editors, despite their indignant conviction that Kraft was lying about the facts and robbing them of their pay, decided not to bring a lawsuit against him, a decision their lawyer endorsed.

Early in 1959 the three editors formed their second book club, The Mid-Century Book Society. Auden's final review for *The Griffin*, "Two Apollonians", had not appeared when the breach occurred at The Readers' Subscription, and it appeared instead in the August 1959 number of the new club's magazine, *The Mid-Century*, under the title "The Creation of Music and Poetry". The three editors ended their connection with their second club late in 1962 after another series of organizational and financial fiascoes, again foreseen by Auden and mostly ignored by his two colleagues. Among the least of the club's troubles was the decision by the Broadway program magazine *Showbill* to drop the club's advertising after having accepted it for many months; this decision puzzled the club's employees until they learned that Gilman Kraft, having acquired *Playbill* in 1957, had now also acquired its only rival, *Showbill*. The staff of the club was unconvinced by Kraft's explanation that he had dropped its advertising only because he could make more profitable use of the space. A further history of The Mid-Century Book Society may be found in *Prose IV*.

AN ELIZABETHAN SONG BOOK

This collection was part of Auden's collaboration with Noah Greenberg and his early-music group the New York Pro Musica (see p. 618), and grew out of a concert of Elizabethan verse and music performed on 30 and 31 January 1954, in which Auden read the text of each song and the group then performed the music. Auden's sleeve notes for the 1955 recording that also resulted from that concert are reprinted in Appendix I.

Auden and Greenberg seem to have planned from the start to produce both a book and a concert. Auden wrote to Norman Holmes Pearson on 3 January 1954 (misdated 1953):

Now, I have a request. Am editing a book of Elizabethan lute-songs for Anchor Books and a textual problem has arisen, over one of the Morley settings. The text is by Nicholas Breton.

Faire in a morne oh fairest morne was ever morne so faire,

I know that the version printed in the Morley song-book differs from the version in *England's Helicon,* so I want to compare them. Could you get a student to copy the E.H. version for me (*not* modernised). If there are more than four stanzas, I only want the first four, i.e. ending

Of Phillida the shepheards Queene, and Coridon the swaine.

Auden submitted the text to Jason Epstein of Anchor Books probably around March or April 1954, with a letter saying: "In the preparation of the text and literary introduction (Noah is doing the musical one) I have collaborated with Mr Chester Kallman, so that the credits should run: Music edited by Noah Greenberg. Text edited by W. H. Auden and Chester Kallman" (Edinburgh University Library).

Anchor published the book on 20 October 1955. A British edition was published by Faber & Faber in May 1957.

THE FABER BOOK OF MODERN AMERICAN VERSE

When Auden visited London from Italy in June 1953 T. S. Eliot seems to have asked him to compile an anthology of modern American verse, with the understanding that it would not include poems by Eliot himself. Auden reported to Norman Holmes Pearson on 17 September 1953: "Eliot wants me to edit a Faber Book of Modern American Verse, so you will be seeing me often I expect when I get back in Dec. What a way to make enemies" (Yale University Library).

He worked on the selection in December 1953 and the early months of 1954; in January he visited Yale where he discussed his choices with Norman Holmes Pearson, and arranged for Pearson to commission students to prepare typescripts and photocopies from books in the Yale library. Pearson had this material ready by early February, and Auden wrote to him on 10 February:

Many thanks for both your letters. I guess the right corpse must be Milton Miles ["J. Milton Miles" is one of four epitaph poems by Edgar Lee Masters included in the book].

Could you send the stuff here plus bill.

Thanks ever so much for your pains. I am completely held up at the moment because the contract terms Faber suggested were so fantastic that I think they must have accidentally miswritten the advance figure.

The contract terms were among the matters Auden raised in a letter to Eliot on 22 March 1954:

I have made all the selections for The Faber Book of Modern American Verse, and nearly finished the pasting up, which leaves the obtaining of permissions and the introduction to do. BUT the contract I was sent made my eyes pop out. If I and Alan Collins [of Auden's agents, Curtis Brown, in New York] understand it correctly, Fabers propose to pay me an advance of 150 pounds out of which I am to pay all copyright fees. Since ALL the poems are copyright, my guessed estimate, confirmed by publishers I have asked, is that the total fees will run around 1500 pounds, so that, on such terms, I should be in debt to Fabers for the rest of my natural life. Before I write a scorcher, please make inquiries.

Eliot assured him that there was no question of the copyright fees being paid out of his advance.

Curtis Brown reported to Faber & Faber on 25 May 1954 that the typescript of the anthology was complete except for introduction. Auden seems not to have written the introduction until early the following year. On 4 March 1955, Charles Monteith at Faber thanked Curtis Brown for the typescript, which seems to have been complete except for the acknowledgements. Faber sent the full typescript, except for the acknowledgements, to the printer on 12 August 1955, but the book was not published until 3 September 1956, the long delay probably resulting from problems in obtaining permissions. At some point Laura Riding refused permission to include her poems, the only refusal that Auden received. An American edition titled *The Criterion Book of Modern American Verse* was published in November 1956.

Public Lectures and Courses

AUDEN taught at Barnard College as an Associate in Religion in the spring term of 1947, but was not listed in the college's printed catalogue.

At Mount Holyoke College in the fall term of 1950 Auden was Florence Purington Visiting Lecturer in English. In the *Mount Holyoke College Bulletin*, Catalogue Number 1950–51 (January 1951), his course is listed as "Studies in Poetry. A critical and interpretive study of certain poets to be selected. Special problems considered." The course was concerned mostly with versification and other technical matters. The *Springfield Daily News* reported on 15 January 1951:

> As a teacher as well as a literary figure, Mr Auden's students have found him a unique and stimulating tutor. Assignments in English 335, "Studies in Poetry," have ranged from translating poems from French and Latin to memorizing long passages from Milton. Mr Auden introduced his class to a type of crossword puzzle in which he gave them [*words missing in the original*]. As a change from assignments of writing serious verse, Mr Auden ran a contest of light verses, and offered the following four lines as a pattern:

> > That the girls at Mount Holyoke
> > Neither drink nor smoke
> > Is a popular myth
> > Believed by girls at Smith.

At Smith College in the spring term of 1953 Auden was William Allen Neilson Research Professor; he taught no courses but gave readings and occasional lectures (see below).

At the Poetry Center of the 92nd Street YM-YWHA in New York, Auden taught a course for adults on twelve Wednesday evenings starting on 19 October 1955; the course was variously referred to as "Form and Style in Poetry" and "Form and Style in Shakespeare's Sonnets".

Auden's unpublished public lectures during this period, other than those in college courses, are described below under "A Lecture Tour in 1952". Published items based on public lectures include *The Enchafèd Flood*, "The Things Which Are Caesar's" (p. 196), and "Portrait of a Whig" (p. 273).

NATURE, HISTORY AND POETRY

Auden delivered versions of this lecture at least four times in the early months of 1950: at Mount Holyoke College on 5 January 1950, under the title "Art and Freedom"; at Fordham University on 15 February 1950, and at Swarthmore College on 9 March 1950, both under the title "Nature, History and Poetry"; and at Barnard College on

11 March 1950, under the title "Freedom and the Artist". Auden wrote to Chester Kallman on 6 January 1950 about the two lectures scheduled for his week at Mount
Holyoke: "The first lecture [this one] was last night and the most severe I have ever
given—a cross between Whitehead and Heidegger—but my Dickens-Firbank one [see
"The Earthly Paradise", below] will be gentler."

On the first three occasions when he delivered this lecture (and perhaps also on the
fourth), he arranged for a three-page mimeographed leaflet to be distributed at the
lecture, with the text of his poem "Prime" on the first page, and copies of early drafts
on the next two pages. (A typescript of the poem and manuscript of the drafts are in
the Mount Holyoke College Archives.) The transcript below incorporates the mimeographed text of "Prime" and its drafts as distributed at Swarthmore; the Mount
Holyoke text of "Prime" is essentially identical except that it also includes a heading
above the title "Prime": "Florence Purington Lecture, January 5, 1950: W. H. Auden,
'Art and Freedom' / A poem with drafts (to be discussed in the lecture)"; no copy of
the version distributed at Fordham is known to exist.

At Swarthmore a sound recording was made of the lecture, and a mimeographed
transcript was prepared by an expert secretary who struggled unsuccessfully with some
of Auden's more obscure formulations; the recording and transcript are in the Swarthmore College Library. The heading of the transcript includes this note: "Mr Auden
has requested that this transcript be kept within the campus, for the use of the students and faculty of Swarthmore College only." Auden evidently never checked the
transcript, and the text below is based on the recording except in a few places where
the recording is damaged and the transcript is the only source. Auden evidently read
the first and last parts of the lecture (from "There are three more questions") from a
written text similar to the 1950 version of "Nature, History and Poetry" (p. 226); these
sections are printed here almost exactly as they were spoken. The paragraphs that immediately follow the poem were evidently spoken *ad lib*, and in this section I have rearranged many passages for the sake of clarity.

President Nason and Ladies and Gentlemen: It is for me a very great pleasure to be back here, and there is one little proof I can give of the genuineness of my feeling for Swarthmore: that I have never been able to change my
bank which, at great inconvenience to myself, is still the Swarthmore Bank.

The remarks I want to make this evening are prompted first of all by two
contemporary considerations. Firstly, the return, all over the world, of either
a direct censorship of the arts, or a wish to censor them. Whereas in the nineteenth century the highbrow artist might be regarded as mad or personally
immoral, there is a tendency now to regard him as a heretic conspirator, at
once unintelligible to the majority and at the same time a member of either
a money-making or political racket excluding the deserving. At the same
time, one notices a vast increase in the number of people, particularly young
people, who, when asked what they wish to do, say "I want to write". It seems
as if writing were to them the only thing they could think of as a free personal
act. Or else they regard it as some kind of magic hygiene of the soul, through
the practice of which they will attain freedom, efficiency, and happiness.

So I would like this evening to try and examine a few problems about the nature of poetry: what the poet actually does. And here I must make two apologies. I must apologize for the first part of what I have to say being rather dull and rather dry, and maybe, it seems, a little off the point. I hope at the end you will see why these things have to be discussed. Secondly, I must apologize for, in the discussion of the poetic present, having to use a poem of my own, which I do not do because I think it is particularly good, but I have to take a poem of my own, because it is only with it that I have the information necessary to make my points.

Now for the rather severe part, which consists of some axioms and some definitions.

Temporal or secular events may be divided into two classes, natural events and historical events.

A natural event is:

(a) a member or class of similar events
(b) occurs necessarily, according to law

An historical event is:

(a) unique; that is to say, a member of a class of one
(b) occurs not necessarily according to law, but voluntarily according to provocation
(c) is the cause of subsequent historical events, in the sense that it provides them with a motive for occurring.

Natural time is the dimension in which natural events occur, and is measured by them. It is cyclical and reversible. Historical time is unilinear, and is created by the occurrence of historical events. Natural events are related by the principle of Identity; historical events, by the principle of Analogy. Of the natural event, it could only be said that it is what it is. Of the historical event, it may be said that it could have been otherwise.

Laws may be divided into two classes, laws-of and laws-for. A law-of is stated in the indicative mood; it indicates that at any moment only one event is possible. About a law-of, it can only be said that its formulation is true or false. A law-for is stated in the imperative mood; it presupposes that at any given instant at least two events are possible, and asserts that one is more probable or preferable. About a law-for, it may be said that its command is just or unjust.

Natural laws are laws-of, and are what the scientist, in time, discovers. The principle of indeterminacy, the discovery that laws-of are statistical, does not change this. It merely means that the variations of, say, the path of neutrons, occur according to no law, and are, from the point of view of the scientist, incomprehensible. Laws-for only apply to historical events, and are what the historian at *a* time judges them by. Of a motive for choosing to occur, with which a law-for provides an event, it may be said that it is good or evil; of the choice itself, that it is right or wrong. A just law is one which provides good motives for choices, not one which compels right choices.

For a law to be discoverable, at least three events, that is to say a plurality, must be known to which it is relatable. Pluralities may be divided into three classes; crowds, societies and communities.

A crowd consists of n members, where n is greater than one, whose sole characteristic in common is togetherness. A crowd has no love for itself or for anything other than itself. It can only be counted; its existence is chimerical. Of a crowd, it can be said either that it is not, but only appears to be, or that it ought not to be.

A society consists of n, a certain finite number of members united in a specific manner into a whole with a characteristic mode of behavior which is different from the behavior of any member in isolation. For example, a molecule of water or a string quartet. A society, that is, has a definite size, a definite structure, and an actual existence. It cannot come into being until neither more nor less of its component members are present and properly related. Add or subtract a member or change their relations and the society ceases to exist, or is transformed into another society. A society is a system which loves itself. To this total self-love, the love of its members is totally subordinate. Of a society it may be said that it is effective in its function or ineffective.

A community consists of n members, all of them of them rational beings united by virtue of a common love for something other than themselves; for example, in contrast to a string quartet, a group of music-lovers. Like a crowd, and unlike a society, the number of members is indefinite. Its character is not changed by the addition or subtraction of any member, and unlike a society it exists not actually, [and unlike a crowd] not by chance, but potentially, so that n may be equal to one. To attain actual existence it must be embodied in societies which express the love which is its *raison d'être*, and of these, there may be an infinite number. The actualization of a community in a society is an order. Of a community it may be said that it is more or less good.

In nature there is only a total system of partial social systems and no community. That is, one cannot say of a natural event that it occurs for the love of anything other than itself. It only enjoys its self-occurrence. The natural social system is therefore fully described in terms of laws-of, and terms like freedom and unfreedom, good and evil, have no relevance. It is only in history that we can speak of communities as well as of societies, of a distinction between an order and a system.

In a system, freedom and unfreedom appear as each other's boundaries, and good and evil as real opposites striving to approach other like positive and negative numbers. Thus, in the case of the string quartet, suppose that a cellist hates Mozart and refuses to play a Mozart quartet. He annuls the other three, and the same would be true vice versa. In a community, unfreedom and evil appear as the denial of freedom and good; that is to say, freedom and goodness are not annulled, but the denial thereby testifies to their existence. For example, suppose we have nine people who prefer beef to mutton, and one person who prefers mutton to beef. Then there is not one community containing a dissonant member, but two communities. The antithesis of a community, therefore, is not another community with a different love but a crowd in the absolute sense, that is to say, an arithmetical plurality of individuals each of whom only loves himself, a chaotic world of pure chance.

Whenever rival communities compete for embodiment in the same society, there is either unfreedom or disorder. In the chimerical case of a society completely embodying a crowd, this would be a state of total unfreedom, that is to say, hell.

Communities, incidentally, can be divided into two classes, closed and open. A closed community is one the members of which are unaware of the existence, real or potential, of rival communities, that is to say, communities united by another love, An open community is one the members of which are aware of the existence of rival communities but have chosen to belong to this one and to reject membership in another. In history absolute closure or absolute openness are hypothetical; every community is more or less closed, less or more open.

A perfect order, that is to say one in which a community were perfectly and completely embodied in a system, could be described in terms of a law-of, but the description would be irrelevant. For a perfect order the relevant description would be: "Love is the fulfilling of the law". Only in Paradise is this the case. Since in historical societies the order is always imperfect, for community and system never coincide, the obligation to approximate to such a coincidence is felt as a command or a law-for.

Man exists concretely as a unity-in-tension of four modes of being: a soul, a body, mind, and spirit.

As a soul and a body he is an individual person; as a mind and spirit, a conscious member of a community. Were man only soul and body, that is to say only an individual, his sole relation with others would be numerical, and a poem could only be comprehensible to its author. Were he only mind and spirit, men would only exist collectively as a system, *Man*, and there would be nothing for poetry to be about.

As body and mind, man is a natural creature; as soul and spirit, an historical creature. Were he only body and mind, his existence would be one of everlasting recurrence and only one good poem could exist. Were he only soul and spirit, his existence would be one of perpetual and absolute novelty and every new poem would supersede all previous poems; or rather, a poem would be superseded before it could be written. Poetry is possible because there is no communal experience which does not come about through the loneliness and vision of the individual, and no separate experience which has not been born in communal experience and revealed to the communal group.

The self-consciousness of man exists as a unity-in-tension of three modes.

Firstly, the consciousness of the self as self-contained, as embracing all of which it is aware in a unity of experiencing. This mode is undogmatic, amoral and passive. Secondly, the consciousness of beyondness, of the ego standing as a spectator over and against both itself and the external world. This mode is amoral, dogmatic, objective. While the good of the first mode is the enjoyment of being, and its evil the fear of non-being, the good of this [second] mode is the perception of necessary relations; its evil, the fear of chance or of non-relation. Thirdly, there is the mode of the ego's consciousness of itself as striving towards, of desiring to transform the self it owns, to realize its potentialities. This mode is moral and active; its good is not present but propounded, its evil the present actuality.

Were the first mode absolute, men would inhabit a magical world of idols in which the image of an object, the emotion aroused by the object, and the word signifying the object were all identical, where past and future, the living and the dead were united. Language in such a world would consist only of proper names which would not be words in the ordinary sense, but sacred syllables. And in the place of the poet there would be magicians, whose task it is to discover and to utter the truly potent spell which can compel what is not, to be. For example, instead of the love poem which expresses the emotion of love, there would be incantations which would compel the beloved to love. It seems not improbable that, historically, poetry was born out of magic of this kind; hence the myth of Orpheus. And wherever this mode of consciousness predominates it can be exploited. Propaganda is the employment of magic by those who do not believe in it against those who do.

Were the second mode of consciousness, of beyondness, absolute, men would inhabit a world which was a pure system of universals. Language would be a kind of algebra and there could only exist one poem of absolute banality expressing the system. Whenever this mode of consciousness is predominant we find a poetry in which poetic forms in the abstract, that is to say, monotonous rhythm and conventional rhymes, tyrannize over the poet and dictate what he says.

Were the third, transcending, mode of consciousness absolute, men would inhabit a purely arbitrary world, the world of the clown and the actor. The ugliest person would be the nicest and vice-versa. In language there would be no relation between seeing and words, all rhymes would be comic, love would rhyme with indifference, and all poetry, therefore, would be nonsense poetry. When this mode of consciousness is predominant we find a wide and theatrical contradiction between what the poet says in his poetry and his life, and a fanatic religion made of the sense of humor.

It is thanks to the first mode of consciousness that every poem is unique. It is thanks to the second that the poet can embody his private experience in a public poem which can be read by others in terms of their private experiences. And it is thanks to the third that he desires to write and the reader desires to read.

The subject matter of a natural scientist is a crowd of disordered natural events at all times. He assumes the crowd to be apparent and attempts to discover the true system concealed beneath its appearance. The subject matter of a poet is a crowd of historic occasions of feelings in the past. He accepts this crowd as real but assumes that it is possible for him to transform it into a community, that is to say, to give it a possible instead of a chimerical existence. The subject matter of the statesman is men, both as natural and historical beings, as they actually are now, existing as crowds, as societies, and as communities. His task is to modify the societies so that they may more completely embody not any possible community but the true community. That is to say, like the poet and unlike the scientist, he is dealing with real, not apparent, disorder. But, like the scientist and unlike the poet, his goal is a true, not a possible order. The temporal category of politics is neither the past of the poet nor the "at all times" of the scientist, but the present moment.

The Muses, then, are, as the Greeks believed, the daughters of Memory. But Memory is not herself a muse. When we recall an occasion of past feeling, we recall the occasion, not the feeling itself. The feeling is, as it were, seen in a mirror; it is no longer ours. Were it not so, it would be impossible for us to detach it from our present existence, to relate it to other emotions, and to embody them in a poem. There are occasions when the recall of the past occasion is accompanied by a repetition of the original emotion. Such are of importance and interest to psychoanalysts but of no practical value to the poet. For poetry is, as Wordsworth says, emotion recollected in tranquillity.

The transformation of a crowd of feelings into a community is effected by translating the former into words which embody the latter. The poem itself is a linguistic society or verbal system. As such it is a natural, not an historical being. Every poem presupposes that the history of language is at an end. Of course, it can sometimes be mistaken, and unfortunate things can happen. For example, owing to changes in meaning, when a poet wrote, "His breath came in short pants", you can see that when it was written he had to presuppose that words would not change their meaning. The poem, therefore, cannot be properly said to exist except when it is being read or remembered. At all other times it is only, as Heidegger would say, "on-hand". But unlike the fleeting occasions of feeling from which it is derived, it is persistently on-hand.

When a poem is read, it orders into a possible community a crowd of past historic occasions of feeling of the reader, not identical with, but analogous to, those of the author. For the reader, as for the author, it is past occasions which are so transformed. The poem has no power of persuasion over the present moment of historical choice. It introduces no novelty of emotion into the reader's "now" other than the feeling which accompanies every such transformation of disorder into order: namely, the feeling we imply that we have when we say that something is beautiful. Language can be used to introduce novel emotion into the present, as for example in pornography, but such use is magical not poetical.

It has been said that a poem should not mean, but be. This is not quite accurate. In a poem, as distinct from any other verbal societies, meaning and existence are identical. Like an image in the mirror, a poem might be called a pseudo-person. That is to say, it has uniqueness and it addresses the reader as person to person. On the other hand, like all natural beings, and unlike historical persons, it cannot lie. It is possible to say of any formulation of a scientific law that it is true or false, because a natural law is not an event, but is a statement of how events occur. To discover its truth or falsehood one has to go to the events themselves. Of a poem it is not possible to say that it is true or false, for one does not have to go to anything except itself to discover whether or no it is, in fact, an order, that is to say, a community of feelings truly embodied in a verbal society. If it is not, if unfreedom or disorder are present, the poem itself reveals it on inspection. We may be, and frequently are, mistaken in a poem, but the cause of the mistake is our self-deception, not the poem.

The poet setting out to write a poem has at his disposal two crowds. The crowd composed of the total number of occasions of past feeling he can recall, and the crowd composed of the total number of words in his vocabulary, and his task is to organize the relevant members of the latter into a society which will embody as many members of the former as it can transform into one community.

The nature of the final order is the outcome of a dialectical struggle between the feelings and the verbal system. Since the system, or society, is of a definite size and structure (that is to say, since any system is finite and the self-love of its members must be totally subordinate to its love of its total self) the verbal system is actively coercive upon the feelings it is attempting to embody. What it cannot embody truthfully, it excludes. As a potential community, since in a community unfreedom is a contradiction, the feelings are passively resistant to all claims of the system to embody them which they do not recognize as just. They decline all unjust persuasions. Similarly the feelings compete, each out of self-love demanding inclusion in a dominant position to which they are not necessarily entitled, and each of the words demands that the system shall modify itself—in its case, but not as a whole, that is to say, that a special exception shall be made for it and for it only. In a successful poem, society and community have become one order. That is to say, the system may love itself because the feelings which it embodies are all members of the same community, loving each other and it. A poem may fail in two ways; or rather, it may exclude too much and become banal, or it may attempt to embody too much in one community of feeling at once and produce disorder.

In writing a poem the poet can work in two ways. Starting from an intuitive idea of the kind of community he desires to call into being, he may work backwards in search for the system which will most justly incarnate that idea. Or, starting with a certain system, he may work forwards in search of a community which it is capable of incarnating most truthfully. In practice, of course, he almost always works simultaneously in two directions, modifying his conception of the ultimate nature of the community at the immediate suggestions of the system, and modifying the system in response to his surer intuition of the future needs of the community.

A system cannot be selected completely arbitrarily, nor can one say that any given form is absolutely necessary. One searches for the one which seems to be just. The laws-of a just system become laws-for the feelings the system claims to embody, which it is their duty to obey. *Ought* always implies *can*. A system whose claims cannot be met is an unjust system which the poet must scrap. He must beware, however, of too hastily rejecting a system as unjust when the fault lies with the inertia and self-love of his feelings, which are always on the lookout for an excuse for not doing the duty which they are capable of doing.

Now, to illustrate what I have been saying, I have to take a poem of my own. I think the simplest thing is, I'll read the whole poem first, and then discuss a few things about [?its history]. The poem is called "Prime".

[*The mimeographed text of the poem and two pages of early drafts were distributed at the lecture; Auden read the poem and referred to the drafts in his comments below. The mimeographed text is here interpolated in the lecture, as in the Swarthmore transcript:*]

Prime

> Simultaneously, as soundlessly,
>   Spontaneously, suddenly
> As, at the vaunt of the dawn, the kind
>   Gates of the body fly open
> To its world beyond, the gates of the mind,
>   The horn gate and the ivory gate
> Swing to, swing shut, instantaneously
>   Quell the nocturnal rummage
> Of its rebellious fronde, ill-favored,
>   Ill-natured and second-rate,
> Disenfranchised, widowed and orphaned
>   By an historical mistake:
> Recalled from the shades to be a seeing being,
>   From absence to be on display,
> Without a name or history I wake
>   Between my body and the day.

Holy this moment, wholly in the right,
   As, in complete obedience
To the light's laconic outcry, next
   As a sheet, near as a wall,
Out there as a mountain's poise of stone,
   The world is present, about,
And I know that I am, here, not alone
   But with a world, and rejoice
Unvexed, for the will has still to claim
   This adjacent arm as my own,
The memory to name me, resume
   Its routine of praise and blame,
And smiling to me is this instant while
   Still the day is intact and I
The Adam sinless in our beginning,
   Adam still previous to any act.

I draw breath; that is of course to wish
   No matter what to be wise
To be different to die and the cost
   No matter how is Paradise
Lost of course and myself owing a death:
   The eager ridge, the steady sea,
The flat roofs of the fishing village
   Still asleep in its bunny,
Though as fresh and sunny still are not friends
   But things to hand, this ready flesh
No honest equal but my accomplice now,
   My assassin to be and my name
Stands for my historical share of care
   For a lying self-made city,
Afraid of our living task, the dying
   Which the coming day will ask.

[*Two mimeographed pages of earlier drafts:*]

Simultaneously as at the instant
Word of the light the gates of the body,
The eyes and the ears open
Into its world beyond,
The gates of the mind, the horn gate, the ivory gate
Swing to, shut off
The nocturnal rummage of its angry fronde,
Crippled and second-rate,
Still suffering from some historical mistake.

             a
Simultaneously, as soundlessly,

          a
Spontaneously, suddenly

                b   b   c
As, at the ⌠vaunt of the dawn, the kind
          ⌡knock
Gates of the body fly open

                    d   c
To its world beyond, the gates of the mind,

             b   e   e
The horn gate and the ivory gate

                              a
Swing to, swing shut, instantaneously

          f
Quell the nocturnal rummage
          f   d
Of its rebellious fronde, ill-favored,

          e   e
Ill-natured and second rate,

Disenfranchised, widowed and orphaned

                         g
By an historical mistake:

                              h   h
Recalled from the shades to be a seeing being,

                         i
From absence to be on display,

                         g
Without a name or history I wake

                         i
Between my body and the day

             a   b   c   d
I draw breath; that is of course to wish
       e   b   f
No matter what to be wise

                              g
To be different to die and the cost
       e   b   f
No matter how is Paradise
    g   c   e   a
Lost of course and myself owing a death:

                              h   i
The eager ridge, the ⎧ steady sea,
                        ⎩ level

    b   d   j
The flat roofs of the fishing village

  j   k
Still asleep in its bunny,

      l   k   j
Though as fresh and sunny still are not friends

            m   h   l
But things to hand, this ready flesh

No honest companion but my accomplice

                  i
For now, my assassin to be:

        n   n
Once more I claim in my name, and yours

   m   o
Stands, my beloved, for that care

Which can neither pretend to be love

        d   o
Nor stop me wishing it were.

No honest companion but my accomplice

                  i
For now, my assassin to be and

        m
My name stands for that pride which because

        n   o
It cannot choose its choice, for

   o   h   p
The joy it hopes for is already there

   n   p
Refuses not to despair

No honest equal but my accomplice now,

            i
My assassin to be and my name

  m   n ⎧   n
Stands for my historical share ⎨ of   care
                              ⎩ in the

$$\left\{\begin{array}{l} \overset{\text{o}}{\text{For a }} \overset{\text{p}}{\text{lying self-made }} \overset{\text{p}}{\text{city, afraid}} \\ \text{Of} \end{array}\right.$$

$$\overset{\text{q}}{\text{Of our living }} \overset{\text{o}}{\text{task, the dying}}$$

$$\text{Which the coming day will } \overset{\text{q}}{\text{ask.}}$$

Actually this poem was written last August, in Italy, but a number of things go back much further than that.

We'll talk first of all about the crowd of occasions of feeling before we talk about the society. In the summer of 1947 I had an idea of writing a series of poems corresponding to the church offices. As you know, Prime is one of the church offices; there are Matins, Lauds, Prime, Tierce, Sext, Nones, and so on. Why I was interested in this was that the offices celebrate historical events, particularly events of the Passion of Christ, and these are repeated daily. So what I had in mind was that it might be possible to write a series of poems, which were to be in some sense of the word—I don't know how—about the relation of history and nature, which is a problem which has fascinated me for at least ten years, and is why I am here at all, talking now. It was just an idea going on in my mind as a possible way of organizing experience one had, and so far—it's nearly three years ago now—this is the only one [of the series] which has actually got itself written.

In regard to this poem: the experience of waking up is something that has always interested me—the problem of return to consciousness and the return of memory and identity, the whole relation of the ego and self. Then, in discussion with, and observation of, others I've always come across a great psychological division between those of us who feel depressed when we wake up and feel better at night and those who feel good in the morning and are depressed at night. One instance of this is that I myself happen to belong to the lot who feel better in the morning, and the bad period for me is in the afternoon between two and four, and one day I have to write a poem about that too. This is a general sort of psychological problem which I could go on observing and talking about indefinitely.

Then there is a general theological problem which interests me and has for some time: to what extent we have any kind of recollection or imagination or intuition of what life was like before the Fall. Now, since the Fall is a condition of human history, as [is shown by] the mythical way in which it is formulated, it seems to me that we cannot imagine an unfallen action, but only the state preceding action; and action, of course, includes not only the physical action but the actual intention of the will. And that, you see, began to link up with the business of waking up.

Now those are the sort of general things that were of most general interest; then, to take it in a more immediate sense, those are the things that are going on in one's mind over some period. All right: what are the major experiences? Breakfasting every morning on the balcony of the simple house I have in Italy in the summer, where, as I take breakfast, I see the sun rising over the mountain one way, and I see the sea the other way. At the same time my bathroom reading consisted of Valéry's *Mauvaises pensées*, which contains some very fascinating observations on the exact problem about waking up and consciousness, under the head of "Laura", the symbol he uses for the dawn. Obviously, I got excited by that kind of thing. So much, for the moment, for the sorts of ideas going into the poem.

Now there is the other side: the verbal society or the verbal system. For a long time now, I've been interested in the possibilities of syllabic metre as one way of achieving a balance between freedom and order. That is to say, I wanted to get away from a conventional pattern of iambics and trochaics, and, at the same time, not to lose the sense of pattern. For a lot of people, this [interest starts from their] reading of Marianne Moore, Horace, and French poetry. Also, apart from the possibilities of irregularly placed internal rhymes (I've marked on the sheet where the internal rhymes are in this particular poem), the line-stops that you make when you read and the rhyme-stops don't coincide but are counterpointed. In the conventional English rhyming schemes, where these two [kinds of stop] coincide and are regular, the effect is more static and logical than when they do not.

Now there comes a problem: are there certain kinds of subjects best related to these sorts of experiments? It seemed to me that for rather fluid states of mind and free associations, for a problem like waking up, this would be the right kind of place [to use these experiments].

I keep a notebook, not a diary, in which I jot down lines, descriptions, and ideas, whenever they occur to me. One day, looking up at the mountain near my house and trying to describe its appearance, thinking "Now what does that look like?", I found my notebook and jotted down the phrase "the eager ridge", which, of course, has a double meaning because the adjective combines physical and mental attributes. Some other time, several years before— that's why you can see how historical feelings are crowds; they are not arranged in order at all—I found I had jotted down about dreams that they were like the Fronde. That, you remember, is the party which rebelled against Mazarin and the centralization that he brought during the minority of Louis XIV; and the Fronde seemed to me a good image for dreams, both as a rebellion and also a rebellion against centralization of the self, which seemed to me what happens during a dream.

Now, to show you the danger of trying to trace things exactly to any one thing: it is true that the particular Italian village [where I have a house] is a fishing village, and it has flat roofs. It is not, however, situated in a bunny, which is a little ravine between sand hills and cliffs; that image actually comes from memories of fishing villages in the south of England. But for the particular picture I wanted to build up it seemed right.

Now, with regard to alterations [in the poem], if you look at the second page of this [mimeographed text] where it begins, "Simultaneously as at the instant / Word of the light and the gates of the body", you can see that I tried to start writing it, thinking that it should be quite free. I very soon got stuck in the way that one does when the form is wrong. I began to think, "It just doesn't come out right". Then I settled finally on what the form should be, which consists of alternating lines of nine syllables and seven syllables, with the fullest elision; that is to say, always eliding between contiguous vowels or through "h"; and with various systems of internal rhymes dotted around [the poem].

I included one alteration in the first verse [in the mimeographed text], to show how often the system helps one to say what one wants. As the line originally ran it was, "as the knock of the dawn"; then I thought, "No, I don't quite like that, because after all the dawn doesn't quite knock. It isn't right". And luckily, because I was using internal rhymes, I suddenly saw the word "dawn", and then a word came into my mind which rhymes in an internal way with it, "vaunt", which has the business of a challenge without the direct physical sense of the word "knock"—which doesn't work with the word "like", though it contains the same idea. There you see an idea suggested by the necessities of the form.

The same occurs in the next [alteration shown on the mimeographed text], where the line originally ran, "The eager ridge, the level sea, the flat roof". I thought, "No, I can't have level and flat; there's not any distinction." Further, if I were to have "eager ridge", which has a double meaning, the word "eager" meaning both sharp and anxious, I must do the same thing for "sea". Here again, the language comes to one's aid. Down below, there is "ready flesh"—and there I found the rhyme [I needed, "steady"].

The chief difficulty was the end. (Please don't think I'm trying to advertise my work in doing this; I have to talk about mine because I know it.) The first version went: "Once more I claim in my name, and yours / Stands, my beloved, for that care / Which can neither pretend to be love / Nor stop me wishing it were". Now this is a case where it's awfully important to have friends you can show your work to. At this point, I showed it to somebody and they said, "Look here, you kept most of the poem dealing with the general problem. Now [at the end] to make it a unique and personal problem is all wrong". I am awfully cross when people say that sort of thing, but then I went away, and thought, oh dear, I must toil away again.

So I started off again. This time it became: "My name stands for that pride which because / It cannot choose its choice, for / The joy it hopes for is already there / Refuses not to despair". No, I thought that won't do; the thing that was right the first time was that after being entirely about myself, it got away from myself. This [new version] just went on entirely about myself. Then I began to believe that the idea I wanted was to go from this personal thing, of calling myself the Adam, to the idea of the two cities, the *civitas dei* and the *civitas terrena*; and then [I gave up that idea] but kept the idea of the city. And that seemed to be right, and so that was finally what came out.

About the last [of the alternations on the sheets], this results from a simple carelessness of being unable to count. The lines now ran: "Stands for my historical share in the care / Of a lying self-made city". However, again, when I showed this to somebody, he pointed out: "You are eliding syllables, aren't you? You have forgotten that 'my historical' elides, and you've got a syllable too many". One has to correct that, because it is just wrong. And so finally, that's how it came out.

There are three more questions that I'd like to raise. Why does the poet write poems? Why does the reader read them? And is the writing or reading of poems morally good, morally bad, or neutral?

I think that just as the scientist has to start off with certain absolute presuppositions, like saying that the world of nature exists, every poet starts off with certain absolute presuppositions or dogmas, whether he is aware of them or not. Firstly, he presupposes absolutely that the historical world exists, consisting of unique events and persons, each a member of a class of one. Secondly, he presupposes absolutely that these events happen, or these persons act, voluntarily through mutual provocation, not necessarily according to law. Thirdly, he assumes—presupposes absolutely—that, though unique, these events and persons are nevertheless comparable. Whereas natural things are comparable by identity, as when we say that all normal human bodies have ten fingers, historical persons are comparable by analogy, and these analogies are potentially infinite in number. Fourthly, he presupposes that the existence of such a world of historical beings is a good. And that, therefore, any addition to their number, and to the complexity of the analogical relation, is also good.

The office of the poet then, is a creative act analogous to God's activity in creating man in His own image. His act is analogous to, not imitative of, God's activity. Imitation would be possible only if man were identical with God; that is to say, if the unity of existence and essence in man were one of identity, in which case, like God, he would be able to create *ex nihilo*. In man, however, unity of existence and essence is a unity-in-tension; thanks to the unity he can create voluntarily, that is to say, out of motive, not necessity, but he can only create analogically, that is to say, out of already–existing materials.

It is, strictly speaking, untrue to say that a poet should not write poems unless he must. Strictly speaking, it can only be said that he should not write them unless he can. The ordinary statement is sound in practice, because only in those who can, and when they can, is the motive genuine.

In those who profess the desire to write poetry and at the same time exhibit a complete incapacity to do so, it is frequently the case that their desire is not creation but self-perpetuation. That is to say, a refusal to accept their own mortality, just as there are parents who do not really wish to beget children, persons analogous [to] but other than themselves, but to prolong their own existence in time. The symptom of this desire is that they identify their children with themselves. It is well known what the consequences of such an identification can be. The sterile impossibility of such an attempt both in parenthood and in art is expressed in the myth of Narcissus, When the poet speaks, as he sometimes does, of achieving immortality through a poem, he does not mean that he hopes, like Faust, to live forever, but that he hopes to rise from the dead. In poetry, as in other matters, the law holds good that he who would save his life must lose it. Unless the poet sacrifices his feelings completely to the poem, so that they are no longer his but the poem's, he will fail.

Adam was created in the image of God; then he sinned and was expelled from Paradise. His fall effaced and obscured, but did not totally destroy, the image he had been. Fallen man retains a unity-in-tension of existence and essence; but, whereas, in prelapsarian man this unity-in-tension was one of perfect balance and harmony, in him it is one of unbalance and discord, for which he feels guilty, knowing that he ought not so to be, and feels a nostalgia for his former state, even if he cannot imagine accurately what it could have been, knowing only that it must have been balanced and harmonious. Evil does not exist positively, but is the deprivation of good. That is to say, evil has no essence of its own. Essence is what evil destroys, but it cannot create or destroy existence, even its own. Of Satan, therefore, it might be said that his existence is absolutely chimerical. He exists, but he has lost all essence; hence his insatiable hunger for souls. Further, it is good that Satan exists, but evil that he exists chimerically as Satan, instead of perfectly as Lucifer, first among the Sons of God.

The materials out of which a poet creates are his historical feelings which are what, in his fallen state, they are, namely, witnesses to his knowledge of good and evil. When we say that poetry is beyond good and evil, we simply mean that a poet can no more change the facts of what has been felt than, in the natural order, parents can change the inherited physical characteristics which they pass on to their children. Censorship and eugenics stand or fall together, the judgment good-or-evil applies only to the intentional movement of the will.

Of our feelings in a given situation, which is the joint creation of our intention and the response favorable or hostile to the external factors in that situation, it cannot be said that they are good or evil, only that they are appropriate or inappropriate, given our intention and given the response. Of a recollected feeling, it cannot be said that it is now appropriate or inappropriate, because the historical occasion out of which it arose no longer exists. A poem is an attempt to embody such recollected feeling in a verbal situation to which all the feelings so embodied are appropriate. Of a poem, therefore, we say that it is beautiful or ugly, according to the degree of success or failure it has in reconciling contradictory feelings in an order of mutual propriety.

Every beautiful poem presents several analogies. Firstly, an analogy of forgiveness of sins; again, an analogy, not an imitation, because it is not evil intentions which are repented of and pardoned, but contradictory feelings which the poet confesses and surrenders to the poem in which they are reconciled. A poem is a natural object and therefore, like all natural objects, like an atomic bomb or anything else, is a potential cause of either good or evil effects. It presents [firstly] an analogy of the divine creation of man in His own image, the free granting of existence to a free creature; secondly, to the Paradisal state in which freedom and law, system and order, are united in harmony; thirdly, to the means of repentance and forgiveness by which fallen man can regain that state.

The effect of beauty is good, therefore, to the degree to which, through its analogies, the goodness of existence, the possibility of paradise, and the historical duty of repentance are recognized. Its effect is evil to the degree that beauty is taken for an imitation, that is to say, as identical with good, so that the artist regards himself as God, and the pleasure of beauty as the joy of Paradise and the conclusion drawn that since all is well in the work of art all is well in history. But all is not well there.

I'd like to conclude with two quotations: the first, a description, maybe, of the art of the poetic process, is from Virginia Woolf; the second, a prayer which all people who either are artists or who love art might do well to remember, by Donne.

This is Virginia Woolf:

> There is a square; there is an oblong. The players take the square and place it upon the oblong. They place it very accurately. They make a perfect dwelling-place—very little is left outside. The structure is now visible; what is inchoate is here stated. We are not so various or so mean. We have made oblongs and put them upon squares. This is our triumph; this is our consolation.

And Donne:

> That learning, thine ambassador,
> From thine allegiance we never tempt;
> That beauty, paradise's flower
> For physic made, from poison be exempt;
> That wit, born apt high good to do,
> By dwelling lazily
> On nature's nothing, be not nothing too;
> That our affections kill us not, nor die,
> Hear us, weak echoes, O thou ear and cry.

THE EARTHLY PARADISE

Auden gave a talk with this title as the second of his two Florence Purington lectures at Mount Holyoke College, 11 January 1950 (the first was "Art and Freedom", described above). A somewhat confused report appeared in the *Mount Holyoke News*, 13 January 1950:

The topic of Mr Auden's lecture was "The Earthly Paradise". His study of the subject was based on aspects of Charles Dickens' *Pickwick Papers* and Ronald Firbank's *The Flower Beneath the Foot.*

Both authors Mr Auden described as mythological writers on the basis that the reader of their works wishes that the stories might continue forever and that the characters might appear in other books.

The purpose of the discussion of *Pickwick Papers* and *Flower Beneath the Foot* was to show Adam's idea of the Garden of Eden in Mr Dickens' book and Eve's idea of the Garden of Eden in Mr Firbank's book.

Mr Auden began his talk by speaking of the self and the ego as seeking self-sufficiency, enjoyment, and the approval of others. The self and the ego are troubled in the world by sufferings of shame and guilt from a lack of sex, knowledge, and rest, and from the feeling of the disapproval of others. Their eternal dream is for self-satisfaction and the approval of others.

In beginning his discussion of the idea of the Garden of Eden as seen through the works of Firbank and Dickens, Mr Auden spoke first of space and the setting of Eden. Apparently, space was to serve in two functions, that of a protective element and also an unlimited element.

The people in the Garden of Eden were completely identical with their names, and such appellations as Augustus Sandgrass and the Honorable Mrs Chillywater were entirely applicable to the character of the people so named in the works of the authors under discussion.

Clothes in the imagined Garden of Eden were based on two ideas. The men dressed in untidy garb, for they believed that the character of each person was unchangeable so that one could dress in what might please him. The women believed in changing their clothes in order to change their inner selves.

Society as a whole was a Utopian group, in which class status and race made little difference. This was illustrated by an argument [in *The Flower Beneath the Foot*] between a Negress and a duchess over the same seat in an opera house. The only personalities to be excluded in the class of inhabitants in the supposed Eden were hypocrites, such as Dickens' Mr Stiggins.

Mr Auden concluded his lecture with the comment that the hero of *Pickwick Papers* and the heroine of *Flower Beneath the Foot* were forced to leave the Garden of Eden and to face the realistic world. The literature, therefore, is not that of the escape type, for each of these people has left his innocent and protective society to assume a better understanding of life and an improved state of mind.

This lecture may have been similar to one Auden delivered in New York in 1951 under the title "Dingley Dell and the Fleet". This is known only from a brief second-hand report in George H. Ford's *Dickens and His Readers* (1955): Auden "argued that Mr Pickwick represents, in his early stages, a pagan god wandering imperviously through the world; later, through suffering, the god is transformed into a human creature" (p. 13).

THE MINISTRY OF THE LAYMAN

Auden was the speaker in a regular series of Layman's Sunday talks at the Protestant Episcopal Church of the Epiphany, New York, 21 October 1951. His talk used much of the same material that he had written a year earlier for "The Things Which Are Caesar's" (p. 196). The *New York Herald Tribune* printed this report on 22 October (I have removed quotation marks and instances of "Mr Auden said" or "he said"):

As laymen we are mixing with others. Our neighbors may not be Christians, or they may be of other denominations. But the more we pray for unity, the more possible it is for God's will to be. When one church attacks another, it is not the fault of the priesthood, it is our fault much more.

If we are Christians we live in two communities. One is the Church of Christ, the other is the historical community of our neighbors. Unconsciously we may begin to adopt non-Christian views. It was never more important for the layman to know some theology, to know what they mean when they recite the Creed.

It is important for us to be completely honest with ourselves about our religious experience—what it is. One might say that the typical experience of people in the Middle Ages was one of God's nearness.

Now our dominant experience is of God's absence, of His distance. We are false if we do not admit this. The danger is of despair and unbelief. But for our time, the distance of God may be something He wishes us to learn.

The layman inherits the task of thinking in local, immediate and concrete terms. He is dealing with temporary things rather than absolute ends. In terms of the precepts of God, he must love God and his neighbor and he must use the gifts which God has entrusted to him.

The layman does his job, not to do good, but because he enjoys it. In this sense, the commandment of God to man is to be happy. But we are not to make idols of ourselves, but rather find faith in the living Christ. Eternal happiness is the only thing we are to consider.

A slightly different version, by Auden's friend Geoffrey Grigson, appeared in the *Sunday Times* (London), 28 October 1951:

If we are Christians, the position in which we find ourselves is living in two communities, the community of the mystical body of Christ and the community of our neighbours. This can make us unconsciously adopt non-Christian views. So as laymen we need more than ever to know some theology and understand our profession of faith. In the Middle Ages the typical experience was of God's nearness. Now it is of God's absence and distance, which may induce despair and unbelief; a situation in which our layman's duty is to accept the present in its fullness, not making an idol of ourselves or history or science.

We could use as our motto Sydney Smith's "Trust in God and take short views." We should love God and our neighbours, not with the deliberate aim of doing good, but because we enjoy it. So God's commandment is to be happy. The thing we have to consider is eternal happiness.

A Lecture Tour in 1952

A firm of concert and lecture agents set up the first of Auden's organized lecture tours, which took him to colleges and universities in the eastern and central United States from around 10 October to 10 December 1952. The firm, National Concert and Artists Management, New York, promoted the tour with a glossy folded sheet headed "W. H. Auden, Poet, Playwright, Critic, Librettist". A descriptive list of "Lecture Subjects" was presumably adapted from Auden's notes:

The Poet and His Poems

Auden's own story of how he writes, how he gets ideas, how he develops them, and the literary influences that have shaped his career. He will give a statement of his credo generally and tell what he thinks the poet's role should be in today's world. If his sponsors wish, he will spend the final ten minutes reading from his own works or, if preferred, will devote the entire lecture period to readings.

The Writing of Poetry

This lecture covers some of the same material included in *"The Poet and His Poems"*, but there is more emphasis upon technique and the lecture is designed for groups with serious interest in writing.

The Hero in Modern Poetry

The warrior hero, the knight-errant, the lover and the Byronic rebel have ceased to be the heroes celebrated in modern poetry. Today's poets celebrate instead, the individual from any class or occupation who has resisted de-personalization in a world where the pressures to become de-personalized are very strong. Poets discussed by Auden in this lecture include Yeats, Frost, Eliot, Lawrence and Cummings.

Music and Poetry

Exposure of the fallacy that poetry is like music. Auden's definition of the true nature of poetry. Poetry is a structure of reflections; music a structure of choices. Music as an imitation of immediate experience of our own bodies and the decisions of our own wills. The distinction between chant and song, the nature of opera, etc.

The Dynamo and the Virgin

The theme for this lecture is taken from Henry Adams and develops the thesis that man belongs simultaneously to two worlds, i.e., the rational world of the dynamo, the world of the masses and weakened relations, and, also, to the historical world of the Virgin, the world of free and analogical relations describable by language. Here the author of "The Age of Anxiety" undertakes to define the complexities and conflicts of our time.

The Nature of Comedy

What is comedy, its history in literature, how presented by various generations and groups of writers.

In "The Dynamo and the Virgin" (above) I have tentatively emended "fear and analogical" to "free and analogical", although this reading is not quite parallel to the earlier phrase "the masses and weakened relations".

The following further details appeared in reports in campus newspapers at the some of the colleges where Auden spoke.

The Poet and His Poems. Auden delivered this lecture at Indiana University on 28 October 1952; part of the report in the *Indiana Daily Student* follows:

In discussing the reasons for a person's becoming a poet, Mr Auden stated that it was not because of economic stability or friendly associations with publishers.

"A publisher of today would just as soon see a burglar enter his office as a poet," he quipped.

He said that often journalists conceive the idea that poets are wise in subjects outside their fields. Poets do not necessarily feel things more strongly than anyone else, he said. They recollect their emotions and try to establish a pattern which will make sense of their feelings.

"Any girl whose boyfriend starts writing her love poetry should become suspicious," Mr Auden said. "He is more likely thinking of his emotions rather than of her."

To make sense of these feelings, a poet will formulate a crowd of historical experiences and then will organize them into a community. The poet effects this transition by incorporating these into a verbal structure. At this point he must be cognizant of the limitations imposed by the nature of a language, Mr Auden said.

He compared the relationship of a poet and language to marriage. The union of a poet—the man—and a language—the woman—begets a poem.

The inspiration for a poem must be judged by oneself, and sincerity can be applied only to the poem, not the author, said Mr Auden.

The last fifteen minutes of Mr Auden's lecture was devoted to his reading of several of his poems.

He read three poems entitled, "Mountains," "Lakes," and "Woods."

"There should be two more in the series, but they aren't written," he shyly admitted.

The audience chuckled at the final reading of the evening ["Under Which Lyre"] . . .

He delivered the lecture again at Northwestern University on 29 October 1952; the *Daily Northwestern* reported the next day:

"Poets are not people whose feelings are any stronger than anyone else," British-American poet W. H. Auden last night told an overflow crowd at Tech auditorium.

The poet merely attempts to relate emotions to others, he explained.

He went on to discuss some of the essentials of a poem, notably sincerity and form.

Commenting on sincerity, he said that "all poets have had periods when they thought what they were writing was phony."

He stressed the essentials of the proper form of a good poem, though he said:

"A poem is like a biological thing in that the symmetry isn't mathematical."

"The poet's conscious job is to exercise what 18th century critics called judgment. He has to reject nonsense."

The poet "has to assume the history of language is at an end," he said. He said that time often changes the meaning of words.

He also delivered this lecture at Marquette University on 2 November 1952. The *Marquette Tribune* reported on 6 November (slightly emended):

The poet disagreed with the popular beliefs that poets are unable to see the world as it really is, or who feel things more deeply than their fellow man.

"Poets do not feel more strongly than others," Auden said. "It's just that poets are interested in relating experiences in order to give them meaning.

"Many people think that poets are idlers, yet poets are always being asked for opinions outside of their field as if they were wise men," he said. "I wish I could say that this opinion is justified. I'm afraid I can not," he added.

Auden defined a poet as a man who belonged to both the natural order and the historical order. The poet is in the natural order because he is a human being. He is in the historical order because he makes choices which affect history. "A poet is interested in historical events and the writing of a poem is an historical act," Auden explained.

Many readers wonder what the actual experience of the author is in connection with a poem he has written. Auden noted the case of Emily Brontë, who wrote many love poems about imaginary people who were based on little tin soldiers.

"If it were not possible to imagine big events from simple ones, we could not understand *Macbeth* unless we had committed a murder," he said.

A poet uses historical experiences which he attempts to convert into a community of definite size and structure, by admitting them into a verbal society, Auden explained. A poet has a wide range of "poetic universes" from which he chooses. He is under an obligation to find words which conform to the laws of the poetic universe, Auden added. This is often difficult because of the limits of language itself.

Auden stressed the importance of language and the "natural order of words" to the poet. A poet must assume that the history of the language in which he writes is at an end. Auden then cited some of the classic examples of beautiful poems which have grown to sound ridiculous because of the changes in the meanings of English words.

Although a poem can be measured, Auden explained, if it's perfectly symmetrical it will be without music and movement. "A poem, like a face, is not absolutely, mathematically symmetrical," he said.

Auden also pointed out there may be a certain moral occupational hazard for poets as people in that they don't have to believe anything; they only have to entertain belief as a possibility. "Every successful, beautiful work of art is analogous, but not identical to life," he added.

This lecture seems to have been substantially the same as one he delivered earlier in the year, for example at Sweet Briar College, in Sweet Briar, Virginia, on 27 February 1952, reported in the *Sweet Briar News* on 6 March:

Mr Auden introduced his topic as "What I have learned about the nature of the world and man through writing poetry." He then analyzed what he felt writing poetry means—how it is done, the nature of a poem, and the purpose of a poet, pointing out that writing a poem is like organizing a community or modeling and reading a face.

Forming a community (or poem) is . . . "a historical act—not merely done of necessity, but provoked by motives." A poet writes for fun— "to give pleasure, gain approval of others, and get cash"; he wishes to make something which is unique and, when read, a "quasi person."

Mr Auden stated several requisites for writing poetry: the poet himself must have experienced things himself to be able to write; the occasion, not the emotion, can be remembered; one must assume that the history of the language is ended and the words' meanings will remain the same; and he must be willing to follow the "laws" of each poem once they are set up.

There are, in theory, two ways of approaching a poem . . . One may either start with the idea of a kind of poem and work back to find the most suitable system of composition or vice versa. However, he states that in practice it works both ways and that once a poem is begun, like a community, it seems to take hold of its author and develop along its own chosen path.

Mr Auden warned his large audience that poems must not be judged comparatively. "They must be judged in the light of themselves. Poems are only good and bad versions of themselves." Also he warned that saying a "poet has a poetic soul is all nonsense. A poet is one who writes verses."

The Hero in Modern Poetry. Auden delivered versions of this lecture from 1951 through 1954. Much of the material that he incorporated into the lecture at different times may be found throughout his essays during the same years, particularly his "Speaking of Books" column in *The New York Times Book Review*, 20 December 1953, and in the three broadcasts published in 1955 under the title "The Dyer's Hand".

On 17 January 1951, at Mount Holyoke College, he delivered his final Florence Purington lecture under the title "The Concept of the Hero in Modern Poetry". The *Mount Holyoke News* reported on 19 January (slightly emended):

The hero and freedom were defined in natural and historical significance. The natural hero, stated Mr Auden, does great deeds, which others cannot do and, therefore, is envied.

Historical freedom makes time important to the hero. He is free to reject the desire to play and go ahead with his ambitions.

Mr Auden read selections from the works of William Yeats, Robert Frost, and T. S. Eliot. He analyzed the settings of their poems, the personification of a hero, and the people surrounding the hero.

Although each poet worked from a different perspective, the absence of a body of people and of a liturgical situation stands out. The voice in the poetry does not address the community as a whole or a class or a nation.

The largest group successfully used is limited to twelve. There are no thanksgivings for victory nor public funerals.

In the modern concept the crowd has lost its history and is void of any significance. [Auden] stated that it is not a question poetically of addressing any particular kind of people but of addressing real people.

Concluding his lecture, Mr Auden said that our problem was not in acquiring freedom, but rather in finding direction to give our life meaning.

Auden used the title "The Hero in Modern Poetry" for a lecture at Dartmouth College, 26 February 1952, reported, with some muddle in the concluding paragraphs, in *The Dartmouth* the following day:

> "Modern is that era beginning about 1870, when most of today's explorers—still essentially unchallenged—were born." Some of the men he had in mind are Yeats, Sartre, Pound, Eliot, Frost, and D. H. Lawrence.
>
> "Though the tempo has accelerated," today's writers only "colonize" where the others "explored."
>
> The "hero" in Auden's view is a "recognizable person who can use the pronoun 'I' "—a figure whom the artist and receiver "explicitly or implicitly" identify themselves with.
>
> From this point Mr Auden proceeded to indicate that the goal of the writer as expressed in his hero-ideal is the discovery of the true "I."
>
> Unlike animals, people lack "faces," or real selfness. The poet wants his unique "face" because he expects to achieve a "state of sanctity" in finding it.
>
> Today's heroes generally turn out to be hard-working artist-peasants, stoical and extremely individualistic. They prefer to struggle with nature rather than man, and to transcend convention. They dislike officialdom and dogmatism.
>
> Today's hyperpersonal poets are "quiet in tone; but if loud (like D. H. Lawrence) not because they are addressing themselves to larger audiences but because they are in a temper."

Auden's lecture under the same title at the Aldeburgh Festival on 26 June 1953 was reported the next day in the *East Anglian Daily Times* (the last quotation may be a recollection of a line in "Memorial for the City" rather than a quotation from the lecture itself); I have emended "fateless" to "faceless" and, in the final sentence, "fate" to "face":

> Mr W. H. Auden gave the afternoon talk at the Baptist Chapel. Unlike Mr Betjeman who the day before had flitted impressionistically about the same platform, Mr Auden chose the lectern and stuck stolidly to it. He gave his audience what was, in fact, a closely-reasoned lecture on The Hero in Modern Poetry.
>
> He first defined the hero in poetry from Homer to T. S. Eliot. The hero is a man with a fate of his own, who consciously faces death and gives him a run for his money—in Homeric times while defending the City, and in medieval times, while defending the True City against the barbarians, inspired at the same time by the love of a woman.
>
> By the Romantic period the persona of the poet and the hero have become almost one. The poet himself is the only man who sees through conventional behaviour and is able to be the prophet of the City which is to come.
>
> We are, Mr Auden suggested, in the middle of the modern period in the arts. This started somewhere between the late sixties and eighties of the last century. We are faced, not with the Romantic job of exploring new country, but with the more humdrum task of colonising territory already occupied, if only sparsely.
>
> It is no use attempting to make further revolutionary breaks in the arts: these are in any case geared to social changes which have a momentum of their own. Consolidation is the word now; and Mr Auden confessed himself a counter-

revolutionary as opposed to a reactionary—someone who is prepared to defend the values of a revolution which otherwise will founder.

To illustrate his theme he took four modern poets: Yeats, Frost, Eliot and D. H. Lawrence; and he recited from memory long passages and separate poems to show whom these poets are addressing and who are their heroes.

All seemed to point to the fact that there is now no relation between the City, the true type of Community, and the organisation of society for economic production.

"The problem therefore for each one of us is to avoid the danger of slipping into becoming a member of the public," the faceless public, the huge abstraction which does nothing but suffers everything.

The artist, he implied, must still be his own hero, just as he was in the Romantic period, and "although across his sleep the barbed wire also runs" he must be against all official bodies, affirming that a human being has a face of his own; and ruling his life accordingly.

Auden again used the title "The Hero in Modern Poetry" when he delivered a lecture at Stanford University on 19 October 1954, reported the next day in the *Stanford Daily* (slightly emended):

W. H. Auden . . . told a Tuesday Evening Series audience . . . that two of the most important trends in modern poetry are "the disappearance of a kind of public voice and the disappearance of the public hero."

He began by defining the terms in his topic, "The Hero in Modern Poetry." By modern . . . he meant that period, not merely in poetry, but in other fields as well since before the beginning of the 20th century. "We are living," Auden said, "not in the beginning, but in the middle of something—the change to the modern came before the beginning of the 20th century: between the 70s and the 90s."

Auden then defined the word hero: "All art has as its central subject the celebration of a hero—a real person with a face of his own and a name of his own. The hero is the nearest equivalent of what the human ought to be."

Auden then gave specific examples of the hero in poetry; first was the ancient hero "Achilles—a man who does things no other man can do." Then was the 17th-century hero—"a man with tremendous power of will, whether for good or evil, who by virtue of this will was able to establish sovereignty over others." Finally came the 18th-century hero, "perhaps a man of balance, reasoning, and common sense who defends the city just as the knight-errant defends against the dragon."

Auden then gave examples and contrasted the works of four modern poets whom he considers most important: D. H. Lawrence, Robert Frost, T. S. Eliot, and W. B. Yeats.

Reading "The Circus Animals' Desertion" by Yeats, Auden saw nature viewed as "intended to be brought into order by man." He also added, "Yeats spent the first 48 years being a minor poet so that he could spend the rest of his life being a major poet writing about his life as a minor poet."

In Frost's poetry, Auden pointed out as his second example, "Man and Nature are in direct antithesis to one another. The heroic man—stoic man—is capable of standing up to nature, alone."

These two examples, Auden said, were expressive of the difference between America and Europe: "Europeans grow up in nature which is full of sacred places—nature is a mother," the poet said; "here (in the U.S.) nature is not a mother: it is the dragon against whom St George struggles."

In the early examples of what Auden termed modern poetry he found two types of heroes: first, "the sensitive man who can't act—who passively experiences"; and second, "the brutal, insensitive man." Later, he said, these two disappear and new characteristics of a hero become common, among which is a feeling on the part of the audience of closeness to the hero, a feeling of being intimately addressed.

Mr Auden concluded his lecture by reading a group of seven poems which he called his "Bucolics". . . .

Music and Poetry. This was evidently a version of the aphoristic essay "Some Reflections on Music and Opera" (p. 296). Auden delivered the lecture under the title "Poetry and Opera" at the University of Chicago on 4 November 1952; a report appeared in the *Chicago Maroon* on 7 November:

> Beginning with a differentiation between the senses, Auden pointed out that in the visual sense the seer is entirely passive and that the visual arts represent pure being rather than becoming, while speech, and particularly music, are derived from subjective experience.
>
> Music began in connection with words, as in chants, or dance, but at a point in history, the pattern of words became subordinated to the musical pattern, he said. It was at this point, with the discovery of singing with the open throat and open mouth, that opera began.
>
> Because of this difference between the two arts, Auden said, in writing words for music, much that is right for music is wrong for poetry. Abrupt contrasts, elaboration, breaks in lines, and other treasured properties of poetry must be abandoned. While words are expendable in opera, syllables are not, and since the rhythm of each language is different, translations of operas are usually unsatisfactory.
>
> The poet who is writing for opera must suppress his natural impulse to write poetry, Auden stated. He must avoid complications and intricacies in his libretto, but can use his imagination in the development of operatic plots and characters.
>
> Because opera is a virtuoso art, naturalism is not suitable for it. Auden defined naturalism as "stylized low life instead of stylized high life." The operatic character is, however, well suited to representation of the universal. Because of the singer's obvious enjoyment of his singing in spite of tragic events, opera cannot be pathetic, and for this reason it is difficult to use contemporary subjects for opera. Universality is necessary, Auden claimed, because the sad situation "must be one about which you can afford to be frivolous because you yourself are involved in it."
>
> Slowly-dawning recognition is impossible in opera, he added, "music cannot walk but must jump or run." Nor is self-deception possible. On the other hand, stated Auden, the librettist doesn't have to bother about credibility. All that is necessary is a situation either too funny or too extraordinary for words, so that it is credible that people should sing instead.
>
> The librettist need not worry about his characters staying in character, either: "in opera song can be out of place, but it cannot be out of character." Auden then proceeded to illustrate these statements with examples from his recent collaboration with Stravinsky, *The Rake's Progress.*

In conclusion, Auden stated that if music in the West is an imitation of historical choice, then opera is an imitation of willfulness. "Not only do we feel certain
things, but we insist on feeling them whatever the cost." Opera, said Auden, is the
greatest assertion of human freedom, and it is no coincidence that the development of opera coincided with the development of the liberal movement. "Every
high C helped demolish the theory that we are puppets of economic forces."

The Nature of Comedy. This talk evidently used the same material that Auden had published earlier in "Notes on the Comic" (p. 307). A few additional details occur in reports of similar talks that Auden gave after completing his 1952 lecture tour. He gave
one such talk at Smith College, 10 April 1953, under the title "Some Reflections on
the Comic"; it was reported in the college newspaper *The Sophian*, 14 April 1953:

> Mr Auden defined "comic" as a contradiction arising from a relation between the
> individual or personal, which does not involve the spectator. In order to be comic,
> a subject must not suffer; or if he does, it must be according to his just deserts.
> Suffering can also be ironic as a proof that we are in the truth, and the subject is
> not. The existence of the comic spirit is possible only in a culture which has laws,
> and which permits a strong sense of the individual.
>
> The poet divided humor into three categories: that rising from a situation
> caused by natural elements, that of oral humor, and that of the spirit. In enlarg-
> ing on the third topic, Auden used the characters of Falstaff, Don Quixote, and
> Mr Pickwick as illustrations. He pointed out that there was a contradiction in each
> of the characters, such as the inversion of the symbol of pickpocketing in Falstaff.
> The humor caused by the religious hero Don Quixote comes from a collision with
> the laws of the world, and frequently involves a certain amount of suffering.

Notes on the Rake

Auden and Chester Kallman gave a lecture recital on *The Rake's Progress* for the Metropolitan Opera Guild, in Town Hall, New York, on 28 January 1953, about two weeks
before the American première of the opera. An unsigned report, with the title above,
appeared in *Opera News*, 9 March 1953, and is reprinted in *Libretti*, pp. 616–17.

A Symposium on Art and Morals

A symposium titled "Art and Morals", at Smith College on 23 and 24 April 1953,
opened with a keynote address by Archibald MacLeish, followed by talks by nine other
speakers: Auden, Allen Tate, Lionel Trilling, Ben Shahn, Philip Johnson, Edgar Wind,
Jacques Barzun, George Boas, and W. G. Constable. A transcript of Auden's talk (in
the possession of Margaret Wind) has been slightly emended for the text below. Following the transcript of Auden's talk are his three contributions to the panel discussion that ended the symposium (from a transcript in the Smith College Library).

Ladies and Gentlemen: An interest in the relation of art (and of the beautiful) and morals, of the true and good, inevitably leads either an artist or a
critic into talking nonsense. However, a critic who, realizing this fact, either
explicitly or implicitly avoids it and is content to be either a pure connoisseur

or a pure historian, avoids making a fool of himself; but they pay a price, that they are unreadable. In the course of the next two days you are doubtless going to hear a lot of nonsense, but I hope that we will be able to make it at least reasonably entertaining.

Now what I want to talk about myself could be summed up in the 111th Sonnet of Shakespeare:

> And almost thence my nature is subdu'd
> To what it works in, like the dyer's hand.

What I want to talk about briefly is the kind of biases in relation to morals that arise for an artist in respect of his occupation, of what he does,—just as you might think of the bias the lawyer has or the scientist has, and so on.

All right, let us begin with what is the brute stuff, the brute concern of the artistic imagination. It is the singular, the personal, that which has a face, that which has a proper name. There are various divisions of this; the first one is the numinous or the uncanny; and that may be both the divine and demonic. Secondly, it is the heroic, which may be both the virtuous heroic and the villainous. And then, if you like, you can take the beautiful and the hideous.

What art excludes is the banal, the repetitive, the official, the nameless. It does not necessarily follow, of course, that the imagination says that what is banal should not exist. It simply says that in the world of art you cannot deal with this. In that sense, one might say that in any work of art there are no things. If in a painting the sun appears, it is, as Blake remarked, not just a round disc, the size of a guinea, but a host shouting "Holy, holy!" In music, if you have a musical representation of a storm, it is not a natural storm, it is the wrath of Zeus.

Numbers can appear in art, but not in the kind of way that they appear in your arithmetic books, when you learn about bath taps filling bathtubs. When I think of numbers, I think of counting out rhymes: "Five golden rings, four calling birds, three French hens, two turtle doves, and a partridge in a pear tree." Well, you see, counting does not mean exactly the same in art as it means in mathematics. And certainly, art has no room for the algebraical conception of "any".

The imagination, the artistic imagination, has certain absolute presuppositions. First, that which is living has freedom to choose itself. Fate may circumscribe a man, but a man is not a puppet of fate. He confronts his fate, and this is good in itself. I think one must say that a determinist philosophy is incompatible with art. Whether it is true or false, they are not compatible.

The second presupposition of imagination is that life as we know it appears in finite creatures, is portrayed in material images, in a material medium; that matter as such is a good. I think that therefore a Manichaeist view, whether it is true or false, is not compatible with art.

Now, imagination leads to another faculty, the moral faculty of conscience, the distinction between what is good and what is evil. What imagination does is to exclude the banal and the repetitive. However, though imagination transfigures both the good and the evil in a certain sense, it is false to itself if it blurs the distinction between them. I think you will recognize at once in any work of art that the evil cannot be represented, shall we say, as serene, emotionally serene. It cannot be represented visually as being in perfect proportion. These are both aesthetic judgments, but we would recognize at once that there is something wrong if that were not the case.

Now it is true that if you isolate the artistic imagination in regards to particular acts, the artistic imagination may seem a little flighty. Let us take a question: Should a man commit adultery with another man's wife? Now, let us suppose the couple may visit Mrs Imagination; and they say: "What shall we do?" Mrs Imagination takes up a paper and says: "What is your name?"— "Tristan. Isolde."—"Who is the husband?"—"King Mark."—"Who is King Mark?" Tristan says: "My best friend." Then a further question to Isolde: "What did Tristan do?"—"Tristan killed the hero of my country." Then Mrs Imagination says: "This is most interesting. You must commit adultery." If they look a little doubtful, Mrs Imagination says: "Fine, here is a love potion, just to encourage this." And off they go. What they do not realize is that the moment they have left the office, Mrs Imagination telephones to Melot to make the situation a little more difficult.

However, it could be quite different. Supposing that the man were a sort of Perseus and the girl was Andromeda, and he had saved her from death, and that the husband actually is an absolute monster and a deadly enemy. In that case Mrs Imagination would say; "No, now the marriage bonds must be observed; and we'll conjure up the ghost of an ill father, or anything to arrange it."

There is a third possibility, that they are not very remarkable people. You see, just a Mr and Mrs Smith, and the lover is a Mr Jones; and nobody cares very much about anybody. It is a question of what to do on a wet afternoon. Then Mrs Imagination says: "Go away, I don't care what you do."

Now they might consult another figure,—and now I'm going to put my big foot in my mouth, I'm going to call it "various doctors Science", because there is not one, there is a whole row of them. All right, the couple arrive, and Dr Science number one says (none of them actually ask any questions about their names because after all they are just male and female particles): "Well, I can't tell you; what is right is whatever is the case. You go off and decide what you do, but please call me up and tell me what you do, because I'm preparing a statistical table." The second one says: "Now, my observations in biology show me that sex is a matter of natural drives. Of course, you must commit adultery because you have to do what you feel like doing, and anything else would be wrong." Number three, however, says: "Now, I've studied the history of cultures and the family, and I see that the future of society depends upon keeping the marriage vow. So that must be kept." As the couple looks rather blue, he says: "No, all right—it *is* difficult. Here is a sedative" (as opposed to a love potion).

You see, Mrs Imagination takes the view that one law for the ox and the ass is oppression. Dr Science takes the view that hard cases make bad law. Now some moralists, seeing this rather frivolous aspect of the imagination, have wanted art to suppress its imaginative qualities. That always means denying that actually all human beings have a separate faculty of moral conscience. They want the imagination to take over an activity which properly belongs to the conscience. Now, one way of doing this, of course, is to treat evil as if it were banal; in other words, to exclude it; to have a literature which is only about good people. The other one is to give quite imaginary reasons why people should be good. You remember how Miss Prism talked to her students about the novel she had written: "The good ended happily, the bad unhappily, that is what fiction means."

But now, in fact, because we have in addition to an artistic imagination a moral conscience, it is very often the case that it is only by our imagination first being caught that our conscience is aroused, whether in regard to ourselves or in regard to others. Here I should like to quote a passage by Chesterton about Dickens, where he is explaining why Dickens actually succeeded in getting certain social reforms effected, or contributed very strongly to them. He says: "The boys at Dotheboys were perhaps more bullied, but they were certainly less bored. For indeed how could anyone be bored with the society of so sumptuous a creature as Mr Squeers? We feel vaguely that neither Oliver nor anyone else could be entirely unhappy in the presence of the purple personality of Mr Bumble. So long as Squeers was dull as well as cruel, he was permitted. The moment he became amusing as well as cruel, he was destroyed. As long as Bumble was merely inhuman, he was allowed. When he became human, humanity wiped him out. For in order to do these great acts of justice, we must realize not only the humanity of the oppressed, but even the humanity of the oppressor."

Well, that is the first stage,—the basic division which the imagination makes between the interesting and the boring. Now the moment the imagination actually starts creating a work, something else comes in. Assume that we know what is trivial and that we have excluded that. Now among the important and the interesting, the imagination immediately makes a moral judgment: it is good as these things are, but not good as they are at present. At the moment, they are a disorderly crowd. This world that the imagination is interested in is in some sense first of all a fallen world, being full of inconsistency, disorder, contradiction. At the same time the artist believes that in some sense this is a redeemable world, that these things should become a community, a city, in which all these singular events are members, one of another. And in fact, every successful work of art is very nearly a utopia.

Here I must tell you a little personal story about the first time in my life, at the age of eleven, in 1918, when I became aware of a personal moral problem. From the age of six my whole imaginative life was centered in a particular kind of world about lead mines. We needn't go into psychological reasons for this; any psychoanalyst could tell you about it. Now, I spent a good deal of my imaginative life inventing the Platonic idea of all lead mines. And then I ran into a problem. Because in a lead mine, among other things—I won't bother you with too many of the technical details—one has to have a concentrating mill which separates the lead ore from the rock. I was planning all this out in my mind. And then there was a particular machine which happens to be called the buddle of which there are two varieties. To me, one was more beautiful or more holy than the other. On the other hand, from my reading I knew that the one I didn't like was the most efficient. And here at the age of eleven I was faced with a straight moral problem, that I had to surrender the detail I preferred to the interest of the whole. Now the ordinary conventional psychological explanation about the reality principle won't hold, because it is a fancy world anyway; but the point is here that any world makes its own demands when one realizes that certain things have to be surrendered for the harmony of the whole. And later on in life, when I started to write poetry, I found that this problem came up all the time. That was my first personal experience of it.

In the writing of poetry, which is the only art about which I know anything and therefore it's the only one I can talk about, there are just two things which I should like to say. First of all, that poetry is not written in a trance. On the other hand, the second truth is that you cannot write a good poem simply because you want to; that this business is a fight with the Muse, analogous to the fight between Jacob and the angel. Whether you take a question about form, a particular question about a right word, whatever you like to make it to be,— the angel has to give you these things; the Muse has to. On the other hand, the Muse is always whispering to you, and fifty percent of what the Muse says is rubbish and has to be rejected. What you wait for is for the Muse to speak with authority. The whole conception of moral authority that an artist learns in his work is that the Muse never explains anything, that you either say: "You are not an authority," or: "Yes, you are, and I obey." This conception of authority is a personal thing saying, "Obey!" And either you say: "I won't," or "You are right." The artist's function, as a conscious person, is here a prohibitive one.

Now it is curious how the Muse can assert her authority in a very funny way. In a very excellent anthology of Mr Barzun's, he quotes a letter of Rossini's. In Rossini's opera *Moses in Egypt* there is a famous chorus, where there is a very effective sudden transition from G Minor to G Major. Now in one of Rossini's letters, which Mr Barzun translated, he describes what happened. He was having a terrible row with his girl friend and was rather ill, and by mistake he dipped his pen in the medicine bottle instead of the ink bottle and made a blot. He put sand on it, blew away the sand, and when he looked at the blot it looked like a natural. He got the idea of a change of key. The point is that that blot spoke with authority.

The kind of judgment which is purely the authoritative intensity, unfortunately in life is not always worthy. An artist understands very well things like a fashion law, that you should on the first of May wear a straw hat. Why he likes that is that there is absolutely no reason why you should. It is a purely arbitrary thing which the kind of people you admire do. Of course you may equally well say: "The kind of people I admire don't," and wear a brown derby; but that is just the reverse. On the other hand, what they mind is a thing like a traffic regulation because there is a reason for this outside itself. An artist understands the idea of a vow because a vow is a personal commitment. An artist does not understand the idea of equality, of one law which applies to everybody at all times. In his private life, one might say therefore, the artist is interested in snobs. It is not a question of class, it is a question of people. He likes queer people who stimulate his imagination. He likes people who are rich, he likes people who are beautiful, he likes people who are amusing. Artists do not like people who are doing what I'm doing at the moment— I was just talking about art—because that is a bore.

If I imagined myself, as all of us do, as a dictator, what would I do? I would be a pluralist. Each village would have to have very strict rules. I would have one village where nobody was allowed to drink alcohol. I would have another village, however, where no one was allowed to drink anything else. To the artist every world is a possible world, and in the end this is an extremely skeptical view. There is no one view which is better than another. On the other hand, of course, no artist has any respect for a majority, and in one sense, not even for a minority. The artistic view is a personal authority, and in that sense you might say it is a minority, of course; but one that admits of disobedience.

An artist understands obedience; he understands rebellion. What I think is repugnant to his imagination is any kind of propaganda. Because what propaganda does is to make people unaware of the fact that they are obeying. The effect of propaganda is to make people's obedience a reflex, and that is no fun.

The limitation, if you take the dangers for an artist, is that because the imagination first of all makes the distinction between the interesting (or the unique) and the boring, and secondly because in making its order, it being a possible order, it can exclude things which it does not need at the moment,—the artistic imagination as such has no real conception of time, of repetition; it sees only isolated instances; it foreshortens time. Because it likes crises and novelties, it doesn't mind taking up a cross, but it wants it to be a new cross and a new shape; and the artistic imagination does not understand the idea of taking up the same cross every day. If I say that art has many virtues, imagination does lack humility. What may be invaluable, however, on the other side, is it does have in our time a particular importance: Every work of art that is produced may not be terribly good, but as long as it is being produced at all, a real work of art in itself is an assertion of the value of the personal free-willing faith; and in an age in which the will to enforce the impersonal, the official, seems so strong, maybe that in itself has political importance. Every artist, whether he knows it or not, does pray to the Madonna, and however sinful he may be, at least he does not bow down and worship before the dynamo.

The first of Auden's comments in the concluding panel discussion follows; Auden begins by alluding to the talk by Edgar Wind (who enjoyed an argumentative friendship with Auden) earlier that day:

After the avalanche of the wrath of Jehovah which descended on my head this afternoon, I can only say that my head is bloody but unbowed. Perhaps I should make clear that, as far as I can see, there is practically no difference between Professor Wind's view and my own as to the nature of art. If I may use this word "frivolity"—I use it deliberately in referring to an art to which I am passionately devoted and to which I devote my life. The fact that I do that means that I have to take it lightly. Then, I think, the only difference between us, possibly, is to what degree art may be said to be magic. I take the view, I think, that true art, I might almost say, is a form of magic which consists in disenchantment from the self; that the bad kind of magic is a kind of propaganda by which obedience becomes a reflex. But what art is interested in is an obedience which is really chosen by yourself. In conclusion I should merely like to thank Professor Wind very much. He mentioned, in quoting a poem of mine, the following two lines:

> The dirt, the imprecision, and the beer
> Produce a few smart wisecracks every year.

Well, I think in this year of grace, 1953, "beating about the burning bush" will remain one of those few smart wisecracks which will be memorable.

Auden's second comment, later in the discussion, alludes to the town of Northampton, Massachusetts, the site of Smith College:

I would first like to raise a point about actually what it is possible to write poetry about. Mr MacLeish yesterday quoted Yeats. I think it is very important to see that the rebellion and the troubles took place on a small enough basis for the personal to enter. When Yeats writes of Connolly, MacBride, and so on, he really knew these people personally; when he refers to the Dublin Post Office, it is the Dublin Post Office. It is almost impossible, I think, to write very often about, shall we say, a political situation as we have it at the moment because it takes place on a scale of impersonality of which the imagination can do nothing. If we had a political row in Northampton I could write a poem about it. I do not know really what I would really write, supposing I wanted to, about the [House] investigating committee in Washington, about which I know nothing except I don't like it.

His third comment responds to questions submitted in writing from the audience:

Two questions here, one of which I can't really answer because it is about a painting I haven't seen. "Mr Auden, you said that no artist should portray evil as beautiful. In that case, what is the position of Doré's engraving of Lucifer from *Paradise Lost*"—which I have not seen. But I will answer the second part: "or of *Paradise Lost* itself in which Lucifer is called 'Child of the Morning'?" Well, actually the portrait of Satan as drawn in *Paradise Lost* illustrates very much what I was trying to say yesterday: Satan is so portrayed you can see there is something a little wrong with him. That doesn't mean he isn't an image of great power, but I said that evil always betrays itself by a certain kind of tension, a certain disturbance of balance, of proportion, which I think certainly one finds about Satan in *Paradise Lost*. With regard to the other question I have here: Would I explain why determinism as a philosophy is incompatible with art? Well, simply because, if it is really believed in a very complete sense, then—I do not say it is either right or wrong, but I say that art, I think, will not exist; because in any work of art, nothing exists except things of freedom. That is why I tried to say yesterday that I do not think there are any real things in art.

A Forum on the Ethics of Controversy

The American Committee on Cultural Freedom, an organization of writers and artists secretly funded by the United States Central Intelligence Agency, sponsored an annual series of forums in the 1950s. On 8 April 1954 Auden was one of four speakers at a forum, "The Ethics of Controversy", at the Museum of Modern Art in New York. The other speakers were the sociologist Daniel Bell, the journalist and editor Henry Hazlitt, and the author on Jewish subjects Will Herberg. Auden had originally been invited to speak at a forum on 25 March with the planned title "Anti-Intellectualism and the Intellectuals," but the invitation took a few weeks to reach him, and by the time he agreed, in a letter to the Committee on 10 February, speakers for the forum had already been chosen, and he agreed to speak instead on 8 April. The text of his remarks is taken from a transcript now in the Tamiment Library at New York University (slightly emended). Auden was the third speaker, introduced like the others by Sidney Hook.

Thank you, Professor Hook. I quite agree with you [about the difficulty of talking about the subject], as I don't really know why I am here. I cannot talk about ethics, because I don't really know anything about them. I can only talk a little about aesthetics, which I do know something about—I hope.

Not long ago Senator [Joseph] McCarthy gave a speech at a breakfast, and all the audience shouted. I think it would be very unfair to say that all those people necessarily believed in what McCarthy stands for, what he believes in, but like ordinary human beings—and I think like you and me—they wanted a good performance. And that, it seems to me, is very, very important when we are thinking about any kind of question of politics.

The Committee for Cultural Freedom has put out a series of ten commandments which you have heard about, and which you may have read. They seem to me admirable. I subscribe to every one of them. I would only say that if they were all scrupulously observed I [do not] doubt that we should be living in a Utopia, a rather dull one where the debates might be carried on by IBM machines.

The aesthetic element of combat plays a great role whether it is in the law courts when lawyers are arguing or whether it is in the House of Congress or the House of Parliament. There are certain aesthetic rules, for example, to which Mr Churchill subscribed—and who was one of the great masters of debate—which are very fair. For example, you must be absolutely implacable when people are strong and you must be magnanimous with people when they are weak. That is about the only rule there is. Otherwise you seize every opportunity for weakness.

I entirely agree, first of all, with what Mr [Henry] Hazlitt said that you must be conscientious and get out the facts, but you are allowed to take—I think must take—advantage of any weakness of your opponent, and take full advantage. Again, as Mr Churchill said, "I give no quarter and I bear no malice." That seems to be a very good rule in controversy.

It is a little unfortunate, I think, in our time that in the study of oratory of certain kinds, we seem to be getting more and more in the position where the people who have a talent for that kind of controversy are often apt to be what we call in quotes "demagogues." I wish we could have a few more liberals who were a little more demagogic.

After all, if you take, who should we say, Voltaire, Shaw or Sydney Smith, I wouldn't call any of them exactly fair. One of the nice things about Mr [Adlai] Stevenson is that he makes good wisecracks; he is nice. One likes to read, for example, Sydney Smith talking to the game boss. First of all, he is very well-informed. He then knows how to phrase things in such a way as hits what he says. He is talking about man-traps and about people, the landowner. He says their object is to preserve game. If the lives of their fellow-creatures can be preserved at the same time, they have no objection; if not, the least of God's creatures must fall—the rustic without a soul, not the Christian partridge, not the immortal pheasant, not the rational woodcock or the incomparable hare.

I think Mr Hazlitt was perfectly correct in saying that you should not use arguments with people you do not believe yourself, but it is up to persons in controversies to find the best method of expressing what he has to say to get across to the audience his concern.

Oratory will differ according to the group you are speaking to, the size of it, the nature of the medium—whether it is television, whether it is radio, whether it is the House of Commons, and so on. But it is a job for someone who goes in [for] controversies to know their stuff.

I would simply make a plea for the recovery of the art of oratory.

A Talk on Modern Poetry

Auden lectured at Washington University, St Louis, on 16 October 1955, in the third of four talks by four writers in a series titled "The Writer and His Public". The talk was announced, apparently in error, as "Dingley Dell and the Fleet", but seems to have been made up of elements from Auden's lectures titled "The Hero in Modern Poetry" and other lectures that he had written during the previous few years. The *St Louis Post-Dispatch* reported on the following morning:

> Modern poetry is often called difficult, but the same charge could be made against good poetry of any age, W. H. Auden . . . said here last night.
>
> There are riddles in modern poetry, but this does not necessarily mean the poems are obscure, Auden declared. The test of a good poem is that the reader feels the explanation of the riddle, when given him by a critic, is a natural one, rather than unfair, he continued. . . .
>
> The 48-year old poet declared modern poetry was really begun before World War I, and that men of his generation can only be colonizers, not explorers, in this field.
>
> "The change in the arts has taken place for the same reason as the change in our life: civilization has become more mechanized and complex," Auden said.
>
> Increased mechanization reduces the field about which a poet can write, because it has dehumanized so many processes formerly performed by hand, Auden said. "A poet can write about a man slaying a dragon, but not about a man pushing a button that releases a bomb," he remarked.
>
> Improved technology has helped the artist by making the entire past come alive, through records, books, and films, thus expanding his knowledge of tradition, he said. Formerly an artist could only learn of his immediate past, relying upon the word-of-mouth stories of his elders, he added.
>
> "Now that so many sounds and sights present themselves to the artist in everyday life, he must spend a tremendous amount of time simply in 'not hearing and not seeing,' in order to remain sensitive to important objects," Auden asserted.
>
> "The poet can be sure of only one thing about society: it will never let him earn a living simply by writing poetry," Auden, a lecturer and teacher as well as poet, declared.
>
> Perhaps the day will come, he suggested, when poets will be taught a skilled manual trade, as part of their apprenticeship in the writing craft, so that they can be sure of supporting themselves while writing poetry part-time.
>
> Auden . . . said young poets should spend more time studying practical subjects

such as botany, geology and even cooking, rather than literary criticism, in order to enhance their descriptive powers.

Auden . . . distinguished between verse writers who are poets and historians.

The poet, a figure of classical times, believes fate controls mankind, whom he divided into heroes and churls, Auden declared. The historian, the versifier of the Christian era, sees man as the possessor of free will, and shows in his writing development of character, he said.

The *Oedipus Rex* of Sophocles is an example of the classical style of writing, written in an elevated style about a hero. *Macbeth* shows the poet as historian, for Shakespeare has written essentially a record of the development of a man faced with choices, he pointed out.

Auden . . . quoted Virginia Woolf to express his own evaluation of art. In his quiet but very English voice he said, "This is our triumph; this is our consolation."

Endorsements and Citations

ENDORSEMENTS

In a letter to Jacques Barzun, 22 May 1950, Auden suggested that Barzun's publishers could use a quotation from Auden's review "The Score and Scale of Berlioz" (p. 193) in advertising the book, but, if nothing suitable could be found, he offered this alternative blurb: "To understand the nineteenth century it is essential to understand Berlioz, and to understand Berlioz it is essential to read Professor Barzun" (Columbia University Library). This seems never to have been used.

Newspaper advertisements for James Merrill's play *The Immortal Husband*, at the Theatre de Lys, New York, in 1955 included a phrase from Auden: "The only new play for some time which I have both enjoyed and admired" (quoted from the advertisement in the *New York Times*, 21 February 1955).

CITATIONS

The American Academy of Arts and Letters and the National Institute of Arts and Letters holds an annual Ceremonial in New York at which the winners of prizes and awards are announced. Members of the Academy and Institute write brief anonymous citations for the Institute's Arts and Letters awards; these are printed in the program of the Ceremonial and in the Academy and Institute's annual *Proceedings*. For the Academy and Institute's Ceremonial on 28 May 1952 Auden wrote one of the citations in literature:

To Theodore Roethke, for the vigor and originality of his style, the subtlety of his versification, and his faithful devotion over many years to the art of poetry, both as a producer and as a teacher.

For the Ceremonial on 26 May 1954, Auden wrote two of the citations in literature (the naming of the recipient's birthplace is customary in these citations, but had been omitted in the citation to Roethke):

To Richmond Lattimore, born in Paotingfu, China, for his translations from the Greek into English verse. By his fine scholarship, literary judgment and poetically informed sense of the life of his own language, he makes available to modern readers a deepened awareness of the substance and formal qualities of the original.

To Ruthven Todd, born in Edinburgh, Scotland, in recognition of his scholarly and illuminating studies of early romantic British art and his loving devotion to natural history.

Typescripts of the citations are in the Academy and Institute's archives.

Auden on the Air

THIS appendix lists Auden's radio and television talks, readings, and discussions; other broadcasts almost certainly occurred but have left no trace.

Auden gave a brief talk during the intermission of a dramatized version of Graham Greene's *The Ministry of Fear*, in the anthology series University Theatre, NBC Radio Network, 23 January 1949. The talk was published under the title (probably not Auden's) "The Heresy of Our Time" (see p. 708).

Auden's talk on Thomas Hardy's poetry, broadcast on BBC Third Programme, 16 September 1949, is described in the headnote to the text, below.

Auden's reading of twelve poems at the Museum of Modern Art, New York, was broadcast outside the United States by the Voice of America, 1 March 1950.

Auden read some of his poems, then participated with four others in a symposium "What Is Culture", on All India Radio, Bombay, 1 April 1951.

Auden, Chester Kallman, and Igor Stravinsky were interviewed during the interval of the broadcast of the première of *The Rake's Progress* on RAI, Rete Azzura, 11 September 1951.

Auden and William Kennedy discussed the topic "Tradition and Experiment" in the series *The World in Books*, WEVD radio, New York, 22 December 1951. Vernon Brooks, the cohost of the series with Kennedy, transcribed his recording of the broadcast for publication in the *W. H. Auden Society Newsletter* 17 (March 1998), where it is misdated 24 December 1951.

Auden, Robert Gomberg, and Helen Parkhust discussed the question "Do we expect too much of our children?" on *It's a Problem*, WNBT-TV, New York, 30 January 1952 (and syndicated on NBC television). This half-hour daytime series of round-table discussions dealt with common problems in women's lives.

Auden again appeared on *It's a Problem*, 10 March 1952, discussing with Dr Roma Gans the question "Should parents teach school-age children?"

Auden and Marianne Moore were interviewed by Glenway Wescott on the subject "Poetical Traditions and Modern Forms", *The Writers Meet*, WNYC radio, New York, 3 April 1953. Wescott's impressions of this interview are noted in *Continual Lessons: The Journals of Glenway Wescott, 1937–1955*, ed. Robert Phelps with Jerry Rosco (1990), p. 331.

Auden recorded an extempore talk on *The Rake's Progress* for the BBC probably during a visit to England in June 1952; the talk was broadcast in the BBC Third Programme, 28 August 1953, and a transcript appears in *Libretti*, pp. 620–26.

Auden's talk listed in newspapers as "Rereading *Huckleberry Finn*" and titled on the BBC transcript as "Huck and Oliver" was broadcast in the BBC Third Programme, 27 September 1953. The talk was published in *The Listener* (see p. 756).

Auden made brief, rehearsed remarks on T. S. Eliot in the CBS television series *Omnibus*, 14 February 1954. Further details appear below.

Auden introduced a recording of poems by (and read by) Dylan Thomas, WNBC radio, New York, 3 March 1954.

A discussion with Jack Sterling, occasioned by a book festival in New York, was broadcast in the radio series *Make Up Your Mind*, CBS radio network, 26 March 1954. On the same day, and probably for the same occasion, Auden was heard on a broadcast on WNYC radio, New York, together with Francis Brown, Elizabeth Janeway, and Louis Kronenberger.

Auden delivered a talk on Melville, one of a series of six talks by various authors on American writers, CBC Trans-Canada Radio, 22 December 1954.

In the fourth program in the television series *Writers of Today*, Auden was interviewed by Walter Kerr. This series was filmed in 1955 by the National Educational Television Film Service, and broadcast at various dates during the next few years (e.g. on WCBS-TV, 19 March 1958). Transcribed in *Harvard Advocate* ([1975]).

Auden read from *The Shield of Achilles* on *Anthology*, a series broadcast by the NBC Radio Network, 27 February 1955.

Under the general title "The Dyer's Hand" Auden recorded three lectures for broadcast in the BBC Third Programme, 8, 15, and 22 June 1955. The talks were published in *The Listener* (see p. 768).

Auden's BBC talk "History, Feigned and Real" (on *The Return of the King*, by J.R.R. Tolkien) was broadcast in the BBC Third Programme, 16 November 1955. A transcript and further details appear below.

Auden's contribution to "A Tribute to Ezra Pound on His Seventieth Birthday" was broadcast by the Yale undergraduate radio station, WYBC, New Haven, on 5 December 1955. A transcript and further details appear below.

THOMAS HARDY: AN ASPECT OF HIS POETRY

Auden wrote this talk probably in Italy during the summer of 1949; it was read for him by two BBC announcers, one reading his text, the other reading Hardy's poems, in a broadcast in the BBC Third Programme, 16 September 1949. Published schedules listed the talk as "The Art of Thomas Hardy"; the title on the transcript in the BBC Archives is "Thomas Hardy: An Aspect of His Poetry"; possibly neither title was written by Auden. The following text is very slightly emended from the transcript.

When Thomas Hardy was born, Tennyson had only published one volume and Metternich was still the ruler of Europe; when he died, *The Waste Land* had been out for several years, Stalin was in the Kremlin and Hitler was already making speeches. In 1840 rural England was still the countryside of the eighteenth century, its customs and loyalties as yet undisturbed by the railway boom, and the industrial north was that grim temple to the god of laissez-faire described in the Factory reports; by 1928 the urban or suburban culture which we know had overwhelmed all localities, and the interference of the State in matters of social welfare was taken for granted by the wildest conservative. When the poet was a young man, intellectuals were asking whether Darwin and the Higher Criticism had not made faith in the Christian Creed impossible; in his old age, they were asking whether Freud, Marx and the anthropologists had not made it impossible to believe in the existence of any absolute truth or value.

It is worth while, I think, in reading any poet to keep his historical background in mind, provided that one does not imagine that it can tell us anything about the *value* of his work. No knowledge of his age or his private life can ever enable us to judge that one of his poems is good and another bad, or explain why. It does however help us to understand why he writes this kind of poetry and not that, why he writes about this *subject* rather than that. Again it is important to remember that the history of literature and human history, though interrelated are not identical.

To the young poet it is the former which is the most important, i.e. his problem is not: "How can I describe a changing world?" but rather "How can I see and describe the world of human experience through my own eyes and words rather than those of my predecessors?" As he matures and develops a personal vision and style, his problem shifts: now it is as if the poetic imagination were the constant factor and the world of experience which was moving, and his question becomes: "How can poetry master and express this novel experience of mankind?"

Hardy, like his contemporaries, had first of all to emancipate himself from the diction and versification of Tennyson, Browning, and Matthew Arnold. He does not seem to have shared the interest of Bridges and Hopkins in prosodic innovation, nor to have developed a theory of diction like Doughty. His chief influences seem to have been:

Swinburne, e.g.:

> I need not go
> Through sleet and snow
> To where I know
> She waits for me;
> She will tarry me there
> Till I find it fair,
> And have time to spare from company.

The movement is quite his own, but it is a personal development from the Swinburnian metric.

Browning, e.g.:

> I've laid in food, Dear,
> And broached the spice and brewed, Dear;
> And if our July hope should antedate,
> Let the char-wench mount and gallop by the halterpath and wood, Dear,
> And fetch assistance straight.

And that other Dorsetshire poet, William Barnes, e.g.:

> I, these berries of juice and gloss,
> Sir or Madam,
> Am clean forgotten as Thomas Voss;

Thin-urned, I have burrowed away from the moss
That covers my sod, and have entered this yew,
And turned to clusters ruddy of view,
   All day cheerily,
   All night eerily!

From all three he inherited a liking for complicated stanza forms. Having a strong visual imagination he could learn fluency from Swinburne without inheriting the Swinburnian vagueness: the influence of Browning, on the other hand, seems to me less happy, i.e. one is sometimes conscious in Hardy's poetry as in Browning's of an arbitrary relation between the form of the verse and its content; rhymes and phrases seem forced, e.g. in this stanza from an excellent poem "An Ancient to Ancients":

   In dance the polka hit our wish.
         Gentlemen,
   The paced quadrille, the spry schottische,
   "Sir Roger"—And in opera spheres,
   The "Girl" (the famed "Bohemian"),
   And "Trovatore", held the ears,
         Gentlemen.

One feels that the fifth line only runs as it does because *The Bohemian Girl* did not rhyme with *Gentlemen* and was two syllables short.

   William Barnes, on the other hand, was perhaps the most fruitful influence of all. He liked stanzas which were not only complicated but where the complications necessarily involved the structure of the thought, and many of Hardy's most successful poems are of this type, e.g.:

   "Who's in the next room?— who?
      I seemed to see
   Somebody in the dawning passing through,
      Unknown to me"
   "Nay: you saw nought. He passed invisibly".

   "Who's in the next room?—who?
      I seem to hear
   Somebody muttering firm in a language new
      That chills the ear".
   "No: you catch not his tongue who has entered there".

   "Who's in the next room? —who?
      I seem to feel
   His breath like a clammy draught, as if it drew
      From the Polar Wheel".
   "No: none who breathes at all does the door conceal".

"Who's in the next room?—who?"
  A figure wan
With a message to one in there of something due?
  "Shall I know him anon?"
"Yea he; and he brought such; and you'll know him anon".

This poem also shows Hardy's diction at its best which is when he is simplest and most direct. Unfortunately it is not always so. The poet who could write as impressive a line as: "I see what you are doing: you are leading me on", is also capable of writing like this:

I thought you a fire
On Heath-Plantation Hill,
Dealing out mischief the most dire
To the chattels of men of hire
There in their vill.

I have referred to Hardy's visual imagination. Unobtrusive—he does not indulge in description for description's sake—his sense of the significant detail, the row of raindrops on the gatebar, the coppery sea flinging its lazy flounce at the quay, the wagonette in the rain at the crossroads, etc. is unerring. Hardy is a regional poet in the best sense, i.e. he is not confined to provincial interests, but sees the most general interests in terms of a loved and intimately known locality. Not all, perhaps even few, of the great poets have been topophiles. Dante was; Shakespeare, I think, was not. But topophilia is one of the most characteristic and endearing qualities of Hardy's poetry. When the souls of the slain return from the Boer War they gather at Portland Bill: it is not any clump of trees which say "Life offers—to deny!" but a particular clump, Yellham-Wood. Devotion to place and *pietas*, a reverence for the enduring earth, for the past, for the dead dominate Hardy's sensibility. Living in a period when industrialism was beginning to destroy every way of life that takes time to grow, and to create the rootless restless short-memoried republic of to-day, it is not surprising that so many of his best and most famous poems would be elegiac, for instance the very beautiful series of lyrics called *Poems of 1912–13*, with the epigraph *Veteris vestigia flammae*, of which I will quote one which is less well-known, I think, than some of the others.

The Voice

Woman much missed, how you call to me, call to me,
Saying that now you are not as you were
When you had changed from the one who was all to me,
But as at first, when our day was fair.

Can it be you that I hear? Let me view you, then,
Standing as when I drew near to the town

Where you would wait for me: yes, as I knew you then,
Even to the original air-blue gown!

Or is it only the breeze, in its listlessness
Travelling across the wet mead to me here,
You being ever dissolved to wan wistlessness,
Heard no more again far or near?

Thus I; faltering forward,
Leaves around me falling,
Wind oozing thin through the thorn from norward,
And the woman calling.

These poems transcend their manifest subject; the theme of personal loss reverberates in the ear as a lament for the death of an order.

There is a curious contradiction between Hardy's sensibility which valued the traditional and instinctive, and his views on the nature of evil. The stock adjective for Hardy's work is pessimistic but it is inaccurate and misleading. Let him speak for himself.

The truth should be told and the fact be faced
That had best been faced in earlier years:

The fact of life with dependence placed
On the human heart's resource alone,
In brotherhood bonded close and graced

With loving-kindness fully blown,
And visioned help unsought, unknown.

("A Plaint to Man")

Consciousness the will informing till it fashion all things fair.

(*The Dynasts*)

Poetry, pure literature in general, religion—I include religion in its un-dogmatic sense, because poetry and religion touch each other, or rather modulate into each other; are indeed often but different names for the same thing. . . . must like all other things keep moving, becoming; even though at present, when belief in witches of Endor is displacing the Dar-winian theory and "the truth that shall make you free," men's minds ap-pear to be moving backwards rather than on. . . . It may be a forlorn hope, a mere dream, that of an alliance between religion, which must be retained unless the world is to perish, and complete rationality, which must come, unless also the world is to perish, by means of the interfus-ing effect of poetry. . . . but if it is true, as Comte argued, that advance is never in a straight line, but in a looped orbit, we may, in the aforesaid

moving backward, be doing it *pour mieux sauter*, drawing back for a
spring.

(Preface to *Late Lyrics and Earlier*)

This can only be called pessimistic in contrast to a doctrine of automatic
progress, the elimination of evil by the mere flow of history. To most readers
to-day, its humanist faith in the benevolence of consciousness, its presupposition that sin is ignorance, its romantic faith in the religious efficacy of poetry,
will probably seem, on the contrary, overly optimistic, and rather Victorian.

We may not be able to accept it as an adequate explanation of human life,
but if one compares Hardy's effort to answer the doubts and perplexities of
the latter half of the nineteenth century with some others, one is impressed
by his courage and his wisdom.

There can be no religion without dogma; but a religious obscurantism
which, seeing that a fact may tempt men into heresy, denies the fact, must always be fought and, at a time when opposition still incurred social oppro-
brium, Hardy fought it. Evil may not be merely the interplay of ignorance
and chance, but it is truer to think so with Hardy than to think with the aes-
thetes that evil is merely ugliness.

Consciousness unaided by Grace may be an ineffectual saviour but at least
it is not destructive like deliberate irrationality.

> Deal, then, her groping skill no scorn, no malediction;
> Not long on thee will press the hand that hurts the lives it loves;
> And while she plods dead-reckoning on, in darkness of affliction,
> Assist her where thy creaturely dependence can or may
>   For thou art of her clay.

Hardy knew the country too well and loved the poor too much to take up
either with a genteel Oxonian Platonism or with one of those cults of Pan and
the Athenian deities which so often seem to appeal to the suburbanite and
the rentier.

Nature, for Hardy, was neither an idol which one pretends one worships
but in fact is manipulating, nor so much stuff to be exploited, but that which
requires our love and care and for which we are responsible.

The worst that can be said against Hardy is that, in unguarded moments,
he falls into that most dangerous of all modern heresies, the heresy of pity,
that secular parody of Christian sympathy and compassion. In a poem on the
portrait of a murderess, he writes:

> Would that your Causer, ere knoll your knell
> For this riot of passion, might deign to tell
>   Why since it made you
>   Good in the germ
>   It sent a worm

To madden its handiwork when it might well
  Not have essayed you.

This is an emotion and a reflection none of us who are born after the eighteenth century can escape having, but to indulge it leads—as we have recently been forced to realise—straight to the purge and the gas-chamber, for pity is always concerned with one's own reactions to another, not with their real needs; it denies them, for one's own peace of mind, what one can never really deny oneself, responsibility.

To criticise Hardy in this respect is, of course, not a criticism of his poetry as poetry. There are, for an Englishman, certain moods of nostalgia, certain memories, which he will find expressed superbly by Hardy and only by him. For instance:

Haunting Fingers

A Phantasy in a Museum of Musical Instruments

"Are you awake,
  Comrades, this silent night?
  Well 'twere if all of our glossy gluey make
Lay in the damp without, and fell to fragments quite!"

  "O viol, my friend,
   I watch, though Phosphor nears,
   And I fain would drowse away to its utter end
This dumb dark stowage after our loud melodious years!"

And they felt past handlers clutch them,
  Though none was in the room,
Old players' dead fingers touch them,
   Shrunk in the tomb.

  "'Cello, good mate,
   You speak my mind as yours:
   Doomed to this voiceless, crippled, corpselike state,
Who, dear to famed Amphion, trapped here, long endures?"

  "Once I could thrill
   The populace through and through,
   Wake them to passioned pulsings past their will." . . .
(A contra-basso spake so, and the rest sighed anew.)

And they felt old muscles travel
  Over their tense contours,
And with long skill unravel
   Cunningest scores.

"The tender pat
Of her aery finger-tips
Upon me daily—I rejoiced thereat!"
(Thuswise a harpsichord, as 'twere from dampered lips.)

"My keys' white shine,
Now sallow, met a hand
Even whiter. . . . Tones of hers fell forth with mine
In sowings of sound so sweet no lover could withstand!"

And its clavier was filmed with fingers
Like tapering flames—wan, cold—
Or the nebulous light that lingers
In charnel mould.

"Gayer than most
Was I," reverbed a drum;
"The regiments, marchings, throngs, hurrahs! What a host
I stirred—even when crape mufflings gagged me well-nigh dumb!"

Trilled an aged viol:
"Much tune have I set free
To spur the dance, since my first timid trial
Where I had birth—far hence, in sun-swept Italy!"

And he feels apt touches on him
From those that pressed him then;
Who seem with their glance to con him,
Saying, "Not again!"

"A holy calm,"
Mourned a shawm's voice subdued,
"Steeped my Cecilian rhythms when hymn and psalm
Poured from devout souls met in Sabbath sanctitude."

"I faced the sock
Nightly," twanged a sick lyre,
"Over ranked lights! O charm of life in mock,
O scenes that fed love, hope, wit, rapture, mirth, desire!"

Thus they, till each past player
Stroked thinner and more thin,
And the morning sky grew grayer
And day crawled in.

In this kind of elegiac, for objects, Hardy stands alone. Let his own words—
they are noble ones—be his epitaph. He deserves them:

If I pass during some nocturnal blackness, mothy and warm,
    When the hedgehog travels furtively over the lawn,
One may say, "He strove that such innocent creatures should come to no
harm,
    But he could do little for them; and now he is gone".

SOME REMARKS ON T. S. ELIOT

On 14 February 1954, *Omnibus*, the weekly hour-long CBS television network arts program, devoted the last segment of its broadcast to the Broadway opening of T. S. Eliot's *The Confidential Clerk*. The segment began with Auden's remarks on (as the host Alastair Cooke described it) what Eliot has meant to modern poetry. Auden wrote to Eliot on 22 March 1954: "I had to make my first T.V. appearance on your behalf; I was petrified but managed to remember my quotes." The text below was transcribed from a kinescope recording of the broadcast. Auden apparently spoke from cue cards (possibly from memory) in a single, unedited "take".

Imagine that World War I has just recently ended. A few enterprising spirits own crystal sets, phonographs still have horns and are wound by hand, automobiles have not lost a resemblance to horse-carriages, and Mr and Mrs Smith are worried because they fear their daughter is turning into a flapper.

And imagine further that you are standing on some college campus where intellectual undergraduates walk in the afternoons, excitedly discussing, as they have done since civilization began, their latest revelations in philosophy, politics, art, or what have you.

Well, where fifty years before you might have heard their fathers reciting

> From too much love of living,
> From hope and fear set free,
> We thank with brief thanksgiving
> Whatever gods may be
> That no life lives for ever,
> That dead men rise up never,
> That even the weariest river
> Winds somewhere safe to sea,

now you would hear declaimed with the same gusto:

> They are rattling breakfast plates in basement kitchens,
> And along the trampled edges of the street
> I am aware of the damp souls of housemaids
> Sprouting despondently at area gates.

And, needless to say, far off in their clubs, their poor bewildered papas are grumbling: "Tried to read this T. S. Eliot my son is always talking about. Can't make head or tail of it. Sounds as if the fellow was drunk."

For at the beginning of the twentieth century, poetry had come, as it comes every now and then, to a dead end. For instance, suppose you were a young poet who wanted to write a long dramatic poem on a modern subject. Well, the natural medium that would occur to you would be blank verse, which would sound like, what shall we say, Browning:

> All Balzac's novels occupy one shelf,
> The new edition, fifty volumes long;
> And little Greek books, with the funny type
> They get up well at Leipsic, fill the next.

But you'd have been worried. You'd have thought to yourself, "Oh dear, oh dear, I wish I could think of a more flexible kind of medium."

Then, with what excitement you would have read for the first time a passage like

> Here I am, an old man in a dry month,
> Being read to by a boy, waiting for rain.
> I was neither at the hot gates
> Nor fought in the warm rain
> Nor knee deep in the salt marsh, heaving a cutlass,
> Bitten by flies, fought.

Again, it is one of the pleasures characteristic of our age to enjoy ironic contrast—the putting side by side of opposite characteristics, the sordid and the grand, the extraordinary and the commonplace. Mr Eliot did not, of course, invent this pleasure for us, but he was one of the first to gratify it, in such verses as this:

> Gloomy Orion and the Dog
> Are veiled; and hushed the shrunken seas;
> The person in the Spanish cape
> Tries to sit on Sweeney's knees.

I think, personally, that Mr Eliot is so idiosyncratic a figure that for any poet to allow himself to be directly influenced by him could only result in pale imitation. But indirectly, his sense of technical and emotional discipline, his demonstration that a poet can be at once traditional and modern, has had so immense an influence that one cannot imagine twentieth-century poetry without him.

Mr Eliot has himself perfectly described the poet's task. I quote:

> Trying to learn to use words, and every attempt
> Is a wholly new start, and a different kind of failure.
> Because one has only learnt to get the better of words
> For the thing one no longer has to say, or the way in which

One is no longer disposed to say it. And so each venture
Is a new beginning, a raid on the inarticulate
With shabby equipment always deteriorating
In the general mess of imprecision of feeling,
Undisciplined squads of emotion. And what there is to conquer
By strength and submission, has already been discovered
Once or twice, or several times, by men whom one cannot hope
To emulate—but there is no competition—
There is only the fight to recover what has been lost
And found and lost again and again: and now, under conditions
That seem unpropitious.

To which I can only add that in these unpropitious days Mr Eliot has been one of the lucky few who found.

HISTORY, FEIGNED AND REAL

Auden recorded this BBC talk in New York on 31 October 1955. The BBC edited it down from thirty-one to twenty minutes, and broadcast it in the BBC Third Programme on 16 November 1955. The text below is from a transcript in the BBC Written Archives Centre. All ellipses are reproduced from the transcript. The text is slightly emended, but I have not tried to correct an apparent muddle in the opening of the paragraph that begins "Mr Tolkien's notion".

On 3 June 1955 Auden wrote to Tolkien: "I have, it seems, to give a twenty minute talk on the trilogy for the Third Programme in October. . . . If there is anything in particular that you would like me to say—for instance, you may have heard misunderstandings and misinterpretations of which I am ignorant and for clearing up which, it would be a convenient opportunity—please let me have them. Also, the B.B.C. may want a few 'human' touches—when you started creating your imaginary world, etc., and I don't want to make any foolish guesses." Tolkien's lengthy reply, on 7 June 1955, appears in *The Letters of J.R.R. Tolkien: A Selection*, ed. Humphrey Carpenter (1981), pp. 211–17. Auden responded on 14 June 1955: "Thank you very much for your letter which, apart from its interest to me personally, is exactly the sort of background material I need though I shall try to avoid direct use of it as much as possible since I share your distaste for the 'personal' approach to literature."

The Quest is one of the oldest, hardiest and most popular of all forms of literature. The earliest known epic, Gilgamesh, is a quest; so is the contemporary detective story. Its essential elements are an adventurous journey, a goal to be attained, trials to be endured or obstacles to be overcome in attaining the goal, and a unique hero, the only individual who is capable of success. The goal is generally either a person, like the Sleeping Beauty, or a numinous object like the Golden Fleece. This person or object has sometimes been stolen by evil powers from its rightful owner, sometimes withdrawn or lost because of mistakes or sins committed by those who originally enjoyed it, and sometimes it is just a very long way off, but in all cases it is guarded, by dragons, fire, or what have you, and only he who has the strength and courage to overcome the guardians can win the prize. (In Melville's *Moby Dick* the numinous object and the guardian are one and the same.)

The hero may be of two kinds, one whose heroic arete is manifest from the first, like Hercules, or, like the Third Brother in fairy tales, one who at first appears nobody in particular, the least of men, but whose arete is then revealed as the story proceeds.

The popularity and historical persistence of the Quest is not difficult to explain, for it is the most obvious way in which we can experience our subjective personal experience of existence. Subjectively, for instance, I am aware of time as a continuous irreversible process of change which, if I translate it into spatial terms, becomes naturally enough a journey.

Further, I am conscious in many of my actions of a telos, or goal—this may be a short-term one—like trying to write a sentence which expresses my present thoughts accurately—or a life-long one, the desire to find true happiness or authenticity of being, to become, that is, what I ought to become or what God intends me to become . . . What more natural image for such a telos than a princess or the waters of life?

While every human being shares in the quest for true happiness, not everybody, it would seem, feels called to one particular way of life rather than another, not everybody says it is my destiny to become a surgeon or a philologist. Whether this is the fault of society or an unalterable difference in nature I don't know. I am inclined to believe that *The Magic Flute* expresses a profound truth. Papageno wins Papagena precisely because he is humble enough to know that he is not a hero and that trials by fire and water are not for the likes of him, so that when the Second Priest threatens him with "Either you undergo these trials or you will never win Papagena", he replies: "In that case I'll remain single."

If only some people experience the vocation of talent, even fewer experience a religious vocation, using the term "religious" in the sense of that which is absolutely binding. The point about the religious vocation is that he who experiences it has to do what seems to him and to others to have no relation to his nature or powers. In fact, while the one who is called by his nature must always say, "I want to do this because I believe I shall be more successful at it than at anything else", the one who feels a religious vocation has nearly always to say: "This must be done, alas, by me, but I do not see how I shall be able to do it."

Such a vocation may be for life, as when God called Abraham, or it may be for a moment only, as when a man, by nature physically timid, finds himself in the position of having to plunge into a burning building to rescue a child, because there is no one else to do so. For this kind of vocation, the literary image is the hero whose arete is concealed from view. In *The Lord of the Rings*

Mr Tolkien gives us both kinds. Gandalf the Magician and Aragorn the Warrior King are professionals; they do what their powers entitle them to do and
which therefore they enjoy doing. Frodo, on the other hand, has no wish to
become the Ring-Bearer, but historical circumstances have put him in the position where he feels it to be his duty.

I have suggested that the heroic Quest is a mode of expressing our subjective experience of reality. If I take the opposite viewpoint and, excluding
myself, try to look out at the world as if I were a camera, the reality I see seems
to conflict at almost every point with the standard Quest properties. I observe, for instance, that the vast majority of people have to earn their living
in a fixed place. Journeys of adventure are for holidays only or for those with
independent means. I observe that, though some wars may be called just,
there are no wars between pure White and pure Black, while, at the same
time, I observe that, in most wars, both sides claim that they are Elves and
their enemies Orcs and that the exaltation of military glory has been responsible for more misery and horror in the world than, perhaps, any other
form of idolatry. As for battles between men and monsters, I can see that
there exist some ferocious animals who may attack a man out of hunger or
fear, but none that do so out of malice. A man may have to kill an animal in
self-defence but this is a necessary not a noble deed.

We who have a taste for Heroic Quests have to produce an example of a
Quest which at one and the same time satisfies our sense of the reality of
choice between good and evil and the demands of historical-social reality.
In my opinion *The Lord of the Rings* satisfies both better than any other Quest
I have ever read, and I shall spend most of the rest of my talk in trying to
show why.

If a feigned history is to seem real, it must be shown as the joint product
of individual character and circumstances, neither, that is, as the operation
of a few great men nor as the inevitable result of the play of impersonal forces.
The present must have an intelligible relation to the past, neither inevitable
nor arbitrary, and the future must appear open; that is, characters in this history may make guesses about what will happen which will turn out to be correct, but, in general, the outcome of their actions will be different from what
they either hope or fear.

If we are to have, as the Quest form demands, a historically unreal dualis-
tic conflict between Good and Evil, we must, at least, be convinced that the
Evil side is fundamentally so—it cannot be just a matter of race, culture or
religion—or rather, all the religions we know, however much they may differ,
must agree that this, at least, is evil.

And, secondly, the triumph of Good must appear historically possible not
a magic daydream. Physical and, to a considerable degree, intellectual power
must be shown as what we know them to be, morally neutral in themselves
and effectively real. Physical battles are won by the physically stronger side,

whether good or evil. Lastly, and here the Quest proper differs from the Dream Allegory—the characters and the world they inhabit must convince us of their natural reality—the laws of such a world need not be exactly the same as those of the world we know, but it must be a world of law not wish.

The Lord of the Rings is, I understand, only the concluding portion of a much longer history, already written, of which we get tantalising glimpses in the Appendices to Volume III, and, of course, many references during the story itself. Consequently every person and thing in the story has a past which makes the present intelligible.

Though Good triumphs over Evil so far as the Third Age is concerned, this triumph is not final—there was Morgoth before Sauron and who knows who will arise in the Fourth Age as Sauron's successor? Further, the triumph of Good does not mean the arrival of the Earthly Paradise or the New Jerusalem. All historical change involves the perishing of past good: with the destruction of the One Ring, the Three Elven Rings lose their power. As Galadriel says to Frodo: "If you fail, then we are laid bare to the Enemy. We must depart into the West, or dwindle to a rustic folk of dell and cave, slowly to forget and to be forgotten." Even Frodo, the hero himself, cannot live happily ever after. "'But,' said Sam, and tears started to his eyes, 'I thought you were going to enjoy the Shire for years and years after all you have done.' 'I thought so, too, once. But I have been too deeply hurt, Sam. I tried to save the Shire, and it has been saved, but not for me. It must often be so, Sam, when things are in danger: someone has to give them up, lose them, so that others may keep them.'"

In the matter of the Dark Lord and his Ring, Mr Tolkien shows excellent psychological and, if I may use the term, theological insight. It is unfair, perhaps, to compare his story with Wagner's, because the allegory in *Der Ring des Nibelungen* is only politico-psychological: Wotan is not a real god but only a feudal old gentleman who behaves just as foolishly and badly as everybody else—but a comparison of their similarities and differences may serve to demonstrate what Mr Tolkien has done.

In both cases we have a ring which will grant its wearer the Lordship of the world and which can only be forged by one who renounces love. But the love that Alberich renounces turns out to be only Frau Minne; there is no formal difference between his ruminations and that of a priest who takes a vow of celibacy. Sauron, on the other hand, has long ago rejected not only Eros but Agape. Like the Machiavellian villain, the only relation between persons that he can conceive of is that of Master and Slave. Every apparent show of affection is, for him, a hypocritical strategy of foolish weakness. Acting on this hypothesis he has built up a physical power which is stronger than any which his opponents, unless they use the Ring, can bring against him. The mistakes which he makes and which cause his downfall are inevitable in the sense that, in order not to make them, he would have to cease being Sauron.

Thanks to Alberich's curses, the Ring of the Nibelungs brings misfortune to all who possess it, but, though like Sauron's it carries with it the Lordship of the World, it does not corrupt them.

Even the hero himself, Siegfried, though the bird has told him what the ring is, is no more interested than Bombadil and very nearly gives it back to the Rhine maidens.

Mr Tolkien's notion of what effect such an object would have—one has to imagine some device which is unique so that no copy of it can ever be made and which combines the physical force of the hydrogen bomb with a power to induce mass hypnosis—the effect of such an object would seem to me much more probable, that is, the danger of corruption would be in direct proportion to the arete of the wearer. Bilbo who doesn't know what the ring is, and is by nature a quiet little hobbit whose interests are confined to the Shire and minor poetry, can wear it and suffer little damage. Gandalf and Aragorn and Elrond know that it would be fatal for them to try—hence the burden of the Quest falls on Frodo, and even he, at the very end, is almost overcome by the power of the ring.

My admiration for *The Lord of the Rings* is by now, I hope, quite clear—indeed I regard the book as a touchstone so that, if someone dislikes it, I shall never trust their literary judgement about anything again. Mr Tolkien must forgive me, then, if I say frankly what I do not like. I fear that some of his critics got no further than the first forty pages of Chapter I—well, I nearly got no further myself. I found and still find them shy-making in the extreme. In scenes of high debate like the Council of Elrond and in scenes of epic action, Mr Tolkien is superb, but he seems to have little gift for light comedy. What he gives us, then, is a sort of Y.M.C.A. heartiness. As for Sam Gamgee, the faithful retainer, he is so very very good I want to scream. Only opera can handle such a character directly. If only, I think to myself, Mr Tolkien could have supplied the history and anthropology of the hobbits and then handed over their conversation to that other great inventor of imaginary worlds in this century—also one of my touchstones—Mr Ronald Firbank.

I also think he has been too squeamish about the Orcs and their Black Speech. In an appendix he writes: "Their language was actually more degraded and filthy than I have shown it. I do not suppose that any will wish for a closer rendering, though models are easy to find. Much of the same sort of talk can still be heard among the Orc-minded." Well, I, for one, do wish for a closer rendering. I know Orc-minded people but no one quite as nasty as an Orc. Since Mr Tolkien is a philologist I want from him the Black Speech equivalent of Grose's *Dictionary of the Vulgar Tongue* and expect to find its four-letter words far uglier than any I know or can imagine.

Having made my little objections, let me finish on an appreciative note by quoting two of Mr Tolkien's poems. Success at writing both prose narrative and verse is not as common as the attempt. In the books of one of Mr

Tolkien's literary ancestors and a great favourite of mine, George Macdonald, there are a number of poems though all of them, alas, are bad.

The poems scattered through *The Lord of the Rings* on the other hand are,
all of them, technically interesting, in a wide variety of moods, and many very
evocative. I should have liked to have read one of the verses in Elvish with its
melodious triple rhymes but I am too afraid of muffing the pronunciation.
Here, in alliterative metre, is one of the songs of Rohan:

> From dark Dunharrow in the dim morning
> with thane and captain rode Thengel's son:
> to Edoras he came, the ancient halls
> of the Mark-wardens mist-enshrouded;
> golden timbers were in gloom mantled.
> Farewell he bade to his free people,
> hearth and high-seat, and the hallowed places,
> where long he had feasted ere the light faded.
> Forth rode the king, fear behind him,
> fate before him. Fealty kept he;
> oaths he had taken, all fulfilled them.
> Forth rode Theoden. Five nights and days
> east and onward rode the Eolingas.
> through Folde and Fenmarch and the Firienwood,
> six thousand spears to Sunlending,
> Mundberg the mighty under Mindolluin,
> Sea-kings' city in the South-kingdom
> foe-beleaguered, fire-encircled.
> Doom drove them on. Darkness took them,
> horse and horseman; hoofbeats afar
> sank into silence: so the songs tell us.

And here is one of Bombadil's songs.

> I had an errand there: gathering water-lilies,
> green leaves and lilies white to please my pretty lady,
> the last ere the year's end to keep them from the winter,
> to flower by her pretty feet till the snows are melted.
> Each year at summer's end I go to find them for her,
> in a wide pool, deep and clear, far down Withywindle;
> there they open first in spring and there they linger latest.
> By that pool long ago I found the River-daughter,
> fair young Goldberry sitting in the rushes.
> Sweet was her singing then, and her heart was beating!
> And that proved well for you—for now I shall no longer
> go down deep again along the forest-water,

> not while the year is old. Nor shall I be passing
> Old Man Willow's house this side of spring-time,
> not till the merry spring, when the River-daughter
> dances down the withy-path to bathe in the water.

A Tribute to Ezra Pound on His Seventieth Birthday

"A Tribute to Ezra Pound on His Seventieth Birthday" was prepared by Yale undergraduates for broadcast on the college radio station, WYBC, on 5 December 1955. The broadcast included Auden's remarks, recorded earlier in his New York apartment. The text below is from a mimeographed transcript of the full broadcast in the Yale University Library.

Poets who are influential on their own generation or succeeding generations can be divided into two classes: those whose influence is immediately discernible; for example, I might read a poet and say, "Oh yes, he's been reading Yeats," or "He's been reading Eliot." And there are others whose influence is more indirect. I think there are not many poets one reads and would say at once, "Oh, this poet has been reading Pound." On the other hand, there are very few living poets, even if they are not conscious of having been influenced by Pound, who could say, "My work would be exactly the same if Mr Pound had never lived." His influence has been so all-pervading, so that a poet who may, we'll say, have been influenced by Mr Yeats or Mr Eliot—but then the question is what effect had Mr Pound already had, whether technically or personally, on Mr Eliot or Mr Yeats, and we know that he had.

In my own case I had a curious, I think, example of this, where in the last few years I've gotten interested in certain kinds of rhythmical effects in poets like Wyatt, or even earlier, in the fifteenth century. Now I only realized quite suddenly that probably the start of my interest is through reading Mr Pound's translations of Cavalcanti, where he certainly reproduces some of the effects of Wyatt. Now I wonder whether I should I have noticed these things in Wyatt if I had not already read Mr Pound's translations. In general I think one could say that Mr Pound's prosodic influence in breaking a certain kind of jam into which poetry is always apt to get at one time or another had been immense on poets who write work of a very different kind.

In a second way, his influence has been great in the way in which he has suggested certain reading material. I doubt if people would have gotten interested, we'll say, in writing sestinas, if Pound had not started an interest in Provençal poetry. Some people imagine that to be, as Mr Pound is in a certain sense, a literary poet, that is to say a poet whose imagination is directly stimulated by other literature, is in some way or other inferior to being stimulated by a beautiful face or a beautiful sunset. That of course is all rubbish. The question is what are the results, not the origin of the stimulus. One of Mr Pound's most characteristic and, for my money, most admirable works is the *Homage to Sextus Propertius*. Now no one can conceivably say that this is a translation; it's not in the least like Propertius, and some people have made quite good fun out of the effect. The only thing, of course, is that it's irrelevant. Here is a poem which is very characteristically a Pound poem, extremely beautiful and interesting, of which the original stimulus comes from Propertius. The good thing is that Pound was not a translator in the sense of one who tries exactly to reproduce in English what was said in the original text. There are other people who have done that. One of the great importances of what Mr Pound has done is to take quite defiantly texts out of the other languages and make something exciting and new out of them.

For these three reasons: firstly for the general prosodic influence on all subsequent poets; his indirect effect on their interests; and his own achievement, I think every poet today would like to wish Mr Pound well on his birthday.

Public Letters Signed by Auden and Others

THIS appendix lists letters to the press and other documents signed by Auden but probably not written by him.

A FUND DRIVE FOR THE NEW YORK PUBLIC LIBRARY

A letter appealing for contributions to the New York Public Library (a privately funded institution), signed by fourteen writers, was reported in the *New York Times*, 30 January 1949, under the headline "Volunteers Flock to Library Drive". The story quotes the letter as saying that the Library "is one of the reasons why so many of us choose to work in New York. To supply the steadily increasing demands that we, with many others, make upon its services, it must have additional funds for the purchase of books, for the payment of adequate salaries, for the modernization of equipment." The signers are listed as Maxwell Anderson, Auden, Van Wyck Brooks, Henry Seidel Canby, John Dos Passos, Lewis Mumford, Elmer Rice, Robert Sherwood, John Steinbeck, Allen Tate, Carl Van Doren, Mark Van Doren, Carl Van Vechten, and Glenway Wescott.

EZRA POUND AND THE BOLLINGEN PRIZE

The controversy over the Bollingen Prize in Poetry awarded to Ezra Pound in 1949 by the Fellows of the Library of Congress in American Literature is described in the notes to "The Question of the Pound Award" (p. 101). A two-part article by Robert Hillyer in the *Saturday Review of Literature*, 11 and 18 June 1949, and an editorial in the 11 June number, attacked the award and everyone whom Hillyer imagined was associated, however remotely, with the Bollingen Foundation, which had funded the award. During the next two months, the article prompted dozens of letters to the editor. One such letter, described in the magazine as having been from all the Fellows (with the exception of Paul Green), was quoted in an editorial titled "More on Pound" in the 30 July 1949 issue (I have added Archibald MacLeish to the list of signers, as his name seems to have been omitted through a typesetter's error).

THE LIBRARY OF CONGRESS
WASHINGTON, D.C.

SIR: The Fellows of the Library of Congress in American Letters assert that the decision of the Jury for the Bollingen Prize was arrived at wholly by democratic procedure. We indignantly protest the impugnment through the editorial and articles in *The Saturday Review of Literature* of the integrity of motive of any of the Fellows.

We wish publicly to thank Mr Paul Mellon and the Officers of the Bollingen

Foundation for their generous encouragement of American Letters and to state that they had no part in nor knowledge of the jury's deliberations.

We wish publicly to thank the Librarian of Congress for his courage and wisdom in upholding the principle that a literary jury should have complete freedom of judgment.

Conrad Aiken	Karl Shapiro
W. H. Auden	Allen Tate
Louise Bogan	Willard Thorp
Katherine Garrison Chapin	Robert Penn Warren
T. S. Eliot	Léonie Adams, Consultant in
Robert Lowell	Poetry at the Library of
[Archibald MacLeish]	Congress and Secretary
Katherine Anne Porter	to the Fellows.

A committee of the Fellows (Adams, Bogan, Shapiro, and Thorp) prepared a long statement on the matter, which the Library distributed as a mimeographed press release. A revised version of the statement, together with much other material, was printed in a pamphlet on the controversy published in October 1949 by the magazine *Poetry* in Chicago, titled *The Case against "The Saturday Review of Literature"*. A two-page preface, signed by all the Fellows (again with the exception of Paul Green), described the contents of the pamphlet. Although Auden approved the use of his signature, he evidently contributed nothing to the preface or to anything else in the pamphlet. During the preparations for the pamphlet Léonie Adams wrote to him apparently to ask whether he had written anything about the matter that might be useful; he replied on 16 August 1949, "No, I have written and spoken nothing except the Partisan piece" ["The Question of the Pound Award"] (Yale University Library).

THE KENNETH PATCHEN FUND

In 1950 the American poet Kenneth Patchen asked Auden for help in paying for treatments for rheumatoid arthritis. Auden wrote to Norman Holmes Pearson from Mount Holyoke College on 25 October (Yale University Library):

What are we to do about Kenneth Patchen? (He telephoned to me at your suggestion.) The only rich people I can think of who might help are Bryher [pseudonym of Winifred Ellerman] whom you know and Alice Bouverie [daughter of John Jacob Astor] whom Edith [Sitwell] knows. I'm going to N.Y. this week end and hope to see Edith.

According to K.P., he can't get reduced hospitalisation rates; Is this true, do you think? If so, it's a scandal.

I'm going to make enquiries myself about psychiatrists.

The lawyer Julien Cornell, who was also representing Ezra Pound, became the treasurer of a fund organized in the following weeks by Auden and others. The following undated printed letter was sent out to writers and others known to the organizers, with the reproduced signatures of the signers:

THE KENNETH PATCHEN FUND

Julien Cornell, Treasurer
Central Valley, New York

We should like to call to your attention to the tragic plight of the young American poet, Kenneth Patchen, and urge that you join with us in bringing him the medical treatment which he desperately needs.

Patchen has been crippled for many years from rheumatoid arthritis. He is now bedridden and in constant pain, his means exhausted, unable to earn the livelihood which he had gained from fifteen books and other writings.

The appearance of new drugs, such as cortisone, now makes it possible to restore the creative activity of this gifted poet, who is still a young man and may have many productive years ahead if funds can be secured for hospitalization and treatment.

A substantial sum is needed for prolonged treatment, about $10,000. This case is of special interest to those who are concerned with the creative arts. Will you join us in meeting this emergency, and in so doing help the cause of poetry in these materialistic times?

Please send contributions to Mr Julien Cornell, treasurer of the Patchen Fund, at Central Valley, New York. Please also call this to the attention of your friends.

Yours sincerely,

W. H. Auden   Archibald MacLeish
T. S. Eliot   Thornton Wilder

A very brief letter on the same subject, naming a different recipient for contributions, appeared under the heading "Aid for a Poet" in *The Nation*, 31 March 1951.

THE DYLAN THOMAS FUND

A printed letter appealing for funds for Dylan Thomas's widow and children was sent out by a committee of seven writers shortly after his death. Slightly abridged versions appeared, each under the heading "Dylan Thomas Fund", in the *Nation*, 28 November 1953, and in the *Saturday Review of Literature*, 5 December 1953; the full text appeared in *Partisan Review*, January–February 1954. The treasurer was a lawyer with a special interest in literary clients and literary property.

THE DYLAN THOMAS FUND

c/o Philip Wittenberg, Treasurer
70 West 40th Street, New York, N.Y.

November 10, 1953

Dear Friend,

I am sure you have read in the press of the sudden and tragic death of the great poet Dylan Thomas. Thomas died of encephalopathy at St Vincent's Hospital in New York on November 9th, after an illness of four days. He was only 39 years old. He was attended by one of the finest brain surgeons in New York and everything possible was done to save him.

Thomas' death is an incalculable loss to literature. His work was growing in stature every year. But there is also a personal tragedy—he leaves a widow without means of support and three children—which gravely concerns his friends and admirers.

As spokesmen for a committee of his friends we are making this urgent appeal to you for a contribution to The Dylan Thomas Fund, which we have hastily organized, which will be used to meet his medical bills and funeral expenses and, if the response is as generous as we hope, to tide his family over the next difficult months.

Please send your check to The Dylan Thomas Fund, care of Philip Wittenberg, Treasurer, 70 West 40th Street, New York City. An accounting of disbursements from the Fund will be sent to the contributors at a later date.

For the DYLAN THOMAS FUND COMMITTEE

W. H. Auden	Marianne Moore
E. E. Cummings	Wallace Stevens
Arthur Miller	Tennessee Williams

Thornton Wilder

SPANISH TRIALS DECRIED

Under this headline the *New York Times* reported on 22 February 1954:

Twenty Americans, including writers, educators and religious and labor leaders, have sent a message to Generalissimo Francisco Franco condemning the use of military courts in Spain to try civilians charged with political offenses.

The message, made public yesterday by Norman Thomas, one of the signers, said that on Feb. 5 a court-martial in Madrid sentenced eighteen civilians to prison terms up to fifteen years. At this trial and a subsequent one, it added, the defendants' petitions for trial before civil courts were refused.

Among the signers were W. H. Auden, poet; the Rev. John Haynes Holmes, pastor emeritus of the Community Church; Professor Sidney Hook, chairman of the Philosophy Department at New York University, and Victor Reuther, assistant to the president of the Congress of Industrial Organizations.

Lost and Unwritten Work

THIS appendix describes prose works written by Auden that never appeared and works that he planned to write but never completed.

From the late 1940s onward Auden intermittently planned to collect some of his published and unpublished prose, but he did not complete the project until *The Dyer's Hand* appeared in 1962. At some point Alan Ansen photocopied and retyped some of the published essays that Auden intended to include in this book. Around 1951 and 1952 Auden seems to have focused his attention on a collection of prose essays and aphorisms. The notes on contributors in *Thought*, Spring 1952, reported that he was working on "a commentary on many things called *Thinks*". Around this time, he scrawled a tentative list of contents on the flyleaf of a notebook that he used in 1950–54 (Harry Ransom Humanities Research Center at the University of Texas at Austin):

Hic et Ille
Nature, History and Poetry
The Dyer's Hand
Reflections on the Comic
Pothooks and Hangers
Notes on Opera
Dingley Dell and the Fleet
The Word and the Tribe
The Hero

"Hic et Ille" was probably a version of the notes and aphorisms translated into French as "De droite et de gauche" (p. 323), and partly reused as "Hic et Ille" in *Encounter*, April 1956. "Nature, History and Poetry" survives in two versions (pp. 161 and 226). "The Dyer's Hand" was probably an early version of the broadcast talks given under the same title in 1955 (p. 536). "Reflections on the Comic" was a version of "Notes on the Comic" (p. 307). "Pothooks and Hangers" (Chester Kallman remembered) was a set aphoristic comments on writing; some probably found their way into the section "Writing" in *The Dyer's Hand*. "Notes on Opera" corresponds to "Some Reflections on Opera as a Medium" (p. 250). "Dingley Dell and the Fleet" was a lecture that Auden delivered in 1951 (see p. 654); he used the same title for a lecture that he gave as Professor of Poetry at Oxford, 26 May 1958, and included in *The Dyer's Hand*. "The Word and the Tribe" (the title alludes to Eliot's quotation from Mallarmé in *Burnt Norton*) may have been a set of aphorisms that eventually grew into "The Poet and the City" in *The Dyer's Hand*. "The Hero" corresponds to the lecture "The Hero in Modern Poetry" (see p. 659) and other writings on the same theme, including parts of Auden's introduction to *The Portable Greek Reader* (*Prose II*).

During the late 1940s (as noted in *Prose II*, pp. 506–7) Auden thought he might write a travel book about England, and first planned to do so in collaboration with John Betjeman, later with Chester Kallman. Late in February 1948 Alan Ansen recorded in his journal Auden's comment on the current state of his plans: "Chester and I are planning a travel book on England with things like meetings in bars with peasants who speak with a Southern accent" (Berg Collection).

Auden wrote to Kallman on 29 January 1950: "have to write a programme note for the Philharmonic debut of [Leonard] Bernstein's [symphony] Age of Anxiety". This note did not appear in the program of the New York Philharmonic debut of the work on 23 February 1950, and was perhaps never written.

Auden tentatively accepted a proposal from the Viking Press to write a book about English prosody, but nothing came of it. Pascal Covici wrote to him 4 April 1952: "I was hoping to persuade you to do the little book on prosody this Summer so that we could have it for publication next Spring." Covici wrote again on 11 August 1953: "Some time back, you may remember, you were interested in doing a small book for us on Modern Prosody and then, last year, you agreed to incorporate the five essays from the Portable English Poets with other material into a book tentatively entitled 'The Nature of English Poetry.' How about combining the two into one and calling it 'Modern Prosody, with an Introduction to English Poetry'?" (Viking Press archives)

Auden and Chester Kallman were reported in 1954 to be considering the possibility that they might propose to write a film script about Mozart, but the report may have been based on a confusion (Michele Regine, "Il poetà inglese Auden prende alloggio a Forio", *Il Giornale*, Naples, 9 July 1954).

In 1955 Auden was actively planning a volume that would collect various works by Charles Williams. He wrote to J.R.R. Tolkien on 14 June 1955:

It is curious that you should mention the memorial volume to Charles Williams [presumably *Essays Presented to Charles Williams*, 1947] because I was rather hurt that I was not asked to contribute. When I am in England next year I hope we shall meet and be able to talk about him. I am editing at the moment a sort of Omnibus Williams for an American publisher. (It is maddening that no publishers today issue definitive collected editions so one must do the best one can.) I propose to include

> *History.* The Descent of the Dove. James I.
> *Criticism.* The Figure of Beatrice.
> *Theology.* The Forgiveness of Sins.
> *Fiction.* Descent into Hell.
> *Poetry.* Taliessin through Logres. The Region of the Summer Stars.

Have you any modifications or additions to suggest.

Later in the year, this project seems to either to have been reduced to or replaced by a paperback reissue of Williams's *The Descent of the Dove*, which appeared with an introduction by Auden in 1956 (see *Prose IV*).

TEXTUAL NOTES

The Enchafèd Flood

THIS was Auden's first published book of prose (with the partial exception of the 1939 pamphlet *Education Today—and Tomorrow*, written in collaboration with T. C. Worsley). The dustjacket of the first (Random House) edition includes a description of the book that Auden wrote during a visit to the publisher's office late in October 1949:

> In these three essays Mr Auden discusses the pre-suppositions of romantic and nineteenth-century writers, their conceptions of God, society and the heroic individual through an analysis of their treatment of a single theme, the sea.
>
> The principal works he examines are Coleridge's *The Ancient Mariner*, Lewis Carroll's *The Hunting of the Snark*, Gerard Manley Hopkins' *The Wreck of the Deutschland*, Jules Verne's *Twenty Thousand Leagues under the Sea*, the poems of Baudelaire and Rimbaud and the novels of Herman Melville.

The hyphen in "pre-suppositions" and the mistitling of Coleridge's *Rime of the Ancient Mariner* are both characteristic of Auden's style.

The Page-Barbour Lectures at the University of Virginia were founded in 1907 by Mrs Thomas Nelson Page, who established that each series of lectures would be published by the university in book form. Auden was invited in the summer of 1948 to give the 1949 lectures. He replied to William Weedon, a dean at the university, on 23 September 1948:

> In reply to your letter, it would [be] most convenient for me if the date could be as late in March as possible. I finish a course at the New School in January and may then have to undergo a minor operation, so the later the better for me.
>
> Also, could you be kind enough to send me a few particulars about the Page-Barbour bequest so that I can (a) have a clear idea of what the donor wanted and (b) be able to refer to him at the beginning.

Having chosen a title, Auden prepared his lectures early in 1949. On 9 February 1949, he replied to a letter from Weedon:

> As to your points:
>
> (1) the subtitle should be The romantic iconography, not the Lyric ditto.
> (2) I shall be delighted to dine with you March 22.
> (3) I have no mad desire to wear a tux if I don't have to.

On 15 March 1949 he wrote to William Wranek, the publicity officer of the university:

> Thank you for your letter of March 11th. I am sorry to tell you that there will be no texts of my lectures available beforehand, as the rush to get

them finished and typed will leave no time. The actual titles of the three lectures which are based on Wordsworth's dream in *The Prelude* Book V, ll 50–140, are as follows:—

I	The Desert and the Sea
II	The Stone and the Shell
III	Ishmael—Don Quixote

I would be grateful if you could spread the news that the works which will be discussed and with some familiarity on the part of the audience will be assumed are as follows.

Coleridge.	The Ancient Mariner.
Poe.	Gordon Pym.
Tennyson.	The Voyage of Maeldune.
Melville.	White Jacket. Moby Dick and Billy Budd.
Lewis Carroll.	The Hunting of the Snark.
Baudelaire.	Fleurs du Mal, and the Intimate Journals.
Rimbaud.	Bâteau Ivre.
Hopkins.	The Wreck of the Deutschland.
Jules Verne.	Twenty Thousand Leagues Under the Sea.

He delivered the manuscript to Random House probably on 21 October 1949 and returned during the next few days to write the acknowledgements and the dustjacket description described at the start of these notes (manuscripts of both are in the Syracuse University Library).

Auden delivered the three lectures on 22–24 March 1949. He may have prepared them for publication during the summer, and Alan Ansen probably typed them in the early autumn after Auden returned from Italy. Auden wrote to Christopher Isherwood on 15 October 1949: "I have some lectures I gave in the spring coming out next spring under the title *The Enchafèd Flood* which are too prolix like all lectures but I like bits of them" (Huntington Library). *The Enchafèd Flood* was published by Auden's usual publisher, Random House, on 17 March 1950, but the copyright was retained by the University of Virginia.

The manuscript from which Auden lectured is lost, but Alan Ansen prepared a typed copy of it for his own use, probably after Auden delivered the lectures (Ansen's typescript includes the word "Lacuna" where perhaps a few lines of manuscript were missing, possibly because they were on a lost inserted page, possibly because Auden neglected to write them.) A carbon copy of this typescript is in the Berg Collection; it has Ansen's marginal notes on the differences between the lecture version and the later typescript prepared for book publication. Most of the differences between the two versions are trivial matters of rearrangement or minor rewriting. A few passages omitted from the published version are these:

In the first lecture, the transcript of the original version begins:

It was the intention of the benefactor who founded these lectures that they should be delivered by someone distinguished in his own field upon a subject relevant to the problems and perplexities of the present age. This leaves your speaker this evening at once flattered and embarrassed. For, as a poet, the only subject on which he can speak with authority is the technique of his craft and by no stretch of the imagination can he believe that to be of general relevance, so that he is forced to talk about something else in respect to which he is an amateur. The subject I have chosen is one which for adequate treatment would require a reading and a scholarship of a very different order from my own, and in daring not only to speak on it but also to do so before a distinguished academic audience, I am courting ridicule; I can but hope that to such an effort attaches the same kind of melancholy interest which Doctor Johnson attributed to the spectacle of a female preacher: "It is not done well, but one is surprised that it is done at all."

The topic of these three lectures is a change in sensibility which occurred towards the end of the eighteenth century and has, I believe, continued until now. It is my purpose to investigate the nature of this change by tracing its reflection in the literary treatment of a single theme, the sea. The works with which I shall deal are, primarily, Melville's *Moby Dick* and *White Jacket*, Coleridge's *The Ancient Mariner*, and Lewis Carroll's *The Hunting of the Snark*, and in a subsidiary way certain poems of Baudelaire, Rimbaud, Tennyson, and Gerard Manley Hopkins, but before doing so I must first say something about the treatment of the sea by pre-romantic writers, and I shall begin at the very beginning, with the first chapter of Genesis.

There follows the quotation from Genesis found in the published version on p. 9 (in this edition). In the lecture version, the long quotation from Wordsworth (on the first page of the published version) occurs after the quotation from Baudelaire (p. 14) and begins: "As a starting point for our investigations, I am going to take a passage from the fifth book of *The Prelude*. It is, perhaps . . ."

In the second lecture, under the heading (in the published version) "The Polemical Situation of Romanticism" (p. 33) the lecture version has an introductory paragraph:

In yesterday's lecture, we discussed the relation between the romantic symbols of sea and desert and the social conditions of urbanisation and crowd publics with which the romantic poets were faced. To-night, let us in the same way review the intellectual and ideological situation in order to relate it to the symbols of stone and shell.

In the third lecture Ansen noted a passage that Auden had deleted from his manuscript, immediately after the quotation from Genesis in which Ishmael "became an archer" (p. 63):

Ishmael's characteristics then are:

(1) someone to whom an injustice has been done through no fault of his own; i.e. he is the first born yet he is not the heir but illegitimate. He has been wronged by the position of his mother, that she was a slave, and by

her character, her arrogance which despises the physical inferiority of
Sarah. He has been wronged by his Father who turned them out of the
house and he has been wronged by his Father's wife who has pursued
his mother and himself with jealous hatred.

(2) He is asocial and aggressive and presumably unhappy.

(3) Nevertheless, he is endowed by God with talents which enable him to
survive and prosper. In some way he is a hero.

And in the section headed "Ishmael-Melville", in the paragraph that begins "He begins to move away" (p. 71) the sentence about Bulkington reads in the transcript:
"Next he has a momentary glimpse of the Handsome Sailor Bulkington, the Lame
Shadow who is, physically, what Ishmael would like to be. Bulkington will reappear as
a protagonist in a later work of Melville's under the name of Billy Budd. Here his role
is only to precede Queequeg." (The final version is of this passage is also present in
Ansen's transcript headed "Alternative uncancelled passage . . .")

In the concluding section, the passage from "More remarkable" (in the middle of
the paragraph that begins "Small wonder", p. 90) to the end of the quotation from
Rimbaud, the transcript has only: "Some wrecked on desert islands, some struck hidden reefs, some were crushed in the ice, some broke in the tempest, but the logs of
their voyages are with us to testify to their heroic greatness."

The typescript of the published version is in the University of Virginia Library. It was
prepared by Alan Ansen, with additions in Auden's hand, most of them minor, but including the long footnote to the section "The Polemical Situation of Romanticism"
(p. 36).

The text of the present edition is based largely on the printed text, which was proofread by Auden or Ansen or both. The printed text closely matches the typescript except for a few errors, which are corrected here. The typography of the printed text
(based on the general practice of the typescript) indicates set-off quotations with
smaller type and quotation marks; the text in this edition (as throughout the edition)
uses smaller type indented from both margins, omits the quotation marks, and uses
square brackets around authorially inserted words where Auden interrupts the quotation to do so (that is, on p. 40, the typescript and printed text have " 'Memory,' writes
Hobbes, 'is the World . . .' ").

In the quotations I have corrected a few minor errors that seem to have resulted
from Ansen's misreading of Auden's hand, but I have neither corrected nor noted
Auden's practice of reconstituting quotations by changing tense and number, removing whole phrases, rewriting or inventing connective phrases, and combining phrases
from adjacent or remote sentences. I have restored a few capitalizations from the typescript. I have also corrected a few errors in the layout of quotations and have revised
the layouts of some lists and charts to correspond more closely with Auden's clear intention in the typescript.

In the first lecture, in the section "The Romantic Sea and the Romantic Desert"
(p. 15), the printed text mistakenly places the second stanza of the quotation from
Carmen after the two stanzas from *The Hunting of the Snark*.

In the second lecture, in the section "Romantic Aesthetic Theory" (p. 40), I have
corrected the chapter number in *Moby Dick* (the printed version has LXII for XLII).
After the final quotation in the same section, I have deleted the mistaken attribution

"(Roscommon)" because the lines are in fact from Dryden's version of Boileau's *The Art of Poetry*; the lines are unattributed in Ansen's typescript of the original lectures, but the misattribution appears in the typescript Auden prepared for publication; possibly Auden or Ansen misremembered the original author, but it is more likely that Auden intended to include an additional quotation from the Earl of Roscommon which either he neglected to write or which Ansen skipped over while typing. If this is the case, Auden might have had in mind either the lines he quotes in the introductions to *Poets of the English Language* (p. 135) or such lines as these from Roscommon's "Essay on Translated Verse": "There Sweat, there Strain, tug the laborious Oar: / Search ev'ry Comment, that your Care can find."

Also in the second lecture, in the section "The Ship versus the City", the unattributed quotation from Jules Verne about the *Nautilus* should have an ellipsis after the name of the ship. In the section "The Environment of the Ship" the table is mistakenly laid out in the printed text so that "and to two scales of weather" is treated as part of the same phrase as "The day and the sun", and the two phrases "The degree of visibility" and "The velocity of the wind" are treated as items in the first column of the table above.

In the third lecture, in the section "Ethical Authority", in the paragraph that begins "The inner danger" (p. 60) I have inserted "it" after "because he says" (the word is absent from both typescripts). In the section "The Heroic Action", both typescript versions and the printed version precede the paragraph that begins "There is almost universal" (p. 66) with a paragraph number "(1)" and indent it as if it were part a numbered list, but no further paragraphs in this section have numbers. (In Ansen's transcript of the lecture version, the numbered paragraph is preceded by the heading "Ishmael".) Auden apparently forgot his original intention to answer the question "What is the romantic hero up to?" with a series of numbered points, so I have removed the number and have reformatted the paragraph as ordinary text.

Following the chart (p. 75), in the sentence that begins "Since they are", I have inserted "it" after "are good at"; the word is missing from all texts.

Also in the third lecture in the section headed "Stubb" (p. 78) only the first of the five quotations near the start has a chapter number from *Moby Dick*; the other quotations are from chapters 39, 39 again, 81, and 114, and the remaining unnumbered quotations in the chapter are from chapters 99, 121, and 73; in the last of these (which silently combines phrases from two adjacent sentences) I have corrected an error where Ansen probably misread "afraid" as "fond". In the section "Flask" (p. 80) the quotations are from chapters 48 and 81. In the section "Pip" (p. 81) the first quotation is from chapter 40. In the section "Ahab" the unnumbered quotation is from chapter 37. In the section "The Artist as Don Quixote" (p. 89) I cannot identify the quotation that begins "Nothing was not to be known"; possibly it is not a quotation at all but part of the preceding paragraph, but is set off as quotation in both of Ansen's typescripts (as in the printed version) because Ansen misinterpreted Auden's manuscript. In the same section, the quotation from Melville is from chapter 52 of *Moby Dick* ("lead" is Auden's slip for "conduct").

This sentence, supplied by the university, appears on the page facing the title page of the printed book: "These lectures were delivered at the University of Virginia under the Page-Barbour Foundation on March 22, 23, 24, 1949."

Essays and Reviews

1949–1955

AUDEN's introduction to *Tales of Grimm and Andersen,* published in 1952, was written in 1947, and appears in *Prose II.* "Poetry and Freedom", a lecture published in 1949, was delivered in 1948 and also appears in *Prose II.* See also p. xxxv.

A NOTE ON GRAHAM GREENE

Page 95.

This was an intermission talk for a dramatization of Greene's *The Ministry of Fear* in the NBC radio series *University Theatre,* broadcast 23 January 1949. Auden wrote to Chester Kallman on 18 January: "Am earning an easy fifty bucks next Sunday by introducing for three minutes a dramatisation by N.B.C. of *The Ministry of Fear.*" A transcript of the talk is in the NBC archives. Auden seems not to have written the talk with a view to publication, but it appeared (under the apparently nonauthorial title "The Heresy of Our Time") in the second issue of *Renascence,* a literary journal published by the Catholic Renascence Society at Marquette University; possibly an editor heard the broadcast and asked Auden for the text. The *Renascence* text was reprinted in the British quarterly *The Wind and the Rain* (Summer 1949) under the descriptive title that, for want of anything better, has been used here. I have added some punctuation.

IN MEMORIAM

Page 96.

Theodore Spencer (1902–49), a poet and literary scholar, first met Auden in 1939, probably when Auden visited Harvard. In the early 1940s Auden began asking Spencer to comment on his work, and he and Spencer exchanged long letters (Auden's are now in the Harvard University Archives) about the details of Auden's longer poems. For more about Auden and Spencer, see *Prose II,* p. 471, and Auden's review of Spencer's posthumous poems (p. 154).

PORT AND NUTS WITH THE ELIOTS

Page 97.

Auden wrote to Eliot on 25 March 1950 (almost a year after this review was published): "If by any chance you saw my review last year of *Towards a definition of Culture* in the New Yorker, I hope you didn't think it an act of lèse majesté" (Faber & Faber Archives).

A secretarial typescript with Auden's manuscript corrections and the same title as the printed text is in the New York Public Library Manuscripts and Archives Division. This edition is based on the magazine text, which has corrected quotations, some minor verbal changes, and some additional paragraphing (although I have restored some of Auden's paragraph breaks where the magazine's paragraphs are dauntingly long). I have restored Auden's freer capitalization of Archdeacon and other nouns. Book reviews in the *New Yorker* embed the title of the book reviewed in the text of the review itself, so the editors inserted it in the paragraph that begins "From its rather formidable title," after "latest essay,"; I have restored the typescript version.

The more significant changes from the typescript to printed text are these. In the paragraph that begins "Nor will anyone quarrel" (p. 98) the typescript has "anyone seriously quarrel". In the paragraph that begins "Yet his experiences" the typescript has "less allergic to the" for "less alarmed by that". In the paragraph that begins "Nobody has ever" (p. 99) the typescript has "Eternal Reprobation" for "Predestination". In the paragraph that begins "In a revolutionary" the typescript has "irresponsible" before "witch-hunting". Immediately above the paragraph that begins "The greatest blessing" (p. 100) the typescript has an additional paragraph (perhaps omitted partly because a long handwritten insertion was difficult to decipher):

Rationalized industrialism can produce consumable goods in greater and cheaper quantities than any other system, and since food, housing, clothing, etc., are primary human needs, any attempt to go back to a preindustrial age is a lost cause. Industrial methods applied to education can provide human instruments for a very specific foreknown social function better than any other and when this is required could be applied much more thoroughly and intensively than they are at present. It is only when the problem is one of reproducing complete human beings that the haste and narrowness of the industrial method makes it more inefficient than any other.

In the paragraph that begins "So one could go" (p. 101) the typescript has "America" for "Jefferson", and the first two phrases set out as dialogue (from "*Ichabod*" to "extraordinary noise?" ["cry" in the typescript]) are run-in with the earlier part of the paragraph; the next paragraph in the typescript begins with "You were saying, Sir" and continues as a single paragraph to the end.

The quotations slightly alter Eliot's wording and punctuation.

THE QUESTION OF THE POUND AWARD

Page 101.

Partisan Review, founded in 1934, was for many years the most prominent left-wing little magazine in America, having declared itself in 1937 committed to the revolutionary cause but unobliged to any party or movement. It maintained a left-wing anti-Stalinist line in politics while promoting modernism in the arts. The editors during the late 1940s and early 1950s were varying combinations of William Rahv, William Barrett, Delmore Schwartz, and others. Auden's political and literary reputation made him a valued contributor, but his work for the magazine (starting with

"The Public v. Mr W. B. Yeats" in 1939) almost always contradicted its editorial policy in a more or less understated way.

Auden's article was the first of eight responses, all printed under the same title,
to William Barrett's editorial "A Prize for Ezra Pound" in the preceding issue (April
1949). In February 1949, Pound's book *The Pisan Cantos* had been awarded the first
Bollingen Prize in Poetry by a jury made up of the Fellows in American Letters of
the Library of Congress, a group of advisers to the Librarian of Congress that had
been formed in 1943 when the Librarian was Archibald MacLeish. The terms of the
prize required it to be awarded for a book of poems published in the preceding year.
Because Pound was under indictment for high treason for his broadcasts over Italian radio during the war, and because the book included ugly statements of anti-
Jewish prejudice, the prize predictably aroused controversy (for later developments,
see p. 694). One result of the controversy was the decision by the Library of Congress to transfer the management of the award to Yale University.

A report by Léonie Adams, secretary to the Fellows in American Letters, on the
procedure by which the winner of the award was chosen, indicates that on a preliminary vote, when the committee met in November 1948, Pound received eight
out of fourteen votes; on a second vote, performed by letter, Pound received ten out
of twelve ballots received. One of Auden's friends reported that he opposed giving
the award to Pound; another reported that he voted for it; probably on the first ballot he voted against Pound (and for William Carlos Williams's *Paterson, Book II*) and
on the second voted for him (when Williams no longer had a chance of winning).

Barrett's editorial focused on this sentence in the announcement of the award:
"To permit other considerations than those of poetic achievement to sway the decision would destroy the significance of the award and would in principle deny the
validity of that objective perception of value on which any civilized society must rest."
After expanding on the implications of this argument, Barrett wrote: "The statement of the Bollingen judges shows a laudable intention to reaffirm the validity of
aesthetic principles [after the distortions of Marxist criticism in the 1930s]. Our history, however, would be incomplete if we did not notice that within American literary criticism over the past decade or more there has developed another attitude
which is so obsessed with formal and technical questions that it has time for only a
hasty glimpse at content."

Auden's opening paragraph alludes to the other members of the jury which decided the award; two of those jurors, Karl Shapiro and Allen Tate, were among the
other seven writers who contributed comments. Auden slightly mistitled Baudelaire's "*Une Charogne*". The *New York Post* was then a liberal newspaper with strong
Jewish sympathies; *Der Stürmer* was the notoriously anti-Semitic newspaper published
in Germany from 1923 until 1945.

INTRODUCTIONS TO *Poets of the English Language*

Page 103.

Auden was sole author of the introductions to this five-volume anthology which
he coedited with Norman Holmes Pearson. For the general history of the anthology, see Appendix II. The notes below describe the text of the introductions. Auden

wrote the introductions in Italy during late spring and early summer of 1949 and seems to have posted them on 8 July to Alan Ansen with a request that he type them and send a copy to Pearson. As in Auden's first book for the Viking Portable Library series, *The Greek Reader* (see *Prose II*), the introduction to each volume was followed by a chronological chart (also described in Appendix II). The five volumes were published on 29 September 1950.

Fragmentary drafts of the introductions to the first two volumes are in a notebook now in the Harry Ransom Humanities Research Center at the University of Texas at Austin. A notebook now in the Berg Collection includes some pencilled drafts that seem to have been preliminary notes for the introductions for the first two volumes.

A partial version of the text that Auden originally gave to the Viking Press survives in the form of five galley sheets headed "Sample Pages" that the press mailed out to between twenty and thirty English professors in April 1950 (see Appendix II). These samples contained a page of the chronological chart, a page of William Langland and one of Thomas Hood, a shorter version of the opening "General Principles", and most of the introduction to Volume IV. Many of the changes between the version in the sample pages and the final published versions may have been editorial, not authorial.

The sample version of the "General Principles" differs from the printed text in the following ways (omitting changes in punctuation):

In the section headed "Selection", first paragraph, second sentence: "for example" is lacking. In the sentence about Tennyson, the sample version has "once more admired". The published second paragraph replaces these two paragraphs in the sample:

It is the duty of the anthologist, therefore, to be a slave neither to the dicta of the past nor to present fashion nor to his personal idiosyncrasies. Were this collection, for example, the simple reflection of the taste of one of the editors, it would contain no Shelley; in fact it contains much: in respect of Mrs Browning, on the other hand, we both, after careful consideration, have felt compelled to back our judgment against all comers and exclude her. Whatever these volumes contain is there by our joint consent and the responsibility for any unjustifiable omissions or inclusions rests upon us both.

Thanks to the number of pages at our disposal, which has permitted us to include long poems or extensive passages therefrom as well as lyrics, we have endeavored to give as all-round a representation of each poet's production as possible. In the case of Shakespeare, we have thought that such a representation was more adequately achieved through printing one play complete than through a number of extracts from several.

The section headed "Arrangement" consists in the sample version only of one brief paragraph:

In principle the poetry is presented in its historical order. We have, however, departed from a strict chronology when another kind of grouping seemed to us to make better sense. Thus Vaughan and Traherne appear with George Herbert, not with Rochester, and all the volumes will be found to overlap slightly.

The section headed "Texts" has this briefer version of the opening sentence: "In the first two volumes, where the textual problem arises, we have tried to produce what is called, we believe, a 'diplomatic' text, i.e. the poems are reproduced from original texts without modification except in the following respects:". The list of three items is the same as in the printed version except that, in the third item, the phrase "to the modern reader," is not present.

The section headed "Supplementary Data" is much longer in the sample version than in the published text and is followed by a section headed "A Warning" as follows:

SUPPLEMENTARY DATA

No biographical data on the men and women who wrote the poems, other than the dates of their births, deaths, and principal works, will be found. This omission is deliberate.

Both the editors have taught English literature to students of all ages from seven to seventy, and one has published verses; as a result of these experiences we both feel very strongly that the time has come to take a firm stand against the all too common fancy that, in order to understand a poem fully, to compare it with other poems, whether of the same historical period or others, and to judge it, it is useful or even necessary to know something about its creator's personal history.

All poems, even the most apparently dramatic ones, are autobiographical in the sense that the experience which went into writing them was the experience of the poet himself, of his loves, his fears, his reading, etc.; on the other hand, all poems, even those written in the first person, are impersonal and public objects, detached forever from their parents, for the whole purpose of writing poetry is to convert private experience into a public form which is at any time reconvertible into or comprehensible in terms of the private experience of any reader.

In Coleridge's ode to "Dejection," for example, we have a certain emotional state described. The meaningfulness of the poem depends upon the fact that most men in most ages have on occasions and for many different reasons experienced such a state; its value depends upon the completeness and accuracy with which this state is expressed. The specific cause for its occurrence in Coleridge or in the reader, whether it be opium or an overanxious mother or what-have-you, is irrelevant.

Again, it is no help in understanding the poetry of Keats to know that the particular young lady with whom he was unhappily in love was Fanny Brawne; all that matters is the emotion in the poetry. All of us, of course, are gossips who like to know about our neighbors, whatever their occupation; but gossip, however enjoyable, is not criticism, and its proper place seems rather the tea table than the library or the classroom. If a poet ceases to write at all or ceases to write well, the causes may very probably lie in his private life and, were the reader a doctor or a priest whom the poet came to consult, personal questions would be in order, but the reader is not in this situation. The only occasion where criticism may legitimately investigate the poet's personal history is when it is concerned with the nature of the creative act itself. The relation of Emily Brontë's poems, for example, to her brother and sisters and their imaginary kingdoms of Angria and Gondal, as demonstrated in F. E. Ratchford's book *The Brontës' Web of Childhood*, is, admittedly, of great interest and value. But when such an investigation is possible, it is only valuable if conducted in the greatest detail. The summary biography which is all that the limited space in any anthology allows is perfectly useless. This is not to assert that there are no facts outside the words of the poem we are reading which are relevant to its appreciation; in reading Pope's *Rape of the Lock*, for instance, it is relevant to know the epics of Homer; in reading Dante, to know something of the *Summa*. The test of relevance is the degree to which a significant relation between the facts of the poem and the outside facts can be demonstrated specifically and precisely.

Instead of biographical data, therefore, we have drawn up a chart that, in giving the main social events to the impact of which poets were exposed, and the principal works of literature, philosophy, science, etc., that affected the climate of opinion by which they were surrounded, will be of some help, we trust, toward seeing the poetry in historical perspective.

A WARNING

By their very nature anthologies distort the general picture of poetry which they attempt to present. They are bound to overemphasize the lyric at the expense of the larger, perhaps more important, forms and a purple passage at the expense of a whole design. They must, almost inevitably, favor the minor poet at the expense of the major. A minor poet may have written two or three good poems which are all that any reader needs to know. There is nothing to be gained by reading the rest of his work. For a major poet this is never the case. Granted, even, that the anthologist has impeccable taste and has indeed selected the best poems, this is not enough. The life work of a major writer is a structured whole and not only his best or his better work must be read, but all of it, including the bad.

As for the uses of an anthology, only two are legitimate. It can serve as an introduction to poetry for the young student who has yet to acquire his library, and as a convenient selection for the adult reader who is temporarily parted from his library. Used otherwise it is an encouragement to sloth. The danger of any anthology—and the better the anthology the greater the danger—is that it may give the reader the illusion that here he has all that he needs to read.

(A separate manuscript of "A Warning" in the Harry Ransom Humanities Research Center at the University of Texas at Austin has in the first paragraph "all his best poems" where the sample galleys have "all the best poems" and has a hyphen in "life-work".)

The sample version of the introduction to Volume IV is almost identical to the printed version, except for the misdating of Wordsworth's Preface to 1802 (corrected to 1800 in the published version). The sample version breaks off after the paragraph that begins "The American had not intended" (p. 144).

The text in this edition is based on the published text and incorporates corrections that Auden marked in Alan Ansen's copy (now in the Berg Collection). In the original Volume I the titles "General Principles" and "Introduction to Volume I" have the same weight, and I have followed that example here; I have added from the title page of the book the colon and the subtitle "Langland to Spenser". The introductions to the remaining volumes were each headed "Introduction"; I have added the volume number and, as in Volume I, the poets' names from the title page.

In the introduction to Volume I, in the paragraph that begins "Nor is it true" (p. 114) the opening words are Auden's correction to the printed text's "It is nonsense". In the introduction to Volume III, in the second paragraph (p. 128), which begins "Verse, owing to", Auden deleted "for example," after "Verse," and inserted "to prose" later in the same sentence. In the introduction to Volume V, in the paragraph that begins "So speaks the victim" (p. 150) Auden made two corrections in the second sentence, the first of which may have been misplaced: he seems to have marked "and" to be replaced with a dash, but perhaps intended to insert the dash before the word, as I have done here; he also corrected "he has found" to "yet has found". In the introduction to Volume IV, the translation from Hölderlin by Michael Hamburger was first published in 1943.

Nonauthorial changes in later printings are described in Appendix II.

SIXTY-SIX SESTETS

Page 154.

For Theodore Spencer, see the notes to "In Memoriam" (p. 96) above. The title of this review, like all others in the *New York Times Book Review*, was chosen by a newspaper editor.

The text in this edition has been corrected on the basis of Auden's untitled manuscript, now in the Northwestern University Library. In the third paragraph the newspaper (perhaps with Auden's approval) adds the parenthetical identification of Spencer's professorship. In the paragraph that begins "Such of his sestets" the newspaper places dashes around the phrase that begins "e.g." and in the same phrase has a comma instead of "or" between the two titles; in the same paragraph the newspaper mistakenly treats the phrase "though he is capable of making an admirable epigram" as the end of the preceding sentence, omits the abbreviation "e.g." that introduces the poem, and immediately after the poem treats the concluding phrase of the sentence as a new, separate sentence. In the fifth paragraph, the newspaper has "terrifying" for "unifying". In the penultimate paragraph the newspaper has "profusely and completely" for "profoundly and complexly", and makes nonsense of the closing sentence by omitting "i.e." In the final paragraph the newspaper has "theme" for "Muse". I have restored from the manuscript the opening phrase in the final paragraph ("This is a posthumous volume:") and I have restored the break that begins that paragraph. Otherwise, I have followed the paragraphing in the newspaper.

Auden's quotations slightly alter Spencer's punctuation.

Notebooks of Somerset Maugham

Page 156.

Auden slightly alters Maugham's wording and punctuation. In the fifth paragraph I have tentatively emended "mood word" to "moral". In the paragraph that begins "Of himself as a writer" I have corrected "part of my nose" to "in front of my nose", and in the paragraph that begins "There are indications" I have emended "the suggestions" to "two suggestions" (in all instances, a compositor probably misread Auden's hand). I have also corrected some minor misspellings and omitted the newspaper's arbitrary section breaks.

Firbank Revisited

Page 159.

Early in 1947 Auden had hoped to compile a selection of Firbank's novels for the Viking Portable Library, and *Harper's Bazaar* reported in a contributor's note in October 1947 that he was "preparing an omnibus of Ronald Firbank for New Directions" (see *Prose II*, p. 507). This plan seems to have fallen through when New Directions learned that Gerald Duckworth was publishing a selection of Firbank in Britain, and that it would be less expensive to reprint the British edition than to publish a separate one.

On 25 May 1949, Auden wrote to William Shawn, editor of the *New Yorker*: "Just a line to say that *if* New Directions bring out a Firbank this summer, which I believe they announced, I would very much like to review it for the *New Yorker*." Shawn did not take up his offer, and Auden probably offered a review to the *New York Times Book Review* in the autumn. He wrote to Isherwood on 15 October 1949: "Am just reviewing the new Firbank collection (only five of them alas). Can any writer give one so much pleasure. 'I should like to spank the white walls of his cottage.'"

A manuscript, titled "Eden Regained", is in the Northwestern University Library; I have followed it in making some slight emendations. The manuscript version lacks the second paragraph of the printed text. In the manuscript the paragraph that begins "All that really matters" ends with these phrases, which are absent in the newspaper version:

and overhear such conversations as:

> "The mistress, I presume, is with the scourge," the butler announced, peering impassibly around.
> "Let her lash it," she said. "In this glorious room one is quite content to wait."

In the paragraph that begins "The second is", the manuscript has the sentence "Why not?" before the closing sentence. In the paragraph that begins "Not only is there", the manuscript reads "to limit behavior, but also no law of logic to limit thought: the minds of the characters wander at will". Following the end of the same paragraph, the manuscript continues, quoting approximately from *The Flower beneath the Foot*:

> —Although he's dark, Vi, it's odd how he gives one the impression of perfect fairness!
> —Who's that, darling?
> —Ann-Jules, of course.
> —I begin to wish, do you know, I'd brought pomegranates, and worn something else.
> —What are those big burley-worleys?
> —Pears . . .
> —Give me one.
> —Catch then.
> —Not that I could bear to be married; especially like *you*, Vi!
> —A marriage like ours, dear, was so utterly unworthwhile . . .
> —I'm not sure that I comprehend altogether? . . .
> —Sea-gulls' wings as they fan one's face . . .
> —It's vile and wrong to shoot them, but oh! how I wish your happiness depended, even ever so little, on me.

All the social differences, class, race, age, exist but without causing pride or envy: negresses mix with duchesses, Mohammedans with Christians, Miami Mouth and Olga Blumenghast are neither more nor less enchanting and absurd than their white and gentile neighbors.

Even death exists but as a last performance, without pain or grief:

> —"I want some mauve sweet peas," she listlessly said.
> —"Her spirit soars; her thoughts are in the Champs Elysées," the Countess exclaimed, withdrawing noiselessly to warn the milliners.

This is followed, as in the printed text, by the paragraph that begins "Everyone is welcome".

In place of the printed text's final paragraph, the manuscript has these two paragraphs:

On the other hand, can any reader, in a world as full of hatred, as governessy, as ours, honestly declare that he would not, if he could, exchange it for one in which nothing is disliked but novels "written in hotels with the bed unmade at the back of the chair," and the only task set by the governess is to conjugate I-am-a-Political-Hostess, and one may pass one's days eating *Pointes d'asperges à la Laura Leslie*, frightening the passing bats with a rope of pearls and listening to the inevitable waltz from *The Blue Banana*?

An ideal Christmas present, but not a book for the guest-room; it will "get lost" very soon.

NATURE, HISTORY AND POETRY

Page 161.

This is an unpublished version written in 1949 of an essay published in *Thought* in 1950 (p. 226). Auden wrote it for a special number of *Les Cahiers de la Pléiade*, Summer–Autumn 1950, edited by Jean Paulhan, devoted to the life and work of Saint-John Perse (pseudonym of Alexis Léger), who lived in the United States and with whom Auden was on friendly terms. Apparently Léger wrote to ask Auden to write a piece for the special number; on 16 October 1949 Auden replied:

As to writing about you in the Cahiers de la Pléiade, I haven't the courage. I am so terrified of saying something silly. I don't know what your experience has been, but I always find it so much easier to write about poetry I don't really like than poetry I admire as much as I admire yours. I just want to say "C'est très belle"; everything else sounds irrelevant or, in the case of poetry in another language, presumptuous.

However, he then sent a manuscript to Léger on 7 November 1949 with this cover letter: "I have written these few remarks as my Hommage for the book. If you approve, could you send them on to Monsieur Paulhan, as I don't want to send anything you dislike." Léger sent the manuscript to Paulhan who chose to omit it from the volume because it was not specifically about Saint-John Perse's poems. The manuscript and Auden's letters are in the Fondation Saint-John Perse in Aix-en-Provence.

THEN AND NOW: 1935–1950

Page 164.

Mademoiselle published literary contributions among its articles on fashion; this essay was commissioned for its fifteenth-anniversary issue. Auden wrote to Chester Kallman on 8 November 1949: "Must stop to go back to my Mademoiselle article— a comparison of the young girl of 1935 and the young girl of 1949. Wish you were here to help about movies and popular music." I have retained the breaks in the printed text, which are logical and possibly authorial.

The ubiquitous writer and critic Alexander Woollcott recommended James Hilton's novel *Good-bye, Mr Chips* to its American publisher and praised the book in *McCall's* magazine and elsewhere. Lloyd Douglas was the author of *Magnificent Ob-*

session, The Robe, and other popular novels on religious themes. Bobby Clark, a veteran comic actor, was starring in the Broadway musical comedy *As the Girls Go,* a title sometimes ignored in newspaper stories that referred to "the Bobby Clark show".

JEAN COCTEAU

Page 168.

Flair was a glossy magazine of art and fashion edited by Fleur Cowles which lasted one year as a monthly and another year as an annual. Auden's note on Cocteau appeared in the first number, together with Cocteau's "A Letter to Americans". Auden wrote from New York to Chester Kallman in Italy on 29 January 1950: "No news here whatsoever except the appearance of no. 1 of *Flair* (camp, my dear)".

RELIGION AND THE INTELLECTUALS: A SYMPOSIUM

Page 170.

Auden's contribution to a "symposium" published in *Partisan Review* in three issues in February, March, and April 1950. The contributors were invited to respond to an unsigned "Editorial Statement" (probably by the two coeditors William Phillips and Philip Rahv, the number of coeditors having recently been reduced by internecine warfare) published in the February 1950 issue, which begins: "One of the most significant tendencies of our time, especially in this decade, has been the new turn toward religion among intellectuals and the growing disfavor with which secular attitudes and perspectives are now regarded in not a few circles that lay claim to the leadership of culture." After describing this phenomenon as occurring particularly among intellectuals in English-speaking countries, the statement poses five general questions, from which Auden quoted or adapted some of the italicized headings in his response. An abridged version of these questions follows:

1. From a naturalistic point of view, all events (including those of history) have their causes, and the present revival of religion would not be an exception. What do you think are the causes of the present trend? Is it due to the worldwide failure and defeat of a real radical movement in politics? . . .

2. Granting that social changes or catastrophes may bring people to consider religion more sympathetically, the fact still remains that the trend in question here is one among intellectuals, who have undergone a change in *convictions.* What has happened to make religion more credible than it formerly was to the modern mind? . . . The credibility of certain religious mysteries like the Incarnation and the Trinity would certainly not seem to be changed by any new data, scientific or otherwise; but there may be other parts of religion whose general credibility is changed by fundamental changes in the climate of opinion. . . .

Does this new trend imply that the scientific attitude of mind is being forsaken? Or that drastic limits are being set to it? . . .

3. Religion and culture. Can culture exist without a positive religion? To what extent must this religion be organized as an institution? The distinction has

been made between prophetic and institutional religion: Do you think that enduring values can be carried by the former? . . .

4. Religion and literature. The revival of religion has perhaps been most noticeable in the literary world. Does this imply some special dependence of the literary imagination upon religious feeling and ideas? Is the present emphasis upon myth among literary theorists connected with the renewed interest in religion?

5. Certain writers have attempted to separate the religious consciousness (as an attitude toward man and human life) from religious beliefs. . . . Is this separation possible? Is there a valuable religious consciousness that can be maintained without an explicit credo postulating the supernatural? . . .

As printed, the article is divided into two sections lettered A and B followed by five sections numbered with roman numerals II through VI. I have tried to restore Auden's intended outlining by adding the roman numeral I before the first heading and placing parentheses around the two lettered headings. "*PR*" was the magazine's standard way of referring to itself; I have italicized the abbreviation for the sake of clarity.

The magazine republished the symposium separately as *Religion and the Intellectuals* (1950) as the third in the PR Series of pamphlets.

INTRODUCTION TO *Red Ribbon on a White Horse*

Page 177.

The text in this edition is the first publication of the full text of Auden's introduction to Anzia Yezierska's memoir; the version that appeared in the book published by Charles Scribner's Sons on 11 September 1950 was heavily cut by Yezierska with Auden's consent.

Anzia Yezierska had been famous as a novelist and short-story writer in the 1920s and 1930s but was forgotten and impoverished when she wrote this memoir in the late 1940s. Probably in 1948, after her unfinished manuscript had been rejected by many publishers, Yezierska attended a class at the Union Theological Seminary taught by Reinhold Niebuhr, who encouraged her to get in touch with Auden. She reportedly made an uninvited visit to Auden's apartment, where she browbeat him into finding a publisher and writing an introduction. Auden sent the manuscript to his editor Saxe Commins at Random House, who turned it down in January 1949, saying that its commercial prospects were limited by the profusion of memoirs by Jewish immigrants about their rise to (and sometimes fall from) affluence. Possibly after further rejections, Auden recommended the book to John Hall Wheelock at Scribner, who had edited Auden's edition of Henry James's *The American Scene* in 1946; Scribner accepted the book in November 1949. Auden told Chester Kallman in a letter of 29 January 1950 that he must "go and write an introduction to the autobiography of Anzia Yezierska (one of yours [i.e. Jewish like Kallman]), which I found very moving and have persuaded Scribner to take." Auden agreed to take a small fee of $150 for his introduction, and asked that it not be deducted from Yezierska's advance (half was to be paid by Scribner, half from any future royalties received by the author).

Yezierska's daughter Louise Levitas Henriksen, in her biography *Anzia Yezierska: A Writer's Life* (1988), recalls that her mother "could not bear the rather stately introduction Auden wrote for her book" and felt cheated by Auden's thoughtful and analytic prose, which could not be translated instantly into emotions. "She had evidently expected great poetry lyrically saluting her writing", and wrote Auden an outraged letter asking him to replace his introduction with "about five or six hundred words that express your idea of the book". Her daughter, horrified by the arrogance of Yezierska's letter, suggested that Auden might be asked merely to make some cuts, and phoned him on her mother's behalf to propose this. Auden readily agreed to the cuts, but later that day Yezierska wrote him another angry letter about his introduction. (Henriksen gives a more compressed account in her 1987 "Afterword" to a paperback reprint of *Red Ribbon on a White Horse*.)

Scribner was caught in the middle; Wheelock suggested his own selection of cuts in a letter to Auden on 7 March 1950 (in which he also wrote, "I hope you haven't been having too bad a time with our mutual friend") but Yezierska seems to have preferred her own slightly different list of cuts. Auden wrote in a postcard to Wheelock on 26 April 1950: "Thank you for your letter and the galleys. I think Miss Y is making a mistake about some of the cuts but it is her book and of course she may do as she pleases."

A carbon-copy secretarial typescript of Auden's introduction is in the Scribner archives at Princeton University Library. The text in this edition is based on the printed text, with the addition of the material cut from the typescript. I have slightly emended the punctuation of the restored material, and, in the printed text, have restored Auden's capitalization and some of his punctuation where the Scribner editors misunderstood the text. Following the typescript, I have reduced "the United States" to "the States".

The printed version adds the closing phrase of the first paragraph ("for I have read . . ."), which Auden seems to have written at Scribners' or Yezierska's request. In the paragraph that begins "So long as" (p. 177) the printed version lacks everything starting with "Thus Dr Cushing". In the paragraph that begins "She began life" (p. 178) the printed text mistakenly adds a comma after "a class" (the meaning of the phrase here is "one class per generation"). In the paragraph that begins "The sudden paralysis" (p. 180) the printed text lacks the sentence that begins "If the former". In the paragraph that begins "As she ceased" the printed text lacks the first two sentences and inserts "than in the United States" after "more static societies". The printed text lacks the paragraph that begins "No man naturally" (p. 181). In the paragraph that begins "So, after a fairy tale" the printed text lacks the opening sentence and replaces "she" in the second sentence with "Miss Yezierska". The printed text lacks the paragraph that begins "Miss Yezierska, for instance" (p. 182). The printed text lacks everything from "As an account" to the end, except for one paragraph that was rewritten to serve as the final paragraph of the printed version; the original version was the paragraph that begins "Miss Yezierska's autobiography" (p. 183), revised for the printed version to read:

Miss Yezierska's autobiography is, literally, the story of an early twentieth-century immigrant, but it has a deeper and more general significance today when, figuratively, the immigrant is coming more and more to stand as the symbol for Everyman, for the natural and unconscious community of tradition is rapidly disappearing from the earth.

Auden collected the printed version in *The Dyer's Hand* (1962) under the title "Red Ribbon on a White Horse," with an added epigraph and some minor changes in the text. The epigraph reads: "'Mowing hay by hand! Bless their hearts!'—An American matron on the train between Bologna and Florence". The two changes (also marked in Auden's copy of Yezierska's book, now in a private collection) are these. In the paragraph that begins "The sudden paralysis" (p. 180) the 1962 version has "I think one reason for this may be the dominance" and omits the phrase "because of the unreality of such an attempt". In the paragraph that begins "The Arts Project" the second sentence of the 1962 text begins "Noblest" (not "Noble"). The 1962 text adds the attribution "(Edward Thomas)" to the lines of verse from Thomas's "Home", and in the sentence immediately following the quotation omits the end of the sentence, from "where she went".

The opening paragraph misattributes to the Preamble to the United States Constitution a famous phrase written by Thomas Jefferson for the American Declaration of Independence; surprisingly, this error remained uncorrected even in *The Dyer's Hand* until the 1968 paperback reprint, in which the publishers made the correction without consulting Auden.

In the paragraph that begins "Further, to be called to Hollywood", the Calcutta sweepstake refers to a race at which bettors won famously huge fortunes.

A PLAYBOY OF THE WESTERN WORLD: ST OSCAR, THE HOMINTERN MARTYR

Page 184.

I have retained the many nonstandard hyphenations that were evidently copied from Auden's manuscript. Auden made some trivial alterations in his quotations. I have corrected the compositor's misreading of Lady Brackwell for Lady Bracknell; I have also corrected Bunberry to Bunbury, although the error may have been Auden's.

OF POETRY IN TROUBLED GREECE

Page 188.

Auden and Rae Dalven were on friendly terms, apparently through literary circles in New York. This book was published in December 1949, more than four months before the review appeared; the long interval may suggest that Auden asked to review the book, possibly at Rae Dalven's instigation, rather than having been assigned it by an editor at the time of publication. Auden later wrote an introduction for Rae Dalven's translation of the *Complete Poems of Cavafy*, published in 1961.

I have restored the anthology's spellings of a few Greek names that were apparently miscopied by either Auden or the compositor.

A Guidebook for All Good Counter-Revolutionaries

Page 190.

Auden had contributed to the liberal weekly *The Nation* since 1939 (although he claimed he never read it; see p. 630). The printed version of this review reflects some cuts made by Auden at the request of the magazine's literary editor Margaret Marshall. Auden wrote to her on 22 March 1950: "Thanks for these galleys. Possible cuts I've marked, i.e. One could start at 'Since the *Recollections*', changing *his* to *De Tocqueville* (galley 10). Galley 11. Cut from 'Thus, though every revolution is unique' to 'theft is strenuously forbidden' (galley 12). I should miss the quotations which are so much better than anything one can say, but shall quite understand if you feel you must" (Yale University Library). Some long quotations may have survived these cuts, but the original opening and the second passage mentioned in Auden's letter are lost.

In the paragraph that begins "This is a record" I have tentatively emended the printed by text by deleting the initial "or" in "or on the other hand he believed". Auden's quotations are approximate or worse; the quotation that begins "Our intention" either paraphrases a passage on p. 201 of the original or was taken from a different source. In the quotation that begins "No sooner" I have corrected "scared and dragged"(probably a compositor's misreading of Auden's hand) to "seized and dragged". In the paragraph that follows, "mathematical certainty" is Auden's miscopying of "mathematical exactness".

The title perhaps echoes "A Handbook for Revolutionaries" in the printed text of George Bernard Shaw's *Man and Superman*.

The Score and Scale of Berlioz

Page 193.

Auden wrote to Chester Kallman on 17 February 1950: "Have read the first 200 galleys of Barzun's book on Berlioz. Quite good but O so donnish." For further details of Auden's relations with Barzun see the account of The Readers' Subscription book club in Appendix II.

In the paragraph that begins "Berlioz himself" (p. 195) the second sentence seems fragmentary, and the period between the first and second sentences could perhaps be replaced by a comma. Auden repunctuated his quotations from Barzun. The dialogue between Berlioz and Metternich (from Berlioz's *Memoirs*) is not in Barzun's book and is perhaps quoted from memory.

The Things Which Are Caesar's

Page 196.

The learned monthly *Theology*, published in London by the Society for the Propagation of Christian Knowledge, was edited by Alec Vidler, the distinguished church historian and theologian. Auden's essay was one of six Beecher Lectures delivered at the annual convocation of the Yale Divinity School, where it was announced under the title "The Ministry of the Laity". Auden wrote to Christopher Isherwood on 28 February 1950, "Must now write a lecture for the Yale Divinity School on the nature of the laity—O dear, one should *never* get involved with the religious—their demands are inexhaustible and their rewards very meagre indeed" (Huntington Library). Because Auden was away in Italy during the convocation, his talk was read for him by Norman Holmes Pearson on 19 April 1950. A mimeographed leaflet with the text was made available to those who attended, and it is unclear whether Auden or a member of the audience suggested to Vidler that it might be published.

The essay was longer than most that appeared in the magazine, and was split between two issues (arbitrarily, before the paragraph that begins "Just as Jehovah"). The printed text seems to have been set up from a copy of the mimeographed text marked with revisions by Auden, but it was probably also emended by an editor. The footnote, which is surely Auden's, is not present in the mimeographed text.

As Auden seems to have read proofs of the magazine text and accepted its wording, that text is used here, but I have restored the rows of asterisks that divide sections in the mimeographed version, and have restored some punctuation from the mimeographed text which the magazine either removed or simplified, usually at the expense of clarity. For example, the magazine seems to have eliminated almost all of Auden's parentheses around subordinate clauses; many of these seem to have been intended as aids for Pearson to use when reading complex sentences aloud, but others seem crucial to the sense, and I have selectively restored them. The printed text includes many exceptionally long sentences that appear in the mimeographed text as series of separate sentences, sometimes with connective words such as "and" at the start of the later sentences in a series. Other essays in the magazine are not characterized by such long sentences, so it was probably Auden who put the sentences together when revising the mimeographed text.

In the excerpt from Pindar (p. 200) in Richmond Lattimore's translation (included by Auden in *The Portable Greek Reader*) I have emended a typist's misreadings of words and line breaks and have corrected the misnumbering of the ode as 9 (for 6).

The single-sentence paragraph that begins "While God permitted" (p. 203) is two sentences in the mimeographed text; the mimeographed version has parentheses within the dashes in the opening words, sets "so that it should . . . carried far enough" in parentheses, and follows the closing parenthesis with "nevertheless God reserved" for "He reserved", and makes "Lord of history" the end of the first sentence; the second sentence begins "Thus, when in" in place of the printed text's "so that when".

The obscure first sentence of the paragraph that begins "While the priestly function" (p. 203) is more lucid in the two corresponding sentences of the mimeographed text: "The priestly function of the Jewish nation had been exercised not by any specifically religious acts or preaching to the Gentiles, but by their history as a people. Yet the gradual and continuous development among Jews of the consciousness that God is not to be manipulated by magic nor possessed by reason, but is a Father who loves his children even when they sin, meant for the Apostles and their successors that the history of religion was ended and that their function would be to serve as the instrument by which the truths necessary to salvation, and the means of grace entrusted to them by Christ, are preserved and transmitted to the end of time."

In the paragraph that begins "Whenever and wherever" (p. 206) I have tentatively restored from the mimeographed text "which a mixed calling runs" in place of the printed text's "which a mixed called runs"; neither reading is fully satisfactory, and the printed version may represent an editor's attempt to correct Auden's grammar.

The quotation from Sydney Smith in the closing paragraph slightly alters the source in Lady Holland's *Memoir*: "Take short views, hope for the best, and trust in God."

A typescript made by Alan Ansen, with Auden's manuscript corrections, is in the Berg Collection.

A That There Sort of Writer

Page 210.

Auden sent the manuscript of this review to William Shawn, editor of the *New Yorker*, on 30 April 1950 with a cover letter that suggests it was a commissioned piece: "Herewith my review of the Byron letters. I hope you can decipher it." The magazine prepared a typescript from Auden's manuscript but never published it (the magazine's internal files list the piece as "Killed 12/26/52") and the review appears here for the first time. The text is that of the manuscript in the New York Public Library Manuscripts and Archives Division. I have not corrected (although the *New Yorker* would have done so) Auden's somewhat approximate quotations. In the paragraph that begins "Again, like all" (p. 213) I have inserted "her" after "wasn't going to have". In the paragraph that begins "An extrovert, then" (p. 214) "an abstract" may be a slip for "an abstraction" but the manuscript's usage is not uncommon.

Introduction to *Selected Prose and Poetry of Edgar Allan Poe*

Page 215.

This selection, intended mostly for college students, was published in paperback by Rinehart & Company on 6 December 1950 as number 42 in the Rinehart Editions series. Auden seems to have developed an interest in Poe while compiling the *Poets of the English Language* anthology in 1948 and 1949 in collaboration with Norman Holmes Pearson (see Appendix II). In 1948 Pearson's edition of Thoreau's *Walden* had appeared in the same series, and Auden probably asked Pearson to recommend an edition of Poe to R. P. Hobbs, the head of Rinehart & Company's college division. Hobbs evidently agreed to the book, and Auden reported to Pearson, in a letter probably written in late February 1950:

Have just taken in to Hobbs the list of the selections you will find on the back of this page. It's unfortunate for Rinehart and for the size of the book that Poe's two most important pieces, at least to me, are his longest, i.e. *Gordon Pym* and *Eureka*. As you will see, I tried to make the story selection representative of his various interests. 4 horror tales, one parody of a horror tale, one Detective, one science of the future, and two travel-adventures. The *Marginalia* extracts I am rather pleased with, as I think through them one can give a pretty complete picture of his critical theories. In *The Poetic Principle* I simply could not face putting that last passage of baloney ending up—"for her LOVE"!! It's really *too* unkind to the old thing. And his *letters* to the ladies, my dear, are the most shy-making documents I ever read.

Hope you will approve (and that Baudelaire's shade will, too).

(Auden's letters are in the Pearson papers in the Yale University Library.)

Pearson's reply can be inferred from Auden's response, mailed on 24 February:

Many thanks for your letter. Will certainly add *A dream within a dream.*

I really do *not* like the Cask of A[montillado], or The Masque of the R[ed] D[eath]; as to The T[ell]-T[ale] Heart, I would prefer for the abnormal psychology angle to use *The Imp of the Perverse* which foreshadows Dostoievsky. Suggest using it (The I of the P) and cutting *Mellonta Tauta.*

Do you agree?

"The Imp of the Perverse" appeared in the book, and "Mellonta Tauta" did not. "A Dream within a Dream" was not added to the book until the revised edition of 1956 (see below).

Auden wrote his introduction in Italy probably in May 1950. Hobbs wrote on 2 June to praise the introduction and to confirm that the book had been accepted. Hobbs made one change in Auden's proposed contents: "The Masque of the Red Death" would need to be included because professors insisted on having it. Auden had apparently capitulated earlier to the necessity of including "The Cask of Amontillado". Hobbs also asked Auden for a textual and bibliographical note on Poe, and, knowing that Auden had consulted Pearson, suggested that Pearson might be willing to write one. Auden wrote to Pearson on 6 June:

Just got a letter from Rinehart to-day saying they want a little Poe bibliography. Not only have I no reference books here but I am no Poe scholar and simply don't know the material. Could you possibly collar a bright student with taste and an interest in Poe (but not too great) and get him to make a list of the obvious books? As far as I am concerned, I want the following included.

Biography. The [Arthur H.] Quinn life.
Critical studies. E. A. Poe. Baudelaire.
    L'Eureka de Poe. Valéry. (Variété).
    Edgar Allen [*sic*] Poe. D. H. Lawrence (Studies in Classical [*sic*] American Literature.)
    From Poe to Valéry. T. S. Eliot.

For tact's sake, too, a forthcoming book on Poe by Allen Tate.

Pearson provided a bibliographical note, for which Auden thanked him on 22 July: "You are a *saint.* The bibliography is exactly right. I shall expect to be offered a chair in American letters any day on the strength of it." The book by Tate that Auden mentions in his letter never got written, although Tate published two essays on Poe around this time, but the bibliographical note dutifully predicts that "Allen

Tate's forthcoming critical and biographical study of Poe should be a significant contribution."

After receiving his copies in December 1950 Auden wrote to Pearson: "Am *fuming* with Rinehart. When I said I wanted a poem *To Helen* it never crossed my mind that they wouldn't know which one. As it is they put in the very bad one ['I saw thee once—once only—years ago']." Another mistake was corrected by a slip pasted on the first page: "The publishers regret that the error in the spelling of Poe's middle name, Allen for Allan, which appears on the cover of the book was not discovered until the books had been completely bound. It will be corrected in subsequent printings."

A revised edition published on 27 January 1956 introduced minor changes to the introduction, almost certainly requested by Auden, and major changes to the contents, some suggested by Auden, others probably made by the publishers at the suggestion of college teachers. "Eureka" was dropped; two stories were added ("The Gold Bug" and "Berenice"); Poe's review of Hawthorne's *Twice-Told Tales* was added; the wrong "To Helen" was replaced with the right one ("Helen, thy beauty is to me"), and these poems were added: "Lenore", "Sonnet—To Science", "The Sleeper", and "A Dream within a Dream" (see Auden's earlier decision to include this, noted above).

The 1956 version of the introduction was reprinted in *Forewords and Afterwords* (1973) with changes noted below.

The text of this edition incorporates corrections that Auden marked in a friend's copy of the first edition (in a private collection) and those that were introduced in the 1956 version. Near the end of the paragraph fragment that begins "In isolation, as a prose sentence," (p. 216) the first edition has "nonrealistic", possibly an editor's error, corrected in 1956 to "realistic". (In the marked copy of the first edition Auden placed parentheses around this sentence, but did not correct it, and I have not added the parentheses here.) In the paragraph that begins "Both these types" (p. 217) the first edition has "affecting his life" for the 1956 version's "directing his life".

In the paragraph that begins "Similarly, 'Ulalume'" (p. 219) the second and third sentences of the 1956 text (from "It is an accident" through "out of place.") replace this one sentence from the first edition: "Edward Lear, the only poet, apparently, to be directly influenced by Poe, succeeds with his emotive place names, 'The Hills of the Chankly Bore,' where Poe fails because he selects a subject where the accidental quality of the name is part of the intended effect."

In the third sentence of the paragraph that begins "If Poe never developed" (p. 221) Auden corrected in a friend's copy "such were" to "such are"; the change was not made in the 1956 edition but was incorporated in the reprint in *Forewords and Afterwords* and in the present edition.

In the paragraph that begins "Remembering his behavior" (p. 222) "deadline" is an emendation for "date line". Auden's quotations slightly alter punctuation, italics, and other minor details.

Oddly, the 1956 text adds the date "Capri, June, 1950" below the introduction. This change was presumably made by Rinehart, as Auden never dated his prose pieces in this manner, and he had probably been in Naples or Ischia, not Capri, when he wrote the introduction, which he completed by May 1950, a least a month before the printed date.

In the section headed "The Man", Rufus W. Griswold was the author of a malicious account of Poe and the first editor of his works; Arthur Hobson Quinn's 1941 biography of Poe exposed Griswold's falsifications in detail.

FOREWORD TO *A Change of World*, BY ADRIENNE CECILE RICH

Page 224.

The fourth of Auden's selections for the Yale Series of Younger Poets. Auden wrote to Eugene Davidson at the Yale University Press on 24 July 1950: "I've picked an MS for the *Yale Younger Poets* which I think pretty good. *Forty Poems* by Adrienne Cecile Rich. I have written to her and am writing to a few of the others [who submitted manuscripts], but shall send the Mss back all together to the Yale Press to return. The Postal Problems, still more the packing problems are not easy here" (Yale University Archives).

Between 24 July and 24 August 1950 Auden wrote five letters to Rich, most of them lengthy and detailed comments on individual poems, with requests for improvements that Rich evidently provided. Rich also provided a revised list of contents and, apparently, the final title. Auden's letter of 10 August says in part: "As to the title, I think *Forty Poems* preferable to any other; later books you will have to give titles to but it is always a pity that booksellers want titles for volumes of short poems to which they cannot possibly legitimately apply" (Schlesinger Library, Harvard University).

On 23 September 1950 Auden wrote again to Davidson: "Herewith the Rich manuscript plus a preface. I am really quite pleased with the volume—it is unpretentious but sound and solid." The book was published on 18 April 1951.

NATURE, HISTORY AND POETRY

Page 226.

This is the second of two surviving versions of this essay; for the earlier version, not published during Auden's lifetime, see p. 161. *Thought* was a quarterly magazine published at Fordham University, a Jesuit institution in New York. The editor was Auden's friend, Fr. William J. Lynch, to whom he gave three essays at two-year intervals in the early 1950s; the others were "Notes on the Comic" (p. 307) and "Balaam and the Ass" (p. 444)

The text is based on Auden's marked copy of an offprint from the magazine, with reference in a few places to the manuscript in the Fordham University Library. Some of Auden's section breaks were reduced in the printed text to paragraph breaks; I have restored the original breaks and some of Auden's original punctuation and italicization. The section number "IV", lacking in the printed text, is also restored from the manuscript. The manuscript indicates section breaks by a short horizontal dash, unlike the three stars or x-marks that Auden used in the earlier version of the essay. Following the magazine, and perhaps following Auden's intention for the printed version, I have used a line space to represent these breaks.

In section I, in the third paragraph ("An historical event") he corrected the last word from "recurring" to "occurring" (as in the manuscript).

In section II, in the second paragraph I have restored "in common" from the manuscript; it seems to be required by the sense. In his marked copy of the printed text, in the third paragraph of section II, Auden corrected "A crowd" to "A society" (as in the manuscript). In the paragraph that begins "A community consists" (p. 227) the phrase following "i.e." reads in the manuscript "n may $= 1$" and the printed version may have been the work either of Auden or Lynch.

In section III, in the second paragraph, the printed text has "only by its author"; I have restored the manuscript reading "only to its author". In the paragraph that begins "Man's consciousness of himself", in item (c), I have restored the manuscript's "consciousness of itself" instead of the printed version's "consciousness of self".

In section IV, in the second sentence, I have restored the manuscript's easily mis-read "behind this appearance" for the printed text's "behind its appearances." In the paragraph that begins "The transformation of a crowd", in the sentence that begins "When a poem is read" I have restored the manuscript's "reader's feeling" for the printed text's "reader's feelings". In the last sentence of the same paragraph I have restored "novel" from the manuscript.

In the first sentence of section V, I have restored the manuscript's "feeling" for the printed text's "feelings".

In the first paragraph of section VI, in item (1), I have followed the manuscript and Auden's marked copy of the printed text in restoring "events and analogical" for "events as analogical". In the final paragraph, I have followed Auden's marked copy of the printed text by inserting "as" after "analogous to but".

YOUNG BOSWELL

Page 223.

Auden wrote to Chester Kallman on 25 October 1950: "Am reviewing Boswell's *London Journal* for the New Yorker. According to himself he was very large." The text here is based on the printed text, with Auden's paragraphing and capitalization restored from the manuscript that he submitted to the magazine, titled "Boswell's London Journal" (New York Public Library Manuscripts and Archives Division). I have removed the magazine's addition of the title of the book within the text (in the paragraph that begins "The fascinating story", as "his preface to *Boswell's London Journal* [etc.]"); in the next paragraph, the magazine may also have inserted "which has been admirably . . . Pottle" but the sentiment may have been Auden's. Some other changes of wording between the manuscript and printed text may have been editorial. In the first paragraph, the manuscript has "smoke-room stories" for "anecdotes". In the paragraph that begins "This journal" the manuscript continues the second sentence with "in six-weekly installments", and the manuscript has "decisive" for "crucial". In the paragraph that begins "For the rest" (p. 234) the manuscript has "clap" for "gonorrhea". In the quotation that begins "From having been" Auden misquotes "about at night" for "abroad at night".

SOME DECEMBER BOOKS CHOSEN FOR THE TRADE BOOK CLINIC

Page 237.

Publishers' Weekly, the American journal of the book trade, conducted a monthly Trade Book Clinic in which a small jury from the book trade voted and reported on well-designed books. Auden seems to have been invited by Donald Klopfer at Random House (his regular publisher) to act as a one-man jury in December 1950; Klopfer thanked him on 13 October for accepting the invitation and suggested that he come to New York from Smith College on 7 or 8 December; his deadline was 27 December (Syracuse University Library).

The headnote to Auden's report reads in part: "Since there was no Trade Book Clinic meeting in December, and therefore no balloting to select the best-designed books of the previous four weeks, the distinguished poet, Wystan Hugh Auden, was invited to make the December selections, acting as a one-man jury. When his books are being designed (for example, the recent *Age of Anxiety* and *The Enchafèd Flood* and the forthcoming *Nones*) he makes suggestions to Random House about the format, with the excellent results familiar to the trade." An accompanying photograph shows Auden with the chairman of the Trade Book Clinic, Ray Freiman, the book designer at Random House who had endured Auden's demands for simple, unornamented designs for the three books mentioned in the headnote; *Nones*, then in press, was published in February 1951.

IN AN AGE LIKE OURS, THE ARTIST WORKS IN A STATE OF SIEGE

Page 240.

Auden and Nabokov had been friendly since 1943 when they met in Washington through Isaiah Berlin; in 1945 Auden had helped Nabokov join the United States Strategic Bombing Survey. In 1969 Auden and Chester Kallman wrote the libretto for Nabokov's opera *Love's Labour's Lost*, performed in 1973.

Andrei Zhdanov, a close associate of Stalin, had denounced bourgeois writers in a widely publicized report to the Communist Party in 1946.

In the paragraph that begins "In the first chapter" Auden misquotes "red morocco" as "red velvet", and the remaining quotations silently omit a few words from the originals. The paragraph that begins "Four chapters later" should begin "Five chapters later".

Aeneid FOR OUR TIME

Page 242.

Auden wrote to Margaret Marshall, literary editor of *The Nation*, in the last few days of January 1951: "I shall be pleased to have a shot at Humphries' *Aeneid*" (Schlesinger Library, Harvard University). An incomplete pencil draft of this review is in the Berg Collection. I have corrected a few minor compositor's misreadings of Auden's hand; in the quotation that begins "the stock to come" Auden changed the singular "triumph" to a plural.

A more literal translation of the line that begins "*hoc solum nomen*" might be "Since only the name of spouse stays behind".

Address to the Indian Congress for Cultural Freedom

Page 246.

The Indian Congress for Cultural Freedom, held in New Delhi on 28–31 March 1951, sponsored by the Indian Committee on Cultural Freedom, was one of many cultural initiatives with similar names organized by left-leaning anticommunist intellectuals with funds that ultimately and secretly derived from the United States Central Intelligence Agency and British intelligence services. Western participants in the Indian Congress included Auden, Denis de Rougemont, Stephen Spender, Salvador de Madariaga, Norman Thomas, and James Burnham. A volume containing the brief talks and longer panels at the conference was published in Bombay in August 1951 under the title *Indian Congress for Cultural Freedom, March 28 to 31, 1951*; the Congress was listed as the publisher.

Much of the Congress was devoted to special reports from committees; foreign visitors spoke mostly in the "Open Sessions" on the first and last days. Auden was the fourth of ten speakers on the last day. In the book his talk is titled simply "Address"; it seems to have been printed from his manuscript or typescript; a carbon-copy typescript by Alan Ansen, probably copied from the published version, is in the Berg Collection of the New York Public Library.

Auden wrote to Ursula Niebuhr on 30 May 1951: "India, at least the Congress, was pure Hell and quite useless. To begin with Bombay has total Prohibition and then I was overwhelmed with the decreative power of Public Life. . . . One can lecture to a large audience on a subject about which one knows and in which they have a genuine interest (i.e. in the truth not in the teacher) and one can talk to a small group of friends. Everything else, all 'saying a few words', is vanity and vexation of spirit. I must, however, add that I had flu at the time" (Library of Congress).

Professor Mueller is a misspelling of H. J. Muller who spoke about science and culture on the first day of the Congress. The friend who visited Anna Akhmatova was Isaiah Berlin. For Zhdanov's attack on Akhmatova (in August 1946, not February 1947), see the notes to "In an Age Like Ours, the Artist Works in a State of Siege" (two items above this one).

Some Reflections on Opera as a Medium

Page 250.

Tempo is a learned musical quarterly published in London. Auden wrote to his friend Wayne Cogswell on 30 April [1951]: "have done my series of Pensées for *Tempo*" (Berg Collection). The occasion was the anticipated première of *The Rake's Progress*. Two abridged versions of the essay appeared elsewhere, but with cuts probably imposed by an editor: a heavily cut version of the essay appeared in *The Observer*, 16 September 1951 (five days after the première), as "Reflections on Opera", with the note "This article appears in the current number of the quarterly *Tempo*"; a slightly cut version appeared in *Opera News*, 9 February 1953, as "Opera as a Medium", on the occasion of the American première of *The Rake's Progress*.

Auden prepared an expanded version probably late in 1951; this appeared as "Some Reflections on Music and Opera" (p. 296), and was reprinted with changes in *The Dyer's Hand* (1962). See the notes to the expanded version for details of its later textual history.

The text in this edition follows the generous capitalization of the original.

The performance of *Tristan und Isolde* mentioned in the piece was probably that of 2 February 1948, around the same time that Auden saw Cocteau's *L'Eternel retour* and offered an endorsement of it (see p. 614).

Auden's theatrically extravagant dismissal of his own role as librettist was taken literally by a few readers who seem to have been impervious to irony. Ronald Duncan, a journalist and the librettist of Benjamin Britten's *The Rape of Lucretia*, was offended enough to respond in "An Answer to Auden" published in the monthly magazine *Opera* (November 1951). Duncan wrote, *inter alia*, that during a discussion of these matters with Auden on the night before the première of *The Rake's Progress*, Duncan had dismissed as "sheer nonsense" Auden's argument that the words of a song cannot be poetry. Auden, Duncan said, then "withdrew the meaning I had justifiably taken from his article and clarified it to, 'the librettist's job is to write verses suitable for the musical setting, if they should turn out to be poetry, so much the better, but it should not be his first intention to write it.'"

Auden responded to Duncan in print in the form of a letter to the editor of *Opera* which appeared in the January 1952 issue, headed "Auden Replies". The italicized passages are Auden's inexact quotations from Duncan's piece:

Sir,

First of all I should like to thank Mr Ronald Duncan for his lucid and courteous observations upon my article in *Tempo*. The latter was, of course, deliberately polemic and intended to call forth just such a dialectical opposition as Mr Duncan has provided. By dialectical I mean a discussion in which both parties desire to arrive at mutual agreement. Thus, both Mr Duncan and myself are agreed (*a*) that opera is an art-form of great value, (*b*) that the primary element in opera is vocal, (*c*) that opera libretti should not be entrusted to literary hacks. The difference between us is, simply, that I start from the position "Nothing, however musically or poetically valuable in itself, shall be admitted in opera if it interferes with the singing," and he starts from the position "Everything which is musically or poetically valuable and does not interfere with the singing shall be admitted." Bearing this in mind, I should now like to reply to a few of his points.

I. *To postulate that a credible situation in opera means a situation in which it is credible that someone should sing, is to confine opera to the bathroom. . . . Does a Rake go to a brothel to sing?*

Mr Duncan has misunderstood my use of the word *credible*; I do not mean *actual* but *possible*. All of us have experienced occasions when, had we been possessed of good voices and unafraid of alarming the neighbours, we would have burst forth into an aria. Indeed, when we are drunk enough to ignore both these facts, we sometimes do. Any such occasion I call a credible situation and I think it rather priggish of Mr Duncan to deny the possibility of its arising in a brothel.

There are, on the other hand, a great many occasions when we feel no wish to sing, and asking for a handkerchief is usually one of them. To raise as an objection to the general principle the special case of *Otello*, where a handkerchief is of great emotional importance, is a red herring.

II. *An interlude should be not "a scraping away regardless" but a considered statement relating the preceding scene to the one that follows.*

I never suggested that an orchestral interlude should be either musically valueless or dramatically irrelevant, only that there should always be a practical reason for its existence which should govern its length. The interlude between scenes one and two of the last act of *The Rake's Progress* is exactly that, and I wish there had been more of them elsewhere. Mr Strawinsky would be the first to admit, I think, that, in two or three places, he did not write enough music to allow of smooth scene changes and we should all have enjoyed it if he had taken the opportunity to make some "considered statements" at these places.

III. *"The words of a song cannot be poetry". I consider this sheer nonsense, and told him so, giving the Sixth Donne sonnet as the best example, and his own lyric "Love too frequently betrayed, etc."*

I think there is a fundamental difference between an operatic aria and a *lied* but let us ignore it. Mr Duncan is clearly right in pointing out that the musical imagination of some composers, e.g. Campion, Hugo Wolf, Benjamin Britten, has been stimulated by poetry of a high order to write wonderful music. The question remains however, whether the listener hears more than the music, whether, in fact, he hears the words as words of a poem or, as I am inclined to believe, only as sung syllables. A Cambridge psychologist, P. E. Vernon, once performed the experiment of having a Campion song sung with nonsense verses of equivalent syllabic value substituted for the original; only six per cent of his test audience noticed that anything was wrong. It is precisely because I believe that, in listening to a song as distinct from chant, we hear, not words, but syllables that I am so violently hostile to the performance of operas in translation. Wagner in Italian or Verdi in English always sounds intolerable, and would do even if the poetic value of the translation were higher than that of the original, because the new syllables have no apt relation to the pitch and tempo of the notes with which they are associated. The poetic or dramatic meaning of the words may be what provokes a composer to set them, but it is the values of the syllables which determines the kind of voice line he writes.

As to my own lyric, it is generous of Mr Duncan to praise it, and, since the music for it which Strawinsky wrote is very beautiful, I must conclude that it is successful, but I would never dream of including it in a volume of poems. A reader, coming across it in isolation, could justifiably complain, among other things, that the style is pastiche and the repetition of the word "Weeping" redundant.

It seems, I must add, which should be unnecessary, that my remarks on this subject are addressed to poets who would like to write libretti; to hacks with neither a talent for, nor a taste in poetry, I have nothing to say.

IV. *To say that opera cannot compel our belief in the illusion which it creates on the stage is to deny it the very essentials of being an art at all.*

Here, as in the case of the word *credible*, I think Mr Duncan and myself must attribute different meanings to the words *belief* and *illusion*, for, if he means by them what I mean, then it would follow from the sentence quoted above that, for him, a performance of *Carmen* in which the singer playing José actually stabbed the singer playing Carmen would be as "artistic" as a normal performance, and, that the movie goer who writes abusive letters to the actor who plays a villain is showing genuine artistic appreciation. I'm quite sure, however, that Mr Duncan knows as well as I do that it is not only after the curtain falls that one should remember that it was only play-acting, but that throughout the performance one must be conscious of this, if one is to have the kind of experience which a work of art intends to provide. I prefer opera to more naturalistic dramatic media precisely because in opera it is almost impossible to forget that the proscenium separates two different worlds.

In arguing against the use of contemporary situations as subjects for *opera seria,* I was saying no more than Wordsworth said when he defined poetry as emotion recollected in tranquility, i.e. an immediate contemporary situation is still too firmly attached to its existential origin to be detachable for embodiment in an objective art-form.

Auden's comment on item III was the basis of a section that he added in manuscript to the expanded version of the piece, "Some Reflections on Music and Opera" (see the notes to p. 296).

THE PHILOSOPHY OF A LUNATIC

Page 255.
    The literary editor of the *Observer* was the newly appointed Terence Kilmartin. Auden seems to have asked (or to have been asked) to review this book during a three-week visit with Stephen Spender in London in May 1951. The pseudonymous author (whom I have been unable to identify) seems to have been fairly well known in academic, psychiatric, and theological circles, and was perhaps known personally to Auden or Spender. The title of the review was the subtitle of the book.

ELIOT ON ELIOT

Page 257.
    The book under review was (as Auden's second paragraph implies) the first Theodore Spencer Memorial Lecture at Harvard. Auden's quotations are approximate; in the final paragraph, "which will present" should be "such as to present".

FOREWORD TO *A Mask for Janus,* BY W. S. MERWIN

Page 259.

Auden wrote to Eugene Davidson at the Yale University Press on 30 July 1951: "The Yale Younger Poet manuscripts arrived safely last week. I have found one which seems good, *A Mask for Janus* by William Merwin. It needs, however, quite a lot of cutting, I think, being too long as it stands. I have just written to Mr Merwin to tell him so." Auden also apologized for being unable to write the introduction until October, because he was about to immerse himself in preparations for the pre-mière of *The Rake's Progress.* On 18 August he wrote to Davidson: "Between us Mr Merwin and I have got his manuscript down to a possible size, and I think you can safely announce his book on Sept 1st if that is your day." The introduction seems to have been written in October 1951, and the book was published on 21 May 1952. The footnote at the end is in the original.

KEATS IN HIS LETTERS

Page 262.

For Auden's relations with Lionel Trilling, see the account of The Readers' Sub-scription book club in Appendix II. The book under review was the first volume in the Great Letters series, described in the notes to "Portrait of a Whig" (p. 273). Auden's quotations slightly modify wording and punctuation; I have restored only "petty" (for "pretty") in the quotation that begins "He understands". The square brackets in the quotations were printed as parentheses in the original review.

A REVIEW OF *Short Novels of Colette*

Page 267.

This was the first of Auden's contributions to the monthly bulletin of The Read-ers' Subscription book club, described in Appendix II. The magazine was undated in its early numbers, including this one. Through their common friend Lincoln Kirstein, Auden was on polite but somewhat wary terms with Glenway Wescott, who wrote the introduction to the book.

The review was reprinted in *Perspectives USA,* Spring 1953, an issue guest-edited by Jacques Barzun, one of Auden's fellow editors at The Readers' Subscription; *Per-spectives USA* was a literary and cultural magazine published for propaganda pur-poses by the Ford Foundation. The *Perspectives USA* text slightly alters punctuation and spellings, but the changes seem not to have been made by Auden.

The first published version omits the acute accent in "Chéri" throughout; this is corrected in *Perspectives USA.* Auden's quotations slightly alter punctuation and spelling; I have restored some correct spellings probably misread by the composi-tor. In the original text the phrase "On Copine, an old prostitute:" is italicized, and it is possible that Auden's lost manuscript also italicized the parallel phrase above it, "On Desmond . . . making money".

The World That Books Have Made

Page 270.

An essay written for the front page of the *New York Times Book Review*, a page occasionally given to an essay in place of the customary review. In the paragraph that begins "The what-would-happen-if" I have added a colon after "vastly improve".

Portrait of a Whig

Page 273.

This essay is perhaps the same as, or is based upon, a lecture Auden delivered at Mount Holyoke College, 29 November 1950, titled "Sydney Smith: The Best of Whiggery." *English Miscellany: A Symposium of History, Literature, and the Arts*, was an annual volume edited by Mario Praz and published in Rome for the British Council in the early spring of each year. Auden wrote this essay as the introduction to a volume of Sydney Smith's letters that was projected for the Great Letters Series, edited by Louis Kronenberger, and published in New York by Farrar, Straus and Young. The first volume in the series was Lionel Trilling's selection of Keats's letters, which Auden reviewed in 1951 (p. 262); this and other early volumes listed Auden's selection of Smith's letters as one of the titles in preparation, but the selection never appeared in its planned form; it became instead *The Selected Writings of Sydney Smith*, edited by Auden and published in 1956, with a rewritten introduction (see *Prose IV*); this rewritten introduction was reprinted in *Forewords and Afterwords* (1973) under the title of the earlier version, "Portrait of a Whig".

Some Italian typographic conventions have been anglicized (for example, magazine titles indicated in the printed text by angled quotation marks are italicized instead). In the opening sentence I have (as any native-speaking editor would have done) removed two commas around the phrase "who is the subject of this essay". I have slightly corrected probable compositor's errors in the quotations.

The printed text has "New York" beneath Auden's name at the end; this was presumably added by Mario Praz or an assistant, as Auden seems to have noted the place of composition of prose writings only when they were in the form of letters, greetings, or tributes.

Introduction to *The Living Thoughts of Kierkegaard*

Page 285.

The Living Thoughts Library was a series of selections of individual writers introduced by well-known contemporary authors: the series editor was Alfred O. Mendel, a German emigré who founded the series when he was an editor at the Longmans, Green publishing house; the first volume in the series was Thomas Mann's selection from Schopenhauer, published in 1939. Auden's selection from Kierkegaard was number 23 in the series, published by David McKay on 17 October 1952; following the series convention, the introduction was titled "Presenting Kierkegaard". A British edition, with the introduction titled "Introduction", was published as *Kierkegaard: Selected and Introduced by W. H. Auden* by Cassell, 19 May

1955. Auden reprinted his introduction in *Forewords and Afterwords* (1973) as "Søren Kiekegaard".

I have found no reference in Auden's letters or papers to his work on this selection, and it is possible that the introduction was written as early as 1950 or as late as the first months of 1952. Auden paraphrased Rudolf Kassner extensively in the poems he wrote in 1950, and the quotations from Kassner in this introduction may or may not indicate that it was written around the same time.

A secretarial typescript of the introduction is in the Berg Collection of the New York Public Library; this is presumably a copy of the typescript submitted to the publisher and includes spelling corrections in an unknown hand. The printed text adds the epigraph, the phrase within parentheses in the opening paragraph, and the parenthetical phrase about Cardinal Newman in the final paragraph. Other differences between the typescript and printed version are minor ones of wording and punctuation.

In the section "The Ethical Religion" the phrase "to have no need for friends" is adapted from the *Nicomachaean Ethics*, where Aristotle rejects the argument that the happy man has no need for friends.

Auden organized the excerpts from Kierkegaard in the main body of the book in seven numbered sections, each with an epigraph by another writer. The sections and epigraphs are as follows (the translation from Kassner is almost certainly Auden's own):

I. Prefatory Aphorisms

The knowledge of God is very far from the love of Him.—Pascal

Calculation never made a hero.—J. H. Newman

II. The Present Age

The same new conditions under which on an average a levelling and mediocrising of man will take place—a useful, industrious, variously serviceable, and clever gregarious man—are in the highest degree suitable to give rise to exceptional men of the most dangerous and attractive qualities. For, while the capacity for adaptation, which is every day trying changing conditions, and begins a new work with every generation, almost with every decade, makes the *powerfulness* of the type impossible; while the collective impression of such future Europeans will probably be that of numerous, talkative, weak-willed, and very handy workmen who *require* a master, a commander, as they require their daily bread; while, therefore, the democratising of Europe will tend to the production of a type prepared for *slavery* in the most subtle sense of the term: the strong man will necessarily in individual and exceptional cases, become stronger and richer than he has perhaps ever been before—owing to the unprejudicedness of his schooling, owing to the immense variety of practice, art, and disguise. I meant to say that the democratising of Europe is at the same time an involuntary arrangement for the rearing of tyrants—taking the word in all its meanings, even in its most spiritual sense.—Nietzsche

III. The Aesthetic, the Ethical, and the Religious

It is just his fantastic dreams, his vulgar folly that he will desire to retain in order to prove to himself—as though that were so necessary—that men still are men and not the keys of a piano, which the laws of nature threaten to control so completely that soon one will be able to desire nothing but by the calendar. And that is not all: even if man really were nothing but a piano-key, even if this were proved to him by natural science and mathematics, even then he would not become reasonable, but would purposely do something perverse out of simple ingratitude, simply to gain his point. You will scream at me (that is, if you condescend to do so) that no one is touching my free will, that all they are concerned with is that my will should of itself, of its own free will, coincide with my own normal interests, with the laws of nature and arithmetic. Good heavens, gentlemen, what sort of free-will is left when we come to tabulation and arithmetic, when it will all be a case of twice two make four? Twice two makes four without my will. As if free will meant that!—Dostoievsky

IV. The Subjective Thinker

> The Child's Toys and the Old Man's Reasons
> Are the fruits of the two seasons.
> The Questioner who sits so sly
> Shall never know how to reply. . . .
> He who Doubts from what he sees
> Will ne'er Believe, do what you Please.
> If the Sun and Moon should doubt,
> They'd immediately go out.
> To be in a Passion you Good may do,
> But no Good if a Passion is in you.
>   —William Blake

V. Sin and Dread

> . . . Wilt thou forgive that sinne by which I have wonne
>   Others to sinne, and made their sinne their doore?
> Wilt thou forgive that sinne which I did shunne
>   A yeare or two, but wallowed in a score?
>   When thou has done, thou has not done,
>   For I have more.
>
> I have a sinne of feare, that when I have spunne
>   My last thred, I shall perish on the shore;
> Swear by thy selfe, that at my death thy sonne
>   Shall shine as he shines now, and heretofore;
>   And having done that, thou hast done.
>   I have no more.
>   —John Donne

VI. Christ the Offence

About Christ it is significant, not that he sees, hears and tastes, but that he is made flesh. In Zeus and through him, sight, hearing and taste became sacred. Thus Zeus is an animal as well as being the order of the universe. Over this sight and hearing and taste reigns Number, the sacred number, the sacred teacher, the mystery of Identity. Also fortune.

When Identity reigns, there is still the Teacher. Christ sets up over against the teacher, the Witness, the Example, just as he replaces Identity by the Individual and Fate by the Sacrifice.—Rudolf Kassner

VII. Epilogue

> My God, by God, though I be clean forgot,
> Let me not love Thee, if I love Thee not.
>   —George Herbert

SOME REFLECTIONS ON MUSIC AND OPERA

Page 296.

An expanded version of "Some Reflections on Opera as a Medium" (p. 250). Auden seems to have submitted this in the form of a typescript copy of the earlier piece with some sections added and others deleted, and with some sections inserted at the last minute on separate manuscript pages; no such typescript has survived, but the manuscript additions (marked "insert on p. 2" and "insert on p. 8" are in the *Partisan Review* archives at Boston University. The inserted passages are the two adjacent sections that begin "Man's musical imagination" and "The difference is demonstrated" (p. 297) and the section that begins "There have been several composers" (p. 302). The manuscript pages show slight differences in word-order and punctuation compared to the printed text.

Auden reprinted the piece in *The Dyer's Hand* (1962) as "Notes on Music and Opera", with some additional sentences and sections, minor cuts, minor changes in punctuation, and two added epigraphs: "'Opera consists of significant situations in artificially arranged sequence.'—Goethe" and "'Singing is near miraculous because it is the mastering of what is otherwise a pure instrument of egotism: the human voice.'—Hugo von Hoffmansthal".

In the opening paragraph the 1962 version replaces the one-word sentence "Choice" with: "Our experience of Time in its twofold aspect, natural or organic repetition, and historical novelty created by choice. And the full development of music as an art depends upon a recognition that these two aspects are different and that choice, being an experience confined to man, is more significant than repetition." In the section that begins "Lacking a historical" the 1962 version replaces "the Greek theories of music tried" with "the Greeks, in their theories of music, tried". The 1962 version omits the section that begins "In opera the Heard and the Seen" (p. 301). In the paragraph that begins "Much as I admire" the 1962 version omits the first two sentences. In the paragraph that begins "There have been several" (p. 302) the 1962 version replaces "Wagner in Italian or Verdi in English" with "Wagner or Strauss or English". Between the two final sections, the 1962 text inserts an additional section (beginning with a slight misquotation):

"History," said Stephen Dedalus, "is the nightmare from which I must awake." The rapidity of historical change and the apparent powerlessness of the individual to affect Collective History has led in literature to a retreat from history. Instead of tracing the history of an individual who is born, grows old, and dies, many modern novelists and short story writers, beginning with Poe, have devoted their attention to timeless passionate moments in a life, to states of being. It seems to me that, in some modern music, I can detect the same trend, a trend towards composing a static kind of music in which there is no marked difference between its beginning, its middle and its end, a music which sounds remarkably like primitive proto-music. It is not for me to criticize a composer who writes such music. One can say, however, that he will never be able to write an opera. But, proba-bly, he won't want to.

The Adult Voice of America

Page 302.

In Auden's catalogue of *New Yorker* cartoonists the full names are James Thurber, Sydney Hoff, and William Steig; Auden misspelled Charles Addams. In the para-graph that begins "An Other-directed culture" I replaced commas after "normal skin" and "other personalities" with semicolons.

While the Oboes Came Up, the Bagpipes Came Down

Page 305.

The title, like all others in the *New York Times Book Review*, was the work of an ed-itor. Auden's manuscript, headed "A Composer's World. Paul Hindemith", is in the Morgan Library (the first page was reproduced in the Charles Hamilton auction cat-alogue, New York, 2 May 1974). The text of this edition restores two passages that did not appear in the printed text: in the paragraph that begins "As far as poetry", the long final sentence that begins "Hence the impossibility"; and, in the single-sentence paragraph that begins "Reform will not", the latter part of the sentence following the semicolon. I have also used the manuscript to correct a few minor mis-readings of Auden's hand.

Notes on the Comic

Page 307.

The second of Auden's three biennial essays for *Thought*; the first was "Nature, History and Poetry" (p. 226) and the third was "Balaam and the Ass" (p. 444). A heavily revised version, with many cuts, additions, and other changes, appeared in *The Dyer's Hand* (1962) and may be found in *Prose IV*. The changes are too extensive to be listed here, and the 1962 version may be considered a separate essay rather than a revision of this one.

The typographic layout in the magazine is a chaos of inconsistencies, and I have made minor efforts to regularize it, in some places following the layout of the ver-sion in *The Dyer's Hand* where it makes more sense than the one in *Thought*. I have added rows of stars above the headings "Comic Travesties" (p. 310), "The Comic Contradiction of the Lover vs. the Citizen" (p. 312), and "The Comic and the Witty Contradiction" (p. 313). In the section "The Spoonerism and the Pun" (p. 314) I have corrected a probable compositor's or typist's error: "my sheep" for "thy sheep". I have removed a row of stars above the paragraph that begins "The Satiri-cal Strategy" (p. 316).

OUR ITALY

Page 319.

In the second paragraph, I have added a comma between "at least" and "uncar-tesian". In the paragraph that begins "Hardly. Morals are so lax", in the long sen-tence that begins "It is an essential", I have removed a comma from after "however" and placed it instead after "superficially".

Auden's quotations are approximate; I have let his versions stand except where, apparently, a compositor's misreadings of his hand produced nonsense (for exam-ple, in the extract that begins "What is shared", I have restored "innermost" instead of "innocent").

[HIC ET ILLE]

Page 323.

The original English text of this essay is lost; the text in this edition is a retransla-tion by Richard Howard from the French version prepared by Christine Lalou for *Preuves*, a monthly published in Paris by the Congrès pour la Liberté de la Culture (a counterpart of the Congress for Cultural Freedom; see the note to "Address to the Indian Congress for Cultural Freedom" above). Auden visited Paris on his way to Italy in the first few days of April 1952, when he gave this essay to the magazine; the lost English text was perhaps titled "Hic et Ille" (see Appendix VII). The essay appeared in a special number of the magazine published to coincide with a conference orga-nized by the Congrès in May 1952, "L'Œuvre du XXe Siècle", which Auden also at-tended, and where he spoke in a session titled "Révolte et Communion".

I have divided the essay in two parts, each with a roman numeral; the break be-tween the parts corresponds to the point where the French text uses a large initial capital to begin a section (and where it omits the star that normally indicates a break between sections).

In the section that begins "British English" (p. 330) I have omitted the phrase "Along with French," with which this section begins in the French version; Auden's later version of this section in "Don Juan" in *The Dyer's Hand* refers to "a distinction which, so far as I have been able to discover, can only be made in the English lan-guage," so the phrase about French was probably added (correctly) by the original translator, and Auden may never have noticed it. (See also p. 210.)

Following both the sense and the corresponding passages in "Hic et Ille" in *En-counter*, April 1956, I have attached the sentence "If the effects" (p. 334) to the end of the paragraph that precedes it, instead of (as in the French text) setting it as a separate paragraph that begins a new section; between this newly combined para-graph and the next (that is, after the sentence in question), I have placed a break but no centered stars, following the example of the French text, which places a sim-ilar break before the sentence in question.

Similarly following the French text, I have placed breaks but no centered stars above the paragraphs that begin "*Touchstones*" (p. 330) and "The camera cannot lie" (p. 333).

Some of the material in this essay is adapted from material in "Squares and Oblongs" (*Prose II*, pp. 339–50) and the introductions to *Poets of the English Language*; some of the material was reused in an otherwise different set of aphorisms titled "Hic et Ille", *Encounter*, April 1956 (*Prose IV*) and in various sections of *The Dyer's Hand* (1962), especially "Writing", "Hic et Ille", and "Don Juan". Auden also alludes to the smell of books in "Some December Books Chosen for the Trade Book Clinic" (p. 240).

Some less-familiar and under-identified titles in the catalogue of Auden's nursery library include *Icelandic Legends*, by Jon Arnason (1864); *The Cruise of the Cachalot*, by Frank T. Bullen (not Ballantyne) (1899); *Underground Life; or, Mines and Miners*, by L. Simonin, translated, adapted to the present state of British mining, and edited by H. W. Bristow, F.R.S. (1869); *Machinery for Metalliferous Mines: A Practical Treatise for Mining Engineers, Metallurgists and Managers of Mines*, by E. Henry Davies, F.G.S. (1894; 2nd edn. 1902); *Lead and Zinc Ores of Northumberland and Alston Moor*, by Stanley Smith (1923, when Auden was sixteen years old); *Dangers to Health: A Pictorial Guide to Domestic Sanitary Defects*, by T. Pridgin Teale (1878; Auden owned the 1881 third edition); and *The Edinburgh School of Medicine* (not *Surgery*), by William Nisbet (1802; often reprinted). An earlier version of this list appeared in 1947 in Auden's introduction to John Betjeman's *Slick but Not Streamlined* (*Prose II*, p. 307); a later version is in *A Certain World* (1970).

The French version published in *Preuves* follows; as described above, the roman numeral II in square brackets represents a break in the printed text.

DE DROITE ET DE GAUCHE

« ... *Le titre de la chanson s'appelle:* Yeux d'Eglefin ».

« *Ah ! c'est le titre de la chanson ?* » dit Alice, *s'efforçant de s'intéresser à la chose.*

« *Mais non, vous ne comprenez pas* », dit le Cavalier, *l'air un peu vexé.* « *C'est comme ça qu'on appelle le titre de la chanson. Le vrai litre, c'est:* Le Vieux, Vieux Bonhomme ».

« *Alors, j'aurais dû dire: 'C'est comme ça qu'on appelle la chanson'* », rectifia Alice.

« *Certainement non ! Ça n'a rien à voir ! La chanson s'appelle:* Voies et Moyens, *mais c'est seulement le nom qu'on lui donne, vous comprenez ?* »

(Lewis Carroll. *Alice de l'autre côté du Miroir*).

La critique, c'est la tradition qui se défend contre les trois armées de la Déesse de la Bêtise: l'armée des amateurs qui ignorent la tradition, l'armée des excentriques vaniteux qui croient qu'on devrait supprimer la tradition d'un trait de plume, afin que l'art véritable commence avec eux, et l'armée des académiciens qui croient que maintenir la tradition, c'est imiter servilement le passé.

★ ★ ★

Le souci de relier l'art à la vie, le beau au vrai, le juste au bien, amène presque infailliblement le critique à dire une foule de bêtises; un critique qui ignore ce souci ou le réprime, et se contente d'être un simple amateur ou un historien de l'art, évite de se couvrir de ridicule, mais à quel prix ! Personne ne le lit.

★ ★ ★

Juger d'une œuvre d'art, c'est à peu de chose près la même opération mentale que de juger des êtres humains, et cela exige les mêmes aptitudes: en premier lieu, un véritable amour des œuvres d'art, prompt à louer plutôt qu'à blâmer, et malheureux lorsqu'il se voit contraint à un refus total; en second lieu, une vaste expérience de toutes les activités artistiques; et enfin, la conscience, ouvertement et joyeusement acceptée, de ses propres parti-pris. Certains critiques échouent parce que ce sont des pédants dont l'idéal de perfection est toujours choqué par une réalisation concrète; d'autres, parce qu'ils sont insulaires et hostiles aux étrangers; ces critiques qui, obéissant à leurs parti-pris sans savoir qu'ils en ont, émettent en toute sincérité des jugements qu'ils croient objectifs, sont plus excusables que ceux qui, conscients de leurs parti-pris, n'ont pas le courage d'entrer en lice pour défendre leurs goûts personnels.

★　★　★

Le meilleur critique littéraire n'est pas celui dont les jugements sont toujours justes, mais celui dont les articles vous obligent à lire et à relire les œuvres dont il parle; même lorsqu'il attaque, on sent que l'œuvre est assez importante pour valoir la peine d'être attaquée—par exemple: Nietzsche contre Wagner ou D. H. Lawrence contre Fenimore Cooper. Il y a d'autres critiques dont les louanges mêmes vous ôtent toute envie de lire un livre.

★　★　★

Les étiquettes de « classique » et de « romantique » sont trompeuses pour désigner les deux partis poétiques qui ont toujours existé: l'aristocratique et le démocratique. Tout poète appartient à l'un des deux, bien qu'il puisse changer de parti ou, dans une circonstance particulière, refuser d'obéir au Secrétaire Général du Parti.

> Principe aristocratique en ce qui concerne le sujet: La poésie ne traitera d'aucun sujet matériel qu'elle ne puisse digérer.
> 　　Voilà qui met la poésie à l'abri du didactisme et du journalisme prosaïques.
> Principe démocratique en ce qui concerne le sujet: Aucun sujet matériel ne sera exclu de la poésie si elle est capable de le digérer.
> 　　Voilà qui met la poésie à l'abri des définitions étroites ou fausses de la matière poétique.
> Principe aristocratique en ce qui concerne le traitement du sujet: le poème ne traitera aucun des à-côtés du sujet en question.
> 　　Voilà qui préserve l'unité du poème et l'empêche d'être diffus et informe.
> Principe démocratique en ce qui concerne le traitement du sujet: rien de ce qui peut avoir le moindre rapport avec le sujet traité ne sera négligé.
> 　　Voilà qui préserve la richesse et la variété d'un poème et l'empêche d'être aride et pauvre.

★　★　★

Les termes « jeune » et « vieux » ne peuvent s'appliquer qu'à l'intérieur d'un cycle fermé. Dans toutes les matières au développement historique, telles que l'art ou la civilisation, on ne peut employer que les termes « avant » et « après ». *L'Iliade* précède *l'Enéide*, mais cela ne rime à rien de dire qu'elle est plus vieille. D'autre part, il n'est pas moins absurde de dire que les œuvres d'art sont immortelles; la persistance de l'œuvre d'art n'est pas dans la durée matérielle de l'objet, mais dans la qualité qui lui donne vie pour un spectateur ou un lecteur vivant à une période historique donnée. *L'Iliade*, en 1950, n'est pas identique à *l'Iliade* en 1750, mais elle n'est pas plus vieille.

Le goût de la tradition ne signifie pas une préférence pour l'art ancien, mais une juste appréciation de l'ordre historique, des rapports entre l'ancien, et le moderne.

On peut dire qu'un poème vieillit uniquement lorsque la langue dans laquelle il est écrit subit des transformations, tout en restant, de façon évidente, la même langue.

A proprement parler, le « vieil anglais » devrait s'appeler le « jeune anglais ».

★   ★   ★

Les œuvres d'art sont plus proches entre elles qu'elles ne le sont de leurs créateurs; la bibliothèque d'un poète nous éclaire ses poèmes infiniment plus que son enfance ou ses amours.

★   ★   ★

S'il est vrai, comme cela semble probable, que les expériences de l'enfance marquent plus profondément la personnalité que les expériences de l'âge adulte, la bibliothèque enfantine d'un futur écrivain peut être le guide le plus sûr pour explorer son œuvre; par « bibliothèque », j'entends les livres qu'il a lus avec passion avant d'avoir acquis les premières notions critiques.

Ma Bibliothèque d'enfant.

Fiction: œuvres complètes de Beatrix Potter, *Alice au Pays des Merveilles* et *Alice de l'autre côté du Miroir*, *La petite Sirène* (Hans Andersen), *Légendes d'Islande*, *La Princesse et le lutin* (George Macdonald), *La Rose et l'Anneau* (Thackeray), *L'enfant de la caverne* (Jules Verne), *La croisière du Cachalot* (Ballantyne), *Les aventures de Sherlock Holmes*.

Poésie: *Struwwelpeter. Recueil des Hymnes anglais, Hymnes d'autrefois et d'aujourd'hui.* Les couplets mnémotechniques des *Premiers Eléments du Latin,* de Kennedy.

Livres sérieux: *La Vie souterraine. Outillage des Mines métallifères, Minerais de Plomb et de Zinc du Northumberland et de la lande d'Alston, Métiers dangereux* (Traité victorien sur le travail du plomb), *L'Ecole de Chirurgie d'Edimbourg.*

Lorsque, à l'âge de quinze ans, je commençai à m'intéresser consciencieusement à la poésie, mon goût se forma par la lecture de *Venez à moi*, anthologie composée par Walter de la Mare et qui me semble encore la meilleure introduction possible à la poésie. (Je n'ai jamais eu entre les mains de livre au parfum plus exquis.) Lorsque, quelques années plus tard, je commençai à lire des critiques littéraires, les deux qui me frappèrent le plus—et je n'ai changé d'avis sur aucun d'eux—furent le Dr Johnson et le Professeur W.-P. Ker.

★   ★   ★

Toutes les œuvres d'art: des commandes—du simple fait que l'idée qui incite l'artiste à créer une œuvre donnée, lui « vient » de l'extérieur. Parmi les œuvres manquées parce que leur point de départ était faux ou inadéquat, le nombre des œuvres qu'on se commande à soi-même est plus grand que le nombre des œuvres commandées par un protecteur ou un ami.

La faculté artistique que les critiques néo-classiques appelaient le Jugement est la capacité de distinguer entre le hasard aveugle et la Providence.

Exemple:

« J'étais en train de composer le choeur en sol mineur (la Prière, dans *Moïse en Egypte*), lorsque, soudain, je plongeai ma plume dans ma bouteille de médicament, au lieu de la tremper dans l'encrier; cela me fit faire un pâté, et lorsque (le papier buvard n'étant pas encore inventé) je le séchai à la poudre, il prit la forme d'un bé-carre; ce qui, instantanément, me fit évoquer l'effet que produirait un passage de sol mineur en sol majeur; c'est donc à cette tâche que revient tout le mérite—s'il y en a. »

(Lettre de Rossini à Louis Engel.)

★　★　★

Dans une œuvre d'art, l'effet de surprise n'est « heureux » que si, à la réflexion, il apparaît inévitable au point que toute autre démarche eût provoqué une surprise « malheureuse ». De même, dans la vie, quand nous repensons à un choix mal-heureux, il nous apparaît que le choix heureux eût été plus facile à faire que celui auquel; nous nous décidâmes.

★　★　★

Au cours des siècles, on a introduit dans la cuisine mentale quelques recettes pour économiser la main-d'œuvre—l'alcool, le café, le tabac, la benzédrine, etc. . . .—mais ce sont là recettes grossières, capables d'altérer la santé du cuisinier, et qui fréquemment échouent. La création artistique, au vingtième siècle après Jésus-Christ, n'est guère différente de ce qu'elle était au vingtième siècle avant Jésus-Christ: il faut encore presque tout faire à la main.

★　★　★

Si l'on pouvait créer des œuvres d'art au moyen de la seule « inspiration », c'est-à-dire, automatiquement, au cours d'une transe, la création deviendrait une opéra-tion si ennuyeuse et si pénible que seules de substantielles compensations en argent ou en honneurs pourraient inciter un homme à se faire artiste.

★　★　★

La Pythie prétendait donner à ceux qui la consultaient de bons conseils pour leur vie à venir; elle n'a jamais prétendu donner des récitals de poésie.

★　★　★

Une œuvré d'art qui serait toute en profondeur, d'où l'on aurait totalement exclu tout ce qui est évident et banal, serait infailliblement une œuvre fausse.

★　★　★

Si fort peu de gens, devant une belle construction, demandent le nom de l'archi-tecte, tandis que la plupart, entendant un beau morceau de musique, demandent le nom du compositeur, ce n'est point que la musique soit un art plus personnel, mais seulement que l'architecte doit joindre les fins utilitaires aux fins esthétiques, tandis que la musique n'est que jeu gratuit.

Quand nous voyons un bâtiment, nous savons que, beau ou hideux, il est là dans un but précis; mais lorsque nous entendons un morceau de musique, nous savons que sa seule raison d'être est de plaire, et, s'il nous plaît, nous sentons instinctivement le besoin de dire merci au responsable. En outre, tout art qui, comme la musique ou la poésie déclamée, n'existe que dans le présent et pendant l'audition, nous semble davantage destiné à notre agrément personnel qu'un art visuel qui demeure éternellement—prêt à donner du plaisir au premier passant venu. Mais cette impression ne confère pas, pour autant, un caractère plus personnel à l'acte de l'audition.

⋆   ⋆   ⋆

La sincérité ressemble au sommeil. Normalement, nous devrions admettre que, sans l'ombre d'un doute, nous allons être sincères, et passer outre. Cependant, pour la plupart, nous avons des crises d'hypocrisie comme nous avons des crises d'insomnie; dans les deux cas, le remède est généralement très simple: pour l'insomnie, changer de régime; pour l'hypocrisie, changer de fréquentations.

⋆   ⋆   ⋆

Quel est le poète anglais qui ne s'est pas, une fois ou l'autre, révolté contre une langue où le suffixe « s » rend un nom pluriel et un verbe singulier ?

L'Art exige non seulement des conventions de forme, mais aussi des conventions de rhétorique.

Aucun art ne peut exister sans une convention qui mette au premier plan certains aspects de l'expérience considérés comme importants et qui en rejette d'autres au second plan. Une convention nouvelle est une révolution dans la sensibilité. Elle offre un attrait pour une génération qui l'adopte parce qu'elle donne un sens à certaines expériences jusque-là négligées. A son tour, chaque convention nouvelle, quand elle a achevé son œuvre, devient réactionnaire et a besoin d'être remplacée. Néanmoins, ses effets ne sont pas annulés. La convention suivante les intègre.

Par exemple, la convention de l'Amour selon Pétrarque, qui règne aux débuts de la poésie anglaise du seizième siècle, diffère de la convention provençale primitive. La Dame, plutôt que d'inspirer de nobles actions à un guerrier, est devenue la source des émotions qu'exprime un poète. Alors, la Dame idéale est une dame de réputation irréprochable, mais qui dit: Non; et le poète idéal est un poète de tempérament doux et plutôt passif mais qui, toujours penché sur son propre cœur, est capable d'une émotion profonde et durable. Quand, à cause de son tempérament ou des circonstances, les sentiments du poète sont frivoles ou éphémères, la convention de la gravité de l'Amour l'incite à la plus ennuyeuse des rhétoriques. Elle ne convient guère non plus aux situations où la conduite de la Dame aimée entraîne dans leurs relations autant de haine que d'amour, ou dans celles où la passion de l'amoureux est consciemment et violemment sensuelle. Shakespeare, dans ses premiers Sonnets, et Donne, dans ses premiers poèmes lyriques, luttent avec la convention et la dépassent, mais, cependant, aucun d'eux ne peut écrire comme si l'*Amor*—religion de la fidélité et déification de la bien-aimée—n'avait jamais existé.

Dans la poésie de leurs successeurs, les Poètes Cavaliers—poésie qui se défend contre le bouleversement social, qui ignore délibérément les intérêts du peuple et insiste tout aussi délibérément sur la vie égoïste de loisirs et de plaisir—la roue a accompli un demi-tour et la convention pétrarquienne est renversée. C'est maintenant l'infidélité qu'on recommande, la fidélité qu'on méprise. Mais les sentiments pétrarquiens sont là encore, bien que refoulés; et c'est ce qui donne à l'œuvre de ces poètes (de Rochester en particulier) sa saveur unique. Ils ne sont pas ingénument frivoles, ils le sont avec défi; ils sont débauchés par un violent effort de volonté.

★ ★ ★

Quand un critique décrète qu'un livre est « sincère », nous comprenons immédiatement: (*a*) qu'il n'est pas sincère, (*b*) qu'il est mal écrit.

Il en va d'un style tarabiscoté (celui de Gongora ou d'Henry James, par exemple) comme d'un vêtement excentrique. Bien rares sont les artistes qui peuvent s'en parer, mais alors, quel ravissement pour nous !

Rimes, mètres, stances, etc., sont comme les serviteurs. Si le maître est assez juste pour gagner leur affection et assez ferme pour leur inspirer le respect, le résultat en est une maison heureuse où tout marche à la perfection. S'il est trop autoritaire, les serviteurs donnent leurs huit jours; s'il est trop faible, ils deviennent paresseux, impertinents, ivrognes et malhonnêtes.

Le poète qui compose des « vers libres » est comme Robinson dans son île: il lui faut faire sans aide sa cuisine, sa lessive, son raccommodage, etc. Dans certains cas exceptionnels, cette indépendance virile a des résultats originaux et impressionnants; mais, la plupart du temps, elle aboutit à une saleté repoussante: des cadavres de bouteilles sur le sol non balayé, des draps sales sur un lit défait.

Il y a beaucoup à dire en faveur d'une forme-type, que ce soit le *blank verse*, l'*heroic couplet* ou toute autre forme. Au lieu de courir après une forme personnelle originale, au risque de ne la point trouver, le poète emploie la forme donnée; il pourra alors consacrer tous ses efforts à lui faire exprimer tout ce qu'il a à à dire. A quelques exceptions près, plus un poète est original, moins il considère comme une limitation le fait d'employer la forme commune; en outre, à pratiquer continuellement la même forme, il exercera son esprit à penser aisément et naturellement dans cette forme et deviendra sensible aux variations les plus subtiles dont cette forme est susceptible.

★ ★ ★

S'il était vrai que la plus pure poésie est celle qui se rapproche le plus de la musique, alors la plus, pure de toutes serait la conversation à l'heure du thé; car, dans cette conversation, les mots n'ont aucune signification en eux-mêmes; leur sens réside tout entier dans les modulations vocales de ceux qui parlent. « Quelle belle journée ! » peut signifier, selon le ton de la voix : « Qu'en pensez-vous ? », ou « Admirez-moi ! » ou bien « Venez à mon secours ! » ou encore « Bla-bla-bla ! », « Pouah ! », etc.

★ ★ ★

Grâce à sa puissance mnémotechnique supérieure, la poésie l'emporte sur la prose pour des fins didactiques. Ceux qui condamnent le didactisme doivent, à fortiori, condamner la prose didactique. En vers, au moins (comme le prouvent souvent les slogans publicitaires) le message didactique est moitié moins impudent.

De même, la poésie est certainement égale et probablement supérieure à la prose pour exprimer clairement des idées, car, entre des mains habiles, la forme du vers peut accompagner et souligner la démarche de la logique. En fait, contrairement à ce que croient la plupart des gens qui ont conservé une conception romantique de la poésie, le danger du raisonnement en vers, c'est de rendre les idées *trop* claires et distinctes, plus cartésiennes que de raison. *L'Essai sur l'Homme* de Pope en est un exemple probant.

Par ailleurs, le vers ne se prête pas à la controverse—à la défense d'un fait ou d'une conviction qui a été mis en doute ou contesté—pour la raison que sa nature artificielle entraîne un certain scepticisme au sujet de ses conclusions.

> *Trente jours ont Septembre,*
> *Avril, Juin et Novembre*

est admissible, parce que personne ne conteste les faits. Si, toutefois, il existait un parti constitué qui contestât cette affirmation, ces vers seraient impuissants à le convaincre car, techniquement, on pourrait aussi bien dire :

> *Trente jours ont Septembre,*
> *Avril, Mai et Décembre.*

⋆　⋆　⋆

La théorie d'Edgar Poe sur la nécessité de faire des poèmes courts est en accord avec la révolution industrielle. A mesure que les sociétés s'accroissent, leurs poèmes tendent à se raccourcir. Un paysan écoutera d'interminables poèmes épiques sur la place du village; le lettré des grandes villes lit des sonnets dans sa baignoire.

⋆　⋆　⋆

Il est parfois plus facile de goûter sans mélange un beau poème exprimant des convictions que nous ne partageons pas qu'un beau poème exprimant nos propres convictions, car le scepticisme afférent à la forme poétique en elle-même ne nous trouble que dans la mesure où le sujet traité a une véritable importance pour nous.

La poésie, dans les sociétés primitives—plus statiques dans leur structure et davantage gouvernées par des pratiques rituelles—exprime des choses simples d'une manière contournée; les sentiments sont sans détours, la forme poétique est compliquée et complexe. La poésie de notre société déliquescente et fort peu respectueuse des rites s'efforce de dire brutalement des choses compliquées; les sentiments sont subtils et ambigus, la forme poétique est « le langage de tous les jours ».

⋆　⋆　⋆

Avec le français, l'anglais de Grande-Bretagne est la seule langue qui distingue ce qui est *boring* de ce qui est *a bore*. De même, *barbant* exprime un jugement subjectif qui signifie « ennuyeux-pour-moi »; l'expression « la barbe » a la prétention d'être objective, valable dans l'absolu, un jugement, quoi !

Non pas « barbant », mais « la barbe » : Henry James, les derniers quatuors de Beethoven, les fresques de la Sixtine, par Michel-Ange.

Quelquefois « barbant », mais jamais « la barbe » : Shakespeare, l'Art de la Fugue, de Bach, Degas.

Ni « barbant », ni « la barbe » : Pope, Verdi, Giorgione.

« Barbant » et « la barbe » : Shelley, Brahms, David.

Indiscutablement « barbant », mais n'ayant rien à voir avec « la barbe » : L'heure qu'il est.

Certainement pas « barbant », mais « la barbe » intégrale : l'Eternité.

⋆   ⋆   ⋆

Je rends grâces à mon ami, Chester Kallman, pour avoir inventé une nouvelle classification critique qui m'est d'un précieux secours. On peut classer les œuvres d'art, non seulement en *bonnes* et en *mauvaises*, mais encore en *bonnes*, en *mauvaises* et en *théoriques*.

On saisira mieux la différence d'après un exemple culinaire: la méthode habituelle de cuisson des choux de Bruxelles, dans notre pays, est un exemple de mauvaise cuisine; c'est-à-dire que lu cuisinière anglaise a l'intention de présenter un légume savoureux, mais elle échoue et l'on peut expliquer la raison de son échec: elle les a fait cuire trop longtemps. Certaines sortes de salades que consomment, aux Etats-Unis, les adeptes d'Helen Hokinson sont des exemples de cuisine « théorique »; elles sont agréables à l'œil, elles contiennent toutes les vitamines nécessaires et, si nous pouvions les absorber par les yeux ou les ingurgiter au moyen d'une sonde stomacale, elles seraient parfaites. Malheureusement, elles ont à passer par les papilles du goût, et cela, on n'en a eu cure. Nous ne pouvons dire qu'elles soient un échec, puisqu'on n'a jamais songé à les rendre agréables au goût; et, pour cette raison même, il est impossible de donner un conseil à la cuisinière pour les améliorer.

De la même manière, quand une œuvre d'art est mauvaise, on peut voir quelles furent les intentions de l'auteur et à quel moment il a déraillé; quand c'est une œuvre « théorique », cela devient impossible. Un critique moyen peut toujours déceler l'œuvre d'art manquée, mais le critique le plus expérimenté peut voir, parfois, sa sagacité se relâcher et il peut se laisser prendre par une œuvre d'art « théorique ».

Exemples d'art théorique: Environ la moitié des sonnets de Pétrarque, les romans (pas les poèmes) de Meredith, les tableaux d'Ingres, le Concerto n° 3 de Rachmaninoff.

Pierres de touche.

Que Matthew Arnold préconise l'emploi de fragments choisis de poésie sublime comme modèles pour les poètes et comme critères pour les critiques, c'est fort bien; mais l'ennui, c'est que le sublime se reconnaît trop facilement. Partir du sommet, c'est la même chose que de donner à un enfant la solution d'un problème d'arithmétique: la solution est peut-être juste, mais il ne s'ensuit pas que l'enfant ait compris le raisonnement par lequel on l'a trouvée.

Quand on veut réellement connaître les réactions d'un lecteur devant un texte (même d'un très grand poète), il faut lui proposer des passages auxquels il ne s'attend pas; et, pour les choisir, il faut tenir compte des tendances du goût général dans son pays et à son époque. Par exemple, au dix-neuvième siècle, un passage de Donne aurait été une bonne pierre de touche, parce que la poésie métaphysique n'était guère connue ni admirée; mais à notre époque, la réaction d'un lecteur devant le même passage nous renseignerait fort peu, parce qu'il est de bon ton d'admirer la poésie métaphysique. Il y a quinze ans, Pope aurait pu servir en l'occurrence; aujourd'hui, il est probable que cela ne rendrait pas. Je proposerai les « tests » suivants, en Amérique, en cette année 1951:

1. *L'Iliade*, 2ᵉ moitié du 2ᵉ chant (la liste des bateaux et de leurs équipages).
2. Un dialogue en vers alternés exposant la situation, dans n'importe quelle tragédie grecque.

3. Un passage de Dante, tel que: « *In quel loco fu'ia Pier Damiano . . .* »
4. Spenser: la fin de *La Reine des fées* (le chant VII et le chant VIII inachevé).
5. Dryden: *Panégyrique de la duchesse d'Ormonde.*
6. Dr Johnson: *En mémoire de M. Levet.*
7. William Barnes: *La Petite Sœur.*
8. N'importe quel chant du *Polyalbion* de Drayton, etc.

[II]

Le rapport dialectique entre l'art et la science est le suivant: Ripostant à l'effort de l'art pour répondre à la question: « Qui suis-je ? » par le truisme: « Je suis ce que je suis », la science objecte que mon « unicité » est relative, qu'on peut me considérer en tant qu'enfant de mes parents, en tant que mammifère, etc. Ripostant à cet effort de la science pour noyer le sujet dans ses attributs, l'art objecte que le moi ne peut se réduire à un pur sujet épistémologique, mais qu'il demeure obstinément passionné par sa propre existence.

★   ★   ★

Toute œuvre d'art est une réponse à la même question informulée: « Qui va là ? » et sa réponse est toujours: « *Moi* ».

En art, l'acte et la signification se confondent, et l'intention de l'artiste ou de l'exécutant n'a guère d'importance. S'il y a eu erreur, l'effet est manqué.

Dans un rite religieux, l'acte et sa signification ne dépendent pas de l'exactitude dans l'exécution, mais de l'intention du croyant.

★   ★   ★

Si l'art était magie, si le but d'un chant d'amour était d'inciter la Belle Inhumaine à confier au poète la clé de sa chambre, un magnum de Champagne serait plus beau qu'un sonnet.

★   ★   ★

La propagande est l'emploi de la magie, par ceux qui n'y croient plus, contre ceux qui y croient encore.

★   ★   ★

L'effet de catharsis est produit, licitement, non par les œuvres d'art, mais par les actes rituels d'un culte religieux. Il est produit aussi, moins licitement, par les courses de taureaux, les matches de football professionnel, les mauvais films, la musique militaire et les exhibition monstres où dix mille éclaireuses s'assemblent pour former un étendard vivant.

★   ★   ★

Hamlet n'est un mythe que pour les acteurs. Tout acteur (et toute actrice) se retrouve en Hamlet et désire incarner le rôle; mais, plus grand est son talent, plus désastreux est l'échec. Un grand acteur peut incarner n'importe quel personnage sauf un personnage d'acteur; or c'est bien là ce qu'est Hamlet.

Ayant vu nombre de grands acteurs échouer dans le rôle de Hamlet, je ne puis m'empêcher de penser que c'est une bonne farce que Shakespeare a jouée délibérément à une corporation dont il avait certainement eu beaucoup à souffrir.

* * *

Les préventions de naguère contre le théâtre ne sont pas totalement injustifiées, car la représentation de personnages par des individus en chair et en os donne naissance à des équivoques dangereuses, plus encore chez les spectateurs que chez les acteurs.

Je suis au théâtre où je vois un héros vaillant et bien doué s'effondrer tragiquement des cimes du bonheur au plus profond du malheur, et un personnage stupide et faible s'élever paradoxalement de l'obscurité à la gloire et à la fortune; lors, je me dis: « Quel charmant conte de fées ! Dans la vie réelle, malheureusement pour moi qui suis de la catégorie des faibles, c'est l'homme fort qui conquiert la princesse et le million de dollars; c'est le faible qui meurt dans la pauvreté et le mépris. Mais ce que je vois ici, en somme, ce n'est que du théâtre. Le héros tragique dont nous venons de voir le suicide viendra tout à l'heure saluer le public, et l'imbécile qui a épousé la princesse va rentrer, après la représentation, dans son garni de vieux garçon. »

Si c'est de cette façon que je conçois le théâtre, alors je me suis simplement abandonné à mon rêve de compter parmi les forts et de voir ceux que j'envie réduits à la misère. Pour saisir la vérité que le théâtre prétend illustrer, il me faut, de ma propre initiative, faire un rétablissement que le théâtre est impuissant à m'imposer. L'irréalité (parce que c'est seulement du théâtre) des souffrances tragiques et de la réussite comique prouve, non pas que le héros tragique ne souffre pas réellement ou que le comique n'est pas réellement heureux, mais que la souffrance et le bonheur ne sont pas ce que je me plais à croire qu'ils sont. La vérité tragique blessante est celle-ci: « Ce héros est soit ce que je suis, soit ce que je voudrais être; et l'on me dit ici que, tant que je serai semblable à lui ou que je désirerai l'être, je m'achemine, à mon insu, vers une mort misérable. » La vérité comique blessante se dissimule, du fait que le héros comique est tout aussi heureux quand il n'est rien du tout que lorsqu'il est le mari de la princesse: « Voici un homme que je n'aimerais pas être, ou que j'aurais honte d'être; or on me dit qu'il est béni parce qu'il se trouve heureux dans une situation que je considère comme misérable. Seul celui qui sait accepter la souffrance est, effectivement, l'époux de la princesse. »

* * *

La Musique est l'alcool des damnés (Bernard Shaw).

Le danger de s'identifier avec l'irréel est encore plus grand dans le cas de la musique que dans celui du théâtre. D'une part, l'oreille est un organe passif; d'autre part, la musique est, par excellence, dynamique; elle reflète la volonté et le choix. Ceux qui souffrent d'un manque de propos et de détermination dans la vie peuvent, d'un seul coup, s'abandonner passivement à la musique et, en s'identifient à elle, y mener, par procuration, une vie imaginaire d'affirmation triomphante.

* * *

Une photographie où les poses des personnages sont bien étudiées a toujours l'air artificiel, et une photographie moderne de ce même type, où l'on a employé la pellicule et l'obturateur les plus rapides, paraît encore plus artificielle qu'un daguerréotype très soigné. Un tableau synthétise le déroulement de l'histoire en un instant et la composition est le moyen employé pour effectuer cette synthèse, mais une photographie ne compose rien du tout; elle offre une reproduction exacte d'un instant historique réel qui n'est jamais composé parce qu'il est un déroulement entre le passé et l'avenir.

L'appareil photographique ne peut mentir; mais, puisque la vérité qu'il fixe est la vérité d'un instant éphémère, soustrait au passé et à l'avenir, sa signification est déterminée par le passé et l'avenir que lui attribuent celui qui le sous-titre d'une légende et celui qui la regarde—signification qui ne peut guère manquer d'être fausse. Une photographie nous montre, juché sur un tracteur, un homme au sourire épanoui; mais la raison pour laquelle cet homme-là, dans ce champ-là, souriait, à ce moment-là, elle ne peut nous le dire. Le spectateur peut inventer la raison qu'il voudra, sans crainte d'être contredit.

Il n'existe pas au monde un seul pays, une seule communauté, où un appareil photographique sans parti pris ne puisse prendre deux séries de clichés dont l'une révélerait un paradis et l'autre un enfer.

★　★　★

Sur une photographie, les différences entre un rocher, une colonne de marbre, un chêne, une grenouille et un visage humain ne sont, que des différences de forme et de grain.

D'une hauteur de trois mille mètres, la terre apparaît à l'œil humain telle qu'elle apparaît à l'objectif de la caméra; c'est-à-dire que l'histoire tout entière se réduit aux accidents naturels. Ce qui a le salutaire effet de faire paraître absurdes les malédictions historiques telles que frontières et haines naturelles ou politiques.

D'un avion, je contemple une surface terrestre visiblement continue. Qu'à travers ce territoire, marquée par quelque faible ligne de hauteurs, par une rivière ou même sans le moindre jalon topographique, puisse se dessiner une frontière, et que les hommes vivant en deçà de cette frontière soient censés haïr ceux qui vivent au-delà, refuser tout échange avec eux et qu'ils se voient interdire tout rapport avec eux, voilà qui, de l'altitude où je me trouve, se révèle une absurdité. Malheureusement, cette révélation ne laisse pas de s'accompagner de l'illusion qu'il n'existe point de valeurs historiques.

De cette même altitude, je ne puis distinguer un affleurement de rochers d'une magnifique cathédrale, ni une famille heureuse s'amusant dans une cour d'un troupeau de moutons; si bien que cela ne fait pour moi aucune différence si je détruis d'une bombe la cathédrale, la joyeuse famille ou bien les rochers ou le troupeau.

Si les effets de la distance entre l'observateur et les objets observés étaient réciproques, et que, de même que les objets terrestres s'amenuisent et perdent leur personnalité, de même l'aviateur se sentît rapetisser et désindividualiser, ou bien nous renoncerions à voler, ou bien nous ferions de la terre un paradis.

Ceux qui accusent le cinéma d'avoir un effet moral désastreux, de désunir les familles et d'augmenter la criminalité de la jeunesse, ont peut-être raison, mais pas à cause des arguments qu'ils mettent en avant. Ce ne sont pas les sujets des films (gangsterisme [*sic*], adultères) qui sont les plus nocifs, mais la nature réaliste de ce moyen d'évocation qui encourage une notion fantaisiste du temps. Dans tout art narratif, il faut moins de temps pour raconter une action que pour la faire réellement; mais, dans un roman ou dans une pièce de théâtre—si réalistes soient-ils—

le déroulement du temps est raccourci, c'est-à-dire présenté en perspective. Par exemple, un homme courtise une femme; au théâtre, la scène se déroulera, mettons, en dix minutes; mais l'auditoire aura l'impression que la scène s'est étendue sur une durée de deux heures. Le réalisme absolu de la caméra détruit cette impression: l'illusion de la vie réelle est si grande que les spectateurs partiront convaincus que, dans la vie réelle comme sur l'écran, il faut quarante minutes pour conquérir une femme. Quand, passant du cinéma à la vie, ils s'aperçoivent que cela prend deux heures, ils perdent patience. Faites des films aussi moraux que vous voudrez, par leur sujet et par leur ton, ils seront tout aussi nocifs; car, s'ils s'efforcent d'inculquer le goût de la vertu, ils ne pourront s'empêcher de témoigner que la vertu s'acquiert en quelques minutes. Quand il s'impatiente, l'habitué du cinéma ne crie pas: « Dépêchez-vous ! », il crie: « Coupez ! »

Keeping the Oriflamme Burning

Page 335.

Auden wrote to his friend Noemi Kenmore on 13 April 1952: "Have just finished reviewing Henry Irving for the N.Y." (Berg Collection). His typescript of the review, with his manuscript corrections, is in the New York Public Library Manuscripts and Archives Division; the title is the same as that of the printed text. The date 28 April 1952, pencilled by a *New Yorker* editor on the title page, is presumably when the typescript was received. In the second paragraph, the magazine replaced "Mr Laurence Irving's task is easy" with "of *Henry Irving: The Actor and His World*, the task of his grandson Mr Laurence Irving, is easy". In the paragraph that begins "The play, *The Two Lives*" (p. 336) the editors expanded Auden's simple "Lewes" to "G. H. Lewes, editor of the *Fortnightly Review*" perhaps because, unaware of Lewes's intimacy with George Eliot, they borrowed an irrelevant identification from a reference book. In the paragraph that begins "It is greatly to Mr Laurence Irving's credit" (p. 337) the editors replaced "a New York critic" with "Augustin Daly".

In the paragraph that begins "The next few years" (p. 336), in the last sentence before the quotation, Auden typed "Once agin [*sic*]", then crossed out the second word but neglected to retype it correctly as "again" and the magazine's editors failed to notice the omission.

Auden's quotations include some mostly trivial changes and omissions; in the extract that begins "the angelic visions" (p. 338) I have restored "the descents" (preceded by a comma) in order to undo the nonsense that resulted from the omission.

Sigmund Freud

Page 340.

A note at the end of this piece reads: "Freud's *The Case of Dora, Totem and Taboo, On Dreams*, and his *Autobiography* have been re-issued recently by the W. W. Norton Company.—The Editors." I have emended the magazine's slightly desperate "Zorastro" to "Sarastro".

FOREWORD TO *Various Jangling Keys*, BY EDGAR BOGARDUS

Page 344.

Auden wrote to Eugene Davidson at the Yale University Press on 13 August 1952: "I must apologise for my delay in dealing with the Yale Younger Poet, but I have had a lot of work and kept postponing it. My choice is Mr Edgar Collins Bogardus . . . ; his Ms is entitled *Various Jangling Keys*. I've written him." Auden probably wrote the introduction shortly after this, and the book was published in the Yale Series of Younger Poets on 20 May 1953.

The poet John Crowe Ransom taught his students at Kenyon College to write formal, metaphysical poetry that tended to be sympathetic with Ransom's nostalgic agrarian politics. Under his editorship, the quarterly *Kenyon Review* published poems and essays by his students and friends and by the most serious-minded practitioners of the New Criticism. See also the introduction to *The Faber Book of Modern Verse*.

FOREWORD TO *The Desire and Pursuit of the Whole*, BY FREDERICK ROLFE, BARON CORVO

Page 347.

Auden wrote to Chester Kallman on 5 July 1952: "Am much enjoying re-reading The Desire and Pursuit of the Whole; I love silly jokes like the Anglican clergyman who sings *My Pew* at a tea-party, and ends telephone conversations with *ah river dertchy*." He finished the foreword on 3 September 1952, and the new edition that included it was published by Cassell in London on 14 May 1953; an American edition was issued by New Directions on 15 July 1953. This book had first been published in 1934 with an introduction by A.J.A. Symons which was also included in the 1953 edition. The "blubber-lipped Professor of Greek" was R. M. Dawkins, whom Auden had met at Oxford.

THE RAKE'S PROGRESS

Page 351.

Harper's Bazaar published literary works among its articles on fashion; Auden's poems and essays had appeared there since 1938. This article (in the American edition of the magazine) was timed to appear shortly before the American première at the Metropolitan Opera, 14 February 1953.

T. S. ELIOT SO FAR

Page 352.

The opening sentence reflects Auden's annoyance at the title chosen by Random House for his *Collected Poetry* (1945); he had asked for *Poems 1928–1942*. The work that would make a lie of the title of Eliot's book was *The Confidential Clerk*, which was scheduled to open in August 1953.

In the opening paragraph the quotation marks around "œuvre" were probably added by the magazine.

In the closing paragraph, Harry and John are from Eliot's *The Family Reunion* and Celia and Lavinia are from *The Cocktail Party*. Some of the quotations may have been written from memory; in the one that begins "Maintain themselves" Eliot wrote "the common routine", not "the same routine".

TWO SIDES TO A THORNY PROBLEM

Page 356.

This essay appeared on the front page of the drama section of the Sunday *New York Times* one day before the opening of a production of *The Merchant of Venice* at the New York City Center. It was perhaps commissioned by an editor who knew of Auden's lectures on Shakespeare at the New School in 1946–47. In the extract that begins "Grieve not" I have emended two probable misreadings of Auden's hand ("therein" for "herein" and "bitter eye" for "hollow eye").

CAV & PAG

Page 358.

The title of the piece in the original printing is "Cav and Pag", but in the one instance where the title phrase appears in the text Auden used an ampersand. "Cav & Pag" (with an ampersand) is the title Auden used when he reprinted the piece in *The Dyer's Hand* (1962). Probably an editor at RCA Victor Records replaced the ampersand with "and". The recordings of the two operas were issued together under the catalogue numbers WDM-6106 (45 r.p.m.) and LM-6106 (long-playing). Separate releases of the two operas issued in 1956 included the same essay under the presumably nonauthorial title "Verismo Opera".

The recordings were made in January through March 1953; Auden was presumably commissioned around the same time to write his note. The English translations of Italian words and lines were probably added by an editor at the record company; Auden omitted them in *The Dyer's Hand* in 1962.

One oddity in the text is the italicized "idealists" at the end of the long paragraph that begins "In the *Prologue*" (p. 363). I suspect that Auden intended that a break should follow the end of the paragraph and indicated it with a horizontal line, which a typist or compositor misinterpreted as an italicization of whichever word happened to be above it. If this is correct, then other breaks may have disappeared from other points in the essay.

The 1962 version adds this epigraph: "'If a perfume manufacturer were to adopt the 'naturalistic' aesthetic, what kind of scents would he bottle?'—Paul Valéry". Other changes in the 1962 version include trivial adjustments to punctuation (some followed here) and the following changes in wording. In the paragraph that begins "If the interplay" (p. 362) the original reading "we frequently have with others to hide our real feelings" is altered to "we frequently have to hide our real feelings for others". In the paragraph that begins "About the music" (p. 363) the 1962 version omits "How shall I classify it? I've got it. *Verismo*." In the paragraph that follows, the sentence that begins "There are dull passages" reads in 1962: "There are dull passages in *Cavalleria Rusticana*, e.g. the music of the mule-driving song, but, in the dramatic passages, the very primitive awkwardness of the music seems to go *with* the characters [etc.]". The 1962 version lacks the first sentence in the paragraph that begins "The idea of *verismo* may" (p. 363). In the penultimate sentence, the 1962 version has "it may be ourselves, not the works, that are at fault".

Duse was the actress Eleanora Duse, who urged Giovanni Verga to turn the story "Cavalleria Rusticana" into a play.

THROUGH THE COLLAR-BONE OF A HARE

Page 364.

The title of the review alludes to the wish expressed in Yeats's poem "The Collar-Bone of a Hare" to sail to a mythically blissful island from which one can look back at the "old bitter world" "Through the white thin bone of a hare." I have restored the hyphen in Auden's title, which was presumably removed by a *New Yorker* editor in obedience to the magazine's stylebook. The tone of the review depends on Auden's assumption that readers would remember that Santayana had died a few months earlier.

Auden's typescript is the New York Public Library Manuscripts and Archives Division. I have restored its paragraphing and some of its punctuation, but not the slight changes in wording that Auden accepted in proof. I have corrected, as the magazine's famous fact-checkers surprisingly did not, Auden's misspelling "Otteline" (Lady Ottoline Morrell). The fact-checkers also failed to notice that the Apple of Discord is not in Homer. In the paragraph that begins "The continual reiteration" (p. 367) the phrase "two faculty members" is absent from the typescript; in the final paragraph, the phrase "to my favorite landscape" is also absent from the typescript.

"Earl Stanley Russell", the disreputable older brother of Bertrand Russell, was more widely known as Frank Russell.

TRANSPLANTED ENGLISHMAN VIEWS U.S.

Page 369.

This piece was commissioned for a seventy-fifth anniversary supplement to the *St Louis Post-Dispatch* (titled *The Second American Revolution*), and seems to have been written many months before it was published. The files of Auden's agents (Curtis Brown Ltd) show that Auden agreed around 22 March 1953 to write the piece, and apparently finished it soon afterward; a letter of acknowledgement from an editor at the newspaper on 8 April 1953 apologizes for not replying sooner because the editor was away for a few weeks. Auden apparently read a version of this essay to a Phi Beta Kappa audience at Yale in the late spring of 1953, and reused much of the material in June 1953 in his BBC broadcast "Huck and Oliver" (p. 378), which he wrote from a British perspective instead of an American one.

Auden claims in the original essay to have re-read *Huckleberry Finn* "the other day", which suggests a date shortly before he wrote the piece apparently in March 1953; in the broadcast recorded for the BBC in June 1953 he says he read the book "about six months ago".

Bernard De Voto was the writer and editor who in the late 1940s and early 1950s successfully campaigned to preserve public lands in the American West when private interests sought to take control of them.

In the paragraph that begins "What is to happen? The oldest" (p. 371) I have emended "authority of his eye" to "authority of his age". In the paragraph that begins "A pluralist nation" I have removed an exclamation point at the end of the first sentence (which may perhaps have been a question mark in Auden's manuscript).

VERGA'S PLACE

Page 374.

Although Auden's review discusses only *The House by the Medlar Tree*, The Readers' Subscription book club made the book available to its members only in a two-book package together with Verga's *Little Novels of Sicily*. Auden's quotations are moderately exact; in the first, I have corrected "broadsheet" to "broadside".

Zahl und Gesicht

Page 377.

Auden seems to have begun reading the works of the critic and philosopher Rudolf Kassner in the mid-1940s and became deeply engaged with *Zahl und Gesicht* (1919) around 1950. Other contributors to this eightieth-birthday tribute, edited by Alphons Clemens Kensik and Daniel Bodmer, included Denis de Rougemont, who perhaps introduced Auden to *Zahl und Gesicht*, and T. S. Eliot. The book was published in Erlenbach-Zürich on 9 September 1953.

HUCK AND OLIVER

Page 378.

A rewritten version of "Transplanted Englishman Views U.S." (p. 369), from a British instead of an American perspective. Auden recorded this talk on 30 June 1953 at the offices of the BBC. The magazine text was based closely on a transcript of the broadcast talk now in the BBC Written Archives Centre, omitting Auden's informal transitions ("Now,", "All right"), clearing up some minor verbal missteps, and, in the paragraph that begins "One of the great differences" (p. 378), adding (perhaps in proof) everything in the final sentence following "except enslave it".

In the paragraph that begins "In the States, money" (p. 381) the final sentence could be clarified through the insertion, after "What is shocking", of the phrase "to Europeans in America". Auden's quotations include trivial inaccuracies.

SELECTED ESSAYS OF T. S. ELIOT

Page 382.

Norman Foerster's *American Criticism* was "torn to pieces" in Eliot's essay "Second Thoughts about Humanism". The "earlier edition" mentioned in the final paragraph was the 1932 predecessor of this 1950 edition, which The Readers' Subscription book club offered to its members three years after publication. Auden's quotations include trivial inaccuracies. In the paragraph that begins "If Mr Eliot's other concern" I have emended "overevaulation" to "overvaluation".

THE GREATNESS OF FREUD

Page 385.

This review partly reproduces the argument of "Sigmund Freud" (p. 340). Auden reviewed the second volume of Ernest Jones's biography of Freud in "The History of an Historian" (p. 596). The quotations in the review are trivially abridged and altered.

TRANSLATION AND TRADITION

Page 388.

The first of Auden's many prose contribution to *Encounter*, the monthly of arts and politics begun in 1953, edited by Stephen Spender and Irving Kristol, and sponsored by the British Society for Cultural Freedom, a counterpart of the Congress for Cultural Freedom (see the note to "Address to the Indian Congress for Cultural Freedom", above). Auden's quotations slightly alter the spelling of some of the originals, but the odd-looking quotations from Cavalcanti are almost exactly reproduced from Pound's 1932 version included in the book under review. Auden spelled Remy de Gourmont correctly, without the acute accent (Rémy) mistakenly added by Pound.

SPEAKING OF BOOKS

Page 391.

"Speaking of Books" was a weekly column on the second page of the *New York Times Book Review*, usually written by J. Donald Adams except during interludes when guest columnists appeared instead. The guest columnists who appeared in one such interlude, from mid-November 1953 through mid-January 1954, were Irwin Edman, Lord Dunsany, Justin O'Brien, Joseph Wood Krutch, John Berryman, Auden, Peter Quennell, Mary M. Colum, Horace Reynolds, and Delmore Schwartz.

Winston Churchill's birthday "a few weeks ago" was 30 November.

BALLET'S PRESENT EDEN

Page 393.

This essay was almost certainly written at the request of Auden's friend Lincoln Kirstein, general director of the New York City Ballet, which performed at the City Center of Music and Drama, New York; Kirstein had formed the company as a vehicle for George Balanchine. *Center* was a monthly published by the City Center that lasted slightly more than two years; this essay appeared in its first number. A closely similar version appeared in the souvenir program book of the Ballet's performance of *The Nutcracker* on 2 February 1954. The spellings in the first version are evidently closer to Auden's original (including his characteristic "eg." for "e.g.") and were slightly refined for the corrected version. I have followed most of the spellings of the original version but have incorporated the second version's correction of "Dumas *fils*" to "Dumas" (p. 394).

Marius Petipa commissioned the music for the ballet and began the choreography, which was completed by his assistant Leon Ivanov. The production by the Vic-Wells Ballet was the first performance outside Russia.

FOREWORD TO *An Armada of Thirty Whales,* BY DANIEL G. HOFFMAN

Page 396.

Auden wrote to Eugene Davidson at the Yale University Press on 21 May 1953: "I've selected a Younger Poet for this year, Mr Daniel G. Hoffman. . . . He has got, however, to cut out a number of the poems, but I will be writing to him about that." Auden sent Davidson the final selection of poems and his introduction on 16 August 1953, and the book was published in the Yale Younger Poets Series on 21 April 1954.

WORDS AND MUSIC

Page 399.

Auden wrote to his friend Noemi Kenmore on 4 September 1953: "immersed in a review of Kurt Sach's *History of Rhythm*—he may know something about musical rhythm but he knows nothing about poetry" (Berg Collection).

A MESSAGE FROM W. H. AUDEN

Page 407.

Written for the commemorative booklet sold at a tribute to Dylan Thomas presented at the Globe Theatre, London. The full title of the performance was *Homage to Dylan Thomas: A Programme of Poetry, Drama and Music.* The program was devised by Louis MacNeice, Rupert Doone, and Vera Lindsay, and was presented by the Group Theatre in association with the Institute of Contemporary Arts. Doone was the director of the Auden-Isherwood plays in the 1930s and lived with Auden's friend Robert Medley; probably Doone or Medley, or possibly MacNeice, commissioned this message from Auden.

A CONTEMPORARY EPIC

Page 407.

In the first set of extracts, I have restored lineation that apparently confused the compositor; I have also added the first set of three stars, which were probably omitted because the break occurred at the foot of the page in the magazine. In the prose extract that begins "To get to it" the square brackets replace round ones in the *Encounter* text (the phrase in square brackets is not in David Jones's original).

Auden reviewed a later edition of *Anathemata* in the undated first issue of the *New York Review of Books* in 1963.

THE MAN WHO WROTE *Alice*

Page 413.

Auden's reference to George Macdonald was conceivably the stimulus for the edition of *The Visionary Novels of George Macdonald* for which he wrote an introduction published later the same year (p. 477).

HANDBOOK TO ANTIQUITY

Page 416.

In the opening sentence I have corrected "student" to "students". In the paragraph that begins "In the meantime" I have emended "Phaidias" to "Pheidias" and "Inonia" to "Ionia". In the paragraph that begins "In the first part" I have somewhat regretfully corrected "hybrids" to "hybris".

A CONSCIOUSNESS OF REALITY

Page 419.

Auden cabled to the *New Yorker* from Italy on 21 November 1953, "Glad to review Woolf send New York address am returning shortly" (garbled text emended). He sent a typescript of his review on 18 January 1954 with a cover letter: "Here is my review of the Virginia Woolf diary. I used a copy I was given for Christmas, but would welcome a review copy as well." The typescript, with his manuscript revisions, is titled "A Writer's Diary", and is in the New York Public Library Manuscripts and Archives Division. The printed text, followed here, adds a few words for the sake of clarity or grammar and corrects Auden's quotations. In the second paragraph, the typescript twice capitalizes "Set"; at the end of the paragraph that begins "At the beginning" (p. 421) the typescript has "in my opinion, is, probably, her masterpiece." In the next paragraph, which begins "With the exception", I have emended a quotation by replacing "in which I shall exist" with "in which I shall rest".

The review is reprinted under the same title in *Forewords and Afterwords* (1973).

THE WORD AND THE MACHINE

Page 425.

The magazine text has a break before the paragraph that begins "Anyone whose social position" (p. 426); like other such breaks in *Encounter*, this was probably not authorial.

A European View of Peace

Page 427.

The text in *The Griffin* presumably follows Auden's lost manuscript in using double quotation marks for most extracts from Raymond Aron and single quotation marks for most short phrases that may or may not be direct quotations; this edition follows standard twentieth-century practice in normalizing quotation marks. I have corrected an error in a quotation in the second paragraph, where Auden may have correctly copied "Continental empire" but a compositor misread this as the printed review's "Continental Europe".

England: Six Unexpected Days

Page 431.

Vogue, like *Mademoiselle* and other fashion magazines, published poems and literary essays in every issue; Auden's work first appeared in the American edition of *Vogue* in 1939. This essay was one of six in a feature titled "Travel Memo—9 Countries". The title was probably editorial; in the magazine's table of contents the title above (the title that appeared with the essay) continues with the words "in the Pennines".

I have inserted a break between the itinerary for the sixth day and the concluding paragraph.

The piece records a journey taken during a visit to England in June 1953, the third day of which inspired the poem "Streams". Holyoke is the town in Massachusetts. The friend who brought a store cheese to T. S. Eliot was Stephen Spender. The Victorian visitor quoted in Auden's entry for the fifth day was Thomas Sopwith, from the penultimate paragraph of his *Account of the Mining Districts of Alston Moor, Weardale, and Teesdale* (1833); Auden also quoted this book in his poem "Not in Baedeker". Auden and his Oxford friend Gabriel Carritt stayed at the Lord Crewe Arms in 1930; during his Oxford years Auden was in love with Carritt who remained resolutely heterosexual.

Introduction to *An Elizabethan Song Book*, by W. H. Auden and Chester Kallman

Page 435.

The introduction to this collection was written around March or April 1954; the extent to which Kallman was an actual rather than nominal coauthor is unclear; possibly Auden wrote the entire introduction. The book was published by Anchor Books on 20 October 1955; a British edition was published by Faber & Faber on 24 May 1957. A more detailed history may be found in Appendix II, and the text of a sleeve note to a recording based on its contents may be found in Appendix I.

Balaam and the Ass

Page 444.

Auden told his friend Wendell Stacy Johnson on 18 November 1953, "Am working my Master-Servant lecture into a long essay" (Berg Collection), but he seems not to have finished it until 1954. The original lecture was probably written in the spring of 1953.

This was the third of Auden's biennial essays for *Thought*; the first two were "Nature, History and Poetry" (p. 226) and "Notes on the Comic" (p. 307). Auden also published the essay in *Encounter*; the *Thought* and *Encounter* versions were probably set from different copies of the same typescript (the misspelling in both versions of Aouda from *Around the World in Eighty Days* is probably a typist's misreading of Auden's hand). The verbal differences between the *Thought* and *Encounter* versions suggest that the *Thought* version reflects a later state of Auden's revisions, which he may have made either on separate copies of the typescripts or in proof or both; the *Thought* version also seems to have endured less editorial interference, except for two changes (described below) evidently made by the editor, Fr. William Lynch, for the sake of conformity with Roman Catholic terminology. I have followed the *Thought* version except in undoing these two doctrinal changes and in restoring capitalizations found in the *Encounter* text that seem characteristic of Auden's manner; I have also made some minor corrections as noted below.

The *Thought* version is reprinted in *The Dyer's Hand* (1962) with different minor changes from those in the *Encounter* version; see below for details.

The *Encounter* version has a different subtitle ("On the Literary Use of the Master-Servant Relationship"), lacks the first epigraph, and includes a footnote to section III, linked to the word "characters" immediately after the dramatic dialogue in the middle of the section: "Needless to say, one must add here and throughout what follows: 'Nevertheless, there are not five characters but one person.'" The *Encounter* text also places "five characters" in quotation marks where *Thought* treats only "characters" as a quoted word. Other minor differences between the two versions are described below.

The *Encounter* text adds plain English translations of the non-English quotations, with this footnote: "All translations, which are merely literal, have been made by the editors."

In section IV, in the paragraph that begins "Had man not fallen" (p. 450) *Encounter* has "his wish for freedom" instead of "the wish of his ego for freedom" and "his wish for a *telos*, a" instead of "its wish for a *telos* simply, a" (the 1962 text, followed by this edition, emends the *Thought* text by removing the comma after "simply").

In section V, in the paragraph that begins "Near the beginning of the play" (p. 451) after the quotation, *Encounter* has "Faust's *der Welt*" (probably an editorial correction) for "Faust's *Welt*". The opening of the paragraph that begins "Mephisto describes himself" reflects a correction made for the *Thought* version; the *Encounter* version begins erroneously, "In the Prologue The Lord describes Mephisto as one:", followed by only the second line of the line-and-a-half quotation present in *Thought* (the quotation occurs in the scene "Study", not the Prologue). Later in the same paragraph, *Encounter* erroneously has "possibly" for "passively". In the paragraph that begins "In this lack" (p. 452) *Encounter* has "was always finite" for "is always finite"; places the phrase "so quickly" following "take up another"; and has "idolatry of novelty" instead of "idolatry of possibility" (which better matches the sense of the sentences that follow it).

In section VI, in the paragraph that begins "Don Giovanni is as inconspicuous", in the sentence that begins "It is Leporello", *Encounter* (and the 1962 text in *The*

Dyer's Hand) omits "for existing"; probably this was an editorial improvement. In the paragraph that begins "As in the case" *Encounter* (followed here) omits a confusing comma after "old beau of hers (to him)"; the sentence is further clarified by a revision in *The Dyer's Hand* (see below).

In section VIII, the first sentence begins in the *Encounter* version "Shakespeare's last play, *The Tempest,* is". In the paragraph that begins "As Christ's comment" (p. 462) *Thought* has only "on the commandment" where *Encounter* (followed here) has "on the Seventh Commandment"; probably Auden wrote "Seventh Commandment" but Fr. Lynch deleted the number as the simplest way of accommodating the fact that the Roman Catholic Church numbers the commandment against adultery as the sixth. Later in the same paragraph, I have followed *Encounter* in printing "mortal sins" instead of *Thought's* "capital sins", probably another technical correction by Fr. Lynch. *Encounter*, followed here, has a paragraph break before "Imagination is beyond" (p. 464).

In section IX, in the paragraph that begins "By and large" (p. 468) I have emended "form our subjective" to "from our subjective". In the paragraph that begins "Then in India" (p. 470) *Encounter* has "impersonal. It is now one of *philia*" instead of "impersonal; *philia* is felt by both." In the paragraph that begins "Like Mr Fogg" (p. 471) *Encounter* has "and has not lifted a finger to get what, for him" instead of "and does not lift a finger to help himself, yet he is rewarded with what, for him". The paragraph that begins "The Quest Hero" (p. 471) was probably rewritten for the *Thought* version; the *Encounter* version reads:

The Quest hero often encounters an old beggar or animal who offers him advice: if, too proud to imagine that such apparently inferior creatures could know better than himself, he rejects the advice, it has fatal consequences, but if he is humble enough to listen and obey, he achieves, thanks to their help, his goal. But, however humble he may be, he dreams of becoming a hero; he may be willing to take advice from his inferiors, but he is convinced that, potentially, he is a superior person, a prince-to-be. Bertie Wooster, on the other hand, not only knows that he is a person of no account, but also never dreams that he will become anything else; to his dying day he will, he knows, remain a footler who needs a nanny: at the same time, he is completely without envy of other people who are of some account. He has, in fact, that rarest of virtues, humility, and so he is blessed: it is he and no other who has for his servant the god-like Jeeves.

In the final sentence of the essay, *Encounter* has commas around "on earth".

Both *Encounter* and *The Dyer's Hand* correct the misspelling "Passpartout" invariably used in *Thought*.

The version in *The Dyer's Hand* (1962) is retitled "Balaam and His Ass" (for "the Ass") and has no subtitle. The 1962 text replaces the first epigraph with " 'Am I not thine ass, upon which thou hast ridden ever since I was thine unto this day'—Numbers: XII, 30". The opening sentence omits "is agnatic . . . to say, it", and the second sentence begins "Nor is it erotic". In the paragraph that begins "As in the case" (p. 456) the 1962 text simplifies one of the sentences to: "His Boss will appear as

King Mark, an old disreputable drinking crony of his as Morold, the scandal-mongering neighbors next door as Melot." In the paragraph that begins "Caliban was once" (p. 463) in the sentence that begins "In order to become" the 1962 text has "to work, and limit its playful activity to imagining"; partly following this example, I have emended the 1954 version by removing the comma after "activities". In the paragraph that begins "Mr Fogg, as Jules Verne" (p. 468) the 1962 text has "cannot tell if he is hungry".

THE FREUD-FLIESS LETTERS

Page 472.

The text in *The Griffin* (normalized here) evidently follows Auden's lost manuscript in generally using double quotation marks for quotations and single quotation marks for concepts (e.g. 'safe science'); the paragraph that begins "That Fliess should" inconsistently places single quotation marks around "merely reading his own thoughts into other people". Auden's quotations slightly modify the originals; in the paragraph that begins "Until the break", in the fifth extract, I have corrected "physical" to "psychical". In *The Griffin* the title (but not the rest of the text) has the misspelling "Fleiss".

In the third paragraph from the end, "*fantastica fornicatio*" is Augustine's term for the mind's fornication with its own fantasies, a phrase that Auden learned from Charles Norris Cochrane (see *Prose II*, p. 226).

INTRODUCTION TO *The Visionary Novels of George Macdonald*

Page 477.

The two novels in this collection were *Lilith* and *Phantastes*; the title page describes the book as "edited by Anne Fremantle", an English writer living in America and associate editor of the liberal Roman Catholic weekly *Commonweal* to which Auden intermittently submitted poems and reviews. She was also the editor of later books to which Auden contributed in later years, including *The Protestant Mystics* (1964). Auden wrote to Norman Holmes Pearson on 1 July 1954, "Am writing an introduction for a republishing of *Lilith* and *Phantastes* of George MacDonald [*sic*]. Do you know them" (Yale University Library).

Anne Fremantle's editorship in this instance seems to have been limited to selecting the two novels by Macdonald, excising most of the interpolated poems from *Phantastes*, and commissioning Auden's introduction. The book was published by Noonday Press in New York on 11 October 1954. The introduction is reprinted in *Forewords and Afterwords* (1973) as "George Macdonald".

HOW CRUEL IS APRIL?

Page 481.

Written for a *Times Literary Supplement* special supplement "American Writing Today", at the invitation of the paper's editor Allan Pryce-Jones; the full supplement was reprinted as a book under the same title in 1957 by the New York University Press, 1957, with a new preface by Pryce-Jones and an introduction by Allan Angoff, who, although identified on the title page as the editor of the book, seems only to have regularized spelling and punctuation and added an index prepared by his wife.

Holding the Mirror Up to History

Page 483.

Auden's typescript is in the New York Public Library Manuscripts and Archives Division; in place of a title it names the title and author of the book at the top of the first page. The *New Yorker* editors added "on Tolstoy, *The Hedgehog and the Fox*" at the end of the opening paragraph. The printed text, followed here, slightly revises Auden's grammar and punctuation and corrects his invariable misspelling "Isiah Berlin". A few notable differences include the following. In the second paragraph the typescript has "and not otherwise" after "described". In the paragraph that begins "Some of the theoretical" (p. 486) the typescript has "their behaviour does not seem foolish but understandable" (with "foolish but understandable" as a single attribute, not two different and contrasting attributes); the original phrase was presumably rearranged by an editor, perhaps with little benefit to the prose; the sense is that the uhlans' behavior is merely lunatic, unlike Prince Andrew's foolish but understandable musings. At the end of the same sentence Auden's typescript omits the comma after "inhuman". In the paragraph that begins "Despite the two men's" (p. 486) the typescript attributes the two quotations to "Book X, chapter 39" and "Some Words about *War and Peace*".

The Hero Is a Hobbit

Page 489.

This seems to have been written at around the same time as Auden's similar but longer review of the British edition of *The Fellowship of the Ring*, "A World Imaginary, but Real". This review was reprinted, without the title, in *The Griffin*, March 1955, "by arrangement with the *New York Times*."

A World Imaginary, but Real

Page 491.

Auden's identifications of Tolkien's place-names are Cold War allusions ("East of "Anduin" means east of the Iron Curtain). Dol Guldur is presumably St Petersburg, from which Lenin was forced into hiding after the February Revolution; the fortress of Barad-dûr is the Kremlin; and Minas Tirith is perhaps West Berlin, preserving itself against its captured twin city Minas Ithil (I do not know why the left-wing *New Statesman* would disagree with this identification but not with the others).

The Private Diaries of Stendhal (1801–1814)

Page 494.

Perhaps Auden prepared a set of excerpts instead of a review because he had been commissioned to write a full review for the *New Yorker*, "The Pool of Narcissus" (p. 502). Auden's excerpts are mostly accurate, although they reduce Stendhal's capitals and italics. I have emended a few obvious minor errors that seem to have resulted from a misreading of Auden's hand.

FOG IN THE MEDITERRANEAN

Page 498.

Auden's only contribution to the *Christian Scholar*, the quarterly journal of the Commission of Christian Higher Education of the National Council of the Churches of Christ in the United States of America. The magazine began publication in 1953 (retaining the volume numbering of an earlier quarterly) and was intended for academic readers with religious interests. An editorial note in the issue with Auden's review described a new policy under which the book reviews were devoted to works "not specifically written for the religious audience", reviewed "by persons who view such books from the standpoint of biblical faith."

The magazine, perhaps following Auden's manuscript, listed the title of the book as *The Rebel (L'Homme Révolté)*. I have added the part number to the first part. In part III I have emended the paragraph that begins "Had Mr Camus" by adding the opening word, "Had". In the first sentence of the paragraph that begins "'One can reject'" I have restored to the quotation three words dropped by an obvious oversight, "the sea and". Auden's quotations make trivial alterations to the originals.

THE POOL OF NARCISSUS

Page 502.

A secretarial typescript, evidently made from Auden's manuscript, with the same title as the published review, is in the New York Public Library Manuscripts and Archives Division. The typescript is dated 22 November 1954, presumably soon after the manuscript arrived at the *New Yorker*. I have restored paragraphing removed by the magazine. The magazine (followed here) corrected Auden's spellings and arithmetic (Auden had written that Stendhal's first novel was not published until he was forty-five, not forty-four). In the paragraph that begins "By a very early age" the typescript has "reduplication" for "duplication". In the paragraph that begins "There could be no better" the typescript has "The substitute Stendhal discovered—others may have made it before him, but he was the first to record it—was originality". Henri Beyle used Mocenigo as the name of a kind of literary practice or identity that he aspired to achieve for a few years after 1810.

INTRODUCTION TO *The Faber Book of Modern American Verse*

Page 506.

Auden apparently wrote the introduction to this anthology early in 1955. The book was published on 3 September 1956; a detailed history of the project may be found in Appendix II.

The introduction was first printed in 1955 in the first number of the annual *An-*

chor Review, a magazine in paperback-book format, under the heading "The Anglo-American Difference: Two Views" (the second view was by David Daiches; neither writer's essay made reference to the other). Auden reprinted the text from the anthology, together with some additional material, in *The Dyer's Hand* (1962) under the title "American Poetry"; this version is described briefly below.

A secretarial typescript, with corrections and additions in Auden's hand, is in the archives of the Viking Press, which briefly considered publishing an American edition of the book but decided against it. An American edition was eventually published by Criterion Books.

The text in this edition is that of the anthology, which has slightly heavier punctuation than the typescript and *Anchor Review* versions and was probably repunctuated by a Faber editor.

In the first paragraph, following the typescript and *Anchor Review*, I have corrected "have received" to "have conceived". The second paragraph begins in the typescript and *Anchor Review*: "In the same year, 1855, appeared *Maud, The Song of Hiawatha*, and the first edition of *Leaves of Grass*: no two poets [etc.]".

In the paragraph that begins "Normally, in comparing" the anthology text twice adds "minutes", probably as an editorial clarification of the typescript and *Anchor Review* text. In the paragraph that begins "But in America" (p. 508) the typescript reads "neither the size, condition, or climate of the continent encourage", and *Anchor Review* reads "neither the size, condition, nor climate of the continent encourages". In the paragraph fragment (after a quotation) that begins "the reason for this" (p. 509) the typescript and *Anchor Review* have "not simply because . . . but also because" for "not simply that . . . but also that".

In the paragraph that begins "To be able" (p. 510) the footnote that translates the quotation from Goethe was probably added by a Faber editor; it is absent in all other texts. Immediately after the quotation from Goethe, *Anchor Review* differs from the typescript and anthology text by having the sentence, "Goethe, I presume, was also thinking of the absence of violent political clashes." in place of the sentence fragment that begins "wrote Goethe". In the same sentence, the typescript matches the anthology text but has a parenthesis after the words "I presume": "(since he was a Neptunist)". Later in the same paragraph, *Anchor Review* prints the footnote about 1829 as a parenthesis in the main text, not as the footnote that appears in the typescript (where it is added in Auden's hand) and the anthology.

In the paragraph that begins "What he does not say" (p. 512) *Anchor Review* has "Here in the States" in place of the typescript and anthology's "In the States". The paragraph break before "On the other hand, a British poet" (p. 512) is based on the *Anchor Review* text; the typescript, in an apparent misinterpretation of Auden's manuscript, places the break before the preceding parenthesis ("In this Cambridge-on-Cam . . . Oxford-on-Thames."), while the anthology has no break at all.

The *Anchor Review* text omits the two closing paragraphs about the anthology itself, and, earlier in the text, omits some of the identifications of quotations.

The version in *The Dyer's Hand* (1962) may be found in *Prose IV*. Auden titled the piece "American Poetry" and added as an epigraph the full text (without title) of Robert Frost's poem "The Gift Outright." In the 1962 version the paragraph that begins "To be able" (and which includes the quotation from Goethe) inserts new material after "was a genuine revolution"; the 1962 text omits the footnote at this point, and adds two new paragraphs; a third new paragraph closes with the last part of the original paragraph, from "There is indeed". After the close of the same paragraph, the 1962 text inserts five new paragraphs. The 1962 text omits the two final paragraphs about the anthology itself.

In the paragraph that begins "Normally, in" (p. 507) the first quotation is from Marianne Moore's "England". In the paragraph that begins "There are advantages" (p. 512) "Gambier, Ohio" alludes to Kenyon College where the work of the serious-minded New Critics was published in the *Kenyon Review*; see the notes to the foreword to *Various Jangling Keys*, by Edgar Bogardus (p. 344).

"I Am of Ireland"

Page 514.

A secretarial typescript, dated 9 February 1955, was made by *The New Yorker* from Auden's manuscript and is now in the New York Public Library Manuscripts and Archives Division. The printed text (followed here) contains many minor corrections of quotation and fact; Auden, for example, had originally written that the book contained no letters to Joyce, not "only one".

The paragraph that begins "As yet there has been" (p. 520) alludes to Pound's incarceration in a lunatic asylum, which allowed him to escape the charge of treason based on his wartime broadcasts on behalf of Fascist Italy.

[A Tribute to Paul Claudel]

Page 521.

Claudel died on 23 February 1955; the French text of this tribute was printed under the title "Le salut de trois grands poètes"; the three were T. S. Eliot (whose contribution was datelined London), Auden (New York), and Giuseppe Ungaretti (Rome). The piece was perhaps written in English, and the ellipsis at the end suggests that additional text is lost. The French text reads:

Malgré l'abîme idéologique qui peut séparer un Whitman d'un Claudel, j'ai souvent été frappé par la parenté qu'il me semblait découvrir dans la façon dont ils exprimaient leurs pensées. Et, parfois, jusque dans ces pensées elles-mêmes. Certes, le mysticisme de l'un se réclamait de l'homme, alors que celui de l'autre se réclamait de Dieu. Mais leur intensité commune venait de la même veine et du même coeur. . . .

Authority in America

Page 521.

In the paragraph that begins "My experience of the Popular Front" I have emended "seem probable" to "seems probable".

Senator John Bricker, Republican of Ohio, opposed the New Deal and championed states' rights. The phrase "a bigger bang for the dollar" was familiar from legislative debates on the cost of armaments.

AM I THAT I AM?

Page 527.

The English writer Nigel Dennis lived in New York in the 1930s and 1940s, when he worked for *The New Republic* and *Time*, and became friendly with Auden perhaps through literary circles. I have removed the breaks added by *Encounter* to enliven the page. Auden's quotations include trivial inaccuracies.

This review was reprinted in *The Griffin*, December 1955, "by arrangement with *Encounter Magazine*".

MAN BEFORE MYTH

Page 532.

In the paragraph that begins "After reading" I have inserted "to" after "he is expected", and have corrected obvious errors such as "experiments" for "expedients" in the paragraph fragment that begins "Johnson does not appear". The apparently random use of single and double quotation marks in the printed text has been regularized.

THE DYER'S HAND

Page 536.

The *Listener* was the weekly review published by the BBC; most articles in the front pages were derived from recent broadcasts; the reviews in the back pages were written for the magazine. Auden had reviewed for the *Listener* in the 1930s and a few of his broadcasts had been reprinted there.

This edition gives separate subtitles to each of the three lectures; these are the subtitles of the three broadcasts as listed in the BBC's weekly schedules in *Radio Times*. The separate title of the first lecture is known only from the *Radio Times* listing; the second and third lectures, but not the first, have separate subtitles in the mimeographed scripts in the BBC Written Archives Centre and in the printed texts in the *Listener*.

Auden apparently wrote the lectures in New York in March 1955 (the typescripts are on an American typing paper); he recorded the first two broadcasts at the BBC on 5 April and the third on 7 April. The BBC's mimeographed scripts (each stamped "Speaker's copy") are marked with many of Auden's additions and changes; some of these additions were copied incorrectly in the *Listener*. The *Listener* texts were reprinted with trivial changes in *Anchor Review*, 1957. Auden used the title "The Dyer's Hand" for other, unrelated works, both earlier and later, among them his book of essays published in 1962.

Three significant stages of the text survive: a secretarial typescript made in New York from Auden's lost manuscript; the mimeographed scripts made by the BBC from the secretarial typescript and then revised by Auden; and the text in the *Listener*.

Auden presumably used the lost top copy of the secretarial typescript when recording the broadcasts; he gave a carbon copy to Stephen Spender (with whom he was staying in London), evidently so that Spender might publish it in *Encounter* if the *Listener* did not print it. Spender's copy, annotated by him but with no corrections or other markings by Auden, is now in the Berg Collection (catalogued as "[Lectures on Poetry]").

The mimeographed scripts prepared by the BBC closely match the secretarial typescript, except that Auden's capitalizations are much reduced and the scripts include (as the typescript does not) the text of Yeats's poem at the end of the first lecture. The scripts are heavily marked in Auden's hand, presumably with changes that he made during rehearsals; some changes are typed out and pasted over the earlier text. Some further changes marked on the mimeographed script were made in an unknown hand, probably on the basis of changes Auden made during the recording; these were followed in the *Listener* and are preserved in the present text. The scripts survive in the form of microfilm copies made when the originals were destroyed by the BBC.

The text in the *Listener* is slightly revised from that of the mimeographed script; most of the revisions disentangle confused syntax, and were made either by an editor with Auden's tacit consent or by Auden in a lost set of proofs.

The text in this edition is based on the text in the *Listener*, with minor corrections based on the earlier versions. I have removed the subtitles added by the magazine to break up columns of type; restored much of the paragraphing in the secretarial typescript except where it creates minor nonsense; and restored Auden's capitalizations of "Poet", "Historian", and other nouns.

The false gender of the noun and adjective in "La monde / Est ronde" (p. 554), which excited the derision of Vladimir Nabokov, has a history that may explain the error without excusing it. Auden evidently remembered the rhyme from his childhood reading of Charles Kingsley's *The Water-Babies*, all editions of which from 1863 through the 1920s had this same error and this same rhyme in chapter 2: "*C'est l'amour, l'amour, l'amour / Qui fait la monde à la ronde.*" (The transcript in the BBC Written Archive Centre, followed by *The Listener*, has "La monde" corrected in an unknown hand to "Le monde", but I have retained Auden's intended erroneous reading.)

The following are detailed notes on minor problems in the text. I have not recorded the many clearly authorial revisions marked by Auden and others in the mimeographed scripts, nor have I noted corrections of trivial errors that crept in when the original typescript was copied by the BBC.

Part I. In the paragraph that begins "For him there is little" (p. 536) the typescript (followed here) has "tempest", apparently miscopied as "tempests" in the mimeographed script and the *Listener*. In the same sentence the typescript and mimeographed script have the numbers 1316 and 1000 (no commas); the printed text has "1,316" and "a thousand", although Auden conceivably wrote "one thousand".

In the paragraph that begins "The most obvious difference" (p. 538) Auden seems to have intended the phrase "which may seem trivial" to replace the typescript and mimeographed script's "in themselves quite trivial" but he neglected to strike out the original phrase, so the compositor left in "quite" (which is removed in this edition).

In the following paragraph, which begins "Like the poet", Auden in the mimeographed script (followed here but not in the *Listener*) changed the punctuation after "are alike" from a comma to a semicolon.

In the paragraph that begins "The Historian's method" an editor at the *Listener* (followed here) corrected "usually tells them" to "usually tells stories".

In the paragraph that begins "His stories do not contain riddles" the first sentence reads in the typescript and mimeographed script: "His stories do not contain riddles, but instead are full of contradictions and paradoxes; many of them are funny stories which the poet's never are." Auden deleted everything after the semicolon and replaced it with what became the second sentence of the printed text; unfortunately, his handwritten replacement was only partly legible to the editors of the *Listener* and is even less legible on the smeared microfilm image of the transcript. The *Listener* tried to make sense of Auden's scrawl by printing "To the poet comedy is synonymous with satire, only the inferior as poetry causes laughter; in the historian's tales, on the other hand, it is often the comic character who is superior to the solemn." The words that the *Listener* rendered as "the inferior as poetry" seem to be "the inferior [line break] inferiority", and Auden presumably intended but neglected to delete the first two words after writing the third. The words that the *Listener* rendered "the solemn" are probably "other" (written in tiny letters to fit on the page) followed by "characters" written twice, first very illegibly, then again, slightly less illegibly, above the first instance.

In the paragraph that begins "It is possible to imagine" (p. 543) the third sentence in the typescript and mimeographed script has "choleric and given to venery"; in the mimeographed script the last three words are replaced in an unknown hand by "passionate", which is perhaps not authorial.

Part II. In the paragraph that begins "Mankind needs" (p. 548) the typescript and mimeographed script's "the hybris of each other, who if unchecked" is revised on the script first in Auden's hand to "the hybris of each, for each if unchecked", then in an unknown hand to "the hybris by which each is tempted, for both if unchecked"; this final version, which appears in the *Listener* with a comma after "both", sounds authorial.

In the paragraph that begins "This assumption is necessary" (p. 552) the typescript and mimeographed script have "take place in the first adjective, and Keats would be startled to learn that a slight change in association has made it possible for a student to reply, when asked by a colleague of mine to explicate the lines [two-line quotation] 'The poor dog [. . .]' "; an unknown hand has rewritten this on the mimeographed script, and the altered version was printed in the *Listener* and is followed here.

Part III. In the final sentence of the paragraph that begins "The sense of security" (p. 559) three of the dashes are restored from the typescript and mimeographed script and one dash is emended from the typescript and script's comma; the *Listener* text has a dash, a comma, and two parentheses.

In the paragraph that begins "I suggested in my first" (p. 560) the sense of the first and third sentences is clear if each colon is regarded as introducing a phrase within dashes.

In the paragraph that begins "Before the coming of the machine" (p. 561) in the sentence that begins, "It is quite unjust", the word "quite" is restored from the typescript and mimeographed script.

In the paragraph that begins "This seems a good" (p. 566) an unknown hand, writing on the mimeographed script, has twice changed "drugstore" to "chemist" and "the proprietor suggests" to "he suggests".

Qui è l'uom' felice

Page 569.

Auden wrote this piece for the annual literary magazine published by Gresham's School, Holt, where he was a member of Farfield House in the years listed beneath the instructions. The 1955 number was described as the Quatercentenary Number, and was issued in the summer term, possibly on Speech Day. Auden's instructions, questions, and Auden's answers were all printed on separate pages. The title is from *Purgatorio* XXX: "Here man is happy."

In the fifth paragraph of instructions, I have inserted "as" before "important".

Speaking of Books

Page 571.

Unlike Auden's earlier contribution to the weekly column published under this name (p. 391), which was one of a long series by different guest contributors, this was a solitary interruption to the regular series written by J. Donald Adams.

[Contribution to *Modern Canterbury Pilgrims*]

Page 573.

The book for which Auden wrote this essay contained untitled essays by twenty-three converts to the Anglican Communion. The full title of the book is *Modern Canterbury Pilgrims and Why They Chose the Episcopal Church*, [a list of twenty-two contributors], Edited, with an essay, by James A. Pike. The editor (and author of the twenty-third essay) was the dean of the Episcopal Diocese of New York. The editor acknowledged that the subtitle simplifies the contents by implying that all the contributors joined the Protestant Episcopal Church of the United States of America; some of the contributors joined other churches in the Anglican Communion. The editor's headnote to Auden's essay (the second in volume) describes his career and ends: "He has summarized his essay with the sentence 'The way in is sometimes the way 'round.'"

Auden was working on his essay early in May 1955, and sent it to James A. Pike on 8 May 1955 with a cover letter: "Here is the piece I promised you for your volume *Pilgrims to Canterbury*. I apologise for the state of the Mss: I am the world's worst typists [*sic*]" (Syracuse University Library). Auden wrote to Ursula Niebuhr on 9 June 1955: "I duly did my piece for Dean Pike. I fear it is rather shy-making as all such pieces can hardly help being" (Library of Congress).

The book was published on 21 May 1956 by Morehorse-Gorham, a house that specialized in titles related to the Episcopal Church. A British edition was published on 21 October 1956 by A. R. Mowbray, with this subtitle: "The Story of Twenty-three Converts and Why They Chose the Anglican Communion, Edited by the Dean of New York, With an Introduction by Bishop Stephen Neill."

In the paragraph that begins "At the same time" (p. 574) " 'Crisis' theology" refers to the theology of Karl Barth and his followers that emphasized the absolute judgement of God on human actions, and the absolute inadequacy of the latter.

In the paragraph that begins "Shortly afterwards" (p. 578) the "Anglican layman" was Charles Williams at the Oxford University Press, whom Auden met in July 1937 when he first proposed *The Oxford Book of Light Verse* in 1937 (see *Prose I*, pp. 707–8). In the next paragraph, the second sentence alludes to the events that occurred after Chester Kallman broke off sexual relations with Auden in July 1941.

FOREWORD TO *Some Trees*, BY JOHN ASHBERY

Page 580.

The Yale University Press conducted in-house preliminary readings of manuscripts submitted to the Yale Series of Younger Poets in order to spare Auden, as the series judge, the time required to look at manuscripts with no chance of being chosen. In 1955, John Ashbery's submission was one of those eliminated by an in-house reader. Auden wrote to Eugene Davidson at the Press on 22 May 1955:

Thank you for your letter of May 18. I am very worried because, for the second year in succession [see p. 623], I do not find among the mss submitted to me one that I feel merits publication. It so happens that there is another poet staying here [Chester Kallman], and I asked him to read them also as a check on my own judgement. He came, however, to the same conclusion.

What bothers me particularly is that a young poet (John Ashbury [*sic*]) whom I know personally told me he was submitting a manuscript this year. I have reservations about such of his poems as I have seen, but they are certainly better than any of the manuscripts which have reached me. I don't know how or by whom the preliminary sieving is done at the Press, but I cannot help wondering whether I am receiving the best.

Chester Kallman, who championed Ashbery's work against Auden's doubts, apparently arranged to have a copy of the manuscript sent to Auden in Italy. On 3 June 1955 Auden wrote to Davidson:

Herewith John Ashbury's poems. I have made a few cuts so you will find some gaps in the page numbering. I have also written to Ashbury suggesting that for the sake of the Press, he adopt a less general title than just *Poems*, and have suggested as an alternative *Some Trees*.

Could you let me have the Ms back when you are through with it as I need it to write my introduction.

On 28 July Auden sent Davidson his foreword and the manuscript, adding, "As you will see, there are a number of changes since you first saw it." The book was published on 28 March 1956.

BILE AND BROTHERHOOD

Page 584.

Auden wrote this review in June 1955; the *New Yorker* paid him $300 for it on 7 July 1955 but "killed" the piece in August 1956. He wrote to his friend Noemi Kenmore on 14 June 1955: "Must go back now to a review of Dostoievsky's travel notes about Paris and London: what an old cross-patch he is." On 25 June 1955 he told Howard Griffin that he was writing "a snooty and *very* limey review" of the book. (Both letters are in the Berg Collection.) The American whose foreword introduced the book was Saul Bellow. The text in this edition is based on Auden's typescript in the New York Public Library Manuscripts and Archives Division.

L'HOMME D'ESPRIT

Page 590.

This introduction was written for the English translation of Valéry's *Analects* in the Bollingen Series edition of his complete works in English, under the general editorship of Jackson Mathews. Auden agreed to write the piece during a visit on 29 October 1954 to the University of Washington in Seattle where Mathews was teaching. Mathews wrote to Vaun Gillmor at the Bollingen Foundation on 13 November 1954 that he and Auden had discussed the edition, that Auden wanted to write the introduction to *Analects*, and that Auden should be paid the series's maximum fee of $500. Mathews suggested that the essay should be finished by November 1955, but Auden finished it by early July 1955; a draft of a letter from Mathews to Auden dated 16 July 1955 expresses pleasure at hearing that the work is done, and a draft of a letter from Mathews to Auden dated 30 July 1955 thanks him for the text (Bollingen Foundation papers, Library of Congress). Auden's typescript with his manuscript corrections is in the Jackson Mathews papers at the University of North Carolina at Chapel Hill Library; it is titled "L'Homme d'Esprit: Introduction to the English translation of the Analects of Paul Valéry".

The volumes in the collected edition appeared at leisurely intervals, and *Analects* was not published by Princeton University Press until 30 July 1970; a British edition was published by Routledge & Kegan Paul on 20 August 1970. Auden's introduction was titled simply "Introduction" in the edition, but it also appeared under a title similar to that of the typescript, "Valéry: L'Homme d'Esprit" in *Hudson Review* in 1969. Auden reprinted the text in *Forewords and Afterwords* (1973) as "Un Homme d'Esprit".

The text in this edition is that of the Bollingen Series edition with the restoration of a paragraph break mistakenly omitted by a compositor before "But for poets" (p. 593). The typescript uses the French text of the excerpts from *Analects* where the published text uses the English translation, and the printed text normalizes Auden's grammar (for example, replacing "they are" with "he is" in "everyone knows what they are going to see"). Jackson Mathews slightly changed some of

Auden's references to other writings by Valéry; in the paragraph that begins "He has extremely" (p. 593) Auden wrote "that in dreams, there can be no conditional tense".

Auden's reference to André Gide alludes to the occasion, probably in Paris in 1937, when Gide, at the height of his success, invited Auden, an impoverished free-lancer, to a grand lunch at the end of which he made clear that Auden was to pay the bill.

THE HISTORY OF AN HISTORIAN

Page 596.

Auden reviewed the first volume of Ernest Jones's biography of Freud in "The Greatness of Freud" (p. 385). In the fourth paragraph I have emended a probable misreading by a compositor, "popular feuilletons", to "regular feuilletons". At the end of the fifth paragraph I have emended "true" to "untrue". In the long extract that begins "He felt satisfied" Auden's "factor" is miscopied from "agency"; trivial errors in transcription occur in other quotations. In the paragraph that begins "Taken off his guard (p. 598) the quotation marks around "paraprax" were proba-bly added by an editor. In the paragraph that begins "As Freud's biographer" (p. 600) I have emended "his library gifts" to "his literary gifts". I have regularized Auden's use of single quotation marks for concepts, and have added closing quo-tation marks where required.

Auden's reference to the six Paladins (p. 599) alludes to Ernest Jones's idea of a secret committee of Freud's defenders who, he said, would be like the Paladins of Charlemagne; at first this was the "Council of Five" mentioned in an earlier para-graph but a sixth member was added later. Dr Abraham was Karl Abraham. Dr Eder was David Eder, first secretary to the London Psycho-Analytic Society.

A SELF-POLICING PEOPLE

Page 602.

Geoffrey Gorer and Auden became friendly during the 1940s, when Gorer was living in America. On 9 July 1955, after reading the book reviewed in this essay, Auden wrote Gorer an eight-page letter with detailed comments on the question-naire described in the opening paragraph of the review and on the themes and con-clusions of the book; many of these comments appear in similar form in the review (Sussex University Library).

I have emended the first word from "In" to "On"; Auden may have intended to name only the month, not the exact date, or the compositor may have misread his hand.

REFLECTIONS ON *The Magic Flute*

Page 604.

The magazine in which this piece appeared is described in the note to "Ballet's Present Eden" (p. 393). The magazine printed an editorial headnote to the essay:

"The N.B.C. Opera Theater presented a new production of Mozart's Magic Flute on Sunday afternoon January fifteenth [1956]. Here W. H. Auden, who wrote the libretto for the television production in collaboration with Chester Kallman, discusses some of the problems involved in shaping and clarifying the original libretto and writing a new English version." This essay was probably written around November 1955. For Auden's further comments on his and Kallman's version, see the following item and the text of their introduction and notes to the 1956 edition, published in *Libretti*. I have repaired some illogical paragraphing.

The paragraph that begins "Pamina, for her part" (p. 606) is erratically punctuated, and may be clarified through the substitution of semicolons for commas after "Monostatos", "silence", "past ties," and "curse". I have inserted *"heiligen"* in *"in diesen heiligen Hallen"* (Auden uses the spelling *heiligen*, not the opera's *heil'gen*, in the list of arias at the end of the piece.)

In the paragraph that begins "Beside Papageno" (p. 608) the composer, perhaps confused by Auden's manuscript, made nonsense of the text from "the humility" to "brother of Caliban." The text in this edition attempts to disentangle the following from the magazine's text: "the humility which would accept a Monostatos heroine, Tamina. He is, in fact, clearly a variety of Papagena; no, he demands the brother of Caliban." My reconstruction makes use of all the words in this garble, other than a perhaps superfluous "Monostatos"; I suspect that "no," is not authorial but have let it stand. Later in the same paragraph I have emended "what he likes" to "what he is like".

PUTTING IT IN ENGLISH

Page 609.

This essay, probably written in November or December 1955, appeared in the drama and music section of the Sunday *New York Times*. A headnote reads: "W. H. Auden and Chester Kallman were commissioned by the N.B.C. Opera Theatre to translate 'The Magic Flute' for televising next Sunday. George Balanchine will stage the work and Peter Herman Adler will conduct." An editor or compositor misread "translator" as "transliterator" in the opening sentence and in the paragraph that begins "Whatever liberties". I have slightly reduced the newspaper's obviously excessive paragraphing.

INDEX OF TITLES AND
BOOKS REVIEWED

THIS index includes titles of each of the works printed or described in this edition and the titles and authors of the books Auden reviewed.

Titles of Auden's works that were originally published (or intended to be published) as separate books or pamphlets are printed in LARGE AND SMALL CAPITALS. Titles of books, plays, and operas that Auden edited or reviewed are in *italics*. Titles of Auden's essays and reviews are all printed in roman type, as are the names of authors of books reviewed, the names of persons who were the subjects of his essays, and the names of his coauthors.